FOURTH EDITION

Everyman's

DICTIONARY
OF DATES

Revised by Audrey Butler, M.A.(Oxon.)

This handy reference volume, planned to make useful dates available to the general reader, now contains extensive changes in content to meet the changing world of today. *New articles include:*

Bagdad Pact;Caribbean Federation;C.E.N.T.O.; Central Africa Office; Common Market; Congo; D-Day; E.O.K.A.; Euratom; European Coal and Steel Community; European Free Trade Association; Fifth Republic; Fourth Republic; Ghana; Guinea; Homicide Act; Hovercraft; Independent Television Authority; Jakarta; Katanga; Laos; Madhya Pradesh; National Economic Planning Council; O.A.S.; Pay as you earn; President Kennedy's assassination; Rockets; Rome, treaty of; Rwanda; South-East Asia Treaty Organisation; Space Flights; Telstar; United Arab Republic; Uttar Pradesh; Warsaw Pact; Zeta.

In addition there are new sections of existing articles; e.g. lists of recent Chancellors of the Exchequer under 'Exchequer' and a list of post-World War II peace treaties under 'World War II'. Many existing articles have been rewritten, or largely rewritten, apart from revision entailing addition of material available since the last edition.

Writers, journalists, teachers, students and the general reader, in fact any associated with the printed word in book, newspaper or magazine, will find in this volume an immediate source of reference of facts which it would take much time and research to find out in other ways.

Everyman's

DICTIONARY OF DATES

A Volume in
EVERYMAN'S REFERENCE LIBRARY

Everyman's

DICTIONARY OF
DATES

Fourth edition revised by
AUDREY BUTLER, M.A.(OXON.)

LONDON: J. M. DENT & SONS LTD
NEW YORK: E. P. DUTTON & CO. INC

© Revisions, J. M. Dent & Sons Ltd, 1964
Made in Great Britain
Set by the
Aldine Press · Letchworth · Herts
and printed by
Lowe & Brydone (Printers) Ltd · London
for
J. M. DENT & SONS LTD
Aldine House · Bedford Street · London
FIRST EDITION 1911
Reprinted 1912, 1918, 1924, 1928, 1931
SECOND EDITION 1940
Reprinted 1941, 1942
THIRD EDITION 1954
FOURTH EDITION 1964

PREFACE

THE basic purpose of this work is to make useful dates accessible to the general reader, but even this lowly and utilitarian objective involves a number of intractable problems. It was necessary to try and include most of the 'obvious' events lest the compilers be accused of 'not even putting in the *Battle of Hastings*,' and yet it was clearly desirable to add many matters —such as the *Shoguns*—which are hard to find quickly elsewhere.

To solve the resulting difficulties of selection, the compilers guided themselves by a number of principles. Considerable prominence was given to countries, institutions, and dynasties of universal influence and, amongst these, Britain and her past and present dependencies were accorded a slight pre-eminence. Then room was found for notices (however short) on other countries, cities, provinces, institutions, and families of independent status or historical repute. Thirdly, considerable space was devoted to arts, sciences, philosophy, religion, and invention, and, lastly, a large number of miscellaneous facts have been included on grounds of interest or notoriety.

Broadly speaking there are three types of headings: short entries relating to particular matters, e.g. *coach*; narratives, e.g. *United States of America*; and classified entries, e.g. *Sieges*. The compilers have sacrificed logic and exclusiveness to convenience wherever they thought it was desirable, and they have not hesitated to repeat themselves if necessary.

Generally the classified entries are the longest, then the narratives, so that if the subject sought by the user is not to be found under its own name he should scan likely general headings in that order. The List of Longer Entries (of all types) given overleaf may be helpful in this respect. It should be borne in mind that this is *not* a biographical dictionary, so that in order to look up 'the dates of George V' one must first know whether the individual in question was the King of England or the last ruler of Hanover of that name, and so on.

Everyman's Dictionary of Dates was first planned fifty-three years ago, and has subsequently passed through ten revisions. This fourth edition, while retaining the basic character of its predecessors, is considerably more comprehensive, and there have been extensive changes in content to meet the demands of the fast-changing world of to-day. The lists of classical emperors, etc., remain; in addition, there are now such new entries as *Rockets* and *Space Flights* (with a detailed list of cosmonauts). It is the publishers' belief that this completely revised and enlarged edition of a well-tried favourite reference book will prove a worthy successor to those of the past half-century.

1964   AUDREY BUTLER

LIST OF LONGER ENTRIES

vii

CALENDARS

(1) The present system of Christian dating originated as follows:

(a) The Roman Era began with the foundation of Rome in 753 B.C. By 46 B.C., owing to various imperfections the Roman Calendar had fallen into confusion and Julius Caesar then reformed it.

(b) The year 46 B.C. was therefore made to consist of 445 days, and is called the 'Year of Confusion.' Thereafter each year consisted of 365 days except that *every* fourth year was a leap year. This Julian or Old Style Calendar remained in general use in Europe until 1582.

(c) By 1582 there was a difference of ten days between the Julian and the tropical year. In that year Pope Gregory XIII ordered that 5 Oct. should be called 15 Oct., and that of the end-century (00) years only the fourth should be a leap year. This Gregorian or New Style Calendar is still in use. It was adopted in:

Italy	Flanders		China 1912
France } 1582	German Catholic States } 1583		Bulgaria 1915
Spain	Poland	1586	Turkey 1917
Portugal	Hungary	1587	U.S.S.R. 1917
Prussia	German Protestant States } 1700		Yugoslavia 1919
Switzerland } 1583	Denmark		Rumania 1919
Holland	Japan	1872	Greece 1923

In Sweden the change was made between 1700 and 1740 by the omission of 11 leap-year days.

In Britain (including N. America and the Colonies) the change was made in 1752 (3 Sept. being called 14), and the beginning of the official year was altered from 25 Mar. (which was the date of the vernal equinox when the Julian Calendar was introduced) to 1 Jan. at the same time.

The following is a calendar of secular (mainly political) anniversaries of the Western world, such as can be fixed by the Gregorian calendar. But there are many important popular festivals which cannot be so fixed, such as the American Thanksgiving Day celebrated on the fourth Thursday in Nov. In cases where a Saint's Day has acquired a mainly political significance through his being the patron saint of a country, the day is mentioned here and not in the Roman calendar which follows.

JANUARY
1.
2.
3.
4.
5.
6. Twelfth Night (Old Christmas Day).
7.
8.
9.
10.
11.
12.
13.
14.
15.
16.
17.
18.
19. Robert E. Lee born, 1807. Holiday in southern U.S.A.
20.   1st Pluviôse.
21.
22.
23. Luxemburg National Day.
24.
25. Burns Night.
26. Republic of India proclaimed, 1950. Australia Day.
27.
28.
29.

30. King Charles I executed, 1649.
31.
FEBRUARY
1.
2. Candlemas (Scottish Quarter Day).
3.
4. Ceylon Independence Day.
5.
6. George VI died, 1952. New Zealand Day.
7.
8. Elizabeth II proclaimed, 1952.
9.
10.
11.
12. Abraham Lincoln born, 1809.
13.
14. Valentine.
15.
16.
17.
18.
19.   1st Ventôse.
20.
21.
22. George Washington born, 1732.
23.
24.
25.
26.
27.
28.
29. Leap Year Day.

ix

MARCH

1. St. David.
2.
3.
4.
5.
6. Ghana Independence Day.
7.
8.
9.
10.
11.
12.
13.
14.
15.
16.
17. St. Patrick.
18.
19.
20. Vernal equinox.
21.   1st Germinal.
22.
23.
24. Queen Mary died, 1953.
25. Lady Day (English Quarter Day).
26.
27.
28.
29.
30.
31.

APRIL

1. All Fools.
2.
3.
4.
5. Income tax year ends.
6.
7.
8.
9.
10.
11.
12.
13.
14. Pan-American Day.
15. Otter hunting begins.
16.
17. Syrian National Day.
18.
19.   Primrose Day.
20.   1st Floréal.
21. Elizabeth II born, 1926.
22. Israel State proclaimed.
23. St George's Day and Shakespeare's Birthday.
24.
25. Anzac Day.
26.
27. Sierra Leone Independence Day.
28.
29.
30.

MAY

1. Labour Day (outside U.S.A.).
2.
3. Polish National Day. Japanese Constitution Day.
4.
5.
6.
7.
8.   Victory in N.W. Europe, 1945.
9.
10.
11.
12.   Coronation of George VI, 1937.
13. Old May Day.
14.
15. Whitsunday (Scottish Quarter Day).
16.
17.   Norwegian National Day.
18.
19.
20.   1st Prairial.
21.
22.
23.
24. Commonwealth (formerly Empire) Day.
25. Argentine Independence Day.
26.
27.
28.
29.   Oak Apple Day.
30.   U.S.A. Memorial Day.
31.   Union Day, S. Africa.

JUNE

1.
2. Elizabeth II crowned, 1953.
3.
4.
5. Constitution Day (Denmark).
6.   D-Day, 1944.
7.
8.
9.
10.   Sovereign's (official) birthday.
11.
12.
13.
14.
15.
16.
17. Icelandic Independence Day.
18. Waterloo Day.
19.   1st Messidor.
20.
21. Summer Solstice.
22.
23.
24. Midsummer (English Quarter Day).
25.
26.
27.
28.
29.
30.

JULY

1. Dominion Day, Canada.
2. Belgian Independence Day.
3.
4.   American Independence Day.
5. Tynewald Day (Isle of Man).
6. Old Midsummer Day.
7.
8. Cecil Rhodes Day.
9.
10.
11.
12.
13. Orangemen's Day.
14.   French National Day.
15.
16.
17.
18.
19.   1st Thermidor.
20.
21.
22.
23.
24.
25.
26.
27.
28.
29.
30.
31.

AUGUST

1. Lammas (Scottish Quarter Day).
2.
3.
4. World War I began, 1914.
5. Oyster season begins.
6. Jamaica Independence Day.
7.
8.
9.
10.
11.
12. Grouse and ptarmigan shooting
13.   [begins.
14. Pakistan Independence Day.
15.   Victory over Japan, 1945.
                  Indian Independence.
16.
17.
18.   1st Fructidor.
19.
20.
21.
22.
23.
24.
25.
26.
27.
28.
29.
30.
31. Malaya Independence Day.
     Trinidad Independence Day.

SEPTEMBER

1. Partridge shooting begins.
2.
3. World War II began, 1939.
4. Labor Day (U.S.A.).
5.
6.
7.
8. Maltese National Day.
9.
10.
11.
12.
13.
14.
15. Otter hunting ends.
16.
17. Arnhem Day.   Sansculottide 1.
18.   Sansculottide 2.
19.   Sansculottide 3.
20.   Sansculottide 4.
21.   Sansculottide 5.
22.   1st Vendémiaire.
23. Autumnal equinox.
24.
25.
26.
27.
28.
29. Michaelmas (English Quarter Day).
30.

OCTOBER

1. Nigeria Independence Day.
    Pheasant shooting begins.
2.
3.
4.
5.
6.
7.
8.
9.
10. Uganda Independence Day.
11.
12. Columbus Day.
13.
14.
15.
16.
17.
18.
19.
20.
21. Trafalgar Day.
22.   1st Brumaire.
23.
24. United Nations' Day.
25.
26.
27.
28.
29. Turkish National Holiday.
30.
31. Hallowe'en.

1.
2.
3.
4.
5. Guy Fawkes Day, 1605.
6.
7.
8.
9. Lord Mayor's Day.
10.
11. Martinmas (Scottish Quarter Day).
Armistice, 1918.
12.
13.
14. Prince of Wales born, 1948.
15. Brazilian National Day.
16.
17.
18.
19.
20. Jamaica Constitution Day.
21. 1st Frimaire.
22.
23.
24
25.
26.
27.
28.
29
30.

1.
2.
3.
4.
5.
6.
7.
8.
9.
10. Tanganyika Independence Day.
11.
12.
13.
14.
15.
16. Dingaan's Day (S. Africa).
17.
18.
19.
20.
21. Forefathers' Day (U.S.A.).
1st Nivôse.
22. Winter Solstice.
23.
24.
25. Christmas (English Quarter Day).
26. Boxing Day.
27.
28.
29.
30.
31.

(2) Jewish Calendar

A system by which the beginning, length, and sub-division of the year is fixed. Nothing is certain concerning the calendar in use during biblical times. Later the beginning of a month was ascertained by observation of the new moon, but about the middle of the fourth century a constant calendar was introduced, based on earlier practice.

The day is the period between two successive sunsets although, for calendar purposes, it is computed to commence at the beginning of the seventh hour after noon, i.e. at 6 p.m. The week consists of seven days, ending with the Sabbath, the other days having no special name, but being designated as the first day, the second day of the week, etc. A month is the period between two revolutions of the moon. Ordinarily, twelve months containing alternately 30 and 29 days, make a year, which should therefore contain 354 days. But since the Bible ordains that Passover must be celebrated in the month of *Abib* (the fresh ears of grain) and since vegetable growth is dependent on the sun, it is necessary to adjust this lunar year to the solar one of 365¼ days. This is done by intercalating a month of 30 days before the last month of the religious year seven times during every nineteen years (the Metonic cycle), viz. in the third, sixth, eighth, eleventh, fourteenth, seventeenth, and nineteenth years of each cycle. These intercalary or leap years therefore ordinarily contain 384 days. But there are certain factors which make it necessary to lengthen or shorten the regular year of 354 days and the leap year of 384 days by one day.

The Day of Atonement must not fall on the first or sixth day of the week, nor the seventh day of Tabernacles on Sabbath. Consequently the New Year festival must not fall on the first, fourth, or sixth day. Again, the New Year festival must be celebrated on the day on which the new moon becomes visible; consequently if the lunar conjunction occurs at noon or later the festival is postponed to the next day, since the new moon will be seen only at 6 p.m. or later, which period belongs to the following day. For these and other reasons, the eighth month, *Cheshvan*, sometimes has 30 instead of 29 days (when the year is described as 'redundant') and the ninth month, *Kislev*, 29 instead of 30 days (a 'defective' year). Thus the ordinary year may contain 353, 354, or 355 days and the leap year 383, 384, or 385.

The character of a Jewish year is therefore definitely known by the determination of its first day, that which is to be celebrated as its New Year Festival, and by its length, dependent on whether it is an ordinary or leap year and regular, redundant, or defective (i.e. whether any variation is required in the lengths of *Cheshvan* and *Kislev*). Each of the possible fourteen types of year, seven for ordinary and seven for leap years, is described by a 'characteristic' consisting of three Hebrew letters, the first of which intimates the day of the week on which the New Year festival falls, the second whether the year is regular, redundant, or defective, and the third the day of the week on which the first day of Passover falls. The last is not really necessary and is included in the 'characteristic' only because when the incidence of Passover is known the days of the week on which the principal festivals of the following year fall may easily be ascertained. To these three letters is, of course, added the Hebrew word for 'ordinary' or 'leap' as may be required.

The times when the solstices and equinoxes (*Tekufah*) fall must also be computed, since the petition for rain has to be interpolated in the *Amidah* prayer on and after the sixtieth day from the autumnal equinox. Each *Tekufah* is 91 days 7½ hours distant from another, being a quarter of the 365¼ days which, according to Samuel Yarchinai, make up the solar year. Each *Tekufah* returns to the same day of the week and to the same hour every 28 years, which period is termed a 'greater cycle' or a 'solar cycle.' The calculation of the civil date with which any particular Jewish date corresponds and vice versa, is of a complicated character. There is, however, a mathematical formula (that of Gauss), which gives the date of the Passover in any year; from this that of the next New Year festival may easily be calculated, since the number of days between these two festivals is constant. If the characteristic of the year is ascertained any particular date may then be calculated, as in the following table.

Jew. Year			Tishri		Cheshvan		Kislev			Tebet
	Civil Year								Civil Year	
5681	1920	M.	13 Sept.	W.	13 Oct.	F.	12 Nov.		Sn.	12 Dec.
5682	1921	M.	3 Oct.	W.	2 Nov.	F.	2 Dec.	1922	Sn.	1 Jan.
5683	1922	St.	23 Sept.	M.	23 Oct.	Tu.	21 Nov.		W.	20 Dec.
5684	1923	Tu.	11 Sept.	Th.	11 Oct.	F.	9 Nov.		Sn.	9 Dec.
5685	1924	M.	29 Sept.	W.	29 Oct.	F.	28 Nov.		Sn.	28 Dec.
5686	1925	St.	19 Sept.	M.	19 Oct.	W.	18 Nov.		F.	18 Dec.
5687	1926	Th.	9 Sept.	St.	9 Oct.	Sn.	7 Nov.		M.	6 Dec.
5688	1927	Tu.	27 Sept.	Th.	27 Oct.	F.	25 Nov.		Sn.	25 Dec.
5689	1928	St.	15 Sept.	M.	15 Oct.	W.	14 Nov.		F.	14 Dec.
5690	1929	St.	5 Oct.	M.	4 Nov.	Tu.	3 Dec.	1930	W.	1 Jan.
5691	1930	Tu.	23 Sept.	Th.	23 Oct.	F.	21 Nov.		Sn.	21 Dec.
5692	1931	St.	12 Sept.	M.	12 Oct.	W	11 Nov.		F.	11 Dec.
5693	1932	St.	1 Oct.	M.	31 Oct.	W.	30 Nov.		F.	30 Dec.
5694	1933	Th.	21 Sept.	St.	21 Oct.	Sn.	19 Nov.		Tu.	19 Dec.
5695	1934	M.	10 Sept.	W.	10 Oct.	Th.	8 Nov.		F.	7 Dec.
5696	1935	St.	28 Sept.	M.	28 Oct.	W.	27 Nov.		F.	27 Dec.
5697	1936	Th.	17 Sept.	St.	17 Oct.	Sn.	15 Nov.		Tu.	15 Dec.
5698	1937	M.	6 Sept.	W.	6 Oct.	F.	5 Nov.		Sn.	5 Dec.
5699	1938	M.	26 Sept.	W.	26 Oct.	Th.	24 Nov.		F.	23 Dec.
5700	1939	Th.	14 Sept.	St.	14 Oct.	M.	13 Nov.		W.	13 Dec.
5701	1940	Th.	3 Oct.	St.	2 Nov.	Sn.	1 Dec.		Tu.	31 Dec.
5702	1941	M.	22 Sept.	W.	22 Oct.	F.	21 Nov.		Sn.	21 Dec.
5703	1942	St.	12 Sept.	M.	12 Oct.	Tu.	10 Nov.		W.	9 Dec.
5704	1943	Th.	30 Sept.	St.	30 Oct.	Sn.	28 Nov.		Tu.	28 Dec.
5705	1944	M.	18 Sept.	W.	18 Oct.	F.	17 Nov.		Sn.	17 Dec.
5706	1945	St.	8 Sept.	M.	8 Oct.	Tu.	6 Nov.		W.	5 Dec.
5707	1946	Th.	26 Sept.	St.	26 Oct.	Sn.	24 Nov.		Tu.	24 Dec.
5708	1947	M.	15 Sept.	W.	15 Oct.	F.	14 Nov.		Sn.	14 Dec.
5709	1948	M.	4 Oct.	W.	3 Nov.	F.	3 Dec.	1949	Sn.	2 Jan.
5710	1949	St.	24 Sept.	M.	24 Oct.	Tu.	22 Nov.		W.	21 Dec.
5711	1950	Tu.	12 Sept.	Th.	12 Oct.	F.	10 Nov.		Sn.	10 Dec.
5712	1951	M.	1 Oct.	W.	31 Oct.	F.	30 Nov.		Sn.	30 Dec.
5713	1952	St.	20 Sept.	M.	20 Oct.	W.	19 Nov.		F.	19 Dec.
5714	1953	Th.	10 Sept.	St.	10 Oct.	Sn.	8 Nov.		M.	7 Dec.
5715	1954	Tu.	28 Sept.	Th.	28 Oct.	F.	26 Nov.		Sn.	26 Dec.
5716	1955	St.	17 Sept.	M.	17 Oct.	W.	16 Nov.		F.	16 Dec.
5717	1956	Th.	6 Sept.	St.	6 Oct.	M.	5 Nov.		W.	5 Dec.
5718	1957	Th.	26 Sept.	St.	26 Oct.	Sn.	24 Nov.		Tu.	24 Dec.
5719	1958	M.	15 Sept.	W.	15 Oct.	Th.	13 Nov.		F.	12 Dec.
5720	1959	St.	3 Oct.	M.	2 Nov.	W.	2 Dec.	1960	F.	1 Jan.
5721	1960	Th.	22 Sept.	St.	22 Oct.	Sn.	20 Nov.		Tu.	20 Dec.
5722	1961	M.	11 Sept.	W.	11 Oct.	Th.	9 Nov.		F.	8 Dec.
5723	1962	St.	29 Sept.	M.	29 Oct.	W.	28 Nov.		F.	28 Dec.
5724	1963	Th.	19 Sept.	St.	19 Oct.	Sn.	17 Nov.		Tu.	17 Dec.
5725	1964	M.	7 Sept.	W.	7 Oct.	F.	6 Nov.		Sn.	6 Dec.
5726	1965	M.	27 Sept.	W.	27 Oct.	Th.	25 Nov.		F.	24 Dec.
5727	1966	Th.	15 Sept.	St.	15 Oct.	M.	14 Nov.		W.	14 Dec.
5728	1967	Th.	5 Oct.	St.	4 Nov.	Sn.	3 Dec.	1968	Tu.	2 Jan.
5729	1968	M.	23 Sept.	W.	23 Oct.	F.	22 Nov.		Sn.	22 Dec.
5730	1969	St.	13 Sept.	M.	13 Oct.	Tu.	11 Nov.		W.	10 Dec.

1ST DAY OF EACH MONTH FALLS.

Jew. Year		Shebat		Adar		Ve-Adar		Nisan	
	Civil Year								
5681	1921	M.	10 Jan.	W.	9 Feb.	F.	11 Mar.	St.	9 Apr.
5682		M.	30 Jan.	W.	1 Mar.		—	Th.	30 Mar.
5683	1923	Th.	18 Jan.	St.	17 Feb.		—	Sn.	18 Mar.
5684	1924	M.	7 Jan.	W.	6 Feb.	F.	7 Mar.	St.	5 Apr.
5685	1925	M.	26 Jan.	W.	25 Feb.		—	Th.	26 Mar.
5686	1926	St.	16 Jan.	M.	15 Feb.		—	Tu.	16 Mar.
5687	1927	Tu.	4 Jan.	Th.	3 Feb.	St.	5 Mar.	Sn.	3 Apr.
5688	1928	M.	23 Jan.	W.	22 Feb.		—	Th.	22 Mar.
5689	1929	St.	12 Jan.	M.	11 Feb.	W.	13 Mar.	Th.	11 Apr.
5690		Th.	30 Jan.	St.	1 Mar.		—	Sn.	30 Mar.
5691	1931	M.	19 Jan.	W.	18 Feb.		—	Th.	19 Mar.
5692	1932	St.	9 Jan.	M.	8 Feb.	W.	9 Mar.	Th.	7 Apr.
5693	1933	St.	28 Jan.	M.	27 Feb.		—	Tu.	28 Mar.
5694	1934	W.	17 Jan.	F.	16 Feb.		—	St.	17 Mar.
5695	1935	St.	5 Jan.	M.	4 Feb.	W.	6 Mar.	Th.	4 Apr.
5696	1936	St.	25 Jan.	M.	24 Feb.		—	Tu.	24 Mar.
5697	1937	W.	13 Jan.	F.	12 Feb.		—	St.	13 Mar.
5698	1938	M.	3 Jan.	W.	2 Feb.	F.	4 Mar.	St.	2 Apr.
5699	1939	St.	21 Jan.	M.	20 Feb.		—	Tu.	21 Mar.
5700	1940	Th.	11 Jan.	St.	10 Feb.	M.	11 Mar.	Tu.	9 Apr.
5701	1941	W.	29 Jan.	F.	28 Feb.		—	St.	29 Mar.
5702	1942	M.	19 Jan.	W.	18 Feb.		—	Th.	19 Mar.
5703	1943	Th.	7 Jan.	St.	6 Feb.	M.	8 Mar.	Tu.	6 Apr.
5704	1944	W.	26 Jan.	F.	25 Feb.		—	St.	25 Mar.
5705	1945	M.	15 Jan.	W.	14 Feb.		—	Th.	15 Mar.
5706	1946	Th.	3 Jan.	St.	2 Feb.	M.	4 Mar.	Tu.	2 Apr.
5707	1947	W.	22 Jan.	F.	21 Feb.		—	St.	22 Mar.
5708	1948	M.	12 Jan.	W.	11 Feb.	F.	12 Mar.	St.	10 Apr.
5709		M.	31 Jan.	W.	2 Mar.		—	Th.	31 Mar.
5710	1950	Th.	19 Jan.	St.	18 Feb.		—	Sn.	19 Mar.
5711	1951	M.	8 Jan.	W.	7 Feb.	F.	9 Mar.	St.	7 Apr.
5712	1952	M.	28 Jan.	W.	27 Feb.		—	Th.	27 Mar.
5713	1953	St.	17 Jan.	M.	16 Feb.		—	Tu.	17 Mar.
5714	1954	Tu.	5 Jan.	Th.	4 Feb.	St.	6 Mar.	Sn.	4 Apr.
5715	1955	M.	24 Jan.	W.	23 Feb.		—	Th.	24 Mar.
5716	1956	St.	14 Jan.	M.	13 Feb.		—	Tu.	13 Mar.
5717	1957	Th.	3 Jan.	St.	2 Feb.	M.	4 Mar.	Tu.	2 Apr.
5718	1958	W.	22 Jan.	F.	21 Feb.		—	St.	22 Mar.
5719	1959	St.	10 Jan.	M.	9 Feb.	W.	11 Mar.	Th.	9 Apr.
5720		St.	30 Jan.	M.	29 Feb.		—	Tu.	29 Mar.
5721	1961	W.	18 Jan.	F.	17 Feb.		—	St.	18 Mar.
5722	1962	St.	6 Jan.	M.	5 Feb.	W.	7 Mar.	Th.	5 Apr.
5723	1963	St.	26 Jan.	M.	25 Feb.		—	Tu.	26 Mar.
5724	1964	W.	15 Jan.	F.	14 Feb.		—	St.	14 Mar.
5725	1965	M.	4 Jan.	W.	3 Feb.	F.	5 Mar.	St.	3 Apr.
5726	1966	St.	22 Jan.	M.	21 Feb.		—	Tu.	22 Mar.
5727	1967	Th.	12 Jan.	St.	11 Feb.	M.	13 Mar.	Tu.	11 Apr.
5728		W.	31 Jan.	F.	1 Mar.		—	St.	30 Mar.
5729	1969	M.	20 Jan.	W.	19 Feb.		—	Th.	20 Mar.
5730	1970	Th.	8 Jan.	St.	7 Feb.	M.	9 Mar.	Tu.	7 Apr.

Jew. Year	Iyar	Sivan	Tammuz	Ab	Elul
5681	M. 9 May	Tu. 7 June	Th. 7 July	F. 5 Aug.	Sn. 4 Sept.
5682	St. 29 Apr.	Sn. 28 May	Tu. 27 June	W. 26 July	F. 25 Aug.
5683	Tu. 17 Apr.	W. 16 May	F. 15 June	St. 14 July	M. 13 Aug.
5684	M. 5 May	Tu. 3 June	Th. 3 July	F. 1 Aug.	Sn. 31 Aug.
5685	St. 25 Apr.	Sn. 24 May	Tu. 23 June	W. 22 July	F. 21 Aug.
5686	Th. 15 Apr.	F. 14 May	Sn. 13 June	M. 12 July	W. 11 Aug.
5687	Tu. 3 May	W. 1 June	F. 1 July	St. 30 July	M. 29 Aug.
5688	St. 21 Apr.	Sn. 20 May	Tu. 19 June	W. 18 July	F. 17 Aug.
5689	St. 11 May	Sn. 9 June	Tu. 9 July	W. 7 Aug.	F. 6 Sept.
5690	Tu. 29 Apr.	W. 28 May	F. 27 June	St. 26 July	M. 25 Aug.
5691	St. 18 Apr.	Sn. 17 May	Tu. 16 June	W. 15 July	F. 14 Aug.
5692	St. 7 May	Sn. 5 June	Tu. 5 July	W. 3 Aug.	F. 2 Sept.
5693	Th. 27 Apr.	F. 26 May	Sn. 25 June	M. 24 July	W. 23 Aug.
5694	M. 16 Apr.	Tu. 15 May	Th. 14 June	F. 13 July	Sn. 12 Aug.
5695	St. 4 May	Sn. 2 June	Tu. 2 July	W. 31 July	F. 30 Aug.
5696	Th. 23 Apr.	F. 22 May	Sn. 21 June	M. 20 July	W. 19 Aug.
5697	M. 12 Apr.	Tu. 11 May	Th. 10 June	F. 9 July	Sn. 8 Aug.
5698	M. 2 May	Tu. 31 May	Th. 30 June	F. 29 July	Sn. 28 Aug.
5699	Th. 20 Apr.	F. 19 May	Sn. 18 June	M. 17 July	W. 16 Aug.
5700	Th. 9 May	F. 7 June	Sn. 7 July	M. 5 Aug.	W. 4 Sept.
5701	M. 28 Apr.	Tu. 27 May	Th. 26 June	F. 25 July	Sn. 24 Aug.
5702	St. 18 Apr.	Sn. 17 May	Tu. 16 June	W. 15 July	F. 14 Aug.
5703	Th. 6 May	F. 4 June	Sn. 4 July	M. 2 Aug.	W. 1 Sept.
5704	M. 24 Apr.	Tu. 23 May	Th. 22 June	F. 21 July	Sn. 20 Aug.
5705	St. 14 Apr.	Sn. 13 May	Tu. 12 June	W. 11 July	F. 10 Aug.
5706	Th. 2 May	F. 31 May	Sn. 30 June	M. 29 July	W. 28 Aug.
5707	M. 21 Apr.	Tu. 20 May	Th. 19 June	F. 18 July	S. 17 Aug.
5708	M. 10 May	Tu. 8 June	Th. 8 July	F. 6 Aug.	S. 5 Sept.
5709	St. 30 Apr.	Sn. 29 May	Tu. 28 June	W. 27 July	F. 26 Aug.
5710	Tu. 18 Apr.	W. 17 May	F. 16 June	St. 15 July	M. 14 Aug.
5711	M. 7 May	Tu. 5 June	Th. 5 July	F. 3 Aug.	Sn. 2 Sept.
5712	St. 26 Apr.	Sn. 25 May	Tu. 24 June	W. 23 July	F. 22 Aug.
5713	Th. 16 Apr.	F. 15 May	Sn. 14 June	M. 13 July	W. 12 Aug.
5714	Tu. 4 May	W. 2 June	F. 2 July	St. 31 July	M. 30 Aug.
5715	St. 23 Apr.	Sn. 22 May	Tu. 21 June	W. 20 July	F. 19 Aug.
5716	Th. 12 Apr.	F. 11 May	Sn. 10 June	M. 9 July	W. 8 Aug.
5717	Th. 2 May	F. 31 May	Sn. 30 June	M. 29 July	W. 28 Aug.
5718	M. 21 Apr.	Tu. 20 May	Th. 19 June	F. 18 July	Sn. 17 Aug.
5719	St. 9 May	Sn. 7 June	Tu. 7 July	W. 5 Aug.	F. 4 Sept.
5720	Th. 28 Apr.	F. 27 May	Sn. 26 June	M. 25 July	W. 24 Aug.
5721	M. 17 Apr.	Tu. 16 May	Th. 15 June	F. 14 July	Sn. 13 Aug.
5722	St. 5 May	Sn. 3 June	Tu. 3 July	W. 1 Aug.	F. 31 Aug.
5723	Th. 25 Apr.	F. 24 May	Sn. 23 June	M. 22 July	W. 21 Aug.
5724	M. 13 Apr.	Tu. 12 May	Th. 11 June	F. 10 July	Sn. 9 Aug.
5725	M. 3 May	Tu. 1 June	Th. 1 July	F. 30 July	Sn. 29 Aug.
5726	Th. 21 Apr.	F. 20 May	Sn. 19 June	M. 18 July	W. 17 Aug.
5727	Th. 11 May	F. 9 June	Sn. 9 July	M. 7 Aug.	W. 6 Sept.
5728	M. 29 Apr.	Tu. 28 May	Th. 27 June	F. 26 July	Sn. 25 Aug.
5729	St. 19 Apr.	Sn. 18 May	Tu. 17 June	W. 16 July	F. 15 Aug.
5730	Th. 7 May	F. 5 June	Sn. 5 July	M. 3 Aug.	W. 2 Sept.

(3) The Roman Calendar

The ecclesiastical or liturgical year begins on the first Sunday of Advent, which is the first Sunday next, whether before or after, the feast of St. Andrew the Apostle (30 Nov.). There follow the four weeks of Advent and the Christmas festivals ending with the Epiphany. The ensuing Sundays are the First, Second, etc. after Epiphany. They can never be more than six, and the series is generally interrupted by Septuagesima, the ninth Sunday before Easter, which is followed by Sexagesima and Quinquagesima, which is the next before Ash Wednesday, on which latter day Lent begins. Lent has six Sundays, the two last of which are known as Passion and Palm Sunday. The week beginning with Palm Sunday is called the Great or Holy Week. Easter Sunday, the feast of the Resurrection, upon the date of which the foregoing festivals depend, falls on the Sunday next following the full moon first occurring after 20 Mar.

The weeks between Easter and Trinity Sunday are Paschal time. Forty days after Easter (always on a Thursday) is the feast of our Lord's Ascension, and on the seventh Sunday, or fiftieth day after Easter, Pentecost (Whitsunday) falls. Trinity Sunday follows, on the Thursday after which the Church celebrates the feast of Corpus Christi, and after its Octave day the feast of the Sacred Heart of Jesus. Other moveable feasts are those of the Holy Name (Sunday between 1 and 6 Jan., otherwise 2 Jan.); Holy Family (Sunday within the Octave of the Epiphany); Seven Dolours of our Lady (Friday after Passion Sunday); Patronage of St. Joseph (Wednesday after the Second Sunday after Easter).

The remaining Sundays of the year, which cannot number more than twenty-eight nor less than twenty-three are known as Third, Fourth, etc., after Pentecost.

Concurrently with the above series of celebrations there runs the calendar of festivals fixed to particular days of the month. This varies considerably from country to country, from diocese to diocese, and even between the calendars of certain religious orders. The calendar printed in this volume show all festivals of universal (excepting certain religious orders) observance. There are rules governing the order of celebration when two feasts of different rank coincide. These will be found prefixed to the Roman Missal.

ABBREVIATIONS:

Ab. Abbot.	K. King.
Ap. Apostle.	M. Martyr.
B. Bishop.	P. Pope.
C. Confessor.	V. Virgin.
D. Doctor of the Church.	W. Widow.

JANUARY

1. The Circumcision.
2. Octave of St. Stephen.
3. Octave of St. John.
4. Octave of Holy Innocents.
5. Vigil of the Epiphany. St. Telesphorus, P. M.
6. The Epiphany.
7.
8.
9.
10
11. St. Hyginus, P. M.
12.
13. Octave of the Epiphany.
14. St. Hilary, B. C. D.—St. Felix, M.
15. St. Paul, 1st hermit—St. Maurus, Ab.
16. St. Marcellus, P. M.
17. St. Antony, Ab.
18. St. Peter's Chair at Rome—St. Prisca, V. M.
19. St. Marius and Companions, MM. —St. Canute, K. M.
20. SS. Fabian and Sebastian, MM.
21. St. Agnes, V. M.
22. SS. Vincent and Anastasius, MM.

23. S. Raymund of Peñafort, C.—St. Emerentiana, V. M.
24. St. Timothy, B. M.
25. Conversion of St. Paul.
26. St. Polycarp, B. M.
27. St. John Chrysostom, B. C. D.
28.
29. St. Francis de Sales, B. C. D.
30. St. Martina, V. M.
31. St. Peter Nolasco, C.

FEBRUARY

1. St. Ignatius, B. M.
2. Purification of our Lady.
3. St. Blaise, B. M.
4. St Andrew Corsini, B. C.
5. St. Agatha, V. M.
6. St. Titus, B. C.—St. Dorothy, V. M.
7. St. Romuald, Ab.
8. St. John of Matha, C.
9. St. Cyril of Alexandria, B. C. D.— St. Apollonia, V.M.
10. St. Scholastica, V.
11. Our Lady of Lourdes.
12. The Seven Founders of the Servite Order.
13.

14. St. Valentine, M.
15. SS. Faustina and Jorita, MM.
16.
17.
18. St. Simeon, B. M.
19.
20.
21.
22. St. Peter's Chair at Antioch.
23. St. Peter Damian, B. C. D.
24. St. Mathias, Ap.
25.
26.
27.
28.

Note. In leap year the feast of St. Matthias is kept on 25 Feb.

MARCH

1.
2.
3.
4. St. Casimir, C.—St. Lucius, P. M.
5.
6. SS. Perpetua and Felicity, MM.
7. St. Thomas Aquinas, C. D.
8. St. John of God, C.
9. St. Frances of Rome, W.
10. The Forty Martyrs.
11.
12. St. Gregory the Great, P. C. D.
13.
14.
15.
16.
17. St. Patrick, B. C.
18. St. Cyril of Jerusalem, B. C. D.
19. St. Joseph.
20.
21. St. Benedict, Ab.
22.
23.
24. St. Gabriel the Archangel.
25. The Annunciation.
26.
27. St. John Damascene, C. D
28. St. John Capistran, C.
29.
30.
31.

APRIL

1.
2. St. Francis of Paula, C.
3.
4. St. Isidore, B. C. D.
5. St. Vincent Ferrer, C.
6.
7.
8.
9.
10.
11. St. Leo the Great, P. C. D.
12.
13. St. Hermengild, M.

14. St. Justin, M.—SS. Tiburtius and Valerian, MM.
15.
16.
17. St. Anicetus, P. M.
18.
19.
20.
21. St. Anselm, B. C. D.
22. SS. Soter and Caius, PP. MM.
23. St. George, M.
24. St. Fidelis of Sigmaringen, M.
25. St. Mark the Evangelist.
26. SS. Cletus and Marcellinus, PP., MM.
27. St. Peter Canisius, C. D.
28. St. Paul of the Cross, C.—St. Vitelis, M.
29. St. Peter, M.
30. St. Catharine of Siena, V.

MAY

1. SS. Philip and James, App.
2. St. Athanasius, B. C. D.
3. Finding of the Holy Cross—SS. Alexander, P., and others.
4. St. Monica, W.
5. St. Pius V, P. C.
6. St. John before the Latin gate.
7. St. Stanislaus, B. M.
8. Apparition of St. Michael the Archangel.
9. St. Gregory Nazianzenus, B. C. D.
10. St. Antoninus, B. C.—SS. Gordian and Epimachus, MM.
11.
12. SS. Nereus and others, MM.
13. St. Robert Bellarmine, B. C. D.
14. St. Boniface, M.
15. St. John Baptist de la Salle, C.
16. St. Ubald, Bp. C.
17. St. Pascal Baylon, C.
18. St. Venantius, M.
19. St. Peter Celestine, P. C.—St. Pudentiana, V.
20. St. Bernardine of Siena, C.
21.
22.
23.
24.
25. St. Gregory VII, P. C.—St. Urban, P. M.
26. St. Philip Neri, C.—St. Eleutherius, P. M.
27. St. Bede, C. D.—St. John, P. M.
28. St. Augustine of Canterbury, B. C.
29. St. Mary Magdalen dei Pazzi, V.
30. St. Felix, P. M.
31. St. Angela, V.—St. Petronilla, V.

JUNE

1.
2. SS. Peter and Marcellinus, MM.
3.
4. St. Francis Carraciolo, C.
5. St. Boniface, B. M.

6. St. Norbert, B. C.
7.
8.
9. SS. Primus and Felician.
10. St. Margaret, Queen, W.
11. St. Barnabas, Ap.
12. St. John of St. Facundo, C.—SS. Basilides and others, MM.
13. St. Antony of Padua, C.
14. St. Basil the Great, B. C. D.
15. St. Vitus and others, MM.
16.
17.
18. St. Ephrem, C. D.—SS. Mark and Marcellianus, MM.
19. St. Juliana, V.—SS. Gervase and Protase, MM.
20. St. Silverius, P. M.
21. St. Aloysius, C.
22. St. Paulinus, B. C.
23. Vigil of St. John the Baptist.
24. Nativity of St. John the Baptist.
25. St. William, Ab.
26. SS. John and Paul, MM.
27.
28. St. Irenaeus, B. M.
29. SS. Peter and Paul, App.
30. Commemoration of St. Paul.

JULY

1. The Most Precious Blood—Octave of St. John the Baptist.
2. The Visitation of our Lady—SS. Processus and Martinian, MM.
3. St. Leo II, P. C.
4.
5. St. Antony Zaccaria, C.
6. Octave of SS. Peter and Paul.
7. SS. Cyril and Methodius, BB., MM.
8. St. Elizabeth, Queen, W.
9.
10. The Seven Brethren, MM.
11. St. Pius, P. M.
12. St. John Gualbert, Ab.—SS. Nabor and Felix, MM.
13. St. Anacletus, P. M.
14. St. Bonaventure, B. C. D.
15. St. Henry, C.
16. Our Lady of Mount Carmel.
17. St. Alexius, C.
18. St. Camillus of Lellis—St. Symphorosa and her Sons, MM.
19. St. Vincent de Paul, C.
20. St. Jerome Emilian, C.—St. Margaret, V. M.
21. St. Praxedes, V.
22. St. Mary Magdalene.
23. St. Apollinaris, B. M.—St. Liberius, B. C.
24. Vigil of St. James—St. Christina, V. M.
25. St. James the Apostle—St. Christopher, M.
26. St. Anne, Mother of our Lady.
27. St. Pantaleon, M.

28. St. Nazarius and others, MM.
29. St. Martha, V.—SS. Felix and others, MM.
30. SS. Abdon and Sennen.
31. St. Ignatius, C.

AUGUST

1. St. Peter's chains.
2. St. Alphonsus, B. C. D.
3. Finding of St. Stephen, 1st martyr.
4. St. Dominic, C.
5. Dedication of our Lady of the Snow.
6. The Transfiguration of our Lord— SS. Xystus and others, MM.
7. St. Cajetan, C.—St. Donatus, B. M.
8. SS. Cyriacus and others, MM.
9. Vigil of St. Laurence—St. Romanus, M.
10. St. Laurence, M.
11. SS. Tiburtius and Susanna, MM.
12. S. Clare, V.
13. SS. Hippolytus and Cassian, MM.
14. Vigil of the Assumption—St. Eusebius, C.
15. The Assumption of our Lady.
16. St. Joachim, Father of our Lady.
17. St. Hyacinth, C.—Octave of St. Laurence.
18. St. Agapitus, M.
19. St. John Eudes, C.
20. St. Bernard, Ab. D.
21. St. Jane Frances de Chantal, W.
22. Octave of the Assumption—St. Timothy and others, MM.
23. St. Philip Benizi, C.
24. St. Bartholomew, Ap.
25. St. Louis, K. C.
26. St. Zephyrinus, P. M.
27. St. Joseph Calasanctius, C.
28. St. Augustine, B.C.D.—St. Hermes, M.
29. Beheading of St. John the Baptist —St. Sabina, M.
30. St. Rose of Lima, V.—SS. Felix and Adauctus, MM.
31. St. Raymund Nonnatus, C.

SEPTEMBER

1. St. Giles, Ab.—The Twelve Brethren, MM.
2. St. Stephen, K. C.
3.
4.
5. St. Lawrence Justinian.
6.
7.
8. Nativity of our Lady—St. Hadrian, M.
9. St. Gorgonius.
10. St. Nicholas of Tolentino.
11. SS. Protus and Hyacinth, MM.
12. Holy Name of Mary.
13.
14. Exaltation of the Holy Cross.
15. Seven Dolours of our Lady—St. Nicomedes, M.

16. SS. Cornelius and Cyprian, BB., MM. — SS. Euphemia and others, MM.
17. Stigmata of St. Francis.
18. St. Joseph of Cupertino, C.
19. St. Januarius and others, MM.
20. St. Eustace and others, MM.
21. St. Matthew, Ap.
22. St. Thomas of Villanova, B. C.— SS. Maurice and others, MM.
23. St. Linus, P. M.
24. Our Lady of Ransom.
25.
26. SS. Cyprian and Justina, MM.
27. SS. Cosmas and Damian.
28. St. Wenceslaus.
29. Dedication of St. Michael.
30. St. Jerome, C. D.

OCTOBER

1. St. Remigius, B. C.
2. The Holy Guardian Angels.
3. St. Thérèse of the Child Jesus.
4. St. Francis of Assisi, C.
5. St. Placid and others, MM.
6. St. Bruno, C.
7. The Holy Rosary—St. Mark. P. C. —St. Sergius and others, MM.
8. St. Bridget, W.
9. St. Denys and others, MM.
10. St. Francis Borgia, C.
11.
12.
13. St. Edward, K. C.
14. St. Callistus, P. M.
15. St. Teresa, V.
16. St. Hedwige, W.
17. St. Margaret Mary Alacoque, V.
18. St. Luke the Evangelist.
19. St. Peter of Alcantara, C.
20. St. John Cantius.
21. St. Hilarion, Ab.—St. Ursula and others, VV., MM.
22.
23.
24. St. Raphael, Archangel.
25. SS. Chrysanthus and Darias, MM.
26. St. Evaristus, P. M.
27. Vigil of SS. Simon and Jude.
28. SS. Simon and Jude, App.
29.
30.
31. Vigil of All Saints.

NOVEMBER

1. All Saints.
2. All Souls.
3.
4. St. Charles Borromeo, B. C.—SS. Vitalis and Agricola, MM.
5.
6.
7.

8. Octave of All Saints—The Holy Crowned Martyrs.
9. Dedication of St. John Lateran— St. Theodore, M.
10. St. Andrew Avellino, C.—SS. Try· phon and others, MM.
11. St. Martin, B. C.
12. St. Martin I, P. M.—St. Mennas, M.
13. St. Didacus, C.
14. St. Josaphat, B. M.
15. St. Gertrude, V.
16.
17. St. Gregory Thaumaturgus, B. C.
18. Dedication of the Basilicas of St. Peter and St. Paul.
19. St. Elizabeth, Queen, W.—St. Pontianus, P. M.
20. St. Felix of Valois, C.
21. Presentation of our Lady.
22. St. Cecilia, V. M.
23. St. Clement, P. M.—St. Felicitas, M.
24. St. John of the Cross, C. D.—St. Chrysogonus, M.
25. St. Catherine, V. M.
26. St. Sylvester, Ab.—St. Peter, M.
27.
28.
29. Vigil of St. Andrew—St. Saturninus, M.
30. St. Andrew the Apostle.

DECEMBER

1.
2. St. Bibiana, V. M.
3. S. Francis Xavier, C.
4. St. Peter Chrysologus. B. C. D.— St. Barbara, V. M.
5. St. Sabbas, Ab.
6. St. Nicholas, B. C.
7. St. Ambrose, B. C. D.
8. The Immaculate Conception of our Lady.
9.
10. St. Melchiades, P. M.
11. St. Damasus, P. C.
12.
13. St. Lucy, V. M.
14.
15. Octave of the Immaculate Conception.
16. St. Eusebius, B. M.
17.
18.
19.
20. Vigil of St. Thomas.
21. St. Thomas the Apostle.
22.
23.
24. Christmas Eve.
25. The Nativity of our Lord.
26. St. Stephen, 1st martyr.
27. St. John the Evangelist, Ap.
28. Holy Innocents, MM.
29. St. Thomas of Canterbury, B. M.
30.
31. St. Sylvester, P. C.

(4) **The Orthodox Calendar**

The ecclesiastical year of the Orthodox Church begins on 1st September and it is called 'Indiction.' (See 9 below.) On 14th November fasting before Christmas starts. Christmas Festivals end with Epiphany. Then, one to four Sundays follow (it depends on the date of Easter Sunday) and 'Triodion' and the movable feasts begin, which consist of two parts: (a) a period of four Sundays, which is as an introduction to the Lent before Easter, and (b) the whole period of seven weeks of the Lent. The most important Sundays of the second period are: the first, in which the reintroduction of the Holy Ikons is celebrated. The third in which the Holy Cross is worshipped for spiritual strengthening of those who fast. And Palm Sunday, after which the Great and Holy Week begins. Special services, called the 'Akathist Hymn,' are held in honour of Holy Virgin in the afternoons of the first five Fridays of Lent. Easter falls on the first Sunday after the full moon of the Spring Equinox, but if it happens to coincide with the Jewish Passover it is postponed to the next Sunday. This is one reason for the differences in the dating of Easter Sunday between Eastern and Western Churches. The weeks between Easter and Pentecost are Paschal time. The Ascension of Our Lord is forty days after Easter and always on Thursday. On the fiftieth day after Easter the feast of Pentecost is celebrated and it is followed by Trinity Monday. The Sunday next is the day of All Saints. The first fortnight in August is dedicated to the Holy Mother of God, when special services are held and it is kept as a fasting period.

With the above runs the Calendar of Festivals—given below in abridged form owing to lack of space—fixed to particular days of the months.

CALENDAR OF FESTIVALS

(Proper names transliterated from modern Greek orthography)

JANUARY

1. Circumcision. St. Basil the Great.
2.
3.
4.
5.
6. The Epiphany.
7. St. John the Baptist.
8.
9.
10. St. Gregory, Bishop of Nyssis.
11. St. Theodosius.
12.
13.
14.
15.
16.
17. St. Antonius the Great.
18. St. Athanasius and St. Cyril, Patriarchs of Alexandria.
19.
20. St. Efthymios the Great.
21. St. Maximus the Confessor.
22.
23.
24.
25. St. Gregory the Theologian.
26.
27. Removal of the Holy remains of St. John Chrysostom.
28.
29.
30. St. Basil the Great, St. Gregory the Theologian, and St. John Chrysostom.
31.

FEBRUARY

1.
2. Purification of Our Lady.
3. SS. Symeon and Anna.
4.
5.
6. St. Photius the Great, the Confessor.
7.
8.
9.
10. St. Charalambos.
11.
12.
13.
14.
15.
16.
17.
18.
19.
20.
21.
22.
23. St. Polycarpos Bishop of Smyrna.
24.
25.
26.
27.
28.
29. St. Cassianos.

1. St. Kosmas and Damianus, the Anargyroi.
2.
3.
4.
5.
6.
7. St. Kyriaki.
8.
9.
10.
11. St. Effimia.
12.
13.
14.
15.
16.
17. St. Marina.
18.
19. St. Makrina.
20. St. Elias the Prophet.
21.
22.
23.
24. St. Christine.
25. Assumption of St. Anna.
26. St. Paraskevi.
27. St. Panteleimon.
28.
29.
30.
31.

1.
2. Removal of the Holy remains of St. Stephanos the Protomartyr.
3.
4.
5.
6. The Transfiguration of Our Lord.
7.
8. St. Emilianus, Bishop of Kyzikos.
9. St. Matthias the Apostle.
10.
11.
12.
13.
14.
15. The Assumption of Our Lady.
16.
17.
18.
19.
20.
21.
22.
23.
24.
25.
26.
27.
28.
29. Beheading of St. John the Baptist.
30.
31.

1. Indiction.   St. Symeon the Stylite.
2.
3.
4.
5. St. Zacharias the Prophet.
6.
7.
8. Nativity of Our Lady.
9. St. Joachim and Anna.
10.
11.
12.
13.
14. The Exaltation of the Holy Cross.
15.
16. St. Effimia.
17.
18.
19.
20. St. Efstathius.
21.
22.
23. St. Thecla the Martyr.
24.
25.
26. Assumption of St. John the Evangelist.
27.
28.
29.
30.

1.
2. St. Cyprianus.
3. St. Dionysios the Areopagite.
4. St. Herotheos Bishop of Athens.
5.
6.
7.
8.
9.
10.
11.
12.
13.
14.
15.
16.
17.
18. St. Luke the Apostle and Evangelist.
19.
20. St. Artemios.
21.
22.
23. St. Jacobus the Brother of Our Lord.
24.
25.
26. St. Demetrius.
27. St. Nestorius.
28.
29.
30.
31. St. Stachios the Apostle, first Bishop of Byzantium.

NOVEMBER

1. SS. Kosmas and Damianos.
2.
3.
4.
5.
6.
7.
8. SS. Michael and Gabriel the Archangels.
9.
10.
11.
12.
13. St. John Chrysostom, Archbishop of Constantinople.
14. St. Phillipos the Apostle.
15.
16. St. Matthew the Apostle and Evangelist.
17.
18.
19.
20.
21. Presentation of Our Lady.
22. St. Phillimon the Apostle.
23. St. Amphilochius, Bishop of Ikonium.
24.
25.
26.
27.
28.
29.
30. St. Andrew the Protoklite.

DECEMBER

1.
2.
3.
4. St. Barbara.   St. John of Damascus.
5. St. Savva.
6. St. Nicholas, Bishop of Myra.
7. St. Ambrosius, Bishop of Mediolana.
8.
9. Conception of St. Anna.
10.
11.
12. St. Spyridon, Bishop of Trimythoundos.
13.
14.
15. St. Elefterios.
16.
17. St. Dionysios, Archbishop of Aegina.
18.
19.
20. St. Ignatius.
21.
22. St. Anastasia.
23.
24.
25. The Nativity of Our Lord.
26.
27. St. Stephen, First Martyr.
28.
29.
30.
31.

(5) *The Moslem Era* begins A.D. 16 July 622 (The Hegira).   The year consists of twelve lunar months.

(6) *The Coptic Era* begins A.D. 29 Aug. 284.

(7) *The Parsee Era* begins A.D. 16 June 632.

(8) *The Japanese Era* begins 11 Feb. 660 B.C.

(9) *The Roman Indiction* was a cycle of fifteen years introduced by Constantine for purposes of taxation.   The indictions began on A.D. 1 Sept. 312.

(10) *The Olympiad* was a four-year period used for dating by the Greeks.   The first year of the first Olympiad was 776 B.C.

(11) *The French Republican Era* lasted from 22 Sept. 1792 until 31 Dec. 1805.   The first days of the months of the French Revolutionary Calendar as they occurred in the year I of the Era are shown in the preceding secular Calendar; in calculating Gregorian dates from Republican dates the following must be borne in mind:

(*a*) The Republican Calendar was only in actual use from 26 Nov. 1793 till 31 Dec. 1805.

(*b*) The Republican Year begins with the first Vendémiaire.

(*c*) In leap years a sixth Sansculottide was added in Sept.   Therefore between 28 Feb. and 22 Sept. 1796 it is necessary to *subtract* one day from each date according to the Gregorian Calendar.

(*d*) On the other hand the year VIII was a leap year, whereas the Gregorian year 1800 was not.   Therefore from 23 Sept. 1800 until 31 Dec. 1805 it is necessary to *add* one day to each Gregorian date except in the period 28 Feb.–23 Sept. 1804 (XII), when the clash between the Gregorian and Republican leap years cancels it out.

A

Aachen or **Aix-la-Chapelle**, Germany. Founded by Romans, A.D. 125. Charlemagne made it his capital, 795. He *d.* and was buried here, 814. Liberated by Americans, 20 Oct. 1944. For treaties signed here *see* AIX - LA - CHAPELLE, TREATIES OF.

Aarau, Treaty of, 11 Aug. 1712, ended the Second Villmergen War. Helvetic republic proclaimed at, 1798.

Aargau. Swiss canton in the basin of the River Aare, which had been conquered by the Franks under Clovis (*c.* 465–511), is first mentioned, as a county, 763. Ceded some south-western territory to Berne in the fourteenth century. The canton was subject to the Swiss Confederacy, from 1415. Joined, 1798, the Helvetic Confederation, and from then until 1803 was divided into two cantons of Baden and A. Joined the Sonderbund (separate Catholic confederation), 1845.

Abadan. First refinery of Anglo-Persian, later Anglo-Iranian, Oil Co. at, 1909. Evacuated by British technicians, 29 Oct. 1951. New refinery at Isle of Grain, Kent, opened to replace it, Nov. 1952. Under agreement ratified by the Shah, 29 Oct. 1954, and signed between the Persian Government, British Petroleum Oil Co. (formerly Anglo-Iranian), National Iranian Oil Co., and seventeen leading international oil companies, British technicians returned to A. *See* PERSIA.

Abbaye Prison (Paris), France. Built 1631–5. Massacre at, 2–3 Sept. 1792.

Abbeville, France. Treaties of A. (1) between Henry III of England and Louis IX of France renouncing *continental* Normandy was made at Paris, 28 May 1258, and confirmed in London, 1259. (2) Between Henry VIII and Francis I, 1527.

Abdications of Sovereigns (including forced abdications and 'desertions'):

Diocletian, Roman emperor A.D.	305
Stephen II of Hungary	1131
Albert the Bear of Brandenburg	1142
Wladislaw III of Poland	1206
Pope Celestine V (forced)	13 Dec. 1294
John Balliol of Scotland	1296
Otho (of Bavaria) of Hungary	1309
Edward II of England (forced)	1327
Richard II of England (forced)	29 Sept. 1399
Eric VII of Denmark	1439
Pope Felix V	1449
Charles V, as Emperor of Germany	25 Oct. 1555
,, as King of Spain	16 Jan. 1556
Mary Queen of Scots (forced)	24 July 1567
Christina of Sweden	16 June 1654
John Casimir of Poland (forced)	1668
James II of England (fled)	11 Dec. 1688
Frederick Augustus II of Poland	1704
Philip V of Spain (resumed)	1724
Victor Amadeus of Sardinia	1730
Charles of Naples	1759
Stanislaw II of Poland (forced)	1795
Charles Emmanuel IV of Sardinia	4 June 1802
Francis II of Germany, who became Emperor of Austria	11 Aug. 1804
Charles IV of Spain, in favour of his son	19 Mar. 1808
Charles IV of Spain, in favour of Bonaparte (*see* SPAIN)	1 May 1808
Joseph Bonaparte of Naples (for Spain)	1 June 1808
Gustavus IV of Sweden	29 Mar. 1809
Louis Bonaparte of Holland	1 July 1810
Jerome of Westphalia, Bonaparte	20 Oct. 1813
Napoleon I of France	5 Apr. 1814
Victor Emmanuel of Sardinia	13 Mar. 1821
Pedro IV of Portugal	2 May 1826
Charles X of France	2 Aug. 1830
Pedro I of Brazil	7 Apr. 1831
Dom Miguel of Portugal (fled)	26 May 1834
William I of Holland	8 Oct. 1840
Louis Philippe of France	24 Feb. 1848
Louis Charles of Bavaria	21 Mar. 1848
Ferdinand of Austria	2 Dec. 1848
Charles Albert of Sardinia	23 Mar. 1849
Leopold II of Tuscany	21 July 1859
Bernhard of Saxe-Meiningen	20 Sept. 1866
Isabella II of Spain	25 June 1870
Amadeus I of Spain	11 Feb. 1873
Prince Alexander of Bulgaria (forced)	7 Sept. 1886
Milan, King of Serbia	3 Mar. 1889
Pedro II of Brazil (forced)	15 Nov. 1889
Oscar, of Norway and Sweden, recognized Norwegian independence; Norway as separate state	27 Oct. 1905
Abdul Hamid II, Sultan of Turkey (forced)	27 Apr. 1909
Manoel of Portugal (forced)	4 Oct. 1910
P'u-yi of China	12 Feb. 1912
Nicholas of Montenegro Left his country	1916
Dethroned	Apr. 1918
Nicholas II of Russia	Mar. 1917
Constantine of Greece	12 June 1917

1

Restored   Dec. 1920
Abdicated again   27 Sept. 1922
Ferdinand I of Bulgaria   4 Oct. 1918
Wilhelm II of Germany   9 Oct. 1918
Karl of Austria   11 Nov. 1918
Mohammed VI of Turkey   17 Nov. 1922
George II of Greece (forced)

                               25 Mar. 1924
Hussein, King of the Hedjaz 5 Oct. 1924
Ali, King of the Hedjaz (forced)

                               19 Dec. 1925
Amanullah, Khan of Afghanistan
(forced)   twice in 1929
Alfonso XIII of Spain   11 Apr. 1932
Prajadhipok of Siam   2 Mar. 1935
Hailé Selassié of Abyssinia
Fled   1 May 1936
Restored   5 Apr. 1941
Edward VIII of Great Britain

                               11 Dec. 1936
Zog of Albania   8 Apr. 1939
Carol II of Rumania   Sept. 1940
Regent Miklós Horthy of Hungary
(forced)   15 Oct. 1944
Peter II of Yugoslavia (forced)

                               Nov. 1945
Victor Emmanuel of Italy   9 May 1946
Umberto of Italy   12 June 1946
Simeon of Bulgaria   Sep. 1946
Michael of Rumania (forced)

                               29 Dec. 1947
Wilhelmina of Holland   Sept. 1948
Leopold III of Belgium   July 1951
Farouk of Egypt   26 July 1952
Talal I of Jordan   Aug. 1952
Ahmed Fuad II of Egypt   June 1953

Abduction, defined and punishable in the U.K. under the Criminal Law Consolidation Act, 1861; Illegal Practices Act, 1883; and Criminal Law Amendment Act, 1885.

Aberdeen, Scotland, built *c.* 893, made a royal burgh by William the Lion, 1179. Chartered by Robert the Bruce, 1319. Burned by English, 1336. St. Machars Cathedral, 1357–1527. King's College founded by Bishop Elphinstone, 1494. Marischal College, 1593. The two colleges united, 1860. Cathedral restored, 1869.

Aberystwyth, Wales. Castle founded by Gilbert Strongbow, 1109. Town incorporated by Edward I. Castle used by Charles I as a mint during civil war, and demolished, 1647. College opened, 1872. Welsh National Library, 1911. *See* WALES, UNIVERSITY OF.

Abingdon, Berks. Monastery founded *c.* 675 by Cissa. Burned by Danes *c.* 871. Grammar school founded, 1563. Held by Essex against Charles I, 1645. Defenders put prisoners to death without trial, hence term 'A. Law.'

Abjuration, Oath of, was required to be sworn by all entering on certain public offices after 1688 (but especially up to 1702), denying the claims of the house of Stuart. Regulated by the Promissory Oaths Act, 1868. *See* NONJURORS.

Abjuration of the Realm, a self-imposed sentence of exile following confession of a crime on account of which the criminal had taken sanctuary. A statute of 1593 required Roman Catholics and Dissenters in certain contingencies to forswear the realm, but the whole procedure of sanctuary and A. was abolished in the reign of James I (1603–25).

Åbo, Treaty of, 18 Aug. 1743. Sweden ceded part of Finland to Russia.

Abolitionists (U.S.A.). Party opposed to slavery. First congress, 1774, but party only became active from 1832 onwards. Merged with the Republican Party, 1868.

Abominable Snowman. Footprints described by Col. Howard-Bury, leader of Everest Expedition, 1921, found at 21,000 feet. Further footprints seen in Burma, 1936. F. Smythe photographed footprints in the Himalaya, 1937, but these proved to belong to the bear *Ursus arctos pruinosus.* Tilman found footprints in the Karakorum, 1937. E. Shipton, leader of the Everest Reconnaissance Expedition, photographed and described footprints, Dec. 1951. Similar prints seen by members of Swiss Everest Expedition June 1952.
A special expedition set out in search of the A. S., 1954, but its findings were inconclusive.

Abrantes, Treaty of, 29 Nov. 1807, ratified at Madrid after which it is sometimes named. *See* PORTUGAL.

Abruzzi National Park, nature reserve around the Gran Sasso d'Italia, founded, 1922.

Abydos, Asia Minor, was the eastern end of the pontoon bridge thrown across the Dardanelles by the Persian Army of Xerxes, 480 B.C.

Abydos, Upper Egypt, contains a ruined temple of Seti I, where, in 1817, was found the Table of A., key to the genealogy of early Pharaohs.

Abyssinia. *See* ETHIOPIA.

Academies, from Academia, a grove outside Athens (sacred to the hero Academus). Plato first taught philosophy here, *c.* 387 B.C. Ptolemy Soter founded an academy at Alexandria, 314 B.C. First philosophical academy in France founded by Père Mersenne at Paris, 1635. The following are the principal A. with the dates when they were founded. The A. of Great Britain are also under their various titles.

Ancona, Caliginosi, 1642.
Berlin, Akademie der Wissenschaften, 1700; Architecture, 1799.

Bologna, Ecclesiastical, 1687; Mathematics, 1690; Sciences and Arts, 1712.
Boston, Arts and Sciences, 1780.
Brescia, Erranti, 1626. Brescia Academy, 1801.
Brest and Toulon, Military, 1682.
Brussels, Académie Royale, 1773.
Bucharest, Rumanian Academy, 1866.
Caen, Belles-Lettres, 1705.
Chicago, U.S.A., Sciences, 1865.
Connecticut, Arts and Sciences, 1799.
Copenhagen, Sciences, 1742.
Cortona, Antiquities, 1726.
Dublin, Royal Irish Academy, 1782.
Erfurt, Saxony, Sciences, 1754.
Faenza, Philoponi, 1612.
Florence, Fine Arts, 1270; Platonica, 1474 (dissolved, 1521); Accademia della Crusca, 1582; del Cimento, 1657; Georgofili, 1752 (agricultural); Antiquities, 1807.
Geneva, Medical, 1715.
Genoa, Painting, etc., 1751; Sciences, 1783.
Göttingen, Gesellschaft der Wissenschaften, 1752.
Haarlem, The Sciences, 1760.
Helsinki, Societas Scientiarum.
Istanbul (formerly Constantinople), Academy of, 1851.
Leipzig, Academy of, 1768.
Leningrad, Academy of the U.S.S.R. (formerly the Imperial Academy), 1728.
Lisbon, Portuguese Academy, 1779.
London, Royal Society, 1662 (charter granted); Royal Academy of Arts, 1768; Royal Academy of Music, 1822.
Lyons, Sciences, 1700.
Madrid, Royal Spanish, 1713; History, 1730; Painting and the Arts, 1753.
Mannheim, Sculpture, 1775.
Mantua, Vigilanti (Sciences), 1704.
Marseilles, Belles-Lettres, 1726.
Massachusetts, Arts and Sciences, 1780.
Milan, Sciences, 1719; Academy of, 1838; Architecture, 1880.
Munich, Arts and Sciences, 1759.
Naples, Rossana, 1540; Secretorum Naturae, 1560; Sciences, 1695; Herculaneum, 1755.
Newhaven, U.S.A., Connecticut Academy of Arts and Sciences, 1799.
New York, Literature and Philosophy, 1814; Sciences, 1818; National Academy, 1863.
Nîmes, Royal Academy, 1682.
Oslo, Academy, 1837.
Padua, Poetry, 1610; Academy of, 1779; Sciences, 1792.
Palermo, Fine Arts, 1300; Medical, 1645.
Paris, Académie Française, 1637; Académie Royale de Peinture et de Sculpture, 1648; Académie de Peinture, 1648; Académie des Inscriptions, 1663; Académie Royale des Sciences, 1666; Académie Royale d'Architecture, 1671. All these A. at Paris were suppressed, 1793, and in 1795 one large one, the Institut National, was founded. This in 1816 was split up in four classes by Louis XVIII: (a) Académie Française; (b) Académie des Inscriptions et Belles Lettres; (c) Académie des Sciences; (d) Académie des Beaux-Arts, and in 1832 Académie des Sciences Morales et Politiques.
Parma, Innominati, 1550.
Peking, Academia Sinica (refounded 1949).
Pennsylvania, Academy of Fine Arts, 1805.
Perugia, Insensati, 1561.
Philadelphia, U.S.A., Arts and Sciences, 1749; Natural Sciences, 1812.
Rome, Lincei, 1609; Umoristi, 1611; Fantastici, 1625; Infecondi, 1653; Painting, 1656; Arcadi, 1656; English, 1752; Nuovi Lincei, 1847.
Stockholm, Sciences, 1741; Belles-Lettres, 1753; Agriculture, 1781.
Toulon, Military, 1682.
Trondhjem, Academy, 1760.
Turin, Sciences, 1757; Fine Arts, 1778.
Upsala, Royal Society, 1720.
Venice, Medical, 1701; Academy, 1760.
Verona, Music, 1543; Sciences, 1780.
Vienna, Kaiserliche Akademie, 1487; Sculpture and Arts, 1705; Surgery, 1783; Oriental, 1810; Sciences, 1847.
Warsaw, Languages and History, 1753.
Washington, D.C., Smithsonian Institution, 1846; National Geographical Society, 1888; International Academy of Sciences, Arts and Letters, 1910.

Acadia (Acadie). Name changed to Nova Scotia (q.v.), 1713.

Acarnania, Greece. People of A. engaged in Peloponnesian War, 429 B.C. against Ambracians, conquered by Spartans, 390 B.C.; by Macedonians, 225 B.C. Defeated by Romans, 197 B.C. Subjugated, 145 B.C., and was included in the province of Achaea.

Acclimatization, Society of, Great Britain, established, 1860. French society founded, 1854. Jardin Zoologique d'Acclimatation opened in Paris, 1860. Garden of A. for rearing English birds and fishes opened Melbourne, Australia, 1861. A. societies in New Zealand include those of Auckland (1867) and Otago (1864).

Accountants. Chartered Institute of England and Wales founded, 1880. Chartered Institute of Scotland founded, 1854. Institute established, 30 July 1870. Society established, 1872. Society of Incorporated A. and Auditors founded, 1885.

Accra. Capital of Ghana (q.v.), formerly the Gold Coast, since 1876. Railway to Kumasi completed, 1903. Achimota College, 1925, reconstituted as University College of Ghana, 1948. Anti-Nkrumah bomb outrages in 1961.

Achaeans. Hellenic tribe (or group of tribes) which played a leading part in the wars and migrations of the Heroic Age (second millennium B.C.) and eventually settled on the N. coast of the Peloponnese, where the **Achaean League** of twelve city-states, renewed in 281 B.C., undertook the liberation of its members from Macedonian hegemony. In 251 it was joined by Sicyon, then by Corinth, Sparta, and other cities not strictly belonging to Achaea, defeated the Macedonians and dominated the peninsula until its defeat by the Romans in 146 B.C., after which the Greek mainland became the Roman province (and later the Byzantine theme) of Achaea.

Acoustics. Explained by Pythagoras c. 500 B.C. Galileo's important discoveries, A.D. 1600. Speed of sound discovered by Newton, 1698. Brook Taylor's practical demonstrations of Galileo's theory, 1714. Mersenne's discovery of 1636 explained by Helmholtz, 1862.

Acre, Saint Jean d' (O.T. *Acco*; N.T. *Ptolemais*; Mod. *Akka*). Captured by Arabs, 638. By Crusaders, 1104. By Saladin, 1187. By Richard I after two years' siege, 1191. By Egyptians, 1291. After its capture by the Turks in 1517 it fell into decay. Successfully defended against Napoleon by Sir Sydney Smith, 1799. Captured by Ibrahim, son of Mehemet Ali Pasha of Egypt, 1832. Stormed by Sir Robert Stopford, 4 Nov. 1840, and returned to Turkey, 1841. Occupied by British, 23 Sept. 1918. Awarded to Arabs by U.N., but taken by the Israelis, 17 May 1948, and became part of Israel. *See* CRUSADES.

Acropolis, at Athens, consisted in the second millennium B.C. of fortifications, which together with most of the other buildings on the site were destroyed in the Persian invasion of 480. An early temple to Athene was replaced by the Erechtheum (completed 409 B.C.). The Parthenon (*q.v.*) built, 447–432, and Propylaea, built 437–433. The theatre of Dionysus on the southern slope was converted to a stone structure between 338 and 326 B.C.

Actinometer. Invented by Sir John Herschel c. 1825.

Acton Burnell, Statute of, legislating for the recovery of debt, passed, 1283.

Acts of Parliament or Statutes. Earliest mentioned Provisions of Merton, 1236. Earliest existing statute roll 6 Edward I (Statute of Gloucester).

Actuary. Institute of As. founded,

1848. International Congress, 1898. Scottish Faculty of As. established, Edinburgh, 1856. A. Society of America assembled, 24 Apr. 1890.

Addis Ababa. Founded, 1885. Made capital of Ethiopia by Emperor Menelek, 1892. Treaty with Italy signed at, 1896. Occupation by Italians, 1936. Pillage of by Italians, 19–22 Feb. 1937. Liberated by British, 5 Apr. 1941. University College of founded, 1950. New opera house completed, 1955.

Addled Parliament, 5 Apr.–7 June 1614.

Adelaide. Capital of state of S. Australia. Founded by Col. Light, who arrived 27 July 1837. Free port, 1845. University founded, 1874.

Aden. Taken by Portuguese, 1513, but captured by Turks, 1538. Independent after 1730 till occupied by the E. India Co., 19 Jan. 1839. Control transferred from Indian to British Government, 1927. Crown colony, 1 Apr. 1937. Military operations against the Hadramaut, 1939. Aden Colony (Amendment) Order, 1958, reconstituted the Legislative Council, giving more elected representation. Constitutional talks, concerning A.'s proposed membership of the S. Arabia Federation, opened in London, July 1962, and it was decided that A. should join, Aug. 1962. Riots against the proposed union, 24 Sept. 1962.

Administrations, British (since the beginning of the modern cabinet system).

Sir Robert Walpole, 1721.

George II :

Sir Robert Walpole, 1727.
John Carteret, Lord Carteret, Feb. 1742.
Hon. Henry Pelham, Nov. 1743.
William Pulteney, Earl of Bath, 10–12 Feb. 1746.
Hon. Henry Pelham, Feb. 1746.
Thomas Pelham Holles, Duke of Newcastle, Apr. 1754.
William Pitt, Nov. 1756.
Thomas Pelham Holles, Duke of Newcastle, and William Pitt as Secretary of State, known as the Coalition Ministry, 19 June 1757.

George III :

Thomas Pelham Holles, Duke of Newcastle, 1760.
Earl of Bute, May 1762.
George Grenville, Apr. 1763.
Marquess of Rockingham, July 1765.
William Pitt, Earl of Chatham, Aug. 1766.
Duke of Grafton, Dec. 1767.
Frederick, Lord North, Jan. 1770.
Marquess of Rockingham, Mar. 1782.
Earl of Shelburne, July 1782.
Duke of Portland, Lord North, and Charles James Fox, known as Coalition Ministry, Apr. 1783.
William Pitt, the Younger, Dec. 1783.

Henry Addington, Mar. 1801.
William Pitt, May 1804.
Lord Grenville ('All the Talents' Ministry),
  Feb. 1806.
Duke of Portland, Mar. 1807.
Spencer Perceval, Oct. 1809.
Earl of Liverpool, June 1812.
George IV:
Earl of Liverpool, Jan. 1820.
George Canning, Apr. 1827.
Visc. Goderich, Sept. 1827.
Duke of Wellington, Jan. 1828.
William IV:
Earl Grey, Nov. 1830.
Visc. Melbourne, July 1834.
Provisional government during absence of
  Sir Robert Peel, Nov. 1834.
Sir Robert Peel, Dec. 1834.
Visc. Melbourne, Apr. 1835.
Victoria:
Visc. Melbourne, June 1837.
Sir Robert Peel, Sept. 1841.
Lord John Russell, July 1846.
Earl of Derby, Feb. 1852.
Earl of Aberdeen, Dec. 1852.
Visc. Palmerston, Feb. 1855.
Earl of Derby, Feb. 1858.
Visc. Palmerston, June 1859.
Lord John Russell, Oct. 1865.
Earl of Derby, June 1866.
Benjamin Disraeli, Feb. 1868.
William Ewart Gladstone, Dec. 1868.
Benjamin Disraeli, Earl of Beaconsfield,
  Feb. 1874.
William Ewart Gladstone, Apr. 1880.
Marquess of Salisbury, June 1885.
William Ewart Gladstone, Feb. 1886.
Marquess of Salisbury, July 1886.
William Ewart Gladstone, Aug. 1892
  (Gladstone resigned Mar. 1894), suc-
  ceeded by Earl of Rosebery.
Marquess of Salisbury, June 1895.
Edward VII:
Arthur James Balfour, 12 July 1902.
Sir Henry Campbell-Bannerman, 5 Dec.
  1905.
Herbert Henry Asquith, 16 Apr. 1908.
George V:
Herbert Henry Asquith, Dec. 1910.
David Lloyd George, 7 Dec. 1916.
Andrew Bonar Law, 23 Oct. 1922.
Stanley Baldwin, 22 May 1923.
James Ramsay MacDonald, 22 Jan. 1924.
Stanley Baldwin, 4 Nov. 1924.
James Ramsay MacDonald, 8 June 1929.
James Ramsay MacDonald, 24 Aug. 1931.
Stanley Baldwin, 6 June 1935.
Edward VIII:
Stanley Baldwin, 22 Jan. 1936.
George VI:
Stanley Baldwin, 4 Dec. 1936.
Arthur Neville Chamberlain, 28 May 1937.
Winston Spencer Churchill (Coalition),
  10 May 1940.
Winston Spencer Churchill (without

Labour Party), 26 May 1945.
Clement Richard Attlee, 27 July 1945.
Clement Richard Attlee. 23 Feb. 1950.
Winston Spencer Churchill, 25 Oct. 1951.
Elizabeth II:
Winston Spencer Churchill, 8 Feb. 1952.
Anthony Eden, 7 Apr. 1955.
Harold Macmillan, 13 Jan. 1957.
Earl of Home (Sir A. Douglas-Home),
  19 Oct. 1963.

Admiral. Word derived from the
Arabic *amir* or *emir* (*lord* or *commander*:
cf. *amir-al-bahr*, commander of the sea)
and was first used in England in the
fourteenth century under Edward III,
though the office it denotes is much older.
In the U.S.A. the A. was declared the
'ranking officer' in the navy, 2 Mar. 1867;
rank abolished, 24 Jan. 1873, but revived
in 1899, when Admiral Dewey was
appointed. *See* famous A.s listed under
SOLDIERS AND SAILORS; and SOLDIERS,
SAILORS, AND AIRMEN OF THIS CENTURY.

Admiralty. A commission for discharg-
ing the duties of the Lord High Admiral
whose office certainly dates from 1405.
and probably earlier; it was first placed
in commission, 1628. Administrative
work of the A., whether in commission or
not, was done by the Navy Board in
stituted in 1546; it performed the duties
originally performed by the Keepers of
the King's Ships the first of whom was
appointed in 1214; the Navy Board was
abolished in 1832. The last Lord High
Admiral (1827–8) was the Duke of
Clarence, later William IV. Under proposals made in July 1963 for co-ordinating
the three service ministries, the sovereign
would adopt the title of Lord High
Admiral, which would be revived for
the purpose.

Coastguards, now under the orders of the
Board of Trade, were an A. service from
1858 to 1923. The number of Lords
Commissioners has varied from time to
time, but the last major reorganization was
that of 1929, when the seventh Lord
(Parliamentary and Financial Secretary)
was included in the patent.

For long the A. had no permanent
quarters, but during the Commonwealth
it functioned in York House (where
Villiers Street now is) and remained there
until the reign of James II. Under
William III it moved to the present site,
then known as Wallingford House, Whitehall, which was rebuilt, 1723–5, and a
separate residence for the First Sea Lord
added, 1786–91. From 1786 to 1832 the
Navy Board (*see* above) occupied Somerset House, and their successors could not
all be accommodated in the Whitehall
building until 1873. The newest part of
the A. proper was erected 1891–1906. It

was severely damaged by enemy air action, 16 Apr. 1941, and its signal office ceased for a while to function; consequently a command post known as the A. Citadel was built at the corner of St. James's Park, near the E. end of the Mall.

Admiralty Arch erected, as a memorial to Queen Victoria, 1910.

Admiralty Court ceased to have jurisdiction in naval disciplinary affairs under the terms of the Naval Discipline Act, 1866, its only connection with naval matters being its capacity as a Prize Court as defined by the Judicature Acts of 1873 and 1875. (*See also* PROBATE COURT.) Criminal cases were transferred from it to the Central Criminal Court in 1836.

Admiralty Islands. Discovered by Dutch, 1616. Occupied by Germany, 1885. Seized by Australian troops, 1914, and since 1919 administered by Australia as a mandated territory. Taken by Japanese, 1942; retaken by Americans, 1944.

'Admonition to the Parliament.' Puritan demand for the abolition of episcopacy presented to the House of Commons, 1572. A second pamphlet drawn up and suppressed, 11 June 1573.

Adowa or **Adua**, capital of Tigré, Ethiopia. Ethiopians inflicted crushing defeat on Italians, 1 Mar. 1896. Taken by Italians, 6 Oct. 1935. Recaptured by British and Ethiopian troops, Apr. 1941.

Adrianople (Turk. **Edirne**). Old town enlarged by Emperor Hadrian (*d.* A.D. 138). Constantine I defeated Licinius near, 3 July 323; Valens defeated and slain by Goths, 378; seized by Turks under Murad I, 1361; their capital until 1453; captured by Russians, 20 Aug. 1829; restored, 14 Sept. 1829; occupied by Russians, 20 Jan. 1878. During Balkan Wars, Oct. 1912–Aug. 1913, surrendered to Bulgarians after five months' siege, 26 Mar. 1913; recaptured by Turks, 18 July 1913.

Adrianople, Peace of. Ended Russo-Turkish War, 14 Sept. 1829.

Adulite Monument, an inscription on a marble seat found at Adulis (now Zula or Thulla on the coast of Eritrea near Massawa) referring in Greek to Ptolemy Euergetes, King of Egypt, 246–221 B.C., by Cosmas of Alexandria in the first half of the sixth century A.D.

Advertisements, Book of. A book of ecclesiastical discipline put in force by Archbishop Parker, 1565. It caused great controversy, and is generally taken as marking the beginning of the persecution of Puritans by the Church of England.

Advocate, The Lord, also **King's** or **Queen's** (Scotland). Office created *c.*

1480 by James III. First mentioned as 'Lord' A., 1598.

Advocate General or **King's Advocate** (England). Office vacant since 1872.

Advocate's Library (Edinburgh). Established 1682 by Sir George MacKenzie of Rosehaugh. Absorbed by National Library of Scotland, 1925.

Aediles. Minor Roman magistrates to superintend finance, sanitation, police, etc. First appointed, 494 B.C. A higher rank of A., Curule A., first appointed, 367 B.C. *See* ROMAN REPUBLIC.

Aegina. Ancient island republic in the Saronic Gulf. Independent till *c.* 456 B.C., when it was subjugated by Athens.

Aemilian Way, giving its name to the region of Emilia, was named after its builder, the consul M. Aemilius Lepidus, at whose orders it was begun in 187 B.C.

Aerial Warfare. *See* AVIATION.

Aerodynamics. Chair instituted at Imperial College, London, 1920.

Aeronautical Society of Great Britain. Established, 12 Jan. 1866.

Aeroplanes. *See* AVIATION.

Aether, a putative fine substance first so named by Leibnitz in 1671; a thesis of Kant, 1755, presupposed A., while Thomas Young in 1801 regarded it as the vehicle of light. Michelson and Morley, in 1881 and 1887, tried and failed to find evidence of an A.-drift at the earth's surface.

Affiliation. Process in England governed by the Bastardy Acts, 1845, 1873, and 1923, and the Affiliation Order Act, 1914.

Afforestation. Forestry Act, 1919, provides for acquisition and A. of land in U.K. Amplified by Forestry Act, 1927. Crown forests transferred to Forestry Commission, 1924.

Afghanistan. Invaded by Alexander the Great, 330 B.C. Unsuccessful Roman attempts to subjugate, 305–255 B.C. Tatar dynasty, A.D. 907. Part of Moghul Empire, 1525. Conquered by Persia, 1737. Became independent under Durrani dynasty, 1747. First Afghan War, 1838–42. Massacre of British at, and disastrous retreat from Kabul, 1841–2. Kabul captured by British, Sept. 1842. Britain helps Afghans by naval support against Persia, 1854. Second Afghan War, Sept. 1878–Nov. 1890. Relief of Kandahar, Aug. 1880. Amir Habibullah murdered, Feb. 1919. His son Amanullah invades India, May–Aug. 1919 (Third Afghan War). Treaty, Nov. 1921. Treaty with U.S.S.R., 31 Aug. 1926. Amanullah dethroned, 1929. New constitution, 1931. Kabul University founded, 1932. Frontier villages bombed by British, Aug. 1933. King Nadir Shah assassinated,

Nov. Succeeded by son, Zahir Shah. Joins League of Nations, 1934. Mutual non-aggression pact with Persia, Iraq, and Turkey, July 1937. Admitted U.N.O., 1946. New boundary agreed with U.S.S.R., June 1946. Loan of 100 million dollars from U.S.S.R., 28 June 1956. U.S. grant for the development of civil aviation in A., 29 June 1956.

Africa Company, Royal, or Guinea Company of Merchants, founded under Charles II, 27 Sept. 1672. Abolished 7 May 1821, when the Crown took possession of all its settlements, forts, and trading posts, etc. Other companies for exploiting the African trade had previously been formed under royal protection in 1588, and in the reigns of Charles I and James I.

Africa, German East. *See* TANGANYIKA.

Africa, North. *See* ALGIERS; TUNISIA; MOROCCO; LIBYA; CARTHAGE.

Africa, South. *See* SOUTH AFRICA, UNION OF.

African Coast, Early Settlements, etc.
Portuguese: Ceuta, 1415. Guinea voyages begun, 1426. Senegal River, 1445. Sierra Leone, 1460. Gold Coast, 1469. Fernando Po, 1481. Elmina, 1482. Congo, 1484. Dias discovers Cape of Good Hope, 1486. Vasco da Gama explores S.E. coast on way to India, 1497–9. Sofata occupied, 1505. Mozambique, 1507.
French: St. Louis, 1626.
English: Cormantine, 1618. Fort James, 1663. Cape Coast Castle, 1672.
Dutch: St. Thomé, 1637–48. Cape Town, 1652.
Prussia: Fredericksburg, 1682.

African Exploration (Interior). Bruce, 1768–73, to discover sources of Nile. Mungo Park: (1) 1795; (2) 1805, to discover the course of the Niger. Livingstone, 1840–73, Great African Lakes area. Stanley, 1868–95, in Central Africa, Nigeria, and Congo. Niger Expedition subsidized by Parliament, 1840–1. Richardson explores Sahara, 1845–6 and 1849.

Afrikander Bond. Association of Dutch-speaking S. Africans, formed 1880. After the grant of self-government to the Union of S. Africa in 1907 it was led by Hertzog, and under his leadership took an active part in the rebellion of 1914. This failure greatly weakened it.

Agadir, Morocco. Importance as a port declined after revolution of 1773. Destroyed by earthquake, 29 Feb. 1960.

Agadir Crisis. Germans sent the gunboat *Panther* to A., Aug. 1911, in support of claims in Morocco in order to test the strength of the Anglo-French Entente (*see* ENTENTE CORDIALE). Britain and France united to compel a withdrawal in 1912.

Aga Khan. Hereditary head of the Ismaili Moslems. First A. K. fled from Persia to Bombay in 1836. The third A. K. (1877–1957) was given the status of a First Class Indian Prince, 1916, for political services in World War I. Succeeded by his grandson Karim (*b.* 1936).

Age in law at which a marriage in England is valid was raised to sixteen by an Act of 1929.

Agincourt. *See* BATTLES.

Agra, Uttar Pradesh State, India. Captured by Baber, 1526, when Koh-i-Noor was among the booty. Seat of Mogul Government, 1566–1658. Taj Mahal built, 1632. Stormed by Lord Lake, 17 Oct. 1803. Withstood a long siege in Indian Mutiny during which many important buildings were destroyed, 1857. *See* INDIAN MUTINY.

Agricultural Holdings Acts (Great Britain), granted greater certainty of tenure and compensation for improvements to agricultural tenants in Scotland; passed, 1883; amended, 1900, 1908, and 1913. Act applicable to England and Wales passed, 1922. Consolidating Act for England and Wales, 1948; for Scotland, 1949.

Agriculture, Fisheries and Food, Ministries of. Board of Agriculture set up, 1793. Dissolved, 1822. Reconstituted, 1889. Became the Board of Agriculture and Fisheries, 1903. Raised to ministry status, 1919. Amalgamated with Ministry of Food, 1955. Has important responsibilities under several Acts, the most important being the Agriculture Act, 1947.

Agrigento, Sicily, lies slightly to the W. of the Greek town of Acragas (Lat. Agrigentum), which *fl.* 560–406 B.C., having been founded in 582 as a colony of Gela. Captured and sacked by the Carthaginians, 405, and again in 255; and twice by the Romans, 261 and 210. During the days of its independence as a Greek city it was famous for its architecture, and the approximate dates of construction of its principal temples are as follows:
Demeter, 500 B.C.
'Hera Lacinia,' 460.
'Castor and Pollux,' 338–210.
'Hephaestus,' after 338.
'Concordia', 440 (adapted as a Christian cathedral, A.D. 597).
Heracles, 510.
Zeus, before 405.
Asclepius, before 210.
'Athena,' 488–472.

In A.D. 828 A. was captured from the Greeks by the Saracens, and from them by the Norman Roger I, 1086. The name

'Girgenti' was adopted during the Middle Ages, but the present form came into use, 1928.

Ahmedabad, Bombay State, India. Founded, 1411. Subjugated by Akbar, 1572, it became the capital of the Moslem Kingdom of Gujarat. Stormed by British, 1780. Restored to Mahrattas same year. Reverted to British, 6 Nov. 1818. Earthquakes, 1819, 1868. Serious riots at, 11 Apr. 1919.

Ahmednagar, Maharashta State, India. Founded, A.D. 1494. Emperor Aurungzeb *d.* here, 1707. Seized by the Peishwa, 1759. Ceded to Scindiah, 1797. Taken by Wellington, 12 Aug. 1803. Finally annexed to British possessions, 13 June 1817 under Treaty of Poona.

Ahvenanmaa or **Åland Islands.** Swedish till 1809, when they were ceded to Russia at the Peace of Frederikshavn. Finnish from July 1919. Demilitarization convention, 1921, signed by Great Britain, France, Italy, and all Baltic powers except Russia.

Aigues Mortes, France. First Tour de Constance built twelfth century by Raymond V of Toulouse. Port created by St. Louis (IX), who built the present Tour de Constance, and sailed from here for the Crusades of 1248 and 1270. Walls built by Philippe le Hardi, 1272–5. Meeting of Charles V and Francis I, 1538.

Air. Discovered not to be an element by Priestley, who isolated oxygen in 1774. First vacuum by Torricelli *c.* 1646. First A. pump by O. von Guericke *c.* 1650. First liquefied by Cailletet, 1877. *See also* OXYGEN.

Air Council. Formed, 1917, on model of Army Council to administer Royal Air Force. Air Minister became Secretary of State for Air, 1920. Became subordinate to Minister of Defence, 1946.

Aircraft Carrier. First ship fitted to carry seaplanes, *Hermes,* took part in British naval manoeuvres, 1913. But the *Ark Royal* (sunk 1941) was the first A. C. to be effectively used in action.

Air Force Regiment, Royal, raised, Feb. 1942.

Air Force, Royal, formed in 1917 by amalgamation of the Royal Flying Corps and Royal Naval Air Service (*see under* FLEET AIR ARM).

Airmen of this Century. *See* SOLDIERS, SAILORS, AND AIRMEN OF THIS CENTURY.

Air Laws. Aerial Navigation Act, 1911, regulated civil air transport in Britain. Extended to naval and military areas. 1913. Allied and Associated Powers Civil Aviation Convention, 1919. Air Navigation Acts, 1920 and 1936, regulate all aspects of civilian flying.

Air Mail. *See* AVIATION.

Air Ministry. Instituted, 1922.

Air Pollution. Extensive powers to prevent this available under the Clean Air Act, 1946.

Air-Raid Precautions Act, 22 Dec. 1937.

Air Raids. First offensive use of aircraft by Italians in Libya, 1911, and by Greeks against Turks at Dardanelles, Feb. 1913. First raid on a town by German Zeppelin on Lunéville, 9 Aug. 1914. First on Britain by German aeroplanes, Dec. 1914. First British air raid on German hangars at Düsseldorf, 22 Sept. 1914. In World War II daily German A.R. on Britain began 18 June 1940. Flying bomb attacks started June 1944. Heavy allied raids on Germany from Jan. 1943 onwards. American planes dropped first atom bomb on Hiroshima (*q.v.*), 6 Aug. 1945. *See* AVIATION and WORLD WARS I and II.

Airships. Invented, 1783. Giffard's steam-driven airship first ascended, 24 Sept. 1852. Gas engine introduced, 1872. Santos Dumont's gasoline-driven airship, 1898. First Zeppelin completed, 1900. Britain abandoned development of A. after the ' R.101 ' disaster at Beauvais, 5 Oct. 1930; U.S.A. after the ' Akron,' 4 Apr. 1933, and ' Macon ' disasters, 12 Feb. 1935. The German airship ' Hindenburg ' was burnt out, May 1937, but the ' Graf Zeppelin ' remained in service until 1938.

Aix-en-Provence (Lat. **Aquae Sextiae**). Founded by Romans, 120 B.C. Destroyed by Moors and rebuilt, A.D. 796. University founded, 1409. Captured by Charles V, 1535. Church councils at, 1112, 1374, 1409, 1416, 1585, 1612.

Aix-la-Chapelle (city). *See* AACHEN.

Aix-la-Chapelle, Congress of. To regulate European affairs, 29 Sept.–21 Nov. 1818.

Aix-la-Chapelle, Treaties of:
1. Between France and Spain, 2 May 1668.
2. At end of War of Austrian Succession, 1748.

Ajaccio, Corsica. Bishopric since seventh century. Napoleon *b.* at, 15 Aug. 1769.

Akhwan. *See* SAUDI ARABIA.

Akkerman, Bessarabia (Rum. **Cetatea Alba**). Taken by Russians from Turks, 1770; restored, 1774; ceded to Russia, 1806. Russo-Turkish Treaty of, 4 Sept 1826. Rumanian 1918–40 and 1941–4. Renamed **Belgorod-Dnestrovskiy,** 1944.

Alabama, U.S.A. Explored by De Soto, 1540. Settled by French, 1702. Ceded to Great Britain by Treaty of Paris, 1763. Part occupied by Spain but retaken by U.S.A., 1813. Admitted to the Union as a state, 1819. Constitution of 1901 curtailed voting power of Negroes.

'Alabama' Dispute. A confederate warship equipped, 1862, in England did great damage to U.S. shipping till sunk by U.S.S. *Kearsarge*, 19 June 1864. Treaty of Washington set up a Court of Arbitration, which decided that Britain must pay compensation for damage to U.S.A., Dec. 1871.

Alais. *See* AI ÉS.

Alaska. First visited by Bering, 1741. Under control of Russian American company, 1799. Called Russian America till purchased by U.S.A., 1867. Boundary dispute with Britain settled by arbitration, 1903. Became an incorporated territory, 1912. Admitted to the Union as the forty-ninth state, 3 Jan. 1959.

Albania. Area in dispute between Bulgars and Byzantines till Michael Comnenus founded Despotate of Epirus, in which A. was included, 1204. Passed to the Orsini family, 1318–58. Conquered by Stephen Dushan, 1358. Scanderbeg's defence of A. against Turks, 1444–66. Venetian attempt to prevent conquest, 1466; fails, 1479–81. Finally became a Turkish province, 1748. Formation of Albanian League, 1879. Albanian nationalists support the Young Turks, 1908. Rebellion achieves independence, 1912. Recognized by European powers at London Conference, 29 July 1913. Prince William of Wied in A., 7 Mar.–3 Sept. 1914. Overrun by Austrians and Allies in World War I. Italians claim protectorate over, 1917. Mandated to Italy, 1920. Republic proclaimed with Ahmed Zogu as president, 22 Jan. 1925. Treaty of Tirana with Italy, 1927. Zogu becomes king, 1928. Italian conquest, Apr. 1939. Invaded by Greeks in Italo-Greek War, Dec. 1940. Tirana recaptured from Italians by Albanian partisans, Nov. 1944. 'Electoral' victory of Communists under Enver Hoxha, 5 Jan. 1946. Proclaimed a republic, 11 Jan. 1946. British cruisers fired at in Corfu Straits, 15 June 1946. British destroyers mined in Corfu Straits, Nov. 1946. Customs and currency union with Yugoslavia, 28 Dec. 1946; denounced by A., July 1948. Hague Court of International Justice ordered A. to pay compensation for mined destroyers (*see* above), 1951, but A. failed to do so. Admitted to U.N. 1955. Third Congress of the A. Communist Party, May–June 1956 confirmed its 'Stalinist' character. Since 1960 has been engaged in ideological quarrel with U.S.S.R. Russia broke off diplomatic relations with A., Dec. 1961.

Albany, New York. First European settlement, Fort Nassau, planted by Dutch, 1614; occupied and renamed by English, 1664. Became state capital, 1797.

Albany, Dukes of. Title first created, 1398, for cadets of the Scottish royal house, and so used until 1536; borne by Darnley (*b.* 1545), consort of Mary Stuart, 1565–7; held by James I, Charles I, and James II (*see* ENGLISH SOVEREIGNS AND THEIR CONSORTS); by Ernst August, Bishop of Osnabrück, youngest brother of George I and other Hanoverian princes, intermittently from 1716 to 1827; lastly by Leopold George Duncan Albert, youngest son of Queen Victoria (*b.* 1853), 1881–4, and by his posthumous son, Arthur Charles Edward, who became the last reigning Duke of Saxe-Coburg (abdicated, 22 Oct. 1920).

Albert Canal (Belgium). Antwerp to Liége opened, June 1939.

Albert Memorials. Albert Hall, London, opened by Queen Victoria, 29 Mar. 1871. Memorial in Hyde Park, London, opened, 3 July 1872. Albert Memorial Chapel, Windsor, opened, 1 Dec. 1875. Albert Bridge, Chelsea, opened, 28 Aug. 1873.

Alberta, Canada. Constituted a province, 1905. University opened at Edmonton, 1908. Crude oil pipeline, 1,150 miles long, from Edmonton oilfields to Superior, Wisconsin, U.S.A., completed, 1951. Extended to Sarnia, Ontario, in 1953 (643 miles), making it the longest pipeline then existing in the world.

Albigenses. Neo-Manichean sect, whose beginnings in France were discernible before 1022, and whose doctrines were denounced by councils of Arras (1025), Charroux (*c.* 1028), and Rheims (1049). Name A. first appeared *c.* 1181, derived from Albi, where they were specially numerous. Peter of Castelnau, papal legate sent to extirpate the heresy in the domains of Count Raymond VI of Toulouse, was murdered therein, 1208. Innocent III proclaimed the 'Albigensian Crusade,' 1209. Slaughtered included 20,000 inhabitants of Béziers, many having no connection with A. Raymond VII continued the struggle against the crusaders and Louis VIII; but made peace in 1229, and the persecution of A. was resumed. They disappear from history after the capture of their last stronghold, Mont Ségur, 1245.

Alcantara, Spain. Famous Roman bridge built, A.D. 105; restored, 1860. *See* KNIGHTHOOD, ORDERS OF.

Aldeburgh, Suffolk, was the first corporation in England to have a woman mayor—Mrs. Garrett-Anderson, 1908.

Aldersgate (London). Described as 'Ealdredesgate' *c.* 1000. Gate rebuilt, 1616. Pulled down, 1761.

Aldershot Camp (Hants). Formed, Apr.

1854. Enlarged, 1856. A. Command instituted, 1904. During World War II became a district and part of Southern Command.

Aldgate (London). Gate rebuilt, 1608. Pulled down, 1761. Pump renovated, 1908.

Aldine Press. Instituted by Aldo Manuzio (Aldus Manutius), at Venice, 1490. Italics first used, 1501. Aldus d. 1515. Press continued till 1597, and printed 908 different works.

Aldwych (London). Modern thoroughfare opened by Edward VII, 18 Oct. 1905.

Alençon, France. Castle built, 1026; Seized by William the Conqueror, 1048; by Henry II, 1135; restored to France, 1219. Captured by English, 1424, who were expelled, 1450.

Aleppo, Syria. Founded earlier than 2000 B.C. Taken by the Egyptians, 1460 B.C. Fell to the Crusaders under Baldwin II, A.D. 1124, and to the Tatars under Tamberlaine, 1400. Became Turkish, 1517. Suffered from an earthquake, 1812; a plague, 1827; and a cholera outbreak, 1832. *See* SYRIA.

Alès, in the Cevennes, was an important centre of the Huguenots, captured by Richelieu in 1629, who signed with them the Treaty of A., or *Edict of Grace*, depriving them of political privilege but guaranteeing their liberty of conscience. *See also* CAMISARDS.

Alessandria, Italy. Founded, 1168, and named after Pope Alexander III. Academy founded, 1562. French, 1800–1814. Cathedral built, 1823. Headquarters of Piedmontese during Lombardo-Venetian rebellion, 1848–9.

Aleutian Isles. Explored by Bering, 1768; Cook, 1778. Japanese got a foothold on Attu and Kiska islands, 1942, but were driven off by Americans, 1943.

Alexandra Land. *See* NORTHERN TERRITORY.

Alexandria, Egypt. Founded by Alexander the Great, 332 B.C. Capital of Egypt under Ptolemaic dynasty, 323–9 B.C. Captured by Caesar, 47 B.C. By Augustus, 29 B.C. Rebuilt by Hadrian, A.D. 122. Captured by Persians, 616; by Arabs, 640. Recovered and retaken, 644. Plundered by Crusaders, 1365. Taken by Turks, 1517. Captured by French, 1798. Taken by British under Abercromby and retaken by French, 1801. Taken by British under Frazer, 1807. Bombarded by British fleet, 1882. British naval base in World War II evacuated, June 1942, but re-established, Nov. 1942. Finally evacuated by British, 1947.

Alexandrian Codex. Probably a fifth-century scriptural MS. in Greek presented by Patriarch of Alexandria and Constantinople to Charles I of England, 1628. Transferred to British Museum, 1753.

Alexandrian Library. Said to have been commenced by Ptolemy Soter *c.* 284 B.C. Badly damaged by fire, 47 B.C., and again in A.D. 391. Remains finally disappeared at or immediately after Omar's conquest of Alexandria in A.D. 642.

Algebra. First Greek textbook on this subject by Diophantus of Alexandria *c.* A.D. 350. Name originates in title of an Arabic textbook *c.* A.D. 820, '*Al-jebr wa'l-muquábala*,' by Al-Khwarizmi, which was translated into Latin by Robert o Chester *c.* 1146. Study of A. reintroduced to Europe by Leonardo of Pisa, 1202. Cubic equation first solved by Tartagna, 15.5. Descartes linked A. with geometry in 1637.

Algeciras, Spain. Taken by Moors, 711; by Spaniards under Alphonso XI, 1344. Naval engagements: 1. English and Spanish fleets defeated by French, 6 July 1801; 2. Result reversed, 12 July 1801. Conference at, concerning Moroccan affairs, Jan.–Apr. 1906. Bombarded by Republican warship in the Spanish Civil War, Aug. 1936.

Algiers and Algeria. Africa. City captured from Turks by Ferdinand of Spain, 1509, but lost again, 1530. The seaboard towns of the province remained the headquarters of the Barbary pirates for three centuries thereafter. The city was bombarded by an Anglo-Dutch fleet in 1816, but the pirates were only finally suppressed when the French invaded and conquered the province in 1830. Annexed to France, Feb. 1842. Kabyle rising, 1871. From 1881 departments of Algiers, Oran, and Constantine an integral part of metropolitan France. 'Parti Populaire Algérien' banned by French Government, 1939. Allies land during World War II at A., 8 Nov. 1942. Laws as to the status of inhabitants modified by decree, 7 Mar. 1944, and new franchise laws passed, 5 Oct. 1946 and 20 Sept. 1947, the last enfranchising women. Anti-French political activity revived in A., 1944. Immense deposits of oil discovered at Hassi Messaoud, near Ouazgla, 1952—two large oilfields in production, 1957. 1 Nov. 1954: Nationalist war against France begun in A., with the object of creating an independent Moslem Algerian state. Several rival nationalist groups were involved at the beginning, but by 1957 the F.L.N. (National Liberation Front) was dominant among them, and had assumed political and military leadership of the campaign. 6 Feb. 1956: Europeans rioted when French Prime Minister Mollet visited

A. 13–14 May 1958: Army in A. occupied public buildings and formed a Committee of Public Safety. Commander-in-Chief General Salan announced he had provisionally taken over responsibility for A. His authority confirmed by Pflimlin government in Paris. 23 May 1958: A single Committee of Public Safety for all A. demanded return to power in France of de Gaulle. 1 June 1958: De Gaulle invested as Prime Minister and Salan made Delegate-General in Algeria. Civil government restored there, 12 Dec. 1958, and Salan returned to Paris. Subsequently European discontent set in and in A. there was an abortive European rising against de Gaulle, 24 Jan. 1960. 8 Jan. 1961: A referendum in France and A. approved de Gaulle's Algerian policy, but in A. itself his support was not unanimous. 19 Apr. 1961: Rebellion in A., led by Generals Challe, Zeller, and Salan. Challe surrendered 26 Apr., revolt collapsed 26 Apr., and Salan went into hiding. 28 Apr. 1961: Three French fighting units disbanded for their part in the army revolt, including the 1st Foreign Legion Parachute Regiment. May 1961: From Madrid General Salan founded O.A.S. (q.v.), subsequently responsible for acts of violence in both France and A. 31 May 1961: Generals Challe and Zeller sentenced to fifteen years' imprisonment. 20 May 1961: Franco-Algerian peace talks began at Evian—broke down 18 July. 27 Aug. 1961: Ferhat Abbas replaced as rebel premier by Ben Kheddah. 10 Sept. 1961: O.A.S. tried to assassinate de Gaulle. 11–18 Feb. 1962: Franco-Algerian peace talks in secret somewhere near the Franco-Swiss border. Terms confirmed by French Cabinet, 21 Feb. 1962, and by rebel Algerian 'parliament' meeting in Tripoli, 22–8 Feb. Further Franco-Algerian talks begun at Evian, 7 Mar. 1962. Cease-fire signed, 18 Mar. 1962, to come into force at midday 19 Mar. 1962. Provided for a caretaker administration in A., to be followed by a referendum to decide the country's future within a few months. Serious bloodshed due to O.A.S. attacks in A. and Oran following the cease-fire agreement. O.A.S. weakened by capture of Jouhaud (Mar.) and Salan (Apr.). 17 June 1962: Cease-fire announced between Nationalists and Oran O.A.S. Referendum in A., 1 July 1962. Overwhelming majority voted in favour of Algerian independence, in co-operation with France. Disagreement between various nationalist elements became increasingly evident, Aug. 1962, but rival factions reached settlement, Sept. 1962, and the elections held on 20 Sept. endorsed Ben Bella's single list of 196 candidates. Ben Bella visited U.S.A. and Cuba, Oct. 1962. Nationalization of French-owned estates in A., 1963.

Algoa Bay, S. Africa. So named by Bartholomew Diaz, 1486. First British colonists landed at, 1820.

Alhambra (Arab. *alhamrah,* the red [castle]) at Granada (*q.v.*), built by the Nasride emirs, beginning A.D. 1213, and enlarged during a period extending into the fourteenth century. Part of the building dates from after the Christian reconquest, and was added in the reign of Charles V (1516–55), being started in 1526, but never finished.

Alicante, Spain. Besieged by Moors, 1331; by French, 1709. Bombarded by Cartagenan insurgents, 1 Oct. 1873. Bombed by Franco's aircraft in Spanish Civil War, 25 May 1938.

Alice Springs. Capital of Central Australia territory from 1927 to 1931, when Central Australia once again became part of the Northern Territory (*q.v.*).

Aliens Acts (Great Britain). Jan. 1793. Act to register A., 1795. A. Act, 1905, came into force, 1 Jan. 1906. British Nationality and Status of A. Act, 1918, prohibited naturalization of Germans for ten years after official termination of World War I. New provisions, 1933. All Germans naturalized after 31 Dec. 1932 liable to internment under Regulation 18B in World War II. British Nationality Act, 1948, defined an alien as a person who was not a British subject, a British protected person, or a citizen of the Irish Republic. Since it came into operation, 1 Jan. 1949, British nationality has depended on the possession of citizenship of the U.K. and colonies or of one of the other self-governing countries forming the British Commonwealth. Entry of A. into the U.K. now exercised through Orders in Council made under the A. Restriction Acts, 1914 and 1919 as extended annually by the Expiring Laws Continuance Acts.

Alkmaar, Holland. Besieged by Spaniards under Alva, 1573. Town hall built, 1582. Captured by Duke of York's Dutch expedition, 2 Oct. 1799.

Allahabad, Uttar Pradesh State, Inida. Very anciently a holy place. Great mosque demolished, 1157. Fort built by Akbar, 1583. Occupied by British, 1765. Finally annexed, 1801. Massacre at, during Indian Mutiny, 1857. Univ. founded, 1887. First Indian National Congress held here, 1885.

Allegiance, Oath of. Statutes requiring: Elizabeth, 1559; William and Mary, 1689; Anne, 1701; combined with Oaths of Supremacy (*q.v.*) and Abjuration (*q.v.*);

Victoria, 23 July 1858. Power to modify the oath to enable Jews to sit in Parliament, 23 July 1858; amended, 6 Aug. 1860. Form of affirmation in lieu of oath, 8 Apr. 1859.

All Souls' College (Oxford), founded, 1438 by Archbishop Henry Chichele in memory of those killed in action in the French wars of the period.

Almanacs. Earliest known published by Soloman Jarchus, 1150. First printed A. by Purbach, 1450. Bore a stamp duty in Britain, 1710–1834. British almanac first published, 1828. Almanach de Gotha first published, 1763.

Almeida, Portugal. Taken and lost by Spaniards, 1762. Captured from British by French under Soult, 17 Aug. 1810. Recovered by Wellington, 11 May 1811.

Almeria, Spain, anciently Urci, became a Roman town, 19 B.C. Was a petty kingdom from A.D. 1288 to 1489. The cathedral dates from 1524.

Almohades. Moslem sect and dynasty founded in twelfth century in N. Africa (Berber). Founded by Mohammed Ibn Tumart. He and his successor, Abd-el-Mumin, conquered much of N. Africa and Morocco between 1128 and 1149, and invaded Spain. Christian reconquest of Spain checked by them at Allarcos, 1185, but their decline was rapid after their defeat at Navas de Tolosa, 1212. By 1254 they were pinned into Granada, and the last of the line was murdered in 1269. *See* ALMORAVIDES and SPAIN.

Almoravides. Moslem sect and dynasty founded eleventh century. They conquered Morocco (*q.v.*), and founded Marrakesh *c.* 1080. In 1086 their leader Yusuf-ibn-Tashfin invaded Spain, and after uniting the various Moslem emirates there defeated the Christian Alfonso VI at Zalaca, 1086. After this a decline set in until they were superseded by the Almohades (*q.v.*), who captured Marrakesh in 1147.

Alnwick, Northumb., England. Besieged by Scots, 13 Nov. 1093; taken, 1136; burnt by King John of England, 1215; by Scots, 1448. Castle ceased to be residence of Dukes of Northumberland, 1945.

Alps. Crossed by Hannibal, 217 B.C.; by Romans, 154 B.C.; highest mountain (Mont Blanc) climbed by Paccard and Balmat, 1786; crossed by Napoleon, May 1800. Mont Cenis tunnel through A. commenced, 1857; completed, 25 Dec. 1870. St. Gotthard tunnel commenced, 1872; completed, 29 Feb. 1880. Simplon tunnel completed, 24 Feb. 1905. First flight by airman over A., Sept. 1910. Susten Pass post-road opened, 1946.

Alsace. Came under French occupa-

tion by Peace of Westphalia, 1648. Annexed by Germany, 1871. Returned to France, 1919. Re-annexed to Germany, 1940. Retaken by France, 1945.

Alsatia. Nickname of district around Whitefriars, London, which had certain privileges of sanctuary and consequently became the resort of criminals. Privileges abolished, 1697.

Althing. *See* ICELAND.

Altona, in Schleswig-Holstein, became Danish in 1640. Burnt down during the Dano-Swedish War, 1713. Fiscal and other privileges granted by the Swedish crown withdrawn, 1853. Occupied by troops of the German Confederation, 1864, and became Prussian territory, 1866. Economic amalgamation with Hamburg and Wandsbek began, 1888, but A. retained separate administration and municipal status until 1937.

Altranstadt, Peace of. 1. 24 Sept. 1706, between Charles XII of Sweden and Augustus II of Poland. 2. 7 Mar. 1714, between Louis XIV and the Emperor Charles VI.

Aluminium. Discovered by Sir H. Davy, 1807. Woehler produced A. powder, 1827. First bar made by Deville, 1855.

'Amadis of Gaul.' Romance of uncertain, possibly fourteenth, century, originally written in its present form by Garcia de Montalvo (late fifteenth century). Enlarged, 1492. First printed, 1508, in Spanish. Translated into French by Herberay des Essarts, 1540. Published in English in an abridged form by R. Southey, 1803.

Amalfi, Italy. Important naval power from seventh century. Fleet repulsed a Saracen invasion of Italy, 848. Independence suppressed by King Roger of Sicily, 1131. Town devastated by flood, 1343. Its Code of Sea Laws (*Tavole Amalfitane*) recognized throughout the Mediterranean till 1570.

Amarapura, Burma. Founded, 1783. Capital of Burma till 1823, and from 1837 to 1860.

Amatongaland (Tongaland), part of Natal Province, annexed to Natal, 1897, being previously part of Zululand.

Amazon River, first seen by Europeans under Vicente Yañez Pinzon, 1500. First descended (by Orellana), 1541, from which time the present European name appears to date. First ascended from its mouth as a route to Quito in Bolivia by Pedro Texeira, 1638. 1867: A. opened to the commerce of all nations at certain points.

Amboina, Amboyna, or **Ambon,** Moluccas, Indonesia. Trading station in native kingdom of Tidor. Occupied by Portuguese, 1562; seized by Dutch, 1605, who massacred the English merchants there in 1623. It was in British hands, 1790–1801 and 1810–16, when it was returned to the Dutch. Became part of Moluccas government, 1927. Captured by Japanese, Feb. 1942. Surrendered by Japanese, 1945. Cap. of Moluccas Province since establishment of the Republic of Indonesia (*q.v.*) in 1950.

Amboise, Edict of, 19 Mar. 1563. Conceded freedom of worship to Huguenots.

Amboise, Tumult of, Jan. 1560. Huguenot conspiracy against the Guises suppressed by Catherine de' Medici.

Ambrose, St., *b.* Trèves *c.* 340; *d.* Milan, 397.

Ambrosian Library (Milan). Founded by Cardinal Borromeo, 1602. Opened, 1609.

America, Discovery of. Named in honour of Amerigo Vespucci, a Florentine, who visited land, 1499. Norse colonies established in tenth and eleventh centuries in N. America. Columbus first discovered Cuba, Oct. 1492. Cabot discovered Labrador, 1497. Portuguese under Cabral discovered Brazil, 1500.

American Federation of Labour, founded 1881 by Samuel Gompers, who became its president in 1882, and retained that office intermittently until his death in 1924.

American Literature in English. The following is a list of American authors not now living:

Abbott, John Stevens Cabot (historian), 1805–77.

Abbott, Lyman (editor and miscellaneous writer), 1835–1922.

Adams, Henry Brooks (historian), 1838–1918.

Adams, James Truslow (historian), 1878–1949.

Adeler, Max. *See* CLARK.

Alcott, Louisa May (novelist), 1832–88.

Aldrich, Thomas Bailey (poet and novelist), 1836–1906.

Allen, William Hervey (novelist), 1889–1949.

Allston, Washington (poet and novelist), 1779–1843.

Anderson, Sherwood (novelist), 1876–1941.

Andrews, Elisha Benjamin (economist and historian), 1844–1917.

Artemus Ward. *See* BROWNE.

Atherton, Gertrude Franklin (novelist), 1857–1948.

Babbitt, Irving (critic), 1865–1933.

Bancroft, George (historian), 1800–91.

Bangs, John Kendrick (novelist), 1862–1922.

Beecher, Henry Ward (theologian), 1813–1887. *See* STOWE.

Bellamy, Edward (novelist), 1850–98.

Bemelmans, Ludwig (Austrian-born humorist and cartoonist), 1898–1962.

Benchley, Robert (humorist), 1889–1945.

Bennett, James Gordon (journalist), 1841–1918.

Bierce, Ambrose (story-writer), 1842–*c.* 1914.

Bigelow, John (journalist), 1817–1911.

Bird, Robert Montgomery (dramatist and novelist), 1804–54.

Boker, George Henry (poet and dramatist), 1823–90.

Bradstreet, Anne (poetess), 1612–72.

Bromfield, Louis (novelist), 1896–1956.

Browne, Charles Farrar ('Artemus Ward') (humorist), 1834–67.

Bryant, William Cullen (poet), 1794–1878.

Burroughs, John (writer on nature), 1837–1921.

Cable, George Washington (novelist), 1844–1925.

Cather, Willa Sibert (novelist), 1876–1947.

Catlin, George (ethnologist), 1796–1872.

Channing, William Ellery (critic), 1780–1842.

Child, Francis James (literary historian), 1825–96.

Churchill, Winston (novelist), 1871–1947.

Clark, Charles Heber ('Max Adeler') (humorist), 1841–1915.

Clemens, Samuel Langhorne ('Mark Twain') (humorist), 1835–1910.

Coolidge, Susan. *See* WOOLSEY.

Cooper, James Fenimore (novelist), 1789–1851.

Crane, Stephen (story-writer), 1871–1900.

Crawford, Francis Marion (novelist), 1854–1909.

Crosby, Frances Jane (hymn-writer), 1820–1915.

Cummins, Maria Susanna (novelist) 1827–66.

Curtis, George W. (editor), 1824–92.

Dana, Richard Henry, sen. (poet and critic), 1787–1879.

Dana, Richard Henry, jun. (miscellaneous writer), 1815–82.

Davis, Richard Harding (novelist), 1864–1916.

Day, Clarence Shephard (humorist), 1874–1935.

Dickinson, Emily (poetess), 1830–86.

Dreiser, Theodore (novelist), 1871–1945.

Dunbar, P. L. (Negro poet), 1872–1916.

Dunne, Finley Peter ('Mr. Dooley') (journalist), 1867–1936.

Eddy, Mrs. Mary Baker Glover (Christian Scientist), 1821–1910.

Edwards, Jonathan (theologian), 1703–58.

Eggleston, Edward (novelist), 1837–1902.

Emerson, Ralph Waldo (poet and essayist), 1803–82.

Faulkner, William Harrison (novelist), 1897–1962.

Field, Eugene (journalist and poet), 1850–1895.

Fiske, John (philosopher and historian),

1842–1901.

Fitzgerald, Francis Scott Key (novelist), 1896–1940.

Frost, Robert (poet), 1875–1963.

Franklin, Benjamin (statesman and journalist), 1706–90.

Freneau, Philip (poet), 1752–1832.

Fuller, Sarah Margaret (critic and essayist), 1810–50.

George, Henry (economist), 1839–97.

Gilder, Richard Watson (poet and editor), 1844–1909.

Gildersleeve, Basil Lanneau (philologist), 1831–1924.

Glass, Montague Marsden (story-writer and dramatist), 1877–1934.

Greeley, Horace (journalist), 1811–72.

Grey, Zane ('Western' novelist), 1872–1939.

Habberton, John (author of *Helen's Babies*), 1842–1921.

Harris, Joel Chandler (miscellaneous writer), 1848–1908.

Harte, Francis Bret (poet and story-writer), 1839–1902.

Haskins, Charles Homer (historian), 1870–1937.

Hawthorne, Nathaniel (novelist), 1804–1863.

Hay, John (statesman and poet), 1838–1905.

Hearn, Lafcadio (miscellaneous writer), 1850–1904.

Hemingway, Ernest Miller (novelist), 1899–1961.

'Henry, O.' *See* PORTER.

Herrick, Robert (satirist), 1868–1938.

Holmes, Oliver Wendell (poet and miscellaneous writer), 1809–94.

Howe, Julia Ward (poetess), 1819–1910.

Howells, William Dean (novelist), 1837–1920.

Irving, Washington (miscellaneous writer), 1783–1859.

Jackson, Helen Hunt (poetess), 1830–85.

James, Henry (novelist), 1843–1916.

James, William (philosopher), 1842–1910.

Johnson, James Weldon (Negro poet), 1871–1938.

Lanier, Sidney (poet), 1842–81.

Leland, Charles Godfrey (poet and folk-lorist), 1824–1903.

Lewis, Sinclair (novelist), 1885–1951.

Lindsay, Nicholas Vachel (poet), 1879–1931.

Locke, David Ross ('Petroleum V. Nasby') (humorist), 1833–88.

London, Jack (novelist), 1876–1916.

Longfellow, Henry Wadsworth (poet), 1807–82.

Lowell, Amy Lawrence (critic and poetess), 1874–1925.

Lowell, James Russell (poet and essayist), 1819–91.

Mahan, Alfred Thayer, Admiral (naval historian), 1840–1914.

Marquis, Donald Robert Perry (humorist), 1878–1937.

Mather, Cotton (divine), 1663–1728.

Mather, Increase (divine), 1639–1723.

Melville, Herman (novelist), 1819–91.

Mencken, Henry Louis (critic), 1880–1956.

Miller, Joaquin (poet), 1842–1913.

Mitchell, Margaret Munnerlyn (novelist), 1900–1949.

Mitchell, Silas Weir (novelist), 1830–1914.

Morley, Christopher Darlington (novelist, poet, and essayist), 1890–1957.

Motley, John Lothrop (historian), 1814–1877.

Norris, Frank (novelist), 1870–1902.

Norton, Charles Eliot (writer on Italy, Dante, etc.), 1827–1908.

O'Neill, Eugene Gladstone (playwright), 1888–1953.

Page, Thomas Nelson (novelist and essayist), 1853–1922.

Parkman, Francis (historian), 1823–93.

Pennell, Joseph (art critic), 1857–1926.

Phillips, David Graham (novelist), 1867–1911.

Poe, Edgar Allan (poet and story-writer), 1809–49.

Porter, William Sydney ('O. Henry') (story-writer), 1867–1910.

Prescott, William Hickling (historian), 1796–1859.

Robinson, Edwin Arlington (poet), 1869–1935.

Runyon, Alfred Damon (humorist), 1884–1944.

Santayana, George (philosopher), 1863–1952.

Shaw, Henry Wheeler ('Josh Billings') (humorist), 1818–85.

Sigourney, Mrs. Lydia (Huntley) (poetess), 1791–1865.

Simms, William Gilmore (poet and novelist), 1806–70.

Stedman, Edmund Clarence (poet and critic), 1833–1908.

Stockton, Frank Richard (story-writer), 1834–1902.

Stoddard, Richard Henry (poet), 1825–1903.

Stowe, Mrs Harriet Elizabeth Beecher (novelist), 1812–96.

Stratton-Porter, Mrs. Gene (novelist and naturalist), 1868–1924.

Tabb, John Banister (poet), 1845–1909.

Taylor, Bayard (poet, essayist, etc.), 1825–78.

Thompson, Dorothy (journalist), 1894–1961.

Thoreau, Henry David (naturalist and author), 1817–62.

Thurber, James Grover (humorist), 1894–1960.

Titchener, Edward Bradford (psychologist), 1867–1927.

Twain, Mark. *See* CLEMENS.

Van Doren, Charles Clinton (critic and biographer), 1885–1950.

Van Druten, John William (playwright and novelist), 1901–57.

Wallace, Lewis (religious novelist), 1827–1905.

Ward, Artemus. *See* BROWNE.

Warner, Susan (novelist), 1819–85.

Webster,Noah (lexicographer),1758–1843.

Wetherell, Elizabeth. *See* WARNER.

Wharton, Edith Newbold (novelist), 1862–1935.

White, Richard Grant (Shakespearian scholar), 1822–85.

Whitman, Walt (poet), 1819–92

Whitney, William Dwight (philologist), 1827–94.

Whittier, John Greenleaf (poet), 1807–92.

Wiggin, Kate Douglas (Mrs. Riggs) (novelist), 1856–1923.

Wilson, Thomas Woodrow (historian and essayist), 1856–1923).

Winthrop, Theodore (novelist), 1828–61.

Wise, John (theologian), 1652–1725.

Woolman, John (Quaker essayist), 1720–1772.

Woolsey, Sarah Chauncy (children's writer), 1835–1905.

American Republics. Haiti declared its independence, 1804; Chile, 1810; Colombia, 1811 (from this Venezuela and Ecuador seceded, 1830); Argentine, 1816; Paraguay, 1821; Peru, 1821; Mexico,1821; Central American Confederation, 1828 (from which secession took place as follows: Guatemala, 1839; Costa Rica, 1839; Honduras, 1839; Nicaragua, 1839; Salvador, 1848. All had formed part of Mexico between 1821 and 1823); Bolivia, 1825; Uruguay, 1828 (after successive occupation by Brazilian and Argentine forces); Dominican Republic, 1844; Brazil, 1889; Cuba, 1897; Panama, 1903.

'America's' Cup, The. Cup originally called the Queen's cup, presented by the Royal Yacht Squadron in 1851 and won in that year by the American schooner *America*. Presented to New York Yacht Club by the owner in 1887; it has been called the A. C. ever since.

Amiens, France. Cathedral built, 1220–88. Treaty of A. between Henry VIII, represented by Cardinal Wolsey, and Francis I, signed here, 18 Aug. 1527. Taken by Spanish, 11 Mar. 1597; retaken by French, 25 Sept. 1597. Peace treaty signed, 25 Mar. 1802, between England, France, Spain, and Holland. War again declared, 1803. Germans entered A., 28 Nov. 1870, during Franco-Prussian War. Threatened by Germans, 24 Apr. 1918. Heavily bombed, 19 May 1940. Occupied by Germans, 21 May 1940. Liberated by British, Aug. 1944.

Amiens, Mise of. The award pronounced by Louis XI of France, 23 Jan. 1264, in the dispute between Henry III of England and his barons. *See also* OXFORD, PROVISIONS OF.

Amman, Jordan (Biblical *Rabbath-Ammon*. Gr. *Philadelphia*). Turkish base in World War I. Bombed by British, Mar. and Apr. 1918. Became capital of Transjordan, 1921. R.A.F. base handed over to Jordanian authorities, 1957. *See* JORDAN.

Amoy or **Hsiamen,** China. Trading with A. permitted, 1676. The fort destroyed by English, July 1840. Town captured, 26 Aug. 1841. Port opened by treaty for trade, 26 Aug. 1842. University founded, 1925. Occupied by Japanese, 1938. Returned to China, 1945. A. linked to mainland by two stone embankments, 1956.

Amritsar became the headquarters of the Sikh religious movement, 1574. Golden Temple destroyed, 1761; rebuilt, 1764, and roofed with copper gilt by Ranjit Singh, 1802. The incident now generally known as the 'A. Massacre' took place, 13 Apr. 1919.

Amsterdam, Holland. Founded, 1204. Charter granted, and Old Church built, 1300. New Church, 1408. Dutch E. India Co. established at, 1602. University founded, 1632. Surrendered to Prussians, 1787. To French, 1795. N. Holland Canal built, 1819–25. N. Sea Canal, 1865–95. Occupied by Germans, 14 May 1940. Liberated, 12 May 1945. Canal linking A. with River Waal opened, 1952.

Anabaptists. Said to have been founded by Thomas Münzer *c.* 1520. A. state established under John of Leyden at Münster, 1533–5. Laws against, 1525–1534. *See* BAPTISTS.

'Anabasis.' 1. *See* TEN THOUSAND. 2. Arrian's account (A.D. 166–8) of Alexander the Great's campaigns.

Anaesthetics. Laughing gas first used as anaesthetic by Sir H. Davy, 1800. Ether by Morton, 1846. Chloroform by Sir J. Y. Simpson, 1847. Local A. first used, 1884.

Analyst, Public. A professional association founded in 1874 adopted the designation 'of Public and other As.' in 1907. Appointment of Public As. is now governed by provisions of the Food and Drugs Act, 1955.

Anarchism. First formulated as a modern political theory by Godwin, 1793. Elaborated by Proudhon, 1840. Four anarchists hanged at Chicago, 1886.

Anatolia or **Asia Minor.** Conquered by Cyrus, 546 B.C. By Alexander the Great, 334. Divided between various states,

320–190. Roman province of 'Asia' established, 133. Roman conquest complete, 63 B.C. Administration reorganized by Diocletian, third century A.D. Invaded by Chosroes II of Persia, 616–26. By Arabs, 668. Central A. subdued by Seljuk Turks, 1071–80. Destruction of Seljuk power by Mongols, 1243. Ottoman power established at Brusa, 1307. Final Ottoman conquest, 1481. (For later history *see* OTTOMAN EMPIRE and TURKISH REPUBLIC.)

Anatomical Society of Great Britain. Founded, 1887.

Ancient Buildings, Society for Protection of. Established, 1877.

Ancient Lights. Law passed, 1 Aug. 1832.

Ancona, Italy. Founded by refugees from Syracuse *c.* 390 B.C. Rebuilt by Trajan, A.D. 107. Besieged: 1. by Frederick Barbarossa, 1167. 2. by Christian, Archbishop of Mainz, 1173. Annexed to Papal States, 1532. Captured by French, 1797; by Austrians, 1799; by French, 1801. Restored to Papal States, 1802. Occupied by French, 1832; evacuated, 1838. Bombarded by Austrians, 18 June 1849. A. (with other towns) rebelled against Papacy, Sept. 1860, and has been since part of Italian kingdom. Severely damaged by bombardment, 1943.

Andaman and **Nicobar Islands,** in the Bay of Bengal. A British settlement was made on N. A., 1789, but abandoned. First used as penal settlement, 1858. Transportation ceased, 1921. The Japanese landed in Mar. 1942, and occupied the A. I. until Aug. 1945. The abolition of the penal settlement was announced, Oct. 1945.

Anderida. *See* SUSSEX.

Andorra (officially **Las Valls d'Andorra**). Small semi-independent republic in the Pyrenees. Counts of Foix and Spanish Bishop of Urgel became co-princes of A., 1278. French office of Co-Prince descended through the French monarchy to the President of the French Republic in modern times, and A. is therefore under French protection. Mild revolution occurred in 1933 when franchise was broadened.

Angers, France. Taken from Romans, A.D. 464; fortified *c.* 859–60. Castle completed by Louis IX. Town burnt by King John of England, 1206; taken by Huguenots, 1585; attacked by Vendéan army, 1793. Church of Saint-Serge built, 1050.

Angevins. *See* ENGLISH SOVEREIGNS.

Angkor, Cambodia. Famous Khmer temple at, built *c.* ninth–twelfth centuries.

Anglesey, Wales. Conquered by Romans under Agricola, A.D. 78. Hugh of Chester's attempt to conquer A. frustrated with Viking assistance, 1098. Subdued and organized by Edward I, 1295–8.

Anglia, East, kingdom founded *c.* A.D. 500. Submitted to Egbert of Wessex, 826. Subsequently invaded by the Danes, who held it until forced to submit to Edward the Elder, 918. One of the four great earldoms under Canute.

Anglo-Saxon Chronicle, or more correctly **Chronicles.** Of the six different texts which survive all appear to have been begun in the reign of Alfred the Great, probably after 880, though they incorporate matter taken from much earlier chronicles which were kept up in Northumbrian religious houses from the middle of the seventh to the end of the eighth century. Between them they record events in Britain from A.D. 449 to 1154.

Angola. Discovered, 1486, and colonized by Portuguese. Occupied by Dutch, 1641. Restored to Portugal, 1648. Riots in A. signalled the beginning of an anti-colonial revolution, Feb. 1961.

Angoulême, France. Became English possession by marriage of Henry II with Eleanor of Aquitaine, 1152; annexed to France, 1303; restored to England, 1360; reconquered by French, 1373.

Anhalt, Germany. Separated from Saxony, thirteenth century. Continual subdivision between various petty princes continued till 1800. The remaining duchies of A.-Bernburg and A.-Dessau united, 1863, under Leopold of A.-Dessau. Assisted Prussia in war of 1866. Joined German Empire, 1871. Reigning duke abdicated, 1918. Became a constituent *Land* under the Weimar (*q.v.*) Constitution, 1919. Liberties suppressed by Hitler, 1933. Now mainly in the district of Halle.

Aniline Dyes. Discovered by Unverdorben, 1826.

Anjou, France. Conquered by Henry II of England, 1156; by Philip II of France from King John, 1204; retaken by Edward III and afterwards given up, 1360. Finally annexed to French crown, 1480. Battle of A. or Beaugé, English defeated by French, 22 Mar. 1421.

Ankara or **Angora** (anciently **Ancyra**). Ottoman capital in fourteenth century. Lapsed into insignificance after invasion of Europe until 1919, when Mustapha Kemal Pasha (later Atatürk) set up provisional revolutionary government at A. Became capital of Turkey, 1923. Headquarters of CENTO (*q.v.*) since Oct. 1958.

Annam. Under Chinese rule till A.D. 968, when local monarchy established. Independent, 1428. First French expedition to, 1787. War with France,

1858. French protectorate, 1884. *See* INDO-CHINA and VIET NAM.

Annapolis, Md., U.S.A. U.S. Naval Academy founded, 1845.

Annapolis Royal, Nova Scotia. Settled by French (as Fort Royal), 1605. Taken by English, 1614 and 1710. Ceded to Britain, 1713. Capital of Nova Scotia till 1879. *See* ACADIA and NOVA SCOTIA.

Annapurna. Mountain in Himalayas, N. Nepal. Height 26,493 ft. Was first peak of over 26,000 ft. to be climbed (by Herzog and Lachenal of the French Himalayan Expedition, 3 June, 1950).

Annates, or First Fruits. First year's profits of a living claimed by the bishop. Suppressed in France by edicts, 1406, 1417, 1418, 1463, and 1464. Prohibited in England by Henry IV. Parliament granted them to the crown in 1534, but in 1704 Queen Anne applied them to the augmentation of poor livings. *See also* QUEEN ANNE'S BOUNTY.

Annobon Island, in the Gulf of Guinea, discovered by Portuguese, 1 Jan. 1471. Ceded to Spain, 1778.

Annual Register. A yearly record of public events first published in London, 1759 (for the year 1758). For thirty years Edmund Burke (1729–97) wrote the survey of events.

Ansbach. Grew up round the monastery founded by St. Humbert in the eighth century. Acquired by Burgraves of Nürnberg, 1331; combined with Bayreuth to form a margravate, 1398. Monastery dissolved, 1560. Caroline Wilhelmine, daughter of the Margrave John Frederick (*d.* 1687), married George Augustus, Prince of Hanover (later George II of England), 1705. United with Prussia, 1791; but awarded to Bavaria by Napoleon, 1806.

Anschluss. Political union of Austria and Germany, 12 Mar. 1938.

Antarctica. *See* ARCTIC AND ANTARCTIC REGIONS and QUEEN MAUD LAND.

Antarctic Ocean. *See* ARCTIC AND ANTARCTIC REGIONS.

Anti-Aircraft Command. Established, 1939. Disbanded, 1955.

Anti-Comintern Pact. Between Germany and Japan, 25 Nov. 1936. Joined by Italy, 6 Nov. 1937. By Hungary and Spain, 1939. By Slovakia, Rumania, and Bulgaria, 1941.

Anti-Corn Law League. Founded Manchester, 18 Sept. 1838. Deputies assembled London, 8 Feb. 1842. Corn Laws repealed, 6 June 1846. League dissolved, 2 July 1846.

Antigua, Leeward Islands. Discovered by Columbus, 1493. First English settlement, 1632. Formally ceded to Britain by Treaty of Breda, 1667. Became part of Leeward Islands Federation, 1871. Crown colony, 1898.

Antioch, now **Antakya,** Turkey. Founded 300 B.C. by Seleucus Nicator. Christians first so-called here, A.D. 42. Destroyed by Persians, A.D. 540. Rebuilt by Justinian, 542–5. Conquered by Arabs, 637. Recovered by the Eastern emperors, 966; lost again, 1086. Captured by Crusaders, 1098, and became a Christian principality till 1268, when it was taken by Bibars, Sultan of Egypt. Made part of Syria, 1920, but restored to Turkey, 1939.

Antipopes. *See* PAPACY.

Antiquaries, Society of. Founded, 1572. Dissolved by James I, 1604. Reconstituted, 1707. Charter, 2 Nov. 1751. George III granted the society apartments in Somerset House, 1780.

Anti-Saloon League of America. Founded 1893, in Ohio. Succeeded in 1948 by the Temperance League of America, which merged with the National Temperance Movement in 1950 to form the National Temperance League.

Anti-Slavery Association. *See* SLAVE TRADE.

Antonine Wall, Scotland. Built *c.* A.D. 140–1.

Antwerp, Belgium. Probably founded by Frankish tribes *c.* eighth century. Destroyed by Vikings early ninth century. Rebuilt tenth century. Republic in eleventh century. Citadel commenced, 1567; completed, 1568; burnt by Spaniards, 4 Nov. 1576 ('The Spanish Fury'). Besieged and captured by Parma, 1584–5; Marlborough captured, 6 June 1706; Marshal Saxe captured, 9 May 1746; captured by French, 29 Nov. 1792. Part of Netherland kingdom, 1815–30; bombarded by French, 4 Dec. 1832; cession to Belgium confirmed, 1839; besieged by Germans, 4–6 Oct., surrendered, 9 Oct. 1914. Albert Canal linking A. to Liège opened, June 1939. Occupied by Germans, May 1940. Captured by British, Sept. 1944. Bombarded by German V-weapons, Nov. 1944–May 1945.

Anur or Tarracina, town of the Volsci (*q.v.*) under Roman supremacy, 509 B.C. Stormed by Volsci, 397. Retaken by Romans, 312. Sacked by Goths, A.D. 409, and again, 595. Temple of Jupiter A. built first century B.C.

Anzac. Landing of As. (i.e. Australia and New Zealand Army Corps) in Gallipoli in World War I, 25 Apr. 1915.

Anzio, anciently **Antium,** conquered by Romans, 468 B.C. Revolted and subdued, 338. The beach-head (known to the Germans as the Nettuno beach-head) established here by Allied Forces, 22 Jan. 1944, was maintained until 25 May, when contact by land was made with Fifth Army.

Aosta, Valle d', came into possession of Counts of Savoy, 1032. Gran Paradiso area, set aside as a game reserve by the Crown Prince of Piedmont in 1836, became a National Park in 1920. Minor adjustment of Franco-Italian frontier, 1945; confirmed by treaty, 1947.

Apartheid. *See* COLOUR BAR.

Apollo Belvedere. Found at Porto d'Anzio early in the sixteenth century. Bought by Pope Julius II, 1511. Taken to Paris by French, 1797. Restored to Vatican, 1815.

Apollo of Rhodes. 'The Colossus', wonder of the world, sculpture of Chares of Lindus 292–280 B.C. Overthrown by earthquake, 224 B.C. Broken up, A.D. 653.

Apostles' Creed. *See* CREEDS.

Apothecaries. First apothecary in England traditionally John Falcourt of Lucca, 1362. Licensed by Bishop of London. 1511. Society chartered, 1606 (with Grocers); separately, 1617. House of Lords pronounced that A. could prescribe for a sick patient without the advice of a physician, 1704. 1774: Society of A. limited its membership to those who were practising A. (i.e. medical practitioners). 1815: Act of Parliament gave society power to examine all A. in England and Wales and grant them licences to practise.

Appeal of Felony. *See* BATTLE, WAGER OF.

Appellants or Lords Appellant. The nobles who protested against certain ministers of Richard II in 1387. They caused the death of two of these ministers. In 1388 the L. A. convened the Merciless Parliament.

Appenzell, Swiss canton, settled by Allemanni before A.D. 600. Joined the Confederation, 1513.

Appian Way, Italy. A famous roadway from Rome to Capua via Albano, begun by Appius Claudius Caecus, 312 B.C. and extended to Brindisi via Benevento. Excavations were instituted by the papal court, 1850–3, and part of the road was reopened. Now Strada Nazionale 6.

Apprentices, Statute of, 1562 (England). No person allowed to work at a trade without previously serving seven years' apprenticeship. Repealed, 1814.

Approved Schools, i.e. approved by the Home Office. Term came into use with the passing of the Children and Young Persons' Act, 1933.

Apsley House (London). Built 1771–8 for Baron Apsley, 2nd Earl Bathurst. Bought by the Duke of Wellington, 1820. Presented by 7th Duke of Wellington to the nation, 1947. Opened as museum 1952.

Apulia or Puglie, Italy. Conquered by Rome, 317 B.C. Devastated in Social War, 90–88 B.C. Became part of the Kingdom of the Two Sicilies, 1134; and of Italy, 1861.

Aquileia, Italy. Founded 181 B.C. Very important till destroyed by Attila, A.D. 452. Became a patriarchate in eleventh century. Part of Holy Roman Empire (*q.v.*), then of Austria, until acquired by Italy in 1918.

Aquitaine, E. France. Conquered by Franks, A.D. 507; separate state, 700; united to France, 1137; became part of English crown by marriage of Henry II and Eleanor of A., 1152; province finally lost under Henry VI, 1453.

Arab League. Founded on occasion of pan-Arab conference at Alexandria, 25 Sept.–7 Oct. 1944, when Egyptian, Iraqi, Syrian, Lebanese, and Transjordanian delegates signed a protocol; Palestinian, Saudi Arabian, and Yemenite delegates were also present. The Constitution of the League was signed by representatives of all these countries, 22 Mar. 1945. Tried unsuccessfully to exert pressure on W. German Federal Republic not to ratify its treaty of restitution to Jewish victims of Nazi persecution, Nov. 1952. When Israel attacked Egypt in Oct. 1956 there was no military response from other members of the A. L. and its importance has waned since. In Aug. 1962 the United Arab Republic's strained relations with the A. L. further weakened it.

Arabia. Minaean Kingdom in Jauf, 1200–650 B.C. Sabaean (Sheba) Kingdom from 1500 B.C. Rise of the Himyarite Kingdom, 115 B.C. Abyssinian rule in Yemen, A.D. 525–75. (For later history down to 1917, *see* CALIPHATE; OTTOMAN EMPIRE, etc.) Conquered by Ibn Saud, 1924, and renamed Saudi Arabia (*q.v.*). *See also* JORDAN; KUWEIT; YEMEN; ADEN.

Aragon. Recovered from the Moors, 1131. Continuous southward expansion at the expense of the Moors checked at battle of Alarcos, 1185. Catalonia united with it, 1137. In alliance with Castile to win great victory at Navas de Tolosa, 1212. Valencia united with it, 1238. Moors practically subdued by James I (1213–76). King Ferdinand II of A. married Isabella, Queen of Castile, 1469.

Aragon, Sovereigns of:

Ramiro I	1035–1063
Sancho I	1063–1094
Pedro I	1094–1104
Alfonso I. the Battler	1104–1134
Ramiro II	1134–1137
Petronilla	1137–1162
Alfonso II	1162–1196
Pedro II	1196–1213

Jaime I, the Conqueror	1213–1276
Pedro III	1276–1285
Alfonso III, the Magnificent	1285–1291
Jaime II	1291–1327
Alfonso IV, the Fair	1327–1336
Pedro IV	1336–1387
Juan I	1387–1395
Martin I	1395–1410
Ferdinand I	1410–1416
Alfonso V, the Magnanimous	1416–1458
Juan II	1458–1479
Ferdinand II, the Catholic	1479–1516
(from 1474 Ferdinand V of Castile)	

See further under SPAIN, SOVEREIGNS OF.

Arbitration, Internal Courts of. First established in Denmark, 1795. France, 1806.

Arbitration, Industrial. Purely voluntary in England until 1896, when legislation placed it on a legal footing. Present practice based on the Conciliation Act, 1896, and Industrial Courts Act, 1919.

Arbitration, International Court of. Established at The Hague, 1900. A. Treaty, 1914, between Britain, U.S.A., France, and Spain. Italo-Greek dispute settled by A., 1923. Bulgaro-Greek dispute settled by permanent court of International Justice (*q.v.*), 1924. Ditto Sino-Belgian dispute, 1924, and Franco-Turkish *Lotus* case, 1926. 1951: Court of International Justice awarded Britain compensation against Albania (*q.v.*) for mined destroyers, but Albania ignored the order.

Arc de Triomphe de l'Étoile, Paris. Begun, 1506. Finished, 1836.

Archaeological Association and Institute (London). Established, 1843.

Archangel (Arkhangel'sk), Russia. Founded, 1584. Blockaded by British fleet, 1854. Allied landing against Bolsheviks, 1918; evacuation, 1919. One of the ports of destination on the convoy route to Russia in World War II.

Archbishop. Title first used in the E., 320; in Rome, 420.

Arches, Court of. Sat in St. Mary-le-Bow from *c.* 1085 till removed to Doctor's Commons, 1567. In Lambeth Palace since 1876.

Architectural Societies (London). Institute of British Architects, 1834. Incorporated and made royal by charter, 11 Jan. 1837. Society of Architects founded, 1884: amalgamated with Royal Institute of British Architects, 1925. A. Association founded, 1847. American Institute of Architects, 1857.

Arcos. The All Russian Co-operative Society, London. Raided by Home Office, 12 May 1927. As a result of discoveries there relations with U.S.S.R. broken off, 27 May 1927.

Arcot. Former capital of the Carnatic. Its successful defence by Clive in 1751 was the decisive event in the Anglo-French struggle for India. Taken by Hyder Ali, 1780. Ceded to E. India Co., 1801.

Arctic and Antarctic Regions, principal expeditions before 1912.

Arctic Regions:

Date	Explorer
1496	Sebastian Cabot
1498	John Cabot
1553	Sir Hugh Willoughby and Richard Chancellor
1576 ⎫ 1577 ⎬ 1578 ⎭	Frobisher
1584 ⎫ 1595 ⎭	William Barents
1585 ⎫ 1586 ⎬ 1587 ⎭	John Davis
1602	George Waymouth
1607–11	Hudson
1612–13	Bylot and Button
1614	Bylot and Gibbons
1615–16	Baffin
1631	James
1676	Capt. Wood
1728 ⎫ 1729 ⎬ 1741 ⎭	Bering
1735	Chelyuskin
1773	Phipps and Lutwidge (Horatio Nelson in this expedition)
1778	Cook and Clerke
1806 ⎫ 1822 ⎭	Scoresby
1818	John Ross
1818	Buchan and Franklin
1819–22	Franklin
1819–20 ⎫ 1821–3 ⎬ 1824–5 ⎭	Parry
1824	Lyon
1819 ⎫ 1824–5 ⎭	Parry
1825–7	Franklin
1826–8	Buchan
1829–33	John Ross
1833–5 ⎫ 1836–7 ⎭	Back
1836–9	Dean and Simpson
1845–6	Franklin
1846–7	Rae
1848–9	{ John Ross { Richardson
1848–52	Moore
1849–50	{ Hooper { Saunders
1849–51	Pullen
1850–1	{ John Ross { Penny { De Haven and Kane
1850–4	M'Clure

1850–5	Collinson
1851–2	Kennedy
1851–4	Rae
1852–4	Maguire, Belcher, Kellett, Pullen
1853–5	Kane
1857–9	McClintock
1859–60	Hayes
1870–2	Hall
1871–2	Merriman
1872–3	Green
1875–6	Nares and Stephenson
1879	The *Jeannette*
1880	Leigh Smith
1887	Col. Gilder
1893–6	Dr. Nansen
1893	Peary
1895	Jackson
1897	Andrée
1899	Wellman
1902	Peary, Sverdrup
1909	Peary (discovery of N. Pole, 6 Apr.)
1909–12	Mikkelsen, Amundsen, Stefansson

Capt. Sedoff's Russian expedition started for Franz Josef Land, 1912; returned, 1915, without Sedoff, who, having set out for N. Pole, had perished. Vilkitsky's expedition, 1915. Stefansson's *Karluk*, on Alaskan expedition on behalf of Canadian Government, sank 40 miles from Wrangel Islands, Jan. 1914; in 1915 he discovered new land N. of Prince Patrick Islands; in 1916 more new land W. of Axel Heiberg Islands, and in 1918 he explored Beaufort Sea, disproving existence of Keenan Land. Amundsen's aeroplane voyage toward N. Pole from Spitzbergen, 21 May–15 June 1925. Byrd flew over N. Pole, 1926. In 1928 Sir Hubert Wilkins flew from Alaska to Dead Man's Land, Spitzbergen; in the same year Gen. Nobile made three flights in his dirigible *Italia*, but was wrecked off N.E. Land. He was rescued, but Amundsen, who had joined in the relief expeditions, perished. Gino Watkins on the Greenland ice-cap, 1931. Ushakov expedition N. of Cape Chelyuskin, 1931–2. Soviet exploration of Nordenskjold Island, 1936; French Polar research ship *Pourquoi Pas* sank off Iceland, Sept. 1936; Otto Schmidt's meteorological survey of N. Polar regions, 1937.

Antarctic Regions. Visited by Cook in 1773 and 1774. Land discovered by Bellingshausen (Peter I and Alexander I Lands), 1821; by Capt. Biscoe, Feb. 1831; by Capt. D'Urville, 1838. Ross discovered and explored Victoria Land, 1839–1843; Nares in the *Challenger* first crossed the Antarctic Circle, 1874. Principal expeditions to: Christensen first to set foot on Antarctic continent, 1894; C. E, Borchgrevink landed at Cape Adare, 23 Feb. 1895; second expedition, equipped by Sir George Newnes, reached Cape Adare, 17 Feb. 1899; de Gerlache expedition, 16 Aug. 1897–28 Mar. 1899; German expedition, under Capt. H. Ruser, 11 Aug. 1901; British expedition, under Capt. Scott, 24 Dec. 1901–10 Sept. 1904; Dr. Bruce's Scottish expedition, Jan. 1903–July 1904; Dr. Jean Charcot, French expedition, 1904–5 and 1908–10; Lieut. (later Sir Ernest) Shackleton's expedition, 1907–9; Dr. David, with Mr. D. Mawson and Dr. Mackay, found the S. magnetic pole to be at 72° 25′ S., 155° 16′ E. on 16 Jan. 1909; Capt. Amundsen's expedition, 1910, S. Pole reached, 16 Dec. 1911; Capt. Scott, British expedition, 1910–13, reached S. Pole, 17 Jan. 1912 (Capt. Scott was found dead by a search party, 12 Nov. 1913); Sir Ernest Shackleton's *Endurance* left on 'Farther South' expedition, 1 Aug. 1914; returned, 1916; Shackleton, with *Quest*, started, 1921; reached S. Georgia, where Shackleton *d.*, 5 Jan. 1922; in 1928 Wilkins flew over Graham Land an l proved that it was not part of the main mass of the Antarctic continent; the British Colonial Office, through the 'Discovery Committee,' sent out *Discovery I* on whaling research expedition; *Discovery II* was sent out in 1930 and 1931, and between 1935 and 1937 circumnavigated Antarctic continent; Norwegian expeditions, 1935 and 1937; Byrd expeditions (U.S. Navy), 1928–9; 1933–8; 1939–40; 1946; 1947–50: Dr (later Sir) Vivian Fuchs organized the Falkland Islands Dependencies Survey in the Antarctic; 1957–8: Expeditions from various countries cooperated in Antarctic exploration to mark the International Geophysical Year; 1957–8: Fuchs and Hillary led British Transantarctic Expedition: Fuchs left Shackleton Base on Weddell Sea, 24 Nov. 1957; reached S. Pole, 19 Jan. 1958; Scott Base on McMurdo Sound, 2 Mar. 1958. Fuchs thus became first man to traverse the Antarctic, completing 2,200 miles in ninety-nine days. *See also* QUEEN MAUD LAND.

Arezzo, anciently **Arretium,** an Etruscan city, made a treaty with Rome, 308 B.C. Besieged by Gauls, 283. Defeated in a war with Florence, A.D. 1289, and became a Florentine possession, 1348. Church of St. Francis built, 1322.

Argentaeus, Codex, discovered in the abbey library of Werden, Westphalia, by the topographer Mercator (alias Gerhard Kraemer, 1512–94), and brought to

Prague for the collection of the Emperor Rudolf II (reigned 1576–1611); on the storming of the city by the Protestant faction in 1648, the looted MS. was taken to Stockholm by Count Königsmark. After further vicissitudes it was presented by Marshal de la Gardie to Upsala University, 1669. It represents the earliest (fourth century) text of the Gothic biblical version which was the work of Ulfilas (311–83) (*see also* GOTHS). It was first reproduced in print, 1665.

Argentina. Rio de la Plata visited by Spaniards, 1515. Buenos Aires (*q.v.*) founded 1536 by Pedro de Mendoza, and made part of the Viceroyalty of Peru. Buenos Aires captured by British expedition from Cape Town, 1806, but British surrendered shortly after. Viceroy deposed, 25 May 1810. Independence proclaimed at Congress of Tucuman, 9 July 1816. Independence recognized by Britain and U.S.A., 1823. By Spain, 1842. Intermittent civil war between Unitarians and Federalists won by the former, Unitarian leader Juan Manuel de Rosas (1793–1877) dictator, 1835–52. Buenos Aires became independent republic, 1853, remainder having its capital at Paranà. Reunited, 1859. Constitution modified, 1862, by making Buenos Aires a federal district. War with Paraguay, 1865–70. Federal system completed, 1880. Republic extended to Rio Negro, 1878–80. Patagonia divided with Chile (*q.v.*) by treaty, 1881. Chilean boundary dispute in the Andes settled by arbitration of King Edward VII, 1902. After withdrawing, rejoined League of Nations (*q.v.*), Sept. 1926. Revolution overthrew Radical President Irigoyen, 1930. Pan-American Peace Pact signed at Buenos Aires, 1936. Military *coup d'état* overthrew Conservative (landowners') Government, 4 June 1943. The Minister of War, Peron, arrested and interned on Martin Garcia Island, Oct. 1945; inaugurated president, 4 June 1946, and carried through sweeping radical changes involving considerable nationalization. Agreement to sell British-owned railways to Government of A., 13 Feb. 1947. The 'Andes' agreement ratified, 19 Feb. 1948. After death of Eva Peron (26 July 1952) Peron regime became markedly anti-Catholic. Revolution by dissident factions resulted in Peron's deposition (22 Sept. 1955) and exile, and return to more democratic government. His successor, Gen. Lonardi, deposed, 13 Nov. 1955, and succeeded by Gen. Aramburu. Dr. Frondizi elected President, 23 Feb. 1958. Peso devalued, Oct. 1955. Peron's assets seized, 1957. A. abstained from voting when Cuba expelled from Organization of American States, 31 Jan. 1962. Peronist victories in elections led to army intervention and government crisis, 18 Mar. 1962. Frondizi deposed, and Guido sworn in as new President. One-day army revolt, 22 Sept. 1962. Another anti-Peronist military revolt failed, April 1963, but economic situation in A. increasingly unstable.

Heads of the State (Presidents) from the Establishment of the Republic, 1853:

Urquiza	1853–1860
Derqui	1860–1862
Mitre	1862–1868
Sarmiento	1868–1874
Avellaneda	1874–1880
Roca	1880–1886
Celman	1886–1890
Pellegrini	1890–1892
Pena	1892–1898
Roca	1898–1904
Quintana	1904–1906
Alcorta	1906–1910
Pena	1910–1914
De la Plaza	1914–1916
Irigoyen	1916–1922
Alvear	1922–1928
Irigoyen	1928–1930
Uriburu	1930–1932
Justo	1932–1938
Ortiz	1938–1942
Castillo	1942–1943
Rawson (two days)	June 1943
Ramirez	June 1943–1944
Farrell	1944–1946
Peron	1946–1955
Lonardi (3 weeks)	1955
Aramburu	1955–1958
Frondizi	1958–1962
Guido	1962–1963

Argon, first isolated in 1894 by Lord Rayleigh and Sir William Ramsay.

Arianism. Propounded by Arius (256–336) *c.* 321. Synod of Bithynia upheld him against St. Athanasius, who was banished, 323. Condemned by Council of Nicaea, 325. His doctrines have since been condemned by numerous councils, but were the basis of 'State' churches in the Gothic and Vandal kingdoms (*q.v.*). As an organized creed A. died out before 600.

Arizona. Discovered by Marcos de Niza, 1539; first settled by Spanish missionaries *c.* 1772. Largely ceded as a result of the Mexican War, 1848; the remaining territory, comprising modern A., was acquired by the Gadsden Purchase of 1853, and its present boundaries were fixed in 1863: admitted to the Union, 14 Feb. 1912.

Arkansas, explored by De Soto, 1541, and settled by French, 1686. Purchased by U.S. Government, 1803; organized as a territory, 1819; admitted to the Union, 1836.

Arles, France. Greek colony refounded

by the Romans c. 47 B.C. Roman theatre and amphitheatre built, second century A.D. Became capital of Gaul and an archbishopric in fourth century, and became capital of the kingdom of Provence or Arelate at end of ninth century. Synod of A., 314. Cathedral built, eleventh century, and rebuilt twelfth and fourteenth centuries. Amphitheatre converted into a fortress, twelfth century. Archbishopric abolished, 1790.

Armada, The Spanish. Quitted Lisbon, 29 May 1588; arrived off Lizard, 19 July; Howard met A., 21 July, and kept up running fight until 25 July; A. anchored in Calais Roads, 26 July; met there by Howard and pursued until 22 Aug., though organized fighting ended 30 July.

Armagnacs or Orléanists. The anti-Burgundian (and therefore patriotic) party formed in 1396, first under the leadership of the Duke of Orleans. They played a decisive part in driving the British from France. Their objects being achieved by the Treaty of Arras, 1435, the faction ceased to exist.

'Armed Neutrality.' Confederacy of northern powers against maritime policy of England, commenced by Russia, 1780; its objects defeated, 1781; renewed, 16 Dec. 1800; dissolved after Nelson's victory at Copenhagen, 16 Dec. 1801.

Armenia (Hayastan), Asia. Subject in turn to Assyrians, Medes, and Persians. Conquered by Alexander, 325 B.C. Under Roman influence in early part of Christian era. Christianity introduced by St. Gregory the Illuminator in third century. Finally cut off from Byzantine Empire after battle of Manzikert, 1071. Conquered by Mongols, 1242. Reigning dynasty overthrown by Saracens, 1375. Continually persecuted by Turks. Massacres, 1895–7. In 1918, during the Russian Revolution, an independent 'Republic of Transcaucasia' was formed by union of A. with Azerbaijan and Georgia. This union was dissolved in 1918 when Allies recognized the independence of the Armenian Republic. Occupied by Red Army, 1920, and transformed into a Soviet republic, which in 1922 was included in the Transcaucasian Federal Republic of the U.S.S.R. When this was abolished, 1936, A. itself became a constituent republic of the U.S.S.R.

Arminianism. A doctrine of free will propounded by Jacobus Arminius, who was professor at Leyden University from 1603 till his death in 1609. A. savagely persecuted by Calvinists after the Synod of Dort (q.v.), 1618–19.

Armistice between Germany and Allies signed at Compiègne, 11 Nov. 1918. Between France and Germany at Com-

piègne, 22 June 1940. Between France and Italy, near Rome, 24 June 1940. Between N. Korea and the U.N. forces, 27 July 1953.

Army, British. Oldest English corps, the Yeomen of the Guard (q.v.), founded, 1485. Gentlemen-at-Arms (q.v.), 1509. Honourable Artillery Company, chartered 1537. 1st Foot (Royal Scots), 1633. Household troops established, 1661. Standing armies declared illegal in First Mutiny Act, 1689; Second, 1803. E. India Co.'s army absorbed, 1858. Flogging abolished in peace-time, 1868. A. Act, 1881. Short Service Act, 1870, and abolition of commission by purchase, 1871—part of the Cardwell (Secretary of War, 1868–74) reforms. Haldane's new A. scheme, 1906. Territorial and Reserve forces Act, July 1907. Kitchener's A., 1915. Derby Scheme, 1915. Conscription introduced, 1916; ended, 1918. Territorial A. formed, 1920. Southern Irish regiments disbanded and cavalry regiments reduced, 1922. Field Punishment No. 1 abolished, 1923. Mechanization, 1935. Conscription into militia (q.v.) introduced, 9 May 1939; ended, 1960. White Paper, 1957, set out plans for army reorganization, scheduled to be complete by the end of 1962, which included reducing the number of line cavalry and infantry regiments by amalgamation. See also REGIMENTS OF THE BRITISH ARMY and VOLUNTEERS.

Army Council. When office of C.-in-C. abolished A. C. was set up under the Secretary of State for War, 1904.

Army Plot, a rumoured attempt by the Royal A. to coerce parliament to obey Charles I, 1641.

Arnhem, Holland. Sir Philip Sidney d. at, 1586. Fortified by Cohoorn, 1702. Taken by French, 1795; by Prussians, 1813. Scene of the famous and unsuccessful landing of the British Airborne Divisions and Polish Parachute Brigade, 17–26 Sept. 1944.

Aroostook Dispute. Boundary dispute, 1839, between New Brunswick and Maine, so named on account of the Aroostook River.

Arras, Treaties of. Armagnacs and Burgundians, 1414; France and Burgundy, 20 Sept. 1435; Louis XI and Flemings, 1482. Catholic union between Hainault, Douai, and Artois signed at A., 5 Jan. 1579.

Arrest, Freedom from, a privilege enjoyed by members of Parliament from very early times, confirmed by Edward I, 1290. Recognized by Act of Parliament, 1433. See also PARLIAMENT.

Arromanches, Harbour of. Artificial prefabricated harbour used during Anglo-

American invasion of Normandy, 1944. Prototype constructed in Scotland, 1943. Equipment dispatched across Channel, 6 June 1944, and harbour functioning fully by the end of June.

Arrondissements or sub-prefectures, territorial divisions of French departments, under the administrative system introduced in 1799.

Arson remained a capital crime in England until the passing of the Malicious Damage Act, 1861.

Articles, The Six, statute passed, 1539; repealed, 1547.

Articles, The Thirty-nine, as now printed in the Prayer Book, are based on the Forty-Two Articles of 1553 (see next article), which were revised by Archbishop Parker and submitted to Convocation in 1562, and finally authorized by Parliament, 1571, the Declaration preceding them being drawn up by Archbishop Laud and added in 1628. Subscription thereto ceased to be obligatory on proceeding to a degree at Oxford or Cambridge, 1871.

Articles of Religion (Anglican), other than those mentioned above, were drawn up as follows:
Ten A., 1536.
Institution of a Christian Man (Bishop's Book), 1537.
Thirteen A., 1538.
Necessary Doctrine, etc. (King's Book), 1543.
Forty-two A., 1553.

Articles of War continued to form the legal basis for the discipline of the British Army until the Mutiny Act (*q.v.*) of 1789.

Artificial Silk or **Rayon.** Idea of imitating silk expressed by Réaumur, 1754 ; thread obtained from nitro-cellulose and called A. S. by Audemars in 1855. Process developed by de Chardonnet, 1886.

Artois, northern French province, conquered by Franks in the fifth century, but ruled by the counts of Flanders until they ceded it to the kings of France, 1180, who made it into a county, 1237, but in the fourteenth century ceded it to Burgundy, whence it passed to Austria, but returned to France under the Treaty of the Pyrenees, 1659. In 1789 it became the department of Pas-de-Calais. First artesian well in Europe sunk in A., 1126 (hence the name).

Arts, The Plastic. *See* ENGRAVING and PAINTING for history. The names of eminent performers in these departments, not now living, are:

American:

Abbey, Edwin Austin (painter), 1852–1911.

Cassatt, Mary (painter), 1855–1925.
Copley, John Singleton (painter), 1738–1815.
French, Daniel Chester (sculptor), 1850–1931.
Homer, Winslow (painter), 1836–1910.
Moses, Mrs Anna Mary Robertson (painter), 1860–1961.
Ryder, Albert Pinkham (painter), 1847–1905.
Saint-Gaudens, Augustus (sculptor), 1848–1907.
Sargent, John Singer (painter), 1856–1925.
West, Benjamin (painter), 1738–1820.
Whistler, James Abbott McNeill (painter and etcher), 1834–1903.
Wright, Frank Lloyd (architect), 1869–1959.

Chinese:

Chao Mêng-fu (painter), 1254–1322.
Chien Lung (painter and architect), 1722–96.
Han Kan (painter), *fl.* 600–50.
Hsieh-Ho (painter), *fl.* 450–500.
Ki K'ai-chih (painter), *fl.* 350–400.
Kuo Hsi (painter), *fl.* 1100–50.
Wu Tao-Tzu (painter), *fl.* 700–50.
Wu Wei (painter), 1458–1508.

Dutch:

Brouwer, Adrian (painter), 1605–38.
Cuyp, Aalbert (painter), 1620–91.
Gogh, Vincent Willem van (painter), 1853–90.
Hals, Frans (painter), 1580–1666.
Heem, Jan Davidsz van (painter), 1606–1684.
Hobbema, Meindert (painter), 1638–1709.
Hooch, Pieter de (painter), 1630–c. 1681.
Israels, Josef (painter), 1824–1911.
Jongkind, Johann Barthold (painter and engraver), 1819–91.
Mauve, Anton (painter), 1838–88.
Mesdag, Hendrik Wilhelm (painter), 1831–1905.
Metsu, Gabriel (painter), 1630–67.
Ostade, Adriaan van (painter and etcher), 1610–85.
Ostade, Isaack van (painter), 1621–49.
Rembrandt van Rijn (painter), 1606–69.
Ruisdael, Jakob Isaac van (painter), c. 1628–82.
Terborch, Gerard (painter), 1617–81.
Vandevelde, Adrian (painter and etcher), 1636–72.
Vandevelde, Jan (engraver), 1593–after 1641.
Vandevelde, Willem (I), 1611–93; and (II) (draughtsman), 1633–1707.
Vermeer van Delft, Jan (painter), 1632–75.

English, Scottish, Irish, and *Welsh:*

Abercrombie, Sir Patrick (architect), 1879–1957.

Adam, Robert (architect), 1728–92.

Alma-Tadema, Sir Lawrence (painter), 1836–1912.

Beardsley, Aubrey (illustrator), 1872–98.

Bewick, Thomas (engraver), 1753–1828.

Blake, William (engraver), 1757–1827.

Bonington, Richard Parkes (painter), 1802–28.

Brown, Ford Madox (painter), 1821–93.

Browne, Hablôt Knight ('Phiz') (caricaturist), 1815–82.

Burne-Jones, Sir Edward (painter), 1833–1898.

Chambers, Sir William (architect), 1723–1796.

Clausen, Sir George (painter), 1852–1944.

Constable, John (painter), 1776–1837.

Cooper, Samuel (miniaturist), 1609–1702.

Cooper, Thomas Sidney (painter), 1803–1902.

Cotman, John Sell (painter), 1782–1842.

Cox David (painter), 1793–1859.

Cozens, John Robert (painter), 1752–99.

Crome, John (painter), 1769–1821.

Cruikshank, George (caricaturist and illustrator), 1792–1878.

Epstein, Sir Jacob (sculptor), 1880–1959.

Etty, William (painter), 1787–1849.

Flaxman, John (sculptor), 1755–1826.

Forbes, Stanhope Alexander (painter), 1857–1947.

Frampton, Sir George (sculptor), 1860–1928.

Gainsborough, Thomas (painter), 1727–88.

Gibbons, Grinling (sculptor and wood-carver), 1648–1721.

Gibbs, James (architect), 1674–1754.

Gilbert, Sir Alfred (sculptor), 1854–1934.

Gill, Eric Rowland (sculptor, engraver, and typographer), 1882–1940.

Gillray, James (caricaturist), 1757–1815.

Girtin, Thomas (painter), 1775–1802.

Guthrie, Sir James (painter), 1859–1930.

Hawksmoor, Nicholas (architect), 1661–1736.

Hogarth, William (painter and engraver), 1697–1764.

Hoppner, John (painter), 1758–1810.

Hunt, William Holman (painter), 1827–1910.

John, Augustus Edwin (painter), 1879–1961.

Jones, Inigo (architect), c. 1573–c. 1652.

Keene, Charles Samuel (illustrator), 1823–91.

Kneller, Sir Godfrey (painter), 1646–73.

Landseer, Sir Edwin (painter), 1802–73.

Lavery, Sir John (painter), 1857–1941.

Lawrence, Sir Thomas (painter), 1769–1830.

Leighton, Frederick Leighton, Baron (painter and sculptor), 1830–96.

Lely, Sir Peter (painter), 1618–80.

Lewis, Percy Wyndham (painter), 1884–1957.

Low, David (cartoonist), 1891–1963.

Lutyens, Sir Edwin Landseer (architect), 1869–1944.

Mackintosh, Charles Rennie (architect), 1869–1928.

May, Philip William (illustrator), 1864–1903.

Millais, Sir John Everett (painter), 1829–96.

Moore, Henry (painter), 1831–95.

Morland, George (painter), 1763–1804.

Moser, Mary (painter), 1744–1819.

Munnings, Sir Alfred (painter), 1878–1959.

Nash, John (architect), 1752–1835.

Nash, Paul (painter and theatrical designer), 1889–1946.

Nevinson, Christopher Richard Wynne (painter), 1889–1946.

Opie, John (painter), 1761–1807.

Orchardson, Sir William Quiller (painter), 1835–1910.

Orpen, Sir William (painter), 1878–1931.

Rackham, Arthur (painter and illustrator), 1867–1939.

Raeburn, Sir Henry (painter), 1756–1823.

Rennie, John (architect), 1761–1821.

Reynolds, Sir Joshua (painter), 1723–92.

Romney, George (painter), 1734–1802.

Rossetti, Dante Gabriel (painter), 1828–1882.

Rothenstein, Sir William (painter and etcher), 1872–1945.

Rowlandson, Thomas (caricaturist), 1756–1827.

Scott, Sir George Gilbert (architect), 1811–78.

Scott, Sir Giles Gilbert (architect), 1880–1960.

Sickert, Walter Richard (painter), 1860–1942.

Sisley, Alfred (painter), 1840–99.

Spencer, Sir Stanley (painter), 1892–1959.

Steer, Philip Wilson (painter), 1860–1942.

Stevens, Alfred (sculptor), 1818–75.

Stone, Marcus (painter), 1840–1921.

Stone, Nicholas (sculptor), 1586–1647.

Tenniel, Sir John (cartoonist and illustrator), 1820–1914.

Turner, Joseph Mallord William (painter), 1775–1851.

Vanbrugh, Sir John (architect), 1664–1726.

Varley, John (painter), 1778–1842.

Watts, George Frederick (painter and sculptor), 1817–1904.

Wilkie, Sir David (painter), 1785–1841.

Wilson, Richard (painter), 1714–82.

Wint, Peter de (painter), 1784–1849.

Wren, Sir Christopher (architect), 1632–1723.

Yeats, Jack Butler (painter), 1871–1957.

Flemish:

Breughel, Jan (painter), 1508–1625.

Breughel, Pieter the Elder (painter), 1520-69.
Breughel, Pieter the Younger (painter), 1564-1637.
Eyck, Hubert van (painter), c. 1379-1426.
Eyck, Jan van (painter), c. 1390-1441.
Hoorenbault, Gerard (painter), 1480-1540.
Mabuse, Jan van (painter), c. 1475-1536.
Matsys, Quintin (painter), 1466-1530.
Memlinc, Hans (painter), c. 1430-94.
Rubens, Peter Paul (painter and etcher), 1577-1640.
Teniers the Younger, David (painter), 1610-94.
Van der Weyden, Rogier (painter), c. 1400-64.
Van Dyck, Sir Anthony (painter and etcher), 1599-1641.

French:

Blanche, Jacques Émile (painter), 1861-1942.
Boucher, François (painter), 1703-70.
Bourdelle, Émile Antoine (sculptor), 1861-1929.
Cézanne, Paul (painter), 1839-1906.
Chardin, Jean Baptiste Siméon (painter), 1699-1779.
Claude de Lorraine (painter), 1600-82.
Clouet, or Janet, François (painter), c. 1510-72.
Corot, Jean Baptiste Camille (painter), 1796-1875.
Courbet, Gustave (painter), 1819-77.
Dalou, Jules (sculptor), 1838-1902.
Daubigny, Charles François (painter), 1817-78.
Daumier, Honoré (caricaturist and painter), 1808-79.
David, Jacques Louis (painter), 1748-1825.
Degas, Edgar Hilaire Germaine (painter and engraver), 1834-1917.
Delacroix, Eugène (painter), 1798-1863.
Diaz de la Peña, Narcisse Virgile (painter), 1808-76.
Duvet, Jean (engraver), c. 1485-1561.
Fantin-Latour, Ignace Henri Jean Théodore (painter), 1836-1904.
Fragonard, Jean Honoré (painter), 1732-1806.
Gauguin, Paul (painter and sculptor), 1848-1903.
Géricault, Théodore (painter), 1791-1824.
Greuze, Jean Baptiste (painter), 1725-1805.
Houdon, Jean Antoine (sculptor), 1741-1828.
Ingres, Jean Auguste Dominique (painter), 1780-1867.
Le Brun, Charles (painter), 1619-90.
Lebrun, Elisabeth Vigée (painter), 1755-1842.
Le Nain, Antoine (painter), 1588-1648.
Le Nain, Louis (painter), 1593-1648.

Le Nain, Mathieu (painter), 1607-77.
Maillol, Aristide (sculptor), 1861-1944.
Manet, Édouard (painter), 1832-83.
Matisse, Henri (painter), 1869-1954.
Méryon, Charles (engraver), 1821-68.
Millet, Jean François (painter), 1814-75.
Monet, Claude Oscar (painter), 1840-1926.
Pissarro, Camille (painter), 1830-1903.
Poussin, Nicolas (painter), 1594-1665.
Puvis de Chavannes, Pierre Cécile (painter), 1824-98.
Renoir, Pierre Auguste (painter), 1841-1919.
Rodin, François Auguste (sculptor and etcher), 1840-1917.
Rouault, Georges (painter), 1871-1954.
Rousseau, Henri Julien (painter), 1844-1910.
Rousseau, Pierre Étienne Théodore (painter), 1812-67.
Seurat, Georges Pierre (painter), 1859-91.
Signac, Paul (painter), 1863-1935.
Toulouse-Lautrec, Henri de (painter), 1864-91.
Troyon, Constant (painter), 1810-65.
Utrillo, Maurice (painter), 1883-1955.
Viollet-le-Duc, Eugène Emmanuel (architect), 1814-79.
Watteau, Antoine (painter), 1684-1721.

German:

Altdorfer, Albrecht (painter and engraver) c. 1480-1538.
Carstens, Asmus Jakob (Danish-born painter), 1754-98.
Corinth, Lovis (painter), 1858-1925.
Cornelius, Peter von (painter), 1783-1867.
Cranach, Lucas (painter), 1472-1553.
Dürer, Albrecht (painter, engraver, and etcher), 1471-1528.
Elsheimer, Adam (sculptor), 1578-1610.
Friedrich, Caspar David (painter), 1774-1840.
Grünewald, Matthias (painter), c. 1470-1529.
Holbein the Elder, Hans (painter), c. 1460-1524.
Holbein the Younger, Hans (painter), 1497-1543.
Kampf, Arthur von, 1864-1950.
Kaulbach, Wilhelm von (painter), 1805-1874.
Liebermann, Max (painter), 1847-1935.
Marc, Franz (painter), 1880-1916.
Mengs, Anton Raphael (painter), 1728-79.
Schadow, Johann Gottfried (sculptor), 1764-1850.
Schongauer, Martin (painter and engraver), c. 1445-c. 1499.
Schwind, Moritz von (painter), 1805-71.
Strigel, Bernhardin (painter), 1460-1528.
Wilhelm of Cologne (painter), *fl.* 1358, *d. c.* 1378.

Greek, Ancient:

Apelles (painter), *fl.* 350 B.C.

Lysippus (sculptor), *c.* 336–270 B.C.

Myron (sculptor), fifth century B.C.

Pheidias (sculptor), *c.* 500–432 B.C.

Polyclitus of Argos (sculptor), *c.* 452–412 B.C.

Polygnotus (painter), *fl.* 500–425 B.C.

Praxiteles (sculptor), *fl.* 364–330 B.C.

Scopas (sculptor), *fl.* 395–350 B.C.

Italian:

Alberti, Leone Battista (architect), 1404–1472

Andrea del Castagno (painter), *c.* 1423–1457.

Andrea del Sarto (painter), 1488–1530.

Angelico, Fra Giovanni da Fiesole (painter), 1387–1455.

Bartolommeo, Fra, of S. Marco (painter), 1475–1517.

Bellini, Giovanni (painter), 1422–1516.

Bernini, Giovanni Lorenzo (sculptor, painter, and architect), 1598–1680.

Borromini, Francesco (architect), 1599–1677.

Botticelli, Sandro (painter), 1445–1510.

Bramante da Urbino (architect), 1444–1514.

Brunelleschi, Filippo (sculptor and architect), 1379–1446.

Canaletto, or Antonio Canale (painter), 1697–1768.

Canova, Antonio (sculptor and painter), 1757–1822.

Cellini, Benvenuto (sculptor and jeweller), 1500–71.

Cimabue, Giovanni (painter), 1240–1302.

Correggio, Antonio da (painter), 1494–1534.

Donatello (Donato di Betto Bardi) (sculptor), 1386–1466.

Duccio di Buoninsegna (painter), *c.* 1260–1319.

Ghiberti, Lorenzo (sculptor), 1378–1455.

Ghirlandajo, Domenico (painter), 1449–94.

Giorgione da Castelfranco (painter), 1477–1511.

Giotto (painter, sculptor, and architect), 1266–1337.

Gozzoli, Benozzo (painter), 1421–97.

Guardi, Francesco (painter), 1712–93.

Lippi, Filippino (painter), *c.* 1457–1504.

Lippi, Fra Filippo (painter), 1406–69.

Luca della Robbia (sculptor), 1399–1482.

Mantegna, Andrea (painter), 1431–1506.

Masaccio di S. Giovanni (painter), 1401–1428.

Michelangelo Buonarotti (painter, sculptor, and architect), 1475–1564.

Modigliani, Amadeo (painter), 1884–1920.

Moroni, Giambattista (painter), 1510–78.

Palladio, Andrea (architect), 1508–80.

Perugino, Pietro (painter), 1446–1523.

Piero della Francesca (painter), 1416–92.

Piranesi, Giovanni Battista (engraver), 1720–78.

Pollaiuolo, Antonio (painter), 1432–98.

Raphael of Urbino (painter and architect), 1483–1520.

Sansovino, Andrea (sculptor and architect), 1460–1529.

Sansovino, Jacopo (sculptor and architect), 1486–1570.

Segantini, Giovanni (painter), 1858–99.

Tiepolo, Giovanni Battista (painter), 1696–1770.

Tintoretto (Jacopo Robusti) (painter), 1518–94.

Titian, or Tiziano Vecellio (painter), 1477–1576.

Uccello, Paolo (painter), 1397–1475.

Veronese, Paolo (painter), 1528–88.

Verrocchio, Andrea del (sculptor and painter), 1435–88.

Vinci, Leonardo da (painter and sculptor), 1452–1519.

Japanese:

Cho Denshu (painter), 1351–1427.

Doncho (Korean painter), *fl.* sixth century.

Hidari Jingaró (sculptor), *d.* 1634.

Hishigawa Moronobu (painter of engravings), 1618–94.

Hokusai (painter of engravings), 1760–1849.

Jositsu (painter), *fl.* fifteenth century.

Kosé-no-Kanaoka (painter), *fl.* 850.

Utamaro (painter of engravings), 1754–1806.

Russian:

Bakst, Leon (painter and costume designer), 1866–1924.

Fabergé, Peter Carl (goldsmith and lapidary), 1846–1920.

Kandinsky, Vasily (painter), 1866–1944.

Repin, Ilya Yefimovich (painter), 1844–1918.

Rublyov, Andrea (painter of icons), *c.* 1370–1430.

Scandinavian:

Burgesson, John (Icelandic sculptor), *d.* 1910.

Jensen, Georg (Danish silversmith), 1866–1935.

Milles, Carl (Swedish sculptor), 1875–1955.

Munch, Edvard (Norwegian painter), 1863–1944.

Thorwaldsen, Bertel (Danish sculptor), 1770–1844.

Vigeland, Gustaf (Norwegian sculptor), 1869–1943.

Zorn, Anders Leonard (Swedish etcher and engraver), 1860–1920.

Spanish:

Cano, Alonso (painter, sculptor, and architect), 1601–67.

Fortuny y Carbo, Mariano José Bernardo (painter), 1839–74.

Goya y Lucientes, Francisco José de (painter and etcher), 1746–1828.

Greco, El, or Domenico Theotocopuli (Greek-Spanish painter), 1541–1614.

Murillo, Bartolomé Estéban (painter), 1617–82.

Pradilla, Francisco (painter), 1847–1921.

Ribera, Jusepe de (painter), 1588–1656.

Velázquez, Diego de Silva y (painter), 1599–1660.

Zurbaran, Francisco (painter), 1598–1662.

Various:

Brancusi, Constantin (Rumanian sculptor), 1876–1957.

Ensor, James (Belgian painter), 1860–1947.

Kauffmann, Angelica (Swiss painter), 1741–1807.

Klee, Paul (Swiss painter), 1879–1940.

Meunier, Constantin (Belgian sculptor), 1831–1905.

Mylsbeč, Joseph Wenceslas (Czech sculptor), 1848–1922.

Arts Council of Great Britain, name adopted on 9 Aug. 1946 by the former C.E.M.A. (*q.v.*).

Arts, Society of. London, established, 1754; incorporated, 1847. Edinburgh, established, 1821; incorporated, 1841.

Arya Samaj. Reformist Hindu society founded about 1866 by Dayananda Sarasvati (1825?–82).

Ascalon (modern **Ashkelon**), Israel. Biblical Philistine city. Captured by Saladin, 1187, and by Bibars, Sultan of Egypt, who demolished its fortifications, 1270. *See* CRUSADES.

Ascension Island, discovered on A. Day, 1501, by João da Nova. First occupied by British, 1815, and administered by the Admiralty until 1922, when it was made a dependency of St. Helena.

Ashanti, Ghana. First British expedition to, 1807. Wars with Great Britain: (1) 1863–4; (2) 1873–4; (3) 1895–1900 (relief of Kumasi). Protectorate, 1896; annexed, 1901. Native dynasty restored, 1935. Riots against proposed constitution of Ghana, 1955.

Ashburton Treaty, 1842, settled the frontiers between U.S.A. and Canada.

Ashes, The, non-existent cricket trophy, competed for between England and Australia, first mentioned 29 Aug. 1882.

Ashmolean Museum. Founded, 1683, by Elias Ashmole (1617–92). Its contents separated, 1860, 1886, and 1894, and the bulk of them placed in the present building.

Asiento, The. Contract originally between France and Spain for supplying Negro slaves to Spanish colonies,

1702. Transferred by Spain to Britain, 1713. Twice lost, it was finally restored for remaining period of two years, 1748.

Assam, State of India. Conquered by British, 1826. Tea planting inaugurated, 1835. Separated from Bengal, 1874. United to E. Bengal, 1905–12. Separate province, 1919. Invaded by Japanese, 1944. Sylhet district voted to join E. Pakistan, Aug. 1947. University established at Gauhati, 1948.

Assassinations. The most famous victims of assassination include:

Hipparchus of Athens, by Harmodius and Aristogiton, 514 B.C.

Artaxerxes III of Persia, by Bagoas, B.C. 338.

Philip II of Macedon, by Pausanias, 336 B.C.

Darius III of Persia, by Bessus, 330 B.C.

Julius Caesar, by Brutus and others, 15 Mar. 44 B.C.

Caius Caligula, by a tribune, A.D. 37.

Claudius I, poisoned by his wife, Agrippina, A.D. 41.

Edmund, St., King of E. Anglia, 870.

Edmund the Elder of England, 26 Mar. 946.

Edward the Martyr of England, 18 Mar. 979.

Albert I of Germany, by his nephew John, 1 May 1308.

Edward II of England, 27 Sept. 1327.

St. Thomas Becket, Archbishop of Canterbury, 29 Dec. 1170.

James I of Scotland, by nobles, 21 Feb. 1437.

Edward V of England, July 1483.

James III of Scotland, by nobles, 11 June 1488.

David Rizzio, Mary Stuart's secretary, by Darnley's followers, 9 Mar. 1566.

Lord Henry Darnley, Mary Stuart's husband, by persons unknown, 10 Feb. 1567.

William the Silent, of Orange, by Balthazar Gérard, 12 July 1584.

Henry III of France, by Jacques Clément, 1 Aug. 1589.

Henry IV of France, by Ravaillac, 14 May 1610.

George Villiers, Duke of Buckingham, by John Felton, 23 Aug. 1628.

Gustavus III of Sweden, by Ankarström, 29 Mar. 1792.

Marat, by Charlotte Corday, 13 July 1793.

Paul, Tsar of Russia, by nobles, 24 Mar. 1801.

Spencer Perceval, British Prime Minister, by Bellingham, 11 May 1812.

Abraham Lincoln, President of U.S.A., by Wilkes Booth, 14 Apr. 1865.

Michael, Prince of Serbia, 10 June 1868.

Abdul Aziz, Sultan of Turkey, alleged

suicide, 4 June 1876.

Mehemet Ali Pasha, by Albanians, 7 Sept. 1878.

Alexander II of Russia, 13 Mar. 1881.

General Garfield, President of U.S.A., by Charles Jules Guiteau, *d.* 19 Sept., 2 July 1881.

Chief Secretary for Ireland, Lord Frederick Cavendish, by Fenians, 6 May 1882.

Sadi Carnot, President of France, by Santo Caserio, 24 June 1894.

Nasr-ed-Deen, Shah of Persia, by Mullah Reza a Sayyid, 1 May 1896.

Elizabeth, Empress of Austria, by Luccheni, 10 Sept. 1898.

Humbert I of Italy, by Gaetano Bresci, 29 July 1900.

William McKinley, President of U.S.A., by Leon Czolgosz, *d.* 14 Sept., 6 Sept. 1901.

Alexander I of Serbia and wife, Draga, 11 June 1903.

King Carlos and Crown Prince of Portugal, by Buica and Da Costa, 1 Feb. 1908.

Prince Ito of Japan, 26 Oct. 1909.

Peter Stolypin, Russian premier, 14 Sept. 1911.

Francisco I. Madero, President of Mexico, and Vice-President José Pino Saurez, 23 Feb. 1913.

George I of Greece, 18 Mar. 1913.

Archduke Francis Ferdinand of Austria-Hungary and wife, by Gabriel Princip, 28 June 1914.

Jean L. Jaurès, French Socialist leader, 31 July 1914.

Tsar Nicholas of Russia and family, at Ekaterinburg, by the Bolsheviks, 16 July 1918.

Habibullah Khan, Amir of Afghanistan, 20 Feb. 1919.

General Venustiano Carranza, President of Mexico, 20 May 1920.

Field-Marshal Sir Henry H. Wilson, in London, 22 June 1922.

Dr. Walter Rathenau, German Foreign Minister, 24 June 1922.

Michael Collins, by rebels, near Bandon, County Cork, 22 Aug. 1922.

Gabriel Narutowicz, first President of Polish Republic by Capt. Niewadowski, 16 Dec. 1922.

General J. C. Gomez, first Vice-President of Venezuela, 29 June 1923.

Giacomo Matteoti, Italian Socialist leader, kidnapped by Fascists, body found 15 Aug., 10 June 1924.

Kevin O'Higgins, Vice-President of Irish Free State, 10 July 1927.

Paul Doumer, President of France, by Paul Gargolov, 6 May 1932.

Luis M. Sanchez Cerro, President of Peru, by Abelardo Hurtado de Mendoza, 30 Apr. 1933.

Nadir Shah, King of Afghanistan, by

Abdul Khallig, student, 8 Nov. 1933.

Ernst Roehm, General Schleicher, his wife, and others, by Nazi Party, 30 June 1934.

Engelbert Dollfuss, Austrian Chancellor, by Otto Planetta, 25 July 1934.

Alexander, King of Yugoslavia, and French Foreign Minister Louis Barthou, at Marseilles, by Georgief, 9 Oct. 1934.

Senator Huey Long of Louisiana, by Carl Weiss, 8 Sept. 1935.

Ernst von Rath, German diplomat, by Herschel Grynszpan, in Paris, 7 Nov. 1938.

Professor Cristescu, Iron Guard leader, Armand Calinescu, Premier of Rumania, by Iron Guard, 26 Jan. 1939.

Leon Trotsky, exiled Russian leader, at Coycacán, Mexico, by Jacques Mornard, 21 Aug. 1940.

Darlan, Jean François, Frencn admiral, at Algiers, 24 Dec. 1942.

Benito Mussolini, dictator of Italy, and his mistress, by Italian partisans, 28 April 1945.

Ananda Mahidol, King of Thailand, 9 July 1946.

Mohandas Karamchand Gandhi, by Natheram Jodre, 30 Jan. 1948.

Imam Yahya of the Yemen, 17 Feb. 1948.

Count Folke Bernadotte, United Nations mediator, by Israeli terrorists, at Jerusalem, 17 Sept. 1948.

President Chalbaud of Venezuela, 13 Nov. 1950.

King Abdullah of Jordan, 20 July 1951.

Liaquat Ali Khan, Prime Minister of Pakistan, by Said Akbar, 16 Oct. 1951.

President Somoza of Nicaragua, 29 Sept. 1956.

King Feisal II of Iraq, his family and Prime Minister, by revolutionary nationalists, 14 July 1958.

Mr. Bandaranaike, Prime Minister of Ceylon, by Buddhist extremists, 25 Sept. 1959.

General Rafael Trujillo, dictator of the Dominican Republic, 30 May 1961.

President Sylvanus Olympio of Togo, 13 Jan. 1963.

John F. Kennedy, President of U.S.A., at Dallas, Texas, 22 Nov. 1963.

Assassins, powerful Moslem secret society founded in Syria by Hassan ibn Sabbah (*fl.* 1080), the original 'Old Man of the Mountain' (*Sheikh-el-Jebel*). Massacre of 1255 virtually exterminated the sect.

Assent, Royal, last refused to a parliamentary bill, 1707.

Assignats and **Mandats.** French revolutionary paper currency, first issued, 1790, secured originally on confiscated church and *émigré* property. Over-issue led to serious inflation, and by 1797 they had to be withdrawn.

Assiniboia. Name previously applied to two districts in Canada. First formed, 1835, by the Hudson's Bay Co. and ceased to exist, 1870, on the transference of Rupert's Land to Canada. Second created, 1882, as a provisional district within the North-West Territories, and became part of Saskatchewan in 1905.

Assisi. St. Francis (d. 1226) b. at, 1182. Founded the Franciscan order at, 1209.

Assize Courts. See COURTS, ENGLISH.

Assize of Clarendon, 1166, first legislative direction to employ the jury (q.v.).

Assize of Northampton, 1176.

Assumption of the Virgin Mary established as an article of the Roman Catholic faith by a papal pronouncement ex cathedra, 1950.

Assyria became independent of Babylon (q.v.), seventeenth century B.C.; rose into prominence under Tiglath-Pileser I c. 1120 B.C., who conquered Babylon. Nineveh became capital under Tiglath-Pileser III (745–727 B.C.), whose empire was maintained by Sargon II, 722–705, and Sennacherib, 705–681 (see Bible). Essarhaddon, 681–668, conquered Egypt, but on his death the empire was divided and an alliance of Medes and Babylonians stormed and destroyed Nineveh and overthrew the Assyrian Empire, 612 B.C.

Assyrians (Modern). About A.D. 1400 the Chaldaean Christians of N. Iraq, who had survived the reign of Timur-i-Leng the Mongol, fled to the Hakkiari mountains N. of Mosul. Their tradition stated that they were the descendants of the ancient A., converted to Christianity in the first century A.D. by Thaddaeus. They were affected to some extent by the Nestorian heresy c. 400. Between 1550 and 1750 various sections submitted to Rome as 'Chaldaean Uniates.' The remainder in the face of Moslem pressure and Kurdish massacres appealed for help to the Archbishop of Canterbury, 1843. An Anglican mission came out in 1876. On 10 May 1915 the Mar Shimun (Patriarch) Benjamin of the A. declared war on Turkey, and after fighting Turkish troops and Kurdish irregulars retired into Persian territory. Until the spring of 1917 the A. fought as Russian auxiliaries. Driven out of the Urmiya area they retired to Hamadan, Aug.–Sept. 1918. In the autumn of 1920 the Agha Petros attempted to set up an Assyrian state in the upper valley of the Great Zab River, but failed. Settled in N. Iraq, 1921–30, employed against Kurdish guerrillas. In July 1933 the Malik Yacu attempted to lead a dissident faction of A. into Syria. Turned back by French frontier officials

he came into conflict with Iraqi forces on the Tigris. In Aug. 1933, while Assyrian villages were being looted and their inhabitants massacred by the Kurds, followers of Yacu who gave themselves up were shot at the instigation or with the connivance of the Iraqi generals Beqir Sidqi, Nuri es Said, and Rashid Ali.

Asteroids, designation given to minor planets, 1802, by Sir William Herschel (1738–1822.) First and largest asteroid, Ceres, discovered by Piazzi at Palermo on 1 Jan. 1801.

Astronomer Royal. Office established, 1675.

Astronomical Association, British. First meeting, 24 Oct. 1890.

Astronomical Society, Royal. Founded, 1820. Incorporated, 1831.

Astronomy. Copernicus (founder of present system), b. 1473, d. 1543; Kepler discovered planetary motions, 1609, 1619; Galileo discovered Jupiter's moons, sunspots, 1610; Newton's discoveries, 1666, etc.; Greenwich Observatory, 1675; Halley's observations, 1705, etc.; Herschel's observations, 1781, etc.; Lord Rose completed famous telescope, 1845; Lick telescope erected at Mt. Hamilton, California, 1887; Professor Perrine discovered new satellites of Jupiter, 1904–5, 1908. The work of stellar spectroscopy begun in America in 1872 by Henry Draper (1837–82). Spectra interpreted, 1913; Michelson measured angular diameter of a star, 1920, at the Mt. Wilson Observatory. Jodrell Bank Radio Telescope, largest in the world, completed, 1958.

Asuncion, Paraguay. Founded, 1537.

Aswan or **Assuan,** Egypt. Dam built, 1902. Raised, 1912. Raised again, 1929–31. High Dam commenced, 1955.

Asylum, Right of. Exercised by embassies in Europe, 1862 (Greece) and 1875 (Spain). In twentieth century exercised intermittently in S. America, more recently in Europe. Nov. 1956: Nagy, the Hungarian Prime Minister, sought asylum in the Yugoslav Embassy, and Cardinal Mindszenty, Hungarian primate, in the U.S. embassy (where he still remained, June 1963).

Athanasian Creed. See CREEDS.

Athelney, Somerset. King Alfred fled here in 878–9. The Alfred Jewel found, 1693.

'Athenaeum,' The. Literary weekly founded, 2 Jan. 1828. Absorbed into the Nation, Feb. 1921; amalgamated with New Statesman, 1931.

Athenaeum Club (London). Founded, 1824.

Athens. History: Dracon's legal code, 621 B.C. Reforms of Solon, 594. Tyranny of the Peisistratids, 560–510.

Reforms of Cleisthenes, 508. Persian Wars, 490; 480–479; 468; 450–449. First Delian League, 478–404; second, 377–338. Age of Pericles, 443–429. Peloponnesian War, 431–421; 416–413; 412–404, when A. surrendered to Lysander. Government of the Thirty, 404–403, when the democracy was restored. A. again at war with Sparta, 378–371. Social War, 357–355. Athenian and allied forces defeated by Philip II of Macedon at Chaeronea, 338. Lamian War, 323–322, when A. was occupied by Antipater and compelled to modify her constitution. The democracy restored by Demetrius Poliorcetes, 307. A. included in the Roman province of Achaia, 146. Captured by Sulla, 86 B.C. Philosophical schools closed by Justinian, A.D. 529. A. captured by Latins, 1205, and remained a Latin duchy till 1261. Captured by Turks, 1454; by Venetians. 1466; recaptured by Turks, 1479. Venetians attack and explode the Parthenon, which had been made a powder magazine, 1687; retaken by Turks, 1690. Captured by Greeks, 1822; retaken by Turks, 1827. Became capital of Greece, 1834. Occupied by French and English, 1854–6; by Allies, Dec. 1916. Piraeus modernized, 1929. Germans occupied A., 27 Apr. 1941. British liberated A., 14 October 1944. Fighting between Communists and German forces, 5–30 Dec. 1944.

Ancient Buildings: A. sacked and destroyed by Persians, 480 B.C. City wall, built by Themistocles soon after 479 B.C.; reconstructed by Conon in 393 and by Lycurgus c. 333; enlarged by Hadrian. Erechtheum: building started between 431 and 421; completed, 409; repaired after fire, early fourth century; west front reconstructed, first century A.D. Long Walls: North and Phaleric completed c. 457 B.C., Middle or South c. 445; all destroyed, 404. North and Middle restored, 393; both finally destroyed by Sulla, 86 B.C. Monument of Lysicrates, 335–334. Odeum of Herodes Alticus, c. A.D. 162. Parthenon: begun, 447 B.C.; dedicated, 438; sculptures completed, 432. Propylaea, 437–433. Stadium, c. 330 B.C.; rebuilt c. A.D. 143; restored, late nineteenth century. Stoa of Attalus c. 158 B.C.; restored, A.D. 1955. Temple of Hephaestus, fifth century B.C. Temple of Olympian Zeus: Begun by Hippias c. 520 B.C.; continued, 175–164; completed, A.D. 132. Theatre of Dionysus: site first used for temporary wooden structure, 490 B.C.; permanent stone structure, between 338 and 326; alterations to stage and orchestra under Nero and Hadrian. Tower of the Winds, second or third century.

Atlantic Charter. Declaration of the Four Freedoms issued by President Roosevelt and Winston Churchill from a warship in the Atlantic, 11 Aug. 1941.

Atlantic Flights. *See* AVIATION.

Atlantic Passage Record since the first crossing by a steamer, *Sirius,* in 1838, was held by the *Queen Mary,* 1938, until broken by the *United States,* 7 July 1952, with a time of 3 days, 10 hours, 40 minutes.

Atlantic Telegraph Cable, begun Aug. 1857. First message, 5 Aug. 1858. Subsequently cable broke, and not successfully relaid until 1866.

Atlantic Telephone Cable. First one successfully laid and opened to traffic, 1956.

Atom. First split by Lord Rutherford, 1919.

Atomic Bomb. First detonated experimentally, 16 July 1945; first used operationally at Hiroshima, 6 Aug., and at Nagasaki 9 Aug. 1945.

Atomic Energy Research Establishment. Established at Harwell, Berks., 1945.

Atomic Power. Radioactivity discovered by Becquerel, 1896. Einstein's equation, 1905.

A.T.S. (Auxiliary Territorial Service). *See* WOMEN'S ROYAL ARMY CORPS.

Attainder, Act of. First Bill of A. recorded against Despenser family, 1321. Most famous against Strafford after his impeachment had failed, 1641. Last against Lord E. Fitzgerald for participation in the Irish Rebellion, 1797.

Atterbury's Plot. Abortive Jacobite plot led by Francis Atterbury, Bishop of Rochester (1662–1732) in 1721. Atterbury was banished.

Attorney-General. William de Giselham, first recorded A.-G., 1278. A.-G. has sat in House of Commons since 1673. Ceased to practise at the Bar privately in return for increased salary, 1945.

Auckland. Founded, 1840. Was capital of New Zealand till 1865.

Augmentation, Court of, set up, 1536, under Act of Dissolution. Dissolved, 1553.

Augsburg. Founded by Romans c. 15 B.C. (as **Augusta Vindelicorum**). Free city, 1276. Confession of A. drawn up by Luther and Melanchthon and presented to Charles V at Diet of A., 25 June 1530. Interim of A., 15 May 1548. Religious peace of A., 1555. League of A. against France, 9 July 1686. Annexed by Bavaria, 1806. Heavily bombed, Aug. 1940 and Apr. 1942, by R.A.F.

Augustales, games, sacred to the memory of the Emperor Augustus, held on his birthday, beginning in 11 B.C.

Augusteo, Roman concert hall on the site of the Mausoleum of Augustus, opened in 1908.

Augustinian Canons. Order established consequent on the Lateran synod of 1059.

Auk, Great. Last known specimen killed, 4 June 1844, on the Stack of Eldey, off S.W. Iceland.

Aulic Council. Established by Emperor Maximilian I, 1497, to assist in governing the Holy Roman Empire (*q.v.*).

Auschwitz. *See* OSWIECIM.

Ausgleich (compromise). A treaty governing the joint affairs of the Dual Monarchy, concluded between its several partners, Austria and Hungary, in 1867, and renewed in 1878, 1887, 1902, and 1907.

Australia. N. coast sighted by various Dutch voyagers, seventeenth century. Explored by Capt. Dampier, 1688; by Capt. Cook, 1769–70; Bass and Flinders, 1798. Colonized by English convicts, 1788. Last convicts landed, 1840. Divided into provinces, 1829, 1834, 1850, 1859. New South Wales Constitution, 1842. Australian Colonies Act passed, 1850; granted power to various provinces to draw up own constitution. Goldrush began, 1851. S. Australian Constitution, 27 Oct. 1856. Victoria Parliament opened at Melbourne, 17 Jan. 1867. Commonwealth Bill of A. Constitution, 9 July 1900. First governor-general appointed, 14 July 1900. Extensive shipping disputes, 1924. New Migration Agreement with Britain early in 1925. Seamen's strike, July–Aug. 1925. Federal Parliament opened at Canberra (*q.v.*) by Duke of York, 9 May 1927. Referendum to alter constitution so as to authorize agreements between Commonwealth and States for taking over State debts and loans, 17 Nov. 1928. Financial crises began, 1930; Scullin (Labour) Ministry extending protective duties to curtail imports. Assisted migration from U.K. stopped, 1930. Labour defeated in General Election. 1931. Returned to office under Curtin, 1941. Western A., after referendum, unsuccessfully sought leave to secede from the Commonwealth, 1933–5. Referendum rejected Commonwealth control of aviation and marketing, 1937. Bank Nationalization Act passed, 27 Nov. 1947; declared unconstitutional by Supreme Court, 13 Aug. 1948. Liberal-Country Coalition won elections, 10 Dec. 1949, and subsequently re-elected 1954, 1955, 1958, and 1961. Labour party split on Communist issue, 1954.

Governor-Generals since 1901:

Earl of Hopetoun	1901–1902
Lord Tennyson	1902–1904
Lord Northcote	1904–1908
Earl of Dudley	1908–1911
Lord Denman	1911–1914
Visc. Novar	1914–1920
Lord Forster	1920–1925
Lord Stonehaven	1925–1930
Lord Somers (acting)	1930–1931
Sir Isaac Alfred Isaacs	1931–1936
Lord Gowrie	1936–1944
Sir Winston Joseph Dugan (acting)	1944–1945
H.R.H. the Duke of Gloucester	1945–1947
Sir Winston Joseph Dugan (acting)	1947
Sir William John McKell	1947–1952
Sir William Slim	1953–1960
Lord Dunrossil	1960–1961
Viscount De L'Isle	1961–

Heads of Administrations (Prime Ministers) from 1901:

Barton	1901–1903
Deakin	1903–1904
Watson	(Apr.–Aug.) 1904
Reid	1904–1905
Deakin	1905–1908
Fisher	1908–1909
Deakin	1909–1910
Fisher	1910–1913
Cook	1913–1914
Fisher	1914–1915
Hughes	1915–1923
Bruce	1923–1929
Scullin	1929–1931
Lyons	1931–1939
Menzies	1939–1941
Fadden	(Aug.–Oct.) 1941
Curtin	1941–1945
Chifley	1945–1949
Menzies	1949–

Austria (Ger. **Oesterreich**). Roman provinces of Rhaetia, Noricum, and Pannonia *c.* 33 B.C. Organized as a march (*Ostmark*) of the Holy Roman Empire (*q.v.*) by Charlemagne, 791–6. Created a duchy, 1156. Given by Emperor Rudolf I of Hapsburg to his son Rudolf, 1282. Carinthia annexed, 1335. Defeated twice by Swiss at Zürich, 1358. Annexation of Tyrol, 1363. Leopold III killed by Swiss at battle of Sempach, 1386. Albert V becomes King of Bohemia and Hungary, 1437–40. Created archduchy, 6 Jan. 1453. Recognizes Swiss independence, 1474. Vienna captured by Matthias of Hungary, 1485. A. given to Ferdinand, brother of Emperor Charles V, 1521. Annexation of Bohemia and Silesia, 1526. First Turkish siege of Vienna, 1529. 'Imperial' Hungary ceded to A., 1541. Truce of Adrianople with Turks, 1545. Zapolya renounces Hungary to A., 1570. Thirty Years War (*q.v.*), 1618–48. Peace of Westphalia (*q.v.*), 1648. Hungary conquered from Turks, 1688; acquisition confirmed by Treaty of Carlowitz, 1699. A. saved by Marlborough and Prince Eugene at battle of Blenheim, 1704. War of Austrian Succession, 1741–8. Seven Years War (*q.v.*), 1756–63. French Revolutionary Wars begun 1792. Lombardy and the Netherlands secured by France, 1797. Defeat at battle of Hohenlinden, Dec. 1800. Pact of Lunéville, Feb. 1801. Defeat at battle of Ulm, 1805. At Austerlitz, Dec. 1805. Pact of Pressburg, Dec. 1805. Battle of Wagram, 1809. Battle of Leipzig, 1813. Treaty of Paris, May 1814. Congress of Vienna, 1814–15. The Karlsbad Decrees, 1819. Congress of Laibach (Ljubljana), 1821. Conference of Münchengrätz, 1833. Annexation of Cracow, 1846. Revolution and resignation of Metternich, Mar. 1848. Czech revolt suppressed, June 1848. Hungarian rebellion under Kossuth, Sept. 1848. Windischgrätz suppressed Vienna insurrection, Oct. 1848. Hungarians capitulate to Russians at Vilagos, Aug. 1849. Convention of Olmütz (Olomouc), 1850. Occupation of Rumania, 1854. Austro-Prussian invasion of Denmark, 1864. War with Prussia, 1866. Battle of Sadowa, 3 July 1866. Sardinia annexed Venetia, 1866. The '*Ausgleich*' ('compromise') with Hungary, 1867. Alliance with Russia and Germany (*Dreikaiserbund*), 1873. Renewed, 1881, 1884. Annexation of Bosnia-Herzegovina, 1908. Archduke Franz Ferdinand assassinated at Sarajevo, 28 June 1914. World War I (*q.v.*), 1914–18. *Bundesrepublik* (Federal Republic) declared secession from Dual Monarchy, 12 Nov. 1918. New boundaries settled by Treaty of St. Germain, 10 Sept. 1919. Federal Constitution, Nov. 1920. Rioting, 1927. Dollfuss suppresses Socialists in Vienna by military force, Feb. 1934. Assassinated by Nazis, 25 July 1934. Prince Starhemberg dismissed from cabinet, 1936. Annexed by Germany ('*Anschluss*'), 12–14 Mar. 1938. Russian armies invaded A., 1945, and captured Vienna, 13 Apr. Karl Renner (1870–1950) elected president, 1945, of revived *Bundesrepublik*. General Election, 25 Nov. 1945. Dr. Figl, Chancellor of Socialist-Populist Coalition Government, approved by Allies, 18 Dec. 1945. Agreement with Italy on S. Tyrol, 6 Sept. 1946. Coalition Government returned again by election of Oct. 1949, with increased Christian-Social influence. Last political (i.e. Nazi) prisoners, except those sentenced for civil crimes, freed, Dec. 1951. Restoration by a court of Starhemberg's estates, confiscated by Nazis in 1938, caused Socialist threat to withdraw from Government, Jan. 1952. Populist government re-

turned by General Election, Feb. 1953. Austrian peace treaty signed, 15 May 1955. Last occupation forces left A., Sept. 1955. Coalition governments of Populists and Socialists formed after 1956 and 1959 elections. There were some right-wing gains in the elections held in November 1962.

Austria, Emperors of:

The rulers of the house of Hapsburg (Grand Dukes of Austria) took the title of Emperor of A. on 11 Aug. 1804, and Francis II renounced the crown of the Holy Roman Empire (*q.v.*), 6 Aug. 1806. The following were the Emperors of A.:

Franz II and I		1804–1835
Ferdinand I		1835–1848
Franz Josef		1848–1916
Karl	(abdicated)	1916–1918

Effective Heads of Administration:

The government of the Austrian Empire cannot be compared with the system of responsible government existing in England at the same time. Its heads relied in the last resort upon the emperor, and his personal policy could decide which member of the administration was to be the effective head, regardless of their actual titles of office. The following is a list of the most influential figures in Austrian government. It does not purport to be a list of the holders of one particular office.

Stadion	1806–1809
Von Metternich	1809–1848
Kolowrat	1848
Ficquelmont	1848
Von Pillersdorf	1848
Wessenberg	1848
Schwarzenberg	1848–1852
Bach	1852–1859
Goluchowski	1859–1860
Von Schmerling	1861–1865
Belcredi	1865–1867
Beust	1867–1870
Taaffe	1870–1871
Hohenwart	1871
Von Auersperg	1871–1878
Stremayr	1878–1879
Taaffe	1879–1893
Windischgrätz	1893–1895
Badeni	1895–1897
Gautsch	1897–1898
Von Thun	1898–1899
Clary–Aldringen	1899
Von Körber	1900–1904
Gautsch	1905–1906
Von Hohenlohe	1906
Beck	1906–1908
Biernerth	1908–1911
Gautsch	1911
Stürgkh	1912–1916
Von Körber	1916
Clam–Martinic	1917

Von Seidler	1917–1918
Hussarek	1918
Lammasch	1918

Presidents, since 1920:

Hainisch	1920–1928
Miklas	1928–1938
	(13 Mar.)
Renner	1945–1950
Koerner	1951–1957
Schärf	1957–

Heads of Administration since 1919 (Chancellors):

Renner	Mar. 1919–Oct. 1919
Mayr	Oct. 1919–July 1920
'Proporz' Cabinet	July 1920–Nov. 1920
Mayr	Nov. 1920–May 1921
Schober	July 1921–May 1922
Seipel	May 1922–Nov. 1924
Ramek	Nov. 1924–Oct. 1926
Seipel	Oct. 1926–Apr. 1929
Steeruwitz	May 1929–Sept. 1929
Schober	Sept. 1929–Sept. 1930
Vaugoin	Sept. 1930–Nov. 1930
Ender	Dec. 1930–June 1931
Seipel	18 June 1931–20 June 1931
Buresch	June 1931–May 1932
Dollfuss	May 1932–July 1934
Von Schuschnigg	July 1934–12 Mar. 1938

Seyss-Inquart was nominally chancellor from 12–14 Mar. 1938. After 'inviting' Hitler to annex Austria, he became first governor of *Ostmark*.

Renner	Apr. 1945–Oct. 1945
	(provisional)
Figl	Nov. 1945–1953
Raab	1953–1959
Gorbach	1959–

Austrian Succession, War of the. Broke out, 1741. Ended by Treaty of Aix-la-Chapelle, 1748.

Authorized Version of the Bible, rendered into English by a commission of 47 translators working, 1607–10, and first published, 1611.

Auto-da-fé, or ceremonial burning of heretics by the Inquisition, last performed in Mexico, 1815.

Automobile Association. Founded, 1905.

Autun. Ancient Augustodunum, founded by Augustus, who removed thither the population of nearby Gallic Bibracte. Destroyed, A.D. 240; but rebuilt 340; sacked by Vandals, 406; Burgundians, 414; Huns, 451; Franks, 534; Arabs, 739; Normans, 895; English, 1379.

Auxiliary Territorial Service. *See* WOMEN'S ROYAL ARMY CORPS.

Aviation. Borelli's artificial wings, 1670; Sir George Caley's machine, 1796; Henson's aerostat, 1843; Wenham's aeroplane, 1866; Dr. Pettigrew's elastic screws demonstrated, 1867; Moy's aerial steamer, 1874; Langley's steam-driven model,

1893; Sir H. Maxim's experiments, 1880–1890, 1893–4; Lilienthal killed on gliding machine, 1896; W. and O. Wright's experiments begun, 1900; they first flew, 1903; S. Dumont's aeroplane, 1906; Farman biplane, 1907; Blériot flew across Channel, 25 July 1909; Paulhan's altitude record, Jan. 1910. First air mail service between Hendon and Windsor, 1911. Single-seater planes used solely for fighting first used by British, Dec. 1914. First airship and aeroplane crossing of Atlantic, 1919. First solo transatlantic flight, New York–Paris, by Lindbergh, in just over thirty-three hrs, reaching Paris, 21 May 1927. First jet-propelled plane in service (German), 1944. First pilotless plane to cross Atlantic, Oct. 1947.

Aviation, Ministry of. Established, Oct. 1959.

Avignon. Popes went into residence at, 1309. Purchased from France, 1348. Papal Palace built, 1342–60. Popes left for Rome, 1377. French antipopes at A., 1378–1408. Became an archbishopric, 1475. Annexed by France, 1797.

Avlona. *See* VLÖNE.

Avoirdupois Weight. First Act directing use of, 1532. *See* WEIGHTS AND MEASURES.

Avranches, Concordat of, whereby Henry II of England withdrew all his demands concerning jurisdiction over 'criminous clerks,' and other causes of his disputes with Becket, and in return was absolved of all complicity in the archbishop's murder, 1172.

' Axis,' The. Italo-German alliance of 1936.

Aylesbury Election Case, 1704, or **Ashby v. White.** Decided that the courts would protect any one whose right to vote was wrongfully denied.

Aynthia, Siam. Founded, 1351. Capital till 1782, when it was sacked by Burmese.

Azerbaijan (Persian). Russian attempt to subvert frustrated, 1946.

Azerbaijan (Russian). Soviet republic, 1920. Included in the Transcaucasian Republic, 1922. Since 1936 a constituent republic of the U.S.S.R.

Azores. Discovered by Portuguese under Cabral, 1431–2. First settled, 1444. British allowed temporary naval and air bases under agreement with Portuguese, 12 Oct. 1943.

Azov, Russia. Founded, twelfth century. Taken by Tamerlane, 1395; by Russians, 1696; restored to Turks, 1711. Fortifications demolished, 1739. Ceded to Russia, 1774. Occupied by Germans, 1941; retaken, 1943.

Aztecs. Settled in Mexico (*q.v.*) c. A.D. 1200. Overthrown by Cortes, 1519.

ADDENDA

B

Baalbek, or **Heliopolis,** Syria. Captured by Assyrians, 738 B.C. Became a Roman colony under Augustus (31 B.C.–A.D. 14). Sanctuary built, 150–210. Converted into church c. 330. Captured by Arabs, 635. Dome removed to the 'Dome of the Rock' in Jerusalem c. 710. Walls demolished, 745. Sacked by Mongols, 1400. Earthquake, 1759. Laid waste, 1760–70, by Turks.

Babi. *See* BAHA'I.

Babington's Conspiracy. Anthony B. (1561–86) and others plotted to kill Queen Elizabeth and liberate Mary Queen of Scots. Leaders of plot executed, Sept. 1586.

Babylon (town). Settled about 4000 B.C. by the Sumerians; first mentioned in a cuneiform tablet c. 2700 B.C. Capital c. 2200 B.C. After 1100 B. became subject to or dependent on Assyria until the New Babylonian Empire (620–539) was founded by Nebopaazar. 'New Palace' built, 604. The most important excavations of the city took place, A.D. 1899–1917. The town was destroyed by Sennacherib the Assyrian, 696 B.C., and rebuilt by Essarhaddon, 680–670. Captured by Cyrus, 538.

Babylonia. First mentioned as an independent state c. 2200 B.C. Elamites driven out by Hammurapi (the biblical Amraphel) c. 2037. Kassite conquest of B. c. 1743. Rise of Assyria, 1900–1400. Assyrians became supreme under Shalmanezer I, 1300. First Assyrian Empire reaches its climax under Tiglath-Pileser I c. 1110. Civil war, 824–746, leads to establishment of Second Assyrian Empire by Pul (Tiglath-Pileser III), 745. Pul crowned at Babylon, 729. Merodach-baladan leads rebellion against Assyria, 722–710. Assyrian power destroyed by the Babylonians and Medes c. 610, and end of B.'s independence, 538, by Persian conquest.

Babylonian Captivity. Jewish historical term to describe the period between the capture or destruction of Jerusalem by Nebuchadnezzar, 599 or 586, and the deportation of its inhabitants, to the edict of Cyrus, 538, allowing the tribes of Judah, Benjamin, and Levi to return home.

'Babylonish Captivity.' Name applied by critical contemporaries to the Papacy's residence at Avignon (q.v.), 1309–77.

Bachelor of Arts. Degree first conferred in various universities in the thirteenth century.

Bachelor Tax. Imposed in England, 1695 and 1785.

Bacteria. Discovered by van Leeuwenhoek, 1680. F. J. Cohn (1828–98) founder of modern bacteriology.

Bactria. Old Persian province now part of Afghanistan (q.v.). Conquered by Cyrus c. 540 B.C., by Alexander, 325. After 323 ruled by Seleucids until the beginning of the independent Graeco-Bactrian kingdom (255–140) founded by Diodotos which was conquered by the Scythians, who ruled until A.D. 560.

Badajoz (Rom. **Pax Augusta**), Spain. Originally a Celtic settlement, then a town in Roman times. Capital of a Moorish kingdom, 1031. Besieged very frequently, the most recent being the sieges by the Portuguese, 1385, 1396, 1542, and 1705; the French, 1808–9, and Feb. 1811; the British, May and June 1811. It was finally stormed by British, 6 Apr. 1812. During Spanish Civil War taken by insurgents, Aug. 1936.

Badakhshan visited by Marco Polo, 1272–3, was part of the Graeco-Bactrian kingdom (*see* BACTRIA), and is still largely inhabited by Tajiks, a people who now speak a dialect of Persian: but they are thought to represent the last survivors in their original home of the Aryan-speaking tribes who from this focal area began to spread westward via S. Russia into Europe before the fifteenth century B.C. Little visited by Europeans, even by Russians, until Gen. Wood's expedition, 1837–8. From the thirteenth century until the time of Nadir Shah (*see* AFGHANISTAN) ruled by a local dynasty claiming descent from Alexander the Great. Conquered by the Uzbeks c. 1800; Afghan supremacy was restored, 1859. A common frontier with Afghanistan, leaving B. in Russian territory, was agreed with Britain, 1873. Gorno-B. has been an autonomous region of Tajikstan (q.v.) since 1929.

Baden, Grand Duchy and Republic of, split between several rulers of the Zähringen family till 1771, when it was united under one margrave. Became a Grand Duchy and substantially enlarged, 1806. Constitution granted, 1818. Hecker and Struve established a republic, 1848; grand duke reinstated, 1849. Joined Austria against Prussia, 1866. Joined German Empire, 1871. The Grand Duke Frederick II abdicated and republic declared, 1918. Republican government suppressed by Hitler, 1934. Divided between French and American zones of occupation, 1945. These territories reunited into the *Land* of Baden-Württemberg, 1952.

Baden-Baden, founded as **Aurelia Aquensis** by Hadrian, in the second century A.D. The ruins on Castle Hill (Schlossberg) are of a castle destroyed by the French in 1689, as was the original 'new castle' built in the sixteenth century, of which the extant building is a facsimile. The gaming tables which bulk so large in nineteenth-century fiction were closed in 1872, and the fashionable life of the spa really ceased in 1914, though it remains a popular holiday resort.

Badminton. Seat of the Dukes of Beaufort in Gloucestershire, came into the hands of the Somerset family, 1608; the present building was erected by Henry Somerset (1629–99), first Duke of Beaufort in 1682, one of the finest surviving examples of the Palladian style. The game of B. was invented at B. House *c.* 1870.

Baffin Bay. Discovered by William Baffin, 1616.

Bagdad, Iraq. Founded, A.D. 763, by the Abbasid Caliph Al-Mansur, it reached its highest splendour in the reign of Haroun-al-Rashid (786–809). Besieged and stormed by Persians under Tahir (812–13). Imperial residence moved from to Samara 836–94. Seljuk Sultan Toghrul Beg acclaimed here, 1055. Seljuks ousted, 1181. Kwarismian attack, 1216. Sacked by Hulagu, the Mongol emperor, 1258. Captured by Timur, 1393. Turkish from 1638. Captured by British, 11 Mar. 1917. Became capital of Iraq, 1921. Headquarters of the B. Pact (*q.v.*), 1955–8. Revolution overthrowing the monarchy originated in B., July 1958.

Bagdad Pact. Defensive and economic pact, so called because it was first signed at Bagdad between Turkey and Iraq in Feb. 1955. Subsequently Britain (Apr.), Pakistan (Sept.), and Persia (Nov.) signed it. Organization put on a permanent footing, Apr. 1956. After revolution in Iraq (July 1958) Iraq left the organization which was renamed CENTO (Central Treaty Organization) (*q.v.*).

Baha'i or **Babi.** Followers of an originally Persian sect founded *c.* 1844 by Mirza Ali Mohammed (1819–*c.* 1850) of Shiraz. After the martyrdom of its founder at Tabriz in 1850 the sect spread through the Ottoman Empire, and is still extant to-day, about two-thirds of its adherents being converts from Islam or the descendants of such, the remainder mostly W. Europeans and Americans. The second leader, Mirza Yahya Nuri, left the direction of affairs to his suc-

cessor, who became prominent in the 1860s, Baha'ullah (*d.* 1892); and the fourth was his son, Abdul Baha. Following the deportation of all believers from Bagdad to Constantinople in 1863, a schism arose between the Azali and B. factions. The former were again exiled to Cyprus, and the latter to Acre, 1868. The mission to America was started by Abdul Baha, who himself went there in 1911 and 1914, after being imprisoned in 1907, but released by the Young Turk government, 1908. Knighted by the British crown, 1920, he *d.* 28 Nov. 1921, and was succeeded by Shogi Effendi, his grandson. World congress of B. held in London, 1963.

Bahamas (formerly **Lucayos**). Discovered by Columbus, 1492. The first island colonized was Eleuthera, 1646; then New Providence, 1666. English expelled by French and Spaniards, 1703; re-colonized by English, 1717; reduced by Spain, 1781; restored, 1783, by treaty. Extensive cyclone damage, 1866, 1883, 1945. Duke of Windsor (the former Edward VIII) appointed governor, 1940–1945. Constitution reformed, 1959. General Election, Nov. 1962. Progressive Liberals lost seats to the United Bahamanian Party.

Bahrein. Archipelago in Persian Gulf, independent since the advent of the Khalifa dynasty in 1782; B. was occupied by the Portuguese for the whole of the sixteenth century, they being dispossessed by Arab subjects of the Shah. Entered into treaty relations with the government of India, 1849, and Sheikh Esa bin Ali (reigned 1862–1922) accepted a British political agent and a British adviser. Sheikh Sir Sulman bin Hamad acceded, 1942. B. Petroleum Co. acquired a concession, 1930, and struck oil, 1932.

Baia, formerly **Bahia**, Brazil. Visited by Amerigo Vespucci, 1510. Colonized, 1536. Refounded, 1549, and seat of viceroys of Brazil until 1763.

Bailey or **Old Bailey.** The street in London (first extant reference, 1444–5) in which have stood a succession of courts for the trial of criminals. One, built 1773, was destroyed, 1780; rebuilt, 1785–1786; enlarged, 1808. Rebuilt on site of Newgate Prison, 1902–7.

Bailey Bridge, invented by Donald Bailey, 1941, and successfully used during World War II and since.

Baireuth. *See* BAYREUTH.

Baku, U.S.S.R. Under Persia, 1509–1723. Under Russia, 1723–35. Persia, 1735–1806. Finally annexed by Russia, 1806. Oilworks severely damaged in civil disturbances, 1904–5, 1914–21, and in World War II.

Balaklava or **Balaclava,** anciently *Portus Cymbolorum,* became a Genoese 'factory' in the fourteenth century, and remained so until the Turkish conquest of the Crimea (*q.v.*). Became a garrison town under Catherine the Great (1762–96). Held by British expeditionary force, 1854–6. *See* BATTLES.

Balasore was the first English settlement in India, 1642, and the last (as distinct from the Portuguese and French possessions) of the other European stations; the Danish 'factory' here was sold to the E. India Co., 1846.

Balearic Islands. Colonized by the Phoenicians *c.* fourth century B.C. Conquered by Romans, 123 B.C. By Vandals *c.* A.D. 426. By Moors, 798. Independent Moorish kingdom,1009–1232. Independent Christian kingdom of Majorca, 1276–1349, when it became a dependency of Aragon. *See* MAJORCA and MINORCA.

Balfour Declaration. *See* PALESTINE, MODERN.

Bali. During the period of Moslem expansion in the fifteenth century A.D. many Buddhists and Brahmins fled to B. and the religion of the island is a synthesis of these two faiths both in a more archaic form than any extant elsewhere. Trade relations with the Dutch began in 1597, and some coastal areas came under the rule of the Netherlands in 1845; Dutch rule not firmly established until 1908. B. was captured by the Japanese in 1942, and they remained in possession until 3 Mar. 1946. Together with the island of Lombok, B. joined the E. Indonesian state in Dec. 1946, and the United States of Indonesia when this republic was unified, 1950. Volcanic eruption, Mar. 1963, killed over 1,000 people on B.

Balkan Entente. Between Yugoslavia, Rumania, Turkey, and Greece, signed in Athens, 9 Feb. 1934. Bulgaria signed nonaggression pact with B. E., 31 July 1938. Renewed for seven years, 3 Feb. 1940, but a dead letter after 1941.

Balkan Mountains. Became frontier line of Turkish dominions by Treaty of Berlin, 13 July 1878.

Balkan Wars, Oct. 1912 to Aug. 1913, fall into three divisions: 1. First B. War—the war of the B. League against Turkey in which the League conquered Macedonia, Albania, and a large part of Thrace. Armistice, Dec. 1912. 2. Greece continued the war. The armistice denounced, Feb. 1913, and the other allies continued the war. 3. Second B. War. B. League broke up, June 1913, then followed the war of Serbia, Greece, and Montenegro against Bulgaria, assisted by Rumania, which now intervened, and

Turkey. The first B. War ended by Treaty of London, 30 May 1913; the second by Treaty of Bucharest, 10 Aug. 1913, and by the treaty between Bulgaria and Turkey, 18 Sept. 1913.

Ballarat goldfield was opened up, 1851. The rebellion of miners at Eureka Stockade, 3 Dec. 1854, is the only battle ever fought on Australian soil.

Ballet. The culmination of a long tradition of European dance technique, difficult to trace historically, but perhaps first reaching a form which would be recognizable to-day at the courts of England, Scotland, and France late in the fifteenth century. To this was added the influence of Italian pantomime; the kind of entertainment devised for Catherine de' Medici by her Master of Music Baltazarini (who *d. c.* 1587) *c.* 1555 is the first to be called B. In the classical comedy of seventeenth-century France B. forms an integral part of the entertainment and nowhere did it become finally disengaged from 'legitimate' drama and opera until the mid-nineteenth century. The classical European B. of to-day derives from the Russian school of St. Petersburg, the formative period of which was 1840–80, though the Imperial B. had been founded in 1735, largely under French and Italian tuition. The return impact of Russian dancing on the W. had its greatest force in the years 1910–20, just after the influence of Isadora Duncan (1878–1927) had been felt in St. Petersburg. Nijinsky became Imperial B. Master, 1913. Massine produced his first B., 1917. For English B. history *see* SADLER'S WELLS.

Balloons. Principal experiments, etc., with: Joseph Montgolfier made first fire balloon, 1782. Brothers Montgolfier successfully made an ascent in a fire balloon, 1783. First ascent in balloon filled with hydrogen at Paris by Professor Charles, Aug. 1783. First ascent in England by Vincent Lunardi, Sept. 1784. Channel crossed by Blanchard and Jefferies, 7 Jan. 1785. Nassau balloon left London and descended at Nassau, 1836. Nadar's balloon ascended with fourteen persons, 4 Oct. 1863 (the first balloon with steering apparatus). Glaisher and Coxwell rose to a height of seven miles in a balloon, 5 Sept. 1862. Godard's Montgolfier balloon ascended, 28 July and 3 Aug. 1864. Giffard's experiments with dirigible, 1852. Zeppelin, 1900, 1908. Alberto Santos Dumont's experiments with steerable balloon, July–Oct. 1901; Feb. 1902. B. were used for observation purposes by the French, 1794, but Napoleon disbanded the Balloon Corps, 1798. Used as artillery observation posts in Italian war of Liberation, 1860; American Civil

War (q.v.); in Franco-Prussian War, 1870–1871; and in Spanish-American War, 1898. German Balloon Corps formed, 1884; British Balloon Corps, 1879. B. first used by the Royal Navy at Gallipoli, 1915, and on the western front during World War I; and in mass as a barrage against aircraft, World War II.

Ballot Box. First used in England at election of London aldermen, 1526. Bills authorizing parliamentary voting by ballot thrown out by Lords, 1710; passed, 18 July 1872. First parliamentary election in England by secret ballot at Pontefract, 15 Aug. 1872.

Ballymote, Book of. A MS. in Middle Irish, a miscellany of prose and verse copied in 1391 by the monks of B. in Sligo; first printed in facsimile, 1887.

Balmoral Castle. Purchased by Prince Albert, 1852; present building commenced, 1853; completed, 1855.

Baltic and Black Sea Canal. Projected by Peter the Great, said to have been completed 70 years after his death, afterwards fell into disuse. A deeper canal was proposed, Nov. 1897; begun, 1898; unfinished; estimated cost of whole, £20,000,000.

Baltic and White Sea Canal (length, 142 miles). Begun, Dec. 1931; opened, 1933.

Baltic Entente. Alliance between Estonia, Latvia, Lithuania, and Poland, Mar. 1922.

Baltic Exchange. The Baltic merchants began in Elizabethan times to meet in the Virginia and Baltic inns. In the eighteenth century merchants interested in Baltic trade met in the Baltic Coffee House. The Baltic Club founded, 1823. The association thus formed was united in 1899 with the London Shipping Exchange to form the modern B. E.

Baltic Expeditions. 1. Under Admirals Parker and Nelson, 1801. 2. Under Admiral Gambier and Lord Cathcart, 1807. 3. Under Admiral Napier, 11 Mar. 1854. 4. Under Rear-Admiral Dundas, 4 Apr. 1855.

Baltic Sea. Whole surface frozen over, 1658, 1809. Holstein Canal, connecting River Eider with Baltic, opened, 1785; B. and N. Sea Canal for large vessels, 1891.

Baltic States. Estonia, Lithuania, and Latvia (see all these) proclaimed independent republics, 1918. Inter-Allied Baltic Commission to control frontiers appointed, Nov. 1919. Soviet Union recognized their independence, 1920. All these states granted U.S.S.R. extra-territorial rights, naval and military, Oct. 1939, and were annexed to the U.S.S.R., July 1940. Occupied by Ger-

many, 1941–4, and incorporated in the Reich Commissariat 'Ostland.' Reconquered by the U.S.S.R., 1944–5.

Baltimore, U.S.A. Founded, 1729. Named after the first Lord B. Incorporated, 1796. Greater part of business area destroyed by fire, 1904. Area nearly trebled by inclusion of adjacent districts, 1920. See MARYLAND.

Baluchistan, Asia. Occupied by British successively, 1839, 1840, 1841. British B. incorporated in India, 1887. Became part of Pakistan (q.v.), 15 Aug. 1947. Four states of Kalat, Mekran, Las Bela, and Kharan entered into agreement to form Union of B., 13 Apr. 1952.

Bamberg, Germany. Prince Bishopric founded, A.D. 1007. University existed between 1648 and 1803. Secular power finally abolished, 1806.

Bamburgh Castle. The stronghold of the Bernician (q.v.) kings, built by Ida the Anglian chief, 547; besieged by the Mercian pagan King Penda, 641. Destroyed by Olaf of Dublin, 993. Besieged by William II, 1095. Extensively added to in Norman times, especially under Robert de Mowbray, Earl of Northumberland, 1080–93; and often restored, especially in 1721. Bought by Lord Armstrong and made into almhouses, 1894.

Bampton Lectures in divinity at Oxford founded by Rev. John B. (1690–1751). Begun, 1780.

Banat, the. Originally ruled by Hungary, but under the Austrian crown, 1849–60. Treaty of Trianon, 1920, divided it between Yugoslavia and Hungary.

Banbury, England. Castle erected at by Alexander, Bishop of Lincoln, 1125. Battle of (Wars of Roses), 1469. Surrendered to Charles I, Oct. 1642; besieged, 1643, 1644, and in 1646, when it surrendered to parliamentary forces.

Band of Hope. Started in Leeds, 1847. Organized into the Band of Hope Union, 1855.

Banda Islands discovered (1512) and settled (1520) by Portuguese; occupied by Dutch, 1814, who had expelled the Portuguese, 1580. Formal cession by Britain to Netherlands, 1816. Joined Indonesia, 1950.

Banda Oriental. See URUGUAY.

Bandoeng or **Bandung,** Indonesia, on the island of Java. The Bandoeng Conference, a meeting of Afro-Asian delegates, held here, 18–27 Apr. 1955.

Banff, Scotland. Granted charter by Malcolm IV, 1163; by Robert Bruce, 1324; and Robert II, 1372. Present castle built, 1750.

Banff, Alberta, visited by King George VI and Queen Elizabeth, May 1939.

Bangkok, Siam. Became capital of Siam after Burmese destroyed Aynthia, 1782. The Emerald Buddha chapel built, 1785. Japanese-supported government moved capital to Pechabun, 1943. Returned, 1945.

Bangor, Wales. Bishopric and cathedral reputed founded by St. Deiniol c. 550. Old cathedral destroyed, 1071. Present cathedral dates from 1496 to 1532. Restored, 1869–80. N. Wales University College opened, 18 Oct. 1884.

Bank. Chinese said to have had a paper currency c. A.D. 800. In 808 Lombard Jews established a B. in Italy. Private Bs. existed in Venice in 1270. Bank of St George, Genoa, 1407. The Banco di Rialto was established in Venice, 1584 and 1587—the first public B. in Europe. Banco del Giro, or B. of Venice, established, 1619; B. of Amsterdam, 1609; first B. established in England by Francis Child c. 1603; Bank of Hamburg, 1619– 1873; Riksbank of Stockholm established, 1656; issued the first banknote, 1658.

Bank Amalgamations (British). Completed, 1918, when the 'big five' emerged: Barclays Bank, founded, 1896; Lloyd's Bank, founded, 1865; National Provincial Bank, founded, 1833; Midland Bank, founded, 1836; Westminster Bank, founded, 1836. Gurney & Co., last of the English private provincial Bs., founded, 1809, bought up by Barclays, Feb. 1953. National Provincial proposed take-over of the District Bank, 1962.

Bank Holidays. Established by Sir John Lubbock's Act, 1871. In England they are: Easter Monday; Whit Monday; first Monday in Aug.; 25 and 26 or 27 Dec.; Good Friday. In Ireland (Northern and Republic) the same plus St. Patrick's Day (17 Mar.). In Scotland Christmas Day; New Year's Day; and the first Mondays in May and Aug.

Bank Holidays Act. Introduced by Sir John Lubbock; passed, 25 May 1871.

Bank of England. Founded by William Paterson, who is said to have originated the project in 1691. Incorporated by charter, 27 July 1694. Special privileges: monopoly conferred, 1709; restricted, 1826, 1833. Cash payments suspended, 1797; resumed, 1821. Under Bank Charter is remodelled, 19 July 1844; Bank Charter suspended: 25 Oct. 1847; 12 Nov. 1857; 11 May 1866. Important changes in management, 16 June 1892. Rebuilding begun, 24 Nov. 1924. Nationalized, 1946.

Bank of France. Founded by Napoleon, 1800. Nationalized, 2 Dec. 1945.

Bank of Ireland. Established, 1 June 1783. Irish Banking Act passed, 21 July 1845. Central Bank of Eire established, 1 Feb. 1943.

Bank of Scotland. Set up at Edinburgh by Act of Scottish Parliament, 1695.

Bankruptcy (Great Britain). Court of, established by Act of Parliament, 1831. Important changes in laws regarding B. made, 1861, 1869, 1883, 1890, 1913, 1914, and 1926.

Bankruptcy Acts (U.S.A.). Bill passed by Congress, 19 Aug. 1841; repealed, 3 Mar. 1843. National B. A., 1898; amended, 1903, 1906, 1910, 1917, 1922, and 1926.

Banks, American. Congress chartered the Bank of N. America, 26 May 1781; opened in Philadelphia, 1782; second bank established at Boston, 1784; Bank of U.S.A. established Philadelphia, 20 Dec. 1790; Bank of New York established, 1790; first Bank of the United States chartered, 1791–1811; second, 1816–36.

Bannockburn. See BATTLES.

Baptists (for earlier history of, see ANABAPTISTS). First English Baptist church founded in Amsterdam by John Smyth and Thomas Helwys, 1609–11. Helwys formed first Baptist church in England, London, 1612 (General Baptist, or Arminian). First Particular Baptist (Calvinist) church formed, Southwark, 1633. Confession of Faith published by the seven Particular Baptist churches in London, 1644. Baptist Missionary Society founded, 1792. Baptist Union formed, 1891. Roger Williams formed first regular congregation of B. in America, in Rhode Island c. Mar. 1639. Baptist World Alliance formed, 1905.

Bar, Confederation of the. An anti-Russian coalition of Polish nobles, formed 1768 and dissolved, 1776.

Bar, Trial at, i.e. a trial in the King's Bench division before a full bench of judges, was the usual procedure up to 1285; the last Trial at B. to date was that of Sir Roger Casement, for treason, 1916. Major Arthur Lynch, who commanded the Irish Brigade in Boer employ during the S. African War, had been so tried, 1904.

'Baralong' Case. German prize crew on board American ship killed by crew of British auxiliary 'B.' 19 Aug. 1915. German Government refused to submit case to an international inquiry, and threatened ruthless Zeppelin warfare in retaliation, Dec. 1915.

Barbados, W. Indies. First mention, 1518. Thought to have been visited by Portuguese c. 1536; formally acquired by English, 1625; occupation became complete under Sir William Courteen, 1627; taken by Parliamentarians during Civil War, 1652; bishopric established, 1824. Adult suffrage introduced, 1951.

Barbed Wire invented in America,

1873. B. W. Act, concerning the fencing of land adjoining highways, passed, 1893.

Barbers, as a guild, were incorporated in England, 1461, and separated from surgeons, 1745.

Barcelona, Spain (q.v.). Said to have been built by Hamilcar Barca, third century B.C. Became a Roman colony; conquered by Visigoths, A.D. 415, and Moors, 713. Independent county, 762; incorporated with Aragon, 1164. Cathedral begun, 1298. University founded, 1450. Treaty of B. between France and Spain, 1493. Captured by the French under Vendôme, 1697; by the English under Peterborough, 1706. Taken by the Duke of Berwick (James FitzJames), for Philip V, 1714; by Napoleon, 1808. Restored to Spain by Treaty of Paris, 1814. Execution of Ferrer for conspiracy at, 13 Oct. 1909. Last capital of the republic, 1937. Surrendered to Gen. Franco, 1939.

Barebones Parliament, or Little Parliament, of members, selected from nominees of the congregations in each county. Met, 4 July 1653; dissolved, 12 Dec. 1653. Named after a certain Praise-God B. or P. Barbon (1596?–1679), who attended as member for London.

Barfleur, France. William, son of Henry I of England, wrecked and drowned, in the 'White Ship,' off B., 28 Nov. 1120. Destroyed by English, 1346. French fleet destroyed off B. by Admiral Russell, 19 May 1692.

Bargain and Sale. An obsolete form of real estate conveyance, facilitated by the Statute of Uses, 1535; fell into desuetude after the passing of the Real Property Act, 1845.

Bari (anct. **Barium**), Apulia, first mentioned, 180 B.C. Captured by Saracens, A.D. 812; retaken by Greeks, 885; by Robert Guiscard, 1071. Annexed to Kingdom of Naples, 1558. After Sept. 1943 was temporary seat of Badoglio's provisional government, in which capacity it was bombed by German planes, 3 Dec. 1943; ammunition ships exploded, causing great damage to harbour.

Barking, Essex. Benedictine abbey founded by St Erconwald, 670, burnt by Vikings, 870. All Hallows, B. by the Tower, belonged to the abbey and was built in the seventh century; burnt down, 1087; rebuilt before 1100; rebuilt again in the thirteenth century and largely destroyed by the Luftwaffe, 29 Dec. 1941. N. aisle restored and reopened, 1949.

Barnard Castle (County Durham). Built by Guy Baliol B. (1112–32). Taken from the rebel John Baliol by the crown, 1696.

Barnardo's Homes, Dr. Founded 1866 by Thomas John B. (1845–1905).

Barnourners. Political faction in the U.S.A., active 1844–52.

Baroda, India. See MAHRATTAS.

Barometer. First made by Torricelli, a Florentine, c. 1643. Pascal's experiments, 1646. Aneroid B. said to have been invented by Conté, 1798. The English patent, however, was registered by Vidi for his invention of 1844. Vidi d., 1866.

Baron. 1. Peerage title first used in England after Norman conquest, 1066. First created by patent, 1387. Wensleydale peerage case, 1856, decided that it must be hereditary to carry a seat in the House of Lords (see LORDS, HOUSE OF). This principle amended by Appellate Jurisdiction Act, 1876, and Life Peerages Act, 1958. Further modified by Peerages Act, 1963. 2. County Palatine of Chester had its own Bs. till 1679. 3. Ditto of Durham till 1716. 4. The Cinque Ports still have Bs. elected for life.

Baronet. Order of knighthood instituted by James I of England, 22 May 1611, to replenish his exchequer. The first B. was Sir Nicholas Bacon of Redgrave.

Barons' War. Caused by disputes between Henry III of England and the B. First important engagement, the taking of Northampton for the king by Prince Edward, 4 Apr. 1264; king's army defeated at Lewes, 14 May 1264; De Montfort killed and B. defeated at battle of Evesham, 4 Aug. 1265.

Barrier Act passed by the General Assembly of the Church of Scotland, 1697.

Barrier Treaties. By the first B. Treaty, between Great Britain and the States-General (29 Oct. 1709), 'Great Britain undertook to procure for the Dutch an adequate barrier . . .' to secure Holland against French aggression. The second (29 Jan. 1713) modified the first; by it British undertook to obtain right for Dutch to garrison the frontier fortresses 'from the future sovereign of the Spanish Netherlands.' The third, signed 15 Nov. 1715, was supplemental.

Barrow-in-Furness became industrially important with the discovery of haematite ore locally, 1840. Docks opened, 1867. Incorporated, 1885. county borough, 1888. Heavily bombed, May 1941.

Bartholomew, Massacre of St., at Paris, 24 Aug. 1572.

Bartholomew, St. Old fair held on festival in London, 1133–1855. Hospital of St. B. (London) founded by Rahere, 1123; refounded, 1547; rebuilt, 1730–66. Medical college founded, 1843.

Baseball mentioned by Jane Austen, 1798. Form of B. played in England and America before 1839; modern game said to have been evolved by Doubleday (1819–83). New York Knickerbocker B. Club formed, 1845; Boston Excelsior Club, 1865. First professional team formed, 1871. National league organized, 1876. Rules standardized, 1887. World Series B. Contests began, 1903.

Basel or **Bâle,** Switzerland. Council of, 1431–49. University founded, 1460. Joined Swiss Confederation, 1501. The bishopric abolished, 1529. Treaty between France and Prussia, 22 July 1795. Canton divided into two half-cantons, 1833 (Basel-Stadt and Basel-Land).

Bashkiria. Autonomous republic of R.S.F.S.R., set up, 1919.

Basic English, first word-list of printed, 1929. First dictionary published, 1932. Committee of ministers reported on, 1943, and Government purchased copyright in, 1947.

Basket Ball invented, 1891 by James Naismith.

Basques. See NAVARRE.

Basra, Iraq. Founded by Caliph Omar, 637. Occupied by British, 1914.

Bassein, Burma. Founded c. 1250. Captured by British, 1852.

Bassein, India. Ceded to the Portuguese, 1534. Taken by the Mahrattas, 1739. Taken over by the British, 1818.

Bass Rock. St. Baldred (d. 756) had a hermitage here. It was bought by the English Government, fortified and made into a political prison, 1671, where leading Covenanters were detained. In 1691 four young Jacobites captured the island by a trick and held it against the Williamite forces from June 1691 to Apr. 1694. Fort demolished, 1701.

Bastaards or **Bastards.** See GRIQUAS.

Bastard. See LEGITIMACY ACT.

Bastille (Paris). Built, 1369–83, destroyed, 14–15 July 1789.

Basutoland, S. Africa. Annexed by Britain, 1868. Annexed to Cape Colony, 1871. Rebellion, 1879–80, resulted in its being made a protectorate directly under Britain, 1883. Visited by George VI, 1947. New constitution given royal assent, Sept. 1959.

Bataan, Philippine Is. Famous stand against Japanese by MacArthur's troops, 9 Dec. 1941–9 Apr. 1942.

Batavia. See JAKARTA.

Batavian Republic. Holland was reorganized under this name under French hegemony from May 1795 until June 1806.

Bates's Case. Tried before Court of Exchequer, 1606. John Bates, a Levant merchant, refused to pay excess duty not authorized by Parliament, but four Barons of the Exchequer found against him.

Bath, England. Roman baths begun, A.D. 84. Used until c. 400. Cathedral founded, A.D. 775. King Edgar crowned at B., A.D. 973. Bishopric amalgamated with Wells, 1139. Present abbey, founded 1405–99, superseded cathedral. Grammar school founded, 1552. Roman baths uncovered, partly, 1788, but not excavated. Rediscovered, 1879, and excavated, 1888–90 and 1923. Pump room built as a result of resolution by the corporation of 1705. Rebuilt, 1751 and 1795. National Hospital for Rheumatic Diseases founded, 1738, largely at the instance of Beau Nash (1674–1761). Assembly Rooms destroyed by Luftwaffe, 1942.

Battersea first mentioned in a document of 693. The park was opened, 1853. In connection with Festival of Britain, 1951, Pleasure Gardens opened 28 May.

Battle, Wager of, and **Appeal of Felony.** Last waged in Court of Common Pleas, 1571. Court of Chivalry, 1631. Court of Durham, 1638. As a result of an attempted Trial by Combat in 1818 both were formally abolished, 1819.

Battle Abbey. Founded by William the Conqueror on site of battle of Hastings, 1067. Consecrated, 1094. Its abbot sat in the House of Lords until the Dissolution of the Monasteries (q.v.), 1539. The building, largely demolished in 1839, was severely damaged by fire, 1930.

Battle Abbey Roll, purporting to be a nominal roll of Norman officers present at the battle of Hastings, is a forgery, probably of the fourteenth century.

Battles. See also WORLD WARS I and II and SIEGES. Most famous or important battles are printed in **bold type.** Those described in Creasy's *Fifteen Decisive Battles of the World* are marked ¶.

ON LAND

B. connected with Napoleon are marked N, with Wellington W, with Marlborough M, and with Frederick the Great F.

Aboukir, (1) 25 July 1799 (N)
(2) 8 Mar. 1801
Abu Klea, 17 Jan. 1885
Acs, 2 and 10 July 1849
Adowa, 1 Mar. 1896
Adrianople, (1) 3 July 323
(2) 9 Aug. 378
(3) 20 Aug. 1829
Agincourt, 25 Oct. 1415
Agnadello, 14 May 1509
Aisne (1) 13–28 Sept. 1914
(2) 16–20 Apr. 1917
(3) 27 May–6 June 1918

C

Aiznadin, 13 July 633
Akhalzikh, 24 Aug. 1828
Alamein, 23 Oct.–7 Nov. 1942
Alamo, 24 Feb.–6 Mar. 1836
Alarcos, 1185
Albans, St., (1) 22 or 23 May 1455
  (2) 17 Feb. 1461
Albuera, 16 May 1811 (W)
Albufera, 4 Jan. 1812 (W)
Alexandria, (1) 21 Mar. 1801
  (2) 11–13 July 1882
Alford, 2 July 1645
Aliwal, 28 Jan. 1846
Allia, 16 July 390 B.C.
Alma, 20 Sept. 1854
Almansa, 25 Apr. 1707
Almenara, 28 July 1710
Angora, 28 July 1402
Anjou, 22 Mar. 1421
Antietam, 16–17 Sept. 1862
Antioch, 28 June 1098
Anzio, 22–5 Jan. 1944
¶ **Arbela, 1 Oct. 331** B.C.
Arcis-sur-Aube, 20–21 Mar. 1814
Arcole, 14–17 Nov. 1796 (N)
Ardennes, 16–22 Dec. 1944
Argaum, 29 Nov. 1803
Argentario, 378
Arklow, 10 June 1798
Arnhem, 17–26 Sept. 1944
Arques, 13–28 Sept. 1589
Aspern, 21–2 May 1809 (N)
Aspromonte, 29 Aug. 1862
Assandun (Ashingdon), 1016
Assaye, 23 Sept. 1803 (W)
Asunden (Lake), Jan. 1520
Atbara, The, 8 Apr. 1898
Atherton Moor, 30 June 1643
Atlanta, 22 July 1864
Auerstädt, 14 Oct. 1806 (N)
Aughrim, 12 July 1691
Auneau, 24 Nov. 1587
Austerlitz, 2 Dec. 1805 (N)
Ayacucho, 9 Dec. 1824
Aylesford, c. 455
Badajoz, 6 Apr. 1812 (W)
Balaklava, 25 Oct. 1854
Bannockburn, 24 June 1314
Bapaume, 2–3 Jan. 1871
Barnet, 14 Apr. 1471
Barrosa, 5 Mar. 1811 (W)
Bassano, 8 Sept. 1796
Bastogne, Dec. 1944
Battlefield. *See* SHREWSBURY
Bautzen, 20–21 May 1813 (N)
Baylen, 20 July 1808 (W)
Beaugé. *See* ANJOU
Belfort (siege), 3 Nov. 1870–8 Feb. 1871
Belgrade (siege), 22 July–4 Sept. 1456
Belmont, 23 Nov. 1899
Benevento, 26 Feb. 1266
Bennington, 16 Aug. 1777
Beresina, 26–28 Nov. 1812 (N)
Berlin, 15 Apr.–2 May 1945
Big Bethel, 10 May 1861

Bir Hakim, 26 May–11 June 1942
Bitonto, 27 May 1734
¶ **Blenheim, 13 (2 O.S.) Aug. 1704 (M)**
Blore Heath, 23 Sept. 1459
Blumenau, 22 July 1866
Borghetto, 30 May 1796 (N)
Borisov, 27 Nov. 1812
Borodino, 7 Sept. 1812 (N)
Bosworth Field, 22 Aug. 1485
Bothwell Bridge, 22 June 1679
Bouvines, 27 July 1214
Boxtel, 17 Sept. 1794
Boyne, 1 July 1690
Braíla, 19 June 1773
Brandywine, 11 Sept. 1777
Brechin, 18 May 1452
Brentford, 12 Nov. 1642
Breslau, 22 Nov. 1757 (F)
Briars Creek, 3 May 1779
Brienne, 29 Jan. 1814 (N)
Brunanburh, *c.* **937**
'Bulge, The.' *See* ARDENNES
Bull Run, (1) 21 July 1861
  (2) 29–30 Aug. 1862
Bunker Hill, 17 June 1775
Burlington Heights, 6 June 1813
Busaco, 27 Sept. 1810 (W)
Buxar, 1764
Caen, 25 June–8 July 1944
Calatafimi, 15 May 1860
Camden (U.S.A.), (1) 16 Aug. 1780
  (2) 25 Apr. 1781
Cannae, 2 Aug. 216 B.C.
Caporetto, 24 Oct.–18 Nov. 1917
Carberry Hill, 15 June 1567
Carrhae, 53 B.C.
Cassano, (1) 16 Aug. 1705
  (2) 27–29 Apr. 1799
Cassino, 5 Feb.–8 May 1944
Castalla, 13 Apr. 1813
Castelnuovo, 21 Nov. 1796
Castiglione, 5 Aug. 1796 (N)
Castillon, 17 July 1453
Castlebar, 7 Aug. 1798
Cawnpore, (1) 16 July 1857
  (2) 27–28 Nov. 1857
  (3) 6 Dec. 1857
Cedar Creek, 19 Oct. 1864
Cerignola, 28 Apr. 1503
Cerisoles, 14 Apr. 1454
Ceva, 1796 (N)
Chaeronea, (1) 7 Aug. 338 B.C.
  (2) 86 B.C.
Chalgrove, 18 June 1643
¶ **Châlons, A.D. 451**
Champaubert, 10 Feb. 1814 (N)
Chancellorsville, 2–4 May 1863
Chatalja, 17–18 Nov. 1912
Châteaudun, 18 Oct. 1870
Château Thierry, (1) 13 Feb. 1814 (N)
  (2) 27 June 1918
Chattanooga, 23–25 Nov. 1863
Chebrëiss, 24 July 1798 (N)
Chickahominy, 26 June–1 July 1862
Chickamauga, 19–20 Sept. 1863

Chilianwála, 13 Jan. 1849
Chippewa, 5 July 1814
Citate, 6 Jan. 1854
Clifton Moor, 18 Dec. 1745
Clontarf, 23 Apr. 1014
Cold Harbor, 1 and 3 June 1864
Colenso, 15 Dec. 1899
Corinth, Miss., 3–4 Oct. 1862
Corunna, 16 Jan. 1809 (W)
Courtrai, 1302
Coutras, 20 Oct. 1587
Craonne, 6–7 Mar. 1814 (N)
Crécy or Cressy, 26 Aug. 1346
Crete, 20 May–3 June 1941
Cropredy Bridge, 29 June 1644
Culloden, 16 Apr. 1746
Custozza, (1) 23–25 July 1848
(2) 24 June 1866
Cynoscephalae, 190 B.C.
Czaslau or Chotusitz, 17 May 1742 (F)
Dannevirke, (1) 1331
(2) 23 Apr. 1848
Dego, 14 Apr. 1796 (N)
Delhi, (1) 8 Sept. 1803
(2) 7–16 Oct. 1804
(3) after siege, 14–20 Sept. 1857
Dennewitz, 6 Sept. 1813
Dettingen, 27 June (N.S.) 1743
Devizes, 13 July 1643
Dien-Bien-Phu, Apr.–May 1954
Dieppe, 14 Aug. 1942
Donnington, Glos., 21 Mar. 1645
Dorylaeum, 1097
Douro, 12 May 1809 (W)
Dresden, 27 Aug. 1813 (N)
Dreux, 19 Dec. 1562
Drumclog, 1 June 1679
Drummossie. *See* CULLODEN
Dunbar, (1) 27 Apr. 1296
(2) 3 Sept. 1650
Dunes, 4 (14 N.S.) June 1658
Dungan Hill, 8 Aug. 1647
Dunkirk, (1) *see* DUNES
(2) **(Evacuation of) 29 May–3 June 1940**
Eckmühl, 22 Apr. 1809 (N)
Edgehill, 23 Oct. 1642
Edington, summer 878
Elandslaagte, 21 Oct. 1899
Elchingen, 14 Oct. 1805
Enghien, 3 Aug. (N.S.) 1692
Enslin, 25 Nov. 1899
Espierres, 22 May 1794
Essling. *See* ASPERN
Eutaw, 8 Sept. 1781
Evesham, 4 Aug. 1265
Eylau, 7–9 Feb. 1807 (N)
Fair Oaks, 31 May–1 June 1862
Falkirk, (1) 22 July 1298
(2) 17 Jan. 1746
Famars, 23–24 May 1793
Fehrbellin, 1675
Firozshahr, 21–22 Dec. 1845
Fleurus, (1) 1622
(2) 1 July 1690

(3) 26 June 1794
Flodden Field, 9 Sept. 1513
Flushing, 15 Aug. 1809
Fontenoy, 11 May (N.S.) 1745
Formigny, 1450
Fornovo, 6 July 1495
Fredericksburg, (1) 13 Dec. 1862
(2) *See* CHANCELLORSVILLE
Friedland, 14 June 1807 (N)
Fuentes de Onoro, 3–5 May 1811 (W)
Gaugamela. *See* ARBELA
Gembloux, June 1578
Germantown, 4 Oct. 1777
Gettysburg, 1–3 July 1863
Gitschin, 29 June 1866
Glencoe (S. Africa). 20 Oct. 1899
Gorey, co. Wexford, 4 June 1798
Gravelotte, 18 Aug. 1870
Great Meadows, July 1754
Grochow, 19–20 Feb. 1831
Gross Beeren, 23 Aug. 1813 (N)
Gross Jaegerndorf, 30 Aug. 1757 (F)
Guadalajara, 1937
Guinegatte, 16 Aug. 1513
Gujrát, 21 Feb. 1849
Halidon Hill, 19 July 1333
Hanau, 30 Oct. 1813
Harlaw, 24 July 1411
Hasbain, 23 or 24 Sept. 1408
¶ **Hastings, 14 Oct. 1066**
Hatfield, 632
Hennersdorf, 23 Nov. 1745 (F)
Herrera, 24 Aug. 1837
Hexham, 8 May 1464
Himera, 408 B.C.
Hochkirch, 14 Oct. 1758 (F)
Hochstädt. *See* BLENHEIM
Hohenfriedberg, 3–4 June 1745
Hohenlinden, 3 Dec. 1800
Homildon, 14 Sept. 1402
Idstädt, 25 July 1850
Imjin River, 23–5 Apr. 1951
Ingogo, 8 Feb. 1881
Ingour, 6 Nov. 1855
Inkerman, 5 Nov. 1854
Ipsus, 301 B.C.
Isandlhwana, 22 Jan. 1879
Ivry, 14 Mar. 1590
Jarnac, 13 Mar. 1569
Jemappes, 6 Nov. 1792
Jena, 14 Oct. 1806 (N)
Kalisz, 1706
Kalka, 1224
Katzbach, 26 Aug. 1813 (N)
Kazan, 1552
Kesselsdorf, 15 Dec. 1745 (F)
Khart, 19 July 1829
* Killiecrankie, 27 July 1689
Kilsyth, 15 Aug. 1645
Kirk-Kilisse, 22–24 Oct. 1912
Kissingen, 10 July 1866
Klissow, July 1702
'Knightsbridge' (N. Africa), 28 May–15 June 1942
Kohima, 10 Apr.–18 May 1942

Kolin, 18 Jan. 1757 (F)
Konieh, 21 Dec. 1832
Königgrätz. *See* SADOWA
Kossovo, (1) 1389
  (2) 1448
Krasnoi, 15–17 Nov. 1812
Kulikovo, 1380
Kumanovo, 23–25 Oct. 1912
Kunersdorf, 12 Aug. 1759 (F)
Kurdla, 1795
La Bicocca, 29 Apr. 1522
Laffeldt, 2 July 1747
Laingsnek, 28 Jan. 1881
Landen, 29 (19 O.S.) July 1693
Landshut, Apr. 1809 (N)
Langensalza, 27 June 1866
Langport, 10 July 1645
Langside (Glasgow), 13 May 1568
Lansdown, 5 July 1643
Laon, 9–10 Mar. 1814 (N)
Largs, 1263
Lauffeld, 2 July 1746
Leipzig, 16–19 Oct. 1813 (N)
Lens, 20 Aug. 1648
Leuctra, 371 B.C.
Leuthen, 5 Dec. 1757 (F)
Lewes, 14 May 1264
Lexington, (1) 19 Apr. 1775
  (2) 20 Sept. 1861
Liaoyang, Sept. 1904
Libenau, 25 June 1866
Liegnitz, 15 Aug. 1760 (F)
Ligny, 16 June 1815 (N)
Lincelles, 18 Aug. 1793
Lincoln, (1) 2 Feb. 1141
  (2) 20 May 1217
Linlithgow Bridge, Sept. 1526
Lioppo, 16 May 1860
Lipau, 1434
Lippstadt, 6 Nov. 1632
Lissa. *See* LEUTHEN (F)
Lodi, 10 May 1796 (N)
Lonato, 3 Aug. 1796 (N)
Lüle Burgas, 28–30 Oct. 1912
Lundy's Lane, 25 July 1814
Lützelberg, 10 Oct. 1758
Lützen, (1) 6 (16 N.S.) Nov. 1632
  (2) 2 May 1813 (N)
Magenta, 4 June 1859
Magersfontein, 11 Dec. 1899
Magnano, 5 Apr. 1799
Magnesia, 190 B.C.
Maharajpur, 29 Dec. 1843
Maida, 4 July 1806 (W)
Majuba, 27 Feb. 1881
Malplaquet, 11 Sept. 1709 (M)
Malvalli, 27 Mar. 1799
Mantinea, (1) 418 B.C.
  (2) *c.* 367 B.C.
  (3) 295 B.C.
  (4) 242 B.C.
  (5) 207 B.C.
Manzikert, 1071
¶ **Marathon, 28 or 29 Sept. 490 B.C.**
Marengo, 14 June 1800 (N)

Margus, (1) 285
  (2) 505
Marignano, (1) 13–14 Sept. 1515
  (2) *See* PAVIA
  (3) 8 June 1859
Marne, The, (1) 6–9 Sept. 1914
  (2) **15 July–31 Aug. 1918**
Marston Moor, 2 July 1644
Maserfield, 641
Mechanicsville, or White Oaks, 26 June
  1862
Medina del Rio Seco. *See* RIO SECO
¶ **Metaurus, 207 B.C.**
Metz, 31 Aug. 1870
Milazzo, 20 June 1860
Millesimo, 13–14 Apr. 1796 (N)
Milli Duzov, 1–2 June 1829
Milvian Bridge, 312
Mincio, (1) 29 May 1796 (N)
  (2) 8 Feb. 1814
Minden, 1 Aug. 1759
Möckern, (1) 5 Apr. 1813
  (2) 16 Oct. 1813
Modder River, 28 Nov. 1899
Moeskirch, 5 May 1800
Mohács, (1) 29 Aug. 1526
  (2) 12 Aug. 1687
Mohilev, 23 July 1812
Mollwitz, 10 Apr. 1741 (F)
Monastir, 15–18 Nov. 1912
Moncontour, 3 Oct. 1569
Mondovi, 22 Apr. 1796 (N)
Mons, Aug. 1914
Mons Badonicus *c.* 500
Montebello, (1) 1796 (N)
  (2) 1805
Montebello Casteggio, (1) 9 June 1800
  (2) 20 May 1859
Montenotte, 12 Apr. 1796
Montinirail, 11 Feb. 1814 (N)
Mookerheede, 1574
Morat, 22 June 1476
Morgarten, 15 Nov. 1315
Mortimer's Cross, 2 Feb. 1461
Mount Tabor, 16 Apr. 1799 (N)
Mudki, 18 Dec. 1845
Mukden, 1–9 Mar. 1905
Multan, 7 Nov. 1848
Münchengrätz, 28 June 1866
Munda, 45 B.C.
Muret, 12 Sept. 1213
Murfreesboro, (1) 31 Dec. 1862
  (2) 2 Jan. 1863
Naas, 24 May 1798
Nachod, 27 June 1866
Najara, 3 Apr. 1367
Nantwich, 25–28 Jan. 1644
Narva, 30 Nov. 1700
Narvik, 28 May–10 June 1940
Naseby, 14 June 1645
Navas de Tolosa, 1212
Nedao, 454
Neerwinden, 18 Mar. 1793
Nesbit, 7 May 1402
Neville's Cross, 17 Oct. 1346

Newburn, 28 Aug. 1640
Newbury, (1) 20 Sept. 1643
(2) 27 Oct. 1644
New Ross, 5 June 1798
Newtownbutler, 30 July 1689
Nicholson's Nek, 30 Oct. 1899
Nive, 9–13 Dec. 1813
Nivelles, 10 Nov. 1813
Nördlingen, (1) 27 Aug. 1634
(2) 3 Aug. 1645
Northallerton. *See* STANDARD, THE
Northampton, 10 July 1460
Novara, 23 Mar. 1849
Novi, (1) 15 Aug. 1799
(2) 8 Jan. 1800
Obidos, 17 Aug. 1808
Oltenitza, 4 Nov. 1853
Omdurman, 2 Sept. 1898
Oporto. *See* DOURO
¶ **Orleans**, (1) **29 Apr. 1429**
(2) 11 Oct. 1870
Ormuz, 1622
Orthez, 27 Feb. 1814
Ortona, Dec. 1943
Ostrolenka, 26 May 1831
Otterburn, 15 Aug. 1388
Oudenarde, 11 July 1708 (M)
Oulart, 27 May 1798
Ourique, 25 July 1139
Paardeberg, 16, 18–27 Feb. 1900
Palestro, 31 May 1859
Palo Alto, 8 May 1846
Panipat, (1) 1526
(2) 1556
(3) 1761
Parma, 29 June 1734
Passchendaele, 26 Oct.–10 Nov. 1917
Patay, 18 June 1429
Pavia, 24 Feb. 1525
Pelekanon, 1326
Pelusium, 525 B.C.
Pfaffendorf, 15 Aug. 1760
Pharsalia or Pharsalus, summer of 48
B.C.
Philiphaugh, 13 Sept. 1645
Piacenza, 16 June 1746
Pinkie, 10 Sept. 1547
Pirmasens, 14 Sept. 1793
Plassey, 23 June 1757
Plataea, 479 B.C.
Plevna, July, Sept., and Dec. 1877
Podoll, 26 June 1866
Poitiers, 19 Sept. 1356
Polotzk, 30–31 July 1812
¶ **Poltava, 8 July 1709**
Port Arthur, 21 Nov. 1894
Porto Novo (S. India), 1 July 1781
Prague, 6 May 1757 (F)
Preston, (1) 17 Aug. 1648
(2) 12–13 Nov. 1715
Prestonpans, 21 Sept. 1745
Pultusk, 26 Dec. 1806
Pusan Perimeter, 1 Sept.–1 Oct. 1950
Pyramids, The, 13, 21 July 1798
Pyrenees, The, 25 July–2 Aug. 1813

Quatre Bras, 16 June 1815 (W)
Ramillies, 23 May 1706 (M)
Rathmines, 2 Aug. 1649
Raucoux, 11 Oct. 1746
Ravenna, 11 Apr. 1512
Redinha, 12 Mar. 1811
Resaca de la Palma, 9 May 1846
Rheinfelden, 3 Mar. 1638
Rietfontein, 24 Oct. 1899
Rieti, 7 Mar. 1821
Rio Seco, 14 July 1808
Rivoli, 14–15 Jan. 1797 (N)
Rocroi, 19 May 1643
Rolica, 17 Aug. 1808
Rorke's Drift, 22 Jan. 1879
Rosebecque or Roosebeke, 26 or 27 Nov.
1382
Rossbach, 5 Nov. 1757 (F)
Roveredo, 4 Sept. 1796 (N)
Ruremonde, 18 Sept. 1794
Saarbrücken (an undefended assault), 2
Aug. 1870
Sadowa, 3 July 1866
Sagunto, 25 Oct. 1811
Saint-Antoine, 2 July 1652
Saint-Denis, 10 Nov. 1567
Saint-Dizier, 27 Jan. 1814 (N)
Saintes, 22 July 1242
Saint-Quentin, (1) 10 Aug. 1557
(2) 19 Jan. 1871
Sakaria, The, 23 Aug.–13 Sept. 1921
Salamanca, 22 July 1812 (W)
Salerno, 9 Sept.–1 Oct. 1943
Sangro, 2 Nov.–27 Dec. 1943
Santa Lucia, 6 May 1848
Saragossa, (1) 20 Aug. 1710
(2) 20 Feb. 1809
Sarantoporon, Oct. 1912
¶ **Saratoga, 17 Oct. 1777**
Schwechat, 30 Oct. 1848
Sedan, 29 Aug.–1 Sept. 1870
Sedgemoor, 6 July 1685
Seidlitz, 10 Apr. 1831
Selby, 11 Apr. 1644
Seminara, 21 Apr. 1503
Sempach, 9 July 1386
Seneffe, 11 Aug. 1674
Seringapatam, (1) 15 May 1791
(2) 6 Feb. 1792
Sesia, The, Jan. 1524
Sheriffmuir, 13 Nov. 1715
Shiloh, 6–7 Apr. 1862
Shrewsbury, 21 July 1403
Simancas, 939
Skalitz, 28 June 1866
Smolensk, (1) 16–17 Aug. 1812 (N)
(2) 1941
Sobraon, 10 Feb. 1846
Soissons, 486
Solferino, 24 June 1859
Solway Moss, 24 Nov. 1542
Soor, (1) Sept. 1745 (F)
(2) 28 June 1866
Sorauren, 28 July 1813
Spion Kop, 24–25 Jan. 1900

Spottsylvania, 7–21 May 1864
Spurs, The. *See* GUINEGATTE
Stalingrad, Sept. 1942–Jan. 1943
Standard, The, 22 Aug. 1138
Steenkirk, 23 July (3 Aug. N.S.) 1692
Stoke, 16 June 1487
Stone River. *See* MURFREESBORO
Stow-on-the-Wold. *See* DONNINGTON
Strasburg, 16 Aug. 1870
Suakin, 20 Dec. 1888
¶ **Syracuse, 413** B.C.
Szegedin, 4 Aug. 1849
Tagliacozzo, 1268
Talavera, 27–28 July 1809 (W)
Talikota, 1565
Tannenberg, (1) 1410
  (2) 26–30 Aug. 1914
Tara, 26 May 1798
Tarbes, 20 Mar. 1814 (W)
Tchernaya, 16 Aug. 1855
Teb, El, 29 Feb. 1884
Tel-el-Kebir, 13 Sept. 1882
¶ **Teutoburger Wald,** A.D. **9**
Tewkesbury, 4 May 1471
Thabor, 16 Apr. 1799
Thapsus, 46 B.C.
Tinchebray, 28 Sept. 1106
Torgau, 3 Nov. 1760 (F)
Toulouse, 10 Apr. 1814 (W)
Tournai, 25 Apr. 1794
¶ **Tours, 10 Oct. 732**
Towton, 29 Mar. 1461
Trautenau, 28 June 1866
Trebbia, (1) 218 B.C.
  (2) 17–19 June 1799
Truellas, 22 Sept. 1793
Tudela, 23 Nov. 1808
Ucles, 13 Jan. 1809
Ulm, 20 Oct. 1805 (N)
Valeggio, 25 July 1848
¶ **Valmy, 20 Sept. 1792**
Valteline, 19 Aug. 1812
Valtezza, 27 May 1821
Varna, 10 Nov. 1444
Vilagos, 25 Apr. 1521
Vauchamps, 14 Feb. 1814 (N)
Villafranca, 10 Apr. 1812
Villaviciosa, 10 Dec. 1710
Vilna, 18 June 1831
Vimiero, 21 Aug. 1808 (W)
Vimy Ridge, 9–10 Apr. 1917
Vinegar Hill, 21 June 1798
Vitebsk, 14 Nov. 1812 (N)
Vitoria, 21 June 1813 (W)
Volturno, 1 Oct. 1860
Vouillé, 507
Wagram, 6 July 1809 (N)
Waitzen, 14–17 July 1849
Wakefield, 30 Dec. 1460
Wandiwash, 22 Jan. 1760
Warsaw, (1) 28–30 July 1656
  (2) 17 Apr. 1794
  (3) 4–8 Nov. 1794
  (4) 7 Sept. 1831
  (5) 14–27 Sept. 1939

  (6) 19–28 Apr. 1943
  (7) 1 Aug.–3 Oct. 1944
¶ **Waterloo, 18 June 1815 (N, W)**
Wavre, 18, 19 June 1815
Wawz, 31 Mar. 1831
White Mountain, 1620
White Oak Swamp, 30 June 1862
White Oaks. *See* MECHANICSVILLE
White Plains, 28 Oct. 1776
Wilderness, 5–6 May 1864
Williamsburg, 5 May 1862
Winwaed, 654
Worcester, (1) 23 Sept. 1642
  (2) 3 Sept. 1651
Wörth, 6 Aug. 1870
Wurschen, 21 May 1813
Würtzburg, 3 Sept. 1796
Ximena, 10 Sept. 1811
Yenidje Vardar, 2, 3, 5 Nov. 1912
Yermuk, Nov. 636
Ypres, (1) 19 Oct.–31 Oct. 1914
  (2) 22 Apr.–25 May 1915
  (3) 31 July–10 Nov. 1917
  (4) Sept. 1918
Zallaca, 1086
Zama, 202 B.C.
Zela, 47 B.C.
Zenta, 11 Sept. 1697
Zorndorf, 25–26 Aug. 1758 (F)
Züllichau, 23 July 1759
Zürich, 24–25 Sept. 1799

NAVAL BATTLES

B. connected with Nelson are marked N.

Aboukir. *See* NILE, THE
Acre, 3 Nov. 1840
Actium, 2 Sept. 31 B.C.
Aegadean Isles, 241 B.C.
Aegospotami, 404 B.C.
Aix Roads, 11–12 Apr. 1809
Alexandria bombarded, 11–13 July 1882
Algeciras, 6 and 12 July 1801
Algiers bombarded, 27 Aug. 1816
Altmark (boarding), 15 Feb. 1940
¶ **Armada, 21–30 July 1588**
Basque Roads. *See* AIX ROADS
Beachy Head, 30 June 1690
Bismarck (pursuit and sinking), 22–7 May 1941
Bismarck Sea, 1–3 Mar. 1943
Cadiz, 1587
Camperdown, 11 Oct. 1797
Cartagena, 1588
Champlain, 1814
Chesapeake Bay, 5 Sept. 1781
Copenhagen, (1) 2 Apr. 1801 (N)
  (2) 25 Sept. 1807
Coral Sea, 4–8 May 1942
Coronel, 1 Nov. 1914
Dannoura, 1185
Dogger Bank, (1) 5 Aug. 1781
  (2) 24 Jan. 1915
Dominica. *See* SAINTS, THE

Dover, (1) 19 May 1652
  (2) 2–3 June 1653
Downs, The, 3 June 1666
Dungeness, 1652
Dunkirk, 1666
Falkland Is., 8 Dec. 1914
Finisterre, Cape, (1) 3 May 1747
  (2) 14 Oct. 1747
  (3) 1805
Gibraltar Bay, 13 Sept. 1782
Guadeloupe. *See* SAINTS, THE
Hampton Roads, 8–9 Mar. 1862
Hangö, 27 July 1714
Harwich, 1666
Heligoland, 28 Aug. 1914
Itamarca, 1640
Japan Sea, 14 Aug. 1904
Java, 27–8 Feb. 1942
Jutland, 31 May 1916
Lagos, 18 Aug. 1759
La Hogue, 14–16 May 1692
Lake Champlain, 11 Sept. 1814
Lemnos, 18 Jan. 1913
Lepanto, 7 Oct. 1571
Lissa, 20 July 1866
Macassar Strait, 23–25 Jan. 1942
Malaga, 13 Aug. 1704
Malaya, 10 Dec. 1941
Manila, 1 May 1898
Matapan, 28 Mar. 1941
Messina, 1676
Midway, 3–6 June 1942
Minorca, 1756
Narvik, 10 and 13 Apr. 1940
Navarino, 20 Oct. 1827
Negapatam, 6 July 1782
New Orleans, 25 Apr. 1862
Newport News. *See* HAMPTON ROADS
Nile, The, 1 Aug. 1798 (N)
North Foreland, (1) 2–3 June 1653
  (2) 1 June 1666
  (3) 25–6 July 1666
Oran, 3 July 1940
Passaro Cape, 11 Aug. 1718
Pearl Harbor, 7 Dec. 1941
Philippine Sea, 23–25 Oct. 1944
Plate River, 14 Dec. 1939
Portland, 18–20 Feb. 1653
Quiberon, 20 Nov. 1759
Rosas Bay, 1 Nov. 1809
St. Vincent, (1) 16 June 1693
  (2) 16 Jan. 1780
  (3) 14 Feb. 1797 (N)
Saints, The, 12 Apr. 1782
Santa Cruz, (1) 20 Apr. 1657
  (2) 1797
Salamis, 480 B.C.
Samos, 16–17 Aug. 1824
Santiago, 3 July 1898
Sevastopol bombarded, 17 Oct. 1854
Sinope, 30 Nov. 1853
Sirte, 22–4 Mar. 1942
Sluys, 24 June 1340
Sole or Southwold Bay, 28 May 1672
Taranto, 11 Nov. 1940

Tchesiné, 7–9 July 1770
Texel, 9 Aug. 1653
Trafalgar, 21 Oct. 1805 (N)
Tsu Shima, 27–8 May 1905
Ushant, (1) 27 July 1778
  (2) 1 June 1794
Yalu, 17 Sept. 1894
Yellow Sea (two battles), 10 Aug. 1904
Zeebrugge, 23 Apr. 1918

AIR BATTLES

Britain, 8 Aug.–29 Oct. 1940

Battleship. First ship with turrets the
Rolf Krake designed for Danish Navy by
British Capt. C. P. Coles, R.N., 1860.
First turret ship in action the U.S.S.
Monitor, 9 Mar. 1862. B. design revolu-
tionized by launching of H.M.S. *Dread-
nought*, 1906. German 'pocket B'
Deutschland launched, May 1931. Bs.
obsolescent by 1960.

Bavaria (Ger. **Bayern**). One of the
original 'tribal duchies' of Germany.
Earliest (probably Celtic) inhabitants
subdued by Romans *c.* 10–5 B.C. Ravaged
by Odoacer, A.D. 476–86. Settled by Germanic tribes, 488–520. Conquered by
Franks, 555, and governed by Frankish
dukes till Charlemagne deposed Tassilo
III, 788. Nordgau separated from, 976.
Wittelsbach family take throne from
Henry the Lion, 1180. Duchy divided
till accession of the Emperor Louis the
Bavarian, 1314. Becomes an electorate,
1623. Annexes the Upper Palatinate,
1648. Alliance with France leads to occupation by British and Austrian troops
before battle of Blenheim, 1704. Attempt
to dismember Austria with Prussian help,
leads to defeat and occupation, 1742.
Becomes a kingdom, 1805. Maximilian
grants B. a constitution, 1818. Joins the
German Zollverein, 1833. Allied to
Austria in Austro-Prussian War, 1866.
Makes military convention with Prussia,
Aug. 1866. Joins in Franco-Prussian
War, 1870, against France. Joins German Empire, 1871. Jesuits expelled,
1873. Wittelsbachs deposed and Soviet
Republic proclaimed by Kurt Eisner,
1918. Eisner murdered, Feb. 1919.
Moderate Government re-established by
force 1 May 1919. Attempted Munich
putsch of Hitler and Ludendorff, 8 Nov.
1923, followed by the Peace of Hamburg
negotiated by Gen· von Seeckt. Democratic government abolished by Hitler and
Ritter von Epp installed as governor,
1933. Occupied by American forces,
1945. Separate *Land* government set up
1946. Constitution of 1946 based on
that of 1919, but with greater emphasis
on state rights. 1958 elections resulted
in the Christian Social Union being the
largest single party in B.

Heads of State. From the foundation of the electorate, 1623, until the declaration of the republic, 1918.

Electors:

Maximilian I	1597–1651
Ferdinand Maria I	1651–1679
Maximilian II	1679–1726
Karl Albrecht I	1726–1745
Maximilian III	1745–1777
Karl Theodor I	1777–1799
Maximilian IV (*elector*) and I (*king*)	1799–1825

Kings:

Ludwig I	1825–1848
Maximilian II	1848–1864
Ludwig II	1864–1886
Otto I (incurably insane)	1886–1913
Luitpold (Regent)	1886–1912
Ludwig (Regent 1912–13)	
Ludwig III	1913–1918

Bayeux, Normandy, has a cathedral built from the eleventh to the thirteenth century. Bishopric dates from the fourth century. Taken by Rollo, 890. Pillaged by Henry I of England, 1106. It was the first French town to be recaptured by the Allies in June 1944. Memorial in British war cemetery at B. dedicated, 1955.

Bayeux Tapestry of panoramic scenes embroidered in worsted on a linen ground, and depicting the events of the reign of King Harold II of England, which culminated in the battle of Hastings (*q.v.*), was almost certainly executed shortly after Oct. 1066, probably under the patronage of Odo (*d.* 1097), Bishop of B. and Earl of Kent and half-brother of William the Conqueror. First recorded mention, 1476.

Bayonet. 'Plug B.,' supposed to have been invented at Bayonne *c.* 1647, but in use before; external screw allowing the firelock to be fired without unfixing B., invented by Gen. Hugh Mackay (1640–1692), after battle of Killiecrankie, 1689.

Bayonne, France. Meeting-place of Catherine de' Medici and the Spanish Duke of Alva, 1565. Ferdinand VII of Spain was here induced by his father, the ex-king Charles IV, to abdicate in favour of Napoleon, 2 May 1808. Invested by British, 1814. Convention of B. signed, 10 May 1808.

Bayonne Decree, 17 Apr. 1808. Napoleon ordered seizure of all American vessels.

Bayreut(h), Bavaria, founded 1194, became in 1248 a dependency of Nürnberg (*q.v.*) and later combined with Ansbach to form a principality ruled by a cadet branch of the Hohenzollerns before becoming Prussian in 1791, finally passing to Bavaria, 1810. The Wagner Theatre was opened in 1876, the Opera House proper, 1748.

B.B.C. *See* BRITISH BROADCASTING CORPORATION.

Bear-baiting in Britain banned by Act of Parliament, 1835.

Beaufort Scale, standard for measuring velocity of wind invented, 1805, by Rear-Admiral Sir Francis B., naval hydrographer (1774–1857).

Beauvais, France. Cathedral choir built, 1227–1347. Unsuccessfully besieged by Charles of Burgundy, 1472, owing to valour of Jeanne Lainé (La Hachette). Transepts and tower of cathedral completed, 1547. Tower (the highest in Europe) fell, 1573. Monument to La Hachette, 1850. British airship 'R.101' crashed at B., Oct. 1930. Town badly damaged by German bombing, 1940.

Bec, Normandy, a Benedictine abbey, founded, 1034, by Herlwin, became famous for the school founded there, 1045, by Lanfranc (1005–89), later Archbishop of Canterbury. Though decline set in during the thirteenth century it survived until 1789, and its last prior was Talleyrand (1754–1838).

Bechuanaland. Ravaged by Matabele, 1817. London Missionary Society established at Kuruman, 1818. Boer encroachments after the Sand River convention of 1852. Chief Khama appeals to Britain, Aug. 1876. Southern B. occupied by British, 1878. Boer republics of Stellaland (*q.v.*) and Goshen (*q.v.*) set up, 1882. Boundary convention of Feb. 1884 broken by Boers whose continuing encroachments led to protectorate established, 10 Sept. 1884. Whole country under British protection, 30 Sept. 1885. Southern B. added to Cape Colony, 1895, but rest of B. has remained a British protectorate ever since. Caprivi Appendix, formerly part of German SW. Africa, incorporated in B., 1922. Visited by King George VI, 1947. Bamangwato succession dispute between Tshekedi Khama and Seretse Khama, arising out of the marriage of the latter, resolved, 1951. Royal Commission undertook expedition into Kalahari Desert, to investigate possibilities of cattle-rearing there, 1952. New constitution came into force, 1961.

Bedford, England. Burned by Danes, 1010. B. School refounded, 1552. B. Modern School founded, 1566. Bunyan imprisoned, 1660–72.

Bedford Level, England. The large area of the Fens drained, *c.* 1640, by Cornelius Vermuyden at expense of the third Duke of B. New B. River burst its banks, Feb. 1947.

Bedlam from Bethlehem Hospital founded in London by Simon Fitzmary, 1247. Became madhouse, 1407. Moved to Moorfields, 1676; to Lambeth, 1815; to Beckenham, Kent, 1931.

Béguines. Order of sisters devoted to education, etc., founded at Liège in the twelfth century by Le Bèghe, still existing in some Belgian towns.

Beirut or **Beyrout,** capital of the Lebanon. Destroyed by earthquake in the sixth century. Seized by Ibrahim Pasha, 1832; Egyptian Army totally defeated at, Oct. 1840; massacre at, May 1860. Bombarded during Italo-Turkish war, 1912. Occupied by Allenby's army, 8 Oct. 1918. Captured from French by British, July 1941. Became capital of the independent republic of the Lebanon, 26 Nov. 1941. Moslem quarter of B. in control of anti-Chamoun rebels, May–Nov. 1958.

Belfast, Ireland. Castle built c. 1177; destroyed by Edward Bruce, 1316. B. attacked by Earl of Kildare, 1503, 1512. Town and castle repaired by Hugh O'Neill, who acquired them in 1552. B. granted by James I to Sir Arthur Chichester, 1612, received its charter, 1613. Taken by Gen. Monck, 1648; by Lord Montgomery, 1649. Castle accidentally burnt, 1708. Town made a city, 1888; county borough, 1899. Mayor became Lord Mayor, 1892. University founded as Queen's College, 1845; received royal charter, 1909. Parliament Buildings at Stormont opened, 1932. Queen (then Princess) Elizabeth and the Duke of Edinburgh received freedom of the city, 1949; state visit, 1953.

Belfort, France. Ceded to France, 1648. Famous for its skilful and resolute defence by Col. Denfert-Rochereau, Nov. 1870–Feb. 1871 against the Prussians. The General Delegation for Occupied France was set up here by Fernand de Brinon, 7 Sept. 1940.

Belgae. A mixed Celtic-Germanic group of tribes in NE. Gaul, part of whom migrated to southern Britain c. 75 B.C.

Belgium. Its Celtic inhabitants conquered by Julius Caesar, 51 B.C. Was southern part of Spanish Netherlands, the northern part of which broke away in 1579. A separate kingdom under Spanish ruler, 1598–1621. Ceded to Austria by Peace of Utrecht, 1713. Overrun by the French, 1744–8. Republic, 1787–90. Passed to France by Treaty of Campo Formio, 1797. Restored to Austria, 1814. United with Holland, 1815. Revolution commenced, 25 Aug. 1830; independence acknowledged by Great Powers, 20 Dec. 1830. Treaty between Holland and B. regarding latter's independence signed at London, 19 Apr. 1839, and guaranteed by principal European powers; commercial treaty with Great Britain, 22 Aug. 1862. Neutrality violated by German Army, 4 Aug. 1914. 'Pact of Mutual Guarantee' (for security of Belgian independence) signed at London, 1 Dec. 1925. Serious financial crisis, 1925–6. Equality of Flemish and French languages in public life recognized, 1932. King Albert killed in climbing accident near Namur, 17 Feb. 1934. Leopold III's first wife, Queen Astrid, killed in a motor accident, 29 Aug. 1935. King's speech announced detachment from foreign conflicts, 14 Oct. 1936. Spaak, B.'s first Socialist Prime Minister, May 1938. Albert Canal completed, June 1939. King Leopold and the Queen of the Netherlands addressed an appeal to the belligerents to cease hostilities, 7 Nov. Defence precautions in view of massing of German troops on frontier, Nov. Invaded by Germany, 10 May 1940. Leopold III capitulated, 28 May. B. liberated Sept.–Nov. 1944. Member of Benelux since its inception, 1948. Minor modifications in B.'s favour on Belgian-German frontier, Apr. 1949. Monarchy crisis, 1944–51. 1950: Referendum pronounced narrowly in favour of recalling Leopold III; his return followed by rioting, and in Aug. he delegated his powers to his son, finally abdicating in his favour, July 1951.

Member of the European Community ('the Six'); of the European Coal and Steel Community, 1952; of the European Atomic Community, 1958, and the European Economic Community (the Common Market), 1958. Congo (q.v.) became independent of B., 30 June 1960. King Baudouin married Fabiola de Mora y Aragon, 15 Dec. 1960. Flemings rioted in Brussels over language dispute, Oct. 1962. In the 'Thalidomide' (q.v.) trial at Liège, all five defendants acquitted, 10 Nov. 1962. King and Queen of the Belgians paid state visit to Britain, 1963. See also FLANDERS; HOLLAND, KINGDOM OF; WORLD WAR II; BENELUX.

Kings

Leopold I	1831–1865
Leopold II	1865–1909
Albert I	1909–1934
Leopold III	1934–*1951
Prince Charles, Regent	1944–1950
Leopold III (20 July–10 Aug.)	1950
Baudouin, Prince Royal (since 11 Aug.)	1950
Baudouin I	1951–

* Prisoner of war, May 1940–May 1945.
Prince Charles was Regent from Aug. 1944

C*

to July 1950. Leopold exercised his prerogatives during July and Aug. 1950, but Prince Baudouin took them over in the latter month. Leopold abdicated, 16 July 1951, and Baudouin was enthroned, 17 July 1951.

Belgorod-Dnestrovskiy. *See* CETATEA ALBA.

Belgrade (Serb.-Cr.**Beograd**), Yugoslavia. Roman town of Singidunum, said to have stood on an earlier Celtic settlement. Destroyed by the Avars in the sixth century. Seized by Hungarians from Greeks, 1124, besieged by Turks unsuccessfully, 1444, 1456; captured by Turks, 1522; imperial forces, 1688; Turks, 1690; Prince Eugene, 1717; restored to Turks, 1739; captured by Austrians, 1789; restored to Turks, 1792; surrendered to Serbia, 1867; independence of Serbia declared at B., 22 Aug. 1878; king and queen murdered by army, 10 June 1903; captured by von Mackensen, 7 Oct. 1915; capital of Yugoslavia (*q.v.*) since 1919; bombed by Germans, 6 Apr. 1941; occupied, 12 Apr. 1941; liberated by partisans and Russians, 20 Oct. 1944. Extensive rebuilding, 1945 onwards. Conference of twenty-four uncommitted nations at B., Sept. 1961. *See also* SERBIA and YUGOSLAVIA.

Bell Rock Lighthouse (N. Sea). Built by Robert Stevenson, 1807–11. The rock is famous through Southey's ballad, *The Inchcape Rock.*

Bells. Used in France *c.* 550. In the capitulation of Jerusalem, A.D. 637, the twelfth article stipulated that the Christians 'shall not ring, but only toll their bells.' Prominent among the ritual ob-objects of the Celtic Church, in the sixth century. First mentioned as used in churches in England in seventh century by the Venerable Bede. Largest B. in the world is the 'Tsar Kolokol' of Moscow, cast in 1773. *See also* CURFEW.

Belorussia, Byelorussia. Independent Belorussian republic proclaimed, 1918. Communists established a more limited Belorussian republic, 1921, which became a constituent republic of the U.S.S.R. in 1922. Area increased, 1924–6, by inclusion of territories to the E. Further extended to include the White Russian areas annexed from Poland in the partition of 1939; most of this territory had been ceded to Poland by the Treaty of Riga, 1921. In 1945 B., like the Ukraine, obtained separate representation in the United Nations. In 1951 a dispute arose as to its representation on the Security Council of U.N.

Belorussians are a linguistic rather than ethnic or political group, and their language, which approximates more closely to Ukrainian than to Great Russian, began to be differentiated from the latter during the fourteenth century, when they were subjects of the principality of Lithuania (*q.v.*) from 1315. The Bible in Belorussian was printed, 1517–19. The first Belorussian dictionary appeared in 1870.

Belsen (Hanover). Concentration camp set up in 1933, and taken by British troops, Apr. 1945. Its commandant, Josef Kramer, and eleven of his staff were sentenced to death for torture and murder of prisoners, 17 Nov. 1945.

Belvoir Castle (Leics.). Seat of the dukes of Rutland, built 1808 after a fire had destroyed the previous building.

Benares or **Banaras**, India. Holy City of great antiquity. Sacked by the Moslems, 1194. Annexed by E. India Co., 1775. College opened, 1791. Hindu university opened, 1916.

Benedictine Order. Founded by St. Benedict, 529. Introduced into England, 596. Expelled from France, 1880. Commissioned by Pope Pius X to revise the Vulgate, May 1907.

Benefit of Clergy, by which after Becket's murder (1170) English clerics, and later all who could read, were exempt from *punishment* by a civil court. After 1489 B. of C. could be claimed only once. Ben Jonson escaped gallows by, 1598. Finally abolished, 1827.

Benelux. Customs and currency union of Belgium, the Netherlands, and Luxemburg. Agreement announced, 3 May 1946. Joins Britain and France in Western Union set up under Treaty of Brussels, signed 17 Mar. 1948.

Benevento, Italy. Captured by Romans *c.* 277 B.C.; conquered by Lombards, 571; ceded by Emperor Henry III to Pope Leo IX 1052. Charles of Anjou defeated Manfred of Sicily at B., 26 Feb. 1266. Seized by King of Naples, but restored, 1773; taken by French, 1798; restored to pope, 1815; Napoleon made Talleyrand prince of B., 1806; annexed to Italy, 1866.

Benevolences. Forced loans levied by English monarchs; so called from reign of Edward IV onwards. Parliament declared them unlawful, 1484, but they continued to be levied. Finally declared illegal by Bill of Rights (*q.v.*), 1689.

Bengal, independent, 1340. Annexed to Mogul Empire, 1576. Under British influence after battle of Plassey, 1757. Ceded to E. India Co., 1765. Made chief presidency of India, 16 June 1773. Warren Hastings governor of, 1772–83. Assam annexed to B., 1826–74. Divided into two parts, 1905. This partition revoked, 1911, and B. reconstituted, 1912, Bihar, Orissa, and Chota Nagpur being made a separate province (*see* BIHAR). Serious famine, followed by large-scale epidemics, 1943, led to government inquiry into the provincial administration of B., 1944. Governor took over direct administration of the province, 30 Mar. 1945. E. B. and part of Assam became part of Pakistan, 15 Aug. 1947.

Benghazi, Libya. Occupied by Italians, 20 Oct. 1911. Captured by Australians, 7 Feb. 1941; lost again, 3 Apr.; recaptured, 24 Dec. 1941; lost, 29 Jan. 1942, and finally recaptured by the British, 20 Nov. 1942. *See* WORLD WAR II.

Benin, Nigeria. Unsuccessful attempt by Sir R. Burton to stop human sacrifice, 1863. British expeditions, 1897–9. Placed under British resident, 1899.

Ben Nevis observatory built, 1883; abandoned, 1904.

Berar, India. Formerly part of Hyderabad State, leased by British Government, 1853–1947. Now part of Madhya Pradesh State.

Berchtesgaden, Bavaria. Has salt-mines which have been worked since 1140. Priors of B. made princes of the Empire, 1495. Principality secularized, 1803. The Berghof, B., was a country residence of Hitler, and here he interviewed Neville Chamberlain about the Sudeten crisis, 15 Sept. 1938. Bombed by allied air forces, Apr. and May 1945; the living-quarters of German leaders were destroyed but the solid stone mountain pavilion or 'Eagle's Nest' was undamaged until taken by the French First Armoured Division, 5 May 1945.

Berg, a county of Westphalia from early in the twelfth century, became a duchy, 1380, and passed to the electorate of Bavaria, 1799. Made a Grand Duchy, and handed to Joachim Murat by Napoleon, 1806. Awarded to Prussia by Treaty of Vienna, 1815.

Bergen, Norway. Seaport founded by King Olaf the Peaceful, 1070–5. Hansa merchants used the twelfth-century church of St. Mary from 1408 to 1763. Cathedral founded, 1248: rebuilt, 1537. Germans landed and occupied port, 9 Apr. 1940. Harbour explosion, 1944, destroyed the Bergenhus (seat of the Norwegian kings until the middle of the fourteenth century). It has since been restored. German naval command in Norway surrendered to British and Norwegians, 15 May 1945. Museum founded, 1825. University established, 1946, opened 30 Aug. 1948.

Bergen op Zoom. Fortified, 1576, unsuccessfully besieged by Spaniards, 1588, 1605, 1622. Held by the French from 1795 to 1815.

Berlin, Germany. First became im-portant during reign of Frederick William the Great Elector (*d.* 1688). Seized by Russians and Austrians, Oct. 1760; entered by French after battle of Jena, 1806. Capital of German Empire from 1871 to 1918. B. Congress, 13 July 1878–May 1880; B. Conference, 16 June–1 July 1880. Became capital of Third Reich, 1933. Surrendered to Russians, 2 May 1945, after heavy bombing and fighting had destroyed about 75 per cent of the city proper. Subsequently partitioned into Russian, American, French, and British sectors; from 1948 effectively only into Russian and Western sectors. Its blockade by the Russians, 28 June 1948–12 May 1949, failed in the face of allied air supply. W. Berlin a *Land* of the Federal German Republic, and simultaneously a city, under constitution of 1 Sept. 1950. E. Berlin the capital of the German Democratic Republic since 1949. Riots in Soviet sector (E. Berlin) suppressed, 17 June 1953. Scene of four-power Conference, 26 Jan.–17 Feb. 1954. 13 Aug. 1961: E. Germany sealed off the Berlin border, and began constructing a permanent concrete wall along it, subsequently reinforced with anti-tank barriers, etc. 20 Aug. 1961: U.S. reinforcements entered Berlin. Russia attempted to reserve various air-lanes into Berlin for her sole use. Feb.–Mar. 1962: Anti-communist riots in W. Berlin after callous shooting of a refugee on the E. side of the wall. 22 Aug. 1962: Russians abolished their office of Berlin commandant, and on 23 Aug. Gen. Helmuth Poppe, of the E. German People's Army, was appointed City Commandant of E. Berlin. President Kennedy visited B., June 1963. Khruschev visited E. Berlin shortly afterwards.

Berlin Decrees, 21 Nov. 1806. *See* CONTINENTAL SYSTEM.

Bermudas or **Somers Islands,** Atlantic Ocean. First recorded on map, dated 1511. Visited and named by Juan Bermudez, 1515; settled, 1609, by Sir George Somers. General Assembly first met, 1620. Administration transferred from B. Company to crown, 1684. Colonized in seventeenth century from Virginia, and during the American Revolution by Loyalists. Air and naval bases first leased to U.S.A., Sept. 1940; Tucker and Morgan Islands leased as flying-boat base, 1 Jan. 1941. Women granted vote, 1944. Motor vehicles prohibited, 1908: their use legalized, 1946. Trade unions permitted by legislation of Oct. 1946, and two unions started, 1947. Railways closed down, Apr. 1948. Free primary education introduced, 1 May 1949. Royal naval dockyard closed, 1951. Evacuation by British garrison begun, 1952. Anglo-Franco-American Conference on Main Is., Dec. 1953.

Bern or **Berne.** Joined Swiss League, 1353. The town of B. resisted Rudolph of Hapsburg, 1288; surrendered to French, 12 Apr. 1798; capital of Switzerland, 1848. International Geographical Congress, 1891. Bears have been kept in B. at public expense ever since 1513. *See* COPYRIGHT.

Bernicia. The more northerly of the two Anglian kingdoms which later merged into Northumbria (*q.v.* for list of rulers). Its area roughly corresponded to that of the modern Northumberland and Durham, but it was only a kingdom distinct from Deira (*q.v.*) from 547 to 605 and from 633 to 655. *See also* BAMBURGH.

Berrow's Worcester Journal, the oldest surviving British newspaper, was founded in 1690, but did not acquire the name B. until 1748.

Berwick-on-Tweed. Seaport, municipal borough and administrative county of Northumberland, England. Given up to England by Scotland, 1176; seized by Robert Bruce, 1318; surrendered to English, 1333. Independent of England and Scotland, 1551. Peace of Berwick, between England and Scotland, 1639. Surrendered to Cromwell, 1648; to Gen. Monck, 1659.

Beryllium. Discovered in the form of oxide in the mineral beryl, 1798. Isolated by Wöhler, 1828.

Besançon, France. Became a free city of the empire, 1184. In Spanish hands, 1648–78. Became capital of Franche-Comté (*q.v.*) when that province was ceded to France, 1678.

Bessarabia (Ukrainian **Budzhak**). Region on the W. coast of the Black Sea between the Danube and the Dniestr, called after the Basarab dynasty or else after the Bessi, a Thracian tribe who lived in the area. The Basarab dynasty, Vlach princes descended from Rada Negru, alias Rudolph the Black, became dominant in the fourteenth century A.D., at which time B. meant the whole of what is now Wallachia, and the land between the Dniestr and the Seret (Siretul) Rivers S. of Kishinev (Chisinau), but after 1482 and its conquest by the Turks the name was applied only to the latter area which was disputed between the Turks, the Russians, and the Tatars of Crimea, and comprised what are now the Russian provinces of Akkerman (*q.v.*) and Ismail, and the Rumanian provinces of Dunarea and De Jos. In 1812 the Peace of Bucharest awarded the whole area between the Dniestr and the Pruth (Prutul) Rivers to Russia under the name B. From 1856

to 1878 three southern districts came under the Moldavian principality. A Moldavian Soviet Republic proclaimed, Dec. 1917, never became effective over the whole of its territory, which was in effect eastern Moldavia, i.e. the B. of nineteenth-century terminology. Its people voted by referendum of 27 Nov. 1918 to join Rumania, and this was confirmed by a treaty signed in 1920 by Rumania, Britain, France, Italy, and Japan, but not Russia, with whom negotiations went on until 1924, when they were abandoned. B. was treated as occupied territory by the Rumanian armed forces down to *c.* 1930. The U.S.S.R. delivered an ultimatum to Rumania, 26 June 1940, and reoccupied the region without opposition. In the first rush of the German campaign of 1941 Rumanian forces as allies of Germany reconquered B., but lost it again in 1944, when the provinces of Ismail and Akkerman were joined to the Soviet Republic of Ukraine and those of Kishinev, Bender (Tighina), Beltsk (Balti), Kagulsk (Cahul), Orgeev (Orhei), and Sorok (Soroca) to that of Moldavia. This settlement confirmed by the peace treaty of 1947.

Bessel's Functions, in mathematics, indicate certain relationships between two variables. Introduced by F. W. Bessel, 1817.

Bessemer Process. Invented by Sir Henry Bessemer, 1856.

Beta-Rays. Discovered by Lord Rutherford, 1899.

Bethlehem (modern **Beit-Lahm**), Israel. The village dates from before 1000 B.C. Christian pilgrimage began earlier than 132 (*see* NATIVITY, CHURCH OF THE), but the village was devastated in 1244 and again in 1489.

Béthune, France. Founded in the eleventh century. Ceded to France at the Treaty of Nijmegen, 1678.

Betting. B. Acts of 1853 and 1874, and the B. and Lotteries Act of 1934, regulated B. in Britain until the B. and Gaming Act, 1960, provided for the establishment of licensed B. shops. Ready-money B. on football, as a business, prohibited, 1920. B. Duty imposed, 1926. In 1928 the B. tax was reduced; in 1930 abolished. Tax on dog totalizators and football pools, Nov. 1947. Goverment announced inquiry to be made into the feasibility of a tax on all betting, Apr. 1963. *See also* GAMING AND GAMBLING.

Betting-houses (Great Britain). Suppressed, 1853. Licensed betting shops allowed under the Betting and Gaming Act, 1960.

Beveridge Plan. National insurance

scheme signed by Lord Beveridge (1879–1963), chairman of the Inter-departmental Committee on Social Insurance and Allied Services, 1941–2, and published by H.M. Stationery Office, 20 Nov. 1942. It formed the basis of post-war legislation in the fields of social insurance and social security.

Beverley (E. Yorks.). Its principal church, of the twelfth century, is built on the site of that founded by St. John of B. (c. 640–721), who is also the reputed founder of B. grammar school. A charter of the town is mentioned as having been granted in 925, but is not extant; but one granted between 1120 and 1135 is. Weaving became an important industry early in the fourteenth century. Charters of incorporation were granted, 1573, 1629, 1663, and 1685.

Bhopal. Former Indian princely state, merged into Madhya Pradesh since 1956. Founded by Dost Mohammed Khan, 1723, and concluded a treaty with Britain, 1818.

Bhutan (Bhotian, **Druk-Yul**) was invaded by Tibetans in ninth century A.D. and Indian population driven out. Treaty with E. India Co., 1774. New British treaty, 1826, whereby B. was to pay annual tribute to Britain, was not kept, leading to the annexation by Britain of the Assam Duars, and undertaking by Britain to pay the rajahs of B. an annual subsidy during good behaviour. British envoy to B. imprisoned, 1863, provoking war which terminated, Nov. 1865. System of dual government by temporal and spiritual rulers became virtually extinct in 1885; the temporal ruler elected maharajah, 1907. Treaty with Britain guaranteeing B. security against Chinese aggression, and charging Britain with the conduct of Bhutanese foreign relations, signed, 1910. British representation in B. succeeded by Indian, Aug. 1947. Treaty of friendship with India, 1949; annual subsidy increased to Rs. 500,000. The second maharajah, Sir Jigme Wangchuk, d. Mar. 1952, and was succeeded by his son, Jigme Dorji Wangchuk (b. 1929).

Bible, Translations of. The first translation of the Old Testament into Greek, called the Septuagint, made in stages between 284 B.C. and A.D. 100. Origen's collection of versions, *Hexapla*, commenced, A.D. 231. Psalms believed to have been translated into Old English before Alfred's time. Cædmon's metrical paraphrase of a portion of the B. c. A.D. 670. Bede's St. John (735) and Aelfric's partial Old Testament (990). Division into chapters, often ascribed to Lanfranc (eleventh century), was probably a result of the labours of Hugh de Sancto Caro

(c. 1200–63). Wycliffe's English versions c. 1382 and 1388. The whole Bible divided into verses first in the Geneva version of 1557–60. Tyndale's (New Testament) printed, 1525; Coverdale's (first complete English B.) printed, 1535; Cranmer's B. first authorized, 1539; authorized version published, 1611 (*see* HAMPTON COURT CONFERENCE); revised version, New Testament, 1881; Old Testament, 1884. Dr. James Moffat's translations published: New Testament, 1913; Old Testament, 1924. New version of the New Testament in modern English, 1961. For Latin B., and translations therefrom, *see* separate article, VULGATE.

Bible Society, British and Foreign. Begun, 1803; organized, 1804. American B. S. organized at Philadelphia, 1808; various American B. Ss. amalgamated to form the American and Foreign B. S., 1839. Papal Bull against B. S. issued, June 1816.

Bibliothèque Nationale. The building in Paris which now houses the collection was bought for the purpose by the crown in 1721, having been built in the mid-seventeenth century. The nucleus of the collection is the books owned by Louis XI (d. 1483).

Bicycle. *See* CYCLE.

Bigamy in England is punishable under the Offences against the Person Act, 1866; in Scotland it is merely another form of perjury punishable by statute of 1551; in the U.S.A. the law of B. varies from state to state, but in general it is based on an English statute of 1603.

Big Ben (London). First hung, 1858. Clock in use from 1859. Chimes first broadcast, 1923. Named after Sir Benjamin Hall (1802–67), Commissioner of Works at the time: he became Baron Llanover, 1859.

'Big Bertha.' Nickname given to German long-range gun which fired on Paris during 1918.

Bihar, India. Separated from Bengal, 1911. From Orissa, 1935. Serious riots in 1942 and 1946.

Bilbao, Spain. Founded c. 1300; taken by French, July 1795, and in 1808; bombarded by Carlists, but relieved, 1874; fell to Nationalist forces, 18 June 1937.

Billiards. Known in England in Shakespeare's time. It has been ascribed to Henri Devigne. 1571.

Billingsgate, London. Tolls collected there from tenth century. Opened, 1588, as a landing-place for provisions; free market, 1699; extended, 1848; rebuilt, 1852, 1876.

Bill of Rights. *See* RIGHTS, BILL OF.

Bills of Exchange Act, 1882, codified

existing practice concerning B. of E. in the U.K.

Bills of Exchequer first issued, 1696.

Bills of Sale or **Chattel Mortgages** are regulated by the Acts of 1878 and 1882 in England and Wales only.

Bingen, Rhenish Palatinate, was important for the water-borne traffic of the Rhine as the nearest harbour to the dangerous rapids of Bingerloch until these were cleared by blasting in 1834. The conspicuous statue of Germania—'Die Dame ohne Verhältnisse'—was erected, 1877–83.

Binomial Theorem. First published by Isaac Newton, 1676.

Birdcage Walk. Perhaps really *Bocage W.*, but James I (1603–25) built an aviary there, and the nearby cock-pit was not done away with until 1816.

Birkbeck College. Founded as the London Mechanics' Institute by Dr. George Birkbeck, 1823. Became a constituent college of London University, 1920.

Birkenhead, England. Dock opened, Aug. 1847. *See* LIVERPOOL.

Birmingham, England. Appears in Domesday Book, 1086. Market charters granted, 1166, 1189, 1249, 1295. Sacked by Royalists, 1643. Canal opened, 1767. 'Church and king' riots in, 1791. Town hall built, 1834. Incorporated, 1838. Chartist riot, 15 July 1839. Bright first elected M.P. for, 1857. Became a city, 1889. Office of lord mayor created, 1896. University chartered, 1900. Became a bishopric, 1904. Repertory theatre founded, 1913. Heavily bombed in World War II, 1940–3.

Birobidjan. Town in the Soviet Far East. Capital of the Jewish Autonomous Region. Formerly a small railway station called Tikhon'kaya, it became a town in 1928.

Birth, Concealment of, in Scotland, was considered to be proof of infanticide, a capital offence, until 1803, when it was made punishable by a maximum of two years' imprisonment, as in England and Wales.

Birth Control. First clinic opened, Amsterdam, 1881; first in Britain (in London), 1921.

Bishoprics (England and Wales). Following are dates of foundation of the Anglican sees (not suffragan sees):

Bangor	*c.* 550	Carlisle	1133
Bath and Wells	1139	Chelmsford	1927
Birmingham	1904	Chester	1541
Blackburn	1927	Chichester	1075
Bradford	1919	Coventry	1919
Bristol	1541	Derby	1927
Canterbury	597	Durham	995

Ely	1109	Rochester	604
Exeter	1050	St. Albans	1877
Gloucester	1541	St. Asaph	*c.* 550
Guildford	1927	St. Davids	*c.* 550
Hereford	676	St. Edmundsbury	
Leicester	1919	and Ipswich	1914
Lichfield	669	Salisbury	1075
Lincoln	1067	Sheffield	1914
Liverpool	1880	Sodor and	
Llandaff	*c.* 550	Man	*c.* 1134
London	605	Southwark	1905
Manchester	1847	Southwell	1884
Monmouth	1920	Swansea and	
Newcastle	1882	Brecon	1920
Norwich	1094	Truro	1876
Oxford	1542	Wakefield	1888
Peterborough	1541	Winchester	*c.* 650
Portsmouth	1927	Worcester	*c.* 680
Ripon	1877	York	625

Bishops (U.K.). Earliest British B. *c.* 180. For dates of foundation of sees, *see* BISHOPRICS. In Scotland replaced by superintendents, 1561. Restored, 1573. Abolished, 1638. Abolished in England, 1646. Restored in both countries, 1661. Expelled by Scottish convention, 1689.

Bishops (U.S.A.). Samuel Seabury, Bishop of Connecticut, Nov. 1784, first bishop consecrated for U.S.A. First bishop of New York consecrated in London, 4 Feb. 1787.

Bishops, Seven, committed to the Tower for seditious libel (i.e. opposing the Declaration of Indulgence), but found not guilty at the Bar of the King's Bench, 29 June 1688.

Bisley (Surrey). Scene of National Rifle Association meetings since 1890.

Bismarck Archipelago. Discovered by Dampier, 1699, and named New Britain, but by agreement of 1885 assigned to the German sphere of influence and their name changed to B. A. Occupied by Australian forces, Sept. 1914, and after 1918 attached to the Australian mandated territories in New Guinea. From 1942 to 1945 under military government as to those parts still held by the Allies. New Britain, the largest island, was occupied by the Japanese in 1941, but partly cleared early in 1944.

Bithynia, Asia Minor. Became part of the kingdom of Lydia, 570 B.C., but absorbed with it by the Persian Empire, 546. After recovery of its independence Nicomedia was founded in 264 B.C. The last king of B. bequeathed his state to Rome, 74 B.C. Conquered by Turks, A.D. 1298.

Bizerta, Tunisia, N. Africa (anciently **Hippo Zarytis**). Occupied by French, 1881. Harbour rebuilt, 1890–5. Captured from Germans, 9 May 1943. French military and naval base retained there after Tunisian independence, 1956. Fighting broke out between the French and Tunisians after the Tunisians blockaded the base, 20 July 1961. Heavy damage and casualties. Cease fire, 23 July 1961.

Black Death. Identical with bubonic plague. Supposed to have originated in China. Raged there, 1340–8. In Europe, 1346–9, 1361–2, and 1369. A plague called the B. D. ravaged Dublin, 1866.

Blackfriars Bridge (London). Old bridge, 1760–1860; new bridge opened, 6 Nov. 1869; enlarged, 1909.

Black Friday. 1. 6 Dec. 1745. Young Pretender's entry into Derby announced in London, causing a run on the bank and closing of shops. 2. 11 May 1866. Overend, Gurney & Co., the bankers, stopped payment, causing commercial panic; partners tried for conspiracy to defraud, but acquitted, Dec. 1869.

Blackheath, England. Wat Tyler's men assembled on, 12 June 1381; Jack Cade, 1 June 1450. Cornish rebels defeated at, 22 June 1497.

Black Hole of Calcutta. Suraj-ud-Dowlah, Nawab of Bengal, imprisoned 146 English people in, on 19 June 1756: only twenty-three survived the night there.

Black Monday. Certain Easter Mondays upon which tradition records disasters to the English: 1. 29 Mar. 1209. 500 settlers massacred by Irish at Collenswood, Dublin; 2. 9 Apr. 1357. Black Prince's army sustained terrible losses through a storm; 3. 13 Apr. 1360. In Edward III's army near Paris many men died of cold.

Black Prince. Eldest son of Edward III; *b.* 15 June 1330; at battle of Poitiers, 1356; *d.* 8 June 1376.

Black Rod. Office instituted, 1349.

Black or **Euxine Sea.** Turks exclude all foreign ships from, 1453. Russians obtain right to trade in, 1774; Austria, 1784; France and Britain, 1802. B. S. Conference, 1871.

Blackwall Tunnel, London, begun, 1892; opened, 1897.

Blanc, Mont, highest mountain in the Alps (15,782 ft.). First climbed by Paccard and Balmat, 1786.

Blandford, England. Whole town almost destroyed by fire, 1731.

Blarney Castle, County Cork, Ireland, gave its name to the cant phrase for flattery which cannot be traced—in writing—further back than 1819. Castle stands on the s'·e of one founded by Cormac McCarthy in 1446.

Blasket Islands, County Kerry. Gaelic-speaking stronghold, evacuated July 1953.

Blasphemy. The last considerable English legislation concerning this offence is an Act of 1697, modified by Smith's

Act of 1813, which distinguishes in favour of Unitarians. The last considerable prosecution for blasphemous libel was that of Bradlaugh in 1868.

Bleaching. Artificial B. invented by Dutch early in eighteenth century; first bleach-field in Scotland established at Salton *c.* 1730; introduced into England, 1768; Berthollet's discoveries with chlorine *c.* 1785; Tennant's patent, 1798; Mather's improvements, 1885.

Blenheim Palace (Woodstock, England). Built by Sir J. Vanbrugh at national expense for the first Duke of Marlborough between 1705 and 1722.

Bloemfontein, capital of the Orange Free State, S. Africa. Founded, 1846. Occupied by British, 13 Mar. 1900.

Blois, France. Sold to Louis, Duke of Orleans, 1391; States-General held at, 1576 and 1588; Henry of Guise assassinated at, 23 Dec. 1588.

Blood, Circulation of the. Principal discoveries regarding, due to William Harvey between 1616 and 1628.

Blood's (Colonel) Conspiracy. Attempt to steal crown jewels, 9 May 1671. Col. Thomas B., *b. c.* 1628, *d.* 1680.

Blood Transfusion was practised on animals as early as the seventeenth century. Janssky in 1907 discovered the principle of the four human blood groups which explained earlier failures in practice on human patients. A method of B. T. not direct from artery to artery was discovered in 1916, as was refrigeration. Plasma, as opposed to whole blood, first transfused on a large scale, 1940.

'**Bloody Assize.**' The trials by Judge George Jeffreys (1648–89), in Aug. 1685, after Monmouth's rebellion (*q.v.*).

Blue-Books. Parliamentary and state reports, so called from their blue paper wrappers. These reports first printed in 1681.

Blue-stocking. Term originated *c.* 1750. when a literary circle was established in London, consisting of ladies and gentlemen among whom was a distinguished Mr. Benjamin Stillingfleet, who habitually wore blue stockings.

Board of Trade, founded 1661, but present form dates from 1786, when a permanent committee was constituted by an Order in Council (still in force). Dept. of Overseas Trade absorbed by the Board of Trade after 1945.

Boat Race, Oxford and Cambridge. First held in 1829, this did not become an annual event until 1856. A dead-heat was rowed in 1877. Score to date (1963): Cambridge, 59; Oxford, 48. No race, 1915–19 inclusive. Oxford boat sank, 1951.

Bodleian Library. *See* LIBRARIES, MODERN.

Boeotia, Greece. United under Theban leadership, *c.* 1100 B.C. Victory over Spartans at Leuctra, 371 B.C., gave B. supremacy in Greece till death of Epaminondas at battle of Mantinea, 362 B.C.

Boers. Emigrated from Cape Colony, 1835–7; founded Orange Free State, 1836; Transvaal Republic, 1848. *See* SOUTH AFRICAN WAR; CAPE COLONY; TRANSVAAL, etc.

Boer Wars. First B. War, 1880–1. Virtually ended by the British defeat at Majuba Hill, 27 Feb. 1881. Second B. War, 1899–1902. Concluded by the Peace of Vereeniging (*see under* TREATIES), 31 May 1902.

Bogomils, Old Slavonic for 'God's beloved,' were a sect of heretics in the Balkans first mentioned in Greek sources, 1115. Their leader Basil was interrogated by the Emperor Alexius Comnenus, and then burnt by his orders, 1118. Slavonic sources mention the sect earlier, in the mid-tenth century, as of Manichaean (*see* MANICHAEISM) type. Driven out of Serbia *c.* 1200, they took refuge in Bosnia, where they survived until the Turkish conquest of that province (fifteenth century).

Bogotá, formerly **Santa Fé de Bogotá,** capital of Colombia since 1831, was founded in 1538 and became an episcopal see in 1561, capital of the viceroyalty of New Granada in 1598. In the War of Liberation it was captured by the Royalists, 1816, and retaken by the Republicans, 1819.

Bohemia. Christianity introduced from Moravia during ninth century. Dukedom, A.D. 891. Rulers known as kings soon after. 'Good King Wenceslas' murdered by Boleslav the Cruel, 929. Recognized as a kingdom by emperor, 1088. Reign of Ottokar begins, 1253. Extinction of Przemyslid dynasty, 1306. John of Luxembourg elected king, 1310. Killed at Crécy, 1346. University of Prague founded, 1348. John Hus *b. c.* 1373. Hussites adopt heretical doctrines, 1390 onwards. Hus burned by Council of Constance, 1415. 'The Twelve Years (Hussite) War,' 1419–31. Battle of Taus, 1431. Destruction of the Taborites at battle of Lipan, 1434. Religious Pact of Iglan, 1436. George of Podebrad elected king, 1457. Ferdinand of Hapsburg became king, 1526. Ferdinand had himself declared hereditary ruler of B., so that B. became a permanent Hapsburg appanage, 1547. Toleration of Protestantism promised by Emperor Rudolf's *Letter of Majesty,* July 1609. The *Letter* violated by Ferdinand II. Defenestration of Prague, 1619. Battle of the White Mountain, 1620. Thirty Years War, 1618–48. After Treaty of Westphalia, 1648, history of B. became generally coincident with that of Austria (*q.v.*) until 1918. Pan-Slav congress held in Prague, 1848, and unsuccessful attempt made to reassert the ancient independence of B. Provisional government organized in Paris by Czech emigrants led by T. G. Masaryk in World War I (1914–18). Czechoslovak Republic proclaimed, 14 Nov. 1918, in Bohemia, Moravia, Slovakia, and Ruthenia. Sudeten territories incorporated in Germany, Oct. 1938. With Moravia became the 'Protectorate of B.-Moravia,' and liberties suppressed under Germany, Mar. 1939. Liberated by Russians and Americans, 1945. Sudeten Germans forcibly driven out, 1945–6. *See further under* CZECHOSLOVAKIA.

Rulers of, from the beginning of the historic period, *c.* 922, until 1918.

Princes:

Wenceslas I (Saint), the Good	*c.* 922–*c.* 929
Boleslav I, the Cruel	*c.* 929–967
Boleslav II	967–999
Boleslav III	999–1002
Vladivoj I	1002–1003
Jaromir I	1003–1012
Ulrich I	1012–1037
Bretislav I	1037–1055
Spytihinev II	1055–1061
Vratislav II (King)	1061–1092
Bretislav II	1092–1110
Borivoj II	1110–1120
Vladislav I	1120–1125
Sobeslav I	1125–1140
Vladislav II (as King, I)	1140–1173
Sobeslav II	1173–1189
Conrad Otho I	1189–1191
Wenceslas II	1191–1192

Kings:

Premysl Ottokar I	1198–1230
Wenceslas I	1230–1253
Premysl Ottokar II	1253–1278
Wenceslas II	1278–1305
Wenceslas III	1305–1306
Rudolf I of Hapsburg	1306–1307
Henry of Carinthia	1307–1310
John	1310–1346
Charles I (IV)	1346–1378
Wenceslas IV	1378–1419
Sigismund	1419–1437
Albert of Hapsburg	1437–1439
Ladislas Posthumus	1439–1457
George of Podebrad	1458–1471
Vladislav II	1471–1516
Louis I	1516–1526
Ferdinand I	1526–1564
Maximilian I	1564–1576

Rudolf II	1576–1612
Matthias	1612–1619
Frederick of the Palatinate	*1619–1620
Ferdinand II	*1619–1637
Ferdinand III	1637–1657
Leopold I	1657–1705
Josef I	1705–1711
Karl II (VI)	1711–1740
Maria Theresa	*1740–1780
Karl of Bavaria	*1740–1743
Josef II	1780–1790
Leopold II	1790–1792
Franz I	1792–1835
Ferdinand IV (I)	1835–1848
Franz Josef	1848–1916
Karl III (I)	1916–1918

* Disputed succession.

Bohemian Brethren. *See* MORAVIAN BRETHREN.

Bokhara or **Bukhara,** Asia. Conquered in seventh century by Arabs, under whom it *fl.* until 1220. Seized by Uzbeks *c.* 1500; British envoys murdered at, 1842; war with Russia, 1866–8; treaty with Russia, 1873; Emirate abolished and Soviet regime founded, 1921. In 1924 territory split between the new Soviet republics of Uzbekistan and Turkmenistan.

Bolivia. Conquered by Spain during the sixteenth century, and formed part of the viceroyalty of Peru. Separated from Peru, 1776, and added to the viceroyalty of Buenos Aires. War of Independence, 1810–24; royalists defeated at battle of Ayacucho, and independence granted, 16 Aug. 1825; first constitution adopted, Nov. 1826. Defeated in alliance with Peru in war with Chile, 1879–83. Boundary dispute with Brazil, 1903. Revolution, Sept. 1925. Boundary dispute with Paraguay, 1928, submitted to international arbitration, 1929. Boundary with Argentina determined, 1930. War over Gran Chaco with Paraguay, 10 May 1933–21 Jan. 1936. Resumed diplomatic relations with Paraguay, 26 May 1937. Military *coup d'état*, 13 July 1937. Frontier with Paraguay fixed by arbitration, 10 Oct. 1938. President Villaroel and some ministers lynched by mob, July 1946. Present constitution adopted, 1947. Just before the expiry of his presidential term in 1951 President Urriolagoitia resigned in favour of a junta headed by Gen. Ballivián Rojas. Revolution in April 1952 led to adoption of more left-wing domestic policies by subsequent governments, all supporters of the National Revolutionary Movement which triumphed, 9 Apr. 1952.

Heads of State (Presidents) from the Establishment of the Republic, 1825–6:

Sucre	1826–1828
Santa Cruz	1828–1829
Blanco	1829–1831
Santa Cruz	1831–1839
Velasco	1839–1840
Ballivian	1840–1848
Belzu	1848–1856
Cordova	1856–1857
Linares	1857–1861
De Acha	1861–1865
Melgarejo	1865–1871
Morales	1871–1872
Ballivian	1872–1874
Frias	1874–1876
Daza	1876–1879
Campero	1879–1884
Pacheco	1884–1888
Arce	1888–1892
Bautista	1892–1896
Alonso	1896–1899

Bolivia. *Heads of State—cont.*

Pando	1899–1904
Montes	1904–1908
Villazon	1908–1912
Montes	1912–1917
Guerra	1917–1920
Saavedra	1920–1925
Guzman	1925–1926
Siles	1926–1930
Galindo	1930–1931
Salamanca	1931–1934
Sorzano	1934–1936
Toro	1936–1937
Busch	1937–1939
Quintanilla	1939–1940
Peneranda	1940–1943
Villaroel	1943–1946
Guillen	1946
Gutierrez	1946–1947
Hertzog	1947–1949
Urriolagoitia	1949–1951
Ballivián Rojas	1951–1952
Estenssoro	1952–1956
Siles	1956–1960
Estenssoro	1960–

Bologna, Italy. Roman colony, 189 B.C. University grew out of schools of liberal arts, which *fl.* in eleventh century; first statutes, 1252. Pope Julius II took and entered, 11 Nov. 1506. Taken by French, 1796; by Austrians, 1799; by French, 1800; restored to pope, 1815; taken by Austrians, 16 May 1849, who evacuated, 12 June 1859, and papal legate left. Became part of kingdom of Italy, 1860.

Bolsheviks. That part of the revolutionary Socialist party which professed Marxist Communism and happened to be in a *majority* (bolshestvo) at the end of the Second Congress of the Russian Social-Democratic Labour Party, in 1903, when several delegates had already left the congress. Independent Bolshevik Party founded (calling itself Social-Democratic Labour Party), 1912. Led by Lenin and Trotsky it seized power in Russia in Nov. 1917. Known by name 'Communist Party' ('Bolsheviks') from 1918; word 'Bolsheviks' dropped, 1952, and term now only used in Russia in an historical sense. *See* OCTOBER REVOLUTION; RUSSIA; MENSHEVIKS; COMMUNISM.

Bolton Abbey (W. Yorkshire.) Founded 1121, at Embsay, and transferred to the site in Wharfedale, 1151. Really a priory, not abbey, of Augustinians. Dissolved, 1540.

Bombay, India. Acquired by Portuguese, 1509; given to Charles II of England as marriage portion of Catherine of Portugal, 1661; granted to E. India Co., 1668. University founded, 1857. Visited by Prince of Wales (Edward VII), 8 Nov. 1875. Aden separated from, 1932.

Bomber. The first specialized military aircraft for this purpose was the German Gotha, twin-engined push-biplane, taken into service, 1917.

Bombs of a type similar to the modern mortar-bomb first mentioned in English, 1588. The word was also used to describe *shells*, an expression not used until the middle of the seventeenth century.

Bonaparte. *See* BUONAPARTE.

Bond Street, New. Built, 1721.

Bond Street, Old. Built, 1686, by Sir Thomas Bond, who in 1683 bought and demolished Clarendon House for a building site.

Bonin or **Ogasawara Islands.** Discovered by Quast and Tasman, 1639. British, 1827. Japanese, 1878.

Bonn, Germany. Became residence of the electors and archbishops of Cologne during the Middle Ages. Sacked by Frederick III of Brandenburg, 1689. Became Prussian after 1815. Academy founded, 1777; made a university, 1786; abolished, 1802; restored and enlarged, 1818. Albert (Prince Consort) educated at, from 1837. Occupied by allied troops after World War I until 31 Jan. 1926. Seat of W. German Federal Government, 5 May 1949.

Bonne's Projection. Invented 1752 by the French cartographer of that name, and was adopted by the survey department of the Napoleonic war office, 1803. As, however, it produces a distortion at the edges of a surveyed area such that indirect artillery fire cannot possibly be directed by its aid, maps based on B. P. were abandoned by most European powers before 1918.

Book of Common Prayer. *See* PRAYER, BOOK OF COMMON.

Bordeaux, France. Taken by Goths, A.D. 412; by Clovis, 508; became subject to England in 1154 by reason of the royal marriage in 1151; surrendered to France, 14 Oct. 1453; entered by British troops, 27 Feb. 1814. Temporary seat of French Government, Sept.–Dec. 1914 and 15–30 June 1940.

Bordeaux Mixture invented by Alexis Millerdet (1838–1902) to combat phylloxera and mildew in vines.

Border, The, between England and Scotland, dates in its present form as to the eastern sector from 1018 when the Scots under Malcolm II recovered Lothian, and as to the western sector from the reconquest of Cumberland by the English in 1157 (*see* STRATHCLYDE). It ceased to be a political frontier in 1603. The characteristic desultory state of tribal warfare on the B. was at its height from 1300 to 1600, which was the period which formed the 'B. ballads'; to some extent this state of society persisted during the Anglo-Scottish religious wars of the seventeenth century and the germs of it had existed since the days of the Roman Wall's abandonment *c.* 376. Following are some battles important in the annals of B. warfare.

Halidon Hill, 1333	Hedgeley Moor, 1464
Otterburn, 1388	Flodden, 1513
Nisbet, 1402	Solway Moss, 1542
Homildon, 1402	Ancrum Moor, 1544

Borneo, Indian Ocean. First European resident in B., Francisco Serrão (Portuguese), 1511–21. Visited by Magellan's comrades in 1522. Dutch established trading posts, 1604. Dutch B. became part of Indonesia (*q.v.*) after World War II. The nucleus of British N. B. was territory acquired in 1878 by a syndicate which transferred to the British N. B. Co., chartered, 1881. Sarawak (*q.v.*) became, 1841, the rajahship of Sir James Brooke and his descendants; enlarged, 1861, 1882, 1884, 1890, 1904. British N. B., Sarawak, and the diminished State of Brunei became British protectorates in 1888. Sarawak and British N. B. annexed by British Government, 15 July 1946, to form British B., which now includes Brunei and the island of Labuan, which was first ceded to Britain by the Sultan of Brunei, 1846, and has at various times formed part of British N. B. The whole legal code was revised, 1952. N. B. claimed by the Philippines, June 1962. Revolt in Brunei and parts of Sarawak, Dec. 1962, inspired by nationalists who objected to Brunei's inclusion in the proposed Malaysia (*q.v.*). British troops brought in and revolt crushed within a week. By agreement finally signed 9 July 1963, to form part of Malaysia from 31 Aug. 1963. *See* WORLD WAR II.

Bornu, Kingdom of. First discovered by Europeans, 1823. Partitioned about 1900 between Nigeria, W. Africa (French), and the Cameroons. *See* all these.

Borough. The Municipal Corporations Act, 1835, defined what was and what was not a municipal B., and reformed their constitutions. It was superseded by the Municipal Corporations Act, 1882, and its subsequent amendments, principally the Local Government Acts of 1933 and 1958.

Borough, The. *See* SOUTHWARK.

Borstal. Originally at B., near Chatham, 1902. Made a regular part of prison system, 1908, under heading of B. detention; name changed to B. training, 1948.

Boscobel, parish in Shropshire. Charles II hid in an oak-tree there after his defeat at Worcester in 1651.

Bosnia. Incorporated with Turkey, 1463; rebellion against Turkish rule, 1849–1851 and 1875; occupied by Austria, 1878, and formally annexed by her, 1908. Became part of Yugoslavia, 1918. *See also* HERZEGOVINA.

Bosnia-Herzegovina. A national committee sat at Sarajevo from Oct. 1918, in close touch with the Yugoslav national council at Zagreb. On formation of the state of Yugoslavia (*q.v.*), B.-H. became part thereof. Became one of the Federated Republics of Yugoslavia, 1945.

Bosphorus or **Bosporus** (now **Karadenzi Bogazi**). Placed by the unratified Treaty of Sèvres of 1920 under a League of Nations Commission. *See also* TURKISH REPUBLIC.

Boston (Lincs.). St. Botolph founded a monastery here, 654, which was destroyed by the Danes in 870. In the Guildhall (1450) those subsequently famous as the Pilgrim Fathers were imprisoned, 1607.

Boston, Mass., U.S.A. Founded by John Winthrop, 1630. First American newspaper, *Boston News-Letter*, Apr. 1704 (*see* NEWSPAPERS). Tea chests destroyed in B. Harbour, 16 Dec. 1773. Harbour closed, 25 Mar. 1774; B. besieged by Americans, 1775; evacuated by British, 1776. Great fires at, Nov. 1872, Nov. 1889, and 17 May 1894.

Botanic Gardens (Kew). Established, 1759; enlarged, 1841–65.

Botanic Society's Gardens, Royal (Regent's Park). Established, 1839.

Botany Bay, Australia. Discovered 28 Apr. 1770, by Capt. Cook. Capt. Arthur Phillip, R.N., commissioned to form penal colony here in 1787, but found locality unsuitable (Jan. 1788), and removed to site on which Sydney now stands. Transportation of convicts ceased, 1840.

Boulder Dam on the Colorado River between Nevada and Arizona completed, 1935–6.

Boulogne, France. Sacked by the Normans, 882. Unsuccessfully besieged by Edward III, 1347. Seized by Duke of Burgundy (?1419), seizure confirmed by Treaty of Arras, 1435; united to France, 1477. Treaty between Henry VIII (of England) and Francis I at B., 28 Oct. 1532. Besieged by English, 1492; taken by English, 14 Sept. 1544; restored, 1550. Napoleon I mustered his forces at B. with the intention of invading England, 1803. British defence of, 22–24 May 1940. Liberated by Canadian First Army, 19 Sept. 1944.

'Bounty' Mutiny. H.M.S. *Bounty* sailed in Dec. 1787 to the Society Islands on a scientific mission under command of Capt. William Bligh (1754–1817). On 28 Apr. 1789, in the Indian Ocean, the crew mutinied and put Bligh and eighteen others in an open boat which he sailed to Timor, reaching that island on 9 June. The mutineers returned to Tahiti, which nine of them left in 1790 for Pitcairn Island, accompanied by Tahitian wives and some Tahitian men. Bligh published his narrative of the mutiny and his subsequent voyage, 1792. By 1800 the only grown man, white or brown, left on Pitcairn was John Adams, a seaman who died, 1829. The island had been discovered by Carteret, 1767, but was seldom visited, and the existence of the colony was unknown to the outside world until 1808. By 1856 it had become overpopulated, and the Pitcairners asked to be evacuated to Norfolk Island, which was done, but forty of them shortly returned. In 1950 Bligh's Bible, discovered in the U.S.A., was taken to Pitcairn and presented to the chief magistrate, Parkin Christian, representing the islanders, by a representative of the High Commissioner, Western Pacific.

Bourbon, House of. First Duke of B., 1327. From this house sprang royal families of France, Naples, Parma, and Spain. King Alfonso XIII of Spain, last reigning monarch of this house, abdicated 1931. *See* FRANCE, SOVEREIGNS OF and SICILY.

Bourbonnais, ancient province united to the French crown on the confiscation of the Constable of Bourbon's domains by Francis I in 1527. From 1661 to 1789 held by the house of Bourbon Condé. Became the department of Allier, 1794.

Bourges, capital, under the name of

Avaricum, of the Gallic Biturigan territory. Avaricum was sacked by Julius
Caesar, 52 B.C. The cathedral was built,
1200–60, but not consecrated until 1324.
Pragmatic Sanction of B., 1437. For a
period c. 1440 was capital of France.

Bourse. See EXCHANGES, FOREIGN.

Bouvetoya. Island in the S. Atlantic,
was discovered by the Frenchman Pierre
Bouvet, 1739; in 1825 the British flag was
hoisted. Dispute as to ownership arose
with Norway, 1928, a Norwegian whaling
party having occupied the island since
Dec. 1927. Britain waived all claims,
Nov. 1928. Proclaimed Norwegian territory, 27 Feb. 1930.

Bouvines. See BATTLES.

Bowling. Played in Germany and the
Low Countries, and in England under the
name 'skittles,' since the fourteenth
century. Taken to America in the
the seventeenth century by Dutch
settlers, and played out of doors until
1840. B. alleys opened in Britain, 1959
onwards.

Bowls has been played in England since
at least 1299. Word first occurs in Act
of 1511.

Bow Street. Magistrates' court first sat,
1735; police court building erected
1881, replacing that of 1749, which was
sacked by the Gordon rioters, 1780. The
street was first built up in 1637. Covent
Garden Theatre built, 1858. B. S.
Runners formed the only criminal detection force in London c. 1750–1829,
after which date their functions were
taken over by the police.

Boxers. Chinese secret society founded
1896, encouraged in 1899 by the agents of
the Dowager Empress to provoke anti-
foreign incidents. For Boxer Rising of
1900, see CHINA.

Boxing. First B. booth opened in
London, 1719. Became a legal sport in
England, 1901.

Boxing Day. Officially recognized as a
Bank Holiday, 1874.

Boycott. Term derived from Capt.
Charles B. (1832–97), land agent to Lord
Erne in County Mayo, Ireland, who was
the victim of a B. in 1880, organized by
the Land League (q.v.) in retaliation for
certain evictions.

Boyle's Law. Formulated, 1662, by
Robert Boyle (1627–91).

Boys' Brigade. Founded, 1883, by Sir
W. Smith (d. 1914). Amalgamated with
Boys' Life Brigade, 1926.

Boys' Clubs, National Association of.
Founded, 1925.

Boys' Clubs of America. Founded,
1906.

Boy Scouts. Organization began in 1908,
in the U.K. Adopted by Chile, 1909, the

U.S.A., France, and Scandinavia, 1910,
and ultimately some fifty other countries.
First World Jamboree, 1920. First Chief
Scout, the founder, Sir Robert Baden-
Powell (who became Baron Baden-Powell
of Gilwell in 1929), was b. 1857 and d. 1941;
was succeeded by Lord Somers, and on the
death of the latter in 1944 by Lord Rowal-
lan. Sir Charles McLean became Chief
Scout in Sept. 1959. The movement prohibited in Germany, 1933; and from 1940
in other countries successively as occupied by German troops (except for
France). Restarted in W. Europe in
1945, but not in Poland, Czechoslovakia,
or any Balkan country except Greece.

Brabant, Low Countries. Duchy,
1190, passed through the house of Burgundy to Philip II of Spain. At the
division of the Spanish Netherlands, 1579,
N. B. became part of the United Provinces
and was recognized as belonging to them
at the Treaty of Westphalia (q.v.), 1648.
This is the modern Dutch province of
N. B. S. B. remained Spanish till 1714,
when it was transferred to Austria. When
Belgium was annexed by France at
Treaty of Campo Formio, 1797, S. B. was
further divided into what are now the
Belgian provinces of B. (capital Brussels)
and Antwerp (capital Antwerp (q.v.)).

Bradford existed during the reign of
Edward the Confessor. Weekly market
granted, 1251; confirmed, 1294 and 1481.
Besieged in 1642 and again in 1643 by
royalist forces. First weaving mill
opened, 1798. First returned M.P.s
(two) in 1832, when Mechanics' Institute
was opened. Incorporated, 1847; became county borough, 1888; city, 1897.
First Lord Mayor installed, 1907. Became Anglican bishopric, 1919.

Braganza. Family descended from
Alfonso (d. 1461), son of King John I
(1357–1433), who was made Duke of B.,
1442. The family ruled Portugal (q.v.),
1640–1910, and Brazil (q.v.), 1822–89.

Brandenburg. Frederick of Hohenzollern became margrave of, 1415. Neu-
mark acquired, 1455. Kottbus, 1462.
Züllichen, 1482. Zossen, 1490. Rever-
sion of Prussia secured by agreement,
1569. Ravensberg Mark and Wesel acquired, 1614. Prussia acquired, 1618.
E. Pomerania, 1648–79, from Sweden.
Elector of B. takes title of King in
Prussia, 1701. Henceforth known as
Prussia (q.v.), except for a district,
corresponding to the Altmark, which
became in 1949 a province of the E.
German People's Republic.

Electors of B., 1415–1701:

Frederick I	1415–1440
Frederick II the Iron	1440–1470

Albert Achilles	1470–1486
John Cicero	1486–1499
Joachim I	1499–1535
Joachim II	1535–1571
John George	1571–1598
Joachim III Frederick	1598–1608
John Sigismund	1608–1619
George William	1619–1640
Frederick William, 'The Great Elector'	1640–1688
Frederick III	1688–1713

(From 1701, Frederick I, King of Prussia.)

See further under PRUSSIA, KINGS OF.

Branding, partly as punishment, but chiefly as an indelible means of identification of human beings, was abolished for civilians in England and Wales, 1822; in France, 1832. In England all accused released by Benefit of Clergy (*q.v.*) were branded under a law of Henry VII. B. survived in the British Army after 1822. In 1858 the British Mutiny Act ordered deserters to be branded below the left arm-pit; this Act was repealed in 1879.

Brasenose College (Oxford). Founded, 1509.

Brasilia, capital of Brazil (*q.v.*). Inaugurated, 21 Apr. 1960.

Bratislava (Hun. **Pozsony;** Ger. **Pressburg**). Founded *c.* A.D. 1000. Became capital of 'imperial' Hungary after capture of Buda by Turks, 1541 until 1784. The Hungarian kings were crowned in the cathedral of St. Martin, 1526–1916, and the Hungarian Parliament met in the Landhaus down to 1848. Royal palace burnt down, 1811. Slovak University founded, 1919. Incorporated in Czechoslavakia, 1918. Capital of 'independent' Slovakia, 1939–44.

Brawling in church was punishable under statutes of Edward VI, which replaced the pre-Reformation canon laws on the offence. The B. Act of 1860 applies to places of worship of all denominations; hitherto only the Anglican churches had been so protected since the Reformation.

Brazil. Treaty of Tordesilhas, drawing a dividing line between Spanish and Portuguese colonial interests, giving the southern American continent to Portugal, 1494. Pedro Álvares Cabral landed on the coast of B., 22 Apr. 1500, and formally took possession of the country for the crown of Portugal. Spanish and Portuguese seafarers had probably been to this part of the world years before. Coast explored by André Gonzalves, Amerigo Vespucci, Fernâo de Noronha, Crisfovâo Jacques, and Gonçalo Coelho, the last going as far S. as the River Plata,

1501–2. Treaty of Tordesilhas ratified, 1506. Martin Alfonso de Souza arrived at Pernambuco, 30 Jan. 1530. Appointed first governor-general, 1531. Colonization started effectively. Traffic in African slaves begun, 1532. First permanent settlement on São Paulo coast, São Martin Alfonso, founded by de Souza, the governor-general, where he established first sugar plantation and sugar mill, 1533. B. divided into twelve captaincies, 1534. Tomé de Souza appointed second governor-general by D. João III, 1548. Foundation of the city of Bahia, which becomes capital of B., 1549. São Paulo founded, 1554. French try to establish a foothold on the bay of Guanabara, 1555. Mem de Sá, third governor-general, 1558–72. Founded Rio de Janeiro, 1567, after driving the French back from their foothold. B. partitioned, ruled by two governors from Bahia and Rio de Janeiro, 1572–81. Spanish domination during absorption of Portugal by Spain, 1581–1640. Pará founded, 1615. Dutch settlement between Maranhão and Pernambuco, 1624. Dutch try to colonize parts of B., 1630–61. Their settlements governed by Maurice of Nassau, 1637–44. Portuguese rebellion and Dutch naval victory over the Spaniards at Itamarca result in re-establishment of Portuguese rule, 1640. Dutch expelled during Anglo-Dutch wars of the English Commonwealth, 1654. Manáus founded, 1669. Bandeirantes, who explored and colonized during the whole seventeenth century the western part of the interior, especially the state of São Paulo, found gold in Minas Gerais, 1699. Coffee plant brought to B., 1727. Progress of commercial cultivation only about 100 years later. Bandeirantes found diamonds in Minas Gerais, 1730. The colony is raised to the state of viceroyalty. Rio de Janeiro, being the chief port for trade with Europe, became the capital and seat of the viceroy, 1763. Tiradentes, inspired by the French Revolution, chief of a revolutionary movement for freedom and independence of the Brazilian people, condemned to death, 21 Apr. 1792. Napoleon's invasion of Portugal results in D. João VI moving to B., with the Portuguese royal family, 1808. B. declared kingdom, 1815. D. Joao VI, returning to Portugal, leaves the regentship to his son, D. Pedro, 1821. D. Pedro declared independence of B. and crowned as first Emperor of B. on the field of Ipiranga, 7 Sept. 1822. Independence secured by naval campaign of Lord Cochrane, 1823–1825. D. Pedro I gave the empire its first constitution (1824) which, with an additional Act (1834), remained in force till B. became a republic. War between B. and Argentine, 1825. Settled by British mediation, 1826. D. Pedro I was forced to abdicate in favour of his five-year-old son, 7 Apr. 1831. Regency during which the country was involved in many revolutions, 1831–40. D. Pedro II was declared of age, 1840. His first concern was to appease the country and unite it again. Great social and administrative reforms. Science and arts flourished. Gave incentive for European immigration. Slave trade abolished, 1850. War against Argentine and her dictator, Juan Manuel de Rosas, 1851. War against Paraguay and her dictator, Francisco Solano Lopez, 1865–70. Complete abolition of slavery, 1888. Proclamation of republic, 15 Nov. 1889. Abdication of D. Pedro II, who left the country and went to Europe. He died in Paris, 1891. Republic recognized by Great Britain and U.S.A., 1890. Constitution of first republic, 1891. Civil war, 1893–4. Permanent arbitration treaty with Great Britain, 18 June 1909. B. joins Allies in World War I, Oct. 1917. Begins great industrial revolution, especially in São Paulo, 1920. São Paulo revolt, July 1924. Col. Percy H. Fawcett, British explorer, disappeared in Brazilian jungle, 1925. Civil war broke out, 1930. President of the republic, Dr. Washington Luiz, was captured, and the revolt ended soon after. New constitution: Getúlio D. Vargas was elected president and ruled for fifteen years on steadily increasing totalitarian principles, 24 Oct. 1930. New constitution, 16 July 1934. Unsuccessful revolution in NE., 25–27 Nov. 1935. President Vargas seizes absolute power, closes congress, new constitution, 1937. Nazi rebellion quelled in NE., May 1938. Discovery of petrol in state of Bahia, installation of heavy industry in Volta Redonda, 1939. Broke off relations with Axis states, June 1942. Declared war on Germany and Italy, Aug. 1942. Expeditionary force under Gen. Mascarenhas de Moraes landed in Italy, 1944. Advanced with allied armies till May 1945. Military revolution dismissed Getúlio Vargas, 30 Oct. 1945. After a short military triumvirate Gen. Dutra elected, to become president, 2 Dec. 1945. The five years' plan SALTE: Saude (health), Alimentaçao (food), Transporte, and Energia (power), 1945. Constituted assembly met, 5 Feb. New democratic constitution promulgated, 18 Sept. 1946. Anglo-Brazilian Cultural Convention, 16 Apr. 1947. Communist Party declared illegal, May 1947. Getúlio Vargas returned to power, Jan. 1951. Law of the Free Foreign Exchange Market signed, 5 Jan.; put into force, 21 Feb. 1953. Vargas committed suicide, 24 Aug. 1954. Period of unstable government ended by election of Kubitschek as president, 31 Jan. 1956. During his five-year term of office much social reform and industrialization took place, and the new capital of Brasilia was inaugurated, 21 Apr. 1960. Inflation became a pressing problem. Kubitschek's successor, Quadros, though elected by an unprecedented majority, resigned, Aug. 1961, to be succeeded by Goulart, a left-wing politician. As a result of army opposition to him, a constitutional compromise resulted in creation of a prime minister and parliamentary system, to curb the president's powers. Weak government and accelerated inflation followed. B. reverted to full presidential government, Jan. 1963.

Presidents of the Republic:

Marshal Manuel Deodoro da Fonseca	1890–1891
Marshal Floriano Peixoto	1891–1894
Dr. Prudente José de Moraes Barros	1894–1898
Dr. Manuel Ferraz de Campos Salles	1898–1902
Dr. Francisco da Paula Rodrigues Alves	1902–1906
Dr. Alfonso Augusto Moreira Penna	1906–1909
Dr. Nilo Peçanha	1909–1910
Marshal Hermes Rodrigues da Fonseca	1910–1914
Dr. Wenceslau Braz Pereira Gomes	1914–1918
Dr. Francisco da Paula Rodrigues Alves (died before taking over the Government)	1918
Dr. Delfim Moreira da Costa Ribeiro	1918–1919
Dr. Epitácio da Silva Pessoa	1919–1922
Dr. Arturo da Silva Bernardes	1922–1926
Dr. Washington Luiz Pereira de Souza	1926–1930
Junto Governativa—Triunvirato Militar	1930
Dr. Getúlio Dornelles Vargas	1930–1945
Dr. José Linhares	1945–1946
Gen. Eurico Gaspar Dutra	1946–1951
Dr. Getúlio Dornelles Vargas	1951–1954
Carlos Coimbra da Luz	(3 days) 1955
Nereu Ramos,	1955–1956
Juscelino Kubitschek	1956–1961
Dr. Janio Quadros	(6 months) 1961
Dr. João Goulart	1961–

Brazzaville. Founded by the French explorer, Count P. P. F. C. S. de Brazza (1852–1905) in 1886.

Breda, Holland. Captured from Spaniards by Prince Maurice of Nassau, 1590; retaken by Spaniards, 1625; by Dutch, Oct. 1637. Compromise of B., 1566. Charles II's Declaration from B., 1660. Peace of B., 1667. Taken by French, 1794; French expelled, 1813.

Brehon Laws. Ancient laws of Ireland, going back to the third century (reign of Cormac MacArt), and prevailing until the middle of the seventeenth century. Penalties against submitting to, 1366. Lord Eglinton's Commission for translating and publishing the B. L., 1852; first volume published, 1865; whole work completed, 1901.

Bremen, Germany. 1. City. Principal member of Hanseatic League (q.v.), fourteenth century. Free city, 1646. Taken by Denmark, 1712. Sold to Hanover, 1715. Independence recognized by George II, 1730. Taken by French, 1757. Restored, 1758. Annexed by Napoleon, 1810. Independence restored, 1813. Joined German Empire, 1871. German Zollverein, 1888. Became member state of Weimar Republic (q.v.), 1920. Liberties suppressed by Hitler, 1933. Heavily bombed in World War II and fell to the British Second Army, 23–8 Apr. 1945.

2. Archbishopric. Became an ecclesiastical principality early in the thirteenth century. Secularized and acquired by Sweden, 1648. Territory taken by Denmark, 1712, and sold to Hanover, 1715.

3. Verden from 1405 to 1550 was a free city of the empire, on the River Aller some 23 miles SE. of B. At the Peace of Westphalia (1648) it became Swedish; until 1715 it had the same history as B. Purchase confirmed by Treaty of Stockholm, negotiated by George I of England, 1719.

Brenner Pass first traversed by a carriage-way, 1772, and by railway, 1864–7.

Breslau, now **Wroclaw**, Poland, formerly in German Silesia. Bishopric, tenth century, and from 1163 capital of a duchy of Silesia. Destroyed by Mongols in the thirteenth century, but rebuilt by German settlers, and joined Hanseatic League. Acquired by the Hapsburgs, 1526. Jesuit College founded, 1702. Captured by Frederick the Great, Jan. 1741, and became part of Prussian territory. University established, 1801. Extensively bombed in World War II, and besieged by Russians for nine weeks in 1945. Conceded to Poland for occupation by Yalta (q.v.) Conference. German inhabitants driven out, 1945–6.

Brest. Founded, 1240; in English hands, 1342–97. Last attacked from the sea by the English, 1694. The *Scharnhorst, Gneisenau,* and *Prinz Eugen* in the docks attracted R.A.F. bombing, 1941–2. German garrison surrendered, 19 Sept. 1944 after a six-week siege.

Brest-Litovsk (Rus. or Pol. **Brzesc Nad Bugiem**). A fortress town since 1017; became Lithuanian, 1319; Polish, 1569; Russian, 1795; Polish, 1918. Has been Russian since Sept. 1939, except for German military occupation during World War II. At a synod held here, 1594, the Uniate Church of Ruthenia was brought to the Roman obedience. In 1831 the old town was demolished by the Russians and a fortress built on the site. The Russian and German armies made contact here after the Polish campaign of 1939, 18 Sept.

Brest-Litovsk, Treaty. Imposed on Russia by Germany, 3 Mar. 1918.

Brethren, Church of the. See GERMAN BAPTISTS.

Brethren of the Common Lot or Life. The name given to a brotherhood founded in the Low Countries by Gerard Groote of Deventer, c. 1380. Erasmus was at one of their schools in 'S Hertogenbosch c. 1483. They began to decline in the sixteenth century, and died out in the seventeenth.

Brétigny, Peace of, 8 May 1360. See HUNDRED YEARS WAR.

Bretton Woods Agreement. An International Monetary and Financial Conference at B. W., begun 1 July 1944, and signed its Final Act, 22 July. This was ratified first by the U.S. Congress in 1945.

Bribery of voters in the U.K. is punishable under the Corrupt Practices Act, 1854, and the Representation of the People Act, 1867.

Bridewell (London). Saxon palace on site of a Roman fort. Rebuilt by Henry I. King John held council, 1210. Wolsey rebuilt palace, 1522. Edward VI granted manor-house and palace of B. to the city of London as a house of correction for vagrants, 1552. Destroyed in Fire of London, 1666. Women's prison built after 1666. Rebuilt, 1829. Pulled down, 1864.

Bridgewater Canal. Begun, 1755. Opened, 17 July 1761.

Brighton, England, Originally Brighthelmstone. Pavilion begun, 1784, by Prince of Wales (later George IV) and finished, 1827. Parliamentary borough, 1832; municipal borough, 1854. W. Pier built, 1866. Palace Pier, 1900. University of Sussex opened at, Oct. 1961.

Brindisi, Italy. Ancient Greek colony founded fifth century B.C. Taken from the Sallentini by the Romans, 267 B.C.

Cathedral founded, 1089. Base of Italian fleet in 1866 and of the Otranto Barrage in World War I. Seat of Badoglio's pro-Allied government, Sept. 1943.

Brisbane, Australia. First occupied as penal settlement by Sir Thomas B., 1824. Became capital of Queensland, 1859. University opened, 1911. Chief magistrate became Lord Mayor, 1930.

Bristol, England. Importance as a town began *c.* 1000. Came by marriage into possession of Earl of Gloucester, 1119. Cathedral founded, 1148. First charter, 1171. Recognized as a staple town, 1353. Church of St. Mary Redcliffe built *c.* end of the fourteenth century. Brothers Cabot sailed for N. America from, 1497. Slave trade *fl.*, 1580–1640. Taken by Prince Rupert, 1643; by Fairfax, 1645. Attempt to fire shipping in harbour. 1777. Modern harbour constructed, 1809. Half city burnt in rioting, 1831. University College founded, 1876. University established, 1909; greatly extended, 1926. Heavily bombed during World War II, 1940–3.

Britain. Invaded by Julius Caesar, 55 and 54 B.C., Cunobelin, King of the Catuvellauni *c.* A.D. 5. Invaded and conquered by Romans under Aulus Plautius, A.D. 43–7. Caractacus defeated by Ostorius and deported to Rome, 50. Romans massacred by Boudicca, 60. Boudicca defeated, 61. Christianity said to have been taught, 64. Agricola reforms government and defeats the Picts, 78–85. Hadrian's Wall begun *c.* 122. Antonine's Wall built by Lollius Urbicus, 142, on site of Agricola's field fortifications. Hadrian's Wall strengthened by Severus, 208. Constantine proclaimed emperor at York, 25 July 306. Saxon raids on coastal areas, from beginning of third century onwards. British bishops attend Council of Arles, 314. War with Picts and Scots, 360; invasion of southern B., 367. Driven out, 368. Romans finally quit B. some time shortly before 429, and abandon responsibility for the defence, 446. Anglo-Saxon invasions begin on a large scale *c.* 449. *See* ENGLAND.

Britain, Battle of. Name for the air attack on B. by day, 8 Aug.–29 Oct. 1940, intended to be the first stage of a series of operations culminating in Operation Sealion (*q.v.*), which would have been the seaborne invasion of SE. England. In the phase 8–18 Aug. the Luftwaffe attacked shipping, ports, and later fighter airfields between Harwich and the Isle of Wight. Aug. 13—'Eagle Day' in the German planning time-table—was the date by which it was hoped that all R.A.F.

fighter stations would be out of action. In the second phase up to 5 Sept. similar objectives farther W. and N. along the coast and farther inland to the NW. were attacked by formations relatively stronger in fighters and weaker in bombers. A mass daylight attack on London (7 Sept.) by 350 bombers began the third phase: until 5 Oct. there were thirty-seven more day attacks on London, besides diversionary attacks on other south-eastern targets, the aircraft flying at higher and higher altitudes. The last phase consisted of night attacks on London by fighters and fighter-bombers and lasted until the end of Oct.

'Britannia.' Naval training ship for officer cadets, 1859–1903. The Royal Naval College, Dartmouth, became officially H.M.S. *B.* in 1921. Royal yacht *B.* (4,000 tons) built to replace the *Victoria and Albert,* and completed in Jan. 1954. Has been used by the royal family on several overseas tours: completed a world cruise early in 1957 and was used by H.R.H. Princess Margaret on her honeymoon, 1960.

British Academy. Incorporated 18 Aug. 1902, after foundation in 1901.

British Association for the Advancement of Science. Established, 1831. Kew Observatory presented to, by Queen Victoria, 1842.

British Broadcasting Corporation (B.B.C.). Succeeded B. B. Co., which was formed, 1922, and established, on national footing, 1923; Chelmsford long-wave station opened, 1924. B. B. Co.'s charter expired, 31 Dec. 1926. Daventry stations opened, 1925 and 1927; Chelmsford (short wave), 1927. Chartered Corporation. 1927. Droitwich took over long-wave from Daventry, 1934. Television from Alexandra Palace, 1936. Foreign broadcasts commenced, 1937. Television service reopened, June 1946. By 1958 sound programmes transmitted by over forty medium- and long-wave stations and twelve V.H.F. stations; television over eighteen transmitters.

British Columbia, W. Canada. Discovered by Perez, 1774; visited by Cook, 1778. Made a British colony, Aug. 1858. Vancouver Island incorporated with, 1866. Annexed to Canada, 1871.

British Council. Established, Nov. 1934, and inaugural meeting held, 2 July 1935; Charter granted, 1940.

British Electricity Authority came into existence in 1948, and took over the functions, the plant, and other assets of private and municipal electrical undertakings, as well as those of the Central Electricity Board (set up, 1927). The Electricity Reorganization Act of 1954 changed the title of the B.E.A. to the Central Electricity Authority.

British Guiana first partially settled by Dutch W. India Co. *c.* 1630. Captured by British, 1796, and ceded to Britain, 1814. Constitution of 1928 amended in 1949 and 1953 to provide for greater self-government, but suspended after six months, in Oct. 1953, to prevent Communist subversion of the government. A nominated legislative council took office, 1954. A new constitution approved, 1956, and elections held under it, 1957, resulted in the return to power of the left-wing Dr. Cheddi Jagan, who became Prime Minister. New constitution came into effect, Aug. 1961, giving B. G. full internal self-government. Riots, looting, and severe damage in Georgetown in protest against Jagan's drastic budget proposals, 16 Feb. 1962. British troops called in to restore order. Oct. 1962: constitutional conference on proposed self-government for B. G. opened in London, but broke down owing to disagreements among the B. G. delegates. A General Strike against the government began in B. G. in Apr. 1963. By July it had resulted in chaos and racial hatred and British troops were called in. Strike settled by a T.U.C. mediator, July. Colonial secretary visited B. G. later that month, but situation remained dangerous.

British Honduras or **Belize.** Probably discovered by Columbus, 1502. It was first settled by woodcutters from Jamaica *c.* 1638 and British rights acknowledged by treaty with Spain of 1670, which Spaniards subsequently denounced and made frequent efforts to expel the colony, notably in 1717, 1754, and 1779. The last attempt, which was signally defeated on 10 Sept. 1789, at St. George's Bay, followed the Treaty of London, 1786, by which Britain had specifically yielded the Mosquito Coast in exchange for final recognition by Spain. The colony was self-governing until a superintendent was appointed, 1786. In its final form the self-governing constitution was based on a charter granted 1765. The first lieutenant-governor, taking orders from the governor of Jamaica, was appointed in 1862 and has been assisted by a Legislative Council since 1870. A governor was appointed in 1884 when dependence on Jamaica ended. In Feb. 1948 a dispute arose with Guatemala which inherited Spanish territorial claims on the colony, abortive attempts to settle which had been made in 1857-9 and 1929. A new constitution was promulgated in 1960, and at the elections held on 1 Mar. 1961 the People's United Party, led by George Price, obtained a clear majority. A

hurricane caused extensive damage, and over 300 deaths, 31 Oct. 1961. New constitution, giving B. H. greater self-government, agreed in London, July 1963.

British Industries Fair first held, 1915. Moved to Olympia, 1930, and the Birmingham section for heavy industries begun, 1920. In 1945 organization of the London section of the B.I.F. taken over by the Board of Trade; responsibility transferred to a private company in 1954. After the 1956 fair the London section closed. Birmingham section continued, organized by the Birmingham Chamber of Commerce, and now much wider in its range of goods.

British Legion. Originally the name of numerous now forgotten military organizations in the service of foreign powers or revolutionary movements (e.g. in the Spanish American wars of Liberation *c.* 1810-25), but now usually referring to the combined ex-service organization which was formed 1 July 1921. Royal charter, Apr. 1925.

British Medical Association. Founded, 1832; took its present name in 1856.

British Museum. Grant made by Parliament, 5 Apr. 1753. Old Royal Library presented to, 1757. Building opened, 16 Jan. 1759. New buildings erected, 1823-1847. Elgin Marbles acquired, 1816; Grenville Library, 1847. Reading-room opened, 18 May 1857. Natural history collection removed to S. Kensington, 1881. Foundation-stone of extension laid by Edward VII, 27 June 1907; the extension opened, 1914. Bill published, proposing fundamental changes in the B.M.'s constitution, 31 Oct. 1962. *See also* LIBRARIES and COTTONIAN LIBRARY.

British Standards Institution. Founded as the Engineering Standards Committee, 1901; royal charter, 1929.

British Union of Fascists. Founded by Sir Oswald Ernald Mosley, 1932. It disintegrated at the outbreak of World War II, and after the war Mosley refounded it as the Union Movement (1948).

Brittany. Conquered by Julius Caesar, 57-56 B.C. and called **Armorica** by the Romans. Large influx of Celts from Britain to B. in the fifth and sixth centuries. Independent duchy *c.* 1000. Under Norman suzerainty, 1066. Bestowed as a duchy by Henry II on his brother Geoffrey, 1159. Succession disputed, 1161, 1171, 1186, 1343. By marriage of Charles VIII of France and Anne of Brittany, 1491, united under crown of France. Finally and irrevocably incorporated into France, 1532. Scene of heavy fighting during the allied invasion of Europe, 1944.

Brixham, Devon, scene of William of Orange's landing, 1688.

Broad Bottom Administration. Formed out of a coalition, 24 Nov. 1744. Dissolved by death of the Premier Henry Pelham 6 Mar. 1754.

Broadmoor Institution. State institution for the criminally insane, in Berkshire. Opened, 1863.

Bromberg (Ger.) or **Bydgoszcz** (Pol.). Polish till 1772. Prussian, 1772–1919. Polish, 1919–39. German, 1939–45. Polish since 1945.

Brooklyn, New York. Settled (as Breuckelen) by Dutch, 1636. Incorporated as a city, 1834. Bridge to New York City opened, 24 May 1883. Borough of New York since 1893.

Bruges (Fr.) or **Brugge** (Flem.), Belgium. Capital of Flanders till 1180. Town hall begun, 1376. Belfry, end of thirteenth century. Order of the Golden Fleece instituted here, 1430. Ceased to be an important port after final silting up of the River Zwyn, 1490. Market hall built, 1561–6. Docks and canal built, 1885–95. Greatly extended, 1930–9.

Brumaire, Coup d'État of. On 18 B. of the year VIII (9 Nov. 1799) Napoleon abolished the Directory. *See* FRENCH REVOLUTION, THE GREAT.

Brunei, N.W. Borneo. Treaty between Britain and Sultan of B., 1847. British protectorate, 1888. Administered by a British Resident, 1906–59. Under constitution of 1959 administration entrusted to a Chief Minister, appointed by the Sultan, an Executive Council, and a Legislative Council. Revolt by nationalists against B.'s proposed inclusion in Malaysia, Dec. 1962, was quelled with the aid of British troops. Under agreement signed in London, July 1963, B. did not in fact become a part of Malaysia.

Brunswick (Ger. **Braunschweig**), a fragment of the old tribal duchy of Saxony, which in the tenth century was the fief of one Bruno from whom the name derives. When in 1181 Saxony was dismembered Duke Henry the Lion was allowed to keep that part which he had personally inherited; in 1267 the territory was divided into separate duchies of B.-Lüneburg and B.-Wolfenbüttel under two branches of the house of Guelf. Alternate reunification and repartition took place down to 1735, the most significant partition being that of 1569, which led to the rise of the ducal house of Lüneburg-Celle, from which the electoral house of Hanover (*q.v.*) derived. Dynastically linked to the electorate of Hanover and thus to the crown of England, Brunswick produced two dukes of great military ability, Karl Wilhelm Ferdinand (*b.* 1735, duke from

1780, *d.* of wounds, 1806) and his son, Friedrich Wilhelm (*b.* 1771, killed in action at Quatre Bras, 1815), who in turn served in and often commanded the forces of practically every anti-French coalition, whether under British or Prussian political direction, from the beginning of the Seven Years War (1757) to the Hundred Days of 1815. The duchy was merged in the kingdom of Westphalia, 1806–14. The last descendant of Friedrich Wilhelm, *d.* 1884, and the next heir was the ex-king George V of Hanover's son, whose accession was prevented by the Prussians, who had seized his patrimony in 1866. Two Prussian nominees reigned as dukes until in 1913 Prince Ernest Augustus of Cumberland renounced the throne of Hanover and was recognized as duke on condition of marrying a Hohenzollern princess. He *d.* in Jan. 1953. The ducal house abdicated, 1918, and the territory constituted a free state under the Weimar Republic (1919–33). The Third Reich (1933–45) reduced B. to the status of a mere administrative province, and since 1945 it has formed part of the Lower Saxon *Land.*

Brussels, Belgium. Mentioned in eighth century as *Bruchsella.* Church of Sainte-Gudule completed, 1273. Capital of Low Countries, 1507. Alva's rule, 1567. Union of B., 1578. Bombarded by Villeroi, Aug. 1695. Taken by French, 1701; by Duke of Marlborough, 1706; by Saxe, 1746; by Dumouriez, 1802. Capital of Belgium, 1831. University founded, 1834. Germans occupied city from Aug. 1914 to Nov. 1918. Again occupied by Germans, 17 May 1940. Liberated, 3 Sept. 1944. Serious rioting in B. during the crisis over the monarchy, 1950.

Brussels, Treaty of, signed 17 Mar. 1948, an instrument of the Western Union (*q.v.*) policy. Signatories were Great Britain, France, Belgium, Holland, Luxembourg. Federal Germany and Italy acceded to the Treaty, 1954.

Bubastis (Arab. **Tel Basta**), city of Lower Egypt, famous for its temple of Pasht or Basht, the cat (originally lioness) goddess, the ruins of which were excavated in 1887, the city having been in ruins since shortly after its capture by the Persians, 352 B.C.

Buccaneers. Sixteenth-century associations of piratical adventurers, chiefly French and English. In 1630 they captured Tortuga and used it as a stronghold. In 1655 they helped the Commonwealth Navy to capture Jamaica. In 1685 they defied the Spanish fleet in the bay of Panama. Their last great achievement was the capture of Cartagena, 1697.

Buchan's Predictions. Meteorological

forecasts by Alexander Buchan (1829–1907), made in 1869. Two of his 'cold periods' were 11–14 Apr. and mid May; but records kept during the present century have not supported his hypotheses.

Bucharest (Bucuresti), Rumania. Became capital, 1859. Held by Germans, Dec. 1916–Nov. 1918. Treaty between Rumania and Central Powers, 7 May 1918, nullified, 11 Nov. 1918. Entered by the Russians, 31 Aug. 1944.

Buchenwald, near Weimar. Site of a notorious German concentration camp, opened in 1934. Liberated by the Americans, 11 Apr. 1945.

Buckingham Palace. Built, 1703. Property of Queen Charlotte, 1761. New building occupied by Queen Victoria, 13 July 1837, after extensive alterations, started in 1825, had been completed. New façade, 1913. Art gallery opened to the public, 25 July 1962.

Budapest, Hungary. Buda, capital of Hungary, 1320–1526. Captured by Turks, 1541. Recovered, 1686. Palaces built, 1770. University, 1784. Buda and Pest united as one city, 1872. Occupied by Rumanians, Aug.–Nov. 1919. Prolonged fighting between Russian and German troops in 1944–5; finally captured by the Russians, 13 Feb. 1945. The city was largely rebuilt after World War II, but again suffered heavy damage during the abortive revolt of Oct.–Nov. 1956.

Buddhism. Religious system of Gautama, *b. c.* 560 B.C. He *d. c.* 480 B.C.

Budget Leakages. 1. 1936. Two M.P.s resigned as a result of the inquiry into improper disclosures of B. 2. Nov. 1947. Hugh Dalton resigned as Chancellor of Exchequer after indiscretions before B. speech.

Buenos Aires. Federal capital of the Argentine Republic. City founded, 1535; refounded, 1580. Taken by British, 27 June 1806; retaken by Spaniards, 12 Aug; British attack repulsed 5 July 1807. University founded, 1821. Constitution of province voted, 23 May 1853; independent state, Oct. 1853; reunited to Argentine, Nov. 1859. Jesuits' college burnt by mob, 28 Feb. 1875.

Buffalo, New York. Founded, 1803 as New Amsterdam; got its present name, 1810. Burnt by British, 1813. Incorporated, 1832. President McKinley assassinated at, 5 Sept. 1901. International Peace Bridge, connecting B. with Fort Erie, Canada, opened, 7 Aug. 1927.

Buganda, province of Uganda (*q.v.*). British officials became the *Kabaka's* accepted advisers, 1890. Monarchy in B. preserved and encouraged when Uganda became a British protectorate

(1893). *Kabaka* exiled by British Government on grounds of failing to carry out the 1900 co-operation agreement, 1953. Conference at Namirembe, 1954, results of which approved by British Government and the B. *lukiko,* and *Kabaka* allowed to return, 1955.

Building Societies. List of major English, Welsh, and Scottish Societies, with their dates of incorporation:

England

Barnsley Permanent	1853
Bath: Liberal	1870
Bedford Permanent	1879
Bedfordshire	1924
Bideford	1862
Bingley	1851
Birmingham Citizens Permanent	1889
Birmingham Incorporated	1847
Bournemouth and Christchurch	1934
Bournemouth: Wessex Permanent	1949
Bradford Equitable	1851
Bradford Permanent	1885
Bradford: Provincial	1849
Bridgwater	1921
Brighton: Alliance	1863
Brighton: Citizens Permanent	1905
Bristol Permanent Economic	1853
Bristol and W.	1850
Burnley	1850
Burnley: Borough	1874
Cambridge	1850
Carlisle: Cumberland Co-operative Benefit	1850
Chalfont and District Permanent	1907
Chatham and District Reliance Permanent	1898
Cheltenham and Gloucester	1850
Cheshunt Permanent Benefit	1861
Chislehurst: Lion, 1937	1937
Colchester Equitable	1869
Colchester Permanent	1856
Colne	1866
Coventry Mutual Permanent	1892
Coventry Permanent Economic	1884
Coventry Provident Permanent	1872
Croydon: Vigilant	1864
Darlington	1946
Derbyshire	1859
Dewsbury and W. Riding	1866
Dudley and District Benefit	1858
Eastbourne Mutuality	1877
Earl Shilton	1857
Enfield	1880
Furness and S. Cumberland	1865
Grays	1880
Halifax	1853
Hanley Economic	1854
Harrow	1882
Hastings and E. Sussex	1851
Haywards Heath and District Permanent Benefit	1890
Hemel Hempstead, 1884	1884

Hinckley and Country 1853
Hinckley and Leicestershire Permanent Benefit 1870
Hinckley Permanent 1866
Hove: Sussex Mutual 1872
Huddersfield 1864
Ipswich and District 1876
Ipswich and Suffolk Permanent Benefit 1849
Ipswich: Eastern Counties 1855
Keighley and Craven 1851
Kingston 1865
Leeds and Holbeck 1875
Leeds Permanent 1848
Leek and Moorlands 1856
Leek United and Midlands 1863
Leicester Permanent 1853
Leicester Temperance and General Permanent 1875
Lewes 1870
Liverpool and Provincial 1854
Liverpool Investment 1877
Liverpool: King Edward 1917

London:

Abbey National 1849
Argyle Benefit 1870
Camberwell and S. London 1875
Chelsea 1878
Church of England 1882
City and Metropolitan 1946
City of London 1862
City Prudential 1908
Civil Service 1931
Co-operative Permanent 1884
Equity Permanent 1879
Finchley 1902
Fourth City 1862
Fourth P.O. 1896
Goldhawk Mutuality Benefit 1876
Greenwich Industrial 1852
Guardian 1871
Hastings and Thanet 1849
Hearts of Oak Permanent 1875
Hendon 1926
Holloway and City Terminus 1957
Lambeth 1852
London and Essex 1883
Magnet 1868
Mornington Park 1866
Nalgo 1932
New Cross Equitable 1866
N.W. 1883
Peckham Mutual 1880
People's 1847
Planet 1848
Portman 1881
Property Owners' 1941
Royal Mutuality Benefit 1865
St. Pancras 1937
Shern Hall (Methodist) 1922
South London 1875
South Western 1876
Temperance Permanent 1854
Vigilant 1864

Walthamstow 1877
Westbourne Park 1885
W. London Investment 1879
Woolwich Equitable 1847

Loughborough Permanent 1867
Luton 1866
Macclesfield 1870
Maidenhead 1859
Manchester: Mancunian 1956
Mansfield 1870
Market Harborough 1870
Melton Mowbray 1875
Middleton 1872
Nelson: Marsden 1860
Newbury 1856
Newcastle upon Tyne Globe Permanent 1876
Newcastle upon Tyne: Grainger and Percy 1957
Newcastle upon Tyne: Northern Counties Permanent 1850
Newcastle upon Tyne Permanent 1861
Newcastle upon Tyne: Rock 1865
Newcastle upon Tyne: Universal Permanent 1863
Newport: Monmouthshire and S. Wales 1869
Northampton and Midlands 1888
Northampton Town and County 1848
N. Shields: Mercantile 1895
N. Shields: Permanent 1875
N. Shields: Tynemouth 1855
N. Shields: Tynemouth Victoria Jubilee Permanent 1887
Northwich 1848
Norwich 1852
Nottingham 1850
Old Hill: Rowley Regis and District Benefit 1888
Otley 1848
Padiham 1877
Peterborough Provincial Benefit 1860
Portsmouth, City of 1896
Portsmouth: Hampshire 1866
Ramsbury 1846
Redditch Benefit 1859
Redhill: East Surrey 1903
Reigate: Holmesdale Benefit 1855
Rugby 1866
Saffron Walden Benefit 1849
Scarborough 1846
Skipton 1853
S. Shields Commercial Permanent 1875
S. Shields: Corporation 1866
S. Shields: Eligible and United 1874
S. Shields Nelson Permanent 1877
Stafford Permanent 1867
Stafford Railway 1877
Steyning and Littlehampton 1878
Stockport: Vernon 1924
Stoke on Trent Permanent 1852
Stourbridge: Brierley Hill and Stourbridge Incorporated 1849
Stroud 1850

Bukovina, originally part of Moldavia (*q.v.*), inhabited principally by Slavs of the Ruthenian (Ukrainian) linguistic division, was under Turkish sovereignty ;from 1512 until its occupation by the Russians in 1769, but was taken from them by the Austrians, 1774, to whom it was ceded by Turkey, 1775, becoming part of Galicia until 1849, when it was separated and made a crown land of the Hungarian kingdom. Granted autonomy, 1861. On the collapse of the Hapsburg Empire the Imperial Governor handed over power to a local Ruthenian committee (23 Oct. 1918), but the Vlach element appealed to the Rumanian Government, 27 Oct., whose troops entered and occupied the province, 11 Nov. Sèvres treaty of 1920 recognized all B. as Rumanian territory. Northern B., together with Bessarabia, was ceded to the U.S.S.R. to comply with an ultimatum of 27 June 1940, but was again Rumanian from 1941 to 1944. It was finally ceded to Russia under the peace treaty of 1947 and forms part of the Ukrainian S.S.R.

Bulgaria. For early history *see* BULGARS. Treaty of Berlin set up the principality of B. and the autonomous province of Eastern Rumelia, 13 July 1878. Prince Alexander of Battenberg elected ruler, 1879; after his abdication,

Prince Ferdinand of Saxe-Coburg elected, 7 July 1887. Independence proclaimed, 22 Sept. 1908, and the prince took title of Tsar. Recognition by Turkey and European powers, Apr. 1909. *See* BALKAN WARS and WORLD WAR I. B. entered World War I on German side, Oct. 1915, and surrendered to the Allies unconditionally, Oct. 1918. Tsar abdicated, 3 Oct. 1918, in favour of his son, Boris III. By Treaty of Neuilly, 1919, B. ceded territory to Greece, Rumania, and Yugoslavia. Military *coup d'état,* 1934; from 1935 Boris ruled as virtual dictator. B. gained release from punitive clauses of Neuilly treaty, 1938. Treaty of Craiova, 8 Sept. 1940, ceded S. Dobrudja to B., thus restoring the frontier of 1912. German troops entered B., Mar. 1941. B. invaded Yugoslavia and Greece, Apr. 1941, and occupied Thrace and Macedonia until 26 Aug. 1944, when B. sued for peace with the Western Allies. Tsar Boris II *d.* 28 Aug. 1943. War with Russia lasted 5–8 Sept. 1944, leading to a change of government, 9 Sept., whose first task was to conclude an armistice with Russia which was signed, 28 Oct., by all the Allies. The Bulgarian Army began hostilities against the Axis, and in the final stages of the war marched into Styria and occupied Klagenfurt after the German surrender. (*See* WORLD WAR II.) Plebiscite, held 8 Sept. 1946, was in favour of a republic, which was duly declared, 15 Sept., and its constitution brought into effect, 4 Dec. 1947. General election, 27 Oct. 1946, returned Fatherland Front Government to power.

The peace treaty with the Allies was signed at Paris, 10 Feb. 1947, and a separate treaty with Yugoslavia, 27 Nov. The agrarian opposition was dissolved, 26 Aug., and its leader, Nikola Petkov, sentenced to death and hanged, 23 Sept. 1947. Banks nationalized, 27 Dec. 1947, and finally merged with the National Bank, 9 Mar. 1951. Fatherland Front turned into one mass movement, entirely Communist controlled, Feb. 1948. Twenty-year Treaty of Friendship with Russia signed, Mar. 1948. Under Church Law of 24 Feb. 1949 fifteen Protestant pastors were prosecuted and imprisoned for espionage and treason. The British Government, 2 Apr. 1949, complained that the treaty of 1947 was being violated and protested again, 19 Sept. The International Court of Justice, at the request of United Nations, gave its opinion (against B.), 18 July 1950. Traicho Kostov, deputy Prime Minister, was tried on a charge of Titoism, condemned, and executed, Dec. 1949.

Bulgarian Patriarchate revived, 1953, and first Patriarch since 1393 elected. Georgi Damianov was elected President of the Presidium, 27 May 1950. Deportation of 250,000 Turks began, summer 1950. Collectivization of farming land accelerated, June–Sept. 1951, and virtually complete by 1958. New labour code came into force, 13 Nov. 1951, and new criminal code, Feb. 1952, both based on Russian practice. Trial of several persons accused of spying for U.S.A. opened, 19 Jan. 1953. Student unrest in Sofia at time of Hungarian rebellion, 1956, admitted by the government. Anti-revisionist purge, Jan.–Feb. 1958. Khruschev, Gomulka, and Kadar all visited B., 1958. Damianov d. 1958, and was succeeded by Ganev.

Chervenkov, who had been forced to resign the premiership in 1956, was finally disgraced in Nov. 1961, and the economic difficulties of 1962 were blamed on his 'gross sectarian doctrines and errors.' In Nov. 1962 Yugov, the then premier, was dismissed for alleged 'Stalinism.'

The following is a list of rulers of modern B.:

Rulers of B., 1879–1946 :

Alexander (Prince)	1879–1886
Ferdinand (King 1908)	1887–1918
Boris III	1918–1943
Simeon II	1943–1946

President of the Bulgarian People's Republic:

Neichev	1947–1950

President of Presidium:

Damianov	1950–1958
Dimiter Ganev	1958–

Bulgars, originally a Ural-Altaic people from Central Asia of pastoral and predatory habit, occupied the space between the Urals and the Volga in the fourth century A.D. After splitting (433) into two main groups, one of them formed a strong state on the northern shore of the Black Sea which was destroyed about 560 by the Avars. The other branch, after a period of subjection, first to the Avars and then to the Turks, recovered its independence, 582, and founded a state on the Volga known as Great Bulgaria (Volgaria), which persisted into the thirteenth century despite Russian attempts at conquest (e.g. c. 1020 Yaroslav of Kiev offered the crown of the country to the dispossessed Norwegian king St. Olav in return for his help in conquering it). A faction split off from this state, under pressure from the Khazars, migrated westwards, and crossed the Danube, 679, into Moesia, where they easily conquered

the local population compounded of Illyrians and more recent Slavonic immigrants, who had first appeared in the third century. The Slavonic immigration into Moesia, which became the country now known as Bulgaria, was still in progress, and the Slavonic language was adopted by the B., who soon lost all memory of their original non-Aryan tongue. They threatened to take Constantinople unless the province was formally ceded to them, which the Emperor Constantine IV Pogonatus (668–85) hastened to do. All territory N. of the Danube was lost c. 900, but this was compensated by continual expansion into the Balkans and a southward shifting of gravity at the expense of the Roman Empire; in 811 the Bulgar Khan Krum defeated and slew the Emperor Nicephorus. The Khan Boris (857–88) adopted Orthodox Christianity in 870, and forced his variously Moslem, pagan, and (very few) Catholic subjects to conform. After a period of maximum expansion and power under Simeon (893–927) the Tsar Samuel was defeated by the Emperor Basil II Bulgaroktonos—'the slayer of B.'—in 1014. The whole Bulgar territory was subject to the empire from 1018 until 1186, when the northern part became independent under the Asen dynasty, who in the reign of Ivan II (c. 1230) ruled the whole Balkan peninsula as far W. as Albania and Epirus. The dynasty died out, 1280, and the B., weakened by internal dissension and Mongol invasions, were defeated and subjected to Serbian rule, 28 July 1330, at the battle of Kustendil; this lasted until 1356, but only forty years of Bulgar independence remained before conquest by the Turks and the end of the first Bulgarian kingdom in 1396. The B. remained under Turkish rule until 1878; the 'Bulgarian atrocities' of 1876 led to Russia declaring war on Turkey (1877), and this paved the way for Bulgarian independence. *See further under* BULGARIA.

The following is a list of medieval Bulgar rulers:

Khans:

Krum	c. 802–814
Omurtag	814–c. 830
Malomir (Presiam)	c. 830–852

Princes.

Boris I (Saint)	852–888
Vladimir	888–893

Tsars:

Simeon I, the Great	893–927
Peter	927–969
Boris II	970–971
Samuel	c. 971–1014
Gabriel Roman	1014–1015
Ivan Vladislav	1015–1018

Bulgaria subject to Byzantium 1018–1186
Ivan Asen I 1185–1194
Peter Asen 1185–1195
Kalojan Asen 1195–1207
Boril 1207–1218
Ivan Asen II 1218–1241
Kaliman I 1241–1246
Michael Asen 1246–1254
Kaliman II 1254–1257
Constantine Asen 1257–1278
Ivail 1278–1279
Ivan Asen III 1279–1280
George Terteri I 1280–1282
Smilec 1282
Choki 1282
Theodore Svetslav 1282–1322
George Terteri II 1322
Michael 1322–1330
Ivan Istvan 1330
Ivan Alexander 1330–1365
Ivan Sracimir 1365
Ivan Sisman 1365–1395

Bull-baiting made illegal in Britain, 1835.

Bullfighting. Prohibited in France, 1894; but prohibition openly ignored since 1932.

Bull Moose. Name of a third party formed in 1912 by the supporters of Theodore Roosevelt, in the U.S.A. It ceased to exist, 1916, when Roosevelt declined to stand for it again.

Bundesrat, Federal Council:
1. The supreme executive of the Swiss confederation, seven men elected for four years by the Bundesversammlung (*q.v.*). The vice-president of this body is a first magistrate co-equal with the President of the Confederation, according to the constitution of 1874, modifying that of 1848.
2. Body corresponding to the Privy Council or Cabinet of the N. German League, 1866–71, and of the Hohenzollern 'Second Reich,' 1871–1918; it also partook of the nature of an upper house in a bicameral constitution, as it could veto laws.
3. In Austria, a second chamber of provincial representatives, under the federal constitution of 1929 readopted, 1945.
4. Upper house, W. German Republic, 1949.

Bundestag, German for Federal Diet, was the name (1) of an assembly of representatives of the German League (*Deutscher Bund*), 1815–66 (not a legislative body, more like a Council of Ambassadors); (2) or lower house of the W. German Federal Republic Parliament from 1949.

Bundesversammlung. German for Federal Assembly, name given to the two legislative houses of the Swiss Confederation, the *Ständerat* and the *National-*

rat, when sitting jointly, under the constitution of 1874.

Bunhill Fields (London). Used by Dissenters. Burying ground first used, 1665; John Bunyan buried, 1688; Defoe, 1731; Susannah Wesley, 1742; Isaac Watts, 1748; William Blake, 1827. Opened as a public garden, 1869.

Buonaparte, House of. Following are the principal members of this family: 1. *Joseph, b.* 1768. King of Naples, 1806–8. King of Spain, 1808–13; *d.* Florence, 1844. 2. *Napoléon I, b.* 1769. First Consul of France, 1800. Consul for life, 1802. Emperor of the French, 18 May 1804. Abdicated, Apr. 1814. At Elba, May 1814–Feb. 1815. Landed at Antibes, Feb. 1815. Abdicated again, June 1815; *d.* St. Helena, 5 May 1821. 3. *Lucien, b.* 1775. President of the Council of Five Hundred, 1799. Prince of Canino; *d.* 1840. 4. *Louis, b.* 1778. King of Holland, 1806–10. Father of Napoléon III below; *d.* 1846. 5. *Jerome, b.* 1784. King of Westphalia, 1806–13. Marshal and President of the French Senate under Napoléon III; *d.* 1860. 6. *Napoléon III, b.* 1808. President of French Republic, Dec. 1848. Emperor, 1852. Abdicated, 2 Sept. 1870; *d.* 9 Jan. 1873, at Chislehurst, England. 7. *Eugène Napoléon, b.* 1856. Prince Imperial. Killed at battle of Ulundi, 1879.

Burgos, Spain. Burial place of the Cid, *d.* 1099. Cathedral begun, 1221. Attacked by the Duke of Wellington, 18–19 Sept. 1812; another attempt failed, 18 Oct.; French blew up castle and retired, 12 June 1813. Headquarters of Franco's insurgents, 1936–9.

Burgundy, France. Burgundians, Germanic tribe arrived in SE. Gaul *c.* 411. Region around Worms-Mainz became known as B., but the centre of gravity of Burgundian kingdom shifted to Rhône valley, 475. Conquered by Franks, 534. After death of Charlemagne (*q.v.*) partitioned between France and Lotharingia by Treaty of Verdun, 843. There then arose (1) a *kingdom* of B. (888–1032), dependent on Lotharingia, later in the empire; (2) a *county* of B. (Franche-Comté), which first merged with the duchy *c.* 1470, but in 1483 passed to the empire, and ultimately, with the southern Netherlands, to the crown of Spain; (3) a *duchy* of B., independent *c.* 888–1363, then a fief of France, under duke of the French royal house. On the death of Duke Charles the Bold, 1479, B. became an ordinary province of France.

Burial Acts in the U.K. still wholly or partly in force are those of 1852, 1855, 1879, 1880, 1906, and the Cremation Act, 1902.

Burke's Peerage. Started 1826 by John Burke (1787–1848) and continued by his son, Sir John Bernard Burke (1814–92).

Burlingame Treaty, between U.S.A. and China. Negotiated Washington, 1868; confirmed Peking, 23 Nov. 1869. Authorized mutual immigration, 'The inalienable right of man to change his habitation'; Anson B. (1820–70) was the American representative in China.

Burlington House (London). Built for 1st Earl of Burlington, 1665–8; reconstructed by 3rd Earl, 1716; bought by Government, July 1854. Royal, Linnean, and Chemical Societies' quarters at, 1857. Exhibition rooms date from 1866, 3rd Earl's colonnade removed same year. Royal Academy acquired lease of building and garden behind it, 1867. Royal Academy first opened at, 3 May 1869. New building erected, 1869–72.

Burma. Divided in earliest times into a number of principalities of fluctuating size, among which the two dynasties established at Tagaung play a leading part. According to legend these were succeeded by establishment of a kingdom at Tharakhetara, 483 B.C.–A.D. 84. A new dynasty was established at Pagân, 95. B. Calendar era established by Thenga Raja, 639. Most of B. united under King Anoarahta Soa, who established Buddhism permanently (1044?–1077?). Conquest of Arakan by Alaungsithu, 1103. Pagân captured by Mongols, 1287. Collapse of the Pagân monarchy, 1298. B. divided between two Shan monarchies at Panya and at Sagaing, 1298–1364. Ava founded, 1364. B. in state of civil war under Shan monarchy at Ava until rise of the Burmese Taungu dynasty, 1530–1752. Arrival of Portuguese at Martaban, 1519. B. united under Bureng Naung, 1551–81. Again divided into Pegu and B., 1581–99. Taungu dynasty unites B., 1599. Portuguese expelled from Martaban, 1613. Capital moved to Ava, 1629. Chinese freebooting invasion, 1658–61. Chinese refugee emperor surrendered to a Manchu Army, 1662. Taungu dynasty extinguished at capture of Ava by Talaings, 1752. Alaungpaya reconquers Ava, 1753. Founds Rangoon, 1755. Subdues the whole country, 1758. Invades Siam, 1759. Siam conquered, 1767. Chinese invasions, 1767–9. Amarapura made capital, 1783. First war with Britain, 1824–6. British annex Lower B., 1826. British resident appointed, 1830. Second Burmese War, 1852. Lower B. annexed to Britain, 1853. Accession of Thibaw, 1878. Deteriorating situation led to whole of B. becoming part of the British Empire, 1885, though pacification of Upper B. took several years. Gen. Wolseley's expedition, 1889. B. made a province of British India, 1923. Revolt in Lower B. suppressed, 1930. Separated from India, 1 Apr. 1937. Road to China built, 1936–8. Invaded by Japanese, 8 Feb. 1942. Allies recapture Rangoon, 3 May 1945. Prime Minister (Aung Saw) and several ministers murdered, 19 July 1947 (former Prime Minister U Saw hanged for this crime, 8 May 1948). Becomes independent republic, 4 Jan. 1948. Admitted to United Nations, 19 Apr. Martial law proclaimed, 20 Aug. U Tin Tut, ex-foreign minister, assassinated, 18 Sept. Communists and Karen rebels threaten capital, but defeated by aid of Shan and Chin tribesmen, 1949. Rebellions largely crushed by end of 1951. 1952: B. joined Colombo Plan and was member of the Afro-Asian Conference at Bandoeng, Apr. 1955. Karen rebels' capital, Papuu, recaptured, 1955. Gen. Ne Win took over the government, Apr. 1958. After elections of Feb. 1960 resulted in victory for U Nu, U Nu became Prime Minister, 4 Apr. 1960. Corruption and discontent led to another army *coup d'état*, 1 Mar. 1962, again led by Gen. Ne Win. Nationalization measures followed.

Presidents of Burma:

Sao Shwe Thaik	1948–1952
Sir Ba U	1952–1957
U Win Maung	1957–

Burma Road. Constructed 1936–8 from Lashio to Chungking. Closed by Britain under Japanese pressure, July–Oct. 1940.

Burschenschaft, perhaps the forerunner of all modern nationalistic youth movements, was an association of German undergraduates of all universities, started at Jena in 1817 under the patronage of the Grand Duke of Saxe Weimar. Suppressed by the Carlsbad Decrees of 1833, it was revived in 1848. *See also* WARTBURG.

Burundi, Africa. Independent kingdom created by the granting of independence to Ruanda-Urundi (*q.v.*), on 1 July 1962.

Buryat Mongolia, an autonomous Soviet Socialist Republic set up 1 Mar. 1920.

Bury St. Edmunds, England. Named after St. Edmund, King of E. Anglia, martyred 870, whose remains were transferred hither from Hoxne, 903. Grammar school refounded by Edward VI, 1550. Plague, 1636. Diocese of St. Edmundsbury and Ipswich founded, 1914.

Bydgoszcz. *See* BROMBERG.

Byzantine Authors:

Some earlier B. historians wrote in Latin, e.g. Eunapius (*c.* 400), Olympiodorus and Priscus (*c.* 450), Malchus (*c.* 490), and Zosimus (*c.* 500). Some authors writing in Greek are:

Nonnus, *c.* 400, epic poet.

Procopius of Caesaraea, *b. c.* 500, *d.* after 559, historian.

Jordanes, *fl. c.* 550, historian.

George Pisiaes, seventh century, panegyrist.

Agathias, 522–88, historian.

Andreas of Crete, *c.* 650–720, hymnologist.

Theodorus of Studium, 759–812, epigrammatist.

Theophanes Confessor, *fl.* 800–13, chronicler.

George Syncellus, *d. c.* 800, chronicler.

Photius, 820–91, philologist.

Leo of Salonika (*c.* 829–56), encyclopaedist.

Leo the Deacon, *fl.* 995, chronicler.

Constantine VII Porphyrogenitus (905–959), historian.

Cometas Chartularius, *fl.* 950?, epigrammatist.

Theodosius Diaconus, tenth century, panegyrist.

Michael Psellus, 1018–78, historian.

Christopher of Mytilene, eleventh century, lyric poet.

Anna Comnena, 1083–1145, historian.

Nicephorus Bryennius, late eleventh century, historian.

Johannes Cimmanus, *c.* 1143–85, historian.

John Scylitzes, *d.* after 1081.

Constantine Manasses, *fl.* 1143–80, rhyming chronicler.

Theodorus Prodromus, *d.* after 1159, epic poet.

George Cedrenus, early twelfth-century chronicler.

Nicetas Acominates, *c.* 1140–1220, historian.

George Acropolita, *c.* 1250, historian.

Critobulos of Imbros, late fifteenth century.

Byzantium. *See* CONSTANTINOPLE and ROMAN EMPIRE, EASTERN.

D

ADDENDA

C

Cab. Abbreviation for *cabriolet de place*, invented by Nicolas Sauvage *c.* 1660, became current *c.* 1825. C. first licensed in London, 1823. Hansom C. patented, 1834. Cabmen's shelters established, 1875. London C. Act, 1896, and London C. and Stage Carriage Act, 1907, are still in force together with the London C. Order, 1934. *See also* HACKNEY COACHES.

Cabal. In later Stuart times the term used for the group of politicians who held power. Originally the so-called C. Ministry of 1671. The letters of the word stood for Clifford, *A*rlington, *B*uckingham, *A*shley, *L*auderdale, its principal members.

Cabinet. *See* COUNCIL.

Cabinet, Imperial War. First met, 1917.

Cabinets. *See* ADMINISTRATIONS.

Cable. Hempen Cs. used by British Navy until 1811, when iron Cs. introduced. First successful submarine C. between S. Foreland and Sangatte, 1851. Atlantic C. laid successfully, 5 Aug. 1858. New pattern C. laid to Holland, Dec. 1947. Pacific C. laid, 1962.

Cade's Insurrection. Mob led by Jack C., May 1450. Entered London, 27 June. C. killed, 11 July.

Cadiz, Spain. Traditionally founded by Phoenicians *c.* 1000 B.C. Had become a famous market for metals by seventh century B.C. Captured by Romans *c.* 206 B.C. Remained part of Roman Empire under name of *Gades* till conquest of Spain by Visigoths, A.D. 409–20. Reconquered after Justinian's reconquest of Africa *c.* 535. Taken by Moors, 711. Sacked by Normans, 813, and joined to Castile by Alfonso X, 1262. Spanish fleet destroyed by Drake ('singeing of the King of Spain's beard'), 1587. Sacked by Earl of Essex, 15 Sept. 1596. Bombarded by British, July 1797. Blockaded by Lord St. Vincent, 1797–9. Besieged by French, July 1812. Celebrated constitution of 1812 promulgated here.

Cadmium. Discovered by Strohmeyer, 1817.

Caen, France. Old capital of Normandy and burial-place of William the Conqueror (*d.* 1087) and his queen. Taken by English, 1346, 1417. University founded by Duke of Bedford, 1432. Taken by French, 1 July 1450. Heavily bombed and half destroyed by Allies, 5–9 June 1944. Restored university inaugurated, 1957. *See* WORLD WAR II.

Caerleon on Usk. Site of Roman fortress (Isca Silurum), planned by Sextus Julius Frontinus, governor of Britain A.D. 74–8, about A.D. 75. Excavations, 1926 and 1939, showed occupation at least down to 350, possibly later. Excavations in 1954 discovered a large town on an adjacent site, distinct from but clearly dependent on the fortress.

Caernarvon. *See* CARNARVON.

Caesaraea (Kaisarieh), Israel. Built by Herod the Great, 25–13 B.C. Jewish rising against Romans, A.D. 66. After A.D. 70 capital of Roman Palestine and residence of the procurators, and the ecclesiastical capital until 451. Occupied by Arabs, 638. Taken by Crusaders, 1101; by Saladin, 1187; by Richard Cœur-de-Lion, 1191. Demolished by Bibars, 1265.

Caesaraea Philippi (Banias), Syria. Founded by Philip the Tetrarch, 3 B.C. Taken by Crusaders, 1129, but lost, 1132. Burnt out, 1157.

Caesarean Section, performed at least as early as A.D. 1500, although one tradition asserts that Julius Caesar was delivered by this method, hence the name.

Caesium. Discovered by Bunsen and Kirchloff, 1860.

Cagliari. Traditionally founded by the Phoenicians. Important in Carthaginian and Roman times. Taken by Vandals, 485; by Byzantines, 533; by Saracens, twelfth century. Aragonese from 1326 until 1714. Cathedral begun *c.* 1257. University founded, 1606. *See* SARDINIA.

Cahors, France. Became a banking centre in thirteenth century. Liberties suppressed by French kings, 1316. University founded by Pope John XXII, 1331. United with University of Toulouse, 1751.

Caicos Island, or The Keys. Discovered *c.* 1512. Settled (from Bermuda), 1678. Jurisdiction transferred to Bahamas, 1804; to Jamaica, 1854. Occupied by Loyalists from Georgia, 1775. Became crown colony and Jamaican dependency, 1874.

'Ça ira!' Famous French revolutionary song, traditionally by Ladié, first heard, 5 Oct. 1789.

Cairo, Egypt. Founded by Amr *c.* A.D. 641 as *Masr*. Became independent capital under Ibn Tulun, 868–83. El

Azhar University founded, 941. Re-founded on new site a mile from old by Jauhar el-Kaid, 968, as El-Kahira, eventually corrupted to C. Citadel built by Saladin, 1176. Captured by Turks, 1517. Great earthquake, 1754. Taken by Napoleon, 23 July 1798. Recaptured with British help, 27 June 1801. Capital of Mehemet Ali's independent kingdom, 1811. British occupation, 1882–1946. Anti-British riots, 1919, 1930, and 1952 (26 Jan.).

Cairo Declaration, 1 Dec. 1943, by China, Great Britain, and U.S.A. regarding war aims and the future of Korea and Formosa.

Calabar. Came under British influence, 1884; protection, 1889. Ceased to be known as Old C., 1904.

Calabria, Italy. The *Iapygia* of the Greeks conquered by Romans, 266 B.C.; subdued by Odoacer, A.D. 476; part of the Ostrogothic kingdom of Theodoric, 493; recovered for empire by Belisarius, 536. After 873 C. constituted part of the SW. peninsula. Invaded by Otho I, 968, who defeated Greeks, 969; invaded by Peter of Aragon, 1283; invaded by Sicilians, 1296. Part of kingdom of the Two Sicilies, 1597.

Calais, France. Became important port, tenth century. Taken by Edward III, 4 Aug. 1347; finally taken from the English by the Duke of Guise, 7 Jan. 1558; taken by Spaniards, Apr. 1596; restored, 1598. Captured by Germans after desperate Anglo-French resistance, 22–7 May 1940. Invested, 20 Sept., and taken, 30 Sept. 1944 by Canadian First Army.

Calcium. First isolated in 1808 by Sir Humphry Davy in his electrolytic researches.

Calculating Machines. Constructed by Napier of Merchiston, 1617; Blaise Pascal, 1642; Sir S. Moreland, 1666; Leibnitz, 1671; Visc. Mahon, 1775; Hahn, 1779; Müller, 1784; C. Babbage, 1822. Colmar's arithmometer c. 1850. First cash-adding machine by Burroughs, 1888.

Calcutta, India. Founded, 1687, by Job Charnock, an East India merchant. Fort built, 1696. Confinement of prisoners in Black Hole, 19 June 1756, after capture of town by Dowlah; retaken, 1 Jan. 1757; Anglican bishopric, 1813; centre of British India, 1773–1912.

Calder Hall. British atomic energy station. Construction began, 1949; formally opened by Queen Elizabeth II, Oct. 1956.

Caldey, island off the Pembrokeshire coast. A Cistercian priory was established here in 1929.

Caledonian Canal (Scotland). Building begun, 1804; opened, 1822, but work not complete until 1847.

California, U.S.A. Discovered by Spaniards, 1542; visited by Drake, 1579; subject to Mexico, 1822; occupied by U.S. Army, 1847; ceded to U.S.A., 1848; admitted to Union as a state, 1850. University of C. opened, 1869.

Caliphate. The spiritual and political headship of Islam in succession to Mohammed. The first three 'Orthodox' caliphs were: Abu Bekr, 632–4; Omar I, 634–44; Othman, 644–56. At the murder of Othman a civil war between Ali, elected at Mecca, and Moawiya of the Ommayad House led eventually to the establishment of the Ommayad C., 661, which was in its turn overthrown by the Abbasids, 750, who reached their greatest prosperity under Haroun al Rashid, 786–809, and were destroyed effectively at the capture of Bagdad by Hulagu Khan the Mongol, 1258. A puppet C. under the domination of the Mamelukes continued, however, in Egypt (*q.v.*), 1261, until its conquest by the Turks, 1517. In 1520 the last of these puppets, Al Motawakkil, surrendered his office to the Turkish Sultan Suleiman the Magnificent, and the title was borne by the Turkish sultans till Nov. 1922, when it was made elective in the Turkish imperial family. On 3 Mar. 1924 the C. was abolished by the Turkish parliament.

Caliphs. Following is a list of C. from the death of Mohammed until the extinction of the genuine caliphate at Bagdad in 1258. Those marked 'O' were of the Ommayad House. Thereafter the remainder were Abbasids. Those marked 'B' were dominated by Buweiyid princes and ministers. Those marked 'S' were virtually vassals of the Seljuk Turks.

Abu Bekr		632–634
Omar I		634–644
Othman		644–656
Ali		656–661
Hasan		661
Moawiya I	(O)	661–680
Yezid I	(O)	680–683
Moawiya II	(O)	683–684
Merwan I	(O)	684–685
Abd-el-Melik	(O)	685–705
Welid I	(O)	705–715
Suleiman	(O)	715–717
Omar II	(O)	717–720
Yezid II	(O)	720–724
Hisham	(O)	724–743
Welid II	(O)	743–744
Yezid III	(O)	744
Ibrahim	(O)	744
Merwan II	(O)	744–750
Abul Abbas (as Saffah)		750–754

Al Mansur		754–775
Al Mehdi		775–785
Al Hadi		785
Haroun Al Rashid		786–809
Al Amin ⎱		809–813
Al Mamun ⎰		
Al Mamun alone		813–833
Al Motassim		833–842
Al Wathik		842–847
Al Mutawakil		847–861
Al Muntasir		861–862
Al Mustain		862–866
Al Motazz		866–869
Al Muhtadi		869–870
Al Motamid		870–892
Al Motadid		892–902
Al Muktafi		902–907
Al Muktadir		907–932
Al Kahir		932–934
Ar-Radi		934–940
Al Muttaki		941–944
Al Mustakfi		944–946
Al Muti	(B)	946–974
Al Tai	(B)	974–991
Al Kadir	(B)	991–1031
Al Kaim	(B)	1031–1075
Al Muktadi	(S)	1075–1094
Al Mustazhir	(S)	1094–1118
Al Mustarshid	(S)	1118–1135
Ar Rashid	(S)	1135–1136
Al Muktafi	(S)	1136–1161
Al Mustanjid	(S)	1161–1170
Al Mustadi	(S)	1170–1180
An-Nasir	(S)	1180–1225
Zahir	(S)	1225–1235
Al Mustansir	(S)	1235–1242
Al Mustasim		1242–1258

Callao, Peru. Old city destroyed by earthquake, 1746.

Calotype. Photographic method discovered by Dr. Fox Talbot, 1841.

Calvinists. Named after John Calvin (b. Noyon, 10 July 1509; d. Geneva, 27 May 1564). See EDICT OF NANTES.

Cambodia. The Khmer Kingdom was founded in A.D. fifth century. Rose to its zenith in ninth century. Angkor-Thom completed by Yasovarman c. 900. Angkor-Vat built, twelfth century. Empire reached its greatest extent under Jayavarman VII early in thirteenth century. Angkor abandoned for Lovek in fifteenth century. Lovek abandoned end of sixteenth century. By seventeenth century the Khmer monarchs were puppets alternately under Siamese and Annamese influence. C. became a French protectorate in 1863, when the king's nominal allegiance to the Emperor of Siam ceased. Formal treaty with France, 1884. Siam claimed overlordship of C. in Oct. 1940 (having renounced it in 1867), and in Jan. 1941 Siamese troops invaded C. By a treaty signed 11 Mar. 1941,

N. C. was ceded to Siam, but the territory was restored in 1945. Became Associated State of French Union, 1949. King Sihanouk (acceded 26 Apr. 1941) dismissed his government for pro-Viet Minh activities in 1950, and in June 1952 dismissed the Huy Kantou cabinet and replaced it by one consisting largely of the royal family. He withdrew (with certain high officials) to Thailand, 12 June 1953, in protest against French failure to grant effective self-government. Complete independence from France, Jan. 1955. Sihanouk abdicated, Mar. 1955, in order to become political leader of C.; succeeded by his father, King Norodom Sumarit. When King Norodom d., 30 Apr. 1960, Sihanouk became Head of State without becoming king.

Cambrai, France. Church councils at, 1064, 1303, 1383, 1565. League of C., 10 Dec. 1508; Paix des Dames Treaty, 1529. Captured by the Emperor Charles V, 1544; by French, 1667; cathedral destroyed, 1793; French defeated by British under Duke of York, 24 Apr. 1794; taken by Austrians, 10 Sept. 1798; by British under Sir Charles Colville, 1815; new cathedral, 1825. See BATTLES.

Cambridge, England. Taken by barons, 1215. Residence of Henry II, who repaired castle, 1265. Castle possessed by Cromwell, 1643. Fitzwilliam Museum founded at, 1837.

Cambridge, Mass., U.S.A. Harvard College (q.v.) founded here, 1639. One of the earliest printing presses, if not the earliest, was set up at C., which published the *Bay Psalm Book*, the first book printed in British America, in 1640.

Cambridge University. First charter, 1231; formally recognized, 1318. Records burnt by Wat Tyler, 1381. New statutes, 1570. Refused to admit Francis, a Benedictine monk recommended by James II, 9 Feb. 1687; vice-chancellor deprived of his office in consequence, 27 May 1687; reinstated, 1688. Written examinations introduced, 1772. New statutes, 1856. Religious tests abolished, 1871. Oxford and Cambridge Act, 1882. Present statutes date from 1926. Women admitted as full members, 1947. The following are the principal colleges and halls with the dates of their foundation and their founders:

Ayerst Hall, opened, 21 Apr. 1884; closed, 1896.

Caius (Gonville and Caius College), founded by Edmund Gonville, 1348. John Caius, M.D., in 1557 obtained royal charter.

Cavendish College, founded 1876 by County College Association; closed, Dec. 1891.

Christ's College, founded 1505 by Lady Margaret Beaufort, Countess of Richmond and Derby, mother of King Henry VII.

Churchill College, founded 1959.

Clare College, founded by Richard Badew as University Hall, 1326; refounded, 1338, by Lady Elizabeth, sister of Gilbert, Earl of Clare.

Corpus Christi, founded 1352; owes foundation to two tradesmen's guilds in the town, called the Guilds of Corpus Christi and of the Blessed Virgin Mary.

Downing College, founded by will of Sir George Downing, Bt., dated 20 Dec. 1717; received charter, 22 Sept. 1800.

Emmanuel College, founded 1584 by Sir Walter Mildmay, Chancellor of the Exchequer.

Fitzwilliam House (non-collegiate), founded 1869.

Jesus College, founded 1496 by John Alcock, Bishop of Ely.

King's College. founded 1441 by Henry VI.

Magdalene College, founded 1542 by Thomas. Baron Audley, of Walden. Replaced Buckingham College, founded by Henry Stafford, Duke of Buckingham (1455–83).

Pembroke College, founded 1347 under name of Valence-Mary, who was in reality Mary de St. Paul, widow of Aymer de Valence, Earl of Pembroke. Henry VI was a liberal benefactor, and is known as second founder.

Queen's College, founded 1448 by Margaret of Anjou, wife of Henry VI; refounded 1465 by Elizabeth Woodville, wife of Edward IV.

St. Catherine's College, founded 1473 by Robert Wodelarke, D.D., Chancellor of the University.

College of St. John the Evangelist (St. John's College), founded 1511 by Lady Margaret Beaufort (founder of Christ's College, q.v.).

St. Peter's College (or Peterhouse), founded 1284 by Hugh de Balsham, Bishop of Ely.

Selwyn College, founded 1882, built by public subscription in memory of George Augustus Selwyn, Bishop of Lichfield.

Sidney Sussex College, founded 1596 under will of Lady Frances Sidney, Dowager Countess of Sussex.

Trinity College, founded 1546 by Henry VIII, who combined three other smaller colleges into one, and added to revenues.

Trinity Hall, founded 1350 by William Bateman, Bishop of Norwich.

The following are women's colleges:

Girton College, founded at Hitchin, 1869. Removed to Girton, near Cambridge, 1873. Admitted as a college of the university. 1947.

Newnham College, founded 1871. Amalgamated with association for promoting higher education for women, 1880. Royal charter, 1915. Admitted as college of university, 1947.

New Hall, founded Oct. 1954.

Cambridge University Press. John Siberch became first printer to the University, 1521.

Cambuskenneth Abbey. Founded by, David I of Scotland, 1147. First Scottish Parliament assembled at, 1326.

Camera Obscura. Known to Euclid, 300 B.C., and described by Alhazen of Cairo (d. A.D. 1038), but popularized by Giovanni Battista della Porta, 1569. First used for photographic purposes by Thomas Wedgwood, 1794.

Cameroons, Africa. Colonized by Germans, 1884. Conquered by French and British, 1914–17. Under British and French mandates, 1922. Trusteeship agreements (U.N.O.) made the former British mandate an integral part of Nigeria, 14 Dec. 1946. The French mandate became independent under the name of the Cameroon republic, 1 Jan. 1960.

Camisards. Huguenots of the Cévennes who rebelled after the revocation of the Edict of Nantes (1685). Camisard war, 1702–6, in which the royal forces were commanded successively by Marshals Montrevel, Villars, and Berwick. Jean Cavalier, the chief Camisard leader, d. in 1740, having been made a British brigadier-general in 1735.

Camorra. Secret society founded in Naples jail c. 1820. Entered political field, 1848. Attempt to suppress, 1877. Gained control of Naples municipality, 1900. Became extinct, 1911.

Campbellites (Disciples of Christ). Sect founded by Alexander Campbell (1788–1866) in 1812.

Campo Formio, Treaty of, 17 Oct. 1797, between Napoleon and Austria, by which (inter alia) the republic of Venice was abolished.

Canada. Discovered by John Cabot, 1497. The St. Lawrence discovered by Jacques Cartier, 1535. From hearing Indians make frequent use of the word kanata, a village, he carried away the impression that the name applied to the whole country. Quebec founded by Champlain, 1608. C. explored by La Salle, 1669, 1678. Hudson's Bay Co. founded, 1670. C. given up to England by France, 1763, after war of 1759–60 (see QUEBEC), in which General Wolfe distinguished himself. C. divided into two provinces, 1791; reunited, 1840; again separated on establishment of the Confederation, 1867. British N. America Act for union of C., Nova Scotia, and New Brunswick, under title of Dominion of C., passed 29 Mar. 1867. Territories of Hudson Bay (Manitoba) added, 1869; of British Columbia, 1871; of Prince Edward Island, 1873; of Alberta and Saskatchewan, 1 Sept. 1905. Canadian Pacific Railway opened, 8 Nov. 1885. World War I: Canadian troops landed in Britain, 16 Oct. 1914. Houses of Parliament at Ottawa burnt, 3 Feb. 1916. First treaty with foreign power concluded by a dominion: C. with U.S.A., 29 Dec. 1923. Trade treaty with Australia, 26 Sept. 1924. C. House, London, opened, 29 June 1925. Labrador boundary defined, Mar. 1927. Bennett, Premier, led Canadian delegation to Imperial Conference, Oct. 1930. Canadian sovereignty over Sverdrup Island recognized by Norway, Feb. 1931. Statute of Westminster (*q.v.*) approved, 30 June 1931. Welland Ship Canal between Lakes Erie and Ontario opened, 1932. Liberals under Mackenzie King returned to power, 1935. Royal visit, June 1939. War on Germany declared, 10 Sept. 1939; and on Italy, 10 June 1940. (*See* WORLD WAR II.) U.S.S.R. admits espionage on atomic secrets, 20 Feb. 1946. Privy Council judgment upholding abolition of Appeals to Privy Council, 13 Jan. 1947. Newfoundland entered Dominion, 31 Mar. 1949. C. signed North Atlantic Treaty, 4 Apr. 1949. Princess Elizabeth and Duke of Edinburgh toured Dominion, Oct. 1951; another royal tour (as Queen Elizabeth II), 1957. Conservatives returned to power, 1957, under Diefenbaker, after twenty-two years', Liberal government. Opening of the St. Lawrence Seaway, 1959. Economic crisis, 1959–60. Canadian opposition to British entry into the Common Market, 1961–2. General election, 18 June 1962. Diefenbaker lost overall majority. Austerity programme announced to meet economic crisis, 24 June 1962. Trans-C. Highway opened, 3 Sept. 1962. Diefenbaker government resigned 6 Feb. 1963 after Social Credit members, who had held the balance of power since the previous election, had voted against it on defence. In the General Election held on 8 April the Liberals emerged as the strongest single party, and their leader, Lester Pearson, became Prime Minister. He visited Britain shortly afterwards.

The following are the Governor-Generals since the union:

Lord Monck	1867–1868
Lord Lisgar	1868–1872
Lord Dufferin	1872–1878
Marquess of Lorne	1878–1883
Lord Lansdowne	1883–1888
Lord Stanley of Preston	1888–1893
Earl of Aberdeen	1893–1898
Earl of Minto	1898–1904
Earl Grey	1904–1911
Duke of Connaught	1911
Duke of Devonshire	1911–1916
Visc. Byng of Vimy	1916–1921
Visc. Willingdon	1921–1926
Earl of Bessborough	1926–1931
Lord Tweedsmuir	1931–1935
Earl of Athlone	1935–1940
Visc. Alexander	1946–1952
Vincent Massey	1952–1959
Georges Philias Vanier	1959–

The following are the Prime Ministers of Canada, from 1867:

Macdonald	1867–1873
Mackenzie	1873–1878
Macdonald	1878–1891
Abbott	1891–1892
Thompson	1892–1894
Bowell	1894–1896
Tupper	1896
Laurier	1896–1911
Borden	1911–1920
Meighen	1920–1219
Mackenzie King	1921–1926
Meighen	1926
Mackenzie King	1926–1930
Bennett	1930–1935
Mackenzie King	1935–1948
St. Laurent	1948–1957
Diefenbaker	1957–1963
Pearson	1963–

Canals. For the principal ones in Great Britain and Ireland, *see under* various headings. The following are the most noted C. outside Great Britain, with the dates of their openings:

Albert (Antwerp to Liège)	1939
American Erie	1817
Amsterdam	1876
Amsterdam and N. Sea	1876
Baltic and N. Sea (Kiel Ship Canal)	1895
Bordeaux and Narbonne	1884
Bourbon	1790
Burgundy	1775
Corinth	1893
Du Midi (Languedoc)	1681
Ganges	1854
Hitler (Upper Silesia to Oder)	1939
Holstein	1785
Kattegat and Baltic	1806
Leningrad and Kronstadt	1884
Michigan-Mississippi	1900
Mittelland (Rhine—Ems to Königsberg)	1938
Moscow-Volga	1937
Orleans	1675
Princess Juliana (Netherlands)	1935
Seine et Loire	1791
Twenthe (Zutphen to Enschede)	1936

Welland (Erie to Ontario) 1932
White Sea and Baltic (Archangel
to Leningrad) 1933
See also SUEZ; PANAMA, etc.

Canary or **Fortunate Islands**, NW.
Africa. Granted by Pope Clement VI to
Juan de la Cerda, 1346; partly occupied
by Spaniards, 1402–4; since 1496 under
Spanish rule.

Canberra. Officially became capital of
Australia, 20 Jan. 1910. Foundation
stone laid, 12 Mar. 1923. Parliament
opened by Duke of York, 9 May 1927.

Candia. *See* CRETE.

Candia, War of, 1635–94. *See* CRETE
and VENICE.

Candlemas. Ordered to be observed as
heretofore by Henry VIII, 1539. Forbidden in England, 1548.

Cannes, France. Popularity as a
resort dates from Lord Brougham's visit,
1834.

Canon. The office of C. appears to have
been introduced into the church in the
eighth century, and arose from the desire
to impose something like a monastic rule
on the cathedral clergy.

Canonization was not known before the
tenth century, but some hold that the first
C. was celebrated by Leo III, A.D. 804.
The canonizing of any deceased Christian
without the bishop's consent was prohibited in the ninth century. John XV
was the first pope who exercised the right,
and in A.D. 993 made Udalric, Bishop of
Augsburg, a saint. *Douleia* of 'canonized saints' enjoined by Council of Trent
(1545–63). Added to calendar in recent
times: Joan of Arc, 16 May 1920; Jean
Baptiste Vianny, 1925; John Bosco, 1934;
Sir Thomas More and Bishop John
Fisher, 19 May 1935; Gemma Galgani,
1940. St. Joan of Valois, July 1950.

Canon Law. *See* DECRETALS.

Canossa. Emperor Henry IV submitted to Pope Gregory VII at, Jan.
1077.

Canterbury, England. Walls of the
Roman *Durovernum* were built in the
second century A.D. Evidence of occupation by Anglo-Saxon (Jutish?) settlers
in whose language C. was known as
Cantwaraburh is afforded by remains
datable to the middle fifth century. St.
Augustine arrived from Rome at C., A.D.
596. See founded, 597. Castle taken by
Louis of France, 1216. Kentish rebels
under Wat Tyler left C. for London, 1381.
Cathedral founded by Augustine, 602;
pillaged by Roric, 851; entirely rebuilt by
Archbishop Lanfranc, 1070; choir completed, 1130. Thomas Becket murdered
in choir, 1170. Choir burnt down, 1174;
rebuilt, 1174–84. Shrine to Becket

erected, 1175; demolished and robbed of
its valuable gifts by Henry VIII, 1538.
St. Martin's Church, frequented by
Queen Bertha before the landing of
Augustine, said to be the oldest Saxon
church in England. Chequers Inn for
pilgrims mentioned by Chaucer, built
1400; mostly burnt down, 1865; bombed
and badly damaged, 1 Jan. 1942; this led
to much excavation of devastated area
round the cathedral, c. 1946–52, whereby
the exact ground-plan of the Roman town
was determined, and the probability of
continuous occupation since Roman days
established.

Canterbury, Archbishops of. The following is a list since the foundation of
the see:

Augustine	597–605
Laurentius	605–619
Mellitus	619–624
Justus	624–627
Honorius	627–653
Deusdedit	655–664
Theodore	668–690
Berhtwald	693–731
Taetwine	731–734
Nothelm	734–740
Cuthbert	740–758
Breogwine	759–762
Jaenberht	763–790
Æthelheard	790–803
Wulfred	803–829
Fleogild	829–830
Ceolnoth	830–870
Æthelred	870–889
Plegemund	891–923
Æthelm	923–925
Wulfelm	928–941
Odo	941–958
Ælsine	958–959
Dunstan	959–988
Æthelgar	988–989
Sigeric	990–994
Ælfric	995–1005
Ælfeah or Alphege	1006–1012
Lyfing	1013–1020
Æthelnoth	1020–1038
Eadsige	1038–1050
Robert of Jumièges	1051–1052
Stigand	1052–1070
Lanfranc	1070–1089
Anselm	1093–1109
Ralph de Turbine	1114–1122
William de Corbeuil	1123–1136
Theobald	1139–1161
Thomas Becket	1162–1170
Richard	1174–1184
Baldwin	1185–1190
Reginald Fitz-Jocelin	1191
Hubert Walter	1193–1205
Stephen Langton	1207–1228
Richard Wethershed	1229–1231
Edmund Rich (of Abingdon)	1233–1240

Boniface of Savoy	1240–1270	
Robert Kilwardby	1273–1278	
John Peckham	1279–1292	
Robert Winchelsea	1293–1313	
Walter Reynolds	1313–1327	
Simon de Meopham	1327–1333	
John Stratford	1333–1348	
John de Ufford	1348–1349	
Thomas Bradwardin	1349	
Simon Islip	1349–1366	
Simon Langham	1366–1368	
William Wittlesey	1368–1374	
Simon Sudbury	1375–1381	
William Courtenay	1381–1396	
Thomas Fitzalan	1396–1398	
Roger Walden	1398	
Thomas Arundel	1399–1414	
Henry Chicheley	1414–1443	
John Stafford	1443–1452	
John Kemp	1452–1454	
Thomas Bourchier	1454–1486	
John Morton	1486–1500	
Henry Deane	1501–1503	
William Warham	1503–1532	
Thomas Cranmer	1533–1556	
Reginald Pole	1556–1558	
Matthew Parker	1559–1575	
Edmund Grindal	1575–1583	
John Whitgift	1583–1604	
Richard Bancroft	1604–1610	
George Abbot	1611–1633	
William Laud	1633–1645	
William Juxon	1660–1663	
Gilbert Sheldon	1663–1677	
William Sancroft	1678–1691	
John Tillotson	1691–1694	
Thomas Tenison	1694–1715	
William Wake	1716–1737	
John Potter	1737–1747	
Thomas Herring	1747–1757	
Matthew Hutton	1757–1758	
Thomas Ecker	1758–1768	
Frederick Cornwallis	1768–1783	
John Moore	1783–1805	
Charles Manners-Sutton	1805–1828	
William Howley	1828–1848	
John Bird Sumner	1848–1862	
Charles T. Longley	1862–1868	
Archibald Campbell Tait	1868–1882	
Edward W. Benson	1882–1896	
Frederick Temple	1896–1902	
Randall Davidson	1903–1928	
Cosmo Gordon Lang	1928–1942	
William Temple	1942–1944	
Geoffrey Francis Fisher	1945–1961	
Arthur Michael Ramsey	1961–	

'Canterbury Christmas.' On 22 Dec. 1647, the crier of Canterbury proclaimed that by decree of Parliament the festivities of Christmas and other superstitious revivals should be put down, which command was strenuously resisted.

'Canterbury Tales,' by Geoffrey Chaucer

(1340?–1400); composed c. 1380 and first printed by Caxton, 1477.

Canton, China. King of Portugal obtained right to trade with, 1517. First visited by English, 1634; besieged and taken by Sir Hugh Gough, 31 May 1841; Convention of C., July 1841; bombed, 23 Sept. 1937; captured by Japanese, 21 Oct. 1938. Restored to China, 1945. Taken by Communists, 1950.

Cape Coast, Ghana. Early settlement of Portuguese, 1610, when castle built; taken from them by Dutch, 1642; ceded to England by Peace of Breda, 1667. *See* GHANA.

Cape Province (formerly **Cape Colony**). Cape of Good Hope discovered by Bartholomew Diaz, 1488. Cape Town founded by Dutch, 1652. Colony of Cape Town captured by English, 16 Sept. 1795; restored, 1802; retaken, 9 Jan. 1806. Wars with Kaffirs, 1811–12, 1817–19. Finally ceded to English by Netherlands, 13 Aug. 1814. Arrival of over 5,000 British emigrants, 1820. Kaffirs raided English settlements, Oct. 1834. Third Kaffir War, 1834–5; fourth Kaffir War, 1846–8; fifth Kaffir War, 1850–3. Boers in large numbers crossed Orange River and left colony ('The Great Trek'), 1835. Legislative Council established, 1837. Natal annexed to C. C., 2 Aug. 1843. Government proclaimed its authority over Orange River sovereignty, 3 Feb. 1848. Orange River territory annexed to C. C., Mar. 1851. Representative Government established, 1 July 1853. Orange River territory formed into a free state, Mar. 1854. Discovery of diamonds, 1867–70. Transvaal Republic annexed for protection, 12 Apr. 1877. Transvaal independent as S. African Republic, 1880 (*see* TRANSVAAL). Houses of Parliament opened, 1885. Arrival of Lords Roberts and Kitchener during S. African War (*q.v.*), 10 Jan. 1900. Annexation of Orange Free State (*q.v.*), 28 May 1900; of Transvaal, 3 Sept. 1900. Became a province of the Union of South Africa after the passing of the South Africa Act, 1909. *See* SOUTH AFRICA, UNION OF.

Cape Horn. Sighted by Drake, 1578; so named by Dutch sailors, 1616.

Capet Dynasty. *See* FRANCE.

Cape to Cairo Railway. Northern railhead of southern half Victoria Falls, 1904; Broken Hill, 1906; now Ndola, Northern Rhodesia, or Bukama, Congo: southern railhead of northern half Khartoum, 1905; Sennar, 1910.

Cape Town (Kaapstad). Factory established by Dutch E. India Co., 1652. Occupied by British when Holland became French dependency, 1806; restored by

Treaty of Amiens, 1810; but reoccupied by British, 1814, to whom the province was finally awarded same year. Castle built, 1666; observatory, 1820; university built, 1873.

Cape Verde. Discovered 1443, by Nuño Tristao.

Cape Verde Islands. Annexed to Portugal, 1441–56.

Capital Levy. First recorded demand for a C. L. in Britain made by a private member in the House of Commons in 1914. Remained part of Labour Party programme until 1927 and revived several times since. The 'Special Contribution' levied by the Labour Government in 1948 is the closest approach to a C. L. so far.

Capital Punishment, British law relating to, reformed, 1826 (in the light of Beccaria's *Treatise on Crimes and Punishments,* 1764), when varieties of capital crime reduced from over 200 to treason, arson, piracy, murder only. Royal Commission report, 1866; House of Commons Select Committee report, 1930; Criminal Justice Bill, 1948; White Paper, May 1948; Royal Commission report, 1953. Homicide Act, 21 Mar. 1957, divided murders into capital and non-capital categories.

C. P. in criminal (non-political) cases abolished or discontinued in other countries:

Europe and Asia. Austria, 1950; Belgium, abrogated by disuse, last execution 1863; Denmark, 1930; Finland, 1949; W. Germany, 1949; Iceland, 1944; Israel, 1954; Italy, 1948; Luxembourg, abrogated by disuse, no execution since 1822; Nepal, suspended since 1931; Netherlands, 1870; Norway, 1905; Portugal, 1867; Rumania, 1864; San Marino, 1859; Sweden, 1921; Switzerland, 1942. N.B. Russia abolished C. P., 1947, and reintroduced it, 1950.

U.S.A. C. P. abolished in Maine, 1887; Michigan, 1847; Minnesota, 1911; Wisconsin, 1853. Nine other states have abolished C. P. but subsequently restored it.

South and Central America. Argentina, 1922; Brazil, 1891; Colombia, 1910; Costa Rica, 1880; Dominica, 1924; Ecuador, 1897; Mexico, 1928; Panama, 1903; Peru, abrogated by disuse, no execution for over half a century; Uruguay, 1907; Venezuela, 1863.

Australia. Queensland, 1922.

New Zealand. 1961.

Capitol. *See* ROME.

Capri Island. Residence of Emperor Tiberius, A.D. 27–37. Captured by British, 1806; by French, 1808. Restored to Naples and Sicily, 1814.

Capua, Italy. Alliance with Rome, 338 B.C. Went over to Hannibal, 216 B.C.; captured by Romans, 211 B.C.; captured by Vandals, A.D. 456; destroyed by Saracens, 840; rebuilt, ninth century. Councils at, 391, 1087, 1118. Captured by Caesar Borgia, 24 July 1501; occupied by French, 23 Jan. 1799; surrendered to British, 28 July 1799; capitulated to Sardinian forces, Nov. 1860.

Capuchins. Offshoot of Franciscans, founded by Matteo di Bassi, 1528. Became an independent order, 1619.

Carberry Hill, Midlothian. Mary Stuart and James Bothwell surrendered to the confederate lords of Scotland, 15 June 1567.

Carbolic Acid. Discovered by Runge, 1834.

Carbonari. Secret society, originated in Naples between 1806 and 1814. Spread to the whole of Italy by 1820. Adherence made high treason in Piedmont and Naples, 1821. Active, 1830–1.

Carcassonne, France. Oldest fortifications still existing seventh century. Completed in present form, thirteenth century. Restored late nineteenth century by Viollet-le-Duc. C. occupied by Saracens, 725–c. 750.

Cardiff, S. Wales. Site occupied since first century A.D., when Roman fort established. Besieged by Owen Glendower, 1404. Oldest charter extant, dated 14 Oct. 1338. Second Marquess of Bute began building dock system, 1830. University College of S. Wales and Monmouthshire established at, 1883. Raised to city status, 1905. Castle presented to citizens of C. by Marquess of Bute, 1947. C. made capital of Wales, Dec. 1955.

Cardinals (*see also* CONCLAVE). Term first applied to chief priest of a Roman parish. Pope Stephen III, about A.D. 770, seems to have been the first to select seven bishops out of the Roman see and give them the title of cardinal. The Council of Rome, under Pope Nicholas II, 1059, granted the College of C. the principal voice in the election of a pope. The number in the College of C. was fixed at seventy in 1586. Number increased by Pope John XXIII (1958–63). Style of 'Eminence' conferred by Urban VIII.

Cards, Playing, and Games of Cards. Earliest written allusion quotes a manuscript of 1299 (Italian). Chinese dictionary of seventeenth century claims for China the invention in 1120. They spread rapidly in fifteenth century. Before 1463 C. were manufactured in England, where a duty was first imposed in 1615. Sixpence per pack was imposed, 1710; raised to 1s., 1756; 1s. 6d., 1767;

2s. 1789; 2s. 6d., 1801; lowered to 1s., 1828; 3d. 1862.

Caribbean Federation. Established by the British Federation Act, 1956, and the W. Indies Order in Council, 1957. Lord Hailes took up appointment as first governor-general, Jan. 1958. Jamaica voted to leave it, Sept. 1961. Trinidad decided to leave, Jan. 1962. Federation dissolved, Apr. 1962.

Carinthia (Kärnten), duchy of the Holy Roman Empire and Austrian province. Last independent duke, Boruch, accepted Bavarian suzerainty and baptism, 738. Conquered by Franks under Charlemagne, 791–7. Became part of Ostmark, 811. Part of kingdom of Bohemia, 1270. Acquired by Rudolph of Hapsburg, 1276. Pawned to the counts of Gorizia, but recovered, 1335. Occupied by French, 1809–13; partly by Serbs and Slovenes, 1919 and 1945; by British, 1945. Plebiscite of 1920 awarded few parishes each to Italy and Yugoslavia.

Carlisle, England. *Luguvallium* of Roman Britain, the Celtic *Caer-luel.* Mentioned by Bede under the year 687 as an inhabited 'city.' Sacked by Danes under Halfdan Ragnarsson, 875. Fortified by William Rufus, 1092; diocese of, 1133; grammar school, 1170; Charles II entered, 6 Aug, 1651; surrendered to Young Pretender, 15 Nov. 1745; submitted to Duke ('Butcher') of Cumberland, 15 Dec. 1745. Public-houses and breweries all acquired by state, 1916; Licensing Act of 1921 transferred the wholesale and retail licensed trade of C. to the Home Secretary.

Carlists (Spain). Supporters of Don Carlos of Bourbon's claim to the Spanish throne. Principally to be found among the Basques they fought two civil wars, 1834–9 and 1872–6, and there were abortive short-lived Carlist risings in 1846 and 1848. Finally suppressed, 1875.

Carlsbad (Karlovy Vary), Bohemia. Medicinal hot springs patronized by Emperor Charles IV, 1358; baths founded 1364. Congress of Powers, 1819, to repress Liberal press, etc. Liberated, Apr. 1945, by U.S. troops under General Patton.

Carmelite Order. Founded by Berthold, Count of Limoges, about 1156 on Mt. Carmel; received its first rule from Albert, Patriarch of Jerusalem, 1209; sanctioned by Pope Honorius III, 1226. Driven out of Palestine by the Saracens, 1238. Pope Innocent IV changed the Carmelites from hermits to mendicant friars, 1247. First general chapter held in England, 1247. Nuns affiliated to the order from 1452. Teresa of Avila reformed the Carmelite nuns, 1562.

Carnarvon or **Caernarvon,** Wales. A Roman military station and residence of a Welsh prince till c. 893. Castle built by Edward I, 1284. First English Prince of Wales (afterwards Edward II) b. at, 25 Apr. 1284. Prince of Wales (later Edward VIII) invested at, 13 July 1911.

Carnatic, India. Taken under direct British rule, 1801.

Carnegie Trust Funds. Administered by a corporation set up, 1911, and also by the Carnegie Foundation for the Advancement of Teaching (instituted 1906), both in U.S.A. Carnegie Trust for universities of Scotland was instituted, 1901, and Carnegie United Kingdom Trust, 1914. Carnegie Endowment for International Peace instituted, 1910.

Caroline Islands. First sighted by Portuguese under Diego da Rocha, 1537. Ruled successively by Portugal and Spain, 1537–1899; sold to Germany, 1899. Mandate entrusted to Japan, 1919. Surrendered to United Nations, 1945, and naval base dismantled. Administered by U.S.A. since 1946 as a U.N. Trusteeship.

Carolingian Dynasty. *See* FRANCE.

Carpet-Bagger, absentee political candidate in U.S.A., especially of the 'Reconstruction' period in the S. c. 1865–7.

Carron Iron Works, oldest working foundry in the U.K., founded 1759, primarily for the manufacture of the short naval gun called carronade (invented, 1752). Manufacture changed, 1852, when cast-iron ordnance became obsolete, to lamp-posts, grates, etc.

Cartagena, Spain. Founded by Carthaginian Hasdrubal as capital of Carthaginian Spain c. 227 B.C. Captured by Scipio Africanus the Elder, 210 B.C. Sacked by Goths, A.D. 425, and by Drake, 1588. Republican naval base during war, 1936–9, and bombed several times.

Cartel, term first used in Germany, 1879, to describe a combine of railway material manufacturers. Laws passed in British and American occupation zones of Germany made Cs. illegal, 1947. *See also* TRUSTS.

Carthage. Phoenician city founded near site of modern Tunis c. 700 B.C. Concluded commercial treaty with Rome, 509. Attempt to conquer Sicily defeated at Himera, 480. N. African Empire reached its height, fourth century B.C. First war with Rome (q.v.) (First Punic war), 264–241 B.C. Second Punic War begun, 218, as result of Hannibal's capture of Saguntum in previous year. His victory at Cannae, 216. The destruction of Hannibal's brother Hasdrubal's army at the Metaurus, 207, led to the conquest of Carthaginian Spain by the Romans, and their invasion of Africa resulted in

Hannibal's defeat at Zama, 202. C. accepted terms of peace, 201. In the Third Punic War (149–146 B.C.) the Romans destroyed the city after a three-year siege. Rebuilt, 10 B.C.–A.D. 10 and named Colonia Julia Carthago. Captured by Vandals, A.D. 439, who made it their capital till its reconquest by Belisarius, 533. Finally destroyed by the Arabs. 697

Carthusian Order. Founded by St. Bruno, A.D. 1086; recognized by pope, 1176. In England the Carthusians settled in 1180, and had a famous monastery in London, since called the 'Charterhouse,' founded 1371. Female branch instituted at Salette, France, 1229.

Casablanca, Morocco. Founded fifteenth century by Portuguese. Taken by French, 1907. Conference of allied statesmen at which President Roosevelt demanded unconditional surrender of Axis powers, 14–24 Jan. 1943.

Cashel, Rock of, Tipperary. Fortress built by Cormack MacCarthy, King of Munster, 1127, and cathedral built, 1169.

Casket Letters. Documents relating to the events of 1567 and the murder of Darnley, produced by the Earl of Morton before Commissions at London and York; the originals were lost after 1584 and never recovered. Authenticity doubted by many historians.

Cassel or Kassel, Germany. Fortified, 1526. Refuge for French Protestants after 1685. Taken by French, 1760; besieged by Count Lippe, 1761, and by Prince Ferdinand, who took it, 1 Nov. 1762; fortifications destroyed, 1767; occupied by French, 1806. Capital of kingdom of Westphalia, 1807–13.

Cassino. *See* MONTECASSINO.

Castel Gandolfo. Papal villa near Lake Albano, built by the architect Carlo Maderno (1556–1629) on estate bought by Clement VIII, 1596. It was used by the popes as a summer residence until 1870, and again since 1929, when C. G. was declared part of the Vatican City.

Castile, Spain. First Count Roderic, A.D. 791. Subject to Leon till 1028, when it was seized by Sancho, King of Navarre, who gave it as a kingdom to his son Ferdinand, first King of C., 1039. Alfonso VI captured Toledo, 1085, but severely defeated by the Almoravides (*q.v.*) at Zallaca, 1086. Alfonso VIII defeated by Almohades (*q.v.*) at Alarcos, 1195, but in alliance with Aragon and Navarre won crushing victory at Navas de Tolosa, 1212. Ferdinand and Isabella sovereigns of, 1474. Moors finally driven out, 1492. United with Aragon under Spanish crown, 1504.

Castile and Leon, Heads of State of (from 1033). Though Ferdinand I ranks as the first King of C. proper, this monarchy traced its history back to the Christian remnant which continued to resist at the height of Mohammedan power in Spain. This early history, however, is obscure, and many of the kings mentioned are known merely as names.

C. and L., although often ruled by the same sovereign, were not finally united until 1230, under (Saint) Ferdinand III.

Sovereign	Leon	Castile
Ferdinand I, the Great	1037–1065	1039–1065
Sancho II		1065–1072
Alfonso VI	1065–1109	1072–1109
Urraca	1109–1126	1109–1126
Alfonso VII	1126–1157	1126–1157
Sancho III		1157–1158
Ferdinand II	1157–1188	
Alfonso VIII, the Good		1158–1214
Alfonso IX, the Slobberer	1188–1230	
Enrique I		1214–1217
Ferdinand III, the Saint	1230–1252	1217–1252

Kings of Castile and Leon:

Alfonso X, the Wise	1252–1284
Sancho IV, the Fierce	1284–1296
Ferdinand IV	1296–1312
Alfonso XI, the Avenger	1312–1350
Pedro I, the Cruel	1350–1368
Enrique II, the Bastard, or the Magnificent	1368–1379
Juan I	1379–1390
Enrique III, the Sickly	1390–1406
Juan II	1406–1454
Enrique IV, the Impotent	1454–1474
{ Isabella the Catholic	1474–1504
{ Ferdinand V, the Catholic	1474–1504
(from 1479 Ferdinand II of Aragon)	
Joanna and Philip	1504–1506
Ferdinand V (again)	1506–1516

See further under SPAIN.

Catalonia, Spain. (Sp. **Cataluña;** Cat. **Catalunya.**) Conquered by Moors, 712. By Charlemagne, 788. United with Aragon (q.v.), 1137. Philip IV of Spain attempted to suppress liberties, 1640. Occupation by French, 1640–59, 1694–7. Liberties and cortes abolished by Philip V, 1714. Civil war, 1823. Divided in four provinces, 1833. Granted local autonomy, 1932–4: then declared a federal republic. Supported Republicans in civil war of 1936–9. Deprived of autonomy, 1939.

Catania, Sicily. Founded by Greeks, 729 B.C. Population removed by Hiero I to Leontini, 467 B.C.; returned, 461 B.C. C. plundered by Dionysius I, 403 B.C.

Became subject to Rome, 263 B.C. Cathedral built eleventh–eighteenth centuries; fort, A.D. 1237; university, 1434. Volcanic disasters, 123 B.C., A.D. 1669, 1693. Captured by Eighth Army after heavy fighting, 5 Aug. 1943.

Câteau Cambrésis, Peace of. Between Philip II of Spain and Élizabeth of England of the one part and Henry II of France of the other, 2–3 Apr. 1559. Calais was finally ceded to France by this treaty.

Catechisms, the earliest written schemes extant are those of Kero of St. Gall (eighth century) and Otfried of Weissenburg (ninth century). For early Protestant C. *see* REFORMATION; these provoked the *Summa Doctrinarum* of Peter Canisius, 1566; that of the Council of Trent (*q.v.*); and other C. of the counter-reformation, e.g. those of Bellarmine, 1603; Bossuet, 1687. A modern Roman catechism is the *Schema de Parvo*, 1870. The Calvinists used the *Geneva Catechism*, 1536, and, in Scotland, Craig's, 1592. The Church of England produced a catechism contemporaneously with the Prayer Book in 1549, expanded in the reign of James I; that now in use was compiled by the Assembly of Divines, 1648.

Catharists. Sect of Gnostics, whose heresy penetrated S. France in the tenth century and was eradicated in the fourteenth. *See* ALBIGENSES.

Cathedrals in England. The following are the principal Anglican cathedrals with dates of foundation (F.) and of the major part of the present building (P.).

	F.	P.
Birmingham		1711–1719
Blackburn		1826
Bradford		14th cent.
Bristol	11th cent.	1306–1337
Canterbury	600	1174–1400
Carlisle	1092–1419	
Chelmsford		19th cent.
	F.	P.
Chester	1053	1200–1315
		and 1485–1537
Chichester	1108	1187–1210
Coventry [1]	15th cent.	1956–1962
Durham	995	1104–1133
Ely	673	1100–1327
Exeter	1050	1260–1291
Gloucester	681	1089–1100
		and 1450–1500
Guildford	1936	1936–1961
Hereford	c. 680	1110–1220
Leicester		14th cent.
Lichfield	672	1200–1321
Lincoln	628	1140–1280
Liverpool	1904	1904–

London·		
(1) Westminster		13th–16th
Abbey	618	cent.
(2) St. Paul's	7th cent.	1674–1710
Manchester	1847	19th cent.
Newcastle		1400–1474
Norwich	1094	1274–1446
Oxford	727	1180–1480
Peterborough	667	1118–1237
Portsmouth	1190	1683–1695
Ripon	678	1330–1450
Rochester	601	1080–1137
St. Albans	793	c. 1360
St. Edmundsbury		15th cent.
Salisbury		1220–1258
Sheffield		15th cent.
Southwark	c. 7th cent.	12th cent.
		and 1470–1500
Southwell		1110–1250
Truro	1880	1887–1903
Wakefield		15th cent.
Wells	704	1306–1333
Winchester	c. 7th cent.	12th cent.
		and 1367–1404
Worcester	964	1224–1374
York	627	1227–1361

[1] Original fabric, except for the spire, destroyed by bombing, 14 Nov. 1940.

Cathedrals, Roman Catholic, in England and Wales (O = Opened; C = Consecrated): Birmingham (of St. Chad) (O) 1808, (C) 1841; Brentwood (of the Sacred Heart and St. Helen) (O) 1836, (C) 1869; Cardiff (of St. David). Destroyed by enemy action, 1941. Now rebuilt. (O) 1836, (C) 1887; Clifton (of the Apostles) (O) 1848, (C) 1848; Hexham and Newcastle (of St. Mary) (O) 1844, (C) 1860; Lancaster (of St. Peter) (O) 1799, (C) 1859; Leeds (of St. Anne) (O) 1838, (C) 1904; Liverpool ((old) of St. Nicholas) (O) 1807, (C) 1815; ((new) of Christ the King), 1933; Menevia (Wrexham) (of Our Lady of Dolours) (O) 1857, (C) 1907; Middlesbrough (of St. Mary) (O) 1868, (C) 1911; Northampton (of St. Mary and St. Thomas) (O) 1825, (C) 1864; Nottingham (of St. Barnabas) (O) 1842, (C) 1844; Plymouth (of St. Mary and St. Boniface) (O) 1858, (C) 1880; Portsmouth (of St. John, Evangelist) (O) 1882, (C) 1887; Salford (of St. John) (O) 1848, (C) 1890; Shrewsbury (of Our Lady Help of Christians and St. Peter of Alcantara) (O) 1856, (C) 1891; Southwark (of St. George). Seriously damaged during World War II. Restored since. (O) 1841, (C) 1894; Westminster (of the Most Precious Blood) (O) 1903, (C) 1910.

Cathedrals, Church in Wales. Prior to the disestablishment of 1920 there were only four dioceses in Wales—Bangor, Llandaff, St. David's, and St. Asaph's. On the formation of a disestablished

Anglican Church in Wales, 1920, two new dioceses were created, and existing churches in Brecon and Newport became Cs.

The following are the principal Welsh cathedrals with dates of foundation (F.) and of the major part of the present building (P.).

	F.	P.
Bangor	before 545	1496–1532
Brecon	1923	13th–14th cent.
Llandaff	before 612?	12th cent.
Newport	1921	c. 1150
St. Asaph's	6th cent.	15th cent.
St. David's	before 601 ?	1180

Catholic Apostolic Church (Irvingites). Founded by Edward Irving (1792–1834), who seceded from the Presbyterian Church having been deposed from the ministry. The sect assumed the name C.A.C., 1832. The last of the original 'Apostles' d. 1901.

Catholic Association, Irish. Organized, 1824; Act for its suppression, 1825, but it continued until 12 Feb. 1829, when it was voluntarily dissolved.

Catholic Emancipation from sundry disabilities under the Penal Laws (1665, etc.) was begun in Britain by an Act introduced by Sir George Saville, 1778. This provoked the Gordon Riots (q.v.) and other disturbances in Scotland, and remained a dead letter. In 1791 a further Act was passed for England, and extended to Scotland, 1792. Some disabilities removed from Irish Catholics by Acts of 1774, 1778, 1782, and 1790. More comprehensive was the C. E. Bill which became law in 1829, and also applied to Ireland. The offices of sovereign, regent, lord chancellor, lord keeper (Great Britain), and lord high commissioner (to the Church of Scotland) remain (1963) closed to Catholics. *See* CLARENDON CODE.

Catholic League in France. Organized against Huguenots (q.v.) by the Duke of Guise. *See* HOLY LEAGUE (4).

Catholics, Old. *See* OLD CATHOLICS.

Catholic Truth Society. Established, 1872, revised and enlarged, 1884.

Cato Street Conspiracy. Formed by Arthur Thistlewood, 23 Feb. 1820, to murder Lord Castlereagh and other ministers. Thistlewood executed with four accomplices, 1 May 1820.

Cattaro. *See* KOTOR.

Cavell Memorial. London, 1920; inscription added, 1924; commemorates British nurse, Edith Cavell, executed by German military authorities, 12 Oct. 1915.

Caves of a Thousand Buddhas. Rock-cut shrines of Kansu, China, date from the mid fourth century A.D., but mostly dug out and embellished between 618 and 1276.

Cawnpore, now **Kanpur,** India. Formally possessed by Great Britain, 1801. Besieged by Nana Sahib, 1857; massacre of women and children by mutineers, 6 June 1857.

Caxton, William (c. 1422–91), set up the first printing press in England at Westminster Abbey, 1476.

Cayman Islands. A dependency of Jamaica (q.v.), described by Columbus, 1503, then by William Jackson, 1643. Victualling point for the Commonwealth Navy, 1655.

Celebes was a Portuguese possession, 1545–1000, and finally came into Dutch hands, 1669. Became part of Indonesia, 1950.

Celibacy of the Clergy. Spanish synod of Elvira first council to enjoin it on clergy, A.D. 305; condemned by Vigilantius, a presbyter of Barcelona, A.D. 406; strictly enjoined by council of 649; strictly enforced by Gregory VII, 1073.

Celluloid. Patented in Britain by Parkes, 1855; improvements made in America by Hyatt, 1870.

C.E.M.A. (Council for the Encouragement of Music and the Arts). Set up 1 Jan. 1940. Became the Arts Council of Great Britain (q.v.). 9 Aug. 1946.

Cenotaph (Whitehall, London). Temporary structure, July 1919; permanent, 1920.

Censorship of Drama is exercised by the Lord Chamberlain, whose activities in this sphere began before 1509, at first through a functionary of his department called the Master of the Revels; at intervals up to the complete outlawry of the theatre under the Commonwealth, C. was exercised, on political grounds, by the Star Chamber. The powers of the Lord Chamberlain became statutory by an Act of 1737 under the terms of which the Examiner of Plays was appointed. He was allowed complete discretion until 1843, when the Theatres Act laid down principles on which plays were to be licensed or refused licence, and also permitted the licensing of playhouses, hitherto the prerogative of the crown alone, by other authorities. This law is still in force to-day, though practice has been greatly modified by the findings of a Joint Committee of the Houses of Parliament sitting in 1909 and the pressure of intelligent public opinion as expressed, for instance, in Shaw's preface to *The Showing-up of Blanco Posnet,* 1909.

Theatre clubs are not subject to censorship.

Censorship of Films (Britain). British Board of Film Censors established, 1912.

Census. A C. Bill was introduced into Parliament, 1753, but rejected on the plea that a C. was dangerous to the liberties of free-born Englishmen. The first C. taken in Great Britain, 1801. C. extended to cover British Empire, 1871. In U.S.A. the first C., 1790. National Register made, 24 Sept. 1939.

CENTO. (Central Treaty Organization). Formerly the Bagdad Pact (q.v.). Iraq ceased to take part in the Pact, July 1958, and withdrew formally, 24 Mar. 1959. Headquarters transferred from Bagdad to Ankara, Oct. 1958. Name of organization changed to CENTO on 21 Aug. 1959.

Central Africa Office. New government department instituted, 19 Mar. 1962, under R. A. Butler, the Home Secretary.

Central African Federation. *See* RHODESIA AND NYASALAND, FEDERATION OF.

Central African Republic. Formerly one of the four territories of French Equatorial Africa (Ubangi Shari), became a member state of the French Community, 1 Dec. 1948, and independent, 13 Aug. 1960.

Central Criminal Court. *See* OLD BAILEY.

Central Electricity Authority. *See* BRITISH ELECTRICITY AUTHORITY.

Central Provinces and Berar. *See* MADHYA PRADESH.

Central Treaty Organization. *See* CENTO.

Cetatea Alba, Bessarabia, now part of Soviet Ukraine and renamed Belgorod-Dnestrovskiy. *See* AKKERMAN.

Cetinje, Yugoslavia. Ancient capital of Montenegro (q.v.), founded, 1485. Captured but not held by the Turks, 1683, 1714, 1785. Captured by Austrians, 13 Jan. 1916, and by Serbs, 4 Nov. 1918.

Ceylon. First European landing by Portuguese,1505. First Portuguese settlement, 1517. Taken by Dutch, 1656–8; by English, 1795–6. Ceded to Britain by Treaty of Amiens, 1802. British sovereignty universally recognized, Mar. 1815. Constitutional commission, 1928; proposed constitution modelled on that of L.C.C., which was instituted 1929. Kandy headquarters of Supreme Commander, Far East, in World War II. University of C. established, 1942. New constitution on Parliament model, 1946. C. became a self-governing Dominion within the Commonwealth, 4 Feb. 1948. Bandaranaike, the Prime Minister, assassinated by Buddhist extremists, Sept.

1957. Coup to overthrow government failed, 1961. Governor-general of C., Sir Oliver Goonetilleke, resigned, Feb. 1962, to enable him to answer queries regarding the coup of 1961. Succeeded by Mr. William Gopallawa.

Chaco or **Gran Chaco.** For wars in *see* BOLIVIA *and* PARAGUAY.

Chad. Accepted French protectorate, 1903. Ceased to be a dependency of Ubangi-Shari Colony, 1920. French penetration of the region had begun in 1885. Under its African governor, Felix Eboué (d. 1944), C. was the first French colony to declare for Fighting France, 26 Aug. 1940. Forces based on C. began to raid Axis outposts in the Fezzan, Jan. 1941. In the winter of 1942–3 they completed the conquest of the Fezzan, and the Colonne du Chad or Colonne Leclerc effected a junction with the Eighth Army between Tripoli and Sfax. Member state of the French Community, 28 Nov. 1958. Became an independent republic, 11 Aug. 1960. Member of U.N. since 26 Sept. 1960.

Chalcedon (Turk. **Kadikeui**). Founded as a colony by the Megarians, 685 B.C., but was absorbed by Pergamum (q.v.), whose king bequeathed it to Rome, 133 B.C. Ravaged by the Goths, notably in A.D. 256, and the Persians (616–26). The Council of C., 451, determined the bounds of the sees of Rome and Byzantium, C. being by then virtually a suburb of the latter, though separated from it by the Bosphorus. It was destroyed by the Turks after 1075.

Chaldea. *See* BABYLONIA, where the Chaldeans formed the ruling class from the eighth century B.C. until the death of Labashi Marduk, 556. *See also* UR OF THE CHALDEES.

Chaleurs Bay (Baie des Chaleurs), Canada. Discovered by Cartier, 1535.

'Challenger' Expedition. British scientific expedition under Capt. (later Sir) George Nares left England in the ship *Challenger*, 7 Dec. 1872, and returned, 24 May 1876.

Châlons, Battle of. Name of a battle now believed to have been fought near Troyes, in which Attila, King of the Huns, was defeated by Aetius and Theodoric, A.D. 451.

Chamberlain, Lord. In Britain, one of the chief officers of state from the thirteenth century. Parliament declared he must be a member of the Council *ex officio*, 1406. Remains to-day an officer of very high standing in the royal household. Lord Scarbrough, L.C. 1952–62, was succeeded by Lord Cobbold in Jan. 1963.

Chambers of Commerce. First Chamber of Commerce founded in France, 1599.

The oldest in Great Britain is at Glasgow, incorporated 1 Jan. 1783; Manchester Chamber of Commerce instituted, 1794; London, 1881. New York Chamber instituted, 1768; incorporated, 1770.

'Chambers of Reunion.' Established by Louis XIV of France for the purpose of asserting claims, through old feudal titles, to territories on German frontier, 1679.

Chambre Introuvable (Fr. **Matchless Chamber**). Chamber of Deputies which met, 1815, and which was ultra-Royalist.

'Chambres Ardentes.' French courts originally for trial of nobles. Notably those instituted under Francis I in 1535 for trial of heretics, and revived by Henry II, Oct. 1547. Under Louis XIV a *chambre ardente* tried poisoners, and condemned the Marquise de Brinvilliers in 1676: this court was abolished in 1682; but C. A. for the trial of embezzling farmers of the public revenues operated during the minority of Louis XV.

Champagne, France. Annexed to crown of Navarre by Theobald, 1234; passed to French crown by marriage of Philip IV to Joanna of Navarre, 1284; invaded by Emperor Charles V, 1523; entered by Prussians under Duke of Brunswick, 1792.

Champ de Mars, Paris. First Grand Federation of the, 14 July 1790; the second, 14 July 1791, at which a petition was signed praying for the abdication of Louis XVI. International Exhibitions of 1867, 1878, 1889, 1900, and 1937 held here.

Champlain, Lake, U.S.A. Discovered by Samuel de C., 1609. Scene of British naval defeat by the Americans, 1814.

Chanak. *See* TURKISH REPUBLIC. Occupied by British as a check to Kemalist advance, Sept. 1922; evacuated, Oct. 1923.

Chancellor, Lord High (Lat. *Cancellarius* = Usher or Chief Clerk). Originally an official responsible for preparation of writs and who acted as clerk of the council. Name C. said to have been used first in England during reign of Edward the Elder, 920. Was nearly always a cleric in the Middle Ages, and rose into prominence by administering equity and by presiding for the king over the House of Lords. First recorded as sitting in the chancery as a judge, 1377. Independent jurisdiction existed by 1474. The following are the most notable since Henry VII:

Cardinal Wolsey, 1515.
Sir Thomas More, 1529.
Stephen Gardiner, Bishop of Winchester, 1553.
Sir Francis Bacon, 1617.
Edward Hyde, Earl of Clarendon, 1660.

Anthony Ashley Cooper, Earl of Shaftesbury, 1672.
George, Lord Jeffreys, 1685.
Philip Yorke, Lord Hardwicke, 1737.
Edward, Lord Thurlow, 1778, 1783.
John Scott, Lord Eldon, 1801, 1807.
Thomas, Lord Erskine, 1806.
John Singleton Copley, Lord Lyndhurst, 1827, 1834, 1841.
Henry, Lord Brougham and Vaux, 1830.
Robert Monsey Rolfe, Lord Cranworth, 1852, 1865.
Frederic Thesiger, Lord Chelmsford, 1858, 1866.
John, Lord Campbell, 1859.
Richard Bethell, Lord Westbury, 1861.
Hugh McCalmont Cairns, Lord Cairns, 1868, 1874.
William Page Wood, Lord Hatherley, 1868.
Roundell Palmer, Lord Selborne, 1872, 1880.
Sir Hardinge Stanley Gifford, Lord Halsbury, 1885, 1886, 1895, 1902.
Sir Farrer Herschel, Lord Herschel, 1886, 1892.
Robert Threshie Reid, Lord Loreburn, 1905.
Richard Burdon Haldane, Lord Haldane, 1912, 1924.
Sir Stanley Owen Buckmaster, Lord Buckmaster, 1915.
Sir Robert Bannatyne Finlay, Lord Finlay, 1916.
Frederick Edwin Smith, Lord Birkenhead, 1919.
George, Lord Cave, 1922.
Sir Douglas McGarel Hogg, Lord Hailsham, 1924, 1935.
Sir John Sankey, Lord Sankey, 1929, 1931.
Sir Frederic Herbert Maugham, Lord Maugham, 1938.
Sir Thomas Inskip, Lord Caldecote, 1939.
Sir John Simon, Lord Simon, 1940.
William Allen, Visc. Jowitt, 1945.
Gavin Turnbull Simonds, Lord Simonds, 1951.
David Patrick Maxwell Fyfe, Visc. Kilmuir, 1954.
Reginald Manningham-Buller, Lord Dilhorne, 1962.

Chancellor of the Exchequer. *See* EXCHEQUER.

Chancellor of Ireland, Lord High. Earliest nomination that of Stephen Ridel during Richard I's reign, 1189. Office abolished, 1922.

Chancellor of Scotland, Lord High. Office abolished in 1707.

Chancery. *See* COURTS.

Chandernagore, India. Former French settlement in Bengal, founded 1673. Treaty transferring sovereignty to India, following referendum of 19 July 1949, ratified by French National Assembly, 11 Apr. 1952.

Changkufeng Incident. The hill of C. on the borders of Korea and Manchuria was seized by Japanese troops in order to bring under artillery observation a projected Russian submarine base at Possiet Bay, June 1938. Out of a skirmish between frontier guards there developed a full-scale battle, though neither side declared war. Finally the Japanese withdrew. *See also* NOMANHAN.

Channel Islands. Formed part of the duchy of Normandy when William I conquered England, 1066, and remained English after all other French territories were lost by the English crown. Part of the diocese of Coutances until 1568; then in the diocese of Winchester. Occupied by Germans, July 1940–May 1945. Constitutional reforms proposed for Jersey and Guernsey, 1946. Hague Court confirms British, not French, title, to Minquiers and Ecrehous reefs, 17 Nov. 1953. *See* ABBEVILLE Treaties (1).

Channel Tunnel. First suggested (to Napoleon I) by the French engineer Mathieu, and again after 1825 by English and French railway engineers. A horse roadway was planned by W. Low in 1867, and a model exhibited at the Paris Exhibition of that year. An English C. T. Co., formed in 1872, actually began digging, but work was stopped by the representations of the War Office. These excavations revealed the existence of the Kentish coal-field. The company continued in being, first as the Submarine Continental Railway, 1881, until after 1940. The Paris Chamber of Commerce passed a resolution favourable to it in 1904, as did the Chamber of Deputies later. A British parliamentary committee also reported favourably, 1930, but on 30 June 1930 the House of Commons rejected the project. Renewed interest in scheme after World War II. Since 1960 schemes for both a C. T. and a Channel Bridge have been put forward; Anglo-French committee was established to consider the feasibility of a Channel tunnel or bridge, 1961, and its report was expected to be published towards the end of 1963.

Chantrey Bequest. A fund left by Sir Francis Chantrey (1781–1841) to the Royal Academy for the encouragement of British painting and sculpture. First purchases made, 1877.

Chapel Royal of England existed, as a body of clergy and musicians, in the reign of Edward IV (1461–83), possibly earlier.

Chapel Royal of Scotland, founded by Alexander I (1107–24) at Stirling Castle,

and moved by Mary Stuart (1542–87) to Holyrood Abbey Church.

Charing Cross. The original C. C. was erected by Edward I in memory of his wife Eleanor, 1291, on the site of a former village called C., of which all trace but the name has vanished, immediately S. of Trafalgar Square. This cross was condemned and removed by order of Parliament, 1647. The present reproduction in the courtyard of C. C. Station was erected, 1865.

Charities. In England and Wales the Charitable Trusts Acts, 1853–1939, form the basis of modern charity administration. Charity Commission instituted under the Act of 1853 and reconstituted under the C. Act of 1960.

Charlemagne or **Charles I.** King of the Franks, the son of Pepin and Bertha; *b.* probably A.D. 2 Apr. 742, *d.* 28 Jan. 814. Crowned Emperor of the West by Pope Leo III, 800.

Charleston, S. Carolina. Founded by William Sayle *c.* 1670. (*See* FORT SUMTER.) There was a severe earthquake here in 1886.

Charlotte Amalie, capital of the Virgin Islands, was known between 1921 and 1937 as St. Thomas.

Charlottenburg. Former town of Brandenburg, Germany, incorporated into Berlin, 1920. Grew up round the palace built there in 1696 by Frederick I of Prussia.

Charter, The Great. *See* MAGNA CARTA.

Charterhouse. Corruption of *Chart-reuse.* Carthusian (*see* CARTHUSIAN ORDER) monastery founded in Clerkenwell, London, 1371, but when monasteries were dissolved by Henry VIII it was made a depository for the king's tents and pavilions, until granted to the Duke of Norfolk, 1539. Purchased by Thomas Sutton, who founded a school and hospital, 1611. School transferred to Godalming, Surrey, 1872.

Charters of Corporate Towns, granted by Henry I, gave security to industry and promoted manufactures, 1132; remodelled by Charles II, 1682; the new charter resisted at Nottingham, accepted by Plymouth and other corporations, 1684. Ancient C. restored, 1698; revised by Royal Commission, 1833; altered by Municipal Reform Act, 1835.

Chartism. A movement in Great Britain for extension of political power to the working classes, caused by economic distress. It began in 1836. In 1838 was drawn up by certain 'representatives of the people' the 'People's Charter,' and riots known as Chartist riots were enacted all over the country. By 1848

Chartres 90 Cherokees

extremists dominated the movement, which petered out by 1858.

Chartres, France. Besieged by Normans, 845 and 911. Henry I of England interviewed Pope Innocent II at, 1131; English from 1417 to 1431; taken by Count of Dunois, 1432; besieged by Duke of Condé, 1568. A fire is recorded in the cathedral as early as A.D. 753; extensive rebuilding, 1020–8. Towers built, 1145–1165; main part of present structure finished by 1260.

Chatham, England. Dockyard and arsenal built by Queen Elizabeth, 1588; removed to its present position, 1662. Surprised by Dutch under De Ruyter, 1667. New docks opened, 21 June 1871; additional docks completed, 1883; fortifications enlarged, 1888.

Chatham Chest. Charitable fund established by Sir Francis Drake and Sir John Hawkins in 1588. It was removed to Greenwich, 1802, and the fund incorporated with Greenwich Hospital.

Chatham House, St. James's Square, London, has been since 1923 the headquarters of the Royal Institute of International Affairs, which originated in 1919. An offshoot of Royal Institute of International Affairs is the Council of Foreign Relations in New York. Between 1919 and 1936 similar bodies were developed in Canada, New Zealand, Australia, S. Africa, and India.

Chatham Islands, now under New Zealand administration, were discovered, 1791, by Lieut. W. R. Broughton. Conquered, 1831, by a Maori expedition; the aboriginals virtually exterminated by 1849.

Cheapside, originally Chepe = The Market, was the commercial centre of medieval London. Laws regulating this market were codified under Edward I (1272–1307). Chaucer about 1380 and Lydgate in the early fifteenth century often refer to Chepe.

Cheb (Ger. **Eger**). Acquired by the Holy Roman Empire, 1000. Colonized by Germans under leadership of Bavarian Cistercian abbots, from 1100. Reichstag (q.v.) met at C., 1213, and Imperial Chamber of Princes, 1239. Became part of the kingdom of Bohemia for the first time in 1279, and finally in 1322. Wallenstein murdered in C. castle, 1634. From 1621 to 1918 the district had its own provincial Diet. Thereafter it became a headquarters of the Sudeten German movement. See SUDETENLAND.

Cheka. Name applied to Russian Soviet Secret Police, 1917–22.

Chelsea Hospital or College (London), for old and disabled soldiers of British Army. Foundation stone laid, 1682; building by Christopher Wren opened, 1694.

Cheltenham, England. Priory of Benedictines founded about 790. Edward the Confessor lord of the manor and granted a charter in 1041. The grammar school and almshouses founded, 1578, by Richard Pate. The C. waters were first discovered, 1716. Pump rooms were opened at montpellier and Pittville in 1809 and 1830 respectively. George III visited C., July 1788, to take the waters. The C. College was established in 1840, followed by the Ladies' College, 1854. The town was incorporated in 1876.

Chemistry. In earlier times known as alchemy, inaugurated in Egypt. Diocletian ordered the destruction of all the works of the alchemists, A.D. 297. A licence for practising alchemy was granted to Richard Carter in London, 1476. C. not a science until the seventeenth century. In 1772 Dr. Priestley published his discoveries, which commenced a new era in the science.

Chemnitz. Town in Upper Saxony, renamed Karl-Marx-Stadt with effect from 1 May 1953.

Chequers (Court). Bequeathed to the nation, with a trust fund for its upkeep for the use of successive Prime Ministers, by Lord Lee of Fareham (then Sir Arthur Lee), 1917. First occupied by David Lloyd George, 8 Jan. 1921.

Cheques. Lawrence Childs, a banker, first printed C. c. 1761. Rules with regard to bills of exchange, defined in the Bill of Exchange Act, 1882, also apply to C. By the Cheques Act of 1947 an unendorsed C. which appears to have been paid by the drawer's banker is evidence of receipt by the payee of the sum payable by cheque. Payment by cheque permissible to any employee from 1 Mar. 1963, subject to the employee's agreement.

Cherasco. 1. Armistice of, between Napoleon I and the King of Sardinia, 28 Apr. 1796. 2. Treaty of, between Louis XIII of France and Victor Amadeus of Savoy, 6 Apr. 1631.

Cherbourg, France. Captured by Henry V of England, Aug. 1418; retaken by French, 12 Aug. 1450; harbour-works planned by Vauban, 1686, but not finally completed until 1856; fortifications destroyed by English, Oct. 1758; further harbour-works constructed, 1886; occupied by Germans, 18 June 1940; captured from them by Americans, 25 June 1944.

Cherkassy, Ukraine. Belonged to Kiev in the Middle Ages; Lithuanian in 1362; Polish, 1569, Russian, 1793.

Chernigov, Ukraine. From 1024 to 1239 capital of a Grand Principality. Finally became Russian in 1654.

Cherokees. Tribe of N. American

Indians. Have a written alphabet of eighty-five letters invented by a half-breed, George Guess, in 1821. Disbanded as a tribe to become U.S. citizens, 1906.

Chesapeake Bay, U.S.A. Explored by Capt. John Smith, 1607, who arrived there with colonists. British incursions in, 1779. Comte de Grasse with French fleet arrived at, 30 Aug. 1781, and battle took place between French and English fleets, 5 Sept. 1781. Blockaded by English, 5 Feb. 1812.

Chess. Learnt by the Persians from India, where it was known in the seventh century. Persians' name for it was *shatranj.* In A.D. 950 an Arabic author, Masudi, spoke of the game as having existed before his time. *The Game and Playe of the Chesse,* second book printed by Caxton, probably appeared, 1475. The first important writer on modern C. was the Spaniard, Ruy López de Segura, 1561.

Chester, England. Called by the Britons *Caerleon.* The *Deva* of the Romans, whose XXth Legion was stationed there until the end of the fourth century. From the Britons it was taken by Ethelfrid, King of Northumbria, 607; at this battle, called by the English Legacester, the Britons deployed 2,100 monks of Bangor to pray for victory, of whom the English slew 1,200; Ethelfrid destroyed the town, 614, but presumably not the walls, as these were occupied by a Danish army in 894, which retained it till rebuilt by Ethelfleda, Countess of Mercia, *c.* 908. Britons once more masters *c.* 918, but soon driven out by Edward the Elder (*d.* 924). Taken by parliamentary forces, 1645. Castle attacked by Fenians, 1867. C. cathedral (originally a Benedictine abbey) dates from 1053.

Chicago, U.S.A. Site visited by Joliet and Marquette, 1673; Fort Dearborn built, 1803; Indians massacred the settlers, 1812; fort rebuilt, 1816; C. received first city charter, 1837; almost entirely destroyed by fire, 7–11 Oct. 1871; rebuilt, 1872–3; serious stockyard fire, May 1934.

Chichester, Sussex, England. Site of Roman town, Noviomagus. Cathedral completed *c.* 1108; rebuilt, 1187. City captured by Parliamentarians, 1643; fortifications destroyed, 1648. New theatre opened, 1962.

Children Acts. That of 1908 was introduced into the House of Commons by Visc. (then Sir Herbert) Samuel (*b.* 1870), and much amended by the Children and Young Persons Act, 1933, and the Children Acts of 1948 and 1952. All these acts now administered by the Children's Department of the Home Office, as recommended by the Curtis Committee, appointed to investigate the needs of children deprived of a normal home life, 1945.

Children, National Society for Prevention of Cruelty to, established by Benjamin Waugh (1839–1908) in 1884, and incorporated under royal charter, 1895. It brought about the passing of the Criminal Law Amendment Act, 1885, the Prevention of Cruelty to Children Act, 1889, and the Infant Life Protection Act, 1897.

Chile. Peruvians acquired territory from Indians inhabiting C., 1450. Discovered by Magellan, 1520. Peruvian dominion ceased, 1533. Spanish invasion, 1435–6, driven back. Detached from Peru, 1568. Treaty of Spain and C. fixing boundary, 1722. Chileans declared independence of Spain, 18 Sept. 1810. Constitution established, 25 May 1833. War declared against Spain, 29 Sept. 1865. Treaty with Peru against Spain, 14 Jan. 1866. War with Bolivia and Peru, 1 Mar. 1879. Peace treaty with Spain confirmed, Sept. 1881. Peace treaty with Bolivia, 25 Jan. 1882; war resumed, July 1882. Peace with Peru, 20 Oct. 1883, by which Peru ceded province of Tarapaca. Navy revolted against President, 7 Jan. 1891. Treaty ending territorial dispute between C. and Bolivia signed, 17 Oct. 1905. President dismissed and partially military junta formed, Sept. 1924. Junta upset by new one, 23 Jan. 1925. General strike at Valparaiso, 13 Feb. 1925. President returned, 30 Mar. 1925. New constitution adopted by plebiscite, 30 Aug. 1925. Roman Catholic Church disestablished, 1925. Tacna-Arica plebiscite, 1926. Education made compulsory between seven and fifteen, 1928. Tacna ceded to Peru by treaty, 1929. Military assistance pact with the U.S.A., 1952. Duke of Edinburgh visited C., 1962.

The following are the presidents of C.:

O'Higgins	1818–1823
Freire	1823–1830
Prieto	1830–1841
Bulnes	1841–1851
Montt (Manuel)	1851–1861
Perez	1861–1871
Zanartu	1871–1876
Pinto	1876–1881
Santa Maria	1881–1886
Balmacede	1886–1891
Montt (Jorge)	1891–1896
Errazuriz	1896–1901
Riesco	1901–1906
Montt (Pedro)	1906–1910
Albano	1910
Figueroa Larrain	1910

Luco	1910–1915
Sanfuentes	1915–1920
Alessandri	1920–1924
Altamirano	1924–1925
Codecido	1925
Alessandri (restored)	1925
Borgono	1925
Figueroa Larrain	1925–1927
Ibañez	1927–1931
Opazo	1931
	(1 day only)
Montero	1931
Trucco	1931
Montero (again)	1931–1932
Socialist Junta	1932
Davila	1932
Blanche	1932
Oyanedel	1932
Alessandri	1932–1938
Cerda	1938–1941
Mendez	1941–1942
Rios	1942–1946
Duhalde	1946
Bielech	1946
Videla	1946–1952
Ibañez (again)	1952–1958
Rodriguez	1958–

Chiltern Hundreds. An ancient statute was amended in 1707 to provide that a member of Parliament might resign only provided he held an office of profit under the crown. By the Place Act, 1742, the stewardship of the C. H. and of the manor of Northstead in Yorkshire were accounted offices of profit for this purpose. A steward of the C. H. was first appointed as a pretext for resignation, 1750.

Chimborazo. Volcanic mountain (height 20,660 ft.) in Ecuador. First ascent by Edward Whymper, 1880.

Chimneys. First introduced into England about 1200. Tax on C. called 'hearthmoney' levied, 1662; abolished, 1689.

China. Hsia Dynasty founded, 2205 B.C., and overthrown 1766 B.C. by T'ang, who founded the Shang Dynasty, which lasted until 1122 B.C., and had its capitals at Po, Nao, and Yin. In 1122 Wu Wang founded the Chou Dynasty, and during this epoch a feudal system came into being in China. In 771 B.C. fear of invasion from the W. led to the establishment of the capital at Loyang. The central authority declined and the Feudal States surrounding the capital gradually increased their authority, supported by strong armies. 479 B.C. is the beginning of the period of the seven 'Warring States.' Cavalry introduced into the kingdom of Chao, 307 B.C. China conquered by Ch'in, one of the seven states, and the Chou Dynasty overthrown, 256 B.C. The first emperor of the Ch'in Dynasty, Shih Huang Ti, is said to have ordered the

building of the Great Wall c. 220–210 B.C. Deportation to Shensi of the Chinese feudal nobility c. 220 B.C. The Burning of the Books c. 220 B.C. Death of Shih Huang Ti, 209 B.C. Ch'in Dynasty overthrown by revolution led by Lio Pang, who as the Emperor Kao Ti established the Han Dynasty, 206 B.C. Feudal fiefs made equally divisible among sons, 144 B.C. Accession of the Emperor Wu Ti, 140 B.C. Beginning of the wars against the Huns, 133 B.C. Conquest of Sinkiang, 130–120 B.C. Conquest of S. C. and Canton, 111 B.C. Chinese embassies reach Seleucid Empire, 120–104 B.C. Conquest of Laklang in Korea, 108 B.C. (Japan). Death of Emperor Wu Ti, 86 B.C. Submission of the Hun c. 54 B.C. Usurpation of Wang Mang, A.D. 9, and civil war ending in re-establishment of the Han Dynasty, A.D. 25. Pan Ch'ao organizes Turkestan, 72–102. Huns decisively defeated, 91. Rise of the palace eunuchs, 126–44. Diplomatic contacts with the Roman Empire, 166. Embassy of Emperor Huen to Marcus Aurelius Antoninus. Yellow Turban rising against eunuch government, 184; leads to civil war, end of the Han dynasty, 220, and the period of the Three Kingdoms, 220–65, followed by the Tsin Dynasty. Hun invasions begin again c. 304, leading to the establishment of a Hun kingdom at Loyang, 311, and the Tsin emperors established a new capital at Nanking, 316, and repel Hun attempt to conquer the S. at the battle of Fei Shui, 387. C. reunited under Wen Ti, founder of the Sui Dynasty, 581. This dynasty was overthrown in 618, and authority was re-established by Kao Tsu, who founded the T'ang Dynasty, and consolidated by his son, the Emperor T'ai Tsung. Rule of the Empress Wu Hou, 684–705. Accession of Hsuan Tung, 713. He makes Yang Fei Kuei his mistress, 745. An Lu Shan's rebellion against the royal extravagance, 755, suppressed by Kuo Tzu-i, 766. Weakening of the central power leads to rise of the war-lords, 770–850. Rebellion of the unpaid army in Annam led by Huang Ch'ao, 875, leads to capture of Chang An, 881, and overthrow of the T'angs, 907. The Five Dynasties Period is notable for the introduction of large-scale printing. C. reunited once more by Chao K'uang-yin, who as T'ai Tsu founded the Sung Dynasty, 960. Wars with the Kitans end in abandonment of the Great Wall by the Emperor Chen Tsung and peace, 1004. N. C. conquered by the Kin ('Golden') Horde, 1126, and established the Southern Sung Dynasty at Hang Chou, 1127. Beginning of the Mongol invasions, 1210. Mongols under

Ogotai capture Kai Feng and destroy the Kin state in N. China, 1233. Under Bayan they capture Hang Chou, 1276, extinguish the Sung Dynasty. 1279, and with the accession of Kublai Khan establish the Yüan Dynasty at Peking, 1260. The weakness of the Mongols after Kublai's death, 1294, leads to a Chinese revolt, 1348, which results in the Mongols being driven out of Nanking, 1356, and from Peking, 1368. Chu Yüanchang (Tai Tsu) establishes Ming Dynasty 1368, at Nanking. Yen seizes the throne, 1402, and reigns as Ch'eng Tsu. Capital moved to Peking, 1404, which was completed in its present form, 1422. Great Wall rebuilt, 1406–25. Chinese Army destroyed by Mongols at Huai Lai, 1450. Christianity introduced by Jesuit missionaries, sixteenth and seventeenth centuries, and made considerable progress in court circles. Portuguese ship under Perestrello reaches Canton, 1516. Portuguese driven back from Canton, 1522; Ningpo, 1542; Chüan Chou, 1549. They are allowed to settle at Macao, 1557. Dutch piracies on Chinese coast, 1607. Dutch attack Macao, 1622. Manchus invade Liao-Tung, 1625. Rebellion led by Li Tzu-cheng overthrows Ming Dynasty, 1644. The Ming general, Wu San-Kuei invites the Manchus to enter C., 1644. They defeat Li Tzu-cheng and seize the throne, founding the Manchu Dynasty, 1644. Accession of Kang Tsi (1662–1722) marked period of intellectual progress and great Christian influence at court. His successor, Yung Cheng, began the policy of 'exclusion.' Christians were persecuted. Final surrender of Ming claimants, 1683. Reign of Kao Tsung, 1735–95. English occupy Macao, 1802 and 1808. Admiral Maitland arrives at Macao, 12 July 1838. The 'Opium War' between Britain and C., 1840–2, ends with Treaty of Nanking, 29 Aug. 1842, under which Hong Kong was ceded to Britain. Tai-ping (Christian) rebellion in Kwangsi begins under leadership of Hung Hsiu-chuan, 1850. He is proclaimed king, 1851, and captures Nanking, 8 Mar. 1853. Anglo-French attack on C., 1857, ends Treaty of Tientsin, June 1858, and the Kung-Elgin Peace convention, 1860, by which in return for the management of the Chinese Customs the English and French were to assist in the suppression of the Tai-ping revolt. Korea becomes independent, 1876. Japan attacks C., 25 July 1894, and declares war, 2 Aug. Naval defeat at battle of the Yalu, 17 Sept. Massacre of Chinese at Port Arthur by Japanese, 21 Nov. 1894. Peace Treaty ratified with Japan, 8 May 1895.

Boxer riots, 1900. War between Russia and Japan in Manchuria, Korea, and the Chinese seas, 1904; by the Treaty of Portsmouth, U.S.A., Aug. 1905, Port Arthur and Dalny were leased to Japan; Korea annexed to Japan, 23 Aug. 1910; revolution, 1911–12, abdication of the last Manchu Emperor P'u-yi, 12 Feb. 1912, and the establishment of a republic with Yuan Shih-k'ai as provisional president, 15 Feb. 1912; Republican Parliament opened, 8 Apr. 1912; Yuan Shih-k'ai elected president for five years, 6 Oct. 1912; assassination of Sung-Chiao-jen, the national candidate for the premiership, Apr. 1913; Parliament dissolved, Sept. 1913; rebellion in the S. which was ended by the fall of Nanking, Sept. 1913; 300 members of the Kuomintang deprived of their parliamentary seats for their part in the rebellion in the S., Nov. 1913. In 1915 Yuan organized a campaign with view of reverting to monarchy, but southern provinces revolted and the plan ended with his death in 1916. In 1920 southern provinces declared an independent republic of S. C.; but in 1921 this deteriorated into a loose federation. Parliamentary government abolished by new 'Chief Executive' of northern government, 1924. Nine-Power Customs Tariff Treaty concluded by France's ratification, 12 Apr. 1925. Anti-Japanese riot at Shanghai, 30 May 1925. General strike at Shanghai, and European and Japanese cruiser crews fought rioters, June 1925. Similar rioting and reprisals at Canton, 23 June 1925. Tariff autonomy conceded by powers, 18 Nov. 1925. Civil war begun, Dec. 1925. Peking evacuated by 'Reds,' with Borodin and other Russian advisers, 16 Apr. 1926. March of the southern Nationalists from Hankow toward Shanghai, Oct.–Dec. 1926. Hong Kong boycotted, June 1925–10 Oct. 1926.

1927: Anti-European riots, Jan.; British agreed in principle to abolition of extraterritoriality, 27 Jan.; Cantonese checked by northern troops at Tsientang River, Feb.; general strike at Shanghai, Feb.–Mar.; British agreement with Cantonese at Hankow c. 20 Feb.; British forces arrived at Shanghai, Feb. and Mar.; Cantonese take Shanghai, 21 Mar.; Nanking, 24 Mar.; Communists suppressed by Cantonese with considerable bloodshed, Apr.; Nanking Nationalists, independent of Canton, intervened, June, disputing authority of N. and S.; Nanking troops hard pressed, mid July; Gen. Sun Chuan-fang fighting against Nationalists on the Yangtse, Aug.–Sept.; fierce anti-Japanese riots in Hankow, 5 Sept.; Chiang Kai-shek invaded Shantung, June; Chang Tso-lin counter-attacked, 18 June; Hankow declared war on Nanking, 9 July; Nationalist *coup d'état* at Hankow, 17 July; Nanking Government organized by the Kuomintang, Sept.; hostilities began between Hankow and Nanking Governments, 23 Oct.

1928: Chang Tso-lin routed by Chiang and Feng, and Peking Government ends. Commercial treaties with western powers, Dec.

1929: Disbandment conference, Jan. Kuomintang, third Party Congress, Mar. Japanese evacuate Shantung, May. Chang Fal-kwei's march on Canton, Sept. Feng Yu-hsiang's expedition against Nanking, Oct. Chiang compounds with Feng, and repulses Chang Fat-kwei, Dec.

1930: C. abolishes extra-territoriality, 1 Jan. Yen Hsi-shan and Feng seize Peking, Mar. Civil war, May–July.

1931: Japanese attack in Manchuria, 18 Sept.

1932: Japanese set up puppet republic in Manchukuo, 2 Jan. They occupy Shanghai, 28 Jan. Invade Jehol, 9 Dec.

1933: Japanese offensive N. of the Great Wall, Feb.–Mar. Armistice signed with Japan, but civil war in C. continues. Communists now a strong force in C., and quite independent of the official government.

1935: U.S.S.R. sells Chinese Eastern Railway to Japan, 23 Mar. Chiang Kai-shek President of Executive, 1 Dec.

1936: Chiang captures Canton, 11 Aug.

1937: The Peking 'Incident,' 7 July. War again breaks out between China and Japan. Japanese seize Peking, 8 Aug.; Shanghai, 9 Nov.; Nanking, 12–13 Dec.

1938: Japanese take Tsingtao, 10 Jan. Cut Lunghai Railway, 15 May. Land in force near Hong Kong, 12 Oct. Take Canton, 21 Oct., Hankow, 25 Oct. Burma Road completed, Dec.

1939: Japanese seize Hainan Island, 10 Feb. Britain co-operates in setting up exchange stabilization fund to support Chinese *yen* against Japanese sponsored *yuan*, 8 Mar. Japanese take Nanchang, 27 Mar. Japanese blockade British concession at Tientsin, 14 June.

1940: Britain closes Burma road, 18 July. Reopens, 18 Oct.

1941: C. breaks off relations with Axis, 2 July. Japanese take Hong Kong, 25 Dec.

1943: Cairo meeting (Churchill, Roosevelt, Chiang Kai-shek), 22–26 Nov.

1944: Japanese take Foochow, 5 Oct.

1945: Japanese surrender in C., 12 Sept. At the end of the war Communists in C. extremely powerful.

1946: Open warfare between Communists and Nationalists.

1947: U.S. ambassador, Gen. George Marshall, returns, having failed to conciliate Kuomintang and Communists; blames both sides equally and advises U.S.A. to support neither, Jan. New constitution comes into force, 26 Dec.

1948: Shansi and Honan overrun by Communists, Mar.; Suchow falls to them, Nov.

1949: Chiang Kai-shek 'resigns' from presidency, Jan. On fall of Peking, People's Republic proclaimed there by Communists, 21 Sept. Peking reinstated as capital. National Day (1 Oct.) instituted. People's Republic recognized by U.S.S.R., 2 Oct.; by Burma, 17 Dec.; India, 30 Dec.

1950: No effective Kuomintang administration, or organized resistance by its troops, on mainland. Peking Government recognized by Pakistan, 4 Jan.; Great Britain, 6 Jan. U.S.A. withheld recognition and still (1963) recognizes the government in Formosa as the legal Chinese government. Chiang Kai-shek 'resumed' presidency, in Taiwan (Formosa) (*q.v.*), 1 Mar. Peking troops intervened against the United Nations forces, Oct., in Korea (*q.v.*). Chinese forces invaded E. Tibet, Oct. Catholic University in Peking closed, Oct.

1951: Chinese offensive against U.N. in Korea, 1 Jan; by 4 Jan. Seoul in Communist hands. U.N. counter-attacked on 21 Jan. Further Chinese offensive in Apr. was thrown back by U.N. counter-attack starting 21 May. Chinese driven back across thirty-eighth parallel. Peace talks between Communists and U.N. forces opened at Kaesong, 10 July. Tibet accepted Chinese suzerainty, 23 May.

1952: State Planning Commission established, Nov. Purge of moderates and persecution of Christians went on throughout the year, and by Dec. all foreign Christian educational institutions had been merged in the State system.

1953: Start of first Five Year Plan, which included the organization of the peasants into 'People's Communes.' Cease-fire in Korea signed, 27 July.

1954: New constitution adopted by the First National People's Congress, 20 Sept.

1955: Renewed tension between U.S.A. and Chinese Communists regarding status of the 'off-shore' islands. The evacuation of the Tachen Islands by the Chinese Nationalists was successfully completed, with the help of the U.S. Seventh Fleet, Feb. Russians transferred the Port Arthur naval installations to the Chinese. Conscription introduced in China.

1956: Thirty-letter Latin alphabet adopted, Feb. Aimed to replace traditional Chinese script gradually. Consistent rumours reached West of dogmatic disagreements between C. and Russia. Eighth National Congress of the Chinese Communist Party met in Sept. and adopted a new constitution, which stated: 'Marxism-Leninism is not a dogma but a guide to action.'

1957: Chinese Roman Catholics, under the Archbishop of Shenyang, asserted their independence of Rome. Vatican treated this assertion as one made under duress.

1958: Second Five Year Plan. Concentrated bombardment of Quemoy Straits by Chinese Communists in July and from Oct. onwards. In Dec. it was announced that Mao Tse-tung was to cease to be chairman of the Republic, but would continue to be party chairman. His effective power unchanged.

1959: A rising against Chinese in Lhasa, capital of Tibet, 17 May. Civil war followed. Chinese soon repressed the revolt, and the Dalai Lama fled to India, 3 Mar. Tibetan government dissolved and a preparatory committee for the Tibetan Autonomous Region established, 28 Mar. Liu Shao-ch'i succeeded Mao Tse-tung as Chairman of the Republic, 27 Apr. Nehru reported that the Chinese had seized an Indian outpost, 18 Aug.; there were subsequently numerous border incidents between India and C. Dalai Lama appealed to U.N., 30 Aug.; a U.N. debate on Tibet held on 20 Oct.

1960: A ten-year agricultural programme to cover period 1956–67, adopted in Apr. Differences between Russia and C. appeared to be reconciled in the manifesto following the Moscow conference of international Communists in July.

1961: Disagreements between Russia and C. were apparent. Serious food shortages in C. admitted. These caused an influx of refugees into Hong Kong.

1962: Flood of refugees to Hong Kong so great that it was apparent they were being abetted in leaving C. by the Chinese authorities, May. Thousands turned back at border by British troops. Build-up of Chinese Communist troops on mainland opposite Quemoy and Matsu, June. U-2 from Formosa shot down over C., Sept. Oct.: Border dispute between C. and India flared into open warfare. Chinese made advances into Indian territory. Oct. 18–22: India obtained British and U.S. assistance in form of aircraft and weapons. By 3 Nov. a Chinese breakthrough in the N.E. threatened Assam. Chinese announced a cease-fire from midnight Nov. 20–1. C. supported Cuba in the crisis of Oct.–

Nov.; was again disallowed representation at the U.N., Nov.

1963: India accepted the Colombo Powers' proposals as a basis for negotiation with C. over the border dispute, Jan. Talks in Moscow to try to settle Sino-Soviet ideological differences ended in deadlock, July.

Dynasties, 2697 B.C.–A.D. 1126. Dynasties and Emperors, 1127–1911:

The Five Sovereigns (Legendary Epoch)	2697–2205 B.C.
The Hsia Dynasty	2205–1766 B.C.
The Shang or Yin Dynasty	1766–1122 B.C.
The Chou Dynasty	1122–255 B.C.
The Ch'in Dynasty	255–206 B.C.
The Han Dynasty	206 B.C.–A.D. 220
San Kuo (The Epoch of the Three Kingdoms)	220–265
The Tsin Dynasty	265–420
The Southern Dynasties	420–589
The Northern Dynasties	386–581
The Sui Dynasty	581–618
The T'ang Dynasty	618–907
Wu Tai (The Epoch of the Five Dynasties)	907–960
The Sung Dynasty [1]	960–1279

The Sung Dynasty (Southern Line), 1127–1279:

Kao Tsung (S. Sung)	1127–1162
Hsiao Tsung	1162–1189
Kuang Tsung	1189–1194
Ning Tsung	1194–1224
Li Tsung	1224–1264
Tu Tsung	1264–1274
Kung Ti	1274–1276
Tuan Tsung	1276–1278
Ti Ping	1278–1279

The Mongol (Yüan) Dynasty, 1206–1368 (Imperial title from 1279):

T'ai Tsu (Jenghiz Khan)	1206–1229
T'ai Tsung (Ogqtai Khan)	1229–1246
Ting Tsung (Kuyak Khan)	1246–1251
Hsien Tsung (Mangu Khan)	1251–1260
Shih Tsu (Kublai Khan)	1260–1294
Ch'eng Tsung	1294–1307
Wu Tsung	1307–1311
Jen Tsung	1311–1320
Ying Tsung	1320–1323
T'ai Ting Ti	1323–1328
Yu Chu	1328
Ming Tsung	1328–1329
Wen Tsung	1329–1332
Ning Tsung	1332–1333
Shun Ti	1333–1368

The Ming Dynasty, 1368–1644:

T'ai Tsu (Chu Yuan-chang)	1368–1398
Hui Ti	1398–1402
Ch'eng Tsu	1402–1424

[1] From 1127 the Sung Dynasty controlled a diminishing area of S. C. only.

Jen Tsung	1424–1425
Hsuan Tsung	1425–1435
Ying Tsung	1435–1449
Tai Tsung	1449–1457
Ying Tsung (restored)	1457–1464
Hsien Tsung	1464–1487
Hsiáo Tsung	1487–1505
Wu Tsung	1505–1521
Shih Tsung	1521–1566
Mu Tsung	1566–1572
Shen Tsung	1572–1620
Kuang Tsung	1620
Hsi Tsung	1620–1627
Ssu Tsung	1627–1644

The Manchu (Ch'ing) Dynasty, 1644–1911:

Shih Tsu	1644–1661
Kang Tsi	1662–1722
Yung Cheng	1723–1735
Kao Tsung	1735–1795
Jen Tsung	1795–1820
Hsuan Tsung	1820–1850
Wen Tsung	1850–1861
Mu Tsung	1861–1875
Teh Tsung	1875–1908
P'u-yi	1908–1911

Effective Heads of Administration from 1911 to the Present Day:

Yuan Shih-k'ai: President of the Republic of C., 1911–16.

Sun Yat-sen: President of the Republic of C., 1921–5.

Chiang Kai-shek: C.-in-C., Northern Armies, 1926; Generalissimo of the National Republic of C., 1928; Director-General of the Kuomintang, 1938; President of the National Republic of C., 1943; *effective ruler of the National Republic of C. from 1925, but rule confined to the island of Formosa from 1949.*

Mao Tse-tung: Chairman of the Council of People's Commissars in Communist S. C., 1931; Chairman of the Central People's Council of the People's Republic of C., Sept. 1949; Chairman of the Central Committee of the Chinese Communist Party only since Dec. 1958; *but effective ruler of all C., excluding the island of Formosa from 1949.* (Chairman of the People's Republic since 27 Apr. 1959, Liu Shao-ch'i.) *See also* FORMOSA; KOREA.

Chinese Eastern Railway, a Russian-built extension of the Trans-Siberian Railway, was sold to the Government of Manchukuo in 1935. Since 1945 part of the Chinese system, jointly owned and operated by China and the U.S.S.R.; to revert completely to China in 1975.

Chinese Labour Question. Proposed introduction of C. L. into Transvaal, Jan.

1904; first contingent arrived, 22 June 1904. Blue Book on, issued, 7 Dec. 1905. Debate in House of Lords, 4–10 Mar. 1904. Sir H. Campbell-Bannerman's motion of censure on the Government for allowing C. L. rejected, 21 Mar. 1904.

Chinese Literature.

(All poets unless otherwise indicated.)

Chang Chao, sixteenth century A.D.
Chang Fang-sheng, fourth century A.D.
Chang Tsai, third century A.D.
Ch'en Tzu-lung, A.D. 1607–47.
Ch'en Tzu-ang, A.D. 656–98.
Cheng Hsiao, *c.* A.D. 250.
Cheng-kung Sui, third century A.D.
Chien Wen-ti, sixth century A.D.
Chi Kang, A.D. 223–62.
Chin Chia, first century A.D.
Chü Yuan, 332–295 B.C.
Fu Hsüan, third century A.D.
Hsi Chün (Princess), second century B.C.
Hsieh T'iao, fifth century A.D.
Hsü Ling, A.D. 507–83.
Kung Fu-tze (Confucius the philosopher), 551 478 B.C.
Lao-tze, sixth century B.C., philosopher.
Li Po, A.D. 701–62.
Lu Yu, A.D. 1125–1209.
Lu Yün, fourth century A.D.
Miu Hsi, third century A.D.
Pao Chao, fifth century A.D.
Po Chü-i, A.D. 772–846.
Su Tung-po, A.D. 1036–1101.
Su Wu, *c.* 100 B.C.
Sung Tsu-Lou, second century A.D.
Sung Yü, fourth century B.C.
T'ao Ch'ien, A.D. 365–427.
T'ao Yün, *c.* A.D. 400.
Tsang Chih, sixth century A.D.
Tsao Chic (Prince), A.D. 192–233.
Tsao Sung, *c.* A.D. 900.
Tso Ssu, third century A.D.
Tu Fu, A.D. 712–70.
Wang Chi, *c.* A.D. 700.
Wei Wen-ti (Emperor), A.D. 188–227.
Wu Cheng-en, sixteenth century A.D., novelist.
Wu-ti (Emperor), 157–87 B.C.
Wu-ti (Emperor), A.D. 464–549.
Yang-ti (Emperor), seventh century A.D.
Yüan Chi, A.D. 210–63.
Yuan Chieh, eighth century A.D.
Yuan-ti, A.D. 508–54.

Chinon, France. Geoffrey of Anjou imprisoned in castle of C., 1068–96. Henry II of England *d.* at, 6 July 1189. Arrival of Joan of Arc at, to meet Charles VII, 24 Feb. 1429.

Chios. Anciently one of the more powerful Ionian maritime states, submitted to the Persians, 546 B.C., but liberated by the battle of Mykale, 479, when C. joined the Delian League. Revolted against Athenian domination, 413

B.C.; renewed alliance with Athens c. 403, but finally left the League, 357 B.C. Became part of the Roman Empire, 133. Under Genoese influence from A.D. 1346; conquered by Turks, but given considerable local autonomy, 1566; massacre by the Turks, 1822. C. became Greek territory after the First Balkan War in 1812. Devastated by earthquake, 1881. Used by British and French forces as a base for the Dardanelles operation, 1915. Revolt which led to fall of King Constantine began in C., 1922.

Chitral, NW. Frontier Province, Pakistan, administered as an agency. Virtually independent until 1895, when the British political agent, Dr. Robertson, and an Indian Army garrison were besieged in the fort of C., 4 Mar.–20 Apr., after which C. became a dependency of Kashmir, though still under its own mehtar or prince.

Chivalry, Court of. Species of court-martial for officers, established in Edward III's reign (1327–77), was regulated by Richard II, 1390. Between 1737 and 1955 tried no cases. In 1955 upheld Manchester Corporation's claim that a certain theatre should not display the civic coat of arms.

Chivalry, Orders of. See KNIGHTHOOD, ORDERS OF.

Chlorine. Discovered by Scheele, 1774; experiments of Gay-Lussac and Thénard, 1809; Davy proved it to be an element, and gave it its present name, 1810; apparatus for making C. invented by Smith, 1847; used in warfare by the Germans, Apr. 1915, and the British, Sept. 1915.

Chloroform. Discovered by Liebig, 1831. First used in 1847 by Bell and Simpson.

Chouans were Breton smugglers, at first under the leadership of Jean Cottereau (1767–94), who rose in revolt against the republican government, 1793. Their activities were mainly confined to the departments of Morbihan and Eure. The Vendéans proper, together with peasants of Anjou, Poitou, Maine, and Mayenne, rose in protest against the Convention's conscription decree of Feb. 1793; their Christian Army (later called Royal and Catholic Army) had possession of most of Brittany and Poitou by Sept. 1793, though they could not capture Nantes. Defeated at Châtillon in Oct., and at Savenay in Dec., the C. main body now dissolved but guerrilla warfare continued, supported by royalist infiltration from England, until the failure of the Quiberon expedition, 20 July 1795. State of siege declared at an end, 30 July 1796. In 1815 there was a Vendéan rising, and another in 1832 against the

Orleans monarchy, led by Mme de Berry.

Christ, Disciples of. See CAMPBELLITES.

Christadelphians. Sect founded in the U.S.A., 1848, by an Englishman, John Thomas (b. 1804).

Christchurch, New Zealand. Founded, 1851, by the Canterbury Association.

Christiania. See OSLO.

Christian Knowledge, Society for Promoting. Founded, 1698.

Christian Science. Theory of C. S. discovered by Mrs. Mary Baker Eddy, 1866. Church of Christ Scientist established in Boston, Massachusetts, 1879. Massachusetts Metaphysical College founded at Boston, 1881.

Christmas Island. In the W. Pacific, discovered by Cook, 1777. Annexed by Britain, 1898. Part of the Gilbert and Ellice Islands colony since 1919. Chosen as the site for British H.-bomb tests, 1957, and subsequently used also for American tests.

Christ's Hospital (The Bluecoat School). Founded, 1552, on site of the monastery of the Grey Friars, Newgate Street, London. Charter dated 26 June 1553. Mathematical ward added by Charles II, 1673. First stone of New Hall in London laid, 28 Apr. 1825; opened, 29 May 1829. School moved to W. Horsham, 29 May 1902. New buildings for the girls' school at Hertford (since 1798) opened 23 July 1906.

Chromium. First isolated by Vauquelin, 1797.

Chronicles, Anglo-Saxon. See ANGLO-SAXON CHRONICLES.

Chronometers. Invented by John Harrison, 1726.

Chungking, China, was first opened to external trade, 1891; first became accessible by steamboat, 1898. Capital of China, 1941–5. See BURMA ROAD.

Church Army. Mission of the Church of England, established, 1882.

Church Assembly, Set up in 1920 under the Church of England Assembly Powers Act, 1919.

Church Commissioners. Set up, 1947, to unite Queen Anne's Bounty and the Ecclesiastical Commissioners, and to exercise the functions of both bodies.

Church Union. Formed, 1859.

Church Missionary Society, ounded 1799.

Cid Campeador (real name Rodrigo Diaz de Vivar), c. 1035–99. The title consists of his Arabic nickname, from sayid-lord, and a Spanish word cognate with champion. As the almost legendary champion of Spanish christendom against the Moors he was the subject of a ballad-cycle, *Poema de mio Cid*, composed about 1140; of a drama, *Los Mocedades del Cid*, by Guillen de Castro, 1618, which was the basis of Corneille's tragedy, 1636; and of Southey's *Chronicles of the Cid*, 1808.

Cigarettes. Popularized in England by soldiers returning from the Crimean War. First factory established at Walworth, 1856. Royal College of Physicians report, 'Smoking and Health,' alleged a causal relationship between cigarette-smoking and lung cancer, Mar. 1962.

Cigars. Introduced into Britain *c.* 1812, by soldiers returning from the Peninsular War.

Cimbri. Germanic tribes from the SW. Baltic area, and the Jutland Peninsula. They advanced into Illyricum and defeated the consul Papirius Carbo, 113 B.C.; repulsed by Drusus in Thrace, 112 B.C., were refused an allotment of lands; defeated the consul Junius Silanus, in Gaul, 109; ravaged the country till checked in Thrace by Minucius Rufus, 109; victorious over the consul Aurelius Scaurus, 108; forced their way into Roman Gaul, where they defeated the consul Cn. Mallius and the proconsul Caepio, 105; invaded Spain, 104; driven out by the natives, 103; defeated the proconsul Lutatius Catulus, 102; forced a passage into Italy, were totally crushed by Marius at Vercellae, their league dissolved, 101.

Cincinnati, Ohio, U.S.A. Maj. Doughty, in 1789, built Fort Washington, around which grew the present town. Incorporated, 1819. During invasion of Kentucky in civil war, attempt was made by Gen. Kirby Smith to take C., but he was driven back, 1862.

Cincinnati, Order of. A republican society formed by Americans, 1783; first general meeting, May 1784.

Cinematography. Principle on which C. is based—the persistence of vision—described as early as the second century A.D. and demonstrated by Dr. Peter Mark Roget, 1824. Thaumatrope, 1826. J. A. Plateau's Phenakistiscope, 1833. The principle crudely embodied in the Zoetrope patented by W. G. Horner, 1833. Marey of Paris and Heyl of Philadelphia, by 1870, had both devised cameras for recording consecutive photographs of glass disks. Muybridge of Kingston arranged twenty-four cameras with mechanism for successive exposures, to settle the problem of a horse's motion, 1872. Goodwin (American) invented the celluloid film, 1887. Augustin le Prince granted a British patent for employment of perforated gelatine film, to reproduce a sequence of images taken through a single objective, 1888. William Friese-Greene (1855–1921) of Bristol filed English patent for camera and projector with inter-

mittent movement and a single lens, using ribbon of sensitized celluloid, 21 June 1889. Edison's kinetoscope, on a different principle (no projection), was in use same year. A French patent for a 'cinématographe' taken out by brothers Auguste (1862–1954) and Louis (1864–1948) Lumière, 1895. A film passion-play produced in New York, 1897. First colour films ('Kinemacolor' of Smith and Urban), 1906; followed by 'Technicolor' *c.* 1929; by 'Kodachrome,' 1935. 'Talky' film developed in America, 1928. 'Cinerama,' 1952. 'Cinemascope,' 1953. 'Vistavision,' 1954. 'Todd-AO,' 1955.

Cinque Ports, England. Originally five in number: Dover, Hastings, Hythe, Romney, and Sandwich; Rye and Winchelsea were added by Richard I. Fortified by William I, 1067; Henry III granted privileges to, 1216. Charter surrendered to the crown, 1688.

Cintra, Portugal. Convention of, concluded between Sir Hew Dalrymple and Marshal Junot, 30 Aug. 1808. It caused great unpopularity, and a court of inquiry was held at Chelsea, 17 Nov. 1808. The decision of Sir Hew Dalrymple was upheld.

Circassia, ceded to Russia by Turkey, 1829, but did not finally submit to Russian rule until 1859.

Circulation of the Blood, first demonstrated by Harvey, 1628.

Cirta. *See* CONSTANTINE.

Cisalpine Republic. N. Italian republic set up by Napoleon, 1797. Later known as the Italian republic, and converted into the Napoleonic kingdom of Italy, 1805.

Cistercian Order, founded at Cîteaux by St. Robert, Abbot of Molêsme, 1098.

City Companies. *See* LIVERY COMPANIES.

Ciudad Trujillo, the oldest European town in the Americas, founded, 1496, by Bartholomew Columbus as Santo Domingo. Adopted present name, 1936.

Civil Defence Bill. Passed, June 1939.

Civil List. The revenue awarded to the sovereigns of England in return for the crown lands. From 1697 C. L. fixed by Parliament. Arrears provided for, 2 Mar. 1769; again paid by a vote of the Commons, 9 Apr. 1777. Sir H. Parnell's motion for inquiry into C. L. causes resignation of the Wellington Ministry, 15 Nov. 1830; select committee appointed to inquire into, 2 Feb. 1860. Sums provided: George IV, £845,727; William IV, £510,000; Victoria, £385,000, plus pension list; Edward VII and George V, £470,000; Edward VIII, £410,000, less £40,000 while unmarried; George VI, £410,000 (1937); Elizabeth II, £475,000 (1952).

Civil Rights Bill. Introduced into U.S. Senate, 29 Jan. 1866; passed, 13 Mar. 1866; amended, 1875.

Civil Wars in Great Britain:
King Stephen and Matilda, 1139–53.
King John and Barons, 1215–16.
Henry III and Barons, 1263–5.
Edward II and Barons, 1321–7.
Henry IV and Owen Glendower, 1403–5.
Wars of the Roses (q.v.), 1455–71, also 1485.
Richard III and Henry VII, 1485.
Covenanters and Scottish Episcopalians, 1638–43, 1666, 1679, and intermittently until 1688.
Charles I and Parliament, 1642–6.
Charles II and Parliament, 1650–1.
James II and Duke of Monmouth, 1685.

See also JACOBITES.

Civil War, American, 1861–5.
Civil War, Russian, 1917–22.
Civil War, Spanish, 1936–9.

Clan-na-Gael. Irish terrorist organization, with headquarters in Chicago, founded c. 1883.

Clarendon Code. A series of English statutes designed to establish the political supremacy of the adherents of the Anglican Church and to destroy the power of the Presbyterians. The principal Acts were: Corporation Act, Dec. 1661. Act of Uniformity, May 1662. Conventicle Act, July 1664; Five-Mile Act, Oct. 1665.
The C. C. was called after Edward Hyde, Earl of Clarendon, who was Lord Chancellor, 1661, until banished, 1667.

Clarendon, Constitutions of. Drawn up chiefly by Richard de Lucy at Council of C., near Salisbury, to limit the power of the clergy, 25 Jan. 1164. Abandoned by Henry II at Avranches, Sept. 1172.

Clarendon Press. The original name of the press of the University of Oxford, founded, 1672; printing house erected by Sir John Vanbrugh, 1711–13 (with profits of Clarendon's *History of the Rebellion*, Oct. 1713). New printing offices erected, 1825–30.

Clayton-Bulwer Treaty. Negotiated in Apr. 1850 by John Middleton Clayton for the U.S.A. and Sir Henry Bulwer of Great Britain, superseded by new treaty, Feb. 1902, in which Secretary Hay appeared for U.S.A. and Lord Pauncefote for Great Britain.

Clearing-House. Bankers' C.-H. for exchange of drafts and bills set up in Lombard Street, 1770; joined by Bank of England, May 1804. Railway C.-H. established, 2 Jan. 1842.

Cleopatra's Needles. Two granite obelisks erected by Thothmes III at Heliopolis (c. 1475 B.C.) and re-erected by Augustus at Alexandria. (1) Transferred to London and placed on the Victoria Embankment, 1878. (2) Presented by the khedive to the U.S.A. and erected in Central Park, New York, 1881.

Clerkenwell (London). Grew up round St. John's Church, founded, 1140. C. Bridewell built, 1615; burnt down, 1669, but rebuilt. Succeeded by a House of Detention, 1775. Scene of a Fenian outrage, 1867; closed, 1877.

Cleves (Kleve). County, afterwards duchy, Germany. War of succession, 1609; concluded, 1614. C. given to Elector of Brandenburg; settlement confirmed, 1666. Seized by French, 1757; restored to Germany, 1763. In 1795 Prussia ceded the part on left bank of Rhine to France. Exchanges took place, 1803–15; outcome: France gave up all to Prussia and Holland. Town almost completely destroyed by allied bombing, 1944–5.

Clocks. Chinese claim invention c. 2000 B.C. Water-C. (Clepsydrae) used in ancient Greece, fourth century B.C. Introduced into Rome c. 160 B.C. Earliest C. of mechanical type in Europe, twelfth century A.D. First reliable C. set up in palace of Charles V of France by de Vick, 1379. Law of pendulum first applied to C. by Huygens c. 1657. First manufactured in U.S.A. by Eli Terry, 1800. First successful electric clocks invented by Hope-Jones and Bowell, 1894.

Closure. First authorized in the House of Commons by the Urgency Rules of 1881. Power first vested in Speaker, but transferred to House, 19 Mar. 1887.

Cloth of Gold, Field of the. Abortive conference between Henry VIII of England and Francis I of France, held near Guisnes, 6 June 1520.

Clubs. First heard of in England during Elizabeth I's reign. Shakespeare and his friends met at the Mermaid Tavern. Ben Jonson set up a club at the Devil Tavern. The Rota instituted, 1659; the Kit-Kat, 1700; Beef-steak, 1735; Johnson's, 1764; Almack's, 1765; Athenaeum, 1823; Reform, 1836; Savage, 1857.

Cluny, France. Benedictine abbey, founded, 910. By 1150, 314 European monasteries had embraced Cluniac regime and were completely subject to C. In 1528 the monastery fell into 'commendam'; order abolished, 1790.

Cnossos. *See* KNOSSOS.

Coach. First used in England in mid sixteenth century. Bill to prevent men from riding in coaches as too effeminate, 1601.
Stage-coaches used for public conveyance in England from the mid seventeenth to nineteenth centuries.

Coal seems to have been used for fuel by ancient Britons, but the first proper notice we have is that it was mined in Newcastle, 1233; forbidden to be burnt in England, 1273. Nobility and gentry of

London petition against use of, 1306. Not in general use in England until 1625. C. Commission established by C. Act, 1938, in which the ownership of all C. vested as from 1 July 1942. Mines nationalized as from 1 Jan. 1947.

Coalition of European States against France, generally brought about by British influence:

1. Great Britain, Austria, and Prussia, 1793.
2. Great Britain, Germany, Russia, Naples, Portugal, and Turkey, 1799.
3. Great Britain, Austria, Naples, and Russia, 1805.
4. Great Britain, Prussia, Russia, and Saxony, 1806.
5. Great Britain and Austria, 1809.
6. Prussia and Russia, 1813.

Coalition Governments in Britain, 1757, 1782, 1783, 1852, 1915, 1931, 1940.

Cobalt. Isolated in 1735 by Brandt.

Cobden Club. Founded London, 1866, to spread principles of Richard Cobden.

Coburg, in Franconia (*q.v.*), is first mentioned in documents, 1056, and became a city in 1331. It became the capital of the duchy of Saxe-Saalfeld-C., 1735, and of Saxe-C.-Gotha, 1926. During the nineteenth century members of its royal house succeeded to the thrones of Belgium, Bulgaria, Great Britain, and Portugal. *See* all of these.

Cochin, now in the merged state of Travancore-C., India, was once part of the kingdom of Kerala, where Jews and Christians of St. Thomas settled in the first century A.D.; these communities still exist. Vasco da Gama sighted the coast 1498, and Portuguese settled in C. city, 1502, with the permission of the local kings, independent since the ninth century, to build a fort. The Dutch expelled the Portuguese, 1663. C. became subject to Hyder Ali of Mysore, 1776, but was ceded to the British by Tippu Sahib, 1791. From 1923 to 1935 C., with Travancore and other principalities, was known as the Madras States.

Cochin China. *See* INDO-CHINA.

Cock-fighting. Prohibited by Edward III, 1365; by Cromwell, 1653; and finally in 1849.

Cock Lane Ghost. Sensation caused by fraudulent representations of William Parsons, his wife, and daughter in 1760–1 at Cock Lane, London. Parsons and wife convicted and imprisoned, 10 July 1762.

Cocoa and Chocolate. Cocoa beans first brought to Europe by Columbus, 1494. Cortez found Aztecs using chocolate as a beverage, 1519, and introduced it to Spain. First 'chocolate house' opened in London, 1657. Chocolate as a sweetmeat became popular during the nineteenth century. Purchase tax on chocolate confectionery and biscuits, 1962.

Cocos. *See* KEELING ISLAND.

Code Napoléon. Codification of French civil law was promised by the constitutions of 1791 and 1793, but commissions for this purpose did not begin work until 1800. The task lasted until 1802, and the necessary measures passed by the Assemblies, 1803–4. The name C. N. was suppressed between 1814 and 1852, but the third and final revision appeared in 1816.

Codex Sinaiticus. *See* SINAITICUS, CODEX.

Coelacanths. Group of specialized cross-opterygian fishes. Originally thought to have become extinct 50,000,000 years ago. But one caught off E. London, Cape Province, 1938; second specimen caught near Madagascar, 1952.

Coffee. Introduced to Europe in the seventeenth century. First English coffee-house opened in Oxford, 1650.

Cognac, Treaty of, between the parties to the Holy League of 1526 (*q.v.*).

Coimbra. Capital of Portugal, 1139–1260. Inez de Castro murdered, 1355.

Colchester, England (Lat. **Camulodunum**). Oldest recorded town in Britain. Cunobelinus reigned in C., 5 B.C.–A.D. 43. Became Roman headquarters in Britain, 43. Burnt by Boudicca, 61. End of Roman occupation c. 367. First charter, 1189. Castle surrendered to Fairfax in civil war, 1648.

Cologne (Ger. **Köln**; Lat. **Colonia Agrippina**). Founded c. 37 B.C. by the Ubii. Colony of Roman veterans established there by Agrippina the Younger, A.D. 51. Diet held at by Charlemagne, 782, and made an archbishopric, 785. Joined Hanseatic League, 1201. Cathedral founded by Archbishop Conrad von Hochstaden, 1248. Town established its independence of the archbishop at the battle of Worringen, 1299. C. incorporated with France at the peace of Campo Formio, 1797, but annexed by Prussia, 1815. Cathedral completed, 1880. Garrisoned by British Rhine Army, 1918–25. City heavily bombed and mostly destroyed, 1942–5. Captured by American troops, 7 Mar. 1945.

Colombia. Territory explored by Spanish, 1505–30, and named the Captain-Generalship of New Granada, 1538. Republic of Gran C. formed by uniting New Granada with Venezuela and Ecuador, and whole proclaimed independent of Spain by Simon Bolivar, 17 Dec. 1819. Recognized by Great Britain,

1825. Venezuela split off, 1829. Ecuador, 1830. Republic of New Granada formed, 21 Nov. 1831. United States of C. formed, 1861. Republic of C. formed, 1886.

Colombia. South American republic. Coast traditionally said to have been visited by Columbus, 1502. Area revolted against Spain, 1811, and achieved independence, 1819. Part of Greater Colombia, 1819–30; when Venezuela and Ecuador seceded, C. called itself the Republic of New Granada, 1831–50. Confederacion Granadina, 1858; United States of Colombia, 1863; Republic of Colombia, 1886. Civil war between federalists and centralists, 1889–98. Series of authoritarian regimes, based on army support, since 1953. *See also* PANAMA.

Presidents of the republic since 1898 (when civil war ended with the consolidation of centralized government):

Sanclemente	1898–1900
Marroquin	1900–1904
Reyes	1904–1909
Holguin	1909
Valencia	1909–1910
Restrepo	1910–1914
Concha	1914–1918
Suarez	1918–1921
Holguin	1921–1922
Ospina	1922–1926
Mendez	1926–1930
Herrera	1930–1934
Pumarejo	1934–1938
Santos	1938–1942
Pumarejo	1942–1945
Camargo	1945–1946
Perez	1946–1950
Gomez	1950–1953
Pinilla	1953–1957
Camargo	1958–

Colombo, capital of Ceylon (*q.v.*). First mentioned by European sources, 1346, was taken by the Portuguese, 1517; from them by the Dutch, 1656; surrendered to the British, 1796.

Colombo Plan for Co-operative Economic Development in S. and SE. Asia, published 28 Nov. 1950, in force 1 July 1951, originally intended to be complete, 1957, U.K., Australia, India, Canada, Ceylon, New Zealand, Pakistan, Malaya, and British Colonial territories participating, with Burma, Indonesia, Cambodia, Laos, Viet Nam, Thailand, Nepal, the Philippines, and Japan. Extensions were agreed upon in 1955 (until 1961) and 1959 (until 1966). The U.S.A. is associated with the C. P.

Colonial Development Corporation. Public corporation established under the Overseas Resources Development Acts, 1948 and 1956. Government announced,

July 1962, that the Corporation's title and terms of reference were shortly to be changed.

Colonial Office. Founded as the Council 'for the Plantations,' 1660. Secretary of state for the colonies first appointed, 1854. This marks the C. O.'s emergence as a separate department of state.

Colonies (British), many of which have since had a change of name and status, were declared as such on the dates given below:

Aden, 1839.
African Forts, 1618.
Anguilla, 1666.
Antigua, 1632.
Ascension, 1815.
Australia, S., 1834.
Australia, W., 1829.
Bahama Islands, 1629. Restored, 1783.
Barbados, 1605.
Bengal, 1652.
Berbice, 1803.
Bermudas, 1609.
Bombay, 1662.
British Burma, 1862.
British Columbia, 1858.
British Guiana, 1814.
British Honduras, 1862.
British N. Borneo, 1946.
British Somaliland, 1884.
Canada, 1760.
Cape Breton, 1763.
Cape Coast Castle, 1667.
Cape of Good Hope, 1806.
Ceylon, 1815.
Cyprus, 1878.
Demerara and Essequibo, 1803.
Dominica, 1763.
Elmina and Dutch Guinea, 1871.
Falkland Islands, 1833.
Fiji, 1874.
Gambia, 1843.
Gibraltar, 1704.
Gilbert and Ellice Islands, 1915.
Gold Coast, 1874.
Grenada, 1763.
Hong Kong, 1841.
Jamaica, 1655.
Keeling Islands, 1857.
Kenya, 1920.
Kermadec Islands, 1886.
Labuan, 1846.
Lagos, 1861.
Leeward Isles, 1763.
Madras, 1640.
Malacca, 1795(–1818), 1824, 1946.
Malta and Gozo, 1800.
Mashonaland, 1890.
Matabeleland, 1890.
Mauritius, 1814.
Montserrat, 1632.
Natal, 1843.

Nevis, 1628.
New Brunswick, 1713.
Newfoundland, 1583.
New Guinea, 1884.
New Hebrides (Condominium), 1906.
New S. Wales, 1787.
New Zealand, 1840.
Niger districts, 1886.
Norfolk Island, 1787.
Nova Scotia, 1622.
Orange Free State, 1902.
Pegu, 1852.
Penang, 1786, 1946.
Pitcairn Island, 1898.
Port Phillip, 1840.
Prince Edward Island, 1745.
Prince of Wales Island, 1786.
Queensland, 1860.
Rhodesia, Northern, 1924.
Rhodesia, Southern, 1923.
St. Helena, 1673.
St. Kitts, 1623.
St. Lucia, 1803.
St. Vincent, 1763.
Sarawak, 1946.
Seychelles, 1810.
Sierra Leone, 1787.
Singapore, 1819.
Socotra, 1886.
Straits Settlements, 1826.
Tasmania, 1803.
Tobago, 1763.
Tortola, 1666.
Transvaal, 1901.
Trinidad, 1797.
Tristan da Cunha, 1816.
Vancouver Island, 1781.
Victoria. *See* Port Phillip.
Virgin Isles, 1666.
Windward Isles, 1803.

See also PROTECTORATES, BRITISH.

Colorado was partly acquired by the U.S.A. from France under the Louisiana Purchase, 1803, and partly from Mexico, 1848. Gold was found in 1858, and until 1910 C. was the leading state for the production of this metal. Indian wars, 1860–5. Admitted to the union, 1876.

Colorado Beetle. Potato pest which reached Europe from the U.S.A., 1922. There have been sporadic outbreaks of the pest in Britain since 1933.

Colosseum, Rome. Begun, A.D. 72, by Vespasian. Finished, 80, by Titus.

Colossus of Rhodes. *See* APOLLO OF RHODES.

Colour Bar. C. B. legislation in S. Africa dates from 1912. Subsequent legislation includes the Native Franchise Bill, 1936; the Separate Representation of Voters Act, 1951; and the Separate Representation of Voters Act Amendment 1956. C. B. in S. Africa based on Nationalist Government's policy of 'apartheid,' i.e. 'separatism.' C. B. in the U.S.A. has no basis in legislation and has declined since World War II, due in great measure to the 'desegregationist' rulings of the Supreme Court under the Eisenhower Administrations (1952–60).

Columbia, District of, originally an area of 100 sq. m., was ceded by Virginia and Maryland, 1790–1, divided by the Potomac; but in 1846 Virginia recovered her portion. Congress first met in the district, 1800. By its Act of 1895 the city of Washington (*q.v.*) became co-extensive with the district. Citizens of C. were given the right to vote in national elections by the 23rd Amendment to the U.S. Constitution, 30 Mar. 1962. *See* WHITE HOUSE.

Columbia University (New York, U.S.A.). Founded, 1754, as King's College; reincorporated as C. College, 1784; the title of university adopted, 1896.

Columbus, Christopher (Cristobal Colón), *b. c.* 1446, *d.* 20 May 1506. Voyages:
(1) 3 Aug. 1492–15 Mar. 1493 to San Salvador, Cuba, Haiti.
(2) 24 Sept. 1493–11 June 1496 to W. Indies.
(3) 30 May 1498–Summer 1499. Possibly American mainland.
(4) 9 May 1502–7 Nov. 1504. Gulf of Mexico.

Combat, Trial by, or Wager of Battle does not appear to have been customary in England before 1066, except perhaps in the Danelaw. The custom is of Scandinavian origin, and must have existed before the settlement of Iceland, where it was called 'holmganga' (i.e. before 870); brought to Normandy from Scandinavia and thence to England, where it was condemned by the Church, 1215, and thus fell into desuetude though still legal. An accused murderer challenged his accuser—who shirked the challenge — and was acquitted, 1817; this led to the immediate abolition of Trial by Combat.

Combination Laws. Various measures, repealed 1824, which had the effect of rendering trade unions or manufacturers' associations illegal.

Combined Cadet Force. Name given since 1939 to the Officers' Training Corps, formed Mar. 1908.

Comecon. *See* COUNCIL FOR MUTUAL ECONOMIC AID.

Comédie Française. In 1658 the touring company of Molière (*see* FRENCH LITERATURE) settled in the Rue Guénégaud, Paris, under the name of the Illustrious Theatre, where it had only one serious rival, the Hôtel de Bourgogne players. The two troupes were ordered by Louis XIV to amalgamate in 1680, and moved to the Rue de l'Ancienne-Comédie, 1687, and to the Tuileries, 1771. The company split in 1790 into two rival political groups—Théâtre de la Nation and Théâtre de la République, both of which perished before the Comédie was revived in 1802 by Napoleon, who in 1812 laid down regulations which are still largely binding on the company. The building nearly destroyed by fire, 1900.

Cominform ('Communist Information Bureau'). A body formed at Russian dictation to direct the activities of the Communist parties of Europe. Formation under Gen. Zhdanov announced at Warsaw, 5 Oct. 1947. Yugoslav Communist Party expelled from, 28 June 1948. See COMINTERN.

Comintern ('Communist International'). Founded, 1919. Formally dissolved, 10 June 1943.

Commando, an Afrikaans word for a military unit, mobile column of varying size under a *Commandant* (roughly, lieutenant-colonel); became familiar to the British when the Second S. African War entered its guerrilla phase (1900 onwards), but had been in use since the early nineteenth century. British Cs. were formed from special service battalions, which themselves were made up of companies, once independent, of volunteers from the Army and Royal Marines, first raised in June 1940, and controlled and trained by Combined Operations Command under Sir Roger Keyes, who was succeeded, 27 Oct. 1941, by Lord Louis Mountbatten. Dates of some C. operations are: 4 Mar. 1941, Lofoten; Nov., Beda Littoria and Cyrene; 27 Dec., Vaagsö; 27 Feb. 1942, Bruneval; 28 Mar., St. Nazaire; May, Diego Suarez, Madagascar; 19 Aug., Dieppe; June 1944, Normandy; Oct., Walcheren. Cs. also fought with U.S. Marine formations in Korea (autumn 1950).

On 25 Oct. 1945 the Cs. passed (or rather reverted, since Marines were first raised for this task) to Marine command for all purposes, but in Aug. 1946 a School of Combined Operations was opened under Marine auspices in N. Devon, where training suitable for Cs. is given to other services.

Committee of Imperial Defence, organized, 1890. Abolished on creation of Ministry of Defence, 1946.

Committee of Public Safety.

1. U.S.A. In Massachusetts, 1774.
2. France. In Paris, 6 Apr. 1793.

Committee of Safety. Formed by officers of the army after retirement of Richard Cromwell from the protectorship, 29 Oct. 1659.

Common Carrier, liabilities of, governed by Carriers' Act, 1830; Railway and Canal Traffic Act, 1854; Road and Rail Traffic Act, 1933; and Transport Act, 1947.

Common Council of London has existed since the fourteenth century; the constitution of its court is virtually unchanged from that period (except that members formerly elected by trades are now elected by ratepayers of wards), being unaffected by the Municipal Corporations Acts, 1835 and 1882. Elections take place annually, 21 Dec.

Common Market. Name popularly applied to the European Economic Community (E.E.C.). Came into being, 1 Jan. 1958, following the ratification of the Treaty of Rome (signed 25 Mar. 1957). Headquarters, Brussels. Members (1963) are: Belgium, France, Federal Germany, Italy, Luxembourg, and Italy ('the Six'). Aim: to eliminate the traditional economic frontiers between member states by gradual abolition of customs barriers, and adoption of common policies on agriculture, transport, and commerce. The Treaty of Rome can also be read as implying some kind of eventual political union. 'The Six' are also members of the European Coal and Steel Community (E.C.S.C.), established 1952, and the European Atomic Community (Euratom), established 1958. Greece associated with the Community, 30 Mar. 1961. Britain announced her intention of negotiating for entry to the C. M., July 1961, provided that the interests of the Commonwealth, the other members of the European Free Trade Association (E.F.T.A.), and British agriculture could be safeguarded. Britain formally applied for membership, 10 Aug. 1961, and some other E.F.T.A. and non-committed countries followed her example (e.g. Denmark, Norway, and Ireland). Edward Heath, Lord Privy Seal, chief British negotiator. Talks for entry speeded up, Mar. 1962, but, 28 June, Heath expressed dissatisfaction at proposals so far offered by 'the Six' for safeguarding Commonwealth agricultural exports. Deadlock in negotiations, 28 July 1962. 6 Aug. 1962: Negotiations adjourned, unfinished, until 8 Oct., when they were re-opened. French obstructionist attitude to British entry increasingly apparent, and matters reached crisis after de Gaulle's speech to the French people in Jan. 1963. On 29 Jan. 1963 talks on Britain's entry finally broke down, due to French pressure, with resulting bitterness among the C. M. countries themselves.

Common Penny, The (Ger. **Das gemeine Pfennig**). Tax first levied in the Holy

Roman Empire to raise money for the Turkish Wars, 1471; renewed, 1496; renewed again for the Venetian War, 1512.

Common Pleas, Court of. One of the old common law courts existing as a superior court of record. Merged in the C. P. division of the high court, 1873, and finally transferred to the Queen's Bench Division by an Order in Council, 1881.

Common Prayer, Book of. See PRAYER, BOOK OF COMMON.

Commons, House of. Originated in thirteenth-century practice of calling up knights and burgesses to give information to the government at Westminster. In embryonic form at Simon de Montfort's Parliament, 1265. 'Model' Parliament, 1295. Claimed right to take part in legislation, 1322. Claimed right to originate direct taxation, 1407. Committee of the whole House instituted c. 1600. Privileges confirmed by Petition of Right, 1628, and Bill of Rights, 1689. Franchise and basis of representation altered by Reform Act, 1832. Franchise further extended, 1867, 1884. Power to overrule the House of Lords (q.v.) given by Parliament Act, 1911, and extended by further legislation under the Labour Government, 1949. Franchise extended to women, 1918 and 1928. Further alterations in system of representation, 1945. See PARLIAMENT.

Commonwealth Day. See EMPIRE DAY.

Commonwealth, English. Lasted from 1649 until 1653.

Commonwealth Immigrants Act, 1962. Provided for restrictions on the number of Commonwealth citizens entering the U.K., and enabled undesirables to be deported to their place of origin. Provisions became law during 1962 (May–July).

Commonwealth Institute (London). Built to commemorate Queen Victoria's Jubilee, 1887, and named the Imperial Institute; opened 1893; used as part of London University, 1899; transferred to Board of Trade, 1902; Colonial Office assumed management with Board of Trade, 1907; placed in statutory control, 1916; control transferred to Department of Overseas Trade, 1935; Orders in Council limited the institute's activities to education and public information, under the general direction of the Minister of Education, 1949. Became an independent body once more, 1953. Changed its name to the C. I. under the Commonwealth Institute Act, 1958. Queen Elizabeth II opened the Institute's new buildings in Kensington, Nov. 1962.

Commonwealth Relations Office was separated from the Colonial Office, 1925 (under name of Dominions Office), and

entrusted with relations with the Dominions and the administration of the High Commission Territories of Bechuanaland, Swaziland, and Basutoland (see all these). Adopted present name, July 1947. Posts of Secretary of State for the Colonies and Secretary of State for Commonwealth Relations combined under one individual (Duncan Sandys), 13 July 1962.

Commune of Paris. 1. The name of the City Council of Paris, set up 21 May 1791, and suppressed, 17 July 1794. 2. The revolutionary socialist government set up in Paris, 18 Mar., and suppressed, 28 May 1871. See FRENCH REVOLUTION, THE GREAT.

Communism. Karl Marx (1818–83) issued Communist manifesto, 1848. First volume *Das Kapital* issued, 1867. Communist Party of Great Britain founded, 1920. See INTERNATIONAL; RUSSIA; BOLSHEVIKS.

Comoro Islands. French protectorate from 1886 to 1912 (Mayotte from 1841); then a French colony. Attached to Madagascar for administrative purposes, 1914, and since 1960 part of the Republic of Madagascar.

Compass. Chinese claim to have invented it, 2634 B.C. Once thought that Marco Polo introduced it to Europe, but now considered that Europeans invented it independently during the twelfth century.

Compromise League of certain Dutch and Flemish nobles petitioned Philip II of Spain to cease religious persecution in Netherlands, 1566. Petition rejected.

Comptometer. Invented by Felt, 1884.

Computer. Babbage (1792–1871) investigated the first mechanical C., but first complete one built in America, 1939–44.

Comrades of the Great War (U.K.). Founded, Aug. 1917, and absorbed in the British Legion (q.v.), 1921.

Concentration Camps. Existed in Nazi Germany, 1933–45. See separate articles on BUCHENWALD, DACHAU, etc.

Concepción, Chile. Founded by Pedro de Valdivia, 1550, on a site seven miles NNE. of the present city. Destroyed by earthquakes in 1730 and 1751 but rebuilt.

Conclave, Papal. Papal election by two-thirds majority of cardinals (q.v.), instituted 1179 by Alexander III. Council of Lyons, 1274 (Gregory X), decreed that cardinals should be locked up until the election was completed.

Concord, Book of, a synthesis, together with the Nicene and Athanasian and Apostles' Creeds, of the following Lutheran theoretical works: Luther's Smaller Catechism, 1529; Luther's Larger

Catechism, 1529; Augsburg Confession, 1530; Apology for Melanchthon's Confession, 1530; Luther's Articles of Schmalkald, 1537; Formula of Concord, 1577, made 25 June 1580 by order of Elector Augustus of Saxony.

Concordats. Treaties regarding ecclesiastical affairs between the pope and a temporal power. The following is a selection: Worms between Emperor Henry V and Calixtus II, 1122. Nürnberg between German Electors and Eugenius IV, 1447. Vienna between Emperor Frederick IV and Nicolas V, 1448. Against the Pragmatic Sanction of Bourges between Emperor Charles V and Clement VII, 1526, and again between Ferdinand VI of Spain and Benedict XIV, 1753. 'The Concordat' between Napoleon I and Pius VII, July 1801. Annulled, 1905. Between Frederick William III of Prussia and Pius VII, 16 July 1821. Between Mussolini and Pius XI, 11 Feb. 1929. Between General Franco and Pius XII, 27 Aug. 1953 (to replace that abrogated in 1931). *See also* VATICAN.

Confederate States of America. The following states seceded from the U.S.A.: S. Carolina, 20 Dec. 1860; Mississippi, 8 Jan. 1861; Florida and Alabama, 11 Jan.; Georgia, 19 Jan.; Louisiana, 26 Jan.; Texas, 1 Feb.; Virginia, Apr.; N. Carolina and Arkansas, May.

Jefferson Davis elected president of the Confederation at Montgomery, Alabama, 18 Feb. 1861. Constitution adopted, 11 Mar. 1861. *See* U.S.A.

Confederation, Articles Of (U.S.A.). Signed, 9 July 1778.

Confederation of the Rhine. Formed by Napoleon I, 1806, after abolition of the Holy Roman Empire. Dissolved, 1813.

Confucianism. Ethical and philosophical system evolved during the Han era in China (206 B.C.–A.D. 220), but based on the teachings of Confucius (Chin. *Kung Fu-tze*), 551–479 B.C. System in its original form abandoned after 1912.

Congo. African republic, formerly known as the Belgian Congo, became independent of Belgium, 30 June 1960. The colony originated with the annexation of C. Free State (*q.v.*), 1908. Exchanged territory with Portuguese W. Africa, 1927. Independence found C. divided by political factions. Force Publique mutinied, 6 July 1960. Katanga (*q.v.*) province declared itself independent of the government in Leopoldville and the central government appealed for U.N. help, 11 July. U.N. troops arrived in C., 15 July. Army coup, 14 Sept. Premier Lumumba arrested. He was kidnapped by Katanga tribesmen and murdered, Feb.

1961. Factions held an inconclusive conference in Madagascar, Mar. 1961. President Tshombe of Katanga arrested by central government troops, Apr.; he was released, 24 June, and signed an agreement reuniting Katanga with C., but the Katangese Parliament rejected this, 4 July. The U.N. broke off relations with Katanga, 1 Sept.; on 13 Sept. U.N. announced Katanga's secession at an end. U.N. troops attempted to end the secession by force. Tshombe and Adoula (central government) had reconciliation talks, 20 Dec.; Tshombe agreed to accept Katanga's subordinate status, but situation remained confused. Belgium re-established diplomatic relations with C., 27 Dec. By autumn 1962 the U.N. began putting increasing pressure on Katanga to rejoin C. A military attack was launched against Katanga by U.N. troops, 28 Dec. and on 14 Jan. 1963 Tshombe formally agreed to Katanga's reintegration.

Congo Free State was set up under the auspices of the Association Internationale Africaine after the expeditions of Cameron, 1875, and Stanley, 1877, and internationally recognized by the Treaty of Berlin, 1885. Formally annexed to Belgium, 1908.

Congo, River. Discovered by Diego Cão, the Portuguese explorer, in 1482.

Congregationalists (Independents, Brownists), under their first leader, Robert Browne (1550–1630), emigrated to Holland, 1581, and to Scotland, 1584. Their greatest period of power and expansion was 1645–60. Congregationalist Union of Scotland formed, 1811; of England and Wales, 1831. Combined with Evangelical Union, 1896. C. established in America, 1620; revival, 1730–40. United with the American Christian Church, 1931. Merger agreed with the Evangelical and Reformed Church, 1956.

Congress of Industrial Organizations formed (U.S.A.), as Committee for Industrial Organization, 9 Nov. 1935, by John L. Lewis (*b.* 1880). Joined World Federation of Trade Unions, 1945, but withdrew 25 Jan. 1949. John L. Lewis resigned, 1950, and was succeeded as President by Scottish-born Philip Murray (1886–1952), a steelworker's leader. Walter Reuther (*b.* 1907) became President of the C.I.O. after Murray's death.

Congress of the United States. The first C. met in 1789, in succession to the Continental C. (*q.v.*).

Congresses, Diplomatic. Principal occasions when sovereigns or their representatives have met to settle diplomatic affairs:

Aix-la-Chapelle, 29 Sept.–22 Nov. 1818.

E

Berlin, 13 June–13 July 1878.
Cambrai, 1722–5.
Carlsbad (*q.v.*), Aug. 1819.
Châtillon, 4 Feb.–18 Mar. 1814.
Constantinople, 23 Dec. 1876–20 Jan. 1877.
Ferentino, 1223.
Frankfort, 16–31 Aug. 1863.
Laibach, 1821.
Paris. Jan.–Apr. 1856.
Prague, 5 July–9 Aug. 1813.
Rastadt, 9 Dec. 1797–8 Apr. 1799.
Reichenbach, 27 June 1790.
Soissons, 1 June 1728; moved to Fontainebleau, 18 Dec. 1729; ended by Treaty of Seville, 28 Sept. 1729.
Troppau, Oct. 1820.
Verona, Aug. 1822.
Vienna, 1 Nov. 1814–9 June 1815.

Connecticut. State of the U.S.A., one of the original thirteen. First settled, 1635; written constitution, 1639, confirmed by Charles II, 1662. Replaced by a state constitution, 1818.

Conscientious Objectors. Term came into prominence during World War I. Special measures taken to deal with C. O. in the Military Service Act, 1916; provision also made for them in the Military Training Act, 1939. C. O. in World War II released from further obligations by the National Service (Release of Conscientious Objectors) Act, 1946.

Conscription. Introduced by Jourdan into France, 5 Sept. 1798. Modern system of call up by age groups introduced in Prussia, 1806. Bill for C. introduced into U.S. Congress at suggestion of James Monroe, Secretary for War, 27 Oct. 1814. C. introduced in Austria, 1868; Russia, 1870; Germany, 1871; Italy, 1873. Militia service compulsory in Canada, 1868. Introduced in U.K., Jan, 1916–Dec. 1920, and from 3 June 1939 (*but see* MILITIA). C. of women, 1941–6. C. in U.K. ended in 1962. Germany, Austria, and Bulgaria forbidden C. by peace treaties after World War I, but Germany resumed it in 1935. C. re-established in E. Germany, 1956, and W. Germany, 1957. U.S.A. adopted selective C., 19 Oct. 1940.

Conservative. Word said to have been invented by J. W. Croker, in the *Quarterly Review*, Jan. 1833, as a more appropriate word than Tory (*q.v.*).

Consolidated Fund, first so-called, 1786.

Consols (Consolidated Annuities). An Act of 1731 consolidated certain perpetual and lottery annuities bearing interest at 3 per cent, and these consolidated annuities form the basis of Cs. Rate altered to 2¾ per cent, 1888, and 2½ per cent, 1905.

Constance (Ger. **Konstanz**), Germany,

on the Rhine at its exit from Lake C., in Baden-Württemberg. Became a bishopric in the sixth century. Free imperial city, 1192. Council of C., 1414–18. John Hus burnt here, 1415. Occupied by Austrians, 1548; besieged by Swedes, 1633. Became part of Baden, 1805. Bishopric suppressed, 1821.

Constantine, Algeria, the Rom. **Cirta.** Town destroyed, 311, but rebuilt by Constantine the Great, 312; taken by the Arabs, 710, and the French, 1837.

Constantinople (Turk. **Istanbul**). The ancient Byzantium (founded from Megara, 667 B.C.) rebuilt as capital of the Roman Empire by Constantine the Great, A.D. 330. Embellished by Justinian *c.* 532. Seized by Venetians and Crusaders, Apr. 1204, when it became capital of the Latin Empire of the East. Recaptured by Byzantine emperor, Michael Palaeologus, 1261. Captured by Turks, who made it their capital, 29 May 1453. Ceased to be capital of Turkey, 1923. *See* OTTOMAN EMPIRE; TURKISH REPUBLIC; COUNCILS OF THE CHURCH; ROMAN EMPIRE, EASTERN.

Consulate, The. French regime, lasted from 1799 to 1804.

Consuls (mercantile) were first appointed by Italian republics about 1100. Except for a revival in the sixteenth century the custom died out, only to become universal in the nineteenth century. In 1943 the British Consular Service amalgamated with the Diplomatic Service to form the Consular Service.

Consuls (highest ordinary magistrates in republican Rome). Two in number, they were elected annually and took office on 15 Mar. until 153 B.C., and thereafter on 1 Jan. The office was open to patricians alone until the *Lex Licinia* (367 B.C.) required one Consul to be a plebeian. Cs. were still appointed in the W. until A.D. 534, and in the E. until 541.

Continental Congress first met at Philadelphia, 1774, where all states, except Georgia, sent unofficial delegates to discuss ways and means of resisting the Stamp Act of 1765, and thereafter annually down to 1783.

Continental Drift. Concept put forward in detail by Wegener (1880–1930) in 1910.

Continental System. The name given to Napoleon I's embargo on trade between Britain and Europe. Begun by the Berlin Decrees, 21 Nov. 1806. Britain retorted by establishing a counter blockade by the Orders in Council of 7 Jan. 1807. The Russian tsar's refusal to co-operate with the C. S. led directly to Napoleon's invasion of Russia, 1812, whilst the English system was an essential cause of the American war of 1812.

Contributory Pensions (U.K.). Introduced, 1925. Scope enlarged, 1937. National Insurance Act, 1946.

Conventicle Acts. First passed, 1593. Revised, 17 May 1664. Repeal by Act of Toleration, 1689.

Convention. *See* FRENCH REVOLUTION, THE GREAT.

Convention Parliaments. The two English Parliaments convened without royal authority: (1) 25 Apr. 1660, to restore Charles II. (2) 22 Jan. 1689, to offer the crown to William III and Mary II.

Also the Scottish Parliament convened by William III, 1689, for the same purpose as (2).

Convocation. 1. Of Canterbury, first summoned by Archbishop Peckham, 1283. Practically suspended, 1717–1852. 2. Of York, first summoned *c.* 1300. Met only formally between 1717 and 1852. *See* ENGLAND, CHURCH OF.

Conway Castle. Built by Edward I, 1284.

Cook Islands or Hervey Islands. Discovered by James Cook, 1773; annexed by Great Britain, 1888; by New Zealand, 1901.

Co-operative Movement. Producers' C. started by Robert Owen at New Lanark, 1799, but declined from about 1828. Consumers' C. opened in Toad Lane, Rochdale, Lancashire, 1844–5. Federation of English Cs., founded 1863 as English Wholesale Society. Central C. Union founded, 1869. First C. bank opened, 1872, in England, though such banks had existed in Germany since 1849. C. Party in Britain established 1917; first M.P. elected, 1919.

Copenhagen, Denmark. Grew up round Axelhuus, a fortress built by Bishop Absalon, twelfth century. Became capital of Denmark, 1443. University founded, 1479. Surrendered to Christian I, 1479; to Christian III, 1536. Captured by Charles X of Sweden, 1658. Danish fleet attacked at, by Nelson and Parker, 2 Apr. 1801. Besieged and taken by British, 5 Sept. 1807. Seized by Germans, 9 Apr. 1940; liberated, May 1945.

Coptic Church. Monophysite Christian Church to which the Abyssinians also belong. It separated from the Orthodox, A.D. 451.

Copyhold Tenure. Abolished in England, 1922.

Copyright (Great Britain). First known grant to Richard Pynson, King's Printer, 1518. In 1642 it was ordered that no book be printed without the author's permission. First C. Act came into operation, 10 Apr. 1710, and gave protection to booksellers for 21 years.

Authors protected for a life or 28 years, 1814. For a life plus 7 years, or 42 years at least, 1842. Act of 1911 (life plus 50 years) came into force, 1 July 1912. Modern law (Copyright Act, 1956) came into force, 1 June 1957.

Copyright, International. International C. laws passed in Britain, 1838 and 1852. In U.S.A., 1891. International Convention at Berne, Sept. 1886. Revised at Paris, 1896; Berlin, 1908; Rome, 1928; and Brussels, 1948.

Copyright (U.S.A.). Petition of Dr. D. Ramsay for C., 5 Apr. 1789. Bill passed, 1790. C. Act, 1831, gave sole rights for 28 years, with power to renew for a further 14. Further legislation, 1870, 1874. Act of 1909 granted 28 years after publication, and after expiration another 29 years to author and his heirs. Further legislation in 1928 and 1956.

Cordeliers. 1. *See* FRANCISCANS, MONASTIC ORDER OF. 2. Since early fifteenth century applied to the Récollets or Observant Franciscans. 3. One of the earliest political clubs during the French Revolution, named after the convent in which they met. Many members executed, 24 Mar. 1794. Ordered to be discontinued, 1795.

Cordova, Spain. Occupied by Romans under the Consul Marcellus, 152 B.C. Taken by Visigoths, A.D. 572. Capital of Moorish Spain, 756. Mosque, built eighth to tenth centuries, is now the cathedral. Reconquered by Spanish, 1236. Captured by French, 1808. Plundered by Carlists, 1836.

Corfe Castle, Dorset, England. Dates from the eleventh century. King Edward the Martyr murdered on its site, 978. Captured and sacked by Parliamentarians, 1645.

Corfu (anct. Corcyra), Greece. First colonized from Corinth, *c.* 700 B.C. Allied with Athens, 443 B.C., and so caused the Peloponnesian War. Taken by Romans, 229 B.C. Held by Robert Guiscard, A.D. 1081–5. By Roger, King of Sicily (*q.v.*), 1147–54. Semi-independent till annexed by Venice (*q.v.*), 1386. Attacked by Turks, 1536, 1716–18. Ceded to France, 1797. British protectorate, 1815, till united with Greece, 1863. University suppressed, 1864. Bombarded by Mussolini, 31 Aug. 1923 ('The C. Incident'). British destroyers mined by Albanians in C. Channel, 1946.

Corinth, Greece. Legendary foundation by Sisyphus *c.* 1350 B.C. Reached highest prosperity under tyranny of Cypselus and Periander, 655–582 B.C. Oligarchy restored 581 B.C. War with Athens, 459 B.C. Starts Peloponesian War, 431 B.C. Destroyed by Romans,

146 B.C. Rebuilt by Julius Caesar, 46 B.C. One of earliest Christian churches established at c. A.D. 40. Attacked by Alaric, 395. Captured by Franks, 1205; by Turks, 1458. Held by Venetians, 1687–1715; by Turks, 1715–1822. Destroyed by earthquake, Feb. 1858. C. Canal opened, 1893. New town destroyed by earthquake, 1928. Canal destroyed by Germans during World War II but in service again by 1948. Temporarily blocked by an earthquake, 1953.

Cork, Ireland. Occupies site of a seventh-century monastery. Perkin Warbeck landed at, 1649. Taken from Jacobites, 21 Sept. 1690. Queen's (now University) College founded, 1849.

Corn Laws (English). Passed to raise price of C. Robinson's Act, 1815, only allowed importation when price reached 80s. a quarter. Principle regulated by sliding scale under Act of 1828. Agitation against begun, 1836. New sliding scale introduced, 1842. Suspended, 1847. Repealed by C. Importation Act, which came into force, 1 Jan. 1844. Latter Act repealed, 24 June 1869.

Cornish Language, a Celtic tongue, was virtually identical with Breton until the sixteenth century. The last C. speaker died in the early nineteenth century, but the last recorded use of the language took place about 1780. Extant C. literature consists entirely of miracle plays, in MSS., the earliest of which was written c. 1410, and the latest copied in 1611.

Cornwall, England. The Celtic inhabitants of Dyvnaint (Dumnonia) who had once occupied Devon, C., Somerset, and Dorset, were driven W. of the Parret, and thus cut off from S. Wales, by King Coenwalh of Wessex, 658. Egbert, King of Wessex, began campaign against Cornishmen, 815, until they acknowledged his supremacy, 823. The last war of the Cornish against the W. Saxons was undertaken in alliance with the Danes, 836–7. The allies defeated and slew Æthelhelm, Alderman of Dorset, at Portland, but were finally beaten at Hingston Down by Egbert. Made a duchy vested in the heir to the throne by charter, 1337.

Coronation Oath settled in new form for William and Mary, 1689. Modified, 1706, 1821, 1910, 1937, 1953.

Coronation Stone. See SCONE, STONE OF.

Corporation Acts (U.K.). See CLARENDON CODE and BOROUGH.

Corsica. Successively a Phocaean, Etruscan, Carthaginian, and Roman settlement. Seized by Saracens, tenth century. Given to Pisa by papal bull, 1090. Ceded to Genoa, 1367. Rebellion, 1735, reduced by France for Genoa, 1739. Sold by Genoa to France, 1768. Occupied by British, 8 June 1794. Insurrection, 8 June 1796, led by P. Paoli (1725–1807). Abandoned by British, 22 Aug. 1796. Reoccupied by French, 22 Oct. 1796. Last bandit sentenced to death, 1935. Italian occupation, Nov. 1942–4 Oct. 1943. First part of French territory in Europe to declare for de Gaulle, May 1958.

Cortes, parliaments or 'estates' (of gentry, clergy, and burghers), once the legislative body in each Christian kingdom of the Iberian peninsula. They began to assume some importance at the beginning of the eleventh century, that of Leon being quite powerful in 1020. Their decline set in in the fifteenth century, coinciding with the eclipse of the lesser kingdoms by Aragon and Castile, and the rise of the Hapsburg-Bourbon monarchy. A revived C. in Spain (1812) and Portugal (1822) was simply a name for a constitutional assembly on the French model, and had no real historical continuity. See SPAIN and PORTUGAL.

Corunna, Spain. Armada anchored here on the way to England, 1588. Part of town burnt by Drake and Norris, 1589. Sir John Moore killed at C., 1809.

Corvée. Forced labour. Unsuccessful attempt by Holy Roman Emperor, Joseph II, to abolish, 1775. Abolished in France, 1792. In Egypt, 1888–91.

Cosmic Rays. Experiments indicating existence of C. R. carried out by Rutherford and McLennan from 1903 onwards. Actual discovery attributed to Millikan, 1925.

Cossacks. Took Azov from Turks, 1637. Rising against Poles, led by Hetman Chmielnicki, 1648. Defeated at Khotin by John Sobieski, King of Poland, 1673. Treaty with Charles XII of Sweden, 1707. Mostly hostile to Soviet Government during civil war, 1917–22.

Costa Rica, Central America. First settled, 1502. Revolted from Spain and joined Mexican Empire, 1821. Independent, 1823. Part of Central American Confederation, 1824–39. Boundary dispute with Nicaragua settled, 1888; with Colombia, 1921; with Panama, 1921. Civil war in May 1948 won by President Figueres, who disbanded the armed forces, 1 Dec. Subsequent civil war, in which Nicaragua intervened and invaded C., ended by a C.-Nicaraguan pact signed in Washington, 21 Feb. 1949. Constitution last modified, 1949. Presidents since then are as follows:

Ulate	1949–1953
Figueres	1953–1958

Echandi   1958–1962
Orlich   1962–

Cotopaxi. Volcano in the Andes, in Ecuador, S. America. Height 19,613 ft. Most violent eruption, 1768. First ascent made by Reid and Escobar, 1872.

Cotton. Introduced by Mohammedans into Europe. Manufactured in Spain, thirteenth century. Italy, fourteeenth. England, seventeenth. Bombay, nineteenth. Raw Cotton Commission, 1948–1954, was an experiment in State buying. Cotton industry in England in decline since 1955.

Cottonian Library (England). Founded by Sir R. Bruce Cotton (1571–1631). Placed in Ashburnham House, Westminster, 1731, and partly burned. Formed part of original nucleus of the British Museum, 1753.

Council or Curia Regis. *See also* WITAN. From Norman feudal King's C. sprang (1) *c.* 1100–*c.* 1250 The Common Law Courts (*see under* COURTS). (2) *c.* 1250–1300 The House of Lords (*q.v.*). (3) *c.* 1350 The High Courts of Chancery and Admiralty. (4) *c.* 1460 The Star Chamber. (5) Early Tudor period other conciliar courts. (6) *c.* 1700–30 The Cabinet. (7) 1833 The Judicial Committee of the Privy Council. *See* COURTS and PRIVY COUNCIL.

Council for Mutual Economic Aid. E. European counterpart to the Common Market (*q.v.*) popularly known as 'Comecon.' Formed 1949. Its members in 1963 were the Soviet Union, the German Democratic Republic, Poland, Czechoslovakia, Hungary, Rumania, Bulgaria, and (since June 1962) Outer Mongolia. Albania ceased to be a member in 1962.

Council of Europe. Established 1949 by agreement of the consultative council of the Brussels Treaty Organization. Headquarters, Strasbourg.

Council of Industrial Design. Established by the President of the Board of Trade, Dec. 1944. The Design Centre, Haymarket, London, opened Apr. 1956. Scottish Design Centre opened in Glasgow, 1957.

Council of the Marches. Instituted by Henry VII at Ludlow. Abolished, 1641.

Council of the North. Instituted, 1537, by Henry VIII after the Pilgrimage of Grace (*q.v.*) at York. Abolished, 1641.

Council of the West. Instituted, 1540. Abolished, 1550.

Councils of the Church. All churches recognize the general councils of Nicaea, 325; Constantinople, 381; Ephesus, 431; Chalcedon, 451. The Greek Church recognizes three others in addition: Constantinople II, 553. Constantinople III, 680–1. Nicaea II, 787. The Roman Church another thirteen: Constantinople IV, 869–70. Lateran I, 1123; II, 1139; III, 1179; IV, 1215. Lyons I, 1245; II, 1274. Vienne, 1311–12. Florence, 1438. Lateran V, 1512–17. Trent, 1545–63. Vatican I, 1869–70. Vatican II, 1962–3. Some French authorities substitute for Lyons, Florence, and Lateran V those of Pisa, 1409; Constance, 1414–18; and Basel, 1431–43.

Counter - Reformation. The Roman Catholic reaction to the Reformation (*q.v.*). First definite move organization of the Oratory of Divine Love, 1517. Franciscans (*q.v.*) reformed, 1526. Jesuits (*q.v.*) formally founded, 27 Sept. 1540. Roman Inquisition set up, 21 July 1542. Doctrinal codification carried out by Council of Trent, 1545–63. Establishment of the Congregation *de propaganda fide,* 1622.

Countess of Huntingdon's Connexion, sect of Calvinistic Methodists, founded, 1748, by Selina, Countess of Huntingdon (1707–91), widow of the ninth earl. Chapels were set up at Brighton, 1761; Bath, 1765; Tunbridge Wells, 1769; Worcester, 1773; Spa Fields (Clerkenwell), 1779. A training college, instituted at Trevecca, Breconshire, 1768, was transferred to Cheshunt, Herts., 1792, and to Cambridge, 1906. Spa Fields Chapel moved to Golders Green, 1910. Most of the chapels now served by Congregational ministers.

County Councils created by Local Government Act, 1888.

County Courts established by Act of Parliament, 1846; amended 1924, 1934, and 1955.

County Hall, Lambeth, headquarters of the L.C.C.; foundations laid, 1913; formally opened, 1922.

'Coupon Election.' British General Election of Dec. 1918, which returned Lloyd George's Coalition Government.

Court of Session, supreme civil tribunal of Scotland established, 1532. Sits Oct. 15–Mar. 20 and May 12–July 20.

Courts (English). The following are the dates of the institution and abolition of the principal English C.:

N.B.—C. still in existence in *italics.*

1. Palatine C.: Chester, eleventh century–1830. *Lancaster,* 1351. *Durham,* thirteenth century.
2. Common Law C.: Common Pleas, twelfth century–1875. King's Bench, thirteenth century–1875. Exchequer, Henry I–1875. Exchequer Chamber, 1357–1875.
3. Travelling Commissions: Trailbaston, 1290–1380. *Of Assize, c.* twelfth cen-

tury. *Of Oyer and Terminer*, twelfth century. *Of Gaol Delivery*, twelfth century. General Eyre, *c.* 1150–*c.* 1360.

4. Statutary Civil C.: Wards and Liveries, 1541–1660. Requests, eighteenth century–1846. *County Courts*, 1846. High Commission, 1558–1641. Probate, 1857–1875. Divorce, 1857–75.

5. Statutary Criminal C.: *Central Criminal Court*, 1834. *Justices of the Peace*, 195. *Quarter Sessions*, 1362. Crown Cases Reserved, 1848–1907. *Criminal Appeal*, 1908.

6. Conciliar C.: *House of Lords* (*q.v.*), *c.* 1250. Chancery, *c.* fourteenth century–1875. Requests, 1493–1642. Appeal in Chancery, 1851–75. Admiralty, *c.* 1340–1875. Star Chamber, fifteenth century–1641. *Judicial Committee*, 1833.

In 1875 the Common Law C., and the Cs. of Chancery, Probate, Divorce, and Admiralty were amalgamated into a single High Court of Judicature, from which there was to be appeal to a new Court of Appeal, which took the place of the Exchequer Chamber. In 1880 the Exchequer and Common Pleas Divisions were amalgamated with the King's Bench Division. *See* COUNCIL or CURIA REGIS.

Courts Martial, instituted in England, 1625–49; up to 1640 officers were tried under royal ordinance by Courts of Chivalry (*q.v.*). Military law, largely influenced by continental custom, did not receive parliamentary sanction up to 1689 (*see* MUTINY ACTS), but from that date until the Army Discipline Act, 1879, C. M. administered discipline according to articles of war. The Army Act of 1881 was in force until amended in 1951 and 1955 by legislation prompted by the Lewis Committee, which reported as a result of the trial for mutiny of some two hundred British parachutists in Malaya, Oct. 1946. Naval C. M., also affected by the Lewis report, were hitherto regulated by the Naval Discipline Acts, 1866, 1884.

Covenanters. Supporters of the Solemn League and Covenant (*q.v.*), financed by Richelieu, raised an army, 1639. Negotiated with Charles I, 1640. Beaten at Rullion Green, 1666, and subsequently persecuted, but rose in revolt and defeated Graham of Claverhouse at Drumclog, 1 June 1679. Defeated by Monmouth at Bothwell Brig, 22 June 1679.

Covent Garden Market. The 'Covent' was, in fact, the Abbey of Westminster, and its garden included Long Acre. The whole parcel was granted to John Russell, first Earl of Bedford (1486?–1555) in 1552. The square, with St. Paul's Church (by Inigo Jones), was laid out by the fourth earl, 1631. Piazzas built on N. and E. sides, 1633–4. Market opened, 1634, but present buildings date from 1831. Proposals to move market out of central London, 1963. E. piazza burnt down, 1769. St. Paul's Church burnt down, 1795, and restored according to the original plans; rebuilt, 1872. Theatre dates from 1732: present building opened, 1858.

Coventry, a county from 1451 to 1842, is first mentioned in a document dated 1043, referring to the foundation of a monastery here by King Knut Sveinsson, 1016. The first charter to the town was ssued by Earl Ranulf of Chester, 1155, and a corporation established, 1345, under Edward III. The legend of Lady Godiva was a tradition, first written down in Roger of Wendover's *Flores Historiarum c.* 1235, and has been fixed on to the historical Godgifu (*c.* 1040–80), a pious lady who was the consort of the almost equally pious Earl Leofric of Mercia (*d.* 1057), the mother of Hereward the Wake and grandmother of the earls Edwin and Morcar. The expression 'send to Coventry' is said by Clarendon, in his *History of the Revolution*, 1701, to have originated in the concentration of Royalist prisoners here by the Parliamentarian garrison of Birmingham, 1647. C. became a county borough, 1888. A 'Baedeker' raid by the Luftwaffe, 14 Nov. 1940, destroyed the fifteenth-century cathedral church, and gave rise to the verb *coventrate*, Ger. *coventrieren* = to destroy. Cathedral rebuilding began, 1956, after a winning design submitted (1951) by (Sir) Basil Spence. Consecrated in the presence of Queen Elizabeth II, 25 May 1962.

Cracow, Poland. Founded *c.* 700. University established, 1364. Capital of Poland, 1320–1609. Taken by Charles XII of Sweden, 1702. By Russians, 1768. Annexed by Austria, 1795. Independent republic, 1815. Again annexed by Austria, 1846. Restored to Poland, 1919. Taken by Germans, 6 Sept. 1939, and became centre of German administration of the Government-General of Poland until stormed by Russians, Jan. 1945.

'Cradle of American Liberty.' Faneuil Hall, Boston, erected, 1742. Burned and rebuilt, 1761. Meeting-place of American patriots during revolution.

Crédit Foncier. Created under official patronage in France, 1852, as a real-estate mortgage agency. Empowered to make advances to local authorities for public works, 1860. Its charter will expire in 1980.

Crédit Mobilier. Set up at the same time as Crédit Foncier (*q.v.*) as a chattel mortgage agency. Taken over by the Banque de l'union Parisienne, 1932.

Creeds.

Apostles': Earliest mention by Rufinus, 410.

Athanasian: Ascribed to Hilary, Bishop of Arles, 429–49. No direct connection with Athanasius (c. 326–73).

Athanasius (c. 326–73).

Nicene: Based on C. of Eusebius, 325. Reaffirmed at Council of Constantinople, 381, rest of the present creed except word *filioque* being then added.

Cremation, the commonest form of disposal of the dead in this country until the reintroduction of Christianity, or until c. A.D. 600. C. was not practised thereafter until 1884, by the Society for Promotion of C., founded 1874. The C. Act, 1902, and Home Office regulations laid down in 1903 control C., but do not compel ministers of religion to officiate threat, because some denominations disapprove of the practice.

Cremona, Italy. Founded by Romans, 218 B.C. Destroyed by Vespasian, A.D. 70; by Goths, 540, and by the Lombards, 605. Passed to the Viscontis in the fifteenth century. Under Spanish control from 1535; Austrian from 1814, and Italian, 1859. The cathedral was begun in the twelfth century.

Crespy or **Crespi,** France, **Treaty of.** Between Francis I of France and Emperor Charles V, 17 Sept. 1544.

Crete or **Candia,** Mediterranean Island. Seat of Minoan civilization c. 3500–1100 B.C. (see KNOSSOS). Roman province from 66 B.C. Greeks expelled from Carthage by Hassan retire to C., A.D. 698; Saracens seize and make pirate centre, 823; recovered by Greeks, 960; sold to Venetians, 1205; besieged and finally taken by Turks, 1645–69; various attempts to throw off Turkish yoke, especially, 1866–8; Turkey accepted the powers' ultimatum in 1898 and withdrew its army; palace of Minos and 'Labyrinth' discovered at Knossos, 1899. At the outbreak of the Balkan War Cretan deputies were admitted to the Greek chamber, and the island annexed by Greece, 14 Oct. 1912; formally handed over to Greece by the Treaty of Peace between Greece and Turkey, 1 Nov. 1913; the annexation of C. by Greece acknowledged by the powers, Dec. 1913; revolt under Venizelos against King Constantine, 1917; interesting archaeological discoveries, 1929–30; second Venizelist revolt crushed, 1935; attacked by German airborne troops, 20 May 1941; flight of Greek Government and evacuation of British and imperial forces, 2 June 1941. Germans withdrew, autumn 1944.

Cricket. Said to be a development of

medieval 'club ball.' Word first used, 1598. First club formed (Hambledon Club), 1750. M.C.C. founded, 1787. First Test match played by Australia against England, Mar. 1877.

Crimea, Black Sea. South C. colonized by Greeks in the seventh century B.C. Later belonged to Rome and Byzantium, and from the thirteenth century to Venice and Genoa. Conquered by the Turks, 1475. Annexed by Russia from Turks, 1783; war declared against Russia by England and France, 28 Mar. 1854; allied armies landed, 1854; war concluded, Apr. 1856. Crimean Autonomous Republic formed, 1921. Occupied by Germans, 1941–3. Crimean Autonomous Republic abolished, 1945, after deportation of the Tatar population for alleged collaboration with the Germans. *See* ALMA, BALAKLAVA, INKERMAN, SEBASTOPOL, *under* BATTLES, SIEGES, and WORLD WAR II.

Criminal Investigation Department, (C.I.D.), the detective branch of the Metropolitan Police, was set up, 1878. Its Special Branch, for the protection of state personages and the suppression of terrorism, was established in 1883 to guard against Fenian outrages.

Criminal Laws of England. Committee formed to inquire into their severity, 2 Mar. 1819; two Acts restricting capital punishment, 1820; eight further mitigating Acts passed soon afterwards, chiefly at the instance of Sir Robert Peel, notably five in 1823; Habitual Criminals Act, 1869; Criminal Law Amendment Act (relating to females), 1885; Aliens Act, 1905; Criminal Appeal, 1907; the Prevention of Crime Act, 1908; the Children Act, 1908; the Criminal Law Amendment Act, 1912. Criminal Justice Act, 1948, transferred responsibility for persons 'detained during His Majesty's pleasure' from Home Office to Ministry of Health.

Cripplegate (London). Rebuilt, 1244 and 1491. Demolished, 1760–1. Institute opened, 1896.

Croatia (Hrvatska). Independent Croat kingdom, tenth–twelfth centuries. Linked with Hungary until the middle of the fifteenth century; then under Turkish domination until the beginning of the eighteenth century. Part of Illyria, 1809–13; subsequently part of Austria-Hungary. At the dissolution of the Austro-Hungarian monarchy, the National Assembly of C. and Slovenia proclaimed their independence of Hungary, 30 Oct. 1918. A composite ministry for the Serb, Croat, and Slovene kingdom (Yugoslavia, *q.v.*) was formed, 29 Dec. 1918. National Agrarians under Raditch made bid for autonomy, 1928; Raditch assassinated, 1928; National Assembly abolished by Alexander, King of Yugoslavia, and the country united under a royal dictatorship, Jan. 1929. A considerable degree of autonomy granted to Croats, 24 Aug. 1939. After conquest of Yugoslavia by Germans C. was declared an independent kingdom, 18 May 1941. Crown accepted for the Duke of Spoleto, 20 May, who never went near C. In 1948 the province became a federal republic. *See* SERBO-CROAT LITERATURE.

Crofters. Small landholders in Scotland. Royal Commission appointed to inquire into condition of, 22 Mar. 1883–28 Apr. 1884; Act for their benefit passed, 25 June 1886; amended, 1888. Further safeguards for C. in the Crofters (Scotland) Act, 1955.

Croix de Guerre. French decoration, instituted 8 Apr. 1915.

Crossword Puzzles first became a common newspaper feature in the U.S.A., 1923. *The Times* crossword first appeared, 1930.

Crown Pieces. Gold crown first struck by Henry VIII (1509–47). The first silver crown struck by Edward VI (1547–53). The half-crown originated with Edward VI. Since that reign whole crowns have usually been minted only for commemorative purposes, e.g. Queen Victoria's two jubilees, 1887 and 1897, the Festival of Britain, 1951, and the coronation of 1953.

Crown, Suit against the, made possible by Act of Parliament in 1947. The crown of Great Britain, in the person of the responsible minister, not of the sovereign, can now be sued, as a result of appeals which went to the House of Lords, 1946.

Crusades. Jerusalem was captured by the Seljuk Turks, 1071, but it was not until 1095 that Pope Urban II was roused by the preachings of Peter the Hermit and appeals from Constantinople to consider a crusade. In Nov. 1095 the Council of Clermont invoked Western Europe to defend the Holy Land. The following are the eight great C.:

First: 1096. Led by (a) Walter the Penniless, a Burgundian, (b) Peter the Hermit, (c) Gottschalk, a German monk. These were disorganized bands and met with failure. The military crusade of 1096 divides itself into four sections: (a) Godfrey de Bouillon from the Rhine and N. Germany; (b) Hugh, Comte de Vermandois, and others from Central France, Normandy, and Britain; (c) Bohemond of Taranto from Italy; (d) Raymond, Comte de Toulouse, from Provence, Spain, and Lombardy. Nicaea captured, June 1097, and on 1 July of the same year the Sultan Soly-

man was defeated at Dorylaeum. Antioch taken, 3 June 1098. Jerusalem, 15 July 1099; and Godfrey de Bouillon elected king, 22 July 1099. Battle of Ascalon, 12 Aug. 1099. St. Jean d'Acre (*q.v.*) reduced, 1104.

Second: Louis VII of France and Emperor Conrad III, 1146. Damascus attacked, July 1148.

Third: Commenced by siege of St. Jean d'Acre (*q.v.*), 1189. Emperor Frederick Barbarossa led an army to Cilicia, 1190. Arrival of Richard I of England and Philip Augustus, 1191. Richard won battle of Azotus, captured Jaffa and Caesarea, 1191. Jerusalem reached, 1192.

Fourth: Set in motion by Pope Innocent III in 1200. Started from Venice, 1202. Led by Boniface of Montserrat and the Counts of Flanders and Blois. Diverted by Venetians to attack Constantinople, which was stormed, Apr. 1204, and a Latin empire established there.

Fifth: To assist John of Brienne, titular King of Jerusalem, against the Sultan Saphadin, the successor of Saladin, 1217. Led by Andrew of Hungary, the Duke of Austria, the Earl of Salisbury, etc. Damietta captured by the English, 1219. The Emperor Frederick II obtained a ten years' treaty, including free access to the Holy City, 1228.

Sixth: Christians driven out of Jerusalem, 1238, caused two distinct C. together known as the Sixth. (a) French knights led by Thibaud of Champagne and the Comte de Bretagne; (b) arranged at Council of Northampton, led by Richard, Earl of Cornwall, which in 1240 arranged a treaty similar to that of Frederick II.

Seventh: Proclaimed by the Council of Lyons, 1245. Led by Louis IX (St. Louis) of France who, with William Longsword of Salisbury and others, set out from Cyprus in spring, 1249. Louis taken prisoner at the battle of Mansurah, 1250.

Eighth: Led by Louis IX of France and Charles of Anjou. Louis IX *d.* at Carthage, 2 Aug. 1270.

Crystal Palace. Originally the building of the International Exhibition of 1851. Its re-erection begun at Sydenham, 5 Aug. 1852; opened by Queen Victoria, 10 June 1854; purchased by the Earl of Plymouth to hold in trust for the nation, 1911; destroyed by fire, 30 Nov. 1936; remaining tower removed, May 1941.

Ctesiphon, Iraq. Capital of Parthian Empire *c.* 150 B.C. Captured by Romans, A.D. 116 and 196. Became capital of Persia under Sassanids, fourth century.

Persians defeated at, by Julian the Apostate, 363. Destroyed by Arabs, 637. Scene of a battle between British and Turks, 22 Nov. 1915.

Cuba. Discovered by Columbus, 27 Oct. 1492; colonized by Spaniards, 1511; Havana fortified, 1584; insurrections of slaves, 1844 and 1848; López's expedition against, 1851; revolt for expulsion of Spaniards, 1868–71; frequent other revolts, notably that starting 1895; occupied by U.S.A. after Spanish-American War, 1898–1901, when it became a republic; Gómez insurrection, 1906; Taft of U.S.A. proclaimed provisional governor, Sept. 1906; evacuation of U.S. troops, 1908; further revolutions, interspersed by relatively settled government, 1917, 1924, 1931, and 1933. Fought on allied side, 1941–5. Batista became president for the second time, 1952, and instituted a dictatorship. Revolutionary movement against him initiated by Fidel Castro, July 1953. Rebels overthrew the government at the end of 1958 and Batista abdicated and fled the country, 1 Jan. 1959. Castro instituted a left-wing regime, with drastic land reform, expropriation, and nationalization of foreign assets, and close ties with the Soviet bloc. As a result, he lost much of his initial middle-class support, and during 1960 many Cubans fled to the U.S.A. U.S.A. broke off diplomatic relations with C., 3 Jan. 1961. C. invaded from Florida by anti-Castro forces, 18–20 Apr. 1961; the invasion was crushed, as Cubans did not rise to help them as invaders and Americans had assumed they would. C. expelled from the Organization of American States by a bare two-thirds majority, 31 Jan. 1962. President Kennedy imposed an embargo on all American imports from C., 3 Feb. Severe rationing of foodstuffs and toilet goods in C., Mar. Cubans captured in unsuccessful 1961 invasion sentenced to long terms of imprisonment which could be waived on payment of ransom-money, Apr. Some, their ransom paid by sympathizers in the U.S.A., were freed later that month. A group of anti-Castro Cubans based on Miami raided Havana, 25 Aug. Soviet arms build-up in C. became apparent during latter half of 1962. On Oct. 22 President Kennedy alleged that Soviet offensive-missile sites were being erected in C. and announced a U.S. naval blockade of the island, to start on 24 Oct. Russia retaliated by putting her army on the alert. C. put in state of siege. Security Council of U.N.O. met, 23 Oct. Khruschev suggested a 'Summit Meeting,' 24 Oct., to which Kennedy agreed, but stated that the blockade would continue until the Russian bases in C. were dismantled. On 28 Oct. Khruschev announced that Russia would dismantle the rocket bases in C. and ship them home. Temporary lifting of U.S. blockade, 30 Oct., while U Thant flew to Havana to seek permission to verify that the rocket sites were being removed. Blockade resumed, 1 Nov., as U Thant's talks with Castro were inconclusive. Soviet deputy Premier Mikoyan arrived in C., 1 Nov., and his purpose believed to be to persuade Castro to be less intransigent. On 8 Nov. Russia stated she would allow U.S. Navy to inspect the ships removing the missiles from C. and on 20 Nov. the U.S. blockade was lifted. There was subsequent bitterness between C. and Russia, Castro apparently considering he had been let down by Khruschev. But Castro's appearance as guest of honour at the May Day parade in Moscow, 1 May 1963, indicated a *rapprochement* between the two countries.

Heads of Administration since the end of Spanish Rule (1898).

United States Military Governors:

| Brooke | 1899 |
| Wood | 1899–1902 |

President of the Republic:

| Estrada Palma | 1902–1906 |

United States Provisional Governors:

| Taft | 1906 |
| Magoon | 1906–1909 |

Presidents of the Republic:

Gomez	1909–1913
Menocal	1913–1921
Zayas y Alfonso	1921–1925
Machado y Morales	1925–1933
Provisional Junta	1933
San Martín	1933–1934
Mendieta	1934–1935
Barnet	1935–1936
Gómez y Arias	1936
Bru	1936–1940
Batista	1940–1944
San Martín	1944–1948
Socarras	1948–1952
Batista (again)	1952–1959
Urrutia	(Jan.–July) 1959
Torrado	1959–

(Castro, who (1963) holds the office of Premier and 'Revolutionary Leader', has been the effective ruler of C. since 1 Jan. 1959.)

Cubism. Term first used by Henri Matisse, 1908. Exhibitions at Paris and Brussels, 1911.

Culdees (Irish = Companions of God). Religious community, drawing their inspiration from the rule of St. Chrodigang, Archbishop of Metz from 742 to 766, which they introduced into Ireland and into Scotland before 800; converted into canons regular in the reign of David I, King of Scotland (1107–53) on the recommendation of his mother, St. Margaret (d. 1092). As a separate body, had disappeared by 1300.

Cullinan Diamond, found, Jan. 1905, at Premier Mine, Transvaal. Presented to Edward VII, 1907.

Curaçao. Principal island of the Dutch W. Indies. Discovered by Spanish explorers, 1527. and acquired by the Dutch, 1634.

Curfew. Said to have been introduced in England by William I, 1068, but probably existed earlier. Still resorted to in various areas during periods of civil unrest, e.g. in Cyprus during the E.O.K.A. disturbances, 1956, and in the principal cities in Algeria during the nationalist war there, 1954–62.

Curtis Report. See CHILDREN ACTS.

Curzon Line. Proposed E. frontier of Poland recognized by the Allies in Dec. 1919 on suggestions by Lord C. but not adopted because of Poland's victory over Russia in 1920. The E. frontier awarded Poland in 1945 (agreed by the Allies at Teheran in 1943) is in fact based on the C. L., with some minor modifications in Poland's favour.

Customs. Granted to the crown in 1275. Commissioners appointed, 1671; consolidation of C., 26 Feb. 1787. C. Consolidation Act, 1876, may be regarded as the principal statute relating to C. Custom House, London, founded, 1559; rebuilt, 1718; new (the present) building, 12 May 1817.

Cycle. Four-wheeled velocipede invented in France by Blanchard and Magurier in 1779; pedals applied to a tricycle by a Dumfriesshire blacksmith, McMillan, 1834; rubber tyres, 1868; bicycles made in England by Coventry Sewing Machine Co., 1869; improved by J. K. Starley, 1874; Starley's 'Rover,' with nearly equal wheels, 1885. First C. club, Pickwick Bicycle Club, founded, London, 1870; National Cyclists' Union and Cyclists' Touring Club, 1878. First manufactured in America by A. A. Pope, 1878.

Cyprus. Greeks began to colonize C. before 1200 B.C.; Phoenicians followed, 1000–800 B.C. Subject in turn to Egypt, Assyria, Persia, Greece, and Rome. Arab raids in seventh century. Seized by Richard I of England, 1192, and sold by him to Guy de Lusignan, whose successors ruled C. as independent kings. Made tributary to the Mamelukes, 1426. Catherine Cornaro, widow of James II, ceded C. to Venice, 1489. C. was conquered by Turks, 1570–1; ceded to

Britain by Anglo-Turkish Convention, 4 June 1878; annexed by Britain, 5 Nov. 1914. Crown colony, 1925. Revolt, instigated by union-with-Greece agitators, broke out; British Governor's residence burned down, Oct. 1931; constitution suspended, Nov. Constitutional conference, 1947. Conference dissolved, 1948. Church plebiscite showed overwhelming support for *enosis* (i.e. union with Greece), 1950. Archbishop Makarios persuaded Greece to take the subject to U.N.O.; transfer of British Middle E. headquarters to C., 1954. E.O.K.A: terrorist campaign to promote *enosis* began, April 1955. State of emergency proclaimed, Sept. Archbishop Makarios exiled to the Seychelles, 1956–7. Agreement signed in London by British, Greek, and Turkish premiers, and ratified by Greek and Turkish Cypriots, which provided for C. to become an independent republic within the Commonwealth, 19 Feb. 1959. Makarios became President of C., 14 Dec. 1959. Independence day, 16 Aug. 1960.

Cyrenaica. See LIBYA.

Cyrene. A colony founded from Thera, c. 630 B.C., became a republic about 431. See LIBYA.

Czechoslovakia. British Government officially recognized it as an allied nation, 19 Aug. 1918. Czechoslovakian Republic proclaimed, with Thomas Masaryk as first president, 15 Nov. 1918. Recognized by Austria, 1918; by Hungary, 1919. Frontier dispute with Poland settled, 1924. Diplomatic relations with Vatican suspended, 1925. Arbitration treaty with Poland, 23 Apr. 1925. Masaryk re-elected president, 1927; resigned, 1935; succeeded by Beneš. Masaryk d., 14 Sept. 1937. Germans incorporated Sudeten territories, 1 Oct. 1938. Poland took possession of zone beyond the Olza, 2 Oct.; Beneš resigned presidency, 5 Oct.; Father Tiso appointed minister for Slovakia (autonomous), 10 Oct.; Brody first premier of autonomous Ruthenia, 12 Oct.; Germany and Italy fixed new frontiers, 2 Nov.; Poles invaded Ruthenia, 24 Nov.; Emil Hacha elected president.

Slovakia seceded from the Czechoslovak State and proclaimed itself an independent republic, 14 Mar. 1939. Germany invaded and annexed the whole country and proclaimed protectorates of Bohemia, Moravia, and Slovakia, 15 and 16 Mar.; Hungary occupied Ruthenia, and granted it autonomy, 16 Mar.; Legion formed in Paris, Sept.; anti-German risings, Sept. and Nov.; Czechoslovak National Committee under Beneš formed in Paris, 17 Nov. Provisional

Government recognized by Britain, 21 July 1940.

Ruthenia annexed by Russia, but rest of country recovers independence at surrender of Germany. May 1945, and President Beneš returned to Prague. Communist *coup d'état*, Feb. 1948. Jan Masaryk, Minister for Foreign Affairs, committed suicide. Russia vetoed a U.N. move to inquire into circumstances of Czech coup, Mar. Beneš resigned, June, and *d.*, Aug.

Vladimir Clementis, former Foreign Secretary (forced to resign, Mar. 1950), Rudolf Slansky, secretary of Communist Party (arrested Nov. 1951), and twelve others, mostly Jews, tried *in camera* on charges of Titoist and Zionist conspiracy, 20 Nov. 1952. All but three condemned to death and their execution announced, 2 Dec. President Gottwald died, 15 Mar. 1953. Antonin Zápotocky, Prime Minister, elected President, 20 Mar. W. Oatis, American journalist, condemned on espionage charge in 1951, released under amnesty, 15 May 1953. Unrest reported in C., 1953. Some liberalization since 1957 but Archbishop Beran (detained 1951) still under arrest in 1963. Reported moves against President Novotny, July 1962, whose views generally considered 'Stalinist,' and in May 1963 Novotny reported to be safeguarding his own position by attacking some of his former 'Stalinist' colleagues.

Presidents of C. since 1918:

Masaryk	1918–1935
Beneš	1935–1938
Hacha	1938–1939
(*and President of Bohemia-Moravia, under German 'protection,'* 1939–1945)	
Beneš	1940–1948
(*administration in London,* 1940–1945)	
Gottwald	1948–1953
Zápotocky	1953–1957
Novotny	1957–

Czechoslovak Language and Literature. The sixth-century Byzantine mission of Cyril and Methodius to the Bohemians and other Slavs N. of the Middle Danube gave rise to a certain amount of vernacular church literature, all but a few traces of which have now perished. By the eleventh century the Orthodox church had ceased to exist in the Czech lands, and so until the thirteenth century Czech words only appear written as glosses to Latin texts. But in this century there occur vernacular hymns (e.g. that to St. Vaclav) and, in the next, secular chronicles and romances and religious epics were produced in Czech. In the fourteenth century radical linguistic changes, including a vowel mutation not shared by

any other Slav dialect, took place. The Caroline University founded by the patronage of the Emperor Charles IV, whose reign (1346–78) coincided with the first flowering of Czech culture, gave Bohemia predominance in arts and letters over the whole W. Slav area. A code of spelling reform, *De Orthographia Bohemica*, was published in 1441, the posthumous work of John Hus (1369–1415), the religious reformer who established the dialect of Prague as the literary language. The first printed book in C. was produced at Pilsen in 1468—a *Troan Chronicle*— just six years before Caxton's first English book, *Recuyell of the Historyes of Troye*, came out. Peter Chelcický (1390–1460), theologian and philosopher, was one of the principal Czech authors of the Hussite period; Tolstoy (1828–1910) considered him his inspiration, and edited his works *c.* 1890. *Lexicon Symphonicum*, the first scientific dictionary of the C. L., 1537, the *Elucidation of Grammar* by Jan Blahoslav, 1571, the Kralice Bible, 1579–93, and V. B. Nudozerský's complete Czech grammar, 1603, served to stabilize the language which had finally evolved from its medieval to its modern form before the battle of the White Mountain (1620) began a period of cultural as well as political stagnation, during which German instead of Latin became the official language of the Czech lands (1774) and similarly Magyar replaced Latin in Slovakia. The folksong, however, did flourish in the seventeenth century. So absolute was the dominance of German in the eighteenth century that the leader of the Czech revival, Josef Dobrovský (1753–29), was bound at first to write his early works in German to gain the ear of the literate classes at all. In the first half of the nineteenth century German loan-words were replaced by reviving old native words or by borrowing from Russian or any other suitable Slavonic language. The Czech-German dictionary of Jungmann (see below) was published 1835–9, and ten years later some spelling reforms served further to differentiate the language. Ballads and folk-tales were collected by F. L. Celakovský (1794–1852) and K. J. Erben (1811–70). A prominent satirical journalist of this period was K. Havlíček (1821–56). The Prague National Theatre was founded in 1883.

The Slovak dialects in the later Middle Ages did not undergo the vowel mutation characteristic of Czech (see above), nor did the Slovak people enjoy any degree of political independence, so that Czech early became the literary language of Slovakia, though there exist Slovak glosses to medieval Latin texts. The proto-protestants of the Hussite period in Slovakia used Czech as the medium of disputation and instruction, but their influence was reciprocal so that from *c.* 1400 to 1600 they introduced many slovakisms into what was becoming a common C. L. By contrast the leaders of the counter-reformation in Slovakia produced some church books in Slovak idiom (e.g. a hymnal in 1655). A Latin-Slovak dictionary was printed at Trnava, 1777. J. Bajza (1755–1836) was a prominent Slovak Catholic writer, but Anton Bernolak (1762–1813), a priest from Bratislava, published a Slovak grammar and wrote a polyglot dictionary which was not published until 1825; many Slovaks, and some the most distinguished down to the generation of Kollar and Šafařik (see below), still used Czech as the 'native' literary language. By the middle of the nineteenth century written Slovak was stabilized largely through the efforts of Ludovit Štúr (1815–56), Mihal Miloslav Hadz (1811–70), and Jozef Miloslav Hurban (1817–88), round the dialects of central Slovakia; Štúr published in 1846 a *Treatise on Slovak Speech*, which was reinforced by M. Hattala's Slovak grammar of 1852–65. Since then well-known writers in Slovak (which became an official language, along with Czech and Ruthenian, in the republic of 1918) have been S. Hurban-Vajansky (1847–1916), Pavol Orszagh (1849–1921), and Martin Kukučin (real name Matej Bencur, 1860–1928).

The following is a short list of authors writing in Czech, including some of Slovak birth mentioned above.

Březina, Otokar (Václav Jebavý), 1868–1929, poet.

Čapek, Josef, 1887–1945, dramatist.

Čapek, Karel, 1890–1938, dramatist and journalist.

Čapek-Chod, 1860–1927, novelist.

Čech, Svatopluk, 1846–1908, poet.

Comenius (Komensky), Jan Amos, 1592–1670, educationist.

Dobrovský, Josef, 1753–1829, philologian and historian.

Hálek, Vitězslav, 1835–74, poet and novelist.

Hašek, Jaroslav, 1884–1923, satirist.

Jirasek, Alois, 1851–1930, poet, novelist, and dramatist.

Jungmann, Josef, 1773–1847, lexicographer and historian.

Kollar, Jan, 1793–1852, poet.

Lützow, Count Francis, 1849–1916, historian.

Mácha, Karel Hynek, 1810–36, poet.

Masaryk, Tómaš Garrigue, 1850–1937, logician and sociologist.

Neruda, Jan, 1834–91, poet and critic.

Palacký, František, 1798–1876, historian.

Šafařik, Pavel J., 1795–1861, critic.

Sládek, Josef Václav, 1845–1912, poet and translator.

Vrchlicky, Jaroslav, 1853–1912, poet.

Zeyer, Julius, 1841–1901, poet.

Czestochowa, Poland. Monastery plundered by Hussites, 1430. Defended against Swedes, 1655. Bombed, 1939, but since restored.

ADDENDA

D

Dachau, Upper Bavaria, was the site of a concentration camp, 1933–45.

Dacia. Roman province, partly corresponding to modern Rumania. Conquered by Trajan, A.D. 101–6; Aurelian withdrew Roman forces and left D. to the Goths, forming a new province of same name S. of Danube c. 275; added to Eastern Empire by Gratian, A.D. 379. *See* VLACHS.

Daghestan or **Daghistan,** Asia. Conquered by Peter the Great, 1723; restored to Persia under Tsarina Anne, 1735; reannexed to Russia, 1813. D. autonomous republic formed, 1920.

Daguerreotype. Invented by Louis Daguerre (1789–1851), a French painter, with the help of J. N. Niepce (d. 1833), between 1825 and 1839.

Dahomey, W. Africa. Commercial treaty between King Gezo and France, 1851. Coast blockaded by Britain, 1876. French protectorate, 1863. French expedition to D., 1892, ended in annexation, 1894. Territory of French W. Africa from 1904 and member of the French Community from 4 Dec. 1958. Independent republic, 1 Aug. 1960, and admitted to U.N., 20 Sept. 1960.

Dail Eireann. 1. Name of a Sinn Fein Assembly, which sat in the Mansion House at Dublin, 1919. 2. Since 1922 the name of the Lower House of the Parliament of Irish Republic.

'Daily Courant,' 'Daily Express,' 'Daily Graphic,' 'Daily Herald,' 'Daily Mail,' 'Daily Mirror,' 'Daily News,' 'Daily Sketch,' 'Daily Telegraph,' and **'Daily Worker.'** *See under* NEWSPAPERS.

Dairen, Dalny, or **Talienwan,** Manchuria. Leased by China to Russia as terminus for the Chinese Eastern Railway, 1898. Ceded to Japan by Treaty of Portsmouth, 1905. Restored to China, 1945. *See also* PORT ARTHUR.

Dakar, capital of Senegal. Formal possession taken by French, 1857. Harbour enlarged, 1898, 1912. Cable to Brest laid, 1905. Improvements to naval (especially submarine) base, 1938–40. Free French forces under de Gaulle repulsed by Vichy forces, 23 Sept. 1940. University established, 1957.

Dalai Lama. *See* TIBET.

Dalmatia. Subdued by Statilius Taurus, 23 B.C., and by Tiberius, A.D. 9. Diocletian b. at Salona (Solin) 245, d. at Split, 313. Occupied by Marcellinus, 461. Conquered by Coloman, King of Hungary, 1102–5. Under Venice, 997–1358. Venetian power largely shaken off as a result of the Wars of Chioggia and Negropont (*see under* EUBOEA), 1358–1573. Venetian power reasserted, 1573–1580. Ceded to Austria by Treaty of Campo Formio (*q.v.*), 1797. Made part of kingdom of Illyria by Napoleon, 1805. Ceded to Austria, 1814. N. D. and D. Islands promised to Italy by Pact of London, 1915, but given to Yugoslavia, 1920, not as separate Yugoslav province, but divided into the Croatian districts of Split and Dubrovnik. Italy seized Fiume and Zara, 1920. Annexed whole of D., 21 May 1941. Whole of D. returned to Yugoslavia at German surrender, May 1945. *See* DUBROVNIK; SPLIT; ZADAR.

Dalriada, ancient name of the northern half of County Antrim, home of a Scottish tribe whose eponymous ancestor was called Riada; they migrated across the N. Channel to Kintyre, and founded a new kingdom of D. c. A.D. 500, of which the nucleus was Argyllshire. The D. Scots were defeated in Ireland at Magh Rath, County Down, 637. By their union with the Picts under Kenneth MacAlpin, 843, the kingdom of Alban was founded. *See* SCOTLAND.

Damascus, Syria. Taken by Assyrians after battle of Karkar, 853 B.C. Finally conquered by Assyrians under Tiglath-Pileser III, 733. Captured by Alexander the Great, 333. Taken by Romans, 63 B.C. Captured by Arabs, A.D. 635. Capital of the Caliphate, 661–750. Attacked by Crusaders, 1126 and 1148. Sacked by Mongols, 1260 and 1399. Conquered by Turks under Selim, 1516. Christians massacred at, 1860. Great Mosque burnt, 1893. Severely damaged by fire, 1912. Captured by T. E. Lawrence and the Arabs, 1918. Occupied by French, 1920. Taken by combined Free French and British troops, 21 June 1941. Syrian independence proclaimed at D., 27 Sept. 1941, and D. became the Syrian capital. Coup which ended Syria's first union with Egypt (1958–61) originated in D., Nov. 1961, and that which heralded Syria's second union with Egypt (1963) also started in D.

Danegeld. Tax to buy off attacks by foreign pirates first levied, 991, by Ethelred II. From 991 to 1012, 158,000 silver pounds was so spent. After the murder of Archbishop Aelfheah in 1012 a special tax, called *heregeld*, was levied to pay a standing army. This tax was still collected by the Danish kings Knut, Harald, Hardaknut (1016–42), and by Edward the Confessor, who abolished it in 1051. There is no recorded use of the actual *term* D. before 1066. William I reimposed the *heregeld* tax, under the name D., and his successors continued to collect it until 1163.

Danelaw. Territory in England ceded to Guthrum by Alfred the Great in 878, after the battle of Edington. It was largely reconquered by Edward the Elder, but in 940 Edmund I was forced to cede part of the D. to Olaf Guthfrithson, the Viking king of Dublin. Edred campaigned to reassert his authority in the region, and at his death (955) it was acknowledged throughout the D.

Danes, a Scandinavian tribe unknown to Roman authors, even by name. Their kings play a large part in the English epic *Beowulf*, which is now thought to have an historical basis in various events of the late fifth century A.D. They were then settled in what is now southern Sweden (Scania). As no tradition of conflict with the Angle-kin persists, the D. probably did not move into Jutland and the islands E. of it until these had been vacated by the Angles and allied tribes when they migrated to Britain in the fifth and sixth centuries. The Skjoldung ('Children of Scyld') Dynasty began to dominate the whole Danish group in the eighth century, under Ivar Widefathom, whose uncle Gudröd's (Godred's) reign in Scania can be tentatively dated 720–40. *See* DENMARK, KINGDOM OF, for later history.

Danish Literature. The following is a list of writers in D. (not now living), both inhabitants of Denmark and authors of Norwegian, Faroese, or Icelandic origin. Some medieval D. writers not mentioned here will be found under LATIN LITERATURE, POST-CLASSICAL, because they produced no vernacular work which has survived. The order is that of date of birth.

Christian Pedersen, *d.* 1554, Bible translator.
Poul Helgesen, 1485–1533, Catholic apologist.
Hans Tausen, 1494–1561, Protestant apologist.
Peder Palladius, 1503–60, essayist.
Anders Sørensen Vedel, 1542–1616, translator of Saxo Grammaticus.
Arild Huitfeldt, 1546–1609, historian.
Anders Arreboe, 1587–1637, religious epic poet.

Anders Bording, 1619–77, poet and editor of the first D. newspaper, *Dansk Merkur,* which appeared in 1666.
Princess Leonora Christiana, 1621–98, memorist.
Peder Syv, 1631–1702, philologist.
Thomas Kingo, 1634–1703, poet, hymnographer.
Ludvig Holberg, 1684–1754, historian, poet, playwright.
Hans Adolf Brorson, 1694–1764, lyric poet.
Ambrosius Stub, 1705–58, poet.
Johan Herman Wessel, 1742–85, poet, playwright.
Johannes Ewald, 1743–81, poet, playwright.
Peder Andreas Heiberg, 1758–1841, poet.
Jens Baggesen, 1764–1826, poet, essayist.
Schach von Staffeldt, 1769–1826, poet.
Adam Oehlenschläger, 1779–1850, poet, playwright.
Steen Steensen Blicher, 1782–1848, novelist, poet.
Nikolai Fredrik Severin Grundtvig, 1783–1872, poet, especially song-writer.
Bernhard Severin Ingemann, 1789–1862, novelist, poet.
Carsten Hauch, 1790–82, novelist, poet, playwright.
Johan Ludvig Heiberg, 1791–1860, critic, playwright.
Poul Møller, 1794–1838, novelist, essayist.
Ludvig Bødtcher, 1793–1874, poet.
Christian Winther, 1796–1876, poet.
Henrik Hertz, 1798–1870, playwright.
Emil Aarestrup, 1800–56, poet.
Hans Christian Andersen, 1805–75, fabulist.
Frederik Paludan-Müller, 1809–76, novelist, poet.
Søren Kierkegaard, 1813–55, philosopher.
Meir Aaron Goldschmidt, 1819–87, novelist.
Georg Brandes, 1842–1927, critic.
Holger Drachmann, 1846–1908, poet, novelist.
J. P. Jacobsen, 1847–85, novelist.
Herman Bang, 1857–1912, novelist.
Karl Gjellerup, 185?–1919, novelist.
Henrik Pontopidan, 1857–1943, novelist.
Jakob Knudsen, 1858–1917, novelist.
Gustav Wied, 1858–1914, novelist, playwright.
Viggo Stuckenberg, 1863–1906, poet.
Ludvig Holstein, 1864–1943, poet.
Jeppe Aakjer, 1866–1930, poet.
Gyrithe Lemche, 1866–1945, novelist.
Helge Rode, 1870–1937, poet, playwright.
Karin Michaelis, 1872–1949, novelist.
Johannes Vilhelm Jensen, 1873–1950, novelist.
Harry Søiberg, 1880–1954, novelist.
Johannes Buchholtz, 1882–1940, novelist.
Nils Petersen, 1897–1943, novelist.
Kaj Munk, 1898–1944, playwright.

Jorgen Franz Jacobsen, 1900–38, novelist. Mogens Klitgaard, 1906–45, novelist.

Dannebrog, Danish royal standard, first flown at the siege of Reval, 1219 (*see under* TALLIN). For Order of D., *see under* KNIGHTHOOD, ORDERS OF.

Dannevirke, fortified boundary dike laid out by King Godred of Denmark (*d.* 810) along his frontier with the empire, 808; extended by Thyra, consort of King Gorm the Old (reigned 900–40). Repaired in the nineteenth century, but pulled down by the Prussians after their victory over Denmark in 1864.

Danube, River. Navigation set free by Treaty of Paris, 1856; regulated by Berlin Treaty, 1878; treaty restoring rights to Russia, 1883; Iron Gates Canal opened, 1898; International Commission for regulating navigation, 1904. Danubian Conference, Aug. 1948, at Belgrade, adopted Soviet-sponsored convention, which was not accepted by the W. powers.

Danubian Principalities, The. Moldavia and Wallachia formed into independent states by Convention of Paris, 19 Aug. 1858; united under title of Rumania (*q.v.*), 23 Dec. 1861.

Danzig (Pol. **Gdansk,** by which name it has been known since 1945). Capital of Dukes of Pomerania, 1230. Occupied by Teutonic Knights, 1308; reconquered by Poland, 1455; place of refuge of Charles VIII when driven from Sweden, 1457; an autonomous free city, 1466–1793; seized by Russians and Saxons, 29 June 1734; ceded to Prussia, 1793; surrendered to Napoleon, who declared it a free city again, 26 May 1807; restored to Prussia, 1814. Declared a free city under the protection of the League of Nations by the Treaty of Versailles, 1919; Nazis gained a majority in favour of altering the constitution, but it was too small for the purpose, 1935. Germany annexed D., 1 Sept. 1939. Heavily bombed by allied and Russian air forces in World War II. Ceded to Poland by Yalta agreement. German population driven out, 1945–6.

Dardanelles, Turkey, or **Strait of Gallipoli** (the anct. **Hellespont**). Here Xerxes crossed into Europe, 480 B.C. and Alexander the Great crossed into Asia, 334 B.C. Passage forced by Sir John Duckworth, 19 Feb. 1807; repassed, 1 Mar. 1807; swum by Lord Byron, 1810; Treaty of, signed in London after conclusion of Syrian War, 1841; British and French fleets entered at the Sultan's invitation, 8 Oct. 1853. British and French naval expedition at, 19 Feb.–18 Mar. 1915, was a failure. Land attack, 25 Apr. 1915–8 Jan. 1916; internationalized by the Treaty of Lausanne, 1923; League of Nations agreed to its refortifi-

cation by Turkey, 1936. *See under* TURKISH REPUBLIC and WORLD WAR I.

Darien Scheme, The. A Scottish attempt to colonize the isthmus of D. (Central America), organized by Paterson, the founder of the Bank of England, 1695. Parliament voted supplies, and the expedition sailed on 26 July 1698; arrived after many difficulties, 30 Oct. 1698; left, 18 June 1699; owing to opposition by the Spaniards only a few of those who started arrived back in Scotland, 13 Nov. 1699. In 1715 the sufferers from the scheme received compensation.

Dartford, England. Wat Tyler's insurrection began here, 1381. First paper mill in England said to have been erected here, 1590.

Dartmoor Prison (S. Devon). Founded, Mar. 1806, for the reception of French prisoners of war. It fell into disuse after 1815; reorganized as a convict prison, 1855.

Dartmouth, England, was a borough, and the rendezvous of the fleet destined for the Holy Land, 1190 (*see* CRUSADES). French pirates repulsed at D. after burning Plymouth, 1404; taken after four weeks' siege by Prince Maurice, 1643; retaken by Gen. Fairfax, 1646.

Dartmouth College. *See* ROYAL NAVAL COLLEGE, DARTMOUTH.

Dartmouth College (New Hampshire, U.S.A.). Chartered, 1769.

Darwinism. Charles Darwin's (1809–1882) works, *On the Origin of Species by Means of Natural Selection,* published in 1859, and *The Descent of Man,* 1871, new edition, 1874.

Dauphin. A southern French title, which, according to a condition made by the last lord of Dauphiné when selling that province to Charles, subsequently (1364) Charles V of France, was always to be borne by the eldest son of the French king. The first royal D. was Charles (afterwards Charles VI of France), on his birth, 1368. The last D. was Louis Antoine, Duke of Angoulême, son of Charles X, who assumed the title on 16 Sept. 1824. It was abolished after the revolution of 1830.

Dauphiné, having belonged successively to the Burgundian and Frankish dominions, passed to the empire in 1032, and was immediately ruled by the counts of Vienne, one of whom, called Dolphin, gave his name to the province *c.* 1130. The Emperor Charles IV granted it as a fief to the King of France, 1356, and from 1364 to 1830 it was the customary apanage of the heir to the French throne. Its connection with the empire ceased in the fifteenth century. In 1794 the province was split up into the departments of Isère, Hautes-Alpes, and Drôme.

Davis Cup. International tennis trophy presented by Dwight F. Davis of St. Louis, U.S.A., in 1900 and competed for annually by teams from different countries.

Davis Strait. Separating N. America from Greenland, discovered by John Davis, 1585.

Davy Safety Lamp (for miners). Invented by Sir Humphry Davy (1778–1829) in 1816.

Dawes Plan to provide payments by Germany and to stabilize German currency; settled by a committee of which the U.S. general Charles G. Dawes (1865–1951) was leading member; submitted to Reparations Commission, 9 Apr., and accepted, 17 Apr. 1924. Superseded by Young Plan (*q.v.*) in 1930.

Day of Dupes. 11 Nov. 1630, when Marie de' Medici and Anne of Austria were outwitted by Cardinal Richelieu.

Daylight Saving, the Summertime Act, 17 May 1916, was due partly to the example of Germany which had adopted D. S. earlier in the year, and partly to the efforts of W. Willett (1856–1915), who first proposed such a measure, 1907. The Act was put into force, 21 May 1916, and received the royal assent, 7 Aug. 1925. British summertime lasted continuously from 25 Feb. 1940 to 31 Dec. 1944, and for all but three months of 1945. During these years, and again in 1947, double summertime was in force from Apr. to Oct. Since 1961 the length of summertime has been experimentally extended at both ends of the period.

D-Day, 6 June 1944, when allied troops landed in Normandy to begin the invasion of Nazi-occupied Europe.

Deal, England. Attempted landing by Perkin Warbeck, 3 July 1495. Outpost of Sandwich until 1699, when it was incorporated.

Dean, Forest of (Glos.). Royal demesne for an unknown period, but certainly since before the Norman Conquest. The Charter of the Swainmote, or Verderers Court, was granted by Knut in 1016. Poachers of D. were the last in England to use the bow (down to 1700 or later). The deer, limited to 800 head by an Act of 1668, had dwindled to ten by 1810, and the last were killed by order of the crown in 1850. Charles I granted large tracts to Sir John Wyntour (Winter), the moneylender, who became secretary to Queen Henriette Marie, about 1630; Wyntour recovered the grant after the fall of the Commonwealth, and between 1660 and 1673 practically denuded his tract of trees. An Act to reafforest D. was passed, 1680. Free miners born in the Hundred of St.

Briavels, under a charter of Edward I or Edward II, are entitled to mine in the forest on payment to the crown of 1*d*. per ton royalty. This right is not affected by the Coal Nationalization Act, 1947. Last perambulation by Justices in Eyre 1833. Iron, first worked in prehistoric times, was last worked, 1941.

Debt Conversion, British. First big conversion, 9 Mar. 1888; conversion of National War Bonds, to value of £163,328,133, in 1921. Between 1945 and the beginning of 1957 nearly £6,000 million converted.

Debt, National. *See* NATIONAL DEBT.

'Decameron.' Written by Giovanni Boccaccio (1313–75) between 1348 and 1358.

Deccan, India. *See* INDIA.

Deceased Wife's Sister, Marriage with. Bill to legalize first introduced, 1841. After numerous attempts to get it passed it finally became law in 1908.

Decembrists (Dekabrists.) Conspirators involved in the Russian mutiny of officers at St. Petersburg, 26 Dec. 1825 (14 Dec., Orthodox style). The survivors of those who were neither hanged nor shot were pardoned by Alexander II in 1856, after banishment to Siberia.

Decemviri. Magistrates appointed at Rome in 451 B.C. to draw up a code of laws that would secure the plebeians against magisterial caprice (*see* TWELVE TABLES). New commission appointed for 450–449, but they were forced to resign before the year was ended. In 367 B.C. a permanent board of D. was created to look after the Sibylline Books and to celebrate the Apolline and Secular Games.

Decimal Coinage. Draft Bill to establish D. C. in Britain approved by Chambers of Commerce, 1917. Royal Commission reported adversely, 1920. Government instituted inquiry into cost and effects of a change to D. C., 1961.

Declaration of Human Rights. Drafting begun, 1946, and subscribed, 10 Dec. 1948, by all member states of the United Nations except the U.S.S.R., Czechoslovakia, Poland, Yugoslavia, Ukraine, White Russia, S. Africa, and Saudi Arabia.

Declaration of Independence, 4 July 1776. *See* UNITED STATES OF AMERICA.

Declaration of London. Concerning contraband and blockade, provisionally ratified by European powers and by U.S.A., 1909. Promulgated by Order in Council, subject to vital modifications, 29 Oct. 1914. Withdrawn by Order in Council, 7 July 1916.

Declaration of Paris, signed by powers attending the Congress of Paris, 1856, and since then by all states except Venezuela,

Spain, Mexico, and the U.S.A., renounces privateering and defines contraband of war.

Declaration of Rights (American). Passed by first American Congress at Carpenter's Hall, Philadelphia, Sept. 1774.

Declaration or Bill of Rights (English). The foundation of the Bill of Rights declared amongst other things William and Mary King and Queen of England; passed, 1689.

Declaration of Rights (Irish). Drawn up by Grattan, demanding legislative independence for Ireland; accepted by Irish Parliament, Apr. 1782, and practically confirmed by the English Parliament in the same year. *See* IRELAND.

Declaration of Rights (Virginian). Drafted by George Mason, and presented on 27 May 1776; adopted, 12 June.

Declarations of Indulgence. 1. By Charles II in 1672, by which all Acts against the Nonconformists and Roman Catholics were suspended; this was withdrawn and the Test Act (*q.v.*) passed, 1673. 2. By James II in 1687, similar to the above. 3. By James II in 1688, which was commanded to be read in the churches (*see* SEVEN BISHOPS, TRIAL OF THE). *See also* NONCONFORMISTS.

Decretals. Collection of papal decrees or decretal letters; part of canon law. First collection made by Dionysius Exiguus about A.D. 550; word generally applied to the compilation of Gratian in twelfth century; first official collection, 1210. What are known as the False D. were supposed to have been written between 425 and 450, but had no existence as a whole until about 850.

Defence, Ministry of. Created 5 Oct. 1946; formally instituted, 1 Jan. 1947. Under proposals published in July 1963, the Defence Ministry would become the centre of Britain's defence administration, somewhat on the lines of the U.S. Pentagon, with the ministries of war, air and the admiralty becoming subordinate to it.

Defence of the Realm Act. *See* D.O.R.A.

Defender of the Faith (*Fidei Defensor*). Title conferred on Henry VIII of England by Pope Leo X, 11 Oct. 1521, in recognition of his tract against Luther entitled, ' On the Seven Sacraments, against Martin Luther, the Heresiarch, by the Illustrious Prince Henry VIII.' Continued by Parliament, 1544, and since then borne by all British sovereigns.

De Haeretico Comburendo. *See* HERESY, LAWS CONCERNING.

Deira, a kingdom of the Angles, founded by Aelle (reigned 560–88), son of Iffa; he made his kingdom independent in a

war with the sons of Ida of Bamburgh, paramount king of the Northumbrians. Ethelfrid had united D. with Bernicia (*q.v.*) by 605, and from then onwards, apart from the period 633–55, the two kingdoms were merged into one as Northumbria (*q.v.*).

Delagoa Bay, Mozambique, E. Africa. Awarded to Portugal, 1875.

Delaware, U.S.A. First explored by Hendrik Hudson, 1609. Takes its name from Thomas West, third Baron de la Warr (1577–1618), who entered D. Bay, 1610. Settled by Swedes and Finns, 1638. Dutch from 1655 to 1664, when it was surrendered to the English. This surrender was enforced by the Treaty of Westminster, 1674. Declared itself independent, 1776. Was the first state to ratify the U.S. Constitution in 1787. The state of D. had new constitutions in 1792, 1831, and 1897. In 1682 the territory was leased to William Penn, and was part of Pennsylvania until 1776. D.–Maryland border stabilized and delineated, 1767. Between 1865 and 1907 the thirteenth, fourteenth, and fifteenth Amendments of the Federal constitution were not ratified by D., consequently Negroes did not enjoy civil rights there, though D. fought on the northern side in the civil war.

Delegates, Court of. Established, 1534. Abolished, 1832, and its powers transferred to the Privy Council.

Delft, Holland. Founded by Godfrey le Bossu, 1075. The famous earthenware first manufactured here late in the sixteenth century. Diet of D. agreed to throw off allegiance to King of Spain, 1575. Estates of Holland and Zeeland assembled in congress at D. and signed a new Act of Union, 25 Apr. 1576. Assembly of United Provinces arranged constitution, 13 Jan. 1581. William the Silent assassinated at, 10 July 1584.

Delhi, India. The present city of Old D. dates from the mid seventeenth century A.D. (The Red Fort was built in 1652.) Previously taken by Tamerlane, 1398; by Nadir Shah, 1739; by Mahratta, 1759; possessed by Great Britain, 1804. During Indian Mutiny seized by Sepoys, who massacred the British there, 1857; recaptured, 20 Sept. 1857. Prince of Wales (Edward VII) visited D., 11 Jan. 1876. Queen Victoria proclaimed Empress of India, 1 Jan. 1877. D. became the official capital of India (*see* CALCUTTA) at the Coronation Durbar of 12 Dec. 1911, when the foundation stone of New D., S. of the old city, was laid. New D. was inaugurated as capital of India, 1931. Delhi Conference, 1940. Visited by Queen Elizabeth II, Jan. 1961.

Delos. Smallest of the Cyclades Islands, Aegean Sea. Now known as **Mikra Dili.** Became a great trading centre after the fall of Corinth in 146 B.C. Devastated, 87 B.C., during the Mithridatic War.

Delphi (modern **Kastri**). The oracle of Apollo at D. in Phocis was a holy spot before the Hellenic invasion, the aboriginals having worshipped a mother-goddess here: the Pythia who delivered the oracles was originally her priestess. The fame of the oracle declined after the fifth century B.C., and the treasure-houses in the walled precincts were sacked by the Phocians between 356 and 346 B.C. The Pythian Games (*q.v.*) were held under the protection of the shrine. The last oracle was uttered at the request of the Emperor Julian (reigned A.D. 361-3). The most revealing excavations were made by French archaeologists from 1892 onwards.

Delphin Classics. Collection of Latin authors prepared by thirty-nine scholars in the reigns of Louis XIV and Louis XV. *Ad usum Delfini* (for the use of the Dauphin, *q.v.*). At first under the editorship of Bossuet, and of the Dauphin's tutor, Pierre Huet, later Bishop of Avranches; published, 1674-1730.

Demarcation, Bull of, 1493. Issued by Pope Alexander VI, dividing New World discoveries between the Spanish and Portuguese.

Demerara, British Guiana. Surrendered to British 1781; again taken by Gen. White, 1796; restored to Dutch, Mar. 1802; recaptured by British, 25 Sept. 1803; ceded to Great Britain, 1814.

Democratic Party, in the U.S.A. 'Democrats' became the only familiar title for the party of Jefferson (anti-Federalist), in 1828; it has controlled the government for the following periods: 1801-41; 1845-1849; 1853-61; 1885-9; 1893-7; 1913-1921; 1932-52, and since 1960.

Dendermonde or **Termonde,** Belgium. Famous interview between William the Silent and Counts Horn, Egmont and Hoogstraaten, regarding Flanders's relationship with Spain held, 1566. Sluices opened against Louis XIV, 1667. Captured by Marlborough, 1706.

Denmark, Kingdom of. Danes began to achieve European prominence as searovers during the ninth century. Kingdom consolidated by Gorm the Old, 900-935. Jutland ecclesiastical see established, 948. Harald Bluetooth (936-86) baptized, 965. Defeated by Emperor Otto II, 974. Independence established, 983. Svein (986-1014) besieges London, 994. Conquers Norway and kills King Olaf at battle of Svold, 1000. Knut the

Great (1018-35) loses Norway, 1015. Becomes King of England, 1016. Defeats Swedes and Norwegians at battle of Helge-aa, 1025. Reconquers Norway, 1028. Break-up of Danish Empire, 1035-42. Danes do homage to Emperor Lothair, 1135. Valdemar I (the Great, 1157-82) conquers Rügen, 1168. Valdemar II (1202-41) conquers Estonia, 1219. Is defeated by Germans at Bornhöved, 1227. Christopher II concedes royal prerogative to the estates, 1320. Valdemar III cedes Schleswig to Duke of Holstein, 1326. Defeated by Holsteiners at battle of the Dannevirke (*see under* BATTLES), 1331. Valdemar IV Atterdag (1340-75) successfully defends Scania against Sweden, 1360. Storms Visby, 1361. Defeats the Hanse at battle of Hälsingborg, 1362. Treaty of Stralsund, 1370. Margaret (1387-1412) becomes Regent of Norway and Denmark, and 'Sovereign Lady' of Sweden, 1388. Defeat and conquest of Sweden at battle of Falköping, 1389. Union of Kalmar (*q.v.*), 1397. Eric of Pomerania deposed, 1439, and succeeded by Christopher of Bavaria in all three kingdoms. Christian of Oldenburg elected King of Denmark, Karl Knutson King of Sweden, 1448. Union restored, 1457. Kings of D. become Dukes of Schleswig-Holstein, 1460. Defeated by Swedes under Sten Sture the Elder at battle of Brunkeberg, 1471. Revival of union, 1497. Swedish rebellion, 1521; ends union, 1523. Decisive defeat of Hanseatic League, 1535. Reformation, 1537. Conquest of Dithmarschen, 1559. Wars with Sweden, 1563-70, 1611-13 (Peace of Knaeroed). Christian IV defeated by Tilly at battle of Lutter, 1626. Jutland overrun, 1627. Peace of Lübeck, 1629. War with Sweden, 1644-5. Loss of Scania, Blekinge, and Halland by Treaty of Brömsebro, 1645. Treaty of Roskilde, 1658. Peace of Copenhagen, 1660. War with Sweden, 1676-9 (Peace of Fontainebleau). Treaty of Frederiksborg exempts Swedish vessels from the Sound duties, 1720. Ascendancy of Struensee, 1766. Cession of Oldenburg to Prussia, 1773. Joins the Northern Confederacy against Britain, 1800. Nelson attacks Copenhagen, 1801. British seize Danish fleet, 2-5 Sept. 1807. D. allied with Napoleon, Oct. 1807. Norway ceded to Sweden at Treaty of Kiel, 1814. Holstein estates demand independence, 1844. Christian VIII's 'Open Letter,' 1846. Schleswig incorporated in D., 23 Mar. 1848. German Government formed in Schleswig-Holstein, 24 Mar. 1848. Prussian invasion, 2 May. Truce of Malmö, 26 Aug. 1848. Prussia evacuates Schleswig-Holstein, 1850.

Schleswig made a Danish province, 1863. Austro-Prussian invasion, 1864. Cession of Schleswig-Holstein by Peace of Vienna, 30 Oct. 1864. Constitutional changes, 1866. Self-government given to Iceland (*q.v.*), 1874. Prince Charles elected King of Norway as Haakon VII, 1905. Plebiscite in N. Schleswig, which is returned to D., 1920. First Social Democratic Government, 1924. German invasion, 9 Apr. 1940. German forces surrender, 5 May 1945. D. signed the North Atlantic Pact, 1949. Members of the Council of Europe, 1949. New Succession Law, 1953, admitted sovereign's daughter to the line of succession. Member of E.F.T.A., 1959. Applied for membership of the Common Market (*q.v.*), Aug. 1961, but announced, Jan. 1963, after Britain's application rejected, that she would not join until Britain did, despite reported French overtures.

Denmark, Sovereigns of:

Gorm the Old	*d. c.* 940
Harald Bluetooth	936–986
Svein Forkbeard	*c.* 986–1014
Harald II	1014–1018
Knut the Great	1018–1035
Hardicanute	1035–1042
Magnus the Good (of Norway)	1042–1047
Svein II Astridsson	1047–1074
Harald III (Hein)	1074–1080
Knut IV the Good (Saint)	1080–1086
Olaf Hunger	1086–1095
Eric the Evergood	1095–1103
Nils	1103–1134
Eric Emune	1134–1137
Eric Lam	1137–1147
Svein III	1147–1157
Knut V (for three days)	1157
Valdemar I the Great	1157–1182
Knut VI	1182–1202
Valdemar II the Victorious	1202–1241
Eric Plough-penny	1241–1250
Abel	1250–1252
Christopher I	1252–1259
Eric Klipping	1259–1286
Eric VI Maendved	1286–1319
Christopher II	1319–1326
Valdemar III	1326–1330
Christopher II (again)	1330–1332
Period of civil war	1332–1340
Valdemar IV Atterdag	1340–1375
Olaf	1375–1387
Margaret, Queen	1387–1397
Regent	1397–1412
Eric of Pomerania (of Sweden, D., and Norway)	1397–1439
Christopher III of Bavaria	1440–1448
Christian I (Oldenburg)	1448–1481
John	1481–1513
Christian II	1513–1523
Frederick I (not of Sweden)	1523–1533
Period of civil war	1533–1534
Christian III	1535–1559
Frederick II	1559–1588
Christian IV	1588–1648
Frederick III	1648–1670
Christian V	1670–1699
Frederick IV	1699–1730
Christian VI	1730–1746
Frederick V	1746–1766
Christian VII	1766–1808
Frederick (Crown Prince Regent)	1784–1808
Frederick VI (not of Norway after 1814)	1808–1839
Christian VIII	1839–1848
Frederick VII	1848–1863
Christian IX	1863–1906
Frederick VIII	1906–1912
Christian X	1912–1947
Frederick IX	1947–

Deodand. Objects which had caused human death were forfeited to the crown as Ds. till 1846.

Départements. France divided into eighty-three, 1790. Napoleon divided France into 130 D., but the number of metropolitan D. is now (1963) ninety.

Deposition, Bull of. 1. 1535, issued by Pope Paul III, excommunicating Henry VIII. 2. 1570, issued by Pius V excommunicating Elizabeth I.

Deptford. Henry VIII's dock (established 1512) here used until 1869; Peter the Great (*see* RUSSIA) came here to study shipbuilding, 1689. Royal victualling yard of the Navy established at, 1745.

Deputies, Chamber of. 1. Lower house of French legislature so named under Louis XVIII, 1814. Dissolved by Charles X, 1827, and 16 May 1830. Superseded by National Assembly, 4 May 1848. Restored by Louis Napoleon, 2 Dec. 1851. During the Second Empire (1852–1870) replaced by a 'Corps législatif.' Restored under Third Republic (1871–1940). Replaced by National Assembly, 1946. 2. Lower house of Belgian Parliament so named, 1831. Known as the Chamber of Representatives since 1921.

Derby. The original Anglian settlement was called Northworthige; this was captured *c.* 870 by the Danes, who made it one of their five boroughs, renamed it D., and fixed the county boundaries of Derbyshire. It was retaken by the English, 917. First sent burgesses to Parliament, 1295. Grammar school built, 1554. Silk mills first set up, 1717. Canal opened, 1836. Railway to Nottingham, 1839; to Leeds, 1841. Bishopric created, 1907.

Derby Day, second day of the summer meeting at Epsom, in late May or early June, when the D. Stakes, instituted 4 May 1780, are run for. Until 1891 Parliament adjourned specially on this day.

Despard's Plot, to assassinate George III, 1802. Col. D. and plotters executed, 21 Feb. 1803.

Detroit, U.S.A. First settled by Antoine Cadillac, 24 July 1701. Originally called *La Ville d'Étroit*. Surrendered to English, 29 Nov. 1760; besieged by Pontiac, 9 May 1763; relieved, 12 Oct. 1763; surrendered to Gen. Brock, 16 Aug. 1812. Centre of motor industry since the beginning of the twentieth century.

Deventer, Holland. Taken by Maurice of Saxony from Spaniards, 10 June 1591.

Devil's Island. In the Îles du Salut group, N.W. of Cayenne, French Guiana. Was notorious for its penal settlement, 1854–1938.

Devil's Parliament. Met at Coventry, 1459.

Devonport. *See* PLYMOUTH.

Diamond. Manilius spoke of it, A.D. 16; Pliny said it was known only to kings, A.D. 100, and described six varieties. Mined in India from earliest times till the close of the nineteenth century; S. America from the middle of eighteenth century; S. Africa (discovered accidentally), 1870. Phosphorescence produced by friction discovered by Robert Boyle, 1663; combustibility established by Florentine academicians, 1694. Smithson Tennant demonstrated carbon composition of Ds., 1796. *See also* KOH-I-NOOR and CULLINAN DIAMOND.

Diamond Necklace Affair (France). Queen Marie Antoinette, the Comtesse de Lamotte, the impostor Cagliostro, and the Cardinal de Rohan were implicated, 1785; Rohan's trial, 14 Apr. 1786. The countess was condemned, but escaped; Rohan was acquitted.

Diamond Sculls. Race for amateur single rowers instituted at Henley, 1844.

Dichlorodiphenyltrichloroethane (D.D.T.). First prepared by Zeidler, 1874, but not used as an insecticide until 1939.

Dictionary. A Chinese D. by Hū Shin, containing 10,000 characters, published, 150 B.C.; Italian D. of the Accademia della Crusca published, 1612; Samuel Johnson's D., 1755; Noah Webster's 1828 (now expanded into *Webster's New International Dictionary*, 1936); Sir William Smith's *Dictionary of Greek and Roman Antiquities*, 1842, *Biography*, 1849, *Geography*, 1857; Liddell and Scott's, 1843; Littré's French D., 1863–72; *Dictionary of National Biography*, edited by Leslie Stephen and Sidney Lee, 1885–1900; Funk's, 1893–5; Murray's *New English Dictionary* initiated, 1857; preparation for publishing began, 1879; first fascicle published, 1884; completed 1928; reissued, with supplement, as *Oxford English Dictionary*, 1933.

Dien-Bien-Phu, Vietnam. Scene of the final battle between French and Viet Minh forces in the 1945–54 Indo-China War. The Viet Minh captured the French positions, May 1954, with heavy losses to both sides.

Dieppe, Normandy. Occupied by the English, 1420–35. Bombarded by British, July 1694; 1794; 14 Sept. 1803. Occupied by Germans, Dec. 1870–July 1871, and again 10 June 1940. Anglo-Canadian landing at, 18–19 Aug. 1942. Liberated, 1 Sept. 1944, by same Canadian unit as had landed in 1942.

Diesel Engine. First model built, 1893–1897, by Rudolf Diesel (1858–1913).

Diet. The following are the principal Ds. of the Empire, with their dates:

Augsburg, (*a*) 1530; (*b*) 1555.
Maglione, 1502.
Roncaglia, 12 Nov. 1158.
Speyer, (*a*) 1526; (*b*) 1529.
Worms, (*a*) 1495; (*b*) 1521 (associated with Martin Luther); (*c*) 1547; (*d*) 1578.
See also REICHSTAG.

'Dieu et mon Droit' ('God and my Right'). The parole of the day at the battle of Gisors, 20 Sept. 1198, at which Richard I was present. It first appeared on the Great Seal of Henry VI; discontinued by Queen Anne, but restored by George I.

Diggers' Conference, in Victoria, Australia, was a 'shadow' parliament, which demanded representation on the Legislative Council, 1854.

Dijon, France. Roman *Divonense Castrum*. Capital of Burgundy, 1180. Joined to French crown, 1477. Capitulated to Germans, Oct. 1870.

Dingaan's Day, anniversary of the victory of Pretorius's commando over D. at Blood River, 16 Dec. 1838. Now officially known as the Day of the Covenant. *See* VOORTREKKERS; ZULUS; TRANSVAAL.

Directors' Liability Act (Great Britain). Passed, 18 Aug. 1890.

Directory, French. The Government established in France after the Convention, 27 Oct. 1795; abolished, 9 Nov. 1799.

Directory of Public Worship drawn up by Westminster Assembly of Divines, 1644; accepted by Scottish General Assembly, Feb. 1945.

Disestablishment. For D. of Anglican Church in Ireland, *see* IRELAND; in Wales, *see* WALES, CHURCH OF. The Church of Scotland virtually disestablished itself at the time of its union with the United Free Church in 1929. In France the Roman Catholic Church was disestablished in 1793–1801, and again in 1906.

Dissenters. *See* NONCONFORMISTS and PURITANS.

Dissolution of Monasteries. *See* MONAS-TERIES.

District Councils (England and Wales) established by Local Government Act, 1894.

'Divine Comedy.' Begun probably in 1300 by Dante Alighieri (1265–1321). First printed at Foligno, 1472.

Divine Right of Kings. The doctrine emphasized in opposition to the temporal claims of the Papacy and used as theoretical justification of secular interference in ecclesiastical affairs during and after the Reformation (*q.v.*), and of royal supremacy in secular affairs especially in England by James I (1603–25) and Charles I (1625–49).

Diving Bell. First used in Europe *c.* 1538.

Divorce (Britain). D. Court established, 1857; D. Amendment Act passed, 21 July 1868. D. Commission, 1910. Bill introduced, July 1913. Lord Buckmaster's Bill passed House of Lords, June 1920; passed Commons and received royal assent, 1923. A. P. Herbert's Matrimonial Causes Act gave new grounds for decrees both of nullity and of D.—notably, incurable insanity, 1937; operating, Jan. 1938.

Dniepropetrovsk. Founded (as **Eka-terinoslav**) by Potemkin, 1778.

Dobruja, Bulgaria and Rumania. Ceded to Rumania, 1878 and 1913. To Bulgaria by Treaty of Bucharest, 1918. To Rumania again, 1919. Southern part to Bulgaria, 1940; confirmed by peace treaty of 1947.

Docking and Nicking of Horses Act, 1947. Makes docking of horses illegal (except on veterinary advice).

Doctors' Commons. College for doctors of civil and canon law established by Dr. Harvey, 1567. Charter, 1768. Dissolved, 1857.

Doctors of the Church. SS. Gregory the Great; Ambrose; Augustine of Hippo; Jerome; John Chrysostom; Basil; Gregory Nazianzen; Athanasius.

The foregoing were acknowledged as D. of the C. by the early Middle Ages. The following were so declared, in the years shown, by papal decree:

SS. Thomas Aquinas, 1568; Bonaventure, 1588; Anselm, 1720; Isidore, 1722; Peter Chrysologus, 1729; Leo I, 1754; Peter Damian, 1828; Bernard of Clairvaux, 1830; Cyril of Alexandria, 1833; Cyril of Jerusalem, 1833; John of Damascus, 1833; Hilary of Poitiers, 1851; Alphonsus Lignori, 1871; Francis de Sales, 1877; The Venerable Bede, 1899; Ephrem, 1920; Peter Canisius, 1925; John of the Cross, 1926; Albert the Great, 1931; Robert Bellarmine, 1931.

Dodecanese Islands. Seized by Italy from Turkey, 1912. Greece gave up claim in favour of Italy, 1920. Formally incorporated in Greece, 1948.

Dodo. Last living specimen seen, 1681.

Dog Licence, fixed at 7*s*. 6*d*. per annum, 1878, by Act of Parliament.

Doge. *See* VENICE.

Doggett's Coat and Badge. Thomas Doggett the actor (*d.* 1721) awarded prize of coat and badge to winner of annual race on Thames by six watermen, instituted 1 Aug. 1715, in honour of George I's accession. Money was left to continue the prize.

Dole. Popular name for unemployment benefit, first became current, 1919–1920.

Dollar, Thaler, Taler, originally **Joachimsthaler.** Coins, the currency of the Hapsburg dominions, were so called from the place in Bohemia (Cz. Jachymov), where they were first coined in 1519. Brought into common use in the U.S.A. *c.* 1794, having been officially introduced in 1787.

Dollar Diplomacy. Associated with the Taft administration in the U.S.A., 1908–13, and repudiated by its Democratic successor.

Dolly's Brae, near Newcastle, County Down, was scene of riot, 12 July 1849, between Orange and Catholic factions, involving fatal casualties. Local J.P.s failed to commit Orangemen for manslaughter.

Domesday or Doomsday Book. Compiled as a survey for taxing and administrative purposes and also to obtain general information about his new territories by order of William the Conqueror, 1085–6.

Dominica, largest of the Windward Islands. Discovered by Columbus, 1493; settled by French, 1632; assigned to native inhabitants, 1660; ceded to Great Britain by Treaty of Paris, 1763; French possession, 1778–83; to Great Britain by Treaty of Versailles, 1783; attacked by French, 2 Feb. 1805; finally restored to Great Britain, 1814. Part of the Windward Islands group since 1940.

Dominican Order. Founded by St. Dominic (1170–1221) in 1216, who obtained a bull from Pope Honorius III. First chapter held at Bologna, 1220. In England they were known as Black Friars, and in 1221 set up a house in Oxford by permission of Stephen Langton.

Dominican Republic or Santo Domingo. E. portion of Hispaniola (*q.v.*). Discovered by Columbus, 1492; colony founded by his brother, Bartholomew, 1496. Ceded by Spain to France, 1795. Part of independent state of Haiti (*q.v.*),

1798–1801, French, 1801–3. Part of Haiti again, 1804–8. British helped Spaniards to drive out French, 1809. Assured to Spain by Treaty of Paris, 1814. Declared its independence, as 'Columbia,' 1821. Part of Haiti again, 1822–43. Became the independent D. R., 1844. Once more Spanish, 1861–3. Republic reconstituted, 1865. Customs handed over to U.S.A., 1907. Occupied by U.S. forces, 1916–23. Treaty with U.S.A., 1924. San Domingo, the capital, swept by hurricane, 1,000 people killed, 3 Sept. 1930. Rafael Trujillo carried out *coup d'état* and became dictator of the D. R., 1930. Name of capital changed to Ciudad Trujillo, 1936. Trujillo assassinated, 30 May 1961. Attempted coup by military junta failed, 16–17 Jan. 1962. Rafael Bonnelly sworn in as new President. First free elections since 1924 were held in Dec. 1962, when Juan Besch, a moderate progressive, was elected President. Tension between the D. R. and Haiti was acute, April–May 1963.

Dominions (British). Canada, Australia, New Zealand, S. Africa, and Irish Free State (now Irish Republic) internationally recognized as independent nations at Paris Peace Conference, 1919. Irish Free State received formal independence, 1921. Remainder with Newfoundland given legislative independence under the crown by Statute of Westminster, 1931. Newfoundland's dominion status and constitution suspended by agreement with U.K., 1934. Ireland adopted republican constitution, 1937; dominion status terminated, Apr. 1949, by the coming into force of the Republic of Ireland Act, 1948. By Act of British Parliament D. of India and Pakistan came into existence, 15 Aug. 1947. By the same Act Ceylon received dominion status, Dec. 1947. Small majority in plebiscite in Newfoundland for confederation with Canada, 1948, and joined Canada, 1949. Ghana became a dominion, 1957; Malaya, 1957; Nigeria, 1960; Cyprus, 1961; Sierra Leone, 1961; Tanganyika, 1961; Jamaica, Trinidad and Tobago, and Uganda, 1962. India became a republic, 1950; Pakistan, 1956, and Ghana, 1960, but all remain in the Commonwealth. Nigeria aims to become a republic within the Commonwealth in Oct. 1963. Cyprus has been a republic ever since acquiring dominion status; Tanganyika since December 1962. S. Africa withdrew from the Commonwealth, 1961, and became an independent republic.

Dominions Office. *See* COMMON-WEALTH RELATIONS OFFICE.

Doncaster, England. First charter granted by Richard I, 1194. Charter of 1467 authorized election of a mayor. Conference held here at which Henry VIII granted pardons (later dishonoured) to partakers in the Pilgrimage of Grace (*q.v.*), 6 Dec. 1536. Famous horse race instituted by Col. St. Leger, 1776. County borough, 1926.

Dongan Charter, granted to New York City (*q.v.*) by Thomas Dongan, governor of the city, 1686.

Donnybrook Fair, outside Dublin, was licensed, 1204; abolished, 1855.

D.O.R.A. (Defence of the Realm Acts). First of the series was passed 27 Nov. 1914; extended to supply and sale of liquor, May 1915. Ceased to operate, 31 Aug. 1921; but the D.O.R. (Acquisition of Land) Acts, 1916 and 1920, operated for five years after end of war.

Dorchester (Dorset). Besieged and burnt by the Danes, 1003; fortified by Parliamentarians, 1642–3. The famous Bloody Assizes (*q.v.*) held here, 1685.

Dorchester (Oxon). Cynegils, King of the W. Saxons, baptized here by St. Birinus, A.D. 634. King Athelstan held a great council here, 938, when he granted a charter to the Abbey of Malmesbury. D. was seat of a bishopric, 634–705 and 870–1085.

Dordrecht or Dort, Netherlands. The meeting-place of the States of Holland after their revolt from Spain, 1572. The famous Synod of D., the first general synod of the Protestants, assembled 13 Nov. 1618, and finished 25 May 1619.

Dortmund–Weser–Ems Canal. Stretch of the Ems canalized, 1892–9. The banks breached by the R.A.F., causing complete draining of the canal, 4 and 21 Nov. 1944; 1 Jan. and 3 Mar. 1945.

Douai, France. Taken from Flemings by Philip the Fair, 1297; restored, 1368. Acquired by Spain, 1529. Attempted seizure by Admiral Coligny failed, 6 Jan. 1557; taken by Louis XIV, 1667; surrendered to Marlborough, 26 June, 1710; retaken 8 Sept. 1712; Roman Catholic English College founded at, 1568; re-founded in England at Ushaw and Ware after the French Revolution. There was a Catholic school for English boys at D. (transferred there from Paris, where it had been founded in 1615) from 1818 to 1903, when it moved to Woolhampton, Berks. The D. version of the Old Testament, published here by command of the pope, 1609–10.

Douglas Rebellion. Headed by William, Earl of Douglas, 1451, as a result of the appointment of Sir William Crichton by James II of Scotland. Douglas murdered by James II in Feb. 1452.

Rebellion carried on by relatives, but finally suppressed in 1484.

Dover, England. Originally *Dwyr*, latinized as *Dubris*. King John resigned his kingdom to the papal legate at, 13 May 1213. The Emperor Charles V met by Henry VIII at, 1520. Charles II landed here after his exile, 26 May 1660. Treaty of D. between Charles II and Louis XIV, 1670. New naval harbour opened, 1909. Repeatedly bombarded, 1941–4.

Dover Patrol. Established during World War I to maintain cross-Channel communications (1914–18). Monitors added, 1915. Frequent small raids by enemy, 1915–17. *Broke* and *Swift* defeated six destroyers, Apr. 1917. War memorial to D. P. erected on French coast after World War I destroyed by the Germans during World War II. Rebuilt memorial unveiled, 7 July 1962.

Downing Street (London). Named after Sir George Downing (*c.* 1623–84). No. 10 has been the official residence of the Prime Minister since the time of Sir Robert Walpole. Drastic renovation of No. 10 commenced, Aug. 1960 (not affecting the external appearance). Scheduled for completion by end of 1963.

D'Oyly Carte Opera Company. Richard D'Oyly Carte (1844–1901) in 1875 produced *Trial by Jury*, the first of the works of W. S. Gilbert (1836–1911) and Arthur Sullivan (1842–1900) to be publicly performed; he built the Savoy Theatre, 1881, and the English Opera House (now Palace Theatre, Cambridge Circus), 1891. The company controlled the copyright in words and music of Gilbert and Sullivan operas as long as both existed (down to 1950 in the case of the music). The copyright on Gilbert's lyrics expired in Dec. 1961, and since then the operas have been performed by other theatrical companies. Richard D'Oyly Carte was succeeded in management by his son Rupert (1876–1950).

Draft Riots (New York), to resist drafting of citizens into the Union Army, 1863.

Drama. Comedy said to have been introduced from Megara into Attica *c.* 580 B.C. Theatrical exhibitions first seen in Rome, 364 B.C. Mystery plays, the origin of D. in England, were performed as early as 1136 at Dunstable. The first original secular play extant is Udall's *Ralph Roister Doister*, written about 1531. The servants of the Earl of Leicester obtained in 1574 a patent for performing plays in any part of England, and in 1576 they built a theatre at Shoreditch, which was the first public building of its kind in England. Shakespeare, with others, received a similar patent, 19 May 1603.

The theatres were all closed by a Parliamentary Act on 2 Sept. 1642. In 1737 plays were ordered to be revised and licensed by the Lord Chamberlain. *See* GLOBE THEATRE and under DRURY LANE.

Drama (American). In 1733 there appears a mention of a theatrical performance in New York. A performance of Otway's *Orphans* was enacted in 1750. *The Beaux' Stratagem* was performed by a company of London actors at Annapolis, 1752.

'Drapier's Letters.' In 1722 the English Government gave contract for making Irish copper coinage to a Mr. William Wood, of Wolverhampton. This aroused the resentment of the Irish, which was fanned into fever heat by the appearance of *Drapier's Letters*, by Dean Swift, 1724. The coinage was withdrawn in 1724.

Dreadnought, name of a battleship launched in 1906, the prototype of a class of Royal Naval battleships known as Ds., which continued to be built up to 1914; the first turbine battleships in the world, a distinctive feature was their armament, the only ordnance carried being heavy or superheavy (ten 12-in. or larger pieces) and light (twenty-four 12-pounder pieces).

Dred Scott Case, a test case in the slavery question, arose in 1848, and was finally decided on appeal to the Supreme Court, 1857.

Dresden, Germany. Capital of the Margravate of Meissen, 1270; seat of the Albertine line from 1485. Destroyed by fire and rebuilt in 1685; celebrated congress held by Napoleon, 1812; besieged by the allied armies on 26 Aug. 1813; capitulated after Napoleon had left on 11 Nov. 1813; street fighting during the revolution of 1849; occupied by Prussians, 1866. Saxon republic proclaimed after World War I, Nov. 1918. Bombed and severely damaged by British and American air forces, 13–14 Feb. 1945. Entered by the Russians, 8 May 1945. 'Dresden china' has been made at Meissen (*q.v.*) since 1710.

Dresden, Treaty of, between Frederick the Great and Maria Theresa of Austria, 25 Dec. 1745.

Dreyfus Case (France). Capt. Alfred Dreyfus (1859–1935) sentenced for high treason, Dec. 1894. New trial ordered through Émile Zola's exertions. Dreyfus again found guilty, 1899, but pardoned. Case reopened and Dreyfus declared innocent, July 1906. Dreyfus awarded the Legion of Honour, 1919.

Driving Licences. Procedure governed by the Road Traffic Acts of 1930, 1934, and 1956.

Drogheda, Republic of Ireland. Here

the chiefs of Ulster did homage to Richard II, 1395, and Poyning's Law (*q.v.*) was enacted, 1494. Stormed by Oliver Cromwell and garrison massacred, 11 Sept. 1649. Surrendered to William III, 1690.

Drunken Parliament (Scotland), 1661.

Drury Lane was known as Aldwych Way until the reign of Elizabeth I, when it was an aristocratic quarter taking its present name from Drury Place, a fifteenth-century house owned by the Drury family. The street became increasingly disreputable from about 1690 onwards, until the clearance of the whole neighbourhood when Aldwych and Kingsway were built, 1899–1905. D. L. Theatre Royal is the fourth to be built on this site; the first opened, 1663, and was burnt down, 1672. The second, designed by Wren, opened, 1674. Sheridan and his partners acquired it from David Garrick, 1776; they pulled it down in 1791, and opened the third theatre, 1794, but this was destroyed by fire, 1809. The fourth theatre, opened 1812, is, after Sadler's Wells (*q.v.*), the oldest theatre open in London (1963).

Druses. Reformed Moslem sect in Syria and the Lebanon, whose separate existence dates from the early eleventh century. They led a rebellion against the French, 1925–6, which was crushed with great severity.

Dual Alliance between France and Russia. Began with contacts established 1887; agreement to co-operate in the Far E., 1891; understanding maintained at accession of Nicholas II, 1894; alliance proclaimed, 26 Aug. 1897; pact of mutual assistance between France and U.S.S.R. signed, 2 May 1935.

Dual Monarchy. Name given to the Austrian Empire, formed by the union of Austria and Hungary from 1867 until 1917.

Dublin (Baile - atha - Cliath), Ireland. St. Patrick is said to have visited D. in 448, but the Norsemen are regarded as the real founders of the city (eighth century). D. was sacked by the Danish leader Ragnar, 831, and captured by Olaf the White, 852. Battle of Clontarf fought near, 1014. Christ Church founded by Sihtric, 1038. Possessed by Crovan, King of Man, 1066. The Earl of Pembroke (Strongbow) captured it, 1170. Many citizens murdered by Irish of surrounding hills, Easter Monday, 1209—the day known as 'Black Monday.' Castle completed, 1220. Besieged by Edward Bruce, 1315. Visited by Richard II, 1394. Bull for the foundation of a university published, 1475. Trinity College founded, 1591. Parliament held at D. after lapse of twenty-seven years,

1613. Convocation held to establish the 'Irish Articles,' 1615. Besieged by Marquess of Ormond, 1649. Oliver Cromwell arrived at, Aug. 1649. Attempt to seize the castle by the notorious Col. Blood and others frustrated, 1663. Visit of James II, who held a Parliament, 1688. Catholic pro-cathedral completed, 1825. National University of Ireland founded, 1909. Sinn Fein rebels, in rising that began 24 Apr. 1916, held G.P.O., City Hall, Four Courts, and Stephen's Green G.P.O. burned in last days of Apr. Since the treaty of 1921 the capital of the Irish Free State, since called Eire and Republic of Ireland. Insurgents opposed to treaty took possession of Four Courts, 14 Apr. 1922, and maintained their hold until 30 June, when, after three days' siege (by Free State troops), they wrecked the building by explosion, destroying the records.

Dubrovnik, formerly **Ragusa,** founded in the seventh century by fugitives from the neighbouring town of Epidaurum. In the Middle Ages was a rival of Venice, but its importance declined after 1497, and still further after the disastrous earthquake of 1667. The republic preserved its independence, though under Turkish suzerainty until 1808, when it was incorporated in Dalmatia (*q.v.*).

Duelling. Forbidden in England by an Act of Oliver Cromwell, 1654. Charles II also issued a proclamation against D., 1679. Anti-D. Association formed in England, May 1843; and three articles of war were issued in 1844 to prevent the practice in the Army. Last recorded duel in England was fought at Egham Hill, Surrey, in 1852.

Famous Duels:

Duke of Hamilton and Lord Mohun, both died. 15 Nov. 1712.

S. Martin wounded John Wilkes, M.P. 16 Nov. 1763.

Lord Byron killed Mr. Chaworth. 26 Jan. 1765.

Charles James Fox wounded by Mr. Adam. 30 Nov. 1779.

William Pitt and George Tierney. 27 May 1796.

Henry Grattan wounded Isaac Corry. 15 Jan. 1800.

Lord Castlereagh wounded George Canning. 21 Sept. 1809.

Duke of Wellington and Earl of Winchelsea. 21 Mar. 1829.

Duc de Grammont-Caderousse killed Mr. Dillon, Paris. Oct. 1862.

Don Enrique de Bourbon killed by Duc de Montpensier, near Madrid. 12 Mar. 1870.

Léon Gambetta and De Fortou, neither hit. 21 Nov. 1878.

Gen. Boulanger, seriously, and M. Floquet, slightly wounded, 13 July 1888.

Dukhobors. Russian heretic sect, sprang up during the eighteenth century. From 1755 to 1864 their leaders claimed to be reincarnations of Christ. Migrated to Canada, 1898–9, where their anarchism has since led to frequent conflicts with the Canadian authorities.

Dulwich College. Founded and endowed by Edward Alleyn, 1619. In 1857 the college was reconstituted by special Act of Parliament and formed into D. C. and Alleyn's School (also in Dulwich). New school buildings, 1870.

Duma (Russian). Council of State created, 6 Aug. 1905. Abolished at Oct. Revolution, Nov. 1917.

Dumbarton Oaks, D.C., U.S.A., was the scene of a conference between the U.S.S.R., Great Britain, and the U.S.A., 21 Aug.–27 Sept., and between Great Britain, the U.S.A., and China, 29 Sept.–7 Oct. 1944, the outcome of which was the United Nations Organization (*q.v.*).

Dumfries derived its early importance from a bridge over the Nith, built 1280. John Comyn the Red was here assassinated by Bruce's followers for compounding with the English, 1306. Robert Burns (*d.* 1796) lived in D. for the last five years of his life, and is buried here.

Dunces, Parliament of. Met at Coventry, 1404; also known as Unlearned Parliament, so called because no lawyer had a place in the assembly.

Dundee, Scotland. Taken by English under John of Gaunt, 1385. Sacked by Montrose, 1645. Besieged by Gen. Monk after battle of Worcester, 1651. The town was so greatly reduced in 1669 that contributions were made for its assistance. Visit of Queen Victoria, 1844. Tay Bridge disaster, 28 Dec. 1879.

Dunedin, New Zealand. Founded, 1848. University opened, 1871.

Dungannon Convention. Meeting of Irish Volunteers under Grattan, passed resolution for parliamentary reform for Ireland, 8 Sept. 1785.

Dunkirk or **Dunkerque**, France. Traditionally sprang up round a church built by St. Eloi in the seventh century. Sacked by the English, 1388. Taken by French, 1646; recovered by Archduke Leopold, 1652; given up to the English, 1658; sold to Louis XIV by Charles II, 17 Oct. 1662; bombarded by English, 26 July 1694. Works ordered to be demolished by Treaty of Utrecht, 1713. Duke of York forced to raise siege of, Sept. 1793. Allied troops evacuated from, May–June 1940. Fifty-year Anglo-French Treaty of Alliance signed at D., 4 Mar. 1947. War memorial at D.

unveiled by Queen Elizabeth the Queen Mother, July 1957.

Dunkirk, Treaty of, between Britain and France, signed 4 Mar. 1947 (*see* preceding article).

Dunmow Flitch, first competed for, 1244; names of successful competitors first recorded, 1445.

Dunwich. The residence of the kings of E. Anglia (*q.v.*), and the seat of their bishops, then of the more northerly of the two E. Anglian sees, 673–870. The first E. Anglian church was built here in 627 by order of King Sigeberht (*d.* 637?) for St. Felix (*d.* 648). It began to be swallowed up by the sea in the fourteenth century. As a rotten borough its parliamentary representation was abolished, 1832; it had sent two burgesses to Parliament since 1296. Corporation abolished, 1886.

Duquesne, Fort (Pa., U.S.A). Erected by French, 1754. Futile attempt to capture by Gen. Braddock, 1755; captured by Gen. Forbes and renamed Fort Pitt after the English statesman, 1758.

Durazzo, now known as **Durres** (anct. **Epidamnus** and **Dyrrachium**). Founded seventh century B.C. by settlers from Corinth and Corcyra. Captured by the Romans, fourteenth century B.C. Destroyed by earthquake, A.D. 345. Besieged, 481, 1082, and 1115. Venetian, 1392–1501, and subsequently Turkish (until 1913).

Durban, Natal, S. Africa. Founded, 1824, received its present name, 1835. Salisbury Island naval base built, 1939–1945.

Durham, England. Called by the Normans *Duresme*. Episcopal see, originally at Lindisfarne, then (from 883) at Chester-le-Street, transferred, A.D. 995. Besieged by Duncan of Scotland, 1040; entered by William the Conqueror, 1067. The present cathedral begun, 1092. Headquarters of Edward III and his army, 1327. Battle of Neville's Cross near, 1346. Henry VI visits shrine of St. Cuthbert, 1448. University founded, 1832.

Durham Report by the Earl of Durham on the state of Canada (*q.v.*) after Papineau's rebellion, 1838. Published, 1839.

Düsseldorf, Germany. Made a city, 1288; capital of the duchy of Berg, 1385, passed to the Palatinate, 1609. Taken by Ferdinand of Brunswick, 1758; by French, 6 Sept. 1795; incorporated in Prussia, 1815. Severely bombed, 1943–1945.

Dutch Guiana or **Surinam.** The first European settlement was attempted by the English, 1630. Sugar planters (Dutch and Portuguese) entered the country,

1644. Permanent settlement by English, 1650; capitulated to Dutch, 1666, and exchanged for New Amsterdam (now New York) the following year. Was again in English hands, 1799–1802 and 1804–16.

Dutch and Flemish Literature:

The following is a list of writers (not now living) in the Dutch and Flemish languages, now identical (in their literary form). Except where 'Belgian' is specified the nationality of the writers is Dutch (Netherlands).

Beets, Nikolaas (novelist), 1814–1903.
Bijns, Anna (poet), c. 1494–1575.
Bilderdijk, Willem (poet), 1756–1831.
Bosboom-Toussaint, Anna Louise Gertrude (novelist), 1812–86.
Bredero, Gerbrand (poet, playwright), 1585–1618.
Buysse, Cyriel (Belgian novelist), 1859–1932.
Cats, Sir Jakob (poet), 1577–1660.
Cauwelaert, August van (Belgian poet and novelist), 1885–1945.
Conscience, Hendrik (Belgian novelist), 1812–83.
Coornhert, Dirk Volckertszoon (humanist), 1522–90.
Couperus, Louis (novelist), 1863–1923.
Deken, Agatha (novelist), 1741–1804.
Dekker, Eduard Douwes (publicist), 1820–1887.
Geel, Jakob (critic), 1789–1862.
Gezelle, Guido Pierre Théodore Joseph (Belgian poet), 1830–99.
Heijermans, Herman (novelist and playwright), 1864–1924.
Holst, Henriette Roland (poet), 1869–1953.
Hooft, Pieter (poet, playwright, historian), 1581–1647.
Hurgronje, Christiaan Snouck (orientalist), 1855–1936.
Huygens, Sir Constantine (poet), 1596–1687.
Langendonck, Prosper van (Belgian poet), 1862–1920.

Langendijk, Willem (playwright), 1683–1756.
Ledeganck, Karel Lodewijk (Belgian poet), 1805–47.
Mont, Charles Polydore (Pol) de (Belgian poet, novelist, and essayist), 1857–1931.
Multatuli. See DEKKER.
Potgieter, Everhard Johannes (publicist), 1808–75.
Querido, Israel (novelist, critic), 1873–1932.
Rodenbach, Albrecht (Belgian poet and dramatist), 1856–80.
Sabbe, Maurits (Belgian novelist, dramatist, and critic), 1873–1938.
Staring, Antoni Christiaan Wenand (poet), 1747–1840.
Timmermans, Felix (Belgian novelist and painter), 1886–1947.
Toussaint van Boelaere, Fernand (Belgian novelist), 1875–1947.
Van den Vondel, Joost (poet, playwright), 1587–1679.
Van Eeden, Frederik Willem (poet, novelist), 1860–1932.
Van Lennep, Jakob (poet, novelist), 1802–1868.
Vermeylen, August (Belgian novelist and essayist), 1872–1945.
Woestijne, Karel van de (Belgian poet and essayist), 1878–1929.
Wolf-Becker, Elizabeth (novelist), 1738–1804.

Dutch Republic. See HOLLAND.
Dvinsk (Rus.), **Daugavpils** (Let.). Founded by Livonian knights in 1278. Polish till 1773. Russian, 1773–1919. In Latvian Republic until its annexation by U.S.S.R., 1940. Known as **Dünaburg** until 1893.
Dyarchy. A system of semi-popular government introduced into British India, 1919, as a result of the Montagu-Chelmsford report. Superseded, 1937.
Dynamite. Patented by Nobel (see NOBEL PRIZE), 1867. Manufactured in Ayrshire, 1872.

ADDENDA

E

E.A.M. (Ellenikon **Apelevtherotikon Metopon).** Political (predominantly Communist) committee controlling E.L.A.S. (*q.v.*), which withdrew from Greek territory to Bulgarian Macedonia, 1948.

Earl Marshal of England. This office has been hereditary in the family of Howard, Dukes of Norfolk, since 1672.

Earl Marshal (Mariscal) of Scotland. This office in the fourteenth century became hereditary in the family of Keith, who retained it until its suppression in 1716.

Early Closing. Movement to reduce shop assistants' working hours inaugurated, 1842. Act for E. C. of shops passed, 1919. Amended by Shops Acts, 1928 and 1937.

Early English Text Society. Founded by F. J. Furnivall (1825–1910). First publications, 1864.

Earthquakes. Many recorded in Greek and Japanese history. An earthquake accompanied the famous eruption of Vesuvius in A.D. 79. An earthquake affecting all the known world occurred 6 Sept. 543. The following is a list of the most notable subsequent E. Figures in brackets denote the approximate number of fatal casualties.

Constantinople, 553 or 555
Thrace and Asia Minor, 26 Oct. 740
Syria and Palestine, 746
Glastonbury destroyed, 11 Sept. 1275
Lisbon, 26 Jan. 1531 (30,000)
Shensi, China, 24 Jan. 1556 (830,000)
London (damaged St. Paul's), 6 Apr. 1580
Japan, Aug. and Sept. 1596
Naples, July–Dec. 1631
Jamaica, 7 July 1692
Japan, 30 Dec. 1703 (200,000)
China, Oct.–Nov. 1731
Calcutta, 11 Oct. 1737 (300,000)
Peru, 28 Oct. 1746
Cairo, 2 Sept. 1754
Lisbon, 1 Nov. 1755 (very violent; 60,000)
Messina, 5 Feb. 1783 (60,000)
Aleppo, 1822 (20,000)
Salerno, 16 Dec. 1857 (12,000)
Quito, 22 Mar. 1859
Peru, 13–15 Aug. 1868
Ischia, July–Aug. 1883
Charleston (S.C.), 1886
Japan, 28 Oct. 1891
Assam, 12 June 1897
Mont Pelée, W. Indies, 1902 (20,000)

Kangra (India), 1905 (20,000)
San Francisco, 18 Apr. 1906
Valparaiso, 17 Aug. 1906
Kingston (Jamaica), 15 Jan. 1907
Messina, 28 Dec. 1908 (77,000)
Luristan (Persia), 1909
S. Mexico, 1911
Tokyo and Yokohama destroyed, 1 Sept. 1923 (180,000); same area, 15 Jan. 1924
Horta (Azores), destroyed, 1926
Herzegovina and Dalmatia, 1927
N. Japan and Kamchatka, 16 Feb. 1927
Tajima (Japan), 7 Mar. 1927
Palestine, 11 July 1927
Chile (Talca), Dec. 1928
S. Italy, 23 July 1930
New Zealand, 3 Feb. 1931
Nicaragua, 31 Mar. 1931
Mexico, 3 June 1932
N. China, 19 Sept. 1933
Quetta destroyed, 21 Jan. 1934
Rabaul (New Britain), 2 June 1937
Alaska, 22 July 1937
Anatolia (Turkey), 19–20 Apr. 1938
S. Chile, over 20,000 dead, 26 Jan. 1939
Anatolia, over 45,000 dead, 26–29 Dec. 1939 (also July 1940 and Dec. 1942)
Karachi, Nov. 1945
Dominican Republic, Aug. 1946
N. Peru, Nov. 1946
S. Japan, Dec. 1946
Fukui, Japan, June 1948
Central Ecuador, 5 Aug. 1949
N. Assam, Aug. 1950
El Salvador, 6 May 1951
Turkey, 18 Mar. 1953
Ionian Islands, 12 Aug. 1953
Cyprus, 10 Sept. 1953
Orléansville, Algeria, 9 Sept. 1954
Afghanistan, 10–17 June 1956
Persia, 4 Nov. 1956
Jangchal, Persia, 2–11 July 1957
Persia, 13 Dec. 1957
Agadir, Morocco, 29 Feb. 1960 (12,000)
Persia, 25 Apr. 1960
Chile 21–5 May 1960 (5,000)
S. Italy, 21–2 Aug. 1962
S. Italy and Greece, 28 Aug. 1962
W. Persia, 1 Sept. 1962 (10,000)
Barce, Libya, 21 Feb. 1963 (over 250).
Skopje, Yugoslavia, 26 July 1963 (over 1,000).

East African Federation. Proposed federation of Kenya, Uganda and Tanganyika, planned to come into being at the end of 1963. Zanzibar announced her intention of joining it, July 1963.

East Anglia. Founded by Uffa on basis of existing Anglian settlements, 575. Submitted to Wessex, 826. The last three E. Anglian kings, Ethelweard, Oswald, and the martyred Edmund, were sub-kings or viceroys under W. Saxon protection, but belonged to the old royal house of Uffa. On the re-conquest of the Danelaw about 920 it was administered directly by Ealdormen under the W. Saxon crown. Knut made it one of the four principal earldoms or administrative regions of England (c. 1017), and so it remained until 1066.

Kings of E. Anglia: Uffing Dynasty:

Redwald	593–617
Eorpwald	617–628
State of anarchy	628–631
Sigeberht	631–634
Egric	634–635
Anna	635–654
Ethelhere	654–655
Ethelwald	655–664
Ealdwulf	664–713
Elfwald	713–749
Beorna	749–?
Ethelberht	?–794
Kings of Mercia (*q.v.*)	794–823
Athelstan of Wessex	? 829–? 839
Ethelweard	? 839–? 854
Oswald	? 854–? 856
Edmund (Saint)	? 856–870

Danish Kings:

Guthrum I (Guttorm)	878–890
Eohric (Eric)	890–902
Guthrum II	902–917

East, Empire of the. *See* ROMAN EMPIRE, EASTERN.

Eastern Question, Near. *See* TURKISH REPUBLIC; SYRIA; PALESTINE; EGYPT; CYPRUS; GREECE, MODERN; IRAQ; ARABIA.

East India Company, The Honourable. Incorporated by Queen Elizabeth, 31 Dec. 1600. Charter renewed, 1609. Settlement established at Surat, 1613. Conflict with Dutch E. I. C., 1621–3. Factories established at Canton, 1637, Madras, 1639. St. Helena occupied, 1651. Fort William (Calcutta) founded and Bombay given to H. E. I. C., 1668. Factory at Calcutta established, 1690. A rival New E. I. C. chartered, 1691. New E. I. C. charter extended, 1698. Bengal reorganized by Sir Charles Eyre, 1700. New E. I. C. merged with H. E. I. C., 1708 (*see* SEVEN YEARS WAR). Defeat of Oudh at battle of Buxar, 1764. Clive reforms Indian administration, 1765–7. Annexation of N. Circars, 1766. International complications arising out of the vast economic and political activities of the company led to its being placed under a certain supervision by the Regulating Act,

1773. A government Board of Control to exercise political responsibility set up by Potts India Act, 1784. H. E. I. C.'s trading monopoly became unenforceable and was abolished, 1822. As a result of the Indian Mutiny (*q.v.*) its political and administrative powers were abolished, 1858 (an Act for the better government of India). Company was finally wound up, 1873, its army having been absorbed into the forces of the crown by 1861.

East India Companies, Foreign.

1. Dutch. Founded, 1602.
2. French. Founded, 1604. Refounded, 1664. Dissolved, 1770.
3. Danish. Founded, 1614.
4. Austrian. Founded, 1720. Dissolved, 1727.

In 1621, having together eliminated the Portuguese, the English and Dutch quarrelled, and the Dutch massacred the English at Amboina in 1623. After the virtual blockade of Holland in the Anglo-Dutch wars of 1652–4, 1665–7, the French company was able to take its place and the struggle between it and the English company reached its climax in the Seven Years War (*q.v.*), 1756–63, and the total defeat of the French company. The Danish company never became a political organization, and the Austrians were persuaded by Walpole to dissolve their company.

East London, Cape Province, S. Africa. Site discovered, 1836, by John Baillie; city founded, 1847, and originally known as Fort Glamorgan.

East Prussia. *See* PRUSSIA.

Easter. Method of calculating date of E. settled by Council of Nicaea, 325.

Easter Island (Sp. **Isla de Pascua;** Polynesian **Rapa-nui**), Chile (since 1888). The English pirate Davis claimed to have visited it in 1695: the Dutch admiral Roggeveen did so, 1722. All traditions concerning the colossal E. I. statues, their origin and purpose, perished c. 1850–90 when 'blackbirders' carried off most of the male population to work in the guano islands of Peru. After 1888 survivors were repatriated, but the population was decimated by disease, the ruling class of Polynesians became extinct, and there was a total breakdown of culture. Virtually whole population became Roman Catholic c. 1860. Sheep-farming introduced from Tahiti in the 1870s. The first census was taken, Apr. 1952.

Eboracum. *See* YORK.

Ecbatana. Founded on the site of the modern Hamadan, 700 B.C. Captured, 550 B.C. by Cyrus, who made it the capital and summer residence of the Persian kings, and by Alexander, 330 B.C.

Ecclesiastical Commission. Appointed, 1835. Incorporated, 1836. Amalgamated with Queen Anne's Bounty (*q.v.*), 1947, after which the two bodies together were known as the Church Commission. *See* CHURCH COMMISSIONERS.

Ecclesiastical Courts. *See* HIGH COMMISSION and ARCHES, COURT OF.

Ecclesiastical Reservation. At Diet of Augsburg, 1555, it was decided that all ecclesiastical states secularized before 1552 were to be retained by Lutherans, but any ecclesiastic who changed his faith afterwards was to forfeit his office.

Ecclesiastical Titles Act. Passed, 1851. Repealed, 1871.

Economic Conference, Allies, at Paris, June 1916, under presidency of M. Clementel, French Minister of Commerce, to discuss post-war trade.

Economics and Political Science, London School of. Founded, 1895.

' Economist, The.' *See under* NEWSPAPERS.

Ecuador. After battle of Cajamarca, 1532, Spanish presidency of Quito established. Then became part of the new Gran Colombia republic by declaration of 17 Dec. 1819. Effective Spanish rule ended at battle of Pichincha, 24 May 1822. Constituted separate republic on break-up of the original state of Gran Colombia (*q.v.*), 1830. Devastating earthquake, Aug. 1868. Civil war between clericals and anti-clericals, 1895–6. New constitution, 1906. *Coup d'état,* 9 July 1925. Congress dissolved by junta; financial reforms, 1927. Constitutional forms resumed, 1929. Joined League of Nations, 1934. Concordat with Rome, 1937. Women first voted, 1939. War with Peru in 1941 was terminated by agreement of 29 Jan. 1942, ratified, 22 May 1944, whereby E. ceded Peru half her Amazonian territories. New constitution promulgated, 6 Mar. 1945. First census of population taken, 1950. Naval bases in Galapagos Islands leased to U.S.A., 1942. Indians first represented in Constituent Assembly, 1944. Political crisis when Ibarra regime fell, 7 Nov. 1961. After two days of confusion, Arosemena, a former vice-president with left-wing leanings, who had air force backing, sworn in as the new President.

Presidents since the Establishment of the Republic of E., 1830:

Flores (Juan José)	1830–1834
Rocafuerte	1835–1839
Flores (Juan José)	1839–1845
Roca	1845–1850
Noboa	1851
Urbina	1852–1856
Robles	1856–1859

Civil disturbance	1859–1861
Moreno (Gabriel Garcia)	1861–1865
Carrion	1865–1867
Espinosa	1868–1869
Moreno (Gabriel Garcia)	1869–1875
Borrero (Antonio)	1875–1876
Civil disturbance	1876–1878
Veintemilla	1878–1882
Civil disturbance	1882–1884
Caamano	1884–1888
Flores (Antonio)	1888–1892
Cordero	1892–1895
Civil disturbance	1895–1897
Alfaro	1897–1901
Plaza	1901–1905
Garcia	1905–1906
Alfaro	1907–1911
Estrada	1911
Plaza	1912–1916
Moreno (Alfredo Baquerizo)	1916–1920
Tamayo	1920–1924
Cordova	1924–1925
Civil disturbance: military junta	1925–1926
Ayora	1926–1931
Civil disturbance	1931–1934
Ibarra	1934–1935
Pons	1935
Paez ('Supreme Head of the State')	1935–1937
Enriquez ('Supreme Head of the State')	1937–1938
Borrero (Manuel)	1938
Narvaez	1938–1939
Arroyo del Rio	1940–1944
Ibarra (second term)	1944–1947
Mancheno	1947
Veintimilla	1947
Arosemena	1947–1948
Lasso	1948–1952
Ibarra (third term)	1952–1956
Enriques	1956–1960
Ibarra (fourth term)	1960–1961
Gallegos (two days)	1961
Arosemena (second term)	1961–

Ecumenical or Oecumenical Councils. *See* COUNCILS OF THE CHURCH.

Eddas. Compilations of Scandinavian mythology and legend made in Iceland. The 'Elder' or 'Poetic Edda' compiled *c.* 1200 by an unknown editor. The 'Younger' or 'Prose Edda' *c.* 1230 by Snorri Sturluson.

Eddystone Lighthouse. Built, 1696. Destroyed, 1703. Rebuilt, 1706. Burnt, 1755. Rebuilt, 1759. Burnt, 1770. Rebuilt, 1774. Present edifice opened, 18 May 1882.

E.D.E.S. (National Democratic Greek Army). Right-wing republican partisans ('Andartes'), operating chiefly in the Epirus against Germans and Italians, from about Apr. 1941 to Nov. 1944, under Gen. Zervas, came under allied Mediterranean command, 2 July 1943.

Edessa (now Urfa), Turkey. Ancient

city, originally *Urhai*. Rebuilt by Antiochus IV *c.* 170 B.C. Became capital of an independent kingdom of E. *c.* 132 B.C. Hadrian (A.D. 117–38) made it a Roman dependency. In 216 it became a Roman military colony and the chief frontier fortress of the Near E. Besieged by Persian King Kavad, 503. Withstood a determined siege by Persian King Chosroes, 544–5. Seized by Baldwin of Flanders and became Crusader principality, 1097. Captured by Zenghi Emir of Damascus, 1151. Lapsed into obscurity thereafter.

Edict, Perpetual. Arose out of the custom by which Roman judicial officials announced, by an edict at the beginning of their year of office, the manner in which they intended to administer justice. The form of this E. began to be standardized, *c.* 200 B.C., and was finally fixed into an unalterable code by Salvius Julianus at the order of the Emperor Hadrian, A.D. 132.

Edict of Châteaubriant. By Henry II of France against Calvinists, 27 June 1551.

Edict of Nantes. By Henry IV of France, giving toleration and a number of cities of refuge to the Huguenots (*q.v.*), 13 Apr. 1598. Revoked by Louis XIV, 22 Oct. 1685.

Edict of Restitution. By the Emperor Ferdinand II of Germany, ordaining surrender of certain Church lands, 1629.

Edinburgh. Founded by and named after Edwin, King of Northumbria, *c.* A.D. 617. Part of Northumbria till 936. Robert Bruce held Parliament at E.,1327 and 1328. Replaced Perth (*q.v.*) as Scottish capital, 1437. Pillaged by Henry VIII, 1544 and 1547. John Knox *d.* at, 1572. University established, 1582. Assembly of Convention of States, 10 Dec. 1599. Charles I crowned King of Scotland at, 16 May 1633. Castle surrendered to Cromwell, Dec. 1650. Porteous Riots (*q.v.*), 1736. Young Pretender occupies, 15–17 Sept. 1745. Building of New Town begun, 1767. Anti-Catholic riots, 1779. Scottish National Gallery opened, 21 Mar. 1859. Forth Bridge opened, 4 Mar. 1890. Scottish National War Memorial opened, 1927. Annual international music and dramatic festival inaugurated, 1947.

'Edinburgh Review.' Founded, Oct. 1802. Last issue, Oct. 1929.

Edinburgh University. Founded, 1582, by charter of James VI. Charter ratified by Scots Parliament, 1621. Constitutional changes by Act of British Parliament, 1858. Constitution now depends on the Universities (Scotland) Act of 1889.

Edirne. *See* ADRIANOPLE.

Edmunds Law against polygamy passed by U.S. Congress, 1882.

Education (U.K.). 1. England and Wales. First grant of public money for E., 1820. Privy Council committee on E. formed, 1839. E. department established in two divisions: (*a*) Popular E. (*b*) Development of science and art, 25 Feb. 1856. Royal Commission appointed, 1858. Regulations published, 1860. Royal Commission reported, 1861. New regulations, 1862. Elementary E. Act passed, 9 Aug. 1870. Made compulsory, 1876. Free, 1891. Board of E. established, 1899. E. Act passed, 18 Dec. 1902. Royal Commission on university E. in London, 1909. New E. Act, 1918. R. A. Butler's Act, 1944. Board of E. replaced by a Ministry of E.

2. Scotland. Act to compel all barons and freeholders to send their sons to school, 1494. Act to provide song schools for instruction of music, 1579. Act taxing agricultural land for maintenance of schools, 1633. Act for providing schools, 1696. Elementary E. compulsory, 1872. E. (Scotland) Act, 1945.

3. Ireland. Kildare Place Society for Promoting E. of the poor founded Dublin, 1811. Received parliamentary grant, 1819. Withdrawn and vested in Commissioners of National E., 1833. Gladstone's University Bill thrown out by Commons, 1873. Intermediate E. Act passed, 1878. Compulsory E. Act, 1892. National University of Ireland founded, 1909. Compulsory instruction in Irish language introduced, 1922.

4. N. Ireland. N. Ireland became a self-governing unit, 1920. First E. Act, 1923. Second Act, 1947, follows the pattern of the English Act of 1944.

Education (U.S.A.). E. Act, 1884. Blair E. Bill, Mar. 1886. Compulsory E. Act, 4 Apr. 1892. National E. Association appointed to committee to inquire into system of E., 1892.

See also UNIVERSITIES, and various colleges and academies.

Education, Board of. Constituted, 1899. Superseded by the Ministry of E. under the 'Butler Act' of 1944.

Edward, Lake. Discovered by Stanley, 1889. Agreed by Anglo-German boundary commission, 1902–4, that Lake E. lay within the sphere of influence of the then Belgian Congo.

Edward VI Prayer Book. *See* PRAYER BOOK OF COMMON.

Eger. *See* CHEB.

Egypt, Ancient. The following dates are approximate down to 945; all are B.C. *Earliest Dynasties:* I, 3200–3000; II, 3000–2780. *Old Kingdom:* III, 2780–2720; IV, 2720–2560; V, 2560–2420; VI, 2420–

2270. *First Intermediate Period:* VII and VIII, 2270–2240; IX and X, 2240–2100. *Middle Kingdom:* XI, 2100–2000; XII, 2000–1788. *Second Intermediate Period:* XIII–XVI, 1788–1600; XVII, 1600–1555. *The Empire:* XVIII, 1555–1350; XIX, 1350–1200; XX, 1200–1090; XXI, 1090–945; XXII, 945–c. 745; XXIII, c. 745–718; XXIV, 718–712. *Late Period:* XXV, 712–663; XXVI, 663–525 (from 663 to 610 Egypt was subject to the suzerainty of Assyria); XXVII (Persian), 525–332; meanwhile Egyptian rebellion, which gradually ousted the Persians, established XXVIII, 405–399; XXIX, 399–379; XXX, 379–341. In 332 Egypt was conquered by Alexander the Great, at whose death (323) Ptolemy established the Greek dynasty. This lasted, with varying fortunes, until 30, when Egypt was made a Roman province.

Egypt, Modern. Christianity existed in E., second century A.D. Roman E. conquered by Arabs, 640. Conquered for Moawiya the Ommayad, 658. Conquered by Abbasids c. 750. Coptic revolt crushed, 832. Ruled by Tulunid dynasty, 868–903. Returned to allegiance of Bagdad, 906. Conquered, 969, by the Fatimids, who ruled till 1171, when the country was conquered by Saladin. From 1261 country ruled by Mamelukes (*q.v.*) under nominal caliphs (*q.v.*), until conquered by the Ottoman Empire (*q.v.*) under the Sultan Selim, 1517. Invaded by French under Napoleon, 1798. Expelled by British and Turks. Virtually independent after revolts of Mehemet Ali Pasha, 1831 and 1839. Mehemet Ali made hereditary khedive, 15 July 1841. De Lesseps obtained concession for the construction of the Suez Canal, 1856. Commercial treaty with Britain, 19 Apr. 1861. Suez Canal opened for navigation, 1869. British anti-slavery expedition, 1869, continued by Gordon, Nov. 1874. Britain purchased Suez Canal shares. Government defaulted on loans, 1876, and instigated anti-foreign rioting which led to British bombardment of Alexandria, July 1882, and Arabi's religious war, 24 July 1882. Arabi defeated at Tel-el-Kebir, 13 Sept. 1882. Constitution promulgated, 1883. Anglo-Turkish convention respecting E., 15 July 1887. Special mission to King Menelek of Abyssinia, 1897. Sir F. R. Wingate (1861–1953) appointed C.-in-C. Egyptian Army, 1899. British interests in E. recognized by France (*see* ENTENTE CORDIALE), 1904. Khedive Abbas II deposed as pro-Turkish by British, 1914. British protectorate established, with Hussein Kamil as sultan, 20 Dec. 1914. Hussein *d.*, 9 Oct. 1917. Succeeded by

Fuad. E. declared kingdom, 16 Mar. 1922. Makwar dam opened, Jan. 1926. King Fuad visited England, 1927. Draft Anglo-Egyptian Treaty rejected by Nationalists, Aug. 1927. Anglo-Egyptian agreement on rights in the waters of the Nile, May 1928. Anti-British rioting and neutral ministry formed, Jan. 1936. King Fuad *d.*, Apr. 1936; succeeded by Farouk I (*b.* 11 Feb. 1920). E.'s sovereignty and independence recognized by treaty with Britain, 26 Aug. 1936. Diplomatic relations with Germany severed, 3 Sept. 1939. (*See* WORLD WAR II.) British troops evacuated from Cairo and Alexandria, 1947. Palestine invaded, 15 May 1948. Israeli troops entered Egyptian territory, Dec. 1948. A truce, 7 Jan. 1949, followed by a general armistice, 24 Feb. 1949.

Demand for 'Unity of Nile Valley'—i.e. annexation of Sudan—and evacuation of Canal Zone despite treaty of 1936, made by Nahas Pasha, Dec. 1951. Ismailia police station shelled and stormed by British Army, 25 Jan. 1952. Anti-European riots in Cairo, 26 Jan. *Coup d'état* by Gen. Mohammed Neguib after flight abroad of most of Wafd leaders, 22 July 1952. King abdicated and Prince Ahmed Fuad (*b.* 16 Jan. 1952) proclaimed, 28 July. Government under Ali Maher Pasha took oath, 24 July. Constitution of 1923 revoked, 10 Dec. Agricultural Reform Decree, Sept. 1952, limiting land ownership.

Agreement with Great Britain over status of Sudan signed, 12 Feb. 1953. Republic proclaimed with Neguib as first president, 18 June. Neguib forced to resign all offices, April 1954. Government carried on by a council of ministers until 1956, when Nasser became premier, and subsequently president and virtual dictator of E. E. took over defence of the Suez Canal from Britain, Nov. 1955; Last British troops left E., 31 Mar. 1956. Britain and U.S.A. withdrew offer of financial aid for building of Aswan high dam, July, and Nasser (26 July) nationalized the Suez Canal Co. Hostilities broke out between E. and Israel again, Oct.; Israel invaded E. France and Britain called on both sides to stop fighting; E. ignored the ultimatum and an Anglo-French force occupied Port Said. E. blocked the Suez Canal with sunken ships. E. accepted a cease-fire on U.N. conditions, 7 Nov; Britain and France called on by U.N. to withdraw forces from E. This they agreed to do on 3 Dec. Withdrawal of Anglo-French forces complete by 22 Dec. De Lesseps statue in Port Said blown up by Egyptians, 24 Dec. Suez Canal re-opened to traffic, 30 Apr. 1957. Union of Egypt and Syria proclaimed by Presidents of both countries, 1 Feb. 1958; two countries to be known henceforth as the United Arab Republic. For Egyptian history after 1 Feb. 1958 see UNITED ARAB REPUBLIC. See also SUDAN; SUEZ CANAL; ISRAEL; ARAB LEAGUE; SYRIA.

Eidsvold, Norway. Norwegian constitution drawn up at and signed, 17 May 1814.

Eiffel Tower, Paris. Built, 1887-9.

Eight Articles. Drawn up by Cranmer, Ridley, and Latimer, 1555.

Eighty Club. Established, 1880.

'Eikon Basilike.' Published, 1649.

Einsiedeln, Switzerland. St. Meinrad, the hermit, was murdered here, 861, and an abbey founded on the site of his cell c. 934. Paracelsus b. in E., 1493, and Zwingli a parish priest here, 1516-18.

Eire. For previous history see IRISH FREE STATE. New constitution passed, 14 June 1937. British sold all naval bases in E. to E. Government for £50,000,000, and a trade agreement, 25 Apr. 1938. Douglas Hyde first president, 4 May 1938. Trade agreement with Germany, 13 Nov. 1938. De Valera protested at application of Military Training Act to Northern Ireland, 2 May 1939. Irish Republican Army declared illegal, 23 June 1939. Neutrality in World War II announced, 28 Sept. 1939. Douglas Hyde d. May 1945, and succeeded, 25 June 1945, by Seán Thomas O'Kelly. Clann na Poblachta Party founded by Seán McBride, 1946. Admission of E. to U.N.O. vetoed by U.S.S.R., 1946 and 1947. Dail Eireann reformed, 1947, to consist of 147 members. General Election of 4-10 Feb. 1948 won by Fine Gael and Clann na Poblachta combination, and John A. Costello appointed prime minister. Thereafter see under IRELAND: Republic of Ireland.

Eisteddfod. Welsh festival of the arts, with origins at least as early as the sixth century A.D. but not called Es. before 1450. Modern conception of the E. dates back to the Corwen E. of 1789. National E. of Wales established 1880, and now held annually.

Ekaterinburg (now **Sverdlovsk**). The Tsar Nicholas II was murdered at, July 1918.

Ekaterinoslav. See DNIEPROPETROVSK.

El Alamein. Eighth Army offensive, marking decisive turning-point of World War II, begun there, 23 Oct. 1942.

E.L.A.S. (**Ellenikos Laikos Apelevtherotikos Stratos**), the armed forces of E.A.M. (q.v.), became active against the Germans after June 1941; engaged in civil war, Dec. 1944, 12 Feb. 1945, and again, 1947-9.

Elba, Isle of, Italy. Taken by Nelson, 9 Aug. 1796. Given, 1814, to Napoleon, who escaped from it, 26 Feb. 1815.

Elders of Zion. Their alleged 'Protocols' published in Russia, 1903, 1905, 1907, were said to have been drawn up, 1897. Exposed as a forgery in The Times, 16, 17, 18 Aug. 1921.

Elections (U.K.) See FRANCHISE.

Electoral Commission (U.S.A.). Bill for regulating elections passed Congress, 29 Jan. 1877. E. C. assembled, 1 Feb. 1877.

Electors of the Holy Roman Empire. The highest ranking princes of the H. R. E., to whom was accorded exclusively the right to elect the Holy Roman Emperor. Their position and rights were settled by the Golden Bull (q.v.) of Charles IV, 1356, and their number restricted to seven, viz.: the Archbishops of Cologne, Mainz, and Trier, the King of Bohemia, the Count Palatine of the Rhine, the Margrave of Brandenburg, and the Duke of Saxony. To this number were added, Bavaria 1623, Hanover, 1692. Electoral rights ceased at abolition of H. R. E., 1806, though the title 'Elector' was used by the Duke of Hesse till 1859.

Electricity. Thales of Miletus said to have noticed the magnetic qualities of rubbed amber, 600 B.C. William Gilbert of Colchester (1540-1603) experimented with magnetic needle. Robert Boyle (1627-91) conducted experiments. Experiments of Royal Society, 1676, following observations of Sir Isaac Newton (1642-1727). Francis Hawksbee experimented with mercury, 1705, and published results, 1709. Dufay (1699-1739) distinguished experimentally two kinds of E. Leyden jar invented by Cunaeus, 1745, improved by Sir W. Watson (1715-1787). Royal Society experiments on velocity of E., 1747. Benjamin Franklin (1706-90) presented theory of positive and negative E. and identified lightning with electric spark. John Canton (1715-72) demonstrated induction. Experiments in atmospheric E. by Beccaria (1716-81), with silk by Robert Symmers, 1759. With metals and salts by Sir D. Brewster (1781-1868). With gases by Henry Cavendish (1731-1810). By Galvani, 1790, and Volta, 1800, which led to invention of galvanic battery and voltaic pile. Magnetic action of E. discovered by Oersted of Copenhagen, 1819. Ampère's theory, 1820. Faraday discovered electro-magnetic rotation, 1821. Seebeck discovered thermo-electricity, 1822. Ohm's law, 1827. Weber invented electro-dynamometer, 1832. Induction and transformer elaborated by Faraday, 1831. Lenz's

Law, 1835. Daniell battery, 1836. Grove's battery, 1836. Bunsen battery, 1842. Sir William Thomson (Lord Kelvin)'s inventions, 1851 *et seq.* Siemens dynamo, 1867. Fauré accumulator, 1881. First electric power station in England opened at Godalming, 1881. D.C. and A.C. converter by Salomons and Pyke, 1892. Electric theory of matter by Niels Bohr, 1913. First power station producing E. from nuclear power opened at Calder Hall (*q.v.*), 1956.

Electric Light. Carbon arc first produced by Sir H. Davy, 1810. Staite's patented lamp, 1847. Serrins ditto, 1857. S. Foreland lighthouse lighted by E. L., 1857. Edison and Swan's incandescent lamp, 1878–80. Tungsten filament, 1904. Neon tubes for street advertisements, 1931. Mercury and sodium vapour lamps for street and floodlighting, 1937.

Electric Lighting Act (Great Britain), 1882. Amended, 1888.

Electric Railway. First experiments by Robert Davidson, 1837. Siemens exhibited dynamo traction at Berlin, 1879. Permanent E. R. opened near Berlin, 1882. E. trams at Leytonstone, 4 Mar. 1882. The same Portrush to Bushmills, early 1882. Liverpool overhead E. R., 1893. City and S. London, 1890. Chicago, 1895 (first in U.S.A.). Underground Waterloo to Mansion House electrified, 11 July 1898. Central London line, 27 June 1900. Mersey railway, 1903. Subsequently considerable electrification of English railways; all underground railways electrified, most suburban services, and, since World War II, many main line routes. New underground line from Victoria to Walthamstow started, 1962. Expected to take six years to complete.

Electric Telegraph. *See* TELEGRAPHY.

Electrons. Discovered by Sir Joseph John Thomson (1856–1940), 1897.

Elgin Marbles brought to England *c.* 1812 by Thomas Bruce, Lord E. (1766–1841) and bought for the British Museum (*q.v.*), 1816.

Ely, England. Abbey founded by St. Etheldreda, 673. Burnt by Danes, 870. Re-founded by Ethelwold, Bishop of Winchester, 970. Present building begun, 1083. Resistance of Hereward the Wake, 1068–71. Barons' stronghold taken by Prince Edward, 1267. Cathedral octagon finished, 1328. King's school founded, 1543.

Élysée (Paris). Built, 1718. Became the presidential residence, 1870.

Elzevir or **Elsevier Press.** Founded at Leyden, 1580, by Louis E. (1540–1617). Last representatives of family, Abraham, university printer at Leyden, 1681–1712, and Peter, bookseller at Utrecht, 1665–75.

The firm continued till 1712.

Emergency Powers Act, 1939. Passed, 24 Aug.

Emmet's Insurrection. Headed by Robert E. (1778–1803) in Ireland, 23 July 1803. E. arrested 25 Aug. and executed 20 Sept. 1803. *See* UNITED IRISHMEN.

Emperor of India. Title proclaimed for British sovereigns, 1 Jan. 1877. Dropped, 15 Aug. 1947.

Empire Day inaugurated, 1902, on 24 May, Queen Victoria's birthday. Known as Commonwealth Day since Dec. 1958.

Empire Marketing Board. Formed, 1926. Discontinued, 1933.

Empire Settlement Act passed, 1922.

Empire State Building, New York. Built, 1930–1.

Employers' Liability Act. Passed for seven years, 7 Sept. 1880. Prolonged for one year, 24 Dec. 1888. Between 1889 and 1946 kept alive by Expiring Laws Continuance Acts. In 1946 the E. L. A. was repealed by the Law Reform (Personal Injuries Act) which, together with the National Insurance (Industrial Injuries) Act (1946), effected far-reaching reforms in the field of workmen's compensation.

Employment Exchanges. Instituted 1905 in U.K. under management of local authorities. Transferred to control of Board of Trade, 1909 (when they were known as Labour Exchanges). To Ministry of Labour, 1917.

Ems Telegram from King William of Prussia to Bismarck, July 1870, which, when published by Bismarck, with parts deliberately suppressed, helped to provoke the 1870 war against France.

Encyclopaedia. Speusippus (*d.* 339 B.C.) is alleged to have compiled an E. which has not survived; neither has the work of Varro (*d. c.* 27 B.C.) entitled *Nine Books of Instruction.* The *Natural History* of Pliny the Elder (A.D. 23–79) is virtually an E. The most important medieval Es. in Latin were those of Martianus Capella the African (fifth century), Isidore of Seville (570–636), and the *Speculum Triplex* of Vincent de Beauvais (*d. c.* 1264). At the same time the Arabs both translated Greek Es. and compiled their own, of which the geographical E. by Yaqut ibn 'Abdullah er-Rumi (1179–1229), a bookseller of Greek extraction, is the best known; it quotes the only surviving passages of Ibn Fadhlan's description of Scandinavians (*Rus*) in S. Russia, written in 921. The greatest Chinese E. was compiled in the reign of Yung Lao (*d.* 1425). Pierre Bayles's *Dictionnaire Historique et Critique* (1697) was the first E. of modern European type, of which the first English example was the *Cyclopaedia* of

Epuraim Chambers (*d.* 1740). Diderot and D'Alembert's *Encyclopédie* (1751–72) was based on a translation of it. The *Encyclopaedia Britannica* was first printed, 1768–71; all editions from the 11th (1910–11) onwards produced under American proprietorship. *Chambers's Encyclopaedia* was first edited 1850–68 by Dr. Andrew Findlater. *Everyman's Encyclopaedia*, where conciseness and relatively low cost were combined with scholarship, was first published by J. M. Dent & Sons Ltd in 1911; 4th edition, 1958.

Enderby Land, Antarctica. Visited by John Biscoe, 1831, and named after his employers. Now part of Australian Antarctic Territory.

Enforcing Act (U.S.A.). Passed by Congress, 9 Jan. 1809, for preserving strict neutrality in Napoleonic War. *See* BAYONNE DECREE.

Engagement, The. Agreement between Charles I and the Scots Commissioners in the Isle of Wight, 1647.

England, Church of. Christianity brought to England by Roman soldiers in first century A.D., but Romano-Celtic Church overwhelmed by Anglo-Saxon invasions, although it survived in the W. and in Wales. St. Augustine sent from Rome, 596, and first church founded at Canterbury, 597 (traditionally on the site of a former Romano-Christian basilica). Metropolitan province of Canterbury set up, and that of York planned, by Pope Gregory, 601. Irish Celtic monks had settled at Iona, 563, and begun the evangelization of the N. Church of Northumbria founded by Paulinus, 627; of E. Anglia by Felix, 631; of Wessex by Birinus, 634. Real evangelization of Northumbria work of St. Aidan, an Iona monk, from 635 onwards. Dispute with Celtic Church settled at Synod of Whitby, 664. Synod of Hertford, 673. *Ecclesiastical History* written by Venerable Bede, who *d.* 735. Third province, with archiepiscopal seat at Lichfield, set up by King Offa in Mercia, but it lasted only from 787 to 802. Councils of Clovesho, 747, 803, of Chelsea, 787, of St. Paul's, 1075, of Winchester (ordering clerical celibacy), 1076. Separation of church and lay courts, 1086. Council of Rockingham, 1095; of Westminster, 1102; of London, 1107. Legatine Council at Westminster, 1125. Murder of Becket, 1170. Legatine Council at London, 1237. Convocations organized *c.* 1283. Wycliffe condemned, 1382. Lollard Act, 1414. Papal authority repudiated and Henry VIII declared head of the church, 1534. Visitation of the monasteries, 1535. Suppression of monasteries, 1536 and 1539.

Ten Articles, 1536. Great Bible authorized, 1538. Act of Six Articles, 1539. English Litany, 1544. First Book of Common Prayer, 1549. Clerical marriage permitted, 1549. Second Book of Common Prayer, 1552. Forty-two Articles, 1553. Reconciliation with Papacy by Mary I, 1554. Independence re-established, 1559, by Queen Elizabeth I. Act of Uniformity restored the 1552 Prayer Book but with certain Catholic amendments. Eleven Articles, 1560. Thirty-nine Articles, 1563. Hampton Court Conference (*q.v.*), 1604. Authorized Version of Bible, 1611. Solemn League and Covenant (*q.v.*), 1643. Establishment of Presbyterianism, 1646. Private use of Prayer Book forbidden, 1655. Savoy Conference, 1667. Trial of Seven Bishops, 1688. Establishment of Queen Anne's Bounty (*q.v.*), 1704. Ecclesiastical Commission (*q.v.*) incorporated, 1836. Church Discipline Act, 1840. Oxford Movement begun, 1833; its first phase ended with Newman's conversion to Rome, 1845. Enabling Act endowed National Assembly of Church of England with legislative powers, 1919. Welsh Church disestablishment came into operation, 1920. Lambeth Conferences (held periodically since 1867) increasingly concerned with Christian reunion. Church Assembly proposed a new Prayer Book, 1927, but this was rejected by Parliament, 1928. Archbishop of Canterbury visited Pope John XXIII, Dec. 1960.

See BISHOPRICS; GREAT BRITAIN; BIBLE, TRANSLATIONS OF; PRAYER, BOOK OF COMMON, etc.

English History. *See* BRITAIN. English mercenaries hired by King Vortigern of Kent mutiny, and make their leader Hengest king, *c.* 450. His descendant, Ethelbert of Kent, marries Christian Frankish wife, 550. Arrival of St. Augustine (*see* ENGLAND, CHURCH OF), 597. From 617 the leading English power was Northumbria, but in 730 supremacy of Mercia was established till battle of Ellendun, 821. Egbert, King of Wessex, becomes first king of the English, 829. He defeats first Danish invasion at battle of Hingston Down, *c.* 835. Arrival of the Danish Here (*q.v.*) in England, 864. It storms York, 865. Defeats Alfred the Great at battle of Ashdown, 870. Alfred driven into Athelney, 877. His great victory at Edington and Truce of Chippenham, 878. Treaty of Wedmore (*q.v.*), 878. He publishes compendium of law, 890–92. Promotes learning, 890–901. English Danes conquered by Edward the Elder, 901–25. Athelstan's great victory over Irish, Danes, Norwegians, Welsh, and Scots at Brunanburh, 937. Dunstan, Abbot of Glastonbury, banished, 956. Recalled and made Archbishop of Canterbury, 960–88. Danish victory at Maldon, 991. Danegeld (q.v.) instituted, 991. At death of Ethelred the Unready and Edmund Ironside, 1016, Knut of Denmark (q.v.) becomes king of the English. He visits Rome, 1027; conquers Norway, 1028, and Scotland, 1031. Wessex dynasty restored by Edward the Confessor, 1042. Death of Earl Godwin, 1053. Battle of Fulford, 21 Sept. 1066. Battle of Stamford Bridge, 25 Sept. 1066. Harold II killed at battle of Hastings, 14 Oct. 1066.

Harrying of the North, 1069–70. Lanfranc consecrated Archbishop of Canterbury, 1070. Invasion of Scotland, 1072. Baronial revolt, 1075. Arrest of Odo of Bayeux, 1082. Domesday Book (q.v.), 1085–6. William II's quarrel with Archbishop Anselm, 1093–6. Anselm in exile, 1097. Anselm goes to Rome, 1103. Henry II conquers Normandy, 1106. Investiture (q.v.) compromise, 1105. Civil war and French attacks in Normandy, 1111–25. Prince William drowned, 1125. Matilda marries Geoffrey of Anjou, 1127. Civil war throughout reign of Stephen, 1135–54. Henry II attacks Toulouse, 1159. Constitutions of Clarendon (q.v.), 1164. Juries (see under JURY, TRIAL BY) instituted in some judicial proceedings, 1166. Murder of Becket, 1170. Invasion of Ireland by Strongbow, 1171. Baronial revolt, 1173. Institution of judicial circuits and Eyres (see EYRE, COMMISSIONS OF GENERAL) c. 1175.

Richard I leaves England for Palestine, 1190. Arrives Acre, 8 June 1191. Returns to England, 13 Mar. 1194. French War, 1194–9.

John loses Normandy, 1204–5. Excommunicated, 1209. Reconciled with Papacy, 1213. Battle of Bouvines, 1214. Grants Magna Carta, 1215 (q.v.).

French invaders driven out, 1217. Barons' war begins, 1262. Simon de Montfort killed at battle of Evesham, 1265. Statute of Mortmain (q.v.), 1279. Statute of Wales, 1284. Quia Emptores, 1290. Award of the Scottish crown to John Balliol, 1292. Scottish rebellion, war in Aquitaine, Welsh rebellion, 1295. Model Parliament, 1295. Confirmatio Cartarium, 1297. Treaty of L'Aumône, 1299. Edward of Caernarvon proclaimed Prince of Wales, 1301. Charter of Merchants, 1303. Robert Bruce's rebellion, 1305–7. Battle of Bannockburn, 1314. Hundred Years War begins, 1338. Naval victory at Sluys, 1340. Edward III claims French throne, 1340. Battle of Crécy, 1346. Capture of Calais, 1347. Battle of Neville's Cross, 1346.

Black death, 1346–7. Battle of Poitiers 1356. Death of Black Prince, 1376. Peasants' revolt under Wat Tyler, 1381. Death of Wiclif, 1384. Death of John of Gaunt, 1399. Lancaster's revolt and deposition of Richard II, 1399. Glendower's rebellion, 1400. Persecution of Lollards (q.v.), 1401. Rebellion of Percys, 1403. Hundred Years War resumed, 1415. Battle of Agincourt, 25 Oct. 1415. Rouen captured, 1419. Treaty of Troyes, 1420. Orléans relieved by Joan of Arc, 29 Apr. 1429. Cade's rebellion, 1450. All France, except Calais, lost, 1454. Wars of Roses (q.v.) begin at battle of St. Albans, 22 May 1455. Henry VI deposed after battle of Towton, 1461.

Death of Warwick the Kingmaker at battle of Barnet, 1471. Caxton sets up printing press at Westminster, 1476. Edward V murdered ('The Princes in the Tower'), 1483. Wars of Roses end in death of Richard III (killed at battle of Bosworth, 1485).

Star Chamber Act, 1487. Lambert Simnel's insurrection, 1486–7. Columbus reaches W. Indies, 1492. Cornish rebellion, 1497. Perkin Warbeck's rebellion, 1492–8. Cabot sails from Bristol to N. America, 1492. Battles of the Spurs and of Flodden, 1513. Wolsey becomes Chancellor, 1516. Field of the Cloth of Gold, 1520. Fall of Wolsey, 1529. Henry VIII's church reforms, 1531–40 (see ENGLAND, CHURCH OF). Thomas Cromwell executed, 28 July 1540. Scots defeated at Solway Moss, 1542. War with France, 1544. War with Scotland, 1547. Somerset Lord Protector, 1547. Battle of Pinkie, 1547. First Prayer Book of Edward VI used, 1549. Northumberland Protector, 1550. Second Prayer Book, 1552. Northumberland's attempt to put Jane Grey on throne foiled by Mary I, 1553. She marries Philip II of Spain, 1554. Wyatt's rebellion and execution, 1554. Lady Jane Grey executed, 1554. Reconciliation with Rome, 1554. Persecution of Protestants and burning of Cranmer, Latimer, and Ridley, 1555–6. War with France, 1557. Calais lost, 1558. Acts of Uniformity and Supremacy, 1559. Treaty of Câteau Cambrésis (q.v.), 1559. Court of High Commission (q.v.) set up, 1559. Treaty of Edinburgh, 1560. Hawkins's ships and goods seized in Spain, 1563. Hawkins's fleet attacked at San Juan de Ulloa and pay of Spanish Netherlands Army detained by Elizabeth, 1568. Papal Bull of Deposition issued against Elizabeth, 1570. Dutch rebels seize Brill, 1572. Drake sails round the world, 1576–9. Throgmorton's plot, 1584. Babington's plot, 1587. Execution of Mary Queen of

Scots, 1587. Drake attacks Cadiz, 1587. Defeat of the Armada (*q.v.*), July–Aug. 1588. Essex storms Cadiz, 1596. Foundation of E. India Co. (*q.v.*), 1600. Spanish expedition to Ireland, 1601. *D.* of Elizabeth I and succession to throne as James I of James VI of Scotland, 1603. (*For later history see* GREAT BRITAIN, HISTORY OF.)

English Literature.

The following is a list of famous writers in the English language (excepting American, for whom *see* AMERICAN LITERATURE IN ENGLISH) not now living:

À Beckett, Gilbert, 1811–56, humorist.

Abercrombie, John, 1780–1844, medical and psychological writer.

Abercrombie, Lascelles, 1881–1938, poet.

Acton, John E. E. Dalberg-Acton, Lord, 1834–1902, historian.

Addison, Joseph 1672–1719, poet and essayist.

Aelfric, 955–*c.* 1022, theologian and educationist.

Agate, James Evershed, 1877–1947, dramatic critic.

Aguilar, Grace, 1816–47, novelist and Jewish historian.

Ainger, Canon Alfred, 1837–1904, biographer and critic.

Ainsworth, William Harrison, 1805–82, novelist.

Akenside, Mark, 1721–70, poet.

Aldington, Richard, 1892–1962, poet, novelist, and biographer.

Alexander, Samuel, 1859–1938, philosopher.

Alfred the Great, King, *c.* 849–99, translator.

Alison, Sir Archibald, 1792–1867, historian.

Allen, C. Grant, 1848–99, scientific writer and novelist.

Allingham, William, 1824–89, poet.

Amory, Thomas, *c.* 1691–1788.

Anson, Sir William Reynell, 1843–1914, jurist.

Apperley, Charles James ('Nimrod'), 1779–1843, sporting journalist.

Arbuthnot, John, 1667–1735, satirist (originator of the term 'John Bull').

Archer, William, 1856–1924, translator of Ibsen, dramatic critic.

Armstrong, John, 1709–79, physician and poet.

Arnold, Sir Edwin, 1820–1904, poet.

Arnold, Matthew, 1822–88, poet and critic.

Arnold, Thomas, 1795–1842, historian.

Ascham, Roger, 1515–68, didactic writer.

Ashley, Sir William, 1860–1927, economist.

Ashmole, Elias, 1617–92, antiquarian.

Atterbury, Francis, 1662–1732, controversialist.

Aubrey, John, 1626–97, antiquarian.

Aumonier, Stacy, 1887–1928, short-story writer.

Austen, Jane, 1775–1817, novelist.

Austin, Alfred, 1835–1913, poet laureate.

Austin, John, 1790–1859, jurist.

Aytoun, Sir Robert, 1570–1638, Scots poet.

Bacon, Francis, 1561–1626, philosopher.

Bacon, Roger, *c.* 1214–92, scientist and philosopher.

Bagehot, Walter, 1826–77, writer on economics, politics, and L.

Baillie, Joanna, 1762–1851, Scots poet.

Balfour, Arthur J., Earl of, 1848–1930, statesman and essayist.

Barbour, John, *c.* 1320–95, Scots poet.

Barclay, Alexander, 1475?–1552, poet.

Barham, Richard Harris, 1788–1845, poet.

Baring, Maurice, 1874–1945, poet and novelist.

Baring-Gould, Sabine, 1834–1924, novelist and hymn writer.

Barker, Sir Ernest, 1874–1961, historian and philosopher.

Barker, Harley Granville-, 1877–1947, dramatist and critic.

Barlow, Jane, 1857–1917, novelist.

Barnes, William, 1801–86, lyric poet.

Barrie, Sir James Matthew, 1860–1937, novelist and dramatist.

Barrow, Isaac, 1630–77, divine and mathematician.

Bax, Ernest Belfort, 1854–1926, philosopher and journalist.

Baxter, Richard, 1615–91, theologian and hymn writer.

Beaconsfield, Earl of (Benjamin Disraeli, 1804–81, novelist.

Beaumont, Francis, 1584–1616, dramatist.

Beddoes, Thomas Lovell, 1803–49, poet.

Bede, the Venerable, *c.* 673–735, historian.

Beeching, Henry Charles, 1859–1919, poet and essayist.

Beerbohm, Sir Max, 1872–1956, critic and miscellaneous writer.

Beeton, Mrs. Isabella, 1836–65, cookery writer.

Behn, Aphra, 1640–89, dramatist.

Beith, Maj.-Gen. J. H. *See* HAY.

Bell, Gertrude Margaret, 1868–1926, oriental traveller.

Belloc, Hilaire, 1870–1953, poet, essayist, and historian.

Bennett, Enoch Arnold, 1867–1931, novelist.

Benson, Arthur Christopher, 1862–1925, novelist and essayist.

Benson, Stella, 1892–1933, novelist.

Bentham, Jeremy, 1748–1832, political writer.

Bentley, Edmund Clerihew, 1875–1956, journalist and novelist.

Bentley, Richard, 1662–1742, scholar and critic.

Berkeley, George, 1685–1753, philosopher.

Besant, Annie, 1847–1933, writer on theosophy and India.

Besant, Sir Walter, 1836–1901, novelist.

Betterton, Thomas, 1635?–1710, dramatist.

Binyon, Laurence, 1869–1943, poet and dramatist.

Birkenhead, Lord, 1872–1930, jurist.

Birmingham, George (Canon J. O. Hannay), 1865–1952, novelist.

Birrell, Augustine, 1850–1933, essayist.

Blackie, John Stuart, 1809–95, scholar and man of letters.

Blackmore, Richard Doddridge, 1825–1900, novelist.

Blackstone, Sir William, 1723–80, jurist.

Blackwood, Algernon, 1869–1951, novelist.

Blair, Robert, 1699–1746, poet.

Blake, William, 1757–1827, poet and painter.

Bland, Edith ('E. Nesbit'), 1858–1924, novelist.

Bland, Hubert, 1856–1914, journalist.

Blessington, Marguerite Power, Countess of, 1789–1849, novelist and essayist.

Bloomfield, Robert, 1766–1823, rural poet and miscellaneous writer.

Blunt, Wilfrid Scawen, 1840–1922, poet.

Bodley, J. E. C., 1853–1925, historian of France.

Boece or Boethius, Hector, 1465?–1536, Scottish historian.

Booth, Rt. Hon. Charles, 1840–1916, sociologist.

Borrow, George, 1803–81, miscellaneous writer.

Bosanquet, Bernard, 1848–1923, philosopher.

Boswell, James, 1740–95, biographer.

Bowdler, Thomas, 1754–1825, editor of Shakespeare.

Braddon, Mary Elizabeth (Mrs. Maxwell), 1837–1915, novelist.

Bradley, Francis Herbert, 1846–1924, philosophical writer.

Bradley, Henry, 1845–1923, lexicographer.

Brewster, Sir David, 1781–1868, scientific writer.

Bridges, Robert Seymour, 1844–1930, poet.

Bridie, James (pseudonym of A. H. Mavor), 1888–1951, Scottish dramatist.

Brome, Richard, d. 1652?, dramatist.

Brontë, Anne, 1820–49, novelist.

Brontë, Charlotte, 1816–55, novelist.

Brontë, Emily, 1818–48, poet and novelist.

Brooke, Rupert, 1887–1915, poet.

Brooke, Stopford Augustus, 1832–1916, miscellaneous writer.

Brougham and Vaux, Henry Lord, 1778–1868, essayist, founder of *Edinburgh Review*.

Brown, Horatio, 1854–1926, historian of Venice.

Brown, Dr. John, 1810–82, physician and essayist.

Brown, Peter Hume, 1849–1919, Scottish historian.

Brown, Thomas Edward, 1830–97, poet.

Browne, Edward Granville, 1862–1926, orientalist.

Browne, Sir Thomas, 1605–82, physician and miscellaneous writer.

Browne, Thomas Alexander (' Rolf Boldrewood '), 1826–1915, novelist.

Browning, Elizabeth Barrett, 1806–61, poet.

Browning, Oscar, 1837–1923, historian.

Browning, Robert, 1812–89, poet.

Bruce, Michael, 1746–67, poet.

Bryce, James, Viscount, 1838–1922, historian.

Buchan, John (Lord Tweedsmuir), 1875–1940, novelist and historian.

Buchanan, George, 1506–82, Scottish historian.

Buchanan, Robert, 1841–1901, poet and novelist.

Buckle, George Earle, 1854–1935, editor of *The Times* and biographer.

Buckle, Henry Thomas, 1821–62, historian.

Bullett, Gerald William, 1893–1958, novelist and poet.

Bunyan, John, 1628–88, allegorist.

Burke, Edmund, 1729–97, statesman and political philosopher.

Burnand, Sir Francis Cowley, 1836–1917, humorous writer.

Burnet, Gilbert, 1643–1715, historian.

Burnett, Frances Hodgson (Mrs. Stephen Townsend), 1849–1924, novelist.

Burney, Fanny. See D'ARBLAY.

Burns, Robert, 1759–96, Scottish poet.

Burton, Sir Richard Francis, 1821–90, anthropologist.

Burton, Robert, 1577–1640, humorist.

Bury, John Bagnell, 1861–1927, Roman historian.

Butler, Samuel, 1612–80, satirist.

Butler, Samuel, 1835–1902, philosophical writer and novelist.

Byron, George Gordon, Lord, 1788–1824, poet.

Cædmon, d. c. 680, Northumbrian poet.

Caine, Sir Thomas Henry Hall, 1853–1931, novelist.

Calverley, Charles Stuart, 1831–84, poet and parodist.

Camden, William, 1551–1623, antiquary.

Campbell, Thomas, 1777–1844, Scottish poet.

Campion, Thomas, 1567–1619, poet.

Canning, George, 1770–1827, statesman, poet, and journalist.

Carew, Thomas, 1595–1639.

Carey, Henry, *c.* 1687–1743, dramatist and song writer.

Carlyle, Thomas, 1795–1881, historian and essayist.

Carman, William Bliss, 1861–1929, Canadian poet.

Carpenter, Edward, 1844–1929, 'democratic author and poet.'

'Carroll, Lewis.' *See* DODGSON.

Cary, Henry Francis, 1772–1844, translator of Dante.

Castle, Egerton, 1858–1920, novelist.

Cave, Edward, 1691–1754. Founder of *Gentleman's Magazine.*

Caxton, William, 1422?–91, editor and translator.

Chalmers, Thomas, 1780–1847, theologian.

Chambers, Ephraim, *c.* 1680–1740, published first English encyclopaedia.

Chambers, Robert, 1802–71, historian and scientific writer.

Chapman, George, 1559–1634, dramatist and translator.

Chatterton, Thomas, 1752–70, poet.

Chaucer, Geoffrey, 1340?–1400, poet.

Chesterfield, Philip Dormer Stanhope, Earl of, 1694–1773, letter-writer.

Chesterton, Gilbert Keith, 1874–1936, poet and critic.

Chisholm, Hugh, 1866–1924, editor of *Encyclopaedia Britannica.*

Cholmondeley, Mary, 1859–1925, novelist.

Cholmondeley, Mary, ?–1925, novelist.

Cibber, Colley, 1671–1757, poet, actor, and dramatist.

Clare, John, 1793–1864, poet.

Clarendon, Edward Hyde, Earl of, 1609–1674, historian. *See* CLARENDON PRESS.

Clarke, Marcus Andrew Hislop, 1846–81, novelist.

Clarke, Samuel, 1675–1729, theologian.

Clough, Arthur Hugh, 1819–61, poet.

Cobbett, William, 1763–1835, publicist.

Coke, Sir Edward, 1552–1634, jurist.

Cole, George Douglas Howard, 1889–1959, political writer.

Coleridge, Hartley, 1796–1849, poet.

Coleridge, Samuel Taylor, 1772–1834, poet, philosopher, and critic.

Collins, John Churton, 1848–1908, critic.

'Collins, Tom.' *See* FURPHY.

Collins, William, 1721–59, poet.

Collins, William Wilkie, 1824–89, novelist.

Colman, George, 1732–94, dramatist.

Colvin, Sir Sidney, 1845–1927, editor and biographer.

Congreve, William, 1670–1729, dramatist.

Conrad (Korzeniowski), Joseph, 1857–1924, novelist.

Constable, Henry, 1562–1613, poet.

Coppard, Alfred Edward, 1878–1957, short-story writer and poet.

Corbett, Sir Julian Stafford, 1854–1922, naval historian.

Corelli, Marie, 1855–1924, novelist.

Cory, William (Johnson), 1823–92, poet.

Coryate, Thomas, 1577?–1617, travel writer.

Cotton, Charles, 1630–87, poet and translator.

Courtney, William Leonard, 1850–1928, journalist.

Coverdale, Miles, 1488–1568, translator. *See* BIBLE.

Cowley, Abraham, 1618–67, poet.

Cowper, William, 1731–1800, poet.

Crabbe, George, 1754–1832, poet.

Craik, Dinah Marie, 1826–87, novelist.

Cranmer, Thomas, 1489–1556, liturgist.

Crashaw, Richard, 1612?–49, poet.

Crashaw, William, 1572–1626, poet.

Creighton, Mandell, 1843–1901, historian.

Crockett, Samuel Rutherford, 1860–1914, novelist.

Crosland, Thomas William, 1868–1924, poet and satirist.

Cummings, Bruce ('W. N. P. Barbellion'), 1889–1917, zoologist.

Cunningham, Allan, 1784–1842, poet.

Curzon of Kedleston, Lord, 1859–1925, publicist.

Cynewulf, *fl.* 750, Northumbrian poet.

Dampier, William, 1652–1715, explorer.

Daniel, Samuel, 1562–1619, poet.

D'Arblay, Frances (Burney), 1752–1840, novelist.

Darley, George, 1795–1846, poet.

Darwin, Charles Robert, 1809–82, naturalist. *See* DARWINISM.

Darwin, Erasmus, 1731–1802, botanist and poet.

Dasent, Sir George Webbe, 1817–96, translator.

D'Avenant, Sir William, 1606–68, poet and dramatist.

Davidson, John, 1857–1909, poet.

Davies, Hubert Henry, 1876–1917, dramatist.

Davies, Sir John, 1569–1626, poet.

Davies, William Henry, 1871–1940, poet.

Day, Thomas, 1748–89, miscellaneous writer.

Defoe, Daniel, 1660–1731, journalist and novelist.

Dekker, Thomas, *c.* 1570–*c.* 1632, dramatist and pamphleteer.

De la Mare, Walter John, 1873–1956, poet and novelist.

Delafield, E. M. (Edmée de la Pasture), 1890–1943, novelist.

Delane, John Thaddeus, 1817–79, editor of *The Times.*

De la Ramée, Marie Louise ('Ouida'), 1839–1908, novelist.

De la Roche, Mazo, 1885–1961, Canadian novelist.

De Morgan, William Frend, 1839–1917, novelist.

Denney, James, 1856–1917, Scottish theologian.

De Quincey, Thomas, 1785–1859, essayist and miscellaneous writer.

Dicey, Albert Venn, 1835–1922, jurist.

Dickens, Charles, 1812–70, novelist.

Dickinson, Goldsworthy Lowes, 1862–1932, philosophical writer.

Dilke, Charles Wentworth, 1789–1864, journalist.

Dillon, Émile Joseph, 1855–1933, foreign correspondent.

Disraeli, Benjamin. See BEACONSFIELD.

D'Israeli, Isaac, 1766–1848, miscellaneous writer.

Dixon, Richard Watson, 1833–1900, poet.

Dixon, William Hepworth, 1821–79, historian and traveller.

Dobell, Sydney Thompson, 1824–74, poet.

Dobson, Austin, 1840–1921, poet and essayist.

Dodgson, Charles Lutwidge ('Lewis Carroll'), 1832–98, writer of nonsense and mathematician.

Dodsley, Robert, 1703–64, poet and dramatist.

Donne, John, 1573–1631, poet and divine.

Doughty, Charles Montagu, 1843–1926, traveller and poet.

Douglas, Lord Alfred, 1870–1945, poet.

Douglas, Gavin, 1474–1522, Scots poet.

Douglas, Norman, 1868–1952, Scottish novelist and miscellaneous writer.

Dowden, Edward, 1843–1913, critic.

Dowson, Ernest, 1867–1900, poet.

Doyle, Sir Arthur Conan, 1859–1930, novelist.

Drayton, Michael, 1563–1631, poet.

Drinkwater, John, 1882–1937, poet and dramatist.

Drummond, Henry, 1851–97, theological and scientific writer.

Drummond, William (of Hawthornden), 1585–1649, poet.

Drummond, William Henry, 1854–1907, poet.

Dryden, John, 1631–1700, poet, dramatist, and satirist.

Dugdale, Sir William, 1605–86, antiquarian.

Dunbar, William, 1460?–1520?, Scots poet.

Dyce, Alexander, 1798–1869, scholar and critic.

Dyer, Sir Edward, 1545?–1607, poet.

Earle, John, 1601–65, essayist.

Eddington, Sir Arthur, 1882–1945, scientist.

Edgeworth, Maria, 1767–1849, novelist.

Eliot, George. See EVANS.

Elliot, Jane or Jean, 1727–1805, Scottish song-writer.

Ellis, Henry Havelock, 1859–1939, psychologist.

Elphinstone, Mountstewart, 1779–1859, historian.

Elyot, Sir Thomas, 1490?–1546, miscellaneous writer.

Ernle, Rowland Prothero, Lord, 1851–1937, editor and critic.

Etherege, Sir George, 1635?–91, dramatist.

Evans, Mary Ann ('George Eliot'), 1819–1880, novelist.

Evelyn, John, 1620–1706, diarist.

Faraday, Michael, 1791–1867, natural philosopher.

Farjeon, Herbert, 1887–1945, critic and playwright.

Farnol, John Jeffrey, 1878–1952, novelist.

Farquhar, George, 1678–1707, dramatist.

Fell, Dr. John, 1625–86, critic and editor.

Ferguson, Sir Samuel, 1810–86, Irish poet.

Fergusson, Robert, 1750–74, Scots poet.

Ferrier, Susan Edmondstone, 1782–1854, novelist.

Fielding, Henry, 1707–54, novelist.

Figgis, Darrell, 1882–1925, Irish politician, poet, and novelist.

Finlay, George, 1799–1875, historian.

Firth, Sir Charles Harding, 1857–1936, historian and critic.

Fisher, Herbert A. L., 1865–1940, politician and historian.

Fisher, St. John, 1459–1535, theologian.

FitzGerald, Edward, 1809–83, translator.

Flecker, James Elroy, 1884–1915, poet and dramatist.

Fleming, David Hay, 1849–1931, Scottish historian.

Fletcher, John, 1579–1625, poet and dramatist.

Fletcher, Phineas, 1582–1620, poet.

Foote, Samuel, 1720–77, dramatist.

Ford, Ford Madox (Hueffer), 1873–1939, poet and novelist.

Ford, John (1586–1640?), dramatist.

Forster, John, 1812–76, essayist and biographer.

Fortescue, Sir John, 1394–1476, jurist.

Fortescue, Sir John, 1859–1933, military historian.

Fowler, Henry Watson, 1858–1933, philologist.

Fox, George, 1624–91, Quaker diarist.

Foxe, John, 1516–87, martyrologist.

Francis, Sir Philip, 1740–1818, reputed author of The Letters of Junius (q.v.).

Frankau, Gilbert, 1884–1952, novelist.

Frazer, Sir James George, 1854–1941, anthropology and comparative religion.

Freeman, Edward Augustus, 1823–92, historian.

Freeman, John, 1880–1929, poet.

Froude, James Anthony, 1818–94, historian.

Fry, Roger E., 1866–1934, art critic.

Fuller, Thomas, 1608–61, antiquary and biographer.

Furnivall, Frederick James, 1825–1910,

F*

lexicographer, editor *Oxford English Dictionary*.

Furphy, Joseph ('Tom Collins'), 1843–1912, Australian novelist.

Galsworthy, John, 1867–1933, novelist and dramatist.

Galt, John, 1779–1839, Scottish novelist and writer.

Gardiner, Alfred G. ('Alpha of the Plough'), 1865–1946, journalist and essayist.

Gardiner, Samuel Rawson, 1829–1902, historian.

Garnett, Edward, 1868–1937, critic.

Garnett, Richard, 1835–1906, biographer and writer on literature.

Garvin, James Louis, 1868–1947, journalist.

Gascoigne, George, 1525?–77, poet.

Gaskell, Elizabeth Cleghorn (Stevenson), 1810–65, novelist.

Gay, John, 1685–1732, poet and dramatist.

Geikie, James, 1839–1915, Scottish geologist.

Gibbon, Edward, 1737–94, historian.

Gibbs, Sir Philip Hamilton, 1877–1962, journalist and novelist.

Gifford, William, 1757–1826, critic.

Gilbert, Sir Humphrey, 1539–83, explorer.

Gilbert, William, 1540–1603, scientist.

Gilbert, Sir William Schwenck, 1836–1911, humorist and dramatist.

Gissing, George, 1857–1903, novelist.

Gladstone, William Ewart, 1809–98, statesman and man of letters.

Gleig, George Robert, 1796–1888, military writer.

Glyn, Mrs. Elinor, 1864–1943, Canadian novelist.

Godwin, Mrs. Mary Wollstonecraft, 1759–1797, miscellaneous writer.

Godwin, William, 1756–1836, philosopher and novelist.

Golding, Louis, 1895–1958, novelist.

Goldsmith, Oliver, 1728–74, poet, dramatist, and essayist.

Gordon, Adam Lindsay, 1833–70, Australian poet.

Gore, Bishop Charles, 1853–1932, theologian.

Gosse, Sir Edmund William, 1849–1928, poet, critic, and essayist.

Gould, Gerald, 1885–1936, poet and critic.

Gower, John, 1325?–1408, poet.

Grahame, Kenneth, 1859–1932, writer on child life.

Grattan, Thomas Colley, 1792–1864, miscellaneous writer.

Graves, Alfred Percival, 1846–1931, Irish song-writer.

Graves, Charles Larcom, 1856–1944, essayist and humorist.

Graves, Clotilde Inez Mary, 1863–1932, Irish novelist.

Gray, Thomas, 1716–71, poet.

Green, John Richard, 1837–83, historian.

Green, Thomas Hill, 1836–82, philosopher.

Greene, Robert, 1558–92, poet and dramatist.

Gregory, Augusta, Lady, 1852–1932, Irish dramatist.

Grenfell, Julian Henry Francis, 1888–1915, poet.

Greville, Charles Cavendish Fulke, 1794–1865, diarist.

Greville, Sir Fulke, Lord Brooke, 1554–1628, poet.

Grossmith, George, 1847–1912, miscellaneous writer (*Diary of a Nobody*).

Grote, George, 1794–1871, historian.

Grundy, Sydney, 1848–1914, dramatist.

Guedalla, Philip, 1889–1944, biographer.

Guest, Lady Charlotte, 1812–95, translator.

Guthrie, Thomas Anstey ('F. Anstey'), 1856–1934, humorist.

Haggard, Sir Henry Rider, 1856–1925, novelist.

Hakluyt, Richard, 1552?–1616, collector of voyages.

Haldane, Richard Burdon, 1856–1928, critical philosopher.

Hale, Sir Matthew, 1609–76, jurist.

Hales, John, 1584–1656, theologian.

Haliburton, Thomas Chandler ('Sam Slick'), 1796–1865, Nova Scotian humorist.

Hall, Edward, *c.* 1499–1547, chronicler.

Hall, Margaret Radclyffe, 1886–1943, novelist.

Hallam, Henry, 1777–1859, historian.

Hamilton, Cicely, 1872–1952, dramatist and writer on sociology.

Hamilton, Sir William, 1788–1856, metaphysician.

Hammerton, Sir John Alexander, 1871–1949, editor and critic.

Hammond, John, 1872–1949, economist and journalist.

Hammond, Barbara, *d.* 1961, economist.

Hannay, J. O. *See* BIRMINGHAM.

Hardy, Thomas, 1840–1928, poet and novelist.

Harington, Sir John, 1561–1612, miscellaneous writer.

Harrington, James, 1611–77, political theorist.

Harris, Frank, 1856–1931, journalist and biographer.

Harrison, Frederic, 1831–1923, philosopher.

Harrison, Mary St. Leger ('Lucas Malet'), 1852–1931, novelist.

Harrison, William, 1534–93, chronologist and topographer.

Harvey, William, 1578–1657, physician.

Hawker, Robert Stephen, 1803–75, poet.

Hawkins, Sir Anthony Hope, 1863–1933, novelist.

Hazlitt, William, 1778–1830, essayist and critic.

'Hay, Ian' (John Hay Beith), 1876–1952, novelist.

Headlam, Cecil, 1872–1934, historian.

Heber, Reginald, 1783–1826, poet.

Heber, Richard (a founder of the Athenæum), 1773–1833.

Hemans, Felicia Dorothea, 1793–1835, poetess.

Henley, William Ernest, 1849–1903, poet and critic.

Henryson, Robert, 1425 ?–1506, Scots poet.

Henson, Herbert Hensley, 1863–1947, theologian.

Henty, George Alfred, 1832–1902, writer for boys.

Herbert of Cherbury, Edward, Lord, 1583–1648, philosopher and historian.

Herbert, George, 1593–1633, poet.

Herrick, Robert, 1591–1674, poet.

Herschel, Sir John F. W., 1792–1871, astronomer.

Herschel, Sir William (father of above), 1738–1822, astronomer.

Hervey, John, Lord, 1696–1743, memorialist.

Hewlett, Maurice Henry, 1861–1923, poet and novelist.

Heywood, John, 1497 ?–1580 ?, dramatist.

Heywood, Thomas, 1575–1650, dramatist.

Higden, Ranulf, d. 1364, historian.

Hilton, James, 1900–54, novelist.

Hobbes, Thomas, 1588–1679, philosopher.

Hobhouse, John Cam, 1786–1869, critic.

Hoccleve or Occleve, Thomas, 1368 ?–1450 ?, poet.

Hodgkin, Thomas, 1831–1913, historian.

Hodgson, Ralph, 1871–1962, poet.

Hodgson, Shadworth Holloway, 1832–1912, philosopher.

Hogg, James ('the Ettrick Shepherd'), 1770–1835, poet.

Holcroft, Thomas, 1745–1809, writer of melodramas.

Holdsworth, Sir William, 1871–1943, jurist.

Holinshed or Hollingshead, Raphael, ?–1580 ?, historian.

Holland, Henry Scott, 1848–1918, divine.

Holland, Philemon, 1552–1637, translator.

Holmes, Edmond Gore Alexander, 1850–1936, Irish educationist and poet.

Holtby, Winifred, 1898–1935, novelist.

Hone, William, 1780–1842, miscellaneous writer.

Hood, Thomas, 1799–1845, poet and comic writer.

Hook, Theodore Edward, 1788–1841, novelist and wit.

Hooker, Richard, 1554 ?–1600, theologian.

Hope, Anthony. See HAWKINS.

Hopkins, Gerard Manley, 1844–89, poet.

Hornung, Ernest William, 1866–1921, novelist.

Houghton, Richard Monckton Milnes, 1st Baron, 1809–85, man of letters.

Houghton, William Stanley, 1881–1913, dramatist.

Housman, Alfred Edward, 1859–1936, poet.

Housman, Laurence, 1865–1959, dramatist and poet.

Howard, Henry. See SURREY.

Hudson, William Henry, 1841–1922, essayist and novelist.

Hughes, Thomas, 1822–96, novelist.

Hume, David, 1711–76, philosopher and historian.

Hume, Ferguson Wright, 1859–1932, novelist.

Humphreys, Mrs. Desmond ('Rita'), 1850–1938, novelist.

Hunt, James Henry Leigh, 1784–1859, essayist and poet.

Hutcheson, Francis, 1694–1746, philosopher.

Huxley, Aldous Leonard, 1894–1963, novelist and poet.

Huxley, Thomas Henry, 1825–95, scientific writer.

Hyde, Douglas, 1860–1949, poet in Irish and English and authority on Irish folklore.

Inchbald, Mrs. Elizabeth, 1753–1821, novelist, actress, and dramatist.

Inge, William Ralph (Dean), 1860–1954, theologian.

Ingelow, Jean, 1820–97, poet.

Ireland, William, 1777–1835, Shakespearian forger.

Jacob, Violet, 1863–1946, Scottish poet and novelist.

Jacobs, William Wymark, 1863–1943, short-story writer.

James I of Scotland, 1394–1437, poet.

James VI and I, 1566–1625, miscellaneous writer.

James, George Payne R., 1801–60, novelist.

James, Montague Rhodes, 1862–1936, short-story, etc., writer.

Jameson, Mrs. Anna Brownell (Murphy), 1794–1860, writer on art.

Jeans, Sir James, 1877–1946, astronomer.

Jebb, Sir Richard Claverhouse, 1841–1905, classical scholar.

Jefferies, Richard, 1848–87, naturalist and novelist.

Jeffrey, Francis, 1773–1850, critic and political writer.

Jerome, Jerome Klapka, 1859–1927, novelist and dramatist.

Jerrold, Douglas William, 1803–57, dramatist, etc.

Jevons, William Stanley, 1835–82, logician.

Johnson, Samuel, 1709–84, essayist and lexicographer.

Johnston, Sir Harry Hamilton, 1858–1927, naturalist, linguist, and novelist.

Jones, Henry Arthur, 1851–1929, dramatist.

Jones, Sir William, 1746–94, orientalist and jurist.

Jonson, Benjamin, c. 1573–1637, poet and dramatist.

Jowett, Benjamin, 1817–93, scholar.

Joyce, James, 1882–1941, Irish novelist.

Kaye-Smith, Sheila, 1887–1956, novelist.

Keats, John, 1795–1821, poet.

Keble, John, 1792–1866, poet and divine.

Ken, Thomas, 1637–1711, hymn-writer.

Kendall, Henry Clarence, 1841–82, Australian poet.

Keynes, John Maynard, Lord, 1883–1946, economist.

Kidd, Benjamin, 1858–1916, sociologist.

Kinglake, Alexander William, 1809–91, historian.

Kingsley, Charles, 1819–75, novelist.

Kingsley, Henry, 1830–76, novelist.

Kipling, Rudyard, 1865–1936, poet, novelist, and short-story writer.

Knight, Charles, 1791–1873, cyclopaedist.

Knowles, James Sheridan, 1784–1862, dramatist.

Knox, John, c. 1513–72, Scottish reformer and historian.

Knox, Ronald (Monsignor), 1888–1957, theologian, translator, and miscellaneous writer.

Kyd, Thomas, 1558–94, dramatist.

Lamb, Charles, 1775–1834, essayist and poet.

Lamb, Mary, 1764–1847, miscellaneous writer.

Lampman, Archibald, 1861–99, Canadian poet.

Landor, Walter Savage, 1775–1864, poet, etc.

Lane, Edward William, 1801–76, Arabic scholar.

Lanfranc, Archbishop, c. 1005–89, theologian.

Lang, Andrew, 1844–1912, poet and mythologist.

Langland, William, 1330?–1400?, poet.

Laski, Harold Joseph, 1893–1950, political scientist.

Latimer, Hugh, 1485–1555, reformer and divine.

Law, William, 1686–1761, theologian.

Lawrence, David Herbert, 1885–1930, novelist.

Lawrence, Thomas Edward, 1888–1935, historian and translator.

Layamon, fl. 1200, poet.

Layard, Sir Austin Henry, 1817–94, explorer.

Leacock, Stephen, 1869–1944, Canadian essayist, etc.

Leaf, Walter, 1852–1927, joint translator (with Lang) of Homer.

Lear, Edward, 1812–88, writer of nonsense verse.

Lecky, William Edward Hartpole, 1838–1903, historian.

Lee, Nathaniel, 1653?–92, dramatist.

Le Fanu, Joseph Sheridan, 1814–73, novelist.

Le Gallienne, Richard, 1866–1947, poet, critic, and novelist.

Leighton, Robert, 1611–84, divine.

Leland, John, c. 1506–52, antiquary.

Lemon, Mark, 1809–70, journalist and humorist.

Le Queux, William, 1864–1927, novelist.

Leslie, John, 1527–96, Scottish historian.

L'Estrange, Sir Roger, 1616–1704, journalist and pamphleteer.

Lever, Charles James, 1806–72, novelist.

Lewes, George Henry, 1817–79, philosopher, etc.

Lewis, Alun, 1915–44, poet.

Lewis, Clive Staples, 1898–1963, novelist.

Lewis, Matthew Gregory ('Monk' Lewis), 1775–1818, dramatist and novelist.

Liddon, Henry Parry, 1829–90, divine.

Lillo, George, 1693–1739, dramatist.

Linacre, Thomas, c. 1460–1524, physician and scholar.

Lindsay or Lyndsay, Sir David, 1490–1555, Scots poet.

Lingard, John, 1771–1851, historian.

Littleton, Sir Thomas, c. 1407–81, jurist.

Livingstone, David, 1813–73, explorer, etc.

Locke, John, 1632–1704, philosopher.

Lockhart, John Gibson, 1794–1854, Scottish editor and biographer.

Lodge, Sir Oliver Joseph, 1851–1940, writer on science.

Lodge, Thomas, 1558?–1625, poet and dramatist.

Lovelace, Richard, 1618–58, poet.

Lover, Samuel, 1797–1868, song-writer and novelist.

Low, Sir Sidney James Mark, 1857–1932, historical writer.

Lucas, Edward Verrall, 1868–1938, story-writer and essayist.

Lucy, Sir Henry ('Toby, M.P.' of Punch), 1845–1924.

Lydgate, John, 1370?–1450?, poet.

Lyly, John, 1553–1606, dramatist, etc.

Lynch, Arthur, 1861–1934, Irish miscellaneous writer.

Lynd, Robert, 1879–1949, Irish essayist and critic.

Lytton, Edward Bulwer-Lytton, Lord, 1803–73, novelist and statesman.

Lytton, Edward Robert Bulwer-Lytton, Earl of ('Owen Meredith'), 1831–91, statesman and poet.

Macaulay, Rose, 1887–1958, novelist and poet.

Macaulay, Thomas Babington, Lord, 1800–59, historian and essayist.

MacCarthy, Sir Desmond, 1878–1952, critic.

McCarthy, Justin, 1830–1912, historian and novelist.

MacDonald, George ('Phantastes'), 1824–

1905, poet and novelist.

Mackail, John William, 1859–1945, Scottish classicist.

Mackenzie, Henry, 1745–1831, novelist.

Mackintosh, Sir James, 1765–1832, philosopher and historian.

Macleod, Norman, 1812–72, divine, poet, and miscellaneous writer.

Macpherson, James, 1736–96, poet.

McTaggart, John McTaggart Ellis, 1866–1925, metaphysician.

Mahaffy, Sir John Pentland, 1839–1919, Irish classicist.

Maine, Sir Henry, 1822–88, jurist and historian.

Maitland, Sir Frederic William, 1850–1906, historian.

Maitland, Sir Richard, Lord Lethington, 1496–1586, Scottish poet.

'Malet, Lucas.' *See* HARRISON, MARY ST. LEGER.

Malory, Sir Thomas, *fl.* 1470, romancer.

Malthus, Thomas Robert, 1766–1834, economist.

Manning, Henry Edward (Cardinal), 1808–1892, theologian.

Manning, Robert, of Brunne, *c.* 1264–1338, poet.

Mansfield, Katherine, 1890–1923, New Zealand novelist.

Markham, Mrs. ('Elizabeth Penrose'), 1780–1837, children's writer.

Markham, Sir Clements Robert, 1830–1916, geographer.

Marlowe, Christopher, 1564–93, dramatist.

Marryat, Frederick, 1792–1848, novelist.

Marshall, Alfred, 1842–1924, political economist.

Marston, John, 1575?–1634, dramatist and satirist.

Martin, Sir Theodore, 1816–1909, poet and biographer.

Martineau, Harriet, 1802–76, novelist and economist.

Martineau, James, 1805–1900, Unitarian theologian.

Marvell, Andrew, 1621–78, poet and satirist.

Massey, Gerald, 1828–1907, poet.

Massinger, Philip, 1583–1640, dramatist.

Massingham, Henry William, 1860–1924, journalist and editor.

Masson, David, 1822–1907, biographer and historian.

Maude, Aylmer, 1858–1938, writer on Russia and Tolstoy.

Maxwell, William Babington, 1876–1938, novelist.

May, Sir Thomas Erskine, Lord Farnborough, 1815–86, constitutional jurist and historian.

Meredith, George, 1828–1909, novelist and poet.

Merivale, Charles, 1808–93, historian.

Merrick (formerly Miller), Leonard, 1864–1939, novelist and dramatist.

Meynell, Alice Christiana, 1847–1922, poet and essayist.

Meynell, Wilfrid, 1852–1948, journalist, poet, and essayist.

Middleton, Thomas, 1580–1627, dramatist.

Mill, James, 1773–1836, philosopher and historian.

Mill, John Stuart, 1806–73, philosopher.

Milman, Henry Hart, 1791–1868, poet and historian.

Milne, Alan Alexander, 1882–1956, journalist, novelist, and playwright.

Milton, John, 1608–74, poet.

Mitford, Mary Russell, 1787–1855, novelist and dramatist.

Moffat, Dr. James, 1870–1944, theologian and translator of Bible.

Monkhouse, Allan, 1859–1936, dramatist and novelist.

Monro, Harold, 1879–1932, poet.

Montague, Charles Edward, 1867–1928, journalist and novelist.

Montagu, Lady Mary Wortley, 1689–1762, letter-writer.

Montgomery, James, 1771–1854, poet.

Montgomery, Lucy Maude, 1874–1942, Canadian novelist.

Moore, George Augustus, 1852–1933, dramatist and novelist.

Moore, Thomas, 1779–1852, poet.

Moore, Thomas Sturge, 1870–1944, poet and writer on art.

More, Hannah, 1745–1833, miscellaneous and religious writer.

More, St. Thomas, 1475–1535, historical and political writer.

Morgan, Charles, 1894–1958, novelist and playwright.

Morley, Henry, 1822–94, writer on English literature.

Morley of Blackburn, John, Visc., 1838–1923, statesman and man of letters.

Morris, Sir Lewis, 1833–1907, poet.

Morris, William, 1834–96, poet and artist.

Motteux, Peter Anthony, 1660–1718, translator and dramatist.

Moyes, Mgr. James, 1851–1927, Catholic historian.

Muir, John Ramsay Brice, 1872–1941, historian.

Müller, Friedrich Max, 1823–1900, Anglo-German philologist.

Mulock, Dinah Maria (Mrs. Craik), 1826–1887, novelist.

Munday, Anthony, 1553–1633, poet and dramatist.

Murray, George Gilbert, 1866–1957, classicist.

Murray, Sir James Augustus Henry, 1847–1915, lexicographer.

Murray, Lindley, 1745–1826, grammarian.

Murry, John Middleton, 1889–1957, critic.

Nairne, Carolina Oliphant, Baroness, 1766–1845, Scots poet.

Namier, Sir Lewis Bernstein, 1888–1960, historian.

Napier, Sir William Patrick, 1785–1860, historian and soldier.

Nash, Thomas, 1567–1601, dramatist and novelist.

Neale, John Mason, 1818–66, hymn-writer.

Newbolt, Sir Henry, 1862–1938, poet.

Newman, John Henry (Cardinal), 1801–90, theologian and poet.

Newton, John, 1725–1807, divine and hymn-writer.

Nichols, Robert Malise Bowyer, 1893–1944, poet.

Norden, John, c. 1546–1625, topographer and religious writer.

North, Roger, 1653–1734, historian.

North, Sir Thomas, 1535 ?–1601 ?, translator.

Northcliffe, Alfred Harmsworth, 1st Viscount, 1865–1922, journalist and newspaper proprietor.

Noyes, Alfred, 1880–1958, poet.

Oldys, William, 1696–1761, antiquarian.

Oliphant, Laurence, 1829–88, novelist.

Oliphant, Margaret (Wilson), 1828–97, novelist and historian.

Oman, Sir Charles William Chadwick, 1860–1946, historian.

Oppenheim, Edward Phillips, 1866–1946, novelist.

Orczy, Emmuska, Baroness, 1865–1947, novelist.

Orwell, George (Eric Blair), 1903–50, novelist and essayist.

Osborne, Dorothy (Lady Temple (q.v.)), 1627–95, letter-writer.

O'Shaughnessy, Arthur William Edgar, 1844–81, poet.

Osler, Sir William, 1849–1919, physician and author.

Otway, Thomas, 1652–85, dramatist.

Ouida. See DE LA RAMÉE.

Overbury, Sir Thomas, 1581–1613, character writer.

Owen, Wilfrid. 1893–1918, poet.

Page, Dr. William, 1861–1934, editor of *The Victoria County Histories*.

Paget, Violet ('Vernon Lee'), 1856–1935, art historian.

Pain, Barry Eric Odell, 1864–1928, story-writer.

Paine, Thomas, 1737–1809, pamphleteer.

Painter, William, 1540 ?–1594, translator.

Paley, William, 1743–1805, theologian.

Palgrave, Francis Turner, 1824–97, poet and anthologist.

Pares, Sir Bernard, 1867–1949, historian and Slavonic philologist.

Paris, Matthew, c. 1195–1259, chronicler.

Park, Mungo, 1771–1806, traveller.

Parker, Sir Gilbert, 1862–1932, Canadian novelist.

Parnell, Thomas, 1679–1718, poet.

Parry, Sir Edward Abbot, 1863–1943, miscellaneous author.

Passfield, Sidney James Webb, Baron, 1859–1947, historian and economist.

Pater, Walter Horatio, 1839–94, essayist and critic.

Patmore, Coventry Kersey Dighton, 1823–1896, poet.

Pattison, Mark, 1813–84, scholar and biographer.

Payn, James, 1830–98, novelist.

Peacock, Thomas Love, 1785–1866, novelist, critic, and poet.

Pearse, Padraic, 1879–1916, Irish poet.

Pearson, Karl, 1857–1936, writer on eugenics.

Peele, George, c. 1558–c. 1597, playwright and poet.

Pepys, Samuel, 1633–1703, diarist.

Percy, Thomas, 1729–1811, antiquary and poet.

Phillips, Stephen, 1868–1915, poet and dramatist.

Phillpotts, Eden, 1862–1960, novelist and dramatist.

Pickthall, Marjorie, 1883–1922, Canadian poet.

Pigott, M. H. Mostyn, 1865–1927, satirist.

Pinero, Sir Arthur Wing, 1855–1934, dramatist.

Piozzi, Hester Lynch (Salusbury) (Mrs. Thrale), 1741–1821, miscellaneous writer.

Pollard, Albert Frederick, 1869–1949, historian.

Pollock, Sir Frederick, 1845–1937, jurist.

Pope, Alexander, 1688–1744, poet.

Porson, Richard, 1759–1808, scholar and critic.

Porter, Jane, 1776–1850. novelist.

Powys John Cowper, 1872–1963, novelist.

Powys, Llewellyn, 1884–1939, novelist.

Powys, Theodore Francis, 1875–1953, novelist.

Praed, Winthrop Mackworth, 1802–39, poet.

Prichard, Harold Arthur, 1871–1948, philosopher.

Priestley, Joseph, 1733–1804, chemist and theologian.

Pringle, Thomas, 1789–1834, S. African poet.

Prior, Matthew, 1664–1721, poet.

Prothero, Rowland Edmund. See ERNLE, LORD.

Prynne, William, 1600–69, antiquarian and pamphleteer.

Purchas, Samuel, 1575 ?–1626, compiler of travels.

Pusey, Edward Bouverie, 1800–82, theologian.

Puttenham, Richard, 1520–1601, critic.

Quiller-Couch, Sir Arthur Thomas, 1863–1944, novelist and critic.

Radcliffe, Mrs. Ann, 1764–1823, novelist.

Rait, Sir Robert Sangster, 1874–1936, Scottish historian.

Raleigh, Sir Walter, 1552?–1618, explorer, historian, etc.

Raleigh, Sir Walter Alexander, 1861–1922, critic.

Ramsay, Allan, 1686–1758, poet.

Randolph, Thomas, 1605–35, poet and dramatist.

Rashdall, Dr. Hastings, 1858–1924, theologian.

Rawlinson, Sir Henry, 1810–95, orientalist.

Ray, John, 1627–1705, naturalist.

Rayleigh, John William Baron, 1842–1919, physicist.

Reade, Charles, 1814–84, novelist.

Reid, Thomas, 1710–96, philosopher.

Reid, Sir Thomas Wemyss, 1842–1905, novelist and biographer.

Rhondda, Margaret Haig Thomas, Viscountess, 1883–1958, editor.

Rhys, Ernest, 1859–1946, poet, critic, and editor of *Everyman's Library*.

Ricardo, David, 1772–1823, economist.

Richard of Cirencester, *d. c.* 1401, historian.

Richardson, Dorothy Miller, 1873–1957, novelist.

Richardson, Henry Handel (Ethyl Florence), 1870–1946, Australian novelist.

Richardson, Samuel, 1689–1761, novelist.

Ridgeway, Sir William, 1853–1926, archaeologist.

Ridley, Bishop Nicholas, 1500–55, theologian.

Rigg, James McMullen, 1855–1926, biographer and translator of the *Decameron*.

Robert of Gloucester, *c.* 1260–1300, metrical chronicler.

Roberts, Sir Charles George Douglas, 1860–1943, Canadian poet.

Roberts, Morley, 1857–1942, writer on travel and novelist.

Robertson, Sir Charles Grant, 1869–1948, historian.

Robertson, John Mackinnon, 1856–1933, Shakespearian scholar.

Robinson, Henry Crabb, 1775–1867, journalist and diarist.

Rochester, John Wilmot, Earl of, 1647–80, poet.

Roger of Wendover, *d. c.* 1236, historian.

Rogers, Samuel, 1763–1855, poet.

Rolle, Richard, *c.* 1300–49, mystic.

Roscoe, William, 1753–1831, historian.

Rose, John Holland, 1855–1942, historian.

Rosebery, Archibald, 5th Earl of, 1847–1929, statesman and historian.

Ross, Sir Edward Denison, 1871–1940, orientalist.

Ross, Janet Anne, 1842–1927, writer on Italy.

'Ross, Martin' (Violet Florence), 1862–1915, novelist.

Rossetti, Christina Georgina, 1830–94, poet.

Rossetti, Dante Gabriel, 1828–82, poet.

Rossetti, William Michael, 1829–1919, miscellaneous writer.

Rowe, Nicholas, 1674–1718, playwright.

Rowlands, Samuel, 1570–1630, satirist.

Rowley, William, *c.* 1585–*c.* 1642, dramatist.

Ruskin, John, 1819–1900, writer on art, economics, etc.

Russell, George William ('A. E.'), 1867–1935, Irish poet.

Russell, Sir William Howard, 1820–1911, journalist.

Rutherford, Ernest, Baron, 1871–1937, New Zealand physicist.

Rutherford, Mark. *See* WHITE, W. H.

Rutherford, Samuel, 1600?–61, Scottish theologian.

Rutter, Francis Vane Phipson, 1876–1937, art critic.

Rymer, Thomas, 1641–1713, poet and critic.

Sackville, Thomas, 1536–1608, poet.

Sackville-West, Hon. Victoria, 1892–1962, poet, novelist, and biographer.

Sadleir, Michael T. H., 1888–1957, biographer and novelist.

Saintsbury, George, 1845–1933, critic.

Sala, George Augustus, 1828–95, novelist and journalist.

Sanday, William, 1843–1920, theologian.

Sandys, George, 1578–1644, traveller and translator.

Sandys, Sir John Edwin, 1844–1921, classical scholar.

Savage, Richard, *c.* 1697–1742, poet.

Sayers, Dorothy Leigh, 1893–1957, novelist, essayist, and playwright.

Schiller, Ferdinand C. S., 1864–1937, pragmatic philosopher.

Schreiber. *See* GUEST.

Scott, Charles Prestwich, 1846–1932, 57 years editor *Manchester Guardian*.

Scott, Michael, 1789–1835, novelist.

Scott, Sir Walter, 1771–1832, novelist and poet.

Scott-Moncrieff, Charles Kenneth, 1889–1930, translator of Proust and Stendhal.

Seaman, Sir Owen, 1861–1936, poet, sometime editor of *Punch*.

Sedley, Sir Charles, 1639?–1701, poet and dramatist.

Seeley, Sir John Robert, 1834–95, historian and essayist.

Selden, John, 1584–1654, jurist and scholar.

Seward, Anna, 1747–1809, poet.

Sewell, Anna, 1820–78, novelist.

Sewell, Robert, c. 1845–1925, historian of India.

Shadwell, Thomas, 1642?–92, dramatist and poet.

Shaftesbury, Anthony Ashley Cooper, Earl of, 1671–1713, philosopher.

Shakespeare, William (q.v.), 1564–1616, dramatist and poet.

Sharp, Clifford Dyce, 1883–1935, editor.

Sharp, William (Fiona Macleod), 1856–1905, novelist and poet.

Shaw, George Bernard, 1856–1950, Irish dramatist.

Shelley, Mary Wollstonecraft, 1797–1851, novelist.

Shelley, Percy Bysshe, 1792–1822, poet.

Shenstone, William, 1714–63, poet.

Sheridan, Richard Brinsley, 1751–1816, dramatist.

Sherwood, Mrs. Mary, 1775–1851, children's novelist.

Shirley, James, 1596–1666, dramatist.

Shirley, John, 1366–1456, translator.

Shorthouse, Joseph Henry, 1834–1903, novelist.

Shute, Nevil, 1899–1960, novelist.

Sichel, Walter Sidney, 1865–1933, biographer.

Sidgwick, Henry, 1838–1900, political economist.

Sidney, Albert, 1882–1950, novelist and critic.

Sidney or Sydney, Algernon, 1622–83, political writer.

Sidney, Sir Philip, 1554–86, poet.

Sigerson, Dr. George, d. 1925, Gaelic scholar.

Simpson, Helen de Guerry, 1897–1940, Australian novelist.

Sims, George Robert, 1847–1922, journalist.

Sinclair, Catherine, 1800–64, novelist.

Sinclair, May, 1870–1946, novelist.

Skeat, Walter William, 1835–1912, Anglo-Saxon scholar.

Skelton, John, 1460?–1529, poet.

Skene, William Forbes, 1809–92, historian.

Smart, Christopher, 1722–71, poet.

Smiles, Samuel, 1812–1904, biographer and miscellaneous writer.

Smith, Adam, 1723–90, philosopher and economist.

Smith, Alexander, 1830–67, poet.

Smith, Capt. John, 1580–1631, historian.

Smith, Sydney, 1771–1845, miscellaneous writer.

Smith, Sir William, 1813–93, lexicographer.

Smollett, Tobias George, 1721–71, novelist.

Somerville, Edith Oenone, 1858–1949, Irish novelist.

Somerville, Mary, 1780–1872, mathematician.

South, Robert, 1634–1716, divine.

Southerne, Thomas, 1660–1746, dramatist.

Southey, Robert, 1774–1843, poet and biographer.

Southwell, Robert, 1561?–95, poet.

Speke, John, 1827–64, explorer.

Spelman, Sir Henry, 1564?–1641, historian.

Spencer, Herbert, 1820–1903, philosopher.

Spender, Edward Harold, 1864–1926, journalist and biographer.

Spenser, Edmund, 1552?–99, poet.

Stanhope, Philip, 5th Earl, 1805–75, historian.

Stanley, Arthur Penrhyn (Dean of Westminster), 1815–81, historian, biographer, and theologian.

Stanley, Sir Henry, 1841–1904, traveller.

Stead, William Thomas, 1849–1912, journalist.

Steed, Henry Wickham, 1871–1956, journalist.

Steele, Sir Richard, 1672–1729, essayist and dramatist.

Stephen, Sir James, 1789–1859, statesman and historian.

Stephen, Sir James Fitzjames, 1829–1929, jurist.

Stephen, Sir Leslie, 1832–1904, biographer and critic.

Stephens, James, 1882–1950, Irish story-writer and poet.

Stephens, James Brunton, 1835–1902, Australian poet.

Sterne, Laurence, 1713–68, novelist.

Stevenson, Robert Louis, 1850–94, novelist and essayist.

Stewart, Dugald, 1753–1828, philosopher.

Stillingfleet, Edward, 1635–99, theologian.

Stow, John, 1525?–1605, historian and antiquary.

Strachey, Giles Lytton, 1880–1932, biographer.

Strachey, John St. Loe, 1860–1927, critic and biographer.

Strickland, Agnes, 1796–1874, historical writer.

Strode, William, c. 1600–45, poet.

Strong, Leonard Alfred George, 1896–1958, poet and novelist.

Strype, John, 1643–1737, ecclesiastical historian.

Stubbs, William (Bishop), 1825–1901, historian.

Sturt, George ('George Bourne'), d. 1927, writer on English peasant life.

Suckling, Sir John, 1609–42, poet.

Surrey, Henry Howard, Earl of, 1517?–47, poet.

Surtees, Robert Smith, 1803–64, novelist.

Sutcliffe, Halliwell, 1870–1932, novelist.

Sutro, Alfred, 1863–1933, dramatist.

Swift, Jonathan (Dean), 1667–1745, satirist.

Swinburne, Algernon Charles, 1837–1909, poet.

Symonds, John Addington, 1840–93, historian, etc.

Symons, Arthur, 1865–1945, poet and symbolist writer.

Synge, John Millington, 1871–1909, Irish dramatist.

Tagore, Sir Rabindranath, 1861–1941, Indian poet.

Tate, Nahum, 1652–1715, poet.

Taylor, Jeremy, 1613–67, essayist.

Taylor, John, 1580–1653, the 'water-poet.'

Temperley, Harold William Vazeille, 1879–1939, historian.

Temple, Sir William, 1628–99, essayist.

Temple, William (Archbishop), 1881–1944, theologian and philosopher.

Tennyson, Alfred, Lord, 1809–92, poet.

Thackeray, William Makepeace, 1811–63, novelist.

Thomas, Dylan Marlais, 1914–53, poet.

Thomas, Philip Edward, 1878–1917, essayist and poet.

Thompson, Francis Joseph, 1860–1907, poet.

Thomson, James, 1700–48, poet.

Thomson, James ('B.V.'), 1834–82, poet.

Thrale. *See* PIOZZI.

Tomlinson, Henry Major, 1873–1958, novelist.

Tottel, Richard, *d.* 1594, author of the *Miscellany*.

Toynbee, Arnold, 1852–83, economist.

Toynbee, Paget Jackson, 1855–1932, translator of Dante.

Traherne, Thomas, 1638–74, poet and theological writer.

Trevelyan, George Macaulay, 1876–1962, historian.

Trevelyan, Sir George Otto, 1838–1928, historian.

Trollope, Anthony, 1815–82, novelist.

Tupper, Martin Farquhar, 1810–89, versifier.

Turner, Charles Tennyson, 1808 – 79, poet.

Turner, Walter James Redfern, 1889–1946, poet, novelist, and music critic.

Tynan, Katherine (Mrs. Hinkson), 1861–1931, Irish novelist and poet.

Tyndale, William, *c.* 1490–1536, translator of the Bible.

Tyndall, John, 1820–93, natural philosopher.

Udall, Nicholas, 1505–56, dramatist and scholar.

Urquhart, Sir Thomas, 1611–60, Scottish translator of Rabelais.

Usk, Thomas, *d.* 1388, poet.

Ussher, James, 1581–1656, divine and scholar.

Vachell, Horace Annesley, 1861–1955, novelist.

Vanbrugh, Sir John, 1664–1726, dramatist.

Vaughan, Henry, 1622–95, poet.

Vaux, Thomas, Lord, 1510–56, poet.

Vinogradoff, Sir Paul Gavrilovich, 1854–1925, jurist.

Walkley, Arthur Bingham, 1855–1926, essayist and dramatic critic.

Wallace, Alfred Russell, 1823–1913, naturalist.

Wallace, Edgar, 1875–1932, dramatist and novelist.

Wallas, Graham, 1858–1932, writer on politics.

Waller, Edmund, 1606–87, poet.

Walpole, Horace, 1717–97, miscellaneous writer.

Walpole, Sir Hugh Seymour, 1884–1941, novelist.

Walsingham, Thomas, *d. c.* 1422, historian.

Walton, Izaak, 1593–1683, biographer.

Warburton, William, 1698–1779, theologian.

Ward, Sir Adolphus William, 1837–1924, historian.

Ward, Mrs. Humphry (Mary Arnold), 1851–1920, novelist.

Ward, Thomas Humphry, 1845–1926, art critic.

Warton, Joseph, 1722–1800, critic.

Warton, Thomas, 1728–90, historian of English poetry.

Watson, John ('Ian Maclaren'), 1850–1907, novelist.

Watson, Sir William, 1858–1935, poet.

Watts, Isaac, 1674–1748, poet and theologian.

Watts-Dunton, Walter Theodore, 1832–1914, poet and novelist.

Webb, Beatrice, 1858–1943, economist and political philosopher.

Webb, Mary, 1881–1927, novelist.

Webster, Augusta, 1840–94, poet.

Webster, John, 1580?–1625?, dramatist.

Wells, Herbert George, 1866–1946, novelist and writer on sociology.

Wesley, Charles, 1707–88, hymn writer.

Wesley, John, 1703 – 91, theological writer.

Whiting, John, *d.* 1963, dramatist.

White, Gilbert, 1720–93, naturalist.

White, Henry Kirke, 1785–1806, poet.

White, Percy, 1852–1938, novelist.

White, William Hale (Mark Rutherford), 1831–1913, novelist.

Whitehead, Alfred North, 1861–1947, mathematician.

Whyte, Alexander, 1837–1921, Scottish theologian.

Whyte-Melville, George John, 1821–78, novelist.

Wiclif, or Wycliffe, John, *c.* 1324–84, translator.

Wilde, Oscar O'Flahertie, 1854–1900, poet and dramatist.

Wilkes, John, 1727–97, journalist, M.P.

Wilkinson, Henry Spenser, 1853–1937, war historian.

William of Malmesbury, *b. c.* 1092, *d. c.* 1143, historian.

Williams, Arthur Frederick Basil, 1867–1950, historian.

Williamson, Charles Norris, 1857–1920, novelist.

Wilson, John ('Christopher North'), 1785–1854, miscellaneous writer.

Wilson, (Florence) Romer, 1891–1930, novelist.

Winchilsea, Anne Finch, Countess of, 1661–1720, poet.

Wither, George, 1588–1667, poet.

Wolfe, Humbert, 1885–1940, poet, critic, and biographer.

Wood, Anthony à, 1632–95, antiquarian, etc.

Wood, Ellen (Mrs. Henry), 1814–87, novelist.

Woolf, Virginia, 1882–1941, novelist.

Wordsworth, Dorothy, 1771–1855, diarist.

Wordsworth, William, 1770–1850, poet.

Wotton, Sir Henry, 1568–1639, poet.

Wyatt, Sir Thomas, 1503–42, poet.

Wycherley, William, 1640?–1716, dramatist.

Wyndham, George, 1863–1914, critic.

Yates, Edmund, 1831–94, novelist and dramatist.

Yeats, William Butler, 1865–1939, Irish dramatist, poet, and critic.

Yonge, Charlotte Mary, 1823–1901, novelist.

Young, A. B. Filson, 1877–1938, miscellaneous writer.

Young, Arthur, 1741–1820, writer on agriculture and travel.

Young, Edward, 1683–1765, poet.

Young, Emily Hilda, 1880–1949, novelist.

Young, Francis Brett, 1884–1954, novelist.

Zangwill, Israel, 1864–1926, novelist and dramatist.

English Sovereigns and their Consorts. The names of some kings of the English tribes (notably Offa I) are known when they were still in S. Jutland, fourth century. Cerdic led the tribe which formed the nucleus of the W. Saxon kingdom to England, *c.* 500, and the sixteenth King of Wessex (*q.v.*) was Egbert, first king of all the English, from whom all subsequent English sovereigns are descended, except those in *italics* in the following list:

House of Cerdic

Egbert	802–839	Edmund I	939–946	assassinated
Ethelwulf	839–858	Edred	946–955	
Ethelbald	858–860	Edwy	955–959	
Ethelbert	860–865	Edgar	959–975	
Ethelred I	865–870	Edward the Younger	975–978	assassinated
Alfred the Great	870–899	Ethelred II (the		
Edward the Elder	899–925	Unready)	979–1016	
Athelstan	925–939	Edmund II (Ironside)	1016	

House of the Skjöldungs or of Denmark

Canute the Great	1016–1035	*Harold I* (alone)	1035–1040
Harthacanute }	1035	*Harthacanute* (again)	1040–1042
Harold I }			

House of Cerdic (again)

Edward the Confessor   1042–1066

House of Godwin

Harold II   1066 (killed at Hastings)

House of Normandy

SOVEREIGN		CONSORT
William I (the Conqueror)	1066–1087	Matilda of Flanders, *m.* 1053, *d.* 1084
William II (Rufus)	1087–1100	
Henry I	1100–1135	(1) Matilda of Scotland (grand-daughter of Edmund Ironside), *m.* 1100, *d.* 1119
		(2) Adela of Louvain, *m.* 1121, *d.* 1151
Stephen	1135–1154	Matilda of Boulogne, *m.* 1124, *d.* 1151

House of Anjou or Plantagenet

Henry II	1154–1189	Eleanor of Aquitaine, *m.* 1152, *d.* 1204
Richard I	1189–1199	Berengaria of Navarre, *m.* 1191, *d. c.* 1230
John	1199–1216	(1) Hadwisa or Avis of Gloucester, *m.* 1189, divorced 1200
		(2) Isabel of Angoulême, *m.* 1200, *d.* 1246
Henry III	1216–1272	Eleanor of Provence, *m.* 1236, *d.* 1291
Edward I	1272–1307	(1) Eleanor of Castile, *m.* 1254, *d.* 1296
		(2) Margaret of France, *m.* 1299, *d.* 1308
Edward II (deposed)	1307–1327	Isabella of France, *m.* 1308, *d.* 1358
Edward III	1327–1377	Philippa of Hainault, *m.* 1328, *d.* 1369
Richard II	1377–1399	(1) Anne of Bohemia, *m.* 1382, *d.* 1394
(deposed and murdered)		(2) Isabella of France, *m.* 1396, *d.* 1409

House of Lancaster

Henry IV	1399–1413	(1) Mary de Bohun, *m.* 1380, *d.* 1394
		(2) Joan of Navarre, *m.* 1402, *d.* 1437
Henry V	1413–1422	Catherine of France, *m.* 1420, *d.* 1437
Henry VI (deposed)	1422–1461	Margaret of Anjou, *m.* 1445, *d.* 1482

House of York

Edward IV	1461–1470	Elizabeth Woodville, *m.* 1364, *d.* 1492
(Henry VI (again)	1470–1471)	
Edward IV	1471–1483	
Edward V	Apr.–June 1483	
(murdered in the Tower)		
Richard III	1483–1485	Anne Neville, *m.* 1474, *d.* 1485
(killed at battle of Bosworth)		

House of Tudor

SOVEREIGN		CONSORT
Henry VII	1485–1509	Elizabeth of York, *m.* 1486, *d.* 1503
Henry VIII	1509–1547	(1) Catherine of Aragon, *m.* 1509, divorced 1533, *d.* 1536
		(2) Anne Boleyn, *m.* 1533, executed 1536
		(3) Jane Seymour, *m.* 1536, *d.* 1537
		(4) Anne of Cleves, *m.* Jan. 1540, divorced June 1540, *d.* 1557
		(5) Catherine Howard, *m.* 1540, executed 1542
		(6) Catherine Parr, *m.* 1543, *d.* 1548
Edward VI	1547–1553	
Mary I and Philip (1554)	1553–1558	Philip II of Spain, *m.* 1554, *d.* 1598
Elizabeth I	1558–1603	

House of Stuart

James I	1603–1625	Anne of Denmark, *m.* 1589, *d.* 1619
Charles I (beheaded)	1625–1649	Henrietta Maria of France, *m.* 1625, *d.* 1669
Commonwealth and Protectorate	1649–1660	
Charles II	1660–1685	Catherine of Braganza, *m.* 1662, *d.* 1705
James II (fled)	1685–1688	(1) Anne Hyde, *m.* 1660, *d.* 1671
		(2) Mary of Modena, *m.* 1673, *d.* 1718
William III and Mary II	1689–1694	*m.* 1677
William III alone	1694–1702	
Anne	1702–1714	George of Denmark, *m.* 1683, *d.* 1708

House of Hanover

George I	1714–1727	Sophia of Brunswick, *m.* 1682, *d.* 1726
George II	1727–1760	Caroline of Ansbach, *m.* 1705, *d.* 1737
George III	1760–1820	Charlotte of Mecklenburg-Strelitz, *m.* 1761, *d.* 1818
George IV	1820–1830	Caroline of Brunswick, *m.* 1795, *d.* 1821
William IV	1830–1837	Adelaide of Saxe-Meiningen, *m.* 1818, *d.* 1849
Victoria	1837–1901	Albert of Saxe-Coburg, *m.* 1840, *d.* 1861
Edward VII	1901–1910	Alexandra of Denmark, *m.* 1863, *d.* 1925

House of Windsor

George V	1910–1936	Mary of Teck, *m.* 1893, *d.* 1953
Edward VIII (abdicated)	1936	
George VI	1936–1952	Lady Elizabeth Bowes-Lyon, *m.* 1923
Elizabeth II	1952–Q.D.S.	Philip Mountbatten, Duke of Edinburgh, *m.* 1947

See also the separate kingdoms for the period before 802, viz. BERNICIA, DEIRA, EAST ANGLIA, ESSEX, KENT, MERCIA, SUSSEX, WESSEX.

Engraving on Metal and Stone. First metal plate from which impressions on paper were taken (a *pax* used in the Roman Catholic service) apparently executed, 1452. Early books with metal engravings, the *Kalender*, 1465, and the *Monte Santo di Dio*, 1477. First specialist in engraving, Marcantonio Raimondi (1475–1530). In England the earliest line engravings are in *The Birth of Mankind*, 1540. Earliest English engraver known by name, William Rogers (*fl.* 1580–1610). Mezzotint process invented by Ludwig von Siegen *c* 1642. Introduced into England, 1660, by Prince Rupert, who had seen Siegen at work. Aquatints said to have been invented by Saint-Non (1730–1804) and first used in England, 1780. Lithography invented by Aloys Senefelder, 1796. *See* ARTS, THE PLASTIC.

Engraving on Wood. Practised by Chinese some centuries B.C. Modern process, however, dates from fifteenth century, earliest dated example (1423) being at Memminingen (Germany). Caxton's second edition of *The Game and Playe of the Chesse*, 1476, contains earliest English woodcuts. Breydenbach's *Travels* (1486) contains engravings by Erhard Renwich, which show remarkable advances, especially in shading. The art was revolutionized by Albrecht Dürer (1471–1528) of Nürnberg. In England George, Edward, John, and Thomas Dalziel were very active from 1839 till process blocks began to supersede engraving *c.* 1879.

Enosis. Campaign for the union of Cyprus with Greece, originated, 1912, and continued until the establishment of the Republic of Cyprus in 1960. *See* CYPRUS.

Enrolment compulsory by Statute of Es., 1535.

Ensign, military rank in British infantry units, was superseded by the term second lieutenant, 1871.

Ensign, national flag flown by shipping, is worn according to a convention adopted in 1864.

Entente Cordiale between England and France (partly brought about by the exertions of King Edward VII) and Anglo-French Agreement signed, 8 Apr. 1904. France agreed to recognize Britain's predominant interests in Egypt in return for similar recognition of France's position in Morocco.

Entertainments Tax (Britain). Introduced, 1916. Modified, 1922, and by Finance Acts, 1947, 1953, 1957, and 1960.

E.O.K.A. Nationalist guerrilla force organized in Cyprus, 1954, to fight for *Enosis* (*q.v.*). Disbanded when Cyprus became a republic, 1960.

Ephesus, Asia Minor. Founded *c.* 1000 B.C. Fell under Lydian domination, sixth century. The Artemisium or Temple of Artemis, founded *c.* 750 B.C.; sacked by Cimmerii *c.* 650; rebuilt *c.* 545–425 in the form which was one of the Seven Wonders of the World (*q.v.*). Destroyed by Herostratus, 356 B.C., but restored shortly after. E. became the administrative capital of the Roman province of Asia *c.* 140 B.C., was visited by St. Paul (*see* Acts) *c.* A.D. 56. Temple destroyed by the Goths in A.D. 263. Church councils held at E., 197, 245, 431, 446, 447, 449.

Epirus, Greece. Rose to prominence for a short period during the wars of its King Pyrrhus against the Romans, which ended 275 B.C.

Episcopal Ordination Act (Scotland). Passed, 1662.

'Epistolae Obscurorum Virorum' (*Letters of Lowly Men*), by several humanists, led by Ulrich von Hutten. First published, 1515; enlarged, 1516; vol. ii, 1517. Condemned in a bull of Leo X, published, 15 Mar. 1617.

Epping Forest. Ancient royal forest bought and opened to the public by the City of London, 1882.

Epsom (Surrey). Sulphate of magnesia springs discovered, 1618. Races run at E. from about 1620.

Erastians. A religious sect following the teachings of Erastus (1524–83). Their ideas much advocated at Westminster Assembly, 1643–9.

Erfurt, Germany. Bishopric, 741; ceded to the Elector of Mainz, 1648. Luther lived in the monastery of St. Augustine, 1508–11. Incorporated into Prussia, 1802.

Erie Canal (U.S.A.). Opened, 1825. Deepened, 1907.

Eritrea. Italians purchased Assab, 1870. Occupied Massawa, 1885. Province of E. organized, 1890. Attempt to extend at Abyssinian expense defeated at battle of Adowa, 1896. Amalgamated with Ethiopia in Italian E. Africa, 9 May

1936. British invasion begins, Dec. 1940. Battle of Agordat, Jan. 1941. Battle of Keren, Feb.–Mar. 1941. British occupied Massawa, 8 Apr. 1941. Under British military administration, 1941–8. Abyssinians lay claim to, 1947. Scheme for federation with Ethiopia under Ethiopian crown approved by United Nations, Dec. 1950. New constitution for E. ratified by Emperor of Ethiopia, Aug. 1952, and the federation with Ethiopia became effective, Sept. 1952. *See* ETHIOPIA.

Erzurum, Turkey. Citadel founded *c.* 415 by Theodosius the Younger. Taken by Turks, 1517. By Russians, 1829 and 1878. Armenians massacred at, 1895 and 1915. Captured by Russians, Mar. 1916. Abandoned on Communist orders, Jan. 1918. Reoccupied by Turks, Mar. 1918. Russian propaganda campaign for cession of to Russia begun, 1945.

Escheat. Abolished in England, 1925.

Escorial or **Escurial,** royal establishment outside Madrid consisting of palace, church, monastery, and college within a single precinct, founded by Philip II of Spain, 23 Apr. 1563. Charles V's remains conveyed there, 1574. Building completed, 1584. Philip II *d.* there, 1598.

Esperanto. International language, invented, 1887, by Dr. L. Zamenhof, a Warsaw oculist (1859–1917).

Essex, Kingdom of. Established by the E. Saxons *c.* sixth century. There was not always one ruler, power and territory being sometimes divided, though the kings were of a common dynasty. Between *c.* 600 and 824 the names of fifteen kings are known. As an independent kingdom it came to an end *c.* 830, and was ceded by Wessex to the Danish kings of E. Anglia under the Treaty of Wedmore (*q.v.*), 878. After reconquest of the Danelaw by Edward the Elder, 925, it was placed under an ealdorman. It was never an important kingdom, such influence as it had being derived from its uneasy control of London, which was in E. Saxon hands from at least the beginning of the seventh century until the time of Bede's old age (*c.* 730). Its king Saberht (*d. c.* 616) was converted to Christianity in 604 by Bishop Mellitus (*d.* 634), but his three sons were apostates, if not lifelong pagans. Bede says they were all killed in battle against the W. Saxons (Gewissae), presumably under King Cynegils, but does not say when.

Estate Duty (U.K.). First levied, 1894, on real property.

Estates, Committee of the. Appointed by Scots Parliament, 1640–8.

Este, Italy. Dukes of became dukes of Reggio and Modena (*q.v.*), 1452 and of

Ferrara, 1471. Family of the Estensi died out in Italy, 1803.

Estonia. Two branches of the Finnish group of tribes originating on the Upper Volga—the Ests and the Livs—were settled respectively N. and W. of the Gulf of Riga by the beginning of the Christian era. The Russians from Novgorod built a fort at Tartu, in E., 1036. Danes under Bishop Albert of Riga, who founded Reval, conquered E., 1219. They sold their gains to the Teutonic Knights (*q.v.*), 1346, who amalgamated E. with Livonia. After dissolution of the Teutonic Order, 1560, northern E. passed to Sweden while southern E. went first to Poland until 1629, thence to Sweden, which ceded the whole country to Russia, 1720. Independence proclaimed, 24 Feb. 1918, and recognized by U.S.S.R., 2 Feb. 1920, and by Western Allies, 26 Jan. 1921. The constitution of 1920 made the prime minister the only head of the state. Communist rising, 1 Dec. 1924: all Communist organizations thereupon suppressed. Lapua near-Fascist movement analogous to that in Finland suppressed, 1930, but political instability (there were eighteen cabinets between 1920 and 1934) resulted in Paets, the premier, assuming the presidency and ruling as a dictator from 1934 onwards. He concluded a tripartite Baltic pact with Latvia and Lithuania, 1934–5, and a non-aggression pact with Germany, 22 June 1939, and another with Russia, 28 Sept., but withdrew from the Baltic Entente, 1935. Russian forces marched into E., 18 June 1940, and E. joined the U.S.S.R., as a constituent republic, 6 Aug. Paets was deported to Russia, his fate unknown since, 14 June 1941. The Germans invaded E., Aug, 1941, and remained in occupation of the country, which became part of 'Ostland,' 17 Nov. 1941, until ejected by Soviet troops, Feb. 1945.

Étaples, Treaty of, between Henry VII of England and Charles VIII of France, 3 Nov. 1492.

Etching. First E. on iron by Albrecht Dürer *c.* 1500. *See* ENGRAVING.

Ether. Faraday (1791–1867) discovered its soporific qualities, 1818. First used as an anaesthetic, 1846.

Ethiopia or **Abyssinia.** Present royal house claims descent from Solomon and the Queen of Sheba. Kingdom of Axum *fl.* first–seventh centuries. Christianity introduced by St. Frumentius *c.* A.D. 330. El-Esbaha conquered Yemen, 525–75. Revolution and country divided between Axum and Shoa, 1000. Reunited under the Solomonean dynasty by Tekuno Amtak, 1268. Arrival of the Portuguese

Pedro de Covilha, 1490. Embassy sent to Portugal, 1509. E. and Portuguese wars with Mohammed Grañ, 1528–42, end in Grañ's defeat and death, 1543. Jesuit attempt at conversion of Copts to Roman Catholicism ends in expulsion of Portuguese by King Fasilidas, 1633. Victory of Kassai of Amhara at Gorgora, 1853. He proclaims himself Emperor as Theodore III, 1853. He defeats the Shoans at Debra Berhan, 1855. Defeat by British and suicide of Theodore at Magdala, 1868. Kassai of Tigré proclaimed Emperor as John I, 1872–89. Emperor Menelek (1889–1913) defeats Italians at Adowa, 1896. Lij Yasu (1913–16) excommunicated and deposed, 1916. Regency of Empress Zauditu and Ras Tafari, 1916–30. E. admitted to League of Nations, 1927. Tafari becomes Emperor as Hailé Selassié, 1930. Italian conquest of E., Oct. 1935–May 1936. Italians massacre large numbers in Addis Ababa, Feb. 1937. Reconquest by British and Hailé Selassié begun, Jan. 1941. Completed, Nov. 1941. Treaty with Britain, 3 Feb. 1942, later superseded by treaties of 1944 and 1954, but 1954 treaty declared invalid by Ethiopian Government as from 26 June 1960. Diplomatic relations with Italy resumed, 1951. Federation with Eritrea became effective, Sept. 1952. Hailé Selassié granted a more liberal Constitution on his Silver Jubilee, 1955. Abortive attempt to overthrow the Emperor, Dec. 1960. Ethiopian soldiers part of U.N. force in the Congo, 1960.

Etna, Sicily. 10,758 ft. Several serious eruptions since 476 B.C. These include eruptions in 125 and 43 B.C., and in A.D. 1169 (when Catania was overwhelmed), 1444, 1537, 1553, 1669 (when a twelve-foot abyss was opened up in the mountainside), 1830, 1852, 1879, 1892, 1899, 1910, 1923, and 1928.

Eton College (England). Founded, 1440, by Henry VI and William of Waynflete. Supplementary charter, 1441, when buildings were commenced. Mutinies took place, 1743, 1768, 1783, 1810, and 1832. The 'Montem' procession was abolished, 1846. Damaged by bombing, 1941.

Etruria, Italy. Inhabited by a people speaking a non-Aryan language, who may have come from Asia some time before 800 B.C. and who probably supplied the Tarquin kings to Rome in seventh century B.C. Finally conquered by Cornelius Dolabella, 283 B.C. Received Roman franchise, 91 B.C.

Euboea or **Negropont,** Greece. Struggle between Chalcis and Eretria for leadership of, eighth century. Euboean colonies founded in Chalcidice eighth and seventh centuries B.C. In Sicily and Italy, 760–648. Eretria assists Ionian revolt against Persia, 499. Eretria sacked by Persians, 490. Athenian colony at Histiaea, 445. Athenian influence shaken off, 404. Joins Athenian confederation again, 357. Submits to Macedon, 336; to Rome, 146. Seized by Venetians, A.D. 1204. Conquered by Turks, 1470. Becomes Greek, 1832.

Eupen and Malmédy. Ceded to Belgium by Germany under Treaty of Versailles, 1919.

Euratom. *See* EUROPEAN ATOMIC ENERGY COMMUNITY.

Eureka Stockade. *See* BALLARAT.

European Association. Founded in London by Mazzini and others to promote republicanism in Europe, 1855.

European Atomic Energy Community (Euratom). Constituted, 1 Jan. 1958, to promote a powerful nuclear industry for peaceful purposes among members of the European Economic Community. An agreement signed with Britain on 4 Feb. 1959 provided a basis for co-operation. Britain applied for full membership of Euratom in Mar. 1962, and negotiations to secure her entry started in July 1962, but lapsed after Britain failed to secure entry to the Common Market (*q.v.*).

European Coal and Steel Community. Established, 10 Aug. 1952, to pool the Common Market countries' resources of coal, iron, and steel in a single market. The High Authority has its headquarters at Luxembourg. Britain signed an agreement of association with the E. C. S. C., 21 Dec. 1954. Britain applied for full membership, Mar. 1962, but the negotiations lapsed after her failure to enter the Common Market (*q.v.*).

European Defence Community (E.D.C.). Proposed defensive federation of France, Belgium, Italy, Luxembourg, the Netherlands, and the German Federal Republic. Treaty establishing E.D.C. signed, May 1952, but the French National Assembly rejected it, 30 Aug. 1954, and it was subsequently superseded by the defence arrangements made under the London and Paris agreements (*q.v.*).

European Free Trade Association (E.F.T.A.). Consists of Austria, Denmark, Norway, Portugal, Sweden, Switzerland, and the U.K. ('The Seven'). E.F.T.A. Convention initialled at Stockholm, 20 Nov. 1959. In force after ratification by all members, 3 May 1960. Finland associated with E.F.T.A., 27 Mar. 1961. First tariff reductions between members took place 1 July 1960. When Britain applied for full membership of the Common Market (*q.v.*), on 10 Aug.

1961, Denmark followed suit, and other E.F.T.A. countries prepared to negotiate some form of association with it. Britain's failure to secure entry, in Jan. 1963, was followed by an E.F.T.A. meeting in Lisbon in May 1963, where it was announced (10 May) that industrial tariffs between E.F.T.A. members were to be completely abolished by the end of 1966.

Eurovision. Direct television link-up between various European countries. Developed after 1953, when the B.B.C. coverage of the coronation was relayed successfully to France, Belgium, Holland, and W. Germany. See TELEVISION.

Evacuation (U.K.) of mothers and children from danger areas before World War II began, 1 Sept. 1939.

Evacuation Day (New York, U.S.A.). Anniversary of the British evacuation of New York, 25 Nov. 1783.

Evangelical Alliance of German protestant states, 1608, opposed by Holy Alliance (founded 1609).

Evangelical Alliance, World's. Founded in London, 1846.

Evangelic League. Founded by certain Lutherans and Calvinists against the Emperor Mathias, 1613.

'Evening News.' See NEWSPAPERS.

'Evening Standard.' See NEWSPAPERS.

Everest, Mount, Expeditions to. Gen. C. G. Bruce (1), 1922; (2) 1924 (with Col. Norton). Marquess of Douglas and D. F. McIntyre flew over E., 1933. H. Rutledge, 1933. H. W. Tilman, 1938. Reconnaisance of western approaches by party under E. Shipton, 1951–2. Swiss expedition in autumn of 1952 abandoned, Dec. Climbed by Hillary and Tensing, 29 May 1953. Allegedly climbed by Wang Fu-Chou and two companions (all Chinese), 25 May 1960. Climbed by two members of the U.S. Expedition (James Whitaker and a Sherpa), 1 May 1963.

Everyman's Library. Comprehensive library of the representative works of all time, first published by J. M. Dent & Sons Ltd in 1906.

Evian Conference on refugees, 6–15 July 1938.

Evian Agreement, between France and the Algerian nationalists to end the civil war in Algeria and acknowledge Algeria's independence, signed 18 Mar. 1962.

Evil May Day. 1 May 1517. A riot of London apprentices which arose out of complaints against foreigners and the consequent conspiracy of 30 Apr. 1517.

Evora, Convention of, ended Portuguese civil war, 1834.

Exarch. 1. (of Ravenna). Title of the Byzantine governor of Italy, 584–782. 2. Title of the Patriarch of the Bulgarian orthodox church instituted, 1876.

Excess Profits Duty. Imposed, Sept. 1915 to Mar. 1921.

Excess Profits Tax. Imposed as from 3 Sept. 1939. New scale laid down in R. A. Butler's budget, 6 Mar. 1952. Abolished by Finance Act, 1953; effective, 1 Jan. 1954.

Exchange, Royal (London). Founded by Sir Thomas Gresham 7 June, 1566. Queen Elizabeth I visited it, Jan. 1571, since when it has been called 'Royal.' Burnt, 1666. Rebuilt by Edward German, 1668. Burnt again, 1838. Present building, 1840–4.

Exchanges, Foreign. Name *Bourse* originated with merchant family of Bruges named van der Beurse, in whose house moneychangers met regularly in the fourteenth century. Amsterdam Wheat Exchange was operating in seventeenth century; here there was a currency exchange from 1530 and a stock exchange from 1602. Paris currency exchange, 1556; stock exchange, 1724. Vienna stock exchange founded, 1753; Berlin, 1806.

Exchequer. Originally part of the Council (*q.v.*), it was already a separate department by reign of Henry II (1154–1189), and also distinct from the court of the same name (see COURTS). Chancellor of E. office founded, 1221. E. Office founded, 1399. Chancellor of the E.'s judicial functions ceased to exist after 1735. E. and Audit Department instituted, 1866.

Chancellors of the Exchequer since 1924:

P. Snowden	1924
W. S. Churchill	1924–1929
P. Snowden	1929–1931
N. Chamberlain	1931–1937
Sir John Simon	1937–1940
Sir Kingsley Wood	1940–1943
Sir John Anderson	1943–1945
H. Dalton	1945–1947
Sir Stafford Cripps	1947–1950
H. Gaitskell	1950–1951
R. A. Butler	1951–1955
H. Macmillan	1955–1957
P. Thorneycroft	1957–1958
D. Heathcoat-Amory	1958–1960
Selwyn Lloyd	1960–1962
R. Maudling	1962–

Exchequer, Court of the. See COURTS.

Excise (U.K.). Introduced by Long Parliament, 1643. Sir R. Walpole fails to pass a new E. scheme owing to strong opposition, 1733. Board of Inland Revenue founded, 1849. Transferred to control of the Board of Customs and E., 1909.

Excise (U.S.A.). E. bill on liquor introduced into Congress, 1791. Caused rioting, 1794.

Exclusion Bill to disable the Duke of York (later James II) as a Roman Catholic from succeeding to the throne, introduced, 1679. It was passed three times by the House of Commons, but on each occasion Charles II dissolved Parliament.

Exeter, England. Originally *Isca Dumnoniorum* and a Roman military station. Known to the W. Welsh as *Caer Wisc.* Sacked by Sweyn, King of Denmark, 1003. Made a bishopric, 1050. Retaken by William the Conqueror after a rising in the W., 1068. Cathedral begun, 1112. Made a county corporate, 1537. E. school established, 1629. Captured by Prince Maurice, 1643. Retaken by Fairfax, 1646. Heavily bombed, 1942. The University College of the S.W. (incorporated 1922) was created University of E. by royal charter in 1955.

Exeter Book. Leofric, Bishop of E. from 1050 to 1071, gave this book to the cathedral library. Written before 1050, first transcribed, 1831, first printed, 1842.

Exeter Hall (Strand, London). Built, 1830–1; used for concerts, meetings, etc., till 1880. Demolished, 1907.

Exhibition of 1851, The Great (London). Royal Commission appointed and building begun in Hyde Park, 3 Jan. 1850. Opened by Queen Victoria, 1 May 1851. *See* CRYSTAL PALACE.

Exile, known in British law as Transportation (*q.v.*).

Existentialism, as a philosophy, was expressed in *Sein und Zeit* by Martin Heidegger, 1926; *Gegenwart: eine Kritische Ethik* by E. Grisebach, 1928; *Philosophie,* by Karl Jaspers, 1932; and from *c.* 1940, but especially since 1944, by the plays of Jean-Paul Sartre (*b.* 1905). E. was condemned by the Pope, 1948.

Extradition Laws. Court of Exchequer declared a form of E. L., 1749. Ashburton Treaty with U.S.A., 1842; extended, 1890. With treaty with France, 1843. New Convention with France when exceptions regarding political offences were made, 1852. Present procedure in Great Britain based on the E. Acts of 1870–3. Questions of extradition and right of political asylum came into prominence in 1962, as a result of the Soblen case; and in 1963, as regards Commonwealth citizens, over the case of Chief Enahoro of Nigeria.

Eyre, Lake, Australia. Discovered by Edward E. (1815–1901) in 1840.

Eyre, Commissions of General. (Lat. '*Iter.*') Bodies of commissioners were sent round the kingdom at intervals to investigate the working of the Government and redress grievances, etc. Instituted by Henry II (1154–89). Henry III (1216–72) compelled to promise that they would not be held more often than once in seven years. Famous E. of Cornwall, 1221. E. of Kent, 1313, lasted a year. Declined in reign of Edward III (1327–77), disappeared under Richard II (1377–99).

ADDENDA

F

Fabian Society. An intellectual society of non-revolutionary Socialists, founded in London, 1883.

Factory Acts. First F. Act introduced by Sir Robert Peel the Elder passed, 1802, providing for F. inspectors. Second F. Act, 1819, relating to cotton mills. Lord Althorp's Act, 1833, introduced the half-time principle, and provided for education of children engaged in factories. Sir Robert Peel's F. Act, 1844, provided a 10-hour limit for women and children. Mining Act, 1842, forbade female and child labour in mines. F. Act extension and Workshop Regulation Acts, 1867, included all Fs. in the previous Acts. First F. inspectors appointed, 1833. Crosse's F. and Workshop Act, 1878, amended 1901, 1902, 1908. First women inspectors, 1893. F. and Workshop (Cotton Cloth Fs.) Act, 1911, altered regulations under the Act of 1901. Shops Act, 1912. 'Half-timers' abolished by Education Act, 1918. Children under fourteen prohibited from industrial employment, 1920. Lead Processes Act, 1920. F. Act, 1937, specified (among other things) normal and overtime hours for women and young persons, required certain standards of lighting, heating, ventilation, and safety. *See* MINING ACTS; SHOP HOURS ACT; WORKMEN'S COMPENSATION.

Faenza, Italy. 'Faïence' pottery manufactured at since the end of thirteenth century.

Faeroe. *See* FAROE.

Fahrenheit Scale. Temperature divisions invented *c.* 1712 by G. D. Fahrenheit (1626–1736) of Danzig. Popularly used in Britain, but began to be superseded by Centigrade, 1961.

Fair Isle, the most probable identification of the island known to the ancients as Thule; mentioned by Pytheas (300 B.C.), whose description would fit the F. I., and by Ptolemy, A.D. 150, but the report of the sighting of Thule by Agricola's fleet, about 80, is too bald and rhetorical to be connected with any particular island. For the rest of its history, *see* SHETLAND ISLANDS.

Falaise, France. Treaty of, between Henry II of England, his son Henry, and Louis VII of France, 1174. Besieged by Henry V of England, 1417. Captured from English, 1450. Scene of the celebrated 'gap' in the Normandy battle

through which the German troops escaped, 7–22 Aug. 1944.

Falangists, members of the Falange Español, founded by José Antonio Primo de Rivera (*b.* 1903), 29 Oct. 1933, were Fascists of the radical type. On the outbreak of the civil war the F. were at a disadvantage as their leader was in Government hands, having been arrested, 15 Mar. 1936. He was executed at Alicante, 20 Nov. 1936. Their 'revolutionary' social ideas and vulnerability to foreign (especially Italian) influence rendered them suspect to the native backers of Franco's movement, and they were forced to merge with Conservative groups in 1937. The year 1938 saw the lowest ebb of their fortunes, but Franco himself took over the leadership of the *F. vice* de Rivera. At the end of the civil war they were the only political party tolerated in Spain.

Falciu, Rumania. Peace between Russia and Turkey, 1711.

Falkland Islands (Islas Malvinas), S. America. Discovered by John Davis, 1592. French settlement existed, 1764. Part taken by British, 1765. Ceded by France to Spain, 1767. Spaniards and English ignored each other till 1769–70. Spain yielded by convention, 1771. Argentine settlement, 1829. New British settlement, 1833, and Argentinians expelled. Naval battle between British and Germans, 8 Dec. 1914. Argentine raises claim to, 1946–7; demands reparations, Feb. 1953, after F. I. police, supported by Royal Marines, had removed Argentine subjects and demolished Chilean huts on Deception Islands, F. I. Dependencies.

Family Allowances, first provided in Manitoba, 1915. Now by all Canadian provinces. Family Allowances Act in Great Britain became law, 15 June 1945.

Family Compact. Name given to three agreements between the French and Spanish branches of the House of Bourbon (*q.v.*). (1) 1733, between Louis XV and Philip V against English commerce. (2) Treaty of perpetual alliance signed at Fontainebleau, 25 Oct. 1743; (3) 15 Aug. 1761.

Faneuil Hall. *See* 'CRADLE OF AMERICAN LIBERTY.'

Fanning Island. Annexed by Great Britain, 1888; included in the Gilbert and Ellice colony, 1916.

Fan Vaulting. Earliest example of F. V. is in timber. F. V. in the chapel of Winchester College *c.* 1390. Earliest stone F. V. at Gloucester *c.* 1420.

Far Eastern Republic. Declared its independence of Moscow, 1921. Suppressed, 1922, and annexed to Soviet Russia.

'Farmer's Letters, The.' A series of letters by John Dickinson against English official measures. First appeared in *Pennsylvania Chronicle*, 2 Dec. 1767.

Farne Islands. Inner F. was the hermitage of St. Cuthbert between 664 and 687. He *d.* there and the cell was thereafter inhabited by his disciple Ethelwald (*d. c.* 740). On its site a Benedictine priory was founded, 1082, of which one tower, called St. Cuthbert's, still stands. The famous rescue by Grace Darling took place here, 1838. The whole group of islands was acquired by the National Trust (*q.v.*), 1925, as a bird sanctuary.

Farnese Family. Following are the most distinguished members: 1. Alessandro Farnese, who became Pope Paul III (1534–49). 2. Pierluigi, his natural son. 1st Duke of Parma, 1503–47. 3. Alessandro (1520–89), who completed the famous F. palace at Rome. 4. Alessandro, 3rd Duke, 1545–92, famous Spanish general. 5. Elizabeth, 1692–1766, who married, 1714, Philip V of Spain.

Farnley Wood Plot against Charles II, 1663. Leaders executed, 19 Jan. 1664.

Faroe or **Faeroe Islands,** N. Atlantic. Irish hermits driven out by Norse pirates *c.* 795. More heavily settled by Norse immigrants up to *c.* 900. Annexed to Norway, 1035. Became Danish, 1380. Law-Thing abolished, 1816; restored, 1852; home rule granted, 1948. Occupied by British troops, Apr. 1940–May 1945. Fishing limits around the F. I. extended to six miles, 1959. Danes announced (1962) that they proposed imposing a twelve-mile limit from Apr. 1963.

Farringdon Market (London). Act for establishing of, 1824. Opened, 20 Nov. 1826. Discontinued, June 1892.

Farthing. First coined by Edward I (1272–1307) instead of quartering pennies. Ceased to be legal tender, 31 Dec. 1960.

Fascism. 1. Founded as a politically organized creed by Benito Mussolini, at Bologna, 1919. Total electoral failure, 1920, but some success in general elections of 1921. In Oct. 1922 the Fascists took over the Italian Government by force in the 'March on Rome.' *See* ITALY. 2. In Britain Sir Oswald Mosley's British Union of Fascists (founded 1932)

got notoriety by the use of violence at meetings in London and Oxford, 1936, which led to passing of the Public Order Act, 1936. Revived after World War II as the British Union Movement (1948). The National Socialist Party of Great Britain, founded 1961, held a meeting in Trafalgar Square on 1 July 1962, which resulted in rioting and violence. Four British Fascists were jailed, 15 Oct. 1962.

Fashoda Question. French Major Marchand occupied F. on the Upper Nile, 10 July 1898. As Britain was in process of reconquering the Sudan from the Mahdi's followers, this interference was bitterly resented. After the Dervish defeat at Omdurman (2 Sept. 1898), and further diplomatic exchanges nearly leading to war, Marchand was withdrawn, 11 Dec. 1898.

Fathers of the Church (*Patres Ecclesiastici*).

The Apostolic F. (believed to have been disciples of the Apostles):

Clement of Rome	*fl.* 93–101
Ignatius	*fl. c.* 101
Polycarp	*d. c.* 155
Barnabas	*fl. c.* 120
Hermas	*fl. c.* 150

The principal ante-Nicene F. are:

Justin Martyr	*c.* 100–165
Irenaeus	*c.* 130–202
Clement of Alexandria	*c.* 150–*c.* 216
Tertullian	*c.* 155–*c.* 222
Origen	185–254
Cyprian	*c.* 200–258
Gregory Thaumaturgus	*c.* 213–*c.* 270

The principal post-Nicene F. are:

Eusebius of Caesarea	*c.* 260–340
Hilary of Poictiers	*c.* 403–449
Athanasius	*c.* 296–373
Basil	*c.* 329–379
Cyril of Jerusalem	*c.* 315–386
Gregory Nazianzus	*c.* 328–390
Gregory of Nyssa	*c.* 301–*c.* 394
Ambrose	*c.* 340–*c.* 397
Epiphanius	*c.* 330–403
Chrysostom	*c.* 334–407
Jerome	331–420
Augustine of Hippo	354–430
Cyril of Alexandria	376–444
Leo the Great	*c.* 540–604
Bede	*c.* 673–735
John of Damascus	*d. c.* 752

Fatima, in Portugal, was the scene of a vision in which the Virgin appeared to three country children, and the sun stood still, 1917.

Fatimites. Family claiming descent from Fatima, daughter of Mohammed, who ousted the Aghlabid dynasty from Tunis, and founded an anti-Caliphate at Al-Mehdiya, near Tunis, 909. After repeated attempts Egypt and Syria conquered from Abbasids, 969, and capital moved to Cairo, where the dynasty remained until extinguished at Saladin's conquest of Egypt (*q.v.*), 1171.

Faversham, England. Abbey founded, 1147–9.

Fawkes, Guy. See GUNPOWDER PLOT.

F.B.I. (Federal Bureau of Investigation), set up, 1908, as a branch of the U.S. Department of Justice, independent of State police forces. J. Edgar Hoover (*b.* 1895) became Director of F.B.I., 1924. From 1941 to 1945 F.B.I. detachments accompanied U.S. armed forces in all theatres on counter-espionage duties, and since 1945 the F.B.I. has been most prominent in anti-Communist activities, its agents giving evidence in treason trials, such as that of Alger Hiss in 1950, and before Senate commissions in the purge of fellow travellers.

F.B.I. (Federation of British Industries). Established, 1916; granted royal charter of incorporation, 1924.

Federal Convention (U.S.A.). Representatives of twelve states assembled at Philadelphia, 1787, to prepare a constitution for U.S.A.

Federal German Republic. See GERMANY, FEDERAL REPUBLIC OF.

Federal Reserve System, reform of American finance and banking methods, introduced by Congress, 1913, and modified by the Banking Act, 1935, which led to the creation of the F. R. Board, 1936.

Federal Trade Commission. Set up by the U.S. Government in 1914 to check the growing menace of trusts and monopolies.

Federalist Party (U.S.A.). Advocates of national constitution, 1788. Defeated, 1800, by the election of Jefferson as president. Disbanded, 1820.

Federation of Rhodesia and Nyasaland. See RHODESIA AND NYASALAND, FEDERATION OF.

Fehmic Courts (Femgerichte), ancient native courts of Westphalia, corresponding to the English *Folkmoot* or Scandinavian *Thing*, as opposed to feudal courts of the common European type, first came into prominence, 1180; by the Emperor Charles IV's Westphalian statute of Nov. 1371 they were empowered to try crimes of violence instead of those involving real estate, as hitherto. The Fs. attained the summit of their power, 1430–40, spreading southwards to Switzerland. Reforms took place, 1437 and 1442. F. proceedings were not normally secret; only at periods when the F. had to function in opposition to feudal courts: the only punishment inflicted was death. Jerome Bonaparte's edict of 1811 abolished F. C. The last president

(*Freigraf*) of a F. Court *d.* 1835. Assassination by right-wing terrorists, 1922–4 (e.g. of Walter Rathenau, 24 June 1922), vulgarly called F. murders, had little in common with the original F. court which was a legal, not a self-constituted, body.

Fenian Association. Name (derived from Irish legend) adopted by John F. O'Mahony (1816–77) for the American section founded by him of the Irish Republican Brotherhood, 1858. The main section in Ireland was led by James Stephens (1825–1901) and the name Fs. came to be applied to the whole membership. Attempted raid into Canada, 1866. Abortive attempt at rebellion in Ireland, and outrages in England, 1867. Attempt to blow up Clerkenwell jail, 13 Dec. 1867. Further raids into Canada, 1870. Plot of the 'Irish Invincibles,' 1882.

Fens (U.K.). See also BEDFORD LEVEL. Romans made attempts to drain the F. Unsuccessful attempt to drain Deeping Fen during reign of William I (1066–87). Vermuyden's efforts *c.* 1640. As a whole the major drainage operations in the F. were completed in 1807. Measures to strengthen flood defences announced, Nov. 1947. Extensive flooding, 1 Feb. 1953. Great Ouse River Board started a large-scale flood-protection scheme to prevent recurrences of this, 1954, virtually complete by end of 1962.

Fernando Po, W. coast of Africa. Discovered by Portuguese Fernão do Po, 1472. English settlement, 1827–34. Now part of the Spanish colony of Guinea which, on 30 July 1959, was divided into the districts of F. P. and Rio Muni.

Ferrara, Italy. Ancient city in the Exarchate of Ravenna *c.* A.D. 753–4. Este family (*q.v.*) became rulers, 1208. University founded, 1391. A council which unsuccessfully tried to reconcile Roman and Greek churches held, 1438. Taken by French, 1796. Given to Papacy, 1814. Held by Austrian garrison, 1849–59. Annexed by Sardinia, Mar. 1860.

Ferrers Arrest. George F., M.P. for Plymouth, was arrested by the sheriffs of the City of London for debt, Mar. 1542. After the sheriffs had refused the Commons request that he should be released they were imprisoned for contempt, 28 Mar. 1542, but released on 30th.

Festival of Britain, 3 May–30 Sept. 1951.

Fettmilch Insurrection led by Vincenz F. and others at Frankfort-on-Main against municipal mismanagement, 1612–1616. Leaders executed, 1616.

Feudalism. A medieval system of society based on land in which a division of labour is achieved by committing governmental functions to those prepared to render military protection in return for agricultural and other services. It arose out of the anarchy of western Europe in the eighth and ninth centuries, but never flourished in its pure form in Britain, where the Anglo-Saxons possessed independent institutions of another type. Nevertheless after the Norman Conquest (1066) the principles of feudal organization were introduced, and many Anglo-Saxon customs were reclassified as if they were feudal in nature. The decline of F. began almost immediately after it was introduced here, the principal dates being: Introduction of Judicial Circuits (*temp.* Henry II, 1154–89). Statute *Quia Emptores* (*q.v.*), 1290. Introduction of the Use, fourteenth century. Statute of Uses, 1535. Statute of Wills, 1540. Act for the Abolition of Military Tenure, 1660. The last traces of F. were swept away by the Law of Property Acts, 1922–5.

Feuillants. Religious order in France, founded, 1577, as a reformed branch of the Cistercians by Jean de la Barrière.

Feuillants Club. Founded 1791 by the moderate section of the 'Amis de la Constitution' (organized at Versailles, 1789). So called from their meeting-place, a disused Feuillant monastery. Disbanded, 10 Aug. 1792.

Fez, Morocco. Founded by Idris II, 808. Mosque of Mulai Idris built, 810. Colleges for foreign students built in thirteenth century. Occupied by French, Mar. 1911. Treaty of F. established French protectorate over Morocco, 1912, which terminated 2 Mar. 1956. New town begun, 1916.

F.F.I. (Forces Françaises de l'Intérieur). Designation adopted by all French resistance forces when placed under unified command once the invasion of June 1944 had started.

Fianna Fail (Irish, meaning Soldiers of Destiny), followers of Eamon de Valera (*b.* 1882), organized as a party in 1926; formed government, 1932–48; again, 1951–4 and since 1957.

Fidei Defensor. *See* DEFENDER OF THE FAITH.

F.I.D.O. (Fog, Intensive Dispersal Operation). Device for clearing airfield fog, invented by A. C. Hartley, 1942.

Field-Marshal (U.K.). Rank first conferred by George II on the Duke of Argyll, 1736.

Field of the Cloth of Gold. Conference between Henry VIII and Francis I near Guines, Pas-de-Calais, June 1520.

Fiery Chamber. *See* CHAMBRES ARDENTES.

Fieschi's Plot to kill Louis Philippe of France, 28 July 1835. F. and accomplices executed, 19 Feb. 1836.

Fifth Column. Expression originating in 1936 at the outset of the Spanish Civil War, attributed to the Nationalist Gen. Mola. Used by the Germans in their invasions of Scandinavia and France and the Low Countries, 1940.

Fifth Monarchy Men. Religious anarchical sect founded in England, 1645. Admonished by Cromwell's council, Dec. 1653, and leaders imprisoned, Jan. 1654. Revolted against Charles II, 1661, and leaders executed.

Fifth Republic, France. Constitution came into force, 4 Oct. 1958.

Fifty-one, Committee of. Formed New York, 1774. Favoured a general congress.

Figueras, Spain. Fortress built by Ferdinand VI, 1746–57. Taken by French, 24 Nov. 1794, 2 Mar. 1808, and 19 Aug. 1811. Restored to Spain by Treaty of Paris, 1814. Taken again by French, Sept. 1823.

Fiji Islands, Polynesia. Discovered by Tasman, 1643. Visited by Capt. Cook, 1773. British protectorate, 1874. Constitution regulated by letters patent of 2 Apr. 1937. More self-government conceded under the Fijian Affairs Ordinance, effective from 1 Jan. 1945. Visited by Queen Elizabeth II, Feb. 1963.

Film Institute, British. Founded 1933 and reconstituted, 1948.

'Financial Times.' *See* NEWSPAPERS.

Fingerprints, their classification systematically organized from *c.* 1870 by the police of the Lower Provinces of India, where F. were used as in many parts of Asia for signatures by illiterates. (Chinese documents of the eighth century A.D., so signed, are extant.) First used in England and Wales, 1901. Recording of F. of certain accused persons authorized by Criminal Justice Act, 1948.

Finland (in Finnish **Suomi**). Finns said to have settled in F. during eighth century. Swedish colonies in from eighth century onwards. Swedes under Jarl Birger Magnusson conquer South F. and Tavestehus, 1230–49, and the Finns adopted Christianity. Swedish influence extending to White Sea, 1293. Treaty of Göteborg (Russo-Swedish), 1323. Karl Knutsson sets out from F. to claim Swedish crown, 1448. Russian encroachment, 1470–1530. Finns support Sigismund's claim to Swedish throne, 1598. Overrun by Russian troops, 1710–11. Province of Viborg (Viipuri) ceded to Russia by Treaty of Nystad, 1721. Swedish troops driven out by Russians, 1808. Emperor Alexander recognized as Grand Duke of F. by Finnish estates, 1809. Finnish estates suppressed and national leaders exiled, 1898. Exiles recalled and Diet reopened, 1904. Scheme for reform of representation, 1906. Independence proclaimed, 6 Dec. 1917. Republican constitution adopted, 17 July 1919. Petsamo ceded by Russia and F.'s. independence recognized at Treaty of Dorpat (Tartu), 14 Oct. 1920. Norway frontier agreement, 29 Apr. 1924. Fascist 'Lapua' revolt suppressed, 3–5 Mar. 1932. Non-aggression pact with Russia for ten years, 7 Apr. 1934. Russian invasion, 30 Nov. 1939. Peace with Russia (Viipuri ceded), 12 Mar. 1940. F. joins Axis, June 1941. Britain declares war on F., 7 Dec. 1941. Allied armistice with F., 4 Sept. 1944. Treaties of peace with Allies, by which Petsamo was ceded and Porkkala leased to Russia (returned to F., 1956) as well as territory ceded and leased under the 1940 treaty, came into force, 15 Sept. 1947. Treaty of friendship with Russia, Apr. 1948, and extended in 1955 to cover a period of twenty years. Payment of reparations to Russia completed, 1952. F. associated with E.F.T.A., Mar. 1961. After the General Election of Feb. 1962 the Communists were no longer the largest single party in F. The combined centre and right outnumbered the left-wing representation by twenty-two seats.

Presidents of Finland:

J. K. Ståhlberg	1919–1925
L. Relander	1925–1931
P. E. Svinhufvud	1931–1937
K. Kallio	1937–1940
R. Ryiti	1940–1944
G. C. Mannerheim	1944–1946
J. K. Paasikivi	1946–1956
U. Kekkonen	1956–

Finnish Literature. The following is a list of F. authors, not now living:

Aho, Juhani, 1861–1921, novelist.
Brofeldt (real name of Aho above).
Cajander, P. E., 1846–1913, poet.
Canth, Minna, 1844–97, playwright.
Castron, M. A., 1812–52, philologist.
Haarla, Lauri, 1890–1944, novelist.
Hirn, Yrjo, 1870–1944, translator.
Ivalo, S., 1866–1937, historical novelist.
Järneveldt, Arvid, 1861–1932, novelist.
Jötuni, Marja, 1880–1943, playwright.
Kallas, A., 1878–1947, novelist.
Kivi, Alexis, 1834–72, playwright.
Leino, Einol, 1879–1926, poet.
Lehtonen, J., 1881–1946, novelist.
Linnankosi, Johannes, 1876–1913, poet.
Lönnbohm, A. E. M. (real name of Leino above).
Lönnrot, Elias, 1802–84, folklorist.
Oksanen, A., 1826–99, poet.
Paivärinta, P., 1827–1913, novelist.
Pakkala, T., 1862–1925, novelist.
Peltonen (real name of Linnankosi above).
Sarkia, Kaarlo, 1902–45, novelist.

Stenval, Alexis (real name of Kivi above).
Von Numers, G., 1848–1913, playwright (also in Swedish).

Finns and Finnish Language. As no branch of these people was literate before the Reformation, and as the accounts of them given by their medieval neighbours are all coloured by hostility or contempt or both, a chronological account of their early history is peculiarly difficult, and must partly be reconstructed from such elements as archaeology and foreign loan-words in their language; thus the very frequent Germanic loan-words like *kultu*-gold must from their form have been borrowed before *c.* A.D. 600. The designation F. was not a native one, but bestowed on them by their western neighbours, perhaps by the Balts: Tacitus in the first century A.D. mentions Fenni and Ptolemy mentions Phennoi about a hundred years later: this could be a rendering of a W. Germanic name, cognate with *fen* and meaning 'people from the marshes,' which adequately translates the western F.'s own name for themselves—Suomalaiset. But the first written reference to 'F.' in a Germanic language (King Alfred's preface to Orosius, written *c.* 885 in Old English) clearly means not F. but Lapps, and early Scandinavian sources all refer to Lapps as F.; their name for F. was *Kvaen,* which Alfred in the same work renders 'Quenas': both are merely variants of the Old Norse and Old English words for woman, and may indicate that at the time of their first contact with the Swedes the F., like the Picts, were matriarchal and polyandrous; this would be in the period A.D. 600–800, when the western branch of them was expanding into the present Finland and Estonia, which they had reached from the homeland of the race about the middle course of the Volga, where the Mordvins still speak a language allied to Finnish as do the Ostiaks (Udmurt) of the Kama basin. Credit for reducing Finnish to writing is usually given to Bishop Michael Agricola (*d.* 1557). *See also* ESTONIA ; KARELO-, etc.; LIVONIA.

Fire Brigades and Appliances. First reference to a fire brigade relates to China *c.* 4000 B.C. Egyptian F. B., 2000 B.C. Romans formed F. B. under a *praefectum vigilum c.* 150 B.C. Machine built by Hautsch of Nürnberg, 1657. Flexible hose introduced by Jan Vanderheide. 1672. First fire insurance office founded in London, 1680, and first English fire brigade then organized. Newsham's engine patented, 1700. In eighteenth century all insurance companies had their own fire brigade, and first fire engine acquired by a London insurance company,

1722. London parishes obliged to keep a fire engine by Act of Parliament, 1774. Several private insurance F. B. united, 1825. First steam fire engine invented by Braithwaite, 1829. All London private brigades united, 1833. Metropolitan fire brigade set up, 1865, by which time steam engines had come into general use. Motor fire engines introduced, 1905. National Fire Service started, 1940. Repartitioned into local F. services, 1948.

Fire of London, The Great, broke out, 2 Sept. 1666, and burned until 6 Sept. Previous to this the term 'Great F. of L.' had meant the catastrophe of 1136.

Firearms. Crude cannon in use in Europe by 1300. Edward III used them against the Scots, 1327. First hand-guns made at Perugia, 1364, and at Augsburg by 1380. Wheel lock in use by 1575; flint-locks *c.* 1640. Percussion detonator patented by Forsyth, 1810. Automatic pistols *c.* 1900.

First Empire, in France, the reign of Napoleon I, 1804–14.

First Offenders Act, 1887, repealed by Probation of Offenders Act, 1907, which was amended by the Criminal Justice Acts, 1925 and 1948.

First Republic, in France, 27 Sept 1792 until 1804.

Fisheries, Northern, between Greenland and Barents Sea. English fishermen began to take cod off the Iceland and Newfoundland banks in the sixteenth century, as did the Basques, Bretons, and Portuguese, but all this fish had either to be salted (at sea) or dried (at shore stations). The first steam trawler sailed from Aberdeen, 1882, and thereafter it became possible to bring back fish fresh from northern waters. The first British trawlers worked off Iceland (Faxa Flói) in the 1890s. Anglo-Danish Agreement of 1901 dealt mainly with Icelandic fishery. Owing to a shrinkage of the Arctic ice-cap, which has been going on for about the last sixty years, it became possible for trawlers to work further and further northward, and in 1905 British trawlers began to fish off N. Norway and Bear Island; in 1925 they had begun to work the Spitzbergen waters, and since 1945 have operated, in the very biggest ships, W. of Greenland. More and more British fishing off the Iceland banks led to running disputes with Icelandic Government and fishing interests from 1948 despite the International Fishery Conference which had taken place in 1930. The Anglo-Russian Fishery Convention of 1930 was denounced by the Russians at the end of 1952, after the Hague Court in 1951 had found in favour of Norway as against Britain when the former decided to extend her territorial waters for fishery purposes. Iceland extended her fishing limits to twelve nautical miles, 1958. This led to a dispute with Britain, but agreement was reached, 11 Mar. 1961.

Fitzwilliam Museum, Cambridge. A collection of engravings and books was bequeathed to the university by Richard, Visc. F. of Meryon (1745–1816). The building was begun, 1837; Marlay Galleries added, 1924; McClean MSS. Room, 1925; Courtauld Galleries, 1931; Henderson Galleries and Charrington Print Room, 1936; Graham Robertson Room, 1955. Fairhaven Bequest received, 1948.

Fiume (It.) or **Rijeka** (Serb.-Cr.), Yugoslavia. Part of the Empire, 1471. Joined to Hungary, 1870. Granted to Italy by secret Pact of London, 1915. Seized by Gabriele d'Annunzio, who proclaimed provisional government, 11 Sept. 1919. Recognized by Italy and Yugoslavia as a free city by Treaty of Rapallo, 12 Nov. 1920. Italy takes possession, 27 Jan. 1924. Permanently ceded to Yugoslavia, 1947.

Five Boroughs. Lincoln, Nottingham, Derby, Stamford, and Leicester established as Danish colonies *c.* 850. They retained certain Danish customs ('by-laws') till well into thirteenth century. *See* VIKING AGE.

Five Hundred, Council of. The lower house of the French legislature under the constitution of the year III (1795), the upper house being called the Council of Ancients. Lucien Buonaparte elected president of, 22 Oct. 1799. Dissolved by Napoleon, 10 Nov. 1799. *See* BRUMAIRE.

Five Members of the Long Parliament, Pym, Hampden, Hazelrigg, Strode, and Holles, whom Charles I attempted unsuccessfully to arrest, 4 Jan. 1642.

Five Mile Act. *See* CLARENDON CODE.

Five Power Naval Treaty signed at London, 22 Apr. 1930, between Britain, U.S.A., Japan, France, and Italy restricting the size of their respective navies.

Five-Year Plan (U.S.S.R.). To industrialize Russia. First F.-Y. P., 1928–1933. Second, 1933–8 (completed by 1937). Third, 1938–42, but interrupted by war. Fourth, 1946–50. Fifth, 1951–5. Sixth, 1956–60. Seventh, 1961–5.

Flagellants. Most famous outbreaks of this ascetic sect, 1348–9 and 1417. Condemned by bull of Clement VI, 20 Oct. 1349.

Flamboyant Architecture. *See* GOTHIC.

Flaminian Way from Rome to Rimini was built during the consulship of Flaminius, 220 B.C.

Flammock's Rebellion, led by Thomas F., Michael Joseph, and Lord Audley, defeated at Blackheath, 22 June 1497. Leaders executed, 28 June.

Flanders, Belgium and N. France. Colonized by Franks, 800–2. Annexed to France, 843. Famous for woollen manufactures, 962. Counts of F. refuse to recognize Hugues Capet as King of France, 987. Flemings take part in William I's conquest of England and in Earl Tostig's unsuccessful invasion, 1066. St. Omer first Flemish city to receive a charter, 1127. Zeeland Islands transferred from F. to Holland, 1256. French influence in F. becomes considerable after 1210. Flemings defeat French at Courtrai, 1302. All Englishmen being arrested in F. on French orders, English king retaliates by embargo on F. wool trade, 1336. Rebellion of Jacob van Artevelde of Ghent, 1337. He calls for English assistance, which being given signals the start of the Hundred Years War, 1338. Anglo-Flemish victory over French at Sluys, 1340. Flemings crushed at Ghent, 1349. Victory over the French at Roosebeke, 1382. Acquired by dukes of Burgundy, 1384. Collapse of Burgundians after death of Charles the Bold at Nancy, 1477. Great Privilege (*q.v.*), 1477. Artois annexed by France, 1483. Margaret of Burgundy, Regent of F., supports Lambert Simnel, 1487, and Perkin Warbeck, 1492–6. Abandons Warbeck in return for trading privileges called 'The Great Intercourse' (*q.v.*), 1497. The 'Bad Intercourse,' 1506. French feudal rights in F. surrendered to Emperor Charles V at Treaty of Cambrai, 1529, and remained loyal to Spain when N. half of Spanish Netherlands broke away, 1579. For history after this date, *see* BELGIUM.

Fleet Air Arm. The Royal Naval Air Service fused with Royal Flying Corps, 1918, to form the Royal Air Force, which controlled *all* aviation, even that attached to the fleet. In 1922, an element of the naval air component, thenceforth called the F. A. A., was placed under complete operational and partial administrative and disciplinary command of the Admiralty. In 1937 complete command passed to the Admiralty, and the official (though not the popular) designation was changed to Air Branch, R.N.

Fleet Ditch (London). Covered in, 1733.

Fleet Market (London). Instituted, 30 Sept. 1737. Superseded by Farringdon Market (*q.v.*). Swept away, 1829.

Fleet Marriages (London) occurred in the Liberties of the Fleet and in the Liberty of the Savoy (notably in the Fleet Chapel) from 1614 until abolished by Lord Hardwick's Act, 1753.

Fleet Prison (London), for debtors, existed as early as 1197, possibly earlier.

Burnt by Wat Tyler, 1381. Star Chamber prisoners incarcerated in till 1641. Burnt in Great Fire of London (*q.v.*), 1666. Parliamentary investigation of abuses at, 1726. Burnt by Gordon rioters (*q.v.*), 1780. Abolished, 1842. Demolished, 1844.

Fleet Street was part of the quarter burnt down in 982. In 1228 it was called F. Bridge Street, and F. S. first in 1311. Its connection with printing begins with Wynkyn de Worde (*d.* 1534), who set up his press at No. 32 in 1500.

Flemings in Britain. *See* WEAVING.

Fleur-de-lis. Emblem of the French monarchy. Origin traditionally ascribed to Clovis, A.D. 496. Definitely connected with the monarchy under Louis VII *c.* 1147. Number in the French royal arms reduced to three, 1376.

Flogging and Whipping. Powers of the British courts to pass a sentence of corporal punishment were abolished by the Criminal Justice Act, 1948, both for adults and juvenile offenders.

Florence, Italy. The ancient Roman colony was rebuilt by Julius Caesar, 59 B.C. Baptistery built *c.* A.D. 1100. Independent republic, 1198. Defeated by Siena, 1260. Cathedral built, 1294–8. City partly burnt in rioting, 1304. University founded, 1321. Ponte Vecchio built, 1345. Papal attack repelled, 1375. Revolution of the Ciompi, 1378. Rule of the Albizzi, 1382–1434. Medici come to power, 1434. Library founded, 1444. Rule of Lorenzo de' Medici (the Magnificent), 1470–92. Founds Platonic Academy, 1476. The Pazzi Conspiracy against the Medici, Giuliano killed, Lorenzo escapes, Apr. 1478. Medici expelled, 1494. Death of Savonarola, 1498. Medici restored, 1512; again expelled, 1527. Again restored, 1530. Giovanni de' Medici becomes pope as Leo X, 1513–21. Medici become Grand Dukes of Tuscany, 1569. Accademia della Crusca founded, 1582. End of Medici family, 1737. F. presented by Napoleon to his sister Élise, 1808. Provisional capital of Italy, 1864–71. Heavily damaged during allied capture, 4–11 Aug. 1944.

Florida, U.S.A. Discovered by Ponce de Leon on Easter Day, 1512. Conquered for Spain by Narvaez, 1528, and de Soto, 1539. Santo Augustino sacked by Sir Francis Drake, 1586. Ceded by Spain to Britain in exchange for Cuba at Treaty of Paris, 1763. Again ceded to Spain, 1783. Taken by U.S.A., 1811. Returned to Spain, 1812. Purchased from Spain, 1819. Admitted to union as a state, 8 Mar. 1845.

Florin. First struck in gold at Florence, eleventh century. Silver F. first struck,

1181. Gold F., value 6s., first struck in England, 1343, by Edward III. Silver F., value 2s., struck, 1849, and called 'Godless and Graceless,' because *Dei Gratia* omitted from the superscription. Omission rectified, 1852. The double F. of 1887 was discontinued, 1890. Name 'Florin' disappeared from superscription at accession of George VI.

Flower Shows in England were started by the Royal Horticultural Society of London, 1804.

Fluorine. Isolated by Moisson, 1886. Theory that F. in drinking water could prevent tooth decay demonstrated in the U.S.A. by McKay (1874–1959). Results from three test areas in England, 1962, backed his theory.

Flushing, Holland (Dutch **Vlissingen**). Jakobskerk founded, 1328. Fort dismantled, 1867. Harbour opened, 1873. Occupied by Germans, 1940. Liberated, 1945.

Flying Bombs (Vergeltungswaffe I, pilotless aircraft, jet propelled) were used against London, June–Aug. 1944, and against Antwerp and Liège, 13 Oct. 1944–31 Mar. 1945.

Flying Squadron. Scots political party led by Lord Tweeddale founded c. 1705, and secured settlement of the union question, 1706.

Fog Signals regularized by the International Maritime Code, 1862; revised 1897.

Foix, France. County in the Pyrenees independent from c. 1000 until Count Francis Phoebus became King of Navarre, 1479. His sister married Jean d'Albert and F. passed with Navarre (q.v.) eventually to the Bourbons, and then to the French crown on the accession of Henry IV, 1589. Its counts were co-princes of Andorra (q.v.), and through this marriage Andorra is under the joint suzerainty of France and Spain. At the revolution it became the department of Ariège.

Fokker. Invention by Anton Fokker (1890–1940) of a wireless-directed bombing plane announced, Sept. 1919.

Folk High Schools, Danish rural colleges, inaugurated, 1844, by Nicholas Frederick Grundtvig (1783–1872).

Fommonah, Treaty of. Between Britain and the King of Ashanti, 1874.

Fontainebleau, France. Treaty of F. between Napoleon and Godoy, the minister of Charles IV and the *de facto* King of Spain, 1807. Decree against British commerce, 1810. Napoleon signed abdication at, 6 Apr. 1814. The palace of F. was traditionally founded in the twelfth century, but, as it exists today, was begun by Francis I in the sixteenth century. S.H.A.P.E. (q.v.) has func-

tioned from F. since its inception in 1950.

Foochow, China. Bridge of Ten Thousand Ages built c. 1000. Visited by Marco Polo c. 1290. Opened to British trade, 1842.

Food and Agriculture Organization. Agency of the U.N., established, 16 Oct. 1945, with headquarters in Rome.

Food Control (U.K.). Food Ministry under Lord Devonport formed, 1917. Maximum prices and rationing introduced, Sept. 1917. F. Ministry abolished, 1921. In World War II W. S. Morrison appointed F. Minister, 6 Apr. 1939. Price-fixing orders, 3 and 11 Sept. 1939. F. rationing in Britain began, 1939, and ended, 1954, and in 1955 the Ministry of F. was amalgamated with the Ministry of Agriculture and Fisheries (q.v.).

Fool's Cap Livery, adopted by Count of Egmont, 1563. His servants wore a monk's cowl and F. C. in mockery of Cardinal Granvelle. Many other Dutch nobles followed suit.

Football Association (U.K.). Founded, 1863.

Football League (U.K.). Founded, 1888.

Foraker Act. Passed by U.S. Congress, 1900, establishing self-government in Puerto Rico, and providing for a tariff. Tariff repealed, 1901.

Force Act. Passed by U.S. Congress, 1870, authorizing Federal agencies to interfere in individual states for the maintenance of order in certain cases.

Foreign Enlistment Act (U.K.). 1. 1819. Forbade British subjects to enlist in a foreign service at war with any state friendly to Great Britain. 2. 1870. Forbade, in addition, the export of arms, equipment, etc., to such service.

Foreign Legions. The term 'legion' as a designation for military unit or formation was reintroduced under Napoleon I (*see* FRANCE), e.g. Dombrowski's Polish Legion, which was destroyed in Italy, 1799. F. L. proper, however, differ from the old mercenary regiments, such as the Irish and Scottish brigades of France and Spain in that their ranks are not made up of men all from one state: in this sense the King's German Legion in British service, 1806–15, may be said to be the first, for though its original cadre was from the Royal Hanoverian Army, it attracted recruits from all the minor German states, and even a few Scandinavians. The French 'Foreign Legion' is, in fact, a group of *Régiments Étrangers*, of which the first was raised by Louis Philippe, 9 Mar. 1831; its nucleus was the recently discharged soldiers of the two Guard and four Line regiments of Swiss, disbanded after the revolution of July 1830: between 1871 and 1914 it consisted largely

G

of Alsatians and Lorrainers. In 1854 Napoleon III raised an *ad hoc* legion, mainly Swiss, for the Crimea, and in 1855 Great Britain raised two, one German-Swiss and one Italian, for the same purpose. F. L., including English, Scots, and Irish in some numbers, fought in Spanish interests in the war of French intervention, 1823; the First, 1834–8, and Second, 1872–6, Carlist Wars; and the Civil War of 1936–9 (International Brigade on Republican side and the professional *Tercio*, together with O'Duffy's volunteers, for Franco); also in the Graeco–Turkish wars of 1821–33 and 1897, on the Greek side. The French *Régiments Étrangers* were disbanded, 1940, but reconstituted, 1945. They fought with distinction in Indo-China, 1946–54, and Algeria, 1954–62. On 28 Apr. 1961, the First Foreign Legion Parachute Regiment was disbanded for its part in the abortive army mutiny in Algeria earlier that month.

Foreign Office. Dates as such from 1872, when the redistribution of functions among Secretaries of State resulted in all foreign affairs being concentrated in the hands of one. The combined Foreign Service resulted from the merger of the F. O. and Diplomatic Service, the Commercial Diplomatic Service, and the Consular Service in 1943.

British Secretaries of State for Foreign Affairs since 1924:

J. R. MacDonald	1924
Sir Austen Chamberlain	1924–1929
A. Henderson	1929–1931
Lord Reading	1931
Sir J. Simon	1931–1935
Sir S. Hoare	1935
A. Eden	1935–1938
Lord Halifax	1938–1940
A. Eden	1940–1945
E. Bevin	1945–1951
H. Morrison	1951
Sir A. Eden	1951–1955
H. Macmillan	1955
Selwyn Lloyd	1955–1960
Lord Home	1960–1963
R. A. Butler	1963–

Forest Laws. Introduced into England by William I, who destroyed several villages to make the New Forest, 1079–1085. Their severity was much mitigated by the F. Charter of Henry III, 1217, and the F. courts fell into disuse by the middle of sixteenth century. In 1631–2 they were revived by Charles I as a means of raising revenue, but the outcry which resulted prevented their penal jurisdiction ever being exercised again.

Commissioners of Woods, Fs., and Land Revenues formed, 9 June 1810.

Formigny, Battle of, 1450. English defeated by French, who for the first time had artillery which could outrange the English long-bow.

Formosa or Taiwan, Island of. Colonized by Dutch, 1624. Spanish landed, 1626, and called the island Formosa, but expelled by Dutch. Dutch expelled by Chinese, 1662. Invaded by Japanese, 1874. Ceded to Japan, 1895. Returned to China, 1945. Riots against Chinese maladministration, Aug. 1947. Since 1949 the seat of Kuomintang Government, and the only territory controlled by it. Mutual security pact between U.S.A. and Nationalist China pledged American protection of F. and the Pescadores and implied, at least temporarily, Nationalist renunciation of the Chinese mainland, 1 Dec. 1954. U-2 from F. shot down by Communists over China, Sept. 1962.

Fort Augustus, built at Kilchumin, Inverness-shire, after the 1715 rebellion (*see* JACOBITES), and taken by the Highland Army, 1745. Reoccupied by Hanoverian troops, 1746, and named after the Duke of Cumberland. Benedictine abbey established here, 1876.

Forth and Clyde Canal (Scotland). Begun, 1768. Opened, 1790.

Forth Bridge (rail). Act passed, 1882. Begun, Jan. 1883. Finished, 1889. Opened, 4 Mar. 1890.

Forth Road Bridge. Begun, 1958. Estimated completion date, 1963.

Fort Sumter (U.S.A.), on an island in Charleston harbour, bombarded by Confederates, 12 Apr. 1861. This action is regarded as the beginning of the American Civil War. Captured by the Federal fleet, 1865. Became a national monument, 1948.

Fortune-telling. First specifically mentioned in English law as a form of witchcraft, and therefore a capital offence, in a statute of 1563. Now punishable under the Vagrancy Act of 1924.

Fotheringhay Castle (Northants, England). Founded, 1066. Richard III *b.*, Oct. 1452. Mary Queen of Scots executed, 8 Feb. 1587. Demolished by James I, 1604.

Foundling Hospitals. 1. London (St. Pancras), projected by Thomas Coram. Royal charter, Oct. 1739. Closed, 1926, and hospital transferred to Berkhamsted, Herts. Site secured as public playground, 1934. 2. Dublin, instituted, 1704. Parliamentary inquiry into abuses, 1835.

Fountains Abbey. Founded, 1132, by a body of Benedictine monks who seceded from the Abbey of St. Mary's, York, on land granted them by Archbishop Thurstan, and joined the Cistercians. Abbey dissolved, 1539, and much of the stone used to build F. Hall. In 1946 it was announced that the empty and partially ruined buildings would be restored to use as a Benedictine house, but this proposal was subsequently abandoned.

Four Cantons (Switzerland). Schwyz, Uri, Unterwalden, original members of the Swiss confederation, 1315, and were joined by Lucerne, 1332. *See* SWITZERLAND.

Four Freedoms, peace aims for the Allies, enunciated while the U.S.A. was still neutral, by Franklin D. Roosevelt, 6 Jan. 1941.

Four Power Pact for peace of Europe between Britain, France, Germany, and Italy initialled at Rome, 1933.

Fourteen Points propounded by President Wilson in an address to U.S. Congress, 8 Jan. 1918, as a basis for a peace settlement with Germany. Considered at Allied Supreme War Council, 3 Nov. 1918, when Britain objected to freedom of the seas, Belgium to removal of economic barriers, and Italy to the readjustment of her frontiers on lines of nationality. Reply sent to Wilson same day.

Fourth Party. Independent group of Conservative politicians formed 1880 and led by Lord Randolph Churchill and A. J. Balfour.

Fourth Republic of France. Existed from 24 Dec. 1946 until 4 Oct. 1958.

France (Lat. **Gallia,** Gaul). Conquered by Romans, 121–51 B.C. Frankish incursions began *c.* A.D. 250. Settlement of Visigoths in F., 415–23. Defence of F. by Aëtius against Salian Franks, 425–430. With Frankish and Gothic help he repulses Attila at battle of Châlons (*q.v.*), 451. Collapse of Roman direct authority, 470–6. Clovis, king of Salian Franks, 481, defeats Syagrius at Soissons, 486; the Alemanni, 496; and embraces Christianity, 496. Defeats Alaric, king of the Visigoths at Vouillé, 507; *d.* 511. Merovingian era, 481–716. Collapse of Merovingian power at death of Dagobert, 638.

Charles Martel, Mayor of the Kingdoms, 716. He defeats the Moors at Tours, 732. Pepin becomes king of the Franks, 751. Charlemagne sole king of the Franks, 771. Count Roland killed at Roncesvalles, 778. Charlemagne crowned Roman Emperor at Rome, 25 Dec. 800; *d.* 814. At Treaty of Verdun Carolingian Empire divided into three, 843. Invasions of Northmen begin *c.* 850. They besiege Paris, 885–6. End of the Carolingian House, 987.

Hugh Capet elected king of France, 987. French defeat by William (Con-

queror) at Varaville, 1058. Norman invasion of England, 1066. First Crusade (*q.v.*), 1095. Statutes of the Templars (*q.v.*) drawn up by St. Bernard, 1128. With accession of Henry II of England Aquitaine and Anjou pass to the English kings, 1154. Conquest of Normandy by Philip Augustus, 1200–4. Philip's great victory over the emperor and the Flemings at Bouvines, 1214. Albigensian Crusades, 1208–29. Death of Philip Augustus, 1223. Under Louis IX (St. Louis) F. reached the height of its medieval greatness, 1226–70. Alliance with Scotland and quarrel between Philip IV and Pope Boniface VIII, 1295. Boniface seized at Anagni, 1302. Clement V crowned pope at Lyons, 1305, and fixed his residence at Avignon, 1309 ('Babylonish captivity'). Templars suppressed, 1312.

Hundred Years War (*q.v.*) begins, 1338; interrupted by Treaty of Brétigny, 1360. Resumed, 1369. Truce of Bruges, 1375. Duke of Orléans murdered in Paris, 1407. English resume the war, 1415. Duke of Burgundy murdered, 1419. Treaty of Troyes, 1420. Joan of Arc drives the English from Orléans, 1429, and crowns Charles VII at Rheims, 1430. Treaty of Arras, 21 Sept. 1435. Paris goes over to the French king, 1436. The *Ordonnance sur la Gendarmerie,* 1439. The *Praguerie,* 1440. Battle of Formigny (*q.v.*), 1450. English driven out of all F. except Calais, 1453.

Charles VIII invades Italy, 1494–6. He marries Anne of Brittany, 1491. Captures Naples, 1504. League of Cambrai, 1508. Holy League (*q.v.*), Oct. 1511. Louis XII assumes title of *Pater Patriae,* 1513. Peace and alliance with England, 1514. Concordat of Bologna, 1516, between Francis I and Leo X. Franco-Hapsburg Wars, 1521–59:

1. 1521–6, ending with Treaty of Madrid (battle of Pavia, 1525).
2. 1527–9 ,, ,, Treaty of Cambrai
3. 1535–8 ,, ,, Treaty of Nice
4. 1542–4 ,, ,, Treaty of Crespy
5. 1552–9 ,, ,, Treaty of Câteau Cambrésis

The Wars of Religion (between Huguenots and Catholics):

The First. 1562–3:
    ending with the Peace of Ambroise
The Second. 1567–8:
    ending with the Peace of Longjumeau
The Third. 1569–70:
    ending with the Peace of Saint-Germain

Massacre of St. Bartholomew, 1572, leading to:

The Fourth. 1572–3:
ending with the Peace of La Rochelle
The Fifth. 1574–6:
ending with the Peace of 'Monsieur'
The Sixth. 1577:
ending with the Peace of Bergerac
The Seventh. 1579–80:
ending with the Peace of Fleix
The Eighth. 1585–98:
ending with the Treaty of Vervins, 1598.

Henry of Guise murdered, 1588. Henry of Navarre acceded as Henry IV, 1589, becoming a Catholic in 1593. Sporadic fighting continued till the Treaty of Vervins, 1598. Edict of Nantes, 15 Apr. 1598. War with Savoy, 1600. Henry IV assassinated by Ravaillac, 1610. Rebellion of Condé, 1614. Richelieu, first minister, 1624. Huguenot power broken by capture of La Rochelle, 1628. Treaty of Bärwald, Jan. 1631. War with Spain, 1635. Death of Richelieu, 1642. Mazarin, first minister, 1643. Treaty of Westphalia (q.v.), 1648, whereby F. obtained Metz, Toul and Verdun, and Lorraine.

The first or Parliamentary Fronde, 1648–9. Second or Aristocratic Fronde, 1650–3. English Alliance (Treaty of Westminster), 1654. Peace with Spain at the Treaty of the Pyrenees, 1659. Death of Mazarin, 1661. Louis XIV takes over the government and appoints Colbert finance minister, 1661. French E. India Co. founded, 1664. War of Devolution against Spanish Netherlands, 1667–8. Dutch War, 1672. Revocation of the Edict of Nantes and the Dragonades, 1685. War of the League of Augsburg, 1688–97. Peace of Ryswick, 1697. War of the Spanish Succession (q.v.), 1701–13, ends by Treaty of Utrecht (q.v.), 1713. Death of Louis XIV, 1 Sept. 1715.

Triple Alliance (England, F., and Holland), Jan. 1717. Quadruple Alliance (England, F., Austria, Holland), 2 Aug. 1718. Voltaire visits England, 1733. F. joins in War of the Austrian Succession (q.v.) against Austria, 1740. Britain joins in an alliance with Austria ('The War of Jenkins's Ear'), 1742. Battle of Fontenoy, 1745. Peace of Aix-la-Chapelle, 1748. The Seven Years War (q.v.), 1756–63. Loss of major part of French colonial possessions in America and India, 1759–60. Intervention in the War of American Independence, 1778. British fleet prevented from relieving Yorktown, 1781. Treaty of Versailles, 1783. Meeting of the States-General, 5 May 1789.

The Great French Revolution (q.v.), 1789–92. Monarchy overthrown, 10 Aug. 1792. The First Republic proclaimed, 22 Sept. 1792. Louis XVI executed, Jan. 1793. The Directory came into force, 1795. Napoleon conquers Italy and makes peace with Austria at Campo-Formio, 17 Oct. 1797. Napoleon in the Middle E., July 1798–Aug. 1799, when he returned to France. He overthrows the Directory (Brumaire, q.v.), 10 Nov. 1799. The Consulate. Napoleon First Consul of F., 15 Dec. 1799. Battle of Marengo, 14 June 1800. Treaty of Lunéville, 9 Feb. 1801. The Concordat, 1802. Treaty of Amiens, 1802. Code Civile published, 1804.

The First Empire: Napoleon crowned himself emperor, 2 Dec. 1804. Battle of Ulm, 20 Oct. 1805. Battle of Trafalgar, 21 Oct. 1805. Battle of Austerlitz, 2 Dec. 1805. Holy Roman Empire abolished and Confederation of the Rhine formed, 1806. Battle of Jena, 1806. Treaty of Tilsit, 1807. Battle of Baylen, 1808. Pope Pius VII deported to F., 1809. Russia deserts the Continental System (q.v.), 1810. Retreat from Moscow, 1812. Battle of Leipzig, Oct. 1813. Napoleon abdicated, 11 Apr. 1814. First Treaty of Paris, 1814. Napoleon returns to Paris, 20 Mar. 1815. Battle of Waterloo, 18 June 1815. Second Treaty of Paris, 15 Nov. 1815.

The Restoration: War with Spain, 1822–1827. Capture of Algiers, 1830. Polignac issues the July Ordinances, 1830. Revolution in Paris. Charles X abdicates, 2 Aug. 1830. The July Monarchy: Louis Philippe of Orleans proclaimed king of the French, 7 Aug. 1830. Conquest of Algeria, 1830–2. Revolution breaks out in Paris, 23 Feb. 1848. Louis Philippe abdicates, 24 Feb. 1848.

The Second Republic: Provisional government formed, 25 Feb. 1848. Republic proclaimed, 26 Feb. National Assembly meets, 4 May 1849. Insurrection (in which Archbishop of Paris is killed) put down, 24–26 June 1849. Louis Napoleon Buonaparte (q.v.) elected president by universal suffrage, 11 Dec. 1848. Republic overthrown by Buonaparte, 2 Dec. 1851.

The Second Empire: Napoleon III proclaimed emperor, 2 Dec. 1852. Joins with Britain against Russia in Crimean War, 1854–6. Treaty of Paris, Mar. 1856. Meeting with Cavour at Plombières, 1858. War with Austria, 1859. Battle of Solferino, July 1859. Truce of Villafranca, 11 July 1859.

Franco-Prussian War, 1870–1. Battle of Sédan, 2 Sept. 1870. Revolution in Paris, 3 Sept. 1870.

The Third Republic proclaimed, 4 Sept. 1870. Paris surrenders, 28 Jan. 1871. Proclamation of the Commune at Paris, Feb. 1871. Peace of Frankfort, 10 May. Commune suppressed, 21–28 May 1871. Republican constitution promulgated, 1875. MacMahon's failure, 1877. The Panama scandal, 1888–92. Franco-Russian alliances, 1891, 1896, 1900. Gen. Boulanger flees the country, 1891. The Dreyfus case, 1894–1906.

Anglo-French Alliance (Entente Cordiale), 8 Apr. 1904; Anglo-French treaty regarding Morocco affairs, 1904. Rupture with Vatican, 1904. Separation Law (Church and State), 1906; Devolution of Church Property Bill passed, 1908; New Tariff came into force, 1910; Electoral Reform Bill introduced, 1911; Franco-Moroccan Treaty, 1912; Three Years' Service Bill introduced, 1913. 1914–18; *see* WORLD WAR I. French troops occupied Ruhr, 1922; treaty with Czechoslovakia, 25 Jan. 1924; war in Morocco, 1924–5; Paris Exhibition of Arts, 1925; Bayonne municipal bank failed, involving Stavisky scandal, 30 Dec. 1933.

1934: Stavisky shot himself, 8 Jan.; fierce rioting in Paris, and Albert Prince, judge of appeal, murdered, 6 Feb.; King of Yugoslavia and French Foreign Minister (Barthou) murdered at Marseilles, 9 Oct.

1935: Laval, Foreign Minister, agreed with Italy as to Africa, and guaranteed Austrian independence, 2 Jan.; mutual assistance pact with Russia signed, 2 May; Laval, Prime Minister, 7 June; rioting at Toulon and Brest, 7–8 Aug.

1936: Laval resigned, 22 Jan.; agreement with Britain for neutrality towards Spanish Civil War, 4 Aug.; Léon Blum, Socialist leader, attacked and wounded by Royalists—Royalist Leagues dissolved by decree, 13 Feb.; Popular Front triumphed at elections, 3 May; Archbishop of Rouen deprived by the Pope, 16 May; stay-in strikes began, 26 May; Blum replaced Sarraut as Premier, 4 June; Chamber passed 40-hour week, 12 June; Fascist organizations dissolved, 18 June; devaluation of franc, 1 Oct.

1937: Compromise with Turkey as to Sanjak of Alexandretta, 24 Jan.; Chautemps succeeded Blum, 21 June; Rheims Cathedral reconsecrated, 18 Oct.

1938: Socialist-Radical Government formed by Blum, 13 Mar.; resigned, 8 Apr.; succeeded by Radicals under Daladier; King and Queen of Britain visited Paris, 19–22 July; French citizens prohibited from visiting Italy, Aug.; Daladier, Premier, announced modification of 40-hour week, 21 Aug.; Daladier and Bonnet visited London to confer about

Czechoslovakia, 17 Sept.; Chamber gave Government plenary powers till 15 Nov., 5 Oct.; thirty-two decree-laws appeared, 13 Nov.; general strike failed, 30 Nov.; Ribbentrop, in Paris, signed declaration that no territorial question existed between Germany and F., 6 Dec.; Franco-Italian agreement of 1935 denounced by Italy, 17 Dec.

1939: National Government of Spain recognized, 27 Feb.; President Lebrun visited George VI in London, 21–4 Mar.; Daladier, in a broadcast, rejected Italy's new claims on F., 29 Mar.; trade agreements with Yugoslavia and Rumania came into force, 1 Apr.; President Lebrun elected for a second term, 5 Apr.; Daladier broadcast declaration of support for Greece and Rumania, 13 Apr.; many new decrees, one extending working week from 40 to 45 hours, 28 Apr.; Daladier announced agreement in principle by F., Britain, and Russia against aggression, 11 May; term of Chamber of Deputies extended by two years to June 1942, and 'family code' for premiums on births issued, 29 July; in view of Russo-German agreement, representatives of Britain, Poland, and Rumania met the French Government, 22 Aug.; Daladier broadcast F.'s determination to stand by Poland, 25 Aug.; censorship of press set up, 28 Aug.; railways under military control, 31 Aug.; general mobilization and state of siege proclaimed, 1 Sept.; war on Germany declared, 3 Sept.; Communist Party suppressed, 26 Sept.; agreement for reconstitution of Czech Army signed in Paris, 3 Oct.; Polish gold reserve reached Paris, 24 Oct.; conference between British and French ministers of finance in London, 14 Nov.; new wage and labour decree, shop stewards abolished, 16 Nov.; Army and Navy chiefs attended Supreme War Council meeting in London, 17 Nov.; Plenary Powers Bill passed by Senate, 1 Dec.; British Chancellor visited Paris to discuss joint economic and financial policy, 4 Dec.; agreement announced, 12 Dec.; creation of Institute of Scientific Research announced, 5 Dec.; George VI met President Lebrun during visit to front, 7 Dec.; Yellow Book on 1938–9 international events published, 21 Dec.

1940: Reynaud became Premier, 21 Mar.; German troops entered Paris, 14 June; F. capitulated and accepted armistice terms of Germany and Italy, 22 June. De Gaulle carried on the fight from London, where he organized a Free French force.

Government set up at Vichy, 1 July; diplomatic relations with Britain broken off, 5 July; authoritarian constitution for F., 9 July; Pétain becomes head of state, with Laval as successor, 12 July; German-occupied zone announced, 28 July; Laval Vice-Premier of Vichy Cabinet, 6 Sept.; Laval becomes Foreign Minister, 28 Oct.; Laval dismissed, Flandin appointed Foreign Minister, 15 Dec.

1941: Flandin resigned, Admiral Darlan appointed Vice-Premier and Foreign Minister, 9 Feb.; Darlan announced successor as head·of state to Pétain, 10 Feb.; Darlan forms new Cabinet, 25 Feb.; Breaks off relations with U.S.S.R., 30 June.

1942: Germans occupy Vichy F., 11–12 Nov. French fleet scuttled at Toulon, 27 Nov. Assassination of Darlan, 24 Dec.

1944: Invasion of France by Allies, 6 June. Most of France liberated by Sept. De Gaulle's Committee recognized as Provisional Government, 23 Oct.

1945: Constituent Assembly to draw up new constitution elected, with women voting in F. for the first time.

1946: De Gaulle resigned, Jan. Fourth Republic came into being, 24 Dec. Beginning of Indo-China war.

1947: P. Ramadier Prime Minister, Jan.–Nov. R. Schuman (M.R.P.), Prime Minister. Several government crises and an inflation problem.

1948: Franc devalued, Jan. Coal strike and further devaluation, Oct. Series of unstable governments. De Gaulle's party gained successes at elections, Nov.

1949: France signed North Atlantic Treaty (q.v.), 4 Apr.

1950: State visit of President to London 7 Mar. Schuman Plan mooted, 9 May. Exile of former reigning families repealed, 16 May.

1951: Agreement ceding Chandernagore to India signed, 2 Feb. General Election, 17 June; R. Pleven formed Radical-M.R.P. Cabinet, 11 Aug.

1952: Rioting in Paris on arrival there of Ridgway, the N.A.T.O. commander, May. Government crisis, Dec.

1953: After prolonged period without a government, Laniel became Premier, June. Strike wave, Oct. Assembly voted to continue Indo-China war.

1954: Fall of Dien Bien Phu (q.v.), May. New government led by Mendès-France, June. Geneva conference of foreign ministers, May–July; as a result an armistice ending the Indo-China war signed there on 21 July. French Assembly rejected E.D.C. in Aug., but the London-Paris agreements of Oct.–Nov. laid the foundation of Western Union and ensured F.'s approval to a German contribution to a European defence force. Civil war broke out in Algiers, Nov.

1955: Mendès-France's N. African policy led to his defeat in Feb. Franco-Tunisian Home Rule agreements signed in June. Moroccan sultan, deposed by the French in 1953, restored to his throne in Oct. Saar referendum in Oct. showed a victory for the pro-German parties. Increasingly grave situation in Algeria.

1956: Moroccan independence announced in Mar. Egypt nationalized the Suez Canal in July, and there were high-level Anglo-French talks on the subject in early Oct. Outbreak of the Israeli-Egyptian war again; an Anglo-French force landed at Port Said, 5 Nov., agreed to withdraw without delay at the U.N.'s request, 3 Dec., and the withdrawal was completed by 22 Dec.

1957: F. a signatory to the Treaty of Rome, establishing the Common Market (q.v.), 25 Mar. State visit to Paris of Queen Elizabeth II in April. Algerian situation becoming critical, and it was largely responsible for the fall of successive governments during the year.

1958: The European Economic Community, as established under the Treaty of Rome, came into being, 1 Jan. Growing impatience in the French Army coupled with serious rioting in Algeria led to the collapse of the Fourth Republic, 13 May. De Gaulle accepted an invitation to form a 'Government of National Safety,' 29 May. National Assembly passed a bill for constitutional reforms, 2 June. Talks in Paris between de Gaulle and the British Premier, Macmillan, 29 June. Referendum showed overwhelming support in F. for de Gaulle, 29 Sept. French Guinea became an independent republic, 2 Oct. New constitution in force, 28 Oct. Final ballot in the elections showed decisive victory for the new party Union pour la Nouvelle République, 30 Nov. De Gaulle elected President of the Fifth Republic, 21 Dec. Devaluation of the franc and series of drastic economic measures, 28 Dec.

1959: Premier Debré announced that F. was establishing an atomic testing ground in the Sahara, 4 May. De Gaulle promised Algeria a referendum on its future, to be held not more than four years after the establishment of peace, 4 Sept., but European distrust of de Gaulle's policy there was growing. 384 people killed when a dam burst at Fréjus, 2 Dec. Debré opened the Sahara oil pipe-line, 5 Dec. Macmillan arrived in Paris for talks with de Gaulle, President Eisenhower, and Dr. Adenauer, 18 Dec.

1960: An abortive anti-de Gaulle rising in Algeria, which was put down by the end of the month, 24 Jan. First French atomic test in the Sahara, 13 Feb. Khruschev began an eleven-day tour of F.,

23 Mar. De Gaulle paid a state visit to England, 5–8 Apr. 'Summit' conference opened in Paris, 16 May; broke down, ostensibly over the ' U-2 ' incident, next day. Fruitless talks with the Algerian nationalists, June–July. First German troops arrived in F. for N.A.T.O. training, 26 Oct. Government bill establishing a nuclear force passed, 6 Dec. Government announced 8 Jan. 1961, as the referendum date on Algeria, 8 Dec.; this was followed by five days' rioting in the Algerian cities.

1961: Referendum in F. and Algeria approved de Gaulle's Algerian policy, 8 Jan. Army revolt in Algeria, 19–26 Apr. This was suppressed, and European resistance there to de Gaulle went underground (see O.A.S.). There were bomb outrages by the O.A.S. in F. proper during the year and in Sept. an unsuccessful attempt to assassinate de Gaulle. President Kennedy had talks in Paris with de Gaulle, June.

1962: Franco-Algerian peace talks held in secret near Franco-Swiss border, 11–18 Feb., ended with agreement made at Evian (q.v.) ending the Algerian war and providing for an independent Algeria. Referendum approved de Gaulle's Algerian policy, 8 Apr. Serious O.A.S. outrages occurred in Algeria subsequently, but by the end of June these had petered out. Thousands of Europeans from Algeria returned to F. during the first half of the year. New French government under Pompidou, Apr. Attempt on de Gaulle's life thwarted, May Ex-General Salan sentenced to life imprisonment, May. In July Adenauer paid an official visit to F. A public show of Franco-German reconciliation reached its climax with a Mass in Rheims Cathedral attended by de Gaulle and Adenauer. Unsuccessful attempt to assassinate de Gaulle, 22 Aug. De Gaulle pays first state visit ever made to Germany by a French President, Sept. 4 Oct.: National Assembly passed vote of censure on de Gaulle for violating the constitution. In a television broadcast de Gaulle threatened to resign if a referendum on the proposed new way of electing a president (cause of the censure vote) went against him, on 28 Oct. 5 Oct.: De Gaulle dissolved National Assembly. In the referendum, 28 Oct., de Gaulle got 61·75 per cent of the votes cast, but there were 23·76 per cent abstentions. However, in the General Election, in Nov. 1962, his supporters won an overall majority over all other parties.

1963: De Gaulle made it clear that he neither expected nor wanted Britain in the Common Market (q.v.), 14 Jan.

Subsequently the negotiations for Britain's entry broke down, due to French intransigence, 29 Jan. On 24 Jan. de Gaulle and Adenauer signed the Franco-German 'reconciliation treaty' in Paris. After the initialling of the nuclear Test Ban Treaty in Moscow, de Gaulle announced (29 July) that France would not be a signatory to it.

France, Heads of State.

1. MONARCHY:

Merovingian Dynasty	481–716
Carolingian Dynasty	771–987

Capetian Kings

Hugh Capet	987–996
Robert	996–1031
Henry I	1031–1060
Philip I	1060–1108
Louis VI	1108–1137
Louis VII	1137–1180
Philip II, Augustus	1180–1223
Louis VIII	1223–1226
Louis IX, the Saint	1226–1270
Philip III	1270–1285
Philip IV	1285–1314
Louis X	1314–1316
John I	1316
Philip V	1316–1322
Charles IV	1322–1328

House of Valois

Philip VI	1328–1350
John	1350–1364
Charles V	1364–1380
Charles VI	1380–1422
Charles VII	1422–1461
Louis XI	1461–1483
Charles VIII	1483–1498
Louis XII	1498–1515
Francis I	1515–1547
Henry II	1547–1559
Francis II	1559–1560
Charles IX	1560–1574
Henry III	1574–1589

House of Bourbon

Henry IV	1589–1610
Louis XIII	1610–1643
Louis XIV	1643–1715
Louis XV	1715–1774
Louis XVI	1774–1793

2. FIRST REPUBLIC

Robespierre	1792–1794

3. THE DIRECTORY

Barras	1795–1799
Rewbell	1795–1799
La Révellière-Lépeaux	1795–1799
Carnot	1795–1797
Letourneur	1795–1797
Barthélemy	1797
Merlin	1797–1799

François	1797
Siéyès	1799
Gohier	1799
Roger Ducos	1799
Moulin	1799

4. THE CONSULATE

First Consul.	Napoleon	1799–1804
Second Consul.	Siéyès	1799–1800
	Cambacérès	1800–1804
Third Consul.	Ducos	1799–1800
	Le Brun	1800–1804

5. EMPIRE
House of Buonaparte

| Napoleon I | (abdicated) 1804–1814 |

6. MONARCHY
House of Bourbon (restored)

| Louis XVIII | 1814–1824 |
| Charles X | (abdicated) 1824–1830 |

House of Bourbon-Orléans

| Louis Philippe | (abdicated) 1830–1848 |

7. SECOND REPUBLIC
President: Louis Napoleon

| Buonaparte | 1848–1852 |

8. EMPIRE
House of Buonaparte (restored)

| Napoleon III | (abdicated) 1852–1870 |

9. PRESIDENTS OF THE THIRD REPUBLIC

Adolphe Thiers	1871
Marshal MacMahon	1873
Jules Grévy	1879
Sadi Carnot	1887 (assassinated, 1894)
Jean Casimir-Périer	1894
François Félix Faure	1895
Émile Loubet	1899
Armand Fallières	1906
Raymond Poincaré	1913
Paul Deschanel	1920
Alexandre Millerand	1920
Gaston Doumergue	1924
Paul Doumer	1931 (assassinated, 1932)
Albert Lebrun	1932
Re-elected, 1939. Deposed, 1940	

10. CHIEF OF THE FRENCH STATE

| Marshal Pétain | 1940–1944 |

11. HEAD OF THE FRENCH RESISTANCE

| Charles de Gaulle | 23 June 1940 |

(Recognized as head of the Provisional Government of France, 23 Oct. 1944)

12. PRESIDENTS OF THE FOURTH REPUBLIC

| Vincent Auriol | 1947 |
| René Coty | 1953 |

13. PRESIDENT OF THE FIFTH REPUBLIC

| Charles de Gaulle | 1958 |

Franche-Comté (the *County* of Burgundy, *q.v.*). Acquired by the *dukes* of Burgundy, 1384. Occupied by French,

1482–3. Seized by Louis XIV, 1678, and ceded to France by Treaty of Nijmegen, 1679.

Franchise, Elective (Britain). 1. *Counties:* Under Edward I county M.P.s were elected by freeholders. Conduct of county elections first regulated by statute, 1406. F. restricted to forty-shilling freeholders, 1430 till 1832. 2. *Boroughs.* There was no general statute on borough F. till 1832, voting qualifications depending exclusively on the terms of the borough charter. 3. *From 1832.* The local government F. in respect of both counties and boroughs was, until the passing of the Representation of the People Act, 1945, based on the occupation of rateable property, but that Act assimilated the local government F. with the parliamentary F. by making the normal basis that of residence. Successive classes of the population admitted to the F. by Acts of 1832, 1867, 1884; all males over 21 and females over 30 admitted, 1918; females between 21 and 30, 1929. Business F. of spouses abolished, 1945. University and business F. abolished, 1948.

Franciscans, Monastic Order of. Called also Minorites. Founded by St. Francis of Assisi (1182–1226) in 1212. First came to England, 1220, where they first founded monasteries at Canterbury (1224) and Northampton.

Franco-Prussian War. Lasted from 15 July 1870 until signing of peace on 10 May 1871, although the Paris Commune continued fighting for a few days longer.

Franconia (Franken), a tribal rather than topographical name meaning 'land of the Franks,' though since the Treaty of Verdun, 843, it has meant a duchy comprising the land of the E. Franks, on both sides of the valley of the Main, from which the Franks first set out to conquer Gaul (*see* FRANCE) and the Low countries in the fourth century. Since *c.* 1500 it has been restricted to three counties (Upper, Middle, and Lower F.) centring round Bamberg, Nürnberg, and Würzburg respectively, in north-western Bavaria. These counties were organized in 1837 by the Bavarian crown, which acquired the whole of F., 1803.

Francs were first struck for John of France, 1360, then again in 1576. In 1793 the franc became the monetary unit of France and maintained the same value (*c.* 10*d.* in gold) until 1914, since when it has been devalued several times. Introduced by the Helvetic Republic, 1799. By the kingdom of the Belgians, 1831. De Gaulle 'New' or 'Heavy' F., 1960.

Frankfurt-am-Main, Hesse, was first mentioned by Einhard, A.D. 793. Diets held at, 822, 823, 951, 1015, 1069, 1109, etc. Became place for election of German emperors, 1152. Placed under an interdict during dispute between Louis the Bavarian and Papacy, 1329–49. By the Golden Bull (*q.v.*) declared the principal seat of imperial elections, 1356. Free city, 1372. Joins League of Schmalkalden, 1536. Garrisoned by Gustavus Adolphus, 1631; bombarded by French, 1796; made capital of Grand Duchy of Frankfort, 1810; entered by Prussians, 16 July 1866. Frankfort Peace signed, 1871. Heavily bombed, 1943–5. *See also* FETTMILCH INSURRECTION.

Frankfurt-an-der-Oder, Brandenburg. Incorporated, 1253. Joined Hanseatic League, 1368; taken by Sweden, 1631; Russians, 1759; French, 1806; Russians, 1945.

Franking of Letters (Great Britain). Members of Parliament had the right from A.D. 1660; abolished on institution of penny postage, 10 Jan. 1840. *See* POST OFFICE.

Fredrickshald (now called Halden), Norway. Charles XII of Sweden killed at siege of, 11 Dec. 1718.

Free Church Federal Council. Formed in 1940 by the union of the Free Church Council (established 1892) and the Federal Council (established 1919).

Free Church of Scotland. Formed by opponents of private patronage, 1843. Amalgamated with the Cameronians, 1876. Amalgamated, 31 Oct. 1900, with the United Presbyterian Church, the union assuming the name United F. C.; but a dissentient fraction, popularly called the Wee Frees, substantiated, before the House of Lords, 1904, a claim to the F. C. property. An Act of 1905 appointed a commission to allocate that property. The United F. C. united with the Church of Scotland on 2 Oct. 1929. The F. C., strongest in the Highlands, and stemming from the Wee Frees, is (1963) a relatively small body.

Freemasonry (Britain and general). The first grand lodge in England was established, 1717; in Ireland, 1725; in Scotland, 1736. Freemasons' Hall, London, built, 1775. Pope Clement XII issued a bull of excommunication against freemasons in 1738. Lodges abolished in Germany, 1934.

Freemasonry (U.S.A.). F. was introduced into America in 1730. In 1733 a lodge was established at Boston by Henry Price. First masonic hall built at Philadelphia, 1754.

Free Soil Party (U.S.A.). Founded on 9 Aug. 1848, against extension of slavery in various territories; disbanded, 1854.

Freiburg (Fr. **Fribourg**). Swiss canton, first belonged to the dukes of Zaehringen, one of whom, Bernard IV, founded the city in 1157. On the extinction of this dynasty, 1218, F. passed to the dukes of Kyburg; to the Hapsburgs, 1277–1452; to Savoy until 1477; joined the Swiss Confederation, 1481.

Freiburg - im - Breisgau. Founded, 1120, by dukes of Zaehringen; became separate county, 1218, until it passed to the Hapsburgs, 1369, who retained it until the dissolution of the empire in 1806; ceded to the Grand Duchy of Baden. In French hands, 1679–97.

French Equatorial Africa. First settled 1839. Its four territories became independent republics in Aug. 1960 under the names of Central African Republic, Congo, Chad, and Gabon.

French Fury, The. Francis, Duke of Anjou, in Jan. 1583, occupied Antwerp. The citizens resisted and massacred 2,000 of his troops, besides many officers and nobles.

French Guiana (Cayenne). F. settlement on this coast, at first mainly of buccaneers, began in 1604, and involved a long struggle with the Dutch, which was only finally decided by the transplantation of dispossessed *habitants* from Acadia (*q.v.*) *c.* 1760. Occupied by the Portuguese during the Napoleonc Wars. Convicts were first sent out in 1854, but the attempt to form regular colonies of convicts, as opposed to mere penal settlements, was abandoned, 1864. Became Overseas Department of France, 1 Jan. 1947. Transportation ceased in Apr. 1946

French Guinea. *See* GUINEA, REPUBLIC OF.

French Literature. The following is a list of authors in the F. language, not now living, whether of F., Belgian, Swiss, Canadian, etc., nationality. Among medieval authors writers in the N. F. dialect, the *langue d'œil*, including Anglo-Normans, are in this list. But writers in the S. F. dialect (*langue d'oc*) of this period will be found in the list of PROVENÇAL AND CATALAN authors.

Abbo of Fleury, 945–1004, theologian.
Abélard, Pierre, 1079–1142, philosopher, famous for letters to Héloïse.
About, Edmond, 1828–85, novelist and journalist.
Adam de la Halle ('the Hunchback of Arras'), ?–1286, dramatist.
Adam, Paul Auguste Marie, 1862–1920, novelist.
Aicard, Jean François Victor, 1848–1921, poet and dramatist.
Amiel, Henri Frederic. 1821–81, Swiss philosopher.
Amyot, Jacques, 1513–93, translator.

G*

Andrieux, François Guillaume Jean Stanislas, 1759–1833, dramatist and poet.

Arnauld, Antoine, 1612–94, Jansenist theologian.

Arnault, Antoine Vincent, 1767–1834, dramatist, etc.

Arouet, François Marie. See VOLTAIRE.

Assoucy, Charles Cuypeau d', 1604–c. 1679, poet.

Aubigné, Jean Henri Merle d', 1794–1872, Swiss historian.

Aubigné, Théodore Agrippa d', 1552–1630 historian, poet, etc.

Augier, Guillaume Victor Émile, 1820–1889, dramatist.

Aymeric of Peyrac, ?–1400, chronicler.

Baif, Jean Antoine de, 1532–82, poet.

Baillon, André, 1875–1932, Belgian novelist.

Balzac, Honoré de, 1799–1850, novelist.

Balzac, Jean Guez, Baron de, 1594–1654, miscellaneous.

Banville, Théodore Faullain de, 1823–91, poet.

Barante, Amable Guillaume Brugière, Baron de, 1782–1866, historian.

Barbey d'Aurevilly, Jules Amédée, 1808–1889, novelist and critic.

Barbusse, Henri, 1873–1935, novelist.

Baron, Michel Boyron, 1653–1729, dramatist.

Barrès, Auguste Maurice, 1862–1923, novelist and political writer.

Bartas, du. See DU BARTAS.

Barthélemy, Abbé Jean Jacques, 1716–95, miscellaneous writer.

Basselin, Olivier, ?–1419, song-writer.

Bataille, Henri, 1872–1922, dramatist.

Baudelaire, Charles Pierre, 1821–67, poet and critic.

Bayle, Pierre, 1647–1706, philosopher, critic, and historian.

Bazin, René François, 1853–1932, novelist.

Beaumarchais, Pierre Augustin Caron de, 1732–99, dramatist.

Bellay, Joachim du. See DU BELLAY.

Belleau, Remi, c. 1528–77, poet.

Belloy, Pierre Laurent Beyrette de, 1727–1775, dramatist.

Benoît de Sainte-Maure, twelfth century, poet.

Benserade, Isaac de, 1613–91, poet.

Béranger, Pierre Jean de, 1780–1857, ballad-writer.

Bergerat, Émile, 1845–1923, poet, dramatist, and publicist.

Bergson, Henri Louis, 1859–1941, philosopher.

Bernanos, Georges, 1888–1948, novelist.

Bernard, Charles de, 1805–50, novelist.

Bernard, Paul (Tristan), 1866–1947, novelist and dramatist.

Bernard, St., of Clairvaux, 1090–1153, theologian.

Bernis, François Joachim de Pierre de (Cardinal), 1715–94, miscellaneous writer.

Bertaut, Jean, 1552–1611, satirical and religious poet.

Bertrand, Louis Marie Émile, 1866–1940, novelist.

Beyle, Marie Henri (Stendhal), 1783–1842, novelist.

Bèze, Théodore de, 1519–1605, historian and theologian.

Bisson, Alexandre Charles August, 1848–1912, dramatist.

Blanc, Louis, 1811–82, historian.

Blondel de Nesle, living in 1193, ballad-writer.

Bloy, Léon, 1846–1917, essayist.

Bodin, Jean, 1530–96, sociologist.

Boétie, Étienne de la 1530–63, poet and political writer.

Boileau-Despréaux, Nicolas, 1636–1711, historian and satirist.

Boissier, Gaston, 1823–1908, classical scholar.

Bonstetten, Charles Victor de, 1745–1832, Swiss publicist.

Bossuet, Jacques Bénigne (Bishop), 1627–1704, historian and theologian.

Bouquet, Dom Martin, 1685–1754, historian.

Bourdaloue, Louis, 1632–1704, preacher.

Bourget, Paul Charles Joseph, 1852–1935, poet, novelist, and essayist.

Boursault, Edmé, 1638–1701, dramatist.

Boutroux, Émile, 1875–1921, philosopher.

Brantôme, Pierre de Bourdeille, Seigneur de, 1540–1614, memoir-writer.

Brébeuf, Guillaume de, 1618–61, poet.

Brémond, Henri, 1865–1939, essayist.

Brieux, Eugène, 1858–1932, dramatist.

Brillat-Savarin, Anthelme, 1755–1826, writer on gastronomy.

Broglie, Achille Victor, Duc de, 1785–1870, political writer.

Broglie, Albert, Duc de, 1821–1901, political and historical writer.

Brosses, Charles de, 1709–77, historian and archaeologist.

Brueys, David Augustin de, 1640–1723, dramatist.

Brunetière, Ferdinand, 1849–1906, critic.

Budé, Guillaume, 1468–1540, Hellenist.

Buffon, George Louis Leclerc, Count, 1708–88, scientific writer.

Calmet, Dom Augustin, 1672–1757, divine.

Calvin (Cauvin), Jean, 1509–64, theologian and philosopher.

Cammaerts, Émile, 1878–1955, Belgian poet, theologian, and essayist.

Camus, Albert, 1913–1961, novelist, essayist, and dramatist.

Caro, Edmé, 1826–87, philosopher.

Carton de Wiart, Henry, 1869–1951, Belgian sociologist and novelist.

Casaubon, Isaac, 1559–1614, theologian.

Chamfort, Nicolas Sébastien Roch, 1741–1794, dramatist and miscellaneous writer.

Chapelain, Jean, 1595–1674, poet.

Charles, Duke of Orléans, 1391 – 1445, poet.

Charron, Pierre, 1541–1603, philosopher.

Chartier, Alain, c. 1385–1433, poet, historian, etc.

Chastellain, Georges, c. 1404–75, poet and chronicler.

Chateaubriand, François René, Vicomte de, 1768–1848, miscellaneous writer.

Chaulieu, Guillaume Amfrye, Abbé de, c. 1639–1720, poet.

Chénier, André Marie de, 1762–94, poet.

Chénier, Marie Joseph de, 1764–1811, poet, critic, and journalist.

Cherbuliez, Charles Victor. 1829–99, novelist.

Choiseul-Gouffier, Marie Gabriel, Comte de, 1752–1817, diplomat and scholar.

Chrétien de Troyes, ?–1195, poet.

Christine de Pisan, 1363–1430, poet, historian, etc.

Colet, Louise, 1810–76, poet.

Colette (Madame Henri de Jouvenel), 1873–1954, novelist.

Collé, Charles, 1709–83, poet and dramatist.

Collin d'Harleville, Jean François, 1755–1806, dramatist.

Commines or Commynes, Philippe de, 1455–1509, diplomatist and historian.

Comte, Auguste, 1798–1857, philosopher.

Condillac, Abbé Étienne Bonnot de, 1714–1780, philosopher.

Condorcet, Jean Antoine Nicolas de Caritât, Marquis de, 1743–94, sociologist.

Constant de Rebecque, Henri Benjamin, 1767–1830, novelist and philosopher.

Coppée, François Édouard Joachim, 1842–1908, poet.

Coquillart, Guillaume, 1450–1510, satirist.

Cormenin, Vicomte de ('Timon'), 1788–1868, jurist and pamphleteer.

Corneille, Pierre, 1606–84, dramatist.

Corneille, Thomas, 1625–1709, dramatist.

Coster, Charles de. 1827–79, Belgian story-writer

Courteline, Georges, 1860–1929, novelist.

Crébillon, Claude-Prosper Jolyot de, 1707–1777, novelist.

Crébillon, Prosper Jolyot de, 1674–1762, dramatist.

Crétin, Guillaume, ?–1525, poet.

Crétineau-Joly, Jacques, 1803–75, historian.

Crousez, Jean Pierre de, 1663–1750, philosopher.

Curel, François, Vicomte de, 1854–1928, dramatist.

Curie, Marie (Sklodowska), 1867–1934), physicist.

Cyrano de Bergerac, Savinien, 1619–55, novelist and dramatist.

Dacier, André, 1651–1722, translator.

Dacier, Mme Anne Lefèvre (wife of the above), 1654–1720, translator.

D'Alembert or Dalembert, Jean le Rond, 1717–83, encyclopedist.

Dancourt, Florent Carton, 1661–1725, dramatist.

Daudet, Alphonse, 1840–97, poet and novelist.

Daudet, Léon, 1867–1942, critic, novelist, and journalist.

Daurat, Jean, 1508–88, classicist.

Deffand, Mme du, 1697 – 1780, letter-writer.

Delavigne, Casimir, 1793–1843, dramatist.

Delille, Abbé Jacques, 1738–1813, poet and translator.

Déroulède, Paul, 1846–1914, poet and dramatist.

Desaugiers, Marc Antoine Madeleine, 1772–1827, poet.

Desbourdes-Valmore, Marceline, 1787–1859, poet.

Descartes, René, 1596–1650, scientific and philosophical writer.

Deschamps, Eustache (called Morel), 1338–1415, poet.

Deschanel, Émile Auguste, 1819–1904, man of letters.

Desfontaines, Pierre François (called Guydot), 1685–1745.

Desmarets de Saint-Sorlin, Jean, 1595–1666, philosopher.

Despériers, Bonaventure, c. 1510–1544, translator, etc.

Desportes, Philippe, 1545–1606, poet and translator.

Destouches, Philippe (Néricault), 1680–1754, dramatist.

Diderot, Denis, 1713–84, miscellaneous writer.

Dierx, Léon, 1838–1912, poet.

Dolet, Étienne, 1509–46, printer and translator.

Du Bartas, Guillaume de Saluste, Baron, 1544–90, poet.

Du Bellay, Joachim, c. 1524–60, poet and antiquarian.

Ducis, Jean François, 1733–1816, dramatist.

Duclos, Charles Pinot, 1704–72, historian.

Dudevant, Amandine Lucile Aurore (Dupin), Baronne ('George Sand'), 1804–76, novelist.

Dufresny, Charles Rivière, 1648–1724, dramatist.

Dumas, Alexandre Davy de la Pelleterie (père), 1803–70, novelist and dramatist.

Dumas, Alexandre (*fils*), 1824–95, novelist and dramatist.

Du Perron, Jacques Davy (Bishop), 1556–1618, essayist and poet.

Duruy, Jean Victor, 1811–94, historian.

Du Ryer, Pierre, 1606–68, dramatic poet and translator.

Eekhoud, Georges, 1854–1927, Belgian novelist and critic.

Elskamp, Max, 1862–1931, Belgian poet.

Eluard, Paul, 1895–1952, poet.

Erckmann Chatrian. The compound name of Émile Erckmann (1822–99) and Alexandre Chatrian (1826–90), who collaborated in fiction and drama.

Estienne. The name of a family of printers and scholars who lived in the sixteenth century.

Fabre, Ferdinand, 1830–98, novelist.

Fabre, Jean Henri, 1823–1915, naturalist.

Faguet, Émile, 1847–1916, critic.

Fénelon, François de Salignac de la Mothe (Archbishop), 1651–1715, miscellaneous writer.

Feuillet, Octave, 1821–90, novelist.

Flaubert, Gustave, 1821–80, novelist.

Fléchier, Esprit, 1632–1710, preacher.

Florian, Jean Pierre Claris de, 1755–94, novelist and poet.

Fontenelle, Bernard le Bovier de, 1657–1757, philosopher, etc.

Fournier, Alain, 1886–1914, novelist.

France, Anatole. *See* THIBAULT.

François de Sales (St.), 1567–1622, theologian.

Froissart, Jean, *c.* 1338–1406, chronicler.

Fromentin, Eugène, 1820–76, critic and novelist.

Furetière, Antoine, 1619–88, novelist.

Fustel de Coulanges, Numa Denis, 1830–1889, historian.

Gaboriau, Émile, 1835–73, novelist.

Gaguin, Robert 1433–1501, poet and historian.

Garnier, Robert, *c.* 1545–90, dramatist.

Gassendi, Pierre, 1592–1655, philosopher.

Gautier, Léon, 1832–97, historian.

Gautier, Théophile, 1811–72, poet, novelist, and dramatist.

Genlis, Stéphanie Félicité Ducrest, Comtesse de, 1746–1830, romantic writer.

Gentil-Bernard, Joseph, 1710–75, dramatist and poet.

Gerlache, Étienne Constantin de, Baron, 1785–1871, Belgian historian.

Gerson, Jean Charlier de, 1363–1428, theologian and philosopher.

Gide, André Paul Guillaume, 1869–1951, novelist and dramatist.

Gilbert, Nicolas Joseph Laurent, 1751–80, poet.

Gilkin, Iwan, 1858–1924, Belgian poet, critic, and historian.

Girardin, Émile de, 1806–81, journalist.

Giraud, Albert (A. Kayenbergh), 1860–1929, Belgian poet.

Giraudoux, Jean, 1882–1944, dramatist and essayist.

Gobineau, Arthur de, 1816–82, novelist, historian, etc.

Godeau, Antoine (Bishop), 1605–72, religious poet.

Godefroy, Frédéric Eugène, 1826–97, literary historian.

Gombauld, Jean Ogier de Lussac, 1570–1666, poet.

Gomberville, Marin Le Roy, 1600–74, romantic writer.

Goncourt, Edmond de, 1822–96 ⎞ joint
Goncourt, Jules de, 1830–70 ⎠ novelists.

Gourmont, Rémy de, 1858–1915, journalist and critic.

Gras, Félix, 1844–1901, Provençal poet and novelist.

Gregory of Tours (St.), A.D. 538 ?–93, historian.

Gresset, Jean Baptiste Louis, 1709–77, poet.

Grévin, Jacques, 1538–70, poet.

Gringore, Pierre, *c.* 1475–*c.* 1545, poet.

Guérin, Charles, 1873–1902, poet.

Guérin, Georges Maurice de, 1810–39, poet.

Guillaume de Nangis, ?–*c.* 1300, historian.

Guimond de la Touche, Claude, 1729–60, dramatist.

Guizot, François Pierre Guillaume, 1787–1874, historian.

Gyp. *See* MARTEL DE JANVILLE.

Halévy, Élie, 1870–1937, historian.

Halévy, Ludovic, 1834–1908, dramatist.

Hamilton, Anthony, 1646–1720, poet and story-writer.

Hardy, Alexandre, 1569–1631, dramatist.

Héloise, 1101–71. *See* ABELARD.

Helvétius, Claude Adrien, 1715–71, philosopher.

Heredia, José Maria de, 1842–1905, poet.

Hervieu, Paul Ernest, 1857–1915, novelist and dramatist.

Holbach, Paul Heinrich Dietrich, Baron d', 1723–89, philosopher.

Huet, Pierre Daniel (Bishop), 1630–1721, scholar.

Hugo, Victor-Marie, Vicomte, 1802–85, novelist and poet.

Hugues de la Bachelerie, twelfth century, poet.

Huysmans, Joris Karl, 1848–1907, novelist.

Jacques de Guise, ?–1399, chronicler.

Jacques de Vitry (Bishop), ?–1240, chronicler.

Jaurès, Jean, 1859–1914, publicist.

Jean de Meung (Jean Clopinel), *c.* 1280–?, translator.

Jean de Troyes, living in 1480, chronicler.

Jean le Bel, ?–1370, chronicler.

Jodelle, Étienne, 1532–73, dramatist.

Joinville, Jean, Sire de, *c.* 1224–1317, historian.

Joubert, Joseph, 1754–1824, philosopher.

Jouffroy, Théodore Simon, 1796–1842, philosopher.

Jouy, Victor Joseph Étienne, c. 1764–1846, novelist and dramatist.

Jusserand, Jean Adrien Antoine Jules, 1855–1932, writer on English literature.

Juvénal des Ursins (Archbishop), 1380–1422, historian.

Kervyn de Lettenhove, Joseph, Baron, 1817–91, Belgian historian.

Labaud, Valéry, 1881–1957, poet and essayist.

Labé, Louise ('La Belle Cordière'), 1526–1566, biographer and poet.

Labiche, Eugène, 1815–88, dramatist.

La Bruyère, Jean de, 1645–96, philosopher and moralist.

La Calprenède, Gautier de Costes de, 1614–63, novelist and dramatist.

La Chaussée, Pierre Claude Nivelle de, 1692–1754, dramatist.

Lacordaire, Jean Baptiste Henri, 1802–61, journalist and preacher.

Lacretelle, Jean Charles, 1766–1855, historian.

Lacroix, Paul, 1806–54, novelist and historian.

La Fayette, Marie Madeleine Pioche de la Vergne, Comtesse de, 1634–93, novelist.

La Fontaine, Jean de, 1621–95, fable-writer and poet.

Laforgue, Jules, 1860–87, poet and story-writer.

La Harpe, Jean François de, 1739–1803, dramatist.

Lamartine, Alphonse Prat de, 1790–1869, historian and poet.

Lamennais, Hugues Félicité Robert de, 1782–1854, theologian and journalist.

La Motte, Antoine Houdart, 1672–1731, dramatist and critic.

Laplace, Pierre Simon, Marquis de, 1749–1827, mathematician and astronomer.

La Popelinière, Henri Lancelot Voisin de, ?–1608, historian.

Laprade, Victor de, 1812–87, poet.

La Rochefoucauld, François, Duc de, 1613–80, writer on morals.

Larousse, Pierre, 1817–75, lexicographer.

La Salle, Antoine de, 1398–1462, romantic writer.

Lavedan, Henri, 1859–1940, novelist and dramatist.

Lavisse, Ernest, 1842–1922, historian.

Le Brun, Ponce Denis Écouchard, 1729–1807, poet, etc.

Leconte de Lisle, Charles Marie René, 1818–94, poet.

Lefreuc, Abel, 1862–1952, critic.

Legouis, Émile, 1861–1937, writer on English literature.

Legouvé, Gabriel Jean Baptiste, 1807–1903, dramatist and miscellaneous writer.

Le Maire de Belges, Jean, 1473–1524 ?, historian and poet, etc.

Lemaître, Jules, 1853–1914, critic and dramatist.

Lemonnier, Antoine Camille, 1845–1913, Belgian novelist and critic.

Lerberghe, Charles van, 1861–1907, Belgian poet and dramatist.

Leroux, Gaston, 1868–1927, novelist.

Leroux, Pierre, 1798–1871, philosopher and economist.

Lesage, Alain René, 1668–1747, novelist, author of Gil Blas.

Lorens or Laurent (Frère), thirteenth century, writer on morals.

Loti, Pierre. See VIAUD.

Maeterlinck, Maurice, Count, 1862–1949, Belgian poet, dramatist, and philosopher.

Maintenon, Françoise d'Aubigné, Marquise de, 1635–1719, letter-writer.

Maistre, Joseph, Comte de, 1754–1821, publicist and philosopher.

Maistre, Xavier de. 1763–1852, novelist.

Malebranche, Nicolas, 1638–1715, philosopher.

Malherbe, François de, 1555–1628, poet and critic.

Mallarmé, Stéphane, 1842–98, poet.

Marchand, Léopold, ?–1952, playwright.

Marguerite de Valois-Angoulême (Queen of Navarre), 1492–1549, poetess and tale-teller.

Margueritte, Paul, 1860–1918, novelist.

Margueritte, Victor, 1866–1942, novelist.

Marie de France, twelfth century, poetess.

Marivaux, Pierre Carlet de Chamblain de, 1688–1763, novelist and dramatist.

Marmontel, Jean François, 1723–99, dramatist, poet, and novelist.

Marot, Clément, 1497–1544, poet.

Martel de Janville, Sibylle Gabrielle Marie Antoinette, Comtesse de ('Gyp'), 1849–1932, novelist.

Mary Stuart, Queen of Scots, 1542–87, poetess.

Maspero, Gaston Camille Charles, 1846–1916, Egyptologist.

Massillon, Jean Baptiste, 1663–1742, orator and professor of rhetoric.

Masson, Pierre Maurice Alexandre, 1879–1916, critic.

Maupassant, Guy de, 1850–93, novelist and short-story writer.

Maurras, Charles Marie, 1868–1952, poet, critic, and miscellaneous writer.

Maynard, François de, 1582–1646, poet, etc.

Ménage, Gilles de, 1613–92, scholar.

Mendès, Catulle, 1841–1909, poet, novelist, and dramatist.

Mérimée, Prosper, 1803–70, novelist.

Merrill, Stuart, 1863–1915, poet of American birth.

Meschinot, Jean, c. 1415–91, poet.

Mézeray, François Eudes de, 1610–83, critic.

Michelet, Jules, 1798–1874, historian.

Mignet, François Auguste Marie, 1796–1884, historian.

Mirabeau, Victor Riqueti, Marquis de, 1715–89, economist.

Mistral, Frédéric Joseph Étienne, 1830–1914, Provençal poet.

Mockel, Albert, 1866–1945, Belgian poet and critic.

Molière, Jean Baptiste Poquelin de, 1622–1673, dramatist.

Montaigne, Michel Eyquem, Seigneur de, 1533–92, essayiist.

Montalembert, Charles Forbes René de, 1810–70, historian and political writer.

Montesquieu, Charles Louis de Secondat, Baron de, 1689–1755, sociologist.

Mounier, Emanuel, 1705–50, philosopher.

Murger, Henri, 1822–61, novelist.

Musset, Alfred de, 1810–57, poet and dramatist.

Necker, Jacques, 1732–1804, statesman and miscellaneous writer.

Nerval, Gérard de, 1805–55, poet and novelist.

Nisard, Désiré, 1806–84, critic.

Noailles, Anna, Comtesse de, 1876–1933, poet.

Nodier, Charles, 1780–1844, miscellaneous writer.

Ohnet, Georges, 1848–1918, novelist.

Paris, Alexis Paulin, 1800–81, scholar.

Paris, Gaston Bruno Paulin, 1839–1903, literary historian.

Parny, Évariste de, 1753–1814, poet.

Pascal, Blaise, 1623–62, philosopher and poet.

Pasquier, Étienne, 1529–1615, historian.

Péguy, Charles, 1873–1914, poet.

Perrault, Charles, 1628–1703, writer of fairy-tales.

Philippe, Charles Louis, 1874–1909, novelist.

Picard, Edmond, 1836–1924, Belgian essayist, dramatist, and poet.

Pigault-Lebrun, Charles Antoine Guillaume Pigault de L'Épinoy, 1753–1835, novelist.

Pirenne, Henri, 1862–1935, Belgiàn historian.

Pirmez, Octave Louis Benjamin, 1832–83, Belgian moralist.

Piron, Alexis, 1689–1773, poet, dramatist, and translator.

Poincaré, Jules Henri, 1854–1912, mathematician and philosopher.

Ponsard, François, 1814–67, dramatist.

Prévost d'Exiles, Antoine François, Abbé, 1697–1763, novelist.

Prévost, Eugène Marcel, 1862–1941, novelist and dramatist.

Prévost, Jean, 1901–44, miscellaneous writer.

Proudhon, Pierre Joseph, 1809–65, socialist writer.

Proust, Marcel, 1871–1922, novelist.

Prudhomme, Sully. See SULLY-PRUD-HOMME.

Quinault, Philippe, 1635–88, dramatist.

Quinet, Edgar, 1803–75, philosophical historian.

Rabelais, François, c. 1490–1553, satirist.

Racan, Honorat de Bueil, Marquis de, 1589–1670, poet, dramatist, and biographer.

Racine, Jean, 1639–99, poet and dramatist.

Regnard, Jean François, 1655–1709, poet and dramatist.

Régnier, Henri François Joseph de, 1864–1936, poet and novelist.

Régnier, Mathurin, 1573–1613, poet.

Renan, Ernest, 1823–92, historian and philosopher, etc.

Restif de la Bretonne, Nicolas Edmé, 1734–1806, novelist.

Retz, Jean François Paul de Gondi, Cardinal de, 1614–78, writer of memoirs and pensées.

Richepin, Jean, 1849–1926, poet and dramatist.

Rimbaud, Jean Nicolas Arthur, 1854–91, poet.

Rivarol, Antoine de, 1753–1801, scholar.

Robert de Sorbon, 1201–74, philosopher, founded the Sorbonne.

Rod, Édouard, 1857–1910, Swiss novelist.

Rodenbach, Georges Raymond, 1855–98, Belgian poet, novelist, and critic.

Roland, Marie Jeanne Phlipon, Mme, 1754–93, writer of memoirs and letters.

Rolland, Romain, 1866–1944, novelist, dramatist, and essayist.

Rollin, Charles, 1661–1741, historian.

Ronsard, Pierre de, 1524–85, poet.

Rostand, Edmond Eugène Alexis, 1868–1918, dramatist and poet.

Rotrou, Jean, 1609–50, dramatist.

Roumanille, Joseph, 1818–91, Provençal poet and story-writer.

Rousseau, Jean Baptiste, 1670–1741, epigrammist.

Rousseau, Jean-Jacques, 1712–78, novelist, philosopher, etc.

Royer-Collard, Pierre Pan, 1763–1845, philosopher and politician.

Rutebeuf, c. 1230–80, poet.

Saint-Amant, Marc Antoine, Seigneur de, 1594–1661, poet.

Sainte-Beuve, Charles Augustin, 1804–69, critic, poet, moralist, historian, etc.

Saint-Évremond, Charles de Marguetel de Saint-Denis, Seigneur de, 1613–1703, miscellaneous writer.

Saint-Exupéry, Antoine de, 1900–44, novelist.

Saint-Gelais, Mellin de, 1491–1558, translator and epigrammist.

Saint-Gelais, Octavien de (Bishop), 1466–1502, poet.

Saint-Pierre, Charles Castel, Abbé de, 1658–1743, sociologist.

Saint-Pierre, Jacques Henri Bernardin de, 1737–1814, novelist and traveller.

Saint-Simon, Claude Henri de Rouvroy, Comte de, 1760–1825, philosopher.

Saint-Simon, Louis de Rouvroy, Duc de, 1675–1755, historian.

Sales. *See* FRANÇOIS DE SALES.

Samain, Albert, 1858–1900, poet.

Sand, George. *See* DUDEVANT.

Sandeau, Jules, 1811–83, novelist.

Sardou, Victorien, 1831–1908, dramatist.

Scaliger, Julius Caesar, 1484–1558, philologist.

Scarron, Paul, 1610–60, novelist and satirist.

Scève, Maurice, *c.* 1510–60, poet.

Scribe, Augustin Eugène, 1791–1861, dramatist.

Scudéry, Georges de, 1601–67, dramatist.

Scudéry, Madeleine de (sister of the above), 1607–81, novelist.

Sedaine, Michel Jean, 1719–97, dramatist.

Segrais, Jean Regnauld de, 1624–1701, poet, memoir, and story-writer.

Séverin, Fernand, 1867–1934, Belgian poet.

Sévigné, Marie de Rabutin-Chantal, Marquise de, 1626–96, letter-writer, etc.

Simon-Suisse, Jules, 1814–96, philosopher and journalist.

Situnondi, Jean Charles Léonard de, 1773–1842, Swiss historian.

Sorel, Albert, 1842–1906, historian.

Sorel, Charles, 1602–74, novelist.

Sorel, Georges, 1847–1922, philosopher.

Staël-Holstein, Anne Louise Germaine (Necker), Baronne de, 1766–1817, novelist.

Stendhal. *See* BEYLE.

Sue, Eugène (Joseph Marie Sue), 1804–57, novelist.

Sully, Maximilien de Béthune, Duc de, 1560–1641, memoir-writer.

Sully-Prudhomme, René François Armand, 1839–1907, poet.

Taine, Hippolyte Adolphe, 1828–93, critic and historian.

Tharaud, Jean, 1877–1952, novelist.

Tharaud, Jerome, 1874–1953, novelist.

Thibault, Jacques Antoine Anatole ('Anatole France'), 1844–1924, novelist and satirist.

Thierry, Amédée S. D., 1787–1873, historian.

Thierry, Jacques Nicolas Augustin, 1795–1856, historian.

Thiers, Louis Adolphe, 1797–1877, historian, critic, and statesman.

Thou, Jacques Auguste de, 1553–1617, historian.

Tocqueville, Alexis Clerel de, 1805–59, historian.

Töppfer, Adolphe, 1799–1846, Swiss novelist.

Tristan L'Hermite, François, 1601–55, poet.

Turgot, Anne Robert Jacques, Baron de l'Aulne, 1727–81, philosopher and political economist.

Tyard, Pontus de (Bishop), 1521–1605, poet.

Urfé, Honoré d', 1568–1625, novelist.

Valéry, Paul, 1871–1945, poet and dramatist.

Vauban, Sébastien Le Prestre, Seigneur de, 1633–1707, political economist.

Vauquelin de la Fresnaye, Jean, 1536–1608, poet.

Vauvenargues, Luc de Clapiers, Marquis de, 1715–47, moralist.

Verhaeren, Émile, 1855–1916, Belgian poet.

Verlaine, Paul, 1844–96, poet.

Verne, Jules, 1828–1905, novelist.

Viau, Théophile de (called Théophile), 1590–1626, poet.

Viaud, Julien ('Pierre Loti'), 1850–1923, novelist.

Viélé-Griffin, Francis, 1863–1937, poet.

Vigny, Alfred, Comte de, 1797–1863, poet and novelist.

Villehardouin, Geoffroi de, 1155?–1213?, historian.

Villemain, Abel François, 1790–1870, critic.

Villiers de l'Isle Adam, Philippe Auguste Mathias, Comte de, 1840–89, poet, story-writer, and dramatist.

Villon, François de Montcorbier (called), 1431–85 ?, poet.

Vinet, Alexandre Rodolphe, 1747–1827, Swiss critic.

Voisenon, Claude Henri de Fuzée, Abbé de, 1708–55, novelist and dramatist.

Voiture, Vincent, 1598–1648, poet and letter-writer.

Volney, Constantin François de Chasseboeuf, Comte de, 1757–1820, philosopher and naturalist.

Voltaire (François Marie Arouet de), 1694–1778, poet, dramatist, philosopher, novelist, etc.

Wace, Robert, of Jersey, *fl.* 1170, chronicler.

Zola, Émile, 1840–1902, novelist.

French Revolution, The Great. Jean-Jacques Rousseau (1712–78) did much to prepare France for the revolution by his *Social Contract*. Meeting of the States-General, 5 May 1789, when the Third Estate demanded that the assembly should be composed of one order instead of three. The Third Estate met and took title of National Assembly, 17 June 1789. Louis XVI ordered Three Estates to separate. Led by Mirabeau, they refused, 23 June 1789. Royal troops sent to Paris, July 1789. Necker dismissed by Louis XVI, 11 July 1789. The Bastille (*q.v.*) captured by the mob, 14 July 1789. Mob marched to Versailles and forced royal family to go to Paris, 5 Oct. 1789. Death of Mirabeau, 2 Apr. 1791. Massacre of the Champ de Mars, 17 July 1791. New constitution formed called the Legislative Assembly, 30 Sept. 1791, and the National Assembly dissolved. Mob invaded the Tuileries, 20 June 1792. The monarchy overthrown, 10 Aug. 1792. Dumouriez defeated the Prussians, who issued a manifesto against the French people, at the battle of Valmy, 20 Sept. 1792. National Convention took place of Legislative Assembly, and declared France a republic, 22 Sept. 1792. Louis XVI executed, 21 Jan. 1793. Committee of Public Safety formed, Jan. 1793. England, Holland, Spain, Portugal, Tuscany, Naples, and the Holy Roman Empire joined against France, 1 Feb. 1793. Girondists overthrown, 2 June 1793. Robespierre triumphant, Mar. 1794, but executed, 28 July 1794. Paris mob demands bread, Apr. 1795. Napoleon fires on mob, 5 Oct. 1795. *See* FRANCE.

French Somaliland. French overseas territory acquired by France, 1856–83.

Friedewald, Treaty of, 1552, between Henry II of France and the German Protestant princes, led by Maurice of Saxony.

Friendly Isles. Explored by Capt. Cook, 1773. *See* TONGA.

Friendly Societies (U.K.). First legalized by Act of Parliament, 1793. Registration made compulsory, 1923. Part of F. S. in National Insurance and social security came to an end under the terms of the National Insurance Act, 1946.

Friends, Society of. *See* QUAKERS.

'Friends of the People.' Society formed 1792, to obtain parliamentary reform by constitutional means.

Friesland. From 1579 to 1795 one of the constituent parts of the republic of the United Provinces. William IV became hereditary stadtholder of F. (and all the other provinces) in 1747. Since 1815 a province of the Kingdom of the Netherlands.

Friesland, East. Region in N.W. Germany. A county in the fifteenth century, and later an independent duchy. Passed to Prussia, 1744, and annexed by Napoleon to Holland, 1806. Passed to Hanover, 1815.

Frigate. 1. Single-decked three-masted warship. First was the *Constant Warwick*, launched, 1646, and purchased for the Navy, 1649. Term abolished in the Royal Navy, 1883.

2. A type of all-purpose small warship introduced by Royal Navy in World War II, 1941.

Friuli, Province of, Italy and Yugoslavia. A county founded by the Carolingian emperors *c.* 780. Divided 1500 between Venice and Austria. Rest of it went to Austria at the fall of the Venetian Republic, 1797, and was ceded to Italy in 1866. Small portion ceded to Yugoslavia, 1947. *See* VENETIA.

Frobisher Bay, Arctic Ocean. Discovered by Sir Martin F., 1576.

Froebel System. Educational system founded by F. W. A. Froebel (1782–1852) as expounded in his book, *Die Menschenerziehung,* 1826. Froebel's first kindergarten opened in Switzerland, 1837.

Fronde, The. The First or Parliamentary F. originated in the Paris Parliament, June 1648, against abuses in the Government. Closed with the Treaty of Rueil, 1 Apr. 1649. The Second or Aristocratic F. led by certain nobles under Condé, principally against Cardinal Mazarin, 1650; suppressed, 1653.

Fucino, Lake (anct. **Lacus Fucinus**). Overflow tunnel from, to Liri River, built at orders of Emperor Claudius, A.D. 37. Attempts to reopen it from 1240 onwards failed. Completely drained, 1876.

Fugitive Offenders Act, 1881. Further strengthened by provisions of Act of 1915.

Fugitive Slave Laws, passed by Congress, 1850; repealed, 1864.

Fulda. Abbey founded, 744, by Winfrith (Boniface) of Crediton, Apostle of Germany (680–755), who is buried there.

Fulham (London). Manor given to bishopric of London *c.* 691. First rector appointed, 1242. Bishops of London have resided at F. Palace since 1141, but present building not started until *c.* 1510–1520.

Fustat, the original name of Cairo (*q.v.*).

Futurism. Movement founded by Marinetti, 1909. First Italian futurist exhibition held in Paris, 1911. Transferred to London, 1912. Movement collapsed *c.* 1915.

Fyrd. Divided into two classes, each liable to six months' service in emergency, 894. Assize of Arms, 1181.

ADDENDA

G

Gabelle. Certain taxes levied in France, especially on salt; first levied, 1286; finally abolished, 1790.

Gabon. Discovered by Portuguese, 1485. First French settlement, 1839. Libreville, founded 1848, made capital, 1849. Territory of French Equatorial Africa, 1946; member of the French Community, 1958; independent republic, 17 Aug. 1960.

Gadsden Purchase. In 1853 the U.S. Government bought certain lands from Mexico. The negotiations were managed by Gen. James G. (1788–1858), hence the name.

Gads Hill, Kent. Dickens bought a house here, 1856, and lived in it from 1860 until his death, 1870.

Gaeta, Italy. Besieged by Alphonso V of Aragon, 1435; by Austrians, 1707 (at this siege Charles Edward Stuart was present as a volunteer); by Charles of Naples, 1734; by French, 1806; by Austrians, 1815; by Italian National Party, 1860–1. Pope Pius IX took refuge here, 1848–9.

Gainsborough, England. Marriage of Alfred the Great at, A.D. 868. Destroyed by the Danes, 1013. Church founded by Templars, 1209. Captured from Parliamentarians, 1643.

Galapagos Islands. Discovered, 1535, by Fra Tomas de Balanga, 3rd Bishop of Panama. Annexed by Ecuador, 1832.

Galatia. Ancient district of Asia Minor. The Gaulish or Galatian immigrants who settled there about the third century B.C. were defeated by Attalos I of Pergamum, 230 B.C. The famous 'dying Gaul' statue is a memento of this battle, and from 183 to 166 G. was a mere province of the Pergamite kingdom. Came under Roman rule, 133 B.C.

Galicia, Spain. Settled at some time B.C. by the Gauls (q.v.), after whom it is named. G. became a Roman province, A.D. 137. The Suevi founded a kingdom of G., 411, which was overthrown by the Visigoths, 528. In the eighth century after a short spell of Saracen rule G. was absorbed into the kingdom of the Asturias, and in 1072 was incorporated with Leon and Castile.

Galicia (former Austrian crown-land), named after the principality of Halicz, was settled towards the E. by Ruthenians (q.v.) and towards the W. by Lechs (Poles) in the sixth century A.D. Western G., after being disputed between Poland and Bohemia, finally passed to the former in the tenth century. Eastern G. was converted to Orthodox Christianity and Russian hegemony in the reign of Vladimir the Great of Kiev (d. 1015). G. formed, together with Volhynia, a short-lived independent principality (1199) which was absorbed by Lithuania, 1321, but fell to Poland under Casimir the Great, 1349. In 1371 a Galician Patriarchate, independent of Kiev, was set up, which at the Union of Brest-Litovsk, 1596, transferred its obedience to Rome (see RUTHENIAN CHURCH). The entire Galician territory passed to Austria in the Partitions of 1772 and 1795, and the Polish (less so the Ukrainian) element managed to retain considerable autonomy down to 1918. Western G. was allotted to Poland by the Supreme Allied War Council in 1919 after fighting between Polish and Ukrainian forces. Eastern G. was at first to have self-determination, but in Dec. 1919 the Council put it under Polish protection, the League of Nations finally to decide its destiny in 1944. But in 1923 the Council of Ambassadors recognized this territory as Polish. All G. was occupied by the Russians from Sept. 1939 to July 1941. By treaty of 17 Aug. 1945 all G. E. of the San River passed to the Soviet Republic of Ukraine.

Galilee became part of the Assyrian Empire, 734 B.C., but was given up to the Israelites after their return from the captivity. Under the rule of the Idumean princes Herod the Great (37–4 B.C.) and his son Herod Antipas (4 B.C.–A.D. 39), the former being also King of Judea, but the latter only Tetrarch of G. Under Roman procurators from A.D. 44, G. became the chief refuge of the Jews after their expulsion from Jerusalem, 135. See SAFAD.

It is first described as G. 'of the Gentiles' by Isaiah (740–690 B.C.?), meaning apparently 'surrounded by foreigners,' but by the time of the tetrarchy Greeks, Syrians, and others had infiltrated the province which now extended from the sea of Tiberias to the coast.

In the war of 1948 the territory was fought over by the armies of the Arab League and the Jews, but in the end remained chiefly in Israelite hands, though a large section of its Arab population fled to Jordan.

Gallia Cisalpina or **G. Citerior**, practically identical with the modern regions of Piedmont, Lombardy, and Venetia, was divided into G. Cispadana on the right bank and G. Transpadana on the left bank of the Po respectively. The Gauls penetrated into the Po valley from the N. perhaps as early as the sixth century B.C. A Roman colony was established at Sena Gallica (Senegaglia), 282 B.C., and the whole country reduced, 203–191, the last Gallic tribe to resist being the Boii.

Gallia Transalpina or **Gallia Ulterior**, consisting of G. Narbonensis (Provence), Aquitania (basin of the Garonne), G. Lugdunensis (central plateau), and G. Belgica, which extended up to the Rhine, is dealt with under *France*. G. is not a topographical term but means 'country of the Gauls' (*q.v.*).

Gallican Church. Owing to its independent attitude towards the Roman See, the Church in France was often called the G. C. The Pragmatic Sanction of 1269 provided that the laws of the Church should conform with the common law. Philip IV in 1302 opposed Pope Boniface VIII and imprisoned him; and again in 1438, the Pragmatic Sanction of Bourges aimed at the encroachments of Rome. This last was superseded by the Concordat of Bologna, between Pope Leo X and Francis I. The declaration of the French clergy in 1682 (the Four Propositions) declared the Pope incompetent to interfere in civil affairs. Condemned by Pope Alexander VIII, 1690; by Clement XI, 1706; and by Pius VI, 1794. After many changes the declaration of 1682 was again put into force by Napoleon, 1810. In 1826 the French bishops confirmed this. However, at the Vatican Council, 1869–70, they declared the Pope competent to intervene.

Gallican Confession. Profession of faith of the French Reformed Church adopted at the Synod of La Rochelle, 1571.

Gallipoli, Turkey. Captured by Turks, 1357. British and French armies landed at, Apr. 1854, and proceeded against the Russians. For G. campaign, 1915–16, *see* Dardanelles, *under* WORLD WAR I.

Gallon, standardized for the U.K., 1824, as the volume of 10 lb. of distilled water at 62° F. and 30 in. barometric pressure. The present standard G. in U.S.A. is the archaic wine G. of Queen Anne, standardized in 1707 at 231 c. in.

Gallup Poll invention, of George Horace G. (*b.* 1901), who founded the G. Institute, 1935, which correctly forecast the results of the U.S. presidential elections in 1936,

1940, and 1944, but signally failed to do so in 1948 and 1952.

Galveston, Texas. Settled 1837. Captured by the Federals, 1862, and retaken by the Confederates, 1863. Seriously damaged by fire, 1885, and by the sea, 1900.

Galway, Ireland. Fortified *c.* 1244; surrendered to parliamentary forces, 10 July 1641. Gavazzi riots at, Mar. 1859.

Galway Election. In May 1872 a petition was presented to unseat Capt. Nolan, M.P. for G., owing to alleged intimidation of certain Irish Roman Catholics. The petition was successful, and the Bishop of Clonfert and others were tried but acquitted.

Gambia, W. Africa. Settlement founded by English on initiative of Portuguese in London, 1588. English factory established at, 1620. English right to G. confirmed by Treaty of Paris, 1815; separated from Sierra Leone, 1843; included in W. African Settlements, 1866; again made a separate colony, 1888. Both banks of the G. River came under British control, 1901. Local self-governing bodies set up for Bathurst, 1946, and Kombo district, 1947. Primary education taken over by Government, 1945. New constitutions in 1954 and 1960 increased G.'s self-government. Internal self-government complete since May 1962.

Gaming and Gambling, Laws against (Great Britain). Act of Charles II, 1665, by which persons losing more than £100 at one time were not compelled to pay. An Act of 1710 provided that bonds and other securities won at play were not recoverable, and any person losing more than £10 might sue and recover this amount from the winner. Acts to amend previous laws, 1845 and 1854. The Betting and Gaming Act, 1860, made it clear that no game was unlawful in itself, but only became so if certain rules were broken. *See* BETTING.

Gamma Rays. Discovered by Willard, 1900.

Gandamak, Treaty of, between Britain and Afghanistan, 1879.

Garde Nationale. Troops of indifferent military, but great political, value and chiefly of middle-class origin, first raised, 1789, under La Fayette, in Paris; they helped to crush the Parisian mob in 1795 (13th Vendémiaire), but in 1830 and 1848 declared for the revolutionaries. Disbanded after the suppression of the Commune at Paris, May 1871. *See* FRANCE.

Garden City idea first mooted by Ebenezer Howard (1850–1928) in his book *To-morrow* (1898). First (Letchworth)

G. C. founded, 1903, and second (Welwyn), 1920. *See* SATELLITE TOWNS.

Garhwal, ravaged by Gurkhas, 1803 (*see* NEPAL, *also* SIKKIM), came under British protection, 1814, and was included in United Provinces. Now part of Uttar Pradesh.

Gas (Coal). Illuminating power demonstrated experimentally by Dr. John Clayton, Dean of Kildare, *c.* 1691. Illumination by, first attempted in Cornwall to replace candles and lamps at a factory, 1792. In London it was introduced, 1807, and generally used, 1816. G. flame used for cooking in J. Sharp's ovens, 1835. First practical internal combustion G. engine made by Lenoir, 1860. Used in conjunction with refrigerating plants, 1908. First used for illumination in U.S.A. at Boston, 1823.

Gas Authority, British. Under the G. Act of 1948 took over all G. installations from private or municipal ownership, 1 May 1949, and reorganized them under twelve Area G. Boards. G. Compensation Stock is redeemable, 1990–5.

Gascony, France. *See* AQUITAINE.

Gastein, Convention of, between Austria and Prussia at close of the Schleswig-Holstein War, 14 Aug. 1865.

G.A.T.T. (General Agreement on Tariffs and Trade), signed at Geneva, 1947. Came into force, 1 Jan. 1948.

Gaul. *See* FRANCE.

Gauls. A branch of the Celts, whose language does not survive in a modern or even medieval form. Their main body spread outwards from the Alps and settled widely in Gallia (*q.v.*), Cisalpina, and Transalpina in the fifth century B.C. The La Tène culture of the early Iron Age (500–1 B.C.) represents the peak of Gallic art. In the fourth century they invaded central Italy, taking Rome, 390, unopposed. At the same time elements migrating south-westwards from France reached Galicia (*q.v.*); another section, called Galatai by the Greeks, pressed eastwards and settled in the interior of Asia Minor, 275 (*see* GALATIA). In the second century German tribes, including the Cimbri and Teutones, drove the Gallic Helvetii and allied tribes out of what is now Baden and Württemberg westwards over the Rhine and S. into the Jura. For the history of the western and southern branches, *see* FRANCE and GALLIA CISALPINA. For that of the eastern, *see* GALATIA.

Gavelkind. An ancient English form of land tenure, under which the inheritance was divided equally among all the sons. It existed only in Kent and was abolished by the Law of Property Act, 1925.

Gaza, Palestine. An ancient town mentioned in Genesis (x. 19) and other biblical books. Captured by Alexander the Great, 332 B.C.; ravaged by Saladin, 1170; citadel captured by him, 1187. Captured by Khwarizmians, 1244, and held by Moslems until taken by the French under Kléber, 1799. Taken by the Egyptians under Ibrahim Pasha, 1831; by the British under Allenby, Nov. 1917.

Gaza Strip came into existence as result of the armistice agreement between Israel and Egypt, 1949. The G. S. represents the area of Palestine left in Egyptian hands after the 1948 fighting. Numerous Israeli-Egyptian incidents in G. S., 1949–1956. Israel expelled Egyptian forces from the G. S., Nov. 1956, but in Mar. 1957 Israeli troops withdrew and a U.N. force took their place. Egypt resumed the civil administration of the G. S.

Gdansk. *See* DANZIG.

Gdynia (Pol.), Gdingen or **Gotenhafen** (Ger.). Built by Poles as a Baltic port, 1921–30. Occupied by Germans, 14 Sept. 1939, who then invented the name Gotenhafen. Returned to Poland, 1945.

Geiger Counter. Invented by Rutherford and Geiger, 1908, and developed by Geiger and Müller, 1928.

Gelderland, Holland. Formed part of the Burgundian possessions, 1472–92. Formed part of the Burgundian Circle of the Holy Roman Empire, 1512. Passed to the Emperor Charles V, 1543. Became one of the provinces of the United Netherlands, 1578. Part of the kingdom of the Netherlands, 1815.

Gelnhausen, Compact or **Agreement of,** by the Electors of the Empire to resist the reforms of the Emperor Maximilian, June 1502.

General Agreement on Tariffs and Trade. *See* G.A.T.T.

General Assembly. *See* CHURCH OF SCOTLAND.

General Strike (Britain), 3–13 May 1926.

Geneva (Ger. **Genf**), Switzerland. Republic founded, 1512; allied with Freiburg, 1519, and Berne, 1526; adopted Protestant doctrines, 1535. Calvin (*see* CALVINISTS) went there, 1536, and exiled from, 1538; recalled, Sept. 1541; *d.* at, 1564. G. annexed to France, 1798. Joined Swiss Confederation, 1815. *See* LEAGUE OF NATIONS.

Geneva Conferences. 1. Held by foreign ministers of nineteen countries at Geneva, Apr.–July 1954, to discuss (*a*) unification of Korea, (*b*) a settlement in Indo-China. No settlement was reached over Korea; but an armistice ending the Indo-China war was signed, 21 July. 2. Heads of governments of Britain,

France, Russia, and the U.S.A. met at Geneva, 18–23 July, 1955, first such meeting since Potsdam (1945). General topics discussed. The four foreign ministers subsequently met at Geneva, 27 Oct.–16 Nov., but reached no agreement on any of the topics discussed.

Geneva Conferences (Disarmament). 1. 1927: Sequel of the Washington Conference of 1922, on naval disarmament. Its sequel was the London Conference of 1930. 2. 1932: Came to an abrupt end in Oct. 1933 when Hitler announced Germany's withdrawal from the conference and from the League of Nations. 3. 1962: Between U.N. members, began 14th Mar.; little progress made subsequently, though these discussions probably indirectly influenced the events leading to the Test Ban Treaty initialled in Moscow between the U.S.S.R., U.S.A. and Britain in July 1963.

Geneva Convention. Signed by the representatives of twelve countries, 22 Aug. 1864, and dealt with the treatment of wounded during war. The U.S.A. did not sign the convention. A second conference was held, 1868, but no effect was ever given to the articles signed. On 6 July 1906, a third convention was signed, to which fifty-seven nations became parties in 1929, when paragraphs relating to the civil population were raised. After a preliminary conference, July–Aug. 1946, a new convention was signed in 1949.

Genoa, Italy (Lat. **Genua,** It. **Genova**). Submitted to Romans c. 200 B.C.; a free republic, A.D. 1000. Joins the First Crusade, 1095–9; and Third Crusade, 1191–6. Alliance with Venice, 1238; with the Pope, 1239; with Florence and Lucca, 1251. Quarrel with Venice at Acre, 1256. Defeat at naval battle of Acre, 1258. Assists the Greek Emperor Michael Palaeologus to retake Constantinople from the Latins, 1261. Treaty of Cremona, 1270. Naval battle of Curzola, 1298. War of Chioggia (q.v.), 1350–81. Annexes Corsica from Pisa, 1367. Commercial treaty with the Turks, 1452. Refuses help to the Knights of St. John, 1520. Sacked by Spanish and Italians under Colonna, 1522. Battle of Prevesa, 1540. Sends nominal contingent to fight at battle of Lepanto, 1571. Walls built, 1626–32. Bombarded by French, 1684; by British, 1745. Sells Corsica to France, 1768. Converted into the Ligurian republic under French domination by Napoleon, July 1797. Annexed by France, 1806. Incorporated with Piedmont-Sardinia, 1815. Bombarded by the British fleet, Feb. 1942.

Gentlemen-at-Arms, Honourable Corps of, English royal bodyguard, founded 1509. First went into action as Henry VIII's bodyguard at Guingatte, 1513, then at the siege of Boulogne, 1544. It also took up action stations at St. James's Palace, 1848, in face of an alleged Chartist march on Westminster. Since the nineteenth century a custom has arisen whereby the Government Chief Whip in the House of Lords is also Captain of the Corps. Its present establishment of five officers and thirty-nine other gentlemen dates from 1862.

Geographical Society, American. Established 1852.

Geographical Society, Royal, was founded, 1830. Caused the establishment of a school of geography, the first in an English university, at Oxford, 1899.

Geological Society, Great Britain. Founded, 1807, and incorporated, 1826.

Geophysical Year, International. July 1957–Dec. 1958, during which period observations of the action of natural physical forces on the earth were made by scientists from approximately forty countries at many places throughout the world.

George Cross. Honour instituted, 1940, to reward the performance of deeds of valour by civilians, both men and women. It ranks immediately after the Victoria Cross (q.v.). The G. C. was awarded to the island of Malta (q.v.) on 17 Apr. 1942, in recognition of its gallantry under enemy bombardment.

George Washington Bridge over the Hudson River opened, Nov. 1931.

Georgia, Caucasus (Rus. **Gruzia**; Georgian **Karthveli**). The 'Iberia' of the ancients. Converted to Christianity, 318. Invaded by Tatars, 1236; laid waste, 1386 and 1393–4, by Timur, who was driven out in 1403; invaded by Persians, 1618. The last king was George XIII, who resigned the crown in favour of Paul, Emperor of Russia, 1800; formally annexed to Russia, 1801. Independence of Georgian Soviet Democratic Republic, proclaimed, 26 May, recognized by Moscow Soviet, Aug. 1918. Soviet Socialist Republic proclaimed, 25 Feb. 1921. Member of Transcaucasian Federation, 1922. Federal Constitution adopted, 1923. Became constituent Republic of the U.S.S.R., 1936. Anti-Russian riots in, 1956.

Georgia, U.S.A. Founded by royal charter, granted 9 June 1732; named after George II; State constitution adopted, 5 Feb. 1777. State university at Athens chartered, 1785. One of original thirteen states of the Union. Seceded, 1861; re-admitted to union, 1870. New constitution adopted, 1945.

German Baptists. A sect founded,

1708; settled in some numbers in America early in the eighteenth century. The first congregation there was organized at Germantown, Pa., 25 Dec. 1723; their press in 1743 printed the first Bible to appear in a European language in America. Members were forbidden to own slaves as early as 1782. J. C. Beissel (1690–1768) seceded with his followers, who are now known as the Seventh Day Baptists. Another faction, the Old Order Brethren, who abhorred higher education, seceded, 1880–90, and a Radical or progressive group, 1882. Since 1928 the G. B. have been known as the Church of the Brethren.

German Catholics. A sect in Saxony and Silesia, which seceded from the Church of Rome, 1844, and may be regarded as the forerunners of the Old Catholics (*q.v.*).

German Literature. The following is a list of principal authors in the G., not now living, whether German subjects, Austrians, or Swiss:

Abbt, Thomas, 1738–66, historian.
Alexis, Willibald (Wilhelm Heinrich Häring), 1798–1871, novelist.
Anzengruber, Ludwig, 1839–89, dramatist.
Arndt, Ernst Moritz, 1769–1860, poet.
Arnim, Bettina von, 1785–1859, poetess.
Arnim, Ludwig Achim von, 1781–1831, miscellaneous writer.
Auerbach, Berthold, 1812–82, novelist.
Auersperg, Graf Anton Alexander von, 1806–76, poet.
Avenarius, Ferdinand, 1856–1923, poet and miscellaneous writer.
Bauernfeld, Eduard von, 1802–90, dramatist.
Baumbach, Rudolf, 1840–1905, poet and novelist.
Beer, Michael, 1800–33, dramatist.
Bitzius, Alfred ('Jeremis Gotthelf'), 1797–1854, novelist.
Bleibtreu, Karl, 1889–1928, poet, critic, etc.
Bodenstedt, Friedrich Martin von, 1819–1892, poet.
Bodmer, Johann Jakob, 1698–1783, miscellaneous writer.
Böhme, Jakob, 1575–1624, philosopher.
Börne, Ludwig or Löb Baruch, 1786–1837, journalist, etc.
Brant, Sebastian, 1458–1521, satirist.
Brecht, Bertolt, 1898–1956, dramatist.
Breitinger, Johann Jakob, 1701–76, miscellaneous writer.
Brentano, Clemens, 1788–1842, romantic writer.
Brockes, Barthold Heinrich, 1680–1747, poet.
Büchner, Georg, 1813–37, dramatist.
Büchner, Ludwig, 1824–99, philosopher.

Bunsen, Christian Karl Josias, **Baron von**, 1791–1860, antiquarian.
Burckhardt, Jakob, 1818–97, art historian.
Bürger, Gottfried August, 1747–94, poet.
Canitz, Friedrich Rudolf Ludwig, Freiherr von, 1654–99, poet.
Carossa, Hans, 1878–1956, story-writer.
Chamisso, Adalbert von, 1781–1838, poet and naturalist.
Curtius, Ernst, 1814–96, archaeologist.
Dach, Simon, 1605–59, poet.
Dahn, Julius Sophus Felix, 1834–1912, historian and novelist.
Döblin, Alfred, 1878–1957, novelist.
Droste-Hülshoff, Annette von, 1797–1848, poetess.
Ebeling, Christoph Daniel, 1741–1817, historian.
Ebers, Georg, 1837–98, romance writer.
Eck, Johann Maier von, 1486–1543, theologian.
Eckhart, Johannes (Meister), 1260–1327, mystic.
Ebers, Georg, 1837–98, romance writer.
Egestorff, Georg, pseudonym. *See* OMPTEDA.
Eichendorff, Joseph Karl Benedikt, Freiherr von, 1788–1857, novelist, poet, and dramatist.
Eilhart von Oberge, *fl.* 1170, poet.
Ekkehard of St. Gall, *fl. c.* 930, poet.
Eucken, Rudolf Christoph, 1846–1926, philosopher.
Fallada, Hans, 1893–1947, novelist.
Feuchtwanger, Leon, 1884–1958, novelist, dramatist, and critic.
Fichte, Immanuel Hermann von, 1797–1879, philosopher.
Fichte, Johann Gottlieb, 1762–1814, philosopher.
Fischart, Johann, *c.* 1546–90, satirist.
Fischer, Ernst Kuno Berthold, 1824–1907, philosopher.
Fischer, Johann Georg von, 1816–97, poet and dramatist.
Fleming, Paul, 1609–40, poet.
Fontane, Theodor, 1819–98, novelist and poet.
Forster, Johann Georg, 1754–94, writer on travel.
Fouqué, Friedrich Heinrich Karl de la Motte, 1777–1843, novelist.
Freidank or Vridanc, *c.* 1215–30, poet.
Freiligrath, Hermann Ferdinand, 1810–76, poet.
Freud, Sigmund, 1856–1939, psychologist.
Frey, Jakob, 1824–75, novelist.
Freytag, Gustav, 1816–95, novelist.
Gaudy, Franz von, 1800–40. poet.
Geibel, Emanuel von, 1815–84, poet.
Geiler von Kaysersberg, Johannes, 1445–1510, mystic.
Gellert, Christian Fürchtegott, 1715–69. poet.
George, Stefan, 1868–1933, poet.

Gerhardt, Paul, 1607–76, hymn-writer.

Gervinus, Georg Gottfried, 1805–71, historian of literature.

Gessner, Salomon, 1730–88, poet.

Gleim, Johann Wilhelm Ludwig, 1719–1803, poet.

Goethe, Johann Wolfgang von, 1749–1832, poet.

Gotter, Frederick Wilhelm, 1746–97, dramatist.

Gottfried von Strassburg, c. 1210, poet.

Gottschalk, Rudolf von, 1823–1909, dramatist, novelist, poet, and critic.

Gottsched, Johann Christoph, 1700–66, poet and dramatist.

Götz, Johann Nikolas, 1721–81, poet.

Grillparzer, Franz, 1791–1872, poet and dramatist.

Grimm, Jakob, 1785–1863 } Philologists and folk-
Grimm, Wilhelm, 1786–1859 } lorists; brothers who collaborated.

Grimmelshausen, Hans Jakob Christoffel von, c. 1624–76, picaresque novelist.

Gryphius, Andreas, 1616–49, poet and dramatist.

Gunther, Johann Christian, 1695–1723, poet.

Gutzkow, Karl Ferdinand, 1811–78, novelist.

Häckel, Ernst Heinrich, 1834–1919, biologist.

Hagedorn, Friedrich von, 1708–54, poet.

Haller, Albrecht von, 1708–77, poet.

Hardenberg, Friedrich von, 1772–1801, poet.

Häring, W. H. See ALEXIS.

Hartmann, Karl Robert Eduard von, 1842–1906, philosopher.

Hartmann von Aue, c. 1170–c. 1210, poet.

Hauff, Wilhelm, 1802–27, novelist.

Hauptmann, Gerhard, 1862–1946, dramatist.

Hebbel, Christian Friedrich, 1813–63, poet.

Hegel, Georg Friedrich, 1770–1831, philosopher.

Heine, Heinrich, 1797–1856, poet and dramatist.

Heinrich von Meissen ('Frauenlob'), c. 1250–1318.

Heinrich von Morungen, end of twelfth century, poet.

Heinrich von Veldeke, c. 1170, poet.

Herder, Johann Gottfried von, 1744–1803, poet and philosopher.

Herwegh, Georg, 1817–75, poet.

Hesse, Hermann, 1877–1962, Swiss-domiciled novelist and poet.

Heyse, Paul Johann, 1830–1914, poet and story-writer.

Hillebrand, Joseph, 1788–1862, philosopher.

Hoffmann, Ernst Theodor Wilhelm, 1776–1822, romanticist.

Hoffmann von Fallersleben, August, 1798–1874, poet.

Hofmann von Hofmannswaldau, Christian, 1617–79, poet.

Hofmannsthal, Hugo von, 1874–1929, poet and dramatist.

Hölderlin, Johann Christian Friedrich, 1770–1843, poet.

Holl, Karl, 1866–1926, church historian.

Hölty, Ludwig, 1748–76, poet.

Humboldt, Friedrich Heinrich Alexander von, 1769–1859, traveller and scientist.

Humboldt, Karl Wilhelm von, 1767–1835, critic and philologist.

Hutten, Ulrich von, 1488–1523, poet and controversialist.

Iffland, August Wilhelm, 1759–1814, dramatist.

Immermann, Karl Lebrecht, 1796–1840, dramatist.

Kant, Immanuel, 1724–1804, philosopher.

Kästner, Abraham Gotthelf, 1719–1800, poet.

Kautsky, Karl, 1854–1938, historian of Socialism.

Keller, Gottfried, 1819–90, novelist and poet.

Kerner, Justinus Andreas Christian 1786–1862, poet.

Keyserling, Count (Hermann Alexander), 1880–1946, philosopher and essayist.

Kinkel, Gottfried, 1815–82, poet.

Kleist, Ewald Christian von, 1715–59, poet.

Kleist, Heinrich von, 1777–1811, dramatist.

Klinger, Maximilian von, 1752–1831, novelist.

Klopstock, Friedrich Gottlieb, 1724–1803, poet.

Knapp, Georg Friedrich, 1842–1926, economic historian.

Konrad von Würzburg, 1230 ?–87, poet.

Körner, Karl Theodor, 1791–1813, dramatist and poet.

Kotzebue, August Friedrich Ferdinand von, 1761–1819, dramatist.

Kurz, Hermann, 1813–73, poet, translator and novelist.

Laroche, Sophie von, 1730–1807, novelist.

Lassalle, Ferdinand Johann Gottlieb, 1825–64, economic writer.

Laube, Heinrich, 1806–84, dramatist.

Lavater, Johann Kasper, 1741–1801, Swiss poet.

Leibnitz, Gottfried Wilhelm, Freiherr von, 1646–1716, philosopher.

Leisewitz, Johann Anton, 1753–1806, dramatist.

Lenau, Nikolaus (Nikolaus Franz Niemsch von Strehlenau), 1802–50, poet.

Lenz, Jakob Michael Reinhold, 1751–92, dramatist.

Lessing, Gotthold Ephraim, 1729–81, dramatist and critic.

Liliencron, Detlev, Freiherr von, 1844–1909, poet and novelist.

Logau, Friedrich, Freiherr von, 1604–55, epigrammist.

Lohenstein, Daniel Caspar von, 1635–83, dramatist.

Ludwig, Emil, 1881–1948, biographer.

Ludwig, Otto, 1813–65, poet and dramatist.

Luther, Martin, 1483–1546, hymn-writer and translator.

Mann, Heinrich, 1871–1950, novelist.

Mann, Thomas, 1875–1955, novelist and critic.

Manuel, Niklaus, 1484–1530, poet.

Marx, Heinrich Karl, 1818–83, economic writer.

Mayer, Karl F. H., 1786–1870, poet.

Melanchthon, Philipp, 1497–1560, theologian.

Meyer, Konrad Ferdinand, 1825–98, Swiss novelist.

Miller, Johann Martin, 1750–1814, poet and novelist.

Mommsen, Theodor, 1817–1903, historian.

Mörike, Eduard Friedrich, 1804–75, poet.

Moritz, Karl Philipp, 1757–93, novelist.

Moscherosch, Johann Michael, 1601–69, satirist.

Möser, Justus, 1720–94, historian.

Müller, Maler, 1749–1825, poet.

Müller, Wilhelm, 1794–1827, poet.

Müllner, Adolf, 1774–1829, dramatist.

Murner, Thomas, 1475–1536, satirical poet.

Musil, Robert, 1880–1942, novelist and playwright.

Neidhart von Reuenthal, c. 1180–1250, poet.

Nestroy, Johann, 1801–62, dramatist.

Nietzsche, Friedrich Wilhelm, 1844–1900, philosopher.

Ompteda, Baron Georg von, 1863–1931, novelist.

Opitz von Boberfeld, Martin, 1597–1639, poet.

Oswald von Wolkenstein, 1367–1445, poet.

Pestalozzi, Johann Heinrich, 1746–1827, Swiss educationist.

Puffendorf, Samuel, Baron von, 1632–94, historical and legal writer.

Rabener, Gottlieb Wilhelm, 1714–71, satirist.

Raimund, Ferdinand, 1790–1836, dramatist.

Ramler, Karl Wilhelm, 1725–98, poet.

Ranke, Leopold von, 1795–1886, historian.

Rebhun, Paul, 1500–46, poet.

Reuter, Heinrich Ludwig Christian Friedrich ('Fritz'), 1810–74, story-writer.

Richter, Johann Paul Friedrich, 1763–1825, novelist, etc.

Rilke, Rainer Maria, 1875–1926, lyric poet.

Rittershaus, Friedrich Emil, 1834–97, poet.

Rosegger, Petri Kettenfeier, 1843–1918, novelist and poet.

Rückert, Friedrich, 1788–1866, poet and translator.

Rudolf von Erns, d. 1287, poet.

Sachs, Hans, 1494–1576, dramatist.

Scheffel, Joseph Viktor von, 1826–86, poet.

Schelling, Friedrich Wilhelm Joseph von, 1775–1854, philosopher.

Schiller, Johann Christoph Friedrich von, 1759–1805, poet and dramatist.

Schlegel, August Wilhelm von, 1767–1845, poet, essayist, and translator.

Schlegel, Friedrich von, 1772–1829, novelist, dramatist, and critic.

Schleiermacher, Friedrich Ernst Daniel, 1768–1834, theologian and philosopher.

Schlosser, F. C., 1776–1861, historian.

Schnitzler, Arthur, 1862–1931, dramatist and novelist.

Schopenhauer, Arthur, 1788–1860, philosopher.

Schröder, Friedrich Ludwig, 1744–1816, dramatist.

Schröder, Robert Alexander, 1878–1962, poet, critic, and translator.

Schubart, Christian Friedrich Daniel, 1739–91, poet and musician.

Schweinfurth, Georg August, 1836–1925, ethnologist.

Spengler, Oswald, 1880–1936, philosopher.

Spielhagen, Friedrich, 1829–1911, novelist.

Spitteler, Carl Friedrich, 1845–1924, poet.

Spyri, Johanna, 1829–1901, novelist.

Storm, Theodor Woldsen, 1817–88, poet and novelist.

Strauss, David Friedrich, 1808–74, theologian and biographer.

Sudermann, Hermann, 1857–1928, dramatist and novelist.

Sybel, Heinrich von, 1817–95, historian.

Sylva, Carmen (Elisabeth, Queen of Rumania), 1843–1916, miscellaneous writer.

Tauler, Johannes, c. 1300–61, mystic.

Tieck, Johann Ludwig, 1773–1853, dramatist.

Toller, Ernst, 1893–1939, dramatist and poet.

Treitschke, Heinrich von, 1834–96, historian.

Uhland, Johann Ludwig, 1787–1862, poet.

Uz, Johann Peter, 1720–96, poet.

Voss, Johann Heinrich, 1751–1826, poet.

Wackenroder, W. H., 1773–98, novelist.

Wagner, Wilhelm Richard, 1813–83, dramatist and musician.

Walther von der Vogelweide, c. 1168–c. 1228, poet.

Wedekind, Frank, 1864–1918, dramatist.

Weismann, August, 1834–1914, biologist.

Weisse, C. F., 1726–1804, dramatist.

Wellhausen, Julius, 1844–1918, theologian.

Werner, Zacharias, 1768–1823, dramatist.

Wieland, Christoph Martin, 1733–1813, novelist, poet, and translator.

Wieser, Friedrich, c. 1851–1926, economist.

Wildenbruch, Ernst von, 1845–1909, dramatist.

Winckelmann, Johann Joachim, 1717–68, art historian.

Wolfram von Eschenbach, c. 1170–1220, poet.

Wundt, Wilhelm Max, 1832–1920, psychologist.

Wyss, Johann Rudolf, 1781–1830, novelist.

Zedlitz, J. C. von, 1798–1862, poet.

Zweig, Stefan, 1881–1942, novelist and poet.

German Volga Republic. The region on both sides of the Lower Volga was settled by Germans at the invitation of Catherine the Great, 1760. In 1918 they set up an autonomous workers' commune, which in 1924 was transformed into an autonomous republic forming part of the R.S.F.S.R. As a result of events during the advance of the German Army in 1941, the republic forfeited its autonomy, and its German inhabitants were deported to Siberia. It became part of the Saratov region, 1947, and the 1957 decree on rehabilitation of the deported peoples did not include the Volga Germans.

Germanium. Chemical element discovered by Winkler in 1886.

Germany. For history previous to 12 July 1806, see HOLY ROMAN EMPIRE, also PRUSSIA. Confederation of the Rhine formed under Napoleon's mediation, 12 July 1806. German Confederation formed under Austrian presidency, 1815. N. German Zollverein (q.v.) founded, 1819. S. German Zollverein, 1828–31. Central German Zollverein, 1828. Revolutions, 1848–50. Resumption of the German Diet, 1851. German-Danish War, 1864. Austro-Prussian War leads to the exclusion of Austria from Confederation and the formation of the N. German Confederation under Prussia, 1866. Franco-German War, 1870–1.

German Empire proclaimed at Versailles, 1871. Peace of Frankfort-on-Main, 10 May 1871. First German Imperial Parliament, Mar. 1871. Jesuits expelled, 1872. New code of laws, 1877. Triple Alliance constituted between Austria, Italy, and G., 1883. Togo, Cameroons, and S.W. Africa acquired,

1884; E. Africa, 1885; William II came to the throne, 1888. Bismarck resigned, 1890. Commercial treaties with Central European countries, 1892–4; agricultural union ('Bund der Landwirte') formed, 1893. Kiaochow seized, 1897. Steady rise of Socialism, with strong Marxist tendencies, from 1900 onwards. Expansion of navy by Navy Bill, 1900; G. refused at Hague Conference of 1907 to abate naval building. Morocco crisis between G. and France, 1905, and Agadir incident (q.v.), 1911. War declared on Russia, 1 Aug.; on France, 3 Aug.; on Belgium, 4 Aug. 1914.

World War I (q.v.). Revolution breaks out, Nov. 1918. Kaiser William II flees, 9 Nov. Provisional constitution adopted and Ebert elected president of the republic, Jan. 1919.

The Weimar Republic established, 31 July 1919. Kapp putsch, Mar. 1920. Berlin isolated by a general strike and Kapp put to flight, Apr.–June 1920. G. declared herself unable to meet reparations, July 1922, and French troops occupied Ruhr, 10 Jan. 1923. Mark stabilized by Stresemann, 1924. Partial evacuation of Ruhr, Nov. 1924. Death of Ebert, 28 Feb.; election of President Hindenburg, 26 Apr. 1925. British Rhine Army headquarters moved from Cologne to Wiesbaden, 1925. Locarno Treaty signed, Oct. 1925. Treaty with Soviet, Apr. 1926. Admission to League of Nations, 8 Sept. 1926. Hindenburg re-elected, 10 Apr. 1932. Chancellor von Papen dictator in Prussia, 20 July 1932.

1933: Adolf Hitler became Chancellor, 30 Jan.; legal Government of Prussia deposed, 6 Feb.; Reichstag fire, 27 Feb.; freedom of speech and press abolished, 28 Feb.; Hitler triumphant at polls, 5 Mar.; persecution of Jews began, 8 Mar.; Bavarian Government suppressed, 10 Mar.; Social-Democratic Party suppressed, 23 June; Centre Party wound up, 29 June; notice of withdrawal from League of Nations given, 14 Oct.; Hitler's policy approved by plebiscite, 12 Nov.; President sanctioned law identifying Nazi Party with the State, 1 Dec.; one prisoner sentenced to death at Leipzig for Reichstag fire, others kept in custody, though found innocent, 23 Dec.

1934: Peace pact for 10 years with Poland, 26 Jan.; 90 dissentient Nazis shot, including Schleicher, former Chancellor, and Röhm, chief of the S.A., 30 June; Hindenburg d., and office of president was abolished, Hitler becoming supreme as Führer, 2 Aug.

1935: Saar plebiscite, 13 Jan., returned to G., 1 Mar.; Hitler denounced Treaty of

Versailles, 16 Mar.; Hitler announced G.'s air force equal to Britain's, 3 Apr.; Nazi flag made national flag, and further laws made against Jews, 15 Sept.; Hitler dissolved the Stahlhelm, 8 Nov.

1936: Dr. Goebbels, minister of propaganda, began demand for return of colonies, 17 Jan.; denunciation of Locarno Treaty, 7 Mar.; troops reoccupied Rhineland, 8 Mar.; Austrian sovereignty recognized, 11 July; Olympic Games at Berlin, 1–16 Aug.; period of army service increased from 1 year to 2 years, 24 Aug.; four-year plan for self-sufficiency announced, 9 Sept.; Italy's sovereignty in Abyssinia recognized, 25 Oct.; Edgar André, Communist leader, beheaded at Hamburg, 5 Nov.; Anti-Comintern Pact with Japan, 25 Nov.

1937: Pastor Niemöller arrested, 1 July; Hitler met Mussolini at Munich, 25 Sept.; Duke of Windsor received by Hitler, 22 Oct.

1938: Niemöller sentenced, 2 Mar.; German troops entered Austria, 11 Mar.; union of Austria with the Reich ('Anschluss') proclaimed, 13 Mar.; and ratified by plebiscite, 10 Apr.; Hitler visited Rome, 3 May; labour conscription came into force, 1 July; British Prime Minister visited Hitler at Berchtesgaden for one day's consultation about Czechoslovakia, 15 Sept.; he again visited Hitler at Godesberg, 22 Sept.; Chamberlain flew, 29 Sept., to Munich, where four-power agreement (Britain, France, Italy, and G.) signed, 30 Sept.; in Austria, Nazis stormed Cardinal Innitzer's palace, 8 Oct.; German occupation of the claimed portions of Czechoslovakia completed, 10 Oct.; mass expulsion of Polish Jews begun, 28 Oct.; in revenge for murder in Paris, 7 Nov., of a German diplomat (vom Lat) by a young Jew (Grynzspan), a pogrom was carried on in G., 10 Nov.; Jewish property confiscated, 13 Nov. American ambassador recalled, 4 Nov.; Franco-German agreement, similar to Munich agreement, 6 Dec.

1939: New labour law in force, allowing compulsion to work 10 hours a day, 1 Jan.; decree for semi-military training of all men between 17 and 45, 21 Jan.; Hitler, addressing Reichstag, claimed return of colonies, 20 Jan.; publication of intention to increase submarine fleet to equal fleets of British Empire, 2 Feb.; Air Force reorganized, 3 Feb.; further steps in conscription of labour, 14 Feb.; Roman Catholic faculty at University of Munich closed, 17 Feb.; Czechoslovak (*q.v.*) republic destroyed by G., 15 Mar.; Slovakia a German protectorate after one day's independence, 16 Mar.; far-reaching demands made on Rumania, 18–19 Mar.;

von Neurath appointed 'protector' of Bohemia and Moravia, 18 Mar.; Memel transferred from Lithuania to the Reich by forced agreement, 22 Mar.; Raeder made grand admiral, 3 Apr.; decree making membership of Hitler Youth compulsory for all boys and girls between 10 and 18 where physically fit, 5 Apr.; von Papen appointed minister to Turkey, 18 Apr.; decree for National-Socialist leadership of church administration and for disestablishment in Austria of the Roman Catholic Church, 26 Apr.; Hitler announced annulment of naval treaty with Britain, and of treaty of non-aggression with Poland, 28 Apr.; Poland rejected G.'s demands as to Danzig, etc., 5 May; 'Axis' announced to have become a military pact, 6–7 May; trade agreement with Lithuania, 20 May; military alliance with Italy embodied in treaty, 22 May; non-aggression pact with Denmark, 31 May; non-aggression pacts with Estonia and Latvia, 7 June; German and Italian foreign ministers in consultation at Salzburg, Hitler consulted by them at Berchtesgaden, 11–13 Aug.; Russo-German non-aggression pact signed at Moscow, 23 Aug.; listening to foreign broadcasts made a criminal offence, Poland invaded at 5.30 a.m. and many of its towns bombed, Danzig's return to Reich proclaimed, 1 Sept. (*See* WORLD WAR II.) Hitler replied to Mussolini's suggestion of a conference, that if Britain's proposal was an ultimatum, conference would be useless, 2 Sept.; refusal of Britain's demand for withdrawal from Poland, Britain and France declared war on G., 3 Sept.; G. announced mine-belt S. of the Sound, 13 Sept.; Czech uprising announced, Gdynia surrendered to G., 14 Sept. Warsaw surrendered to G., 28 Sept.; Western Poland annexed, Germans in Latvia invited to return to Reich, 8 Oct.; first shipload of Baltic Germans left Riga for Gdynia, 14 Oct.; repatriation of Germans from Estonia announced, 16 Oct.; Hitler held conference with gauleiters and with ambassadors recalled from Moscow, Rome, and Ankara, 21–22 Oct.; government of occupied Polish territories established at Cracow, Hitler nearly killed in Bürgerbräukeller at Munich by a time-bomb, 8 Nov.; *Bremen* reached Bremerhaven, 12 Dec.; Hitler visited western front, 25 Dec. (for details of the war, *see* WORLD WAR II.)

1940: Invasion of Denmark and Norway, 9 Apr.; and of Belgium and Holland, 10 May; France accepted armistice terms of G. and Italy, 22 June; Tripartite Pact (*q.v.*) with Italy and Japan signed in Berlin, 27 Sept.; German troops began occupation of Rumania, 13 Oct.; Hungary signs pact in Vienna, 20 Nov.; Rumania and Slovakia sign pact, 23 Nov.

1941: New frontier and trade pact with U.S.S.R., 10 Jan.; German troops occupy Bulgaria, which joins Axis (Tripartite) Pact, 1 Mar.; invasion of Yugoslavia and Greece, 6 Apr.; both countries occupied by end of Apr.; flight to Britain of Rudolf Hess, Deputy Führer, 10 May; attack on Russia began, 22 June.

Hitler presumed dead in Berlin, 30 Apr. 1945. Final surrender, 8 May 1945. Four allied commanders-in-chief assumed supreme power and established zones of occupation, 5 June 1945. Potsdam Conference, July 1945. Formation of State governments begun in U.S. zone, Jan. 1946. Fusion of British and American zones begun, Dec. 1946. German Economic Council set up at Frankfort, June 1947. Four-power negotiations in the Council of Foreign Ministers in London broke down on the future of a politically and economically united G., Dec. 1947. Britain, France, and the U.S.A. therefore (1948) integrated their zones politically and economically. Russians leave Control Council, 20 Mar. 1948. Currency reform in Western zones, June 1948, followed by Russian blockade of Berlin (q.v.), 28 June 1948–12 May 1949. Parliamentary Council met in Bonn to begin the task of drafting a constitution for W. G., Sept. 1948. For subsequent history of G. see the next two articles.

Germany, Democratic Republic of (Eastern). German Democratic People's Republic set up in Russian zone, 7 Oct. 1949. The republic is not (1963) recognized by any Western government. Government is run on Communist lines. Pieck (1876–1960) became first President, but real power resided in Ulbricht's hands. Five *Länder* replaced by fourteen districts, 1952. After Stalin's death a more 'liberal' policy begun, June 1953, but after rioting in Berlin and several other cities had had to be crushed by Russian tanks, 16–17 June, a harsher policy was readopted. 'National people's army' created, 18 Jan. 1956. Due to defections to the West, the population of the republic fell by nearly 2,000,000 between 1948 and 1959. After Pieck's death (7 Sept. 1960) the presidency was abolished. Instead a council of state was established whose chairman (Ulbricht) had dictatorial powers. Friction between the republic and the West increased during 1960–1, due to steady flow of refugees to the West through Berlin, and on 13 Aug. 1961 the republic closed the Berlin border and subsequently built a wall along it (20 Aug.). *See also* BERLIN.

Germany, Federal Republic of (Western). A constitution for a Federal Republic in W. G. was approved by the Western Occupying Powers, 12 May 1949, and the republic came into being, with its capital at Bonn, 23 May. First elections to Federal Diet (Bundestag), 15 Aug. First president, Theodor Heuss. First chancellor, Konrad Adenauer, elected, 16 Sept. State of war between Western Powers and G. ended, 1951. Member of the Council of Europe, 1951. Adenauer visited England, Nov. 1951. Reparations agreement concluded with Israel, 1952. Member of the European Coal and Steel Community, 1952. Adenauer's party increased its majority, 1953, despite Socialist campaign based on objections to the federal republic's proposed defence liaison with the West. Adenauer visited Moscow, 1955. Diplomatic relations were established between Russia and the federal republic, and several thousand German prisoners repatriated from Russia. The republic joined Western Union and N.A.T.O., May 1955. Saar reunited to Germany at midnight on 31 Dec. 1956. Member of the European Economic Community, and a principal advocate of the Common Market (q.v.), 1958; also a member of Euratom. Saar reintegrated economically with Germany by 5 July 1959. A foreign ministers' conference at Geneva, attended by representatives of both German republics, failed to reach agreement on reunification of Germany, 1959. Lübke succeeded Heuss as President of the republic, Sept. 1959. German troops arrived in Wales for N.A.T.O. training, Aug. 1961. In elections in 1961 Adenauer's party lost its absolute majority and was obliged to govern with support of the Free Democrats, led by Mende. A limit set to Adenauer's tenure of the chancellorship. Franco-German friendship demonstrated by Adenauer's official visit to France, July 1962, when there was a public ceremony of reconciliation between the two countries. Economic symptoms suggested the coming end of the republic's 'boom' period, summer–autumn 1962. De Gaulle paid successful state visit to the republic, Sept. Oct.–Nov.: Prosecution of editor and staff of the news magazine *Der Spiegel* on treason charges led to a government crisis, when the Free Democrat members of the government resigned, owing to Adenauer's refusal to dismiss Strauss, the Defence Minister. Crisis eventually resolved, Dec., when a new administration, without Strauss, was formed. 1963: Franco-German 'reconciliation treaty' signed in Paris, 24 Jan. In Apr. Adenauer announced he would definitely resign the chancellorship in Oct. or Nov., and subsequently declared Erhard as his successor. The federal republic stated its willingness to sign the nuclear Test Ban Treaty (q.v.), subject to certain conditions being observed, Aug.

Huess d. Dec. 1963.

Gertruydenberg. Conference to end War of Spanish Succession (q.v.) frustrated, 1710.

Gestapo (GEheime STAatsPOlizei), based on an existing organization of the Weimar Republic analogous to the Special Branch of the Metropolitan Police; the G. was first set up in Prussia by Goering, 1933. Other federal states of Germany followed and the separate forces amalgamated into one for the whole Reich under Himmler, 1934. Pronounced a criminal organization, membership of which made one automatically liable to imprisonment, at the Nürnberg trials, 1946.

Gettysburg, Pa., U.S.A. The Federal Army of the Potomac defeated the confederates under Lee and thereby saved the union from defeat in the civil war, 1–3 July 1863. Lincoln's celebrated speech was made in Nov. 1863, at dedication of the cemetery.

Ghana. Came into being, 6 Mar. 1957, on attainment of Dominion status by the former colony of the Gold Coast (q.v.) and the trusteeship territory of Togoland (q.v.). Name is that also held by a powerful medieval W. African monarchy. Link with Guinea, Nov. 1958, and Mali, Dec. 1960. Became a republic, 1 July 1960, with Nkrumah as President. Increasingly authoritarian regime led to unrest in G., especially in Accra, 1961, but despite this, Queen Elizabeth II paid a successful state visit there in Nov. Some lessening of tension with release of several hundred political detainees, 5 May 1962. Attempt to assassinate Nkrumah failed, 1 Aug. 1962. Anglican bishop of Accra expelled for criticizing the government, 13 Aug. 1962. Nkrumah dismisses and jails two ministers, 29 Aug. 1962. After further attempts on Nkrumah's life, a state of emergency proclaimed, Sept. 1962. Bishop of Accra allowed to return to G., Nov. 1962. Another attempt on Nkrumah's life, Jan. 1963. *See also* GOLD COAST.

Ghent, Belgium. Said to have been founded in the fifth century. Given to Count Baldwin IV, 1007; capital of Flanders (q.v.), twelfth century; John of Gaunt b. at, 1340. Insurrection of Jakob van Artevelde at, 1379; rebelled against the Emperor Charles V, 1539; surrendered to Spaniards, 1584; taken by Louis XIV of France, 1698; by Duke of Marlborough, 1706; seized by French, 1793; incor-

porated with Netherlands, 1814; became part of Belgium, 1830 (*see* FLANDERS); occupied by Germans, Oct. 1914–Nov. 1918, and May 1940–Sept. 1944.

Ghent, Convention of, granted the Great Privilege (q.v.), 1477.

Ghent, Pacification of, agreed to expulsion of the Spaniards and the establishment of Protestantism, 8 Nov. 1576.

Ghent, Treaty of, between U.S.A. and Great Britain ratified, 17 Feb. 1815.

Ghetto. Jewish quarter of any city, named after the G. of Rome, instituted, 1556, and demolished, 1885, though Gs. had existed at Valencia, 1239; Frankfort-on-Main, 1462; Venice, 1516. Its counterpart in London was the Old Jewry, a Jewish quarter from 1066 to 1291, where pogroms took place in 1261 and 1264. After the conquest of Poland in 1939 a quarter of Warsaw was walled off by the Germans and designated G. (*Judengasse*); its inmates rose against the Germans, 18 Apr. 1943, and for six weeks engaged Axis forces (mostly Ukrainian S.S. units); the quarter was burnt out and razed to the ground, as was the G. of Bialystok after a similar rising in Sept. 1943, which lasted a fortnight, and involved 40,000 Jewish casualties.

Ghibellines. *See* GUELPHS.

Ghurkas. Predominant ethnic group of Nepal (q.v.), from which were recruited ten regiments of Ghurka Rifles for the army of British India. By an agreement of Aug. 1947, eight of the nineteen Ghurka battalions then in being took service under the British crown, the rest entering the Indian service. In 1952 a dispute arose between the British and Indian Governments over the depots maintained by the former in Indian territory for the recruitment of G., which was settled peacefully. Ghurka families joined their husbands training in England, 1962.

Gibraltar, S. Spain. Taken by Moors, 711; captured by Spaniards, 1462; formally annexed to Spain, 1502; surrendered to combined English and Dutch fleet under Sir George Rooke, 1704; finally ceded to Great Britain by Treaty of Utrecht, 1713; frequently besieged by Spaniards, most famous attempt, 1779–83. Local currency (notes) first issued, 1914. State lottery inaugurated at, 1947.

Gilbert and Ellice Islands, Pacific. British protectorates (1892) annexed to the Crown as colonies, Nov. 1915, and by desire of inhabitants. Ocean Island (annexed 28 Nov. 1900), Phoenix Island (since Mar. 1937), and the Line Islands (annexed 1888) are dependencies, the last only since 1919. Christmas Island (q.v.) is one of the group.

Gilbertine Order, founded in England by St. Gilbert of Sempringham, 1135. Suppressed at the Reformation.

Gin Act, 1736. Imposed duty on G. sold by retail. Repealed, 1743.

Gipsies, Acts against (U.K.). Banished from England, 1531. From Scotland, 1541. Act forbidding intercourse with G., 1562. Acts repealed, 1783.

Girl Guides. Movement founded in 1910 by Lord Baden-Powell as a parallel organization to the Boy Scouts (*q.v.*).

Girls' Public Day School Trust. Founded, 1872; one of the pioneers of girls' public day schools in England and Wales.

'Girl Pat.' British trawler stolen by her master and captured, 19 June 1936, off British Guiana.

Girondists or **Girondins.** A party of moderate republicans led by Danton during the French Revolution, 1791. The earliest members of the party were returned by the votes of the Gironde district of France. Louis XVI formed a Girondist ministry, 1792. They attempted to save the king's life, but failed. On 1 Oct. 1793 many of them were tried before the National Convention, and several executed. The party had disappeared by 1794.

Gisors, Treaty of, 1113. Between Henry I of England and Louis VI of France.

Gladiators (Lat. *Swordsmen*) were originally either performers in funeral games or the victims of funeral sacrifices. Professional G. were first said to have been employed by Marcus and Decimus Brutus at their father's obsequies, 264 B.C. The revolt of G. under Spartacus took place 73–71. Gladiatorial displays were unsuccessfully prohibited by Constantine, A.D. 325, and they were finally abolished by Theodoric, 500.

Glamorgan Treaty, The. Negotiated for Charles I by the Earl of G. with the Roman Catholics, 1644.

Glasgow, Scotland. St. Mungo (Kentigern) founded a bishopric here c. 560. See restored by David, prince of Cumbria, 1115. Present cathedral structure begun, 1175. G. made a burgh of barony c. 1176; made a burgh of regality by James II, 1450. University founded by Bishop Turnbull, 1450–1; endowed by James, Lord Hamilton, 1460, and a new deed of erection granted by James VI, 1577; new buildings opened, 1864. An Act of 1889 placed the entire city in the county of Lanark. Municipal buildings in George Square erected, 1889. Broomielaw bridge built, 1899; George V bridge, 1927. Heavily bombed, 1941–3.

Glastonbury (Somerset). Abbey traditionally said to have been founded by Joseph of Arimathea about A.D. 63. It is historically certain that a British monastery was founded here c. 610, and was replaced c. 708 by a Saxon abbey built by Ina. The Chapel of St. Joseph built, 1101–20; destroyed by fire, 1184. The last abbot, Richard Whiting, was hanged on G. Tor for his adherence to the Roman Catholic faith, 15 Nov. 1539. A lake-village was discovered at G. in 1892, pointing to the existence of Celtic tribes there.

Glencoe, The Massacre of. The Government issued a proclamation in Scotland promising pardon to all who before 31 Dec. 1691 would lay down their arms and promise to live peaceably. One of the heads of clans, Alexander MacIan Macdonald of G., was late in doing so, and he and others of his clan were ruthlessly killed by the Campbells on 13 Feb. 1692.

Globe Theatre (London). Erected by Richard and Cuthbert Burbage, 1599; associated with William Shakespeare; burnt, 1621; rebuilt shortly afterwards; destroyed by Puritans, 1649.

Glorious First of June. Usual name of a naval victory over the French, won by Howe in the open sea off Ushant, 1794. Known in France as the battle of Prairial of the year II.

Gloucester, England. The Roman **Glevum** (later **Claudia Castra**). Founded by Nerva, A.D. 96–8; Abbey of St. Peter founded, 681; fabric of present cathedral erected by Abbot Serlo (1072–1104); first charter granted by Henry II, 1155; incorporated by Richard III, 1483; made a bishopric, 1541; restoration of cathedral, 1873–90 and 1897.

Glyndebourne Festival. An operatic season held annually at Glynde, Sussex, in a private opera house erected by John Christie (1882–1962). First year, 1934.

Goa, India. Discovered, 1498, by Vasco da Gama. Seized, 1510, by Portuguese under Alfonso de Albuquerque, and made capital of their Indian Ocean trading Empire, 1511. St. Francis Xavier visited G., 1542–52. By 1570 it had become one of the wealthiest cities in India, but after 1580, when Portugal was annexed by Spain, it began to suffer from the Anglo-Dutch competition directed against Spain. Its decline continued after Portugal regained her independence, 1640, and by 1843 the Old City was in so ruinous a condition that the capital of the colony was moved to Panjim. In 1946 it was given the status of a metropolitan province. Continuous agitation by Indian politicians for evacuation by the Portuguese from Aug. 1947 onwards. On 18 Dec. 1961 Indian troops invaded G., which surrendered the following day, and was subsequently incorporated in India proper.

Gobelin Tapestry. Called after a family of dyers, who set up dye works in Paris in the fifteenth century, and added tapestry-making in the sixteenth. The business was acquired by Colbert in 1662 for Louis XIV as royal upholstery works. Tapestry-making only, since 1697. Closed during revolutionary and Napoleonic periods, then reopened.

Godesberg was the scene of a conference between Hitler and Neville Chamberlain, 22–24 Sept. 1938.

Godiva Legend. See COVENTRY.

Godolphin Administration. After Lord G., First Lord. 1. Formed, 1684; 2. 1690.

God's Truce. An instrument for suspending hostilities on holy days and seasons used during the Middle Ages. Originated in S. France at the synod of Tuluges, in Rousillon, 1027; confirmed by Council of Clermont, 1095, and other councils. Fell into disuse in the thirteenth century.

'Goeben' and 'Breslau.' German warships which in 1914 escaped from Messina, 6 Aug., into Dardanelles, 10 Aug. Nominally sold to Turkey, 13 Aug. Sank monitor *Raglan*, 20 Jan. 1918. *Breslau* sunk, 20 Jan. 1918. *Goeben* surrendered, Oct. 1918.

Gog and Magog, figures in the Guildhall of London, were perhaps first placed there in the reign of Henry V, but were destroyed in the fire of 1666. Replaced by new figures, 1708, which were seriously damaged in the fire of 29 Dec. 1940. New figures were erected in 1951.

Golconda, India. City and kingdom which *fl.* independently from 1512 until conquered by the Mogul emperor Aurungzebe, 1687, and placed under the viceroyalty of Hyderabad (*q.v.*).

Gold Coast, W. Africa. Possessed by Portuguese, 1481–2; by Dutch, 1642; war between English and Dutch over settlements, 1664–5; Dutch forts and territory purchased by Great Britain, 1871; created a separate crown colony, 1874. Northern Territory added, 1897. Political agitation for dominion status, 1947–57. Became the dominion of Ghana, 6 Mar. 1957. For subsequent history *see* GHANA.

Golden Bull, The, of Charles IV. Issued in its first form at the Diet of Nürnberg, 10 Jan. 1356, and in its final form at Diet of Metz, 25 Dec. 1356. It laid down the major principles of the constitution of the Holy Roman Empire (*q.v.*), confirmed the powers of the Diets, and of the Electors (*q.v.*). It remained in force till 1806.

Gold Rushes. California, 1848; Australia, 1851; S. Africa, 1886; Klondike, 1897.

Gold Standard. First introduced into Britain, 1821. Internationally established when adopted by India, 1893. Abandoned during World War I, 1914–19. Slowly re-established, 1919–28. Finally abandoned by Britain, 1931.

Golf. Game of Scottish origin, dating back at least to the middle of the fifteenth century.

Goncourt. Academy and Prize were founded under the will of Edmond de G., who *d.* 1896 (*see* FRENCH LITERATURE). Academy constituted, 1903.

Good Parliament, 1376. The only medieval parliament in which the Commons made sufficient show of independence to secure reforms in their favour.

Gordon Riots. Caused by an Act, passed in 1778, repealing certain harsh laws against Roman Catholics. On 2 June 1780 Lord George G. headed a mob, which almost succeeded in forcing its way into the House of Commons. During the next few days much property was destroyed, and on 6 June Newgate prison was attacked and many prisoners released. The military soon dispersed the mob, and many of the ringleaders were executed. Lord George G. was acquitted of high treason; but was imprisoned, 28 Jan. 1788, on another account, and *d.* insane in Newgate, 1 Nov. 1793.

Gorizia (Slovene **Gorica;** Ger. **Goerz**). Seat of an important county under the Carolingian Empire, which was divided, 1001, between the county of Friuli (*q.v.*) and the bishopric of Aquileia. Inherited by the Hapsburgs, 1500. The city was founded, 1307. Demanded by Italy as part of the price of her defection from the Triple Alliance, 1915, and entered by King Victor Emmanuel at the head of Italian troops, 9 Aug. 1916. Recaptured by Austrians, 28 Oct. 1917, but awarded in 1919 to Italy, which retained it against Yugoslav claims after 1945.

Gorki, *see* NIJNI NOVGOROD.

Goshen, Land of. Boer republic, set up in southern Bechuanaland, 1882, and dissolved, 1884.

Gothenburg or Göteborg, Sweden. Founded, 1609–11, by Charles IX of Sweden, who introduced Dutch settlers to build it as a 'by-pass' to the Danish-held Sound. Destroyed by the Danes, 1611. Under the Treaty of Knäred Danes occupied Alvsborg, 1613, until indemnified. Dutch financiers raised indemnity and after the departure of the Danes G. was refounded, 1615–20. Successful defence against Danes, 1789.

Gothic Architecture. The transition

stages leading from Roman to pure G. are given in the following chronological table. After the middle of the sixteenth century the practice of G. A. died out gradually, but its influence extended to the end of the seventeenth century, and was partially revived in the eighteenth.

Norman, or Romanesque, 1066–1154.

Transitional from Norman to Pointed, 1154–89.

Early English, First Pointed, or Lancet, 1189–1272.

Transitional from Early to Complete Pointed, 1272–1307.

Geometrical Pointed, 1307–27.

Flowing, or Curvilinear, 1327–77.

Transitional from Geometrical and Flowing (sometimes classed together as Decorated, or Middle Pointed) to stiff and hard lines, 1377–99.

Third Pointed, Rectilinear, or Perpendicular, 1399–1546.

Flamboyant, 1450–1600 (mainly on Continent).

The **Gothic language**, said by Procopius (d. c. 560) in his book, *The Vandal War*, dealing with events of 530–40, to be identical with the Vandal and Gepidic languages, is preserved in the Ostrogothic dialect of Moesia, the Arian bishop Ulfilas (d. 383) having translated considerable passages of the scriptures into Moeso-Gothic: he wrote in a self-invented script, compounded of Greek, Latin, and Runic (q.v.) letters. Squinting Wilfred the Swabian, author, in a work written c. 840–2, says that in his time Gothic was still spoken along the Danube, and a few snatches of the language appear in a tenth-century MS. from Salzburg. Ostrogothic survivors, tributary to the Tatars in the Crimea, are mentioned, and recognizable Gothic words cited, by the Imperial ambassador to Constantinople Ghislain de Busbecq, c. 1550.

Goths. First known to history as settlers on the middle Vistula in first century A.D. According to their own tradition they had arrived there from Sweden (probably the Island of Gotland), via Pomerania. About A.D. 150 they migrated again south-eastward to the N. shore of the Black Sea and the Crimea. In the third century they invaded the Roman province of Moesia on the lower Danube; they conquered Dacia and raided Thrace, 321, but were beaten off by the Emperor Constantine. Their king, Hermanaric (the Eormanric of Old English Jörmunrekr of Old Norse, poetry) d. c. 370, after conquering numerous other German tribes as well as Slav and Estonian neighbours. Thereafter, *see* OSTROGOTHS and VISIGOTHS.

Gotland (island in Baltic). Not improbably, as the name implies, the former home of the Goths (q.v.), but they must have left the island about or just before the birth of Christ. St. Olaf introduced Christianity there, 1030. Island acknowledged Swedish suzerainty after battle of Roma, 1288. King Birger Magnusson repulsed, 1313. Island conquered by Danish king Waldemar, 1361. Reconquered by King Karl Knutsson of Sweden, except Visborg, 1449. Ravaged by constant wars between Sweden and Denmark till 1526. Finally passed to Sweden, 1644–5.

Göttingen, Germany. Joined Hanseatic League (q.v.) c. 1360. Captured by Tilly, 1626. By Saxons, 1632. University founded, 1734, by George II of England. Opened, 1737.

Gowrie Conspiracy, 5 Aug. 1600. The Earl of G. and his brother, Alexander Ruthven, attempted to murder James VI of Scotland at G. House. An alarm was raised, however, and the two brothers were killed.

G.P.U., O.G.P.U. (Rus. State Political Department), new designation for the Cheka, adopted 1922–34, after which the name was changed to N.K.V.D. (q.v.).

Graeco-Turkish Wars. 1. 1897, broke out 18 Apr., the result of anti-Christian excesses and anti-Turkish risings in Crete (q.v.), then part of the Ottoman Empire, but claimed by Greece. British Liberals supported Greece, and a small company of British volunteers fought on the Greek side, as did a Garibaldini unit of Italian volunteers; British Conservatives favoured Turks. On 9 Apr. Greek *Andartai* (partisans) raided a Turkish blockhouse on the Pindus frontier and captured its garrison. A similar raid in the same area was repulsed, 12 Apr. Turks entered Larissa, 23 Apr. Greeks defeated in Epirus, but won battle in Thessaly, 29 Apr. Turkish mountain position of Imaret-Grimbovo stormed, 12–15 May. Greek volunteers who had been landed in Crete before the outbreak of war (Feb.) were withdrawn, 9 May, under pressure from the Concert of Europe, and the terms finally settled at Constantinople, 6 Dec., included only slight frontier adjustments and the payment by Greece of £4,000,000 indemnity. Turks evacuated Thessaly, June 1898.

2. 1921–2. Greek offensive in Asia Minor, 23 Mar. 1921. Greeks defeated near Eskishehr, Apr. 1921; resumed offensive from Ushak and Brusa, July 1921; entered Eskishehr, 20 July. Turks fell back on Sakaria River; Greeks heavily defeated, Sept. 1921; retired on Eskishehr and repulsed Turkish attacks at Afion

Karahissar, Oct. 1921. Main Turkish offensive opened, 26 July 1922; Greeks in headlong flight, Aug.–Sept. 1922; Mudania Armistice, Oct. 1922, terminated the war.

'Graf Spee, Admiral.' German 'pocket' battleship engaged and crippled by three British cruisers off River Plate, took refuge in Montevideo, 14 Dec. 1939; scuttled by order of Hitler, 17 Dec.; captain committed suicide, 20 Dec.

Graham Land. Discovered by John Biscoe, 1832. Proved to be an island by Sir H. Wilkins, 1928.

Gramophone (American 'phonograph': its modern successor currently known as a 'record-player'), which was invented by Edison, 1877, was perfected by E. Berliner, 1888. Electrical recording first practised, 1920.

Granada, Spain. Invaded by the Moors, A.D. 745. Wall of the Alhambra built c. 1019. Part of the Arab kingdom of Murcia, 1229–38. Fell into hands of Abu Abdullah Mohammed Ibn al Ahmar, who formed the kingdom of G., 1238. Alhambra Palace begun, 1213. Captured by Christians, 1492.

Grand Alliance. 1. Against France, began with the Treaty of Vienna, May 1689, between the emperor and the Dutch. It came to include Spain, Holland, Sweden, Savoy, and Great Britain. Renewed at The Hague, 1696; ended, 1697.

2. Concluded at The Hague, 7 Sept. 1701, between England, Holland, and the empire; joined by Prussia, 20 Jan. 1702; by Portugal, 16 May 1703; by Savoy, 25 Oct. 1703. It dealt mainly with the conquest of Spain. *See* SPANISH SUCCESSION, WAR OF.

Grand Juries (England). Abolished, except for a few minor exceptions, 1933.

Grand National horse race at Liverpool instituted, 1839.

Grand Remonstrance. *See* REMONSTRANCE, THE GRAND.

Grantham, England. Mentioned as a Royal Demesne in Domesday Book, 1085. Incorporated by Edward IV, 1463. Captured by royalists, 1642–3.

Grattan's Parliament. The Irish parliament, whose legislative independence was granted, May 1782, through the exertions of Henry G. (1746–1820). It came to an end, 2 July 1800.

Gravelines, France. Founded by Henry Count of Flanders, 1160. Defeat of French by Spanish Army, 1558. Defeat of Spanish Armada (*q.v.*) by the English at, 1588. Taken by French, 1658, and ceded to them, 7 Nov. 1659.

Gravesend, England. Mentioned in Domesday Book, 1085. Burned by the French, 1380. Incorporated, 22 July 1562. Princess Pocahontas *d.* at G., 1617.

Great Britain, History of (For previous history *see* ENGLISH HISTORY; SCOTLAND; ENGLISH SOVEREIGNS. G. B. formed by union of the crowns of England and Scotland, 10 Apr. 1603. Toleration for Catholics, July 1603. Hampton Court Conference and peace with Spain, 1604. Gunpowder plot discovered, 5 Nov. 1605. Plantation of Ulster, 1607. Defence treaty with Holland, 1608. Bacon impeached, 1621. War with France, 1624–9. Petition of Right, 1628. Dissolution of Parliament and beginning of the personal rule of Charles I, 1629. Charles attempts to introduce C. of E. Prayer Book into Scotland, 1637. The Ship Money trial (R. *v.* Hampden), 1637. Scots sign the National Covenant, 1638. First Bishops' War begins, May 1639. The Long Parliament meets, 3 Nov. 1640. Root-and-Branch Petition, Dec. 1640. Strafford beheaded, Star Chamber and High Commission abolished, May 1641. Irish Rebellion, Oct. 1641. Grand Remonstrance, Nov. 1641. Charles I attempts to arrest the Five Members, Jan. 1642. Civil war begins, Aug. 1642. Charles I surrenders to Scots, May 1646. Scots begin Second Civil War, Apr. 1648. Pride's purge, Dec. 1648. Charles I beheaded, 30 Jan. 1649. England declared a Commonwealth, 29 May 1649. Scots defeated at Dunbar, Sept. 1650. Charles II defeated at Worcester, Sept. 1651. First Navigation Act, Oct. 1651. War with Holland, 1652–4. Cromwell became Protector, 1653. War with Spain, 1656–9. Oliver Cromwell *d.*, 3 Sept. 1658. Long Parliament restored, 7 May 1659. Richard Cromwell resigns the Protectorship, 25 May 1659. Convention Parliament called by Monck, 15 Apr. 1660. The Restoration, 25 May 1660. Charles II sells Dunkirk to France. Act of Settlement, 1662. Second Naval War with Holland, 1665–7. Great Plague, 1665. Fire of London, 1666. Secret Treaty with Louis XIV, 1667. Secret Treaty of Dover, 1670. The 'Popish Plot,' 1678. Habeas Corpus Act, 1679. Charles II dismisses the Oxford Parliament, 1681. Discovery of the Rye House Plot, 1683. Monmouth's rebellion defeated at Sedgemoor, July 1685. James II's Declaration of Indulgence, 2 Apr. 1687. Reissued, 4 May 1688. Trial of the Seven Bishops, 29–30 June 1688. William III lands at Torbay, 15 Nov. 1688. Bill of Rights, Oct. 1689. James II defeated at battle of the Boyne, July 1690. War with France, 1690–7. Massacre of Glencoe, 1692. French naval defeat at La Hogue, 1692. National Debt established, 1693. Bank of England, 1694. Press censorship ends, 1695.

Treaty of Ryswick, 1697. Partition Treaties (*q.v.*), 1698–1700. War of the Spanish Succession, 1701–13. Parliamentary Union of England and Scotland, 1 May, 1707. Treaty of Utrecht, 1713. Jacobite rising, 1715; Septennial Act, 1716. S. Sea Bubble, 1720. War of Jenkins's Ear, 1739–48. Jacobite Rebellion in Scotland, 1745. Defeated at Culloden, 16 Apr. 1746. Treaty of Aixla-Chapelle, 1748. Seven Years War (*q.v.*), 1756–63. American Stamp Act, 1765. Royal Marriage Act, 1772. Boston Assembly threatens secession, 1772. The Boston Tea-party, 1773. First congress of American colonies, 1774. Quebec Act, 1774. War of American Independence begins with battle of Lexington, 19 Apr. 1775. American Declaration of Independence, 1776. British defeat at battle of Saratoga, Oct. 1777. France declares war on Britain, 1778. Spain, 1779. British capitulation at Yorktown, 1781. Independence of U.S.A. recognized at Peace of Versailles, 1783. War with France (*q.v.*), 1793–1802. Treaty of Amiens, 1802. War with France (*q.v.*), 1803–14, 1815. 'Battle of Peterloo,' 1819. Six Acts, 1819. Castlereagh commits suicide, 1822. First Burma War, 1824. Trade unions legalized, 1825. First steam locomotive railway opened, 1825. Catholic emancipation and Metropolitan police established, 1829. Reform Act passed, 1832. Municipal Corporations Act, 1835. Chartist agitation, 1838–9. Penny postage introduced by Rowland Hill, 1840. Chartist riots, 1842. Factory Act, 1844. Repeal of Corn Laws, 1846. Oregon Treaty with U.S.A., 1846. Great Exhibition, 1851. Crimean War, 1854–6. Peace of Paris, 1856. Divorce legalized, 1857. First Atlantic cable laid, 1857. Ionian Islands ceded to Greece, 1863. Second Reform Act, 1867. Queen Victoria proclaimed Empress of India, 1877. Gladstone defeated on Home Rule Bill, 1886. Local Government Act, 1888. S. African War, 1899–1902. *Entente Cordiale* between Britain and France, 8 Apr. 1904. Anglo-Japanese alliance, 1905. Lords reject Lloyd George's finance bill, Nov. 1909. Parliament Act, 1911. Coal Mines Act, 1912. National Insurance Act, 1912. World War I (*q.v.*), 1914–18. Welsh Church disestablished, 1920. U.S.S.R. recognized, 1 Feb. 1924. Property legislation, 1925. Contributory pensions introduced, 1925. General Strike, 3–13 May 1926. Relations with U.S.S.R. broken off, 27 May 1927. Derating scheme introduced, Mar. 1928. Diplomatic friction with Egypt, Apr. 1928. Illness of George V, 1929. Kellogg Pact, July 1929. Two million unemployed by Dec. 1929. Landslide' election for a 'National' government, Oct. 1931. Anglo-German naval agreement, June 1935. League of Nations Union Peace Ballot, 27 June 1935. Hoare-Laval proposals *re* Abyssinia, 9 Dec. 1935. Hoare succeeded by Eden as Foreign Secretary, 22 Dec. 1935. George V *d.*, 20 Jan. 1936. Edward VIII abdicated, 10 Dec. 1936. Coal royalties expropriated, 1937. Coronation of King George VI, 12 May 1937. Eden resigned Foreign Secretaryship, 20 Feb. 1938. Royal visit to Paris, 19–22 July 1938. Chamberlain sees Hitler at Munich, 17 Sept., Godesberg, 22 Sept. Munich agreement, 29 Sept. 1938. Hire Purchase Act came into force, 1 Jan. 1939. Premier and Lord Halifax visit Rome, 11–14 Jan.; Sir S. Cripps expelled from Labour Party for his 'Popular Front' campaign, 25 Jan. French president visited Britain, Mar.; British guarantee to Poland, 31 Mar.; to Greece and Rumania, 13 Apr.; Military Training Act, 27 May; Anglo-French proposals to U.S.S.R., 27 May; Anglo-Polish Mutual Assistance Pact, 24 Aug.; British ultimatum to Germany, 1 Sept.

World War II (*q.v.*), 3 Sept. 1939–12 Sept. 1945. Churchill forms coalition government, 10 May 1940. Roosevelt and Churchill issue Atlantic Charter, 11 Aug. 1941. Twenty-year Treaty of Alliance with U.S.S.R., 26 May 1942. Azores agreement with Portugal, 12 Oct. 1943. Education Act, 1944. Labour Party leaves Churchill government, 26 May 1945. General Election, 5 July 1945. Labour government returned (*see* NATIONALIZATION; WESTERN UNION; UNITED NATIONS ORGANIZATION, etc.

Bank of England nationalized, Mar. 1946; Civil aviation, Aug. National Insurance Act, 1946. National Health Service Act, 1946. Coal nationalized, 1 Jan. 1947. Royal tour of S. Africa, Feb.–Apr. 1947. Princess Elizabeth married Lt. Philip Mountbatten, created Duke of Edinburgh, 20 Nov. 1947.

1948: Transport nationalized, 1 Jan. Argentine trade treaty signed, 12 Feb.; Danish trade agreement signed, 22 Feb.; fifty-year treaty of mutual aid with France and Benelux (*q.v.*) signed, 17 Mar.; British Medical Association finally agreed to co-operate with National Health Service, 28 May; second atomic pile (Harwell) began working, 3 July; last German prisoners of war leave, 12 July; Prince Charles *b.*, 14 Nov.

1949: Nationalization of gas and electricity undertakings; Lynskey Tribunal reported, 25 Jan.; General Election in Northern Ireland won by Unionists, 9

H

Feb.; lumbar sympathectomy performed on king, 12 Mar.; clothes rationing ended, 15 Mar.; N. Atlantic Treaty signed, 5 Apr.; Republic of Ireland Act (1948) came into force, 18 Apr. (*see under* IRELAND); London dockers struck, 27 June–25 July; Parliament Act passed under 1911 Act procedure, Sept.

1950: General Election returns Labour Party with majority of eight, 23 Feb.; London dock strike, 19 Apr.–1 May; protest with France and U.S.A. to Russia against arming of E. German police, 23 May; Korean War broke out, June; Princess Anne *b.*, 15 Aug.; British troops in action in Korea, 6 Sept.; Cresswell colliery disaster, 26 Sept.

1951: A. Bevan changed from Health to Labour Ministry, 17 Jan.; Iron and steel nationalized, 15 Feb.; H. Morrison Foreign Secretary, 9 Mar., *vice* E. Bevin, Lord Privy Seal (*d.* 14 Apr.); A. Bevan, J. Freeman, and H. Wilson resigned, 21–24 Apr.; defence of Imjin River fords by 1st Bn. Gloucestershire Regt. in Korea, 22–25 Apr.; Festival of Britain opened, 3 May; Commonwealth Defence Ministers' Conference in London, 21 June; operation performed on king, 23 Sept.; five Councillors of State appointed, 27 Sept.; General Election, 25 Oct., returned Conservative majority of sixteen.

1952: King George VI died, 6 Feb.; Queen Elizabeth II proclaimed, 8 Feb.; repeal of Acts nationalizing iron and steel and road transport; new libel law came into force, 1 Dec.

1953: State visit of Marshal Tito, Mar.; Queen Mary *d.*, 24 Mar.; Queen Elizabeth II crowned, 2 June, and news reached London that Hillary and Tensing had climbed Everest (*q.v.*); Queen and Duke of Edinburgh started extensive Commonwealth tour, Nov.

1954: Food rationing in Britain ended; Eden represented Britain at Geneva talks, Apr.–July, and played a leading part in securing a settlement in Indo-China, July; agreement with Egypt provided for evacuation of Suez by the British; oil dispute with Persia settled, Aug.; London-Paris agreements evolved a new defence formula for W. Europe, Sept.–Oct.; Television Act provided for an alternative commercial television service.

1955: Twenty-six-day national newspaper strike; Churchill resigned the premiership, 5 Apr., and succeeded by Eden; at general election in May Conservatives increased their majority; meeting of heads of government (including Eden) at Geneva, July; Attlee resigned as Labour leader, and granted an earldom, Dec. He was succeeded by Gaitskell. First I.T.A. programmes.

1956: Bulganin and Khruschev visited Britain, Apr.; last British troops left Suez, June; Anglo-French bombing of Egypt, 31 Oct. (*see* EGYPT; SUEZ CANAL); Anglo-French military action in Egypt, 5–6 Nov. Reintroduction of petrol rationing, Dec. Withdrawal of Anglo-French troops from Egypt complete by 22 Dec.

1957: Eden resigned premiership for health reasons, 3 Jan.; was succeeded by Macmillan; Commonwealth prime ministers' conference in London, June; Rent Act came into force, July; Ghana (Mar.) and Malaya (Aug.) became Dominions; worsening economic situation and considerable government unpopularity; royal state visits, to Denmark, Portugal, and France.

1958: Macmillan made a highly successful Commonwealth tour; inflationary pressures continued, and on 19 Sept. the Bank Rate raised from 5 per cent to 7 per cent (highest since 1920). State visit to the Netherlands.

1959: Macmillan visited Moscow, Feb.; White Paper gave details of Cyprus settlement, Feb.; income tax reductions in Budget, Apr.; five-year trade agreement signed with Russia, May; printing strike, 22 June–6 Aug.; Queen started N. American tour, June; Street Offences Act came into force, Aug.; Eisenhower visited London, Aug.; Conservatives increased their majority at general election, Oct.; initialling of agreement setting up the European Free Trade Association, in which Britain was a leading member in Stockholm, Nov.

1960: Prince Andrew *b.*, 19 Feb.; Macmillan attended abortive Summit conference in Paris, May; Princess Margaret married Antony Armstrong-Jones (later Lord Snowdon), 6 May; Selwyn Lloyd became chancellor of the exchequer, July; Archbishop of Canterbury visited the Pope, Dec. Farthing ceased to be legal tender, 31 Dec.

1961: Queen left on tour of India and Pakistan; Commonwealth prime ministers' conference in London, Mar., during which S. Africa announced her intention of withdrawing from the Commonwealth; Surtax concessions in Budget, Apr.; Betting and Gaming Act in force, May; state visit to Italy; President Kennedy visited London, June; 'wages pause' begins, July, and tax increases contained in the 'Little Budget'; Britain applied for membership of the Common Market, Aug.

1962: Government unpopularity shown by a series of by-election reverses, and sweeping Cabinet changes, involving the resignation of Selwyn Lloyd, made in

July; vote of no confidence defeated; disturbances at meetings of right-wing 'Nazi' groups, June–Aug.; Soblen, convicted for spying for Russia by the U.S.A., landed in Britain, July, and died there, Sept.; Common Market negotiations adjourned unfinished, Aug., to be resumed in the autumn. British banknotes (up to £50) could be spent abroad for first time since Sept. 1939, 30 Aug. Commonwealth prime ministers' conference opened in London, 10 Sept. Its final communiqué, published 19 Sept., approved of Britain's proposed resumption of Common Market (q.v.) negotiations, but expressed certain anxieties about the subject. Macmillan (20 Sept.) stated Britain's intention of pursuing negotiations. One-day national rail strike, 3 Oct. (first since 1926). Labour Party emerged as against Britain's entering the Common Market on the existing terms (party conference vote, 3 Oct.). Financial policy eased: earlier post-war credit repayments, and easier bank loans (3 Oct.), and purchase tax on cars cut from 45 per cent to 25 per cent (5 Nov.). Government set up independent tribunal under Lord Radcliffe to inquire into the security aspects raised by the Vassall spy case, 13 Nov. Contracts of Employment Bill published, 12 Dec. In Dec. premier Macmillan visited France and had inconclusive talks with de Gaulle. He then met President Kennedy in the Bahamas. The result was the Nassau Agreement, under which it was agreed that Britain should depend for her nuclear weapons on Polaris missiles, not Skybolt.

1963: Worst winter since 1947 and unemployment highest since then. Electricity cuts due to a combination of weather and unofficial 'work to rule.' Lord Hailsham to be minister with special responsibilities for tackling unemployment in N.E. England, 9 Jan. Common Market talks reopened in Brussels, but French obstructionism soon apparent. Hugh Gaitskell, leader of the Labour Party, d. 18 Jan. Talks on Britain's entry to the Common Market broke down, 29 Jan. On 31 Jan. Macmillan announced that Great Britain had offered her bomber force to N.A.T.O. Harold Wilson elected leader of the parliamentary Labour Party, Feb. Substantial tax cuts in the Apr. Budget. Radcliffe report on Vassall case censured various elements of the press. Government suffered heavy losses in local elections, May. Commonwealth Economic Conference opened in London, 13 May. Relations with Nigeria embittered by the Enahoro affair, which had started in Dec. 1962, but reached major proportions,

April–May. Belgian State visit to London, 14 May. The Profumo affair broke on the public with the resignation of John Profumo, Minister of War, 7 June. In a vote of confidence on 17 June the government obtained the unusually low majority of 69, many Conservatives abstaining. Macmillan announced a judicial inquiry under Lord Denning into the security aspects of the Profumo affair, 21 June. The Ward trial, July–Aug.; Ward d. from an overdose of drugs, 3 Aug. (see TRIALS AND CAUSES CÉLÈBRES). Philby sought asylum in Moscow, 29 July, and was granted Soviet citizenship; the British Government had stated earlier that he was the 'third man' in the Burgess and Maclean affair. The Peerages Bill received the royal assent, 31 July. G. B. initialled the nuclear Test Ban Treaty in Moscow, 25 July; and signed it on 5 Aug.

Macmillan resigned the premiership for health reasons, 18 Oct. 1963; 14th Earl of Home succeeded him, 19 Oct., disclaimed his peerages on 23 Oct., and was returned to the Commons for Kinross on 7 Nov.

Great Council of Peers. See MAGNUM CONCILIUM.

Great Intercourse, 1495. Commercial treaty between Henry VII of England and Philip of Burgundy relating to trade with Flanders.

Great Plague. In London and Derbyshire, 1665.

Great Privilege (Groote Privilegie). On 3 Feb. 1477 a congress of the Netherlands met at Ghent (the first regular assembly of the States-General of the Netherlands). The Duchess Mary, then regent, granted to this assembly a charter known as the G. P. on 11 Feb. 1477. It has been called the 'Magna Carta of Holland,' and was largely a restoration of ancient rights.

Great Schism. After the return of the Papal Court from Avignon, 1378. Urban VI was elected pope, but the French Party elected Clement VII as a rival. The two parties continued to elect rival popes until 1409, when Gregory XII at Rome was deposed and Alexander V and John XXIII successively elected in his place. As Gregory XII refused to recognize his successors there were therefore three rival popes until 1415, when at the Council of Constance John XXIII was deposed and Gregory XII resigned. Martin V was then elected pope at Rome in their stead in 1417. This is generally called the end of the G. S., though a French anti-papacy continued (as successors to Clement VII) till 1429. See PAPACY.

Greece, Ancient. Earliest settlements known at Tiryns and Mycenae, c. 3000 B.C. Minoan supremacy in the Aegean, *c.* 2300–1400. Achaeans' invasion of G., *c.* 1270–1250. They attack Egypt, 1223. And sack Troy (The Iliad), *c.* 1180. Dorians overrun G., *c.* 1100–1000. Ionian settlements of Asia Minor, *c.* 1040. Athenian monarchy made elective, 683. Sparta threatened by the First, 736–716, and the Second, 650–630, Messenian wars introduces the Reforms of Lycurgus *c.* 610. Ionia falls under the power of Croesus of Lydia, 560–546, when Lydia was conquered by the Persians under Cyrus. Persian Darius invades Thrace, 516. Ionian revolt, 499. Helped by Athens, 498; defeated at naval battle of Lade, 494. Persian invasion of G., 491; battle of Marathon, 490. Second Persian invasion, 480. Battle of Thermopylae and Salamis, 480. Battles of Plataea and Mycale, 479.

Delian confederacy formed under Athens, 478. Battle of the Eurymedon, 466. Athenians attack Egypt, 459. Delian Treasury moved to Athens, 454. Thirty years' peace between Athens and Sparta signed, 445. Peloponnesian War begins, 431. Battle of Pylos (Sphacteria), 425. Battle of Amphipolis, 422. Peace of Nicias, 421. Athenian expedition to Syracuse, 415, and final defeat at, 18 Sept. 413. Decelean War, 413. Resumption of Peloponnesian War, 412. Battle of Aegospotami, 405. Surrender of Athens, 404. Sparta supreme in G., 404; till overthrown by Thebes at battle of Leuctra, 371. Thebes collapses after death of Epaminondas at battle of Mantinea, 362. Philip becomes king of Macedonia, 359. Checked by Athenians at Thermopylae, 352. Demosthenes delivers First Philippic, 351. Battle of Chaeronea, 338. Philip forms Pan-Hellenic League at Corinth, 338. Murdered, 336. Alexander the Great puts down Theban revolt, 335. Alexander conquers Persian Empire and dies, 323. Aetolian League founded, 323. Achaean League revived, 281. Romans defeat Macedon at Cynoscephalae, 197. Macedon conquered and made a Roman province, 146. Rest of G. conquered the same year. Remained a Roman province until the Turkish Conquest, A.D. 1440–1460. *See* ROMAN EMPIRE; OTTOMAN EMPIRE; GREECE, MODERN.

Greece, Modern. For previous history *see* GREECE, ANCIENT; ROMAN EMPIRE; OTTOMAN EMPIRE; ROMAN EMPIRE, EASTERN. War of independence began, 25 Mar. 1821, and practically ended in the battle of Navarino, 20 Oct. 1827, when the Egyptian fleet was destroyed by Britain, France, and Russia. On 7 May 1832, G. declared independent kingdom under British, French, and Russian protection. New constitution, 1843. War with

Turkey (*see* GRAECO-TURKISH WARS (1)). Otto I (ex-prince of Bavaria) expelled, 1862. Ionian Islands (*q.v.*) incorporated, 1863. The powers compelled Turkey to withdraw her forces from Crete, 1898, and Crete was granted autonomy under a Greek prince; Balkan Wars (*q.v.*), Oct. 1912–Aug. 1913; Salonika captured by the Greeks, 9 Nov. 1912; King George of G. murdered, 18 Mar. 1913; Crete ceded to G., Nov. 1913; Venizelos (pro-Ally), Premier, 1914–15, invited allied troops to Salonika, Oct. 1915. Constantine repudiated invitation and Venizelos resigned, Oct. 1915. G. refused Allies' bribe of Cyprus, Oct. 1915. Bulgarian invasion, Aug. 1916. Cretan revolution under Venizelos, Sept. 1916. Allies bombarded Athens, 1 Dec. 1916. Constantine abdicated, June 1917, and succeeded by Alexander, who *d.* 1920. Constantine king again, 1920–2. Graeco-Turkish War (*q.v.* (2)), 1921–2. Republic proclaimed, 25 Mar. 1924. Royalist revolt in Athens, 9 Sept. 1935; end of the republic, 10 Oct. 1935; plebiscite, and restoration of King George II, 3 Nov. 1935. Venizelos *d.* in Paris, 18 Mar. 1936; parliamentary government suspended after *coup d'état* by Gen. Metaxas, 4 Aug. 1936. Annual conference of Balkan Entente held at Athens, 15–17 Feb. 1937; Graeco-Turkish agreement of friendship and neutrality, 27 Apr. 1938; the king visited London, Oct.–Nov. 1938; King Zog of Albania took refuge in G., 8 Apr. 1939; announcement of British support against aggression, 13 Apr. 1939; trade agreement with Britain, 12 July 1939; agreement with Italy to withdraw troops from Albanian frontier, 30 Sept. 1939. Cruiser *Helle* torpedoed by Italian submarine, 15 Aug. 1940; Italian ultimatum, 3 a.m., and invasion of G., 5.30 a.m., 28 Oct. 1940; Greek forces thrust back Italians into Albania, 1940. Death of Gen. Metaxas, Jan. 1941; Alex. Korizis Premier, 29 Jan. 1941; British troops landed in G., Mar. 1941; German invasion, 6 Apr. 1941; Korizis committed suicide, 18 Apr. 1941; Tsouderos Premier, 19 Apr. 1941; removal of Government to Crete, 23 Apr. 1941; occupation of Greek mainland by Germans completed, 2 May 1941. Withdrawal of German troops, Sept. 1944.

Communists start civil war, 12 Oct. 1944. Truce negotiated, Dec., and peace agreement signed, 12 Feb. 1945. Monarchy restored by plebiscite, 1946; and Communist rising. King George II *d.*, Apr. 1947; succeeded by Paul I. Partisan Gen. Markos proclaims Soviet Republic of G. from Radio Tirana, 16 Aug., and announces 'Free Greek'

Government, 24 Dec. 1947. Annexation of Dodecanese, 7 Mar. 1948; total defeat of Communists as a result of Papagos's military campaign against them, Aug. 1948. G. joined N.A.T.O., 1951. Papagos resigned the appointment of Chief of Staff in protest at government inefficiency, 30 July 1952, and formed new party, the Greek Rally, which came to power in the election of Nov. He dominated Greek politics until his death in 1955. From 1953 Greek politics increasingly influenced by Cyprus (*q.v.*) question. Problem resolved by the Zürich and London Agreements of 1959 to which G. was a party. Karamanlis succeeded Papagos, Oct. 1955, and remained premier until 1963. Princess Sophia married Don Juan of Spain in Athens, May 1962. Incident in London involving Queen Frederika, Apr. 1963, temporarily jeopardized proposed state visit to London, later that year. Karamanlis resigned, June, when King Paul insisted on making the visit, and was succeeded by Pipinelis. The state visit to Britain in July was marked by a number of hostile demonstrations by left-wing elements. *See* U.N.S.C.O.B.

Kings of Modern Greece:

Otto (Prince Otto of Bavaria)	1833–1862
George I (Prince William of Denmark)	1863–1913
Constantine I	1913–1917
Alexander	1917–1920
Constantine I (again)	1920–1922
George II	1922–1923
Republic	1924–1935
George II (again)	1935–1944
Regency	1944–1946
George II (again)	1946–1947
Paul I	1947–

Greek Authors, Classical, of whom complete works or fragments survive:

Aeschines, 389–314 B.C., orator.
Aeschylus, 525–456 B.C., tragedian.
Agathon, c. 448–400 B.C., tragedian.
Alcaeus, *fl.* 606 B.C., lyric poet.
Anacreon, 570–c. 485 B.C., lyric poet.
Apollonius Rhodius, c. 222–180 B.C., poet and grammarian.
Appian (Roman of Alexandria who wrote in Greek), second century A.D., historian.
Archilochus, *fl.* c. 700 B.C., lyric poet.
Archimedes, 287–212 B.C., mathematician.
Aristarchus of Samos, c. 280 B.C., mathematician and astronomer.
Aristophanes, c. 445–c. 385 B.C., comic poet.

Aristotle, 384–322 B.C., philosopher.
Arrian, c. A.D. 95–c. 170, historian and philosopher.
Asclepiades of Samos, third century B.C., lyric poet.
Aurelius, Marcus, A.D. 121–80, philosopher.
Bacchylides, *fl.* c. 460 B.C., lyric poet.
Bion, c. 280 B.C., bucolic poet.
Callimachus, c. 305–c. 250 B.C., poet and grammarian.
Corinna, *fl.* c. 500 B.C., lyric poetess.
Critias of Athens, d. 403 B.C., orator.
Democritus, c. 460–361 B.C., natural philosopher.
Demosthenes, c. 384–322 B.C., orator.
Dio Cassius, c. A.D. 150–235, historian.
Diodorus Siculus, late first century B.C., historian.
Diogenes Laertius, second or third century A.D., biographer.
Dionysius of Halicarnassus, *fl.* c. 30 B.C., historian and rhetorician.
Epictetus, *fl.* c. A.D. 55–138, philosopher.
Epicurus, 341–270 B.C., philosopher.
Epimenides, sixth century B.C., poet.
Euclid, c. 330–283 B.C., geometer.
Euripides, c. 484–407 B.C., tragedian.
Galen, A.D. 130–200, physician.
Heliodorus of Emesa, third century A.D., romantic writer.
Heraclitus of Ephesus, c. 540–c. 475 B.C., philosopher.
Herodas, third century B.C., dramatist.
Herodotus, c. 484–424 B.C., historian.
Hesiod, ? c. 700 B.C., didactic poet.
Hippocrates, c. 460–377 B.C., physician.
Homer, *fl.* ? between 810 and 730 B.C., epic poet.
Isaeus, c. 420–c. 350 B.C., orator.
Isocrates, 436–338 B.C., rhetorician.
Lucian, c. A.D. 125–90, satirist.
Lycophron, *fl.* 285–247 B.C., grammarian and poet.
Lysias, 458–380 B.C., orator.
Menander, 342–292 B.C., comedian.
Mimnermus, *fl.* c. 634–600 B.C., elegiac poet.
Moschus, *fl.* c. 150 B.C., bucolic poet.
Pausanias, second century A.D., geographer.
Pindar, 518–442 B.C., poet.
Plato, c. 428–347 B.C., philosopher.
Plutarch, c. A.D. 46–after 120, biographer and philosopher.
Polybius, c. 204–122 B.C., historian.
Sappho, b. c. 612 B.C., poetess.
Simonides of Amorgos, *fl.* c. 664 B.C., iambic poet.
Simonides of Ceos, c. 556–467 B.C., lyric poet.
Sophocles, 496–406 B.C., tragedian.
Stesichorus, c. 640–c. 555 B.C., lyric poet.
Strabo, c. 63 B.C.–c. A.D. 24, geographer.
Theocritus, c. 310–c. 267 B.C., bucolic poet.

Theognis, *b. c.* 540 B.C., elegiac poet.
Theophrastus, *c.* 370–286 B.C., philosopher.
Thucydides, *c.* 464–*c.* 402 B.C., historian.
Tyrtaeus, *fl. c.* 685–668 B.C., poet.
Xenophon, *c.* 430–*c.* 356 B.C., historian.

See also BYZANTINE AUTHORS.

Greek Fire, pre-eminently a naval weapon, but also used in sieges, was invented by Callinicus of Heliopolis, a Syrian in the employ of the Emperor Constantine Pogonatus (648–85); this so-called 'wet fire' (because the liquid when it came in contact with water was self-igniting) is the true G. F. as used during the Crusades; incendiary mixtures used as ammunition for ballistae, etc., are mentioned by G. authors of tactical manuals as early as the fourth century, B.C., but all had to be ignited before discharge.

Greek Orthodox Church. First signs of disunion between the Greek and Roman Churches in A.D. 385, when celibacy of priests was enforced, and a demand that the Pope should be recognized as supreme, and doctrinal differences were raised. In A.D. 484 the two Churches separated for a period of 40 years. In 734 the Greeks condemned image worship (Iconoclastic Controversy). The final separation may be said to be the Great Schism of 1054, when Pope Leo IX excommunicated the patriarch of Constantinople. Several attempts were made to bring about a reconciliation, but without success. The most important by the Emperor John Palaeologus II at the Council of Ferrara, 1438. The 'Orthodox Confession' was drawn up in 1643.

Greenback Party, advocating that treasury notes, as opposed to bank-notes, should be the sole legal tender of U.S.A., *fl.* 1874–84.

Greenland. Original Scandinavian settlement, begun in 982, died out *c.* 1480. Visited by Frobisher, 1577. Danish settlements re-founded, 1721. Large deposits of lead ore discovered at King Oskar Fjord, 1948. Mutual defence of G. arranged by agreement with U.S.A. signed, 27 Apr. 1951. On 5 June 1953 G. became an integral part of the Danish kingdom (had been a colony since 1261), with same rights and measure of self-government as the rest of Denmark.

Greenville, Treaty of. Between U.S.A. and the NW. Indian tribes, 3 Aug. 1795.

Greenwich, London, celebrated for its hospital and observatory (*see* succeeding articles). A palace was built here by Humphrey, Duke of Gloucester, in 1428, and later came into Henry VI's possession. It was a favourite residence of the Tudors; Mary I and Elizabeth I were *b.* there, and Edward VI *d.* there. Charles

II started to rebuild it, but in 1694 William and Mary gave up residence and decided on its conversion to a sailors' hospital.

Greenwich Hospital (England). Founded, 1694, on the site of G. Palace. Opened, 1705. Ceased to be a pensioners' hospital, 1869. Became Royal Naval College, 1873.

Greenwich Observatory (London). Built, 1675, by Wren. Opened, 1675–6. Removed to Herstmonceux, 1947.

Gregorian Chants. Named after Pope Gregory I (540–604), who is traditionally said to have added extra tones to the Ambrosian Chants then in use.

Grenada, W. Indies. Discovered by Columbus, 1498; colonized by French, 1651; ceded to England by Treaty of Paris, 1763; recaptured by French, 1779; restored to England by Treaty of Versailles, 1783. 'Brigands' War,' 1795. Massacre of governor and loyal subjects, 1796. Placed under Governor of Windward Islands, 1885, and declared a crown colony, 1876. Constitution suspended, 18 June 1962, because of the financial activities of the chief minister.

Grenadiers. A few G. were first attached to the French *Régiment du Roi* in 1667. Formed into companies in 1668–70. Evelyn in 1678 mentions them. The British Grenadier Guards (First Foot Guards) were organized in 1660. They received their present name in 1815 after Waterloo, as a result of the conspicuous part taken by them in defeating the G. of the French Imperial Guard. G. in the German Army derived prestige from the traditions of the Prussian G., the élite infantry units of the Seven Years War and other mid eighteenth century campaigns, most of which had been raised by King Frederick William I (reigned 1713–40). About 1942 most German infantry units began to be designated G., e.g. *Panzer-grenadier* (lorried infantry) regiments.

Gresham's Law, or the proposition 'Bad money drives out good,' was formulated in 1560 by Sir Thomas G. (1519–79), founder of the Stock Exchange (*q.v.*), and of the school at Holt which bears his name (*see* PUBLIC SCHOOLS).

Gretna Green, Scotland. After the abolition of Fleet marriages (*q.v.*) in 1754, those in England wishing to marry clandestinely, crossed the border to G. G. to take advantage of the Scotch marriage laws. By a law passed in 1856, these marriages were invalid unless one of the parties had resided in Scotland for three weeks.

Grey Friars. Franciscan monastery established in London, 1224. Afterwards Christ's Hospital (*q.v.*).

Greyhound Racing. The National Greyhound Racing Club was set up in Britain in 1927, exercising a rigid control over the standards of G. R.

Griquas, a tribe of Hottentot-Boer half-castes, otherwise known as Bastards, who had been leading a nomadic life S. of the Orange River, were persuaded by the missionary Anderson to settle under their leader Barend Barends N. of the river and W. of what is now Kimberley, in 1808. This settlement centring on Griquatown (formerly Klaarwater) was the nucleus of the present Griqualand W. Treaty relations with the British Government, 1834. After the diamond rush of 1867 political pressure on the Griqua community was exerted both by the Orange Free State to the E. and the diggers of Kimberley, and the G. petitioned the crown of Britain to take over the country, which was done, 27 Oct. 1871. Griqualand W. became a crown colony in July 1873, was annexed to Cape Colony, 1877, and incorporated therein, 1880.

Among the Griqua leaders of the pre-Anderson era had been a half-caste named Adam Kok I (1710–95), whose grandson, Adam Kok II, was a companion of Barend Barends, and in company with him trekked eastwards in 1820 into the southern part of the present Orange Free State, where they and their followers settled for some forty years S. of the Modder River. Adam Kok II *d. c.* 1835, and his son, Adam Kok III, who entered into treaty relations with Britain, 1843, succeeded him. Under pressure from Orange Free State these G., led by Adam Kok, trekked over the Drakensberg Mountains (1861–3) to the present E. Griqualand, with its capital Kokstad; its founder *d.,* 1876, one year after its annexation to Cape Colony.

Grisons (Ger. **Graubünden**; It. **Grigioni**; Romansch **Grischun**). Largest of the Swiss cantons. The Raetians living about the sources of the Rhine and Inn were conquered by Rome in 15 B.C., and the district formed the nucleus of Raetia Prima. Christianity was introduced, 400. Conquered by the Franks, 536, who entrusted civil government to the Bishop of Chur. In 806 Charlemagne separated the civil power and placed it under a count. The 'Grey League' from which the canton takes its name was founded, 1395, as a defensive union of rural communities about the size of the Old English hundred; this *Graubund* joined in federation with the League of God's House (founded, 1367), and the League of Ten Laws (founded, 1436) to form the Free State of Ten Leagues, which became more and more closely associated

with the original Swiss Confederation from 1497 to 1524. In 1794 Veltlin (Valtellina) seceded, and was attached by Napoleon to the Cisalpine Republic, 1797, since when it has been Italian with a short interval of Austrian hegemony. The rest of G. joined the Helvetic Republic, 1797, but regained its independence in 1803. Finally adhered to the Swiss Confederation, 1854. Romansch was admitted as an official language in the canton, 1803, and in Switzerland as a whole, 1938.

Groats. First coined, 1351. Discontinued, 1662. Revived, 1838. In Scotland first issued, 1358. In Ireland, 1460. Last coined in Great Britain, 1856, except for a special issue coined for Maundy money. *See* MAUNDY THURSDAY.

Groningen, Holland. Joined Hanseatic League (*q.v.*) *c.* 1282. Part of United Netherlands, 1594.

Ground-nuts Scheme, Tanganyika, launched early in 1947; reorganized under the Overseas Food Corporation, 1950; Overseas Food Corporation wound up, 1955.

Guadalcanal. One of the largest and most important of the Solomon Islands (*q.v.*). It is remembered as the scene of a protracted campaign against the Japanese, who landed powerful forces there in summer 1942. American and Australian forces were landed shortly afterwards and drove the Japanese out by 9 Feb. 1943.

Guadalupe-Hidalgo, Treaty of. Between U.S.A. and Mexico, signed, 2 Feb. 1848.

Guadeloupe, W. Indies. Discovered by Columbus, 1493, colonized by France, 1635; captured by Britain, 1759; restored to France, 1763; ceded to Sweden, 1813; restored to France, 1814. Became an Overseas Department of France, 19 Mar. 1946. Its dependency, St. Martin, was simultaneously occupied by the French and Dutch, but amicably partitioned 1648.

Guam. *See* LADRONES.

Guardians of the Poor. Abolished, 1929, by Local Government Act. *See* POOR LAWS.

Guatemala, Central America. Declared independent of Spain, 1821, and joined Central American Federation. Left the C.A.F., 1839. Carrera defeats Federalists at La Arada and becomes president under new constitution, 1851. Boundary treaty with Britain, 1859. Life president, 1854–65. Liberals depose President Cerna and expel Jesuits, 1871. President Barrios killed in invasion of Salvador, 1885. Dictatorship of President Cabrera, 1898–1920, of Ubico, 1931–44. Common boundary with Salvador and Honduras agreed, Mar. 1936. From Feb. 1948 to

May 1951 the frontier with British Honduras was closed as part of the recurrent claim, dating from Spanish colonial days, that this is Guatemalan territory. Arbenz's regime, 1951, instituted a left-wing policy and became increasingly pro-Communist. Land reform operative, 1953. Nicaraguan diplomats expelled, 19 May 1954. Nationalist, anti-Communist rebels under Col. Castillo Armas entered G. from Honduras, allegedly with the backing of Nicaragua and United Fruit Company, 18 June. Arbenz resigned, 27 June, in favour of a junta, and fled to Argentina. The junta negotiated an armistice in Salvador, 29 June, and admitted Castillo Armas, who subsequently became President. He was assassinated, 1957, and a period of military rule was ended when, under the terms of the new constitution of 1956, Ydigoras Fuentes was elected President, 1958. There was an anti-Communist coup d'état, Apr. 1963.

Presidents from the Promulgation of the 1851 Constitution:

Carrera	1851–1865
Cerna	1865–1871
Granados	1871–1873
Barrios (Justo Rufino)	1873–1885
Sinibaldi	1885
Barillas	1885–1892
Barrios (Jose Maria Reina)	1892–1898
Cabrera	1898–1920
Herrera	1920–1921
Orellana (Jose Maria)	1921–1926
Chacon	1926–1930
Palma	1930
Orellana (Manuel)	1930–1931
Andrade	1931
Ubico	1931–1944
Vaides	1944
Triumvirate	1944–1945
Arevalo	1945–1951
Arbenz	1951–1954
A junta	1954
Castillo Armas	1954–1957
Gonzalez Lopez (provisional)	1957
A junta	1957–1958
Ydigoras Fuentes	1958–1963

Guatemala City, capital of the preceding and before that of a Spanish colonial province, was founded, 1776, on the destruction of the previous capital, Antigua, in the earthquake of 1773.

Guelph, Welf. Surname of the dukes of Saxony since the eleventh century, and thence surname of the Hanoverian royal family of Great Britain. Proclamation changing name to Windsor, July 1917.

Guelphs and Ghibellines. Two factions caused by the rivalry between emperor and pope, after the death of Henry V in 1125. The Ghibellines, or emperor's party, took their name from Waiblingen, a castle in Württemberg, Italianized into Ghibellino. The G. or papal party had their name from Welf, the name of many princes of the House of Bavaria. The first outbreak of hostilities between the two parties occurred in 1154, when the Emperor Frederick Barbarossa made an expedition into Italy. After the Hohenstaufen defeat at Tagliacozzo, 1268, the struggle began to lose its real force. In the fifteenth century the names died out of current politics, but were temporarily revived during the French campaigns in Italy at the beginning of the sixteenth century.

Guernica, Spain. Famous because on 27 Apr. 1937, during the Spanish Civil War, it was heavily bombed by German planes supporting the Falangists.

Guernsey, Channel Islands. Probably granted to abbot of Dol by Childebert the Merovingian, A.D. 550. Became part of Normandy on its formation in tenth century. Its fortress, Castle Cornet, held out against the parliamentary forces, 1643–51. French made ineffectual attempts to land, 1779 and 1780. Occupied by Germans, 1 July 1940–9 May 1945. Constitution modified by Reform Law of 1948, which took effect from 1 Jan. 1949.

Gueux ('Beggars'). During the revolt of the Netherlands against Spain a confederacy of nobles drew up, in 1565, a 'Compromise' (see COMPROMISE LEAGUE) which in Apr. 1566 they presented to the regent, Margaret of Parma. The demonstration caused some alarm, but she was reassured by a councillor: 'Madam, is your Highness afraid of these beggars?' The 'Beggars of the Sea', under de la Marck, did much damage to the Spanish fleet, and captured Brill in 1572.

Guiana, S. America. British occupy Surinam, 1630–67. Dutch occupy Paramaribo, 1640. French in Cayenne, 1664. Dutch cede Georgetown and Berbice to British, 1781. Returned to Dutch, 1783. Finally became British, 1814. See also BRITISH GUIANA; DUTCH GUIANA; FRENCH GUIANA.

Guides, Girl. See GIRL GUIDES.

Guildford, England. Abbots Hospital founded, 1619. Diocese, 1927. Cathedral founded, 1936; consecrated, 1961. Assizes transferred to Kingston, 1930.

Guildhall, London. An important hall has stood on this site since the eleventh century. A new building was erected, 1411–26, but much of this was destroyed in an air raid on 29 Dec. 1940. A new Great Hall was completed in 1954 to the designs of Sir Giles Gilbert Scott.

Guillotine. Supposed to have been invented by Joseph Ignace Guillotin

(1738–1814), but in fact he merely recommended the use of the instrument, long known to the Scots and in certain parts of the N. of England. It was first used to execute a highwayman in Paris, 25 Apr. 1792.

Guinea. Gold coin first used in England, 1664. Last issued, 1813.

Guinea, Republic of, formerly French Guinea. Britain recognized France's rights in the area, 1882. Made a separate colony from Senegal, 1891. Boundaries finally settled, 1899. The territory voted to leave the French Community in the referendum of 28 Sept. 1958, and became an independent republic on 2 Oct. 1958. Agreement of unity with Ghana (Nov. 1958) and Ghana-Mali (Dec. 1960).

Guinea, Portuguese. Discovered by Nuno Tristao, 1446, and made a separate colony of Portugal, 1879.

Guinea, Spanish. Acquired by Spain at the end of the fifteenth century.

Guines, Treaty of. *See* CLOTH OF GOLD, FIELD OF THE.

Gun-cotton. Discovered by Braconnot, 1832. Put to practical use by Schönbein (German), 1845. First manufactured in England, 1847.

Gundulph Bible, a Vulgate MS. copied in Amsterdam, was brought to England by G., a monk of Bec, from which abbey he followed Lanfranc of Pavia to Caen, and later (1070) to Canterbury. In 1077 he became Bishop of Rochester, and his Bible was kept in the cathedral until 1540, when it disappeared. In Mar. 1952 it was rediscovered in a library at San Marino, California.

Gunpowder. The precise era of the invention and application of G. is doubtful but it was clearly known before the middle of the fourteenth century, and, before the end of the same, the use of artillery was familiar to the states of Germany, Italy, Spain, France, and England. G. is said to have been discovered by Berthold Schwartz of Brunswick *c.* A.D. 1320, although Roger Bacon mentions its composition in a work published, 1216.

Gunpowder Plot. Originated by Robert Catesby early in 1604, to blow up the Houses of Parliament. In July 1605, Guy Fawkes was commissioned to commit the deed, and 5 Nov. 1605, the day on which Parliament was to meet, was the day chosen. Catesby was killed during the course of his flight from the Government officers. Fawkes and other leaders executed, Jan. and Feb. 1606.

Gupta. A famous dynasty under which India reached great prosperity, A.D. 320–480.

Guy's Hospital (London). Founded by Thomas Guy, 1721.

Gwalior, India. City and state founded by Mahadji Sindhia, 1769. Under British influence, 1782. British intervention, 1843. It became the nucleus of the Union of Minor States, known as Madhya Bharat, formed 15 June 1948. with G. city as its capital.

ADDENDA

H

Haarlem, Holland. Besieged by Duke of Alva and the Spaniards, Dec. 1572–July 1573.

Habeas Corpus Act (Great Britain). Passed, 1679, to prevent illegal imprisonment; extended to cases other than criminal, 1816. In Scotland the Wrongous Imprisonment Act, passed 1701, is equivalent to the English Act; Irish Act passed, 1781–2.

Hackney Coaches. First used in London, 1625. Laws regarding hire of, 1831, 1853, 1869. The London Cab Order, 1934, regulates the London taxi service, the modern equivalent of H. C.

Hadfield's (James) attempt to assassinate George III at Drury Lane Theatre, 15 May 1800. Tried and acquitted, 26 June 1800.

Hadrian's Wall (England). Designed by the Emperor Hadrian during his visit to Britain in A.D. 122, but the work was executed largely by the legate Aulus Platorius Nepos, 122–6. Extended from the Tyne to the Solway Firth; repaired by Severus about 208. Wall abandoned, A.D. 383.

Hague, The, or **'s Gravenhage,** Holland. Founded, 1248. Spanish supremacy abjured at, 1580; the de Witts killed, 1672; captured by French, 19 Jan. 1795; evacuated by the French, Nov. 1813; the Permanent Court of Arbitration at The H. established in 1899; the Palace of Peace at The H., instituted by the Carnegie Foundation for the Permanent Court of Arbitration, inaugurated Aug. 1913. Academy of International Law founded, Jan. 1914. Permanent Court of International Justice founded, 1920. Bombed by Germans, 1940, and the R.A.F., 1945.

Hague, The, Peace Conferences at. (1) Met, 18 May 1899; Arbitration Court instituted, Apr. 1899; (2) met 15 June–18 Oct. 1907.

Hague, The, Treaties of. (1) Between England, France, and Holland to enforce Peace of Roskilde (q.v.), 21 May 1659; (2) between England and Holland, July 1659; (3) between England, France, and Holland, Aug. 1659; (4) between Great Britain and Holland, 23 Jan. 1668; receives name of Triple Alliance after Sweden joins, 25 Apr. 1668; (5) between Portugal and Holland, 7 May 1669; (6) between the Emperor, Holland, and Spain against France, 25 July 1672; (7) Grand Alliance (q.v.) renewed, 1696; (8) second Triple Alliance (q.v.), 4 Jan. 1717; (9) between Spain, Savoy, and Austria, 17 Feb. 1717; (10) convention between Great Britain, Austria, Holland, and Sardinia against France and Spain, 26 Jan. 1748; (11) between France and Holland, 16 May 1795.

Haifa, Israel. Developed commercially since c. 1890. Harbour completed, 1933. Town severely damaged by terrorist sabotage of Shell refinery, 30 Mar. 1947. Since Israel's independence (1948) the oil pipe-line from Kirkuk has been cut, and the refining of oil curtailed.

Haileybury and Imperial Service College (Herts., England). Founded 1806 by the E. India Co., originally occupied Hertford Castle, but removed to its present site, 1809. When the company in 1858 was taken over by the crown the college fell into neglect. In 1862 it was reopened as a public school, and incorporated, 1864. The Imperial Service College was amalgamated with it in 1942.

Hainaut (Hainault, Henegouwen) acquired as part of a dowry by Baldwin, Count of Flanders, 1051; passed to Bavaria, 1345; Burgundy, 1433; Austria, 1477; Spanish Netherlands, 1555; France, 1659; Austrian Netherlands, 1714. Became French province, 1794; was ceded to the United Netherlands, 1814; became Belgian province, 1830.

Hair-powder Tax. In Great Britain, 1795. Repealed, 1869.

Haiti. Once signified the W. Indian island of Hispaniola (q.v. for early history). Now the name of the western portion of the island. Jean Jacques Dessalines, an ex-slave, proclaimed himself Emperor of H. (reviving for the whole island the original or native name), 1804; assassinated, 1806. Henri Christophe, in the N., proclaimed life-president, 1807. Rival Government, headed by Alexandre Pétion, formed at Port-au-Prince, 1807–18. Christophe proclaimed king, 1811; crowned 1812; committed suicide, 1820. Pétion's successor, Jean Pierre Boyer, seized Christophe's dominion, drove Spaniards from eastern portion, and ruled the whole island, 1822–43. For subsequent history of eastern portion, *see* DOMINICAN REPUBLIC. H. proper proclaimed an empire by Faustin

Soulouque, 1849; republic restored, 1859. Many revolutions since. U.S.A. intervened, 1915. Treaty with U.S.A., 1916, brought H. under U.S. protection. U.S. marines left, 15 Aug. 1934. New constitutions, 1935 (amended 1939, 1944), 1946, 1950, and 1957. *Coup d'état*, 10 May 1950, led by Col. Paul Eugène Magloire, who was the first president (Oct. 1950) to be elected by universal *direct* suffrage. U.S. fiscal control of H. finances ceased, 1947. Magloire attempted to stay in power when his term of office ended, 1956, but was forced to resign. A period of political upheaval and army rule ended with Duvalier's election as President, Sept. 1957. Britain and U.S. concerned at blatant corruption by the Duvalier regime, and the attempts to extort money from foreigners residing in H., 1961–2. Tension with the Dominican Republic (*q.v.*) temporarily threatened Duvalier's regime, Apr.–May 1963.

Heads of State since the Establishment of the Republic, 1804. The head of the state is a president. Several of the earlier presidents, however, awarded themselves royal titles. These are given, where important. This practice was discontinued after the time of Soulouque.

Dessalines	('Emperor')	1804–1806
Christophe	('King')	1807–1820
Pétion		1807–1818
Boyer		1818–1843
Rivière-Hérard		1843–1844
Guerrier		1844–1845
Pierrot		1845–1846
Riché		1847
Soulouque	('Emperor')	1847–1859
Geffrard		1859–1867
Salnave		1867–1869
Nissage-Saget		1870–1874
Domingue		1874–1876
Boisrond-Canal		1876–1879
Salomon		1879–1888
Légitime		1888–1889
Hyppolite		1889–1896
Simon Sam		1896–1902
Nord Alexis		1902–1908
Simon		1908–1911
Leconte		1911–1912
Auguste		1912–1913
Oreste		1913–1914
Zamor		1914
Théodore		1914–1915
Guillaume Sam		1915
Dartiguenave		1915–1922
Borno		1922–1930
Roy		1930
Vincent		1930–1941
Lescot		1941–1946
Estimé		1946–1950
Magloire		1950–1956
Military junta		1957
Duvalier		1957–

Half-crown. *See* CROWN PIECES.

Half-pay in British Forces. Army *permanent* H.-P. first granted, 1698. Abolition of *retired* H.-P., 1884.

Halicarnassus. City of Asia Minor on S.W. coast of Caria, founded by Dorians from Troezens and Argos. Became subject to Persia, sixth century B.C. The satrap Lygdamis obtained power as tyrant; his daughter and successor, Artemisia I, present with Xerxes at Salamis, 480 B.C. H. was a member of the Delian League until the Peace of Antalcidas restored it to Persian suzerainty, 387 B.C. The satrap Mausolus (377–353 B.C.) made himself independent. His wife and successor, Artemisia II, built the Mausoleum *c*. 352 B.C. H. was destroyed by Alexander, 334 B.C.

Halifax, Nova Scotia. Founded, 1749; garrisoned by British troops until 1906; explosion in harbour caused 5,800 casualties, 16 Dec. 1917.

Halifax Fisheries Award. One of the articles of the Treaty of Washington (*q.v.*), 1871, provided for a commission to inquire into the value of the fishery privileges allowed to the U.S.A. by the treaty; met at Halifax, Nova Scotia, 5 June 1877. Great Britain awarded $5,500,000 for fishing privileges for twelve years.

Halifax Law (summary trial and execution by guillotine for certain types of larceny) arose in Halifax, Yorkshire, in the fifteenth century and was last enforced in 1650.

Hall Marks (Britain).
1. The London assay office established by statute, 1300. The earliest marks of this office now known date from 1390. The date letter series begins, 1478. Its marks were:
1478–1697: A crowned leopard's head. 1697–1719: Britannia. 1719–1820: A crowned leopard's head. 1820 to now: Leopard's head uncrowned.
2. The Chester office probably existed before 1300. Date letter series begins, 1701. Its marks were:
1300–1701: A shield with three sheaves and a dagger. 1701–19: As before, halved with three English leopards. 1719: The London leopard's head was added. In 1779 the old shield was readopted. In 1839 the London mark was dropped. Office closed, 1962.
3. The Birmingham office opened, 1773. Its mark is a crown.
4. The Sheffield office opened, 1773. Its mark is an anchor.
5. The Edinburgh office was in existence 1485, from which its earliest marks date. The date letter series begins, 1681. Its mark is a three-towered castle on a rock.
6. The Glasgow office instituted, 1819.

Its mark is the fish, tree, bell, and bird of the Glasgow arms.

7. The Dublin office was in existence by 1500. Date letter series begins, 1638. Its mark is a crowned harp. From 1730 a figure of Hibernia was added to denote payment of a tax. The tax was abolished 1890, but the figure is still in use.

8. The following offices have also existed:

(a) Exeter date letter series begins, 1544. Mark, a three-towered castle. Office closed, 1883.

(b) Newcastle founded, 1423. Date letter series begins, 1658. Mark is three towers on a shield. Office closed, 1864.

(c) Norwich founded, 1423. Date letter series begins, 1565. Marks are a crowned rose, and a shield with a gate tower over an English leopard. Office closed, 1697.

(d) York founded, 1423. Date letter series begins, 1562. Marks are: a fleur-de-lys and a crowned leopard's head halved with each other, and a cross charged with five leopards. Office closed, 1857.

The Excise Duty Mark (the sovereign's head in profile) was used between 1784 and 1890. The heads of both sovereigns were used in the year 1935 only.

Halle, Saxony. Part of Archbishopric of Magdeburg from 968. Member of Hanseatic League, 1281–1478; passed to Brandenburg, 1648. Cathedral built, 1520–36. Martin Luther University founded, 1694; incorporated with University of Wittenberg, 1817.

Hallé Orchestra. Established in 1857 n Manchester by Sir Charles Hallé (1819–1895).

Halley's Comet observed, 1682, by Edmund Halley (1656–1742), who correctly predicted its reappearance in 1758. Again appeared 1835 and 1910; next expected appearance, 1986. The comet which appeared in 1066, 1456, 1531, and 1607 was almost certainly H. C.

Hambledon (Hants). Traditional birth-place of cricket (q.v.).

Hamburg, Germany. Founded by Charlemagne, A.D. 808; bishopric, 831; archbishopric, 834; made a free imperial city, 1189; allied with Lübeck, 1241; Bank of, founded, 1619; peace of, 1762; occupied by French, 1806; annexed to France, 1810; evacuated by French on approach of Russians, 1813; freed from French, 1814; joined German Confederation, 1815; one-third of the town destroyed by fire, 1842; new constitution granted by the senate, July 1860; joined the N. German Confederation (q.v.), Aug. 1866; joined the Zollverein, Oct. 1888; cholera epidemic, 1892; university founded, 1919; constitution revised, 1921;

free city privileges abolished by Nazis, 1934. Dock area mostly destroyed by allied bombing, 1942–3. Captured by British troops, 3 May 1945. Flooding caused over 150 deaths and severe damage, 16–17 Feb. 1962. See HANSEATIC LEAGUE.

'Hampshire,' The. British armoured cruiser on the way to Russia mined and sunk off Marwick Head in the Orkneys, Lord Kitchener and staff perishing, 6 June 1916.

Hampton Court Conference. Held at H. C., 12–18 Jan. 1604, between the Church party and the Puritans. The only substantial result was the decision to translate the Bible.

Hampton Court Palace (Middlesex, England). Built by Cardinal Wolsey, and presented by him to King Henry VIII, 1526; Edward VI b. there, 12 Oct. 1537; enlarged by Christopher Wren for William III, 1694, when the famous chestnut avenue was planted; vine planted, 1768; state apartments opened to public, 1837; excavation of ancient moat completed and restoration, 14 Oct. 1910. Severe fire damage to first-floor apartments in Clock Court, November 1952.

Hampton Roads Conference between Lincoln and Seward for the Federal Government and Confederate vice-president Stephens, 3 Feb. 1865.

Hanaper Office of the Court of Chancery founded c. 1670. Abolished, 1842.

Hangchowfu. Described (as Kinsai) by Marco Polo, who visited it c. 1280. Capital of Sung dynasty, 1127–1278. Held by Taiping rebels, 1851–4. Nationalist stronghold in civil war, 1926. Captured by Japanese, 1937; by Communists, 1949.

Hankow, China. Founded during Ming dynasty (1300–1644). Sacked and largely destroyed in the Taiping rebellion, 1851–1854. Opened to European trade, 1862. Occupied by Japanese, 1938; by Nationalists, 1945; by Communists, 1949.

Hanover, Germany. Made an electorate, 1692. Elector George acquired Celle by marriage, 1705. Became King of Britain, 1714. Acquired Bremen and Verden from Sweden, 1715. Made a kingdom, 1814. Acquired E. Friesland, 1815. At accession of Victoria crown of H. went to Ernest Augustus, hitherto deputy-elector of H. and Duke of Cumberland, 1837, because Salic Law obtained in H. Joined Austria in the Austro-Prussian War of 1866, and annexed by Prussia, 26 Sept. 1866. George, fifth Elector and first king of that name, succeeded his father in 1851. He d. in 1878.

Hanover, House of. *See* ENGLISH SOVEREIGNS AND THEIR CONSORTS.

Hanover, Treaties of. 1. Between England, France, and Prussia, signed, 3 Sept. 1725, to oppose the secret Treaty of Vienna (20 Apr. 1725) between Spain and Austria, who pledged themselves to assist in the restoration of the Stuarts, joined by Holland, 9 Aug. 1726; by Sweden, 26 Mar. 1727; by Denmark, 18 Apr. 1727. 2. Between George II and Maria Theresa, 24 June 1741. 3. Between H. and England, 1834.

Hanoverian Succession. Established by law, 12 June 1701; arranged that the Princess Sophia of Hanover and her heirs should succeed to the British throne after the death of Queen Anne, provided the latter *d.* without issue.

Hansard. Re3ord of parliamentary debates, begun by Luke Hansard (1752–1828), a printer. The name 'Hansard' was dropped from the *Parliamentary Debates* between 1889 and 1943, but restored in the latter year as the result of a House of Commons Select Committee's recommendation.

Hanseatic League, or Hansa. Never had a formal beginning. Hamburg and Lübeck in alliance, 1241. First meeting of Hanse towns (The Wendish Group), 1256. Gothland association existed in 1229 when it negotiated a treaty with the Russians, but was subsequently absorbed by the H. L. Was given privileges in England, 1237. The Free Counter at Bruges established, 1309. At Bergen, 1343. Wars with Denmark, 1361–70. Lübeck recognized as head of the H. L., 1418. Baltic trading monopoly broken by Peace of Copenhagen, 1441. Novgorod counter closed, 1494. Bruges counter closed, 1540. Last general assembly held, 1669. Counters at Bergen closed, 1775; London, 1852; Antwerp, 1863.

Hapsburg or Habsburg, House of. Family called after H., in Switzerland, which they came to in 1028. Rudolf of H. elected Holy Roman Emperor, 1273. Austria and Styria acquired soon after. Carinthia and Carniola, 1335. Tirol, 1363–4. Franche - Comté, 1493 (lost, 1555). Württemberg and Breisgau, 1520 (lost, 1534). Bohemia, Moravia, Croatia, Silesia, and Christian Hungary, 1526. Rest of Hungary reconquered from the Turks, 1650–99. Netherlands, 1712 (lost, 1797). Milan, 1714 (lost, 1797). Banat of Temesvar, 1718. Craiova and Serbia, 1718 (lost, 1739). Parma, 1735 (lost, 1748). Tuscany, 1737 (lost, 1801). Silesia lost, 1742. Galicia, 1772. Lublin, 1795 (lost, 1809). Venetia, 1797 (lost, 1805). At Vienna Congress (1814–15) Hs. obtained Tuscany,

Modena, Parma, Milan, Venetia, which were all lost, 1859–66, and permanently acquired Trento and Salzburg. Through marriages with the houses of Burgundy and Spain the Emperor Charles V was also King of Spain, but at his death the Spanish and the Germanic lands descended in different branches of the family until the extinction of the Spanish Hs., 1700 (*see* SPANISH SUCCESSION). The death of the Emperor Charles VI, 1740, extinguished the true Austrian branch, but through the marriage of his daughter Maria-Theresa with Prince Charles of Lorraine the family was known as H.-Lorraine. At abolition of the Holy Roman Empire (*q.v.*), 1806, the Hs. took the title of Emperor of Austria. They ceased to reign in Austria and Hungary, 1918.

Hara-Kiri. Japanese form of honourable suicide required on certain occasions. H. became customary during the Middle Ages. Abolished officially, 1868, but was practised by a number of Japanese officers during World War II.

Harar or Harrar, Ethiopia. Became seat of Arab government of Zelia, 1521. Occupied by Egyptians, 1875–85. Conquered by Ethiopian Emperor Menelek II, 1887. Seriously damaged by bombing, 1935. Captured by British forces, Mar. 1941, and this signalled the beginning of the collapse of Mussolini's colonial empire.

Harfleur, Normandy. Captured by Henry V of England, 1415. English expelled, 1433. Recaptured by English, 1440. Driven out by Dunois, 1450. Sacked by Huguenots, 1562.

Harleian Collection. Valuable MSS., books, and pamphlets, whose collection was started by Robert Harley (1661–1724), 1st Earl of Oxford, and continued by his son. Much of it was acquired from Lady Oxford in 1753 by the British Museum.

Harper's Ferry, W. Va., U.S.A. The scene of John Brown's celebrated raid before the American Civil War, 16 Oct. 1859.

Harrow School. Founded by John Lyon, 1571. Originally intended for education of poor boys of the parish. Original red-brick school house built, 1608–15. Mutinies at, 1771 and 1815. Chapel built, 1857.

Hartford, Conn., U.S.A. Settled by the Dutch, 1633, by the English, 1635. First named Newton, but changed to H. in honour of the birthplace in England of Samuel Stone, one of the leaders of the settlers.

Hartford Conventions. 1. 20 Oct. 1779, to inquire into the depreciation of continental paper money. 2. 15 Dec. 1814, to deliberate upon security and defence.

Harvard University (U.S.A.). Founded by the general court of Massachusetts Bay Colony, 10 Oct 1638, and subsequently named H. College after Rev. John Harvard (*b.* 1607), who went to America in 1637, and bequeathed in 1638 his library and a sum of money towards the foundation of the college at Cambridge (*q.v.*), Mass. Charter granted, 1650. Transformed into a university, 1780. Under control of state until 1865, since when it has been self-governing.

Harwich, Essex, England. Danes defeated off, A.D. 885; incorporated, 1318, and charter further extended, 1604; Isabel, queen of Edward II, landed at, 1326; Dutch fleet defeated by Duke of York near, 3 June 1665. Parkeston Quay erected, 1882.

Hastings, Sussex. One of the Cinque Ports, supposed to have been founded by H. (*Hásteinn,* anglicized to *Haesten*), a Danish pirate, *c.* A.D. 893. King Athelstan established a mint here. H. was a borough before 1086. The battle of H. so called was not fought here but six miles inland on the London road; William's army halted at H. on the night of 13–14 Oct. 1066, preceding the battle. Importance as a port declined after English loss of Normandy in 1204. Burned by French, 1377 and 1380.

Hastings, Warren, Trial of. Commenced before the House of Lords, 12 Feb. 1788; lasted until 23 Apr. 1795.

Hatfield, Council of (England). Held to declare the orthodoxy of the English Church regarding Monothelite heresy; also accepted the decrees of the five first general councils, 17 Sept. 680.

Hatfield House (Herts., England). Old Palace built *c.* 1496 by Archbishop Morton, Henry VII's minister. Later it passed to the crown and James I gave it to Robert Cecil, Earl of Salisbury, in exchange for Theobalds. Substantial rebuilding was undertaken between 1607 and 1611, leaving the H. H. that can be seen today.

Hatteras Expedition. The Confederate forts at H. Inlet (U.S.A.), attacked by Federal army, under Gen. Butler, and a small fleet, 28 Aug. 1861; Confederates, under Maj. W. S. G. Andrewes, surrendered on following day.

Havana. *See* CUBA.

Havana, Declaration of, published by Pan-American Conference, 30 July 1940.

Havre, France. Originally *Havre de Notre-Dame de Grâce.* Founded by Louis XII, 1509; given to Queen Elizabeth by Huguenots, 1562; besieged and captured by Montmorency, 1563; bombarded unsuccessfully by English, 1678, 1694, 1759, 1794, 1795.

Hawaian or **Sandwich Islands.** Shipwrecked Spaniards settled here, 1527. Juan Gaetano made landfall, 1555. Rediscovered by Capt. Cook, 1778. Cook murdered by the natives here, 1779. Constitution granted by reigning king, 1840; independence guaranteed by Great Britain and France, 1844; revolution at, 1893, when reigning Queen Liliuokalani (*d.* 11 Nov. 1917) was deposed. Republic proclaimed, 1894; annexed to U.S.A., 1898. Territory of Hawaii constituted, 1900. First request to be made a State of the Union, 1903. Became a state of the Union, 1959.

Hawkers or **Pedlars,** Acts respecting, in Great Britain. Pedlars Act, 1871, by which they were placed under surveillance of the police; extended, 1881. H. Act, 1888, required a yearly licence.

Hayastan. *See* ARMENIA.

Haymarket Square Riot by anarchists in Chicago, 1886.

Hay-Pauncefote Treaty. Between Britain and U.S.A., 1901, to amend Clayton-Bulwer Treaty regarding canal scheme between Atlantic and Pacific.

Head Act (Ireland), 1465, permitting wholesale slaughter of the Irish.

Headmasters' Conference. *See* PUBLIC SCHOOLS.

Health Centre. The first H. C. to be set up under the National Health Service Act, 1946, was opened at Stoke Newington, 14 Oct. 1952.

Health, Ministry of. Established by Act of 1919, superseding the Local Government Board and the National Insurance Commissions. First minister appointed, 1920. Responsible for the central administration of the National Health Service since its inauguration in 1948.

Hearth or Chimney Money. A tax on every hearth introduced in England, 1663. Abolished, 1689.

Hearts of Steel (Ireland). Protestant tenants of Tyrone and Antrim formed this society, 1772.

Heavy Hydrogen (Deuterium). Discovered by Urey in 1931.

Heavy Water. Discovered by Urey in 1931.

Hebdomadal Board (Oxford). Instituted, 1631.

Hebdomadal Council, supplanted preceding, 1854.

Hebrides. Settled and Christianized by the Scots of Dalriada, sixth century. Immigration from Norway begun *c.* 800. H. subjugated by Harald Fairhair, King of Norway, *c.* 875, and granted to the Jarls of Sudreyar (Lords of the Isles, *q.v.*), who remained Norwegian vassals until 1266. Thereafter *see under* SCOTLAND.

Heidelberg, W. Germany. University founded by Elector Rupert I, 1385; reconstituted by Charles Frederick, Grand-Duke of Baden, 1803. H. plundered by Tilly, 1622, by the Swedes, 1633, and by the Imperialists, 1635; sacked by the French, 1688 and 1693.

Hejaz, Arabia. Sherif Hussein of Mecca proclaimed independent of Turkey, June 1916. Recognized as King of the H., 29 Oct., and enthroned, 4 Nov. After unsuccessful war with Ibn Sa'ud, King Hussein abdicated, 1924. After the Saudi capture of Mecca, 1925, Hejazi independence was extinguished. Annexation recognized by Britain, 1927. *See* SAUDI ARABIA.

Hejira. The name given to Mohammed's flight from Mecca to Medina, A.D. 622, *See* CALENDAR (5), p. xxiv.

Helicopter. First constructed, 1872; first successful model (built by Crocker and Hewitt) flown, 1918. Used extensively for air-sea rescue during and since World War II. Used by G.P.O. to collect and deliver mail in E. Anglia, 1948. H. freight service introduced in Britain, 1949. Experimental flights from outer London to Festival of Britain site made in summer of 1952 proved this site unsuitable for H. landing ground. First heliport opened in London, 1959.

Heligoland (Frisian island off mouth of Elbe) was a place of pilgrimage for the Angles and Frisians in heathen times, containing sacred groves in which were temples of Forseti and the mother goddess Herta. The former building was destroyed by St. Ludger, first Bishop of Münster (*d.* 809), after the Northumbrian missionary St. Willibrord (688–739) had made unsuccessful attempts to convert the heathen crowds who resorted thither, *c.* 690. Ceded to Britain, 1814. Exchanged for certain German E. African possessions, 1890. Fortress blown up by British, 1945–7. Displaced inhabitants demonstrated in favour of reoccupation, 1951. Formally returned to W. German Republic, 1 Mar. 1952.

Helium. Discovered in the sun by Sir Joseph Lockyer (1836–1920), 1868. Onnes (1853–1926) of Leyden succeeded in liquefying it, 1908.

Helsinki or **Helsingfors,** Finland. Founded by Gustavus I of Sweden in sixteenth century; made capital of Finland instead of Åbo, 1812; bombarded by allied fleets, Aug. 1855; Diet convoked by Alexander II, 1863; bombed by Soviet aircraft during Russo-Finnish wars, 1939–40 and 1941–4. *See* FINLAND.

Helvetic Confession. First H. C. drawn up, 1536, by the Swiss theologians assembled at Basel. H. C. at Zürich, 1566, formed basis of union between Calvin's party and the Zürich reformers.

Henley-on-Thames Regatta, first held, 1839.

Heralds' College of Arms. Founded by Richard III of England, 1483.

Herculaneum (It. Ercolano). Damaged by a severe earthquake, A.D. 63. H. was destroyed by the eruption of Vesuvius, 79, as described by Pliny the Younger (62–*c.* 120). Excavations on a small scale began, 1719, and were continued more ambitiously, 1927–30.

Hereford was a Mercian outpost in A.D. 600, but was retaken by the Welsh, who in 1055 destroyed a castle built by Ralph, the Norman earl installed by Edward the Confessor. Chartered as a city by Richard I, 1189. The cathedral, founded 680, was also destroyed, 1055, but a new Norman building was finished in 1140. Other portions built between 1220 and 1500. The Mappa Mundi in the cathedral library is the oldest extant example of its kind, executed *c.* 1300. *See also* THREE CHOIRS' FESTIVAL.

Heregeld ('Army Tax'), levied after the murder of Archbishop Alfheah in 1012, to pay Danish mercenaries who had deserted from Knut's army. Abolished, 1051.

Heresy, Laws concerning (England). In 1382 provided that sheriffs should arrest 'persons certified by the bishops to be heretics.' By the *De Haeretico comburendo* Act, 1401, the bishops themselves were empowered to punish H. This Act was enlarged, 1414. In 1533 an Act declared that offences against the See of Rome were not H. The Bill of the Six Articles, 1559, defined various heretical acts. Punishment of death for H. abolished, 1677.

Heretics. The following are some of the better known sects regarded as heretical by the Roman Catholic Church.

Gnostics. Appeared in first century A.D., but had pre-Christian origins. Among the principal exponents were Simon Magus (first century); Marcion, Basilides, and Valentinus (second century), Mani (third century).

*Montanists. c.*156 Montanus proclaimed himself prophet of the Spirit. Tertullian joined the sect *c.* 202, and it lingered on in Africa and the E. until *c.* 400.

Monarchians. (*a*) Dynamists (or Adoptionists) founded by Theodotus of Byzantium *c.* 190–200; died out in the middle of the third century; (*b*) Sabellians (or Patripassians or Medalists) arose *c.* 215 with the arrival of Sabellius in Rome. Condemned at Council of Nicaea, 325.

Donatists. Followers of Donatus, Bishop of Carthage, in opposition to Majorinus, 311; opposed by Pope Melchiades, 313, the Council of Arles, 314, and finally condemned by the Council of Carthage, 411. The sect disappeared after the Saracenic invasion of Africa.

Arians. Commenced at Alexandria in 313, when Arius (*c.* 250–336) quarrelled with the Bishop Peter. Condemned at Nicaea, 325, and lost its hold after the Second Council of Constantinople, 381. Its continuation among the barbarian kingdoms was of political rather than doctrinal significance.

Pelagians. Pelagius began to preach, *c.* 405, at Rome. Doctrine condemned at Councils of Carthage, 418, and Orange, 529. The Semi-Pelagians, founded by Cassian (*c.* 360–*c.* 435), Abbot of St. Victor; condemned at Orange, 529.

Nestorians. Nestorius (*d. c.* 451), a disciple of Theodore of Mopsuestia (*c.* 350–428) was condemned at the Councils of Ephesus, 431, and Chalcedon, 451. His doctrines already preached by Diodorus of Tarsus (*d. c.* 392). The sect survives in the E.

Monophysites. Principal teachers were: Eutyches (*c.* 378–*c.* 454), Dioscurus (*d.* 454) who was condemned at Chalcedon, 451, and Timothy Aelurus (*d.* 477). The teaching survives among the Copts and Syrian Jacobites.

Monothelites. The doctrine first appears *c.* 622 in an address delivered before the Emperor Heraclius by Paul, head of the Acephali; but the principal exponent was Sergius (*d.* 638), patriarch of Constantinople. Monothelitism was finally condemned at Constantinople, 680–1.

Modernism. Condemned by papal decree *Lamentabili*, 3–4 July 1907, and by the encyclical *Pascendi*, 8 Sept. 1907. Chief exponents: A. Loisy (1857–1940) in France and G. Tyrrell (1861–1909) in England.

Heritable Jurisdictions Act abolished hereditary jurisdictions in Scotland, 1746, as a result of the 'Forty-Five.'

Hermandad (Sp. brotherhood), a defensive alliance of Castilian and Aragonese cities, formed *c.* 1250, and reinforced, 1295. Ceased to exist *c.* 1550.

Hertogenbosch (Fr. **Bois-le-Duc**), Netherlands. Became a fortified town, 1184. Taken by the Duchy of Brabant, 1629. In French hands, 1794–1814.

Herzegovina. United with Bosnia (*q.v.*), 1326; formally ceded to Turkey, 1699, by Peace of Carlowitz; rebelled against Turkish rule, 1875; occupied by Austrians, Aug. 1878; formally annexed to Austria-Hungary, 7 Oct. 1908; became part of Yugoslavia, 1918.

Formed, with Bosnia, one of the federal republics of Yugoslavia, 1945.

Hesse, Germany. Became a principality, 1292. Divided into four, 1567. By 1622 there were three H.s, viz. H.-Darmstadt, H.-Homburg, H.-Cassel. The two latter annexed by Prussia, 1866. H.-Darmstadt became a republic, 1919. Its liberties were suppressed by Hitler, 1933. The province, reunited, formed part of American occupation zone in 1945, and subsequently a federal unit of the W. German Republic.

Hexham (Northumberland). The early English abbey church is on the site of the church of St. Andrew, which St. Wilfrid founded 673. It was the seat of a Northumbrian bishopric associated with the sub-kingdom of Bernicia (*q.v.*). The see finally merged into that of Lindisfarne, 821, and was absorbed by that of Durham. A district called Hexhamshire surrounding H. was under the jurisdiction of the Archbishop of York, as County Durham was of the Earl Bishop, until 1545.

Hibbert Lectures on theology founded, 1878.

High Church Party. Term first used in England *c.* 1703, and referred to the party who opposed the Dissenters (*see* NON-CONFORMISTS), and enforced the laws made against them.

High Commission, The Court of. Established by Queen Elizabeth I, 1559, to investigate ecclesiastical cases; abolished by the Long Parliament, July 1641. James II in 1686 revived it, but it was finally abolished by the Bill of Rights in Dec. 1689. A similar court existed in Scotland, 1608–38.

Highland Garb Act forbade the wearing of H. dress, 1746. *See* TARTAN.

High School, term denoting, in U.S.A., school maintained by the states from *c.* 1850. Similar institutions in Canada were first opened in Prince Edward Island, 1860; Nova Scotia, 1864; Quebec, 1870; Ontario, 1871; British Columbia, 1876; Manitoba, 1880–90; New Brunswick, 1884; Saskatchewan, 1907.

Hii. Alternative name for the island of Iona (*q.v.*).

Hindenburg Line. *See* WORLD WAR I.

Hire Purchase Act (Britain) came into force, 1 Jan. 1939, since which date various amending Acts have been passed.

Hiroshima, Japan. Atom bomb dropped at H., 6 Aug. 1945.

Hispaniola. Name given to the island that now contains Haiti and the Dominican Republic, by Columbus, on his discovery thereof, 1492. Santo Domingo, first European town in western hemisphere, founded by Bartholomew Columbus, 1496. Negroes, introduced 1505, soon displaced native population. Western portion, invaded by French buccaneers, ceded to France by Treaty of Ryswick, 1697; negroes of western portion rose against whites, 1791. Eastern portion ceded by Spain to France, 1795. Toussaint l'Ouverture quelled British invaders, 1798; crushed mulatto revolt, 1799; completed conquest of whole island, but was deported by the French, 1801. French had to leave, 1803. Eastern portion reoccupied by Spain, 1816–21; for later history, see HAITI and DOMINICAN REPUBLIC.

Hitler Youth (Hitlerjugend), official National Socialist (see NATIONAL SOCIAL-ISM) youth movement initiated in 1926 and made virtually compulsory for all 'Aryan' children in Germany, 1936.

Hittites. Invaded Asia Minor c. 2300 B.C. Rose to greatest power under Shubi-luliumash c. 1385 B.C. Fell c. 1170 B.C.

Hoare-Laval Pact, proposing for Abyssinia unacceptable terms as the price of peace with Italy, signed Dec. 1935. See ETHIOPIA.

Hohenstaufen, a famous German family who, as Holy Roman Emperors (q.v.), 1138–1254, conducted a controversy with the Papacy until the male line was extinguished by the murder of Conradin in 1268.

Hohenzollern. Name of the Swabian family which became successively Electors of Brandenburg (q.v.), kings of Prussia (q.v.), and German emperors. The regime of the senior branch ended in Germany, Nov. 1918, and the last H. to have ruled Prussia d. 4 June 1941, but the Sigmaringen branch continued on the throne of Rumania (q.v.) till abdication of King Michael, 30 Dec. 1947.

Holland House, Kensington, built, 1608–10, by Sir Walter Cope. Henry Richard Vassall Fox, third Baron H. (1773–1840), nephew of Charles James Fox, made H. H. a headquarters of the Whig Party from 1800 until his death. Owing to severe damage during World War II it has since been largely demolished.

Holland, Kingdom of. (Now properly **Kingdom of the Netherlands.**) Became a separate entity after the Spanish victory at Gembloux, 1578, had driven the Catholic Netherlanders to make terms and instituted the Union of Arras, 1579 (see BELGIUM). The Northern Protestant provinces repudiated Spanish sovereignty in the Act of Abjuration, 26 July 1581. William I of Orange assassinated, 1584. Jacob van Oldenbarneveldt in power, 1586–1618. Spanish naval defeat at Gibraltar, 1607. Truce of Antwerp, 1609. English threat to Dutch shipping by

passing the Navigation Act, 1651. Wars with Britain, 1653–4, 1666–7. Joins Triple Alliance against France, 1668. War against France and Britain, 1672–8. Joins the League of Augsburg against France, 1685. William of Orange becomes King of Britain, 1689. Treaty of Ryswick, 1697. Joins in War of Spanish Succession (q.v.) against France, 1701–13. Office of Stadhouder declared hereditary in the family of Orange, 1747. French Republican army marched into H., 1794; William V expelled, 15 Jan. 1795; declared a kingdom with Louis Bonaparte as king, 5 June 1806; abdication of Louis, 1 July 1810. United to France, 9 July 1810. House of Orange restored under William Frederick, 1 Dec. 1813; H. and Belgium united by Treaty of London, 14 June 1814; William placed on throne as King of the Netherlands, 15 Mar. 1815. Separated from Belgium (see BELGIUM), 12 July 1831; peace concluded between H. and Belgium, 19 Apr. 1839; William Frederick abdicated; William II succeeded, 1840; William III, 1849; Wilhelmina crowned (after queen-mother's regency), 1898. Struggles against Socialism became acute, 1903. The series of wars in Achin (E. Indies), spread over more than thirty years ended, 1904. Allied Powers imposed rigorous conditions on imports, and over 1,000,000 Belgians sought refuge, 1915–18. Universal suffrage and proportional representation introduced, 1917. Ex-Kaiser sought refuge, 10 Nov. 1918; French demand for his extradition refused, 10 Jan. 1920. Gold standard abandoned, 1936. Crown princess married Prince Bernhard of Lippe Biesterfeld, 7 Jan. 1937; heiress born (Princess Wilhelmina Beatrix), 31 Jan. 1938. Rhine customs agreement with France and Belgium, 3 Apr. 1939. German invasion, 10 May 1940. Dutch military surrender, 14 May 1940, but royal family fled to Britain. Ex-Kaiser William II d. at Doorn, 4 June 1941. General strike against Germans proclaimed as British airborne forces land at Arnhem, 17 Sept. 1944. British land at Walcheren, 1 Nov. 1944. Member of Benelux (q.v.), 1946. Queen Wilhelmina abdicated, 4 Sept. 1948. (She d. Nov. 1962). Member of N.A.T.O., 1949. Dispute with E. Indies nationalists settled by establishment of the Republic of Indonesia, 1950. Member of the European Coal and Steel Community, 1952; the Common Market (q.v.), 1958, and Euratom, 1958. Sporadic fighting with Indonesians over possession of Dutch (W.) New Guinea ended with an agreement signed on 15 Aug. 1962 between H. and Indonesia whereby the U.N. was to have control of W. New Guinea from Oct. 1962, and Indonesia to have complete ownership from 1 May 1963. *See* NEW GUINEA. Following is a list of sovereigns of the Netherlands:

William I [1] (*d.* 1843)	1815–1840
William II	1840–1849
William III	1849–1890
Wilhelmina	1890–1948
Juliana (*b.* 1909)	1948–

[1] 'I' means first *king*. He would have been the sixth Stadhouder of that name.

Holloway. Prison for women built, 1849–51.

Holy Alliance. Signed at Paris, 26 Sept. 1815, between the rulers of Russia, Prussia, and Austria. It was offered for signature to the other powers, and all except Great Britain signed.

Holy Island (Lindisfarne). St. Aidan (*d.* 651) founded a priory, 635, which was destroyed, 793 (*see* VIKING AGE). Lindisfarne with Hexham (*q.v.*) was one of the two episcopal sees associated with Bernicia (*q.v.*) under the house of Bamburgh. St. Oswald's head was buried here after he had been killed in action against the pagan Mercians, 642. After about ninety years of actual harassing, or the threat of it, by Scandinavian pirates (*see* VIKING AGE) the first monastery was abandoned in 883 (*see* DURHAM). Benedictines from Durham re-established a cell on H. I., 1082.

Holy Leagues, The. 1. Formed in 1511 between Pope Julius II, the Emperor Maximilian I, Henry VIII of England, and Ferdinand, King of Aragon, to crush France; dissolved, 1513. 2. Formed by Pope Clement VII in 1526 against the Emperor Charles V; France, Venice, and Milan were also in the league. 3. Formed by Pope Pius V, Spain, and Venice against the Turks, 1570. 4. Formed by the Catholic party against the Huguenots in 1576, also known as the Catholic League. 5. Formed by Catholic princes of Germany under Maximilian of Bavaria in 1609 as a counterblast to Protestant Union of 1608. 6. Formed by Pope Innocent XI, the Emperor, Poland, Venice, and Russia, against the Turks in 1684.

'Holy Maid of Kent.' Elizabeth Barton, during Henry VIII's reign. Urged on by the Catholics she prophesied the violent death of the king if he married Anne Boleyn. She and her confederates executed, 1534.

Holy Places. *See* CRUSADES. Dispute over their custody ultimately caused war in Crimea (*q.v.*), 1854.

Holy Roman Emperors. (Rivals and Anti-Caesars in *italics*)

Charles I (Charlemagne)	800–814
Louis I (the Pious)	814–840
Lothar I	840–855
Louis II (in Italy)	855–875
Charles II (the Bald)	875–881
Charles III (the Fat)	882–887
Guido (in Italy)	887–894
Lambert (in Italy)	894–896
Arnulf	896–899
Louis the Child	899–901
Louis III of Provence (in Italy)	901–911
Conrad I	911–915
Berengar (in Italy)	915–918

Saxons

Henry I (the Fowler)	918–936
Otto I. King of the E. Franks	936–962
H. R. Emperor	963–973
Otto II	973–983
Otto III	983–1002
Henry II (the Saint)	1002–1024

Salians

Conrad II (the Salic)	1024–1037
Henry III (the Black)	1037–1056
Henry IV	1056–1106
Rudolf of Swabia	1077–1081
Hermann of Luxemburg	1081–1093
Conrad of Franconia	1093–1106
Henry V	1106–1125
Lothar II	1125–1138

Hohenstaufen

Conrad III	1138–1152
Frederick I (Barbarossa)	1152–1190
Henry VI	1190–1197
Philip ⎫ as rivals Otto IV ⎭	1197–1208
Otto IV, alone	1208–1212
Frederick II	1212–1250
Henry Raspe ⎱	1246–1247
William of Holland ⎰	1247–1256
Conrad IV	1250–1254
Interregnum	1254–1257
Richard of Cornwall ⎱ *Alfonso of Castile* ⎰	1257–1272
Rudolf I of Hapsburg	1273–1291
Adolf of Nassau	1292–1298
Albert I of Hapsburg	1298–1308
Henry VII of Luxemburg	1308–1313
Louis IV of Bavaria	1314–1347
Frederick of Austria	1314
Charles IV of Luxemburg	1347–1378
Günther of Schwartzburg	1347
Wenzel of Luxemburg	1378–1400
Rupert of the Palatinate	1400–1410
Sigismund of Luxemburg	1410–1437
Jobst of Moravia	1410

Hapsburgs

Albert II	1438–1440
Frederick III	1440–1493
Maximilian I	1493–1519
Charles V	1519–1558
	(Abdicated 25 Oct.)
Ferdinand I	1558–1564

Maximilian II	1564–1576
Rudolf II	1576–1612
Matthias	1612–1619
Ferdinand II	1619–1637
Ferdinand III	1637–1657
Leopold I	1658–1705
Joseph I	1705–1711
Charles VI	1711–1740
Charles VII of Bavaria	1742–1745
Francis I of Lorraine	1745–1765
Joseph II	1765–1790
Leopold II	1790–1792
Francis II	1792–1806
	(Abdicated)

NOTE. Francis I was elected as husband of Maria Theresa of Austria because no woman had ever held the throne. Charles VII is therefore the only true exception to the permanent Hapsburg tenure beginning in 1438.

Ferdinand I and his successors were never crowned by the Pope.

Holy Roman Empire. Leo III crowns Charlemagne Roman Emperor at Rome, 25 Dec. 800. Civil war, 840, leads to Partition of Verdun, 843. Deposition of Charles the Fat, 887. Henry the Fowler defeats the Magyars at battle of the Unstrut, 933. Magyars finally defeated by Otto I on the Lech, 955. Otto I crowned emperor of the H. R. E. of the German nation by John XII, 963. Henry III reforms Papacy at Synod of Sutri, 1046. Choice of popes transferred from H. R. Emperor to the cardinals, 1059. Hildebrand (Gregory VII) denounces Lay Investiture (q.v.), 1075. Henry IV submits to Gregory VII at Canossa, 1077. War of Investiture, 1077–1122. Concordat of Worms (Investiture Compromise), 1122. Elective principle asserted at election of Lothar, 1125. Frederick Barbarossa begins war with Lombard cities, 1158. Defeated at battle of Legnano, 1176. Peace of Constance, 1183. Frederick II leaves Sicily for his Peaceful Crusade, 1228. Papal deposition of Frederick II at Council of Lyons, 1245. Hohenstaufen defeat and destruction battle of Tagliacozzo, 1268. Election of Rudolf of Hapsburg, 1273. He conquers Austria from Bohemia, battle of the Marchfeld, 1278. First Union of Swiss Cantons, 1307. Battle of Morgarten, 1315. Charles IV establishes Electoral Constitution of the H. R. E. by the Golden Bull, 1356. John Hus burned by Council of Constance, 1415. Bohemian (Hussite) War, 1419–36, ends with Compact of Iglan, 1436. Turkish raids begin after battle of Kossovo, 1448. Maximilian fails to introduce effective reforms at Diets of Worms, 1495. Augsburg, 1500. After

battle of Mohacs (1526) Turks besiege Vienna, 1529. Charles V rejects confession of Augsburg, 1530. Formation of League of Schmalkalden (Protestant), 1530. Truce of Frankfort, 1539. Protestant defeat at battle of Mühlberg, 1547. Interim of Augsburg, 1548. Peace of Augsburg, 1555. War of Dutch Liberation begins, 1572. Union of Utrecht, 1579. Counter Reformation, 1551–1620. Defenestration of Prague, 1618. Thirty Years War, 1618–48. Wallenstein becomes Imperial C.-in-C., 1625. Dismissed, 1630. Tilly sacks Magdeburg, 1631. Defeated by Swedes at battle of the Breitenfeld, 1631. Wallenstein defeated and Gustavus Adolphus of Sweden killed at battle of Lützen, 1632. Wallenstein murdered, 1634. Peace of Westphalia (q.v.), 1648. Repulse of the Turks from Vienna, 1683. War of Spanish Succession (q.v.), 1701–14. Treaty of Utrecht, 1713. Treaty of Rastatt, 1714. Pragmatic Sanction guaranteed by Prussia, 1728. War of Austrian Succession, 1740–2. Second Silesian War, 1744–5. Peace of Aix-la-Chapelle (q.v.), 1748. Seven Years War (q.v.), 1756–63. Napoleon forms Rhenish Confederation, 12 July 1806. Francis renounces crown of H. R. E., 6 Aug. 1806. See AUSTRIA.

Holyrood Abbey and Palace (Edinburgh). Abbey founded, 1128, by David I of Scotland. The palace was built in 1501 by James IV of Scotland; destroyed by English, 1544, but immediately rebuilt; Rizzio murdered at, 1566; burned by Cromwell's troops, 1650; rebuilt by Charles II, 1670–9. The monastery was dissolved at the Reformation, and the chapel became the parish church until James II made it a chapel royal (1687). H. has been in ruins since 1768.

Home Guard came into being as a voluntary force, May 1940, some local bands having been formed spontaneously before Eden's broadcast call for volunteers on 14 May. Members reached their peak—about two million men in a thousand battalions and A.A. batteries—about June 1943. The force stood down, 1 Nov. 1944, and was disbanded, 31 Dec. 1945. Re-formed, Jan. 1952. Placed on a reserve basis, 1956. All activities suspended, 1957. See also VOLKSSTURM.

Home Rule. See IRELAND.

Homestead Act. 1. New Zealand, passed 1885, providing land for emigrants free of charge. 2. Western Australia, similar Act, 1893.

Homestead Act (U.S.A.). Passed by Congress, 1862, by which every U.S. citizen of the age of 21 years was entitled to claim a certain portion of unappropriated land.

Homicide Act, 21 Mar. 1957. Established categories of capital and non-capital murder.

'Homilies, Book of.' The Convocation of 1542 decided to publish it for the guidance of preachers. First published, 1547; reprinted, 1560. Second book published, 1563.

Homs (Hims), Syria, the Roman city of Emesa, was taken by the Saracens, A.D. 636, and by the Crusaders, 1098. Ibrahim Pasha defeated the Turks at, 1832. *See* FIRST CRUSADE.

Honduras, republic of Central America. Discovered by Columbus, 1502. First settlements, 1524 (Spanish). Independent of Spain, 1821. Independent of the Federation of Central America, 1838. Frequent wars with other states till 1876, and several civil wars, notably in 1883 and 1903. Pan-American Highway completed, 1943. New constitution came into force, 1957.

Honduras, British. *See* BRITISH HONDURAS.

Hong Kong, China. Occupied by British, 1841. Ceded to Britain at Treaty of Nanking, 1842. Kowloon added, 1860. Chinese Government grant 99-year lease of other mainland areas, 1898. University opened, 1912. Bombed by Japanese, 21 Feb. 1939. Captured by Japanese, 7–25 Dec. 1941. Liberated, 30 Aug. 1945. Considerable influx of refugees from China, from 1950 onwards, resulted in refugees being turned back at border by British, 1961–2. Typhoon, 3 Aug.–1 Sept. 1962, caused severe damage and over 100 fatal casualties.

Honourable Artillery Company (H.A.C.). Founded 1537 in London as a guild for Trained Band instructors. In 1638 some members of it migrated to America and founded the Ancient and H. A. C. of Boston (Mass.).

Hops. First introduced from Netherlands into England c. 1525. Prohibited temporarily, 1528, because certain physicians thought them harmful.

Horse Guards, Royal. Present regiment raised by Earl of Oxford in 1661, out of the remains of Cromwell's New Model. Their headquarters, in Whitehall, London, erected, 1758.

Hospitallers, Knights. *See* MALTA, KNIGHTS OF.

Houghers. Irish rebels, 1711–13. When they reappeared a special Act was passed against them, 1784.

Hovercraft. First public service began between Rhyl and Wallasey, 20 July 1962.

Hubertusburg, Treaty of, 1763, between Prussia and Austria at end of Seven Years War. By it the Empress Maria Theresa finally ceded Silesia to Frederick the Great.

Hudson Bay Territory or Prince Rupert's Land, NW. America. Discovered by Cabot, 1498; revisited and explored by Hudson, 1610; Hudson's Bay Co. formed, 1670; English factories at captured by French, 1685; restored by Peace of Utrecht, 1713; part of territory became British Columbia (*q.v.*), remainder was purchased by Canada, 1858; formal transfer to the Dominion, 19 Nov. 1869. Most of the H. B. T. has formed part of the North-West Territories (*q.v.*) since 1918.

Huguenots. The name originated between 1510 and 1535 at Geneva, when those in favour of an alliance with Freiburg were called *Eidgenossen* ('partakers of an oath'), a popular French adaptation having introduced association with the personal name Hugues. They joined themselves with the Bernese, who had declared for the reformed religion. The name gradually came to be attached to the French Protestants. *See* BARTHOLOMEW, MASSACRE OF ST., and FRANCE.

Hull (Kingston-upon-), England. Chartered by Edward I, 1299. Further charter, 1381. Made a county, 1440. Defences built, 1541. Manor granted, 1552. Incorporated, 1576. New charter, 1688. Made a county borough, 1888. University college founded, 1927; reconstituted as the University of Hull, 1954.

Human Rights. *See* DECLARATION OF HUMAN RIGHTS.

Humane Society, Royal, founded, 1774.

Humble Petition and Advice. The second paper constitution of the English Protectorate, 1657. It arranged for future government in the event of the death of Cromwell. The petition collapsed on the dissolution of Parliament by Cromwell in 1658.

Hundred Associates, The. Cardinal Richelieu, in 1627, annulled a charter of the Trading Co. of New France in America belonging to a family of Huguenots, and organized a company known as the H. A., to drive out the Huguenots and colonize the district.

Hundred Years War, 1338–1453. France assists Scotland against England, 1334. All Englishmen in Flanders arrested, 1336. Rebellion of Jacob van Artevelde of Ghent, 1338. Edward III renews claim to the French crown, 1340. Naval battle of Sluys, 1340. English sack Poitiers, win battle of Crécy and Neville's Cross, 1346; capture Calais, 1347. Black Death, 1347–50. Battle of Poitiers, 1356. The *Jacquerie*, 1358. Peace of Brétigny, 8 May 1360. War resumed, 1369. English driven out of most of France by Bertrand de Guesclin, 1369–1375. Peasants revolt in England, 1381. Duke of Orleans murdered by Burgundy, 1407. England resumes war again, 1415. Harfleur captured and battle of Agincourt, 1415. Burgundy murdered, 1419. Treaty of Troyes, 1420. Joan of Arc relieves Orleans, May 1429. Dauphin crowned at Rheims, 1430. Joan of Arc burnt, 28 May 1431. Burgundy changes sides at Treaty of Arras, 1435. *Ordonnance sur la Gendarmerie*, 1439. *La Praguerie*, 1439–43. Battle of Formigny, 1450. English driven out except at Calais by 1453.

Hungarian Literature. The following is a list of prominent Hungarian authors not now living:

Ady, Endve, 1871–1915, poet.
Arany, Janos, 1817–82, poet.
Babits, Mihaly, 1883–1941, poét.
Balassi, Balint, 1554–94, poet.
Bessenyei, György, 1747–1811, dramatist.
Csiky, Gregor, 1842–91, dramatist.
Döbrentei, Gabor, 1786–1851, philologist.
Eötvös, Baron József, 1813–71, poet.
Fejer, György, 1766–1852, historian.
Jókai, Maurus, 1825–1904, novelist.
Jozsef, Attila, 1906–37, poet.
Kazinczy, Ferenc, 1759–1831, literary reformer and critic.
Kemény, Baron Zsigmund, 1816–75, novelist.
Kisfaludy, Károly, 1788–1830, poet and dramatist.
Kosztolanyi, Dezsö, 1885–1939, poet.
Miksáth, Kálmán, 1847–1910, novelist.
Molnar, Ferenc, 1878–1952, dramatist.
Petőfi, Sandor, 1823–49, poet.
Szigligeti, Ede (József Szatmáry), 1814–1878, dramatist.
Vörösmarty, Mihály, 1800–55, poet and dramatist.

Hungary. The Hungarians or Magyars crossed the Carpathians, A.D. 889. Were driven out of Germany after battle of Unstrut, 933, by Henry the Fowler. Last invasion of Germany defeated by Otto I at the Lech, 955. Converted by King Stephen to Christianity, 1000. Stephen II abdicates, 1131. Invaded by Mongols, 1226. Turkish slave raids begin after their capture of Adrianople, 1361. Defeat of Christian confederacy by Turks at the first battle of Kossovo, 1389, and of crusades at Nicopolis, 1396. Rise of John Hunyadi, 1437. His victory at the Haemus, 1444. Defeated at Varna, 1444. Decisive defeat by Turks at second battle of Kossovo, 1448. Election of Matthias Corvinus to the throne, 1458. Invades Bohemia, 1468. Seizes Vienna, 1485. Conquest of H. at battle of Mohacs, 1526. Treaty of Torok, 1606.

Turks repulsed at second siege of Vienna, 1683. Prince Eugene reconquers H., 1683–99. Peace of Carlowitz, 1699. Maria Theresa appeals to the Hungarians against Prussia, 1741. Rebellion against Hapsburg rule, 1848. Defeated by Jellaçic at battle of Schwechat, 30 Oct. 1848. Capitulation of Villagos, 14 Aug. 1849. The *Ausgleich*, Feb. 1867. (For events during the war of 1914–18 *see* WORLD WAR I.) Declared a republic, 1918; succeeded by Bela Kun's Communist dictatorship, Mar. 1919. Invaded by Rumania, Soviet gave place first to Socialist Government under Peidel and then to presidency of Archduke Joseph, Aug. 1919; Archduke Joseph resigned and Admiral Horthy became governor, 1920; ex-King Karl tried to regain throne, Mar. 1921, but was removed by Allies, Oct. 1921. 'Numerus clausus' law against Jews, 1925. French banknote forgery scandal, 1925–6. Claimed zones in Czechoslovakia (Ruthenia and S. Slovakia), and occupied them in own time, Oct. 1938.

1939: Russia severed diplomatic relations in view of H.'s. entry into Anti-Comintern Pact, 2 Feb.; National-Socialist Party suppressed, 24 Feb.; fighting on Slovakian border, 24–25 Mar.; agreement with Slovakia reached, 31 Mar.; withdrawal from League of Nations, 11 Apr.; Count Teleki concluded negotiations with Germany in Berlin, 2 May; Jewish Restrictions Bill passed, 3 May; Government victory at elections, 28–29 May; frontier clashes with Rumania, July–Aug.; diplomatic relations with Russia resumed, 24 Sept.; Count Csaky demanded revision of Treaty of Trianon, 29 Nov.

1940: Cession by Rumania of half Transylvania by 'Vienna Award,' 30 Aug.; signed Axis Pact, 20 Nov.; friendship pact with Yugoslavia, 12 Dec.

1941: Death of Count Csaky, 25 Jan.; Laszlo Bardossy appointed Foreign Minister, 15 Feb.; suicide of Count Teleki, Bardossy became Premier, 3 Apr.; diplomatic relations with Britain broken off, 8 Apr.; invasion of Yugloslavia, 11 Apr.; war declared on Russia, 27 June (*see* WORLD WAR II).

1946: Republic proclaimed, 1 Feb.

1947: Communists with Soviet assistance destroy Smallholders' Party, Feb.; ratification of peace treaty, June; came into force, 15 Sept.

1948: President Tildy resigns, Aug.; successor, Szakasits—resigns, 1950.

1949: Cardinal Mindszenty sentenced to life imprisonment; beginning of systematic persecution of the Roman Catholic church in H.

1950: E. Sanders, British subject, arrested, November, sentenced at Budapest to 15 years for espionage, Feb. 1950; released, Aug. 1953. Dissolution of large monasteries and convents, Sept.

1953: Imre Nagy replaced Matyas Rakosi as Prime Minister, 4 July; this indicated some liberalization of government policy.

1955: Nagy replaced by Hegedus, and pressure again applied, Apr.

1956: Budapest mob demanded withdrawal of Russian troops from H. and return of Nagy, 23 Oct. Nagy became Premier, 24 Oct.: Reformed government, including non-Communists in it. Mindszenty released. H. renounced the Warsaw Pact, 1 Nov. Russian troops advanced to crush the rebels, 4 Nov. Budapest heavily bombed by Russian planes. Nagy replaced by pro-Soviet Kadar, and took refuge in Yugoslav Embassy, but was subsequently abducted by the Russians. Mindszenty sought asylum in U.S. Embassy. Revolt over by mid Nov. and thousands of refugees fled to W. Europe.

1957–8: Policy of severe repression followed. Many executions. Announcement that Nagy had been executed for 'high treason,' June 1958. Khruschev visited H., April 1958.

1959: Law of 6 Apr. gave State greater control over Church.

1960–3: Increasing liberalization noted. In Sept. 1961 there was a government reshuffle and Kadar became Premier (instead of Münnich) as well as party leader. Amnesty for many political prisoners, 1962. Release of several Catholic church leaders.

Huns. A Turanian group of tribes which invaded Europe in fourth and fifth centuries, and were defeated at battle of Châlons, 451. After this they were probably absorbed in other nations moving in from the E.

Hussars, light cavalry of Hungarian origin, first raised by Matthias I (Corvinus), 1458. For the dates of conversion of British Light Dragoon regiments to H., see under REGIMENTS OF THE BRITISH ARMY.

Hussites. The followers of John Hus (b. c. 1373) who was burned as a heretic by the Council of Constance, July 1415. Led by Ziska they carried out the 'Defenestration of Neustadt,' 1419, and took up arms to prevent Catholic reconquest. Establishment of Tabor, 1420, and the split between the Taborites and the Calixtines. Death of Ziska, 1424. Rise of Procopius the Great, 1425. Victory over Cesarini at battle of Tauss, Aug. 1431. Annihilation of Taborites by

Calixtines at battle of Lipan, 1434. Maintained a position of semi-independence until battle of the White Mountain, 1620.

Hyde Park (London). Originally belonging to Westminster Abbey it became crown property, 1536. Opened to public, 1670. Serpentine formed, 1730–3. Underground car park for 1,100 cars opened, 15 Oct. 1962.

Hyderabad, India. At the conquest of the Deccan by Aurungzebe, 1687, H. became the residence of the governor of the Deccan. By 1748 this official under the title of the Nizam of H. had made himself virtually independent of the Moguls. He ceded the Circars to the French, 1755. Defeated by Marathas at battle of Kurdla, 1795. Accepted permanent British alliance. 1799. Acquired Berar from the Marathas, 1804. Ceded Berar to British so that its revenues could support the H. contingent in British Army, 1853. Loyal to Britain, 1857; new treaty, 1860. At division of India, 15 Aug. 1947, delayed accession. Indian troops entered the State and set up military government, Sept. Standstill agreement with India, Nov. 1947. Nizam appeals to the United Nations, Aug. 1948. On 1 Dec. 1949 the State acceded to the Indian Union. Redrawing of state boundaries in 1956 meant that H. was partitioned between various units, and the Nizam became a private Indian citizen.

Hydro-electric Power. First Hydro-electric station in the British Isles begun in 1883, in N. Ireland.

Hydrogen. Discovered by Paracelsus c. 1500; experiments by Boyle, 1672; proved to be an element by Cavendish, 1766; presence in water was discovered by Watt and Cavendish, 1781.

Hydrogen Bomb. U.S. Atomic Energy Commission announced on 16 Nov. 1952 that tests involving 'thermo-nuclear weapons' had taken place on Eniwetok Atoll, Marshall Islands. This was generally taken to mean that explosions felt in the Pacific area 1–4 Nov. had been caused by the detonation of a H. B. Marshal Voroshilov claimed Russia had H. B., Nov. 1953. H. B. first officially detonated by U.S.A. in the Marshall Islands on 1 Mar. 1954. Russia detonated her first H. B. in Sept. 1954. U.S.A. exploded a H. B. 200 miles above Johnston Island, in the Pacific, on 9 July 1962, and this was subsequently admitted to have caused a new radiation belt around the earth.

Hypnotism, first investigated in modern times by Paracelsus (1493–1541). Used therapeutically by Mesmer, 1774 (whence mesmerize). Brought into disrepute by

Cagliostro (1743–95). The word H. was coined by Dr. Braid of Manchester, 1841.

Hythe, one of the original *Cinque Ports* (*q.v.*) under Edward the Confessor (1042–1066), lost its maritime importance with the silting up of the River Leman, whose estuary once extended from H. to Lympne. Its ancient liberties were conferred by King John, 1205. The infantry of Picton's Light Division, which gained distinction in the Peninsular War, was largely trained here *c.* 1809, at which time the Royal Military Canal from H. to Rye was cut. The Small Arms School, as it was first called in 1919, was founded at H. as the School of Musketry, 1853.

I

Ice Hockey. Canada's national sport. Has developed rapidly since the formulation of rules in 1879. Played increasingly in Britain since 1927.

Iceland. Discovered by Irishmen at the beginning of ninth century. Colonized by Norwegians *c.* 870–90. (*See* VIKING AGE.) First Parliament (*Althing*), 930. Christianity officially adopted, 1000. Inhabitants acknowledged sovereignty of Norway, 1262–4. United to Denmark with Norway, 1380; at separation of Norway and Denmark in 1814 became part of Denmark. New constitution, 1874; modified, 1903; women enfranchized, 1915. Danish-Icelandic Federal Constitution, making both I. and Denmark free and independent states under the same sovereign, 1 Dec. 1918. Under Acts passed 1928, this arrangement to be terminable in 1943 if notice given by either Government not later than 1940. Occupied by British troops, 10 May 1940. As a result of separation from Denmark crown prerogatives assumed by the *Althing*, 16 May 1941. Sveinn Björnsson elected Regent of, 17 June 1941. American troops landed, July 1941. Declared a republic and Sveinn Björnsson elected president, 17 June 1944. Signed North Atlantic Treaty (*q.v.*) 1949, and under its provisions agreed to U.S. forces being stationed in I., 30 June 1958. The Icelandic Government declared that I.'s fishery limits were to be extended from four to twelve miles as from 11 Sept. 1953. This caused a prolonged dispute with Britain, which ended on 11 Mar. 1961, when Britain withdrew her objections to the twelve-mile limit.

Presidents of Iceland since 1944:

Sveinn Björnsson   1944–1952
Asgeir Asgeirsson   1952–

Icelandic Language and Literature. At the time of the Settlement (*see above*) W. Norse, the language of Norway and its overseas dependencies, had only just begun to differentiate itself from other Scandinavian dialects, and by the end of what philologists call the Viking Norse period (1100) the difference between it and E. Norse (Danish and Swedish) was marked, but not to the point of unintelligibility, and for practical purposes the language of Norway, Iceland, Faeroe, Orkney, Shetland, Greenland, a large part of the Hebrides and certain smaller areas in England, Scotland, and Ireland was identical down to the thirteenth century. The succeeding centuries down to 1500 are the period known as Literary Norse, because the oldest surviving MSS. in Scandinavian languages were written then, and mostly in Iceland, so that both Literary Norse and Viking Norse are also called Old I., or, according to a different system of terminology, Old (W.) Norse. During this period Norwegian became differentiated from I. and the insular dialects of the N. Atlantic, and Scandinavians in the British Isles, whether W. Norse or Danish, fused their language with Old English, or were linguistically submerged by the Gaels. But as long as Norway remained a separate political unit, and as long as minor Scandinavian princes maintained themselves in the British Isles (say until 1263), the acknowledged masters of the arts of prose narrative and of poetry over the whole area were Icelanders, and by *c.* 1000 it was exceptional to find a court-poet (Skald) who was not a native of that republic. With few exceptions the authors of the greater I. sagas are unknown, so that most of the names to whom definite works, extant or lost, can be ascribed are those of Skalds: and though some of the earlier of these were Norwegians, all have here been included under I. When during the later Middle Ages the influence of continental, and particularly of French, styles and schools became predominant in the Scandinavian peninsula, biography, history, and elaborate epigrammatic verse in the native tradition were still practised in Iceland itself. The following are some Old I. authors:

Ari Thorgilsson, ?–1148, historian, poet, and editor.
Arnor Jarlaskald, *d.* 1067?, poet.
Egil Skallagrimsson, 900–83, poet.
Einar Fostri, *fl.* 1430.
Einar Gilsson, *fl.* 1350.
Einar Jinglescale (Skalaglamm), *fl.* 1130–1160, poet.
Eysteinn Asgrimsson, *fl.* 1350.
Eyvind Finnson, the Plagiarist (Skaldaspillar), *fl.* 935–70, poet.
Gunnlaug Serpentstongue (Ormstungu), *fl. c.* 991, poet.
Halldor Skvaldri, *fl.* 1110.

Hallfred Vandradaskald, *fl.* 995–1000, poet.

Jon Arason, 1484–1551, poet and historian.

Kormak Ogmundsson, 937–65, poet.

Saemundr Jonsson, 1056–1133, poet and editor.

Sighvat Thordarson, *fl.* 1015–30, poet.

Snorri Sturluson, 1179–1242, historian.

Stuf Thordarson, *fl.* 1050.

Sturla Thordarson, 1214–84, poet.

Thjodolf of Kvin, *fl.* 870, poet.

Thorarin Praisetongue (Loftungu), *fl.* 1040, poet.

Thorarin Stuttfeldr, *fl.* 1110.

Thord Sigvaldi's Skald, *fl.* 1000–30, poet.

Thormod Kolbrunarskald, ?–1030, poet.

The 'modern' period of I. L. and L. is not easily defined owing to the slow rate and steadiness with which the language evolves and the unbroken continuity of the literary tradition. For purposes of convenience it may be possible to say that modern I. letters begin with the Reformation and the introduction of the printing-press, as in the rest of Northern Europe, but neither printing nor Protestantism made that impression on the intellectual life of the country which is apparent in Britain or in the other Scandinavian lands: partly because the art of copying had been sedulously practised on a large scale for many centuries, and a large literate laity and a vernacular devotional literature already existed. But the last of the Catholic bishops of Holar, Jon Arason (*see above*), may be regarded as also the last of the older poets in the skaldic tradition, and it was he who in 1525 brought the first printing-press to Iceland. It was not used to produce the first vernacular version of the New Testament (which was printed at Copenhagen in 1540), but in 1584 this press at Holar printed the first I. edition of the entire Bible. The following is a list of modern I. authors not now living:

Andresdottir, Herdis, ?–1939, poet.

Andresdottir, Olina, ?–1935, poet.

Benediktsson, Einar, 1864–1940, poet.

Bjarklind, Unnr, ?–1946, novelist.

Bjarnason, Johann, 1866–1945, poet.

Breithfjörth, Sigurthr, 1798–1846, poet.

Briem, Valdimar, 1848–1930, poet.

Egilsson, Sveinbjörn, 1791–1852, translator.

Einarsson, Eindridi, 1851–1939, playwright.

Einarsson, Halfdan, 1732–85, historian.

Erlingsson, Thorsteinn, 1858–1914, poet.

Frithjonsson, Guthmundr, 1869–1944, poet and novelist.

Gislason, Thorsteinn, ?–1938, poet.

Gröndal, Benedikt, 1826–1907, poet.

Guthmundsson, Guthmundr, ?–1919, poet.

Hallgrimsson, Jonas, 1807–45, poet and novelist.

Hofstein, Hannes, 1861–1922, poet.

Jochumsson, Matthias, 1835–1920, poet and translator.

Jonasson, Jonas, 1856–1918, novelist.

Jónsson, Finnr, 1858–1934, philologist.

Jonsson, Hjalmar, 1796–1875, poet.

Jónsson frá Vogi, Bjarni, ?–1927, poet.

Kamban, Guthmundr, 1888–1945, novelist and playwright.

Kvaran, Einar, 1859–1938, novelist.

Magnússon, Guthmundr ('Jon Trausti') 1873–1918, novelist and poet.

Magnússon, Jon, ?–1944, poet.

Olafsson, Eggert, 1726–68, poet.

Olafsson, Pál, 1827–1905, poet.

Olafsson, Stefan, 1620–88, poet.

Pálsson, Gestr, 1852–91, novelist.

Pálsson, Gunnar, 1714–68, poet.

Petursson, Hallgrimr, 1614–74, hymnographer.

Sigurjonsson, Johann, 1880–1919, playwright.

Sigurthardottir, Olöf, ?–1933, poet.

Sigurthsson frá Arnaholti, Sigurthur ?–1939, poet.

Stefánsson, Jon, 1851–1915, novelist.

Stefánsson, Stefán, 1853–1927, poet.

Sveinsson, Brynjolfr, *fl.* 1643.

Thomsen, Grimr, 1820–1906, poet.

Thorarinsson, Bjarni, 1786–1841, poet.

Thorlaksson, Jon, 1743–1819, translator.

Thoroddsson, Jon. 1819–68, poet.

Thorsteinsson, Steingrimr, 1831–1913, poet.

Vidalin, Paul Jónsson, 1666–1727, poet.

Vigfusson, Guthbrandr, 1828–89, historian and philologist.

Iceni revolted under Boudicca, A.D. 61.

'Ich Dien.' Motto of John of Luxemburg, King of Bohemia, found on his helmet after the battle of Crécy, 26 Aug. 1346. Thereupon adopted as the motto of the Prince of Wales by the Black Prince.

Icolumcille. *See* IONA.

Iconoclasts (Gk. 'Image Breakers'). Name given in the eighth century to those who opposed the use of images in the Church. The Emperor Leo the Isaurian issued edicts against images in A.D. 726 and 730. Images allowed in churches, 787. Images restored in the E., 843.

Idaho. State of the U.S.A. Territory formed, 1863; present limits defined, 1868; state admitted to Union, 1890.

Identity Cards (Britain). Issued 30 Sept. 1939 and following days. Abolished, Apr. 1952.

Ido, adapted from Esperanto, 1907.

Iglau, Treaty of, 1436, ended the war of the Emperor Sigismund against Hussites (*q.v.*).

Ijsselmeer. Remnant of Zuider Zee formed by irruption of N. Sea through W. Frisian coastline in thirteenth century. Bill for reclamation became law, 1918. Work begun, 1923. Wieringer Polder completed, 1930; wrecked, 1945; restored, 1946. NE. Polder completed, 1942; E. Flevoland, 1957.

Illinois, U.S.A. Explored by Jacques Marquette, Jesuit missionary, and Louis Joliet, representing the Government of New France, 1673. By treaty passed to English, 1763, ceded to U.S.A., 1783; admitted into the Union as a state, 3 Dec. 1818. Present constitution adopted, 1870.

Illyria (more properly **Illyricum**). Greek colonies on coast, sixth century B.C. Country except Dalmatia annexed by Romans, 168 B.C. Dalmatia also annexed, A.D. 9. At partition of empire fell to Byzantium, 379. The Napoleonic 'Kingdom of I.' formed 1809 and attached to 'Kingdom of Italy'; ceded to Austria, 1814.

'Imitatio Christi' (*The Imitation of Christ*). Generally held to be the work of Thomas à Kempis (c. 1379–1471). First printed at Augsburg c. 1471. Translated into English at least as early as 1438 (MS. now in Magdalen College, Oxford).

Immaculate Conception. Established as an article of the Roman Catholic faith by the bull *Ineffabilis Deus*, 8 Dec. 1854.

Impeachment. The first recorded exercise of the power was in 1376, when an attack was made on Richard Lyons and Lord Latimer by the 'Good Parliament.' Fell into disuse owing to the more general employment of Acts of Attainder until the I. of Sir Giles Mompesson, 1620. By Act of Settlement, 1701, a royal pardon cannot be pleaded in bar of I. Last I., 1806.

Imperial Airways. Formed, Mar. 1924; report of Government inquiry into affairs, 8 Mar. 1938; British Overseas Airways Corporation took over I. A. and British Airways, 26 Nov. 1940.

Imperial College of Science and Technology, S. Kensington; part of University of London formed by the fusion in 1907 of the City and Guilds Technical College, Royal College of Science (founded 1881), and the Royal School of Mines (founded 1851).

Imperial Conference of Premiers of Great Britain and Self-Governing Dominions. Resolution of Colonial Conference of 1907 to hold such conferences every four years. First meeting of I. C. held in London, 1911. The second, due in 1915, was postponed; but Imperial War Conferences were held in 1917 and 1918; and the I. C., as originally constituted, met in 1921, in 1923, in which latter year there sat concurrently an Imperial Economic Conference to discuss overseas trade development and economic questions generally, Oct.–Nov. 1923. Meetings of, 1926 and 1930, chiefly concerned with intra-imperial relations; meeting in 1937 with extra-imperial affairs. Since 1937 superseded by **Prime Ministers' Meetings,** taking place, since 1944, whenever the occasion has demanded, but always in London. The last of these took place in Sept. 1962, when the Common Market (*q.v.*) was the chief topic for discussion.

Imperial Defence College. Formed in London, 1927.

Imperial Institute. *See* COMMONWEALTH INSTITUTE.

Imperial War Museum. Founded, 1917.

Inauguration Day, U.S.A. 20 Jan., the day on which (at four-year intervals) the newly elected President takes the oath of office.

Incas (Peru). The Inca dynasty was probably established in Peru in A.D. thirteenth century. Tupac Inca Yupanqui conquered Chile c. 1450. Huayna Capac conquered Quito c. 1490. Accession of Atahualpa, 1525. He massacred many I., 1532. Was seized and murdered by Pizarro, 1533.

'Incident, The.' The name given to a supposed plot to assassinate the Earls of Hamilton, Argyll, and Lanark in 1641.

Incitement to Disaffection Act, 1934, enables the police, on leave given by a High Court judge, to search the premises of persons suspected of endeavouring to seduce members of H.M. forces from their allegiance.

Income Tax first imposed in Great Britain, 1799, at rate of 2s. per £ on incomes over £200. Discontinued during Peace of Amiens, and again in 1815. Reintroduced by Peel in 1842 at 7d. in the £. 'Pay-as-you-earn' (P.A.Y.E.) system instituted, 1943.

Income Tax (U.S.A.). First enacted by Congress, 1 July 1862. Act of 3 Mar. 1865 increases tax. Act of 2 Mar. 1867 imposed tax to be levied until 1870. Bill renewed for one year, 14 July 1870; repealed, 26 Jan. 1871. Reimposition in 1894 was adjudged unconstitutional. An amendment to the constitution in 1913 enabled re-establishment of the tax.

Incumbered Estates Act (Ireland). Passed 28 July 1849. First Court of Commissioners sat in Dublin, 24 Oct. 1849.

Indemnity Acts (Britain). Usually passed to relieve servants of the Crown of the consequences of any illegal act done by them in an emergency. Originated, 1715.

Independence Day, 4 July, public holiday in U.S.A. since 1776.

Independent Labour Party. Formed at Bradford, 1893. Dominated Labour Party (*q.v.*) until 1914. Seceded, 1932, under James Maxton (1885–1946). Last seat won away from Clyde, 1935. Last won a Clyde seat, 1946. Last I.L.P. M.P. joined Labour Party, 1948.

Independent Television Authority. Set up under the Television Act of 1954 to provide television services additional to those provided by the British Broadcasting Corporation (*q.v.*). The I.T.A. was instituted for an initial period of ten years, but the Pilkington Report of 1962 recommended its continuance in a modified form, and this the government accepted.

Independents. *See* CONGREGATIONALISTS; *also* NONCONFORMISTS.

'Index Expurgatorius.' Part of the Prohibitory Roman Index (*see* following entry); a list of books to be expurgated before being sanctioned to be read. First printed, 1601.

'Index Librorum Prohibitorum' (*List of Prohibited Books*). Drawn up by the Council of Trent, submitted for papal approval, and published, 1564; it is revised and brought up to date by the 'Congregation of the Index,' and underwent modifications under Leo XIII. An early list had been previously drawn up by the university of Louvain, and the first Roman Index was issued in 1557 and 1559 under Paul IV.

India. Punjab invaded by Alexander the Great, 327–325 B.C. Rise of Asoka and annexation of Baluchistan from Seleucus Nicator *c.* 250 B.C. Kushan invasions, A.D. 150. Kushan decline *c.* 330. Rise of Guptas under Samudragupta, 340. Conquest of Gujarat from Sassanids by Chandragupta, 400. First Mohammedan raid, 664. I. split into numbers of small states till the conquest of the Punjab by Mahmud of Ghazni, 1000–1. Afghans conquered most of the country, 1206–10, and founded the 'Slave Dynasty,' which *fl.* till 1250, and declined on Tamerlane's invasion, 1398. Marco Polo visits I. *c.* 1290–3. Formation in S. I. of Vijayanagar, fourteenth century. Vasco da Gama reaches I., 1498. Defeat of Egyptians at Diu by Francisco d'Almeida, 1509. Albuquerque's viceroyalty and establishment of Portuguese trading empire, 1509–15. Baber's invasion, 1525, and establishment of Mogul Empire (1525–50), which reached its peak under Akbar, 1556–1605. Destruction of Vijayanagar at battle of Talikota, 1565. Accession of Jehangir, 1605. Dutch blockade of Goa, 1606. Death of Jehangir and accession of Shah Jehan, 1629. Reign of Aurungzebe, 1659–1707. Invasion of Nadir Shah from Persia, 1739. Rise of Marathas, 1720 onwards. Clive's defence of Arcot, 1751. Cession of Northern Circars to French, 1753. Suraj-ud-Dowlah's capture of Calcutta (*q.v.*), 1756. Seven Years War, 1756–63. Battle of Plassey, 1757. French defeat at battle of Wandewash and Marathas capture Delhi, 1760. First Mysore War, 1767–9. Warren Hastings governor of Bengal (*q.v.*), 1772. Second Mysore War, 1780. Arrival of French fleet under Suffren, 1782. Third Mysore War, 1790. Capture of Pondicherry, 1793. Fourth Mysore War, 1799. Storming of Seringapatam and death of Tipu Sahib, 1799. Treaty of Bassein (*q.v.*), 1802. Maratha Wars, 1802–5. E. I. Co.'s trading monopoly abolished, 1813. Nepal War, 1814. Pindari War, 1817–1818. First Burma War, Dec. 1825–Feb. 1826. Measures against Thugs (*q.v.*) and Suttee (*q.v.*), 1829. Mysore rebellion, 1830. First Afghan War, 1837–42. Sind War, 1843. First Sikh War, 1845–6. Annexation of Sattara, 1848. Second Sikh War, 1848–9. Annexation of Punjab, 1849. Second Burma War, 1852. Railway built from Bombay to Thana, 1853. Treaty with Afghanistan, 1855. Persian War, 1856. Indian Mutiny (*q.v.*), 1857. Assumption of Government of I. by the crown, 1858. Queen Victoria proclaimed Empress of I., 1 Jan. 1877. Frontier War, 1897–8. Prince and Princess of Wales (afterwards George V and Queen Mary) toured I., 1905–6. Mohmand incursions, joined by the Afghans, 1908. Reform schemes adopted, 1909. Seditious Meetings Act, 1907, re-enacted as a permanent measure, with some modifications, 1911. Act limiting the number of hours of labour in textile factories to twelve, 1911. Government of I. Bill passed, June 1912, by which the seat of government was transferred from Calcutta to Delhi, and changes were made in the constitution of Bengal and Assam. Schemes for the establishment of universities, 1912–13. World War I: Indian Expeditionary Force sent to France, Aug.–Sept. 1914; in action, 28 Oct. 1914, at Neuve-Chapelle; mixed division sent to E. Africa, Sept. 1914; two divisions infantry and one cavalry brigade sent to Egypt, Oct.–Nov. 1914; Indians co-operate with Japanese at Tsingtau, Nov. 1914; Indians in Mesopotamia from 31 Oct. 1914. Indian National Congress demanded self-government for I., 1917. Delhi and Punjab disturbances and martial law in Punjab, Apr. 1919. Amritsar riots, in which Brig.-Gen.

Dyer ordered troops to fire on the mob, 13 Apr. 1919; Indian Legislature established, 1919. House of Commons adopts findings of Hunter Report, 8 July 1920. Permanent Advisory Council of Princes inaugurated, 8 Apr. 1921; Council of State and Legislative Assembly inaugurated, 8 Apr. 1921. Dyarchy suspended in Bengal, 1925. Hindu-Moslem strife in Calcutta, Apr. 1926. Council House at New Delhi opened, 18 Jan. 1927. Fatal communal riots at Dehra-Dun (United Provinces), 28 Sept. 1927. Simon Commission landed, Feb. 1928; its report was published in 1930. Round Table Conference met in London, Oct. 1930; second conference, 1931. Gandhi visited England, Oct.–Nov. 1931.

1932: Third civil disobedience campaign—Gandhi arrested, 4 Jan.; terrorism in Bengal, Feb.; Government award as to representation published, 17 Aug.; Gandhi approved compromise, 24 Sept.

1933: Extensive prosecutions of Communists for treason, Jan.; Congress meeting at Calcutta prevented by police; Gandhi released, 1 May; re-arrested, 1 Aug.; released, 23 Aug.; Gandhi transferred charge of Congress to Nehru.

1934: Communist Party of I. declared unlawful, July; 54-hour week passed; Gandhi successful in forcing the hands of the caste Hindus in favour of the depressed classes in scheme of representation, Sept. See ROUND TABLE CONFERENCES.

1935: Earthquake destroyed Quetta (see EARTHQUAKES); Government of I. Bill, providing for development of a popular constitution, became law, 2 Aug.; expedition against Mohmands drove them back, 18 Sept.; government of Alwar State taken over by Indian Government for fifteen years, 27 Sept.

1936: Legislative Assembly passed motion to terminate Ottawa trade agreement, 30 Mar.; religious riots in Bombay, 15–18 Oct.; Congress rejected new constitution, 28 Dec.

1937: Completion of election to legislative assemblies, 20 Feb.; provincial autonomy began, and Burma and Aden separated from I., 1 Apr.; new viceroy's speech boycotted by Congress, 13 Sept.

1938: Minor engagements on NW. Frontier throughout year; announced in Dec. that Ottawa trade agreement would not be continued after 31 Mar. 1939.

1939: Moslem League at Patna disapproved Federation scheme, already disapproved by Congress, 2 Jan.; Subhas Chandra Bose re-elected President of Congress at Bombay—a victory for opponents of Federation, 29 Jan.; thirteen right-wing members of Working Committee, including Pandit Nehru, resigned

from Congress, 22 Feb.; Indian budget presented to Legislative Assembly, duty on raw cotton doubled, 28 Feb.; Congress at Tripuri passed resolution of adherence to Gandhi's party, 12 Mar.; approval by Chamber of Princes for its reorganization enlarging the Standing Committee and placing it on a regional basis, 13 Mar.; new trade agreement with U.K., till 31 Mar. 1942, signed after two years' negotiations, 20 Mar.; the new tariff bill rejected by Central Legislature, 15 Apr.; Council of State passed tariff bill a second time, 18 Apr.; Bose resigned presidency of Congress after interview with Gandhi. Rajenda Prasad succeeded, 29 Apr.; new Congress Working Committee announced, 1 May; Bose announced formation of a new left *bloc* under his leadership, 3 May; Congress debated their attitude towards the war, Gandhi calling on the British to implement their declarations of faith in democracy. 8–14 Sept.; Working Committee of Moslem League declared that Federal scheme, now suspended, should be altogether abandoned, as they did not endorse the 'Federal objective,' 18 Sept.; the viceroy stated the Allies' war objects, and announced that at the end of the war the Government would consult the several communities and parties and interests in I., 17 Oct.; Congress Working Committee resolved that the viceroy's statement was wholly unsatisfactory and asked for a declaration of war aims. Ministries of Bombay, Madras, and Bihar resigned, 27–31 Oct.; resignation of ministry of United Provinces, 3 Nov.; ministry of Orissa resigned, viceroy announced that the parties having met had totally failed to agree, 5 Nov.; ministry of Central Provinces resigned, 9 Nov.; at Allahabad the Congress Working Committee reaffirmed their demand for 'recognition of I.'s independence,' 23 Nov.; first contingent of Indian troops reached France, 27 Dec.

1940: Finance Bill rejected by Central Legislative Assembly, 19 Nov.; Finance Bill certified by viceroy, 21 Dec.

1941: Customs union with French I. established by treaty, 28 Jan.

1942: Cripps mission's proposals rejected by Congress. See WORLD WAR II.

1946: Constituent Assembly for I. first met, 9 Dec.

1947: I. given Dominion status and Pakistan (*q.v.*) separated from it, 15 Aug.; massacres and migrations in the Punjab, Aug.–Oct.; Moslem revolt in Kashmir, Oct.; Customs Union with French I. denounced.

1948: Assassination of Gandhi, 30 Jan.; Patiala Union of Rajput States inaugurated, July; Nehru prime minister, Sept.; Hyderabad (*q.v.*) occupi d by Indian troops, 13 Sept.

1949: Constituent Assembly passed Act conferring interim powers on Central Government, Jan.; I.'s relation to Commonwealth defined and agreed, 27 Apr.; Hindi declared official language (but this not to replace English *in practice* until 1965; legislation subsequently introduced for extending use of English after 1965).

1950: Rajendra Prasad elected president, 24 Jan.; republic proclaimed, 26 Jan.; U.N. mediator between I. and Pakistan over Kashmir (*q.v.*) question appointed, 22 Aug.

1952: French settlement of Chandernagore incorporated in I., 9 June.

1953: Premier of Pakistan arrived in New Delhi to discuss Kashmir problem, 15 Aug.

1954: All remaining French settlements transferred to I., 1 Nov. (formal cession treaty, 1956).

1955: Attempted assassination of Nehru, Mar.; treaty of friendship with Egypt signed in Cairo, Apr.; I. a leading member of the Afro-Asian Conference held at Bandoeng, 18–27 Apr., and established herself as spokesman for the 'uncommitted nations'; Nehru visited Moscow, June; Marshal Bulganin and Mr. Khruschev made a goodwill tour of I., Nov.

1956: Acts dividing I. into fourteen states and six centrally administered territories came into force, Nov.; Nehru visited U.S.A. for talks with President Eisenhower, Dec.

1959: Dalai Lama of Tibet (*q.v.*) given political asylum in I., 31 Mar.; Indian President took over the government of Kerala and dismissed its Communist ministry, July.

1961: Queen Elizabeth II and Duke of Edinburgh visited I., Jan.; Indian forces invaded Goa (Portuguese possession in Indian subcontinent), 18 Dec.; it surrendered, 19 Dec.

1962: Sporadic local fighting in disputed areas of the Chinese-Indian border from Jan. onwards led to cooler relations with China; general election in Feb. returned Nehru's Congress party, but with a reduced majority; I. suggested self-government within the Indian republic for the Nagas, Aug.; Nehru visited London and played a leading part in the Prime Ministers' Conference, Sept.

Border dispute with China flared into open fighting when Chinese invaded Indian territory and made advances along her frontiers, 18–22 Oct. India sought and received British and American military aid in form of weapons and aircraft, Oct.–Nov. Krishna Menon dismissed from

Defence Ministry, and subsequently left government altogether, Nov.

By 19 Nov. the Chinese breakthrough was threatening Assam, but the Chinese then announced a ceasefire beginning midnight, 20–1 Nov. India and Pakistan agreed to discuss the Kashmir problem again, 29 Nov.

1963, Jan: India accepted the Colombo powers' proposals as a basis for negotiation with China over the border dispute. Apr.: Further inconclusive talks with Pakistan about Kashmir. Talks finally broke down, 16 May. Renewed threat from China, July–Aug.; motion of no-confidence in Nehru tabled in Indian parliament.

India, Governors-General (or Viceroys) of:

Warren Hastings, 1774.
Sir John Macpherson, 1785.
Marquess Cornwallis, 1786.
Sir John Shore, 1793.
Marquess Cornwallis, 1796.
Sir Alured Clarke, 1798.
Marquess Wellesley, 1798.
Marquess Cornwallis, 1805.
Sir George Barlow, 1805.
Earl of Minto, 1807.
Marquess of Hastings, 1813.
Hon. John Adam, 1 Jan.–1 Aug. 1823.
Lord Amherst, 1823.
Hon. W. Butterworth Bayley, 1828.
Lord William Bentinck, 1828.
Sir Charles Metcalfe, 1835.
Earl of Auckland, 1836.
Earl of Ellenborough, 1842.
Viscount Hardinge, 1844.
Marquess of Dalhousie, 1848.
Earl Canning, 1856.
Earl of Elgin, 1862.
Sir John Lawrence, 1864.
Earl of Mayo, 1869.
Lord Northbrook, 1872.
Earl Lytton, 1876.
Marquess of Ripon, 1880.
Earl of Dufferin, 1884.
Marquess of Lansdowne, 1888.
Earl of Elgin, 1894.
Lord Curzon, 1899.
Earl of Minto, 1905.
Lord Hardinge, 1910.
Lord Chelmsford, 1916.
Earl of Reading, 1921.
Lord Irwin, 1926.
Earl of Willingdon, 1931.
Marquess of Linlithgow, 1936.
Viscount Wavell, 1943.
Earl Mountbatten, 1947.

India, Dominion of, Governors-General of:

Earl Mountbatten, 15 Aug. 1947–21 June 1948.
Mr. Rajagopalachari, 21 June 1948–24 Jan. 1950.

Indian Mutiny. Began at Meerut, 10 May 1857; at Lucknow (*q.v.*), 30 May; Delhi taken, 20 Sept.; rebels defeated at Agra, 10 Oct.; Lucknow relieved, 17 Nov.; Gwalior captured, 19 June 1858.

Indian National Congress. First met, 1885. Combined with the Moslem League in a declaration for Indian Home Rule, 1916. *See* INDIA above.

Indian Territory, former name of Oklahoma (*q.v.*).

Indian Union, President of. Dr. Rajendra Prasad, 1950–

Indiana. First settled by French, who had trading posts *c.* 1672. Made part of Canada by Quebec Act, 1774. Passed into American control, 1779. Indian Wars, 1785–95. Territory partitioned from North-Western Territory, 1800. Reduced to its present limits by further partitioning, 1809. Admitted to the Union as state, 1816. Revised constitution, 1851. Invaded by Confederate troops, June 1863.

Indo-China. French influence in Tongking and Annam (*q.v.*) dates from the seventeenth century. Cochin-China was invaded by French and British forces, 1861. Annam and Tongking proclaimed a French protectorate, 1884, and finally united to Cambodia, 1887, at the instigation of Jules Ferry (1832–93). Paul Bert (1833–86) founded system of indirect rule in I.-C. The local Vichy Government surrendered to the Japanese, 1941, who ejected them in favour of Viet Nam republican authority, Mar. 1945. Peace between re-established French authorities and Viet Minh lasted 6 Mar.–19 Dec. 1946. French military operation began in Tongking, Oct. 1947. A treaty between the Emperor Bao Dai and the French republic, signed 8 Mar. 1949, theoretically marked the end of the French colonies in I.-C. and the beginning of Viet Nam 'independent within the French Union.' In Jan. 1950 China and the U.S.S.R. recognized the rival government of Ho Chi Minh. Viet Minh invaded kingdom of Laos, hitherto immune from war, 14 Apr. 1953. France suffered increasing reversals in her fight against the Communists in I.-C., culminating in the defeat at Dien Bien Phu (*q.v.*) in May 1954; and events in I.-C. actually caused the fall of several postwar French governments. As a result of the Geneva Conference, an armistice ending the I.-C. war was signed there on 21 July 1954, and this in fact marked the end of French authority in the area. *See also* CAMBODIA and VIET NAM.

Indonesia, formerly **Netherlands E. Indies.** Republic of I. proclaimed by Sukarno and Hatta on 17 Aug. 1945, but not recognized by the Dutch, who, except for a brief period during the Napoleonic wars, had controlled the territories concerned since *c.* 1620. The Dutch countered by sponsoring a number of autonomous states. Sporadic fighting, interspersed by negotiations, between Dutch and Indonesian nationalists, 1945–1950. A conference called by India, Jan. 1949, proposed that power over the whole area be handed over to an Indonesian government by 1 Jan. 1950. The United States of I. were officially inaugurated in Aug. 1950. Netherlands - Indonesian Union dissolved, 1954. Bandoeng Conference, Apr. 1955; this established I. as one of the principal 'uncommitted nations.' Military conspiracy in Java, 1957, and attempt to assassinate President Sukarno. I.'s claims to W. New Guinea, made since 1950, resulted in armed clashes between Dutch and Indonesians, 1961–2. Under agreement signed between Holland and I., 15 Aug. 1962, W. New Guinea was transferred to Indonesian control on 1 May 1963. I. encouraged the nationalist revolt in Brunei, Dec. 1962, and in 1963 asserted ultimate claim to Australian New Guinea. I. protested against proposed federation of Malaysia (*q.v.*), July–Aug. *See* NEW GUINEA; HOLLAND.

Indulgence, Declaration of, allowing liberty of conscience, 1687. A second declaration was issued in 1688. *See* SEVEN BISHOPS.

Indulgences. Commenced in the Roman Catholic Church *c.* A.D. 800 by Pope Leo III. In the twelfth century they were given principally as rewards to the Crusaders. Clement V in 1313 instituted the public sale of I. Leo X's abuse of the issue of I. led amongst other things to the publication of Luther's theses at Wittenberg, 1517.

Industrial Design, Council of. *See* COUNCIL OF INDUSTRIAL DESIGN.

Industrial Revolution, British, took place *c.* 1740–1840. Arnold Toynbee first used the term, 1884.

Infallibility, Papal, defined by Vatican Council, 1870.

Information, Ministry of, formed, Sept. 1909, from publicity department of Foreign Office, largely reduced 1945, and succeeded by:

Information, Central Office of, in Apr. 1946.

Ingolstadt, Germany. Danube diverted to pass it, 1363. University was founded, 1472. City fortified, 1539.

Inland Revenue, Board of, originated in the Commissioners of Stamps, appointed, 1694. Commissioners of Taxes appointed, 1719. Consolidated Board of Stamps and Taxes established, 1834. Commissioners of Excise absorbed, 1849.

Excise matters transferred to Customs Board, 1908.

Innsbruck, Tirol (*q.v.*). Became a city, 1232. Taken by Maurice of Saxony, 1552. By Bavarians, 1703. By French and Bavarians, 1805. University founded, 1669.

Inns of Court and Chancery.

Lincoln's Inn moved to present site, 1415, but existed 150 years earlier. To it were attached the following Inns of Chancery: Thavies', 1550-1769; Furnival's, 1406-1890.

Gray's Inn. Established *c.* 1295. Freehold of present site acquired, 1733. Inns of Chancery: Staple, end of fourteenth century; Barnards, *c.* 1440-1894.

Inner Temple. Established by 1326. Freehold of present site acquired, 1609. Inns of Chancery: Cliffords, 1345; Clements *c.* 1460.

Middle Temple. See INNER TEMPLE. Separate by 1404. Inn of Chancery: New Inn, 1485.

Serjeants' Inn. Fleet Street, 1443-1758. Chancery Lane, 1416-1876.

Only Lincoln's Inn, Gray's, and the Inner and Middle Temple now exist as organizations.

Inquisition or Holy Office of the Church of Rome. Was constituted when the imperial rescripts of 1220 and 1224 were adopted into the ecclesiastical criminal law in 1231. The direction of the court was entrusted chiefly to the Dominican Order, 1233, when the bishops of S. France also were instructed by Pope Gregory IX. It operated principally in the Latin countries, and in the Spanish and Portuguese possessions. In Spain it became largely a political instrument wielded by the Spanish kings.

Institute of International Affairs, Royal. *See* CHATHAM HOUSE.

Instrument of Government. Passed by English Parliament, 16 Dec. 1653, constituting Oliver Cromwell Lord Protector of England. It also arranged that parliaments should be triennial.

Insulin for diabetes introduced 1921 by Dr. Banting (1891–1941) of Canada.

Insurance (Great Britain). The earliest record of any life policy being issued was on 15 June 1523, at the 'Office of Insurance within the Royal Exchange.' First fire insurance office opened in London, 1680. The first general I. company was established in 1696 under the name of the 'Amicable Contributionship for the I. of Houses'; it was using 'Hand-in-Hand' as subtitle in 1706, and under that name it lasted till absorbed by the Commercial Union Assurance Co. Ltd., 1905. The oldest *life* I. office was the 'Society of Assurance for Widows and Orphans,' started in 1699. Life As-

surance Companies Act passed, 1870, by which all companies before starting had to deposit a sum of £20,000 with the Court of Chancery.

Insurance (U.S.A.). The first I. company was established in Boston, Mass., by the Sun I. Co. (English), 1728. The first fire I. policy was issued in Hartford, Conn., 1794. First accident I. company established at Hartford, Conn., 1863.

Interdict. The most famous are those issued (1) against Poland by Gregory VII after the murder of Bishop Stanislaus, 1080; (2) against Scotland by Alexander III, 1181; (3) against France by Innocent III, 1200; (4) against England under King John by Innocent III, 1208; (5) against England under Henry VIII by Paul III, 1535.

Interim of Augsburg. A system of doctrine issued by the Emperor Charles V, May 1548, attempting to reconcile religious differences.

International. *First:* Developed from I. Working Men's Association formed by Marx and Engels, 1864.

Second: Held its First World Congress at Paris, July 1889.

Third: Identical with Comintern (*q.v.*).

N.B. *The Socialist International* was formed in 1951, being a descendant of the Second International (*see above*).

International Bank for Reconstruction and Development, popularly known as the 'World Bank,' established by the Bretton Woods Agreement (*q.v.*) in 1944.

International Justice, Permanent Court of. Established, 1920. Superseded after 1945 by the **International Court of Justice.**

International Labour Office. Established at Geneva in 1919 at same time as League of Nations. In 1946 the I.L.O. became a specialized agency associated with the U.N.

International Monetary Fund. One of the institutions established by the Bretton Woods Agreement (*q.v.*) of 1944. It came into existence in Dec. 1945.

Interpol (International Criminal Police Commission). Established, 1923, in Vienna.

Invalides, Hôtel des (Paris). Established by Louis XIV for wounded soldiers, 1670. Dome built, 1693. Endowed by Napoleon I, 1811. His remains deposited at, 1861.

Invasions of British Isles. From the Norman Conquest, the following are the principal invasions of the British Isles:

William the Conqueror, 1066.
The Irish, 1069.
The Scots, 1091.

Robert of Normandy, 1103.
The Scots, 1136.
Empress Maud, 1139.
Ireland, by Fitz-Stephen, 1169.
Ireland, by Edward Bruce, 1315.
Queen Isabel, 1326.
Duke of Lancaster, 1399.
Queen Margaret, 1462.
Earl of Warwick, 1470.
Edward IV, 1471.
Queen Margaret, 1471.
Earl of Richmond, 1485.
Lambert Simnel, 1487.
Perkin Warbeck, 1497.
Ireland, by Spaniards and Italians, 1580.
Ireland, by Spaniards, 1602.
Duke of Monmouth, 1685.
William of Orange, 1688.
Ireland, by James II, 1689.
James Stuart, the Old Pretender, 1708.
Second invasion of Pretender, 1715.
Glenshiel, by Spaniards and Jacobites, 1719.
Young Pretender, 1745.
Ireland, 1760.
Wales, by the French, 1797.
Ireland, by the French, 1798.
Channel Islands, by the Germans, 1940.

Inventions Board set up by Admiralty, July 1915, to encourage and co-ordinate scientific effort for naval uses.

Investiture, Lay. The power of a lay sovereign to control the appointment of ecclesiastical dignitaries. Condemned by Gregory VII (Hildebrand), 1075. Urban II forbade ecclesiastics to do homage to any layman even in respect merely of temporalities, 1095. Holy Roman Emperor surrendered his rights of I. at the Concordat of Worms, 1122. *See also* REFORMATION.

Iodine. Discovered by Courtois at Paris, 1811.

Iona, Hii, Y, Icolumcille. Monastery founded by St. Columba (Columcille, 521–97), a native of Donegal, A.D. 563. The last synonym commemorates him. I. was an episcopal see from the ninth century until 1507, when the title and boundaries were changed to that of 'The Isles' (and later to 'Sodor and Man' the present designation: *see* LORD OF THE ISLES): the see depended on Trondhjem (*q.v.*) from *c.* 1000 to 1263. Since 1938 the I. Community (founded by the Rev. George MacLeod, a Church of Scotland minister) has restored the ancient monastery buildings.

Ionian Islands, Mediterranean. In 1081 Corfu and Cephalonia were seized by Robert Guiscard. Corfu became Venetian property, 1386. Ceded to France, 1797. Seized by Russia and Turkey, 1799, when they were formed into the republic of the Seven United Islands. Restored to France by Treaty of Tilsit,

1807. After Napoleonic Wars, 5 Nov. 1815, formed into the United States of the I. I. under British protectorate. Incorporated with Greece by treaty, 14 Nov. 1863. *See* CORFU.

Iowa, U.S.A. Territory formed 1838 by partition of Wisconsin Territory and its boundaries reduced to present limits on formation of state, 1846. Formally annexed to France, 1682; after exploration, 1673 and 1680. Part ceded to Spain, 1762; retroceded to France, 1800. Purchased by U.S.A., 1803. Constitution of 1857 still pertains.

Ipswich, England. First charter, 1200. Incorporated, 1464. Reincorporated, 1665.

Iran. *See* PERSIA.

Iraq. Conquered from Turkey by British forces, 1914–18. Entrusted to Great Britain as a mandate, 1919, and name officially adopted, 1921, when Feisal became first king of I. Constitution defined by Organic Law, June 1924. New treaty with Great Britain extending period of previous treaty to twenty-five years or until I.'s admission to League of Nations, Jan. 1926. Anglo-Iraqi treaty, June 1930. Mosul agreement between Turkey and Britain, 6 June 1926. Joined League of Nations, 4 Oct. 1932. British mandate ended, 3 Oct. 1932. King Feisal *d.* 8 Sept. 1933; succeeded by his son Ghazi. Compulsory military service introduced, 1934–5.

1935: I.-Mediterranean oil pipe-line inaugurated, 14 Jan.; tribal revolts, Mar. and May.

1937: Non-aggression pact with Iran, Turkey, and Afghanistan, 9 July (Pact of Saadabad).

1939: King Ghazi killed in motor accident; succeeded by his infant son, Feisal II; regent, Amir Abdul Ilah, 4 Apr.

1940: Bagdad railway completed, 17 July.

1941: Pro-German Rashid Ali el Gailani assumed premiership by *coup d'état*, 3 Apr.; Regent Abdul Ilah deposed, 11 Apr.; British troops arrived in I., 19 Apr.; clash between Iraqi rebel and British troops at Habbaniyah, 2 May; revolt collapsed, 30 May; flight of Rashid Ali, 31 May; armistice and reinstatement of regent, 1 June.

1944: Organic Law (*see above*) modified to allow king to dismiss Government.

1945: I. signed U.N. Charter, 26 June.

1946: Electoral Law modified.

1947: All British forces withdrawn from I. except for two R.A.F. bases.

1948: Treaty of alliance and mutual assistance with Britain initialled, 15 Jan., but repudiated.

1950–1. Mass exodus of Iraqi Jews to Israel.

I

1952: New thirty-inch pipe-line from Kirkuk to Banias (Syria) finished, 19 Nov.

1953: King Feisal enthroned, 2 May.

1955: I. signed the Bagdad Pact with Turkey. This was later joined by Persia, Pakistan, and Britain. Remained on friendly terms with Britain throughout Suez crisis of 1956–7.

1958: Following the creation of the United Arab Republic (14 Feb.) the kings of I. and Jordan (q.v.) united their two kingdoms in the 'Arab Federation.' An armed left-wing coup d'état on 14 July, led by Major Kassem, overthrew the Hashemite monarchy. King Feisal, his family, and ministers were assassinated, and a republic was established, which had at first close links with both the United Arab Republic and the Soviet bloc. The union with Jordan was declared null and void.

1959: I. formally withdrew from the Bagdad Pact, 24 Mar. Unsuccessful attempt to assassinate Kassem, 7 Oct., was followed by large-scale treason trials and purges.

1960: Cooling in I.'s relations with the United Arab Republic. Jordan recognized Kassem's regime, Oct.

1961: I. claimed Kuwait (q.v.), 25 June; British forces landed in Kuwait on 2 July, but had been withdrawn by 10 Aug.; Kassem accused 'imperialists' of fostering Kurdish revolts in N. I.

1963: Pro-Nasser, anti-Communist coup, 8 Feb. led by Colonel Arif. Kassem shot after a summary military trial, 10 Feb. I. joined the United Arab Republic, 17 Apr. but subsequent government crises and reshuffles in I. itself indicated that the union had many influential opponents.

See also ASSYRIANS.

Ireland. Until the arrival of St. Patrick from Rome in A.D. 432 the history of I. is not at all well documented. The five chief kingdoms of I. in the fifth century were: Ulster, Leinster, Meath, Connaught, and Munster. According to Celtic tradition, Tara was the chief residence of the Irish kings in ancient times, a central monarchy being established here, and 150 monarchs reigned till it was destroyed in 563. In the tenth century the famous Brian Boru brought the country into subjection to his rule; he was killed at Clontarf, where the Scandinavian power in I. was finally destroyed, 1014 (see VIKING AGE). After his death various dynasties disputed the over-lordship of I. Much-needed church reforms put in hand at Synod of Kells, 1152. When Strongbow invaded I. Roderick O'Connor, High King of I., did homage to Henry II, and at Synod of Cashel Henry enforced papal claims on

Irish Church, 1172. I. divided into a series of virtually independent palatinates by the Anglo-Normans. Division of English pale into counties by King John, 1212. Statute of Kilkenny, forbidding inter-marriage of Anglo-Normans and Irish, 1367. Richard II landed with armed force, 1394. Poynings' Law, 1494. Insurrection of Tyrone, 1601. Maguire's rebellion (Ulster Civil War) to expel English, great massacres, 23 Oct. 1641. Oliver Cromwell subdued the whole land with great cruelty, 1649–50. Landing of the deposed James II, 1689. Landing of William III, 14 June 1690. Battle of Boyne, 1690. Treaty of Limerick (q.v.), 3 Oct. 1691. Irish Parliament declared independent (see GRATTAN'S PARLIAMENT), 1782. Act of Union, which joined English and Irish Parliaments, 1 Jan. 1801; followed by Robert Emmet's insurrection, 23 July 1803. Act of Catholic Emancipation, 1829. Daniel O'Connell's great agitation for repeal of Act of Union commenced, 1842; trial of O'Connell, 15 Jan. 1844. Irish famine; subsequent decades saw large-scale Irish emigration to the U.S.A., 1846. The 'Dolly's Brae' (q.v.) affray, 1849. Disestablishment of Anglican Church in I., 1869. Murder of Lord Frederick Cavendish, chief secretary for I., and T. H. Burke, permanent under-secretary, in Phoenix Park, 6 May 1882. Gladstone's first Home Rule Bill brought and defeated, Mar. 1886; Gladstone's second Home Rule Bill passed by Commons, but thrown out by Lords, 1893. Augustine Birrell's Irish Council Bill thrown out, 1907. Irish Land Act, Aug. 1907; Irish Universities Act, 1908; Irish Land Act, Dec. 1909. Home Rule Bill introduced by Asquith, 11 Apr. 1912; second reading moved by Churchill, 30 Apr., carried by 372 votes to 271 on 9 May; committee stage begun, 11 June; in Ulster there was an anti-Home Rule movement led by Sir Edward Carson, and on 28 Sept. a covenant was signed by Ulster men at Belfast against the bill; the bill was twice passed by the Commons and twice rejected by the Lords between 1 Jan. and 14 Aug. 1913. A Home Rule Bill was placed on statute book in 1914, with suspensory clause for duration of World War I. A hopeless rebellion, 'organized' by Sinn Fein ('Ourselves Alone'), broke out, 24 Apr. 1916. Irish Convention met, 25 July 1917; report, Apr. 1918. After the war, Home Rule Act was superseded by Government of Ireland Act, 1920, the greater part of Ulster electing to remain united with Great Britain. The Republicans or Sinn Fein Party rejected the Act, and a state of war between I. and England existed until a peace treaty was signed, 6 Dec. 1921, by which the Irish Free State (*q.v.*), with Arthur Griffith as president, was set up in southern I. British evacuated 1921. Boundary (between Northern and Free State I.) Commission appointed, 1924; its report suppressed and superseded by consent, 1925. *See* IRELAND, NORTHERN; FENIAN ASSOCIATION; IRELAND, LORDS LIEUTENANT OF. For events between 1921 and 1948 *see* IRISH FREE STATE *and* EIRE.

Republic of Ireland, brought into existence by R. o. I. Act, 1948, which came into operation, 18 Apr. 1949. Sean T. O'Kelly, second president of Eire, continued, as first president of the republic, to hold office until 1959, when he was succeeded by the veteran of Irish politics, Eamon de Valera. In 1961 the Republic announced her intention of applying for full membership of the Common Market (*q.v.*), but after Britain's application for membership had been rejected, 1963, I. was forced to reconsider her own position. President Kennedy visited I., summer 1963.

Ireland, Lords Lieutenant and Lords Deputy of:

1172. Hugh de Lacy
1173. Richard, Earl of Pembroke
1176. Raymond le Gros
1177. Prince John
1184. Lord Justices, no Lord Deputy
1189. Hugh de Lacy
1199. Meyler FitzHenry
1203. Hugh de Lacy
1204. Meyler FitzHenry
1205. Hugh de Lacy
1215. Geoffrey de Marisco
1308. Piers Gaveston
1312. Edmund le Botiller
1316. Roger de Mortimer
1320. Thomas Fitzgerald
1321. John de Bermingham
1327. Earl of Kildare
1328. Prior Roger Outlow
1332. Sir John d'Arcy
1337. Sir John de Cherlton
1340. Prior Roger Outlow
1344. Sir Raoul de Ufford
1346. { Sir Roger d'Arcy
       { Sir John Moriz
1348. Walter de Bermingham
1355. Maurice, Earl of Desmond
1356. Thomas de Rokeby
1357. Almaric de St. Amand
1359. James, Earl of Ormonde
1361. Lionel, Duke of Clarence
1367. Gerald, Earl of Desmond
1369. William de Windsor
1376. { Maurice, Earl of Desmond
       { James, Earl of Ormonde

1380. Edmund, Earl of March
1385. Robert, Earl of Oxford
1389. Sir John Stanley
1391. James, Earl of Ormonde
1393. Thomas, Duke of Gloucester
1395. Roger de Mortimer
1398. { Reginald Grey   } Lord
       { Thomas de Holland } Justices
1398. Sir John Stanley
1401. Thomas, Earl of Lancaster
1413. { Sir John Stanley
       { Sir John Talbot
1420. James, Earl of Ormonde
1423. Edmund, Earl of March
1425. Sir John Talbot
1427. Sir John Grey
1428. Sir John Sutton
1431. Sir Thomas Stanley
1438. Lionel, Lord de Wells
1446. John, Earl of Shrewsbury
1449. Richard, Duke of York
1461. George, Duke of Clarence
1470. Tiptoft, Earl of Worcester
1472. George, Duke of Clarence (again)
1478. John de la Pole, Earl of Suffolk
1483. Gerald, Earl of Kildare
1484. John de la Pole, Earl of Lincoln
1488. Jasper, Duke of Bedford
1494. Henry, Duke of York (afterwards Henry VIII)
1496. Gerald, Earl of Kildare
1521. Thomas, Earl of Surrey
1529. Henry, Duke of Richmond
1560. Thomas, Earl of Sussex
1599. Robert, Earl of Essex
1603. Charles, Lord Mountjoy
1622. Henry, Visc. Falkland
1629. Thomas, Earl of Strafford
1643. James, Marquess of Ormonde
1647. Philip, Lord Lisle
1649. Oliver Cromwell
1657. Henry Cromwell
1662. James, Duke of Ormonde
1669. John, Lord Robartes
1670. Lord Berkeley of Stratton
1672. Arthur, Earl of Essex
1677. James, Duke of Ormonde
1685. Henry, Earl of Clarendon
1687. Richard, Earl of Tyrconnel
1692. Visc. Sydney of Shepey
1695. Lord Capell of Tewkesbury
1700. Laurence, Earl of Rochester
1703. James, Duke of Ormonde
1707. Thomas, Duke of Pembroke
1709. Thomas, Earl of Wharton
1710. Thomas, Duke of Ormonde
1713. Charles, Duke of Shrewsbury
1717. Charles, Duke of Bolton
1721. Charles, Duke of Grafton
1724. Lord Carteret
1731. Lionel, Duke of Dorset
1737. William, Duke of Devonshire
1745. Earl of Chesterfield
1746. William, Earl of Harrington
1751. Lionel, Duke of Dorset

1755. William, fourth Duke of Devon·
shire
1756. John, Duke of Bedford
1761. George, Earl of Halifax
1763. Earl of Northumberland
1765. Earl of Hertford
1767. George, Visc. Townshend
1772. Simon, Earl Harcourt
1777. Earl of Buckinghamshire
1780. Earl of Carlisle
1782. { Duke of Portland
      { Earl Temple
1783. Earl of Northington
1784. Duke of Rutland
1787. Marquess of Buckingham (the Earl
Temple, appointed 1782)
1790. Earl of Westmorland
1795. { Earl Fitzwilliam
      { Earl Camden
1798. Marquess Cornwallis
1801. Earl of Hardwicke
1806. Duke of Bedford
1807. Duke of Richmond
1813. Visc., afterwards Earl, Whitworth
1817. Earl Talbot
1821. Marquess Wellesley
1828. Marquess of Anglesey
1829. Duke of Northumberland
1830. Marquess of Anglesey (again)
1833. Marquess Wellesley
1834. Earl of Haddington
1835. Visc., afterwards Marquess of,
Normanby
1839. Lord, afterwards Earl, Fortescue
1841. Earl de Grey
1844. Lord Heytesbury
1846. Earl of Bessborough
1847. Earl of Clarendon
1852. Earl of Eglinton
1853. Earl of St. Germans
1855. Earl of Carlisle
1858. Earl of Eglinton (again)
1859. Earl of Carlisle (again)
1864. Lord Wodehouse (Earl of Kim·
berley)
1866. Marquess of Abercorn
1868. John, Earl Spencer
1874. James, Duke (formerly Marquess)
of Abercorn
1876. Duke of Marlborough
1880. Earl Cowper
1882. John, Earl Spencer
1885. Henry Herbert, Earl of Carnarvon
1886. Earl of Aberdeen
1886. Marquess of Londonderry
1889. Earl of Zetland
1892. Lord Houghton (afterwards Earl
of Crewe)
1895. Earl Cadogan
1902. Earl of Dudley
1905. Earl of Aberdeen (again)
1915. Lord, afterwards Visc., Wimborne
1918. Visc. French of Ypres
1921. Visc. FitzAlan

Ireland, Northern (*see also* ULSTER).
King George V opened Parliament, 1921.
Sir James Craig, later Visc. Craigavon,
first Prime Minister of N. I.
1922: James, Duke of Abercorn, appointed first Governor; Civil Authorities
(Special Powers) Act, emergency measure,
delegated Parliament's order-keeping
functions to executive, widened courts of
summary jurisdiction's authority as well
as scope of punishments capital and
corporal, placed upon accused in certain
cases onus of proving innocence, and gave
police unlimited right of entry. Land
Purchase Commission closed down, 1 Apr.
1925: General Election returns another
Unionist Government.
1926: 'Londonderry' Act established
popular control of education.
1928: Franchise conferred on women;
'special powers,' which had been kept
alive annually, enacted for a further five
years.
1930: Court of Criminal Appeal established.
1933: 'Special powers' made permanent.
1935: Lord Carson *d.*, 22 Oct. By
Summary Jurisdiction Act (Northern I.)
judicial functions taken away from Justices of the Peace and vested in Resident
Magistrates.
1937: King George VI visited Belfast;
and border custom-houses burnt by
I.R.A., 28 July; large increase in unemployment.
1939: I.R.A. proclamations found dis-
played in all towns, 15 Jan.; unity with
the U.K. in European war announced,
4 Sept.; emergency budget introduced,
11 Oct.
1940: Death of Lord Craigavon. 24
Nov.; S. M. Andrews appointed premier,
25 Nov.
1943: Sir Basil Brooke (later Visc.
Brookeborough) Prime Minister.
1945: Earl Granville appointed
governor. King George VI visited N. I.
1946: Reciprocal welfare (National Insurance, etc.) arrangements with Dominions authorized.
1947: Northern I. criminal jurisdiction
extended.
1948: Health Services Act (Northern I.)
passed. Mental Health Act (Northern I.)
passed. Roads Act settled responsibility
for upkeep of trunk roads on Northern I.
Government.
1947: Unionist Government again
returned to power.
1949: Ireland Act (U.K. Parliament)
further defines N. I.'s constitutional
position.
1951: Earl Granville reappointed
governor, Sept.

1952: Lord Wakehurst appointed governor.

1953: Queen Elizabeth II visited N. I.

1954: I.R.A. raided Armagh barracks.

1955: Lord Chandos appointed chairman of the Advisory Development Council for N. I. Unemployment in N. I. now considerably higher than the U.K. average.

1957: I.R.A. campaign of violence reopened in N. I.

1958: Unionist Government returned at General Election (all N. I. administrations since 1921 have been Unionist).

1962: I.R.A. called off its terrorist campaign in N. I., Feb. Customs relaxations with the Irish Republic, Sept.

1963: Lord Brookeborough resigned premiership; succeeded by Captain Terence O'Neill.

Irish Free State. (For early history *see* IRELAND.) Civil war, 1921–3. Griffith *d.*, 1922. Michael Collins murdered, 1922. Cosgrave president, 1922. I. F. S. Agreement Act, 1922, enforced Treaty of, 6 Dec. 1921, conferring Dominion status on Ireland. I. F. S. Constitution Act, 1922. First Governor-General, Timothy Healy, 1922. British soldiers attacked at Queenstown, 21 Mar. 1924. Protection adopted, 1924. Fianna Fail Party formed, 1926. Kevin O'Higgins (Minister of Justice) murdered, 10 July 1927. Republicans renounced abstention from Dail and took their seats, 12 Aug. 1927. General Election caused a stalemate, 20 Sept. 1927. Oaths of allegiance to king, and appeals to Privy Council abolished, 1933, by de Valera's administration; Somerville murdered, 24 Mar. 1936. University representation abolished, 12 Dec. 1936. Name changed to 'Eire' (*q.v.*), a 'sovereign independent and democratic state' with directly elected president, 30 Apr. 1937.

Irish Republic. Sinn Feiners declared themselves 'the Provisional Government of the I. R.' in 1916. *See* IRELAND.

Irish Republican Army (I.R.A.). Formed in 1920 to fight for complete independence of the whole of Ireland. Active until the end of 1921; and in Northern Ireland and England in 1938 and 1939 in terrorist bombing. Declared illegal by the Government of Eire, 23 June 1939. After World War II the I.R.A. became active again in both N. Ireland and England. Its campaign of violence in N. Ireland, which entered its last phase in 1957, was called off in Feb. 1962.

Irish Volunteers. Formed by Sinn Feiners, Sept. 1913, following a famous speech by John Redmond in that year. In Nov. 1915 they joined forces with the Citizen Army, and thereafter planned rebellion against British Government.

Iron and Steel Federation (British), set up, Apr. 1934; replacing National Federation of Iron and Steel Manufacturers (established 1918).

Iron Cross. Prussian Order instituted by Frederick William III in 1813 for service in the War of Liberation; revived (by William I), 19 July 1870, and again in the war of 1914, and by Hitler in 1939.

Iron Crown of Lombardy, containing a circlet said to have been made from one of the nails of the Cross, *c.* 591. Used by all emperors who were kings of Lombardy, including Napoleon I, crowned at Milan, 26 May 1805.

Iron Curtain. Description, used in Mar. 1946 by Winston Churchill to denote the barrier separating Communist and non-Communist states in Europe, which has passed into popular usage.

Iron Mask, The Man in the. An unknown prisoner of the Bastille, supposed to have been imprisoned, 18 Sept. 1698, and who almost certainly *d.* 19 Nov. 1703. Public notice first attracted to the case by the *Mémoires secrets pour servir à l'histoire de Perse*, published Amsterdam, 1745–6.

Iroquois. Name given by the French to one of the great confederations of N. American Indians. The I. reached the height of their power *c.* 1720; they always sided with the English against the French and fought on the English side in the War of Independence.

Isfahan, Ispahan, capital of Persia, A.D. 1587–1800. Masjid-i-Shah (Royal Mosque) built *c.* 1600; Masjid-i-Juma (Friday Mosque) begun, 760; completed eleventh century; rebuilt, seventeenth century; Palace of Forty Pillars remodelled, 1700; Madrasseh - i - Shah Husain, 1710; Maidan-i-Shah (Royal Square) and Chahar Bagh (Four Gardens Avenue) laid out, 1600–23. Sacked by Afghans, 1722, and ceased to be royal residence, 1749.

Islam. *See* MOHAMMEDANISM.

Ismailis. Moslem sect, founded in the mid eighth century.

Israel. (For history prior to 1948 *see* PALESTINE, ANCIENT *and* PALESTINE, MODERN.) State proclaimed, 14 May 1948, and immediately recognized by U.S.A. Admitted to United Nations, 11 May. Transjordan Arab Legion reached Old Jerusalem, and Egyptian Army entered Beersheba, 20 May 1948. Armistice, June–Oct. 1948 (but fighting, 10–18 July). United Nations mediator Count Folke Bernadotte murdered, 17 Sept. Jews overrun Negeb and destroy Palestinian Arab Army in Galilee, Nov. 1948.

King Abdullah makes peace with Israelite Government, Dec. 1948. Truce with Egyptian forces, 7 Jan. 1949. General armistice with Arab League signed at Rhodes, 24 Feb. 1949. Separate armistices with Jordan (confirmed), Mar.; Lebanon, Apr.; Syria, 20 July. Large-scale exodus of Arabs from I., 1949 onwards; equally large influx of Jews from all over the world. Knesset (legislative assembly) first met, 8 Mar. 1949. Israelite forces occupy Aquaba, 1950. Chaim Weizmann, first president (*b.* 1874), *d.*, 9 Nov. 1952. His successor, Izhak Ben-Zvi (*b.* 1884), elected, 8 Dec. Treaty with W. German Federal Republic concluded, 1952. I. invaded Egypt (*q.v.*) and occupied Sinai peninsula and Gaza strip, Oct. 1956. Anglo-French intervention and arrival of U.N. forces in area followed. I. had withdrawn from most of the territory gained by Jan. 1957. Premier Ben Gurion announced capture of Adolf Eichmann, a leading Nazi war criminal, May 1960; he was tried in I., 1961, and execute d there, 1962. President Ben-Zvi *d.*, Apr. 1963.

Istanbul. See CONSTANTINOPLE.

Istria. Conquered from the Illyrians by Rome, 177 B.C.; from the Ostrogoths by Byzantium, A.D. 539. Incorporated in the kingdom of Lombardy by Charlemagne, 788. Under Dukes of Carinthia (*q.v.*), 1173, and Patriarchs of Aquileia, 1209. In the fourteenth century partitioned between Venice and the Hapburgs. By Treaty of Campo Formio, 1797, the whole peninsula came to Austria, which retained it until 1918 except during Napoleon's 'Illyrian Kingdom' (1805–9), who developed Pola as a naval base. After 1918 the greater part of it was incorporated in Italy. After 1947 most of it, except for Trieste, went to Yugoslavia.

Italy. (For early history of I. *see* ROME.) Odoacer deposed the last W. emperor, 476. Invasion of I. by Theodoric, King of the Ostrogoths, A.D. 489. Reign of Theodoric, 493–526. Power of Goths overthrown, 553. Lombard invasion under Alboin, 568. Charlemagne's invasion, 774; he was crowned emperor at Rome, 800. Hildebrand (Gregory VII) becomes pope, and the great struggle between Guelph and Ghibelline (*q.v.*) begins, 1073. During the fourteenth and fifteenth centuries I. was split up between five principal powers (*see under* titles of various duchies, Ferrara, Venice, etc.). Invasion of Charles VIII of France, 1494. Louis XII assumed titles of King of Naples and Duke of Milan, 1499. Treaty between him and Ferdinand of Spain, Ferdinand to have Calabria and Apulia, and Louis the remainder of Neapolitan

kingdom, 1501. France and Spain at war in I., 1502. French driven out of I. by Holy League, 1513. Francis I conquered Milan, 1515; lost it, 1521; captured at battle of Pavia, 1525. Emperor Charles V sacked Rome and made Pope prisoner, 1527. After another campaign, Francis renounced Italian claims at the Peace of Cambrai, 1529. Charles took possession of Milan for Spain, 1535, and Naples came to be governed by Spanish viceroys for 200 years. Savoy again independent, 1574. Francis, with allies, warred against Spain in Northern I., 1635–59; Neapolitan revolt under Masaniello, 1647. Austrian predominance assured by end of reign of Louis XIV. Sicily, wrested from Spain, exchanged by Savoy for Sardinia; Duke of Savoy took title King of Sardinia, 1720. Bourbons established in the Two Sicilies (kingdom of Naples), 1734–5; obtained Parma and Piacenza, 1748. Forty-five years of peace ended, 1793. Napoleon Bonaparte entered I., 1796 (*see* BUONAPARTE); crowned himself King of I., 1805. By Congress of Vienna, 1815, I. was reorganized, and French rule ended. States of central I. annexed to kingdom of Victor Emmanuel, Mar. 1860. First Italian Parliament met at Turin, Feb. 1861, and Victor Emmanuel proclaimed King of I. Emancipation of I. completed by Victor Emmanuel's triumphal entry into Rome, 2 July 1871. I. joined Germany and Austria in Triple Alliance, 1882; seized Massawah on Red Sea, 1885, and established colony of Eritrea. Set up a protectorate over Somaliland, 1889–92. War with Ethiopia, 1896, and (29 Feb.–1 Mar.) the disaster of Adowa. Assassination of King Umberto, 29 July 1900, by an anarchist. War with Turkey on the question of Tripoli, 29 Sept. 1911, ended by the Treaty of Lausanne, 18 Oct. 1912; Electoral Reform Bill passed, May 1912. Socialist rising in the N. suppressed, June 1914 (*see* WORLD WAR I). Protectorate over Albania (*q.v.*) proclaimed, 20 June 1917. D'Annunzio seized Fiume (*q.v.*), Sept. 1919 (*see* RAPALLO). Fascisti's first success, in suppressing Bologna riots, Nov. 1920. Fascisti 'march on Rome,' 28 Oct. 1922; came into office, 31 Oct. Venice Conference with Austria, 8 Oct. 1922. Corfu occupied, 31 Aug. 1923 (*see* JANINA). Soviet Republics recognized, 27 Feb. 1924. Murder of G. Matteotti by Fascisti, 10 June 1924. New electoral system, also subordination of the press, 1925. First instalment of the code of 'the Corporative State' passed, Apr. 1926; labour organized into syndicates, 1926; treaties with Spain, Rumania, Yemen, Greece, Albania, and Germany, 1926.

Pacts with France, 3 Dec. 1927; with Turkey, 1 June 1928; and with Greece, 22 Sept. 1928. Italo-Albanian Alliance, 22 Nov. 1927. Vatican established as a sovereign state, 7 June 1929. Scheme whereby all male Italians from 8 to 55 were soldiers, 18 Sept. 1934. Fighting with Ethiopia (*q.v.*) began at end of 1934. Sanctions against I. by 50 countries began, 18 Nov. 1935. Chamber of Deputies replaced by National Assembly of Corporations, 23 Mar. 1936.

1937: Pact with Yugoslavia, 25 Mar.; Mussolini visited Hitler, 25 Sept.; adherence to German-Japanese Anti-Comintern Pact (formed 1936), 6 Nov.

1938: D'Annunzio *d.*, 1 Mar.; provisional agreement with Britain, 16 Apr.; Hitler in Rome, 3 May; report issued by Ministry of Popular Culture, embodying racialism and beginning the Italian persecution of Jews, 14 July; Mussolini conferred at Munich with Chamberlain and Hitler concerning Czechoslovakia, 29 Sept.; Anglo-Italian agreement came into force, 16 Nov.; I. denounced Franco-Italian agreement of 1935, 17 Dec.

1939: Lord Halifax and Neville Chamberlain made an official visit to Rome, 11–13 Jan.; 60,000 men called up for training from 1 Feb., 25 Jan.; Fascist Grand Council reaffirmed adhesion to Berlin-Rome Axis, 21 Mar.; Mussolini spoke in Rome on twentieth anniversary of the Fascist March, reiterating demands on France as to Tunisia, Jibuti, and Suez Canal, 26 Mar.; I. invaded Albania after bombarding ports, 7 Apr.; King Zog fled to Greece, 8 Apr.; the King of I. accepted the Albanian crown, 13 Apr.; foreign ministers of Germany and I. met at Milan and confirmed the Axis as a military pact, 6–7 May; military alliance with Germany signed in Berlin, 22 May; German and Italian foreign ministers met at Salzburg, and Count Ciano saw Hitler at Berchtesgaden, 11–13 Aug.; at Bologna, Mussolini reaffirmed non-participation in the war, but derided attempts to restore governments destroyed by Germany, 23 Sept.; agreement with Germany for repatriation of Germans from S. Tirol signed at Rome, 21 Oct.; Britain's *de facto* recognition of I.'s annexation of Albania, 21 Nov.; the *Telegrafo* strongly supported Finland against Russia, 29 Nov.; Count Grandi appointed President of Chamber of Fasci and Corporations, 30 Nov.; Grand Council affirmed I.'s interest in Balkans, 8 Dec.

1940: I. declared war on Allies, 10 June (*see* WORLD WAR II); France accepted armistice terms of Germany and I., 22 June; mutual assistance pact with Germany and Japan (Tripartite Pact), 27

Sept.; ultimatum and invasion of Greece, 28 Oct.; Marshal Badoglio resigned, 6 Dec.

1941: Marshal Graziani resigned; war declared on Yugoslavia, 6 Apr.; crown of 'independent' Croatia (*q.v.*) offered to House of Savoy, 18 May; Dalmatia annexed, 21 May; war declared on Russia, 22 June.

1943: Mussolini overthrown and succeeded by Badoglio, 25 July; surrender to Allies, 9 Sept.; I. declared war on Germany, 13 Oct.

1944: King Victor Emmanuel III transfers royal power to Prince Umberto as Lieutenant-General of the Realm, 5 June.

1945: Mussolini executed by partisans, 28 Apr.

1946: Communal elections, 10 Mar.–5 Apr.; king abdicates in favour of Umberto, 9 May; referendum and general elections to Constituent Assembly, 2 June, led to proclamation of I. as a republic, 11 June, and departure of King Umberto, 13 June; Constituent Assembly met, 25 June, elected Enrico de Nicola as provisional president of the republic, 28 June.

1947: Peace treaty signed with Allies at Paris, 10 Feb.; Lateran treaties adopted as part of constitution, July; Luigi Einaudi (*b.* 1874) elected president, 10 May; peace treaty finally ratified, 6 Sept.; Istria ceded to Yugoslavia.

1948: British-French-U.S. proposal to return Trieste to I., 20 Mar.; Christian Democrat victory in general elections, 18–19 Apr.

1949: Italy entered N.A.T.O.

1951: Cabinet reconstituted, July; Italian forces (permitted under the terms of the peace treaty of 1947) put at disposal of N.A.T.O. (five Italian divisions). Italian admiral appointed to N.A.T.O. naval command in Mediterranean.

1952: Death of Carlo Sforza (*b.* 1873), republican leader, 4 Sept.; I. entered the European Coal and Steel Community.

1953: General Election, 9 June, returned Christian Democrats again with reduced majority. Shortly afterwards de Gasperi (the leading figure in post-war Italian politics) resigned. He *d.* the following year.

1954: Italy and Yugoslavia settled their nine-year-old dispute over Trieste (*q.v.*), Oct.

1955: Gronchi succeeded Einaudi as president of the republic.

1956–8: Decline of Communism in Italy; drive to bring prosperity to S. Italy. Italy signed Treaty of Rome (25 Mar. 1957) and as a result became one of the full members of the Common Market (*q.v.*) on 1 Jan. 1958. when the European Economic Community came into being; and also became a member of Euratom. State visit to London of President Gronchi, Mar.

1962: President Segni elected, May.
1963: Christian Democrat losses in the General Election, Apr.
See also TRIESTE.

Italian Literature. The following is a list of prominent I. writers not now living:

Alamanni, Luigi, 1495–1556, poet and satirist.
Alberti, Leone Battista, 1404–72, humanist.
Aleardi, Aleardo, 1812–78, poet.
Alfieri, Vittorio, Count, 1749–1803, poet and dramatist.
Algarotti, Francesco, Count, 1712–64, critic.
Amari, Michele, 1806–89, orientalist and historian.
Amicis. *See* DE AMICIS.
Ammirato, Scipione, 1531–1601, historian.
Angiolieri, Cecco, *c.* 1260–*c.* 1312, poet.
Aretino, Pietro, 1492–1556, dramatist.
Ariosto, Lodovico, 1474–1533, poet and dramatist.
Arnaboldi, Alessandro, 1827–98, poet.
Azeglio Massimo Taparelli, Marchese d', 1798–1866, novelist.
Bandello, Matteo, *c.* 1485–1561, writer of tales.
Baretti, Giuseppe, 1719–89, miscellaneous writer.
Basile, Giovanni Battista (Count of Morone), seventeenth century, writer of tales.
Beccaria, Cesare, 1735–93, legist.
Belli, Giuseppe Gioacchino, 1791–1863, poet.
Bello, Francesco, *c.* 1450–1505, poet.
Bembo, Pietro (Cardinal), 1470–1547, poet and historian.
Bentivoglio, Ercole, 1506–73, poet.
Bentivoglio, Guido (Cardinal), 1579–1644, historian.
Berchet, Giovanni, 1783–1851, poet.
Berni, Francesco, *c.* 1497–1535, poet.
Betti, Ugo, 1892–1953, dramatist.
Bisticci, Vespasiano da, 1421–98, biographer.
Boccaccio, Giovanni, 1313–75, writer of tales and poet.
Boiardo, Matteo Maria, *c.* 1440–94, poet.
Bruni, Leonardo, 1369–1444, biographer.
Bruno, Giordano, 1548–1600, poet.
Campanella, Tommaso, 1568–1639, poet.
Carducci, Giosuè, 1836–1907, poet.
Caro, Annibale, 1507–66, poet and translator.
Casa, Giovanni della, 1503–56, poet.
Casanova de Seingault, Giovanni Jacopo,

1725–98, diarist and adventurer.
Casti, Giovanni Battista, 1724–1803, poet.
Castiglione, Baldassare, 1478–1529, author of *The Book of the Courtier*.
Cavalcanti, Guido, *c.* 1250–1300, poet and philosopher.
Cellini, Benvenuto, 1500–71, artist and autobiographer.
Cena, Giovanni, 1870–1917, novelist and poet.
Cesarotti, Melchiore, 1730–1808, poet.
Chiabrera, Gabriello, 1552–1637, poet.
Cino da Pistoia, *c.* 1268–1337, poet.
Cinzio. *See* GIRALDI.
Coletta, Pietro, 1775–1831, historian.
Colonna, Vittoria, 1490–1547, poetess.
Compagni, Dino, ?–1324, chronicler.
Coppetta, Francesco, 1510–54, poet.
Costanzo, Angelo di, 1507–*c.* 1591, poet and historian.
Croce, Benedetto, 1866–1952, philosopher and critic.
Dall' Ongaro, Francesco, 1808–73, poet.
D'Annunzio, Gabriele, 1863–1938, poet and novelist.
Dante Alighieri, 1265–1321, poet.
Davila, Enrico Caterino, 1576–1631, historian.
De Amicis, Edmondo, 1846–1908, novelist, writer of travel books, etc.
Deledda, Grazia, 1875–1936, novelist.
De Sanctis, Francesco, 1818–83, critic.
Ficino, Marsilio, 1433–99, humanist.
Filelfo, Francesco, 1398–1481, humanist.
Filicaja, Vincenzo da, 1642–1707, poet.
Fogazzaro, Antonio, 1842–1911, novelist.
Folengo, Teofilo ('Merlino Coccaio'), 1491–1544, macaronic poet.
Foscolo, Ugo, 1778–1827, poet.
Galileo Galilei, 1564–1642, scientist.
Giannone, Pietro, 1676–1748, historian.
Gioberti, Vincenzo, 1801–52, philosopher.
Giordani, Pietro, 1774–1848, miscellaneous writer.
Giraldi, Giovanni Battista (Cinzio), 1504–1573, writer of tales.
Giusti, Giuseppe, 1809–50, poet.
Goldini, Carlo, 1707–93, dramatist.
Gozzi, Carlo, Count, 1720–1806, dramatist.
Gozzi, Gasparo, Count, 1713–86, poet and essayist.
Gregory I, Pope, 540–604, theologian.
Guarini, Giovanni Battista, 1537–1612, poet and dramatist.
Guicciardini, Francesco, 1483–1540, historian.
Guidiccioni, Giovanni, 1500–41, poet.
Guinizelli, Guido, *c.* 1230–76, poet.
Jacopone da Todi, *c.* 1230–1306, poet.
Lanzi, Luigi, 1732–1810, art historian.
Latini, Brunetto, 1230–94, poet.
Leopardi, Giacomo, 1798–1837, poet and philosopher.

Lorenzo de' Medici, 1449–92, poet and patron of letters.

Machiavelli, Niccolò, 1469–1527, historian and political writer.

Maffei, Scipione, Marchese di, 1675–1755, archaeologist.

Maggi, Carlo Maria, 1630–99, poet.

Mamiani, Terenzio, 1799–1885, miscellaneous writer.

Manzoni, Alessandro, 1785–1873, poet and novelist.

Marino, Giovanni Battista, 1569–1625, poet.

Mazzini, Giuseppe, 1808–72, patriot.

Meli, Giovanni, 1740–1815, poet.

Metastasio (Trapassi), Pietro, 1698–1782, poet and dramatist.

Michelangelo, Buonarotti, 1475–1564, poet.

Molza, Francesco Maria, 1489–1544, poet.

Monti, Vincenzo, 1754–1828, poet.

Muratori, Lodovico Antonio, 1672–1750, editor and historian.

Niccolini, Giovanni Battista, 1782–1861, dramatist.

Oriani, Alfredo, 1852–1909, novelist.

Parini, Giuseppe, 1729–99, poet.

Pascoli, Giovanni, 1855–1912, poet.

Pellico, Silvio, 1789–1854, poet and dramatist.

Petrarca, Francesco (Petrarch), 1304–74, poet.

Petrarca, Francesco, 1304–74, poet.

Pindemonte, Ippolito, 1753–1828, poet.

Pirandello, Luigi, 1867–1936, dramatist.

Pius II, Pope (Aeneas Sylvius Piccolomini), 1405–64, humanist.

Poliziano (Angelo Ambrogini), 1454–94, poet and dramatist.

Polo, Marco, 1254–1324, traveller.

Pontano, Giovanni, 1426–1503, statesman, diplomatist, and poet.

Prati, Giovanni, 1815–84, poet.

Pulci, Luigi, 1432–84, poet.

Redi, Francesco, 1626–98, physician and naturalist.

Romagnosi, Giovanni Domenico, 1761–1835, philosopher.

Rosmini-Serbati, Antonio, 1797–1855, philosopher.

Rossetti, Gabriele, 1783–1854, translator.

Rucellai, Giovanni, 1475–1525, poet.

Sacchetti, Franco, c. 1330–99, writer of tales.

Sannazaro, Jacopo, 1458–1530, poet.

Sarpi, Pietro (Fra Paolo), 1552–1623, natural philosopher.

Serao, Matilde, 1856–1927, novelist.

Sforza, Count Carlo, 1873–1952, political writer and philosopher.

Stampa, Gaspara, 1523–54, poet.

Straparola, Giovanni Francesco, d. c. 1556, story-writer.

Tansillo, Luigi, 1510–68, poet.

Tasso, Bernardo, 1493–1569, poet.

Tasso, Torquato, 1544–95, poet.

Tassoni, Alessandro, 1565–1635, poet.

Telesio, Bernardo, 1509–88.

Testi, Count Fulvio, 1593–1646, poet.

Thobez, Enrico, c. 1870–1925, critic.

Tiraboschi, Girolamo, 1731–94, historian.

Todi, Jacopone da. See JACOPONE DA TODI.

Tommasèo, Niccolò, 1802–74, essayist.

Tozzi, Federigo, 1883–1920, novelist.

Trissino, Giovanni Giorgio, 1478–1549, poet and diplomatist.

Troya, Carlo, 1784–1858, historian.

Uberti, Fazio degli, c. 1310–c. 1370, poet.

Valle, Pietro della, 1586–1652, traveller.

Vanini, Lucilio (Guilio Cesare), c. 1585–1619, poet.

Vasari, Giorgio, 1511–74, biographer.

Verga, Giovanni, 1840–1922, novelist.

Verri, Count Alessandro, 1741–1816, poet.

Vico, Giovanni Battista, 1668–1744, philosopher.

Villani, Giovanni, c. 1275–1348, historian.

Villari, Pasquale, 1827–1917, historian.

Vinci, Leonardo da, 1452–1519, artist, and writer on painting and natural philosophy.

Zanella, Giacomo, 1820–88, poet.

Zeno, Apostola, 1688–1750, playwright.

I.W.W. (Industrial Workers of the World). Founded, 1905.

J

Jack the Ripper. Between 1887 and 1889 eight women were murdered and mutilated in the E. end of London by a criminal popularly nicknamed 'J. the R.,' who was never caught.

Jacobins. Members of an extremist political club, formed during French Revolution, originally known as *Club Breton*, founded at Versailles, 1789, by members of States-General. Later called J. because of their meetings in a building in the Rue St. Honoré, Paris, which belonged to the Dominican Order. Practically dissolved at the death of Robespierre, 1794; formally closed, 9 Nov. 1794.

Jacobites. Followers of the exiled Stuarts. Name first adopted after revolution of 1688, especially in the Irish war of 1689–90 between Williamites and J.

Insurrection of 1715. An attempt to set James Edward Stuart, son of James II, on the throne after Queen Anne's death, 1714. Earl of Mar (John Erskine, 1675–1732) set up James's standard at Braemar, 6 Sept. 1715. Indecisive battle against the Duke of Argyll at Sheriffmuir, 13 Nov. James landed at Peterhead, 22 Dec., but re-embarked with Mar in Feb. 1716 (O.S. 1715) and left for Avignon, France.

1719: Highland rising began Apr. under George Keith (the last Earl Marshal of Scotland, 1693?–1778), but only Mackenzies and Macraes 'came out.' Ended June in drawn battle at Glensheil. Some 300 Spanish troops sent to support the Highlanders laid down their arms.

Rebellion of 1745. Led by Charles Edward Stuart, son of James Edward, who gained victory at Prestonpans, 21 Sept. Reached Derby, 6 Dec. (*see* BLACK FRIDAY). Defeated at Culloden by ('Butcher') Cumberland, 16 Apr. 1746. It led to the abolition of heritable jurisdictions in Scotland, 1746.

Last Jacobite executed (Dr. Archibald Cameron), 7 June 1753.

The last Stuarts: James Francis Edward: 'James III'—*The Old Pretender*, 1688–1766. Charles Edward: 'Charles III'—*The Young Pretender*, 1720–80. Henry Benedict Maria: 'Henry IX'—*Cardinal York*, 1725–1807. James Fitzjames, Duke of Berwick: *Marshal of France and political adviser to the Old Pretender*, 1670–1734.

Jacquerie. A rebellion of French peasants in 1358. Word taken from 'Jacques Bonhomme,' the name given by the nobles to the peasants; finally suppressed at battle of Meaux, 9 June 1358.

Jaffa, Israel (Arab., *Yafa*; Gr., *Joppa*). Within the Roman province of Syria from 64 B.C. Captured by Crusaders, 1099. Incorporated as a fief in the kingdom of Jerusalem, 1100. Captured by Saladin, 1187. Recaptured by Crusaders under Richard I, 1190. Sacked by Bibars, 1267. Captured by Napoleon, 1799; and by British, 1917. Centre of Arab nationalism until 1948. Administration united with that of Tel-Aviv in Oct. 1949.

Jaipur, India. The capital, formerly at Amber, was transferred to J. city, newly founded in 1728. The maharaja, Sir Man Singh, ceded his powers to the Indian Union, 8 Mar. 1948, having ascended the throne in 1922. Bicameral legislature was set up in 1944. J. joined the Rajasthan Union, 30 Mar. 1949.

Jakarta, Indonesia. City of NW. Java founded by the Dutch as **Batavia** in 1619. Headquarters of Dutch E. India Co. Occupied by British troops, 1811–16. Name reverted to J. after 1945.

Jamaica. Discovered by Columbus, 1494; possessed by Spaniards, 1509; British expedition sent out by Cromwell conquered J., 1655; ceded to England by Treaty of Madrid, 1670; insurrection of negroes, Oct. 1865; new constitution framed, 1866; earthquake at Kingston destroying practically whole town, 14 Jan. 1907. Strikes, Apr. and May; mobs fired on, 7 June 1938. Various defence sites leased to U.S.A., Nov. 1940. New constitution, 1944. Announcement of ten-year development plan, 31 Jan. 1946. W. Indian University College opened a medical faculty, 18 Oct. 1948. Royal charter, 10 Jan. 1949. Further faculties opened, 1949 and 1950. Member of Caribbean Federation (*q.v.*), 1956; new constitution, 1959. Referendum on whether or not to stay in Federation produced a majority against, Sept. 1961. Constitutional talks in London followed. As a result, J. became a self-governing Dominion, 6 Aug. 1962, the independence celebrations being held in the presence of Princess Margaret, representing the Queen.

Jameson Raid. An invasion of the

Transvaal by the forces of the British S. Africa Co., 31 Dec. 1895–2 Jan. 1896. The leader was Dr. Jameson, who was tried in July 1896 under the Foreign Enlistment Act (q.v.) and sentenced to imprisonment.

Jamestown, Virginia. Named after James I by English settlers who landed, 13 May 1607.

Janina (Alb.), **Ioannina** (Gr.), or **Yannina** (Turk.), Epirus. Murder of Gen. Tellini and other Italian members of boundary commission in Albania, Aug. 1923. Result was the 'Corfu Incident' (q.v.), Sept. 1923. Siege of, by Greeks in Second Balkan War, 25 Nov. 1912–6 Mar. 1913.

Janissaries. Troops originally recruited exclusively from Christian children for the Ottoman Army. First raised by Sultan Orkhan c. 1330. Reorganized by Murad I c. 1360. Insurrection of, 14 June 1826, resulted in their destruction.

Jan Mayen Island, Arctic Ocean. Sighted by Hudson, 1607. Said to have been rediscovered by Jan Mayen, 1614. Annexed to Norway, 1929.

Jansenists. Religious sect founded after death of Cornelius Jansen (1585–1638) in France. His work *Augustinus* (published, 1640) led to the foundation of the Port Royal (q.v.) community. It was condemned in 1642, and the controversy led to Pascal's *Provincial Letters*, 1656–7; continual persecution and the practical dissolution of the movement in 1713, though the ideas of the J. continued to influence French Catholicism into the nineteenth century.

Japan. (Traditional date of the foundation of the Japanese Empire by the Emperor Jimmu, 11 Feb. 660 B.C. This date is, however, discredited.) Japanese missions visit Korea, A.D. 57, 107. War with Korea under the Empress Jingu early third century. Arrival of Wani as tutor in Chinese to the imperial family, 405. Japanese naval defeat by Koreans, 516. Buddhism introduced, 552. Religious and political rivalry of the Soga and Nakatomi clans, 554–93. Issue of the Code of Shōtoku Taishi, 604. First embassy to China, 607. Death of Shōtoku Taishi, 621. Soga overthrown by Nakatomi-no-Kamatori, 645. The Taikwa or Great Reform Edict introduced a new system of Land Tenure, 646. The Taiho edict sets up administration on Chinese model 702. Nobility reorganized on Chinese model, 707.

Nara founded, 710. Fujiwara family in power, 710–59, and from 782 to 1068. Capital moved to Nagaoka, 784. To Heian (Kyoto), 794. Wars against the Ainu in N. J., 782. Ainu subdued, 812.

Rise of the Taira clan, 937–40. Rise of the Minamoto clan, 961–5. Decline of the Fujiwara with the rise of the Cloistered Emperors, 1087–1156. Taira supremacy, 1156–85. Taira clan overthrown by Minamoto Yoritomo at naval battle of Dannoura, 1185.

Kamakura made capital of the Shogun (q.v.) Yoritomo, 1185. Hojo family became regents on behalf of the Minamoto Shoguns, 1205. Defeat of the Mongol invasions, and Mongol fleet destroyed in a storm ('Divine Wind'), 1281. End of the Hojo regency and the destruction of Kamakura, 1333.

Establishment of a Northern Court at Kyoto and a Southern Court at Yoshino and civil war between them, 1336–92. With the settlement of the dynastic dispute power passes to the Shoguns of the Ashikaga family, who move the capital to Muromachi, a suburb of Kyoto, 1392. The Onin Civil War, 1467–77. Total collapse of government and civil war, 1480. Portuguese reach J., c. 1542. Order restored by Nobunaga, 1568. Hideyoshi destroys power of western feudatories, 1577. First Christian persecution, 1587.

Yedo founded, 1590. Hideyoshi's unsuccessful invasion of Korea, 1592. Jyeyasu establishes himself by defeat of the Toyotomi clans at Sekigahara, 1600, and by storming Osaka, 1615. 'Law of the Military Houses,' 1615. Spaniards expelled, 1624. Shimabara rebellion, 1637. Japanese forbidden to go abroad, 1638. Portuguese expelled, 1638. All other Europeans expelled, 1640, except Dutch, who were confined to Deshima, 1641. Beginning of the Nito School of Historians, 1660. The 'Genroku' period, 1688–1703. Relaxation of edicts against western learning, 1716. Famine and rioting, 1783–6. American Commodore Perry compels the Shogun to conclude commercial treaty, 1854. End of Shogunate, 1867, and rise in real power of the emperor.

Universal military service introduced, 1872. Expedition against Formosa, 1874. Meiji Constitution granted, 11 Feb. 1889. War with China, 25 July 1894. By first Treaty of Shimonoseki China cedes Formosa and Liaotung, 17 Apr. 1895. By Second Treaty Russia, France, and Germany take Japanese gains except Formosa, 8 May 1895. Anglo-Japanese alliance, 1902. Russo-Japanese War, 8 Feb. 1904. Russian defeat on land at battle of Mukden, 1–9 Mar. 1905. At sea in battle of Tsushima, 27–28 May 1905. Treaty of Portsmouth, 5 Sept. 1905. J. establishes protectorate over Korea, 18 Nov. 1905. Emperor of Korea abdicates, 1907. Annexation of Korea, 1910. On Allied side in World War I, 1914–18, and received various German colonies as mandated territories, 1919.

Manhood suffrage introduced, 1925. Premier Inukai assassinated, 1932. Invasion of Jehol and J. leaves League of Nations, 1933. U.S.S.R. sells Chinese E. railway to J., 1935. Military revolt in Tokyo, 26–29 Feb. 1936. Anti-Comintern Pact with Germany, 25 Nov. 1936.

1937: 'The Peking Incident,' 7 July. (For War in China, see CHINA.)

1938: Hostilities with U.S.S.R. at Changkufeng, July–Aug.

1939: Annexation of Spratley Island despite French claims, 31 Mar.; hostilities with U.S.S.R., May–Sept.

1940: Japan joins the Axis, 27 Sept.

1941–5. See WORLD WAR II.

1945: Atomic bomb dropped on Hiroshima, 6 Aug.; Atomic bomb dropped on Nagasaki, 9 Aug.; J. surrendered unconditionally, 14 Aug.; Gen. MacArthur enters Tokyo, 8 Sept.; Allied Control Council created by Moscow agreement, 28 Dec.

1946: New constitution published, 6 Mar.

1947: New constitution in force; elections held; 'democratization' of J. on W. lines, and growth of Japanese Communist Party.

1951: Peace treaty signed at San Francisco between J. and representatives of forty-eight countries, 8 Sept.; ratified by the Japanese Diet, 26 Oct.; Security Treaty with U.S.A. ratified, 26 Oct.

1952: Serious Communist rioting at Tokyo, 1 May; after this Communist power in J. went into apparent decline.

1955: Left-wing and right-wing Socialists combined into one party, Oct.; Democrats and Liberals formed the Liberal-Democratic Party, Nov. Consequent stabilization of internal politics.

1956: J. became a member of U.N.O., 18 Dec.

1959: Japanese Crown Prince married a commoner, 10 Apr.

1960: Violent demonstrations in Tokyo against the Kishi Government and the security treaty with the U.S.A., 26 May, led Japanese Government (16 June) to ask President Eisenhower to put off his proposed visit to Japan indefinitely, as it could not guarantee his safety there. Ikeda succeeded Kishi as premier, 18 July. Head of the Japanese Socialist Party assassinated, 12 Oct. Victory of Liberal-Democratic Party at General Election in Nov.

Jarrow, County Durham. The Venerable Bede was associated with the Benedictine abbey founded here, 682, by Benedict Biscop (628–90).

Jassy (Rum. **Iasi**) was a centre of Greek as well as Vlach culture, and capital of Moldavia, in the sixteenth century. Here Alexander Ypsilanti (1792–1828) proclaimed the independence of Greece, 1821, but his forces were defeated by the Turks, and he fled into exile.

Java, Indonesia. Dutch rule began, 1619. Occupied by British, 1811. Regained by Dutch, 1816. Primary education introduced, 1872. Javanese admitted to local affairs, 1903. People's council created, 1918. Given full legislative powers, 1925. Conquered by Japan, Feb.–Mar. 1942. Became part of the republic of Indonesia, 1950. See INDONESIA.

Jedburgh, Scotland. Abbey founded by David I, 1118–47. Burned by English, 1544–5.

Jena, Germany. First documentary mention of, A.D. 863. Granted municipal rights in thirteenth century. Came into hands of the Saxon Wettin dynasty, 1331, and was an independent dynasty known as Saxe-Jena, 1672–90. Came by inheritance to the principality of Saxe-Weimar, 1741, whose ruler, Karl August (reigned 1775–1828), was a great patron of the arts and of J. University (founded 1558). Battle of J., between Napoleon I and the Prussians, 14 Oct. 1806.

Jenkins's Ear (War of). The otherwise unremarkable Robert Jenkins, master of the brig *Rebecca*, had his ship boarded off Havana, 9 Apr. 1731, by Spanish coastguards, who, Jenkins alleged, cut off the ear in question. He complained to his own Government with no result, but in 1738 was called to the bar of the House of Commons, where he repeated his story, which was used as a *casus belli* for the war of 1739–42. Jenkins *d.* 1745.

Jericho. The walls traditionally destroyed by Joshua were excavated *c.* 1900, and in 1920 and 1930, and would appear to have been continuously occupied from 2000 to 1600 B.C., the outer works dating from *c.* 1800 B.C. Further investigations since World War II have proved that J. existed as early as 3000 B.C.

Jersey. United to the English crown 1066. Occupied by Germans, June 1940–9 May 1945. British military government lasted, 12 May–25 June 1945. Legislative reforms, 1948. See CHANNEL ISLANDS.

Jerusalem (Arab. **al Qds,** colloquially **'Udes).** Letters signed by the ruler of 'Urusalim,' and written *c.* 1375 B.C., are extant. Taken by David *c.* 1050 B.C. Hezekiah repels Assyrian siege, 701 Destroyed by Nebuchadnezzar, 586. Rebuilt by Nehemiah, 445. Taken by Alexander the Great, 332. Temple de stroyed by Antiochus Epiphanes, 168. Rebuilt by Maccabees c. 150. J. taken by Pompey, 65. Temple plundered by Crassus, 54. Rebuilt by Herod, 35–34. Sacked by Titus, A.D. 70. Captured by Arabs, 637. Occupied by Crusaders, 1099–1244 (see CRUSADES). Captured from Turks by Allenby, 1917. University on Mt. Scopus formally opened, 1 Apr. 1925. British evacuate, 1948. During the Israelite-Arab War of 1948–9, Jordan forces occupied the Old City and Israelite forces the New, which the Knesset proclaimed as the capital of Israel, 23 Jan. 1950.

Jervaulx Abbey (Yorks). Founded, 1156. Last Abbot hanged, 1537.

Jesuits (Society of Jesus). Founded, 1534, by Ignatius Loyola (1491–1556). Constitutions approved by papal bull, 1540. First colleges in Portugal, 1542; France (at Billom), 1545; Paris, 1550. Expelled from France, 1594. Restored, 1603. Again expelled, 1764; again restored, 1814. Again expelled, 1880. Expelled from England, 1579, 1581, 1586, 1602, 1829. Suppressed by Pope Clement XIV, 1773. Restored by Pius VII, first in Russia, 1801, then in the Two Sicilies, 1804; completely, 1814. Today (1963) permitted establishments in most countries outside the Communist bloc, but position doubtful in Mexico and Cuba.

Jet Propulsion. Basic principles first stated by the French engineer, René Lorin, 1913. In 1930 Sir Frank Whittle, then a R.A.F. cadet, began work on gas turbines, which received official support from the Air Ministry, 1937. His first J. P. aircraft flew, 14 May 1941. Independent experiments started by the German, Heinkel, 1939, and the J. P. Heinkel 53B was flown on 27 Aug. that year.

Jew, the Wandering. First mentioned in the Chronicle of St. Alban's Abbey, 1228.

Jews in England. Mentioned in ecclesiastical documents as early as A.D. 740. Came to England in large numbers after the Norman Conquest (1066). Riots against them in 1189 at coronation of Richard I. Driven from England by Edward I, 1290; but from 1580 to 1640 Portugal was conquered by and annexed to Spain, and a great many Jewish refugees from Portugal, some of them marranos—i.e. descendants of persons who had pretended to embrace Christianity in face of persecution by the Spanish and Portuguese authorities, 1480–98—were engaged in clandestine trade with Portugal, encouraged by the English Government. Many of them were settled in Bristol and London between 1590 and 1600. This *fait accompli* was acknowledged, and J. officially readmitted by Cromwell, 1656. Bill passed to naturalize J., 1753, repealed, 1754. Allowed to obtain freedom of City of London, 1832. Act to relieve J. elected to municipal offices from taking oaths, 1845; extended when they were admitted to Parliament, 1858. Universities Tests Act, 1871, enables J. to graduate at the universities. First admitted to House of Lords, 1885. Considerable influx of J. to Britain from E. Europe, 1880–1910; from Nazi Germany, 1933–8. Two hundred and fiftieth anniversary of the opening of the Sephardic synagogue, Bevis Marks, celebrated, 19 Dec. 1951.

Jibuti, French Somaliland. Founded by French, 1888.

Johannesburg, Transvaal. Founded, 1886, and probably named after Johannes Meyer, the Mining Commissioner of that time. Jameson Raid (q.v.) organized at, 1895. Bishopric of J. created, 1922. Made into a city, 1928.

John Bull. Personification of the English nation. Name and character first popularized in 1712 by John Arbuthnot, an anti-Whig pamphleteer.

John o' Groats House, N. Scotland. Said to be named after a Dutchman who settled here in 1489.

Johns Hopkins' University. Founded by a gift from Johns Hopkins, of Baltimore, made 1867. Opened, 1876. The present buildings are on a site outside Baltimore, Maryland, U.S.A., presented by the city in 1902.

Johore, former Unfederated Malay State, entered into treaty relations with Britain, 1885. Accepted an adviser, 1914. Became a member state of the Malay Federation, 1948.

Joinville, Treaty of, 1584, between Philip II of Spain and Henry of Guise.

Jordan (formerly **Transjordan**). Conquered by Moslem armies, 637. Hashimite Kingdom established when, after the expulsion of the Emir Feisal from Syria (1920), his brother, Sharif Abdullah, was dissuaded from invading Syria again (which he threatened to do, Apr. 1921) by being recognized as emir of the territory E. of J., between Es Salt and Ma'an. An independent, though mandated, state, proclaimed by the British, 1923. Boundary with Nejd province of Saudi Arabia fixed by Treaty of Hadda, 1925. Treaty of Feb. 1928 provided for greater local autonomy. Question of union with Iraq debated in Parliament, 18 Dec. 1935. Britain recognized complete independence by treaty of 22 Mar. 1946. Name changed to J. officially, 17 June 1946, but not in general use until June 1949. In the war with Israel, 1948, J. conquered c. 2,000 square miles of Arab Palestine, and subsequently annexed this, Apr. 1950. New Anglo-Jordan treaty signed at Amman, 15 Mar. 1948. King Abdullah murdered, 20 July 1951, and succeeded by his son, the Emir Tallal, 6 Sept., who visited King Ibn Sa'ud in that month. Tallal deposed and succeeded by his son, Emir Hussein (b. 1936), 11 Aug. 1952. Hussein enthroned, 2 May 1953. J. refused to consider revision of 1948 treaty with Britain, and would not join Bagdad Pact, 1955. In Mar. 1956, Glubb, the British Commander-in-chief of the Arab Legion, was dismissed. Egypt, J., and Syria established joint military command under Egyptian leadership to meet any emergency, 25 Oct. 1957. During the Suez crisis, 1956–7, British influence in J. reached its lowest ebb. In Jan. 1957, Egypt, Syria, and Saudi Arabia agreed to pay J. the equivalent of the annual subsidy Britain had been paying her under the 1948 treaty, which was terminated officially, 4 Feb. 1957. All British military and air bases handed back to J. by May 1957. Subsequently Egyptian influence in J. waned. The kings of J. and Iraq (q.v.) united their kingdoms in the 'Arab Federation,' 14 Feb. 1958; this lapsed after 14 July 1958. and was officially dissolved, 1 Aug. 1958. King Hussein married a British woman, Antoinette Gardiner (Muna al Hussein), in May 1961, as his second wife; a son and heir was born in 1962. Pro-Nasser demonstrations in J. following the establishment of the new United Arab Republic (q.v.) in Apr. 1963. These were rapidly suppressed by the Jordanian army.

Juan Fernandez Island, Pacific. Discovered in sixteenth century by Juan Fernandez. The famous Alexander Selkirk lived here, 1704–9. Occupied by Spain, 1750, and passed to Chile in 1810.

Judicature Acts passed 1873, 1875, and 1925. The Act of 1925 consolidated Acts, 1873–1910, and has been amended by the Administration of Justice Act, 1928. *See* COURTS, ENGLISH.

Judiciary of the U.S.A. Supreme Court organized, 1789; Court of Claims established, 1855; Circuit Court of Appeals established, 1891. Women admitted to practise in the Supreme Court, 15 Feb. 1879.

Jülich. Occupied in Roman times, the medieval city was chartered in the thirteenth century, ruled from 1336 by margraves, and from 1386 by dukes; captured by Maurice of Orange, 1610,

during the J.-Cleves succession dispute (1609–14). Became part of Prussia, 1814, having been included in the French Empire since 1801. Fortifications demolished, 1860. Scene of heavy fighting between the Americans and the Germans in Feb. 1945. *See* CLEVES.

'Junius, Letters of.' A series of seventy political letters signed 'Junius,' which appeared in the *Public Advertiser* between 21 Jan. 1769 and 21 Jan. 1772. The printer and publisher, H. S. Woodfall, was prosecuted in Dec. 1769 for a certain letter which appeared against King George III, but acquitted. Sir Philip Francis (1740–1818) reputed to have been the author. Claims have also been made for the authorship of Burke, Wilkes, Horace Walpole, etc.

Jury, Trial by. Use of juries first appears in compilation of Domesday Book (q.v.), 1085–6. Established as a method of trial by Henry II, 1154–89, in civil cases. In criminal cases, c. 1215, as a result of abolition of trial by ordeal. Introduced by Act of Parliament for civil cases in Scotland, 1815. Grand Juries abolished for most purposes, 1933.

Justice of the Peace. Knights to keep the peace appointed by royal proclamation in England, 1195. *Custodes Pacis* appointed by Simon de Montfort, 1262–4. Regular provision for their appointment made by an Act of 1327. Known as J.P.s since 1362. Commissions of the Peace finally settled, 1590. Their administrative powers transferred to County Councils by Local Government Act, 1888. Women have been eligible to become J.P.s since 1919.

Justice, Royal Courts of. From the Norman Conquest to 1873, situated at Westminster Hall. Then reorganized and transferred to the present building in the Strand.

'Justification,' The, of William of Orange. In 1567 the Council in Spain declared William (the Silent) of Orange an outlaw if he did not surrender himself for trial. William's reply was his 'J.,' published in 1568, and sent to all the courts of Europe.

Justinian's Legislation. The following are the principal legal works issued at J.'s orders:

Codex Vetus, 529.
The Fifty Decisions, 529–31.
The Digest or Pandects, 533.
The Institutes, 533.
Codex Repetitae Praelectionis supersedes the Codex Vetus, 534.
The Novels, 534–65.

Jutland. N. Slesvig ceded to Prussia, 1864, but returned to Denmark after a plebiscite, 1920.

Juvenile Offenders Acts. Act for instituting a prison for the correction of J. O., 1838. Act for committal to reformatories, 1854. J. O. Act, 1901. By the Act of 1908, separate courts set apart for trial of children. Children and Young Persons Act of 1933 provided for less formal court procedure. Criminal Justice Act of 1948 made various changes in the procedures for dealing with delinquent juveniles.

K

K-2, Himalayas, otherwise known as Mount Godwin-Austen. First climbed, 31 July 1954, by an Italian expedition.

Ka'aba (Mecca). Present building erected, 1626, but so as to preserve the essential features of the original building and some part of the fabric of the mosque which the Caliph Mahdi left unfinished at his death (A.D. 785). The holy black stone 'cube' built into the wall of the pre-Islamic shrine was carried off by raiders, A.D. 930, but restored, A.D. 952.

Kabul, Afghanistan (q.v.). Captured by Tamerlane, 1394; by Nadir Shah, 1702. Made capital of Afghanistan, 1774. Captured by British, 1839. Lost and British massacred, 1841. Retaken by Pollock, Sept. 1842. Cavagnari, resident British agent, murdered, 1879. Insurrection at, 1928. University established, 1932.

Kaffir Wars with British: 1779–81, 1789–93, 1799–1802, 1811–12, 1817–19, 1834–5, 1846–8, 1850–3.

Kaffraria, S. Africa. British colony from 1847 till 1865, when it was joined to Cape Colony.

Kaleidoscope. Invented, 1817, by Sir David Brewster.

Kaliningrad, U.S.S.R. Founded as Koenigsberg by Teutonic Knights c. 1255. University founded, 1544. Rebuilt, 1844. First came into possession of Brandenburg-Prussia, 1618 (see PRUSSIA). Annexed by U.S.S.R. and name changed to K., 1945, in which year the university was abolished.

Kalmar, Union of, June 1397. Norway, Sweden, and Denmark united dynastically by Queen Margaret of Denmark under a Danish dynasty. Sweden (q.v.) seceded from the Union when Gustavus Vasa was elected king of Sweden at the Diet of Strängnäs, 6 June 1523. See KIEL, TREATY OF.

Kamakura, Japan. See JAPAN.

Kamchatka, Asiatic Russia. Discovered by Cossacks, A.D. 1690; in Russian possession, 1697; visited by Bering, 1728; unsuccessful attempt made on fort of Petropavlovsk by combined British and French fleets, 1854.

Kampala, Uganda. British flag hoisted at K. fort, 1 Apr. 1893. Proposed as future administrative capital of Uganda, 1958. Raised to status of city, Oct. 1962.

Kandahar, Afghanistan. Capital of Afghanistan, 1747–74. Held by British from 1839 until 1842; finally evacuated by British, Apr. 1881. See AFGHANISTAN.

Kansas, state of the U.S.A. The greater part of the territory was acquired by the Louisiana Purchase, 1803; more territory taken over from Mexico, 1850. The K.-Nebraska Act, 1854, regulated the boundaries of these two states, allowed local option in the slavery question. In 1861 the state was admitted to the Union, and acquired a constitution.

Kappel, Switzerland. First Peace of, between the Forest Cantons and the Zwinglian Party, June 1529; second Peace of, 11 Oct. 1531. after Zwingli had been killed in battle there.

Karachi, Pakistan. Founded, 1843. Became capital of Pakistan (q.v.), 1947.

Karelo-Finnish S.S.R. (Fenno-Carelia or **Soviet Karelia**) occupies the area of the White Sea, and is populated chiefly by Finns. Ethnically and geographically was no different from Finland; the frontier between the two countries merely marks the eastward limit of Swedish conquest (thirteenth century), which determined the limits of the Grand Duchy of Finland Known under the tsars as Olonets Province it became the Karelian Autonomous Soviet Socialist Republic, July 1923. The present designation and constitutional status were assumed, 31 Mar. 1940, when all territory ceded by Finland (q.v.) to the U.S.S.R. was included. But in 1946 the areas containing Vyborg (see under VYBORG) and Käkisalmi were transferred to the Russian R.S.F.S.R.

Karen Rebellion, 1947. See BURMA.

Kariba Hydro-electric Scheme. Building of the dam begun, 6 Nov. 1956; opened by Queen Elizabeth the Queen Mother, 17 May 1960.

Karl-Marx-Stadt. See CHEMNITZ.

Karlsbad Decrees, 1819. Issued against liberalism in Germany at Congress of K at the instance of Metternich.

Kashmir, India. Jammu dynasty of Gulab Singh established by British influence, 1846. The Hindu prince of this dynasty reigning at the separation of Pakistan from India (15 Aug. 1947) did not at once accede to either dominion In Oct. Moslems from NW. Frontier Province began raiding K., ostensibly in support of Moslem populace against Hindu rule. The Maharajah acceded to

India on 27 Oct., and Indian troops were flown to occupy Srinagar. The K. Congress leader, Sheikh Abdullah, was released from prison in Sept. 1947 to become Prime Minister. Throughout 1948 an undeclared war was fought, ostensibly between Pathan irregulars and the Kashmiri Moslem force known as Azad K. on the one side and the K. State forces on the other: actually both sides were supported by regular Pakistani and Indian troops respectively. A United Nations' Commission arrived in Aug. 1948, and a cease-fire was arranged on 1 Jan. 1949. Maharajah Sir Hari Singh resigned, and was succeeded as regent by Karan Singh, 1951. Constituent Assembly of Indian-occupied K., by Abolition of Landed Estates Act, 1950, limited agricultural holdings to twenty-three acres, and resolved, 1952, to elect a head of the state. Karan Singh was sworn in as Sadi-I-Riyasat. (Re-elected for a further five years, 1957.) Sheikh Abdullah arrested, replaced by more pro-Indian Ghulam Mohammed, 9 Aug. 1953. Dispute has continued to embitter relations between India and Pakistan, and in 1962 there were indications that pro-Moslem elements in K. were prepared to seek Chinese help in their efforts to throw off Indian rule. Following the Chinese invasion of India's frontiers in Oct. 1962, Pakistan and India agreed to reopen talks on K., but the talks broke down, 16 May, 1963.

Kassel, Germany. *See* CASSEL.

Katanga, richest state in the Congo Republic (*q.v.*). It declared itself independent of the central government of the Congo, 11 July 1960, and appealed for closer links with Belgium. President Tshombe of K. was held under arrest by the central government, Apr.–June 1961. He was released after signing an agreement to reunite K. with the Congo, but on 4 July 1961 the K. Parliament rejected this. On 1 Sept. the U.N. broke off relations with K. U.N. stated that K.'s secession was at an end, and attempted to terminate it by force, 13 Sept. Heavy fighting followed in the Elizabethville area. A cease-fire was arranged in Dec., but the situation remained confused; but efforts by the U.N. during 1962 to end the secession peacefully did result in a cease-fire being signed on 16 Oct. between K. and the central government, which envisaged the eventual integration of the K. gendarmerie into the central government army. When this appeared ineffective, the U.N. pressed for sanctions against K. (11 Dec.), and on 28 Dec. launched another military attack, in an attempt to force the province's integra-tion. On 14 Jan. 1963 the Katangan power appeared broken, and Tshombe agreed to K.'s re-integration with the rest of Congo.

Katrine, Loch, Scotland, has supplied Glasgow with water since 1859. Works started, 1854. Further works completed, 1896.

Kazakhstan Republic, created 1920. Became a constituent republic of the U.S.S.R., 1936. Its territory formerly was included in Siberia and Russian Turkestan (*q.v.*). Kazaks not reconciled to this regime emigrated to Sinkiang (*q.v.*), Kansu, and Chinguin in western China. In 1950 they fled again into Tibet, ultimately reaching Kashmir. In 1952 those who did not wish to settle in Kashmir accepted the offer of the Turkish Government to let them settle permanently in Turkey.

Kazan, Russia. Captured by Russians, 1552, from Tatars who founded it, mid thirteenth century, and made it their capital, 1445. Destroyed during the Cossack mutiny of Pugachev, 1774, and rebuilt by Catherine II. Capital of Tatar Soviet Republic since 1920.

Kebuga Triangle. Formerly part of German E. Africa, assigned to Portugal, 1919.

Kedah, former Unfederated Malay State. The ruling house converted to Islam *c.* 1500. Known since 1516 to the Portuguese, who attacked it, 1611. English traders dealt with K. merchants in the seventeenth century, but the Dutch obtained a concession, 1641, and drove out the English company, 1683. In order to gain British aid in a war with Selangor (*q.v.*), 1771, the sultans of K. made overtures to the British, who, in 1786, obtained the cession of Prince of Wales Island. By treaty of 1791 the government of K. was subsidized by the E. India Co. The country was partitioned by the Siamese, who conquered it, 1821, which explains the present independence of Perlis (*q.v.*). By treaty between Siam and Britain, 1909, the whole territory, except Setul, was transferred to British suzerainty. A British adviser was accepted by the sultan, 1923. Penang fell to the Japanese, 15 Dec. 1941. K. adhered to the Malay Union, 1946, and the Malay Federation, 1948.

Keele, University of. Formerly the University College of N. Staffordshire. Granted charter, 1962.

Keeling, or Cocos, Islands. Became British protectorate, 1856. Became a Territory under the authority of the Commonwealth of Australia, 23 Nov. 1955.

Kelantan, former Unfederated Malay

State. Conquered by Mahmud, last Sultan of Malacca, who reigned, 1488–1511. Became temporarily independent under a prince from Johore at end of sixteenth century. British adviser accepted by treaty of 1910. Adhered to Malay Union, 1946, and Malay Federation, 1948.

Kellogg Pact. For 'outlawry of war.' Signed by representatives of fifteen nations, 27 Aug. 1928; called after its negotiator, Frank B. Kellogg (1856–1937), U.S. ambassador in London, 1923–5. Eventually fifty-nine nations signed it; but it had little practical effect on international politics.

Kenilworth (England). Castle founded by Geoffrey de Clinton c. 1120. Given by Queen Elizabeth to the Earl of Leicester, 1563.

Kenilworth, Dictum or **Ban of,** 31 Oct. 1266, enacted that all who took up arms against the king should pay the value of their lands for five years.

Kensington. Holland House built, 1608–10. Serpentine formed, 1733. K. Gardens generally opened to the public, early nineteenth century. Victoria and Albert Museum established, 1857. Natural History Museum, 1881. New buildings for Victoria and Albert Museum, 1899. Science Museum organized, 1909.

Kensington Palace. Originally Nottingham House. Bought by William III from the second Earl of Nottingham, 1689. Queen Victoria b. at, 1820. London Museum opened at, 1951. Princess Margaret and the Earl of Snowdon in residence there since 1960.

Kent, Kingdom of. The arrival of Hengest and Horsa in K. as *foederati* in the service of the British king Vortigern is said by the early chroniclers to have taken place during the reigns of Martian and Valentinian III, Roman emperors of the E. and W., and is thus dated between 449 and 455. Though the Germanic settlers in K. are called Jutes by Bede, their leaders Hengest and Horsa are not so called anywhere. But the laws of Ethelberht, written down late in the sixth century, show a social organization and system of land tenure different from that of other Old English kingdoms; money, weights, and measures, and the administrative divisions of the kingdom also differed, and there were linguistic differences common also to the settlers in SE. Hants and Wight who were also described by Bede as Jutes. From c. 580 to his death Ethelberht was 'Bretwalda,' or paramount king of all the Anglekin S. of the Humber. The kingdom was coterminous with the modern county, and appears at an early stage to have been divided as the county still is into E. (of the Medway) and W. K., since alone among English kingdoms at this date it had two dioceses—Canterbury, founded in 597, and Rochester, in 600. Ethelberht's son Eadbald relapsed into paganism on his accession, but was quickly reconverted by Bishop Laurence (d. 619). In the next reign the Kentishman Ithamar was the first native Englishman to be appointed to an episcopal see (Rochester, 644). Between 673 and 685 a second code of law, which survives, was issued by King Hlothere, in whose reign there were two destructive invasions, one by the Mercians c. 675, and one by the W. Saxons under Caedwalla and his brother Mull, beginning in 685. The men of K. burnt Mull alive, 687, and in 688 Caedwalla retired into Wessex. In 694 Ine, the powerful King of Wessex, exacted £30,000 as weregild for his late kinsman Mull. Wihtred's (*see* list of rulers below) laws are extant; at his death the kingdom was divided and Eadberht (d. 748) and Alric shared it with Ethelberht II. After c. 780 K. ceased to have any real independence, and if native kings ruled they did so only as the clients first of Mercia, then (after 825) of Wessex.

Rulers of, c. 449–860:

Hengest	*fl.* 449–*d.* 488
Oisc	?
Octa	?
Eormenric	?
Ethelberht I	c. 560–616
Eadbald	616–640
Eorcenberht	640–664
Egbert I	664–673
Hlothere	673–685
Eadric	684–686
State of anarchy	686–694
Wihtred	694–725
Eadberht	725–748
Ethelberht II	748–762
Kent divided among several kings, subject to Mercia	762–798
Cuthred of Mercia	798–805
Baldred (*probably subject to Mercia*)	805–823
Ethelwulf of Wessex	825–839
Athelstan of Wessex	839–c.840
Ethelwulf of Wessex (*again*)	856–858
Ethelberht of Wessex	858–860

Kentish Petition, The. Drawn up by William Colepeper, chairman of the Quarter Sessions at Maidstone, 1701, against the peace policy of the Tory Party. It was signed by the deputy lieutenants, twenty justices, and a large number of freeholders.

Kentucky, U.S.A., was originally part of Virginia, and its early history is closely connected with that of W. Virginia and Tennessee (*q.v.*). Settlement made by

Daniel Boone, 1775. Admitted to the Union, 1792.

Kenya. Prospected in 1880 by the Imperial E. Africa Co., which was chartered, 1885. Protectorate over coastal area leased from Sultan of Zanzibar (*q.v.*) set up under name of British E. Africa, 1895. Came under Colonial Office administration, 1905. First British settler, Maj. Fay, on the Kinangoj Plateau, 1906. At this time large tracts of agricultural land were conveyed from Kikuyu families to Europeans: the former treating the bargain as a lease, the latter as a freehold sale. United with Zanzibar Protectorate, renamed K., and made a colony, 1920. Kikuyu Central Association formed, 1922; proscribed, 1939. Jubaland ceded to Italy, 1924. Part of Uganda added, 1926. Customs Union with Uganda and Tanganyika, 1927. Gold discovered, 1931, in native reserve. Ordinance permitting removal of natives from, 1932. Kenya African Union founded, 1944. Executive Council reorganized, 1946. Northern boundary agreement with Ethiopia, 1947. Mau-Mau (*q.v.*) disturbances among Kikuyu tribe led to Royal Commission, Oct. 1952, and proclamation of state of emergency. Trial of Jomo Kenyatta, (*b.* 1896) and four other defendants, Kenya African Union leaders, on charge of administering unlawful oaths, Dec. 1952–Mar. 1953. Kenyatta was found guilty and sentenced to life imprisonment. By 1957 the Mau-Mau terror was virtually over. The Lyttelton Constitution of 1954 was declared unworkable in 1957. After 1957 there were informal talks with African leaders on the future of K. Many European settlers left the country. At elections in Feb. 1961 K.A.N.U. (supporting a future centralized K. and acknowledging Kenyatta as its real leader) returned as the biggest single party. Kenyatta freed, 14 Aug., and attended constitutional talks in London, Feb. 1962, which ended in Apr., when Britain and the two major parties in K., K.A.N.U. and K.A.D.U., agreed on a draft constitution for a future self-governing dominion of K. Malcolm MacDonald succeeded Sir Patrick Renison as governor of K., Nov. 1962. Kenyatta's K.A.N.U. party won an overwhelming victory in the General Election, 27 May 1963. Announced that K. to be independent by 31 Dec. 1963.

Kerch (anct. **Panticapaeum**), town in the E. Crimea. Founded by Greeks, sixth century B.C. Capital of the Bospor Kingdom, from the fifth century B.C. to the fourth century A.D.; then

Byzantine, Tatar, and Turkish. Russian since 1774. Destroyed during Crimean War and 1941–3.

Kerguelen Islands, Indian Ocean. Discovered by Kerguélen-Trémarée (1745–97), 1772; annexed by France, 1893.

Ket's Rebellion. Instigated by Robert Ket, a Norfolk tanner, in July 1549. The rioters met at Norwich, but were soon disbanded. Ket, defeated at Dussindale, 26 Aug., was executed, 7 Dec. 1549.

Kew, Surrey, England. Royal Botanic Gardens founded, 1759; open to the public since 1840.

Keys, House of. *See* TYNWALD.

K.G.B. (Russian abbreviation for **Committee of State Security**). Name of Soviet security service since 1953.

Khalifa. Title taken by Abd'allah at Taashi, the successor of the Mahdi. He was defeated by Kitchener at Omdurman, 1898, and killed at Om Debrikah, 1899.

Khartoum, Sudan. Founded *c.* 1822 by Mehemet Ali; defended against the Mahdi, 1884–5, by Gen. Gordon, who was killed there, 26 Jan. 1885; after the battle of Omdurman, 2 Sept. 1898, K. was recovered from the Khalifa (*q.v.*).

Khedive, Persian word meaning prince, conferred as an hereditary title by the Turkish sultan on the rulers of Egypt (*q.v.*), 1867, and borne by them till 1914.

Khyber Pass, Afghanistan. Twice crossed by British Army during first Afghan War, 1841, 1842, and again in the second Afghan War, Nov. 1878. The Treaty of Gandamak, 1879, stipulated that the pass should be fully controlled by the British authorities, and these rights were acquired by the Dominion of Pakistan, 1947.

Kiakhta, Treaty of. Between China, Russia, and Outer Mongolia, for settlement of boundaries, 1915.

Kiaochow, now usually known as **Tsingtao.** Seized by Germans, 1897; ceded to Japan, 1919; restored to China, 1922, and again in 1945.

Kiel, founded, 1240; chartered, 1242; joined Hansa, 1248. Naval base developed *c.* 1890–1914 and 1934–9. Heavily bombed by the British, 1941–4.

Kiel Canal. Completed in July 1914.

Kiel, Treaty of, ceding Norway to Sweden, between Great Britain, Sweden, and Denmark, 14 Jan. 1814.

Kiev, Ukraine. According to the *Chronicle of Nestor* was founded by the Slav brothers, Kiy, Shchek, and Khoriv, 864. but seized by the Rus (Swedes), Askold and Dir, same year (*see* VIKING AGE). Capital of Russian Varangian principality by A.D. 880. Became centre of Russian Christianity after baptism of Vladimir, 988. Said to have had four hundred churches and eight markets by Thietmar, Bishop of Merseburg (975–1018). Captured by Andrei Bogolyubski, 1169. Destroyed by Tatars under Batu, 1240. Passed to Lithuania, 1320. Sacked by Crimean Tatars, 1483. Obtained the 'Magdeburg Right' (Civil Liberties), 1499. Ceded to Poland, 1569. Poles driven out, 1654. Elective magistracy instituted, 1667. Annexed by Russia, 1686. Dubno Contract Fair moved to K., 1797. In 1869 a hoard of Roman and central Asiatic coins, the profits of trading caravans in Varangian times, was discovered. Rebellion at, 1905. Ukrainian Rada at, Feb. 1917. Stormed by Communists, Dec. 1919. Occupied by Poles, May–June 1920. Bitter fighting at, and serious damage, 1941–3. See WORLD WAR II.

Kilimanjaro, highest mountain in Africa. First climbed, 1889.

Kilkenny, Statute of. Forbade amongst other things (1) marriage between English and Irish; (2) Englishmen to use Irish names or wear Irish apparel; passed, 1367.

Kilmainham Treaty, Apr. 1882, between Gladstone and Parnell, by which the latter promised to assist in the restoration of order in Ireland. It was abortive because of the Phoenix Park murders (q.v.), which immediately followed.

Kimberley, S. Africa. Relieved, 15 Feb. 1900, after a three-month siege in S. African War.

King's Bench Prison (London). Burnt during Gordon Riots, 7 June 1780; rebuilt, 1781; demolished, 1880.

King's Champion, an office dating from the reign of William I, involves tenure by service of the manor of Scrivelsby in Lincolnshire, and has been discharged by the family of Dymoke since 1377. The earliest written claim to perform the service is dated 1327. The last Champion actually to challenge all comers at the coronation banquet to deny the sovereign's title was the Champion of George IV in 1820. As the banquet has not been held since then successive sovereigns have granted the Champion the right to carry the standard either of England or of the Union.

King's Counsel. Title first granted in England by James I in 1604 to Sir Francis Bacon.

King's Cup. Aeroplane race instituted, 1922.

King's Evil or **Scrofula.** Supposed to have been cured by the touch of the sovereign. The custom was maintained from the time of Edward III, but fell into disuse with the accession of George I in 1714.

Kings of England and Great Britain. See ENGLISH SOVEREIGNS AND THEIR CONSORTS.

King's Prize for rifle shooting instituted, as Queen's Prize, 1860.

Kingston, Jamaica (q.v.). Founded 1693 after earthquake (1692) had destroyed Port Royal; became commercial capital on destruction of Port Royal by fire, 1703. Almost totally destroyed by earthquake, 1907.

Kingston-upon-Thames, Surrey. Incorporated in the time of Henry II; but first extant charter dated 1200. Saxon kings crowned here. Castle captured by Henry III during Barons' War, 1264. Gen. Fairfax made it his headquarters during civil war, 1647.

Kirghizstan became an autonomous republic, 1926, and a constituent member of the U.S.S.R., 1936. Its inhabitants, the Kara-Kirghiz and Kirghiz Kazaks, recognized Russian suzerainty in 1864 and 1810 respectively.

Kit-Cat Club, founded c. 1703 in London as a literary society, grew into a club patronized by influential supporters of the Hanoverian succession. Dissolved, 1720.

Kleve. See CLEVES.

Klondike gold rush began, 1896.

Klosterzeven, Convention of, concluded by the Duc de Richelieu (1696–1788) and the Duke of Cumberland (d. 1760), respectively for the French and Anglo-Hanoverians, 1757.

Knighthood, Orders of. The following are the principal historical orders (many not now extant), with the dates of their foundations:

GREAT BRITAIN

Bannerets, said to have been in existence, 1282.

Bath, 1399; renewed, 1725.
British Empire, 1917.
Garter, c. 1346–8.
Indian Empire, 1877.
Royal Victorian Order, 1896.
St. Michael and St. George, 1818.
St. Patrick, Ireland, 1783.
Star of India, 1861.
Thistle, 1687.

FOREIGN

Albert (Saxony), 1850. Albert the Bear (Anhalt), 1382 traditionally; revived, 1807 and 1836. Alcantara (Spain), 1156. Alexander Nevsky (Russia), 1725. Amaranta (Sweden), 1645. Andrew, St. (Russia), 1698. Anna, St. (Bavaria), 1784. Anne, St. (Russia), 1735. Annunciation (Italy), 1362 traditionally. Anthony, St. (Bavaria), 1382. Apostolic Order of St. Stephen (Hungary), 1764. Aviz, St. Benedict of (Portugal), 1147; became a spiritual order, 1162.

Bavarian Crown (Bavaria), 1808. Bear (Austria), 1213. Black Eagle (Prussia), 1701. Blood of Our Saviour (Austria), 1608.

Calatrava (Spain), 1158. Catherine, St. (Russia), 1714. Charles III (Spain), 1771. Charles XIII (Sweden and Norway), 1811. Charles Frederick (Baden), 1807. Christ (Portugal), 1317. Crescent (Turkey), 1801. Crown (Rumania), 1881.

Dannebrog (Denmark), 1219 traditionally; revived, 1671. De la Scaura (Spain), 1320. Ducal House (Oldenburg), 1838.

Elephant (Denmark), 1693. Ernest (Saxe-Coburg), 1690.

Falcon (Iceland), 1921. Faustin, St. (Haiti), 1849. Ferdinand, St. (Spain), 1811. Fidelity (Denmark), 1732. Francis Joseph (Austria), 1849. Frederick (Württemberg), 1830.

George, St. (Austria), 1470. George, St. (Bavaria), 1729. George, St. (Russia), 1769. George of Alfaura, St. (Spain), 1201. Golden Fleece (Spain and Austria), 1429.

Henry the Lion (Brunswick), 1834. Hermingilde, St. (Spain), 1814. Hubert, St. (Bavaria), 1444.

Iron Cross (Prussia), 1813. Iron Crown (Austria), 1805. Iron Helmet (Hesse), 1814. Isabella, St. (Portugal), 1801. Isabella the Catholic (Spain), 1815.

James, St. (Portugal), 1310. James of Compostella, St. (Spain), 1175. John, St. (Prussia), 1812. John of Malta, St. (Austria), 1043.

Legion of Honour (France), 1802. Leopold (Austria), 1808. Leopold (Belgium), 1832. Lily of Aragon (Spain), 1410. Louis (Bavaria), 1827. Louisa, St. (Prussia), 1814.

Maria Louisa (Spain), 1792. Maria Theresa (Austria), 1757. Maurice, St. (Italy), 1434. Maximilian (Bavaria), 1853. Medjidie (Turkey), 1852. Mercy (Spain), 1261. Merit (Prussia), 1740. Michael, St. (Bavaria), 1693. Military Merit (Russia), 1792.

Netherlands Lion, 1815. Nicani-Iftihar (Turkey), 1831.

Olaf, St. (Norway), 1847. Our Lady of the Conception (Portugal), 1818. Our Lady of Mercy (Spain), 1218. Our Lady of Montesa (Spain), 1317.

Palatine Lion (Bavaria), 1768. Polar Star (Sweden), 1748.

Red Eagle (Prussia), 1734. Redeemer (Greece), 1833. Rosary of Toledo (Spain), 1212.

Saviour (Spain), 1118. Saviour of the World (Sweden), 1561. Savoy (Italy), 1815. Seraphim (Sweden and Norway),

1280. Sincerity (Prussia), 1705. Slaves to Virtue (Austria), 1662. Stanislaus (Russia), 1765. Star (Rumania), 1877. Starry Cross (Austria), 1668. Swan (Prussia), 1449. Sword (Sweden and Norway), 1525.

Teutonic Order (Austria), 1191. Theresa (Bavaria), 1827. Tower and Sword (Portugal), 1459.

Ulrica (Sweden), 1734.

Vasa (Sweden and Norway), 1772. Vladimir (Russia), 1782.

White Eagle (Russia), 1713. White Falcon (Saxe-Weimar), 1732. William (Netherlands), 1815. Wing of St. Michael (Portugal) 1172.

Knights of Columbus. Roman Catholic men's lay organization, founded U.S.A., 1882.

Knights of Labour. A labour association founded at Philadelphia, U.S.A., 1869. First general assembly held, 1878.

Knights Hospitallers. See MALTA, KNIGHTS OF.

Knights Templars. See TEMPLARS.

Knights' War, The, 1522–3, waged by the knights of Germany under Franz von Sickingen and Ulrich von Hutten, who espoused the Lutheran cause against the empire.

Knossos. Ancient city of Crete, originating before 4000 B.C.; neolithic beds contain pottery, stone implements, and idols; copper utensils from *c.* 3000 B.C. Its great palace (*c.* 2000 B.G.), whose complicated structure may have given rise to the legend of the Labyrinth, was destroyed by fire *c.* 1800 B.C., but immediately rebuilt. This second Minoan civilization was somehow destroyed in fourteenth century B.C. In twelfth and eleventh centuries B.C. Achaean culture superseded Minoan and K. ceased to be the principal city. Excavations by Sir Arthur Evans, 1900–8, and his account of them published, 1921–36. His account questioned by experts, 1961.

Koenigsberg. See KALININGRAD.

Koh-i-Noor Diamond. Owned by Nadir Shah, 1739. Given to Queen Victoria by E. India Co., 1850.

Kopparberg, range of mountains and province in Sweden; the capital is Falun, where the K. Mining Co., founded 1284, still has its headquarters, and operates a copper mine.

Koran. Mohammed wrote none of the *suras* (chapters) himself. Some portion of his teaching would appear to have been written down as early as 615, and revised by him later; the remainder was collected after his death in 632 by Zaid ibn Thabit, his last secretary. (*See* MOHAMMEDANISM.) Translated into Latin, 1143.

Korea (Tai-Han: in Japanese, **Chosen**). A Chinese possession from *c.* 200 B.C. Anti-Japanese riots, 1882. Treaties with Britain, 1883; Russia, 1888. Invaded by Japan, 1894. Independence proclaimed 1895. Russo-Japanese Treaty to maintain independence, 1897. Became scene of much fighting in Russo-Japanese War, 1904. Recognized as a Japanese dependency by Treaty of Portsmouth, 1905. Annexed by Japan, 1910. Prominent Koreans tortured and imprisoned, 1911. Abortive revolt suppressed with great cruelty, Mar.–July 1919. NW. coast swept by tidal wave, 1923. 'Extension of local self-government' announced, 1930. Russia, Britain, the U.S.A., and Nationalist China agreed that in due course K. was to resume her independence, Nov. 1943. Divided into Russian and American occupation zones, divided by the 38th parallel of latitude, Sept. 1945. Russian-American talks about the unification of the country broke down, May 1946. Elections were held in May 1948 in the American zone, and in July Syngman Rhee was elected first President of the Republic of K., which was proclaimed on 15 Aug., when U.S. military government ceased. N. of the 38th parallel a Korean People's Republic (K.P.R.), claiming authority over the whole country, was proclaimed in Pyongyang, 12 Sept. 1948. K.P.R. troops crossed the 38th parallel and invaded the southern republic of K., hereinafter called R.O.K., 25 June 1950. The Security Council of the U.N. demanded a N. Korean withdrawal and asked member countries to help it enforce its demands, 27 June. First U.S. troops landed in K., 30 June; MacArthur made Supreme Commander of the U.N. forces in K., 7 July. 1st Battalions of the Middlesex and Argyll and Sutherland regiments from Hong Kong were the first non-American U.N. forces to reach the theatre of war (29 Aug. 1950), where existing forces had been driven into a small perimeter round Pusan, out of which they broke, 15 Sept., when the U.S. X Corps from Japanese bases landed at Inchon and captured Seoul, 28 Sept. 3rd Battalion Royal Australian Regiment joined British units in 27th Commonwealth Brigade, Oct. R.O.K. units crossed the 38th parallel, 1 Oct., and U.S. troops, 9 Oct. By the end of Oct. U.N. troops had almost reached the Manchurian border, but on 26 Nov. Chinese troops, which had apparently been in K. since about 25 Oct., counter-attacked at several points. U.N. retreat terminated at Imjin River, end Mar. 1951. Gen. Matthew B. Ridgway replaced Gen. MacArthur, 11 Apr. 1951.

Truce talks suggested by Malik, Russian delegate to U.N. Security Council, began 10 July 1951. Gen. Ridgway had orders to break these off if no result had been achieved by the end of the year, but in the event he sought and obtained leave to extend them, first for a month, then indefinitely. First British Commonwealth Division formed, 28 July. N. Korean and Chinese peace negotiators produced a (defective) list of U.N. prisoners held by them, 18 Dec. The British Maj.-Gen. Harrison was appointed Deputy Commander, 8th (U.N.) Army, 21 Dec. Riots broke out against U.S. and R.O.K. guards at Koje Island prison camp, 18 Feb. 1952. Gen. Mark Clark appointed to succeed Gen. Ridgway, 28 Apr. Prisoners on Koje subjected to screening. Gen. Clark effectively assumed command, 7 May. Rhee re-elected President of S. Korea, Aug. 1952. Eisenhower, U.S. president-elect, toured U.N. front, 2–5 Dec., declaring he wished to seek 'an honourable end to fighting.' Armistice eventually signed, 27 July 1953. U.S.A. and S. Korea signed mutual defence pact, 9 Aug. Geneva Conference discussed K., Apr.–June 1954, but failed to agree on measures for reunifying the country. Syngman Rhee re-elected President again in 1956 and 1960, but there was a popular revolt against his regime in Apr. 1960 and Rhee was forced to resign and leave the country. In June the constitution was amended, and the President's powers drastically reduced. There were incidents on the frontier between N. and S. Korea in July 1963, resulting in some American loss of life.

Kotor (It. **Cattaro**), a small Adriatic republic in the Middle Ages, absorbed by Venice, 1420. Ceded to Austria, 1814. Occupied by Italians, Nov. 1918, but ceded to Yugoslavia, 1919. Became part of the Federal Republic of Montenegro, 1945. Had severe earthquakes, 1563 and 1667.

Kowloon, China. The peninsula ceded to Britain, 1861, by the terms of the Convention of Peking, 1860. Further adjacent area leased to Britain for ninety-nine years by China, 1898. K. forms part of the Crown Colony of Hong Kong (*q.v.*).

Krakatoa. Volcano in E. Indies, which had a celebrated eruption in 1883.

Kremlin (Rus. **Kreml'**). A citadel, especially that of Moscow, which once (in the early fifteenth century) comprised the whole area of the city. It contains within fortified walls the cathedral of Uspensky (1474) and other contemporary churches and palaces. Has been the seat of government for all Russia except for the period 1703–1917. Closed to the public during Stalin's regime, but reopened, 1955.

Kriegspiel. Marshal Keith (1693–1788), a Scottish officer in the Prussian employ, invented a form of K., but its present form was evolved by von Reisswitz, 1824.

Kronstadt, Russia. Founded by Peter the Great, 1703; K. Canal, 1884.

Ku-Klux-Klan. A secret society said to have been founded in Tennessee in 1865. It gradually came to have farreaching powers, but was disbanded, Mar. 1869, and had entirely ceased to exist by 1871. The second organization of this name was started by W. J. Simmons in 1915, at a meeting near Atlanta, Georgia. Like its predecessor, it opposed negroes and stood for white Protestant domination in politics. It reached the height of its power in 1928, and was revived again after World War II by Dr. Samuel Green (1945). Meetings of the K. were said to have been held in Birmingham, Alabama, during the racial riots there in May 1963.

'Kulturkampf.' Name given to the conflict between Bismarck and the Roman Catholic Church in Germany, 1871–87.

Kuomintang. Chinese radical republican party formed, Aug. 1912, to carry out political programme of Sun Yat-sen, who was its chairman till his death in 1925. By 1928 it was dominated by Chiang Kai-shek, who by defeating Chang Tso-lin at Peking made it the only party in China (*q.v.*), apart from the Communists, who originally formed part of the K., but were expelled in 1927.

Kurds. Since 1920 divided between Turkey, Iraq, and Persia. Turkish K. rebelled following abolition of the caliphate, 1925. Iraqi K. have at-

tempted (often with Soviet help) to assert their independence, 1922–3, 1944–1945, and 1960–2, and after the overthrow of the Kassem regime in Feb. 1963 were placated by the new government with offers of considerable local autonomy.

Kurile Islands, formerly Japanese territory, awarded to the U.S.S.R. in 1945 as the price of her participation in the war against Japan, under the terms of the Yalta agreement (*q.v.*).

Kutchuk-Kainardji, Treaty of, between Catherine II of Russia and the Sultan Abdul Hamid I, signed, 1774. By this treaty Turkey gave up the Crimea, Azov, and Taganrog.

Kuwait, or **Kowait,** Persian Gulf. Turkish attempt to occupy prevented by British, 1897. Under British protection, 1899. Britain recognized the sheikh of K. as an independent ruler, under British protection, 1914. Wahabi attack repulsed with British help, 1919. Boundaries fixed by Treaty of Mohammerah, 1921. Further Wahabi attacks, 1927–8. Oil concession granted half to Anglo-Iranian Co., half to American Gulf Oil Co., 1934. Development of oilfield greatly accelerated by Anglo-Persian oil dispute, 1951, and new agreement (3 Dec.) provided for equal division of profit between ruler and concessionaires, now known as the K. Oil Co., a joint British-American enterprise. Iraq (*q.v.*) claimed K., 25 June 1961. British troops landed to protect her, 2 July, but had all been withdrawn by 10 Oct. A constitutional monarchy was instituted, Dec. 1961, to come fully into force by 1963, K. being recognized as fully independent.

Kyoto, founded A.D. 793, was the capital of the Japanese Empire until 1868.

L

Labour Day, in Europe, usually 1 May, perhaps because on that date in 1889 the Second International first proposed a workers' festival for all countries. In Great Britain it is held on the first Sunday after 1 May The meeting in Hyde Park was first heid, 1892. L. D. in the U.S.A. is the first Monday in September, and began in certain western states in 1882, but was federally adopted in 1894. Canada also celebrates L. D. on the first Monday in Sept.; in New Zealand it is observed on the third Monday in Oct.

Labour Exchanges. Established by Robert Owen in England, 1832–4. Previously established at Cincinnati by Josiah Warren. New Act for L. E. 1909. Name subsequently changed to Employment Exchanges (q.v.).

Labour, Ministry of. Established, 1916. Renamed Ministry of L. and National Service, 19 Dec. 1938.

Labour Party of Australia, founded, 1891.

Labour Party of Great Britain. Arose out of the L. Representation Committee, appointed by representatives of the I.L.P. (q.v.), the Fabian Society, and the Trades Union Congress, 27 Feb. 1900. It took the name L. P. about the time of its successes at the polls, Jan. 1906. In office, 22 Jan.–4 Nov. 1924, and 8 June 1929–24 Aug. 1931. Branches disaffiliated for not expelling Communists, Mar. 1927; T.U.C. broke off relations with Russia, 8 Sept. 1927. I.L.P. disaffiliated itself from, 30 July 1932. Obtained control of London County Council, 8 Mar. 1934. Abandoned support of non-intervention in Spain, 28 Oct. 1936. Leaders entered Government, 10 May 1940. Left it, 26 May 1945. Victorious at General Election, 5 July 1945. Held office, 27 July 1945–Oct. 1951. C. R. Attlee (now Lord Attlee) was leader of the party, 1935–55; he was succeeded by Hugh Gaitskell, who d. in Jan. 1963, Harold Wilson being elected new leader the following month. L. P. conference passed vote condemning Britain's entry into the Common Market (q.v.) on the terms as then proposed, 3 Oct. 1962.

Labour Party of New Zealand, first returned members to Parliament, 1890.

Labourers, Statutes of, were all passed in the reign of Edward III, and were the result of disturbed social conditions which followed on the Black Death of 1348. The most important were those ot 1349 and 1351; all attempted to fix the agricultural wage at the level of 1347.

Labrador. Visited by Norsemen (who called it Helluland) in the tenth or eleventh centuries; possibly sighted and even visited by Cabot, 1498; visited by the Portuguese Cortereal, 1510; explored by Frobisher, 1576; rediscovered by Hudson, 1610; the peninsula ceded to Britain by France in 1763. The part that drains into Hudson Bay belonged to the Hudson's Bay Co. Remainder given to the province of Quebec by Act of 1774. Newfoundland recovered its strip by Act of 1809. Part of this strip, from Ance Sablon to 52° N., restored to Quebec (Lower Canada), 1825. The Hudson's Bay Co.'s part surrendered to Canada, 1869. Newfoundland, under letters patent of 28 Mar. 1874, exercised jurisdiction along Atlantic coast. The remainder, under order in council of 18 Dec. 1897, was constituted Ungava, an unorganized territory of Canada, annexed to Quebec, 1912. In 1927 the Privy Council decided that Newfoundland was entitled to all that part that drained into the Atlantic. When Newfoundland acceded to the Dominion of Canada, 1949, all L. was automatically brought into the confederation.

Labuan. Ceded to Britain by Sultan of Brunei, 1846.

Laccadive Islands. Discovered by Vasco da Gama, 1499; acquired by Britain, 1877; part of India since 1947.

Lado Enclave, surrounding the town of L. on the White Nile, was Egyptian territory from 1878, when Gen. Gordon founded it, to 1885, when it passed to the then Belgian Congo. In 1909 it became part of the Anglo-Egyptian Sudan (now the Sudanese Republic); part was transferred to N. Uganda in 1914.

Ladrones or **Mariana Islands,** Pacific Ocean. Discovered by Magellan c. 1521. Guam, the largest, ceded to U.S.A. by Spain, 1898; remainder sold to Germany, 1899; mandated to Japan, 1919. Scene of heavy fighting in World War II, particularly Guam. U.S.A. took over administration of the formerly Japanese mandated islands as a trusteeship for the U.N., 18 July 1947.

Ladysmith, S. Africa. Founded, 1851. Relieved by Sir R. Buller after siege of 121 days during S. African War. 28 Feb. 1900.

Lagos, Nigeria (*q.v.*). District ceded from native king, 1861. Created a separate government, 1863; part of British W. African Settlements from 1866; of Gold Coast, 1874; made a colony, 1886; part of southern Nigeria, 1906, being renamed the colony (as distinguished from the protectorate) of southern Nigeria. Capital of both colony and protectorate of all Nigeria, 1 Jan. 1914, and of the independent dominion since 1960.

Lahore, Pakistan. British Council of Regency established at, 1846. Became capital of Punjab, 1849. Earthquake, 1905. Destructive rioting at, Oct.–Nov. 1947.

Laissez-faire, laissez-aller, or, more correctly, *laisser-passer*, a phrase denoting a government policy of non-interference in economic matters. Its origin is usually attributed to Legendre, who *c.* 1680, in an interview with Colbert regarding government interference with commerce, stated: 'Laissez-faire, laissez-aller.'

Lambeth Articles. Drawn up by Archbishop Whitgift, 1595. They embraced the doctrines of Calvinism and were disapproved by Parliament; again rejected at Hampton Court Conference, 1604.

Lambeth Bridge, built, 1862; demolished, 1929; new bridge opened, 1932.

Lambeth Conferences, of bishops of the Anglican communion from all over the world, originated in a letter from Bishop Hopkins of Vermont in 1851, followed by a request from the Church in Canada, 1865. The following conferences have been held, with their presidents and numbers of bishops present:

(1) 1867.	Archbishop Longley	76
(2) 1878.	Archbishop Tait	100
(3) 1888.	Archbishop Benson	145
(4) 1897.	Archbishop Temple	194
(5) 1908.	Archbishop Davidson	242
(6) 1920.	Archbishop Davidson	252
(7) 1930.	Archbishop Lang	307
(8) 1948.	Archbishop Fisher	326
(9) 1958.	Archbishop Fisher	310

Lambeth Palace (London), residence of the Archbishops of Canterbury since 1197, consists now largely of buildings erected, 1430–90, though the chapel, largely damaged in the air raids of 1941, was built *c.* 1230. Sacked in Wat Tyler's rising, 1381.

Lambeth Walk, street in L. of no great antiquity celebrated in street songs current in the nineteenth century, printed versions of which appeared in 1899 and 1924. It inspired a song-and-dance number in the musical comedy 'Me and My Girl,' 1937, and the dance invented for this purpose became popular. 1938.

Lambeth Ware. Pottery was first made in L. *c.* 1630, and figures of artificial stone were modelled at Goade's works from 1760. Doulton pottery was first produced in the Vauxhall Walk, L., by the firm of that name, in 1815. Their factory was partly gutted by German air action, 1941, but other parts continued to function.

Lampeter, Cardiganshire, the seat of St. David's College, establishment for training priests of the Episcopal Church in Wales before ordination, which was founded, 1822, and affiliated to Oxford and Cambridge.

Lancaster, England. Castle supposed to have been built by Agricola, A.D. 124; present structure begun by Roger de Poictou *c.* 1094; restored by John of Gaunt in the fourteenth century; burnt by Scots, 1322 and 1389. L. received its first charter, 1193. 'Lancashire witches' tried here, 1612. Given the title and dignity of a city, 1937.

Lancaster, Duchy of. Settled on John of Gaunt and his heirs by royal charter, 1362. Annexed to the crown by Edward IV, 1461. The court of the county was abolished by the Judicature Act of 1873.

Lancers did not exist in Europe until the fourth century A.D., when the Roman Army adopted as part of its equipment the stirrup without the use of which no horseman can handle a lance. The knight of medieval times was pre-eminently a lancer and his equipment and technique derived from the Byzantine armoured L. called, cataphractes, the lance continuing to be the decisive cavalry weapon until about 1600, when the dragoon's pistol began to replace it. Thereafter only the Cossacks and Poles among European cavalry retained the lance, but such was the success of the latter in the French employ under Napoleon (1807–15) that first French (1811) and later other cavalry units readopted the lance (British in 1816) and often with it some characteristic features of Polish cavalry dress. Lancer regiments in the German Army were called by the Polish name *ulani* (in German *Uhlanen*); though not all German cavalry regiments were so called, all were in effect L. until 1918. The last British lancer unit to use the weapon in action was probably the 21 L. against the Mohmand rebels in the 1914–18 war; in Sept. 1918 the 2nd Indian L. used it on the Turks at Lejjun, Palestine. Its use was abolished in the British Army in 1927. The Polish cavalry still used the lance in the Russian war of 1920, and in the German war of 1939.

Lancers, square dance of five figures, a form of quadrille (*q.v.*) invented in Paris, 1836; brought to London, 1850.

Land League. Founded in Ireland by Michael Davitt, 1879, for the purchase of land; Act of Parliament against, 1881.

Land Registry established by Act of 1862; re-formed by L. Transfer Act, 1875, L. Transfer Act, 1897, and L. Registration Act, 1925.

Landsknechte, term used for German dismounted mercenaries employed in France (Lansquenets), Italy, and occasionally England in the sixteenth century. Word first applied to units raised by the Emperor Maximilian in (S.) Germany, 1492.

Land Taxes, payable in the U.K. under an Act of 1798: four new taxes, introduced in 1910, were abolished in 1920.

Languedoc, France. Eastern L. annexed to French crown, 1229. Western L. (county of Toulouse), 1271. Estates first convoked, 1302. Civil war in L., 1561–98. Protestant rebellion, 1620–2. Replaced by the eight departments of Haute-Loire, Lozère, Ardèche, Aude, Tara, Hérault, Gard, and Haute-Garonne, 1791.

Laocoön, The. Famous ancient sculpture discovered at Rome, 1506, and placed in the Vatican by Julius II. Napoleon brought it to Paris, 1796. Restored, 1814. Fragments of a similar group found in a cave at Sperlonga, 1957.

Laon, France. Seat of a bishop, 515–1790. Present cathedral founded in twelfth century. Napoleon repulsed at, by Blücher and Bülow, Mar. 1814; surrendered to Germans, 9 Sept. 1870. Formed S. pivot of the Hindenburg Line in World War I.

Laos, independent kingdom in SE. Asia. French protectorate, 1893; independent sovereign state within the French Union, 1949. Invaded by Vietminh forces, 1953, aided by Pathet-Lao (pro-Communist Laotian group). Agreement for cessation of hostilities reached at Geneva, 1954; Vientiane Agreements signed between royalist government and Pathet-Lao leader, Nov. 1957. Disturbed internal political situation, 1958–1960; Pathet-Lao recommenced war with foreign Communist support, and made substantial inroads into L., Dec. 1960. After a year's negotiations, agreement to form coalition between three rival groups in L. (right-wing, neutralist, and Pathet-Lao) indicated an early end to the civil war, 1962, but in spring 1963 fighting again broke out between the rival groups and tension built up in the area once more.

La Paz, Bolivia. Founded, 1548. Bishopric established, 1605. Rose against Spaniards, 1809. Became *de facto* capital of Bolivia, 1898.

La Plata, Argentine. Founded, 1882.

Lascaux Caves, the greatest gallery of palaeolithic art discovered hitherto, were first entered in modern times, 1940. Its paintings may have been executed some 100,000 B.C.

Latakia. Separated from Syria under French influences, 14 May 1932, but formally reunited, 12 Jan. 1942.

La Tène, an old Celtic settlement at the northern end of the lake of Neuchâtel, in Switzerland. It was inhabited from *c.* 250 to 100 B.C., first brought to the notice of archaeologists in 1858, and excavated after 1881. The period of prehistory named after it by archaeologists is that following the Hallstadt culture, and is alternatively called the Later Iron Age; it extends from 550 to 15 B.C.

Lateran, St. John (Rome). Palace and church rebuilt in twelfth century. Church entirely rebuilt by Sixtus V, 1586.

Lateran Treaty, 11 Feb. 1929. *See* PAPACY.

Latin Literature, Classical: (principal authors of whom works or fragments survive):

Andronicus, Livius, *fl.* 240 B.C., epic and dramatic poet.

Aufidius Bassus, first century A.D., historian.

Bassus, Caesius, *fl.* A.D. 60, lyric poet.

Caecilius Statius, *d. c.* 168 B.C., comic poet.

Caesar, C. Julius, 102–44 B.C., historian.

Calpurnius Sienlus, T., first century A.D., pastoral poet.

Cato, M. Porcius, 232–147 B.C., historian and writer on agriculture.

Cato, P. Valerius, first century B.C., poet and grammarian.

Catullus, C. Valerius, 84–*c.* 54 B.C., poet.

Catulus, Q. Lutatius, *d.* 87 B.C., orator and poet.

Cicero, M. Tullius, 106–43 B.C., orator, philosopher, etc.

Cinna, C. Helvius, *d.* 44 B.C., poet.

Columella, L. Junius Moderatus, writer on agriculture and arboriculture.

Commodianus, *fl. c.* A.D. 250, poet.

Cornificius, *fl. c.* 85 B.C., rhetorician.

Curtius Rufus, Q., *fl.* A.D. 41–54, rhetorician.

Ennius, Q., 239–170 B.C., epic poet.

Eumenius, *c.* A.D. 260–*c.* 312, panegyrist.

Fabius Pictor, Q., *b. c.* 254 B.C., historian.

Festus, S. Pompeius, second century A.D., grammarian.

Figulus, P. Nigidius, *c.* 98–45 B.C., polymath.

Flaccus, L. Valerius, *fl.* A.D. 70, epic poet.

Florus, second century A.D., historian.

Frontinus, *c.* A.D. 40–103, writer on aqueducts and military stratagems.

Fronto, M. Cornelius, *c.* A.D. 100–70, grammarian and rhetorician.

Gellius, Aulus, *c.* A.D. 123–65, miscellaneous writer and grammarian.

Graltius, first century A.D., didactic poet.

Hirtius, Aulus, *c.* 90–43 B.C., historian.

Horace (Q. Horatius Flaccus), 65–8 B.C., poet.

Justinus, second century A.D., historian.

Juvenal (D. Junius Juvenalis), *c.* A.D. 50–*c.* 130, satirist.

Livy (T. Livius), 59 B.C. – A.D. 17, historian.

Lucan (M. Annaeus Lucanus), A.D. 39–65, epic poet.

Lucilius, Gaius, *c.* 180–*c.* 102 B.C., satirist.

Lucretius Carus, *c.* 99–55 B.C., philosopher and poet.

Lupus, P. Rutilino, *fl.* A.D. 30, rhetorician.

Maecianus, L. Volusius, second century A.D., writer on weights and measures.

Manilius, first century A.D., astronomer and poet.

Martial (M. Valerius Martialis), *c.* A.D. 40–*c.* 104, poet.

Mela, Pomponius, first century B.C., geographer.

Naevius, Gnaeus, third century B.C., epic poet and dramatist.

Nemesianus, M. Aurelius Olympius, third century A.D., poet.

Nepos, Cornelius, first century B.C., historian.

Ovid (P. Ovidius Naso), 43 B.C.–A.D. 17, poet.

Pacuvius, M., *c.* 220–130 B.C., tragic poet.

Paterculus, C. Velleins, 19 B.C.–*c.* A.D. 40, historian.

Pedianus, Q. Asconius, *c.* 9 B.C.–*c.* A.D. 76, grammarian.

Persius Flaccus, A., A.D. 34–62, satirist.

Petronius, *d.* A.D. 66, romance writer and satirist.

Phaedrus, *b. c.* 30 B.C., fabulist.

Plautus, T. Maccius, *c.* 254–184 B.C., comic poet.

Pliny the Elder (C. Plinius Secundus), A.D. 23–79, polymath.

Pliny the Younger (C. Plinius Caecilius Secundus), A.D. 61–*c.* 113, panegyrist and letter-writer.

Propertius, S. Aurelius, *c.* 50–*c.* 16 B.C., elegiac poet.

Publilius Syrus, first century B.C., mimeographer.

Quadrigarius, *fl.* 100–78 B.C., historian.

Quintilian (M. Fabius Quintilianus), *b. c.* A.D. 40, rhetorician and critic.

Sallust (C. Sallustius Crispus), 86–34 B.C. historian.

Seneca, L. Annaeus, *c.* 4 B.C.–A.D. 65, Stoic philosopher.

Seneca, M. Annaeus, *c.* 55 B.C.–*c.* A.D. 41, rhetorician.

Silius Italicus, Tib. Catius Asconius, *c.* A.D. 25–*c.* 101, epic poet.

Solinius, C. Julius, third century A.D., geographer.

Statius, P. Papinius, *c.* A.D. 61–96, poet.

Stilo Praeconinus, L. Aelius, *c.* 154–74 B.C., philologist.

Suetonius Tranquillus, C., *fl.* A.D. 110, historian.

Tacitus, P. Cornelius, *c.* A.D. 55–*c.* 120, historian.

Terence (P. Terentius Afer), *c.* 195–159 B.C., comic poet.

Tibullus, Albius, *c.* 54–19 B.C., elegiac poet.

Valerius Maximus, first century A.D., historian.

Varro, M. Terentius, 116–27 B.C., antiquary and writer on agriculture.

Virgil (P. Vergilius Maro), 70–19 B.C., poet.

Latin Literature: chief post-classical authors:

Abélard, Pierre (French), 1079–1142, philosopher, theologian, and poet.

Adam of Bremen (German), *d. c.* 1076, historian.

Adam of St. Victor (French), 1130–80, hymn-writer.

Adamnan, St. (Irish), 642–704, biographer and topographical writer.

Aeneas Sylvius. *See* PICCOLOMINI.

Albertus Magnus, Albert of Cologne, or Albrecht von Böllstadt (German), 1193–1280, scientific writer, philosopher, and theologian.

Alcuin (Northumbrian), 735–804, educational writer and theologian.

Aldhelm, St. (Wessex), *c.* 640–709, poet and ecclesiastical writer.

Anselm, St. (Italian), 1033–1109, philosopher and theologian.

Ascham, Roger (English), 1515–68, educational writer.

Asser (Welsh), *d. c.* 910, biographer.

Bacon, Roger (English), 1214–92, philosopher.

Bede, the Venerable (Northumbrian), *c.* 673–735, historian.

Bernard of Clairvaux, St. (French), 1090–1158, poet, theologian, and mystical writer.

Boccaccio, Giovanni (Italian), 1313–75, poet.

Bourne, Vincent (English), 1695–1747, poet.

Buchanan, George (Scottish), 1506–82, historian.

Calvin, John (French), 1509–64, religious reformer.

Cheke, Sir John (English), 1514–57, classical scholar.

Coffin, Charles (English), 1676–1749, poet.

Columba, St. (Irish), *d.* 597, poet.

Corippus, Flavius Cresconius (African), *fl.* 550–80, poet.

Dante Alighieri (Italian), 1265–1321, poet and political writer.

Duns Scotus, Johannes, or John the Scot (probably English), *d.* 1308, philosopher and theologian.

Einhard (German), *c.* 770–840, historian.

Ekkehard of Saint Gall (German), *d.* 973, poet.

Erasmus Desiderius (Dutch), 1466–1536, humanist and critic.

Estienne, Charles, or Stephanus Carolus (French), 1504–64, anatomist.

Florence of Worcester (English), *d.* 1118, chronicler.

Fortunatus, Verantius (Italian), *fl.* 569, poet.

Fulbert of Chartres (French), *d.* 1029, hymn and didactic writer.

Geoffrey (Norman Welsh) of Monmouth, or Geoffrey Arthur, *c.* 1100–54, chronicler.

Geoffrey of Vinsauf (Norman), *fl.* 1200, poet.

Gerard, John (English), 1564–1637, autobiographer.

Gerbert (Pope Sylvester II) (French), 999–1003, philosopher, theologian, and mathematician.

Gildas, St. (British), *c.* 516–70, moralist.

Giraldus Cambrensis, or Gerald de Barri (Norman-Welsh), *c.* 1147–1220, historian and topographical writer.

Godescalc of Orbais (Frankish), *fl.* 730, hagiographer.

Gregory I, Pope St. (Roman), *d.* 604, theologian and spiritual writer.

Gregory of Tours, St. (Frankish), *d.* 594, historian.

Grève, Philippe (French), *d.* 1236, hymnwriter.

Grossetête, Robert (English), *c.* 1175–1253, theologian and scholar.

Guido delle Colonne (Sicilian), thirteenth century, novelist.

Heiric of Auxerre (French), *c.* 834–*c.* 881, poet.

Henry of Huntingdon (English), 1080–*c.* 1150, historian.

Hildebert (French), *d.* 1134, poet.

Hrabanus Maurus (German), 784–856, theologian and pedagogic writer.

Hroswitha (German), *d. c.* 1000, poetess and playwright.

Isidore of Seville, St. (Spanish), *c.* 560–636, encyclopaedist.

John of Salisbury (English), *c.* 1115–80, philosopher and historian.

Johnson, later Cory, William (English), 1823–92, poet.

Jónsson, Arngrimr (Icelander), 1568–1648, historian.

Jónsson, Finnur (Icelander), 1704–89, ecclesiastical historian.

Jordanes (Romano-Gothic), *fl. c.* 550, historian.

Langton, Stephen (English), *d.* 1228, scriptural writer.

Liutprand (Lombard), *c.* 922–73, historian.

Luther, Martin (German), 1483–1546, religious reformer.

Magnusson, Arne (Icelander), 1633–1730, historian.

Map, Walter (English), *c.* 1140–*c.* 1210, poet and anecdotal writer.

Martin of Braga, St. (Spanish), *d.* 580, moralist.

Matthew of Vendôme (French), eleventh–twelfth century, poet.

Melanchthon (Philipp Schwarzerd) (German), 1497–1560, theologian and philologist.

Nennius (Welsh), *fl.* 840, chronicler.

Newton, Sir Isaac (English), 1642–1727.

Notker Balbulus (German), 840–912, poet and historian.

Olaus Magnus or Olaf Stora (Swedish), 1490–1558, historian.

Owen, John (English), *d.* 1622, poet.

Paulus Diaconus (Lombard), *d. c.* 799, historian.

Pecham, John (English), *c.* 1240–92, poet, biographer, and letter-writer.

Peter Damian, St. (Italian), 1007–72, moralist.

Petrarca (Petrarch), Francesco (Italian), 1304–74, poet and moralist.

Piccolomini, Aeneas Sylvius (Italian), *d.* 1464, humanist and critic. He became Pope Pius II.

Poggio Bracciolini, Giovanni Francesco (Italian), 1380–1459, historian.

Poliziano, Angelo (Politian) (Italian), 1454–94, poet.

Pontano, Giovanni (Italian), 1426–1503, poet.

Prudentius, Aurelius Clemens (Spanish), 348–*c.* 405, poet.

Reuchlin, Johann (German), 1455–1522, critic and grammarian.

Richard of Bury (English), 1286–1345, bibliophile.

Sannazaro, Jacopo (Italian), 1458–1530, poet.

Santeul, Claude de (French), 1628–84, poet.

Santeul, Jean de (French), 1630–97, poet.

Saxo Grammaticus, *fl.* 1140–1206 (Danish), historian.

Scaliger, Jules-César (French), 1484–1558, philologist, critic, and classical scholar.

Scaliger, Joseph Justus (French), 1540–1609, classical scholar.

Simeon of Durham (English), *fl.* 1130, historian.

Spagnoli, Giovanni Battista (Italian), 1448–1516, poet.

Theodulf (Spanish), *d.* 821, poet and theologian.

Thomas Aquinas, St. (Italian), 1226–74, philosopher, theologian, and poet.

Thomas of Celano (Italian), *d. c.* 1251, poet.

Torfaeus (Thormodur Torfason), (Icelander), 1636–1719, historiographer.

Verecundus (African), *d.* 552, ecclesiastical writer.

Vergil, Polydore (Italian), *c.* 1470–*c.* 1555, miscellaneous writer.

Vincent of Beauvais (French), *d.* 1264, encyclopaedist.

Walafrid 'Strabo' (German), 807–49, poet and theologian.

William of Malmesbury (English), *d.* 1143 ?, historian.

Wipo (French), eleventh–twelfth century, historian.

Wycliffe, John (English), 1324–84, religious writer.

Latitudinarians. A school of theologians in England which grew up after 1688. They were the forerunners of the nineteenth century Broad Church Party.

Latvia. Consisted in the Middle Ages of three provinces: Courland or Kurland, Livonia or Livland, and Zemgale or Semigallia; came under the domination of the Teutonic Order and of (German) prince-bishops, 1158. Under Polish rule from 1562 to 1795, except for Livonia, which was ruled by the Swedes from 1629 to 1721. From 1795 to 1918 L. was merely one of the Baltic provinces of Russia. Independent republic proclaimed, 18 Nov. 1918. Seizure of dictatorial powers by K. Ulmanis, 15 May 1934. 50,000 German Balts 'recalled' by Hitler left L., Oct.–Dec. 1939. Latvian-Soviet Pact, 5 Oct. 1939. After ultimatum presented, 16 June, Russian troops entered L. without resistance, 17 June. Latvian S.S.R. admitted to Soviet Union, Aug. 1940. German occupation of L. complete, July 1941. First Latvian units in German employ left for eastern front, 18 Sept. 1941. Reconquered by the Soviet Union, 1944–5.

Presidents of L.:

Jānis Čabste	1922–1927
Gustaus Zenigals	1927–1930
Alberts Kviesis	1930–1936
Kārlis Ulmanis	1936–1940

Laureate, Poet. The first poet laureate proper was appointed by Queen Elizabeth in 1591. The following is a list of the poets laureate:

Edmund Spenser	1591–1599
Samuel Daniel	1599–1619
Ben Jonson	1619–1637
Vacant from	1637–1660
Sir William Davenant	1660–1668
John Dryden	1670–1689
Thomas Shadwell	1689–1692
Nahum Tate	1692–1715
Nicholas Rowe	1715–1718
Laurence Eusden	1718–1730
Colley Cibber	1730–1757
William Whitehead	1757–1785
Thomas Warton	1785–1790
Henry James Pye	1790–1813
Robert Southey	1813–1843
William Wordsworth	1843–1850
Alfred Tennyson	1850–1892
Alfred Austin	1896–1913
Robert Bridges	1913–1930
John Masefield	1930–

Lausanne Conference, of Britain, France, Italy, Belgium, and Germany, 1932, ended war debts (with one exception as to Germany) as between those parties, but U.S.A. would not assent.

Lausanne, Treaty of. *See* TURKISH REPUBLIC.

League of Nations. Covenant of the L. accepted by Allies, 28 Apr. 1919; subscribed by the signatories of the Treaty of Versailles, 28 June 1919; came into force, 1 Jan. 1920. President Wilson's action in committing U.S.A. to participation repudiated in the presidential election of 1920. L. Council's first meeting, Paris, 16 Jan. 1920. First meeting of Assembly, Geneva, 15 Nov.–18 Dec. 1920; Permanent Court of International Justice established, Sept. 1919. In July 1922 Council approved mandates for Togoland, Cameroons, Tanganyika, Palestine, and Syria. Fourth Assembly, Sept. 1923, advised conference of ambassadors in Italo-Greek dispute over Janina murders. Geneva Protocol for Arbitration, Security, and Disarmament prepared by Fifth Assembly, 1924. Council reorganized and Germany entered the L., 8 Sept. 1926.

1933: Sir Eric Drummond replaced as secretary-general by Joseph Avenol (France); Japan and Germany gave notice of withdrawal, 27 Mar. and 4 Oct. respectively.

1934: Russia joined, 18 Sept.; Afghanistan joined, 27 Sept.; Ecuador joined, 28 Sept.

1935: Paraguay gave notice of withdrawal, 24 Feb.; Council denounced Italy as aggressor, sanctions following, 5 Oct.; Hoare-Laval plan for Abyssinia shelved by Council, 19 Nov.

1936: Secretariat removed to new palace, Feb.; Turkey asked leave to re-fortify Dardanelles (*q.v.*), 10 Apr.; Italian delegation left Geneva, 12 May; Guatemala announced decision to withdraw, 15 May; Emperor of Abyssinia addressed Assembly, 30 June; Eden told Assembly that Britain would not recognize Italy's conquest—France agreed, 1 July; sanctions against Italy ended, 15 July.

1937: Egypt joined, 24 May; new hall occupied, Japan's action in China condemned, 28 Sept.

1938: Appeal by Spanish Government against non-intervention agreement, 11 May; Council left members free to recognize Italian Government in Abyssinia, 12 May; announced to Assembly that all foreign combatants on Republican side were to be withdrawn from Spain immediately, 21 Sept.

1939: Dr. Wellington Koo, on behalf of China, urged members to enforce sanctions against Japan, 17 Jan.; Hungary and Peru gave notice of withdrawal, 11 Apr.; Albania gave notice of withdrawal, 13 Apr.; Spain gave notice of withdrawal, 7 May; Lord Halifax made statement concerning obligations undertaken by his Government to resist forcible solutions, 23 May; the Mandates Commission considered the British plan for Palestine, 15–18 June; publication of British Government's communication to secretary-general as to German acts of aggression, 12 Sept.; announcement that I.L.O. continued to function, 22 Sept.; announcement that instead of Assembly meeting the fourth committee of the Nineteenth Assembly would meet on 4 Dec., 18 Nov.; L. Council met 10 Dec., and Assembly, 11 Dec., to receive Finnish appeal for assistance against Russia. The U.S.S.R. refused to discuss the cessation of hostilities, 12 Dec., and was expelled from the L., 14 Dec. Bruce Report for international co-operation in economic affairs adopted, 12 Dec.

Final meeting, 8 Apr. 1946. Existence formally terminated, 31 Aug. 1947.

League, The, in full the Holy Catholic L., was organized by the Duc de Guise (1550–88) in 1576 to prevent the accession of Henry of Navarre (Henri IV), the Protestant claimant to the throne of France.

Lease-Lend. Bill introduced into both Houses of U.S. Congress, 10 Jan. 1941. Passed by Senate, 9 Mar.; by Representatives, and signed by President, 11 Mar. 1941. L.-L. officially terminated, 20 Aug. 1945.

Lebanese Republic. Made a state separate from Syria, under French mandate, 1920. Occupied by British and Free French forces, 1941. Independence proclaimed at Beirut, 26 Nov. 1941. Beshara el Khoury elected president, 21 Sept. 1943. Agreement with French Committee of Liberation, 27 Dec. Transferred administrative power to L. Government, with effect 1 Jan. 1944. All foreign troops evacuated by 1956.

Revolt by Moslem elements against President Chamoun, May 1958; in July U.S. troops landed in the L. R. at Chamoun's request. When Chamoun's term of office ended (Sept.) Fuad Chehab succeeded him, and internal peace was restored. American troops all withdrawn by end of Oct. 1958.

Leeds, Yorks, England. Captured by parliamentary forces under Gen. Fairfax, 1643; incorporated, 1626, and again in 1673, after the charter had been forfeited. Borough, 1889; city, 1893. University founded as a college, 1874; granted university status, 1904.

Leeward Islands (British). U.S.A. acquired base at Antigua, Nov. 1940. Ministerial government introduced, 1956; new constitution, 1960. *See also* ANTIGUA; NEVIS; VIRGIN ISLANDS.

Leghorn (It. **Livorno**), first mentioned, 891, was under the dominion of Pisa in the fourteenth century, but *c.* 1400 passed to France, and was sold to the Genoese, 1407. They sold it to the Florentines, 1421, whose Medici princes extended and fortified the port, 1550, and opened it to ships of all nations, 1606. It was a free port from 1691 to 1867. There was a severe earthquake in 1741. During the allied Fifth Army's offensive in July 1944 L. was heavily bombed and shelled with considerable damage to the town, and before withdrawing on the 10th the Germans and Fascist Republicans carried out extensive demolition of port installations.

Legion of Honour created by Napoleon I, 1802.

Legitimacy. The Legitimacy Act of 1926 provided for legitimation of children by subsequent marriage of parents. The Act of 1959 carried this process further by enacting that marriage legitimized a person even if the father or mother was married to a third party when the illegitimate person was born.

Legitimists, word now applied to any partisans of monarchy, or of a particular branch of a royal house as against another branch (cadet) or republican regime, but only current since 1830, when it was coined to describe those royalists who supported the senior Bourbon as opposed to the cadet Orléans branch of the French royal house.

Leicester, England. In Old English, *Legerceastre.* Site of Roman *Ratae* on the Fosse Way. Seized by the Danes, A.D. 874. Incorporated by King John, 1199. Cardinal Wolsey *d.* at the abbey, 1530. Captured by royalist forces, May 1645, when the castle was dismantled; retaken by parliamentary forces under Fairfax, June 1645. University College became the University of L., 1957.

Leipzig, Germany. First mentioned in 1015. L.'s fair first mentioned, 1268. University founded, 1409. L. Conference between Luther, Eck, and Carlstadt, 1519. L. Book Fair instituted, 1545. During the Thirty Years War (1618–48) it was five times besieged and taken; captured by Prussian Army, 1756; allied armies entered the city after defeat of Napoleon, 16–19 Oct. 1813. Centre of town largely destroyed by allied air attack, 4 Dec. 1943, and following days. Further heavy air attacks, Feb. 1945. Occupied by the First American Army, 17 Apr. 1945.

Lemnos (Modern Gk. Limni) was captured from the Venetians by the Turks, 1478. Mudros Bay on the S. coast of L. was used as an allied base from 1915, and here the Turks signed an armistice, 30 Oct. 1918. British troops expelled or captured the German garrison, 16 Oct. 1944.

Lend-Lease, *see* LEASE-LEND.

Leningrad. Formerly St. Petersburg and Petrograd (*qq.v.*). So renamed, 22 Apr. 1924. Kirov assassinated at, 1934. Besieged by Germans, 21 Aug. 1941–18 Jan. 1944.

Leon, Spain. Kingdom founded tenth century A.D. First united with Castile, 1037. Finally, 1230.

Kings of Leon. See under CASTILE.

Leopoldville, Congo, founded by Stanley, 1882.

Letters of Marque. Licences first granted, 1295, permitting seizure of an enemy's ships or property. Abolished by Treaty of Paris, 1856.

Lettres de Cachet. Warrants of imprisonment granted by the kings of France from about the fourteenth century. Abolished by National Assembly, 1 Nov. 1789.

Levant Company, The. Founded 1581. Chartered by Queen Elizabeth I for trade with Middle E., 1592. British Government took over consular representation from L. C. in Turkey, 1803. Company dissolved, 1825. A new company started, 1918.

Levellers. Ultra-republican party in the parliamentary army during the civil war, 1647. In 1649 it brought about a mutiny, but was suppressed. The leader was Lieut.-Col. John Lilburne (1618–57).

Leyden or **Leiden,** Holland. University founded 1575 by William of Orange in commemoration of the citizens' defence of the town against the Spaniards from Oct. 1573 to Oct. 1574.

Lhasa, Tibet (*q.v.*). Became capital of Tibet in seventh century. Became seat of the Dalai Lama, 1641. The Potala built, 1641–1701. Occupied by the Chinese, Mar. 1959. The Dalai Lama fled to India.

Liampo. *See* NINGPO.

Liberals. Covenanters termed 'Whigamores,' 1679; name Whig came to be fastened on all Scottish Presbyterian zealots, then on English politicians who opposed court and treated Nonconformists leniently. Terms Whig and Tory came into use, 1679–80, and more advanced Whigs and reformers first named L. in a derogatory sense (meaning French revolutionary) *c.* 1820. Last held office, 1918. Dissatisfaction with both Government and Labour Opposition led to greatly increased Liberal vote during by-elections, 1961–2.

Liberia, W. Africa. A negro republic, originally of liberated slaves. Founded by the American Colonizing Society, 1821; republic constituted, 1847. Boundaries determined by Anglo-Liberian (1885) and Franco-Liberian (1892, 1907, 1910) agreements. In 1911 a small exchange of territory with Sierra Leone took place. Customs laws codified, 1907. Criminal code enacted, 1914. Customs laws revised, 1940. Air bases leased to U.S.A., 31 Mar. 1942. Lease-lend aid granted to L., 8 June 1943. W. V. S. Tubman elected President, 1943; re-elected, 1952, 1955, 1959. U.S. Public Health service mission entered L., Nov. 1944. Manhood suffrage granted natives, 1945. 'Americo-Liberian' female suffrage granted, 1947. President Tubman paid state visit to Britain, 1962.

Liberum Veto was written into the Polish constitution in the first half of the seventeenth century. First exercised, 1652; and abolished, 1791.

Libraries, Ancient. Chaldean L. said to have existed as early as 1700 B.C. First public library founded at Athens by Pisistratus, 540. Founding of the great Alexandrian library by the first of the Ptolemies, 284; partially destroyed when Julius Caesar set fire to the city in 47. First library in Rome brought from Macedonia by Aemilius Paulus, 167. Library at Constantinople founded by Constantine, *c.* A.D. 355.

Libraries, Modern. The following are the most famous L., with the dates of their foundation:

Austria. Vienna: Imperial Library, founded by Frederick III *c.* 1440.

France. Paris: Royal Library, now the Bibliothèque Nationale, founded by Francis I *c.* 1520.

Canada: Parliamentary Library, Ottawa, founded, 1849.

Denmark: Royal Library, Copenhagen, founded, 1661.

Germany. Berlin: Royal Library, founded, 1659. Dresden: Royal Library, founded, sixteenth century. Munich: Royal Library, founded by Duke Albert V of Bavaria, sixteenth century. Stuttgart: Royal Library, founded, 1765.

Great Britain and Ireland. Library Association of the U.K., founded, 1877. Aberystwyth: Welsh National Library, founded, 1911. Cambridge: University Library, founded, fifteenth century, enlarged by George I, 1715. Dublin: King's Inns' Library, founded, 1787; Trinity College Library, founded, 1601. Edinburgh: Advocates (now Scottish National) Library, founded, 1682; University Library, founded, 1580. St. Andrews: University Library, founded, 1456; London: British Museum (*q.v.*), 1757; Royal Society Library, founded, 1660; Royal College of Physicians' Library, founded, 1518; London Library, founded 1840; University of London Library, founded *c.* 1838. Oxford: Bodleian Library, founded, 1598; Radcliffe Library, founded under the will of Dr. Radcliffe, 1714, opened, 1749. Manchester: Chetham Library, founded, 1653, claims to be first free library in England.

Holland. Royal Library, The Hague, founded, 1798.

India. Imperial Library, Calcutta, founded, 1903.

Italy. Florence: library, founded by Niccolo Nicoli, 1436; Mediceo-Laurenziana, 1571; Marucelliana, 1703; Nazionale (amalgamation of Magliabechiana and Palatina), 1861. Rome: Biblioteca Casanatense, founded, 1701; Vatican Library, founded by Pope Nicholas V, 1446, enlarged by Sixtus V, 1588; Vittore Emanuele Library, 1875.

Portugal. Lisbon: Bibliotheca Naçional, founded, 1796. Oporto: Municipal Library, founded, 1833.

South Africa. Cape Town Library, 1818 (holds copyright privilege for Cape Province).

Spain. The Escorial's library, founded soon after the building, which began, 1562. Salamanca: University Library, founded, 1254.

U.S.A. Baltimore: Enoch Pratt Free Library, 1857; Johns Hopkins University, 1876; Peabody Institute Library, 1857. Boston: Public Library, 1885–1905. California: Leland Stanford University Library, 1891. Chicago: John Crerar Library, 1894; Newberry Library, 1887; University Library, 1892. Harvard University Library, 1638. Massachusetts: Amherst College Library, 1821. Michigan: University

Library, 1837. New Haven: Yale College Library, 1701. New Jersey: Princeton University, 1746. New York: Astor Library, opened, 1854; Columbia University, 1763; Lenox Library, 1870. Pennsylvania: Lehigh University Library, 1877; State Library, 1777; University of Pennsylvania, 1749. Washington: Bureau of Education, 1868; Geological Survey, 1882; House of Representatives Patent Office, 1836; Library of Congress, 1800.

Libya. Originally a Greek name signifying the N. African littoral, not including Egypt. The Romans at first applied the name Africa to L. and the territory W. of the Gulf of Sirte together. After the Jugurthine War of 106 B.C. L. proper, known as the Regio Tripolitana, was annexed to the province of Africa, but under Diocletian (emperor, A.D. 284–305), the name L. was reintroduced and the western part named Marmarica. In 476 the Vandals (*q.v.*) conquered the whole of the diocese of Africa, including L. It was recovered by Count Belisarius in 534, and remained part of the *Praefectura Africae* until its conquest by the Arabs, 647. In the fifteenth century it was conquered by the Turks, who granted a measure of local independence, 1711, but proclaimed the country a vilayet, 1835. Seized from Turks by Italians, 1911. Italian conquest recognized at Treaty of Ouchy, 18 Oct. 1912. 'Pacification' by Italian forces under Marshal Balbo in 1925 necessitated a treaty with Egypt, signed 6 Dec. 1925, whereby the Bay of Sollum was ceded to Egypt in return for the Oasis of Jarabub, a Senussi stronghold, occupied by Italian forces, 7 Feb. 1927. Large-scale immigration schemes from Italy, 1930–40. Scene of much fighting in World War II, it was finally conquered by British, Feb. 1943. Cyrenaica and Tripolitania were occupied by the British and the Fezzan by the French, under guarantee of eventual independence pledged by United Nations in 1945. Libyanization of public services took place gradually during the next six years. In June 1949 the British Government recognized Mohammed Idriss es Senussi as Emir of L., and by his constitution, promulgated 18 Sept. 1949, a Federal State came into being with alternating capitals at Benghazi and Tripoli. On 24 Dec. 1951, sovereignty was formally transferred to the Emir Mohammed Idriss. Treaty of friendship with Britain signed, 29 July 1953. Agreement allowing U.S. use of Libyan air bases, 9 Sept. 1954. Franco-Libyan Treaty; providing for evacuation of the Fezzan by the French, 10 Aug. 1955. Severe earthquake destroyed the town of Barce, 21 Feb. 1963.

Licensing Laws (Britain). The present law founded on Consolidation Act of 1826. In 1830 an Act empowering publicans to take out beer licences without applying to the magistrates. Wine and Beer House Act of 1869 regulated 'off licence' houses. Act of 1872 amended, 1874, restricted issue of new licences, and shortened hours for the sale of liquor. Act of 1902 increased penalties for drunkenness, convicted habitual drunkards, and compelled clubs to be registered. Act of 1904 mainly dealt with compensation for withdrawal of licences. Children Act, 1908, prohibited presence in bars of children under 14; and it and L. (Consolidation) Act, 1910, restricted sale of liquor to such. 'Permitted Hours' system established, 1921. Sale to persons under 18 restricted by Act of 1923. Further provisions in Acts of 1933 and 1934. The principal L. Act in Scotland embodying all previous ones passed, 1903. Licensing Act, 1949, made minor amendments; but Licensing Act, 1961, increased permitted hours of drinking in public houses, and selling hours in off-licences, and introduced principle of local option to Wales in respect of Sunday opening of public houses there. Scottish L. L. amended by Licensing Act (Scotland), 1961. *See also* LOCAL OPTION.

Lichfield (Staffs), England. The Mercian See founded here in the seventh century, by St. Chad, first Bishop of L. Cathedral dates from thirteenth century. Besieged by parliamentary army, 1643. Statue of Dr. Samuel Johnson erected, 1838.

Lick Observatory (California). Founded by James L. (1796–1876), who left a sum of money for the purpose. Interesting discoveries made here concerning the Jupiter satellites, 1905.

Lidice, Czechoslovakia. After assassination of Heydrich, the German Protector of Bohemia and Moravia, the Germans destroyed the village, 10 June 1942, killed all the adult males, shot the women or sent them to concentration camps, and sent the children to German foster-homes or concentration camps. Village rebuilt after 1945.

Liechtenstein, Principality of. Named after the L. family, who acquired the county of Vaduz, 1699, and the lordship of Schellenberg, 1713. Became a principality, 1719. Preserved its independence at extinction of the Holy Roman Empire, 1806. Joined the Germanic Confederation, 1815, but at the latter's dissolution again retained its independence, 1866. Entered currency union with Switzerland, 1921, and customs union, 1924.

Liège (Flem. **Luik**), Belgium. Cathedral founded, 712. Captured by Charles the Bold, 1467; by the French, 1691; by the English under Marlborough, 1702; by French, 1794; university founded, 1817; occupied by Germans, Aug. 1914 and May 1940. Bombarded with V-weapons by Germans, 1944–5.

Lifeboat. The first L. patented, 1785, by Lionel Lukin, an Essex coachbuilder. Henry Greathead, *c.* 1789, also patented one, and is generally regarded as the inventor of the L. First steam-propelled L. designed, 1890; first with motor power, 1904.

Lifeboat Institution, Royal National. Founded in 1824 through the exertions of Sir William Hillary and Thomas Wilson, M.P. for the City of London.

Life Guards. *See under* REGIMENTS.

Lighthouses. One at Sigeum on the Hellespont preceded the Pharos at Alexandria which was erected *c.* 280 B.C. A Phoenician one at Coruña was re-established *c.* 1634, and modernized in 1847. The oldest extant is at Cordonan at the mouth of the Gironde, built 1584–1611. The first Eddystone one, mainly of wood, erected, 1696, by Henry Winstanley, was destroyed, 1703, by a storm in which the architect lost his life. Rudyerd's, 1706, was destroyed by fire, 1755. Smeaton's, 1759, though burnt, 1770, was rebuilt and lasted till 1877; demolished then because of wear in rock foundation. Douglass's, farther out, completed, 1882. Northern Lighthouse Board instituted by Act of Parliament, 1786. In America an Act of Congress dated 1789 provided for the building of L. *See also* TRINITY HOUSE.

Light, Velocity of, determined by Römer, 1675; more accurately by Michelson, 1926.

Ligurian Republic. Set up at Genoa by Napoleon on 6 June 1797. Annexed to France, 1805.

Lille, France. Founded in the eleventh century by counts of Flanders. Mortgaged to France, 1305; became part of Burgundy, 1369; captured by Louis XIV, 1667; by the Duke of Marlborough, 1708; restored, 1713; bombarded by Austrians, 1792.

Lillibullero or **Lilliburlero**, words published in 1687, attributed to Lord Wharton (1648–1715), and set to Purcell's (1658–1695) arrangement of an old Irish tune. British Commando units adopted the tune as a march during World War II.

Lima, Peru (*q.v.*). Founded, 1535, by Pizarro, who was murdered here in 1541. University founded, 1551. Severe earthquake, 1746.

Limburg. Dutch province, part of a county founded in Carolingian times, which became a duchy in the twelfth century, and passed to Brabant in 1228, then to Burgundy (q.v.), and thus to the Austrian Netherlands, 1713. Included in the kingdom of the United Netherlands, 1815, it was partitioned in 1839, when the western portion became **Limbourg** or **Limburg,** Belgian province, whose coalmines were first exploited in 1920.

Limerick, Ireland. Incorporated, 1195. Taken by Ireton, 1651; invested by English and Dutch, Aug. 1690; again invested and surrendered, Oct. 1691. The cathedral founded, 1142; rebuilt, 1490.

'**Limericks.**' Earliest known, appeared in print c. 1820. Popularized through publication of Edward Lear's *Book of Nonsense,* 1846.

Limousin, anct. province of France centring on Limoges, came into English hands, 1152, as the dowry of Eleanor of Aquitaine, bride of Henry II. Restored to France, 1369. Partitioned into the departments of Corrèze, Haute-Vienne, Creuze, and (parts of) Charente, Dordogne, 1791.

Limousins, name given to a clerical party, a group of cardinals native to the above region, dominant at the papal court of Avignon, 1342–78.

Lincoln, England. Bishop of L. present at Council of Arles, 314. Castle commenced by William I, 1068. Cathedral built between 1068 and 1501. Fight known as 'Fair of Lincoln,' 1217. Five Parliaments held here between 1301 and 1386. Besieged by parliamentary army under the Earl of Manchester, 1644.

Lincolnshire Insurrection, The. Was largely the outcome of the dissolution of the monasteries and of fiscal oppression. It originated in Oct 1536 and had been largely suppressed by the end of that month.

Lindisfarne. *See* HOLY ISLAND.

Linnean Society (London). Founded, 1788, by Sir J. E. Smith; incorporated, 1802; named after Carl Linnaeus, the Swedish botanist (1707–78).

Lion League. Formed by the knights against the tax instead of personal service levied by Albert IV of Bavaria, 1488.

Liquor Control. The L. Traffic Central Board instituted, 1915. Bill to substitute Commission, 1919. State Management Districts Department of Home Office created by Licensing Act, 1921. *See also* LICENSING LAWS.

Lisbon. Conquered by Moors, A.D. 716. Retaken by the Portuguese with English assistance and cathedral built, 1147. Vasco da Gama embarked from Belem, 1497, and monastery of Belem commenced, 1500. Made capital of Portugal, 1506. Seized by Spaniards under Alva, 1580.

Retaken by Braganza, 1640. Almost totally destroyed by earthquake, 1 Nov. 1755. Cathedral rebuilt, 1756–7. Held by French, 1807–8. University founded, 1911 (that founded in 1290 was transferred to Coimbra, 1537).

Lithography. Invented by Alois Senefelder (1771–1834) c. 1796. *See* ENGRAVING.

Lithuania (Lith. **Lietuva**). The inhabitants of Baltic stock appear to be identical with the Galindae and Sudeni mentioned by Ptolemy c. A.D. 150 as inhabiting this area; their own name for themselves was *Litva* or *Lituvininkai,* at the time when, with the closely related tribes of Letts and Old Prussians, they first came in contact with literate Russians in the E. and Germans in the W. respectively. The tribes of Lithuanian speech were first politically united under Mindaugas, Grand Prince from 1236 to 1263. His most prominent successors were Gediminas (1316–41), Algirdas (1345–77), and Vestutis, the last heathen ruler, who was murdered after being taken prisoner by the Teutonic Knights, 1382. The latter's son, Vytautas the Great, allied with Poland to smash the Teutonic Knights at the first battle of Tannenberg (1410); the alliance became a union when the marriage (1386) of the Grand Prince Jogaila to the Polish princess Jadwiga (1369–99) by which he became King Jagiello (Wladislaw II) of Poland (q.v.), and converted the Lithuanians to Christianity. The joint power of L. and Poland now extended to the Black Sea and their legislatures were merged at the Union of Lublin, 1569, from which time L. shared the history of Poland, its partitions, and suppression. Except for Memel (Klaipeda) most of L. fell to Russia, and became known as the Government of Kovno, 1795. Independence was proclaimed at Vilnius (Vilna), 16 Feb. 1918. A Constituent Assembly met, 15 May 1920, the republic was recognized by the Western Powers, and admitted to the League of Nations, Sept. 1921, which was then administering the Memel province, but handed it over to L., 15 Jan. 1923, in the face of strong German protest, both local and national. All ties with Russia were formally dissolved by the Treaty of Moscow, 12 July 1920. Vilnius, regarded as the capital, was only the seat of government up to Jan. 1919, when it had to be evacuated in the face of advancing Bolshevik forces, from whom it was recaptured (Apr. 1919), not by Lithuanians, but by Poles, who regarded it as Polish territory. Thus for practical purposes Kaunas became the capital and there the University of Vytautas the Great was founded, 16 Feb.

1922. Autonomy granted Memel province, 8 May 1924. Dictatorship under President Smetona from 1926. Concordat with Vatican signed, 27 Sept. 1927. L. signed a non-aggression pact with Russia, 7 July 1933. (*See* MEMEL for the German occupation of Klaipeda.) Pact of Mutual Assistance, 10 Oct. 1939, allowed Russian garrisons at certain points and the country was totally occupied by the Red Army, 15 June 1940. A Communist-dominated Seimas (parliament) elected, 15 July, applied for membership of the U.S.S.R. which was granted to the Socialist People's Republic of L. (Leituvos Tarybine Socialistine Respublica), 3 Aug. German occupation was complete within a few days following 22 June 1941. The Russians reconquered L., 1944–5. There was Lithuanian resistance to both Germans and Russians, and during 1956–7 reports of considerable unrest in L.,

especially among the student population.

Little Entente (Czechoslovakia, Yugoslavia, and Rumania). Formed, Aug. 1920. Scope enlarged, 1922 and 1923.

Liverpool, England. Founded by King John, 1199. Made a free borough, 1229. Attacked by Prince Rupert, 26 June 1644. King's Dock built, 1785. Queen's Dock, 1786. Clarence Dock, 1830. Waterloo Dock, 1834. Victoria and Trafalgar Docks, 1836. University College founded, 1880. Made a city and diocese, 1880. Mersey railway tunnel open, 1886. Chief magistrate made Lord Mayor, 1893. Independent university set up, 1903. Anglican cathedral founded, 1904. Lady Chapel completed, 1910. Roman Catholic cathedral founded, 1930. Mersey road tunnel opened, 1934. Severe bombing by the Germans, 1941.

Livery Companies of London. So called: not all have livery. In order of precedence; with earliest date at which each is known to have existed (E.), and date of incorporation (I.). Names in square brackets are of extinct companies. Names marked 'N L' are of companies that have no livery:

	E.	I.
1. Mercers	1172	1393
2. Grocers	1345	1428
3. Drapers	1180	1365
4. Fishmongers	1321	1364
5. Goldsmiths	1180	1327
6. Skinners	1272	1327
7. Merchant Taylors	1267	1327
8. Haberdashers	1371	1448
9. Salters	—	{ Reign of Edward III
10. Ironmongers	1364	1463
11. Vintners	1321	1437
12. Clothworkers	1480	1528

The above are the 'Great Companies.'

	E.	I.
13. Dyers	1188	1471
14. Brewers	1345	1438
15. Leather-sellers	1372	1444
16. Pewterers	1348	1473
17. Barbers	1308	1462
18. Cutlers	1285	1416
19. Bakers	1155	1486
20. Waxchandlers	1358	1483
21. Tallowchandlers	1363	1462
22. Armourers and Braziers	{ Reign of Edward II }	1453
23. Girdlers	1180	1448
24. Butchers	1180	1605
25. Saddlers	1216	1395
26. Carpenters	1333	1477
27. Cordwainers	1272	1439
28. Painter-Stainers	1466	1581
29. Curriers	1272	1606
30. Masons	1356	1677
31. Plumbers	1365	1611
32. Innholders	{ 1327 as Hostelers }	1515

33.	Founders	.	.	.	.	.	.	1365	1614
34.	Poulters	.	.	.	.	.	.	1345	1504
35.	Cooks	.	.	.	.	.	.	1311	1482
36.	Coopers	.	.	.	.	.	.	{ Reign of Edward II }	1501
37.	Tylers and Bricklayers		.	.	.	.		? 1502	1568
								E.	I.
38.	Bowyers	.	.	.	.	.	.	1488	1621
39.	Fletchers	.	.	.	.	.	.	1371	None
40.	Blacksmiths		.	.	.	.	.	1325	1571
41.	Joiners	.	.	.	.	.	.	1309	1571
42.	Weavers	.	.	.	.	.	.	{ Not later than reign of Edward I }	{ Reign of Henry I }
43.	Woolmen	.	.	.	.	.	.	? 14th cent.	Unknown
44.	Scriveners		.	.	.	.	.	1357	1617
45.	Fruiterers		.	.	.	.	.	1416	1606
46.	Plaisterers	.	.	.	.	.	.	—	1502
47.	Stationers	.	.	.	.	.	.	? 1403	1556
48.	Broderers		.	.	.	.	.	—	1561
49.	Upholders		.	.	.	.	.	14th cent.	1626
50.	Musicians	.	.	.	.	.	.	{ 1350 as Minstrels }	1604
51.	Turners	.	.	.	.	.	.	1310	1604
52.	Basket-makers		.	.	.	.	.	1422	? None
53.	Glaziers	.	.	.	.	.	.	1328	1638
54.	Horners	.	.	.	.	.	.	1376	1638
55.	Farriers	.	.	.	.	.	.	1272	1685
56.	Paviours	.	.	.	.	.	.	{ Before 1479 }	{ 1673 (withdrawn) }
57.	Loriners	.	.	.	.	.	.	1260	1711
58.	Apothecaries		.	.	.	.	.	1511	1617
59.	Shipwrights		.	.	.	.	.	1456	1605
60.	Spectacle-makers		.	.	.	.	.	? 1628	1629
61.	Clockmakers		.	.	.	.	.	1627	1631
62.	Glovers	.	.	.	.	.	.	14th cent.	1638
63.	[Combmakers]		.	.	.	.	.	—	? 1650
64.	Feltmakers		.	.	.	.	.	1180	1667
65.	Framework Knitters		.	.	.	.		—	1657
66.	[Silk-throwers]		.	.	.	.	.	—	? 1629
67.	[Silkmen]	.	.	.	.	.	.	—	—
68.	[Pinmakers]		.	.	.	.	.	—	? 1636
69.	Needle-makers	.	.	.	.	.	.	{ Reign of Henry VIII }	{ Common-wealth }
70.	Gardeners	.	.	.	.	.	.	1345	1605
71.	[Soap-makers]		.	.	.	.	.	—	? 1638
72.	Tinplate Workers		.	.	.	.		{ 1469 as Wiredrawers }	1670
73.	Wheelwrights		.	.	.	.	.	—	1670
74.	Distillers	.	.	.	.	.	.	—	1638
75.	[Hatband-makers]		.	.	.	.	.	—	? 1638
76.	Patten-makers		.	.	.	.	.	14th cent.	1670
77.	Glass-sellers		.	.	.	.	.	—	1664
78.	[Tobacco-pipe Makers]		.	.	.	.		—	? 1663
79.	Coach and Coach-Harness Makers			.	.	.		—	1677
80.	Gunmakers	.	.	.	.	.	.	—	1638
81.	Gold and Silver Wyre Drawers			.	.	.		1423	1623
82.	[Longbow-string Makers]		.	.	.	.		—	—
83.	Playing-card Makers	.	.	.	.			—	1628
84.	Fan-makers		.	.	.	.	.	—	1709
85.	[Woodmongers]	.	.	.	.	.	.	—	—
86.	[Starchmakers]		.	.	.	.	.	—	? 1632
87.	[Fishermen]	.	.	.	.	.	.	—	? 1687
88.	Parish Clerks	N L	.	.	.	.	.	1233	1442

89. Carmen	.	.	.	.	.	.	1516	1524
90. [Porters]	.	.	.	.	.	.	—	—
91. Watermen and Lightermen	N L	.	.	.	.	Unknown	None
92. [Surgeons]	.	.	.	.	.	.	—	? 1308
Not num- bered { Solicitors	N L	.	.	.	.	1908	None
Master Mariners	.	.	.	.	.	1926	1930

Livingstonia Mission. Suggested by Dr. Livingstone, the explorer (1813–73), for the abolition of slavery on the E. coast of Africa; expedition first fitted out in 1875, and settled at Cape Clear. Moved to Bandawé, 1883.

Livonia (Let. **Vidzeme;** Est. **Libmaa**), territory since at least the beginning of the Christian era inhabited by and named after the Livs, a Finnish tribe related to the Estonians; subject to and converted to Christianity by the Teutonic Order (*q.v.*), after whose decline it submitted to Polish suzerainty, 1561, until 1629, when it passed to Sweden; Russian territory from 1721. In 1918 partitioned between Estonia and Latvia. *See* LATVIA and ESTONIA.

Lloyd's Marine Intelligence Department. Originally in a coffee-house kept by Edward L. (*c.* 1648–1713) in seventeenth century; moved from Tower Street to Lombard Street, 1691; to Royal Exchange, 1774; parliamentary inquiry into management of, 1810; incorporated, 1871. Moved to Leadenhall Street, 1928; further new building opened by Queen Elizabeth the Queen Mother, 1957.

Lloyd's Register of Shipping had its origins in Lloyd's coffee-house (*see* previous article) *c.* 1760; became an independent organization, 1834.

Load Line. *See* PLIMSOLL.

Loango, W. Africa, partitioned by the Berlin Conference, 1885, between Congo Free State (later Belgian Congo), Angola (Portuguese E. Africa), and French Equatorial Africa.

Local Defence Volunteers (L.D.V.). *See* HOME GUARD.

Local Government (U.K.). Municipal corporations made elective by ratepayers in Scotland, 1832. In England, 1835. County Councils set up 1888. Urban and Rural District Councils set up, 1894. Franchise extended to all parliamentary electors, 1945.

Local Government Board (U.K.). Superseded the Poor Law Board, 1871. Replaced by Ministry of Health, 1919.

Local Option as to the granting of licences to sell liquor became law in Scotland under the Temperance Act, 1913, but was not introduced in practice until 1920. An attempt to introduce the system in England had failed, 1895.

The principle of L. O. was applied in Wales, under the Licensing Act of 1961, to determine whether public houses should open or not on Sundays, the decision being determined by a majority vote in each county and county borough.

Locarno Treaties, 16 Oct. 1925. Three treaties: 1. Mutual guarantee by Germany, Belgium, France, Great Britain, and Italy. Denounced by Germany, 1936. 2. France and Poland, against Germany should she break the peace. 3. France and Czechoslovakia, similar to 2.

Lochaber Hydro-Electric Power Scheme begun, 1926.

Lofoten Islands, Norway, raided by British forces, 6 Mar. and 29 Dec. 1941.

Logarithms invented, 1614, by John Napier (1550–1617).

Lollards. Name applied, after his death, to the followers of Wyclif (1324–1384). In 1395 they presented a petition to Parliament protesting against abuses in the Church. In 1401 the statute *De Haeretico Comburendo* was passed against them, and on 12 Feb. 1401 William Sawtrey, the first victim, was burnt at the stake for his views. Persecution continued spasmodically, Sir John Oldcastle being one of the most famous victims in 1417. After this date the sect lost its importance.

Lombardy, Italy. Occupied by the Lombards or Langobards, A.D. 568. Joined by Charlemagne to his empire, 774. From 843 ruled by its own kings until 1337, when it passed to the dukes of Milan. Became part of Spain under Charles V, 1529. Fell to Austria, 1714. After Napoleon's campaign and his downfall it was restored to Austria, 1815. Annexed by Savoy, 1859.

London and Paris Agreements (1954) evolved a formula to supersede the defensive arrangements which E.D.C., rejected by France, had been intended to cover. All the W. countries concerned in these agreements had ratified them by May 1955.

London Airport, Heathrow, opened, 1946.

London Bridge. Originally built of wood, the first bridge of which we have documentary evidence (963) was wrecked by Olaf the Saint, when a mercenary in the service of Ethelred II, 1014. Another was built, destroyed by a hurricane in 1091, not rebuilt till 1120, and burnt down, 1136. A temporary structure followed. A new (stone) one commenced, 1176, and completed, 1209. It suffered frequently from fire, and was restored. Toll discontinued, 27 Mar. 1782. Present bridge commenced, 15 Mar. 1824, and opened by William IV, 1 Aug. 1831, when the old structure was demolished; widening begun, 1902; new footways opened, 28 Mar. 1904.

London, City of. Said to have been founded before A.D. 43. Burned by Boudicca, 61. Fortified, 350–69. Destroyed by Danes, 839. Tower of L. commenced, 1078. First charter granted to city, 1079. First mayor appointed, 1089. Privileges granted by the regent, Prince John Lackland, 1191. Divided into wards, and aldermen appointed, 1242. Chief magistrate known as 'Lord Mayor' since 1354. Royal proclamations against further building, 1580 and 1611. Great Plague, 1665. Great Fire, 1666. Street lamps first used, 1677. Charter forfeited, 1682; restored, 1689. Great fires caused by German raids, Dec. 1940 and May 1941. Right to send two M.Ps. to Parliament abolished, 1948.

London Conference on naval armaments opened, 22 Jan. 1930. Treaty concluded between five powers—Great Britain, U.S.A., France, Italy, and Japan—22 Apr. 1930.

London County Council. County of L. formed by Local Government Act, 1888, and L.C.C. set up to administer the same area as was served from 1855 onwards, by the Metropolitan Board of Works, whose powers the L.C.C. inherited. First met under the chairmanship of the Earl of Rosebery, 21 Mar. 1889. For the first 18 years of its existence it was dominated by the Progressive Party. In 1895 there was a tie, and the Progressives retained control only by means of co-opted aldermen. The School Board for L. was abolished, 1903, and its powers given to the L.C.C. In 1896 irregularities, not involving corruption, were discovered in the Works Department. Nevertheless the Progressives afterwards had good majorities, until 1907. In that year their opponents, who had begun as the Moderate Party, and had changed their name to Conservative during the popularity of khaki, adopted the name Municipal Reform and won the election easily, 2 Mar. They immediately abolished the Works Department. They retained power until 8 Mar. 1934, when they were beaten by the Labour Party, who have retained power at every succeeding election up to the present day (1963). The County Hall was opened in 1922 to house about 4,000 of the 8,300 or so officials of the central administrative staff. The method of representation was altered by the Representation of the People Act, 1948. Abolition of L.C.C. and substitution of a Greater London Council (as from 1965) recommended in a Government White Paper, 1961, and a Bill (the London Government Bill) providing for this was introduced, 1962.

London, County of. Defined by Local Government Act of 1888, and a county council formed. Formed into 28 municipal boroughs by L. Government Act, 1899. Changes proposed in White Paper, 1961.

Londonderry (Irish **Doire**), locally still called Derry, and so called by all English speakers until its colonization in the seventeenth century by the Irish Society of London. Grew up round a monastery founded in A.D. 546 by St. Columba. The twelfth-century cathedral church was demolished, 1600. Besieged, 19 Apr.–30 July 1689, by Jacobites. Catholic-Protestant faction fights, 1920. U.S. naval base opened, 5 Feb. 1942.

Londonderry Air, traditional Irish tune, first printed, 1855.

London, Diocese of. Following is a list of bishops since 1044:

William, 1051
Hugh d'Orivalle, 1075
Maurice, 1086
Richard de Belmeis I, 1108
Gilbert Universalis, 1128
Robert de Sigillo, 1141
Richard de Belmeis II, 1152
Gilbert Foliot, 1163
Richard Fitzneal, 1189
William de Santa Maria, 1199
Eustace de Fauconberg, 1221
Roger Niger, 1229
Fulk Basset, 1242
Henry de Wengham, 1260
Henry de Sandwich, 1263
John de Chishull, 1274
Richard Gravesend, 1280
Ralph de Baldock, 1306
Gilbert Segrave, 1313
Richard de Newport, 1317
Stephen de Gravesend, 1319
Richard de Bintworth, 1338
Ralph de Stratford, 1340
Michael de Northburg, 1355
Simon de Sudbury, 1362
William Courtenay, 1375
Robert de Braybroke, 1382
Roger Walden, 1405
Nicholas Bubwith, 1406
Richard Clifford, 1407
John Kemp, 1421
William Gray, 1426

Robert FitzHugh, 1431
Robert Gilbert, 1436
Thomas Kemp, 1450
Richard Hill, 1489
Thomas Savage, 1496
William Wareham, 1502
William Barons, 1504
Richard FitzJames, 1506
Cuthbert Tunstall, 1522
John Stokesley, 1530
Edmund Bonner, 1540
Nicholas Ridley, 1550
Edmund Bonner, 1553
Edmund Grindal, 1559
Edwin Sandys, 1570
John Aylmer, 1577
Richard Fletcher, 1595
Richard Bancroft, 1597
Richard Vaughan, 1604
Thomas Ravis, 1607
George Abbot, 1610
John King, 1611
George Mountain, 1621
William Laud, 1628
William Juxon, 1633
Gilbert Sheldon, 1660
Humfrey Henchman, 1663
Henry Compton, 1675
John Robinson, 1714
Edmund Gibson, 1723
Thomas Sherlock, 1748
Thomas Hayter, 1761
Richard Osbaldeston, 1762
Richard Terrick, 1764
Robert Lowth, 1777
Beilby Porteous, 1787
John Randolph, 1809
William Howley, 1813
Charles James Blomfield, 1828
Archibald Campbell Tait, 1856
John Jackson, 1869
Frederick Temple, 1885
Mandell Creighton, 1896
Arthur Foley Winnington-Ingram, 1901
Geoffrey Francis Fisher, 1939
John William Charles Wand, 1945
Henry Montgomery Campbell, 1956
Robert Wright Stopford, 1961

'**London Gazette.**' *See* NEWSPAPERS.
London Library. Founded 1840, and opened, 3 May 1841. Reading-room opened, 15 May 1843. Removed from 40 Pall Mall to Beauchamp House, St. James's Square, 1845. Rebuilt, 1896.
London Museum. Founded, 1910, and opened at Kensington Palace, 1912. Transferred to Lancaster House, St. James's, 1913–14, but closed in 1939. Reopened at Kensington Palace, 1951. Is devoted to historical and social life of London from the earliest times. In 1962 it was announced that the L. M. was to amalgamate with the Guildhall Museum to form the Museum of London in a new

building to be erected in the City.
London, Pact of. Between Britain, France, and Russia, who mutually engaged not to conclude peace separately, Sept. 1914. A secret agreement, signed 26 Apr. 1915, by the Allies and Italy, comprising the terms on which Italy would enter the war on the side of the Allies. Published by British Government, 30 Apr. 1920. *See* FIUME.
London Passenger Transport Board. Established, 1933. Duties taken over in 1948 by the **London Transport Executive**, established under the Transport Act of 1947, the latter being an agent of the British Transport Commission, and, under the reorganization which took place in railway administration in 1962–3, by the **London Transport Board.**
London, Tower of. The present White Tower, the earliest part of the structure, was built by William the Conqueror *c.* 1078. In 1140 Stephen used the tower as a residence. In Henry III's reign (1216–1272) the regalia were removed to the tower. The famous attempt to steal the crown jewels by Col. Blood from the tower, 9 May 1671.
London, Treaties of. 1. Between England and Holland, signed 1674, ending war of 1672. 2. Between England, France, and Russia, during Greek War of Independence; contracting parties bound themselves to take action for the purpose of securing the independence of Greece under Turkish suzerainty; signed, 1827. 3. Between Great Britain, France, and Holland, providing for the erection of the Flemish and Walloon provinces into an independent kingdom; signed 1833. 4. Between Austria, France, Great Britain, Prussia, and Russia, confirming the treaty of 1833. 5. Between England, France, Russia, Austria, and Turkey, after conclusions of Syrian War; it provided that the Bosphorus and Dardanelles should be closed to ships of war (also known as the Treaty of Dardanelles); signed, 1841. 6. Between Austria, France, Great Britain, Prussia, Russia, and Sweden, settling the succession to the Danish throne; signed, 1852. 7. Treaty of L., 30 May 1913, ending the First Balkan War. 8. Treaty of L. (Naval), defined relative strengths of fleets of the powers, 1936. *See also* LONDON AND PARIS AGREEMENTS.
London University. Institution in Gower Street (now University College) founded, 1828. King's College founded as a rival institution, 1829. University chartered by William IV, 28 Nov. 1836: students from both existing colleges to sit for examinations conducted by the university. Amended charter, 1858.

Degrees granted to women, 1878. University of London Acts, 1898 and 1926. New buildings in Bloomsbury begun, 1933; completed, 1936.

Schools of the University. Bedford College, Birkbeck College, Imperial College of Science and Technology, King's College, London School of Economics and Political Science, Queen Elizabeth College, Queen Mary College, Royal Holloway College, Royal Veterinary College, School of Oriental and African Studies, School of Pharmacy, University College, Westfield College, Wye College; the medical schools associated with the following hospitals: Charing Cross, Guy's, King's College, London, Middlesex, Royal Dental, Royal Free, St. Bartholomew's, St. George's, St. Mary's, St. Thomas's, University College, Westminster; the British Postgraduate Medical Federation (14 federated institutes and one associated institute); the London School of Hygiene and Tropical Medicine; the Lister Institute of Preventive Medicine; also King's College Theological Department, New College, and Richmond College (all theological schools of the university).

The university also maintains a number of institutes, some of which cater only for post-graduate students.

Queen Elizabeth the Queen Mother was installed as Chancellor of the University of London in Nov. 1955.

Long Island, first settled 1636. L. I. City created, 1870, and officially absorbed by New York City (borough of Queens), 1898.

Long Parliament. The fifth Parliament summoned by Charles I; met, 3 Nov. 1640 (*see* PRIDE'S PURGE); dissolved forcibly by Oliver Cromwell, 20 Apr. 1653; recalled twice, and finally declared itself dissolved, 16 Mar. 1660.

Lonsdale Belt first awarded, 1911, by Hugh Cecil Lowther (1857–1944), fifth Earl of L.

Lord of the Isles. Title of the rulers of the Western Isles of Scotland. First conferred by David I of Scotland on Somerled of Argyll, 1135. Somerled's line supplanted by Iain MacDonald of Islay, 1346. The Ls. of the I. were intermittently vassals of Norway until the Treaty of Perth, 2 July 1266, when Haakon of Norway surrendered his claims. Title forfeited to Scottish crown, 1493, and became an apanage belonging to the heir male of the Scottish crown in 1540, which it has since remained.

Lord Privy Seal. Office first held by laymen in reign of Henry VIII (*q.v.*). Specific duties abolished, 1884, and position now generally held by a senior member of the Cabinet.

Lord's Day Observance Society. Founded, 1831.

Lords, House of. Earliest extant writ is dated 1265. Mitred abbots excluded, 1536. Abolished by Commons, 6 Feb. 1649. Cromwell recalled a selection of peers to be called House of Lords, 20 Jan. 1658. House of Lords constituted as before 1649 reassembled, 25 Apr. 1660. Sixteen Scottish peers elected by their order added under Act of Union, 1707. Crown's power to create peers used to secure a Tory majority, 31 Dec. 1711. Twenty-eight Irish peers, elected for life, added, 1801; no election of Irish peers has taken place, however, since the Irish Free State Act of 1922. Proxy voting waived since 1868. L. of Appeal added by Appellate Jurisdiction Act, 1876. Parliament Act restricting Lords' veto to a delaying power of two years became law, 18 Aug. 1911. New bill to restrict delaying power to one year became law in 1948. Life Peerages Act, 1958, empowered the sovereign to create men and women life peers and peeresses. Labour Party agreed to join a Select Committee to consider the reform of the House of Lord, Jan. 1962. This published its report in Dec. 1962, recommending that hereditary peers should have the option of remaining commoners (in which case they could stand for election to the Commons), though their heirs would be free to revive the title. In 1963 the government announced that legislation to make these recommendations law would be enacted before the end of the present Parliament, giving effect to this, and the Peerages Bill became law on 31 July 1963.

Loreto or **Loretto,** Italy. Virgin Mary's house reputed to have been miraculously translated from Nazareth to L., 1295. The Holy Image was taken to France, 1796; but restored, 1803. Pope John XXIII made a pilgrimage to L. on the eve of the opening of the Ecumenical Council, Oct. 1962.

Lorraine, founded as kingdom of Lotharingia, A.D. 843. Duchy of L. given to King of Poland, 1736. Incorporated in France, 1766. Thereafter changed hands in same manner as Alsace (*q.v.*).

Lorraine, Cross of. Carried by Joan of Arc in the fifteenth century, and adopted as an emblem of French resistance to the Germans by de Gaulle in 1940. From 1958 onwards he used it as his political emblem in France.

Los Angeles, California, settled in 1781, became the Mexican capital of California, and was seized by a U.S. naval force in 1846. U.S. city charter granted, 1850. Aqueduct 233 miles long from Sierra Nevada mountains built through Mojave desert to L. A., 1913.

Lost Ten Tribes of Israel, not accounted for after the deportation of the original twelve Israelite tribes to Media by the Assyrians, 722 B.C. Frequently 're-discovered,' e.g. by Antonio de Monte-zinos, 1644, in America, but first in England by John Sadler, 1649. The doctrine of the British Israelites was first developed by Richard Brothers (1757–1824).

Louisbourg, Nova Scotia. Fortified by French, 1713. Taken by British, 1745. Restored to France, 1748. Again captured by British, 1758. Finally ceded to Britain, 1763.

Louis d'Or. Gold coin in use in France, 1641–1795.

Louisiana, U.S.A. Originally claimed for France by the explorer La Salle (1643–1687), who named the territory after Louis XIV. Handed over to the Mississippi Co. (see MISSISSIPPI SCHEME), 1719. Ceded to Spain by England, 1762; to France, 1800. Sold to U.S.A. by Napoleon, 1803; admitted as a state, 1812. Present constitution, 1921. Huey Pierce Long's governorship, 1931–5.

Lourdes, France. Virgin Mary appeared to a peasant girl, Bernadette Soubirous, 11 Feb. 1858. Church declared the facts to be authentic, 1862. The basilica, over the spring which is said to have suddenly come to light at the time of the miracle, erected, 1876. St. Bernadette canonized, 1933. Underground basilica consecrated, 1958.

Lourenço Marques, Portuguese E. Africa, founded as a Portuguese factory, 1544.

Louvain (Flem. **Leeuwen**), Belgium. University founded, 1426; suppressed, 1797; refounded, 1817, and designated the Catholic University, 1835. Seriously damaged by Germans in 1914 and 1940.

Louvre, The (Paris). Present building started in 1541 by Francis I. Formerly a royal palace, now a museum and picture gallery; enlarged during reign of Louis XIV (1643–1715).

Loyalists, United Empire, migrated to Canada, 1783, from United States. See ONTARIO.

Lübeck, Germany. Founded by Saxons, A.D. 1143; held by French, 1806–14; joined N. German Confederation, 1866. Relinquished status as free city, 1937. Heavily bombed by R.A.F., 1942. See HANSEATIC LEAGUE.

Lucca, Italy. Originally *Luca*. Since at least the eleventh century the cathedral of St. Martin has contained the *Volto Santo* (Holy Face), a wood-carving of Christ attributed to His contemporary, St. Nicodemus. Made a Roman colony, 177 B.C.; independent republic from 1369 to 1797; made a principality by Napoleon,

1805; passed to Spain, 1815; ceded to Tuscany, 1847.

Lucerne (Luzern), Switzerland. Joined Swiss Confederation, 1332.

Lucknow, India. Ancient city. Capital of Oudh, 1775; besieged during the Indian Mutiny, 1 July 1857; reinforced by Gen. Havelock, 25 Sept. 1857; relieved by Sir Colin Campbell, 17 Nov. 1857; final capture by him, 19–22 Mar. 1858. University founded, 1920. Now the capital of Uttar Pradesh state.

Luddite Riots. Broke out first in Nottinghamshire in Nov. 1811. The name L. originated with one Ned Ludd a worker who is said to have broken some machinery some years before. Renewed, July 1816, when much damage was done.

Luftwaffe, German Air Force which had existed in fact since at least 1933, first officially mentioned in a proclamation by Goering, Mar. 1935. Post-war L. came into being, 1956.

Lundy Island, bought by A. L. Christie, 1917. His coins, not being legal tender, were withdrawn from currency, 1927.

Lunéville, Peace of. Signed between Germany and France, 9 Feb. 1801, confirming the Treaty of Campo Formio.

Lupercalia, ancient Roman festival, celebrated on 15 Feb., until its abolition, A.D. 494, when Pope Gelasius I decreed its replacement by the Christian Lady Day (2 Feb.).

Lusaka. Capital of N. Rhodesia since 1935.

Lusatia (Wend. **Lužica**; Ger. **Lausitz**), principally inhabited by the Wends (q.v.), was one of the Bohemian crown lands for the period 1160–1360. It was acquired by the Electors of Saxony, 1620. All but a part of Upper L. was ceded to Prussia, 1815. Since 1949 has formed part of the People's Republic of Eastern Germany, province of Saxony, with the exception of a portion which lies E. of the R. Neisse, and which has belonged to Poland since 1946.

'Lusitania.' Unarmed Cunard liner sunk by German submarine off Old Head of Kinsale, 7 May 1915. 1198 passengers and crew, including 124 Americans, were drowned, and the sinking influenced the U.S.A.'s subsequent decision to enter the war on the allied side.

'Lutine,' H.M.S. A 32-gun ship wrecked in a storm off Vlieland, Netherlands, 9–10 Oct. 1799, with specie on board to the value of £1,175,000. Dutch claimed the wreck, and not until 1823 did the Dutch Government acknowledge that Lloyd's were entitled to half. Much had already been taken. Operations on Lloyd's behalf began 1857. By 1859 they had received £22,162 6s. 7d. Operations

K*

resumed, May–June 1938, when some bars of gold were recovered.

Lutterworth (Leics.), England. Wyclif was rector at the church here, 1374–1384. The church, containing many relics of the reformer, was carefully restored, 1867–9.

Luttrell or **Louterell Psalter.** Illuminated MS. of *c.* 1340. Acquired for the nation, 1929.

Lützen, Germany. Wallenstein defeated by Gustavus Adolphus (who was killed), 1632; allies by Napoleon, 1813.

Luxemburg (in the local Franconian dialect **Letzeburg**). Settled by Franks, A.D. 459. Independent county, 963. Became Burgundian territory, 1443. Then Hapsburg, 1482; Spanish, 1555; French, 1684–97; Spanish until 1714; Austrian until 1795; then French again until allotted to the United Netherlands at Congress of Vienna, 1815, and garrisoned by Prussia. Seceded from Belgium, 1839, losing thereby Belgian L. Constitution granted, 1848. In 1867, by Treaty of London, it was declared an independent grand duchy, and the Prussians withdrew. The fortifications were at the same time demolished. Occupied by the Germans, 1914–18. Declared free of all German ties by Treaty of Versailles, 1919. Joined Belgian Customs Union, 1921. Invaded by Germany, 10 May 1940; liberated, 1944. Joined Western European Alliance, 1948; Benelux, 1948. Constitutional revision of 1948, abolished L.'s 'perpetually neutral' status. Joined N.A.T.O., 1949. Signed Treaty of Rome, 1957, and member of the E.E.C. since its inception on 1 Jan. 1958.

Lvov. Founded *c.* 1250. Became Polish, 1340. From 1848 centre of the Ukrainian national movement. Part of Austria, 1772–1918, and then Polish until 1939, when it was annexed by the U.S.S.R.

Lydia, Asia Minor. Before 700 B.C. known as Maeonia. Conquered by Persians, 546. Independent, 334, but after a period of Syrian and Pergamite domination became part of the Roman province of Asia, 133.

Lynne River Flood Disaster. On the night of 15–16 Aug. 1952 the E. and W. L. Rs. burst their banks, and wrecked the town and harbour of Lynmouth, Devon, causing some twenty deaths by drowning.

Lyons, France. Roman colony of Lugdunum founded, 43 B.C. Burnt, A.D. 59; by Romans, 197. Made capital of Burgundy (*q.v.*), 478. United to French crown, 1312. The silk-weaving industry was introduced by Italian refugees about the second decade of the fourteenth century; it was fostered by Charles VII, Francis I, Henry II, and Henry IV. In 1793 refused to acknowledge National Convention, and was besieged for 70 days and destroyed. Its name was also changed to Ville-Affranchie. Capitulated to Austrians, Mar. 1814 and July 1815. Important centre of French resistance movement, 1940–4; liberated from the Germans by French and American troops, 3 Sept. 1944.

M

M.1. First British motorway intended to link London and Birmingham. First section officially opened, Nov. 1959.

'Mabinogion, The.' Title of a collection of eleven medieval Welsh folk-tales found in *The White Book of Rhydderch* (*c.* 1300–25) and *The Red Book of Hergest* (*c.* 1375–1425) and other MSS.

Macadamization of Roads. Named after J. L. McAdam (1756–1836). First used in England between 1810 and 1816. Word 'Tarmac' registered, 1903.

Macao, China. Portuguese settled at, 1557. Declared a free port, 1845. British and Chinese prevent coolie trade, 1873. Treaty with China, 1 Dec. 1887, confirmed Portuguese rights to the territory.

Macassar, Celebes, Indonesian Republic. First Dutch settlement, 1607. Massacre, 1618. Dutch government established at, 1667. Seized by Japanese, Feb. 1942.

Macedonia, peopled by Grecian tribes, became united under one government *c.* 700 B.C. Capital: first, Aegae; then, Pella. Persians subdued it *c.* 490 B.C.; its king, Alexander I, compelled to help invasion of Greece by Xerxes. Recovered independence after battle of Plataea, 479 B.C. Prospered under Archelaus (*d.* 399 B.C.). Civil wars till accession, 359 B.C., of Philip II, who became leader of Greece. His son, Alexander the Great, ruled 336–323 and was succeeded by Antipater (*d.* 319 B.C.). Civil wars ensued; security regained under Antigonus Gonatos, 277–239 B.C. Conquered by Rome, 168 B.C.; became a Roman province, 143 B.C.; later, part of Eastern Roman Empire (*q.v.*). Overrun by Slavs at end of sixth century A.D. Dominated by Bulgarians, ninth–eleventh centuries. Mission of Cyril and Methodius, *c.* 860, led to Macedonian, first among Slavonic languages, being reduced to writing in the Cyrillic and Glagolithic scripts invented by the missionaries. Eleventh-century MSS. (Codex Zagrophenic, etc.) still extant. Thereafter the language was not written until *c.* 1764, when the first Macedonian dictionary was published. Byzantine rule re-established, early eleventh century. Included in Serbia in fourteenth, fell to Turks in fifteenth. Claimed by Greece, Serbia, and Bulgaria in nineteenth; and was in a continuous state of civil war till 1903, when the Bulgarians rose and the Turks were massacred. The Balkan League's victory over Turkey, 1912–13, and the defeat of Bulgaria, resulted in division of M. between Greece, Bulgaria, and Serbia, 1913. Macedonian recognized as a separate nationality and language at AVNOJ session of 29 Sept. 1943, and Macedonian Republic set up, as a constituent part of Yugoslavia, 2 Aug. 1944. Civil war started by Communists with Yugoslav and Bulgarian assistance in Greek M., 1945. *See* GREECE, MODERN and BULGARIA.

McGill University of Canada, founded by James McG. of Glasgow (*d.* 1813). Incorporated, 1821 and 1852. Women's college added, 1899.

Machu Pichu, ancient Peruvian city of the Andes, built *c.* A.D. 800, rebuilt in the sixteenth century after having been abandoned once. Site rediscovered, 1911, by Hiram Bingham who, in 1948, formally opened a new highway to the city, named after him.

M'Naughten Rules, the answers to a set of questions put to the judges as a body by the House of Lords following the acquittal on grounds of insanity of Daniel M'N., who in 1843 shot dead Sir R. Peel's private secretary. The maintenance of the M'N. R. (with one exception) was recommended in the report (published 1924) of the Atkin Committee, set up in 1922 following the case of Ronald True, similarly acquitted.

Madagascar. Appears on Arab charts of twelfth century. Visited by Diego Diaz (Portugal), 1500. Granted, 1642, by Louis XIV to the Compagnie de l'Orient. French massacred by natives, 1672. Britain took possession, 1814; French returned after 1815. British ascendancy 1810–28; English missionaries at work by 1820; Capt. Owen, R.N., surveyed coast, 1823–5. Under Queen Rànavàlona I missionaries were persecuted and trade hampered, 1829. Europeans returned to Antananarivo after 1853. King Radama I, friendly to Europeans, murdered, 1863. Grandidier explored interior, 1865–70. French territory invaded by natives, Tamatave bombarded by French, 1883, the year of accession of Queen Rànavàlona III. French protectorate practically established, 1885; recognized by Britain, 1890. Hova dynasty suppressed, Queen Rànavàlona III (1861–1916) exiled to Algeria, and M. made a French colony, 1896. Occupied by British to forestall Vichyite collaboration with Germans,

May–Sept. 1942. French resumed administration, 1944. Hova rebellion, 1946. Member of the French Community, 14 Oct. 1958, and became an independent republic within the Community, 26 June 1960. Admitted to the U.N., Sept. 1960.

Madeira, Atlantic. Porto Santo discovered, 1418; Mitrelf, 1420, by João Gonçalves Zarco. Colonized by Portuguese, 1431. Occupied by British, 1801 and 1807–14, in trust for Portuguese crown. Unsuccessful rebellion against Portuguese rule, Apr.–May 1931.

Madhya Pradesh, India. Present state came into existence, 1 Nov. 1956, with the merger of the states of Madhya Bharat and Vindhya with most of the former Central Provinces (renamed M. P. from 1947 onwards), excluding the Mahratta-speaking districts of the latter. The Central Provinces had been part of British India since 1861, having previously been part of the Mahratta kingdom.

Mad Parliament, 1258. It appointed the committee which drew up the Provisions of Oxford (q.v.).

Madras, India (q.v.). City and state. English established themselves in, 1644; city captured by French, 1746; restored to English, 1748; besieged by French, 12 Dec. 1758.

Madras Mutiny, among European officers of the E. India Co.'s army, broke out, 1809.

Madrid, Spain. Founded by Moors in tenth century as *Medina Majerit.* Taken by Ramiro II, King of Leon, 939, but not permanently conquered until 1083. First charter, 1202. Cortes first held there, 1309. Treaty between Charles V and Francis I, 1526. Declared capital of Spain by Philip II, 1561. Captured from French by allied forces under Wellington, 1812. University of M. was established by the removal of that of Alcalá to the capital, 1836–7. Town wall razed, 1878. Made a bishopric, 1885. Great hurricane, 13 May 1886. National Library and Museum finished, 1892. Industries, hitherto neglected, and especially the tobacco industry, established in 1890s. Great fire in working-class quarter, 10 May 1908. Occupied by Franco, 29 Mar. 1939.

Madrigal Society of London. Founded by John Immyns, 1741.

Mafeking Night, 18 May 1900, when the news reached London that M. had been relieved after a seven-month siege by the Boers.

Mafia, Sicilian secret society, similar in nature to the Camorra (q.v.), founded at some time between 1800 and 1825. Its period of greatest activity and power was from 1860 to 1870, and in the 1890s its influence spread to the U.S.A., where a large number of immigrants to New York were of Sicilian origin. The Fascists claimed to have crushed the organization in 1928, but there was a recrudescence of violence and extortion in Sicily after World War II, and by 1962 the Sicilian authorities were admitting this to be the work of the M. and were seeking the assistance of the central government to suppress it. In Nov. 1962 the Italian Chamber of Deputies authorized a commission of inquiry into M.

Magdeburg, German Democratic Republic. Founded by Charlemagne, A.D. 805; destroyed by the Wends, 924, and refounded shortly afterwards by Editha; made seat of a bishopric, 968; joined Luther, 17 July 1524; joined League of Schmalkalden (q.v.), 1531; surrendered to Maurice of Saxony, Nov. 1551; besieged in vain by Wallenstein, 1629; sacked by Tilly, 1631; annexed to kingdom of Westphalia, 1803; restored to Prussia, 1814. Severely damaged by allied bombing during World War II and part of the German Democratic Republic since 1949.

Magellan, Straits of, discovered, 1520, by the Portuguese navigator, Ferdinand M. (1480–1521).

Maginot Line. Eastern fortifications of France, constructed 1928–34. Named after André Maginot (1877–1932), minister of war.

Magna Carta or **The Great Charter** of England. The barons compelled King John to grant it at Runnymede, 15 June 1215.

Magnum Concilium or Great Council of Peers last met at York, 1640.

Mahdi. *See* SUDAN.

Mahrattas. First appear in Indian history in the middle of seventeenth century. Defeated by Afghans, Jan. 1761. From 1780 onwards they were continually at war with the British and their allies. Of their leaders the Peishwa of Poona was compelled to accept a British alliance in 1802, the Gaekwar of Baroda in 1803, the Scindiah and the Bhonsla of Nagpur in 1804, the latter being then forced to cede Berar to the Nizam of Hyderabad (q.v.). War nevertheless continued intermittently and culminated in the submission of the Holkar of Indore in 1817, the British annexation of Poona in 1818, and the abolition of the Peishwaship. The claimant to this office, Nana Sahib, later played a leading part in the Indian Mutiny (q.v.). Satara was annexed in 1848. Nagpur in 1853.

Maiden, beheading machine used in

Scotland and in some northern English boroughs (*see* HALIFAX LAW) in the Middle Ages. That of Edinburgh was first used, 1561; last used, 1710.

Maiden Castle, earthwork in Dorset surrounding a site inhabited from *c.* 2000 B.C. until the inhabitants were forcibly evacuated by the Romans, *c.* A.D. 70. It was systematically excavated by Sir R. E. M. Wheeler, 1934–7.

Maine, French province up to 1789, with capital at Le Mans. From *c.* A.D. 800 was ruled by counts who were themselves vassals of the counts of Anjou (*q.v.*). United with Anjou under the Angevins, 1110. English territory, 1154–1204. It belonged to the Count of Provence, 1246–1328, then passed again to the French crown. It returned permanently to the French crown in 1481. M. became a province *c.* 1600.

Maine, U.S.A. First permanent settlement, at Pemaquid, 1623. Western territory, known as province of M., 1635, from 1651 to 1820 a detached part of Massachusetts. The present state of M. founded, 1820; boundary dispute with Great Britain settled, 1842.

Mainz or **Mayence**, Germany. Of Celtic origin; Roman military station called Moguntiacum dates from 13 B.C.; cathedral built, A.D. 975–1009; head of the confederacy of Rhenish cities, thirteenth century; in French possession, 1797–1814; by Congress of Vienna, 1814–1815, ceded to Hesse-Darmstadt; declared a federal fortress, 1870. Heavily damaged during fighting in 1945.

Majorca (Sp. **Mallorca**), Mediterranean, conquered by the Romans, 123 B.C.; by the Vandals, A.D. 423; by the Moors, 790; became a Moorish kingdom, 1009; independent Christian kingdom 1276–1349, when finally annexed by Aragon. M. favoured the cause of Charles in the War of the Spanish Succession, but submitted to Philip V of Spain, 1715; held by the insurgents during the civil war of 1936–9.

Major-General. Term first used in technical military sense (commander of infantry of an army), early seventeenth century. Rank was instituted in Britain with special sense by Oliver Cromwell in 1655, after he had quarrelled with his first Parliament. Each M.-G. was to govern a district. This scheme was dropped in 1657.

Malacca, Malaya (*q.v.*). Settled by Portuguese, 1511, who held it until 1641, when the Dutch seized it and, in turn, held it until 1795, when the English took possession; restored to the Dutch by the Peace of Amiens, 1801; exchanged with Britain for Sumatra, 1825; made part of

Straits Settlements, 1867. Incorporated in the Malayan Union, 1947, and in the Malayan Federation, 1948.

Malaga, Spain. Captured from Moors by Ferdinand and Isabella, 1487. Sacked by French, 1810. Captured by Franco's forces, 8 Feb. 1937.

Malaya. Main treaties establishing British predominance made with Perak, 1874; Selangor, 1874; Negri Sembilan, 1896; Pahang, 1888. These states were federated in 1896. By treaty with Siam, Siamese suzerainty over Kelantan, Trengganu, Kedah, and Perlis ceded to Britain, 1909. Johore came under British influence after 1815, and ceded Singapore to Britain, 1819. Penang was purchased from Kedah, 1786. Malacca ceded by the Dutch, 1825. Japanese invasion began, 8 Dec. 1941. *See* MALAYAN FEDERATION, MALAYAN UNION, and all the separate states and territories mentioned above.

Malayan Federation, including all former British colonies and protectorates in the Malay Peninsula and Islands, excluding the colony of Singapore, inaugurated its Legislative Council, 24 Feb. 1948. Communist rebellion broke out, May 1948. Only hard core of terrorists left by 1955; amnesty offer made by Malayan Government, 1955; withdrawn, 1956. The M. F. became a self-governing Dominion within the British Commonwealth, 31 Aug. 1957.

Malayan Union. Proposal for reorganization of M. states and colonies published 22 Jan. 1946. Union inaugurated, 1 Apr. 1946. Proposals for greater local autonomy published, 24 July 1947. Union came to an end, 1 Feb. 1948.

Malaysia. A proposed union of the Malayan Federation, Singapore, N. Borneo and Sarawak, and Brunei. The Prime Minister of Malaya held talks in London on its formation, July 1962. Agreement was reached that M. would come into existence on 31 Aug. 1963, Brunei subsequently deciding not to join it. In Aug. 1963 Britain agreed that the U.N. should investigate the feelings of the peoples of the peoples of Sarawak and N. Borneo towards M.; it thus seemed likely that M. would not come into being on the date envisaged.

Maldive Islands. British protectorate having treaty relations with Ceylon (*q.v.*). A new constitution established a sultanate, 1932, which was abolished in 1952 when the M. I. became a republic. Sultanate restored, 1954. New treaty with Britain, giving greater self-government, signed, 14 Feb. 1960.

Mali, independent African republic since 22 Sept. 1960. For previous history *see* SUDAN: *French Sudan*.

Malines or **Mechelen**, Belgium. Made a separate fief, 754. Passed to Philip the Bold of Burgundy, 1384. Became archbishopric, 1559. Sacked by Spaniards, 1572. Bombarded in World War I and accidentally bombed by Americans in World War II.

Mall, The, began to have houses built along the N. side, 1650–60.

Malmédy, Belgium, together with Eupen became Prussian in 1814, but both were ceded to Belgium in 1919.

Malta, G.C. Phoenicians colonized the island, sixteenth century B.C.; Greeks dispossessed them, 736 B.C.; driven out by Carthaginians c. 500 B.C. Became finally Roman, 201 B.C. St. Paul shipwrecked at, first century A.D. Fell to Vandals, then Goths, in the fifth century; liberated by Belisarius, 533, and nominally united with E. Empire. Arabs drove out the Greeks, 870, and made M. a centre of piracy. Count Roger of Sicily drove Arabs from, 1090; conquered by Spain, 1282; given by the Emperor Charles V to the Knights of the Order of St. John of Jerusalem, 1530, who owned the island until 1798, when the French took possession; the Maltese rebelled, and after much fighting the island was recognized as British by the Congress of Vienna, 1814–1815. Constitution granted, 1887; revised, 1903. Elected Legislative Assembly granted under the constitution of 1921. Dispute between Church and State begun, 1929. British Government expostulated with the Vatican, May 1930. Constitution suspended, 1930. Royal Commission of Inquiry, 1931. Constitution restored, 1932; suspended, 2 Nov. 1933. Maltese superseded Italian as language of courts, 1934. Constitution revoked, 12 Aug. 1936. Proposal for new constitution announced, 29 July 1938; promulgated, 26 Feb. 1939. Severely damaged by Italian and German bombing in the years 940–3. Island awarded the George Cross by King George VI, 17 Apr. 1942. Granted new constitution, Sept. 1947. Maltese premier Mintoff suggested 'integration' with Britain, 1955. This was generally welcomed in London and supported by a majority in a referendum in M. on 11–12 Feb. 1956. Later Mintoff's relations with Britain deteriorated and in Apr. 1958 he and his government resigned. A state of emergency was proclaimed in the island, and tl e Governor took over its administration. On 15 Apr. 1959 the 1947 constitution was revoked, and an interim constitution took its place. New constitution proposed, 1961, and at a General Election on 17–19 Feb. 1962 the Nationalist (led by Olivier) came to power. Mintoff's Socialists, who were opposed by the Catholic Church, were heavily defeated. The new 'State of Malta' came into being, 4 Mar. 1962. M.'s financial situation continued grave, and a government inquiry into the working of Bailey (Malta) Ltd. proposed, Apr. Olivier visited London, July–Aug. 1962. At the end stated that M. now wanted independence within the Commonwealth. Britain had refused his request for a further £8¾ million financial aid. Olivier had further talks in London in Dec. 1962. Britain offered to give Malta financial aid to assist emigration from the island, May 1963. There were further talks in London between the British Government and the representatives of all the Maltese parties, July 1963. These were adjourned, unfinished, on 30 July, and Britain announced that M. would become independent by Apr. 1964.

Malta, Knights of. Known also as the Order of the Knights of St. John of Jerusalem, the Knights of Rhodes, and the Hospitallers; founded by one Gerald or Gerard in a hospital at Jerusalem c. 1070; sanctioned by Pope Paschal II, 1113; Frederick Barbarossa took the Order under his protection, 1185; captured Rhodes, 1310, which they held until 1523; Charles V presented them with the island of M. (q.v.), 1530, which they surrendered in 1798, when the Order became a charitable religious institution, establishing its headquarters at Rome in 1878. The modern English Order of St. John is a purely secular and philanthropic institution, incorporated by charter in 1888.

Malvern Festival. Founded, 1929, but not held since World War II.

Mamelukes. The Turkish M. under Kutuz seized the government of Egypt, 1250. They were superseded by the Circassian M., 1390, and the latter ruled till the Ottoman conquest of 1517.

Man, Isle of. Ruled by Welsh kings from sixth to ninth centuries, when the Norwegians conquered the island; ceded to the kings of Scotland, 1266; inhabitants placed themselves under protection of Edward I of England, 1290; kingdom granted to Sir John Stanley, 1406; surrendered to parliamentary army, 1651; fell by inheritance to the Duke of Atholl, from whom it was purchased by the British Government after prolonged negotiations (1765–1829).

Manchester, England. There was a Roman fort, called *Mancunium* or *Mamucium*, in the Castleford district of M., founded c. A.D. 79 during Agricola's conquest. In the Middle Ages it was called *Mamecestre*. Captured by Edwin, King of Northumbria, 620; King Edward the

Elder sent forces to repair and man it, 923; first charter granted, 14 May 1301; during civil war Fairfax captured it, 1643; walls and fortifications removed, 1652; Peterloo Massacre at, 1819; Owens College opened, 1851. Victoria University, founded 1880 by royal charter, consists of Owens College (founded 1846) only: University College (Liverpool), which had been admitted, 1884, and Yorkshire College (Leeds), which had been admitted, 1887, having since joined Liverpool and Leeds Universities respectively. M. Ship Canal built, 1887–94. Badly damaged by bombing in World War II.

Manchuria or **Manchukuo.** Conquered China (*q.v.*), 1644, and founded the Chinese dynasty that reigned there till 1911; the occupation of M. by Russia (*q.v.*) was to cause the Russo-Japanese War, 1904–5. Made into a state separate from China, 18 Feb. 1932, by Japan (*q.v.*), who installed the former emperor of China, Pu Yi, as emperor (under the name of Kang Teh) of Manchukuo, 1 Mar. 1934. Joined Anti-Comintern Pact, 16 Jan. 1939. Manchukuo State abolished, 1945, and all industrial enterprises requisitioned by Nationalists as 'enemy property,' 1946. Controlled by Communists since 1949.

Mandalay, built as the capital city of Burma by King Thebaw *c.* 1860. Captured by British, 1885. Largely destroyed by fire, 1892. Held by Japanese, 8 May 1942–13 Mar. 1945, during which time British bombers rendered almost total the destruction begun by Japanese planes and artillery.

Mandates. British M. ended in Iraq, 1932. French in Syria, 1936. British in Palestine, 1948.

Manhattan Island, U.S.A.. Purchased for Dutch W. India Co. by Peter Minuit, 1624.

Manichaeism. A dualistic religion ascribed to Mani (*c.* 215–77). Numerous Persians converted, 241 onwards. Spread to Roman Empire, 280–440. From it are descended the Bogomil, Paulician, Catharist, and Albigensian (*q.v.*) doctrines.

Manila, Philippine Islands. Founded by Legaspi, 1571. Attacked by British, 1762. Spanish squadron destroyed by U.S. Navy, May 1898. Occupied by the Japanese, 2 Jan. 1942. Retaken by the Americans in desperate fighting between 5 and 24 Feb. 1945. It ceased to be the capital of the Philippines in 1960, being replaced by Quezon.

Manila Conference. Held 6–8 Sept. 1954, on S.E. Asia defence, and ended with the signing of the South East Asian Collective Defence Treaty.

Manitoba Province. Known as Red River Colony from 1812 and administered by Hudson Bay Co. (*see under* HUDSON BAY TERRITORY) till 1869. Became a province of Dominion of Canada, 1870. University of M. founded at Winnipeg, 1877. Enlargements of boundaries, 1881, 1912.

Mansion House (London). The official residence of the Lord Mayor; building begun, 1739.

Mantua, Italy. Ruled by the Gonzagas, 1328–1708. Taken by French, 1797; by Austrians, 1814; surrendered to Italy, 1866.

Maori Wars. 1. Between the settlers of New Zealand and the natives, 1843–7; it resulted in the definition of boundaries. 2. Boundary disputes caused war, 1863–Aug. 1864. 3. In consequence of a massacre of whites by natives, July 1869–Jan. 1870.

Maquis (Corsican dialect for Italian **Macchia**). Mediterranean heath, hence hilly country covered by it; since the Napoleonic Wars synonym for outlawry, phrase popularized by romances of Prosper Mérimée (1803–70); applied to young Frenchmen who took to the hills to avoid forced labour after the occupation by the Germans of 'Vichy' France, Nov. 1942, and became a loose synonym for F.F.I. (*q.v.*).

Marathon, in Attica, scene of the defeat of the Persians by Athenians and Plataeans, 490 B.C. Of the several monuments, some inscribed, which survived and were described by Pausanias, A.D. 110, only the burial mound of the 192 Athenians killed in the action is now known.

Marble Arch (London). Originally erected in front of Buckingham Palace by Nash, 1828. Moved to present site, 1851.

Marine Corps (U.S.A.). Established by Congress in Nov. 1775; became a permanent arm of the service by the Act of 11 July 1798.

Marketing Boards for agricultural products. Established under Act of 1933; bacon, hops, milk, pigs, potatoes, eggs, etc.

Marlborough House (Pall Mall), built by Wren, 1709, for John Churchill, first Duke of M., who died there, 1722. Occupied by Queen Mary, 1936–53, and given to the nation by Queen Elizabeth II, 17 Feb. 1959, for use as a Commonwealth Centre.

Marlborough, Parliament of, 1267, after the Barons' War (*q.v.*).

Maronites, Syrians who adopted Christianity in the fifth century, abandoned Monothelite heresy, 1182, when they adhered to the Church of Rome, though they left it again temporarily for the period 1382–1445.

Maroon (from Spanish **Cimarron, a run-**

away slave especially in the Caribbean). The Ms. of Jamaica, who lived in the interior mountains, were in a more or less permanent state of rebellion against the English from the occupation in 1655 till the Maroon War of 1796, most of the survivors of which were transported to Nova Scotia and Sierra Leone.

Marprelate Controversy. Caused by certain writings against episcopacy by Elizabethan Puritans, 1587–9; supposed to have been written by John Penry, who was executed in 1593.

Marquesas Islands, the first European to sight which was the Spaniard Mendaña de Nera, 1594, were not all known to navigators until 1701. Became a French protectorate, 1842. Overseas territories of the French Community since 1958; form a part of French Polynesia.

Marriage Laws (Britain). Lord Hardwicke's Act of 1753 provided that Ms. must be performed in the parish church, with the exception of those of Jews or Quakers. This Act superseded by the Marriage Act of 1823. Dissenters' M. Act, 1836, permitted Dissenters to marry in their own chapels or churches or enter into a civil contract by giving notice to the registrar. M. Act of 1886. Acts for subsidiary purposes, 1898, 1899, 1901, 1903, 1905 (amended 1924), 1906. Deceased Wife's Sister's M. Act, 28 Aug. 1907. Further Acts of a minor character, 1908, 1912, 1915, 1916. Deceased Brother's Widow's M. Act, 28 July 1921. Age of M. Act (making void Ms. of persons under 16), 10 May 1929. Marriage Act, 1931, legalized marriage as a civil contract with various categories of person formerly within the prohibited degrees. *See also* DIVORCE.

Married Women's Property Act, 18 Aug. 1882, abolished the rule whereby upon marriage a woman's property passed at law to her husband. Amended, 1884, 1893, 1907.

Marseillaise, The, national anthem of the French Republic, was partly written and composed in 1792 by Rouget de Lisle, an officer stationed at Strasbourg. Originally called *Chant de guerre pour l'Armée du Rhin.* Brought to Paris by certain soldiers from Marseilles, and sung by them as they advanced to the storming of the Tuileries, 30 July. It was forbidden under the Restoration and Second Empire, and again became the national song during the Franco-Prussian War of 1870.

Marseilles, France. One of the oldest towns in France, originally known as *Massalia* or *Massilia.* Captured by Julius Caesar, 49 B.C.; became a republic, A.D. 1112; treacherously surrendered to Henry IV; shortly after it finally lost its

independence. The Old Port district destroyed by the Germans, 1943. The port itself blown up by the Germans, 23 Aug. 1944.

Marshall Islands came under German protection, 1885. Mandated to Japan, 1920. Overrun by U.S. forces, 1944. Put under U.N. trusteeship, 1946. U.S.A. appointed U.N. trustee, 19 July 1947.

Marshall Plan or **European Recovery Programme (E.R.P.).** Original proposal made by George M. (1880–1959), U.S. Secretary of State, in speech at Harvard University, 5 June 1947. Benelux countries consult, 14 June. Anglo-French consultations, 17–23 June. Interim Aid Bill signed by President Truman, 17 Dec. 1947. Convention for European Economic Co-operation (16 nations) signed at Paris, 16 Apr. 1948. This was the foundation of O.E.E.C. (*q.v.*), although the M. P. itself came to an end in 1952.

Marshalsea Prison, in what is now the Borough High Street, Southwark, was built at some time between 1327 and 1377, and was first used to confine those who 'broke the King's peace' within a certain radius of Westminster Palace; then it housed those convicted of piracy and other maritime crimes. It became specifically a debtors' prison *c.* 1560, but at some time the site was changed because the M. prison where the father of the novelist Charles Dickens was imprisoned, 1824–5, was farther down the Borough High Street, was united with the King's Bench and Fleet prisons in 1842, and was demolished, 1887.

Martello Towers. Built as English coast defences at the end of the eighteenth century, after the model of a fort on Cape Mortella, bombarded unsuccessfully by British in 1794.

Martinique. Discovered by the Spaniards, 1493. Settled by French, 1635. Slavery abolished, 1860. An overseas dept. of France since 1946.

Maryland, U.S.A. Explored by John Smith, 1608. First settled by Capt. William Claiborne, 1634. Named after Henrietta Maria, queen of Charles I. Representative government established, 1638; parliamentary commissioners took possession of the Government, 1652, but it was restored to the governor, 1658; a Protestant association overthrew the Government, which was Roman Catholic, 1689; declared a free state, 1776; Confederate army entered M. after crossing the Potomac, 30 Aug. 1862. Present constitution dates from 1867.

Marylebone Cricket Club, better known as M.C.C., first so called in 1787, when an already existing club began to play in Dorset Square, M.

Mason and Dixon Line, drawn by two

English surveyors, M. and D., who in settlement of a dispute between the proprietors of the various colonies demarcated the boundary between Maryland and Pennsylvania, 1763–7. This line and its westward continuation became from 1820 onwards the boundary between 'slave' and 'free' states and the phrase and its abbreviation 'Dixie' achieved greatest currency in the Civil War (1863) period.

Mashonaland, S. Rhodesia. Placed under British protection, 1888; powers of administration granted to British S. Africa Co., 1889.

Massachusetts, U.S.A. Explored by Gosnold, 1602; Champlain, 1604; John Smith, 1614. Settled by English Puritans, Nov. 1620, who sailed over in the *Mayflower.* First constitution framed, 1780; amended, 1820. Constitution of U.S.A. adopted, 1788.

Master of the King's Musick, an office instituted, 1660, was conferred on Sir Arthur Bliss, 17 Nov. 1953.

Masulipatam, India. English settlement founded, 1611. Held by Dutch, 1686–90. Given to French by Nizam of Hyderabad, 1750. Captured by British under Forde, Apr. 1758.

Matabeleland, Rhodesia. Ceded to the British S. Africa Co., 1889. Matabele rebellion, 1896; ended by Rhode's mediation, Aug. 1896.

Matterhorn (Switzerland). Summit first reached, 14 July 1865. First winter ascent of the N. face made by two Swiss climbers, 4 Feb. 1962.

Maudheim, base of Anglo-Scandinavian Antarctic expedition, 1950. The wintering party left M. in the research ship *Norsel,* 15 Jan. 1952, *en route* for Europe.

Mau-Mau, a conspiracy among the Kikuyu tribe aiming to dominate first it and then all other Africans in Kenya (*q.v.*) with a view to seizing power in Kenya and expelling or killing all Europeans and Asiatics. Its organization and collection of arms began about 1944. Its existence became known to the authorities in 1950. Its first large-scale outbreak of cattle-maiming occurred 25 Sep. 1952 at Timau. First Europeans killed, 2 Oct. Trial of Jomo Kenyatta, Dec. 1952–Mar. 1953. Kenyatta found guilty of managing M.-M. and sentenced to life imprisonment. Lari massacre of nearly 100 loyal Kikuyu, 26 Mar. 1953. The White Paper published 23 Feb. 1954 set out the findings of a parliamentary delegation which visited Kenya 8–26 Jan. By 1957 M.-M. had been crushed and the state of emergency was declared at an end. Kenyatta was freed in Aug. 1961 and immediately acknowledged as one of Kenya's national leaders. Both he and

Mboya condemned the recrudescence of oath-taking which was reported in Kenya in 1962 and which was alleged in some quarters to herald a revival of M.-M.

Maumbury Rings, late Neolithic or early Bronze Age (*c.* 1800 B.C.) fortification converted during the Roman occupation (after A.D. 200) to an amphitheatre which was excavated 1908 and 1913.

Maundy Thursday. The Thursday before Good Friday, also known as Holy Thursday, on which day alms are still given to the poor in the form of 'M. money' by the sovereign.

Mauritania, independent Islamic republic in W. Africa, made a French protectorate, 1903, a 'Civilian Territory,' 1904, and a colony, 4 Dec. 1920. From Nov. 1958 M. was a member of the French Community, and it became an independent republic on 28 Nov. 1960.

Mauritius, Indian Ocean. Discovered by the Portuguese between 1505 and 1512; occupied by the Dutch, and named M. after Prince Maurice of Orange, 1598; abandoned by Dutch, 1710; occupied by French, 1715; captured by English, 1810; formally ceded to England by Treaty of Paris, 1814.

Mausoleum. Named after the tomb erected for King Mausolus of Halicarnassus, in Caria (377–353 B.C.), by his widow, Queen Artemisia II, *c.* 352 B.C.

Mayas, a race based on Yucatan in Central America. The first M. Empire lasted from the second to the eighth centuries A.D. The second empire was founded A.D. 1000, and was still flourishing at the time of the Spanish conquest.

May Day, in pagan times was an almost universal feast in Europe, taking place at or soon after the vernal equinox, as the Roman Floralia did. Tolerated in England from the time of Augustine's mission until 1644, when it was banned, but revived in 1661. *See also* LABOUR DAY.

'Mayflower,' The. Sailed from Plymouth, England, 6 Sept. 1620. The M. compact was signed off Cape Cod, 2 Nov., and the Pilgrim Fathers (*q.v.*) landed in Massachusetts, 16 Dec. 1620. Society of M. Descendants founded, 1894. On 20 Apr. 1957 *Mayflower II,* a replica of the first ship, sailed from Plymouth to Cape Cod, in connection with the 350th anniversary of the first permanent English settlement in N. America (at Jamestown, Virginia). She reached Cape Cod on 12 June.

Maynooth College (Ireland). Founded, 1795, by Irish Parliament for education of candidates for Irish Roman Catholic priesthood. Endowment, continued after Union, increased, 1846. By Irish Church Act, 1869, which disestablished Pro-

testantism in Ireland, M. grant was withdrawn as from 1 Jan. 1871, a capital sum
14 times the annual amount being granted
as compensation.

Mayor as a title for the chief dignitary
of a city first appears in England c.
A.D. 1100.

Meal Tub Plot, 1679. Pretended conspiracy against the Duke of York originated by Dangerfield.

Mecca (Arab. **Om al Kora**). Known to
Ptolemy in the second century A.D.
Expelled Mohammed, 622, who returned
and captured it, 630. Captured by
Wahabis, 1803, but ceded to Mehemet
Ali, pasha of Egypt, 1833. Captured
again by Wahabis under Abdul Aziz ibn
Sa'ud, 13 Oct. 1924, who was proclaimed
king of the Hejaz here, 1926.

Mecklenburg, Germany. Became
duchy, 1348. Lutheranism became state
religion, 1549. Partitioned, 1611. Repartitioned into M.-Schwerin and M.-
Strelitz, but with joint diet, 1701. Serfdom abolished, 1819. Joined N. German
Confederation, 1866. From 1934–45 a
state of NE. Germany; since 1945 part of
the Russian Zone and subsequently
divided into various administrative
districts of the German Democratic
Republic.

Media, in NW. Iran, became independent of Assyria c. 708 B.C., and overthrew the Assyrian Empire, 612. Amalgamated with Persia, 560. Became part
of the Macedonian Empire, 331. After
624 the north-western portion became
independent and remained so, under the
name of Atropatene, until the first century
A.D. The remainder thereafter was
alternately in the possession of Persia,
Syria, and Parthia.

Medici Family. Chiefs of the Florentine
Republic from 1434. Contributed to the
restoration of literature and the arts in
Italy. Cosimo de' M. (1389–1464) was
the first chief. Lorenzo de' M. ruled,
1469–92; he was the father of Pope Leo X.
Caterina de' M. became Queen of France,
1547; Maria de' M., 1600. The family
became extinct, 1737.

Medina (Arab. 'the city'), in full
Medinat Rasul Allah, was the residence of
Mohammed in A.D. 622. He d. and was
buried here, 632.

Medina del Campo, Treaty of, 1489.
By it Henry VII of England betrothed his
infant son Arthur to Catherine of Aragon.

Meissen, Saxony, a castle founded here
by Henry I, 929, as the nucleus of a
margravate (border county) established,
966, which became part of the electorate
of Saxony, 1423. The manufacture of
porcelain began, 1710. Some leading
designers were Hörold (1720–35), Kändler

(1735–56), Count Marcolini (1774–1813).
Most so-called 'Dresden' ware, 1710–
1863, was made at M.

Melbourne, Australia. Site first occupied, 1835. Named M., 1837. Made a
diocese, 1849. Became capital of Victoria, 1851. University founded, 1854.

Melfi, Apulia, founded, A.D. 304,
became capital of the Norman duchy of
Apulia, 1044. Its cathedral, built in
1155, was almost totally destroyed in the
earthquake of 1851.

Mellifont (County Meath), first Cistercian
abbey in Ireland, founded, 1142, by St.
Malachy (1094–1148). Ruins excavated,
1884–5.

Melos (It. **Milo**), island in the Cyclades,
taken by Athenians, 416 B.C.; by Turks,
1566. The statue of Venus called 'of
Milo' found here, 1820.

Melrose Abbey (Scotland). Founded by
David I in 1136; partly destroyed by
English in 1322 and 1385; reduced to ruin
by Lord Hertford, 1545.

Memel (Lith. **Klaipeda**). Founded,
1253. Detached from Germany by
Treaty of Versailles, 1919. Given conditionally to Lithuania (which had, in
fear of Polish intervention, annexed the
place in Jan.), 1923. Annexed by Germany, 22 Mar. 1939; by U.S.S.R., 1945.

Menai Straits. Telford's suspension
bridge open, 1826 (reconstructed 1940).
Stephenson's tubular bridge, 1850.

Mendelianism. Theory of heredity
propounded between 1860 and 1884 by
G. J. Mendel (1822–84) while abbot of
the Augustinian monastery at Brno in
Czechoslovakia.

Menin Gate (Ypres, Belgium). Unveiled
by Lord Plumer, 24 July 1927.

Mennonites, pacifist Protestant sect,
successors to the Anabaptists, formed c.
1537, taking their name from the preacher
Menno Simons (1492–1559). Several
colonies of M. formed in S. Russia, 1786,
and the first Mennonite congregation
established at Germantown, Pennsylvania, 1683. In 1871 considerable
numbers settled in Kansas and Minnesota.

Mensheviks (Rus. **menshinstvo,** minority), a wing of the Russian Social Democratic Party, founded, 1903. Suppressed,
1922.

Mercator. Gerhard Kremer, *alias*
Gerardus M., born at Rupelmonde, 5 Mar.
1512. His 'Projection' for maps was
published, 1568. He d. 2 Dec. 1594.

Merchant Adventurers, The. A guild of
traders established in Brabant, 1296.
The branch in England received the title
by patent of Henry VII, 1505; incorporated, 1553. Became known as the
Hamburg Company, 1578; dissolved,
1808.

Merchants, Charter of. Granted in 1303 by Edward I to foreign merchants.

Merchants, Statute of. *See* ACTON BURNELL, STATUTE OF.

Merchant Shipping Acts. Consolidating Act, 1854; this superseded by the Act of 1894 which remains the principal Act on the subject, various amendments and additions having been made to it since it became law.

Merchant Taylors' School (London). Founded, 1561; school house destroyed during Great Fire of 1666; rebuilt, 1671–4; rebuilt on new site, 1873–4; rebuilt, Northwood, Middlesex, 1931–3.

Mercia. Anglian kingdom, founded 500–50 in central England. Rose to supremacy *c.* 730, which lasted through the reigns of Ethelbald and Offa, and ended by the defeat of Coenwulf at Ellendun, 821, after a period in which it was tributary to Wessex. Completely absorbed in Wessex, 825–9. It was finally conquered by the Danes, 874, and split into English (SW.) and Danish (NE.) Mercian earldoms; reunited in 1016 under Knut, the territory ceased to be an administrative unit in 1066.

Mercia, rulers of, c. 593–874:

Creoda	*d. c.* 593
Pybba	*c.* 593–*c.* 606
Cearl	*c.* 606–*c.* 626
Penda	626–655
Peada	655–656
Oswy (of Bernicia)	656–659
Wulfhere	659–675
Ethelred	675–704
Cenred	704–709
Ceolred	709–716
Ethelbald	716–757
Beornred	757
Offa	757–796
Ecgfrith	796
Coenwulf	796–821
Ceolwulf I	821–823
Beornwulf	823–825
Ludeca	825–827
Wiglaf	827–829
Egbert (of Wessex)	829–830
Wiglaf (restored)	830–839
Beorhtwulf	839–852
Burgred	852–874
Ceolwulf II	874

Merciless (or Wonderful) Parliament. Summoned in 1388 by the Lords Appellant after the defeat of Richard II. It condemned eight of Richard's supporters to death.

Merit, Order of, instituted, 1902.

Mermaid Tavern (Cheapside), first mentioned, 1464. M. Club founded, reputedly by Sir Walter Raleigh, 1603. Burnt down, 1666.

Merovingians, Frankish dynasty, reigning 448–751. *See* FRANCE.

Mersey Tunnel (railway) opened, 1886; road tunnel opened, 1934.

Mesopotamia. *See* IRAQ.

Mesopotamian Campaign, Commission of Inquiry into the. Set up, July 1916; reported, 26 June 1917.

Messina, Italy. Founded by Greeks *c.* eighth century B.C. Taken by the Saracens in the ninth century A.D. and in 1072 by the Normans. Ruled by Spain, 1282–1713. Devastated by plague, 1743; by earthquake, 1783 and 1808.

Metaphysics, Institute of International. Opened at Paris, 1919.

Meteorological Office set up, 1855. Transferred from Board of Trade control to that of the Royal Society, 1867. Since 1919 administered by the Air Ministry.

Methodists. Name first given to followers of John and Charles Wesley at Oxford, 1729; Wesleyan Methodist Society founded by John Wesley, 1739; first conference, 1744; conference constituted supreme authority, 1784; Dr. Coke constituted 'bishop' of the American M., 1784; death of Wesley, 1791, after which the sect split up; union of many divisons into the 'United Methodist Church,' 1907; Enabling Bill for union of Wesleyan, Primitive, and United M. passed, 1929; final denominational vote, 1931. Reunion became effective, 1932. Proposals for a two-stage reunion with the Church of England published, 25 Feb. 1963.

Methuen Treaty. Negotiated by Sir Paul M., English ambassador in Portugal, 1703. It reduced the duty on Portuguese wines to the detriment of French wines, thus helping to form the upper-class English habit of port drinking. Annulled, 1836.

Metric System. Became the legal system in France, 1795. Though not in commercial use the system was made legal in the U.K. by an Act of 1864. Revived interest in M. S. in Britain, 1960 onwards, owing to Britain's policy of closer links with Europe.

Metronome, invented *c.* 1814.

Mexico. In 1519 Hernando Cortes (1485–1547), the Spanish adventurer, landed at Vera Cruz, and conquered the land, 1521. In 1540 M. was united with other American territories and called New Spain. Declared itself independent of Spain, and Gen. Iturbide made emperor, May 1822. Proclaimed a republic, 1824. War with the U.S.A. regarding boundary dispute, May 1846–19 May 1848, when a peace treaty was signed. War with France, 1862–7. Emperor Maximilian shot, 1867. Revolution in 1910–11, during which President Diaz was dethroned and Señor Madero was elected the new president, Oct. 1911. After the murder of President Madero, 1913, Huerta became president. Venustiano Carranza, as head of the Constitutional forces, set up federal governments, Sept.–Oct. 1913; established his seat of government at Vera Cruz, 1914; was recognized as president, 1915. New constitution promulgated, 9 Feb. 1917. In 1920 rebellion under Obregon broke out, and Carranza was assassinated. P. E. Calles succeeded Obregon as president, 1924; campaign against Roman Catholic Church begins; foreign priests and nuns expelled, 1926; churches closed, 1929–31; abortive rebellion, 1930; hurricane on W. coast, Sept. 1933; Cardenas becomes president, 1934; Calles driven into exile, 1936. Between 1937 and 1941 various negotiations with the U.S.A. and Great Britain concerning ownership and control of Mexican oil resources. Trotsky murdered at Coycacán, 21 Aug. 1940. M. declared war on the Axis powers, 2 June 1942; final report of the Mexican-American commission for economic co-operation issued, 1945; President Truman visited M., 1947; Mateos elected President of M., 1958; President Kennedy visited M., 1962.

Heads of State, from 1821. (All presidents, except where otherwise indicated):

Iturbide	(Regent)	1821–1822
	(Emperor)	1822–1823
Victoria		1824–1829
Pedraza		1829
Guerrero		1829
Bustamante		1829–1832
Pedraza		1832
Santa Anna		1833–1836
Bustamante		1836–1841
Santa Anna		1841–1842
Bravo		1842–1843
Santa Anna		1844
Herrera		1844–1846
Paredes		1846
Santa Anna		1846–1847
Herrera		1848–1851
Arista		1851–1853
Santa Anna	(Dictator)	1853–1855
Alvarez		1855–1856
Comonfort		1856–1857
	(Dictator)	1857–1858
Juarez		1858–1863
Zuloaga		1858
Miramon		1859–1861
Maximilian	(Emperor)	1864–1867
Juarez		1867–1872
Lerdo		1872–1876
Diaz		1877–1880
Gonzalez		1880–1884
Diaz		1884–1911

Mexico. *Heads of State—cont.*

Madero	1911–1913
Huerta	1913–1914
Carranza	1914–1920
Obregon	1920–1924
Calles	1924–1928
Portes Gil	1928–1930
Ortiz Rubio	1930–1932
Rodriguez	1932–1934
Cardenas	1934–1940
Camacho	1940–1946
Alemán Valdes	1946–1952
Cortines	1952–1958
Lopez Mateos	1958–

Mexico City. Founded as Tenochtitlan by Aztecs (*q.v.*) *c.* A.D. 1325. Captured by Spaniards, 1521. Cathedral begun, 1573.

Michelson-Morley Experiment. Albert Abraham Michelson (1852–1931) and Edward Williams Morley (1822–94) performed an experiment in 1887 to determine the velocity with which the earth moved through the ether. Its negative results led to the hypothesis on which the theory of relativity (*q.v.*) is based.

Michigan, U.S.A. Discovered by French, 1618, and settled by French missionaries, 1671. Detroit founded, 1701; possessed by British, 1763; by Americans, 1796; erected into an independent territory, 1805; fell into the hands of the British, Aug. 1812; reconquered by Gen. Harrison, 1813; admitted to the Union as a state, Jan. 1837; new constitution adopted, 1908.

Microphone, invented by E. Berliner (1851–1929), 1877.

Microscope. The first compound M. said to have been made by Janssen, a Dutchman, 1590. It was not, however, of much practical use until the achromatic lens was invented *c.* 1758.

Middelburg, Holland. St. Nicholas Abbey founded, 1106. Bell-tower rebuilt, 1718. Flooded and seriously damaged in fighting on Walcheren, Nov. 1944.

Midway Islands, discovered and annexed to the U.S.A., 1859. Made an American reservation, 1903. Japanese fleet defeated by U.S. Navy off M., June 1942.

Midwives Act (Great Britain), 1902, provided that no woman should use title of midwife without being certified; and that after 1 Apr. 1910 no woman, except in emergency, should attend cases unless under direction of a qualified medical man.

Mikado, title of the emperors of Japan (*q.v.*), the first of whom is supposed to have begun his reign, 660 B.C.

Milan, Italy (Lat. Mediolanum). Taken from Gauls by Romans, 222 B.C.; Constantine's edict in favour of Christians,

A.D. 313; sacked by Huns, 452; by Goths, 539 head of Lombard League from 1167; ruled by Visconti family, 1227–1447, by Sforza family, 1450–1535; from 1535 to 1713 under the rule of Spain, then of Austria; after Napoleonic wars restored to Austria, 1815; capital of Austro-Italian kingdom until 1859, when it became part of Italy; present cathedral founded, 1386; and completed, 1805–13. Seriously damaged by allied bombing, 1943.

Mildenhall Treasure, a hoard of Roman silver-ware found near M. in Suffolk, 1942–3, presumed to have been buried for safety by the occupants of a villa during Pictish raids in the fourth century A.D.

Mile. English statute M. legalized, 1593.

Military Training Act, 1939, compelling every male subject between 20 and 21 to undergo 6 months' training and then to be 3½ years in auxiliary force. Superseded by National Service (Armed Forces) Act, 3 Sept. 1939, and National Service Act, 1947.

Militia (Great Britain). M. statutes, 1661–3; general M. Act passed, 1802; M. Reserve Act, 1867; M. Enlistment Act, 1875; title of M. abolished on introduction of Territorial and Reserve Force Act, 1907; superseded by Special Reserve (1908); Special Reserve renamed M., 1921, but it remained a merely nominal force. The conscripts under the Military Training Act, 1939, were termed M. *See* FYRD.

Militia (U.S.A.). Bill for the organization of the M. passed House of Representatives, 27 Mar. 1792.

Millbank Prison (London). Erected 1813–16; closed 1890; demolished, 1903; on the site now stands the Tate Gallery (*q.v.*).

Milo, Venus of. *See* MELOS.

Minnesota, U.S.A. Explored by two Huguenots, Groseilliers and Radisson, 1658–9; formally possessed by French, 1671; divided between Spain and Great Britain, 1762–3; visited by Jonathan Carver, 1766; part of territory of Indiana, 1800; purchased by U.S.A., 1803; territory of M. created, 1849; admitted to the Union, 11 May 1858.

Minorca, Mediterranean. Captured by English, 1708, during War of Spanish Succession, ceded to England by Treaty of Utrecht, 1713; recaptured by French 1756 (as a result of which the English executed Admiral Byng); restored to England by Treaty of Paris, 1763; recaptured by French and Spaniards, 1781; ceded to Spain, 1782; retaken, 1798, but restored to Spain by Treaty of Amiens,

1802. At the end of the Spanish Civil War the island surrendered bloodlessly to Nationalists, 9 Feb. 1939.

Mint (Great Britain). Regulations for the government of the M. made by King Athelstan *c.* A.D. 928; by Act of Parliament the present M. was founded on Tower Hill, 1811; new constitution, 1815; complete change in administration, and a master, deputy master, and comptroller appointed, 1850; office of Chancellor of the Exchequer amalgamated with that of master, and the office of deputy master and comptroller combined, 1870. Ms. established at Sydney, Australia, in 1855, at Melbourne, Australia, 1872, and at Pretoria, S. Africa.

Mint (U.S.A.). The earliest M. was established at Boston, 27 May 1652. The power of coinage was exercised by several states from 1778 until the adoption of the National Constitution. M. established at Rupert, Victoria, 1785. Establishment of a M. by Act of Congress, 1795, at Philadelphia.

Minton porcelain, first made by Thomas and Herbert M. at Stoke-on-Trent, 1796.

Misericordia, Confraternity of the. Florentine volunteer ambulance service, raised, 1244, or, according to some, not until 1292. Records destroyed in floods of 1557. From 1425 to 1430 merged with the charitable Guild of Sta. Maria del Bigallo. Present constitution dates from the latter year. Primarily intended to function during plagues, the last of which (cholera) occurred in 1855.

Missal. Ordered to be used in all Roman Catholic churches by Council of Trent (*q.v.*), 1570. Revised, 1604, 1634, 1884.

Mississippi, U.S.A. The lower course of the river discovered by de Soto, 1541; visited by La Salle, 1682; territory of M. created, 7 Apr. 1798; admitted to the Union as a state, 1817; new constitution, 1890. Federal enforcement of anti-segregation at State University at Oxford, Mississippi, led to riots and fatalities, Sept.–Oct. 1962.

Mississippi Scheme. A proposal to develop Louisiana (*q.v.*), the country on the borders of the M. The scheme was the idea of John Law (1671–1729), who floated a company in 1717. The scheme was not a success, and in July 1720 the bubble broke.

Missouri, U.S.A. Originally called Upper Louisiana. Ste. Geneviève said to have been founded, 1735; by Treaty of Paris, 1763, territory passed to the English; ceded to U.S.A., 1803; admitted into the Union as a state, 10 Aug. 1821;

suffered from dissensions during Civil War of 1861; new constitution, 1945.

Missouri Compromise, The. In 1818 the inhabitants of the M. territory petitioned for admission into the Union as a state; a bill was introduced into Congress, 13 Feb. 1819. A question of the abolition of slavery in the territory caused the bill to be delayed until a compromise was agreed, 2 Mar. 1820; this still led to much discussion, and it was not until 27 Feb. 1821 that a final compromise was adopted, and M. admitted to the Union as a state.

Mithraism, a branch of Zoroastrianism (*q.v.*). Introduced into Rome from Asia Minor, 68 B.C. It *fl.* in Britain, mainly as a cult in garrison stations, throughout the Roman occupation, and a temple to Mithras was excavated in London in 1953. M. ceased to exist in the W. with the victory of Theodosius in 394, when it was superseded by Christianity.

Moabite Stone, The. Now in the Louvre, Paris. Discovered by Rev. F. Klein at Dibon in 1868.

Modena, Italy. Ruled by the Estes, 1288–1860. Made a duchy, 1452; duke expelled by French, 1796; restored, 1814; finally expelled and duchy incorporated in Italy, 1860.

Mohammedanism. Mohammed (571–632) began to preach between A.D. 600 and 610. He fled to Medina in 622.

Mohawks or **Mohocks, The.** A club of wealthy young London men about town who committed such outrages that on 18 Mar. 1712 they were the subject of a royal proclamation.

Moldavian Republic. Constituted 2 Aug. 1940 as the thirteenth Soviet Socialist Republic. Occupied almost immediately on outbreak of war in June 1941 by German and Rumanian forces, until May 1944. The former M. Autonomous Soviet Republic was created within the Ukraine, 1921. *See* BESSARABIA.

Molony Report, 25 July 1962, recommended the establishment of a Consumers' Council in the U.K. to safeguard shoppers' interests.

Molly Maguires, in Ireland, an anti-landlord society which *fl.* 1835–55. In America, an Irish-led terrorist society which attempted to dominate the Pennsylvanian coal-mining area, 1862–77.

Mombasa, Kenya. Originally an Arab town in E. Africa, was first visited by the Portuguese, 1498. Sacked (1500) and occupied by them, 1505. Retaken by Arabs, 1698. Included in British E. African protectorate, 1896. Linked by rail to Uganda, 1895–1901.

Monaco. An independent principality on the Mediterranean, ruled by the Grimaldi family since 1297; made a French protectorate, 1644; Menton and Roquebrune annexed by Sardinia, 1846; became part of Italy, 1859; sold to Napoleon III, 1861. Until 1911 the Prince of Monaco was an absolute ruler; in that year constitution providing for universal manhood suffrage was adopted. By a treaty of 1918, succession to the throne of M. must be approved by the French Government. Rainier III became Prince of M. in 1949; he married Grace Kelly, an American film actress, in 1956. A 'good neighbour' treaty was signed between France and M., 23 Dec. 1951. In Jan. 1959 Prince Rainier suspended temporarily certain articles of the constitution; restored, 1962. In Jan. 1962 Pelletier, the Gaullist Minister of State (Premier), was summarily dismissed by Rainier; treaty of friendship renounced by France, 11 Apr., and customs barriers erected by the French on the French-M. border, 12 Oct. 1962. Talks with France reopened, Nov. Women in M. given the vote, Dec. French restrictions eased, Feb. 1963. Final agreement with France on all points in dispute, 18 May 1963.

Monasteries (England). M. on the Celtic pattern certainly existed in SW. and NW. Britain in the fifth century. The first monastery in England with Benedictine influence appears to have been erected about A.D. 597 by St. Augustine. A large number, belonging to many different orders, grew up in England. In 1535, during Henry VIII's reign, a commission was issued for the visitation of the M. In 1536 an Act was passed for the suppression of the religious houses with an income of less than £200. The large houses were suppressed in 1539.

Mongolia, Outer, People's Republic of. Chinese province, 1686–1911. Chinese officials expelled by the chiefs, 1911. Again a Chinese province, 1919–21. Communist revolution and proclamation of a People's Government, Mar. 1921. Treaty with U.S.S.R., Nov. 1921. Republic proclaimed, 1924, on death of Khan Bogdo Gezen. New currency introduced, 1925. Mutual assistance agreements with U.S.S.R., 1934 and 1936. Dispute with and defeat of Japanese, Sept. 1939 (*see* NOMANHAN and CHANGKUFENG incidents). New constitution, 1940. Plebiscite confirmed desire for independence, 30 Oct. 1945, and independent Outer M. recognized by China, 5 Jan. 1946, further guaranteeing it in Sino-Soviet Treaty of Feb. 1950. Treaty of unity and mutual aid between Outer M. and U.S.S.R. signed, 27 Feb. 1946;

further treaties with Russia, 1952 and 1960. Five-year plan adopted, 1947. Modified Cyrillic alphabet introduced, 1946.

Monmouth's Rebellion. Originated by James, Duke of Monmouth (1649–85), who landed on 11 June 1685 at Lyme Regis. He was defeated at Sedgemoor, 6 July 1685, and executed, 15 July.

Monopolies. In 1597 Parliament protested to Elizabeth against grants of M. The Parliaments of Charles I protested still more strongly, and by an Act of 1624 most of these M. were abolished, and in 1639 the whole system was done away with. In more modern times, the Monopolies and Restrictive Practices Act, 1948, which established the Monopolies and Restrictive Practices Commission, was a Government attempt to check M. and restrictive arrangements in industry and trade.

Monroe Doctrine. Proclaimed by President James M. (1758–1831) of the U.S.A. in his message to Congress on 2 Dec. 1823. In the words of M. himself, the doctrine was that the U.S.A. 'should consider any attempt on their [the foreign Powers'] part to extend their system to any portion of this [the American] hemisphere as dangerous to our peace and safety.'

Montagnards or **Montagne,** extremist republican wing in the French National Convention c. 1792–5.

Montana, first settled, 1809. Organized as a territory, 1864. Admitted to the Union as a state, 1889.

Mont Blanc (France and Italy). In 1760 Saussure offered a reward for a practicable route to the summit. Two guides in June 1786 gained it. Saussure reached the top himself in 1787. Construction of the M. B. tunnel begun, 1959; completion expected by 1963.

Mont de Piété or **Monte di Pietà.** Institutions founded for lending money to the poor at low interest, first established at Orvieto, 1463, and Perugia, 1467.

Montecassino, oldest monastic house in Europe, founded by St. Benedict, A.D. 529. Sacked by Lombards, 585; destroyed by Saracens, 884, and by allied air forces and shell-fire, Feb.–May 1944; occupied by Polish forces, 18 May 1944. Restored after each event: during the restoration of 1950–6 an urn believed to contain remains of St. Benedict and his sister Scholastica (missing since c. 1550) rediscovered. Abbey formally reopened, 1956.

Montenegro (Serb.-Cr. **Crnagora**). The history of M. as an independent state begins with the battle of Kossovo, 1389; Cetinje made capital, 1484; captured by the Turks, 1623, 1687, and 1714; fresh war with Turkey, 1853; peace finally restored, Nov. 1858; Turkish supremacy recognized, Sept. 1862; declared independent of Turkey by Treaty of San Stefano, 3 Mar. 1878; first Montenegrin Parliament assembled at Cetinje, Oct. 1906; Prince Nicholas assumed title of king, 28 Aug. 1910. During the first Balkan War, Oct. 1912–May 1913, M. allied with Bulgaria, Serbia, and Greece against Turkey; during the second Balkan War, June–Aug. 1913, M. allied with Serbia and Greece against Bulgaria, Rumania, and Turkey. King Nicholas fled the country in face of Austrian invasion, 1916. *See* YUGOSLAVIA, with which M. was united, 1918. Capital moved from Cetinje to Podgorica (renamed Titograd), 1945.

Montessori Method. Education system founded, 1906–9, by Maria Montessori (1870–1952).

Montevideo, Uruguay. First settlement made, 1726; taken by the English, 1807; in 1828 it was made the capital of Uruguay or Banda Oriental. German warship *Graf Spee* driven into M., Nov. 1939.

Montreal, Canada. Originally **Ville Marie.** Founded by French settlers, 1642; captured by British, 8 Sept. 1760; by Americans, 12 Nov. 1775; recaptured by British, 15 June 1776. McGill College founded, 1813; made a university by royal charter, 1821; new charter granted, 1852. Bishopric founded, 1850. Great fire destroyed the greater part of the town, 8–9 July 1852. Christ Church, the Anglican cathedral, destroyed by fire, 10 Dec. 1856. M. University founded, 1878.

Montyon Prizes. Awarded each year by the French Academy for examples of disinterested goodness. The fund for this purpose was bequeathed by the Baron de M. (1733–1820.).

Moravia. Occupied in early period successively by Boii (Celts); Quadi (Teutons); Rugii and Heruli, fifth century; soon displaced by Slavs; they sided with Charlemagne in suppressing the Avars on the E., end of eighth century; received part of Avars' territory. Allied with Bulgars and Byzantine Empire c. 850. Converted to Christianity by Cyril and Methodius, 863. King Svatopluk extended dominions to the Oder and the Gran. Magyars entered at his death, 894. From 1029 usually incorporated with Bohemia. On death of Louis II at battle of Mohácz came under rule of Austria, 1526; made a separate crown land, 1849. Became part of Czechoslovakia, 1918. Some territory ceded to Germany and Poland, Oct. 1938; part of the German protectorate of Bohemia-Moravia, 15 Mar. 1939 until liberated in 1945.

Moravian Brethren or **Moravian Church.** A religious sect founded in the E. of Bohemia *c.* 1457; first synod held, 1467. It grew out of the Hussites. In 1749 the British Parliament passed Acts to encourage their settlement in the English-American colonies.

Moriscos. Moors who remained in Spain after their final conquest in 1492, and who were finally expelled by Philip III, 1609–10.

Morley-Minto Reforms introduced in India by Lord Morley (1838–1923), Secretary of State, and the fourth Earl of Minto (1847–1914), Viceroy, 1909.

Mormons, The, or **Latter-Day Saints.** A sect founded by Joseph Smith (1805–44). *The Book of Mormon* was first published at New York in 1830. The first church was founded on 6 Apr. 1830 at Fayette; moved to Kirtland, Ohio, Jan. 1831. Their headquarters at Salt Lake City founded, 1847, by Brigham Young.

Morocco (Arab. **Maghreb,** 'Far W.'). Occupied by Berbers since at least 1200 B.C. Conquered by Arabs, A.D. 682. Successful Berber revolt, 739. Idrissi dynasty (Arab) 788–988 founded, Fez, 808. Almoravide (*q.v.*) (Berber) rule, 1061–1149. Marrakesh founded, 1062, by Yusuf Ben Tashfin. Almohade (*q.v.*) (Moorish) rule, 1149–1269. Marinid (Tribal Berber) dynasty established, 1269. Yakub II subdues Spain, 1269–86. Ali V takes Tlemcen, 1337. Fall of Marinids, 1360–1471. Wattassi dynasty (1471–1548) loses coastal towns to Spanish and Portuguese. Portuguese driven out by Saadi dynasty (Arab), 1550–1668. Conquest of Timbuktu end sixteenth century. Present Filali (Berber) dynasty seized Marrakesh, 1668. Unification under Moulay Ismail, 1672–1727. French conquest of Algeria, 1830, resulted in wars, 1844 and 1859. 'Capitulation' granted to Britain, 1886. Spaniards take Tetuan, and Ifni ceded to them, 1860. Special British Embassy, 1892. Britain relinquishes her interests to France, 8 Apr. 1904. Tangier crisis, 1905. Algeciras Conference, 1906, drafted Act of Algeciras, 7 Apr. French occupy Casablanca, 1907. Mulai Hafid takes throne, 1908. Agadir crisis, 1911. Mulay Yusuf became sultan, 1912. Spanish and French protectorates established by treaty of Fez, 30 Mar. 1912. Anglo-Franco-Spanish Convention, 18 Dec. 1923, defined the status of Tangier (*q.v.*). Abd-el-Krim's rebellion against Spanish, 1923–6. Sidi Mohammed proclaimed sultan, 18 Nov. 1927. Ifric occupied and effectively annexed by Spaniards, 1934. British capitulations abolished, 1937, in French zone. Government reformed and re-organized, 21 June 1947. France and the Sultan terminated the treaty of Fez, 2 Mar. 1956; Spanish protectorate ended, 7 Apr.; and the international status of Tangier was abolished, 29 Oct., thus making M. a completely independent sovereign monarchy by the end of that year. Sultan took title of king as from Aug. 1957. Hassan II succeeded to the throne, 26 Feb. 1961.

Mortmain, Statute of, 15 Nov. 1279. It forbade any person to buy or sell or under cover of any gift, term, or other title, to receive any lands or tenements in such a way that such lands and tenements should come under the ownership of a corporation without royal licence. A second Statute of M. was passed in 1391.

Moscow, Russia. Founded *c.* 1147; captured by the Tatars (i.e. by Toktamish, Khan of the Golden Horde), 1382; burnt by the Khan of the Crimea, 1571; the city was burnt by the inhabitants in 1812, when Napoleon entered, and he was forced to leave it. Ceased to be Russian capital on founding of St. Petersburg, 1712. At distribution of coronation gifts, 2,000 people crushed to death, 18 May 1896. Again made capital, 1917.

Mosul. Finally included in Iraq by Treaty of Angora, 5 June 1926.

Mountains, First Ascents of:

Etna (Sicily), Emperor Trajan, approximately A.D. 100.

Titlis (Switzerland), four peasants, 1744.

Mont Blanc (France-Italy), M. G. Paccard and J. Balmat, 1786.

Gross Glockner (Austria), five local men, 1800.

Jungfrau (Switzerland), J. R. and H. Meyer, 1811.

Ararat (U.S.S.R.), Parrot, 1829.

Finsteraarhorn (Switzerland), J. Leuthold, 1829.

Piz Bernina (Switzerland-Italy), J. Coaz, 1850.

Monte Rosa, Dufourspitze (Switzerland), five British, 1855.

Dom (Switzerland), J. Ll.-Davies, 1858.

Aletschhorn (Switzerland), F. F. Tuckett, 1859.

Gran Paradiso (Italy), J. J. Cowell, 1860.

Monte Viso (Italy), W. Matthews, 1861.

Weisshorn (Switzerland), J. Tyndall, 1861.

Les Ecrins (France), E. Whymper, 1864.

Grandes Jorasses (France-Italy), E. Whymper, 1865.

Aig Verte (France), E. Whymper, 1865.

Matterhorn (Switzerland), E. Whymper, 1865.

Elbruz (Caucasus), D. W. Freshfield, A. W. Moore, C. C. Tucker, 1868.

Cimone della Pala (Italy), E. R. Whitwell, 1870.

Meije (France), E. B. de Castelnau, 1877.

Grand Teton (U.S.A.), N. P. Langford, J. Stevenson, 1872.

Grand Dru (France), C. T. Dent, 1878.

Chimborazo (Ecuador), E. Whymper, 1880.

Mt. Cook (New Zealand), W. S. Green, 1882.

Aig du Géant (France-Italy), four Signori Sella, 1882.

Kabru (Himalaya), W. W. Graham, 1883.

Kilimanjaro (Kenya), Hans Meyer, 1887.

Ushba (Caucasus), J. G. Cockin, 1888.

Aconcagua (Chile-Argentine), M. Zurbriggen, 1897.

Mt. St. Elias (Alaska), Duke of Abruzzi, 1897.

Mt. Kenya (Kenya), H. J. Mackinder, 1899.

Ruwenzori (Central Africa), Duke of Abruzzi, 1906.

Trisul (Himalaya), T. G. Longstaff, 1907.

Mt. McKinley (Alaska), Parker-Browne expedition, 1912.

Mt. Robson (Canada), W. Foster, A. H. McCarthy, C. Kain, 1913.

Mt. Logan (Alaska), A. H. McCarthy, 1925.

Illampu (Bolivia), German-Austrian expedition, 1929.

Kamet (Himalaya), Kamet expedition, 1931.

Nanda Devi (Himalaya), British-American expedition, 1936.

Annapurna (Himalaya), French expedition, 1950.

Everest, E. P. Hillary (New Zealand) and Tensing (Nepal), 29 May 1953.

Nanga Parbat (Himalaya), H. Buhl (Austria), 3 July 1953.

K-2 (Himalayas), Italian expedition, 31 July 1954.

Kangchenjunga, British expedition, 25 May 1955.

Manaslu (Nepal), Japanese expedition, 1956.

Lhotse, Swiss expedition, 1956.

Broad Peak, Austrian expedition, 1957.

Rakaposhi, British-Pakistani expedition, led by M. Banks, 1958.

Mozambique. Discovered by Vasco da Gama, 1498. Colonized by Portuguese from 1505. Large areas chartered to the M. Co., and the Nyasaland Co., 1891, and the Zambesi Co., 1892. Vatua rebellion and siege of Lourenço Marques, Aug. 1894. Vatuas broken by battles of Marracuene, Coolela, and Chaimite, 1895. Gazaland reconquered, 1897. Transport from Transvaal regulated by the M. Convention, 1909. Charters of the Nyasaland Co. fell in 1928, and of the M. Co., 1942.

Mudania Convention. *See* GRAECO-TURKISH WARS.

Mufti, Grand, office abolished in Turkey, 1924. The office of M. of Jerusalem was instituted, 1922.

Muggletonians. A religious sect which was founded in England *c.* 1651 by John Reeve and Lodowick Muggleton.

Mugwumps, faction of the Republican Party in the U.S.A., first so called, 1889.

Mukden (Chin. **Shenyang**), Manchuria, largely burnt out in the Boxer rising of 1900. Russians defeated by Japanese, Mar. 1905. Besieged by Communists, 1947, and taken by them from Kuomintang, Oct. 1948.

Munich or München, Germany. Capital of Bavaria (*q.v.*). Supposed to have been founded, A.D. 962, by Henry of Saxony; taken by Gustavus Adolphus of Sweden, 1632; by Austrians, 1704, 1741, 1746; by French, 2 July 1800; university founded, 1826. Scene of first National Socialist *putsch,* 8 Nov. 1923. M. Conference on Czechoslovakia, 30 Sept. 1938.

Munitions, Ministry of. British Government set up a M. of M., June 1915. Abolished, 1920, and succeeded by the Disposal Board.

Münster, Westphalia, by 1186 had grown into a town; declared for the reformed faith, 1532; famous during 1535 for the Anabaptist disturbances, when the Roman Catholic bishop was expelled, but returned after besieging the city the same year.

Münster, Treaty of. Also known as the Treaty of Westphalia (*q.v.*), 1648.

Murmansk, founded, 1915, as Romanovna-Murmane, allied base in the abortive Archangel expedition of 1918–19. Besieged by Finns and Germans, 1941–4. Capital of province of same name, whose area was increased by the session of Petsamo (*q.v.*), 1945.

Muscat, Persian Gulf. Occupied by Portuguese, 1508. Driven out by the Sultan of Oman, 1650, who made it his capital, 1741.

Musical Composers. The following are the most celebrated of the world's M. C. (not now living) with their dates:

American:

Buck, Dudley, 1839–1909

Chadwick, George Whitefield, 1854–1931

De Koven, Henry Louis Reginald, 1859–1920

Foster, Stephen, 1826–64

Gershwin, George, 1898–1937

Griffes, Charles Tomlinson, 1884–1920

Herbert, Victor (*b.* Irish), 1859–1924

Loeffler, Charles Martin Tornov (*b.* French), 1861–1935

MacDowell, Edward Alexander, 1861–1908
Nevin, Ethelbert Woodbridge, 1862–1901
Paine, John Knowles, 1839–1906
Parker, Horatio William, 1863–1919
Schelling, Ernest, 1876–1939
Sousa, John Philip, 1854–1932

Austrian:

Berg, Alban, 1885–1935
Bruckner, Anton, 1824–96
Czerny, Karl, 1791–1857
Dittersdorf, Karl Ditters von, 1739–99
Fall, Leo, 1878–1925
Goldmark, Karl, 1830–1915
Haydn, Franz Josef, 1732–1809
Kreisler, Fritz, 1875–1962
Lanner, Josef, Franz Kar , 1801–43
Mahler, Gustav, 1860–1911
Mozart, Wolfgang Amadeus, 1756–91
Pleyel, Ignaz Josef, 1757–1831
Schubert, Franz Peter, 1797–1828
Strauss I, Johann, 1804–49
Strauss II, Johann, 1825–99
Suppé, Franz von, 1819–95
Wolf, Hugo, 1860–1903

Belgian:

Benoît, Pierre Léopold Léonard, 1834–1901
Des Prés, Joaquin, c. 1450–1521
Dufay, Guillaume, c. 1400–74
Franck, César August, 1822–90
Gossec, François Joseph, 1734–1829
Grétry, André Ernest Modest, 1741–1813
Jannequin, Clément, c. 1475–1560
Lassus, Roland de (Orlando di Lasso), c. 1532–94)
Lekeu, Guillaume, 1870–94
Ockeghem, Jean de, c. 1430–c. 1495
Tinel, Edgar, 1854–1912
Verdelot, Philippe, c. 1530–c. 1567
Vieuxtemps, Henri, 1820–81
Willaert, Adrian, c. 1480–1562

British:

Arne, Thomas Augustine, 1710–78
Attwood, Thomas, 1765–1838
Balfe, Michael William, 1808–70
Bateson, Thomas, c. 1575–1630
Bax, Sir Arnold Edward, 1883–1953
Benedict, Sir Julius, 1804–85
Bennett, Sir William Sterndale, 1816–1875
Bishop, Sir Henry Rowley, 1786–1855
Blow, John, 1649–1708
Boyce, William, 1710–79
Bridge, Frank, 1879–1941
Bridge, Sir John Frederick, 1844–1924
Bull, John, c. 1562–1628
Burney, Charles, 1726–1814
Butterworth, George Sainton Kaye, 1885–1916

Byrd, or Byrde, William, 1543–1623
Campion, Thomas, 1567–1619
Carey, Henry, c. 1687–1743
Cellier, Alfred, 1844–91
Clarke, Jeremiah, 1673–1707
Coleridge-Taylor, Samuel, 1875–1912
Cowen, Sir Frederick Hymen, 1852–1935
D'Albert, Eugene Francis Charles, 1864–1932
Davies, Sir Henry Walford, 1869–1941
Delius, Frederick, 1862–1934
Dibdin, Charles, 1745–1814
Dowland, John, 1563–1626
Dunstable, John, d. 1453
Elgar, Sir Edward, 1857–1934
Farnaby, Giles, c. 1565–c. 1640
Field, John (Irish), 1782–1837
German, Sir Edward, 1862–1936
Gibbons. Orlando, 1583–1625
Greene, Maurice, 1695–1755
Gurney, Ivor, 1890–1937
Handel, George Frederick, 1685–1759 (b. Germany)
Harty, Sir Herbert Hamilton (Irish), 1879–1941
Henschel, Isidor Georg (Sir George) (b. German), 1850–1934
Heseltine, Philip ('Peter Warlock'), 1894–1930
Holst, Gustav Theodore, 1874–1934
Hullah, John Pyke, 1812–84
Humfrey, Pelham, 1647–74
Ireland, John, 1879–1962
Lehmann, Liza (Mrs. Herbert Bedford), 1862–1918
Locke, Matthew, c. 1630–77
MacCunn, Hamish (Scottish), 1868–1916
Macfarren, Sir George Alexander, 1813–1887
Mackenzie, Sir Alexander Campbell (Scottish), 1847–1935
Miles, Philip Napier, 1865–1935
Monckton, Lionel, 1862–1924
Morley, Thomas, 1557–1602
Nares, James, 1715–83
Novello, Ivor (Davies), 1893–1951 (Welsh)
O'Neill, Norman Houston, 1875–1934
Ouseley, Sir Frederick Arthur Gore, 1825–89
Parratt, Sir Walter, 1841–1924
Parry, Joseph, 1841–1903
Parry, Sir Charles Hubert Hastings, 1848–1918
Purcell, Henry, 1659–95
Ronald, Sir Landon, 1873–1938
Rootham, Cyril Bradley, 1875–1938
Sharp, Cecil James, 1859–1924
Somervell, Sir Arthur, 1863–1937
Stainer, Sir John, 1840–1901
Stanford, Sir Charles Villiers, 1852–1924
Sullivan, Sir Arthur Seymour, 1842–1900
Tallis, Thomas, c. 1505–85

Taverner, John, c. 1495–1545
Tomkins, Thomas, 1573–1656
Tosti, Sir Francesco Paolo (b. Italian), 1846–1916
Tovey, Sir Donald Francis, 1875–1940
Tye, Christopher, c. 1500–72 or '73
Vaughan Williams, Ralph, 1872–1958
Wallace, William Vincent, 1812–65
Warlock, Peter. See HESELTINE, PHILIP
Weelkes, Thomas, c. 1575–1623
Wesley, Samuel, 1766–1837
Wesley, Samuel Sebastian, 1810–76
White, Robert, c. 1535–74
Willbye, John, 1574–1638
Wood, Charles, 1866–1926

Czech:

Dvořák, Anton, 1841–1904
Fibich, Zdĕnek, 1850–1900
Hammerschmidt, Andreas, 1611–75
Janáček, Leoš, 1854–1928
Kozeluch, Leopold Anton, 1754–1818
Nedbal, Oscar, 1874–1930
Smetana, Bedřich, 1824–84
Suk, Josef, 1874–1935

Danish:

Buxtehude, Diderik, 1637–1707
Gade, Niels Vilhelm, 1817–90
Hartmann, Johan Peter Emil, 1805–1900
Horneman, Christian Frederik Emil, 1841–1906
Lassen, Eduard, 1830–1904
Nielsen, Carl August, 1865–1931

Dutch:

Isaak, Hendrick, 1450–1517
Obrecht, Jakob, 1430–1505
Röntgen, Julius, 1855–1934
Sweelinck, Jan Pieterszoon, 1562–1621

Finnish:

Kajanus, Robert, 1856–1935
Melartin, Errki Gustav, 1875–1937
Sibelius, Jean, 1865–1957

French:

Alkan (Morhange), Charles Henri Valentin, 1813–88
Auber, Daniel François Esprit, 1782–1871
Audran, Edmond, 1840–1901
Benoist, François, 1794–1878
Berlioz, Hector, 1803–69
Bizet, Georges, 1838–75
Boëllmann, Léon, 1862–97
Boïeldieu, François Adrien, 1775–1834
Bourgault-Ducoudray, Louis Albert, 1840–1910
Bruneau, Louis Charles Bonaventure Alfred, 1857–1934

Campra, André, 1660–1744
Caplet, André, 1879–1925
Chabrier, Alexis Emmanuel, 1841–94
Chausson, Ernest, 1855–99
Couperin, François, 1668–1733
David, Félicien César, 1810–76
Debussy, Claude, 1862–1918
Delibes, Léo, 1836–91
Dukas, Paul, 1865–1935
Duparc, Henri, 1848–1933
Erlanger, Camille, 1863–1919
Fauré, Gabriel Urbain, 1845–1924
Godard, Benjamin Louis Paul, 1849–95
Goudimel, Claude, 1510–72
Gounod, Charles François, 1818–93
Guilmant, Félix Alexandre, 1837–1911
Halévy, Jacques Fromental Élie, 1799–1862
Hérold, Louis Joseph Ferdinand, 1791–1833
Indy, Paul Marie Théodore Vincent d', 1851–1931
Lalo, Victor Antoine Édouard, 1823–92
Lecocq, Alexandre Charles, 1832–1918
Lesueur, Jean François, 1760–1837
Lully, Jean Baptiste, 1632–87
Magnard, Albéric, 1866–1914
Massenet, Jules Émile Frédéric, 1842–1912
Méhul, Étienne Nicolas, 1763–1817
Messager, André Charles Prosper, 1853–1929
Monsigny, Pierre Alexandre, 1729–1817
Offenbach, Jacques, 1819–80
Onslow, George (Anglo-French), 1784–1853
Philidor, François André, 1726–95
Pierné, Henri Constant Gabriel, 1863–1937
Planquette, Robert, 1848–1903
Rameau, Jean Philippe, 1683–1764
Ravel, Maurice Joseph, 1875–1937
Reyer (Rey), Ernest, 1823–1909
Roussel, Albert, 1867–1937
Saint-Saëns, Charles Camille, 1841–1921
Satie, Erik (Alfred Eric Leslie), 1866–1925
Séverac, Joseph Marie Déodat de, 1873–1921
Thomas, Charles Louis Ambroise, 1811–1896
Widor, Charles Marie Jean Albert, 1844–1937

German:

Bach, Carl Philipp Emanuel, 1714–88
Bach, Johann Christian, 1735–82
Bach, Johann Sebastian, 1685–1750
Beethoven, Ludwig van, 1770–1827
Brahms, Johannes, 1833–97
Bruch, Max, 1838–1920
Cornelius, Peter, 1824–74
Draeseke, Felix, 1835–1913
Flotow, Friedrich, Freiherr von, 1812–1883

Franz, Robert, 1815–92
Gluck, Christoph Willibald, 1714–87
Goetz, Hermann, 1840–76
Graupner, Christoph, 1683–1760
Handl, Jakob, 1550–91
Hasse, Johann Adolf, 1699–1783
Hassler or Hasler, Hans Leo, 1564–1612
Henselt, Adolf von, 1814–99
Hiller, Johann Adam, 1728–1804
Hoffman, Ernst Theodor Amadeus, 1776–1822
Hummel, Johann Nepomuk, 1778–1837
Humperdinck, Engelbert, 1854–1921
Jensen, Adolf, 1837–79
Karg-Elert, Sigfried, 1877–1933
Keiser, Reinhard, 1674–1739
Kirchner, Theodor, 1824–1903
Kücken, Friedrich Wilhelm, 1810–82
Kuhnau, Johann, 1660–1722
Lachner, Franz, 1804–90
Lortzing, Gustav Albert, 1801–51
Löwe, Johann Karl Gottfried, 1796–1869
Marschner, Heinrich August, 1795–1861
Mendelssohn-Bartholdy, Jakob Ludwig Felix, 1809–47
Meyerbeer, Giacomo, 1791–1864
Moscheles, Ignaz, 1794–1870
Moszkowski, Moritz, 1854–1925
Mottl, Felix, 1856–1911
Naumann, Johann Gottlieb, 1741–1801
Neukomm, Sigismund von, 1778–1858
Nicodé, Jean Louis (b. Polish), 1853–1919
Nicolai, Karl Otto Ehrenfried, 1810–49
Pachelbel, Johann, 1653–1706
Raff, Josef Joachim, 1822–82
Reger, Max, 1873–1916
Rheinberger, Josef Gabriel, 1839–1901
Scharwenka, Ludwig Philipp, 1847–1917
Scharwenka, Xaver, 1850–1924
Schreker, Franz, 1878–1934
Schumann, Robert, 1810–56
Schütz, Heinrich, 1585–1672
Spohr, Ludwig, 1784–1859
Steibelt, Daniel, 1765–1823
Strauss, Richard, 1864–1949
Telemann, Georg Philipp, 1681–1767
Vogler, Georg Josef, 1749–1814
Volkmann, Friedrich Robert, 1815–83
Wagner, Wilhelm Richard, 1813–83
Weber, Karl Maria Friedrich Ernst von, 1786–1826

Hungarian:
Bartók, Béla, 1881–1945
Dohnanyi, Ernö, 1887–1960
Erkel, Ferenc, 1810–92
Heller, Stephen, 1814–88
Joachim, Joseph, 1831–1907
Lehár, Ferencz (Franz), 1870–1948
Liszt, Franz, 1811–86
Mosonyi, Michael Brandt, 1814–70

Italian:
Abbatini, Antonio Maria, c. 1595–1677
Allegri, Gregorio, 1582–1652

Arditi, Luigi, 1822–1903
Bellini, Vincenzo, 1801–35
Boccherini, Luigi, 1743–1805
Boito, Arrigo, 1842–1918
Bononcini or Buononcini, Giovanni Maria, 1642–78
Bossi, Marco Enrico, 1861–1925
Busoni, Ferruccio Benvenuto, 1866–1924
Caccini, Giulio, 1545–1618
Carissimi, Giacomo, 1605–74
Catalani, Alfredo, 1854–93
Cavalieri, Emilio di, c. 1550–1602
Cavalli, Pietro Francesco, 1602–76
Cherubini, Maria Luigi Zenobio Carlo Salvatore, 1760–1842
Cimarosa, Domenico, 1749–1801
Clementi, Muzio, 1752–1832
Corelli, Arcangelo, 1653–1713
Donizetti, Gaetano, 1797–1848
Durante, Francesco, 1684–1755
Frescobaldi, Girolamo, 1583–1643
Gabrieli, Andrea, 1520–86
Gabrieli, Giovanni, 1557–1612
Gagliano, Marco da, c. 1575–1642
Geminiani, Francesco, 1687–1762
Gesualdo, Carlo, Prince of Venosa, 1560–1613
Jommelli, Niccolò, 1714–74
Legrenzi, Giovanni, 1625–90
Leo, Leonardo, 1694–1744
Leoncavallo, Ruggiero, 1858–1919
Locatelli, Pietro Antonio, 1693–1764
Lotti, Antonio, 1667–1740
Marcello, Benedetto, 1686–1739
Marenzio, Luca, 1553–99
Martucci, Giuseppe, 1856–1909
Mercadante, Giuseppe Saverio Raffaele, 1795–1870
Merulo, Claudio, 1533–1604
Monteverdi, Claudio, 1567–1643
Paer, Ferdinando, 1771–1839
Paesiello or Paisiello, Giovanni, 1741–1816
Paganini, Niccolò, 1782–1840
Palestrina, Giovanni Pierluigi da, 1525–1594
Pergolese, or Pergolesi, Giovanni Battista, 1710–36
Piccinni, or Piccini, Niccolo, 1728–1800
Pinsuti, Ciro, 1829–88
Puccini, Giacomo, 1858–1924
Respighi, Ottorino, 1879–1936
Rossini, Gioacchino Antonio, 1792–1868
Sacchini, Antonio Maria Gaspare, 1734–1786
Salieri, Antonio, 1750–1825
Sarti, Giuseppe, 1729–1802
Scarlatti, Alessandro, 1660–1725
Scarlatti, Domenico, 1685–1757
Sgambati, Giovanni, 1841–1914
Spontini, Gasparo Luigi Pacifico, 1774–1851
Steffani, Agostino, 1654–1728
Stradella, Alessandro, 1642–82
Tartini, Giuseppe, 1692–1770

Traetta, Tommaso, 1727–79
Vecchi, Orazio, c. 1550–1605
Verdi, Giuseppe, 1813–1901
Viadana (Grossi), Ludovico, 1564–1645
Vicentino, Nicolà, 1511–c. 1576
Zingarelli, Nicolà Antonio, 1752–1837

Norwegian:

Grieg, Edvard Hagerup, 1843–1907
Selmer, Johan Peter, 1844–1910
Svendsen, Johan Severin, 1840–1911

Polish:

Chopin, Frédéric François, 1810–49
Godowsky, Leopold, 1870–1938
Moniuszko, Stanislaus, 1819–92
Noskowski, Zymunt, 1846–1909
Paderewski, Ignacy Jan, 1860–1941
Szymanowski, Karol, 1882–1937

Russian:

Arensky, Antonin Stepanovitch, 1861–1906
Balakirev, Mily Alexeievitch, 1837–1910
Borodin, Alexander Porfirievitch, 1833–1887
Cui, César Antonovitch, 1835–1918
Dargomijsky, Alexander, 1813–69
Glazunov, Alexander Constantinovitch, 1865–1936
Glinka, Mikhail Ivanovitch, 1804–57
Kastalsky, Alexander Dmitrievitch, 1856–1926
Liadov, Anatol Constantinovitch, 1855–1914
Liapunov, Serge Mikhailovitch, 1859–1924
Mussorgsky, Modest Petrovitch, 1839–1881
Napravnik, Eduard (b. Czech), 1839–1916
Prokofiev, Sergei, 1891–1953
Rachmaninov, Serge, 1873–1943
Rebikov, Vladimir Ivanovitch, 1866–1920
Rimsky-Korsakov, Nicolas Andreievitch, 1844–1908
Rubinstein, Anton, 1830–94
Scriabin, Alexander Nicolaievitch, 1871–1915
Taneiev, Alexander Sergeievitch, 1850–1915
Taneiev, Serge Ivanovitch, 1856–1915
Tchaikovsky, Peter Ilyitch, 1840–93

Spanish:

Albeniz, Isaac, 1860–1909
Bretón, Tomás, 1850–1923
Chapí, Ruperto, 1851–1909
Granados Campina, Enrique, 1867–1916
Pedrell, Felipe, 1841–1922

Sarasate, Pablo de, 1844–1910
Victoria, Tomás Luis de, c. 1535–1611

Swedish:

Hallén, Johan Andréas, 1846–1925
Hallström, Ivar, 1826–1901
Sjögren, J. G. Emil, 1853–1918

Swiss:

Huber, Hans, 1852–1921

Musical Festivals. Festival of the Sons of the Clergy in St. Paul's Cathedral, annual since 1698. Three Choirs Festival held annually in cathedrals of Gloucester, Hereford, and Worcester, in succession, from 1715. Birmingham Festival began, 1768; held at irregular intervals till 1912. Norwich Festival held at irregular intervals since 1770. Crystal Palace Handel Festival began, 1857; irregular, and then triennial. Leeds Festival instituted, 1858; held again, 1874; since then, triennial. Edinburgh International Festival instituted, 1947. Aldeburgh, Suffolk, festival instituted, 1948. In U.S.A. festivals began at Boston and Worcester, 1858; Cincinnati, 1873. Bach Festival at Bethlehem, Pennsylvania, 1900. Berkshire Festivals, established at Pittsfield, Massachusetts, 1918, were in 1931 transferred to Library of Congress, Washington. The Boston Symphony Orchestra acquired Tanglewood, Berkshire, Massachusetts, as permanent festival home in 1937. In Germany the Lower Rhine Festival, dating from 1817, was the most important. Salzburg Festival founded 1870; held annually since 1920.

Mutiny Acts, the legal basis of military law and hence of the existence of a standing army in the U.K., were passed annually from 1689 to 1881, when they were merged in the Army Acts, still passed annually.

M.V.D., executive forces of the Ministry of the Interior of the U.S.S.R., and including frontier and security troops of all arms, and warders and administrative personnel of forced-labour camps, as well as the secret police force, known until 1945 as the N.K.V.D. (*q.v.*), and after 1953 as the K.G.B. (*q.v.*).

Mysore, India. Continually at war with the British, 1760–99. In 1799 Tipu Sahib finally defeated; M. made to accept a subsidiary alliance and to cede Coimbatore to British, and Kurnool to Hyderabad, 1801. State completely annexed by British, 1834, but retroceded to a native rajah, 1881. Joined the Indian Union and introduced responsible government, Dec. 1947.

ADDENDA

N

Nagasaki, Japan. From 1640 the Dutch were the only European nation permitted to trade with Japan, and they were allowed only one trading post on Deshima, near N. This continued till Japan was opened to trade, 1859. City mostly destroyed by atomic bomb, 9 Aug. 1945.

Nairobi, Kenya. Founded, 1898. Granted royal charter, 30 Mar. 1950.

Namur, Belgium. Captured by Louis XIV in 1692; recaptured in 1695 by William III; in French possession, 1702–1712; bombarded by allies, 1704; subsequently in possession of different powers, and assigned to Belgium, 1830.

Nancy, France. Captured by Charles the Bold, 29 Nov. 1475; lost by him, 5 Oct. 1476; captured by French, 1633 and 1670; restored to Duke Leopold, 1697; became French possession, 1766; put to ransom by the Prussians, 1870.

Nanking, China. Capital of China, 1368, till abandoned by Yung-lo, 1405. Captured by British, 1842. By Taipings, 1853. Railways to Tientsin and Shanghai opened, 1909. Became capital again, 1928. Stormed and sacked by Japanese, Nov. 1937. Became capital of Wang Ching Wei's Japanese-sponsored government, 1940–5. Officially ceased to be Chinese capital after Communist victory in 1949.

Nantes, France. Of Roman origin. In possession of Clotaire I, A.D. 560; held by Normans, 843–936; communal constitution granted by Francis II, 1560; scene of Carrier's *noyades*, 1793.

Nantes, Edict of, by which the Huguenots were permitted to exercise their own religion, was published on 15 Apr. 1598 by Henry IV of France. Its revocation on 24 Oct. 1685, by Louis XIV, drove many of the Protestants into exile.

Naples, Italy. The Romans subdued the territory in 326 B.C.; it fell into the hands of the Goths, but they were driven out by Belisarius in A.D. 536; Charles of Anjou in possession, 1266; great massacre of the French at Palermo known as the Sicilian Vespers (q.v.), 1282; separated from Sicily (q.v.), 1303; reunited with Sicily, 1442; annexed to Spain, 1504; insurrection headed by Masaniello, 1647; possessed by Austria, 1713; recovered by Spain, 1734; invaded by French Republican Army, 1789; by Napoleon, 1806; restoration of the Bourbons, 1815; incorporated in the kingdom of Italy, 1860. *See also* WORLD WAR II.

Narbonne, France. A considerable time before the Roman invasion of Gaul, N. was a famous city. In 118 B.C. the first Roman colony in Gaul was founded under the name of *Narbo Martius*; seized by the Visigoths, A.D. 413; by Saracens after a two years' siege, 719; retaken by Pepin le Bref, 759; united to French crown, 1507; Cinq-Mars arrested at for conspiracy, 1642.

Narvik, formerly Viktoriahavn, was connected with the ironstone mines in northern Sweden (Kiruna, etc.), 1903. Four German destroyers sunk in N. fiord, 13 Apr. 1940; town captured by Allies, 28 May, but abandoned, 10 June.

Nassau, Germany. Early occupied by the Alamanni, who were defeated by Clovis towards the close of the fifth century; became part of German kingdom, 843; annexed to Prussia, 1866.

Natal, S. Africa. Discovered by Vasco da Gama on Christmas Day, 1497, hence the name; declared part of British dominions, 1843; formally annexed to Cape Colony, 31 May 1844; declared a separate colony, 15 July 1856; Zululand annexed to, 1897; Boers finally driven from, 1900. An original member of the Union of S. Africa, 1910.

National Anthems. The following are the titles (if any), first lines (in the original language), with names of the author of the words (W.) and composers of the tunes (T.) and dates, where known, of the principal N. A. of various countries:

Abyssinia. *See* ETHIOPIA.

Albania: 'Rveth Flamurit le per bashkuar' poet and composer unknown.

Argentine: 'Oid, mortales, el grito sagrado Libertad'; (W.) Vicente López y Planes, 1813; (T.) José Blas Parera, revised by Juan P. Esnaola.

Armenia: (W.) Sarmen; (T.) Khatchaturian, 1945.

Australia: 'Advance, Australia fair'; (W. and T.) Peter Dodd McCormick and W. W. Francis, before 1916 (broadcast, but not actually adopted as a N. Anthem).

Austria (imperial): 'Gott erhalte Franz den (or 'unsern') Kaiser'; (W.) Leopold Haschka; (T.) Haydn, 1797.

Austria (Nazi): *Lied der Jugend*, 'Ihr Jungen schliesst die Reihen gut'; (W. and T.) Hermann Leopoldi, c. 1933.

Austria (republic, 1920–9): 'Deutsch-

Oesterreich, du herrliches Land, wir lieben dich'; (W.) Karl Renner; (T.) Kienzl, 1920.

Austria (republic, 1945): 'Land der Berge, Land am Strome'; (W.) Paula Preradovic; (T.) W. A. Mozart.

Bavaria: 'Bayern, mein Heimatland'; (W.) F. Beck; (T.) F. Lachner, 1848; also 'Gott mit dir, du Land der Bayern'; (W.) Michael Öchsner; (T.) F. M. Kunz.

Belgium: La Brabançonne, 'Qui l'aurait dit de l'arbitraire' (now 'Après des siècles d'esclavage'); (W.) Jenneval, 1830; (T.) François van Campenhout, 1830 (real name, Louis Alexandre Hippolyte Dechez).

Belgium (Flemish): De Vlaamsche Leeuw; (W.) H. van Peene; (T.) Karel Miry.

Bolivia: 'Bolivianos, el hado propicio'; (W.) Ignacio de Sanjinés; (T.) Benedetto Vincenti.

Brazil: 'Ouviram do Ypiranga as margens placidas'; (W.) Joaquin Osorio Duque Estrada; (T.) Francisco Manoel da Silva.

Brazil (earlier): 'Seja um pallio luz'; (W.) M. Albuquerque; (T.) Léopold Miguez.

Bulgaria: until 1946, Shoumi Maritza; (W.) Mereček; (T.) Gabriel Šebek; since 1946, 'Bulgaria mila', words and tune by various authors.

Burma: 'Nang-gan-daw-Thachin'; (W. and T.) M. B. Saya Tin, 1930.

Canada: The Maple Leaf for Ever, 'In days of yore, from Britain's shore'; (W. and T.) Alexander Muir, 1867.

Canada (French): 'O Canada: Terre de nos aïeux'; (W.) Adolphe Basile Routhier, 1880; (T.) C. Lavallée (adapted from the priests' march in Mozart's Magic Flute).

Chile: Dulce patria, 'Ha cesado la luncha sangrienta'; (W.) Eusebio Lillo, 1847; (T.) Carnicer, 1828.

China: 'Tsung-kuoh hiung li jüh dschou tiän'; (W. and T.) unknown, 1912.

China (Nationalist): The Song of Kuomintang; (W.) Sun Yat-sen; (T.) Ch'eng Mao-yün, 1928.

China (People's Republic): 'The March of the Volunteers'; (W.) Tien Han; (T.) Nieh Erh.

Colombia: Oh! Gloria inmarcesible, 'Cesó la horrible noche'; (W.) Rafael Núñez; (T.) Orestes Sindici, c. 1905.

Costa Rica: 'Noble patria, tu hermosa bandera'; (W.) José Maria Zeledón; (T.) Manuel Maria Gutiérrez, 1821, in use from 1853.

Cuba: Himno Bayamés, 'Al combate corred bayameses'; (W. and T.) Pedro Figueredo, 1868.

Czechoslovakia: Combination of 'Kde domov muj'; (W.) Josef Kajetán Tyl; (T.) Škroup, 1834, and 'Nad Tatrou sa blyska'; (W.) Janko Matúska, 1844; (T.) traditional; first officially used 1919.

Denmark: 'Kong Kristian stod ved højen mast'; (W.) Johannes Ewald; (T.) J. E. Hartmann (from opera Fiskerne), 1780; also 'Der er et yndigt land'; (W.) Adam Oehlen schläger; (T.) H. E. Krøyer, twentieth century, and 'Dengang jog drog afsted'; (W.) F. Faber; (T.) J. O. E. Horneman, twentieth century.

Dominican Republic: 'Quisqueyanos valientes, alcemos'; (W.) Emilio Prud'-homme; (T.) José Reyes, 1900.

Ecuador: Salve! Oh patria, mil veces, 'Indignados tus hijos del yugo'; (W.) Juan Léon Mera; (T.) Antonio Neumann, 1866.

Egypt. See UNITED ARAB REPUBLIC.

Eire. See IRELAND, REPUBLIC OF.

England. See GREAT BRITAIN.

Estonia: 'Mu isamaa, mu önn ja röön'; (W.) J. Jannsen, 1865; (T.) Pacius, 1848.

Ethiopia: 'Etiopia hoy, des yibalish'; (W.) by a group of Ethiopian scholars, 1930; (T.) M. K. Nalbadian, 1925.

Finland: Maamme, 'Oi maamme suomi synnyiumaa'; (W.) J. L. Runeberg (originally in Swedish), 1843; (T.) Pacius, as for Estonia. A second tune by Pacius was also adopted.

France: La Marseillaise, 'Allons, enfants de la patrie' (W. and T.) Rouget de Lisle, 1792.

Germany (imperial): 'Heil dir im Siegerkranz'; (W.) Heinrich Harries, 1790, adapted by B. G. Schumacher, 1793; (T.) as for Great Britain; also, after 1870, Die Wacht am Rhein, 'Es braust ein Ruf wie Donnerschall'; (W.) M. Schneckenburger, 1840; (T.) Carl Wilhelm, 1854.

Germany (Nazi): Horst Wessel Lied, 'Die Fahne hoch, die Reihen dicht geschlossen'; (W.) Horst Wessel; (T.)? Bohemian comic song; in use 1933–45.

Germany (republic): 'Deutschland, Deutschland über alles'; (W.) H. A. Hoffmann von Fallersleben, 1841; (T.) Haydn, as for Austria.

Great Britain: 'God Save the Queen'; c. 1740; (W.) unknown; (T.) Henry Carey.

Greece: 'Se gnorizo apo ten kopsi tu spatjie ten tromere'; (W.) Dionysius Solomos, 1824; (T.) N. Mántzarios; in use since 1873.

Guatemala: 'Guatemala feliz!'; (W.) J. Joachin Palma; (T.) Rafael Alvarez, in use from 1896.

Haiti: La Dessalinène, 'Pour le pays, pour les ancêtres'; (W.) Justin Lhérisson; (T.) Nicolas Geffard, 1903.

Hawaii: 'Hawaii ponoi'; (W. and T.) ?

Kalakana, king of Hawaii, c. 1880.

Holkar's Dominions. *See* INDORE.

Holland: 'Wilhelmus van Nassuwe'; (W.) Philip van Marnix, c. 1570; (T.) unknown, first published, 1626; also 'Wien Neerlands bloed in d'aderen vloeit'; (W.) Hendrik Tollens; (T.) Jan Wilms, 1820.

Honduras: 'Compatriotas, de Honduras los fueros'; (W.) Augusto C. Coello; (T.) Carlos Hartling.

Hungary: *Himnusz*, 'Ysten áldd meg a Magyart'; (W.) F. Kölcesey, 1823; (T.) F. Erkel, 1845; usually followed by *Szózat*, 'Hazádnak rendületlenül légy hive óh magyar'; (W.) Michael Vörösmarty, 1836; (T.) Benjamin Egressy, 1844.

Iceland: 'O Gud vors land'; (W.) Mathias Jochumsson, 1874; (T.) Sveinbjørn Sveinbjørnsson.

India: 'Jana Gana Mana'; (W.) Sir Rabindranath Tagore. In addition, 'Bande Matram' by Bankin Chandra Chatterjee is honoured as a national song.

Indonesia: *Indonesia Raja*; (T.) W. R. Supratam, 1928.

Indore: 'Prabho prarth ana parisa amuchi'; (W.) ?; (T.) Jad.

Iran. *See* PERSIA.

Iraq: (monarchy) *Royal Salute* (march); (W.) none; (T.) A. R. Murray. Republican choice not yet made final.

Ireland, Republic of: 'A Soldier's Song' adopted as (Free State) N. Anthem, 1926. (W.) P. Kearney, 1907–10; (T.) P. Heaney, 1926.

Israel: *Hatikvah* (*Hope*), 'While even yet unchanged'; (W.) Hebrew: N. H. Imber; English: Nina Salaman; (T.) ? 1936.

Italy: *Inno di Garibaldi*, 'All' armi, all' armi, si scopron le tombe'; (W.) L. Mercantini; (T.) A. Olivieri, 1858.

Italy (Fascist): *La Giovinezza*, 'Sù, compagni in forti schiere'; (W.) Marcello Manni; (T.) G. Castaldo after Giuseppe Blanc, 1921.

Italy (Republic): *Inno di Mameli*, 'Fratelli d'Italia'; (W.) G. Mameli; (T.) M. Novara, 1847.

Japan: *Kimagayo*; (W.) ninth century; (T.) Hayashi Hirokami, revised by F. Eckert, 1880.

Jewish. *See* ISRAEL.

Jugoslavia. *See* YUGOSLAVIA.

Latvia: 'Dievs, sveti Latviju'; (W. and T.) Karlis Baumanis.

Lebanon: 'Kullu na lil watan'; (W.) R. Nachleh; (T.) M. El-Murr, 1926.

Liberia: 'Salve, Liberia, salve!'; (W.) President Warner; (T.) Olmstead Luca, 1860.

Liechtenstein: 'Oben am deutschen Rhein lehnet sich Liechtenstein'; (W.) H. H. Jauch, 1850; (T.) as for Great Britain.

Lithuania: 'Lietuva, tévyné mùsu'; (W. and T.) Vincas Kudirka, 1918.

Luxemburg: *Ons Hémecht*, 'Wò d'Uolzécht duréch d'Wisen zét'; (W.) Michel Lentz, 1859; (T.) J. A. Zinnen.

Malta: *Tifhíra lil Mâlta*, 'Int sabíha, Mâlta tâna'; (W.) Giovanni Antonio Vassalla; (T.) Bersaglieri song adapted, twentieth century. After 1942: 'Lil din l'art Helwa'; (W.) C. Psaila; (T.) R. Samut.

Mexico: 'Mexicanos, al grito guerra'; (W.) Francisco Gonzáles Bocanegra; (T.) Jaime Nunó, 1854.

Montenegro. *See* YUGOSLAVIA. Does not seem to have contributed to the federal anthem.

Nepal: 'May glory crown our illustrious sovereign'; (W. and T.) unknown, 1952.

New Zealand: 'God defend New Zealand'; (W.) Thomas Bracken; (T.) J. J. Woods, not consistently used until 1940. ('God Save the Queen' also used.)

Newfoundland: 'When sun rays crown thy pine-clad hills'; (W.) Sir Charles Cavendish Boyle; (T.) Hubert Parry. (This does not displace 'God save the Queen.')

Nicaragua: 'Hermosa soberana'; (W.) Blas Villatas; (T.) A. Cousin; after 1917 (W.) Salomón Ibarra Mayorga; (T.) unknown.

Norway: 'Ja, vi elsker dette landet'; (W.) Bjørnson; (T.) Nordraak, 1859.

Orange Free State: 'Heft, Burgers, 't lied der vrijheid aan'; (W. and T.) Hamelberg.

Pakistan: No decision yet made.

Palestine. *See* ISRAEL.

Panama: 'Alcanzamos por fin la victoria'; (W.) Gerónimo de la Osa; (T.) Santos Jorge, 1903.

Paraguay: 'Paraquayos, Republica ó muerte'; (W.) Francisco Acuna de Figueroa; (T.) Francés Dupey.

Persia: 'Shāhanshān—a mā Zandah bādā'; (W.) S. Afsar; (T.) Najmi Moghaddam, c. 1934.

Peru: 'Somos libres, seámos lo siempre'; (W.) José de la Torre Ugarte; (T.) José Bernardo Alcedo, 1821.

Philippine Islands: 'Tierra adorada (*Marcha nacional filipina*); (W.) José Palma; (T.) Julian Felipe, c. 1898.

Poland: 'Jeszcze Polska nie zgineta'; (W.) Josef Wybicki; (T.) ? Kleofas Oginski, 1795, newly harmonized by K. Sikorski, 1948.

Portugal (royal): 'O patria, O rei, O povo'; (W. and T.) Pedro I of Brazil, formerly Pedro IV of Portugal, 1822.

L

Portugal (republic): 'Heiros do mar'; (W.) Lopez de Mendoça, 1890; (T.) Alfredo Keil; used since 1910.

Prussia: 'Borussia'; (W.) G. R. Duncker; (T.) Spontini, 1818; also 'Ich bin ein Preusse'; (W.) Bernhard Thiersch; (T.) A. H. Neithardt, 1826.

Rumania (royal): *Traeasca Regele in pace si onor*; (W.) V. Alexandir; (T.) E. A. Hübsch, 1861.

Rumania (republican): *Te slavim Romania*, 1951.

Russia (imperial): 'Bozhe Tsarya khrani'; (W.) W. A. Zhukovsky, 1833; (T.) Lvov, 1833.

Russia (Soviet to 1944): *L'Internationale*, 'Debout, les damnés de la terre'; (W.) Eugène Pottier (translated into Russian, last in 1932); (T.) Pierre Degeyter.

Russia (Soviet, after 1944): *Gymn Sovietskogo Soiusa*; (W.) Sergey Mikhalkov and I. Registan; (T.) A. V. Alexandrov, c. 1942.

Salvador: 'Saludemos la patria orgullosos'; (W.) Juan J. Cañas; (T.) Juan Aberte.

Scotland: 'Scots wha ha'e wi' Wallace bled'; (W.) Robert Burns, 1793; (T.) traditional.

Serbia: *Srpska Himna*, 'Bože pravde, it što spase'; (W.) J. Djordjewič; (T.) Davorin Jenko, 1872.

Siam: 'Taurasoen Barami'; (W. and T.) unknown.

S. Africa (Union): 'Die Stem van Suid-Afrika'; (W.) J. C. Langehoven, (T.) M. L. Villiers.

Spain (royal): *Marcha real*; (W.) none; (T.) unknown German composer, 1770; also *Hymno de Riego*; (W.) unknown; (T.) Huerta.

Spain (republic): *Marcha grandera*.

Sweden: 'Du gamla, du fria, du fjällhöga Nord'; (W.) R. Dybeck; (T.) traditional, 1844.

Switzerland: 'Rufst du, mein Vaterland'; (W.) J. H. Wyss, 1811, with French and Italian translations; (T.) as for Great Britain; also *Schweizerpsalm*, 'Trittst im Morgenrot daher'; (W.) L. Widmer; (T.) Josef (Father Alberik) Zwyssig, 1841.

Transvaal: 'Kent gij dat volk vol heldenmoed'; (W. and T.) Catherine Félicie van Rees.

Tunisia: *Marche beylicale*; (W.) none; (T.) by an Italian composer, 1881–3, adapted by Sidi-Sadock.

Turkey: 'Korkma! Sönmez bu safaklarda yüzen al sancak'; (W.) M. Akif; (T.) Zeki; officially adopted 1921.

United Arab Republic: (march) 'Ha ni au be au da to samil ma kam'; (W.) unknown; (T.) ? Verdi.

Uruguay: 'Orientales, la patria ó la tumba!'; (W. and T.) Juan Coppetti.

U.S.A.: *The Star-spangled Banner*, 'Oh say, can you see, by the dawn's early light'; (W.) Francis Scott Key, 1814 (T.) John Stafford Smith; officially adopted 1931; earlier 'Hail Columbia' (W.) J. Hopkinson; (T.) Fyls, c. 1800.

U.S.S.R. *See* RUSSIA.

Venezuela: 'Gloria al bravo pueblo'; (W.) Vicente Salias; (T.) Juan Lan daeta, after 1810.

Wales: 'Mae hen wlad fy nhadau' ('Land of my fathers'); (W.) Evan James, English, John Owen; (T.) J. James.

Westphalia: 'Ihr mögt den Rhein, den stolzen, preisen'; (W,) E. Ritterhaus (T.) Johann Peters.

Württemberg: 'Preisend mit viel schönen Reden'; (W.) J. Kerner, 1826; (T. traditional.

Yugoslavia: A compound of the Serbian hymn 'Bože pravde' (*see* SERBIA), th Croatian hymn 'Lijepa naša domovino' (W.) Antun Mihanoic; (T.) Lichtenegger and the Slovene hymn 'Naprej zastav Slav'; (W.) Simon Jenko; (T.) Davorin Jenko.

Zanzibar: National march for military band by Sir Donald Francis Tovey.

National Art Collections Fund. Founded, 1903. Prominent in 1962 in its successful efforts to secure a Leonardo da Vinci cartoon for the nation.

National Assembly, 1789–91. *Se* FRENCH REVOLUTION.

National Assistance Act, 1948, was in tended to replace by a new principle system which hitherto had been based o successive modifications of the Eliza bethan Poor Laws (*q.v.*).

National Book League. Founded, 1944, as the successor to the National Book Council (founded, 1924).

National Debt (Great Britain). Origin ated in the reign of William III, and wa introduced by Charles Montagu, Earl o Halifax (1661–1715) on 15 Dec. 1692 Became a permanent institution, 1694. Deadweight debt on 31 Mar. in years named: 1914, £649,770,091; 1939, £8,279,839,000; 1960, £27,735,375,000.

National Dental Service provided fo under N. Health Service Act, 1946, whic came into operation 5 July 1948. In 1951 new regulations placed a considerably greater part of the expenses on the patient, e.g. half the cost of dentures and the first £1 of any fees due in respect of treatment.

National Economic Planning Council. Envisaged by Selwyn Lloyd, then Chancellor of the Exchequer, July 1961; established Jan. 1962.

National Gallery (London). Founded, 1824. Present building completed, 1838; enlarged, 1860, 1869, 1876, 1886, and

'30; N. Portrait Gallery founded, 1856,
tablished at S. Kensington, 1869;
moved to Bethnal Green Museum,
⅃85; transferred to new buildings
⅃joining N. G., 1896.

National Gallery of British Art. *See*
⅃TE GALLERY.

National Governments, coalitions in the
.K. which came to power in Aug. 1931
⅃d Nov. 1935, and which continued in
⅃ice during World War II, being, how-
'er, largely reconstituted in the spring
1940. It continued in office until 1945.

National Guard (France). Introduced
to Paris during French Revolution,
⅃ly 1789; superseded by present military
'stem, 1870.

National Guard (U.S.A.). Founded,
⅃03.

National Health Service Act was evolved
om proposals made in the White Paper
' Feb. 1944. It became law in 1946, but
d not come into operation until 5 July
⅃48. Charges for medicine, etc., supplied
⅃der this Act first made, June 1952.

National Insurance. An insurance
⅃ainst ill health and unemployment,
⅃troduced in 1911, and came into force,
⅃ July 1912. Unemployment insurance
⅃came compulsory, 8 Nov. 1920; and
⅃cts passed 1920–34 were repealed or
⅃nsolidated by Act of 1935. As to
⅃alth insurance, Acts passed 1920, 1922,
⅃24, and 1928 were repealed by a con-
⅃lidating Act, 1936. Entire structure of
'. I. in Britain changed by the Act of
⅃46 (*see* next article).

National Insurance Act, 1946, based on
⅃commendations made in the report of
⅃e Beveridge Committee, 1942, and de-
⅃eloped in a White Paper of Sept. 1944,
⅃pealed all previous legislation on the
⅃bject of unemployment, etc., insurance,
⅃d pensions, and became law, 1946.

National Parks and Access to the
⅃untryside Act, 1949, set up the National
⅃arks Commission with powers to
⅃signate national parks and areas of
⅃tstanding beauty in England and
⅃ales. Ten national parks had been
⅃tablished by 1962, and several smaller
⅃eas of outstanding natural beauty.

Nationality Act, British, replaced a
⅃evious Act of the same name, passed in
⅃14, and was enacted, 30 July 1948.

Nationalization. Sankey Commission
⅃nanimously recommended N. of minerals
⅃d Mr. Justice Sankey himself recom-
⅃ended state ownership, 1919. Coal
⅃oyalty Owners expropriated, Mar. 1937.
The following is a list of principal
⅃easures of N. taken since 1944. A=date
⅃ passing of the Act. V=date when the
⅃dertaking vested in the crown, etc.
⅃=date repealed.

	A	V	R
Bank of England:	14 Feb. 1946	1 Mar. 1946	
Cable and Wireless:	6 Nov. 1946	1 Jan. 1947	
Coal-mines:	12 July 1946	1 Jan. 1947	
Railways and Canals:	6 Aug. 1947	1 Jan. 1948	
Road Transport:	6 Aug. 1947	27 Jan. 1948 (Executive appointed)	May 1953
Civil Aviation:	1 Aug. 1946	8 Aug. 1946 (Boards appointed)	
Electricity:	16 Aug. 1947	1 Apr. 1948	
Gas:	1948	1 May 1949	
Iron and Steel:	1949	—	1953

National Physical Laboratory. As from
1 Apr. 1918, the Department of Scientific
and Industrial Research, appointed by
Order in Council, 28 July 1915, has been
responsible for maintenance of N. P. L.,
which was founded in 1899.

National Playing Fields Association.
Founded, 1925; chartered, 1933.

National Register. 1. Taken, 15 Aug.
1915. 2. Register taken and identity
cards issued, 29 Sept. 1939. Closed,
1952.

**National Research Development Corpor-
ation.** Set up by the Development of
Inventions Act, 30 July 1948.

National Savings Certificates first issued,
Feb. 1916.

National Security Council, U.S.A.,
established by the National Security Act,
1947 (since amended). The Central
Intelligence Agency (C.I.A.) is under the
Council's direction.

National Service, Ministry of. Set up, on
the failure of the Derby scheme of voluntary attestation, as a temporary recruiting
expedient, 1917, and dissolved after the
war. Revived as part of Ministry of
Labour and N. S., 19 Dec. 1938. N. S.
Handbook issued, Jan. 1939.

National Socialism (Germany). A pan-
German party with the title N. Socialist
Labour Party was founded in Bohemia
in 1912, but had no direct traceable connection with that which Anton Drexler
founded at Munich in 1919, and called
simply German Labour Party (Deutsche
Arbeiter Partei). This was used by
Hitler as the nucleus of his N. Socialist
German Labour Party (N.S.D.A.P. for
short in German). It adopted a detailed
pan-German nationalist programme, with
some vague socialist tenets, 1920, **and**

from 1933 to 1945 was the only permitted party in the country, though the German Nationalist Party of Hugenberg which it absorbed was for a time allowed some vestige of independence.
National Temperance League. *See* ANTI-SALOON LEAGUE.

National Theatre, Great Britain. Sir Laurence Olivier agreed to become its first director, Aug. 1962. First season opened in Old Vic theatre, 1963.

National Trust, founded by Octavia Hill and others, 1895. Status confirmed by N. T. Acts of 1907, 1919, 1937, and 1939. The N. T. for Scotland was founded in 1931.

Nativity, formally appointed to be observed on 25 Dec. by the Synod of Salzburg, 800, but this was in fact only confirmation of practice general since *c.* 690.

Nativity, Church of the, at Bethlehem. St. Helena (*c.* 250–330), mother of the Emperor Constantine, built a church here in 325, over a cave first mentioned as the scene of the N. by Justin Martyr in 155, and which was shown to Origen in 215. St. Helena's building was burnt, probably in the Samaritan rising of 529; but by order of the Emperor Justinian (reigned 527–65) a church was built on the same site. On the Moslem conquest of Palestine the church was given special protection by command of the Caliph Omar (*c.* 640). From then until 1947, except for the period 1099–1187, the site was in Moslem hands; since 1947, in Israel.

N.A.T.O. (North Atlantic Treaty Organization). N. Atlantic Treaty (*q.v.*) signatories set up permanent council of ministers' deputies, May 1950. Defence Committee decided on a permanent integrated force on a war footing on the European mainland, Sept. 1950. General Eisenhower appointed Supreme Commander, and Field-Marshal Montgomery appointed Deputy-Commander Land Forces, Dec. Their headquarters, S.H.A.P.E., became operational, Apr. 1951, with seven divisions under command at that time. Turkey and Greece joined N.A.T.O., 1952. Admiral Sir A. Power appointed first Commander Channel Command, Feb. 1952. Lord Ismay, Secretary-General, Oct. 1952. Lisbon Conference, Feb. 1952, laid down programmes until 1955. Eisenhower released at his own request, 1 June 1952, and succeeded by Gen. Matthew B. Ridgway. Admiral Lord Mountbatten appointed C.-in-C. Mediterranean, Dec. 1952. German Federal Republic joined N.A.T.O., Oct. 1954 (effective 9 May 1955), and German units thereafter included in N.A.T.O. forces.

Secretaries-General of N.A.T.O.:

Lord Ismay	1952–1957
Paul-Henri Spaak	1957–1961
Dirk Stikker	1961–

Supreme Commanders of N.A.T.O.:

General Eisenhower	1950–1952
General Ridgway	1952–1953
General Gruenther	1953–1956
General Norstad	1956–1962
General Lemnitzer	1962–

Naturalization Act (Great Britain Passed, 1870; a treaty with U.S.A. wa entered into the same year, by which bot countries pledged themselves to recogniz claims of N.

Naval Discipline Acts begin in Englan with the N. Laws of Olèron, 1194. Henry VIII codified Sea Laws, 1530. The Act of 1866, amended by that of 1884, and further revised in 1957, is still in force.

Naval Limitation Conference (at Geneva —Great Britain, U.S.A., and Japan-failed to come to any agreement, 4 Au 1927. *See* LONDON CONFERENCE.

Navarre. United all Basques tenth eleventh centuries. United with Aragor 1076–1134. Vizcaya and Guipúzcoa ar nexed by Castile *c.* 1200. Frenc dynasty took throne, 1285. Spanish N annexed by Castile, 1512. French N united when Henry of N. ascended Frenc throne as Henry IV, 1589. Spanish N was a viceroyalty till 1833. *See* SPAIN.

Navigation Laws (Great Britain). Olive Cromwell in 1650 excluded all foreig ships without a licence from trading wit the plantations of America. The N. Ac of Cromwell passed, 1651. Act providin that all colonial produce should be ex ported in English vessels, 1660. Colonie prohibited from receiving goods in foreig vessels, 1663. N. Act of Charles II, 167: extended Cromwell's Act and ruined th Dutch Navy. N. Act repealed, 1826, bu a new code of regulations still prevente free trade. These laws abolished, 184: 1846, and 1849. Coasting trade of Britai thrown open to foreign vessels, 1854.

Navy, Royal (British). Alfred the Grea built a fleet to resist the Danes, 897 Richard I equipped a large fleet for th crusades, 1189; Edward III defeated th French at Sluys, 1340; Henry V increase the number and size of the ships, 1413–22 Henry VII built the *Great Harry.* 1488 the English N. defeated the Armada, 1588 the *Sovereign of the Seas* launched, 1637 the first British frigate built. 1649; firs steamer built for the Royal N., 1814; screw propeller introduced, 1845; reserve volun teer force established, 1859; first ironcla t the N. built, 1860; Royal School of aval Architecture established, 1864; rst armour-clad turret ship built, 1868; reech-loading guns manufactured for the I., 1881; torpedo cruiser built, 1887; first ritish submarine launched, 1901; 13·5-1. guns replace 12-in. on *Orion* class, 1912; 5-in. on *Queen Elizabeth*, 1915–16; 18-in. n monitors, 1917–18. All big ships quipped with seaplanes, 1919–20. Esti-nates, 1921–2, 56 new ships under con-truction. Between 1929 and 1937, esides many smaller craft, 47 new ruisers were ordered. In 1936 two new attleships were ordered, in 1937 three. *See* WORLD WARS I and II, and BATTLES. Tumber of Royal N. ships in commission leclared to be exceeded by total U.S.S.R. trength, Mar. 1953. Work begun on a uclear-powered submarine, 1958. Com-leted, 1963.

Navy, U.S.A. On 13 Oct. 1775 Con-ress authorized the fitting out of a gun-arrying vessel. This was the beginning f the U.S. N. Board of Admiralty stablished, 1779. Other vessels fitted ut, 1775. In 1794, the N. having fallen nto neglect, Congress voted a sum of noney 'for creating a small N.' In Jan. 813 an Act was passed authorizing the uilding of 4 gunboats and 6 frigates. In Iar. 1813 another Act provided for the uilding of 6 sloops of war. Since then he N. has steadily increased. Eighteen lreadnought battle-cruisers, 12 other more owerful ships, with 12-in. and 16-in. guns, under construction, 1920. The N. n 1937 comprised 15 capital ships and 27 cruisers. Two more capital ships vere on order, and 10 cruisers. 1938: 4 pattleships, 4 cruisers; half of these being eplacements. 1939: 2 battleships, 2 ruisers, 8 destroyers, 8 submarines, 9 uxiliary vessels. *See* WORLD WARS I nd II, and BATTLES. In 1962 the U.S. Navy was probably the most powerful sea orce in the world, though numerical omparison is impossible, as exact Russian naval figures are not known.

Nazi Party. *See* NATIONAL SOCIALISM.

Neanderthal, valley near Düsseldorf, Germany, giving its name to a primitive uman, or near-human, race, a skull of ne of its members having been found here, 1856.

Nebraska, territory ceded by France to Spain, 1762, returned to France, 1801, and orming part of the Louisiana (*q.v.*, 1803) Purchase. Territory organized, 1854; tate admitted to Union, 1867. Single-chamber legislature introduced, 1937.

Negri Sembilan, former Federated Malay State, is largely populated by the descendants of Sumatrans who immi-grated in the sixteenth century. Domin-ated by Johore (*q.v.*), 1641–1773. British intervention in local politics first invited, 1874. A confederation of smaller states gave N. S. its present extent, 1895. Since 1948 part of the Malayan Federation.

Negropont. *See* EUBOEA.

Nejd. *See* SAUDI ARABIA.

N.E.P. (New Economic Policy). The revolution having led to economic break-down in Russia, Lenin introduced the N.E.P. as a temporary capitalist dilution of Soviet socialism, 1921–8.

Nepal. Conquered by Harisinha-Deva, 1324. Jayastithi-Malla (1386–1429) in-troduces caste system. Divided into four states, 1429–1768. Conquered by Ghurkas, 1768–70. War with China, 1790–2. Treaties with British, 1792–1801. First Ghurka War, 1814–16, ended in cession of Kumaon province to British India. British residency established at Katmandu, 1817. Jung Bahadur Rana seizes power ('The Kot Massacre'), 18 May 1845. Rana family consolidated their power and established new system of government, 1845–56. Ghurkas assist British in Indian Mutiny, 1857. Treaty with Britain recognized independence of N., 1923. The Prime Minister and C.-in-C. Sir Juda Shumshere Jung Bahadur Rana took office, 1932. Retired and entered religion, 1945. New treaty with Britain, 1950. His successor, Mohun Shumshere Rana, in Dec. 1950 found himself at odds with King Tribhuvana, who fled to India. The Ranas en-throned the infant Crown Prince Gijanen-dra; but King Tribhuvana, with the support of the Nepalese Congress Party and of the Indian Republic, returned in Feb. 1951, and was reinstated; the Ranas were ousted, and a mainly Nepalese Congress Party government took office. Mohun Shumshere Rana left the country, Dec. 1951. King Mahendra succeeded his father, 14 Mar. 1955. New constitu-tion promulgated, Feb. 1959. Rebellion put down, Feb. 1962.

Netherlands. *See* FLANDERS; HOLLAND; BELGIUM.

Neuchâtel, Switzerland. Originally *Novum Castellum,* whose original posses-sors took the name of count mid twelfth century; under Prussian rule from 1707 to 1857, with the exception of the years 1806–14, when Napoleon granted it to Marshal Berthier; became a full repub-lican member of the Swiss Confederation, 1857.

Neuilly, Treaty of, by which Bulgaria, after World War I, gave up all claims to Macedonia and Thrace, signed 27 Nov. 1919.

Nevada, first settled, 1849. At first part of the territory of Utah which was set up, 1850 (see UTAH), but made a territory on its own, 1861, and became a state, 1864.

Nevis, Nievis, or **Mevis,** Leeward Island, formed with St. Kitts and Anguilla into a presidency, 1882. Discovered by Columbus, 1493. Granted to the Earl of Carlisle, 1627, and colonized from St. Kitts, 1628. Devastated by the French, 1706, and again captured by them, 1782, but restored by the Treaty of Versailles in the following year. Administered with St. Kitts, Anguilla, and Sombrero. Ministerial government since 1956. New constitution, Jan. 1960.

New Brunswick, Canada. Discovered by Cabot, 1497; colonized by French, 1630 and 1672; ceded to Britain, 1713, and in 1784 separated from Nova Scotia and made a separate colony; by British N. America Act was incorporated with the Dominion of Canada, 1867.

New Caledonia, Pacific, was discovered by Capt. Cook, 1774; closely explored by d'Entrecasteaux, 1793; claimed by France, 1843; British claim withdrawn, 1853. Became an Overseas Territory, 1954.

Newcastle upon Tyne, England. Named after castle erected 1080 by Robert Curthose; besieged by William Rufus, 1095; present castle built, 1172–7; besieged by Scots under Gen. Leslie, 1644; bishopric founded, 1882. Tyne Bridge opened, 1928.

New Deal. Name given to policy of Franklin D. Roosevelt, President U.S.A., adumbrated during his first presidential campaign at Atlanta, 22 May 1932.

New Delhi. See DELHI.

New England, U.S.A. Visited by Sir Humphrey Gilbert, 1583; and by Bartholomew Gosnold, 1602; Puritans sailed in the *Mayflower*, and founded settlement, 1620. See MASSACHUSETTS and MAINE.

New Forest, England. Already a forest when Canute issued his Laws at Winchester, 1016. William I extended its area, 1079, and enforced the Forest Laws more harshly.

Newfoundland. Discovered by John Cabot, 24 June 1497. Visited by five Anglo-Portuguese expeditions, 1500–5. Formally annexed to England by Sir Humphrey Gilbert, Aug. 1583. Island divided between English and French at Treaty of Ryswick, 1697. Wholly given to Britain by Treaty of Utrecht, 1713, certain fishing rights being reserved to the French. These gave rise to continual disputes which were not settled till the Anglo-French Convention of 1904. N. was one of the Dominions given independent status under the Statute of Westminster, 1931, but owing to bankruptcy

the government was surrendered to commission nominated by the Britis Treasury, 18 Dec. 1933. National Con vention to consider future governmen elected, 1946. Negotiations with Canad 1947. Referendum, June 1948, on th following alternatives: 1. commission government for five years; 2. confeder: tion with Canada; 3. responsible gover: ment as in the period 1855–1933. N clear majority, but choice 1 eliminate and two alternatives put to a secon referendum in July. Confederation chose by a small majority. Royal assent give in Canadian Senate, 18 Feb. 1949, t terms of Union, and in House of Lord 23 Mar. 1949 to amendment of British N America Act and N. became part of the Dominion of Canada on 31 Mar.

Newgate Prison (London). In exis tence at least as early as 1190. Being rebuilt when burnt down in the Gordor Riots (q.v.), 1780, and building completed 1783. Executions took place here in public, 1783–1868. Demolished, 1902–3.

New Guinea. Probably sighted by Antonio d'Abreu (Portuguese), 1512 First visit by Europeans: either Jorge d Menesis (Portuguese), 1526, or Alvaro d Saavedra (Spanish), 1528. E. Ind: Co. made a settlement in Geelvink Ba: 1793; but in 1814 British Governmer admitted claims of Holland. Dutc proclaimed sovereignty over western ha of island, 1848. Remainder divide between Britain (S.) and Germany (N. 1884. The British part, called Papus was placed under the Commonwealth c Australia in 1906. In 1914 the Germa territory was occupied by Australia forces. Petroleum discovered, 1919. Civ administration of former German territor appointed by Commonwealth, 1921, unde League of Nations mandate of 192(Scene of much fighting in World War I (q.v.). On 15 Aug. 1962 Holland and Indonesia signed an agreement in New York settling the future status of Dutch New Guinea. The United Nations took control of the territory from Oct. 1962, prior to its being handed over to Indonesia on 1 May 1963.

New Hampshire, U.S.A., first settled 1623, founder member of the Union signatory of the Declaration of Inde pendence (q.v.). Has a pre-revolutionar; university in Dartmouth College, Hanove (founded, 1769).

New Haven, Conn., U.S.A. Originall; *Quinnipiac.* First settled by Englis; Puritans, 1637. Collegiate school o Connecticut removed to N. H., 1716 This later became Yale University Attacked by British, 5 July 1779. In corporated, 1784.

New Hebrides. First visited by the Spaniard de Quiros, 1606. Then by Bougainville, 1768, and Cook, 1774. Franco-British naval commission set up to protect British and French subjects in, 1887; succeeded by condominium, 1906.

New Jersey, U.S.A., discovered by John Cabot, 1497; settlements made in early seventeenth century by Dutch taken by British, 1664. Founder member of Union. New constitution, 4 Nov. 1947, provides that with effect from 1950 election of governors is to be quadrennial.

New Jerusalem Church. See SWEDEN-BORGIANS.

New Mexico, U.S.A., organized as a territory, 1850, admitted to the Union, 1912, as state which, however, consisted only of the rump of the territory, which had ceded large areas to Texas, Utah, and Colorado (1861), and out of which the whole of Arizona was carved 1863). First Spanish settlement, 1598. For the Mexican War, ending Feb. 1848, after which Mexico ceded N. M., see TEXAS.

New Model Army. The name given to the new parliamentary force raised by Cromwell and Fairfax, 15 Feb. 1645.

New Orleans, Louisiana, U.S.A. Founded, 1718; possessed by Spain, 1763; fell to France, 1800, and purchased from her as part of the Louisiana Purchase, 1803; attacked by British, Dec. 1814, who were repulsed, 8 Jan. 1815; surrendered to the Federals, Apr. 1862.

New South Wales, Australia. Named, 1770, by Capt. Cook. Colony established by transported prisoners, 1788. Transportation ceased, 1840. Gold discovered at Bathurst, 1851. Responsible government, 1855. See AUSTRALIA.

Newspapers. In the fifteenth century in some German towns news-sheets were issued in the form of letters. The first official paper was issued in Venice in 1566, and was known as the *Notizie Scritte*, published by order of the Venetian Government. First English newspaper: H. G. Aldis (*Cambridge History of English Literature*) says of the printer, Nathaniel Batter: 'He is said to have issued a *Courant, or Weekly Newes from Foreign Parts* as early as Oct. 1621; but his first entry of *A Currant of Newes* in the (Stationers') registers is dated 7 June 1622, and this publication must very shortly afterwards have assumed a regular periodical issue, for "Number 24" is entered on 26 Mar. 1623.' The *Publick Intelligencer* first issued by Nedham as a bi-weekly, 1659; after his flight abroad, Oliver Williams issued another with the same title. *Cambridge History* says of Sir

Roger L'Estrange: 'His two periodicals, *The Intelligencer* and *The News* (31 Aug. 1663 to 29 Jan. 1666), were . . . in 1664 paged and numbered together as one periodical.' The *London Gazette* was started by Henry Muddiman, 7 Nov. 1665. In 1662 a press censorship was started and continued until 1695. First English daily newspaper, the *Daily Courant*, existed from 1702 until 1735. A tax of one halfpenny on N. introduced, 1712, increased by stages to fourpence in 1815; in 1836 reduced to one penny, and abolished altogether, 1855. The following famous London daily papers have ceased to exist:

Morning Chronicle, 28 June 1769–2 Mar. 1865.
Morning Post, Nov. 1772–30 Sept. 1937 (absorbed by *Daily Telegraph*).
Globe, 1803–5 Feb. 1921.
Standard, 21 May 1827–16 Mar. 1916.
Daily News (founded by Charles Dickens), 21 Jan. 1846–31 May 1930.
Pall Mall Gazette, 7 Feb. 1865–27 Oct. 1923.
Echo, 8 Dec. 1868–31 July 1905.
Daily Chronicle, 6 Mar. 1871–31 May 1930.
Westminster Gazette, 31 Jan. 1893–31 Jan. 1928 (absorbed by *Daily News*).
Daily Graphic, Jan. 1890–16 Oct. 1926.
News Chronicle, May 1930–17 Oct. 1960 (incorporated into the *Daily Mail*).
Star, 17 Jan. 1888–17 Oct. 1960 (absorbed by the *Evening News*).

London daily papers still existing, with dates of first issues:

The Times, 1 Jan. 1788 (had been running three years as the *Daily Universal Register*).
Morning Advertiser, 8 Feb. 1794.
Guardian, started in Manchester, 1821, as the *Manchester Guardian*; changed its name to *Guardian* in 1959 and began printing a London edition.
Daily Telegraph, 29 June 1855.
Evening Standard, 11 June 1860.
Evening News, 26 July 1881.
Financial Times, 1888.
Daily Mail, 4 May 1896.
Daily Express, 24 Apr. 1900.
Daily Mirror, 2 Nov. 1903.
Daily Sketch, started in Manchester, 1909; printed in London from 1925.
Daily Herald, 15 Apr. 1912.
Daily Worker, 1930 (suppressed under Defence Regulations, Jan. 1941–Sept. 1942).

Weekly papers, with dates of first issues:
Observer, 4 Jan. 1801.
Sunday Times, 20 Oct. 1822.
Spectator, 5 July 1828 (original *Spectator*, 1 Mar. 1711–20 Dec. 1714).

Economist, 1843.

News of the World, 1 Oct. 1843.

Sunday Citizen (originally *Reynolds' Newspaper*, then *Reynolds News*), 5 May 1850.

People, 16 Oct. 1881.

Sunday Pictorial, 1915 (renamed *Sunday Mirror*, Apr. 1963).

Sunday Express, 29 Dec. 1918.

New Statesman and Nation (amalgamated), 21 Feb. 1931.

John O' London's Weekly, 1919–54; revived, 1959.

Time and Tide, 1920.

} these merged after the issue of 27 Dec. 1962.

Sunday Telegraph, 5 Feb. 1961.

Newspapers (U.S.A.). The first newspaper issued in America was in 1690 at Boston. Its title was *Public Occurrences*. It, however, only lasted a day owing to its too outspoken nature. The first permanent paper was the *Boston News-Letter*, which was issued in Apr. 1704. The first daily paper was the *Pennsylvania Packet or General Advertiser*, afterwards known as the *Daily Advertiser*, first issued in 1784.

New York City, New York. Settled by the Dutch and named N. Amsterdam, 1624; captured by English and the name changed to N. Y., 27 Aug. 1664; surrendered to the English during War of Independence, 15 Sept. 1776; British evacuated, 25 Nov. 1783; temporary national capital, 1789.

New York State, U.S.A., coast first explored by Verrazano, 1524, and hinterland by Samuel de Champlain (from Canada), 1609. The British Col. Nicolls took possession in the name of the Duke of York, 1664. Founder state of the Union.

New Zealand. Discovered by Tasman, 1642; surveyed by Capt. Cook, 1769; ceded to Great Britain by Treaty of Waitangi, 1840, and colonized the same year; self-government granted, 1852; Wellington made capital, 1865; called Dominion of N. Z., 1907. Dunedin Exhibition, 1926; visit of Duke and Duchess of York, 22 Feb.–24 Mar. 1927. Earthquake, Feb. 1931. Labour Party won majority for first time in General Election, 27 Nov. 1935. New trade treaty with Canada, 2 Oct. 1937. Social Security Act passed, 1938. War on Germany declared, 3 Sept. 1939; and on Italy, 11 June 1940. Flogging and death penalty abolished, except for treason, 1941. Statute of Westminster adoption Bill passed, 28 Nov. 1947, and New Zealand Constitution (Amendment) Act, 1949, repealing the New Zealand Constitution (Amendment) Act of 1957, was then

enacted. Referendum in favour of peacetime conscription held, Aug. 1949. In Dec. 1949 the Labour Party was defeated after 14 years in office. Financial crisis, 1952. Queen Elizabeth II visited N. Z., 1953–4. Labour Party returned to power again, Nov. 1957. Defeated, 1960. N. Z. problems regarding her exports to Britain should Britain join the Common Market were the principal topics, 1961–2. Visited by Queen Elizabeth II and the Duke of Edinburgh, 1963. To adopt decimal coinage, 1967.

Prime Ministers since the Granting of Dominion Status, 1907:

Ward	1906–1911
Mackenzie	1911–1912
Massey	1912–1925
Coates	1925–1928
Ward (again)	1928–1930
Forbes	1930–1935
Savage	1935–1940
Fraser	1940–1949
Holland	1949–1957
Holyoake	(2 months) 1957
Nash	1957–1960
Holyoake (again)	1960–

Governor-Generals since 1917 (Date of Establishment of the Office):

Earl of Liverpool	1917–1920
Viscount Jellicoe	1920–1924
Sir Charles Fergusson	1924–1930
Lord Bledisloe	1930–1935
Viscount Galway	1935–1941
Sir Cyril Newall	1941–1946
Lord Freyberg	1946–1952
Lord Norrie	1952–1957
Viscount Cobham	1957–1962
Sir Bernard Fergusson	1962–

Niagara Falls. Discovered, 1678, by a French priest. Blondin was the first to cross them on a tight-rope, 1859. Rainbow bridge opened, 1941.

Nicaea (Turk. **Isnik**) in Bithynia (*q.v.*), built 316 B.C. under the name of Antigonea, name changed by order of the Macedonian Gen. Lysimachus (*d.* 281). Chosen as capital by the Sultan Soliman 1078; taken by the Franks in the First Crusade, 1096. After the capture of Constantinople by the Latins, 1204, was the temporary capital of the Eastern Empire. The scene of the First Ecumenical Council, 325, when the Nicene Creed was formulated, and the Seventh, held in 787, which dealt with the Iconoclast controversy.

Nicaragua, Central America. Discovered by Columbus in 1502; explored by Gil Gonzalez De Avila, 1522; declared itself independent, 1821; joined Federal Union of the five Central States, 1823; separate republic, 1838; independence acknowledged by Spain, 1865; war with Honduras, Feb.–Apr. 1907. In 1916 U.S. Government purchased canal route and naval bases in Fonseca Bay and Corn Island by Bryan Chamarre Treaty, Feb.–June. America supervised elections of, 1928, 1930, 1932. Managuo earthquake, 1931. New constitution, 1950. President Somoza assassinated, Sept. 1956; succeeded by his son, Luis Somoza, who was re-elected for a six-year term, 1957.

Nice, France. Founded by the Phocaeans of Marseilles *c.* 600 B.C.; Saracens repulsed, A.D. 729; burnt by Saracens, 880; attached to Savoy from 1388; attacked by Francis I and Barbarossa, 1543; captured by Duke of Guise, 1600; by Catinat, 1691; restored to Savoy, 1696; besieged by French, 1705, and captured; by Treaty of Utrecht was again restored to Savoy, 1713; again captured by French, 1795, who owned it until 1814, when it reverted to Savoy. Finally ceded to France after a plebiscite, 1860.

Nice, Truce of. Between Charles V and Francis I for ten months from June 1538.

Nicobar Islands, ceded by Holland to Britain, 1869, and administered in one unit with the Andaman Islands, being used like them as a penal settlement by the government of British India. Occupied by the Japanese, Mar. 1942–Sept. 1945. Now, with the Andamans, a province of India, since 1947.

Nicosia, Cyprus. Pillaged by the Mamelukes, 1426. Fortified by the Venetians, 1567. Taken by the Turks, 1570, and 20,000 Christians massacred in street fighting. Earthquake, 1741. British flag raised over N., 1878. Capital of the Republic of C. since 1960.

Nidaros. *See* TRONDHJEM.

Nigeria. Includes what was formerly the Niger Coast (or Oil Rivers) Protectorate, formed, 1844. Remainder of N. acquired by British United African Co., 1879–86. Constituted, 1 Jan. 1900; Lagos (*q.v.*) added, 1906. Governments of Southern and Northern N. amalgamated, 1 Jan. 1914. Legal status of slavery abolished by Slavery Ordinance, 1917. Legislative Council instituted, 1923. Visit of Prince of Wales, 1925. Parliament of newly reformed constitution first met, 29 Jan. 1952, under the N. (Constitution) Order in Council, 1951. Its failure subject of Whitehall conference, July 1953, and Lagos conference, Jan. 1954. N. made a federation, under a Governor-General, 1954. After negotiation with the British Government N. became a Dominion within the Commonwealth, 1 Oct. 1960. Visited by Queen Elizabeth II, 1961. Anglo-Nigerian defence pact, in force since 1960, ended by mutual agreement, 21 Jan. 1962. Strained relations with Britain due to the Enahoro affair, Mar.–May 1963. N. became a republic within the Commonwealth, Oct. 1963.

Nijmegen, Gelderland province of the Netherlands, was a residence of the Frankish emperors in the ninth century A.D. Devastated in the allied attack by air and ground forces, Sept. 1944.

Nijni Novgorod (now Gorki) under protection of Suzdal, 1221. Ceased to elect its prince, 1390. Annexed to Moscow, 1392. Fair established at Makaryev, 1641. Repels attack by Stenka Razin 1667. Fair moved to N. N. city, 1817. Revived after revolution, 1923, but abolished finally, 1930. Renamed, 1932.

Nîmes, France. Taken by Romans, 121 B.C. Made a military colony under Augustus. Amphitheatre built, first-second century A.D. Belonged to Toulouse, A.D. 1185–1207. Catholics massacred by Protestants, 1567. Trestaillons and his bandits massacred Bonapartists, 1815.

Nineveh, adjoining the modern Mosul, in Iraq, became the capital of Assyria under Sennacherib (704–681 B.C.). Destroyed, 612, by combined forces of Babylonians, Medes, and Scythians. The deserted site was first investigated by western archaeologists early in the nineteenth century, and the Frenchman P. E. Botta began excavations, Dec. 1842. He was followed by A. H. Layard in 1845, who in 1847 discovered the palace of Sennacherib and largely uncovered its ruins, 1849–51. Further excavation by Hormuzd Rassam and Sir H. C. Rawlinson, 1849–54. New expedition under George Smith of the British Museum, 1873–4. H. Rassam again, 1876–7. Pre-Assyrian sites investigated, 1931–2 by M. E. L. Mallowan.

Ningpo, formerly **Liampo,** was a Portuguese 'factory,' 1522–45. Occupied by British, 1841–2.

Nitroglycerine first produced by Sobrero, 1846.

N.K.G.B., the Soviet security service, 1943–6. It had essentially the same functions as its predecessor, the N.K.V.D. (*q.v.*).

N.K.V.D. (Narodnij Kommissariat Vnutrennich Djel=People's Commissariat for Internal Affairs), designation of the Russian Home Office and its internal security forces, but not of the ordinary urban police ('militia') from 1934 to 1943. In 1943 it was divided into two commissariats, the N.K.V.D. and the N.K.G.B. (*q.v.*), the latter being responsible for state security.

Nobel Prize. Founded by Alfred N.

L*

(1833–96), the inventor of dynamite, to be awarded annually for excellence in learning and the furtherance of universal peace. First awarded, 1901.

Nomanhan, on the borders of Inner and Outer Mongolia, was the scene of a six weeks' undeclared war between Mongolian, Japanese, and Russian troops in 1939. The Japanese and Inner Mongolian forces had to retire, and the incident led to the Russo-Japanese non-aggression pact of 1941.

Non-Compounders. The extremist section of the Jacobite Party formed c. 1692. Were prepared to restore James II unconditionally.

Nonconformists and Nonconformity, the religious attitude of Dissenters in England. Word first used in this sense c. 1563, but gaining wider currency at the Restoration, especially with the passing of the Act of Uniformity, 1662. Some disabilities were suspended by Charles II's Declaration of Indulgence, 1672, and by James II's Declaration of Indulgence of 1687. They were accorded freedom of worship by Toleration Act, 1689, but excluded from municipal office by the Occasional Conformity Act, 1711, which was itself repealed, 1718. The Schism Act, 1711, excluded N. from schools and was also repealed, 1718. Political disabilities of N. removed, 1828. Admitted to universities, 1871. During the sixteenth and seventeenth centuries the essence of Nonconformity was the particularism of numerous sects, but in 1730 a phase of amalgamation and consolidation set in which may be said to have culminated in the reunion of the Methodist Church in 1932, previously split into three factions. *See also* FREE CHURCH FEDERATION.

Non-Intervention Committee of European powers to watch conduct of civil war in Spain, first met in London, 9 Sept. 1936.

Nonjurors. Clergy in Britain who refused the oath of allegiance to William and Mary. An Act of 1 Aug. 1689 required them to take the oath within six months or suffer deprivation. In Scotland all the bishops refused and episcopacy was abolished.

Nordic Council. Assembly of elected representatives from the Scandinavian parliaments (Denmark, Norway, Sweden, Finland, and Iceland), established, 1952, to foster closer co-operation between their countries. Passport regulations between the Scandinavian countries abolished, 1952.

Norham, Conference of. Between Edward I and the competitors for the crown of Scotland, June 1291. The question of the disposal of the Scottish crown was settled, Nov. 1292.

Normandy, France. Rollo appointed first duke, A.D. 912; united with the crown of England under William the Conqueror (Duke of N.), 1066; united to crown of France, 1204; English claim formally renounced, 1259; conquered by Edward III, 1346; by Henry V, 1418; English finally driven out, 1449. Invaded by Allies, 6 June 1944. *See* WORLD WAR II.

North Atlantic Treaty signed at Washington, 4 Apr. 1949, between Britain, Canada, the U.S.A., France, Belgium, Holland, Luxemburg, Norway, Denmark, Iceland, Italy, and Portugal. Greece and Turkey were admitted to the treaty, 1951 (effective, 1952), and the German Federal Republic, 1954. *See* N.A.T.O.

'North Briton' Newspaper. Instituted by John Wilkes. 'Number 45,' the issue dated 23 Apr. 1763, was publicly burnt by the hangman, 3 Dec. 1763, as containing a libel against the king. *See* WILKES'S CASE.

North Carolina, U.S.A. Coasts said to have been discovered by Cabot, 1498; first settled, unsuccessfully, 1585–6; named after Charles II of England, who, in 1663, granted the region to certain of his courtiers; permanently settled by English, 1670; made a royal province, 1728; declared itself independent of Great Britain, May 1775; state constitution adopted, 1 Dec. 1776. Seceded, 20 May 1861; readmitted to the Union, 25 May 1868. Present constitution dates from 1876.

North Dakota, U.S.A., part of the old territory of Dakota, organized as such, 1861. Admitted to the Union, 1889. First settlements took place c. 1766. *See also* SOUTH DAKOTA.

Northern Fisheries. *See* FISHERIES, NORTHERN.

Northern Ireland. *See* IRELAND, NORTHERN.

Northern Territory, Australia, formerly **Alexandra Land,** originally part of New S. Wales (*q.v.*), but annexed to S. Australia, 1863. Placed under direct Commonwealth rule, 1911. Divided into N. Australia and Central Australia, 1926, but united under a single administration by an Act of 1931. Northern Territory (Administration) Act, 1947, established a legislative council in the N. T. Coast first explored by P. P. King, 1818, by J. C. Wickham, 1838, and J. L. Stokes, 1339. Interior explored by A. C. Gregory, 1855. Overland telegraph line completed, 1872, to Darwin, capital of N. T.

North German Confederation, league of German states established, 1867, under Prussian leadership. Dissolved in the German Empire, 1871.

North Pole. First reached, 6 Apr.

909, by the American Robert E. Peary.
See ARCTIC AND ANTARCTIC REGIONS.

North Sea Fisheries Convention. Entered
into by Great Britain, Germany, Holland,
Belgium, and France on 6 May 1882;
supplementary convention signed, 16
Nov. 1887.

North Sea Outrage. On the night of 21
Oct. 1904 the Russian Baltic Fleet fired
on some English fishing boats in the N. S.
An international commission of inquiry
was held on the affair from 22 Nov. 1904
to 25 Feb. 1905.

**North Staffordshire, University College
of.** Founded, 1949, and opened at Keele
Hall, near Stoke-on-Trent, 1950. Subsequently granted full university status,
1962, as Keele University (q.v.).

North, The Council of the. Instituted
in 1536 by Henry VIII originally to try
persons connected with the Pilgrimage of
Grace (q.v.); abolished by Long Parliament, 1641.

Northstead, Manor of, in Yorkshire, has
a stewardship in the gift of the crown, the
holding of which by the Place Act, 1742,
is not compatible with membership of the
House of Commons, and is thus used as
formal excuse for resignation of an M.P.
See CHILTERN HUNDREDS.

Northumbria, Kingdom of. See BER-
NICIA and DEIRA.

Kings of c. 547–c. 913 :

Bernicia:

Ida	547–559
His elder sons	559–586
Ethelric	586–593
Ethelfrith	593–617
Edwin (of Deira)	617–632
Eanfrith	632–633
Oswald	633–642
Oswy	642–670

Deira:

Aelle	560–588
Ethelric (of Bernicia)	588–? 593
Ethelfrith (of Bernicia)	? 593–617
Edwin	617–632
Osric	632–633
Oswald (of Bernicia)	633–642
Oswine	642–651
Ethelwald	651–655
Oswy (of Bernicia)	655–670

Kings of all N.:

Ecgfrith	670–685
Alfrith	685–704
Eardwulf I	704–705
Osred I	705–716
Cenred	716–718
Osric	718–729
Ceolwulf	729–737
Eadberht	737–758
Oswulf	758
Ethelwald Moll	759–765

Alhred	765–774
Ethelred I	774–779
Elfwald I	779–788
Osred II	788–790
Ethelred I (restored)	790–796
Osbald	796
Eardwulf II	796–808
Elfwald II	808
Eardwulf II (restored)	808–810
Eanred	810–840
Ethelred II	840–844
Raedwulf	844
Ethelred II (restored)	844–848
Osberht	848–866
Elle	866–867
Egbert I	867–872
Ricsige	873–876
Egbert II	fl. 876
Eadwulf	?–913

North-West Frontier Province.
Created by the British administration in
India, 25 Oct. 1901. Merged into West
Pakistan Province, 1955.

North-West Mounted Police, raised,
1873; title changed to Royal Canadian
Mounted Police, 1920. Mechanized, 1953.

North-West Territories of Canada,
formed from the former Northern Territory and Rupert's Land, and divided into
the districts of Keewatin, MacKenzie, and
Franklin by Order in Council of 16 Mar.
1918. Under N.-W. T. Act, 1952, government is in the hands of a commissioner,
who acts on instructions from the
Governor in Council or the Minister of
Northern Affairs and National Resources.

Norway. Battle of Hafursfjord, 872,
and N. united for the first time under
Harald Fairhair. First Norwegian settlement in Iceland, 874. Rolf the Ganger's
expedition against Normandy, 876.
Erik Bloodaxe king, 930. Haakon the
Good comes from England and is made
king at Trondhjem, 935. Erik Bloodaxe
goes to England, 939, and is killed there,
950. Battle of Rastarskalf, 955. Death
of Haakon the Good after battle of Stord,
961. N. ruled by Jarl Haakon of Lade,
970–95. Christianity introduced, 998.
Death of King Olaf Tryggvason at battle
of Svold, 1000. N. under Swedish and
Danish rule till battle of Nesjar and
election of St. Olaf as king, 1015. He
makes alliance with Sweden, 1019.
Defeated by Knut (Canute) of Denmark
at Helge-Aa, 1027. N. conquered by
Denmark, 1027–8. Death of St. Olaf at
battle of Stiklestad, 29 July 1030.
Danes driven out by King Magnus the
Good, 1035–6. Harald Hardrada king,
1047. Killed at Stamford Bridge, 1066.
Norwegian crusading expedition, 1107–
1110. After Haakon IV, 1217–63, N.
declined into chronic civil war (for

history down to this point *see* VIKING
AGE). It was finally united with Sweden
under the Danish crown by the Union
of Kalmar (*q.v.*), 1397. Despite Sweden's
defection N. remained under Danish
rule till virtually cut off from Denmark by the British blockade, 1794–
1814. As a reward for Swedish participation in the war against Napoleon I it
was proposed that Denmark should cede
N. to Sweden (Treaty of Kiel, 14 Jan.
1814). The Norwegians called a national
convention which drew up and signed a
parliamentary constitution at Eidsvold,
17 May 1814, and then accepted the
suzerainty of the Swedish crown.
Separated from Sweden, Oct. 1905.
Haakon VII elected to the throne, 18 Nov.
1905. Women eligible as M.P.s, 1915.
Prohibition introduced, 1919. Christiania
renamed Oslo, 1 Jan. 1925. Spitzbergen
(Svalbarth) annexed, 14 Aug. 1925.
Prohibition on a national scale abolished,
1926. First Labour Government, 1928.
Greenland awarded to Denmark by
International Court of Justice, 5 Apr.
1933. Oslo Commercial Convention with
Sweden, Finland, Denmark, Belgium,
Luxemburg, and Holland, May 1937.
Part of Antarctica annexed, 14 Jan. 1939.
Declarations of neutrality, 2 Sept. and 26
Dec. 1939. *Altmark* incident, 17 Feb.
1940. Attacked by Germany, 9 Apr.
Battles of Narvik, 10 and 13 Apr. Cessa-
tion of hostilities, 11 June 1940. Liberated,
8 May 1945. Signed North Atlantic
Treaty (*q.v.*), 1949. Fishing dispute with
Great Britain settled in favour of N. by
Hague International Court, 1951. Mem-
ber of Nordic Council, 1952. Death of
Haakon VII and accession of Olaf VI (*b.*
1903), 1957. Member of European Free
Trade Association (*q.v.*), 1959.

Rulers of c. 839–1349 ; 1905–51:

Halfdan the Black	c. 839–c. 860
Harald I Fairhair	c. 860–933
Erik Bloodaxe	930–935
Haakon I the Good	935–961
Harald II Greyskin	961–970
(Jarl) Haakon of Lade	970–995
Olaf I Tryggvason	995–1000
(Jarls) Erik and Svein	1000–1015
Olaf II, Saint	1015–1030
Svein Knutsson	1030–1035
Magnus I, the Good	1035–1047
Harald III, the Stern	1048–1066
Olaf III, the Quiet	1067–1093
Magnus II	1067–1069
Magnus III, Barelegs	1093–1103
Haakon	1093–1095
Olaf IV	1103–1116
Eystein I	1103–1122
Sigurd I, the Pilgrim	1103–1130
Magnus IV, the Blind	1130–1135

Harald Gille	1130–1136
Sigurd II, Mund	1136–1155
Inge	1136–1161
Eystein II	1142–1157
Haakon, II, the Broad- shouldered	1161–1162
Magnus V	1162–1184
Sverre	1184–1202
Haakon III	1202–1204
Anarchy	1204–1217
Haakon IV, the Old	1217–1263
Magnus VI	1263–1280
Erik	1280–1299
Haakon V	1299–1319
Magnus VII	1319–1343
Haakon VI	1343–1380
Olaf V	1381–1387
Margaret (Lady of N.)	1387–1389
Eric of Pomerania	1387–1439

(*See further under* DENMARK, KINGS OF
1439–1814: SWEDEN, KINGS OF, 1814–
1905.)

Modern Norway:

Haakon VII	1905–1957
Olaf VI	1957–

Norwegian Language and Literature
From the Union of Kalmar down to the
end of the nineteenth century the written
language of Norway, both for official and
artistic purposes, was Danish; therefore
some N. authors have been listed under
Danish Literature *supra*. There are two
modern idioms: the urban, or *riksmål*,
developed from the Danish, which is the
official idiom, and the rustic, or *landsmal*,
now generally called *nynorsk*. The
progress of the language was assisted by
Dølen, the first newspaper to be printed
in it (1858), under the editorship of
Aasmund Olafsen Vinje (1818–70).
The following are mainly *riksmål*
authors not now living (those marked *
wrote *nynorsk*):
Johan Sebastian Welhaven, 1807–73,
poet.
Henrik Wergeland, 1808–45, poet.
Peter Christen Asbjørnsen, 1812–85,
folklorist.
Jørgen Moe, 1813–82, folklorist.
Henrik Ibsen, 1828–1906, playwright.
Bjørnstjerne Bjørnson, 1832–1910, play-
wright.
Amalie Skram, 1846–1905, novelist.
Camilla Collett, 1849–1906, novelist.
* Arne Garborg, 1851–1924, novelist.
Gunnar Heiberg, 1857–1929, playwright.
Knut Hamsun, 1859–1952, novelist.
Nils Collett Vogt, 1864–1937, poet.
Hans E. Kinck, 1865–1926, novelist and
poet.
Tryggve Andersen, 1866–1920, novelist.
Sigbjørn Obstfelder, 1866–1900, poet.
Niels Kjaer, 1870–1924, essayist.

Vilhelm Krag, 1871–1933, poet.
* Olav Duun, 1876–1939, novelist.
Sigrid Undset, 1882–1949, novelist.
* Olaf Aukrust, 1883–1929, poet.
Olaf Bull, 1883–1933, poet.
Olav Nygard, 1884–1924, poet.
Sigurd Christiansen, 1891–1947, novelist.
Ronald Fangen, 1895–1946, novelist.
Rudolf Nilsen, 1901–29, poet.
Nordahl Grieg, 1902–43, poet.
Jonas Lie, 1833–1908, novelist.
A. L. Kielland, 1849–1906, novelist.
* Jens Tvedt, 1857–1935, novelist.

Norwich, England. First mentioned in *Saxon Chronicle,* 1004, when sacked by Svein. Cathedral founded, 1096. Charter, 1158; extended, 1194. Cathedral completed *c.* 1500. Chief magistrate made Lord Mayor, 1910. Carrow Bridge open, 1923. New city hall, 1938.

Nottingham, England. One of the five Danish boroughs, 868. Fortified by Edward the Elder, 922–4. Seized by Svein, 1013. Parliaments held at N., 1334, 1337, 1357. Incorporated, 1448–9. Charles I set up standard at, 1642. Castle dismantled, 1644. Goose Fair instituted under Queen Anne, 1702–14. Suffragan Bishopric, 1870. University College opened, 1881. Made a university, 1948.

Nova Scotia. Discovered by John Cabot, 1497; partly colonized by the French, as 'Acadia,' 1598; French settlements destroyed by English from Virginia, 1614; granted by James I to William Alexander, Earl of Stirling, 1621; ceded to France by Treaty of Breda, 1667; captured by English, 1689; restored to France by Treaty of Ryswick, 1697; Port Royal captured by English under Gen. Nicholson, 1710; formally ceded to England by Treaty of Utrecht, 1713; became part of the Dominion of Canada, 1867.

Novaya Zemlya, archipelago off the N. coast of Russia, explored by Stephen Borough, 1556, and Baron Nordenskjold, 1895–97. Also by H. J. Pearson, 1895–97, and O. Ekstam, 1900–3.

Novgorod (formerly **Veliki Novgorod** ('N. the Great'), founded by Scandinavians, traditionally, 862, but probably on the site of an existing Slav settlement. Though it acknowledged princes of the house of Rurik it was virtually an independent republic of merchants, and obtained a charter from Yaroslav the Wise, 997, which was regarded as the basis of its liberties, of which it was deprived by the Muscovite Ivan III, 1478. It was burnt to the ground by Ivan IV (the Terrible), 1570.

Noyon, Treaty of. Between Charles of Spain and Francis I, signed 1516; by it Francis gave up all claims to

Naples, and France's right to Milan was acknowledged.

N.R.A. (U.S.A.). National Recovery Administration appointed under National Industrial Recovery Act, 1933, empowered to promulgate codes for industry. It imposed conditions as to child labour, minimum wages, and maximum hours. The U.S. Supreme Court held codes unconstitutional, 18 Feb. 1935.

Nubia. *See* SUDAN.

Nuclear Reactor. Harwell, Berks, built 1947, was the first British N. R.; the first American N. R. was built at the University of Chicago in 1942.

Nuclear Test Ban Treaty signed, Moscow, between the U.S.A., U.S.S.R. and Great Britain, 5 Aug. 1963.

Nudens or **Nodens,** the Celtic deity Nudd or Ludd, worshipped at Lydney in Gloucestershire, where a temple of the first century A.D. has been excavated.

Nürnberg (Ger.: anglicized as **Nuremberg,** which form is also current in other non-German countries), Germany. Made an Imperial Free City, 1219. Embraced Protestantism *c.* 1525. Annexed by Bavaria, 1806. First Nazi Party congress, 1933. Mostly destroyed by allied bombing in World War II.

Nürnberg Laws, anti-Semitic code decreed by the Nazi Government, Sept. 1935.

Nürnberg Trials, international trials of war criminals, lasted from Nov. 1945 to Oct. 1946.

Nyasaland, E. Africa. Visited by Bocarro, 1616. By Dr. Livingstone, 1859. African Lakes Co. established, 1878. British Consuls established, 1883. Rhodes obtains charter for British S. Africa Co. to develop N., 1884. Protectorate established, 1891. Suppression of slave trade, 1893–7. John Chelembwe's revolt, 1915. Joins Central African Committee, 1944. United with the Rhodesias in Central African Federation, 1953, but African population, led by Dr. Hastings Banda, continued to agitate strongly against federation. Rioting and casualties in N., Mar. 1959; Dr. Banda was arrested and the Colonial Secretary alleged a massacre plot by the Nyasaland African Congress. Commission of inquiry appointed; published its report, 23 July. Dr. Banda released, 1 Apr. 1960. Conference on N., July–Aug. 1960, completely successful. Banda's Malawi Congress Party won control of the N. Legislative Assembly, Aug. 1962. Constitutional Conference in London, Nov. 1962, ended with agreement that N. should be self-governing from Feb. 1963. The federation issue was not discussed, but in Dec. 1962 the British Government acknowledged N.'s right in principle to secede from the federation. *See also* RHODESIA AND NYASALAND, FEDERATION OF.

Nylon. Discovered by Du Ponts, U.S.A., 1927.

Nyon Conference to end submarine piracy in Mediterranean: Britain, France, Greece, Yugoslavia, Turkey, Egypt, Albania, Russia, Rumania, and Bulgaria, 11–14 Sept. 1937.

O

Oak Apple Day, anniversary of the restoration of Charles II to the English throne, 29 May 1660. The oak leaves sometimes worn on this occasion commemorate his hiding in an oak-tree when a fugitive from Worcester, 6 Sept. 1651.

O.A.S. (Organisation de l'Armée Secrète). Clandestine, ultra-right-wing organization founded by General Raoul Salan, in Madrid, in May 1961, after the failure of the anti-Gaullist rising in Algiers. Its object initially was to keep Algeria French, and though weak in France itself it had strong support in Algeria. Used violence to pursue its aim and was responsible for bomb outrages in both Algeria and France. After Algerian independence, in July 1962, the O.A.S. transferred its activities entirely to France, concentrating on destroying the Gaullist regime by force and attempting to assassinate de Gaulle. General Salan was captured, Apr. 1962, and sentenced to life imprisonment for treason, May 1962. Bidault, the political leader of the anti-Gaullist movement, settled in exile in Brazil, Apr. 1963. This marked the end of real O.A.S. influence, although the movement was still capable of organizing attempts upon de Gaulle's life.

O.A.S. (Organization of American States). Charter adopted, 30 Apr. 1948. Cuba expelled from the O.A.S., 31 Jan. 1962; in Oct. 1962 the O.A.S. backed President Kennedy's blockade of Cuba (*q.v.*). Inquired into the dispute between Haiti (*q.v.*) and the Dominican Republic, Apr.–May 1963.

Oaths, Parliamentary. Oath of supremacy, imposed on M.P.s, 1534; oath of allegiance, 1610. In 1678 no member could take his seat until the O. of allegiance, supremacy, and abjuration were taken. By Act of 1829 Roman Catholics could use special form of oath; provision made for Jews, 1858. In 1866 the three O. were combined in one, and in 1868 the form included all religious denominations. O. Act of 1888 allows an affirmation in lieu of the oath.

Oberammergau (Germany). Passion play commemorates a plague of 1633. The decision to produce a play every ten years was taken in 1634. The last production was in 1960.

Observer Corps, Royal. An O. C., composed of special constables, was raised in 1925 under War Office auspices, but operational command in 1927, and administration in 1939, passed to the Air Ministry. Operationally controlled by Fighter Command, the O. C. was given the title Royal in Apr. 1941. It stood down, 12 May 1945, and was reconstituted on a spare-time basis, 1 Jan. 1947.

October Club. A Tory club, instituted 1710.

October Revolution. So called because it occurred in Oct., according to the Julian Calendar. Kerensky's government overthrown and the Communists established in power, 7 Nov. 1917 (25 Oct., Old Style).

Oddfellows. A friendly society bearing this name was formed at Manchester in 1810, and the movement spread to U.S.A. in 1819, where a Grand Lodge of O. was formed, 1821. This severed its connection with the parent organization at Manchester, 1842, but established a branch at Montreal, which became the first Oddfellow Lodge of Canada, 1843.

Oder–Neisse Line. Has formed the boundary between Germany and Poland since 1946, and all Germans formerly living E. of it have been deported W. of it.

Odessa, Ukraine. Disputed between Lithuania and Tatars, fourteenth–sixteenth centuries. Captured by Turks, 1764. By Russians, 1789. Finally occupied by Russians, 1791. Inhabitants supported the 'Potemkin' rising, 1905. Occupied by the Rumanians, 1941–4, becoming the capital of Transnistria during that time.

O.E.E.C. (Organization for European Economic Co-operation) became effective in the passing by Congress of the Economic Co-operative Act, Apr. 1948, with the object of restoring the European economy by the end of 1951. Convention signed in Paris, setting up a permanent constitution for O.E.E.C., 16 Apr. 1948. After Marshall Aid ended, 1952, O.E.E.C. continued as a permanent instrument of European Economic co-operation. Spain joined it, 1959. In Dec. 1960 the organization was reconstituted as the **O.E.C.D. (Organization for Economic Co-operation and Development.)**

Offa's Dyke, built *c.* 785 as a boundary between his dominion and the Welsh (whom he defeated, 779) by O., King of Mercia, who reigned *c.* 755–94, abdicated, and *d.* at Rome, 796.

Ohio, U.S.A. First explored by La Salle *c.* 1680; N. of the O. River was held by French until 1763, when it was surrendered to the English; unofficially admitted to the Union as a state, 1803; entrance made official retroactive to 1803, 8 Aug. 1953.

Oil Rivers Protectorate. *See* NIGERIA.

Oklahoma, then known as the Indian country, was extensively settled from 1866 onwards by government purchase of land from the Choctaw, Cherokee, Creek, Chickasaw, and Seminole Indians. Organized as a territory, 1890, and admitted as a state to the Union, 1907.

Old Age Pensions (Britain). First proposed in 1772 by Francis Maseres, and again in 1787 by Mark Rolle, M.P.; other schemes proposed, notably by W. E. Gladstone's royal commission in 1893, but nothing was done until passing of O. A. P. Act, 1908, which came into force on 1 Jan. 1909. Amended 1911, 1914, and 1924. Widows', Orphans', and Old Age Contributory Pensions (Voluntary Contributors) Act, 1 July 1937. Since 1946, covered by the provisions of the National Insurance Act (*q.v.*).

Old Bailey. A court held in a house on 'Balehill' is mentioned in Stow's *Survey of London*, 1603. Sixty persons attending the court, including two judges and the Lord Mayor, *d.* of jail fever from the adjacent Newgate Prison (*q.v.*), 1780. The present Central Criminal Court occupies the site of the old sessions and part of the former Newgate Prison, demolished to make way for it, 1902.

Old Catholics. Those Catholics who refused to accept the doctrine of papal infallibility proclaimed at the Vatican Council of 1870. They met first at Nürnberg; and at Munich in 1871 resolved to become connected with the Jansenists (*q.v.*) of Utrecht. Numbers declined after 1875. Dogmatic base of all groups of O. C. contained in the Declaration of Utrecht (1889). The O. C. of Germany in communion with the Catholics of E., 1930, and with the Church of England, 1931. Polish archbishop of the O. C. re-entered Roman Church, Apr. 1948.

Old Contemptibles, name applied to the (predominantly Regular) British Expeditionary Force of Aug. 1914. In Sept. a B.E.F. Routine Order quoted the Kaiser Wilhelm II on 'Gen. French's contemptible little army,' but without giving chapter and verse: no one has ever established when (or whether) this phrase was actually used, and in 1925 the ex-Kaiser denied that he had ever done so. The B.E.F. Order did not quote in the original, and it may be a mistranslation for 'contemptibly small.'

Oldenburg, Germany. Independent county, 1180. United with Denmark, 9 June 1667. Ceded to Russia, 16 Oct. 1776. Made an independent duchy under Frederick of Holstein-Gottorp, 22 Mar. 1777. Acquired Wildeshausen from Hanover, 1803. Permanent alliance with Prussia, 1834. Joined Zollverein, 1852. Joined German Empire, 1871. Became a republic, 1918. Since World War II has formed part of the *Land* of Lower Saxony.

Old Vic. A theatre called the Coburg was built on this site in the Waterloo Road, 1818. In the middle nineteenth century it became a music hall, but classical concerts were given there from 1880 onwards, and in 1914 regular performances of Shakespeare's plays were produced under Lilian Baylis (1874–1937). Association with Sadler's Wells (*q.v.*) began, 1929. Rendered unusable in the 1939–45 war, the auditorium was renovated and performances recommenced, 1950. Dramatic School closed, 1952. The last performance by the O. V. company was given in the theatre, June 1963. The theatre was due to reopen, autumn 1963, as the temporary home of the new National Theatre (*q.v.*) under the directorship of Sir Laurence Olivier.

Olive Branch Petition, by moderate Americans to avert civil war. Presented, July 1775, to George III, who took no notice of it.

Olmütz, Convention of. Austro-Prussian agreement of 1850, reviving Austrian influence in Germany at the expense of Prussia, and regarded by the latter as 'the humiliation of Olmütz.'

Olympia, Greece. The site of the original Olympic games. The earliest building is the temple of Hera, *c.* 1000 B.C. The method of calculating time by Olympiads or quadrennial periods between celebrations of the games, reckoned from 776 B.C., was first adopted *c.* 264 B.C. After the year A.D. 394 the games were discontinued, and in 426 the temple destroyed. The Olympic games were revived at a meeting of delegates from various nations, 16 June 1894. Games were held at Athens, 1896; Paris, 1900; St. Louis, 1904; London, 1908; Stockholm, 1912; Antwerp, 1920; Paris, 1924; Amsterdam, 1928; Los Angeles, 1932; Berlin, 1936; London, 1948. The meeting in 1940 should have been at Tokyo, but in 1938 the venue was altered to Helsinki; owing to the Russo-Finnish War this meeting did not take place, nor did the one for 1944. That of 1952 was held at Helsinki. That of 1956 held at Melbourne; of 1960, held at Rome. The 1964 O. G. will be held in Tokyo.

Olympiad. *See* OLYMPIA.

Omaha Beach. Code-name for the stretch of beach from the Vire R. to Port-en-Bessin, where the U.S. 5th Corps landed on D-Day, 6 June 1944, and from which they only narrowly averted being dislodged by the defending Germans.

Omnibus. The first O. to ply in London was run by Mr. G. Shillibeer, 1829. The London General O. Co. was founded, 1856. First double-decker appeared, 1904; last horse-bus, 1911. Electric trolley-buses from 1911 onwards; diesels increasingly used after 1955.

Ontario, Canada. First settled by the French in the late seventeenth century; British territory from 1763; its prosperity founded by loyalist emigrants from the U.S.A. after the latter had declared its independence; made into a separate province in 1791, and known as Upper Canada, but in 1867 it again received its original name.

Opera. First O. proper was *Dafne*, 1597, by Peri and Rinuccini; first O. whose music survives complete was *Euridice*, 1600, by the same collaborators.

Opium War. Between China and Britain, 1840–2.

Oporto, Portugal. Originally *Portus Cale*, the origin of the name *Portugal*, to which in the fifth century a new northern quarter, the *Castrum Novum* of the Alani, was added. Captured by Visigoths, A.D. 540; by the Moors, 716; recaptured by Christians, 997; captured by the Duke of Wellington, 12 May 1809; besieged by Dom Miguel, 1832–3. The thirteenth-century cathedral occupies the site of a church built by Theodomir, king of the Visigoths, 589, to house the relics of St. Martin of Tours (316–97).

Optional Clause, otherwise Article 36, paragraph 2, of the Statutes of the Court of International Justice, providing for reference of justiciable disputes to the court, signed, 19 Sept. 1923.

Oradour - sur - Glane, Haute - Vienne, France, scene of a notorious German atrocity, 10 June 1944, when the men of the town were all shot and the women and children driven into the church, which was then set on fire.

Oran, a Spanish settlement established in 1509, was finally abandoned, 1792, and occupied by the French, 1831. French fleet attacked after ultimatum by Admiral Somerville, 3 July 1940, in the harbour of Mers-el-Kebir at O. Scene of violent O.A.S. (*q.v.*) disturbances, Mar.–June 1962, until agreement was reached between the Oran O.A.S. and the Algerian Nationalists on 20 July.

Orange Free State, S. Africa. Inhabited by the Dutch Boers, 1836; annexed to British crown, 1848; given up to the Boers, 1854; became part of British Empire after Boer War as the Orange River Colony, 1902; granted responsible government, 1907; joined Union of 1910 as the O. F. S.

Orange, House of. Came to principality of O. (S. France), 1393. Philibert of O. given lands in Netherlands by Emperor Charles V, 1522. These lands passed to William of O.-Nassau (William the Silent), 1544. The family held the offices of Stadhouder and Captain- and Admiral-General of the Netherlands, 1577–1650 and 1672–1702. William III was King of England, 1688–1702. William VI became King William I of the Netherlands, 1815. *See* HOLLAND, KINGDOM OF.

Orangemen, The. A term applied to Protestants in Ireland in 1689; the first Orange lodge instituted, 21 Sept. 1796; all Orange societies suspended, 1813–28; in 1836, however, they were exceedingly strong, and in 1869 their grand master was arrested for violating the Party Procession Act.

Oratory of St. Philip Neri, Congregation of the (or Oratorians). A Roman Catholic order founded, 1556, by Philip Neri (1515–95); confirmed by papal bull, 1575, and again in 1612; first congregation in England established, 1847.

Ordainers, The Lords. Consisted of earls, barons, and bishops, appointed in Mar. 1310; they were formed for the purpose of reforming the laws of the realm.

Ordeal, Trial by. O., together with compurgation, was the commoner form of assessing the value of evidence in pre-Conquest English law-courts: for instance, the weight of red-hot iron to be carried by an accused person pleading not guilty is laid down by the Laws of Athelstan (between 925 and 940), as 3 lb. Queen Emma Aelfgifu, widow of Ethelred, was so tried for adultery, and acquitted, 1043. Trial by O. was abolished in England, 1215–19 (except for Trial by Battle, which was not formally abolished till 1819). It survived longer on the Continent, and unofficially, in the form of witch-ducking, much longer in England. Directions for the latter procedure are preserved in a document by the ninth-century German bishop, Hincmar. A case of Trial by O. was reported from Charleston, N. Carolina, 26 Feb. 1951.

Orders in Council (Britain). First issued in eighteenth century. 'The O. in C.' were issued in 1807 in reply to Napoleon's Berlin Decrees (*see under* CONTINENTAL SYSTEM).

Orders of Knighthood. *See* KNIGHTHOOD, ORDERS OF.

Ordnance Board existed before 1660,

but the 'ordinance' relating to the calibre of artillery from which it takes its name is no longer extant. Recognized as a civil department of state, 1683. Divided into separate military and civil branches, 1689. The Master-General of the O. ceased to be a member of the Cabinet, 1828. The duties of the O. B. were transferred to the War Department, 1855.

Ordnance Survey was formed in 1791, to make a map on the scale of 1 inch to 1 mile of the whole of Great Britain. This task was completed for England, except the six northern counties, 1840. Its establishment was doubled, 1880, after being transferred from the War Department, 1870. Cultivated area of England completely mapped on scale of 1:2500 by 1890.

Oregon. Name first applied to whole area of modern O. and Washington. Columbia River discovered by Capt. Gray, 1792. Fur trading post established on river, 1811. Dispute between Britain and U.S.A. about boundary between Canada and U.S.A. from the Lake of the Woods to Pacific arose, 1816. Fixed along 49° N. by provisional treaty of Nov. 1818 between Lake of the Woods and the Rocky Mountains. Area comprising the modern states of Idaho, O., Washington, and the southern half of British Columbia in joint Anglo-American occupation till 49° N. boundary extended to Queen Charlotte Sound by treaty of 1846. Government of territory organized, 1848. Admitted as state of the Union, 1859. Vancouver Island given to Canada by arbitration, 1872.

Oriental and African Studies, School of, opened by King George V, 23 Feb. 1917. Charter issued, 5 June 1916. African branch added, 1938.

Orissa. *See* BIHAR.

Orkney Islands, N. of Scotland. Possessed by Northmen in ninth century; formally subject to the Norwegian crown, 1098; pledged by Christian I of Denmark for the payment of the dowry of his daughter Margaret, betrothed to James III of Scotland in 1468; the money was never paid, so the islands passed to the Scottish crown. Denmark renounced all claims to the O. I., 1590. Great damage by severe gales, 1952.

Orléanists. A French political party who supported the royal claims of the house of Orléans, founded shortly after the French Revolution; after the revolution of 1848 it practically ceased to exist

Orléans, France. Originally *Civitas Aureliani.* Vainly besieged by Attila, A.D. 451; captured by Clovis, 498; entered by Joan of Arc, 29 Apr. 1429; besieged by the Duke of Guise, 1563; held

by Huguenots, 1567–8; surrendered to Henry IV of France, 1594; occupied by Prussians, 1815 and 1870.

Orsini Affair. Felix O. and accomplices attempted the life of Napoleon III, 14 Jan. 1858, and were subsequently executed. The plot had been arranged in London, and the French protested so strongly in London that the British Government introduced a propitiatory bill into Parliament, and so was forced to resign.

Orthodox Eastern Church. *See* GREEK ORTHODOX CHURCH and CALENDAR.

Orvieto, Italy. Captured by Belisarius, A.D. 539; Pope Hadrian IV resided at, 1157; cathedral commenced before 1285; town became part of kingdom of Italy, 1866.

Osborne House (Isle of Wight). Purchased by Queen Victoria, 1845; Queen Victoria *d.* there, 1901; presented to the nation by Edward VII as a convalescent home for officers, 1902; Royal Naval College at Osborne opened, 1903. State and private apartments now open to the public.

Osborne Judgment. Disallowing a forced political levy on trade union members, handed down by the House of Lords, 1909. Largely nullified by the Trades Union Act of 1913.

Oslo, Norway. Founded by Harald Hardrada, 1047. King Sigurd the Crusader buried here, 1130. Burnt down, 1624. Rebuilt by Christian IV of Denmark, who renamed it Christiania. Reverted to older name, 1925. Occupied by Germans, 9 Apr. 1940–May 1945. City Hall opened, 1951.

Oslo, Convention of, a free trade convention between the 'O. Powers'— Belgium, Luxemburg, the Netherlands, Sweden, Norway, and Denmark, signed, Dec. 1930. Finland adhered, Feb. 1933.

Ossewabrandwag. Extremist Afrikaner political party, deriving its political inspiration from the Voortrekkers (*q.v.*) of 1836. Supplanted the Broederbond Party *c.* 1935, and achieved its maximum influence and membership, 1941.

Osteopathy formulated by Andrew Taylor Still (1828–1917), an American doctor, 1874. British School of O. founded, 1917. London College of O. founded, 1946.

Ostrogoths. Soon after A.D. 370 the eastern portion of the hitherto united Gothic tribes came under the supremacy of the Huns (*q.v.*). A raid of the under King Radagais penetrated into Italy as far as Florence, 406. Ostrogothic bands fought in the army of Attila at Châlons-sur-Marne, 451, but after the death of the Hunnish king regained their liberty of action. They sued the Empire for permission to settle in Pannonia (*q.v.*), which was granted in the second half of the fifth century. Their king, Theodoric (Dietrich, 454–526), became a figure of Germanic legend, and founded an Ostrogoth kingdom in Italy *c.* 500, having first, in the service of the eastern emperor Zeno, reconquered Dalmatia and the Danube lands from the mutinous western Gen. Odoacer, himself probably a Goth. He married his daughter to Alaric II, king of the Visigoths (*q.v.*), effecting a reunion of the E. and W. Goths, who again separated at his death. Under his grandson and successor Athalaric the Ostrogoth kingdom came to an end, 555. The chief source for their history is *De origine actibusque Getaram*, a summary, made in 551, by the Gothic monk Jordanes, of a lost work of the same title by the senator Cassiodorus.

Oswiecim, Poland (Ger. **Auschwitz**). The Germans began the construction of a camp here in 1941. By Mar. 1945 a million and a half persons, mostly Jews, had been killed in O. 'destruction camp' by various branches of the S.S. (*q.v.*). The commandant and other S.S. officers were tried and executed at Warsaw for crimes against humanity in 1947.

Otranto, anciently **Hydruntum,** taken from the Byzantines by the Norman, Robert Guiscard, 1068. The Romanesque cathedral was consecrated, 1088. Taken by the Turks, 1480. The castle of O., subject of Walpole's novel published in 1764, was built in 1450.

Ottawa, Canada. Discovered by Champlain, 1613; first permanent settlement, 1826; originally known as Bytown; name changed to O., 1854, when it was incorporated as a city; made capital of Canada, 1858; first Parliament opened at, 1865. *See* CANADA.

Ottawa Conference between Britain and the Dominions (except Irish Free State) agreed upon trade preferences, Britain to raise tariffs against other countries, 1932.

Ottoman Empire. *See* OTTOMAN RULERS and TURKISH REPUBLIC. Ertogrul (*d.* 1288) obtains lands near Ankara from Seljuks (*q.v.*), and later moves to Sugut. Osman conquers Karaja Hissar, 1295. Orkhan takes Brusa, 1326; Karasi, 1338; Gallipoli, 1355. Foundation of the Janissaries by Orkhan, 1326–59. Murad I takes Ankara and Adrianople, 1361. Adrianople becomes capital, 1367. Acquires Kutahiah, 1381. Overthrows the allied Balkan forces at battle of Kossovo, 27 Aug. 1389. Bayazid I besieges Constantinople; takes Salonika, 1395. Recognized as Sultan of Rum by caliph, 1396. Defeated and captured by Tamerlane at battle of Ankara, 1402. Revival

of Os. under Mohammed I, 1413–21. Murad II defeats John Hunyadi at Kossovo, 1448. Mohammed II takes Constantinople, 29 May 1453. Organizes government and army, 1455–80. Naval victory over Venice, 1499. Selim I (the Grim) drives Bayazid II from throne, 1512. Persians defeated, 1515. Syria and Egypt annexed. 1516–17. Assumes caliphate, 1517. O. E. reaches its greatest extent under Soliman I (the Magnificent or the Lawgiver), 1520–66. He annexes Belgrade, 1521. Destroys Hungarian Army at battle of Mohacs; conquers most of Hungary, 1526–47. Bagdad captured from Persians, 1534. Kheir-ed-Din Barbarossa's naval victory over allied Christians at Prevesa, 1538. Peace with Persia, 1555. Unsuccessful attack on Malta, 1563–5. Naval defeat at battle of Lepanto, 1571. First capitulations granted to Britain, 1580. First serious Janissary revolt, 1591. They murder Osman II, 1622; Ibrahim, 1648. The Kiuprili family become chief ministers, 1648. Siege of Vienna marks beginning of O. decline, 1683. Kiuprili supremacy ends, 1703. Defeat of Russia, 1710. Phanariot Greeks given governorships of Moldavia and Wallachia, 1710–1821. Austrian reconquest of Hungary, 1680–1718. Belgrade passes to Austria by Treaty of Passarowitz, 1718. Popular rising of Patrona Khalil, 1730. Treaty of Belgrade, 1739. Persian war, 1743–6. Women's faces ordered to be veiled, 1755. Russians conquer the Crimea, 1771. Treaty of Kuchuk-Chainardji, 1774. War with Napoleon, 1798–1802. Unsuccessful British attack on Constantinople, 1807. Treaty of Bucharest, 1812. Beginning of Serbian independence, 1817. Greek rising begins, 1821. Mahmud II destroys Janissaries, 1826. Turko-Egyptian fleet destroyed at Navarino, 1827. French occupy Algiers, 1830. Greece independent by Treaty of London, 1832. Treaty of Unkiar Skelessi, 1833. Governorship of Egypt (*q.v.*) made hereditary, 1840. First Straits Protocol, 1841. Hatti-Sherif of Gulhané, 1842. Crimean War, 1854–6. Hatti-Humayun, 1857. The Lebanon agreement, 1861. Abdul Aziz establishes the Bulgarian Exarchate, 1870. The 'Bulgarian Atrocities,' 1876. War with Russia, 24 Apr. 1877. Treaty of San Stefano, 3 Mar. 1878. Cession of Cyprus to Britain, 4 June 1878. Berlin Treaty, 13 July 1878. Decree of Muharram gives the Turkish debt administration to European delegates, 1881. Bulgaria autonomous, 1885. Armenian revolts and 'massacres.' 1894–6. War with Greece, 1897. Germans begin the 'Bagdad-Berlin' railway, 1899. Macedonian insurrections, 1901–3. Austria annexes Bosnia. Bulgaria declares independence, 1908. Young Turk Revolution and dethronement of Abdul Hamid II, 1909. Italian aggression, 1911; and annexation of Tripoli and Dodecanese, 1912. *See* BALKAN WARS and WORLD WAR I. Sultanate abolished, 1 Oct. 1922. Caliphate abolished, 3 Mar. 1924. For later history *see* TURKISH REPUBLIC.

Ottoman Rulers. Those marked 'A' abdicated. Those marked 'M' were murdered. Those whose reigns were ended by the Janissaries are marked 'J.'

Osman I ('Ottoman')	1288–1326
Orkhan	1326–1359
Murad I	1360–1389
Bayazid I	1389–1403
Sultan	1396
Interregnum	1403–1413
Mohammed I	1413–1421
Murad II	1421–1451
Mohammed II (the Conqueror)	1451–1481
Bayazid II (A)	1481–1512
Selim I (the Grim)	1512–1520
Caliph	1517
Soliman I (the Magnificent or the Lawgiver)	1520–1566
Selim II (the Sot)	1566–1574
Murad III	1574–1595
Mohammed III	1595–1603
Ahmed I	1603–1617
Mustafa I (imbecile)	1617
Osman II (J M)	1618–1622
Mustafa I (again) (J A)	1622–1623
Murad IV	1623–1640
Ibrahim (J M)	1640–1648
Mohammed IV (J A)	1648–1687
Soliman II	1687–1691
Ahmed II	1691–1695
Mustafa II (J A)	1695–1703
Ahmed III (J A)	1703–1730
Mahmud I	1730–1754
Osman III	1754–1757
Mustafa III	1757–1773
Abdul Hamid I	1773–1789
Selim III (J A)	1789–1807
Mustafa IV	1807–1808
Mahmud II	1808–1839
Abdul Mejid I	1839–1861
Abdul Aziz (A)	1861–1876
Murad V (insane)	1876
Abdul Hamid II (A)	1876–1909
Mohammed V	1909–1920
Mohammed VI (A)	1920–1922
Abdul Mejid II (as caliph only)	
(A)	1922–1924

Oudh, India. Became independent of Mogul *c.* 1732. War with the British, 1759–64, ended in defeat at battle of Buxar, 1763, and acceptance of subsidy at treaty of alliance, 1764. Half

territory ceded to Britain, 1801. Completely annexed, 1856. Formed, with Agra, the United Provinces (*q.v.*), 1902. Part of Uttar Pradesh since 1949.

Outward Bound Schools. Sea school opened, 1941. O. B. Trust formed, 1946. Mountain school opened, Eskdale, 1950. Training courses started for girls, 1951.

Owens College (Manchester). Founded from a bequest by John Owens (*d.* 1846). Opened, 1851. Extended, 1873. *See* MANCHESTER.

Oxford City, England. Mentioned in the *Anglo-Saxon Chronicle*, 912. Empress Maud besieged in, 1142. Charter, 1199. Mad Parliament held at, 1258. Made a bishopric, 1542. Occupied by Charles I, 1644–6. Charles II holds Parliament at, 19–28 Mar. 1681. Growth of the motor industry transformed Oxford into an industrial city, 1925–38. Revolutionary replanning proposals (the Sharp report) published, 1948. Road through Christchurch Meadow agreed by Government after protracted negotiations, 1961.

'Oxford Group.' A movement started by Frank Buchman (an American) (1878–1961). Having become a Lutheran pastor, 1902, he formed a First Century Christian Fellowship at Oxford, 1921, with which he toured S. Africa, 1929, where the S. Africans dubbed the party 'the O. G.' Considerable objection was made by O. University when the organization applied for registration as a non-profit making limited company under above title, 1939. Popularly known as 'Moral Rearmament' rather than the O. G. since World War II.

Oxford Movement. Founded, 1833, by Newman and others for reforming the Church of England along Catholic lines. When Newman was converted to Rome, 1845, the O. M. lost its initial impetus; nevertheless, its views on matters of liturgy and theology have had a penetrating and lasting effect upon Anglicanism everywhere.

Oxford, Provisions of. Drawn up by Simon de Montfort, 1258, and annulled, 1261, by Henry III.

Oxford University. Schools founded early twelfth century. Vacarius lectured on Roman law at O., 1149. University as a corporate body dates from late twelfth or early thirteenth centuries. A migration from O. to Cambridge traditionally started the latter university, 1209. Earliest known charter, 1214. Recognized as a *Studium Generale* by the Pope, 1296. Famous Town and Gown Riot, 1354. University reorganized, 1571. Given right to representation in the House of Commons, 1604. New statutes, 1636, 1854, 1877, 1926. Women admitted to degrees, 1920. Parliamentary representation abolished, 1948.

The following are the colleges, halls, and societies, with dates of foundation and the names of their founders:

All Souls, 1438. Henry VI and Archbishop Chichele.

Balliol. *c.* 1263. John and Devorguilla Baliol.

Brasenose, 1509. William Smyth, Bishop of Lincoln and Sir R. Sutton.

Campion Hall, 1896. Richard Clarke.

Christ Church, 1546. Henry VIII.

Corpus Christi, 1517. Richard Foxe, Bishop of Winchester.

Exeter, 1314. Walter Stapeldon, Bishop of Exeter.

Greyfriars, 1953.

Hertford, 1740. Richard Newton. Dissolved, 1805.
1874. T. C. Baring, M.P.

Jesus, 1571. Queen Elizabeth I.

Keble, 1868. Erected by subscription as a memorial to John Keble.

Lady Margaret Hall (Women), 1878.

Linacre Society, 1692.

Lincoln, 1427. Richard Fleming, Bishop of Lincoln.

Magdalen, 1458. William Waynflete, Bishop of Winchester.

Mansfield, 1886.

Merton, 1264. At Merton.
1274. At Oxford. Walter Merton, Bishop of Rochester.

New, 1379. William of Wykeham, Bishop of Winchester.

Nuffield, 1937. Lord Nuffield.

Oriel, 1326. Adam de Brome and Edward II.

Pembroke, 1624. Thomas Tesdale and Richard Wightwick.

Queen's, 1340. Robert Eglesfield.

Regent's Park, 1886.

Ruskin, 1899.

St. Benet's, 1897.

St. Antony's, 1950. M. Antonin Besse.

St. Catherine's (as a society), 1868. Refounded as a college, 1962.

St. Edmund Hall, 1270.

St. Hilda's (Women), 1893.

St. Hugh's (Women), 1886.

St. John's, 1555. Sir Thomas White.

St. Peter's Hall, 1929.

Society of Home Students (Women), 1879. Renamed St. Anne's College, 1952.

Somerville (Women), 1879.

Trinity, 1554. Sir Thomas Pope.

University, 1249. William of Durham.

Wadham, 1612. Dorothy and Nicholas Wadham.

Worcester, 1714. Sir Thomas Cooke.

Oxford University Press. Founded, 1585.

Oxygen. First obtained, 1727, by Stephen Hales. First described by J. Priestley, 1774. Word 'O.' first used by Lavoisier *c.* 1775.

P

Pacific Islands in British Possession. *See* GILBERT AND ELLICE ISLANDS; PITCAIRN ISLAND; SOLOMON ISLANDS; TONGA ISLANDS, *etc.*

Pacific Ocean. First sighted from Panama by Balboa in Sept, 1513. Magellan sailed, 1520, through the strait named after him, and gave the ocean its name.

Padua, Italy (Lat. **Patavium**), came under Roman supremacy, 215 B.C.; sacked by Attila, A.D. 452; under rule of the Franks, 774; university founded by the Emperor Frederick II in 1222, and the present buildings date from 1493 to 1552; the town was conquered by the Venetians in 1405, who ruled it until 1797, when it was taken by the French; ceded to Austria, 1814; incorporated with kingdom of Italy, 1866.

Paestum (now **Pesto**). Greek colony of Poseidonia, founded by Sybarites, *c.* 600 B.C. Became subject to Rome, 273 B.C. Sacked by Saracens, 871, and partially dismantled by Normans *c.* 1055. Eventually abandoned during sixteenth century. Temple 'of Peace,' built second century B.C., excavated, 1830. Temple 'of Ceres' built *c.* 530 B.C. Temple of Poseidon built, sixth century B.C. Other remains accidentally uncovered, 1943; excavated since 1945 under auspices of the Neapolitan Museum.

Pagan, anct. ruined city of Upper Burma. Capital of the country from 849 to 1287, when it was sacked by Kublai Khan.

Pahang, former Federated Malay State. Became British protectorate, 1888. Invaded by Japanese, 1942. Joined Malayan Union, 1946, and Malayan Federation, 1948.

Painting. P. on canvas known at Rome, A.D. 66, and to Bede, A.D. 735. The brothers Van Eyck founded Flemish school of P. in oil, 1415. Royal Academy founded, 1768. Modern movements are: Impressionism, 1831; Neo-Impressionism, 1886; Post-Impressionism, 1890; Fauvism, 1906; Cubism, *c.* 1908; Futurism, 1911; Expressionism, 1908; Dadaism, *c.* 1920; Surrealism, 1925. For list of eminent painters, *see* ARTS.

Pakistan. Name first coined, 1933. Agitation in favour of a separate Moslem state in India begun by All India Moslem League, 1938. P. became independent dominion with the Quaid-i-Azam Mohammed Ali Jinnah as first Governor-General,

14 Aug. 1947. Jinnah *d.* 12 Sept. 1948. Succeeded by Khwaja Nazimuddin, 14 Sept. 1948–17 Oct. 1951, and then by Ghulam Mohammed, 19 Oct. 1951. Liaquat Ali Khan (assassinated 1951) was first Prime Minister, who was succeeded on his death by the former Governor-General, Khwaja Nazimuddin. New constitution tabled in Parliament, Dec. 1952, to include compulsory religious instruction for all children of Moslem parents, total prohibition of liquor, gambling, and prostitution. Country made a federation of two units—E. and W. P.—Nov. 1954. Joined Bagdad Pact (later CENTO, *q.v.*), Sept. 1955. Proclaimed an Islamic Republic within the Commonwealth, 23 Mar. 1956. Internal situation, unstable since assassination of Liaquat Ali Khan, became increasingly so from 1956 onwards. On 7 Oct. 1958 President Mirza declared martial law in P., abolished all political parties, and abrogated the constitution. Handed his powers over to Field Marshal Ayub Khan, 28 Oct. Ayub Khan's tenure of presidency confirmed by ballot held in Feb. 1960. Ayub Khan announced new constitution, Mar. 1962; elections for Parliament held, Apr. 1962, and Parliament assembled, June 1962. P. objected to W. aid for India against China, Nov. 1962. British Colonial and Commonwealth Secretary, Duncan Sandys, visited P., Nov. India and P. agreed to discuss Kashmir, 29 Nov., but the talks broke down in May 1963.

Governor-Generals of Pakistan, 1947–56 :

Quaid-i-Azam Mohammed Ali
Jinnah	1947–1948
Khwaja Nazimuddin	1948–1951
Ghulam Mohammed	1951–1955
Iskander Mirza (acting)	1955–1956

Presidents of Pakistan, from 1956 :

Iskander Mirza (provisional)	1956–1958
Mohammed Ayub Khan	1958–

Palace Court instituted, 1631; abolished, 1849.

Palatinate (Ger. **Pfalz**). First Count Palatine, 945–96. P. given to Otto of Bavaria, 1215. Became independent at division of Wittelsbach possessions, 1255. Received electoral vote under Golden Bull, 1356. Divided into four, 1410. Re-

220. Julius III, 1550–5
221. Marcellus II, 1555 (Apr.)
222. Paul IV, 1555–9
223. Pius IV, 1559–65
224. St. Pius V, 1566–72
225. Gregory XIII, 1572–85
226. Sixtus V, 1585–90
227. Urban VII, 1590 (Sept.)
228. Gregory XIV, 1590–1
229. Innocent IX, 1591 (Oct.-Dec.)
230. Clement VIII, 1592–1605
231. Leo XI, 1605 (Apr.)
232. Paul V, 1605–21
233. Gregory XV, 1621–3
234. Urban VIII, 1623–44
235. Innocent X, 1644–55
236. Alexander VII, 1655–67
237. Clement IX, 1667–9
238. Clement X, 1670–6
239. Bl. Innocent XI, 1676–89
240. Alexander VIII, 1689–91
241. Innocent XII, 1691–1700
242. Clement XI, 1700–21
243. Innocent XIII, 1721–4
244. Benedict XIII, 1724–30
245. Clement XII, 1730–40
246. Benedict XIV, 1740–58
247. Clement XIII, 1758–69
248. Clement XIV, 1769–74
249. Pius VI, 1775–99
250. Pius VII, 1800–23
251. Leo XII, 1823–9
252. Pius VIII, 1829–30
253. Gregory XVI, 1831–46
254. Pius IX, 1846–78
255. Leo XIII, 1878–1903
256. St. Pius X, 1903–14
257. Benedict XV, 1914–22
258. Pius XI, 1922–39
259. Pius XII, 1939–58
260. John XXIII, 1958–63
261. Paul VI, 1963–

See also ROME and INVESTITURE.

Papal States. Temporal rule of the Papacy began with the bestowal of the Exarchate of Ravenna, hitherto administered from Byzantium, on Pope Stephen II (752–7). Greatly reduced in extent, 1859, and suppressed, 1870. In 1929 a successor to this state, known as the Vatican (*q.v.*) City was recognized as a sovereign power by concordat with Italy.

Paper. Said to have been invented in China, A.D. 105, by Tsai-Lun.

Papua. *See* NEW GUINEA.

Papworth Village Settlement, begun 1917.

Parachute first used by a human being from an aircraft (balloon), Paris, 22 Oct. 1797.

Paraguay. Explored by Juan Diaz de Sotis, 1515. By Irala, Ayotas, and Garay, 1519–32. First settlement founded by Pedro de Mendoza, 1537. Further exploration by Cabeza de Vaca, 1541–2. First Jesuits arrive, 1557. Foundation by Father Diego de Torres of the Jesuit Missionary State in P. ('The Reductions'), 1608–11. Natives exempt from service, 1611. Printing presses introduced, 1705. Civil war between the Spanish planters and the Jesuits, 1723–5. Rebellion of the *Comuñeros* led by Mompox, 1726–35. Jesuit rule abolished, 1767. Declaration of P.'s independence from Spain, 1811, and Francia's dictatorship, 1814–40. New constitution, 1844. War with Brazil, Argentina, and Uruguay, 1865–70. New constitution, 1870. Brazilian occupation, 1870–6. War with Bolivia, 31 July 1932–12 July 1935. Frontier with Bolivia fixed by arbitration, 10 Oct. 1938. Civil war, Mar.–Aug. 1947, resulted in victory of Colorados. Immigration virtually forbidden, 1948; but allowed to 10,000 families of Italians, 1951–4. Stroessner became President, 1954, and established a dictatorship.

Heads of Administration since the Establishment of the Republic, 1811:

Triumvirate	1811
Junta	1811–1813
Consulate	1813–1814
Dictator:	
Francia	1814–1840
Junta	1840–1841
Consulate	1841–1844
Presidents:	
Lopez (Carlos Antonio)	1844–1862
Lopez (Francisco Solano)	1862–1869
Triumvirate	1869–1870
Presidents:	
Rivarola	1870–1871
Jovellanos	1871–1874
Gill	1874–1877
Uriarte	1877–1878
Barreiro	1878–1880
Caballero	1880–1886
Escobar	1886–1890
Gonzalez (Juan Gaulberto)	1890–1894
Morinigo (Marcos)	1894
Eguzquiza	1894–1898
Aceval	1898–1902
Carballo	1902
Escurra	1902–1904
Gaona	1904–1905
Baez	1905–1906
Ferreira	1906–1908
Navero	1908–1910
Gondra	1910–1911
Jara	1911
Rojas	1911–1912
Pena	1912
Navero	1912
Schaerer	1912–1916

Paraguay. *Heads of Administration—cont.*

Franco (Manuel)	1916–1919
Montero	1919–1920
Gondra	1920–1921
Paiva	1921
Ayala (Eusebio)	1921–1923
Ayala (Eligio)	1923–1924
Riart	1924
Ayala (Eligio)	1924–1928
Guggiari	1928–1931
Navero	1931–1932
Guggiari (again)	1932
Ayala (Eusebio)	1932–1936
Franco (Rafael)	1936–1937
Paiva	1937–1939
Estigarribia	1939–1940
Morinigo (Higinio)	1940–1948
Frutos	1948
Gonzalez (Juan Natalicio)	1948–1949
Rolon	1949
Lopez (Felipe Molas)	1949–1950
Chavez	1950–1954
Pereira	1954
Stroessner	1954–

Paratroops, first demonstrated by Russians, 1936. First used by Germans in Holland, May 1940. Development of British P. from 1942 onwards.

Paravanes. Introduced into British Navy, 1916, but made obsolete by the development of asdic.

Parents' National Educational Union (P.N.E.U.), founded by Charlotte Mason, 1888.

Paris, France. First mentioned by Caesar under title of *Lutetia Parisiorum.* In 52 B.C. it became a Roman town of some importance; Clovis made it his capital, A.D. 508; between 1180 and 1223 the cathedral of Notre-Dame was commenced and the University of P. founded; revolution of P. headed by Étienne Marcel, 1358; reconstruction of the city under Napoleon III, 1851–70; fell to German Army, 1871 and 14 June 1940; liberated by Fighting French forces under Leclerc, Aug. 1944. Considerable growth of population and rebuilding since 1945. *See* FRANCE and BASTILLE.

Paris, Declaration of. Drawn up at the Congress of P. in 1856. It settled four important points of international law.

Paris, Treaties of. 1. Between France, Spain, and England, by which the Seven Years War was ended and Canada ceded to England, signed Feb. 1763. 2. Between Britain and the American Commissioners, recognizing American independence, 3 Sept. 1783. 3. Between the allies, after the abdication of Napoleon in May 1814. 4. After the close of Napoleon's final campaign in Flanders, 20 Nov. 1815. 5. Between Russia, Turkey, England, France, and Sardinia at the close of

the Crimean War, signed 30 Mar. 1856. 6. Between England and Persia: amongst other things it abolished the slave trade in the Persian Gulf, signed 3 Mar. 1857; 7. Terminating the Spanish-American War, 10 Dec. 1898.

Parliament (*see also* LORDS, HOUSE OF; COMMONS, HOUSE OF; FRANCHISE). In Jan. 1265 there was a meeting (summoned by Simon de Montfort) of citizens and burgesses, together with knights of the shire; but until 1295 there appears, despite frequent summons to the burgesses to attend, to have been for the most part only one legislative chamber. Acts of P. were first printed in 1501. First P. of Great Britain met, 23 Oct. 1707. Septennial Act became law, 7 May 1716; first P. of the U.K. of Great Britain and Ireland, 1801; Roman Catholic Relief Act, 1829; Reform Act, 1832; Houses of P. destroyed by fire, 16 Oct. 1934; new buildings commenced, 1840; new House of Lords completed, 15 Apr. 1845; new House of Commons completed, 4 Nov. 1852; Act for enabling Jews to sit, 1858; Parliamentary Elections Act (as to corrupt practices), 1868; Ballot Act, 1872; closure adopted, 1882; P. Act, 1911, made five years instead of seven maximum length of a P., and curtailed powers of House of Lords, as did that of 1949. Act of 1948 abolished plural voting, by abolishing University and business franchises. Labour Party agreed to join select committee on reform of the House of Lords, Jan. 1962. Report published, Dec. Government announced intention of legislating to implement the report's main recommendations, May 1963, and the resultant Peerage Bill became law, 31 July. *See* LORDS, HOUSE OF.

Parma, duchy of, created 1545, for Pierluigi Farnese, natural son of Pope Paul III. Conquered by the French, 1796. Assigned to Marie Louise, wife of Napoleon, after 1815. Became part of the kingdom of Italy, 1859.

Parnell Commission. Caused through facsimile reproduction in *The Times* of 18 Apr. 1887, of a letter purporting to have been written by Charles S. Parnell (1846–1891): it excused the Phoenix Park murders (*q.v.*). Further and similar letters having been produced (July 1888) by defendants in F. H. O'Donnell's libel action against *The Times*, the Government (Aug. 1888) appointed a special commission, before which the forger Richard Pigott (who committed suicide in Madrid, 1 Mar. 1889) broke down, and which reported, 13 Feb. 1890. It acquitted P. on all charges.

Parthenon at Athens, building begun,

447 B.C.; dedicated, 438; sculptures completed, 432. Converted into a Christian church, fifth century, and into a mosque, A.D. 1456. Blown up, 1687. Sculptures removed by Lord Elgin, 1801.

Parthia, anct. W. Asian kingdom. Controlled a considerable empire between 250 B.C. and A.D. 224 when the country was annexed to Persia.

Partition Treaties between William III, representing England and Holland, and Louis XIV, attempted to settle the devolution of the Spanish dominions at the death of the reigning King Charles II. 1. 2 Oct. 1698. By this treaty Spain, its colonies, and the Netherlands were to go to the Electoral Prince of Bavaria, Milan to the Archduke Charles of Austria, Naples, Sicily, and other Italian possessions to the Dauphin. This arrangement was frustrated when Charles II left all the Spanish dominions to the Electoral Prince by a will, published 14 Nov. 1698, and the Electoral Prince *d.*, 6 Feb. 1699. 2. 11 June 1699. The Archduke Charles to have the Electoral Prince's share. The Dauphin to have the same as before, plus Milan. This treaty was ratified, 13 Mar. 1700. It was frustrated because the Austrian emperor refused ratification, and Charles II, by a will signed 7 Oct. 1700, gave all the territories to the Duke of Anjou (grandson of Louis XIV). Charles II *d.* 1 Nov. 1700. Louis XIV accepted the Spanish offer, 12 Nov. Acceptance publicly announced, 16 Nov. 1700. *See* SPANISH SUCCESSION, WAR OF.

Passau, Agreement of. Between the Protestant states of the empire and the Roman Catholics; signed, 29 July and 15 Aug. 1552.

Paston Letters, The. A series of letters written to or by the Ps., a Norfolk family, between 1422 and 1509; they give an invaluable insight into English life of the fifteenth century.

Patagonia. Since 1881 part of Argentina (*q.v.*).

Patent Laws (Britain). First granted for exclusive privilege of printing books, 1591; properties and rights of inventors first protected in 1623; this law was repealed and a new Act passed known as the P. Act in 1883; amended, 1885, 1886, 1888, 1901, 1902, 1907, 1919, 1928, 1932, and 1946. Important changes contained in new Act, which was passed 1949 and came into operation, 1 Jan. 1950. Bill to develop useful inventions introduced, 1948.

Patent Laws (International). A select committee of the House of Commons in 1872 recommended international protection of patents; in 1873 at Vienna, and in 1878 at Paris, international congresses

met, and on 20 Mar. 1883, an 'International Convention for the Protection of Industrial Property' was signed at Paris; most of the civilized countries of the world signed this.

Patent Laws (U.S.A.). First P. Act passed by Congress, 10 Apr. 1790; revised, 1793; all previous laws repealed and new one passed, 1837. Terms of Ps. extended by Act of 1861. Whole system revis⁀d and codified, 1870. Right to have incomplete invention protected withdrawn, 1910.

Pavia, Italy (anct. **Ticinum**; later **Papia**). Founded by the Ligurii. Taken from the Lombards by Charlemagne, 774. Taken by the Viscontis, 1359. Sacked by the French, 1500. Charles V captured Francis I of France here, 1525. Annexed by Austria, 1714. Became part of a united Italy, 1859. Church Councils held at P., 1081, 1160, 1423.

Pawnbrokers' Act, 1922, enforced registration and licensing of all P. shops in England.

Pay As You Earn (P.A.Y.E.), part of modern British income tax system, was introduced in 1944.

Peace Ballot, conducted by the League of Nations Union, secured 11,640,066 British votes for adherence to the League, and 10,500,000 for all-round reduction of armaments, 27 June 1935.

Peace Conferences (International). *See also* HAGUE. 1. Met at The Hague, 1899; arbitration court formed at the conference, and founded 29 July 1899. 2. Met at The Hague, 15 June–18 Oct. 1907. 3. Inter-Allied and Associated Powers held first plenary session, in Paris, on 18 June 1919. Draft treaty handed to German delegates, 7 May 1919. After the treaty was ratified further conferences were held at San Remo, Apr. 1920, and at Hythe, May, and Spa, June 1920, to discuss reparations, disarmament, mandates, and the Adriatic question. For P. C. with Turkey *see* TURKISH REPUBLIC. 4. A Peace Conference held in Paris in 1946 resulted in peace treaties between the Allies and Italy, Hungary, Rumania, Bulgaria, and Finland being signed and ratified in 1947. The treaty with Austria, however, was the subject of several years' negotiations and was not signed until 1955.

Peace Preservation (Ireland) Acts. In continuation of the policy of an Act passed in 1847 (whereby the Lord Lieutenant was given special powers, notably to 'proclaim' any district, after which possession of arms or ammunition therein was illegal), the first P. P. Act was passed, 1856. It was kept alive by re-enactments till 1880, an amending Act having been passed in

1870. New Act, for five years, passed, 1881. Succeeded by Criminal Law and Procedure Act, 1887.

Peacham's Case. Edmund P., rector of Hinton St. George, Somerset, convicted of high treason despite Lord Chief Justice Coke's written opinion in his favour, 1516.

Pearl Harbor, American naval base in the Hawaiian Islands. Dredging of P. H. completed, 1912; dry dock opened, 1919. Japanese attack on P. H., 7 Dec. 1941, brought the U.S.A. into World War II on the allied side.

Peasants' Revolt. Accelerated by enforcement of poll-tax (1379). Rebels suppressed after breaking into Tower of London, 15 June 1381.

Peasants' War. 1. France. *See* JACQUERIE. 2. Germany: Decay of feudal protection, together with continuance of feudal tyranny, led to a P. League which rose in the Rhine countries in 1502, and to another rising in Württemberg in 1514. Great insurrection began in Swabia, 1524, and spread through S. Germany. Demands of P. set out in 12 Articles issued by insurgents of Swabia, Easter, 1525; Under the Anabaptist Münzer, they were overwhelmed by Philip of Hesse at Frankenhausen, 15 May 1525.

Peckham Health Centre, opened, 1926. New building opened, May 1935. Closed owing to lack of funds, 1951.

Peculiar People. Evangelical Protestant denomination founded, 1838, by John Banyard. For origin of name, *see* Deut. xiv. 2 and xxvi. 18.

Peep-of-Day Boys. Irish Protestant secret society, founded *c.* 1785.

Peine Forte et Dure, form of torture to extort plea or evidence, authorized in England, 1406. Last recorded instance, 1741. Abolished, 1772.

Peking or **Peiping,** capital of China. Captured by Khitan Tatars, A.D. 986; recaptured by Chinese in twelfth century; again captured by Tatars, 1151; first settlement of foreigners in 1860; Boxer riots and the siege of the legations, 1900. Capital of China from 1421 until 1928, when Chiang Kai-Shek removed the government to Nanking and renamed Peking Peiping. Occupied by Japanese, 1937–45. Surrendered to the Communists, 1 Feb. 1949, and re-established under its original name of Peking as the capital of China, 1 Oct. 1949.

Pelagians. The followers of Pelagius (*c.* 360–420), a British theologian, who was summoned before a synod of bishops at Jerusalem, 415, where he successfully defended his views. Pope Innocent, however, in 416 upheld the opponents of Pelagius, amongst whom was St. Augus-

tine of Hippo. The doctrine of Pelagianism finally condemned, 418, by the Western Church, and in 431 by the Eastern Church.

Penal Servitude, as punishment for felony, substituted for transportation in English law, 1853–7. Abolished, 1948.

Penang (*see* MALAYA). Ceded to E. India Co. by Rajah of Kedah, 1785. Made a penal settlement, 1796. Made separate presidency, 1805. Incorporated with Singapore and Malacca, 1826. Capital of Straits Settlements, 1837–1936. Joined Malayan Union, 1946, and Malayan Federation, 1948.

P.E.N. Club founded, 1921.

Penicillin. Discovered, 1928, by Sir Alexander Fleming (1881–1955).

Peninsular War, The (1808–14). Between France and England, begun in consequence of the alliance between Spain and England, July 1808, when the Duke of Wellington, then Sir Arthur Wellesley, was dispatched to the peninsula with troops; there were two campaigns, and the British Army was forced to evacuate the country in Jan. 1809. A fresh force was landed in Apr. 1809; the war had commenced with the battle of Vimiero, 21 Aug. 1808, when Wellington defeated Junot, and ended with the battle of Toulouse, 10 Apr. 1814, when Wellington defeated Soult (*see* PORTUGAL and SPAIN).

Pennsylvania, U.S.A. Founded by William Penn, who in 1681 obtained a grant of land in America from Charles II. In Sept. 1682 Penn embarked on the *Welcome* for America, and landed on 28 Oct. of the same year; as one of the thirteen original colonies it became a state of the Union, 1787.

Penny. First mentioned in Laws of King Ine (*fl.* 689–726), King of Wessex. Halfpennies not coined before the late ninth century. Copper pence first struck, 1797; bronze substituted for copper, 1860.

Pennymite and Yankee War, 1769. Between Connecticut settlers and the Pennsylvanians.

Pensions, Ministry of, created, 1916. Merged with the Ministry of National Insurance, to form the M. of P. and National Insurance, 1953.

Pentagon Building (Washington, D.C., U.S.A.), built 1941–3. Claimed to be the world's largest office building.

Peonage, made illegal in New Mexico, 1867.

Perak, former Federated Malay State, made treaty (1765) with Dutch, who first established factories there, 1650. Ceded Dinding and Pangkor Island to Britain by treaty of 1826, but these were returned, 1934–5. Joined Malayan Union 1946, and Malayan Federation, 1948.

Perceval Administration. Spencer P. (1762–1812) at the head. Formed, Oct. 1809; dissolved on assassination of P. in the lobby of the House of Commons, 11 May 1812.

Pergamum. Said to have been founded by Aeolian Greeks; a place of some importance by 420 B.C. Ruled by Philetaerus, 283–263; Eumenes I, 263–241; Attalus I, 241–197; Eumenes II, 197–159; Attalus II, 159–138; Attalus III, 138–133. The last three made alliances with Rome, who greatly enlarged their kingdom, and to whom it was bequeathed in 133 B.C.

Perlis, former Unfederated Malay State, became subject to Siam, 1821, and independent, 1841. By treaties of 1909 and 1930 the ruler of P. accepted British protection and the services of a British adviser. Joined Malayan Union, 1946, and Malayan Federation, 1948.

Persia (Iran). Establishment of Achaemenid dynasty when Cyrus defeated Medes at battle of Pasargadae, 550 B.C. Reached their zenith under Darius I, 522–485. Xerxes I was defeated by Greeks at Salamis, 480. The dynasty fell with the conquest of P. by Alexander the Great, 331, and the assassination of Darius III. At Alexander's death, 323, P. was ruled by the Seleucids until conquered by the Arsacid (Parthian) dynasty, 129. Scythian invasions repelled by Mithridates the Great, 123–90. Defeat of Crassus at Carrhae, 53. Phraates IV enters into a treaty of dependency with Rome, 4 B.C. Arsacids overthrown by the Sassanids under Ardashir I, A.D. 226. Unsuccessful wars under Sapor I (240–73) with Rome. Perso-Roman wars under Sapor II (310–379) take on a religious aspect. Sassanids reach their greatest power under Kavad I, 488–531. Chosroes I, 531–79. Defeat and destruction of Sassanids by Arabs at battles of Kadisiya, 637, and Nehavend, 641. Population converted to Islam, eighth century. P. divided and in confusion until conquered by the Mongols under Hulagu, 1256. Mongol rule continued till death of Tamerlane, 1404. After civil wars Safavid dynasty seized power, 1499. Defeat of the Uzbegs, 1510. War with Turkey, 1514–55. Zenith of Safavids under Shah Abbas I, 1587–1628. Russian and Turkish invasions, 1722–7. Nadir Shah overthrows Safavids, 1736. Invades India, 1738. Bokhara and Khiva, 1740. Nadir assassinated, 1747. Zand dynasty, 1750–94. Kajar dynasty takes the throne, 1794. Treaty of Tehran with Britain, 1814. Defeated by Russia in war for Georgia, 1812–28. Invasion of Afghanistan, 1837–8. Anglo-Russian agreement fixes spheres of influence in P.,

1907. Constitutional revolution, 1909. Last Kajar Shah deposed and succeeded by Reza Shah Pahlevi, 1925. Anglo-Russian action forces Reza to abdicate, 1941, in favour of his son, Mohammed Reza Pahlevi (b. 1919). The ex-Shah d. in S. Africa, 1944. Soviet-supported rebellion in Azerbaijan breaks out, 16 Nov. 1945. Government troops drive Soviet puppet government from Azerbaijan, 11–13 Dec. 1946. And from Kurdistan, 15 Dec. 1946. Tudeh Party dissolved, 5 Feb. 1949. Supplemental agreement on oil royalties negotiated with Anglo-Iranian Oil Co., 1949, but withdrawn by Majlis, 26 Dec. 1952. Shah offers entire crown lands (800 villages) for sale to tenants, Jan. 1951. Prime Minister, Gen. Razmara, murdered, 7 Mar., and succeeded by Dr. Mussadeq, Apr., who passed measures nationalizing the Anglo-Persian Oil Co. The last British technicians left Abadan in Oct. 1952, the Hague Court having declared in July that it had no competence to deal with the dispute. Renewed Anglo-American proposals rejected by Mussadeq, 30 Aug., and diplomatic relations with Britain suspended, 22 Oct. 1952. Mussadeq's bill for extension of his plenary powers passed, Jan. 1953. Shah and queen fled to Bagdad on failure of royalist putsch, 16 Aug. 1953, but royalist Gen. Zahedi became Prime Minister, and Shah returned. Mussadeq imprisoned, September. Oil dispute settled, 1954; British technicians returned. P. joined Bagdad Pact (later CENTO, q.v.), 1955. Shah married Farah Diba as his third wife, 1959, and a son and heir was born, Oct. 1960. Economic difficulties caused government crisis, July 1962. Earthquake in W. P. on 1 Sept. 1962 caused 10,000 deaths. In Jan. 1963 the Shah received overwhelming support in a referendum envisaging drastic land reform, etc. Women voted for the first time.

Persian Authors, Classic.
Avicenna (Abu Ibn Sina), 980–1036, philosopher and physician.
Firdausi, Abulkasim Mansur, c. 950–1020, poet.
Hafiz, Shamseddin Muhammed, d. c. 1390, poet.
Jalaluddin Rumi, 1207–73, poet.
Khayyám, Omar, d. 1123, poet.
Saadi, d. 1291, poet.
Zoroaster, c. seventh century B.C., poet and prophet.

Perth, Scotland. Said to have been founded by Agricola, A.D. 70. Made a royal burgh by William the Lion, 1210;

besieged and captured by Robert Bruce, 1311; captured by Edward III, 1335; retaken by Scots, 1339; after 1437, the year of the murder of James I, P. was no longer capital of Scotland; captured by Montrose, 1644; by Cromwell, 1651; Old Pretender proclaimed at, 16 Sept, 1715.

Peru, Spanish Viceroyalty of. Conquered by Pizarro, 1531–4. Lima founded, 1534. Manco Inca's unsuccessful revolt, 1535. Pizarro killed, 1541. 'New Laws' according liberty to Indians, 1542. Execution of Inca Tupac Amaru, 1571. Viceroyalty of New Granada separated from P., 1739. Viceroyalty of the River Plate separated from P., 1776. Condorcanqui's rebellion, 1780.

Perugia, Italy. Originally *Perusia.* Captured by Pope Leo X from the Baglioni, 1520; occupied by French, 1797; by Austrians, 1849; united to kingdom of Italy, 1860.

Peruvian Republic. Independence proclaimed, 28 July 1821. Declared independent of Colombia, 26 Jan. 1827. Constitution proclaimed, 21 Mar. 1828. United with Bolivia, 1835–9. Joined with Bolivia against Chile in the 'Nitrate War,' 1879. Defeated and forced to cede the province of Tarapaca to Chile, 1883. Tacna-Arica dispute with Chile amicably settled, 3 June 1929. War with Colombia, 1932–4. Skirmish with Ecuador, 1941. Declared war on Germany and Japan, Feb. 1945. Women fully enfranchised, 1955. Presidential elections, June 1962, produced an inconclusive result. P. army deposed President Prado and set up a military junta, 18 July, promising free elections within a year. Change in junta leadership, Mar. 1963.

Heads of State since the Establishment of the Republic, 1821:

Protector:

San Martin	1821–1822

President:

Aguero	1823–1824

Protector:

Bolivar	1824–1826

Presidents:

La Mar	1827–1828
Gamarra	1829–1833
Orbegosa	1833–1836
Santa Cruz (Peru united with Bolivia (*q.v.*))	1836–1839
Gamarra	1839–1841
Menendez	1841–1845
Castilla	1845–1851
Echenique	1851–1854
Castilla	1855–1862
Pezet	1862–1865

Prado (Mariano Ignacio)	1866–1868
Balta	1868–1872
Pardo (Manuel)	1872–1876
Prado (Mariano Ignacio)	1876–1879
Pierola	1879–1881
Calderon (Francisco Garcia)	1881–1883
Iglesias	1883–1885
Cacares	1886–1890
Bermudez	1890–1894
Cacares	1894–1895
Pierola	1895–1899
Romana	1899–1903
Candamo	1903–1904
Calderon (Serapio)	1904
Pardo (Jose)	1904–1908
Leguia	1908–1912
Billinghurst	1912–1914
Benavides	1914–1915
Pardo (Jose)	1915–1919
Leguia	1919–1930
Ponce	1930
Cerro	1930–1931
Elias	1931
Jimenez	1931
Ocampo	1931
Cerro	1931–1933
Benavides	1933–1939
Prado (Manuel)	1939–1945
Bustamante	1945–1948
Odria	1948–1950
Noriega	1950
Odria	1950–1956
Prado (Manuel)	1956–1962
Military Junta	1962–

Peter I Island, in the Antarctic Ocean, sighted by the Russian admiral Bellinghausen, and named by him in 1821, was first visited by Europeans in 1929 when a Norwegian party took possession on behalf of the King of Norway; proclaimed Norwegian territory, 23 Apr. 1931.

Peterborough, England. Originally called *Medehamstede.* In 655 Saxulf, a monk, founded a monastery there, and the name was altered subsequently to *Burgus sancti Petri*; cathedral founded, 656; destroyed by Danes, 870; the present building founded, 1117, and was consecrated, 4 Oct. 1237. See founded by Henry VIII, 1541. Cathedral despoiled by Cromwell, 1643.

Peterloo Massacre at St. Peter's Field, Manchester, 16 Aug. 1819.

Peter's Pence. A tax levied on the English by the popes, and probably dating from the eighth century; it is mentioned in a letter of Canute's, dated 1031, from Rome to the English clergy; in 1534 the tax was abolished by Henry VIII.

Petition of Right. Presented to Charles I by Parliament, 28 May 1628; it asked for a reform of various constitutional abuses. Until the Crown Proceedings Act, 1947, a P. of R. was the only way in which the subject could obtain legal relief against the crown.

Petrograd. St. Petersburg (*q.v.*) renamed Aug. 1914 to remove any suggestion of German influence. Name changed to Leningrad (*q.v.*), 1924.

Petsamo (Fin.), **Petchenga** (Rus.). A port in the Barents Sea, together with a small province named after it, E. of Lake Inari. It did not form part of the Grand Duchy of Finland (*q.v.*), but was ceded to the Finnish republic by the U.S.S.R. under the Treaty of Dorpat, 24 Oct. 1920. The treaty of 1940 secured the Russians access to the port and freedom of movement across the province, but that of 1944 ceded both to the U.S.S.R. outright.

Pharmaceutical Society. Founded, 1841; incorporated, 1843. Membership became automatic and compulsory for all qualified chemists and druggists, 1933. Constitution revised by granting of a supplementary charter, 1953, and the coming into operation of the Pharmacy Act, 1953.

Phi Beta Kappa. Oldest American college fraternity, formed at William and Mary College, Williamsburg, Virginia, 1776. Women eligible since 1876.

Philadelphia, Pa., U.S.A. Founded by William Penn, 1682. Free public library founded by Benjamin Franklin, 1731. Was capital of Pennsylvania and of United (at first Federal) States until 1800.

Philippine Islands. Discovered by Magellan, who was killed there, 1521. Occupied by Spaniards, who built Manila, 1564–71. Destructive earthquake, 1599. Manila badly damaged by earthquake, 1862. Admiral Montojo's fleet destroyed at battle of Manila, 1 May 1898. Ceded to U.S.A. by Treaty of Paris, 10 Dec. 1898. Assembly for self-government opened by Taft, Secretary for War, 16 Oct. 1907. Granted local autonomy, 1916. Council of State created by executive orders, 1918 and 1928. U.S. Congress declares P. I. independent as from 1945 (but this in fact delayed by World War II), 24 Mar. 1934. Commonwealth of the Ps. inaugurated, 14 Nov. 1935. Japanese attack and occupy Manila, 2 Jan. 1942. Siege of Bataan, 5 Jan.–1 May 1942. Surrender of Corregidor, 6 May 1942. Americans land in P. I., 20 Oct. 1944. Final liberation, 6 Aug. 1945. Republic of the Philippines came into being 4 July 1946. Claimed W. Borneo, 1962.

Phoenicia conquered by Egyptians *c.* 1600 B.C. Became independent again *c.* 928 B.C. Hegemony of Tyre lasted until 876 B.C., when Phoenician cities became tributary to Assyria and thereafter to other great powers; but the colony of Carthage (*q.v.*) was founded *c.* 700 B.C.

Phoenix Park Murders. Lord Frederick Cavendish, Chief Secretary for Ireland, and T. H. Burke murdered by irresponsible terrorists in Dublin, 6 May 1882.

Phosphorus. Discovered, 1669, by Dr. Brandt, of Hamburg.

Photography. In the sixteenth century the action of light on chloride of silver was known, but it was not until *c.* 1802 that Thomas Wedgwood (1771–1805) published his *Account of a Method of copying Painting upon Glass, and of making Profiles by the Agency of Light upon Nitrate of Silver*; in 1819 Sir John Herschel improved Wedgwood's method, and in 1824 Louis J. M. Daguerre produced photographic plates, afterwards known as daguerreotypes; the first *negative* was produced by Talbot in 1839; celluloid roll films introduced by George Eastman, 1889; telephotography invented by T. R. Dallmeyer (1859–1906) in 1891; direct colour P. by the Lumière Autochrome Plate, patented, 1904.

Photogravure. Invented by Klietsch (1841–1926), 1895.

Physicians, Royal College of (London). Charter granted through exertions of Dr. Linacre, Henry VIII's physician, in 1518.

Pianoforte or **Hammerklavier** developed by modification of the harpsichord by Bartolomeo Cristofori (1655–1731).

Piarists, founded soon after 1597 by St. Joseph Calasanctius (1556–1648).

Pietists began to hold meetings, 1670, of German Lutherans under Jakob Spener (1625–1705). Community at Herrnhut founded by Nikolaus Ludwig, Graf von Zinzendorf (1700–60).

Pilgrimage of Grace. The name given to the insurrection caused by the dissolution of the monasteries and the agrarian injustices resulting from enclosures; it originated in Yorkshire and Lincolnshire in 1536; the leaders were executed in Mar. 1537.

Pilgrim Fathers, *émigré* Puritans from Lincolnshire, left England, 1608, for Leyden, sailed from Delftshaven, July 1620; from Southampton, 5 Aug.; from Plymouth, Devon, 6 Sept.; landed at Plymouth, Massachusetts, 16 Dec. 1620.

Pilgrim Trust founded, 1930.

Pillory, offences punishable by defined, 1266, in 'Statute of the P.' Limited to cases of perjury and subornation, 1816; last used, 1830; and finally abolished in England, 1837. Abolished in France, 1832; in state of Delaware, 1905; in rest of U.S.A., 1839.

Piltdown Man's skull partially dug up, 1912, and further skull fragments found, 1915. It was decided that Piltdown Man must have lived some 50,000 years ago. Detailed technical examination by

M

modern methods, 1953–4, resulted in the
'discovery' being exposed as a fraud,
1955.

Piraeus. See ATHENS.

Pisa, Italy (anct. **Julia Pisana** or **Julia
Obsequeus**). Independent republic by
the eleventh century; leaning tower built,
1173–1350; power crushed by Genoa in a
naval battle off Melovia, 1284; university
founded, 1343; subject to Florence, 1405
becomes independent under French protection, 1494; retaken by Florence, 1509;
mob attempted to destroy cathedral as a
protest against execution of Ferrer, 17
Oct. 1909.

Pitcairn Island. Discovered by Carteret, 1767; occupied by mutineers from
the *Bounty,* 1790, and not visited by
anyone else from the outside world until
1808. Population removed to Tahiti,
1831, but returned to P. I., 1832. Removed to Norfolk Island, 1856, but
several soon returned. Duchess of
Gloucester visited P. I., 1947. Original
P. I. Bible returned to P. I., 1949.
Administrative reforms, 1952. *See*
'BOUNTY' MUTINY.

Pittsburgh, Pa., U.S.A., began to grow
c. 1785 on the site of Fort Pitt (formerly
Fort Duquesne, which was built, 1754).

Plastics. First plastic (celluloid) discovered by Alexander Parkes, 1865.
Considerable developments since 1920,
and especially since 1939.

Platinum. Discovered, 1538, in Spain;
first found in 1741 in England by Brownrigg.

Player Piano invented, 1842.

Plebiscite, originally a law enacted by
the Plebs (*see* ROME) in their own
assembly, the *comitia tributa,* established
449 B.C., as opposed to the Senate. Such
laws came to be valid for the whole nation
by the *Lex Hortensia,* 286 B.C. For
modern Ps. *see* CARINTHIA; GREECE,
MODERN; ITALY; SAARLAND; SILESIA.

Plebs under King Servius Tullius (578–
534 B.C.) acquired some constitutional
rights and the obligation of military
service. Office of Tribune of Plebs
instituted, 493.

Plimsoll Line, compulsory load-line,
obtained, 1876, by the efforts of Samuel
P. (1824–98).

Plombières. The Pact of P. was signed
by Napoleon III and Cavour, 1858. *See*
FRANCE and ITALY.

Pluralism forbidden in England by Act
of 1529 in certain cases. Also by the
Acts of 1837 and 1885, which have more
the effect of amalgamating parishes.

Plural Voting in Great Britain completely abolished by Representation of
the People Act, 1948.

Plymouth, England, was frequently
attacked by the French during the fourteenth and fifteenth centuries. First
English town to be incorporated by Act of
Parliament, 12 Nov. 1439. Witnessed
the departure of Drake on his expedition
round the world, 1577; of the Elizabethan
fleet in the encounter with the Spanish
Armada, 1588; and of the *Mayflower,*
1620. Three separate towns of Devonport, East Stonehouse, and P. amalgamated under the name of P., 1914.
Severely damaged by German bombing,
1941.

Plymouth Brethren. Religious sect
founded *c.* 1830 at P.; John Nelson
Darby (1800–82) is generally regarded as
the founder.

Pola. *See* ISTRIA.

Poland, Kingdom of. First appears as
independent state, tenth century. Mieszko
I (962–92) converted to Christianity.
Boleslaw III divides P. between his sons,
1138, but country reunited by Casimir II
(1177–94). Teutonic Knights settle in
Kulm, 1208. Mongol invasion. 1241; P.
again divided. P. reunited under
Wladislaw Lokietek, 1306. Kingdom
revived, 1320. First Diet, 1331. Casimir the Great, 1333–70. Personal union
with Lithuania, 1386. Witowt and
Jagiello (Wladislaw II) defeat Teutonic
Knights at Tannenberg, 1410. Union of
Horodlo, 1413. Prussia acquired from
the Knights by Treaty of Thorn, 1466.
War with Turkey, 1485 onwards. Escheat of Masovia and Warsaw, 1526.
Religious dissensions, 1550–64. Decrees
against heretics, 1564. Political union
with Lithuania (Union of Lublin), 1 July
1569. Interregnum, 1572–3, following
which monarchy becomes elective. Election of Henry of Valois, 1573. Reign of
Stephen Báthory, 1575–86. University
of Vilna founded, 1579. Sigismund III
tried for treason by a Court of Inquisition,
1592. Creation of the Uniate Church,
1596. Right of deposition recognized,
1607. War with Russia, 1608–18. Defeat of Turks at battle of Czoczim, 1621.
Cossack rebellions, 1640–9. Bogdan
Khmelnitzki recognized as Hetman of the
Cossacks at Zborow, 1649. Khmelnitzki
defeated at battle of Beresteczko, 1651.
War with Russia, 1651–64. Loss of
Ukraine and Smolensk to Russia at
Truce of Andrussov, 1667. John
Sobieski rescues Vienna from the Turks,
1683. Peace of Karlowitz, 1699. Attempt by Czartoryski family to reform
constitution, 1735–60. Confederation of
Radom, 1767. Russian influence
attacked by Confederation of Bar, 1768.
First Partition of P., 1772. Constitu-
tion reformed, May 1791. Russians
abolish the reforms, 1792. Second Par-

tition, 1793. Kosciuszko proclaims national insurrection, Mar. 1794. Russians suppress Kosciuszko, 1794. Third Partition, 1795–6. King Stanislaw abdicates, 1795, and *d.* in Russia, 1798. Napoleon creates Grand Duchy of Warsaw, 1806–15. Congress of Vienna creates a kingdom of P. under the Russian crown, usually called 'Congress P.,' 1815. Suppressed, 1831, following the rising of 1830. Rising in Russian provinces of P., 1863. (Separate government until 1864.)

Kings of Poland, 962–1795:

Partitional Period of Rival Duchies, 1138–1305:

Poland, Republic of. The risings of 1830 and 1863 (*see* preceding article) had really been in support of the republic, which was at last proclaimed, Nov. 1918. Independence guaranteed under Versailles Treaty, 1919. Wars of aggrandizement with Lithuania, western Ukraine, and Soviet Russia, Apr. 1919–Mar. 1921 (*see* RUSSIA). Constitution voted, 17 Mar. 1921. Czechoslovakia frontier dispute settled, 1924. *Coup d'état*, with bloodshed, by Marshal Pilsudski, 12 May 1926. Non-aggression pact with Germany, 1934. Less liberal new constitution introduced, Apr. 1935; Marshal Pilsudski *d.*, 12 May 1935. Took possession of zone in Czechoslovakia beyond the Olza, 2 Oct. 1938.

1939: Ribbentrop (German foreign minister) had discussions in Warsaw with Col. Beck (Polish foreign minister), 25–7 Jan.; demands regarding Danzig presented by Germany, 21 Mar.; British support for P. promised in Parliament, 31 Mar.; Col. Beck visited London, 3 Apr.; Hitler announced annulment of non-aggression treaty with P., 28 Apr.; Col. Beck in the Seym rejected Hitler's claims on Danzig and the 'Corridor,' 5 May; Hitler's 16-point plan transmitted by radio, 31 Aug.; Germans invaded P. at 5.30 a.m., 1 Sept.; Soviet Russian troops crossed into P. at 4 a.m., Brest-Litovsk fell, 17 Sept.; Soviet troops reached Hungarian frontier, President Moscicki with his Government entered Rumania, thousands of Polish troops fled into Lithuania, 19 Sept.; Soviet troops reached Ruthenia, Germans retreating before Soviet advance, 21 Sept.; Fourth Partition of P. between Germany and Russia announced from Moscow, 22 Sept.; surrender of Warsaw and fall of Modlin, final partition of P. agreed between Germany and Russia, 28 Sept.; President Moscicki resigned, new Polish Government (recognized by Britain and France) formed in France under presidency of Wladyslaw Raczkiewicz with a Cabinet under Gen. Sikorski, 30 Sept.; Hela peninsula garrison surrendered, completing Polish subjection, 1 Oct.; Poznan and Pomerelia annexed to Germany, 19 Oct.; first meeting of People's Assembly (elected 22 Oct.) of western Ukraine and western White Russia, 28 Oct.; Polish Government in exile protested to the League of Nations, 1 Nov.; Gen. Sikorski made generalissimo in place of Smigly Rydz, 9 Nov.; first meeting of new Cabinet held at Angers in France 23 Nov.; deportation of Czech and Austrian Jews, and removal of Polish Jews to Jewish Reserve near Lublin, Oct. and Nov.; Polish National Council formed at Angers, 15 Dec.

1940: Russians massacre 12,000

Polish officers at Katyn c. May. Polish Government established in London, 21 June.

1941: Sikorski visits Moscow, Nov.; a new Polish army organized in Russia.

1943: Warsaw ghetto rising, 18 Apr.–1 June.

1944: Poles rise against Germans in Warsaw, 1 Aug. Russians refuse help, 20 Aug. Rising crushed, 2 Oct. Poles forced to concede Curzon Line to Russia at Moscow Conference, 9–19 Oct.

1945: Russians enter Warsaw, 11 Jan. Communist-dominated Government of National Unity established, 28 June. Russo-Polish frontier treaty, 17 Aug. Large-scale deportations of Germans from new Polish territories in the W.

1946: Persecution of Mikolajczyk's Peasant Party, Mar.–June.

1947: Government intimidation leads to Socialist-Communist victory at elections, 19–22 Jan. Flight of Mikolajczyk to Britain, 26 Oct.

1948: Gomulka (Premier) expelled from Communist Party, 4 Sept. Socialist and Communist parties merged, Dec.

Peasants' Party merged with Communists, 1949; P. withdraw from the International Monetary Fund, 1950, and from U.N.E.S.C.O., 1952. Election of Nov. 1952 returned 99·8 per cent National Front (i.e. Communist) candidates. By the revised constitution of July 1952 the presidency fell into desuetude, being replaced by a Council of State, the first chairman of which was Alexander Zawadski. Persecution of the Catholic Church; Wyszinski, primate of P., imprisoned, 1953–6. Workers and students rioted in Poznan, June 1956; 'liberal' elements gained control of the Communist regime in P.; Gomulka became the real ruler of Poland, Oct. 1956. Wyszinski released and visited Rome to receive his cardinal's hat, 1957; increasing contacts with W. Europe and greater religious freedom. By 1961 this freedom was again being curtailed, and Wyszinski made vigorous public protests, condemning the State's atheism, notably in Aug. 1962.

Presidents of Poland from 1918:

Pilsudski ('Chief of the State')	1918–1922
Narutowicz (assassinated after five days of office)	1922
Wojciechowski	1922–1926
Moscicki	1926–1939
Bierut	1947–1952

Heads of Administration in Poland from 1918:

Parliamentary government in P. proved unstable from the outset, and between 1922 and 1926 governments changed constantly. After the *coup d'état* by Pilsudski in 1926 parliamentary government in the sense known in Britain ceased to function. The following were the effective heads of administration in P.:

Pilsudski	1918–1922
Paderewski	1919–1921
Pilsudski	1926–1935
Smigly-Rydz	1935–1939

From 1939 to 1945 the Polish Government was in exile. Heads of administration in London were:

Sikorski	1939–1943
Mikolajczyk	1943–1945

The real ruler of Poland, since 1947, has in fact been the individual holding the position of first secretary of the Communist party; a position held by Gomulka since 1956.

Polish Literature. The following are some P. authors, not now living:

Fredro, Count Aleksander, 1793–1876, dramatist.

Krasicki, Ignatius, 1735–1801, poet and critic.

Kraszewski, Jósef Ignacy, 1812–87, novelist, historian, and critic.

Kraszinski, Zygmunt, 1812–49, dramatist.

Mickiewicz, Adam, 1798–1855, poet.

Niémcewicz, Julian Ursin, 1757–1841, poet, dramatist, and novelist.

Orzeszkowa, Eliza, 1842–1910, novelist.

Przybyszewski, Stanislas, 1868–1927, novelist.

Reymont, Ladislas Stanislas, 1867–1925, novelist.

Sienkiewicz, Henryk, 1846–1916, novelist.

Slowacki, Juljusz, 1809–49, poet and dramatist.

Tetmajer, K., 1865–1939, poet.

Wyspianski, S., 1869–1907, poet and playwright.

Zapolska, Gabriela, 1860–1921, dramatist.

Police. In Britain the modern police force derives from Sir Robert Peel's reorganization of the Metropolitan Police Force, 1829.

Political Uniforms. Prohibited in Britain by Public Order Act, 1936.

Poll-Tax. Levied in England, 1377, 1379, and 1380. The latter was a cause of Wat Tyler's rebellion in 1381; revived, 1513; finally abolished. 1689.

Polotsk, independent principality from the tenth century, absorbed by Lithuania, 1307. Retaken by Ivan the Terrible, 1563. Became Polish 1582; and finally Russian, 1772.

Polygamy. *See* MORMONS and UTAH, where it was forbidden by the Edmunds-Tucker Act of 1887.

Pompeii, Italy. Entirely destroyed by eruption of Vesuvius, 24 Aug. A.D. 79; in 1763 systematic excavations were commenced. Further considerable excavations from 1861; especially in 1921, 1941, and 1956–7.

Pondicherry, first settled by French, 1674. Transferred to India *de facto*, 1 Nov. 1954; cession formally recognized by treaty 28 May 1956.

Pontefract Castle (Yorks). Built *c.* 1069; Richard II murdered at, 10 Feb. 1400. Castle dismantled, 1649.

Poor Laws (Britain). Overseers were appointed for parishes, 1601; the word 'guardian' first used in this connection in a bill introduced into the Commons, 11 May 1735, by William Hay (1695–1755); first systematization of unions of parishes accomplished by Gilbert's Act, 1782, by which the relief of the poor was entrusted to visitors and guardians appointed by the justices. Poor Law Commission, 1832–3; Poor Law Board appointed, 1834; dissolved, 1846; Poor Law Amendment Bill passed, 1834; amended, 1836, 1838, 1846, 1868; New Poor Law Act passed, 1889; amended, 1890. Overseers abolished by Rating and Valuation Act, 1925, as from 1 Apr. 1927; boards of guardians by Local Government Act, 1929, as from 1 Apr. 1930: these Acts transferred care of poor to the local authorities. Whole system abolished, 1948.

Poor Persons' Legal Aid, provided by the Poor Prisoners' Defence Act, 1930, in criminal cases, and in civil cases by the Legal Aid and Advice Act, 1949, which came into operation, 1951.

Popish Plot. Imaginary Roman Catholic plot against Charles II, invented by Titus Oates. He deposed before Sir E. Berry Godfrey, 28 Sept. 1678. Godfrey was murdered, 14 Oct. 1678. Oates convicted of perjury, May 1685. Reinstated, 1688.

Popular Front, suggested by Comintern, 1935. (*See* FRANCE and SPAIN.) Sir Stafford Cripps suggested a similar combination in England, which led to his expulsion from the Labour Party, Apr. 1939. The P. F. campaign was then abandoned.

Port Arthur. Massacre of Chinese by Japanese, 21 Nov. 1894; surrendered by Russian garrison to Japan, 1 Jan. 1905. In 1945 China and Russia agreed to joint use of P. A. for next thirty years; but this arrangement abandoned under the Sino-Russian treaty of 1950, and P. A. was handed over to China in 1955.

Porteous Riots. Caused by the hanging of a smuggler in Edinburgh, 1736; Capt. P. ordered the military to fire on the rioters and killed many; he was sentenced to death, but respited; the mob, however, seized him afterwards and hanged him.

Portland, Me., U.S.A., first settled, 1632. Capital of Maine, 1820–31.

Portland Vase recovered from a tomb in the seventeenth century; bought by Sir William Hamilton from the Barbarini family, 1770, and sold by him to the Duchess of P., who lent it to the British Museum, 1810. Broken by a maniac, 1845, but repaired. Auctioned by the Duke of P., 1929, but withdrawn. Sold to the British Museum, 1946.

Port of London Authority set up under the P. of L. Act, 1908.

Porto Bello, Panama, built on site of earlier settlement called Nombre de Dios (1502), which was sacked by Drake, 1572. P. B. was built, 1584, and sacked by Henry Morgan, 1668, and John Spring, 1680. Captured by the English for the last time, 1739.

Port Royal des Champs (France). Convent founded, 1204, by Mahaut de Montmorency. It became a Bernardine house with the privilege of receiving laity desiring retirement. The nuns moved to Paris, leaving P. R. to the lay community, 1626. Schools founded, 1643. The house supported the Jansenists (*q.v.*). Some nuns returned, 1648. Schools suppressed by royal order, 1660. Society reconstituted under the 'Peace of Clement IX,' 1669. Angélique Arnauld (1624–84) abbess, 1678. On Louis XIV's suppression of Jansenism the nuns were dispersed and the buildings demolished, 1709.

Portsmouth. Granted its first charter, 1194. Importance as a naval dockyard dates from *c.* 1545. Became seat of a diocese, 1924, and a city, 1926. Scene of the assassination of the Duke of Buckingham, 1628, and the marriage of Charles II to Catherine of Braganza, 1662. Heavily bombed during World War II.

Port Sunlight founded, 1888.

Portugal. Conquered by Carthaginians under Hamilcar Barca, 241–230 B.C. By Romans, 193–178 B.C. Lusitanian revolt, 154–150 B.C. Rebellion of Viriatus, 146–139 B.C.; of Sertorius, 80–72 B.C. First mention of Christianity, A.D. 250. Invasion of Goths, Alans, and Vandals, 409–10. Swabian kingdom established in N. P., 410–29. Oporto sacked by Visigoths, 456. Swabian kingdom incorporated in Visigothic kingdom by Leovigild, 585. Visigoths converted to Christianity, 586–610. Collapse of Visigothic kingdom in the Moorish invasion, 710–12. Moors conquer P., 712–16. Ommayad rule established, 755. Christian reconquest begun c. 747. Rise of the Cordovan monarchy, 796–812. Viking raids, 844–60. Battle of Simancas, 939. P. overrun by Almanzor, 987–8. Viking raids under St. Olav, 1017. Christian conquest of Coimbra, 1064. Henry of Burgundy first Count of P., 1095. Portuguese independence from Leon established at, by Alfonso Henrique at battle of São Mamede, 1128. He wins great victory over Moors at Ovrique, and takes title of king, 1139. Anglo-Portuguese conquest of Lisbon, 1147. Papacy recognizes Portuguese monarchy, 1179. Almohade (q.v.) invasion, 1191. Quarrel with the Church and deposition of Sancho II, 1248. Moors finally driven out, 1249. Treaty of Badajoz with Castile, 1267. Treaty of Alcañices, 1297. Foundation of the Order of Christ, 1319. Victory with Castilians over the Moors at the battle of the Salado, 1340. Ines de Castro, mistress of Pedro, the heir to the throne, murdered by Coelho, 7 Jan. 1355. Civil war ensues, 1355–7. Castilian War, 1369. Burgundian dynasty ends, 1383. Spanish claimant murdered, 1383. John of Avis made regent, Nov. 1383. Proclaimed king, 6 Apr. 1385. Castilians decisively defeated at battle of Aljubarrota, 14 Aug. 1385. Anglo-Portuguese Alliance at Treaty of Windsor, 9 May 1386. John marries Philippa of Lancaster, 1387. Peace with Castile, Oct. 1411. Capture of Ceuta, 1415. Final peace with Castile at Treaty of Medina del Campo, 1431. Trading stations established on African coast, 1448–9. Braganza rebellion suppressed at battle of Alfarrobeira, 1449. Tangier captured, 1471. Bartholomew Dias rounds the Cape of Good Hope, 1488. Covilhã and Paiva visit Abyssinia, 1489. Treaty of Tordesilhas fixes Spanish and Portuguese spheres of discovery, 7 June 1494. Legal reforms of Manoel I, 1498–21. Vasco da Gama reaches India, 1498. Cabral discovers Brazil, 22 Apr. 1500. Trading empire established in Indian Ocean, 1501–1508. Egypto-Indian fleet defeated by Almeida at Diu, 2 Feb. 1509. Goa made capital of Portuguese India by Albuquerque, 1510. Molucca dispute with Spain, 1517–29. Inquisition introduced, 1536. Loss of most of the N. African possessions at battle of Alcazar-Kebir, 1578. End of the house of Avis, 28 Jan. 1580. P. seized by Philip II of Spain, June 1580. Dutch and British reduce most of the Far Eastern possessions, 1595–1620. Independence re-established by John IV, 1 Dec. 1640. Anglo-Portuguese Treaty, 1654. Catherine of Braganza marries Charles II of England, and Bombay becomes British, 25 Apr. 1662.

Castelo Melhors palace revolution, 1662. The Methuen Treaty (q.v.), 1703. P. enters the War of Spanish Succession (q.v.), 1703. Absolute government established, 1706. Pombal's Ministry, 1750–1777. Lisbon earthquake, 1 Nov. 1755. The Tavora trials, 1758–9. War with Spain, Feb.–June 1801. French invasion, 1807. Junot entered Lisbon, 30 Nov., royal family fled to Brazil. Sir Arthur Wellesley arrived at Oporto, July 1808 (see PENINSULAR WAR). Masséna defeated by British and Portuguese, at Busaco, 27 Sept. 1810. Wellington at Torres Vedras, Oct. 1810. Retreat of Masséna, defeated at Fuentes de Oñoro, 5 May 1811. Popular rising began at Oporto, 29 Aug. 1820. Inquisition abolished. Single-chamber constitution, 1822; modified by the king, 1823. Bicameral Legislature instituted, 1826. Dom Miguel, absolutist regent, proclaimed king, 4 July 1828. Capitulation of Miguel at Evora, 26 May 1834. Constitution of 1822 revived after Sept. coup d'état, 1836. Another revolution, May 1846. Oporto revolutionary junta surrendered to British and Spanish forces, June 1847. Another rising, Apr. 1851. Constitution much amended, 1852. King Pedro V d. of cholera, 11 Nov. 1861. Slavery in colonies abolished, 1869. Conspiracy for an Iberian republic, July 1872. Dispute with Britain as to Shiré highlands (Africa), 1889. Military rising in Oporto, Bank of P. suspended payment, 1891. Constitution further democratized, 1901. Insurrection of peasants at Fundào, Jan. 1903. Government manipulation of elections manifest, 1906; assassination of King Carlos I, 1 Feb. 1908; revolution, Aug. 1910; King Manoel escapes to England, Oct. 1910; Dr. Manoel de Arriaga appointed first president of the new republic, 1911. P. joined war on Allies' side, 1916. Coup d'état by Dr. Paez, 1917; elected president, 1918; assassinated, Dec. 1918. Royalist rising suppressed, 1919. Radical revolution suppressed, 10 Dec. 1923. Unsuccessful Radical revolution, June 1925. Angola Bank scandal, Dec. 1925. Successful revolution under Gen. Gomes da Costa, 28 May 1926. Oporto rebels bombarded by Government, 5 Feb., and military coup d'état failed, 12 Aug. 1927. Gen. Carmona elected president, 23 Mar. 1928. Professor Antonio de Oliveira Salazar became Finance Minister, 1928, and Prime Minister with dictatorial powers, 1932. New constitution, 1933.

1939: Treaty of friendship with Spain, 18 Mar.; Anglo-Portuguese alliance reaffirmed by P., 22 May; by Britain, 26 May; announcement of neutrality in World War II, 2 Sept.; note received from

Brazil that that country would cease to be neutral if P. threatened with invasion, 11 Oct.; link of currency shifted from sterling to dollar, 14 Nov.

1940: Anglo-Spanish-Portuguese commercial agreement signed, 24 July; treaty of friendship with Spain signed, 30 July.

Dutch and Australian troops moved into Portuguese Timor (*q.v.*), 18 Dec. 1941, whereat P. protested despite her agreement of 4 Nov. to accept British protection from the Japanese, who landed 20 Feb. 1942, and occupied the whole territory until 9 Sept. 1945.

1943: Agreement with Allies for use of the Azores against the Germans.

Joined the North Atlantic Treaty Organization, 1949.

General Election, 1951, allowed the nomination of opposition candidates for the presidency, but was so managed that Dr. Salazar's protégé was returned virtually unopposed. Similarly, in 1958, the chief opposition candidate withdrew from the contest shortly before the election, alleging political pressure. Political unrest increased from 1960 onwards. On 23 Jan. 1961 armed passengers seized control of the Portuguese liner *Santa Maria*, in the name of the opposition to Salazar; the liner was surrendered on 2 Feb. On 18 Dec., after protracted and fruitless negotiations with P., Indian forces invaded Goa, P.'s principal Indian colony; it surrendered the following day. The nationalist rebellion in Angola, which had begun in Feb. 1961, led to much destruction and many deaths, and to a rethinking of Portuguese colonial policy, as expressed in suggestions made in 1962 for administrative changes. Licensed prostitution abolished, 1 Jan. 1963. *See also* ANGOLA; GOA.

The following is a list of Portuguese authors not now living:

Alcoforado, Marianna, 1640-1723, author of *Letters of a Portuguese Nun*.

Barros, João de, 1496?-1570, historian.

Bocage, Manuel Maria Barbosa de, 1765-1805, poet.

Braga, Joaquim Theophilo, 1843-1924, historian and poet.

Camoens, Luis de, 1524-80, poet.

Castello Branco, Camillo de, Viscount, 1825-90, novelist and dramatist.

Castilho, Antonio Feliciano de, Viscount, 1800-75, poet.

Castro, Eugenio de, 1869-1944, poet.

Deus, João de, 1830-96, poet.

Ferreira, Antonio, 1528-69, poet and dramatist.

Garrett, João Baptista da Silva Leitão de Almeida, Viscount, 1799-1854, poet, dramatist, and novelist.

Portugal. *Portuguese Authors—cont.*

Goes Damião de, 1502-74, historian.

Herculano de Carvalho e Araujo, Alexandre, 1810-79, historian and poet.

Lopez, Fernão, 1380?-1460?, chronicler.

Macedo, José Agostinho de, 1761-1831, poet.

Nascimento, Francisco Manoel de, 1734-1819, poet.

Oliveira Martins, Joaquim Pedro de, 1845-94, historian.

Pascoais, Teixeira de, 1877-1952, poet.

Pinto, Fernão Mendes, 1509-83, adventurer.

Queiroz, José Maria Eça de, 1843-1900, novelist.

Resende, Garcia de, 1470-1536, poet.

Sá de Miranda, Francisco de, 1485?-1558, poet and dramatist.

Vicente, Gil, 1465?-1536?, dramatist.

Kings of Portugal, 1139-1910:

Burgundian Dynasty:

Alfonso I	1139-1185
Sancho I	1185-1211
Alfonso II the Fat	1211-1223
Sancho II	1223-1248
Alfonso III	1248-1279
Diniz	1279-1325
Alfonso IV	1325-1357
Pedro I the Severe	1357-1367
Ferdinand	1367-1383
Civil War	1383-1385

Aviz Dynasty:

John I	1385-1433
Edward	1433-1438
Alfonso V the African	1438-1481
John II	1481-1495
Manoel I	1495-1521
John III	1521-1557
Sebastian	1557-1578
Henry	1578-1580
Under Spanish Suzerainty	*1581-1640

Braganza Dynasty:

John IV	1640-1656
Alfonso VI	1656-1683
Pedro II	1683-1706
John V	1706-1750
Joseph	1750-1777
Pedro III	1777-1786
Maria I the Mad	1777-1816
John VI	1816-1826
Pedro IV	1826
Maria II	1826-1828
Miguel	1828-1834
Maria II (again)	1834-1853
Pedro V	1853-1861
Luiz I	1861-1889
Carlos I	1889-1908
Manoel II (*d.* in exile in England, 1932)	1908-1910

* *See* Spanish kings, Philip II, III, and IV

Presidents of the Republic:

Manoel de Arriaga	1911–1915
Teofilo Braga	May–Oct. 1915
Bernardino Machado	1915–1917
Sidonio Paez	1917–1918
Admiral de Canto e Castro	1918–1919
Antonio de Almeida	1919–1923
Manuel Gomes	1923–1925
Bernardino Machado	1925–1926
Marshal Antonio Carmona	1926–1951
Marshal Francisco Higino Craveiro Lopez	1951–1958
Rear - Admiral Americo de Deus Rodrigues Tomas	1958–

Positive Rays discovered, 1886, by Goldstein.

Post Office (Britain). The first English postmaster of whom there is any account is Sir Brian Tuke, mentioned *c.* 1533; in 1619 Matthew de Quester was appointed 'Postmaster-General of England for foreign parts'; new postal system organized by the Common Council of London, 1649; rates of postage and rights and duties of postmasters settled by Parliament, 1657; Act for erecting and establishing a P. O. passed, 1660. *Penny Post* instituted in London and suburbs by William Dockwra, 1680; annexed to the crown revenues department, 1690: new Penny Postage Law introduced through exertions of Rowland Hill, 1839: adhesive stamps invented by James Chalmers, 1834, first issue, 6 May 1840; new general P. O. at St. Martin's-le-Grand opened, 1830; extensions, 1873, 1891; public office removed to King Edward Street, 1910. Pillar boxes first erected (at St. Helier, Jersey), 1852. The red cylindrical pattern generally adopted, 1876. Act of 1959 made provision for considerable further capital development by the P.O. Biggest robbery suffered by the P. O. took place in a hold-up of the Glasgow–London mail train in Buckinghamshire, Aug. 1963, when over £2,500,000 was stolen.

Post Office Life Assurance Scheme initiated, 1864. Abandoned for lack of support, 1928.

Post Office Savings Bank established in Britain, 1861.

Potassium. First isolated by Davy in 1807.

Potato introduced into Britain from America by Sir Walter Raleigh in sixteenth century. Crop failure caused famine in Ireland, 1846 and 1847.

Potsdam Agreement, result of conference between Churchill, Attlee, Truman, and Stalin at P., 16 July–1 Aug. 1945.

Poynings' Law. Called after Sir Edward P. (1459–1521), lord-deputy of Ireland; passed, 13 Sept. 1494; this law made the Irish legislature subordinate to and completely dependent on the English Privy Council. Repealed, Apr. 1782.

Poznan (Pol.) or **Posen** (Ger.). Town known as the seat of an episcopal see from 968, which became fused with that of Gniezno in the twelfth century. Province or voivodship ceded to Prussia in first and second partitions of 1772 and 1793 (*see* POLAND). Assigned to Poland by Treaty of Versailles, 1919. Annexed by Germany, Sept. 1939. Reassigned to Poland, 1945.

Praemunire, Statutes of, passed, 1353 and 1392, for the purpose of restricting papal authority in England.

Praetorian Guard, regular but extralegionary cohorts, nine of which were raised by Augustus, 2 B.C. Their barracks NE. of the Palatine at Rome were laid out in the reign of Tiberius (A.D. 14–37). The corps was disbanded by Constantine, 312.

Pragmatic Sanctions. 1. 1385. Against papal interference in the French Church. **2.** Of Bourges, 1438, imposed limits on papal authority in France; temporarily annulled, 1461. **3.** 1713. Securing the succession of Maria Theresa to the Austrian lands. Ratified by Prussia, 1728. By majority of other German states, 1735. Prussia's disregard of the P. S. caused the War of the Austrian Succession (*q.v.*). **4.** Of Naples, 1759, when Charles II of Spain made Naples over to his third son.

Prague, Czechoslovakia. Founded *c.* 600. Became a bishopric, 973. Rebuilt by Charles IV, 1348. Captured by Swedes, 1648. By French, 1741. By Prussians, 1744. Treaty of P. ended Austro-Prussian War, 23 Aug. 1866. Germans seized P., 15 Mar. 1939. Liberated, 10 May 1945.

Prayer, Book of Common. First P. B. of Edward VI, 1549; second P. B. of Edward VI, 1552. Revised, 1559; suppressed, 1645; restored, 1660; and revised, 1662. A further revision, completed 1927, was placed before Parliament, passed by the Lords, but rejected by the Commons. Steps taken to initiate revision of certain parts of the prayer book since 1960. *And see* PROTESTANT EPISCOPAL CHURCH.

Preference, Imperial. I. P. on articles produced in and consigned from the British Empire instituted by Finance Act, 1919; extended by Finance Acts, 1925 and 1926. Whole subject discussed at Imperial and Imperial Economic Conferences, Oct.–Nov. 1923. Australia gave Canada P., 1924. I. P. much weakened by Commonwealth economic development after World War II; and its vestiges would presumably disappear if

Britain ever entered the Common Market (*q.v.*). *See also* TARIFFS.

Premium Bonds. Form of government savings bond introduced by Harold Macmillan, then Chancellor of the Exchequer, in the Budget of 1956.

Premonstratensians. Order founded by St. Norbert *c.* 1120, and following the Augustinian Rule.

Pre-Raphaelite School of Painting. Founded *c.* 1850 by John Everett Millais (1829–96), William Hunt (1827–1910), Dante Gabriel Rossetti (1828–82).

President of the Council, Lord. Became a political office, 1680.

Press Association, The. Founded, 1868. *See also* REUTERS NEWS.

Pretoria. Founded, 1855, by Marthinus Wessels Pretorius (1819–1901). Became capital of Transvaal (*q.v.*), 1860. Surrendered to Lord Roberts, 1900. Became administrative capital of Union of S. Africa, 1909. University founded, 1930.

Pride's Purge. The name given to the expulsion and arrest of certain members of Parliament who opposed the trial of Charles I. Col. Pride, at the head of two parliamentary regiments, on 6 Dec. 1648, effected the 'purge.'

Prime Minister. This office existed in England, *de facto*, from 1710, but its existence was first officially recognized and its holder given a definite precedence, 1905. A deputy P. M. (R. A. Butler) was officially named for the first time, 13 June 1962. *And see* ADMINISTRATIONS.

Prime Ministers' Meetings. *See under* IMPERIAL CONFERENCE.

Primitive Methodism. *See* METHODISTS.

Primrose League. Conservative association founded, 1883, in memory of Disraeli.

Prince Edward Island, Canada. Discovered by Cabot, 1497; possessed by French, 1603; captured by Great Britain from French, 1758; admitted to Dominion of Canada, 1873.

Princeton. University founded, 1746. Moved from Elizabethtown to P., 1756.

Printing, Origins of. Practised by the Chinese in very early times (*see* ENGRAVING); the origin of the present system seems to be very doubtful, though recent evidence points not to Gutenberg (1397–1468), once accepted as the first printer from movable type, but to Laurens Coster of Haarlem, who printed from wood blocks in 1440. Gutenberg, however, appears to have been the first European to make a practical business of P. from movable types.

Privateering. *See* LETTERS OF MARQUE.

Privy Council (England). By an Act passed, May 1612, P. Councillors took precedence after Knights of the Garter; dissolved on the demise of the crown; in 1679 the council was remodelled and the P. Councillors by this Act held office for six months after the sovereign's death. (*See* COUNCIL.) The whole P. C. has not met except at an accession since 1839, when Queen Victoria's impending marriage was declared in Council.

Prize Money originated in England before 1243. Paid for the last time in the Royal Navy, 1945.

Probate Court began separate existence under Judicature Act, 1873.

Probation for first offenders first introduced in Massachusetts, 1878. Became legally recognized in England under the Probation of Offenders Act, 1907.

Production, Ministry of, set up, 1942. Merged with Board of Trade (*q.v.*), 1945.

Profiteering. Act to check excessive profits passed, Aug. 1919. Attempts to stop P. during World War II by Prices of Goods Act, 1939, and the Goods and Services (Price Control) Act, 1941.

Profits Tax. First introduced as a temporary tax, and called the National Defence Contribution, by Neville Chamberlain, 1937.

Prohibition. Voting in Scotland in connection with Scottish Temperance Act, 1920, resulted as a whole in the maintenance of existing conditions, although certain towns and districts voted for and received complete 'local veto,' and others suffered a reduction in the number of licences. P. introduced in Sweden, 1922, and in modified form in Norway, 1922. Abolished in Finland, 1932, in Norway, 1946, in Sweden, 1955. P. in America lasted from 1920 until 1933. P. virtually total in India from 1950 onwards; but by 1962 being relaxed in some areas, e.g. the Punjab. *See* U.S.A., CONSTITUTION OF.

Promenade Concerts, first given in Queen's Hall, 10 Aug. 1895, and continued there until the hall's destruction by bombing, 1941. Since then held in the Albert Hall.

Propaganda or De Propaganda Fide. An institution of the Roman Catholic Church at Rome, founded for the propagation of the Roman Catholic faith originally by Pope Gregory XIII (1572–84), but more fully developed by Gregory XV, 1622.

Propaganda, Ministry of. Established in Germany under Goebbels, 1936–45.

Propagation of the Gospel, Society for, founded by royal charter, 1701.

Protectorates, British (several of which have since had a change of status). Basutoland,* 1868; Bechuanaland,* 1895; Brunei, 1888; Johore, 1914; Malay

---

* Nominally not P., but High Commission Territories.

States, Federated (Perak, Selangor, Pahang, Negri Sembilan), 1874; Malay States, Unfederated (Kedah, Perlis, Kelantan, Trengganu), 1909; N. Borneo, 1881; Nyasaland, 1891 (called British Central Africa until 1907); Solomon Islands, 1893; Somaliland, 1884; Swaziland, 1890; Tonga Island, 1899; Uganda, 1894; Zanzibar, 1890.

Protestant Episcopal Church. American form of Anglicanism, introduced into Virginia, 1607. Movement for union of all its American branches began *c.* 1784. Its first bishop (of New York) consecrated *in London*, 1786. Its prayer book revised, 1789, 1892, 1928.

Protestantism. *See* REFORMATION.

Provençal and Catalan Writers.

Aldobrandini of Florence, Provençal (Italian), thirteenth century.
Anellier, Guillaume, Provençal, *fl. c.* 1280.
Aribau, Carlos, Catalan, 1798–1862.
Bernard of Ventadour, Provençal, mid twelfth century.
Bertran de Born, Provençal, *c.* 1170–1200.
Brueys, Claude, Provençal, 1570–1650.
Brunetto Latini, Provençal (Italian), thirteenth century.
Carner, José, Catalan, *b.* 1554.
Cortete, François de, Provençal, 1571–1655.
Costa y Llebera, Miguel, Catalan, 1854–1922.
Daniel, Arnaut, Provençal, late twelfth century.
Favre, Abbé, Provençal, 1729–83.
Folquet of Marseilles, Provençal, *c.* 1150–1231.
Gaillard, Augor, Provençal, 1530–95.
Ganos, Gaston Pey de, Provençal, *fl.* 1565.
Ganulin, Faidit, Provençal, late twelfth century.
Girant of Borneil, Provençal, twelfth century.
Goudelin, Pierre, Provençal, 1579–1649.
Guimerá, Angel, Catalan, 1849–1924.
Iglesias, Ignacio, Catalan, 1871–1928.
Lull, Ramon, Catalan, *c.* 1235–1315.
Maragall, Juan, Catalan, 1860–1911.
Marcubru, Provençal, *fl.* 1140.
March, Ausias, Catalan, 1379–1459.
Metge, Bernat, Catalan, ? 1350–after 1410.
Mila y Fontanals, Manuel, Catalan, 1818–1884.
Mistral, Frédéric, Provençal, 1830–1914.
Mutaner, Ramon, Catalan, 1265–1336.
Peter of Auvergne, Provençal, twelfth century.
Rigaud, Auguste, Provençal, 1760–1835.
San Jordi, Jordi de, Catalan, end fourteenth century–before 1430.
Satoly, Nicholas, Provençal, 1614–75.

Verdagner, Mosén Jacinto, Catalan, 1845–1902.
Vidal de Besalù, Raimon, Provençal, mid twelfth–early thirteenth century.
Vidal of Toulouse, Peire, late twelfth century.
William IX, count of Poitiers, Provençal, eleventh century.

Provisors, Statute of, passed, 1350, to prevent papal pretensions to the disposition of ecclesiastical benefices in England.

Prussia. *See* BRANDENBURG. Albert of Hohenzollern, Grand Master of the Teutonic Knights, converts P. into a secular duchy, 1525. Treaties of mutual succession with Silesia, 1537. Pomerania, 1571. Arrangement of Gera, 1599. P. comes under Brandenburg as a Polish fief, 1618. Poland renounces suzerainty at Treaty of Wehlau, 1657. Defeat of Swedes at Fehrbellin, 1675. Frederick of Brandenburg crowned king of P., 18 Jan. 1701. By Treaty of Stockholm with Sweden acquires W. Pomerania, 1720. P. guarantees Pragmatic Sanction (*q.v.*), 1728. Frederick the Great invades Silesia, 1740. Obtains Silesia by Treaty of Berlin, 1742. Second Silesian War, 1744–6. Treaty of Aix-la-Chapelle, 1748. Frederick invades Saxony and starts the Seven Years War, 1756–63. Austria finally recognizes Prussian acquisition of Silesia at Treaty of Hubertusburg, 1763. First Partition of Poland, 1772. Declaration of Pilnitz against French revolutionaries, 1791. Second Partition of Poland, 1793. Third Partition of Poland, 1795. Joins Northern Confederacy against Britain, 1800. Occupies Hanover, 1801. Defeated by Napoleon at Jena and Auerstädt, 1806. Congress of Vienna gave P. large additions in Rhineland and Saxony, 1815. Organizes the Zollverein (*q.v.*) 1818 onwards. War with Denmark, 1848. Convention of Olmütz, 1850. Austro-Prussian attack on Denmark, 1864. Austro-Prussian War, 16 June–26 July 1866. Franco-Prussian War, 19 July 1870. King William I proclaimed German Emperor at Versailles, 18 Jan. 1871. (*See* GERMANY.) Proclaimed a republic, 9 Nov. 1918. Nazis take over by force, 20 July 1932. P. liquidated by Allied Control Council, Feb. 1946. Of the territory called P. at its greatest extent, E. P. was joined to Russia in 1945, W. P. (Pomerelia) to Poland at the same date. Now, of the remaining territory, Brandenburg and Sachsen-Anhalt remained in the Soviet zone, as provinces, while the more westerly territory was divided so as to include the former Rhenish P. with other lands.

Kings of Prussia:

Frederick I	1701–1713
Frederick William I	1713–1740
Frederick II	1740–1786
Frederick William II	1786–1797
Frederick William III	1797–1840
Frederick William IV	1840–1861
William I (became German Emperor, 1871)	1861–1888

Public Debt. *See* NATIONAL DEBT.

Public Health Acts in England and Wales passed 1848, 1875, 1936.

Public Order Act, banning political uniforms, etc., passed, 1936. Resurgence of fascist groups in Britain, 1962, led to this act being enforced again for the first time for several years, and suggestions that it should be strengthened were put forward.

Public Prosecutor. Office separated from that of Solicitor to the Treasury 1908.

Public Schools (British), for boys: with their dates of foundation. For this purpose 'public school' is defined as one of the establishments whose principals attend the Headmasters' Conference, which first met, 1869, annually until 1879, thereafter biennially.

1. *England and Wales:*

Abingdon. Re-endowed, 1563. But a school existed as part of the abbey (founded, 675) down to the Reformation
Aldenham, 1597
Alleyn's, 1619
Allhallows, Rousdon, 1515 (grammar school since 1614)
Ampleforth, 1802
Ardingly, 1858
Arnold, Blackpool, 1870
Ashville College, Harrogate, 1877
Bablake, 1344; refounded, 1560
Bancroft's (Draper's Company, Woodford Green), 1737
Barnard Castle, 1883
Beaumont College, Windsor, 1861
Bedford existed in reign of Henry II (1133–89), but probably much older. Royal licence, 1552
Bedford Modern, endowed, 1566
Berkhamsted, between 1509 and 1547
Birkenhead, 1860
Bishop's Stortford, 1868
Blackburn, Queen Elizabeth's, 1509 re-established, 1567
Bloxham, 1860
Blundell's, Tiverton, 1604
Bolton, 1524
Bootham, 1823
Bradfield College, 1850
Bradford Grammar School, 1548

Brecon, Christ College, 1541
Brentwood, 1557
Brighton College, 1845
Bristol Grammar School, 1532
Bromsgrove, 1553; refounded, 1693
Bruton, King's School, 1519 (suppressed, 1538–50)
Bryanston, 1928
Canford, 1923
Carlisle Grammar, 1170; refounded, 1541
Caterham, 1811
Charterhouse, 1609–27
Cheltenham, 1841
Chester, King's School, 1541
Chigwell, 1629
Christ's Hospital, 1552
City of London, 1442
Clayesmore, 1896
Clifton, 1862
Coventry, King Henry VIII School, 1545
Cranbrook, 1520
Cranleigh, 1863
Culford, 1881
Dartmouth (R.N.C.), 1905. Absorbed Osborne, 1921
Dauntsey's, 1543
Dean Close, Cheltenham, 1884
Denstone, 1868
Douai, Woolhampton, 1818–1903 at Douai. Refounded successor to school of St. Edmund, Paris, 1615–1793
Dover, 1871
Downside, *c.* 1605
Dulwich, 1619
Durham, 1414
Eastbourne, 1867
Elizabeth College, Guernsey, 1563
Ellesmere, 1879
Eltham, 1842
Ely, King's School, *c.* 1000; re-endowed, 1541
Emanuel, 1594
Epsom, 1853
Eton, 1440
Exeter, 1333; refounded, 1633
Felsted, 1564
Forest School, 1834
Framlingham, 1864
Giggleswick, 1512
Gresham's, Holt, 1555
Haberdasher's Aske's, Elstree, 1690
Haileybury, 1862; absorbed Imperial Service College, (founded 1912), 1942
Harrow, 1571
Hereford Cathedral School, before 1381
Highgate, 1565
Hulme's Grammar School, Manchester, 1887
Hurstpierpoint, 1849
Hymer's College, Hull, 1889
Ipswich, 1400
Jersey, Victoria College, 1852
Kelly College, 1867
King Edward's, Birmingham, 1552
King's, Canterbury, 600

King's College School. 1829
Kingston Grammar, 1561
Kingswood, 1748
Lancaster Royal Grammar, before 146^
Lancing, 1848
Latymer, Hammersmith, 1624
Leeds Grammar, 1552
Leighton Park, 1890
Leys, Cambridge, 1875
Lincoln, c. 1090
Liverpool College, 1840
Llandovery, 1848
Lower School of John Lyon, Harrow, 1876
Lytham, King Edward VII's, 1908
Macclesfield, King's School, 1502
Magdalen College School, Oxford, 1478
Maidstone Grammar, 1549
Malvern, 1865
Manchester Grammar, 1515
Marlborough, 1843
Merchant Taylors', Crosby, 1670
Merchant Taylors', Northwood, 1561
Mill Hill, 1807
Monkton Combe, 1868
Monmouth, 1615
Mount St. Mary's, 1842
Newcastle under Lyme, High School, 1874
Newcastle upon Tyne, Dame Allan's, 1705
Newcastle upon Tyne, Royal Grammar, 1545
Norwich, before 1256; refounded, 1547
Nottingham High School, 1513
Oakham, 1584
Oldham, Hulme, 1611
Oundle, 1556
Owen's, 1613
Perse School for Boys, 1615
Plymouth College, 1854 (as Mannamead)
Pocklington, York, 1514
Pontypool, Jones's, W. Monmouthshire, 1614
Portsmouth Grammar, 1732
Radley, 1847
Ratcliffe, 1844
Reading, 1125
Repton, 1557
Rochester, King's, 1542
Rossall, 1844
Royal Masonic, Bushey, 1789
Rugby, 1567
Rydal, 1885
St. Albans, between 948 and 1097
St. Bees, 1583
St. Benedict's, 1902
St. Dunstan's, 1446
St. Edmund's, Canterbury, 1749
St. Edward's, Oxford, 1863
St. John's, Leatherhead, 1851
St. Lawrence College, 1879
St. Olave's and St. Saviour's Grammar. St. Olave's (1561) was united to St. Saviour's (1559), 1899
St. Paul's, 1509

St. Peter's, York, 627
Sebright, 1620
Sedbergh, 1525
Sevenoaks, 1418
Sherborne, 705–9; refounded, 1550
Shrewsbury School, 1552
Silcoate's, Wakefield, 1820
Solihull, 1560
Stamford, 1532
Stockport, 1487
Stonyhurst, 1794 (from Flanders where founded, 1593)
Stourbridge, King Edward's, 1430
Stowe, 1923
Sutton Valence, 1576
Taunton, 1847
Taunton, King's College, 1293
Tonbridge, 1553
Trent, 1866
Truro, 1879
University College School, 1830
Uppingham, 1584
Wakefield Grammar, 1591
Warwick, 914; refounded, 1545
Wellingborough, 1595
Wellington College, 1859
Wellington School, 1842
Westminster School, before 1339; refounded, 1560
Whitgift, Croydon, 1596
Whitgift, Croydon, Middle School, 1857
Winchester, 1394
Winchester, Peter Symond's, 1607
Wolverhampton Grammar, 1512–15
Woodhouse Grove, Bradford, 1812
Worcester, King's School, 1541
Worcester Royal Grammar, 1291
Wordsworth's, Bishop, Salisbury, 1890
Worksop, 1895
Wrekin, 1880
Wycliffe, 1882
Wycombe, High, Royal Grammar, 1545–1553
York, Archbishop Holgate's Grammar, 1546

2. Scotland:

Daniel Stewart's, Edinburgh, 1855
Edinburgh Academy, 1824
Fettes, 1870
George Heriot's, 1628
George Watson's, 1723
Gordonstoun (ex-Salem), 1934
Loretto, 1827
Glasgow Academy, 1846
Merchiston Castle, 1833
Robert Gordon's, 1729
Strathallan, 1912
Trinity College, Glenalmond, 1847

3. Northern Ireland:

Campbell College, Belfast, 1894
Portora Royal, Enniskillen, 1608
Royal Academical Institution, Belfast, 1810

4. *Isle of Man:*

King William's College, 1668

5. *Republic of Ireland:*

St. Columba's College, Rathfarnham 1843

Public Trustee office opened, 1908, under Official Trustee Act, 1906.

Public Works Loan Board created, 1817. Regulated by P. W. L. Act, 1897, and Local Authorities Loan Act, 1945.

Puerto Rico, formerly **Porto Rico,** discovered by Columbus, 1493; explored by Ponce de Léon, 1508. Ceded to U.S.A. by Spain, 1898. Constitution established by 'Jones Act,' 1917; amended, 1947. Governor elected quadrennially, from 1948. Considerable emigration to U.S. mainland since 1930. National agitation led to an attempt on President Truman's life, 1950.

Pullman Coaches. Invented by G. M. P. of New York (1831–97). First car built, 1859.

Punjab. Invaded by Alexander the Great, 326 B.C. Devastated by Genghiz Khan, A.D. 1221. Ruled by Mogul emperors, 1556–1707. Sikh kingdom under Ranjit Singh, 1799–1820. *See*

SIKHS. War against the British, 1845 and 1848–9, who annexed P., 1849. Lieutenant-Governor appointed, 1859. Severe plagues between 1896 and 1910. Provincial autonomy introduced, 1937. Communal rioting began, Mar. 1947. Partitioned between India and Pakistan, 14 Aug. 1947, into E. and W. P.

Purchase Tax imposed first by the Finance Act, 1940. Came into effect, 21 Oct. 1940.

Puritans. Name first derisively given to Anglicans who, between 1564 and 1569, wished to purge the established ecclesiastical system from so-called popish abuses. Earliest P. thus a party within the established Church. In the later seventeenth century the term came to be applied to dissenters outside the Church of England, e.g. Congregationalists, Baptists, Quakers, etc.

Pythian Games, originally held every nine, later every four, years. Regulated by Amphictyonic Council after 586 B.C. Coincided with the third year of each Olympiad (*see under* OLYMPIA). Laurel wreath first awarded to victor, 582.

Pyx, Trial of the, dates from the reign of Edward I (1272–1307).

ADDENDA

Q

Qatar, state in the Persian Gulf; its relations with Britain governed by the treaty of 3 Nov. 1916.

Quadi, a tribe living to the E. of the Marcomanni, and classified by Latin writers as 'Suevi,' i.e. nomadic Germans. They rebelled against Rome, A.D. 167, and again, 171, but were finally crushed, 173.

Quadrille. 1. Country dance of French origin, introduced into England, 1818. 2. Card game, became fashionable in England *c.* 1726, and remained so until the introduction of whist (*q.v.*) into upperclass families.

Quadruple Alliance. 1. England, France, Austria, Holland, 1718. 2. Britain, France, Portugal, and Spain, 1834.

Quakers or **Society of Friends.** Founded by George Fox between 1647 and 1666; the name 'Quaker' was given to the sect by Mr. Justice Bennet, 1650, who was admonished by Fox to tremble at the word of the Lord; first meeting-house was opened in London, 1650. Q. in America, 1656. Their 'affirmation of the truth' was declared by Act of Parliament to be sufficient in place of the usual oaths in courts of justice, 1696; and for municipal offices, 1828 and 1837. Nobel Peace Prize awarded jointly to the American Friends' Service Committee and the Friends' Service Council, in recognition of Quaker work for international reconciliation, 1947.

Quantum Theory. First expounded by Max Planck, 1900. Applied by Niels Bohr, 1913, to gases and the frequency of light emitted. New Q. T. evolved by de Broglie, 1924.

Quarter Sessions. Established, 1363. Regulated, 1831.

'Quarterly Review.' First published by John Murray to counteract the Whig *Edinburgh Review,* Feb. 1809. Edited till 1824 by William Gifford (1756–1826).

Quebec, Canada. Town and province. Town founded by Champlain, 1608; captured by Britain, 1629; restored to France, 1632; finally captured by British under Gen. Wolfe, 13 Sept. 1759; formally ceded to Britain by Treaty of Paris, 1763; the 'Quebec Act' of 1774 gave the French-Canadians the right to exercise their customs, laws, and religion. Province united with Ontario, 1841. Separated and made a province of the new dominion, 1867. Boundary extended, 1912.

Queen Anne's Bounty. Instituted in 1703 for the relief of the poor clergy. Queen Anne devoted the funds arising from first fruits and tithes which were at her disposal to this object. United with the Ecclesiastical Commissioners, 1947, since when functions of both bodies have been exercised by the Church Commissioners, instituted that year for the purpose.

Queen Charlotte Island. *See* BRITISH COLUMBIA.

Queen Mary Land, in Antarctica, was discovered by the Australasian Antarctic Expedition of 1911–14. The Shackleton expedition took possession of Q. M. L. for the British crown, 1912.

Queen Mary's Army Auxiliary Corps. Formed, 1917. Disbanded, 1920.

Queen Maud Land in Antarctica, is Norwegian territory, with effect from 14 Jan. 1939. The Anglo - Scandinavian Antarctic expedition was based there, 1949–51.

Queen Victoria Memorial (Buckingham Palace). Unveiled, 16 May 1911.

Queensberry Plot. In Mar. 1703 a pardon was granted to the Jacobites who would take the oath to Queen Anne; Lord Lovat took advantage of the pardon, but his name was forged to a letter which would have led to disgrace and perhaps death; the fraud was discovered, and the Duke of Q., who was a party, had to resign his office as High Commissioner.

Queensberry Rules of boxing drawn up by eighth Marquess of Q., 1867.

Queensferry was the site of the earliest bishopric in Scotland from 681 to 685.

Queensland, Australia. Visited by Captain Cook, 1770. Explored, 1823. Divided from New S. Wales, 1859.

Queens of England. *See* ENGLISH SOVEREIGNS AND CONSORTS.

Quetta, Pakistan. British Residency established at, 1876. Disastrous earthquake, 31 May 1935.

Quia Emptores, a statute passed in 1290 to stop the practice of subinfeudation.

Quintuple Treaty, guaranteeing Belgian integrity, signed by Austria, France, Great Britain, Russia, and Prussia, 1839.

Quoits originated in the fifteenth century. Still played in Scotland and N. England.

343

R

R. 101. *See* AIRSHIPS.

Rack. This instrument of torture is thought to have been introduced into England by John Holland, Duke of Exeter (1352–1400). Its use was declared illegal in 1628.

Radar (for Radio Detection and Ranging). The principle—that of reflected short range wireless waves—became generally known shortly after 1920. The Appleton Layer from which waves are reflected was discovered in 1928. Sir Robert Watson-Watt projected aircraft detection apparatus, 1935, and first R. station in world set up in Britain. Range increased to 150 miles, 1938. Belt of coastal systems almost complete in 1939. Cavity magnetron invented, 1940. Germans captured intact Coastal Command anti-submarine R. set, 1942, enabling U-Boats to carry counter-device which was defeated, 1943, by new shorter-wave detection beam carried in aircraft.

Radcliffe College (Cambridge, Mass., U.S.A.). A college for women, founded 1878, and part of Harvard University; named after Annie R., the first woman who left money to Harvard University.

Radiation. Theory first developed by Max Planck (1858–1947), 1900.

Radical. The word applied to a political party was probably originated by a speech by Charles J. Fox in 1797, when he referred to the necessity for 'R. reform.'

Radioactivity discovered, 1896, by Henri Becquerel (1852–1908).

Radiometer invented, 1873–6, by Sir W. Crookes.

Radium. Mme Marie Curie's investigations, on her taking the principle of radioactivity as subject for her doctorate degree, led her and her husband (1859–1906) to the discovery, in 1898, of R. Its burning effect on human tissue accidentally discovered by Becquerel, 1901; and a 'Laboratoire biologique du R.' was established in Paris in 1906; similar laboratory in London in 1909. Mme Curie (1867–1934) and André Debierne isolated metallic R. from its chloride in 1910.

Ragged Schools, first opened in Portsmouth, 1820. R. S. Union founded, 1844, by Earl of Shaftesbury (then Lord Ashley). Discontinued after the Education Act, 1870 (*q.v.*). *And see* SUNDAY SCHOOLS.

Railways (Britain). First line opened for passenger and general traffic was Stockton–Darlington, 1825. Also authorized in that year was the Canterbury–Whitstable Railway, closed 1 Dec. 1952. Except for metropolitan R., grouped in four main systems: London, Midland, and Scottish; London and N. Eastern Railway; Great Western Railway; and the Southern Railway by Act of 1921 as from 1 Jan. 1923. Metropolitan systems were united under the London Passenger Transport Board as from 1 July 1933 (replaced by London Transport Executive, 1948, renamed the London Transport Board, 1963). All R. were nationalized by Act of 1947 as from 1 Jan. 1948. as British R. under railway executive. Considerable closures of branch lines forecast by the chairman of the Transport Commission, Dr. Beeching, 1962, and further details of these were announced in his report, published Apr. 1963. New structure of railway boards established, 1963.

Rajasthan, a union of Indian states approximately the same as the former Rajputana. First nine states united, Apr. 1948. Jaipur, Jodhpur, Bikaner, and Jaisalmer then joined union, and formal inauguration celebrated, 30 Mar. 1949. Redrawing of state boundaries, 1956.

Rand. *See* TRANSVAAL, SOUTH AFRICA.

Ranelagh pleasure garden at Chelsea laid out, and wooden rotunda built, 1742. Decline set in *c.* 1788. Closed down, 1804.

Ranelagh polo club, Barnes, founded, 1894.

Rangoon, made Burmese capital, 1752, on site first inhabited, A.D. 746, near Shwe Dagon Pagoda; this building last modified in sixteenth century A.D. E. India Co. factory established, 1790. Town rebuilt, 1841. Captured by British, 1852. First bombed by Japanese, 4 Jan. 1942. Civilian evacuation ordered, 21 Feb.; abandoned by troops, 7 Mar.; Japanese marched in next day. Reoccupied by British and Indian troops, 3 May 1945. Instrument of surrender for all imperial Japanese forces in Burma signed here, 13 Sept. 1945.

Rapallo, Treaty of. 1. Between Italy and Yugoslavia. Settled Italo-Yugoslav frontiers, Nov. 1920. 2. Between Germany and the Soviet Union, for the mutual renunciation of reparations and the re-establishment of diplomatic and economic relations, 18 Apr. 1922.

Rationing. *See* FOOD CONTROL.

Ravenna. Became seat of W. Empire, 404; conquered by Belisarius, 540, and seat of the exarchs of the E. Empire from 553 until 752, when it was sacked by the Lombards. Pepin forced the Lombard king to bestow the exarchate on the Pope, 756. Subject to Venice, 1441; again part of the papal states, 1509.

Reading. Danish Army under Ivar and Ubbe quartered here, 871. Abbey founded, 1121; consecrated, 1164. University college became University of R., 1926.

Receiver in Bankruptcy. The Official R.'s department was established in 1914, and its administration regulated by Acts of that year, of 1926, and of 1929.

Rechabites, Independent Order of, established, 25 Aug. 1835; inspired by a Jewish sect of pastoral ascetics of the same name who *fl.* tenth century B.C.

Recife, or **Pernambuco,** Brazil. Founded, 1537. Occupied by Dutch, 1624–54, when it was recaptured by the Portuguese.

Reconstruction, Ministry of. Established 21 Aug. 1917, for purpose of submitting to Parliament a policy of reconstruction in acute post-war problems. Wound up, May 1919.

Record Office (London). Founded on the recommendation of a committee of the House of Commons, which first met in 1800; the report of this commission was published, 1837, and resulted in the Public R. O. Act of 1838; the publication of the Calendars of State papers was commenced in 1856.

Red Cross. As a result of the efforts of the Swiss Henri Dunant (1829–1910) the Geneva Conference, 1863–4, by the Convention of 1864, set up the International R. C. with its headquarters at Geneva. The British R. C. Society was founded, 1870, and incorporated, 1908. The American National R. C. was founded, 1881, and reincorporated, 1893.

Red River Settlement in the present Manitoba province was made on land sold to Thomas Douglas, the fifth earl, of Selkirk (1771–1820) by the Hudson's Bay Co., 1811. Wars between the settlers, landless dispossessed Highland crofters, and the local half-breed population. took place, 1814 and 1815. Treaty with Indians purchasing more land, 1817. Intermittent fighting with local inhabitants, who were led by the North-West Fur Co., continued up to its amalgamation with the Hudson's Bay Co., 1821.

Red Sea Expedition, sent by Wellesley

from India to expel the French from Egypt, 1800.

Reform Acts. 1. The 'Great' R. Act introduced by Lord J. Russell, 1 Mar. 1831, but defeated on amendment. Reintroduced, June 1831, but rejected by the Lords. Introduced a third time, Dec. 1831, but amended out of recognition by the Lords. Government persuaded William IV to threaten wholesale creations of peers, 15 May 1832. Passed by Lords, 4 June, and received royal assent, 7 June 1832. 2. The Second R. Act passed by Disraeli's Government, 1867, conferred household and lodger franchise in boroughs. 3. The Third R. Act by Gladstone, 1884, made household and lodger franchise uniform in U.K. It was followed by a drastic Redistribution of Seats Act, 1885. *See* REPRESENTATION OF THE PEOPLE ACTS.

Reformation. Martin Luther (1483–1546) issues the 95 Theses at Wittenberg in protest against the sale of indulgences, 31 Oct. 1517. He refuses to recant before Cardinal Cajetan at Augsburg, 12 Oct. 1518. He disputes with Eck at Leipzig, 27 June–16 July 1519. He burns papal bull of excommunication, 10 Dec. 1520. Lutherans outlawed by Edict of Worms and Luther retires to the Wartburg, May 1521. Zwingli carries out a R. in Zürich, 1519–25; killed in battle, 1531. Leo X bestows title of 'Defender of the Faith' on Henry VIII, Feb. 1522. Luther's translation of the New Testament appears, Sept. 1522. Philip of Hesse joins the R., 1523. R. in Sweden, Denmark, and Lüneburg, 1527. Henry VIII of England proclaimed Supreme Head of the Church in England, Feb. 1531. Act of Supremacy in England, 1534. Dissolution of the English monasteries, 1536–9. Calvin goes to Geneva, 1536, and his movement supersedes Zwinglianism as the main Protestant force in Switzerland. Cardinal Contarini's attempt at reconciliation, 1540. Calvin organizes the Geneva church and Knox begins R. in Scotland, 1541. Cardinal Beaton murdered in Scotland, 1546. The *Interim* of Augsburg, 15 May 1548. First English Act of Uniformity and Prayer Book, 9 June 1549. Second English Act of Uniformity and Prayer Book, Jan. 1552. Treaty of Passau annuls *Interim*, 2 Aug. 1552. Queen Mary I's counter-R. in England, 1553–8. Religious peace of Augsburg, 25 Sept. 1555. First Covenant signed in Scotland, Dec. 1557. Elizabethan Act of Supremacy, 8 May 1559. Issue of the Gallican Confession by the French Calvinists, May 1559. Scots Parliament abolished papal jurisdiction, Aug. 1560. Knox established Scottish Church, 1561. Netherlands Confession of Faith, 1562. Queen Elizabeth I excommunicated, 25 Feb. 1570. Thirty-nine Articles sanctioned, 1571. Massacre of French Protestants (St. Bartholomew), 23–24 Aug. 1572. Presbyterian system established in Scotland, 1592. Hooker publishes his *Ecclesiastical Polity*, 1594. Edict of Nantes grants toleration to the Huguenots, 13 Apr. 1598. Authorized Version of the Bible appears, 1611. Calvinist Synod of Dort, 1618–19.

Regency Acts (Great Britain). 1. 1751, on death of Frederick, Prince of Wales, appointing Princess of Wales regent in the event of George II's death before the Prince of Wales (i.e. George III—to be) was 18. 2. 1765, on the recovery of George III from his first attack of mental disease. 3. 1788, during the second mental attack of George III. 4. 1810, when the mind of George III finally gave way. 5. 1830, Duchess of Kent appointed regent during minority of Victoria should the latter succeed to the throne before the age of 18. 6. 1837, provided for the carrying on of the Government by lords justices in the event of the Duke of Cumberland, the heir-presumptive, being abroad. 7. 1840, on the marriage of Queen Victoria with Prince Albert; it enacted that in the event of Victoria's demise, and any child of hers succeeding to the throne under the age of 18, Prince

Albert should act as regent. 8. 1910, appointed Queen Mary regent in the event of a child of George V's succeeding to the throne before the age of 18. 9. Acts providing for a regency in the event of the Sovereign dying and leaving an heir who is a minor have subsequently been passed at the beginning of the reigns of George VI and Elizabeth II, the most recent being the Act of 1953, designating the Duke of Edinburgh as regent, should a regency arise during the minority of Queen Elizabeth II's children.

Regent's Park, London. Laid out by John Nash for the Prince Regent, 1812. Park opened to the public, 1838.

Regicides, The. Those who tried and condemned Charles I in 1649; the Bill of Indemnity in 1660 ordered severe penalties against the R.

Regiments of the British Army (U.K. Establishments). The following is a list of British Cavalry and Infantry R. of the line and of the Household, with the dates when they were first raised, the numbers they bore up to 1881, and an account of their reorganization, 1958–61.

Household Cavalry:

First Life Guards, 1660, and Second Life Guards, 1661: Amalgamated, 1922. Each became a *regiment* (not troop as before), 1788.
Horse Guards, 1661 (Ex-Cromwellian Crook's Regiment).

		Horse		*Dragoon Guards*			*Dragoons*	
1	1661	Tangier – – – – –	– – – – – – – –		– –	1	1693	Royals
2	1678	– – – – – – 1	1746	King's		2	1691	Scots Greys
3	1685	– – – – – – 2	1746	Queen's Bays		3	1685	King's Own– – – –
4	1685	– – – – – – 3	1746	Prince of Wales's		4	1685	Queen's Own – –
				(3/6) *				
5	1685	– – – – – – 4	1788	(4/7)		5	1685	Disbanded, 1799
6	1685	– – – – – – 5	1788	Inniskilling (5/6		6	1689	Inniskilling (5/6
				Dragoon Guards)				Dragoon Guards)
7	1685	– – – – – – 6	1691	Carabiniers (3/6)		7	1690	Queen's Own – – –
8	1688	– – – – – – 7	1788	(4/7)		8	1693	– – – – – – – –
						12	1715	– – – – – – – –

		Light Dragoons			*Hussars*			*Lancers*		
3	1715	– – – – – – –	3	1859						
4	1715	– – – – – – –	4	1859						
						5	1859	Re-raised (16/5)		
7	1715	– – – – – – –	7	1805						
8	1715	– – – – – – –	8	1822						
9	1715	– – – – – – – – – – – – – –				9	1806			
10	1715	– – – – – – – 10		1806						
11	1715	– – – – – – – 11		1840						
12	1768	(Prince of Wales's)	– – – – – – – – – –			12	1806			
13	1715	– – – – – – – 13		1861						
14	1715	– – – – – – – 14		1861						
15	1759	– – – – – – – 15		1806						
16	1759	– – – – – – – – – – – – – – –				16	1806	(16/5)		
17	1759	– – – – – – – – – – – – – – – –				17	1806	(17/21)		

* 3rd Carabiniers since 1929.

Light Dragoons		*Hussars*		*Lancers*

18	1763	– – – – – – – 18	1807	
19	1759	19	1861	Ex-East India Company's 1st, 2nd, and 3rd European Cavalry
20	1759	20	1861	
21	1760	21	1861	– – – – – – – – 21 1896 (17/21)
22	1760	Disbanded 1799		
23	1781	– 23 1816 Disbanded
				27 Raised 1941

Foot Guards:

Scots Guards (Third Foot Guards), 1641.
    Totally destroyed at Worcester, 1651.
    Re-raised, 1661, in Scotland. On British Establishment, 1707.

Grenadiers (First Foot Guards). *Émigré* regiment raised, 1656; re-formed, 1660.

Coldstream (Second Foot Guards). Monk's Regiment (1650) entered Charles II's service, 1660.

Irish Guards, 1902.

Welsh Guards, 1915.

No.	Date Raised	Title in 1881
1	1633	Royal Scots.
2	1661	Queen's Royal West Surrey.
3	1665	Buffs (East Kent).
4	1680	Lancaster.
5	1685	Northumberland Fusiliers.
6	1673	Warwickshire (now Royal Warwickshire Fusiliers).
7	1685	Royal (English) Fusiliers.
8	1685	King's Liverpool.
9	1685	Norfolk.
10	1685	Lincolnshire.
11	1685	Devon.
12	1685	Suffolk.
13	1685	Somerset Light Infantry.
14	1685	West Yorkshire.
15	1685	East Yorkshire.
16	1688	Bedfordshire and Hertfordshire.
17	1688	Leicestershire.
18	1684	Royal Irish.
19	1688	The Green Howards.
20	1688	Lancashire Fusiliers.
21	1678	Royal Scots Fusiliers.
22	1689	Cheshire.
23	1689	Royal Welch Fusiliers.
24	1689	South Wales Borderers.
25	1689	King's Own Scottish Borderers.
26	1689	1st Cameronians (Scottish Rifles) (*see* 90).
27	1690	1st Inniskilling Fusiliers (*see* 108).
28	1694	1st Gloucestershire (*see* 61).
29	1694	1st Worcestershire (*see* 36).
30	1702	1st East Lancashire (*see* 59).
31	1702	1st East Surrey (*see* 70).
32	1702	1st Duke of Cornwall's Light Infantry (*see* 46).
33	1702	1st West Riding (*see* 76).

No.	Date Raised	Title in 1881
34	1702	1st Border (*see* 55).
35	1701	1st Royal Sussex (*see* 107).
36	1701	2nd Worcestershire (*see* 29).
37	1702	1st Hampshire (*see* 67).
38	1702	1st South Staffordshire (*see* 80).
39	1702	1st Dorset (*see* 54).
40	1712	1st South Lancashire (Prince of Wales's Volunteers) (*see* 82).
41	1719	1st Welch (*see* 69).
42	1743 ?	1st Black Watch (*see* 73).
43	1741	1st Oxford and Buckinghamshire Light Infantry (*see* 52).
44	1741	1st Essex (*see* 56).
45	1740	1st Sherwood Foresters (*see* 95).
46	1741	2nd Duke of Cornwall's Light Infantry (*see* 32).
47	1741	1st North Lancashire (*see* 81).
48	1741	1st Northamptonshire (*see* 58).
49	1741	1st Royal Berkshire (*see* 66).
50	1755	1st Queen's Own Royal West Kent (*see* 97).
51	1755	1st King's Own Yorkshire Light Infantry (*see* 105).
52	1741	2nd Oxford and Buckinghamshire Light Infantry (*see* 43).
53	1755	1st Shropshire Light Infantry (King's) (*see* 85).
54	1755	2nd Dorset (*see* 39).
55	1755	2nd Border (*see* 34).
56	1755	2nd Essex (*see* 44).
57	1755	1st Middlesex (*see* 77).
58	1750	2nd Northamptonshire (*see* 48).
59	1755	2nd East Lancashire (*see* 30).
60	1755	King's Royal Rifle Corps (formerly Royal Americans).
61	1756	2nd Gloucestershire (*see* 28).
62	1757	1st Wiltshire (*see* 99).
63	1756	1st Manchester (*see* 96).
64	1756	1st North Staffordshire (was 2nd/11th till 1758) (*see* 98).
65	1756	1st York and Lancaster (*see* 84).
66	1756	2nd Royal Berkshire (*see* 49).
67	1756	2nd Hampshire (*see* 37).
68	1756	1st Durham Light Infantry (*see* 106).
69	1756	2nd Welch (*see* 41).

No.	Date Raised	Title in 1881
70	1758	2nd East Surrey (*see* 31).
71	1766	1st Highland Light Infantry (*see* 74).
72	1778	1st Seaforth Highlanders (*see* 78).
73	1786	2nd Black Watch (*see* 42).
74	1787	2nd Highland Light Infantry (*see* 71).
75	1787	1st Gordon Highlanders (*see* 92).
76	1787	2nd West Riding (*see* 33).
77	1787	2nd Middlesex (*see* 57).
78	1793	2nd Seaforth Highlanders (*see* 72).
79	1793	Cameron Highlanders.
80	1793	2nd South Staffordshire (*see* 38).
81	1793	2nd North Lancashire (*see* 47).
82	1793	2nd South Lancashire (*see* 40).
83	1793	1st Royal Irish Rifles (*see* 86).
84	1793	2nd York and Lancaster (*see* 65).
85	1794	2nd Shropshire Light Infantry (King's) (*see* 53).
86	1799	2nd Royal Irish Rifles (*see* 83).
87	1793	1st Royal Irish Fusiliers (*see* 89).
88	1793	1st Connaught Rangers (*see* 94).
89	1794	2nd Royal Irish Fusiliers (*see* 87).
90	1794	2nd Cameronians (Scottish Rifles) (*see* 26).
91	1794	1st Argyll and Sutherland Highlanders (*see* 93).
92	1794	2nd Gordon Highlanders (*see* 75).
93	1800	2nd Argyll and Sutherland Highlanders (*see* 91).
94	1800	2nd Connaught Rangers (*see* 88).
95	1816	2nd Sherwood Foresters (*see* 45).
96	1800	2nd Manchester (*see* 63).
97	1798	2nd Queen's Own Royal West Kent (*see* 50).
98	1824	2nd North Staffordshire (*see* 64).
99	1824	2nd Wiltshire (*see* 62).
100	1858	1st Leinster (*see* 109).
101	1861	1st Munster Fusiliers (*see* 104).
102	1861	1st Dublin Fusiliers (*see* 103).
103	1861	2nd Dublin Fusiliers (*see* 102).
104	1861	2nd Munster Fusiliers (*see* 101).
105	1861	2nd King's Own Yorkshire Light Infantry (*see* 51).
106	1861	2nd Durham Light Infantry (*see* 68).
107	1861	2nd Royal Sussex (*see* 35).
108	1861	2nd Inniskilling Fusiliers (*see* 27).
109	1861	2nd Leinster (*see* 100).

No.	Date Raised	Title in 1881
	1800	1st Rifle Brigade; 1805, 2nd Rifle Brigade, up to 1816 known as 1st and 2nd Battalions, 95th regt. (*q.v.*); 1855, 3rd Rifle Brigade; 1857, 4th Rifle Brigade.

Nos. 101–109 were formerly the European element of the E. India Co.'s Army.

Changes effected in the reorganization of the army, 1958–61.

Apr. 1958: The West Yorkshire Regiment (Prince of Wales's Own) *and* The East Yorkshire Regiment (The Duke of York's Own) *became* The Prince of Wales's Own Regiment of Yorkshire.

May 1958: The Devonshire Regiment *and* The Dorset Regiment *became* The Devonshire and Dorset Regiment.

June 1958: The Bedfordshire and Hertfordshire Regiment *and* The Essex Regiment *became* 3rd East Anglian Regiment (16th/44th Foot).

July 1958: The East Lancashire Regiment *and* The South Lancashire Regiment (The Prince of Wales's Volunteers) *became* The Lancashire Regiment (Prince of Wales's Volunteers).

Sept. 1958: The King's Regiment (Liverpool) *and* The Manchester Regiment *became* The King's Regiment (Manchester and Liverpool).

Oct. 1958: 4th Queen's Own Hussars *and* 8th King's Royal Irish Hussars *became* Queen's Royal Irish Hussars.

Nov. 1958: 3rd The King's Own Hussars *and* 7th The Queen's Own Hussars *became* The Queen's Own Hussars.

Nov. 1958: The Oxfordshire and Buckinghamshire Light Infantry *changed its name to* 1st Green Jackets (43rd and 52nd).

Nov. 1958: The King's Royal Rifle Corps *changed its name to* 2nd Green Jackets (The King's Royal Rifle Corps).

Nov. 1958: The Rifle Brigade *changed its name to* 3rd Green Jackets (The Rifle Brigade).

Jan. 1959: The Royal Scots Fusiliers *and* The Highland Light Infantry (City of Glasgow Regiment) *became* The Royal Highland Fusiliers (Princess Margaret's Own Glasgow and Ayrshire Regiment).

Jan. 1959: The South Staffordshire Regiment *and* The North Staffordshire Regiment (The Prince of Wales's) *became* The Staffordshire Regiment (The Prince of Wales's).

Jan. 1959: 1st King's Dragoon Guards *and* Queen's Bays (2nd Dragoon Guards) *became* 1st The Queen's Dragoon Guards.

Mar. 1959: 4th Royal Tank Regiment

and 7th Royal Tank Regiment *became* 4th Royal Tank Regiment.

June 1959: The Royal Berkshire Regiment (Princess Charlotte of Wales's) *and* The Wiltshire Regiment (Duke of Edinburgh's) *became* The Duke of Edinburgh's Royal Regiment (Berkshire and Wiltshire).

Aug. 1959: The Royal Norfolk Regiment *and* The Suffolk Regiment *became* 1st East Anglian Regiment (Royal Norfolk and Suffolk).

Oct. 1959: The King's Own Royal Regiment (Lancaster) *and* The Border Regiment *became* The King's Own Royal Border Regiment.

Oct. 1959: The Queen's Royal Regiment (West Surrey) *and* The East Surrey Regiment *became* The Queen's Royal Surrey Regiment.

Oct. 1959: The Somerset Light Infantry (Prince Albert's) *and* The Duke of Cornwall's Light Infantry *became* The Somerset and Cornwall Light Infantry.

Oct. 1959: 3rd Royal Tank Regiment *and* 6th Royal Tank Regiment *became* 3rd Royal Tank Regiment.

June 1960: The Royal Lincolnshire Regiment *and* The Northamptonshire Regiment *became* 2nd East Anglian Regiment (Duke of Gloucester's Own Royal Lincolnshire and Northamptonshire).

July 1960: 5th Royal Tank Regiment *and* 8th Royal Tank Regiment *became* 5th Royal Tank Regiment.

Sept. 1960: 9th Queen's Royal Lancers *and* 12th Royal Lancers *became* 9th/12th Royal Lancers (Prince of Wales's).

Feb. 1961: Seaforth Highlanders (Ross-shire Buffs, The Duke of Albany's) *and* The Queen's Own Cameron Highlanders *became* The Queen's Own Highlanders (Seaforth and Cameron).

Mar. 1961: 3rd Battalion Grenadier Guards *was suspended* (1st and 2nd Battalions remaining unchanged).

Mar. 1961: The Buffs (Royal East Kent Regiment) *and* The Queen's Own Royal West Kent Regiment *became* The Queen's Own Buffs, The Royal Kent Regiment.

Regional Commissioners appointed, Feb. 1939, but never assumed their functions, which would have become operative only in the event of successful invasion.

Registers, Parish, were regularly kept in France from about 1308, but in England only since 1538. From 1837 they record only baptisms, marriages, and deaths.

Registrar-General first appointed, 1836, to conduct census and carry on **Registration of Births, Marriages, and Deaths,** which was first generally enforced in England by the Registration Act, 1837,

and extended to Scotland, 1855, and Ireland, 1864. Consolidating Act, 1874, gave rise to the General Registry, Somerset House. Optional shortened form of birth certificate issued, from 1947, which omitted details of parentage.

Regium Donum (royal gift). Originally an annual grant to Nonconformist bodies in Britain and Ireland by the king. In 1690 William III made a grant of £1,200 a year to the Presbyterian ministers in Ireland; which, interrupted, 1711, was resumed, 1715, with amount increased to £2,000. Further increases, 1784 and 1792; and a special grant of £45,000 in 1868. Ceased on passing of Irish Church Act, 1869. This grant was also paid to English Nonconformist clergy from 1721, but withdrawn by mutual consent in 1857.

Regius Professor. All these chairs endowed by Henry VIII, 1546, except that of Modern History at Oxford which George I founded, 1724.

Regulating Act. Introduced by Lord North in 1773 to cause the British Government to interfere in the administration of India.

Regulating Act. Passed by Parliament, 1774, for the subversion of the charter of Massachusetts.

Reichsrat, or Imperial Council, second chamber of several European legislatures, but especially the Upper House of the German legislature, set up under the Weimar Constitution, 1919, as a council of Federal republics; it survived, in theory at least, until 1945.

Reichstag, a modern form of the Imperial Diet (*q.v.*), revived under the régime of Bismarck as the legislature of the N. German Confederation (1867) and then of the German Empire (Reich: 1871). The name and the institution continued little altered under the Weimar Constitution of 1919; though the power of the Upper House (Reichsrat, *q.v.*) was curtailed, the R. never had the initiative as the English Commons in Parliament have had, and in 1933 it yielded to Hitler practically without a struggle. Following the R. elections of 5 Mar. 1933 the trial of certain persons, alleged agents of the Comintern, took place on charges of arson in that they caused the fire whereby the R. building was burnt out, 27 Feb. 1933.

Relativity, Theory of. Einstein's paper on the Special Theory of R. published, 1905. On the General Theory, 1915.

Remonstrance, The Grand. A petition drawn up by Parliament against the cruelty and injustice of Charles I; presented, 1 Dec. 1641.

Remonstrants. The Dutch Protestants

who, in 1610, after the death of Arminius, presented to the Holland and Friesland states a remonstrance in which the doctrines of Calvinism were repudiated; their confession of faith was drawn up in 1621; they were bitterly persecuted, 1625–52, and received official recognition, 1795.

Renaissance. The great cultural movement in Europe after the Middle Ages, representing the emergence of the modern age. It was much more than a revival of old forms, as its name might imply, and its span is such that it is impossible to fix it with dates. The following, however, are relevant: Cimabue's *Madonna della Trinità* completed, 1260. Roger Bacon's *Opus Majus* completed, 1266. Dante completed *La Vita Nuova*, 1292, and *De Monarchia*, 1313, and *Divina Commedia*, 1321. Boccaccio finished the *Decameron*, 1353. Manuel Chrysoloras lectures on Greek at Florence, 1396. Lorenzo Valla, humanist, *b.* 1405, *d.* 1457. Printing reaches Italy, 1456. St. Mark's, Venice, completed, 1484. St. Peter's, Rome, commenced, 1513.

Rennes, capital of Brittany from the ninth century, became an episcopal see in the fifth century. Burnt down and radically replanned, 1720. Second trial of Dreyfus took place here, 1899.

Rent Restriction Acts. Tenants of houses of £30 rateable value protected by Act of Dec. 1915. Extended to £70, Apr. 1919. Security of tenure extended, 1923 and 1925. Extended to £100 in London and £75 outside, 1939 and 1942. Rent tribunals established under the Furnished Houses (Rent Control) Act, 1946. Housing Repairs and Rent Acts of 1954 allowed house-owners to raise rents in order to enable them to spend more on repairs. Rent Act of 1957 drastically cut the number of houses protected by R. R. and subsequently gave rise to some hardship, especially in London and the major industrial cities, a point which was underlined by the Rachman affair, which came to light in 1963.

Reparations. Germany's reparation debt put at £6,600,000,000, 1920. Allied ultimatum, 1921. Germany applied for reductions, Dec. 1921. Moratorium granted, Jan. 1922. London Conference, Aug. 1922. Abortive negotiations among Allies, 1922. French and Belgian forces advanced into the Ruhr, Jan.–Feb. 1923. German passive resistance in Ruhr, Feb.–Sept. 1923. (Lord Curzon's speech, Imperial Conference, 5 Oct. 1923.) Dawes Plan (*q.v.*), 1924. Young Plan (*q.v.*), 20 Jan. 1930. Obligations cancelled, 1932.

Representation of the People Acts. Women over 30 enfranchized, 1918. Extended to all women over 21, 1928. Extension of local franchise, 1945. Act of 1948 abolished plural voting.

Republican Party was formed in 1828 when a faction seceded from the Democratic Party. Modern R. P. really dates from 1854, however, beginning as a union of elements opposed to slavery. First National Convention held, 1856. First R. president — Abraham Lincoln — elected, 1860. Dwight D. Eisenhower, R. candidate, elected president, 1952; held office until 1960, since when the Democrats have filled the presidency.

Resale Price Maintenance. The Restrictive Trades Practices Act, 1956, outlawed collective price maintenance in Britain.

Rescissory Act. Passed by Scottish Parliament, 1661; it was proposed by Sir Thomas Primrose with the object of annulling the Acts establishing Presbyterianism in Scotland.

Restoration, in English context, means the return of Charles II, his family, and court to England in 1660, and his coronation. The 'R. Period' in English literature and arts is usually taken to mean the whole epoch from then until, say, 1700, but *not* to cover the reign of Queen Anne. In French history, means the R. of the Bourbons, and the reigns of Louis XVIII and Charles X (1814–31).

Resurrectionists, *c.* 1826–30, provided anatomical specimens for surgeons, especially in Scotland, by robbing graves; after Burke and Hare were hanged, 1829, for murdering people as an easier alternative to digging, public attention was directed to the R., and an Act of 1832 required licences to be procured for the dissection of human bodies. This did nothing to increase the legitimate supply of specimens (officially the only source was the hangman), and the practice continued for some time after this.

Réunion or **Bourbon,** Indian Ocean. Discovered, 1513, by Portuguese navigator, Pedro Mascarenhas; formally possessed by French, 1643; attacked and captured by British, 1810; restored to France, Apr. 1815. Became an overseas department of France, 1946.

Reuters News (originally **Telegraph Agency**), founded by Baron Julius Reuter (1816–99), who in 1849 at Aachen began to transmit commercial intelligence by pigeon post, and transferred his agency, now working by electric telegraph, to London, 1851. Became a limited liability company, 1865, and a private trusteeship, 1918. In 1947 the company became the joint property, together with the Press Association, of British, Australian, and New Zealand newspaper concerns, joined in 1949 by the Press Trust of India.

Reval. *See* TALLIN.

Revolutionary Tribunal, The. Established in Paris, Oct. 1793, for the trial of criminal cases; it was suppressed, 31 May 1795.

Reykjavik, capital of Iceland. The first settler on the site of the town was Ingolf, who landed in 874. *See* ICELAND.

Rhaetia, Central Alpine region conquered by the Romans, 15 B.C., and organized, as a province. Enlarged by addition of Vindelicia, late first century A.D. Divided into R. Prima and R. Secunda in the reign of Diocletian, A.D. 284–305. R. Prima corresponded to the present Swiss cantons of Grisons, St. Gall, Appenzell, Thurgau, Glarus, parts of Zürich and Schwyz, the Austrian provinces of Vorarlberg and Tirol, and the Italian province of Bolzano. R. Secunda, or Vindelicia, consisted of Swabia and Bavaria N. to the Danube and E. to the Inn. *See* articles on all of the above provinces.

Rheims or **Reims,** France. *Durocortorum* mentioned by Julius Caesar as the capital of the *Remi*; Clovis baptized at, 496; from 1179 to 1825 the sovereigns of France were crowned here. Cathedral built between 1211 and 1430; restored, 1877 *et seq.*; ruined by German bombardment, Sept. 1914; restored and consecrated, 18 Oct. 1937; reopened, 10 July 1938. Ceremony of Franco-German 're-conciliation' held at Rheims, in presence of Adenauer and de Gaulle, July 1962.

Rhine, Confederation of the. *See* CONFEDERATION OF THE RHINE.

Rhineland, or Rheinland, a German region corresponding to Rhenish Prussia (*see* PRUSSIA). Demilitarized under terms of Versailles Treaty; French efforts to form a separatist R. state finally failed in 1924. The demilitarized zone was reoccupied by the Wehrmacht, 7 Mar. 1936. Heavily bombed by the Allies, 1942–5.

Rhode Island, U.S.A. Explored by the Dutch, 1614; commonwealth of R. I. founded, 1636, by Roger Williams; further settlements in 1638, 1643; patent for the government of the settlement granted, 1644; first General Assembly met, 1647; patent confirmed by Cromwell, 1655; charter granted by Charles II, 1663; ratified National Constitution of U.S.A., 29 May 1790. Present constitution dates from 1843.

Rhodes, Dodecanese Islands. Early settled by Dorians. Enrolled in Delian League, fifth century B.C. Revolted from Athens, 412. City of R. built, 408. Great prosperity from 330 onwards. Successful resistance to Demetrius Poliorcetes, 304. Colossus completed, 280;

destroyed, 224. In alliance with Rome, 180–160. Sacked by C. Cassius, 43. Finally ruined by earthquakes, A.D. 155. Occupied by Saracens, 653–8 and 717–18. Conquered by Knights of St. John, 1309. Turkish siege, 1480. Turkish conquest, 1522. Occupied by Italians, 1912 (*see* DODECANESE ISLANDS). Given to Greece, 1947.

Rhodesia. Named after Cecil Rhodes (1853–1902), who founded the British S. Africa Co.; chartered, 1889. The company administered all R. till 1 Oct. 1923, when Southern R. (*q.v.*) received responsible government, and 1 Jan. 1924, when Northern R. (*q.v.*) became a crown colony. Northern and Southern R. federated with Nyasaland, 1 Aug. 1953.

Rhodesia and Nyasaland, Federation of. Came into being in Aug. 1953 despite African opposition, which was particularly strong in Nyasaland (*q.v.*). First Prime Minister, Sir Godfrey Huggins (later Lord Malvern). Sir Roy Welensky succeeded him in 1956. In Feb. 1961 a new draft constitution for the Federation angered many white elements and a White Paper in June 1961 proposed amendments to the draft which in turn angered the Africans. Further amendments, in favour of the Africans, proposed by Britain, 28 Feb. 1962. Welensky visited London, and on his return he dissolved the Federal Parliament and called a General Election for 25 Apr. to give him a mandate to hold the Federation together by force if necessary. African leaders denounced him, but his party returned with a big majority. Developments in Nyasaland and N. Rhodesia in 1962–3 severely undermined the Federation, and Welensky strongly criticized the British Government's decisions to allow the secession of these two constituent parts. In 1963 he visited S. Africa and had talks with Verwoerd. The Victoria Falls Conference, 28 June–4 July 1963, agreed that the Federation should be wound up by the end of the year.

Rhodesia, Northern. Capital moved from Livingstone to Lusaka, 28 May 1935. Decision to give more responsibility to government of Northern R. at London Conference of E. African Governors, Nov. 1947. Constitutional Conference, 1960. New constitution, 1962. First elections under it, Oct. 1962; Kaunda party, which opposed federation, gained great successes, and a coalition government of the two major African parties was formed. In Mar. 1963 Britain agreed in principle to N. Rhodesia's right to secede from the Federation.

Rhodesia, Southern. Franchise extended to adult male British subjects and married women, July 1928. Beit bridge over Limpopo River opened, 31 Aug. 1929. Free trade with S. Africa ended, 18 Feb. 1935. Work begun on railway line connecting Salisbury with Lourenço Marques, Portuguese East Africa, begun, Dec. 1952; completed, 1954. New constitution promulgated, Dec. 1962; opposed by African parties. Zapu party banned in S. R., Sept. 1962, and on the 22nd set up a 'government in exile' in Tanganyika. Sir Hugh Foot resigned as British representative on U.N. Trusteeship Council, Oct. 1962, owing to disagreement with Britain's official policy towards S. R. U.N. voted for suspension of S. R.'s new constitution, 31 Oct. 1962. In Nov. the S. R. United Federal Party pledged an end to racialism in the country, but it was defeated in the elections in Dec., which were won by the Rhodesia Front, led by Winston Field. Field subsequently visited London (1963), to press for immediate independence for S. Rhodesia.

Richborough, the Roman *Rutupiae*, was the beachhead of Claudius's invasion, A.D. 43. A monumental building in honour of the Emperor Domitian, final conqueror of Britain, was erected, 85. Signs of Roman occupation continue into the early fifth century. The port was heavily fortified *c.* 287–93 against Saxon pirates. In modern times the port, practically deserted since the fall of Rutupiae, was used for military purposes almost exclusively as an embarkation port for troops and as train ferry base. In 1943–4 units of the Mulberry harbour and the cross-channel petrol supply pipe, 'PLUTO,' were made at R.

Ridolfi Conspiracy. A Roman Catholic plot instigated by Roberto R., in which the Duke of Norfolk was involved, against Queen Elizabeth, 1571. It arose out of the papal bull *Regnans in Excelsis* against Queen Elizabeth, 25 Feb. 1570. Norfolk was executed with others, June 1572.

Rievaulx Abbey (Yorks). Founded by Cistercians, 1131.

Rifle. Invention of spiral groove attributed among others to J. Koller of Vienna, fifteenth century. Such a rifled weapon is recorded at Guastalla (Italy), 1476. Occasionally found, especially among French troops, in seventeenth century. Introduced by Swiss colonists into America, 1721. A R. factory existed in Pennsylvania, 1754. The British 95th Regiment armed with the Baker R., 1800. General introduction of breachloading Rs. into Prussian Army, 1841–8. Smooth bores abolished in British Army *c.* 1852. Magazine Rs. used in American Civil War, 1861. Lee-Enfield R. introduced to Britain, 1895; British Army

changed to Belgian FN.30 Rs., 1954.

Riga, founded, 1201, by Bishop Albert of Livonia, seat of an archbishopric from 1225. Joined Hanseatic League, 1282, with the same privileges and laws as Hamburg. Came into possession of the Teutonic Knights, 1330, adopted Protestant faith (Lutheran), 1522. Free City of the Empire from the decay of the Teutonic Knights' dominions (1561) until 1582, when it became Polish. Passed to Sweden, 1621; to Russia, 1710; to Latvia, 1919. *See* TREATIES. Leased to U.S.S.R. as military base, 3 Oct. 1939; taken by Germans, 1 July 1941; by Russians, 13 Oct. 1944.

Rights, Bill of (Britain), Oct. 1689. confirmed the Declaration of R. made to William and Mary, Feb. 1689. It affirmed the liberties of the subject and settled the succession.

Rights, Bill of (U.S.A.). The collective name given to the first ten amendments to the U.S. Constitution passed together, 15 Dec. 1791.

Rights of Man, Declaration of. Proclaimed by the French National Assembly, 4 Aug. 1789.

Rio de Janeiro, Brazil. Discovered, 1502, by Coelho. City founded, 1566. Capital of Brazil, 1822.

Rio de Janeiro, Treaty of, 2 Sept. 1947, for the mutual defence of the Americas.

Riot Act (Britain), **1714.**

Ripon, Treaty of, 1640; ended the war between England and Scotland; peace was finally concluded in London, Aug. 1641.

Road Traffic Act, 1962, increased provisions against drunken driving, etc.

Robot (from Czech *robotnik*—worker), a term invented by Karel Čapek in his play *R.U.R.,* 1923. *See* CZECH LITERATURE.

Rochelle, La, France. Became part of English possessions by marriage of Henry II to Eleanor of Aquitaine; taken by Louis VIII of France, 1224; ceded to England, 1360; retaken by France, 1372; resisted siege as Huguenot stronghold, 1573; besieged (1627) and taken by Richelieu, 1628; modern harbour opened, 1890.

Rochester, England. Bishopric founded, 604, by St. Augustine; present cathedral founded, 1077–1107; earliest city charter, 1189; castle of very early construction, captured by King John, 1215; besieged in vain by Simon de Montfort, 1264; captured by Wat Tyler, 1381.

Rockefeller Foundation, endowed by John Davidson R. (1839–1937). Chartered, 1913.

'Rocket, The.' Steam locomotive built by Stephenson, which in Oct. 1829 won the Rainhill competition, and so inaugurated the use of locomotives on the Liverpool and Manchester Railway.

Rockets. As a firework and missile, invented by the Chinese, twelfth–thirteenth centuries A.D. A small rocket missile used by the British in India at the end of the eighteenth century. Modern interest in Rs. dates from c. 1920. First flight of a liquid-propelled R. made at Massachusetts, 1926. Germany did much work on Rs. after 1933 and Rs. were used against Britain from 1944 until 1945. Subsequent research carried out on space Rs. and military Rs. by America and Russia. First man in space was a Russian, 12 Apr. 1961; he orbited the earth; an American made a sub-orbital flight in May. Both countries developed military Rs. Russians claimed to have an anti-missile missile, July 1962; later that month the American anti-missile missile successfully intercepted an Atlas long-range missile. Russia reported to be ahead of the U.S.A. in work on anti-missile missiles, May 1963. See also SPACE FLIGHTS.

Roman Catholics in England. Absolved from allegiance to Henry VIII by Pius III, 1535, to Queen Elizabeth I by Pius V, 1570. Excluded from the throne, 1689. Laws against repealed, 1780, 1791. Catholic Emancipation Act, 13 Apr. 1829. Episcopate re-established 1850.

Roman Emperors before the division of the Empire. Dates of accession only:

Augustus	27 B.C.	Tacitus	275
Tiberius	A.D. 14	Florian	276
Caligula	37	Probus	276
Claudius	41	Carus	282
Nero	54	Carinus } Numerian }	284
Galba } Otho } Vitellius }	68	Diocletian (abdicated 305)	284
Vespasian	68	Maximian associated with Diocletian	286
Titus	79		
Domitian	81		
Nerva	96	Constantius } Galerius }	305
Trajan	98	Severus	306
Hadrian	117	Constantine the Great	306
Antoninus Pius	138	Licinius	307
Marcus Aurelius	161	Maximin	308
Commodus	180	Constantine the Great } Licinius } Maximin } Galerius } Maxentius } Maximian }	Jointly 309
Pertinax } Didius Julianus } Niger }	193		
Septimus Severus	193		
Caracalla } Geta }	211	Constantine alone	323
Macrinus	217		

Elagabalus	218
Alexander Severus	222
Maximin I	235
Gordian I and II } Balbinus } Pupienus }	238
Gordian III	238
Philip	244
Decius	249
Gallus	251
Aemilian } Valerian } Gallienus }	253
Gallienus alone	260
Claudius II	268
Aurelian	270
Constantine II } Constantius II } Constans }	337
Constantius II alone	353
Julian	361
Jovian	363
Valens } Valentinian I }	364
Valentinian I } Gratian }	367
Gratian } Valentinian II }	375
Theodosius the Great	379–95

See also ROMAN EMPERORS (LATER WESTERN) and ROMAN EMPIRE, EASTERN.

Roman Emperors (Later Western). (Usurpers in italics.) (See also ROMAN EMPERORS.)

Honorius	393–423
Constantine III	407–411
Constantius III	421
John	423–425
Valentinian III	425–455
Maximus	455
Avitus	455–456
Majorian	457–461
Severus	461–465
Anthemius	467–472
Olybrius	472
Glycerius	473
Julius Nepos	473–480
Romulus	475–476

NOTE: Romulus surnamed Augustulus is wrongly known as the last R. Emperor in the W.; he was never recognized in the E., and Julius Nepos survived him.

Roman Empire. Organization of by Augustus, 30 B.C.–A.D. 14. Defeat of Romans by Germans under Arminius, A.D. 9. Annexation of Mauritania, 41–2. Of Britain, 43–5. Boudicca's rebellion in Britain, 61. Batavian rising, 69–71. Fortification of the German frontier, 96. Empire reaches its widest extent under Trajan, 98–117. The *Perpetual Edict of Julius Salvianus* drawn up c. 130. Germanic invasion of Italy, 161. Beginning of serious praetorian interference in central government, 193. *Constitutio Antoniniana* extends Roman citizenship to all freeborn subjects, 212. Defeat of Emperor Valerian by Sapor I of Persia, 260. Defeat of the Goths at Nish, 269. Diocletian organizes the R. E. into two great circumscriptions (Eastern and Western), 285. Britain independent under Carausius, 286–93, and under Allectus, 293–6. Constantine legalizes Christianity by the *Edict of Milan*, 313. Defeat of Emperor

Valens by Visigoths at Adrianople, 378. Definite partition of the Empire at death of Theodosius the Great, 395.

Roman Empire, Eastern, or Byzantine Empire. The name given to that part of the R. E. whose capital was at Constantinople and which continued after the end of the Western Imperial line in A.D. 476. For previous history *see* ROME, ROMAN EMPIRE, etc. First schism between Eastern and Western Churches begins, 484. Justinian closes Athens University, 529. Belisarius reconquers N. Africa, 533–4. Invades Italy, 535–40. Narses makes Italy a Byzantine province, 552–5. Hagia Sophia Cathedral consecrated, 563. War with Persia, 572–91. Persians conquer Syria and Palestine, 614; Egypt, 618–19. Heraclius recovers Jerusalem, 629. Arabs under the Caliph Omar defeat Byzantines at battle of the Yarmuk, 634; take Damascus, 635; Jerusalem, 638; Egypt, 639–40; Tripoli, 647; Cyprus, 649. They begin conquest of N. Africa, 670. Arab siege of and defeat at Constantinople, 673–7. Arab raids on Constantinople, 717–19. Lombards take Ravenna from Byzantines, 751. The Iconoclastic controversy, 726–842. Arabs take Crete, 826; and invade Sicily, 827; and S. Italy, 838. Cyril and Methodius convert the Bulgars, 864. Basil I recovers S. Italy, 867–80. Arabs expel Byzantines from Sicily, 902. Saracens attack Salonika, 904. Romanus I (Lecapenus) extends Byzantine Empire to the Euphrates, 920–44. Crete reconquered, 961; and Cyprus, 964–6. Victorious wars under John Zimisces and Basil II (Bulgaroktonos—' Kill-Bulgars ') against Bulgars, 971–1025. Conquest of Armenia, 1045. Disastrous defeat of Romanus IV (Diogenes) by Seljuk Turks at Manzikert and loss of central Anatolia, 1071. Norman invasion of the Balkans, 1081–5. Alexius Comnenus defeats Petchenegs at Leburnium, 1091; and the Cumans at Adrianople, 1095. (*See* CRUSADE (FIRST), 1096–9.) Commercial agreements with Venice, 1126. Venetian merchants excluded, 1171. Seljuks defeat Manuel I at Myriokephalon, 1176. Cyprus becomes independent, 1184. (*See* CRUSADE (THIRD), 1189–93, and CRUSADE (FOURTH) which, led by Venice, captures Constantinople and establishes a Latin Empire, 1204.) (*See* TREBIZOND.) Theodore Lascaris established at Nicaea, 1208. Vatatzes expels Latins from Anatolia, 1224; and captures Salonika, 1246. Michael VIII Palaeologus retakes Constantinople and overthrows Latin Empire, 1261. Osman I (Ottoman) defeats Byzantines at battle of Baphaion, 1301. He takes Brusa, 1326. John VI Cantacuzene, Turkish-supported candidate for imperial

throne, 1347–54. First Turkish settlement in Europe, 1353. Turks take Adrianople, 1357. John V visits the W. to get aid against the Turks, 1366. Final loss of Anatolia, 1390. Defeat by Turks at battle of Nicopolis, 1396. First Turkish siege of Constantinople, 1422. Turks storm Constantinople and bring the Eastern R. E. to an end, 29 May 1453. *See* OTTOMAN EMPIRE.

Eastern Roman Emperors from the Foundation of Constantinople, A.D. 330.

(Usurpers in italics. The *Basileus Autocrator's* name is given always in capitals. Constantine II and Constans I are not included, as they never exercised effective power in the E.)

Constantinian Dynasty:

CONSTANTINE I, the Great	d. 337
CONSTANTIUS	337–361
JULIAN, the Apostate	361–363
JOVIAN	363–364
VALENS	364–378

Theodosian Dynasty:

THEODOSIUS I, the Great	379–395
ARCADIUS	395–408
THEODOSIUS II	408–450
MARCIAN	450–457

Leonine Dynasty:

LEO I	457–474
LEO II	474
ZENO	474–491
Basilicus	475–476
ANASTASIUS I	491–518

Justinian Dynasty:

JUSTIN I	518–527
JUSTINIAN I	527–565
JUSTIN II	565–578
TIBERIUS II	578–582
MAURICE	582–602
Theodosius, Co-Emperor	590–602
PHOCAS	602–610

Heraclian Dynasty:

HERACLIUS I	610–641
Constantine III	613–641
Heracleonas	638–641
CONSTANTINE III	641
HERACLEONAS	641
CONSTANS II	641–668
Constantine IV	659–668
Heraclius	659–681
Tiberius	659–681
CONSTANTINE IV, Pogonatus	668–685
JUSTINIAN II, Rhinotmetus	685–695
Leontius	695–698
Tiberius III, Apsimar	698–705
JUSTINIAN II, Rhinotmetus	705–711
Tiberius	706–711
PHILIPPICUS, Bardanes	711–713
ANASTASIUS II, Artemius	713–716
THEODOSIUS III	716–717

Isaurian Dynasty:

LEO III, the Isaurian	717–740
Constantine V	720–740
CONSTANTINE V, Coprony-	
mus	740–775
Leo IV	750–775
LEO IV, the Chazar	775–780
Constantine VI	776–780
CONSTANTINE VI	780–797
IRENE	797–802
NICEPHORUS I	802–811
STAURACIUS	811
MICHAEL I, Rhangabe	811–813
LEO V, the Armenian	813–820

Amorian Dynasty:

MICHAEL II, the Amorian	820–829
Theophilus	821–829
THEOPHILUS	829–842
MICHAEL III, the Drunkard	842–867
Basil I	866–867

Macedonian Dynasty:

BASIL I. the Macedonian	867–886
Constantine	869–880
Leo VI	870–886
Alexander	871–912
LEO VI, the Wise	886–912
Constantine VII	911–913
ALEXANDER	912–913
CONSTANTINE VII, Por-	
phyrogenetus	913–919
ROMANUS I, Lecapenus	919–944
Constantine VII	919–944
Christopher Lecapenus	921–931
Stephen Lecapenus	924–945
Constantine Lecapenus	924–945
CONSTANTINE VII, Por-	
phyrogenetus	944–959
Romanus II	c. 950–959
ROMANUS II	959–963
Basil II	960–963
Constantine VIII	961–1025
BASIL II, Bulgaroctonus	963
NICEPHORUS II, Phocas	963–969
Basil II	963–976
JOHN I, Tzimisces	969–976
BASIL II, Bulgaroctonus	976–1025
CONSTANTINE VIII	1025–1028
ROMANUS III, Argyrus	1028–1034
MICHAEL IV, the Paphla-	
gonian	1034–1041
MICHAEL V, the Caulker	1041–1042
ZOE and THEODORA,	
Porphyrogenetae	1042
CONSTANTINE IX, Mono-	
machus	1042–1055
THEODORA, Porphyrogen-	
eta	1055–1056
MICHAEL VI, Stratioticus	1056–1057
ISAAC I, Comnenus	1057–1059

Ducas Dynasty:

CONSTANTINE X, Ducas	1059–1067
Michael VII	c. 1060–1067
MICHAEL VII, Parapinaces	1067–1068
ROMANUS IV, Diogenes	1068–1071

Michael VII	1068–1071
MICHAEL VII, Parapinaces	1071–1078
NICEPHORUS III, Botan-	
iates	1078–1081

Comnenian Dynasty:

ALEXIUS I, Comnenus	1081–1118
Constantine, Ducas	1081–1090
John II	1092–1118
JOHN II, Calojohannes	1118–1143
Alexius	1119–1142
MANUEL I	1143–1180
Alexius II	1172–1180
ALEXIUS II	1180–1183
Andronicus I	1182–1183
ANDRONICUS I	1183–1185

Angelus Dynasty:

ISAAC II, Angelus	1185–1195
ALEXIUS III	1195–1203
ALEXIUS IV	1203–1204
Isaac II	1203–1204
ALEXIUS V, Murtuphlus	1204

Latin Emperors:

Baldwin I	1204–1205
Henry	1206–1216
Peter of Courtenay	1216–1217
Robert	1221–1228
Baldwin II	1228–1237
John of Brienne	1228–1237
Baldwin II (alone)	1237–1261

Lascarid Dynasty (Nicaean Empire, 1204–1261)

THEODORE I, Lascaris	1204–1222
JOHN III, Ducas Vatatzes	1222–1254
THEODORE II, Lascaris	
Vatatzes	1254–1258
JOHN IV, Ducas Vatatzes	1258

Palaeologan Dynasty:

MICHAEL VIII, Palaeologus	1258–1282
Andronicus II	1272–1282
ANDRONICUS II	1282–1328
Michael	1295–1320
Andronicus III	1325–1328
ANDRONICUS III	1328–1341
JOHN V	1341–1347
JOHN VI, Cantacuzene	1347–1355
John V	1347–1355
Matthew Cantacuzene	1348–1355
ANDRONICUS IV	1376–1379
John VII	1376–1390
JOHN V	1379–1390
Andronicus IV	1379–1385
Manuel II	1386–1391
JOHN VII	1390
JOHN V	1390–1391
MANUEL II	1391–1425
John VII	1399–1412
John VIII	1423–1425
JOHN VIII	1425–1448
CONSTANTINE XI, Palae-	
ologus	1448–1453

Roman Empire (Later Western). The Vandal mercenary Stilicho seizes power, A.D. 395. Alaric's first invasion of Italy, 401–3. Capital moved to Ravenna, 401–3. Assassination of Stilicho, 408. Rome three times besieged by Alaric, 408–10. Visigoths (q.v.) settle in Gaul, the Vandals and Suevi in Spain, 415–23. Vandals (q.v.) invade and settle N. Africa, 429–42. Aetius defeats Huns at battle of 'Châlons' or the Catalaunian Fields (probably near Troyes), 451. Odoacer rules Italy, 473–89; Italy conquered by Theodoric the Ostrogoth, 489–93. Belisarius reconquers Italy, 536–49. Byzantine rule established, 552–5.

Roman Republic. Foundation of Rome, 753 B.C. Expulsion of the Tarquin dynasty, 510. First dictatorship. 501. Enactment of the XII Tables, 451–450. Rome sacked by the Gauls, 390. Final subjection of the Latin League, 338. Publication of the *Jus Flavianum*, 304. *Lex Hortensia* gives the plebs concurrent power of legislation by plebiscite, 267. First Punic War with Carthage is indecisive, 264–241. Conquest of Sardinia, Corcyra, and Lombardy, 241–218. Second Punic War, 218; ends with defeat of Hannibal at Zama, 202. Conquest of Syria, 190; Macedon, 168. In Third Punic War Carthage is destroyed, 149–146. Greece conquered, 146. Rise and fall of the Gracchi, 135–123. Marius defeats the Cimbri and Teutones, 106–101. The Social War, 91. Sulla crushes the Marians, 88. Defeats Mithradates of Pontus, 84. Institutes the proscriptions, 82. Resigns dictatorship, 79. *Lex Cornelia*, 67. First Triumvirate (Caesar, Pompey, Crassus), 63. Caesar conquers Gaul, 58–51. He crosses the Rubicon, Jan. 49. He defeats Pompey at Pharsalus, 48. Is murdered, 15 Mar. 44. Second Triumvirate (Octavius, Antony, Lepidus), 43. Defeat of Antony at Actium, 2 Sept. 31. Octavius changes his name to Augustus, 16 Jan. 27.

Romantic Movement, as a conscious literary school, had its first English manifesto in the preface to the *Lyrical Ballads* (the second edition, of 1800) by Wordsworth. The word *romantic* when given a literary connotation is of English origin, but was first introduced into the German language by Novalis c. 1795, and as used by him and Wieland and reintroduced into English by Coleridge, Southey, etc., came to have the anti-classical and medievalizing association of the R. M. which is largely the result of interaction between English, French, and German literature and philosophy; its influence on and derivation from the literature of the Mediterranean countries is negligible. France was drawn into the R. orbit last

of the three, and Mme de Staël's *De l'Allemagne*, 1813, shows the origin of French R. ideas. R. traditions lasted longer in France than elsewhere, at least until the 1850s, perhaps because of the longevity and continued vigour of the chief French R. poet, novelist, and playwright, V. Hugo, who did not die until 1885. The R. heyday in Germany and England may be said to have come to an end c. 1832 with the deaths of Scott and Goethe.

Rome, City of. (*See also* ROMAN REPUBLIC; ROMAN EMPIRE, etc.; also PAPACY and ITALY.) Traditionally founded, 753 B.C. Capitol founded c. 614. Sacked by Gauls, 390. Aqua Appia built, 312. Aqua Julia, 33. Pantheon, 27. Colosseum begun, A.D. 72. Trajan's column, 114. Charlemagne crowned at, 25 Dec. 800. Sacked by Saracens, 846. By the Emperor Arnulf, 896. By the Normans under Guiscard, 1084. Taken by Barbarossa, 1167. University founded, 1245. Rienzi's republic at R., 1347. St. Peter's new cathedral begun, 1513. Completely sacked by the Spaniards, 1527. Consecration of St. Peter's, 1626. Walls restored, 1749. Proclaimed a republic by the French, 1798. Restored to Pope, retaken, and restored, 1799–1801. Annexed to Napoleon's kingdom of Italy, 1808. Restored to Pope, 1814. Garibaldi's Roman republic suppressed by French, 1848–9. Became capital of Italy, 1870. Papal temporal authority restored in Vatican City, 1929.

Rome, Treaty of, signed, 25 Mar. 1957, between Belgium, France, Federal Germany, Italy, Luxemburg, and the Netherlands, which instituted the European Economic Community, the members of which were to form the Common Market (q.v.).

Roses, Wars of the. Collective name for the English Civil Wars which broke out in 1455 and ended at battle of Bosworth, 1485. Red Rose = Lancaster; White Rose = York.

Rosetta Stone, inscribed c. 200 B.C.; dug up, 1779. True contents recognized, and demotic text partially translated, 1816, by Dr. Thomas Young (1773–1829). The whole deciphered, 1822, by Jean François Champollion (1790–1832). Ceded to Britain, 1801.

Rosicrucians. Although there is no contemporary evidence for their existence in the Middle Ages, Rosicrucian tracts published soon after 1600 claim the existence of Rosicrucian societies in the fourteenth century. They first became widely publicized by Johann Valentin Andreae (1586–1654).

Roskilde, Roeskilde, was capital of

Denmark until 1443. Most of the Danish kings from Harald Gormsson (d. 986) onwards are buried here in the cathedral which was consecrated, 1084, but the present building was erected, 1191–1200.

Rostock, founded, 1160, by the Polish Prince Pribislav, across the river from a Wendish castle, joined the Hanseatic League, 1218. Burnt out, 1677. Became part of Duchy of Schwerin, 1695. Fell to Russians, May 1945.

Rostov-on-Don. Founded by Slavs in 862, R. is first mentioned in a document of 988; was an independent principality from the tenth to the fourteenth century; assimilated by the Grand Duchy of Moscow, 1389. Fortified, 1761. Changed hands four times in the Second World War, the last time in Feb. 1943, when the retreating Germans destroyed most of the older buildings.

Rosyth was the residence of Margaret, sister of Edgar Atheling, wife of King Malcolm Canmore; she d. 1093. The naval base here was first laid down, 1903. Put on maintenance basis, 1925–39. Port of assembly for the Norwegian expedition, May 1940.

Rotary International, founded, 1905, in Chicago by P. P. Harris (d. 1947). New York R. Club founded, 1909. First non-American R. Club in Dublin, 1911. British Association of R. Clubs formed, 1914; known as the R. I. in Great Britain and Ireland since 1938.

Rotterdam, Holland. John I in 1299 granted various privileges to burghers of, and this date marks the origin of the present town; Erasmus b. at, 1467; plundered by Spaniards, 1572. Heavily bombed by the Germans, May 1940, and town centre destroyed; rebuilt since 1945.

Rouen, France. Originally *Ratuma*, latinized as *Rotomagus*. An archbishop's see in A.D. 260; became capital of Normandy, 912; death of William the Conqueror at, 1087; Joan of Arc burned at, 1431; sacked by Huguenots, 1562; occupied by Germans, Dec. 1870–July 1871 and June 1940–Aug. 1944. Much damage caused by fighting in the city during its liberation, 1944.

Round Table Conferences (in London). Three were concerning government of India: first, Nov. 1930–Jan. 1931; second, Oct.–Dec. 1931; third, Nov.–Dec. 1932. Besides these, a Burma R. T. Conference was held, Nov. 1931–Jan. 1932, and there was a Malta R. T. Conference, 1955.

Rowton Houses named after Lord R. (M. W. L. Corry, 1838–1903) in 1892. Much modernized since World War II.

Royal Academy of Arts (London). Originally the Society of Incorporated Artists, founded by Hogarth c. 1739;

first exhibition held, 21 Apr. 1760; the present institution founded, Dec. 1768, with Sir Joshua Reynolds as president; first exhibition held at Burlington House, 3 May 1869. The following are the presidents, with their dates of inauguration:

Sir Joshua Reynolds, 1768.
Benjamin West, 1792.
James Wyatt, 1805.
Benjamin West, 1806.
Sir Thomas Lawrence, 1820.
Sir Martin A. Shee, 1830.
Sir Charles Eastlake, 1850.
Sir Edwin Landseer, 1866.
Sir Francis Grant, 1866.
Sir Frederick Leighton, 1878.
Sir John Everett Millais ⎫ 1896.
Sir Edward John Poynter ⎭
Sir Aston Webb, 1919.
Sir Frank Dicksee, 1924.
Sir William Llewellyn, 1928.
Sir Edwin Lutyens, 1938.
Sir Alfred Munnings, 1944.
Sir Gerald Kelly, 1949.
Sir Albert Richardson, 1954.
Sir Charles Wheeler, 1957.

Royal Air Force. Formed by Act of Parliament, 1 Apr. 1918, by amalgamation of the R. Naval Air Service and R. Flying Corps.

Royal Bounty, part of the Civil List, was fixed at £13,200 in 1837. Payment from R. B. to subjects whose wives are delivered of three or more children at one birth discontinued, 1957.

Royal Commissions (with unofficial names).

1887. First Report of R. Commission to inquire into Civil establishments and offices of State.—Ridley.
1909. Canals and Waterways.—Shuttleworth.
1910. Electoral systems.—Cavendish.
1910. Trade relations between Canada and the W. Indies.—Balfour of Burleigh.
1910. Church of England.—Vaughan Williams.
1912. Civil Service.—MacDonnell.
1912. Public Records.—Pollock.
1912. Divorce and matrimonial causes.—Gorell.
1913. University education in London.—Haldane.
1914. Indian finance and currency.—Chamberlain.
1917. Dominions.—Vincent.
1919. Awards to inventors.
1920. Income tax.—Colwyn.
1921. Wheat supplies.—Crawford.
1922. Honours.—Dunedin.
1924–6. National Health Insurance.—Lawrence of Kingsgate.
1925. Food prices.—Geddes.
1926. Coal industry.—Samuel.

1926. Indian finance and currency.—Hilton Young.

1926. Lunacy and mental disorder.—Macmillan.

1926. Cross-river traffic in London.—Lee of Fareham.

1927–8. Agriculture in India.—Linlithgow.

1929. Police powers and procedure.—Lee of Fareham.

1929. Local government.—Onslow.

1929–31. Civil Service.—Tomlin.

1931. Transport.—Griffith-Boscawen.

1931. Labour in India.—Whitley.

1931. Licensing (Scotland).—Mackay.

1931–2. Unemployment Insurance.—Holman Gregory.

1932. Licensing (England and Wales).—Amulree.

1933. Lotteries and betting.—Rowlatt.

1934–6. Dispatch of business at Common Law.—Peel.

1935. University of Durham.—Moyne.

1935. Merthyr Tydfil.—Lowry.

1936. Tithe rent charge in England and Wales.—Fischer Williams.

1936. Private manufacture of and trading in arms.—Bankes.

1936–7. Safety in coal-mines.—Rockley.

1937. Local government in Tyneside area. Newton Scott.

1937. Palestine.—Peel.

1937–8. Geographical distribution of the industrial population.—Barlow.

1939. Rhodesia-Nyasaland.

1939–44. Workmen's Compensation.—Hetherington.

1944–6. Equal pay.—Asquith.

1944–9. Population.

1946. Awards to inventors.

1946–8. Justices of the Peace.—Du Parcq.

1947–9. The press.—Ross.

1949–51. Betting, Lotteries, and Gaming.—Willink.

1949. Capital punishment. Rendered report, 23 Sept. 1953.

1950. Taxation, foreign compensation.

1951–5. Marriage and divorce.

1952. Kenya.

1953–4. Scottish Affairs.—Balfour.

1953–5. Taxation of profits and income.—Cohen.

1954–7. Law relating to mental illness.—Percy.

1955. Civil Service.—Priestley.

1956–8. Common land.—Jennings.

1957–60. Doctors' and dentists' remuneration.—Pilkington.

1959–61. Local Government in England and Wales.

1959–61. Local Government in Greater London.—Herbert.

1960–1. Police.—Willink.

1961–2. Press.—Shawcross.

Since 1950 the increasing use of committees in investigating controversial subjects of general concern has tended to lessen the number of R. C.

Royal Exchange (London). *See* EXCHANGE, ROYAL.

Royal Flying Corps. *See* ROYAL AIR FORCE.

'Royal George,' flagship of Admiral Kempenfelt, sank suddenly in Portsmouth harbour, 29 Aug. 1782.

Royal Hospital (Chelsea). *See* CHELSEA HOSPITAL.

Royal Institution of Great Britain. Founded, 1799. R. charter, 1800. Act of Parliament, 1810.

Royal Marriage Act arose out of the marriages of the Duke of Cumberland (1745–90) and the Duke of Gloucester (1743–1805) to Mrs. Horton and Lady Waldegrave respectively. By this Act, passed in 1772, all descendants of George II, other than the issue of princesses married into foreign R. families, must obtain the sovereign's consent before marriage, which is otherwise void. It would seem, however, that a descendant of George II over 25 years of age may marry without the royal consent on giving twelve months' notice to the Privy Council, provided Parliament in the interim makes no objection.

Royal Military Academy, founded at Woolwich, 1741. In 1946 it amalgamated with the R. M. College, which was established at Sandhurst in 1813; the R. M. College buildings date mostly from 1911.

Royal Naval Air Service. *See* FLEET AIR ARM.

Royal Naval College. Opened at Osborne, 1903; closed, 1921. Another, at Greenwich, 1873. Another, at Dartmouth, 1905. Age of entry raised to 16, 1948.

Royal Regiment of Artillery formed, 24 May 1716.

Royal Society. Originated, 1660. Incorporated, 22 Apr. 1662.

Ruanda Urundi, annexed by Germany as part of German E. Africa, 1884, was awarded to Belgium, as mandatory of the League of Nations, 1919. United administratively to the then Belgian Congo, 1925. Trusteeship territory from 1946. Became independent on 1 July 1962 as the two states of Rwanda (*q.v.*) and Burundi (*q.v.*). In serious economic difficulties at the time independence was granted.

Rugby League. Seceded 1895 from Rugby Union (*q.v.*). First known as Northern Union, and took its present name in 1922.

Rugby School (England). Founded by Laurence Sheriff, 1567. Rebuilt, 1809. Thomas Arnold, headmaster, 1828–42. Rugby football originated here in 1823.

Rugby Union, founded, 1871, by adherents of a game played according to rules similar to those codified at R. School (see above) in 1846. The characteristic R. U. tactic of *carrying* the ball was first adopted by W. W. Ellis, in 1823. New rules, 1953.

Rumania. Came into existence by the union of Moldavia and Wallachia under Alexander Cuza, 23 Dec. 1861. Cuza succeeded by Charles of Hohenzollern, 22 Feb. 1866. Independent of Turkey, 13 July 1878. Proclaimed a kingdom, 26 Mar. 1881. Alliance with Austria, 30 Oct. 1883. Balkan Wars, 1912–13. Crushed by German-Austrian offensive, 1–9 Dec. 1916. Bessarabia proclaims union with R., 9 Apr. 1918. Treaty of Bucharest with Germany, 9 May 1918. Transylvania proclaims union with R., 30 Nov. 1918. Treaty of Bucharest annulled by treaties of St. Germain, 10 Sept. 1919 and Trianon, 4 June 1920. R. acquires N. Bukovina, 1920. Joins Little Entente, 17 Aug. 1920. Bratianu ministry scandals, 1924. First accession of King Michael, 20 July 1927. Ex-Crown-Prince Carol ordered to leave England, 1928. He is elected king instead of Michael (his son), 8 June 1930. Premier Ion Duca murdered by Iron Guard, 29 Dec. 1933. Joins Balkan Pact, 9 Feb. 1934. Coalition government under Patriarch Miron Cristea, Feb. 1938. Cristescu (leader of Iron Guard) shot, 26 Jan. 1939. Trade agreement with Germany, 23 Mar. 1939. Britain and France promise support against aggression, 13 Apr. 1939. Premier Galinescu assassinated by Iron Guard. 21 Sept. 1939. Bessarabia and N. Bukovina ceded to U.S.S.R., 28 June 1940. S. Dobrudja to Bulgaria, 21 Aug. 1940. Vienna Award cedes half of Transylvania to Hungary, 30 Aug. 1940. Antonescu appointed leader (*Conducator*), 5 Sept. 1940. Second accession of King Michael, 6 Sept. German military occupation, Oct. 1940. Axis pact signed, 23 Nov. R. attacks U.S.S.R., 22 June 1941. Britain declares war on R., 7 Dec. 1941. Russians invade R., 2 Apr. 1944. King Michael overthrows Antonescu dictatorship, 23 Aug. 1944. Declares war on Germany, 25 Aug. 1944. Russians capture Bucharest, 31 Aug. 1944. Russians force Communist government on King Michael, Nov. 1945. King Michael abdicates under duress and R. proclaimed a People's Republic, 30 Dec. 1947. First constitution of the Rumanian People's Republic, 13 Apr. 1948; this superseded by a second of 24 Sept. 1952 which strengthened the Communist grip on the country. Ex-King Carol *d.* Apr. 1953.

Kings of Rumania, 1881–1947:

Carol I	1881–1914
Ferdinand	1914–1927
Michael	1927–1930
Carol II	1930–1940
Michael (again)	1940–1947

See also BESSARABIA; VLACHS; MOLDAVIAN REPUBLIC.

Rump. M.P.s remaining after Pride's Purge (*q.v.*).

Runes. The earliest decipherable runic inscriptions to which a date can be assigned are at Vimose, Fynen, Denmark, and date from *c.* A.D 250. R. spread to Norway before 300, and thence to Sweden; they spread to the W. Germanic area (Germany, eastern France, and England) during the fifth century. Early R. found in the Rhineland all date from 450 to 550. The Franks casket (Anglian, probably Northumbrian work) was inscribed with R. before 650, and R. were extensively used in England until *c.* 860. The Old English *Rune Song,* a versified ABC of R., must have been composed before 900, though the only MS. known, burnt in 1731, was of the eleventh century. No examples from Denmark are found between 600 and 800, but after that date a lapidary style was developed, especially for gravestones, of which large numbers down to *c.* 1050 are extant. This style was adopted in Sweden, notably by Asmund (*fl.* 1025–50), a Christian missionary of English origin, who was also a monumental mason. The runic alphabet achieved its final form in Scandinavia *c.* 1100, and was in use in the N. generally for certain purposes, until the Reformation. In remote parts of Sweden runic calendars and almanacs were in use until the eighteenth century. As to the origin of R., according to Marstrander they were first adapted by Gothic traders or mercenaries on the Black Sea from the Greek alphabet: this would imply A.D. 150 at earliest. The theory of Von Freisen derives them from a N. Etruscan alphabet current in Noricum, and adapted by the Marcomanni of Bohemia: this could have happened *c.* A.D. 1. Descriptions by Tacitus (A.D. 55–120) of German divination by lot appear to imply the existence of R.

Russia. Rurik comes from Sweden, and his successors found the principality of Kiev, 864. Vladimir of Kiev marries Anna, a Byzantine princess, 988. Is baptized, and sets about conversion of R., 990–1015. Conversion continued by Jaroslav, 1015–54. Sack of Kiev and foundation of Vladimir by Andrew Bogolinski of Suzdal, 1169. R. overwhelmed by Mongols at the battle of the Kalka, 1224, and of the Oka and the Sit,

1238. Batu established Empire of the Golden Horde, 1242. The reign of Alexander Nevski, 1252–63. Moscow becomes the leading feudatory under Ivan Kalita, 1328–41. Rise of Lithuania, 1315–77. Dimitri Donskoi defeats the Golden Horde at Kulikovo, 1380. The Horde is attacked by Tamerlane, 1390–4. Ivan the Great (1462–1505) proclaims himself tsar and overthrows the Golden Horde, 1480. He conquers Kazan, 1487. Russo-Polish War, 1512–22. Ivan the Terrible conquers Astrakhan, 1554. Boris Godunov regent, 1588. End of the dynasty of Rurik, 1598. The 'False Dimitriy,' 1605–6. The Time of Troubles, 1606–13. Michael Romanov elected tsar, 1613. Treaty of Stolbova with Sweden, 1617. Serfdom of the peasantry legally established, 1649. Alexis takes Smolensk, 1654. Treaty of Vilna with Poland, 3 Nov. 1656. Treaty of Kardis with Sweden, 1661. Beginning of the Raskol (schism) in Russian Church, 1666. Truce of Andrussov with Poland secures Smolensk and Kiev, 1667. Peter the Great captures Azov from Turks, 1696. He destroys the Streltzi (Musketeers), 1698. Is defeated by Swedes at battle of Narva, 1700. He founds St. Petersburg, 1703. He decisively defeats Charles XII of Sweden at Poltava, 8 July 1709. He obtains Baltic provinces from Sweden by the Peace of Nystad, 10 Sept. 1721. R. obtains S. Finland from Sweden by Treaty of Aabo, 1743. R. enters Seven Years War (q.v.) against Prussia, 1757. Peace with Prussia, 1762. First Partition of Poland, 1772. Treaty of Kuchuk Kainardji with Turkey, 1774. R. obtains N. Black Sea coast by Treaty of Jassy, 1792. Second Partition of Poland, 1793. R. suppresses Kosciuszko's rising in Warsaw, Mar. 1794. Third Partition of Poland, 1795. R. defeated at Zürich, 1799. Defeat at Austerlitz, 1805; at Eylau, 1807. Treaty of Tilsit, 9 July 1807. Napoleon's invasion of R., May–Dec. 1812. Congress of Troppau, 1820. Frontier treaty with U.S.A., 1824. Treaty of Adrianople with Turkey, 1829. Straits Convention, 1841. Poland made a Russian province, 1847. Assists Austrians to crush Hungarian nationalists at Vilagos, 13 Aug. 1849. Crimean War, 1853–6. Serfs emancipated, 3 Mar. 1861. Hereditary priesthood abolished, 1869. Russo-Turkish War, 1877–8. Murders of prominent ministers: Bogolepoff, 1901; Sipyagin, 1902; Plehve, 1904. Russo-Japanese War, 1904–5. Revolt in St. Petersburg, Jan. 1905. In Sebastopol, Oct. 1905. First Duma meets, 10 May 1906. See WORLD WARS I and II and U.S.S.R. for subsequent history.

Russian Literature. The following is a list of Russian authors not now living:

Aksakov, Ivan, 1823–86, poet and miscellaneous writer.

Aksakov, Serge Timofieievitch, 1791–1859, novelist.

Andreiev, Leonid Nicolaievitch, 1871–1919, novelist.

Artsibashev, Mikhail Petrovitch, 1878–1927, novelist.

Bakunin, Mikhail, 1814–76, anarchist writer.

Baratinsky, Evgen Abramovitch, 1800–1844, poet.

Bashkirtsev, Marie, 1860–84, diarist.

Batiushkov, Constantine, 1787–1855, poet and translator.

Bely, Andrey, 1880–1934, novelist and poet.

Belinsky, Vissarion, 1811–48, critic and philosopher.

Blok, Alexander Alexandrovitch, 1880–1921, poet.

Bunin, Ivan Alexeyevitch, 1870–1953, poet and novelist.

Chekhov. See TCHEKHOV.

Delvig, Anton Antonovitch, 1798–1831, poet.

Derzhavin, Gabriel Romanovitch, 1743–1816, poet.

Dmitriev, Ivan Ivanovitch, 1760–1837, poet.

Dolgorukaia, Princess Natalia, 1713–70, memoir writer.

Dostoevsky, Fedor Mikhailovitch, 1822–1881, novelist.

Fadeyev, Alexander Alexandrovitch,, 1901–56, novelist.

Gogol, Nikolai Vasilievitch, 1809–52 novelist.

Gontcharov, Ivan Alexandrovitch, 1812–1891, novelist.

Gorky, Maxim (the pen name of Alexei Maximovitch Pyeshkov), 1868–1936, novelist.

Griboiedov, Alexander Sergeievitch, 1798–1829, dramatist.

Grigorovitch, Dmitri Vasilievitch, 1822–1900, novelist.

Herzen (or Gertsen), Alexander Ivanovitch, 1812–70, novelist, etc.

Jukovsky, Vasili, 1786–1852, poet, translator, and miscellaneous writer.

Kantemir, Antiochus Dmitrievitch, 1708–1744, poet and satirist.

Karamzin, Nikolai Mikhailovitch, 1766–1826, historian.

Katkov, Mikhail, 1820–87, journalist and editor.

Kheraskov, Mikhail Matvieievitch, 1733–1807, epic poet.

Khomiakov, Alexis, 1804–60, poet and theologian.

Kirieievsky, Ivan Vasilievitch, 1806–56, critic.

Koltzov, Alexis Vasilievitch, 1808–42, poet.

Korolenko, Vladimir Galaktionovitch, 1853–1921, novelist.

Kostomarov, Nikolai Ivanovitch, 1817–1885, historian.

Kovalevsky, Sonya, 1850–1901, novelist.

Krylov, Ivan Andreievitch, 1768–1844, fabulist.

Kuprin, Alexander Ivanovitch, 1870–1938, novelist.

Lermontov, Mikhail Yurevitch, 1814–41, poet.

Leskov, Nikolai Semenovitch, 1831–95, novelist.

Lomonosov, Mikhail, 1711–65, poet and prose writer.

Lukin, Vladimir Ignatievitch, 1757–1824, dramatist.

Maïkov, Apollonius Nicolaievitch, 1821–1898, poet.

Merezhkovsky, Dmitri Sergeievitch, 1866–1941, poet.

Nékrasov, Nikolai Alexeievitch, 1821–77, poet.

Nestor, c. 1050–c. 1100, historian.

Nikitin, Ivan Savitch, 1826–61, poet.

Novikov, Nikolai, 1744–1818, prose writer and social reformer.

Ostrovsky, Alexander Nicolaievitch, 1823–1886, dramatist.

Pasternak, Boris, 1890–1960, poet and novelist.

Ozlerov, Ladislas, 1769–1816, poet and dramatist.

Pisemsky, Alexis, 1820–81, novelist and dramatist.

Pokrovsky, Maxim N., 1868–1932, Soviet historian.

Polevoy, Nicholas, 1796–1846, historian and miscellaneous writer.

Polotsky, Simeon, fl. seventeenth century, poet and dramatist.

Pososhkov, Ivan, c. 1673–1726, reformer and miscellaneous writer.

Prokopovitch, Feofan, 1681–1736, ecclesiastic reformer, controversialist, author of prose works and poems.

Pushkin, Alexander Sergeievitch, 1799–1837, poet.

Pyeshkov, Alexei Maximovitch. *See* GORKY.

Radishtchev, Alexander Nikolaievitch. 1749–1802, prose writer.

Remisov, A., 1877–1957, novelist.

Romanovna, Princess Dashkov, 1743–1810, prose writer and editor, for some years president of the Academy of Science.

Saltykov, Shtchedrin. Mikhail Evgrafovitch, 1826–89, novelist.

Sologub, Fedor (pseudonym of Fedor Kuzmitch Tchernikov), 1863–1927, novelist and poet.

Soloviev, Sergei Mikhailovitch, 1820–79, historian.

Soloviev, Vladimir Sergeievitch, 1853–1900, philosopher.

Sumarokov Alexis Petrovitch, 1718–77, dramatist.

Tatishtchev, Vasili Nikititch, 1685–1750, author of literary and scientific works.

Tchadaev, Peter Yakovlevitch, 1793–1855, writer and critic.

Tchekhov, Anton, 1860–1904, dramatist and novelist.

Tchernishevsky, Nikolai, 1828–89, critic, philosopher, and novelist.

Tiutchev, Fedor Ivanovitch, 1803–76, poet.

Tolstoy, Alexei Nikolaievitch, 1883–1945, novelist.

Tolstoy, Alexis Constantinovitch, 1817–1875, novelist, etc.

Tolstoy, Leo Nikolaievitch, 1828–1910, novelist, etc.

Trediakovsky, Vasili, 1703–69, poet and prose writer.

Turgenev, Ivan Sergeievitch, 1818–83, novelist.

Yesenin, Sergei, 1895–1925, poet.

Zhukovsky, Vassili Andreievitch, 1783–1852, poet.

Russian Secret Police. Tsarist designation, Okhrana; since the revolution, *see* CHEKA, M.V.D., N.K.G.B., N.K.V.D., etc.

Russian Tsars. The R. rulers from 864 till 1169 were Grand Princes of Kiev. From 1169 to 1328 they were Great Dukes of Vladimir, and from 1328 till 1480 Grand Dukes of Muscovy. Ivan the Great proclaimed himself tsar, 1480. This list therefore begins with him.

House of Rurik:

Ivan III (the Great)	1462–1505
Vassili III	1505–1533
Ivan IV (the Terrible)	1533–1584
Theodore I	1584–1598

House of Godunov:

Boris	1598–1605
Theodore II	1605
Interregnum	1605–1613

House of Romanov:

Michael	1613–1645
Alexis	1645–1676
Theodore III	1676–1682
Ivan V	1682–1689
Sophia (regent)	1682–1689
Peter I (the Great)	1682–1725
Catherine I	1725–1727
Peter II	1727–1730
Anne	1730–1740
Ivan VI	1740–1741
Elizabeth	1741–1762
Peter III	1762
Catherine II (the Great)	1762–1796
Paul	1796–1801
Alexander I	1801–1825
Nicholas I	1825–1855
Alexander II	1855–1881
Alexander III	1881–1894
Nicholas II (abdicated)	1894–1917

N

Ruthenia. Ruthenians, or Little Russians, or Ukrainians, are a linguistic division of the Slavs, the most southwesterly of the E. Slav group, whose language was identical with that of the other E. Slavs (Great Russians, White Russians) until *c.* 1240. All alike spoke Old Russian. From 1321 to 1772 the greater part of R. was under Lithuanian, then under Polish, dominion, while from 1772 to 1917 it was divided under Russian, Austrian, Hungarian, and occasionally Turkish suzerainty. In 1918 the easternmost province of the newly set up Czechoslovak Republic was named R., or Sub-Carpathian Russia. In 1938 it was isolated by the defection of the Slovaks from the republic, and was occupied by the Hungarian Army and annexed to Hungary. In 1945 the Ukrainian S.S.R., which had already acquired the territories of Galicia from Poland and N. Bukovina and Bessarabia from Rumania, obtained the cession of the province from Czechoslovakia. Now known as Transcarpathian Ukraine, it is politically united to the rest of the Little Russians for the first time in history. *See* UKRAINE.

Ruthenian Church is a name for the Uniate Catholic Church (Catholics of Slavonic rite but Roman allegiance), whose followers are spread over Polish, Russian (especially in Galicia), Czechoslovak, and Rumanian territory. The Little Russians, for the most part, became Christian during the reign of Vladimir the Great of Kiev (980–1015), and at the time of the schism, 1054, sided with the Greek faction. But after numerous overtures they became attached to the Roman allegiance by the union of Brest-Litovsk, 1594. Persecution by the Soviet authorities, and an attempt to force the R. C. into allegiance to the Eastern Patriarchs began with the absorption of Galicia by the U.S.S.R. in 1939, and was greatly intensified after the reconquest of territory from the Germans in 1944. In 1946 about 3½ million members of the R. C. in Soviet territory withdrew their allegiance to Rome, under duress, and submitted to the Orthodox Patriarchate in Moscow.

Rutland. English county, dating from the thirteenth century, whose absorption into Leicester was recommended, 1961; but this proposal was abandoned, 1963.

Ruthven, Raid of. A *coup d'état* which involved kidnapping the boy James VI of Scotland from his guardians, the Duke of Lennox and the Earl of Arran; this was done by the Earls of Gowrie and Mar, Lord Lyndsay of the Byres, and the Master of Glamis, in 1582.

Rwanda, Africa. Independent republic created by the granting of independence to Ruanda-Urundi (*q.v.*) on 1 July 1962.

Rye House Plot. A conspiracy formed in 1683 to assassinate Charles II and the Duke of York; the plot was frustrated soon after its origin.

Ryswick, Treaty of, 1697. Ended the war between France and the coalition composed of England, Spain, Brandenburg, Holland, and the Empire.

S

S.A. **(Sturmabteilungen).** National Socialist (*q.v.*) 'assault detachment' formed about 1922 for the purpose of breaking up meetings by rival parties, etc. Dissolved, 1923, following the Munich *putsch*; refounded, 1925. Banned by the Brüning Government, Apr. 1932, but re-legalized by Papen, June 1932. Its chief of staff, Roehm, shot, 30 June 1934, when the influence of the formation ceased to predominate in Nazi politics. Goering became its commander. One infantry division (S.A. Infantry Division *Feldherrnhalle*) was formed entirely of S.A. men in 1939, and served in Poland and the west. Otherwise there was no force analogous to the Waffen S.S. In 1944 the S.A. was called on to provide a cadre of instructors for the Volkssturm (*q.v.*).

Saarland (for earlier history *see* PALATINATE) was placed under control of League of Nations from 10 Jan. 1920 by Treaty of Versailles (*see end* of WORLD WAR I) for fifteen years, viz. until 1935, when prescribed plebiscite decided for return to Germany. From May 1945 occupied by French troops. New Landtag, elected Oct. 1947, passed constitution making S. an autonomous state, economically united to France, Nov. 1947: ratified by French National Assembly, Feb. 1948. Total coal output until A.D. 2000 pledged to France in return for political autonomy, Mar. 1950. Agreement on future status of S. signed by France and Federal Germany, 23 Oct. 1954; this rejected by the Saarlanders in a referendum, Oct. 1955. Widespread agitation for unification with Federal Germany resulted in France and Federal Germany signing an agreement in Oct. 1956, in accordance with which S. returned to Germany on 1 Jan. 1957. Completely reintegrated with Germany economically by 5 July 1959. Serious coal-mining disaster at Voelklingen, Feb. 1962; over 280 dead.

Sacco and **Vanzetti** were accused of a double murder committed, 15 Apr. 1920, in U.S.A. Trial began, 31 May 1921, verdict of guilty given, 14 July. Celestino Madeiros confessed to the murder, 18 Nov. 1925. Judge Thayer refused re-trial and sentenced S. and V. to death, 9 Apr. 1927. Sentence executed, 23 Aug. 1927.

Sadler's Wells Opera Company began playing in S. W. theatre, 1931, but was on tour permanently from 1940 to 1945 while the theatre was closed. Proposal to move the company from the present theatre (in Islington) caused protests, 1962.

Safad, Safed, N. Galilee, Israel. After 1492 became centre of Jewish learning and the residence of Isaac Luria ben Salomon (Ashkenazi) (1534–72) and other Cabbalistic scholars. First Palestinian printing-press installed, 1563. Severe earthquake, 1837.

Sahara crossed by Europeans: Hornemann, 1798–1800; Oudney, Denham, and Clapperton, 1822–4; Laing, 1826; Caille, 1828; Davidson, 1836; Richardson, 1845; Barth, 1850–5; Rohlfs, 1865–7; Nachtigal, 1869–70; Lenz, 1880; Flatters (perished), 1881; Buchanan, 1922, all with animal transport. Laperrine lost his life attempting to fly across the desert, 1919. First motor-car crossing by B. Kuhn de Prohuk, 1920.

St. Albans, England. Present town, containing many ancient buildings, and near site of Roman *Verulamium*, is called after St. Alban, a Roman soldier martyred there, A.D. 303. Monastery erected c. 793; dissolved, 1539. Abbey (cathedral since 1877) consecrated, 1115. Battles at during Wars of the Roses: (1) 22 May 1455; (2) 17 Feb. 1461.

St. Albans, The Council of. Held Aug. 1213.

St. Andrews, Scotland. Royal burgh after 1140. Cathedral commenced in 1162; consecrated, 1318; desecrated by Protestant mob, 1559. University founded, 1411. Robert Bruce held his first Parliament at, 1309. Golf club instituted, 1754.

St. Bartholomew, St. Barthélemy Island, was first settled by Frenchmen from St. Kitts in 1648. Taken by English, 1689, and restored to France, 1697. Retaken, 1746, restored, 1748. Ceded to Sweden, 1785, but bought back, 1878.

St. Bernard Pass. Great S. B. P. contains the hospice of St. Bernard of Mentone (923–1108), built 962, and served by Augustinian canons since thirteenth century. Hospice handed over to French, 1947; since closed. Crossed by Napoleon's army, 15 May 1800. Carriage road opened, 1895. Little S. B. P. used by Hannibal's army(?), 218 B.C.

St. Gothard Pass. First opened to wheeled traffic, 1820–4. Railway (and tunnel) constructed, 1872–82.

St. Helena, Island of, S. Atlantic. Discovered by the Portuguese on St. Helena's Day, 21 May 1502; possessed by E. India Co., 1659; Napoleon *d.* at, 1821; certain Boer prisoners during S. African War sent there, 1900-2; British troops withdrawn from, which caused protest from inhabitants, 29 Oct. 1906; island of Ascension annexed to, 1922.

St. James's Palace, London. Built by Henry VIII, 1530-6. Extended by Charles II, 1668; by George IV, 1827. Official residence of the sovereign from 1698 until 1837.

St. John, Knights of. *See* MALTA, KNIGHTS OF.

St. Kilda. Sold by The Macleod, 1779; bought back, 1871; evacuated by remnant of population, 1930.

St. Kitts, W. Indies. Discovered by Columbus, 1493. Ceded to Britain, 1713.

St. Lawrence Seaway. Complex of dredged channels, locks, and Great Lakes, linking centre of the American mainland to the Atlantic Ocean for sea-going vessels, started 1954, opened officially by Queen Elizabeth II, 26 June 1959.

St. Louis, U.S.A. Named after Louis IX of France, and founded in 1764 by Laclède. Possessed by Spain, 1768; by U.S.A., 1803.

St. Lucia, Windward Islands. Discovered by Columbus, 1502. French, 1635. English settlement established, 1639; captured by English, 1664; English evacuated, 1667. Finally ceded to Britain, 1814.

St. Paul's Cathedral (London). A church built in the early seventh century, traditionally on the site of a demolished Roman basilica, was burnt down in 1087. Bishop Maurice undertook the construction of a new cathedral, which was completed about 1287; in 1561 the spire was struck by lightning and considerable damage done. About 60 years later Inigo Jones was entrusted with the task of restoration, but in 1666, after its destruction by the Great Fire, Christopher Wren was commissioned to rebuild the cathedral; in 1675 the foundation-stone of the new building was laid, and the whole was completed, 1710. A 'dangerous structure' notice, in regard to the dome, served by the City of London, 6 Jan. 1925. Eastern part of cathedral thereupon cleared for five years while the building was made safe. Damaged by bombing, 1940-1; restored and renovated at the end of the war. W. front cleaned, 1962-3.

St. Paul's School (London). Founded by Dean Colet in 1509; the school-house was destroyed by fire, 1666, and rebuilt by Wren; removed to Hammersmith, Apr. 1884.

St. Peter's (Rome). Church originally erected by the Emperor Constantine about A.D. 319 on the site of a chapel built over the tomb of St. Peter by Pope Anacletus at the beginning of the second century; the present church was designed by the architect Bramante, and in 1506 the first stone was laid by Pope Julius II; building began in earnest, 1513; the church was consecrated, 18 Nov. 1626.

St. Petersburg, Russia. Founded by Peter the Great, 27 May 1703; became seat of government, 1712; Peace of, between Russia and Prussia, signed 5 May 1762; treaty of alliance signed at, between Bernadotte and the Emperor of Russia, Alexander, 24 Mar. 1812. *See* PETROGRAD and LENINGRAD.

St. Pierre and Miquelon Islands. First occupied by French, 1635; fortified, 1700. They have been in British hands for the following periods: 1702-63; 1778-83; 1793-1802; 1803-14. Governor appointed, 1921.

St. Sophia, Constantinople. Founded in the fourth century by Constantine; rebuilt by Theodosius (415) and Justinian (538-68); Mohammedan mosque, 1453-1927; museum since 1927.

St. Thomas, Virgin Islands. *See* CHARLOTTE AMALIE.

Sakhalin. First settled by Russians, 1855, and Russian sovereignty extended over whole island, 1875; partitioned with Japan, 1905; penal settlement abolished, 1907; northern half occupied by Japanese, 1917-25; whole ceded to Russia, 1945.

Salamanca, Spain. Captured by Hannibal, 222 B.C.; Moors expelled from, 1055; university founded, 1243; library of the university founded, 1254; cathedral begun, 1513; defeat of French by Wellington, 1812.

Salem, Mass., U.S.A. Founded, 1626; settlement under Endicott, who gave the place its present name, 1628; famous witchcraft trials, 1692. Incorporated, 1836.

Salerno, Italy. University, traditionally founded in the ninth century, and said to be the oldest in Europe; closed by order of Napoleon, 1811. S. beach was the scene of bitter fighting in Sept. 1943, when British and American forces fought to establish a beachhead there.

Salette-Fallavaux, La, France. Miracle at, 19 Sept. 1846. Missionaries of Our Lady of La Salette founded, 1852.

Salisbury, England. Founded, 1219, when the clergy were removed by Bishop Poore from Old Sarum (*q.v.*). Present cathedral built, 1220-58, except the spire, The close was fortified in 1331. Spire built *c.* 1330–60. Walls of Old Sarum demolished, 1608. S. incorporated, 1611. Cathedral destructively restored, 1782–1791. Spire repaired and summit rebuilt, 1950–1.

Salisbury (England), **Councils held at.** 1. Summoned by William the Conqueror to take the oath of allegiance to himself, 1086. 2. Summoned by Henry I to swear to the succession of Prince William (1103–20), 1116. 3. National councils, 1296, 1328, 1384.

Salk Vaccine, against poliomyelitis, was developed by the American scientist Jonas Salk in 1954.

Salona (Serb.–Cr. **Solin**). Sacked by Avars, 639. *See also* SPLIT.

Salonika, Greece. Rebuilt by Cassander on the site of Therme and named Thessalonika, 315 B.C.; surrendered to the Romans,168 B.C.; made a free city, 42 B.C.; St. Paul preached there, A.D. 52; taken by the Saracens, 904; by the Normans of Sicily, 1185; by the Turks, 1430; Young Turk revolution broke out here, 1908; captured by the Greeks, 8 Nov. 1912, during the First Balkan War. Assigned to Greece by Treaty of London, 30 May 1913. French and British troops entered, 5 Oct. 1915. Venizelist revolutionaries here declared war on Germany and Turkey, 23 Nov. 1916. Great fire, 18 Aug. 1917. French and British forces used S. as base for their operations against Bulgaria until end of World War I. *See* GREECE, MODERN and WORLD WAR I.

Salt Lake City, U.S.A. Founded by the Mormons (*q.v.*), 1847. Became a city, 1851.

Salvador, El. Conquered, 1526, by Spaniards under Pedro de Alvarado, who built capital San Salvador, 1528; formed part of Guatemala colony until 1821, of Mexico until 1823, and of Central American Federation, 1823–39; became independent, 1841. New and more liberal constitution, 1950. U.S.A. sent a military mission to train S.'s armed forces, 1954. Rivera, a supporter of the U.S. alliance, elected President, 1962.

Salvation Army, The. Founded by William Booth, 1865.

Salzburg, Austria. The S. music festival was founded in 1870; it became an annual event from 1920 onwards.

Samaria. City founded by King Omri (*c.* 887–876 B.C.), and extended by Ahab (*c.* 876–853 B.C.), kings of Israel. Destroyed by Assyrians, 721. Colonized by Alexander, 331. Burnt down, A.D. 66; but rebuilt, mostly by Herod the Great (39–34 B.C.), who renamed it Sebaste. Twentieth-century excavations have revealed the remains of Ahab's palace.

Sam Browne Belt. Named after its in-

ventor Sir Samuel Browne (1824–1901). The British Army discarded it for field service after 1939, but it is still worn with service dress.

Samoan Islands, Pacific. Visited by the Dutch, 1721–2; by Bougainville, 1768; Christianity introduced, 1830; independence recognized by European powers, 1889. Treaty of 1899 divided Pacific Islands between England, Germany, and the U.S.A.; W. Samoa ceded to Germany and Tutuila to U.S.A. W. Samoa was mandated to New Zealand, 1920. Swain's Island ceded to the U.S.A., 1925, and considered an integral part of American Samoa.

Samos, Aegean island, colonized by Ionian Greeks, eleventh century B.C. Oligarchy overthrown, 535; tyranny of Polycrates, 535–522; then subject to Persia until 479, when it regained independence and joined the Delian League. Seceded in 440, but reduced by Athens and became tributary to her. Under Spartan domination, 404–394; again subject to Persia from 387 until its recovery by Athens, 366. Subsequent history uncertain until given by Rome to Eumenes II of Pergamum (*q.v.*) in 189 B.C. Genoese colony, A.D. 1346–1560; then Turkish until 1834, when it became a virtually independent principality. Annexed to kingdom of Hellenes, 1912. British forces landed, but withdrew, together with Italian garrison, Sept. 1943.

Sanctions. Use of term became current in present sense, 1919. S. were first applied, 1921: at Düsseldorf by the French, and later, in 1935, against Italy. Suggested use against Katanga, 1961–2.

Sanctuary, Right of. Abolished by law in 1624, so far as felons were concerned, although debtors were able to take refuge in London and elsewhere until the end of the seventeenth century.

Sandhurst. *See* ROYAL MILITARY ACADEMY.

Sandwich Islands. *See* HAWAIIAN ISLANDS.

Sandringham, Norfolk. Estate purchased by the Prince of Wales, 1862. House rebuilt, 1871. King George VI *d.* here, 6 Feb. 1952.

San Francisco, California. Formerly *Yerba Buena.* Spanish mission arrived at, 27 June 1776; American settlement, 1836; name changed to present one, 1847; discovery of gold, 1849; subject to U.S.A., 1850; disorder in and vigilance committee appointed, 1851; earthquakes at, 1868, 1872, and 1906.

San Francisco Conference opened, 25 Apr. 1945. Broke up, July 1945.

San Marino City founded, A.D. 885.

Republic reputedly dates from second half of fourth century A.D. Treaty relations with Italy established, 1862; treaties of friendship, 1897 and 1953. Constitution, though technically inviolate, dominated by Fascist regime from 1923 to 1943. Neutrality violated by Germans and by British, Sept. 1944. Communist infiltration led to a government crisis, and a provisional government was set up of anti-Communists, supported by Italy. Government coalition confirmed in office by 1959 elections.

Sans Souci (Potsdam), built and laid out by G. W. von Knabelsdorff for Frederick the Great, 1745–7.

Santa Cruz de Teneriffe. Spanish fleet destroyed by Blake, 1657; attacked by Nelson, who here lost his arm, 1797.

Santiago, Spain. Sacked by Moors, A.D. 995, who held it till taken by Ferdinand III, 1235; captured by French, 1809; restored, 1814.

Santo Domingo. *See* DOMINICAN REPUBLIC.

Sarajevo Crime. Archduke Franz Ferdinand, heir of Emperor Francis Joseph, and his consort Sophia, Duchess of Hohenberg, were assassinated in S., 28 June 1914.

Sarawak. By cession from the sultanate of Brunei (*see* BORNEO). James Brooke became Rajah of S., 24 Sept. 1841. Independence recognized by Britain, 1863. British protectorate, 1888. End of absolute rule proclaimed, Feb. 1941. Japanese invasion began, 16 Dec. 1941. Oilfields recaptured by Australian 9th Division, June 1945. Ceded by Rajah Sir Charles Brooke to Britain, Feb. 1946. Vote in favour of cession by Council Negri, 17 May 1946. Proclaimed a crown colony, 1 July 1946, and has administratively formed a part of British Borneo since that time. New constitution, 1956. To form part of Malaysia (*q.v.*) from 31 Aug. 1963.

Sardinia, Island of. Conquered by Vandals (*q.v.*), 435. Conquered by the Byzantines *c.* 540. Conquered by Saracens, tenth century. Successful revolt against Saracens, 1052, and acquired by Norman kingdom of Naples *c.* 1060. Came under Hohenstaufen rule, 1189. To Aragon, 1323. Placed under Spanish viceroys, 1478–1713. To Austria, 1713. To Duke of Savoy, 1720, who then took the title of King of S. *See* SARDINIA, KINGDOM OF and SAVOY.

Sardinia, Kingdom of. At the acquisition of S. by the dukes of Savoy (*q.v.*), the latter proclaimed themselves kings of S., 1720. Deprived of their mainland territories by Napoleon, 1796, but reinstated with Genoa added by Congress of Vienna, 1814. Merged in Italy when the kings of S. became kings of Italy, 1861.

Sardinian Convention, 1855, between Britain, France, and Sardinia, by which the King of Sardinia agreed to furnish troops for the Crimea.

Sargasso Sea. First observed by Columbus, 1492.

Sark (Sercq) became fief of English crown, 1066. Demilitarized and occupied by Germans, 1 July 1940. Raided by British Commando, night 3–4 Oct. 1942. German garrison capitulated, 9 May 1945. British military government functioned until 25 Aug. 1945. New harbour opened, 23 June 1949.

Sarum, Old, became seat of bishopric, formerly at Sherborne, in 1078. A cathedral, begun 1067, was burned down, 1092. See removed to New Sarum (i.e. Salisbury), 1219. Parliamentary borough abolished, 1832.

Saskatchewan, province of Canada (*q.v.*). Name means 'Rapid River' in the language of the Crees, who before 1869 were almost the sole inhabitants. In the 1870s a settlement began, partly by half-breeds who took part in Riel's second rebellion, 1885. Constituted a province, 1905. University of S., at Saskatoon, incorporated, 1907. Introduction of a state health service provoked a doctors' strike, July 1962, eventually settled by mediation.

Satellites. First four man-made earth S. put into orbit were Sputnik I, 184 lb., 4 Oct. 1957; Sputnik II, 1118 lb. 3 Nov. 1957 (both Russian); Explorer I, 31 lb., 31 Jan. 1958, and Vanguard I, *c.* 3 lb., 17 Mar. 1958 (both from the U.S.A.). *See also* ROCKETS and SPACE FLIGHTS.

Satellite Towns. First to be built was Welwyn Garden City (1920). Seven S. T. round London projected under New Towns Act, 1946. Work begun on the first of these (Stevenage), 1947. *See* GARDEN CITY.

Saudi Arabia. Nominally a dependency of Turkish Empire from 1871. As Nejd, consisted of two emirates, Eastern and Western Nejd, until 1892, when Eastern defeated and absorbed Western. Ibn Saud, who seized the emirate in 1905, annexed province of Hasa, on the Persian Gulf, 1914. Inactive during World War I, by 1920 he had annexed parts of Asir; in 1921 Hail and other places. He subdued the new kingdom of Hejaz, 1925; proclaimed King of Hejaz, 1926, and Sultan of Nejd, 1927. The enlarged realm, in 1932, was named S. A. British missions helped train Saudi armed forces, 1947–51. New agreement with Arabian American Oil Co., Jan. 1951, provided for 50–50 division of profits. Ibn Saud *d.* 9 Nov. 1953; succeeded by his son, Saud ibn Abdul-Aziz. U.S.A. obtained lease of base at Dharan, 1957. Relations with the United Arab Republic (*q.v.*) deteriorated after 1958. In Nov. 1960 S. A. broke off diplomatic relations with the United Arab Republic, claiming that Yemeni and the United Arab Republic forces were launching an aggressive attack on her, but the dispute was settled in Apr. 1963. Prince Feisal, the new Prime Minister, announced the end of slavery in S. A., 6 Nov. 1962. King Saud was reported to be seriously ill, and visited Europe for medical treatment, 1963.

Saurashtra, India. Confederation of former princely states of W. India set up, Mar. 1948. Merged into Bombay State in the reorganization of 1956.

Savannah, U.S.A. Taken by British, 1778. Americans and French repulsed, 1779. British evacuation, 1782. First steamship (the *Savannah*) to cross the Atlantic sailed from S. to Liverpool, 1819.

Savings Banks. First suggested by Defoe, 1697, but first practical scheme started by Rev. J. Smith, who instituted a S. bank for his parish, 1799. Post Office S. bank established, 1861. In U.S.A. first S. B. at Boston and Philadelphia, 1816. New York, 1819.

Savoy. Duchy founded by Umberto Biancamano, 1034. Piedmont acquired by marriage, 1056. The dukes of S. became kings of Sardinia (*q.v.*), 1720. The district of S. was annexed by France, 1792, but returned to Sardinia, 1814. In 1860 it was finally ceded to France.

Savoy Conference, The. For the purpose of discussing changes in the liturgy of the Church of England (*q.v.*); it was attended by Church and Puritan parties, and sat, 15 Apr.–24 July 1661.

Savoy Palace (London). Built by Peter of Savoy, 1245; burnt by Wat Tyler, 1381; restored by Henry VII; used as a hospital till eighteenth century; finally taken down, 1817. The chapel survives, having twice been considerably restored.

Saxony. Ancient tribal duchy in NW. Germany broken up, 1180. The name survived in districts of Lauenburg (annexed to Hanover, 1680) and Wittenberg, which with Thuringia and Meissen became under Frederick of Meissen the nucleus of the modern S. in E. Central Germany, 1423. Ravaged by Hussites, 1429–1430. S. divided between Ernestine and Albertine families at Partition of Leipzig, 1485. John Frederick (Ernestine) forced to transfer the electoral title to the Albertine branch (capitulation of Wittenberg), 1547. Treaty of Naumburg results in foundation of the five Thuringian duchies, 1554. Devastated in Thirty Years War, 1618–48. Augustus the Strong, Elector of S., elected King of Poland, 1697. Polish connection continues till 1762. S. joins the *Fürstenbund*,

1785. Frederick Augustus I assumes title of king, 1806, and becomes Duke of Warsaw, 1807. Half S. annexed by Prussia, 1815. New constitution, 1831. Revolutions, 1848–9. In alliance with Austria against Prussia, 1866. Last king abdicates 9 Nov. 1918. Republican constitution adopted, 1 Nov. 1920. Nazis seize power, 1933. Since 1945 the name 'S.' has appeared in the names of three German *Länder*, two in the German Democratic Republic and one, Lower S., in the German Federal Republic.

Scala, La (Opera House, Milan), completed, 1778; restored, 1878, 1922; severely damaged, 1943; reopened, 1947.

Scapa Flow. Admiral Reuter scuttled interned German fleet, 21 June 1919. German submarine penetrated the basin, 14 Oct. 1939, and sank the battleship *Royal Oak* with the loss of 810 lives.

Schism Act, The, 1714. Replaced by Occasional Conformity Act, 1719.

Schleswig-Holstein. Convention of Gastein, 1865, provided that H. should be under Austrian occupation and S. under Prussian; by the Treaty of Prague, 1866, Austria resigned her rights; it was stipulated that North S. should be reunited to Denmark if the people wished it; nothing was done, however, and the two countries were organized as a single Prussian province, 1867. After plebiscites of the inhabitants of North and South S., North S. was assigned to Denmark, and renamed South Jutland, 1919. German population of H. and South S. greatly increased by influx of displaced East Germans, 1945–6.

Schmalkalden, League of. Formed by the Protestants of Germany, who met at the town of S. on 22 Dec. 1530. It was finally organized in Dec. 1531.

Schneider Trophy. First race, 1913. Annual till 1927, when it became biennial; the trophy was won outright by Britain in 1931, and there have therefore been no contests since.

Schools, Brothers of the Christian. A Roman Catholic congregation for the education of the poor, founded, 1679, and organized by the Abbé de la Salle in France, 1683; Pope Benedict XIII acknowledged the order, 1725.

Scientific and Industrial Research, Department of, originally a committee of the Privy Council, appointed by Order in Council, 28 July 1915. Charters, 23 Nov. 1916 and 27 Apr. 1928. Department of Scientific and Industrial Research Act, 1956.

Scientists. Among the most prominent are:

Abbe, Ernst, 1840–1905
Abel, Sir Frederick Augustus, 1827–1902

Agassiz, Alexander, 1835–1910
Ampère, André Marie. 1775–1836
Aquinas, St. Thomas, 1225–74
Archimedes, 287–212 B.C.
Aristotle, 384–322 B.C.
Arrhenius, Straute Augustus, 1859–1927
Avogadro, Amedeo, 1776–1856
Bacon, Roger, c. 1214–94
Baird, John L., 1889–1946
Banting, Frederick Grant, 1891–1941
Berthelot, Marcelin, 1827–1907
Black, Joseph, 1728–99
Bohr, Niels, 1885–
Bose, Sir Jagadis Chandra, 1858–1937
Boyle, Hon. Robert, 1627–91
Bragg, Sir William, 1862–1942
Braun, Wernher von, 1912–
Bunsen, Robert, 1811–99
Cavendish, Henry, 1731–1810
Copernicus, Nicolaus, 1473–1543
Crookes, William, 1832–1919
Curie, Marie, 1867–1934
Curie, Pierre, 1859–1906
Dalton, John, 1766–1844
Darwin, Erasmus, 1731–1802
Darwin, Charles, 1809–82
Davy, Sir Humphry, 1778–1829
Descartes, René, 1596–1650
Dewar, Sir James, 1842–1923
Dyson, Sir Frank, 1868–1939
Eddington, Sir Arthur, 1882–1944
Edison, Thomas, 1847–1931
Ehrlich, Paul, 1854–1915
Einstein, Albert, 1879–1955
Euclid, 330 ?–280 B.C.
Fabre, Jean Henri, 1823–1915
Faraday, Michael, 1791–1867
Fleming, Sir Alexander, 1881–1955
Galileo, Galilei, 1564–1642
Gauss, Karl Friedrich, 1777–1855
Haeckel, Ernst, 1834–1919
Haldane, John B. S., 1892–
Haldane, John Scott, 1860–1936
Herschel, Sir William, 1738–1822
Hipparchus of Nicaea, 160–125 B.C.
Humboldt, Alexander von, 1769–1859
Huxley, Thomas Henry, 1825–95
Huxley, Julian, 1887–
Jeans, Sir James, 1877–1946
Joliot-Curie, Pierre, 1900–58
Kepler, Johannes, 1571–1630
Lavoisier, Antoine, 1743–94
Leibnitz, Gottfried Wilhelm, 1646–1716
Lodge, Sir Oliver, 1851–1941
Low, Archibald Montgomery, 1888–1956
Marconi, Marchese Guglielmo, 1874–1937
Mayer, Julius Robert, 1814–78
Newton, Sir Isaac, 1643–1727
Nobel, Alfred Bernhard, 1833–96
Ohm, Georg Simon, 1789–1854
Paracelsus, Theophrastus, 1493–1541
Pascal, Blaise, 1623–62
Pasteur, Louis, 1822–95
Piccard, Auguste, 1884–1962
Poincaré, Jules Henri, 1854–1912

Priestley, Joseph, 1733–1804
Robinson, Sir Robert, 1886–
Röntgen, Wilhelm Konrad, 1845–1923
Ross, Sir Ronald, 1857–1932
Rutherford, Lord, 1871–1937
Salk, Jonas Edward, 1914–
Saussure, Horace Bénédicte de (physicist), 1740–99
Siemens, Werner S., 1816–92
Thomson, Sir Joseph John, 1856–1940
Vinci, Leonardo da, 1452–1519
Volta, Count Alessandro, 1745–1827
Wallace, Alfred Russell, 1823–1913
Watson-Watt, Sir Robert, 1892–
Watt, James, 1736–1819
Whittle, Sir Frank, 1907–
Wilson, Charles Thomson Rees, 1869–1959

Scilly Islands (Sillinae). Conquered by Athelstan, 938. Given to the abbey of Tavistock by Henry I. Became crown property on dissolution of monasteries, 1539; leased to Francis Godolphin, 1571; civil power granted him, 1593; Godolphin leases ended, 1830; leases granted by Duchy of Cornwall to Augustus John Smith, 1834; his successors, the Dorrien-Smiths, in 1920 surrendered all except Tresco, Samson, and Tean. Exemption from income tax ended by Finance Act, 1953.

Scone, Stone of, taken to Westminster by Edward I, 1296. Taken away by Scottish Nationalists on Christmas Eve, 1950. Handed to the curator of Arbroath Abbey, Apr. 1951. Returned to Westminster Abbey, Feb. 1952.

Scotland. St. Columba founds Iona and begins the conversion of the Picts, 563. Rise of the Scots under Constantine I, 789–820. Kenneth McAlpine unifies south S. and founds kingdom of S. proper, 832–60. Malcolm I conquers Strathclyde (q.v.), 946. Malcolm II conquers Lothian, 1018. Duncan killed by Macbeth, 1040. Macbeth defeated by Siward and Malcolm Canmore at Dunsinane, 1054, and killed, 1057. Malcolm Canmore becomes king, 1058. He does homage to William I of England, 1070. David defeated by English at battle of the Standard, 1138. Malcolm IV subdues Galloway, 1160. Defeat of Haakon of Norway at battle of Largs, 1263. Acquisition from Norway of Hebrides and Isle of Man at Treaty of Perth, 1266. Margaret, the ' Maid of Norway,' dies, 1290. Edward I awards throne of S. to John Baliol, 1292. Franco-Scots alliance, 1295. Wallace defeats English at Stirling Bridge, 1297. Wallace defeated at battle of Falkirk, 1298. Wallace captured, 1304. Robert Bruce crowned king, 25 Mar. 1306. Accepted by clergy, 1310. Defeats Edward II at

Bannockburn, 1314. Edward Bruce invades Ireland, 1315–18. Anglo-Scots truce, 1323. Battle of Halidon Hill, 1333. David II captured at Neville's Cross, 1346. David released by Treaty of Berwick, 1357. Robert II, first of the Stuarts, succeeds to the throne, 1371. Battle of Chevy Chase (Otterburn), 1388. James I murdered at Perth, 1437. James II killed at Roxburgh, 1460. James III annexes Orkneys and Shetlands, 1471. James III murdered, 1488. James IV killed at battle of Flodden, 1513. Knox begins Reformation, 1541. Defeat at battle of Solway Moss, 1542. English sack Edinburgh, 1544. Henry VIII of England instigates the murder of Cardinal Beaton, 1546. Knox flees to France, 1547. The Covenant signed, 1557. Treaty of Berwick, 1560. Papal jurisdiction abolished, 1560. Mary Queen of Scots marries Darnley, 1565. Rizzio murdered, 1566. Darnley murdered, 1567. Mary flees to England, and is imprisoned by Elizabeth, 1568. James VI takes over government, 1578. He signs the second Confession of Faith, 1581. Mary beheaded at Fotheringhay, 1587. Presbyterianism established, 1592, but king reintroduces episcopacy, 1597. James VI becomes King of England as James I, 1603. Charles I authorizes new book of canons, 1635. First Bishops' War, 1637. National Covenant, 1638. Second Bishops' War, 1639–40. The Solemn League and Covenant, 1643. Covenanters' rebellion defeated by Monmouth at Bothwell Brig, 1679. Jacobites defeated at Killiecrankie, 1689. Massacre of Glencoe, 1692. Legislative Union with England, 1707. *See* ENGLISH HISTORY and GREAT BRITAIN, JACOBITES, etc.

Scotland, Sovereigns of :

Constantine I	789–820
Kenneth I (McAlpine)	832–860
Donald	860–863
Constantine II	863–877
Eocha	881–889
Donald I	889–900
Constantine III	900–942
Malcolm I	942–954
Indulf	954–962
Dubh	962–967
Cullean	967–971
Kenneth II	971–995
Cuilean	967–971
Kenneth II	971–995
Constantine IV	995–997
Kenneth III	997–1005
Malcolm II	1005–1034
Duncan	1034–1040
Macbeth	1040–1057
Lulach	1057–1058

Malcolm III (Canmore)	1058–1093
Donald Bane	1093
Duncan II	1094
{ Donald Bane (again)	1094–1097
{ Edmund	1094–1097
Edgar	1097–1107
Alexander I	1107–1124
David I	1124–1153
Malcolm IV	1153–1165
William the Lion	1165–1214
Alexander II	1214–1249
Alexander III	1249–1286
Margaret (' the Maid of Norway ')	1286–1290
Interregnum	1290–1292
John Baliol	1292–1296
Interregnum	1296–1306
Robert I (Bruce)	1306–1329
David II (Bruce)	1329–1371
Robert II (Stuart)	1371–1390
Robert III	1390–1406
James I	1406–1437
James II	1437–1460
James III	1460–1488
James IV	1488–1513
James V	1513–1542
Mary (Abdicated)	1542–1567
James VI	1567–1603

James VI became James I of England, 1603. *See* ENGLISH SOVEREIGNS AND THEIR CONSORTS.

Scotland, Church of. Founded by John Knox (1505–72) and Andrew Melville (1545–1622). First Assembly ratified Confession of Faith, 20 Dec. 1560. Act of Scottish Parliament establishing the C. of S. passed, 1592. Episcopacy finally abandoned, 1690. Union with United Free Church of Scotland, 3 Oct. 1929.

Scotland Yard, the London palace of the Scottish kings, was demolished soon after 1603. Last Scottish sovereign to use it had been Queen Margaret Tudor (*d.* 1541). Police office set up, 1829, which moved to New S. Y. and became H.Q. Metropolitan Police, 1891.

Seal of England, Keeper of the Great. First keeper, Richard, a chaplain, 1116; joined to Lord Chancellorship, 1563.

Seal of the United States, Great. Design adopted by Congress, 20 June 1782.

S.E.A.T.O. *See* SOUTH-EAST ASIA TREATY ORGANIZATION.

Sebastopol. A town in the Crimea, built in 1784; famous for the eleven months' siege by the English and French in 1854–1855, after which it was largely rebuilt, and the siege by the Germans, 1941–2, which also resulted in widespread destruction of the town.

Second Empire. Dec. 1852–4 Sept. 1871. *See* FRANCE.

Second Republic. 24 Feb. 1848–Dec. 1852. *See* FRANCE.

N*

Secretary of State (U.S.A.). First appointment (that of Thomas Jefferson) made, 1789.

Secretary of State for Scotland appointed under terms of the Act of Union, 1707, but office abolished in 1746, when its duties devolved on the Home Secretary. In 1827 these were delegated to the Lord Advocate; Secretaryship created, 1885, and office of S. of S. re-established, 1926.

Sedan Chairs. First used in England, 1581; in general use, 1649.

Sederunt, Act of, 1532. James V of Scotland conferred on the Scottish Court of Session the power to regulate Courts of Law by means of A. of S. Power confirmed, 1540.

Seditious Meetings Act. Introduced by William Pitt in 1795. It prohibited the meeting of more than 50 persons (except county and borough meetings duly called) for the consideration of petitions or addresses for reform in Church or State. S. M. and Assemblies Bill, 1817.

Selangor, state of the Federation of Malaya. Reigning dynasty established, 1743; entered into commercial treaty with E. India Co., 1818; accepted British resident and protection, 1874.

Self-Denying Ordinance. A measure introduced into the Long Parliament on 9 Dec. 1644. It was to enact ' that no member of either House of Parliament should during the war enjoy or execute any office or command, military or civil.' Rejected by the Lords, it was modified to enact merely that within 40 days all members of either House should resign any office bestowed by the then existing Parliament, and was passed 3 Apr. 1645. Thus Essex and other Presbyterians were removed and replaced by Cromwell's nominees, and since, under the Ordinance as finally passed, reappointment was allowed, Cromwell became cavalry commander.

Seljuk, Turkish dynasty, was descended from eponymous chieftain who *fl.* 950 *as* first Moslem Emir of Bokhara. His grandson, Toghrul Beg, became Shah of Persia, and established new capital at Merv, 1040; he captured Bagdad, 1055. Toghrul Beg's successor, Alp Arslan, defeated and captured the Emperor Romanus at Manzikert, 1071. On death of Malik Shah (1092) the S. domains were split among four branches of the dynasty the last of which was supplanted by the Ottomans *c.* 1300.

Selsey, original seat of the S. Saxon bishopric, founded by Wilfrid of Ripon *c.* 683, removed to Chichester, 1079.

Semaphore invented by Edgeworth, 1767; adapted by Chappe, 1794; by Sir G. Murray, 1795; Sir H. Popham's system

adopted by Royal Navy for sea service, 1816, but replaced by Pasley's system, 1827. Present system not fully evolved until 1890.

Senate, Roman, first mentioned, 509 B.C., as having 300 members, all patricians; plebeians admitted shortly before 401 B.C. It existed, though largely deprived of effective power, as long as the Western Roman Empire (*q.v.*).

Senegal. First European explorer in modern times was Jean de Béthencourt (1406). French factories established, 1626, but displaced by English; returned, 1677; again displaced by British, 1720–63: this settlement confirmed, 1783; abandoned between 1789 and 1815, the colony was re-established and re-explored, 1824. Dakar (*q.v.*) founded by Gen. Faidherbe, who landed, 1852, and became governor, 1854. Member of the French Community from 25 Nov. 1958. S. became an independent republic on 20 Aug. 1960, after having been a partner (with the Sudan) in the Federation of Mali from Jan. 1959 until Aug. 1960. It became a member of the U.N., 29 Sept. 1960. Attempted coup by the Premier failed, 17 Dec. 1962. President took over the government.

Seoul made capital of Korea (*q.v.*) by King Ni Taijo (*fl.* A.D. 1392). Scene of heavy fighting during the Korean War, 1950–1.

Septennial Act, passed, 1716, in force until 1911.

Sepulchre, Church of the Holy, Jerusalem. The first building, commissioned by Constantine, 326, was combined with other small early churches in one building at the time of the Crusades (*q.v.*). Largely rebuilt, 1799 and 1810. East dome damaged in earthquake, 1927. Rockefeller Foundation undertook repairs as result of Harvey Report (1932). Damage caused in battle between Arab Legion (Jordan Army) and Israeli forces, 1947–8, and in the fire of 1949.

Sepulchre, Knights of the, received papal sanction, 1113.

Serbia. Serbs settled in present S. *c.* 610–40. Zhuponiya period, sixth to ninth centuries. Visheslav dynasty early ninth century to 890. Bulgarian supremacy, 890–924. Yovan Vladimir captured by Bulgars, 989. Michael Voislavich king, 1077. S. united and independent under Nemanyich dynasty, 1159–1331. Zenith under Tsar Stephen Dushan, 1331–55. After great Turkish victory at Kossovo Polje (The Field of Blackbirds) S. becomes tributary to Turks, 15 June 1389. Despotate of S., 1389–1459, suppressed by Sultan Mohammed II, 1459. S. a Turkish Pashalik, 1459–1805. Karageorge storms Belgrade, 1805. Limited international recognition of Treaty of Bucharest, 1812. Turkish reconquest, 1813–15. Miloš Obrenović frees S., 1815–17. Becomes hereditary prince, 1830. Milos abdicates, 1839. Alexander Karageorgević elected prince, 1842. International guarantee by Treaty of Paris, 1856. Miloš Obrenović returns, 1858. Succeeded by Michael, 1860. Michael murdered, 1868. Milan elected prince, 1868. Regency till 1872. War with Turkey, 1876–8. Full independence recognized by Treaty of Berlin, 1878. Proclaimed a kingdom, 1882. War with Bulgaria, 1885–6. Milan abdicates, 1889. Alexander Obrenović deposes the regents, 1893. Assassination of Alexander and Queen Draga, 1903. Peter Karageorgević elected king, 15 June 1903. Austria annexes Bosnia, 1908. For later history *see* BALKAN WARS; WORLD WAR I; YUGOSLAVIA. Part of Yugoslavia since 1918.

Serbo-Croatian Language, spoken in the western half of the Balkan peninsula since its penetration by the Slavs in the seventh century A.D. Now the language of Yugoslavia (*q.v.*), except for its constituent republics of Macedonia and Slovenia. Through the second half of the Middle Ages, and down to the end of the eighteenth century, S. was little used as a literary language and the purest artistic tradition were transmitted orally in a wealth of ballads and folk-tales. Ivan Gundulic of Dubrovnik (1589–1638), who wrote pastoral comedy and romantic epic, somewhat influenced by Italian models, is the most considerable writer of the period. In the eighteenth century the search for Russian patronage induced writers to use an admixture of Church Slavonic with the native idiom which had an unfortunate aesthetic effect. The struggle against this influence, comparable with that of French in some western literatures of the same period, was led by Dositej Obradovic (1742–1811), and later with much greater success by Vuk Stefanovic Karadzic (1787–1864), who was a grammarian and philologist; his Serb Grammar was published, 1814, and his Serb Dictionary, 1818, besides which he revised and simplified S. orthography and collected and edited the popular ballads, a collection of which appeared posthumously in nine volumes, 1891. A Serb, he was the pupil of Kopitar the Slovene (*q.v.*), and an example to the Croat Ljudevit Gaj (1809–72), who introduced a phonetic method of spelling Croat dialects in Latin script corresponding to that used by Vuk Karadzic for spelling Serb dialects in Cyrillic script. His newspaper *Danica Ilirska* was suppressed by Austro-

Hungarian censor, 1843. At a congress of Yugoslav scholars in Vienna, 1870, the principle was established of one standard dialect as the literary medium, whether written in the Roman or the Cyrillic alphabet.

Seringapatam. British defeated Tipu Sahib of Mysore, 15 May 1791. In a later war S. was stormed by Madras Army and Tipu killed, 4 May 1799. *See* MYSORE.

Serjeant at Law. This rank became obsolete in 1873.

Settlement, Act of, 1662. Relating to the forfeiture of estates by Irish rebels. Repealed, 1689. Restored, 1690.

Settlement, Act of, 1701. Secured the succession to the throne to the house of Hanover in default of Protestant heirs to the house of Stuart.

Seven Bishops. *See* BISHOPS, SEVEN.

Seven Years War, 1756–63.

1756: Anglo-Prussian alliance, 16 Jan. Franco-Austrian alliance, 1 May. Britain declares war on France, 15 May. Black Hole of Calcutta, 19 June. French take Minorca, 28 June. French take Oswego (Canada), 14 Aug. Prussia invades Saxony, 29 Aug. Saxon Army capitulates, 15 Oct.

1757: Clive takes Calcutta, 2 Jan. Russia, Poland, Sweden, and the Empire declare war on Prussia, 10 Jan. Austrians defeat Prussians at Kolin, 18 June. Clive wins victory at Plassey, 23 June. French defeat British at Hastenbeck, 26 July. Russians and Swedes invade Prussia, Aug.–Sept. British capitulate at Kloster Zeven, 8 Sept. Great Prussian victories at Rossbach over French and Imperialists, 5 Nov.; at Leuthen over Austrians, 5 Dec.

1758: British agree to finance Prussia, 13 Apr. French defeated at Krefeld, 23 June. British take Louisburg, 24 July. Prussians defeat Russians at Zorndorf, 25 Aug. Austrians defeat Prussians at Hochkirch, 14 Oct. British conquer Pittsburgh and French Senegal and Clive forces Dutch in India to surrender at Chinsura, Nov.

1759 (*Annus Mirabilis*): British take Masulipatam, 7 Apr. British defeat French at Minden, 1 Aug. Austro-Russians defeat Prussians at Künersdorf, 12 Aug. British capture Quebec, 18 Sept. British destroy French fleet at Quiberon, 20 Nov. Prussians defeated at Maxen, 21 Nov.

1760: Decisive French defeat in India at Wandewash, 22 Jan. Prussians defeated at Landshut, 23 June. Prussian victory at Liegnitz, 15 Aug. British capture Montreal, 8 Sept. Prussian victory at Torgau, 3 Nov.

1761: British victory at Patna, 15 Jan. British take Pondicherry, 16 Jan. Franco-

Spanish alliance (Third Family Compact), 15 Aug. Austro-Russian invasion of Prussia, Oct.–Dec.

1762: Britain declares war on Spain, 4 Jan. British clear the W. Indies, Jan.–Apr. British cease to subsidize Prussia, Apr. Sweden and Russia make peace with Prussia, May. Prussia defeats Austrians at Bürkersdorf, 21 July. French capitulation at Kassel, 1 Nov. Truce between Prussia, Austria, and Saxony, 24 Nov.

1763: Peace of Paris between Britain, France, Spain, and Portugal, 10 Feb. Peace of Hubertusburg between Prussia and Austria, 15 Feb.

Seville (anct. **Hispalis**; Latin **Julia Romula**), taken by Julius Caesar, 45 B.C., became Roman colony. Taken, A.D. 411, by Vandals, 441 by Visigoths, 712 by Moors. Reconquered 1248 by Castilians. Building of cathedral lasted 1402–1519, though some parts like the Sacristy (1532) were added later, and parts of the older Moorish mosque were incorporated, such as the Orangery and the quadrangular Giralda tower (1184). Other buildings include Alba Palace, 1483; University, 1502; Town Hall, 1527–64; and Exchange, 1583.

Sèvres porcelain first manufactured, 1756. Treaty of S. signed, 10 Aug. 1920.

Sewing-machine first built by Thomas Saint, 1790 (for shoemakers); for tailoring by Madersperger, 1814; B. Thimonier, 1830; Walter Hunt, 1834; Elias Howe, 1845; I. M. Singer, 1851; A. B. Wilson, 1852.

Seychelles, discovered by Portuguese, 1505. Explored by French, 1742 and 1744, and captured by the British, 1794. Ceded to Britain, 1814. Politically separated from Mauritius (q.v.), 1897; letters patent granted, 1903. Leaders of Arab revolt in Palestine exiled here, 1937. Archbishop Makarios of Cyprus banished to S., 1956–7.

Shakers (United Society of Believers in Christ's Second Appearing) founded c. 1747 in England. Moved to America, 1774. Community of Mt. Lebanon, New York State, founded 1787.

Shakespeare's Works. Shakespeare was b. in 1564 and d. in 1616. First collected edition of his works, 1623, in folio. The first plays produced about 1590, in which Shakespeare himself took part; the Globe Theatre, Southwark, was the scene of most of the early productions. Shakespeare's plays with conjectural dates of composition are: *Titus Andronicus* and *Love's Labour 's Lost*, 1590; *The Two Gentlemen of Verona*, 1591; *Henry VI*, *The Comedy of Errors, Romeo and Juliet*, and *A Midsummer Night's Dream*, 1592;

Richard II and *Richard III*, 1593; *King John*, 1594; *The Merchant of Venice* and *The Taming of the Shrew*, 1596; *Henry IV*, *Henry V*, and *The Merry Wives of Windsor*, 1598; *Julius Caesar*, 1598–9; *Much Ado about Nothing* and *As You Like It*, 1598–1600; *Twelfth Night*, 1600; *All 's Well that Ends Well*, 1601; *Hamlet*, 1602; *Troilus and Cressida*, 1603; *Othello* and *Measure for Measure*, 1604; *Macbeth* and *King Lear*, 1606; *Timon of Athens*, 1607; *Pericles* and *Antony and Cleopatra*, 1608; *Coriolanus*, 1609; *Cymbeline*, 1610; *The Winter's Tale* and *The Tempest*, 1611; *Henry VIII*, 1612. Poems, with dates of publication: *Venus and Adonis*, 1593; *The Rape of Lucrece*, 1594; *The Passionate Pilgrim* (partly Shakespeare's), 1599; *The Phoenix and the Turtle*, 1601; Sonnets, and *A Lover's Complaint*, 1609.

Shanghai first settled by Europeans under terms of Treaty of Nanking, 1842. Central Bank of China opened, 1928. Battles between Kuomintang and Japanese, 1932 and 1937. Occupied by Japanese, 1938, and International Settlement taken over by them, 1941. Treaty rights of European powers abandoned, 1947. S. captured by Communists, 1949. Heavily bombed by Formosa Nationalists, 1949–50.

Shan States annexed to Burma, 1885. Council of Chiefs instituted, 1922; combined with Wa States into single S. State, 1947.

Sheerness. A royal dockyard in Kent, made by Charles II in 1663; taken by the Dutch under De Ruyter in 1667; Nore mutiny here, 1798; modern dockyard made in 1814.

Sheffield, England. First charter, 1297. Famous for knife-making in fourteenth century. Steelworks since nineteenth century. Borough, 1843; city, 1882. University founded, 1905. Diocese of S., 1914. City severely damaged by gales, Feb. 1962.

Sheriffs became important in English provincial administration c. A.D. 1000, and more so after 1066. Yearly tenure of office introduced, 1100; confirmed, 1258. Ceased to command county militia, 1557. Modern practice regulated by Sheriffs' Act, 1887.

Sherman Act (U.S.A.), against trusts, passed 1890 at instance of John S. (1823–1900).

Shetland Islands. Written sources state Scandinavian settlement began c. A.D. 800, but contact with Scandinavia probably much earlier than this. Early Norse form of S. place-names indicates occupation before 700. Annexed to Norway, A.D. 875. Came under Scottish rule, 1466. Excavations at Jarlshof,

Sumburgh, 1951–2, indicate the islands were inhabited in the first century A.D. by people who kept (and ate?) horses. This proves the S. pony was *not*, as previously thought, introduced from Norway.

Ship. Roman ' *corvus* ' in use, 260 B.C. Light galleys became standard Mediterranean warships after battle of Actium, 31 B.C. Large warships built in England, 1413. Success of galleasses at battle of Lepanto, 1571. *Royal George* launched, 1756; *Victory* 1765. Earliest iron ship built at Foss (Yorkshire), 1777. Transatlantic packets began, 1816. First genuine clipper, 1832. First power boat, 1786. First paddle steamer, *Charlotte Dundas*, 1801. First screw steamer, *Archimedes*, 1839. Twin-screw ship, *Flora*, 1862. Steam turbine, *Turbinia*, 1894. First Diesel and electric ship, *Wandal*, 1903. First gas-turbine driven ship, 1948. First nuclear-powered vessel, the U.S. submarine *Nautilus*, completed her trials, 1955.

Ship-money was first levied by Ethelred, 1007. Specifically forbidden by Petition of Right, 1628, but declared legal by a majority of judges of the Court of Exchequer, 1637. Abolished by statute, 1641.

Shipping, Ministry of, formed, 1916, wound up, 1919.

Shoguns of Japan. Originally a military C.-in-C. the first shogun was Otomo Otomaro, 794. When Yoritomo became shogun in 1192 the shogun was the political ruler of Japan. The shogunate was itself under a regency, 1205–1333. The office was held by the Ashillaga family, 1338–1500. Oda Nobunaga seizes shogunate, 1568. Succeeded by Hideyoshi, 1582. With the appointment of Iyeyasu in 1603 the office became hereditary in the Tokugawa family until its abolition, 1867. The following are the Tokugawa S.:

Iyeyasu	1603	Yoshimune	1716
Hidetada	1616	Iyeshige	1745
Iyemitsu	1622	Iyeharu	1760
Iyetsuna	1651	Iyenari	1786
Tsunayoshi	1680	Iyeyoshi	1838
Iyenobu	1709	Iyesada	1853
Iyetsugo	1713	Iyemochi	1858

Yoshinobu (Kei-Ki) 1866–7.

Shop Hours Acts (Britain), 1886, 1892, 1893, 1899, 1904.

Shops Acts, 1911, 1912, 1928, 1934, 1937.

Shops and Offices Act, 1963, legislated to improve working conditions of white-collar workers.

Shoreditch (London). First public theatre in England built here, 1576.

Siam. *See* THAILAND.

Siberia. Explored by Russians in 1483. Tatar khanate, whose capital was Sibir

on the Irtish, formed in sixteenth century. Russian conquest begun by Yermak, 1579. Tobolsk built on site of Sibir, 1587. Traders reached Sea of Okhotsk, 1639. Russians reached the Amur, 1651. Treaty of Nertchinsk established boundary between Russia and China, 1689. S. first used as place of banishment, 1710. Sakhalin (*q.v.*) occupied, 1853. Petropavlovsk abandoned, 1855. Convention of Aigun, making the Amur boundary between Russia and China, 1857. Country between Ussuri and the sea secured by Treaty of Pekin, and Vladivostok founded, 1860. Construction of Trans-Siberian Railway begun, 1891. Russia occupied Liaotung peninsula and established Port Arthur and Dalny, 1895. Trans-Siberian Railway was completed, partly through Chinese territory, in 1896. The Russo-Japanese War, 1904–5; Port Arthur fell, Jan. 1905, and Japan gained footing on mainland. Exile system abolished, 1914. A new line made the Trans-Siberian Railway complete on Russian territory, 1916. In the struggles that began in Nov. 1917, the Bolsheviks of S. were driven out by Czechs. Britain and France landed contingents at Vladivostok, Aug. 1918, and followed by Japanese, 12 Aug.; on the fall of Chita, 6 Sept., Bolshevik Government disappeared from S. The leader of the reaction, Admiral Koltchak, became dictator after a *coup d'état* at Omsk, 18 Nov. On the resurgence of Bolshevism, Koltchak lost Omsk in Nov. 1919; he was caught and shot, 7 Feb. 1920. Organization into Soviet Republics, 1922–3.

Sicilian Vespers. Massacre of the French began, 30 Mar. 1282.

Sicily. The Phoenicians founded colonies here in 735 B.C., and the Greeks 200 years later; made a Roman province, 241 B.C.; taken by Belisarius, A.D. 535; by Saracens, 832; in Norman possessions, 1072–1194; made one kingdom with Naples, 1130; Charles of Anjou King of the Two Sicilies, 1266; 'Sicilian Vespers,' massacre of French at Palermo, 1282; became a Spanish dependency, 1501; revolution in, 1848; Garibaldi landed at Marsala, 1860; defeated Neapolitans at Milazzo, 1860; annexation with Sardinia and arrival of King Victor Emmanuel, 1860; annexation to kingdom of Italy, 1860; earthquake at Messina, 1908. In World War II Germans driven out by British, American, and Canadians, 10 July–17 Aug. 1943. *See also* NAPLES.

Sieges:

Acre, 1189–12 July 1191; 16 Mar.–20 May 1799; Apr.–24 June 1832; 3–4 Nov. 1840.
Adrianople, Oct. 1912–26 Mar. 1913.
Alesia, 52 B.C.

Algeciras, 1342-4.
Algiers, 1682-3; 26-27 Aug. 1816; 14 June-5 July 1830.
Almeida, 17 Aug. 1810.
Amiens, 1597.
Ancona, Oct.-13 Nov. 1799.
Antwerp, 1584-5; Dec. 1832; 1914.
Arras, 1640.
Avignon, 10 June-13 Sept. 1226.
Badajoz, 1385; 1396; 1542; 1705; Mar. 1811; Apr. 1812.
Bagdad, 1258.
Barcelona, 1471; 1697; 1705; 1706; Sept. 1714.
Bataan, Jan.-Apr. 1942.
Belgrade, 1456; Aug. 1521; Aug. 1717; Oct. 1789.
Belle Isle, June 1761.
Bergen-op-Zoom, 1588; 1622; Sept. 1747; Mar. 1814.
Berlin (blockade), June 1948-May 1949.
Berwick, 1296; 1333; 1481.
Besançon, 1668; 1674.
Bethune, 1710.
Bilbao, 1835; 1874; 1937.
Bois-le-Duc, 1601; 1603; 1794.
Bologna, 1506; 1796; 1799.
Bomarsund, 1854.
Bonn, 1689; 1703.
Bordeaux, 1451; 1453.
Bouchain, Aug.-Sept. 1711.
Boulogne, Sept. 1544.
Breda, 1625; Feb. 1793.
Brescia, 1512; 1849.
Breslau, 1807.
Brisach, 1638.
Brussels, 1695; 1746.
Budapest, July 1541; Sept. 1686; Dec. 1944-13 Feb. 1945.
Burgos, Sept.-Oct. 1812; June 1813.
Cadiz, 1812.
Calais, Sept. 1346-Oct. 1347; 1558, 1596; 22-7 May 1940.
Calvi, 1794.
Candia, 1667-9.
Capua, 211 B.C.; 1501; 1799.
Cartagena, 1706; Nov. 1873-Jan. 1874.
Chalus, 1199.
Charleroi, 1672; 1690.
Charleston, U.S.A., 1780; Aug. 1863-Feb. 1865.
Chartres, 1568.
Cherbourg, 1418; 1758.
Chester, 1643-6.
Chillon, 1536.
Chitral, Mar.-Apr. 1895.
Ciudad Rodrigo, June-July 1810; 1812.
Colchester, June-Aug. 1648.
Como, 1127.
Compiègne, 1430.
Condé, 1676; 1793; 1794.
Coni, 1691; 1744.
Constantinople, 1453.
Copenhagen, 1658; 1801; 1807.
Cordova, 1012.

Corfu, 1536; 1716-18.
Corinth, 1205; 1209.
Cracow, 1702; 1794.
Cremona, 1702.
Cumae, 553.
Danzig, 1734; 1793; 1807; 1813-14.
Delhi, 1857.
Dien Bien Phu, Apr.-May 1954.
Douay, 1710.
Dresden, 1756; 1760; 1813.
Drogheda, 1649.
Dublin, 1170; 1500; 1649.
Dunkirk, 1646; 1793.
Edinburgh, 1093; 1296.
Edinburgh Castle, 1571.
Exeter, 1136.
Famagusta, 1571.
Flushing, Aug. 1809.
Fredrikshald, 1718.
Gaeta, 1707; 1734; Nov. 1860-Feb. 1861.
Genoa, 1684; 1747; 1800.
Gerona, 1808-9.
Ghent, 1706.
Gibraltar, 1704; 1779; 1782-3.
Glatz, 1622; 1742; 1807.
Gloucester, Aug.-Sept. 1643.
Göttingen, 1760.
Granada, 1491-2.
Groningen, 1594; 1678.
Haarlem, Dec. 1572-July 1573.
Harfleur, 1415.
Heidelberg, 1688.
Herat, 1837-8; 1856.
Humaitá (Paraguay), 1868.
Ismail, 1770; 1790.
Janina, 1913.
Jerusalem, c. 1400 B.C.; 588 B.C.; A.D. 70; 637; 1099.
Kandahar, 1521; 1839-42.
Kars, 1855.
Kehl, 1796-7.
Khartoum, 1884-5.
Kimberley, Oct. 1899-Feb. 1900.
Komárom or Komorn, 1849.
Ladysmith, Nov. 1899-Feb. 1900.
La Motte, 1634.
Landau, 1702; 1703; 1793.
Landrecies, 1712; 1794.
Leipzig, 1547; 1642.
Leith, 1560.
Leningrad, 21 Aug. 1941-18 Jan. 1943.
Lerida, 1647; 1707; 1810.
Leyden, 1574.
Liège, 1468; 1702; 1914.
Lille, 1708; 1792.
Limerick, 1651; 1690-1.
Londonderry, 1689.
Lucknow, 1857.
Luxemburg, 1795.
Lyons, 1793.
Madrid, 1936-9.
Maestricht, 1579; 1673; 1703; 1748; 1793-4.
Mafeking, Oct. 1899-May 1900.
Magdeburg, 1631; 1806.

Mainz, 1689; 1793.
Malaga, 1487.
Malta, 1565; 1798; 1800; June 1940–Nov. 1942.
Mannheim, 1793.
Mantua, 1796–7.
Messina, 1282; 1719; 1848.
Metz, 1552–3; 1870.
Missolonghi, 1822; 1823; 1825–6.
Mons, 1691; 1709; 1746; 1792.
Montargis, 1427.
Montauban, 1621.
Montevideo, 1807; 1814.
Namur, 1692; 1695.
Naples, 1495; 1799; 1806.
Nice, 1705.
Numantia, 134–133 B.C.
Olivenza, 1811.
Olmütz, 1741; 1758.
Orleans, 1428–9; 1563.
Ostend, July 1601–Sept. 1604; 1706; 1745; 1798.
Oudenarde, 1708.
Padua, 1509.
Pampeluna or Pamplona, 1813.
Paris, 885–6; 1594; Sept. 1870–Jan. 1871.
Pavia, 1525; 1655.
Pekin legations, 1900.
Perpignan, 1542; 1642.
Phalsbourg, 1814; 1815; 1870.
Phillipsburg, 1644; 1676; 1688; 1734; 1799–1800.
Plevna, 1877.
Pondicherry, 1748.
Port Arthur, 1904.
Prague, 1741–4.
Quebec, 1759.
Quesnay, 1793–4.
Rheims, 1359.
Rhodes, 1306–9; 1480; 1522.
Richmond (Va.), 1864–5.
Riga, 1700; 1710.
Rochelle, 1573; 1628.
Rome, 1527; 1849.
Romorantin, 1356.
Rouen, 1419; 1449; 1591.
Roxburgh, 1460.
Saguntum, 219 B.C.
Saint-Quentin, 1557.
San Sebastian, 1813.
Saragossa, 1710; 1808; 1809.
Schweidnitz, 1762; 1807.
Scio, 1822.
Scutari, 1913.
Sebastopol, Oct. 1854–Sept. 1855; 1941–1942.
Seringapatam, 1792; 1799.
Seville, 1248.
Silistria, 1854.
Smolensk, 1611; 1812.
Stalingrad, Aug.–Nov. 1942.
Stralsund, 1715.
Strasbourg, 1870.
Tarragona, 1813.
Temesvar, 1716.

Thérouanne, 1303; 1479; 1513.
Thionville, 1792.
Thorn, 1703.
Tobruk, Apr.–10 Dec. 1941; 18–20 June 1942.
Toledo, 1936.
Tortosa, 1810–11.
Toulon, 1707; 1793.
Toulouse, 844; c. 848; 1229.
Tournai, 1340; 1513; 1581; 1667; 1709; 1792.
Tunis, 1270; 1535.
Turin, 1640; 1706.
Valencia, 1812.
Valenciennes, 1677; 1793; 1794.
Vannes, 1342.
Venice, 1849.
Verdun, 1792; 1916.
Vicksburg, 1863.
Vienna, 1529; 1683; 1848.
Warsaw, 1831; 1939; 1944.
Westerplatte, 1939.
Xativa, 1246; 1707.
Xeres, 1262.
York, 1644.
Ypres, 1648; 1794.
Zürich, 1544.
Zutphen, 1586.

Siegfried Line. 1. (Or **Hindenburg Line**.) German line of defence in France in Sept. 1918. 2. German fortifications, properly called the West Wall, stretching from the Dutch to the Swiss frontiers, partly on the E. bank of the Rhine, completed, 1939.

Sierra Leone, Dominion of. Discovered, 1462, by the Portuguese navigator, Pedro de Sintra. Became a settlement for freed slaves, 1786. British colony of S. L. originated in sale of land by native chiefs to some English settlers, 1788. Crown colony, 1808; protectorate, forming the hinterland of the colony, 1896. New constitution, 1958. Became an independent member of the British Commonwealth, 27 Apr. 1961.

Sikhs, religious order founded by Nanak (1469–1539). Became politically independent of the Moguls, 1764. Ranjit Singh became overlord of the confederation of Sikh states, 1805; in 1849 the Punjab, home of all S., came under British rule. Patalia and E. Punjab Union, a Sikh state forming part of the republic of India, was set up, 5 May 1948, but reorganized as the Punjab, 1956. Sikh agitation against alleged Indian discrimination, 1961–2.

Sikkim suffered in eighteenth century from aggression by Nepal (*q.v.*), which was ended by alliance with Britain against Nepal (1814). Site of Darjeeling sold to British for 180,000 Rs., 1835. In Aug. 1947 the dominion of India entered into the same treaty relations with S. as formerly had obtained between S. and Britain.

Silchester, Hants, formerly **Calleva Atrebatum**, was laid out as a Roman town in the first century A.D. Excavated 1890–1909, 1938–9, and 1954.

Silesia. Mutual succession pact between Hohenzollerns (of Prussia) and the Piasts (Rulers) of S., 1537. Last Piast dies and S. seized by the emperor as a Bohemian fief, 1675. Hohenzollern claims renounced in return for Schwiebus, 1686. Schwiebus returned to Austria, 1694. Seized by Frederick the Great of Prussia, 1740. Cession to Prussia finally recognized by Austria, 1763. After plebiscites Teschen ceded to Czechoslovakia and Upper S. partitioned between Germany and Poland, 1920. Teschen taken by Poland, 1938. S. east of the Neisse taken by Poland, 1945, and the German population expelled.

Silk. Silkworms introduced into Europe from China in 552 by two Persian monks; manufactured in Italy, Spain, and S. France, 1510; first S. mills in England, 1604; formerly all S. was brought from abroad.

Silver Coinage. Until Dec. 1920 contained 92·5 per cent silver. Coinage Act, 1920, authorized 50 per cent only. New Coinage Act of 1946 did not legally abolish S. as coinage, but for all practical purposes meant that S. coins were to be replaced by cupro-nickel.

Simplon Pass, Switzerland. Road built by Napoleon, 1800–7. Tunnel built, 1898–1906.

Sinaiticus, Codex, incomplete Greek MS. of Old and New Testaments and some other writings, on vellum. Probably copied in Egypt or Palestine c. 350. Tischendorf (1815–74) found the MS. in the monastery of St. Catherine, Mt. Sinai, 1844 and 1859; he published it in facsimile type, 1862. Photographic reproductions appeared, 1911 and 1922; about 340 leaves of MS. were bought for the British Museum from the Soviet Government, 1933.

Sind, Scinde, annexed to British India, 1843. Autonomous province of Pakistan, 1947–55, when it was integrated into W. Pakistan.

Singapore, the old Malay city, *fl.* in the fourteenth century A.D., but had been destroyed by 1391. Settlement founded by Sir Stamford Raffles, 1819; placed under Bengal Government, 1823; part of Straits Settlements, 1836–1946. British land forces in Malaya retired into S., 30 Jan. 1942. Japanese landed on S. Island, 8 Feb. 1942; garrison surrendered, 15 Feb. Reoccupied by British forces, 5 Sept. 1945. S. now became a separate

Crown colony, distinct from Malayan Union and from Malayan Federation. It had become an important naval base between the two world wars; its new airport opened, 1955, and (1963) it is at present the defence headquarters of the U.K. armed forces in the Far E. An agreement reached in London in Apr. 1957 provided for an internationally self-governing S. and the creation of a S. citizenship. This new constitution came into force in June 1959. A referendum on 1 Sept. 1962 produced a majority in favour of an autonomous S. within the projected Malaysia (*q.v.*).

Sinkiang, formerly Chinese Turkestan, became a separate province at the territorial reorganization of the Manchu Empire, 1882. Russian influence increased steadily from 1911 until 1941, by which date S. was virtually another Soviet republic. In 1942 the Governor declared his allegiance to China, and Chinese control became more effective; but Russian-sponsored Turki-Kazakh revolt, 1944, resulted in virtual home rule, 1946. In 1949 the local civil and military authorities declared for Mao Tse-tung or left the country. S. given the official name of the S. Vighur Autonomous Region of the Chinese People's Republic, Oct. 1955.

Sinking Fund first adopted, 1716, increased, 1727; exhausted, 1786, and new fund started. S. F. on new principle started, 1792; modified by Vansittart, 1813. Legislation on S. Fs. repealed, 1866; another new fund started, 1875; modified by Lloyd George, 1910. Other S. Fs. started by Baldwin, 1923, and Churchill, 1928.

Sinn Fein, Irish nationalist movement, formed about 1905, which, in the period before 1922, aimed at economic and political separation from England. After 1923 S. F. became one of the established Irish political parties.

Sino-Japanese Agreement. Signed, 16 May 1918, to counteract common danger of German penetration towards Eastern Russia.

Sistine Chapel, built for Pope Sixtus IV, 1473–81; Michelangelo painted the ceiling 1508–12, and the E. wall, 1534–41.

Skoda steel works, Brno. Renamed Vladimir Ilyitch Lenin Works, Dec. 1951.

Slavery. Abolition of, in British colonies in 1833, and owners compensated; S. in British possessions terminated following year; the abolition in U.S.A. announced, 1861.

Slave Trade. In England began, 1562; abolished, 25 Mar. 1807.

Slovakia. Under Hungarian domination until 1918, when the Slovaks united with the Czechs of Bohemia, Moravia, and Silesia to form Czechoslovakia (q.v.). Nominally independent as a German satellite, 1938–45. A province of Czechoslovakia again, 1945–8, when it was divided into six administrative regions.

Slovene Literature. Following are some Slovene authors of the modern period:

Jurij Dalmatin, *fl.* 1584, translator (Old Testament).
Tomaz Hren, 1560–1630, theologian.
Matthias Kastelic, 1620–88, theologian.
Marko Pohlin, 1735–1801, grammarian.
Leopold Wolkmer, 1741–1815, fabulist.
Anton Linhart, 1757–95, dramatist.
Valentin Vodnik, 1758–1819, poet.
Jernej Kopitar, 1780–1844, philologist.
Matthias Čop, 1797–1835, critic.
France Preseren, 1800–49, poet.
Janez Blajvajs, 1808–81, essayist.
F. Levstik, 1851–87, popular lyricist.
S. Jenko, 1835–69, lyricist.
J. Stritar, 1836–1923, poet and critic.
J. Jurjic, 1844–81, novelist.
S. Gregorcic, 1844–1906, lyricist.
Stanislas Skrabec, 1844–1918, critic.
I. Tivcar, 1851–1923, novelist.
J. Kersnik, 1852–97, short stories.
A. Askerc, 1856–1912, novelist.
I. Cankar, 1856–1918, short stories.
Zofka Kveder, 1878–1926, novelist.
Prezhikov Voranc, 1893–1950, poet.

Slovenes migrated from the western Carpathians to the valley of the Drava (Drau) about A.D. 600. Threatened by the Avars they appealed for protection to the Franks, to whom they became subject about 790, first under the counts of Friuli and dukes of Carinthia, then, from 1056 onwards, under the counts, later dukes, of Styria. From 1260 to 1282 they formed part of the kingdom of Bohemia (Ottakar II); then passed under Hapsburg dominion, which was finally consolidated in 1335. No major political change took place until 1918 (*see* YUGO-SLAVIA). Their language became separated from Croatian between A.D. 600 and 900, and its earliest written monument, the Freising Leaves, dates from the eleventh century. New Testament rendered into Slovene by Primoz Trubar (1508–86), 1582. First grammar, 1584, by Adam Bohoric, and quadrilingual dictionary, 1592, printed at Wittenberg.

Slovenia is historically speaking an ethnic, not a geographical, term, denoting the land of the Slovenes (*q.v.*). In 1918 S. was formed out of Lower Styria, Carniola, and a small part of Carinthia. The term went out of official use in the internal reorganization of Yugoslavia, 1922, the nearest geographical equivalent being the Banat of the Drava. In 1945 the Federal Republic of S. was constituted, including the same area as in 1918, but including parts of Istria and Venezia Giulia, subject to United Nations decisions concerning Trieste (*q.v.*) territory.

Smallpox. *See* VACCINATION.

Smithfield. A cattle market in 1150 till 11 June 1855; a meat market, 1 Dec. 1868. Famous as a place of Protestant martyrdom, notably during the reign of Mary Tudor, 1553–8.

Smithsonian Institution endowed by bequest of James Smithson (1765–1829) dated 1826. Formally organized, 1846, first buildings completed, 1854.

Smyrna (Turk. Izmir), founded by Greeks *c.* 1000 B.C.; passed into possession of Colophon and thence into the Ionian confederation, *c.* 690 B.C.; captured by Lydians, 630 B.C.; besieged by Timur-i-leng, A.D. 1402; taken by Turks, 1424; occupied by Greek Army, 1919; awarded to Greece (for a trial period of five years) by Treaty of Sèvres, 1920; Greeks expelled, 1922; awarded to Turkey by Treaty of Lausanne, 1923.

Soane Museum (13 Lincoln's Inn Fields). Formed by Sir John Soane; opened, 1833.

Social Credit, the economic theory of C. H. Douglas (*b.* 1879), enunciated in his books *Credit Power and Democracy* and *Economic Democracy*, 1920, and *Social Credit*, 1933. S. C. parties in Canada owe their existence to this doctrine; that of the province of Alberta gained 51 seats in the provincial legislature out of a total of 57, 1948. In the provincial general elections of July 1952 the S. C. Party was successful for the first time in British Columbia, defeating the Liberals and the Socialist Party (C.C.F.). Since that date the party has continued to dominate in Alberta and British Columbia, and held the balance in the Canadian Parliament after the 1962 election. When its members voted against Diefenbaker in Feb. 1963, his government resigned, and in the ensuing elections, which resulted in the return of a Liberal government, the S. C. party's representation fell.

Society Islands, so named in honour of the Royal Society, his patrons, by James Cook, 1769. Windward Islands annexed by France, 1880; Leeward Islands annexed, 1885.

Sofia, anciently **Serdica,** occupied by the Romans, A.D. 29; sacked by the Huns, 447; taken by Bulgars, 808; conquered by Turks, 1382; liberated, 1877; became Bulgarian capital, 1878; university founded, 1904.

Sokol movement (Panslav athletic youth clubs) founded, 1861, by Miroslav Tyrs (1832–84).

Soldiers and Sailors. The following is a selective list of outstanding military and naval commanders prior to 1900. Where not otherwise specified, their distinction is specifically military.

Alexander the Great, 356-323 B.C., Greek.

Attila the Hun, *c.* 400-53.

Belisarius, *c.* 505-65, served Byzantium, probably *b.* in Illyria.

Blake, Robert, 1598-1657, English soldier and sailor.

Blücher, Gebhard Leberecht von, 1742-1819, Prussian.

Caesar, Gaius Julius, 102-44 B.C., Roman.

Charles XII of Sweden, 1682-1718.

Clive, Robert, 1725-74, English.

Condé, Louis II de Bourbon, 1621-86, French.

Cromwell, Oliver, 1599-1658, English.

Drake, Sir Francis, *c.* 1545-96, English sailor.

Prince Eugene of Savoy, 1663-1736, French *b.* but served the Empire.

Frederick II the Great of Prussia, 1712-1786.

Garibaldi, Guiseppe, 1807-82, Italian.

Genghiz Khan, 1162-1227, Mongol Emperor.

Gordon, Charles George, 1833-85, British.

Grant, Ulysses Simpson, 1822-85, American.

Grenville, Sir Richard, *c.* 1541-91, English sailor.

Gustavus VI Adolphus of Sweden, 1594-1632.

Hannibal, 247-*c.* 183 B.C., Carthaginian.

Henry V of England, 1387-1422.

Howard of Effingham, Baron Charles, 1536-1624, English sailor.

Howe, Earl Richard, 1726-99, English sailor.

Hunyadi, John Corvinus, *c.* 1387-1456, Hungarian.

Jackson, Thomas Jonathan, 1824-63, American.

Jones, John Paul, 1747-92, Scots-born American sailor.

Marlborough, John Churchill, Duke of, 1650-1722, English.

Napoleon I Bonaparte, 1769-1821, French.

Nelson, Horatio, Viscount, 1758-1805, English sailor.

Ney, Michel, 1769-1815, French.

Peter I the Great of Russia, 1672-1725.

Roberts, Frederick Sleigh, 1st Earl, 1832-1914, British.

Rupert of Bavaria, Prince, 1619-82 (served England).

Ruyter, Michael Adriaanszoon, 1607-1676, Dutch sailor.

Tamberlane (Timur Beg), 1335-1405, Mongolian.

Tilly, Johann, Count von, 1559-1632, Flemish born, served the Empire.

Turenne, Henri de la Tour d'Auvergne, Vicomte de, 1611-75, French.

Tromp, Martin Harpertszoon, 1597-1653, Dutch sailor.

Wallace, Sir William, *c.* 1272-1305, Scots.

Wallenstein, Albrecht von, 1583-1634, *b.* Bohemia, served the Empire.

Washington, George, 1732-99. American.

Wellington, Arthur Wellesley, Duke of, 1769-1852, British.

Wolfe, James, 1727-59, English.

Wolseley, Garnet, Viscount, 1833-1913, British.

Xerxes, *c.* 519-465 B.C., Persian.

Soldiers, Sailors, and Airmen of this Century. The following is a list of military, naval, and air commanders not now living, but noted for their service since 1900.

American:

Fairchild, M. S., 1894-1950, general (air force).

Marshall, George, 1880-1959, general.

Patton, George Smith, 1885-1945, general.

Pershing, John Joseph, 1860-1948, general.

Stillwell, Joseph W., 1883-1946, general.

Australian:

Blamey, Sir Thomas, 1884-1951, field marshal.

Hobbs, Sir Talbot, 1864-1938, general.

Monash, Sir John, 1865-1931, general.

Bolivian:

Hans Kundt, 1860-1939, general.

British:

Alanbrooke, Alan Francis Brooke, 1st Viscount, 1883-1963, field marshal.

Allenby, Edmund Henry Hynman, Viscount, 1861-1936, field marshal.

Beatty, David, 1st Earl, 1871-1936, admiral.

Birdwood, William Riddell, 1st Baron, 1865-1951, field marshal.

Carton de Wiart, Sir Adrian, lieutenant-general, 1880-1963.

Chetwode, Sir Philip, 1st Baron, 1869-1950, field marshal.

Cunningham, Sir Andrew, 1st Viscount, 1883-1963, admiral.

Cunningham, Sir John, 1885-1962, admiral.

Dundonald, Douglas, 12th Earl, 1852-1935, general.

Freyberg, Sir Bernard Cyril, 1st Viscount, 1890–1963, general.

Gough, Sir Hubert de la Poer, 1870–1963, general.

Haig, Douglas, 1st Earl, 1861–1928, field marshal.

Hamilton, Sir Ian, 1853–1947, general.

Horne, Henry Sinclair, Lord, 1861–1929, general.

Ironside, Sir William Edmund, 1st Baron, 1880–1959, field marshal.

Jellicoe, John Rushworth, 1st Earl, 1859–1935, admiral.

Keyes, Roger John Brownlow, 1st Baron, 1872–1945, admiral.

Kitchener, Horatio Herbert, Earl, 1850–1916, field marshal.

Lawrence, Thomas Edward, 1888–1935, lieutenant-colonel.

Maud, Sir F. S., 1864–1917, general.

Methuen, Paul, 3rd Baron, 1845–1932, field marshal.

Milne, G. F., 1st Baron, 1866–1948, field marshal.

Mountevans, Sir Edward, 1st Baron, 1881–1957, admiral.

Plumer, Herbert, Viscount, 1857–1932, field marshal.

Rawlinson, Henry Seymour, 1st Baron, 1864–1925, general.

Townsend, Sir Charles, 1861–1924, general.

Trenchard, Hugh Montague, first Viscount, 1873–1956, Marshal of the R.A.F.

Wavell, Archibald, 1st Baron, 1883–1950, field marshal.

Wingate, Francis Reginald, 1861–1953, general.

Wingate, Orde Charles, 1903–44, major-general.

Ypres, John French, 1st Earl of, 1852–1925, field marshal.

Finnish:

Mannerheim, Baron, Carl Gustaf Emil von, 1867–1948, marshal.

French:

Brocard, Félix, 1885–1950, general (air).

Darlan, Jean L. X. F., 1881–1942, admiral.

Degoutte, J. M. J., 1866–1938, general.

Foch, Ferdinand, 1851–1929, marshal of France.

Gallieni, Joseph, 1849–1916, general.

Gamelin, Maurice Gustave, 1872–1958, general.

Giraud, Henri, 1879–1949, general.

Joffre, Joseph C., 1852–1931, marshal of France.

de Lattre de Tassigny, Jean-Joseph-Marie, 1889–1952, marshal of France.

Leclerc de Hautecloque, Philippe, 1902–1947, marshal of France.

Lyautey, Louis H. G., 1854–1934, marshal of France.

Manoury, Michel Joseph, 1847–1934, general.

Marchand, J. B., 1863–1934, general.

Nivelle, Robert G., 1856–1924, general.

Pétain, Philippe, 1856–1951, marshal of France.

Sarrail, Maurice P. E., 1856–1929, general.

German:

Bock, Fedor von, 1880–1945, colonel-general.

Bülow, Karl von, 1846–1921, general.

Falkenhayn, Erich von, 1861–1922, general.

Fritsch, Werner von, 1880–1939, colonel-general.

Goering, Hermann, 1893–1946, field marshal.

Guderian, Heinz, 1889–1954, colonel-general.

Hindenburg und Beneckendorf, Paul von, 1847–1934, field marshal.

Hipper, Franz von, 1863–1932, admiral.

Kesselring, Albert, 1885–1960, field marshal.

Kluck, Alexander von, 1846–1934, general.

Kluge, Günther von, 1882–1944, field marshal.

Liman von Sanders, Otto, 1855–1929, general.

Ludendorff, Erich, 1865–1937, general.

Mackensen, August von, 1849–1945, field marshal.

Paulus, F., d. 1957, field marshal.

Rommel, Erwin, 1891–1944, field marshal.

Rundstedt, Gerd von, 1875–1953, field marshal.

Seeckt, Hans von, 1866–1936.

Tirpitz, Alfred von, 1849–1930, grand admiral.

Greek:

Kondylis, George, 1879–1936, general.

Metaxas, John, 1871–1941, general.

Papagos, Alexander, 1883–1955, marshal.

Italian:

Aosta, Amadeo Umberto Duca d', 1898–1942, general.

Badoglio, Pietro, 1871–1956, marshal.

Balbo, Italo, 1896–1940, marshal.

Cadorna, Luigi, Count, 1850–1928, general.

Diaz, Armando, marshal, 1861–1928.

Graziani, Rodolpho, Marchese de, 1882–1955, marshal.

Japanese:

Togo, Heihachiro, Count, 1847–1934, admiral.

Tojo, Hideki, 1884–1948, general.

Paraguayan:
Estegarribia, José Felix, 1888–1940, general.

Polish:
Pilsudski, Josef, 1867–1935, marshal.
Sikorski, Wladyslaw, 1881-1943, general.
Smigly-Ridz, Edward, 1886–?1939, marshal.

Rumanian:
Avarescu, Alex, 1859–1938, general.

Russian:
Alexeiev, Mikhail 1857–1918, general.
Brussilov, Alexei, 1853–1926, general.
Budenny. Semyon Mikhailovitch, 1883–1919, marshal.
Krylenko, Nikolai Vasilievitch, 1885–1938, general.
Nikolai Nikolaievich, Grand Duke, 1956–1929, general.
Rennenkampf, Paul, 1854–1918, general
Samsonov, Alexander, 1859–1914, general.
Tolbukhin, Fyodor, 1894–1949, marshal.
Tukhachevski, Mikhail Nikolaievitch, 1893–1937.

South African:
Cronje, Piet Arnoldus, 1835–1911, general.
Botha, Louis, 1862–1919, general.
Smuts, Jan Christian, 1870–1950, rebel field marshal.
De la Rey, Jacobus, 1847–1914, commandant-general.
De Wet, Christian Rudolf, 1854–1922, general.

Turkish:
Fevzi Chakmak, 1876–1950, marshal.
Mustapha Kemal Pasha (Kemal Atatürk), 1880–1938, marshal.

Yugoslav:
Mihailovich, Draza, 1893–1946, general.

Solemn League and Covenant. Drawn up by Scots against Charles I's religious interferences, 1638. Agreed by English parliament, 1643. Declared illegal, 1661.

Solomon Islands, first visited by Alvaro de Mendaña *c.* 1568, then by Carteret, 1767, and sighted by Bougainville, 1768. British protectorate recognized by treaties with Germany, 1886 and 1893, extended to more northerly islands, 1898–9: further islands transferred from German protectorate, 1900. Remaining German protected islands (Bougainville, etc.) captured by Australian forces, 1914; mandated to Australia, 1918. Japanese invaded, Jan. 1942. American counter-attack began, Aug. 1942. Operations taken over by Australian forces, Dec. 1944; reconquest of islands virtually complete by July 1945.

Somalia (formerly Italian Somaliland), conquered by Portuguese in the sixteenth century, and by the Sultan of Zanzibar, 1866, became an Italian protectorate by treaty, 1889. Further territory leased from Zanzibar, 1892, and bought outright, 1905. Kisimayu leased from Britain, 1905. Frontier with Ethiopia defined, 1897, and readjusted by convention ratified 16 May 1908. Southern half of colony became crown colony, 1910; Juba-land ceded by Britain. 1925, in accordance with secret agreement of 1915; uniform administrative system set up, 1927; Raheita acquired from French Somaliland (*q.v.*), 1935; S. incorporated in the government of Italian E. Africa, 1936; conquered by British, 1941 (Feb.–May); status not defined by Italian peace treaty of 1947, but territory occupied by British troops from 1941 to 1 Apr. 1950 was handed over to Italians, United Nations trusteeship to expire in 1960. On 1 July 1960 S. became an independent republic, formed by the merger of S. with British Somaliland (see next article). Protested against inclusion of a Somali minority in the proposed independent Kenya, 1962–3.

Somaliland, British. Made a British protectorate, 1884; Dr. Donaldson Smith's expeditions, 1894 and 1900; Mullah defeated by British at Berbera, 1899; British and Ethiopian expedition, 1902; further fighting in 1903 and 1904; Mullah finally defeated, 1920, and *d.* in Ethiopia, 1921. Conquered by Italians, Aug. 1940. Regained, Mar. 1941. Merged with Somalia, 1 July 1960, to form an independent Somali republic.

Somaliland, French, annexed, 1864. Jibuti–Addis Ababa railway completed, 1917. Raheita territory ceded to Italy, 1935. Declared for Fighting French, 28 Dec. 1942. Overseas territory of France since the end of World War II.

Somerset House. Founded, 1549, on the site of some old churches. Its founder, the Protector Somerset, was executed, and his house fell to the crown; demolished in 1775, and a new building erected. The E. wing forms King's College, and was built, 1833.

South Africa, Republic of, formerly the **Union of.** Union formed, 31 May 1910, with Botha as premier. Rebellion began Sept., ended Dec. 1914. S. African Military Command terminated, 1 Dec. 1921, when responsibility for defence devolved on the Union. Anti-Asiatic measure in Parliament; Colour Bar Bill passed, May 1926.

1927: Agreement with Indian Government as to Indian immigration announced, 21 Feb.; rush to Grasfontein diamond fields, 4 Mar.: Governor-General became deputy of the king only, 1 July; acute controversy over the Flag Bill, involving riot at Bloemhof, 30 Sept.; agitation finally laid to rest by the agreement of Oct.

1930: Prince of Wales visited S. and E. Africa; native and coloured riots at Worcester, Cape Province; Riotous Assemblies Bill to deal with political agitation passed, Feb.; women enfranchised.

1933: S. A. off the gold standard. Economic difficulties led to the establishment of a Hertzog-Smuts coalition.

1934: Status of the Union Act.

1936: Representation of Natives Act secured to Cape aborigines 4 members of Senate and 3 of House of Assembly, and 2 members of the Provincial Council (none of these might be natives).

1938: United Party's victory in General Election, 20 May; protests by English-speaking inhabitants against omission of national anthem at military reviews, May–June; Oswald Pirow, minister of railways and defence received by king, 8 Nov.; interviewed Hitler, 24 Nov.; interviewed Mussolini, 28 Nov.; in Brussels, 1 Dec.; at The Hague, 2 Dec.; back in England, 4 Dec.; interviewed Chamberlain, 7 Dec.; centenary of the Great Trek celebrated, Dec.

1939: Asiatics Land and Trading Bill read a third time in House of Assembly (segregation foreshadowed), 2 June; British Government appointed Sir Edward Harding as High Commissioner for Basutoland, Bechuanaland Protectorate, and Swaziland, 18 July; announcement that Union Government would take over administration of eastern portion of the Caprivi Zipfel from the mandated territory of SW. Africa as from 1 Aug., 28 July; Gen. Hertzog moved declaration of neutrality, but Gen. Smuts's amendment declaring war on Germany carried by 80 to 67, so the Hertzog ministry resigned, 4 Sept.; Gen. Smuts formed ministry, 5 Sept.; the two opposition chiefs, Gen. Hertzog and Dr. Malan, in conference at Pretoria to arrange amalgamation of their groups, 23 Nov.

1940: War declared on Italy, 11 June.

1947: Visit of King George VI, Feb.–May.

1948: Daniel François Malan (1874–1959) became prime minister as leader of the Nationalist Party with support of Afrikaner Party under N. C. Havenga, 4 June. *Apartheid* the basis of government domestic policy.

1949: Merger of Afrikaner Party and nationalists. Natives Representative Council abolished. Separate Representation of Voters Act passed. Group Areas forbade native, Asiatic, or coloured (half-caste) South Africans to own or occupy property in ' European ' quarters. Citizenship Act required five years' residence in S. A. as qualification for citizenship. Virtual incorporation of SW. (former German) territory, July.

1952: Supreme Court ruled Malan's disenfranchisement of Cape coloured votes illegal. Malan threatened its with replacement by a ' political ' supreme court, which first sat in secret, Aug., and was declared unconstitutional by the Supreme Court. Secession first publicly discussed in Natal. First political general strike by non-white unions, 26 June 1950. Civil disobedience campaign by united African, Asiatic, and coloured political bodies began, 26 June 1952.

1954: Malan retired, 1954; succeeded by Strijdom (*d.* 1958), an avowed republican.

1957: Delimitation Commission laid down revised membership for House of Assembly. *Die Stem* made S. A.'s sole national anthem, 2 May. Minister of External Affairs, Eric Louw, told journalists in London that S. A. intended to become a republic eventually: she might or might not remain in the Commonwealth.

1958: Strijdom *d.*; succeeded by Dr. H. F. Verwoerd. S. A. returned to full membership of U.N.O., which she had abandoned earlier owing to U.N. criticism of her *apartheid* policy. Franchise extended to all Whites over the age of 18.

1960: Increasing unrest among African element in S. A.; measures to restrict political freedom of all government critics; in a referendum among White voters as to whether S. A. should become a republic, 5 Oct., 850,458 were in favour, and 775,878 against. Senate Act passed.

1961: S. A. announced her intention of leaving the Commonwealth, 16 Mar.; her membership ended, 31 May, and she then became an independent republic. Trials of Africans and liberal Europeans on charges of subversion took place, 1961–2.

1962: During this period several persons were sentenced to confinement to their homes for periods of several years, as potential enemies of the state. U.N. called for sanctions against S. A. as a protest against S. A.'s racial policies, Nov.

1963: Sir Roy Welensky, Premier of the Rhodesian Federation, had talks in S. A. with Dr Verwoerd, May.

Governor-Generals of the Union of South Africa, 1910–61:

Viscount Gladstone	1910–1914
Earl Buxton	1914–1920
H.R.H. Prince Arthur of Connaught	1920–1924

Earl of Athlone	1924–1931
Earl of Clarendon	1931–1937
Sir Patrick Duncan	1937–1943
N. J. de Wet (acting)	1943–1945
G. B. van Zyl	1946–1950
Dr. E. G. Jansen	1951–1959
C. R. Swart	1960–1961

State President of the Republic of South Africa since 1961:

| C. R. Swart | 1961– |

See also CAPE PROVINCE; ORANGE FREE STATE; TRANSVAAL.

South African War. 1899: Ultimatum sent by Boers, 9 Oct. Lord Roberts appointed C.-in-C. after British reverses, 23 Dec.
1900: Relief of Kimberley, 15 Feb.; Cronje's surrender at Paardeberg, 27 Feb.; relief of Ladysmith, 28 Feb.; relief of Mafeking, 17–18 May; Transvaal Republic annexed to Great Britain, 1 Sept.; formally annexed, 25 Oct.
1902: Peace of Vereeniging, 31 May.

Southampton. A Roman town (Clausentium) and a Jutish port (Hamwih) existed in the suburbs of modern S., but the first town on the present centre was built shortly before 1066. Present system of wharves, due to Southern Railway dock extension scheme, begun 1927. The University College became S. University in 1952.

South Australia was surveyed by Tasman, 1644, and Flinders, 1802. Murray River explored, 1828. First settlement made, 1834, at the instance of Maj. Baron and under the auspices of Edward Gibbon Wakefield. Province proclaimed, 28 Dec. 1836. Copper discovered, 1842 and 1845. Constitution adopted, 1856. Became a state of the Australian Commonwealth, 1901.

South Carolina, U.S.A., first permanently settled as proprietary government, 1670. Charleston founded, 1680. Became a crown colony, 1729 (*see also* NORTH CAROLINA). Seceded from Union, 1800. Present constitution dates from 1895.

South Dakota, U.S.A., first explored by brothers Verendrye, 1743. First permanent building by white men, 1794. Sold to U.S.A. by France, 1803, as part of Louisiana Purchase. Dakota Territory created, 1861. Gold struck in the Black Hills, 1874. Intensive agricultural settlement begun, 1879. Separated from N. Dakota and admitted to Union, 1889.

South-East Asia Treaty Organization (S.E.A.T.O.). Arose from the South-East Asia Collective Defence Treaty, S.E. Asian counterpart to the N. Atlantic Treaty (*q.v.*), signed in Manila, 8 Sept. 1954,

between Britain, the U.S.A., Australia, New Zealand, Pakistan, France, Thailand, and the Philippines, for their 'continuous and effective self-help and mutual aid.' The organization's headquarters was established at Bangkok in Feb. 1955.

South Pole. First reached, 16 Dec. 1911, by the Norwegian, Roald Amundsen. Scott reached it 17 Jan. 1912. *See* ARCTIC AND ANTARCTIC REGIONS.

South Sea Bubble. The financial scheme under which the S. S. Co. (incorporated 1710) offered in 1720 to pay off the national debt and to buy up the irredeemable annuities granted in the two previous reigns, Parliament accepted the offer, and a number of other bubble companies competed. Shares rose to fantastic prices and then slumped, the stock of the S. S. Co. which had risen to 1,000 falling to 135. Sir Robert Walpole went far to restoring credit by arranging to assign £9,000,000 S. S. stock to the Bank of England, a like amount to the E. India Co., and to repay the bonus of £7,500,000 which the Government had received.

Southwark, though retaining its identity as a borough, was annexed to the city of London, 1327. Became the city ward of Bridge Without, 1550. Diocese of S. created, 1905.

South-West Africa (formerly German SW. Africa). Mandated to Union of S. Africa by League of Nations, 17 Dec. 1920. Legislative Assembly established by constitution of 1925, and representation in S. African Parliament granted, 1949. In July 1949 the Union of S. Africa informed the United Nations that no further mandate reports would be submitted, and it was henceforth virtually incorporated in the Union.

Sovereigns when first minted (1503) were worth 22s. 6d., later 10s. and 11s. In 1817 the value was fixed at £1, which remained constant until 1917, when they were recalled by the bank. In 1949 some 100,000 S. were minted in order to preserve the art and craft of gold coining. Some Italian jewellers, accused of coining S. in Switzerland, acquitted on the plea that S. were not legal tender and their product ranked as jewellery, Aug. 1952. A small number were made in 1953 to mark the coronation of Queen Elizabeth II; some were also made in 1957.

Sovetsk. *See* TILSIT.

Soviet. *See* U.S.S.R.

Spa, in Belgium, where mineral springs were discovered in 1326, gave its name to an establishment for curative waters. Was German G.H.Q. in 1918, seat of the

Armistice Commission, 1918–19, and venue of a conference, 1920, on German disarmament and reparations.

Space Flights. Up to 1 Aug. 1963 9 men and 1 woman had successfully orbited the earth, and in addition two others had made successful sub-orbital flights. Details are as follows:

Date	Name	Nationality	Number of Orbits	Flight Time
12 Apr. 1961	Yuri Gagarin	Russian	1	1 hr. 48 min.
5 May 1961	Alan Sheppard	American	Sub-orbital	15 min.
21 July 1961	Virgil Grissom	American	Sub-orbital	15 min.
6 Aug. 1961	Gherman Titov	Russian	17	25 hrs. 18 min.
20 Feb. 1962	John Glenn	American	3	4 hrs. 56 min.
24 May 1962	Malcolm Scott Carpenter	American	3	4 hrs. 56 min.
11 Aug. 1962	Andrian Nikolaev	Russian	64	94 hrs. 25 min.
12 Aug. 1962	Pavel Popovich	Russian	48	70 hrs. 59 min.
3 Oct. 1962	Walter Schirra	American	6	9 hrs. 13 min.
15 May 1963	Gordon L. Cooper	American	22	34 hrs. 21 min.
14 June 1963	Valery Bykovsky	Russian	82	119 hrs. 54 min.
16 June 1963	Valentina Tereshkova	Russian	49	70 hrs. 50 min.

Spain (*Hispania*). Occupied (south of the Ebro) by Carthaginians, 238–210 B.C.; after which the country was slowly subjugated by Rome. S. was divided into two provinces after the second Punic War, and into three by Augustus. Overrun by the Vandals, Alans, and Suevi, A.D. 409. Visigoths overrun S. and establish kingdom, 416–18. Vandals migrate to Africa, 429. Visigothic state overthrown and S. conquered by Arabs, 711–18. Abdurrahman (I) founds the Ommayad caliphate of Cordova, 755, which reaches its zenith in the reign of Abdurrahman III (912–61). Christian reconquest begins in earnest under Sancho I of Leon, 962. Civil war destroys caliphate, 1031. Alfonso VI of Castile takes Toledo, 1085. Moslem revival under Almoravides (*q.v.*), 1086. Aragonese defeat at Fraga, 1134. Alfonso VII of Castile takes Cordova, 1146. Moslem revival under Almohades at battle of Alarcos, 1185. Great Christian victory at Navas de Tolosa, 1212. Moors confined to Granada by 1257. Permanent union of Aragon and Valencia, 1309. Moslem defeat at battle of the Salado, 1340. French expel Pedro the Cruel from Castile and substitute Henry of Trastamara, 1366. English expel Henry and restore Pedro, 1367. Henry defeats Pedro at Montiel, 1369. John I of Portugal defeats Castilians at Aljubarotta, 1385. Union of Aragon and Castile under Ferdinand and Isabella, 1479. Granada conquered, 2 Jan. 1492. Treaty of Tordesillas, 1494. Cortez conquers Mexico, 1519–21. Victory over French at Pavia, 1525. Treaty of Câteau Cambrésis, 1559. Spanish sack of Antwerp, 1576. Annexation of Portugal, 1580. English defeat of the Armada, 1588. Portugal again independent, 1640 (*see* PARTITION TREATIES). War of Spanish Succession, 1701–13. Treaty with France against Britain (' First Family Compact '), 1733. Second Family Compact, 1743. Third Family Compact, 1761 (*see* SEVEN YEARS WAR). S. at war with Britain, 1779–83. Alliance with France and war with Britain, 1796. Destruction of Franco-Spanish fleet at battle of Trafalgar, 21 Oct. 1805. Insurrection against French occupation begins, 1808. French driven out by Wellington, 1812. Revolution, 1820, suppressed by French, 1823. First Carlist War, 1830–40. Espartero regent, 1841. Driven out by Narvaez, 1843. Espartero recalled, 1847. Second Carlist War, 1872–6. War with U.S.A., 1898. Campaign in Melilla, 1909; insurrection at Barcelona, 1909; general strike and martial law, 1916; serious rioting, 1919; mutiny in army, 1920; military revolution, 1923; directorate formed, Sept. 1923. Riff War in Morocco, 1924–5 (*see* MOROCCO). Martial law abolished, 17 May 1925. Military revolution suppressed, 7 Sept. 1926; new National Consultative Assembly opened, 10 Oct. 1927; Gen. Primo de Rivera, dictator, resigned, 28 Jan. 1930; *d.*, 16 Mar. Revolution and flight of King Alfonso, Mar. 1931; Alcala Zamora elected president, 10 Dec. 1931; monarchist risings in Madrid and Seville suppressed, 13 Aug. 1932.

1934: General strike in Madrid, 22 Apr.; Federal Republican State of Catalonia proclaimed, and crushed by bombardment, 6–7 Oct

1936: General election victory for Popular Front, 16 Feb.; Manuel Azaña formed Cabinet, 19 Feb.; President Zamora deposed, 7 Apr.; Azaña elected president, 10 May; civil war began in Morocco, 18 July; Gen. Mola set up Insurgent Government at Burgos, 24 July; seaplanes brought Insurgent reinforcements from Morocco, 26 July; Algeciras bombarded by Republican warships,

7 Aug.; Insurgents captured Badajos, 14 Aug.; Largo Caballero formed government, and Insurgents captured Irun, 4 Sept.; Republicans evacuated San Sebastian, 13 Sept; the Alcazar of Toledo blown up by Republican forces, but Insurgent defenders continued to resist, 18 Sept.; Republicans withdrew from Alcazar after two months' siege, 28 Sept.; Gen. Franco, head of Insurgent Government, 30 Sept.; Republican Government granted autonomy to Basque provinces, 1 Oct.; Republican Government moved to Valencia, 7 Nov.; Franco recognized by Germany and Italy, 18 Nov.

1937: Britain banned volunteers, 9 Jan.; Insurgents captured Malaga, 8 Feb.; food ships ran blockade of Bilbao, 20–23 Apr.; Guernica, ancient Basque capital, destroyed by Insurgents, who captured Durango, 27 Apr.; Juan Negrin, premier in place of Caballero, 15–17 Apr.; German warship shelled Almeria in reprisal for bombing (29 May) of the *Deutschland* near Balearic Isles, 31 May; Bilbao given up to the Insurgents, 19 June; Santander surrendered to Insurgents, Basque president flying to Bayonne, 26 Aug.; Gijon and Oviedo taken by Insurgents, 21 Oct.; Russia rejected part of British plan as to volunteers, 22 Oct.; Insurgents captured remaining Asturian villages, 23 Oct.; British plan accepted by Russia, 16 Nov.

1938: Insurgents surrendered Teruel, 8 Jan.; Insurgent advance on Cordova front, 31 Jan.; stern note from Britain to Franco as to sinking of British ships, 5 Feb.; Teruel reoccupied by Insurgents, 22 Feb.; Insurgent advance beyond Teruel, 24 Feb.; new Insurgent offensive in Aragon, 9 Mar.; reached Catalan frontier, 27 Mar.; entered Lerida, 3 Apr.; Catalonia cut off, 15 Apr.; Republican line broken N. of Teruel, 25 Apr.; Republican troops driven into France going back to Barcelona, 16 June, etc.; Non-Intervention Committee agreed on British plan, 5 July; Franco made great advance on Teruel-Sagunto front, 17 July; Republican reverse on the Ebro, 7 Aug.; Republicans that had crossed Ebro captured, 8 Aug.; Republican offensive in Lerida, 9 Aug.; Franco rejected British plan, 21 Aug.; fierce fighting on Ebro front throughout Aug. and Sept.; imminent withdrawal of all foreign combatants on Republican side announced, 21 Sept.; 10,000 Italians left, 15 Oct.; Republican left continued retreat on the Ebro, 4 Nov.; struggle for Ebro ceased, 18 Nov.; advance into Catalonia along 100-mile front by Franco, 23 Dec.

1939: Insurgents captured Artesa, 4 Jan.; Insurgents captured Falset, 12 Jan.; Insurgents captured Valles, 14 Jan.;

Republican Government left Barcelona for Gerona, 24 Jan.; fall of Barcelona to Nationalists, 26 Jan.; the Cortes met (for the last time) at Figueras, 3 Feb.; fall of Gerona to Insurgents, 4 Feb.; President Azaña entered French territory, 5 Feb.; mass exodus of refugees into France, 5–11 Feb.; British warship *Devonshire* conveyed an agent of Franco's to Minorca, 8 Feb.; Minorca surrendered to Insurgents, 9 Feb.; Insurgent drive reached French frontier, 9–10 Feb.; resignation of President Azaña, 16 Feb.; recognition of Franco S. by Greece, Rumania, Turkey, and Yugoslavia, 22 Feb.; by Netherlands, 23 Feb.; by France and Britain, 27 Feb.; by Australia, 28 Feb.; by Eire, Switzerland, Poland, Egypt, Bolivia, Brazil, Peru, Argentina, and Lithuania all in Feb.; Negrin, his foreign minister, del Vayo, and 'Col. Lister' (i.e. the Soviet Gen. Stern) of the International Brigades, arrived Toulouse, 6 Mar.; Franco declared blockade of Republican S., 8 Mar.; final surrender of Communist Party, 11 Mar.; fall of Madrid after a siege of more than two years, 28 Mar.; Valencia fell, 29 Mar.; martial law in Madrid, the art treasures returned by the League of Nations, 30 Mar.; Cartagena fell, 31 Mar.; U.S.A. recognized Franco S., 1 Apr.; Nationalist Government announced from Madrid the end of the civil war, 2 Apr.; end of the Non-Intervention Committee, 20 Apr.; ex-King Alfonso's property restored to him, 24 Apr.; Franco as 'Caudillo' issued extensive decrees for reconstruction, 27 Apr.; notice of withdrawal from League of Nations, 7 May; return (from France) of the gold of the Bank of S., 27 July; further strengthening of the army and revival of the Gibraltar command, 20 Aug.; S.'s neutrality in the European war decreed, 5 Sept.; Church reinstated in national budget, 1 Nov.

1940: Non-aggression treaty with Portugal, 30 July; Sr Companys executed, 20 Oct.; death of ex-President Azaña, 4 Nov.

1941: Death of ex-King Alfonso XIII, 28 Feb.

1942: The Cortes was re-established, but on corporative lines, July.

1947: Referendum declared in favour of monarchy, 6 July.

1951: Franco's daughter and son-in-law, and his foreign minister, toured Arab countries on goodwill mission.

1952: American economic and technical aid accepted.

1953: Concordat signed in Rome, 27 Aug., to replace that of 1851, denounced by the Republicans in 1931; defence treaty with U.S.A., allowing American bases in S., signed 26 Sept.

1957: Government reconstituted, 25 Feb., with Franco remaining at its head; Cortes informed, July 1957, that the monarchy would be restored on Franco's death or withdrawal from power.

1961–2: Industrial unrest culminating in a strike wave in Apr.–May 1962. Franco accused disruptive elements, including some Catholic clergy, of fomenting trouble; Don Juan Carlos married Princess Sophia of Greece, 14 May; severe floods in Barcelona area due to torrential rain caused over 400 fatal casualties and heavy damage, 26–7 Sept.

1963: Execution of Julian Grimau, Communist police chief of Barcelona during the civil war, caused world-wide protests, Apr.

Spain, Sovereigns of, from the Union of Castile and Aragon, 1479, under Ferdinand of Aragon and Isabella of Castile.

Isabella	*d.* 1504
Ferdinand	*d.* 1516

House of Hapsburg:

Charles V (Emperor) I	1516–1556 (abdicated)
Philip II	1556–1598
Philip III	1598–1621
Philip IV	1621–1665
Charles II	1665–1700

House of Bourbon:

Philip V	1700–abdicated 1724
Luis	Jan.–Aug. 1724
Philip V (again)	1724–1746
Ferdinand VI	1746–1759
Charles III	1759–1788
Charles IV	1788–1808 (abdicated)
Ferdinand VII	1808
Joseph Bonaparte	1808–1812 (abdicated)
Ferdinand VII (again)	1813–1833
Isabella II	1833–flees 1868
Interregnum	1868–1874
Alfonso XII	1874–1885
Alfonso XIII	1886–abdicated 1931

Spanish Literature. The following is a list of Spanish (and of Spanish-speaking S. American) authors not now living:

Aguilera, Ventura Ruiz, 1820–81, poet.

Alarcón, Juan Ruiz de, *c.* 1581–1639, dramatist.

Alarcón, Pedro Antonio de, 1833–91, prose writer of tales, etc.

Alemán, Mateo, 1547–*c.* 1613, prose writer, author of the popular *Guzman de Alfarache.*

Alfonso X, the Learned, of Castile and Leon, 1226–84, poet and patron of letters.

Álvarez Gato, Juan, *fl.* fifteenth century, poet.

Álvarez Quintero, Joaquin, 1873–1944, dramatist.

Álvarez Quintero, Serafín, 1871–1938, dramatist.

Argensola, Bartolomé Leonardo de, 1562–1631, historian and poet.

Argensola, Lupercio Leonardo de, 1559–1613, poet and dramatist.

Avellaneda, Alonso Fernandez de, seventeenth century, author of false Don Quixote.

Avilia, Juan de, 1500–69, mystic and prose writer.

Ayala, Adelardo López de, 1828–79 poet, and dramatist.

Ayala, Pero López de, 1332–1407, poet and prose writer.

Ayala, Ramón Pérez de, 1880–1962, poet, critic, and novelist.

Balmes y Uspia, Jaime, 1810–48, controversial writer.

Bazan, Emilia Pardo de, 1851–1921, novelist.

Becquer, Gustavo Adolfo, 1836–70, poet and tale writer.

Benavente y Martinez, Jacinto, 1866–1954, dramatist.

Berceo, Gonzalo de, 1198?–1264?, poet.

Boscan Almogavér, Juan, *c.* 1490–1542, poet and prose writer.

Bretón de los Herreros, Manuel, 1796–1873, dramatist.

Caballero, Fernán (pseudonym of Cecilia Böhl von Faber), 1797–1877, novelist.

Cadalso y Vázquez, José de, 1741–82, poet and dramatist.

Calderón de la Barca Henao de la Barreda y Riaño, Pedro, 1600–81, poet, dramatist, and prose writer.

Campoamor y Campoosorio, Ramón de, 1817–1901, poet.

Carrasquilla, Tomás, 1851–1941, Colombian novelist.

Castillejo, Cristobal de, *d.* 1556, poet.

Castro y Bellvis, Guillén de, 1569–1631, dramatist.

Cervantes Saavedra, Miguel de, 1547–1616, author of *Don Quixote,* poet, dramatist, and prose writer.

Cota de Maguaque, Rodrigo, *fl.* late fifteenth century, poet.

Cruz y Cano, Ramón de la, 1731–95, dramatist.

Dario, Rubén, 1867–1916, Hispano-American poet.

Diaz de Castillo, Bernal, *fl.* second half sixteenth century, historian of the conquest of Mexico.

Echegaray y Elizaguirre, José, 1832–1916, dramatist.

Encina, Juan de, 1468–c. 1529, poet and dramatist.

Ercilla y Zuñiga, Alonso de, 1533–94, poet.

Espinel, Vicente Martínez, 1551–1624, poet and novelist.

Espronceda, José de, 1810–42, poet and miscellaneous writer.

Estébanez Calderón, Serafín, 1799–1867, miscellaneous prose writer.

Feijoo y Montenegro, Benito Jerónimo, 1677–1764, prose writer and critic.

Figueroa, Francisco de, d. 1620, poet.

Galdos, Pérez, 1842–1920, novelist.

Gallego, Juan Nicasio, 1777–1853, poet.

Gana, Alberto Blest, 1830–1920, Chilean novelist.

García de la Huerta y Muñoz, Vicente Antonio, 1734–87, dramatist.

García Gutiérrez, Antonio, 1812–84, dramatist.

Garcilaso de la Vega. See VEGA, GARCILASO DE LA.

Garcilaso the Inca, 1539–1616, Inca b., historian.

Gómez de Avellaneda, Gertrudis, 1816–73, poet, dramatist, and novelist.

Góngora y Argote, Luis de, 1561–1627, poet.

Gracián, Baltasar, 1601–58, prose writer, Jesuit epigrammatic moralist.

Granada, Luis de, 1505–88, mystic and religious writer.

Guevara, Antonio de, c. 1480–1545, chronicler and moralist.

Guevara, Luis Velez, 1570–1644, dramatist.

Harzenbusch, Juan Eugenio, 1806–80, dramatist.

Herrera, Fernando de, 1534–97, poet and critic.

Ibañez, Vicente Blasco, 1867–1928, novelist.

Iriarte y Oropesa, Tomás de, 1750–91, fabulist.

Isidore of Seville, St., c. 560–636, encyclopaedist and Doctor of the Church.

Isla y Roja, José Francisco de, 1703–81, humorous prose writer.

Jáuregui y Aguilar, Juan Martínez de, c. 1570–c. 1641, poet and translator.

Jimenez, Juan Ramón, 1881–1958, poet.

Jove-Llanos, Gaspar Melchior de, 1744–1811, poet, dramatist, and prose writer.

Juan de la Cruz, 1542–91, mystic, poet, and prose writer (St. John of the Cross).

Juan Manuel, Infante, 1282–1349, poet and miscellaneous writer; his chief prose work was El Conde Lucanor, a collection of tales.

Larra, Mariano José de, 1809–37, miscellaneous prose writer.

Listay Aragon, Alberto, 1775–1848, poet.

López de Gómara, Francisco, 1519–60, historian of the conquest of Mexico.

Lorca, Federico García, 1899–1936, poet.

Loyola, St. Ignatius, 1491–1556, author of the Exercitia Spiritualia and the Constitutiones. See also JESUITS.

Lucena, Juan de, fl. fifteenth century, prose writer.

Lully, Raymond ('Ramon Lull'), 1235–1315.

Luzán Claramunt de Suelves y Gurrea, Ignacio, 1702–54, critic and poet.

Machado y Ruiz, Antonio, 1875–1939, poet and dramatist.

Machado y Ruiz, Manuel, 1874–1947, poet and dramatist.

Manrique, Gómez, 1412–91, poet.

Manrique, Jorge, 1440–79, poet.

Mariana, Juan de, c. 1535–1623, historian.

Martínez de la Rosa, Francisco, 1789–1862, poet, dramatist, and novelist.

Martínez de Toledo, Alfonso, 1398–1466?, prose writer and moralist.

Meléndez Valdés, Juan, 1754–1817, poet and dramatist.

Melo, Francisco Manuel de, 1611–66, prose writer.

Mena, Juan de, 1411–56, poet.

Mendoza, Diego Hurtado de, 1503–75, poet and scholar.

Mesonero Romanos, Ramón de, 1803–82, miscellaneous prose writer.

Mistral, Gabriela (Lucila Godoy y Alcayaga), 1889–1957, Chilean poet and prose writer.

Molinos, Miguel de, c. 1640–96, author of the Spiritual Guide.

Montemayor, Jorge de, c. 1520–61, author of the prose pastoral, Diana Enamorada.

Morales, Ambrosio de, 1513–91, historian.

Moratín, Leandro Fernández de, 1760–1828.

Moreto y Cabaña, Agustin, 1618–69, dramatist.

Naharro, Bartolomé Torres, fl. early sixteenth century, dramatist.

Nebrija, Elio Antonio de, 1444–1522, humanist.

Nuñez de Arce, Gaspar, 1833–1903, poet and dramatist.

Padilla, Juan de, 1468–1522?, poet.

Palacio Valdés, Armando, c. 1854–1938, novelist.

Paravicino y Arteaga, Hortensio Félix, 1580–1633, poet.

Pereda, José María de, 1833–1906, novelist.

Pérez, Andrés ('Francisco Lopez de Ubeda'), fl. early seventeenth century, picaresque novel writer.

Pérez, Antonio, 1540–1611, miscellaneous writer.

Pérez de Guzmán, Fernán, 1378–1460, poet and historian.

Pérez de Hita, Ginés, fl. early seventeenth century, historical novelist.

Pérez de Montalban, Juan, 1602–38, dramatist.

Pérez Galdós, Benito, 1843–1920, novelist and dramatist.

Ponce de León, Luis, 1529–91, poet.

Pulgar, Hernando de, 1436–92?, historian.

Quevedo y Villegas, Francisco Gómez de, 1580–1645, poet and prose writer.

Quintana, Manuel José, 1772–1857, poet, dramatist, and prose writer.

Rivas, Duque de. See SAAVEDRA.

Rodo, José Enrique, 1872–1917, Uruguayan essayist.

Rojas, Fernando de, *fl.* late fifteenth century.

Rojas Zorrilla, Francisco de, 1607–48, poet and dramatist.

Rueda, Lope de, *c.* 1510–65, dramatist.

Ruiz de Alarcón, Juan. See ALARCON, JUAN RUIZ DE.

Ruiz, Juan, *fl.* fourteenth century, poet.

Saavedra, Angel de (Duque de Rivas), 1791–1865, poet and dramatist.

Samaniego, Félix María de, 1745–1801, fabulist.

San Martin, Juan Zorrilla, 1855–1931, Uruguayan poet.

Sancho IV, *d.* 1295, author of *Castigos y Documentos*, and patron of letters.

Santillana, Iñigo Lopez de Mendoza, Marqués de, 1398–1458, poet and prose writer.

Sarmiento, Martín, 1695–1772, prose writer and critic.

Selgas y Carrasco, José, 1824–82, poet.

Sem Tob, *fl.* fourteenth century, author of a collection of proverbs and maxims in verse.

Silvestre, Gregorio, 1520–70, poet.

Solis y Rivadeneira, Antonio de, 1610–86, dramatist and historian.

Tamayo y Baus, Manuel, 1829–98, dramatist.

Teresa, St., 1515–82, poet and prose writer.

Tirso de Molina, *c.* 1584–1648, poet, dramatist, and prose writer.

Torre, Alfonso de la, *fl.* fifteenth century, didactic prose writer.

Torre, Francisco de la, 1534?–94, poet.

Unamuno, Miguel de, 1864–1936, novelist.

Urrea, Pedro Manuel de, 1486–1530?, poet.

Valdés, Armando P. See PALACIO VALDÉS.

Valdés, Juan de, *c.* 1500–44, mystic, scholar, and prose writer.

Valera, Juan de, 1824–1905, novelist and critic.

Vega Carpio, Lope Félix de, 1562–1635, poet, novelist, dramatist, and miscellaneous writer.

Vega, Garcilaso de la, 1503–36, poet.

Velez Guevara, Luis. See GUEVARA, LUIS VELEZ.

Villamediana, Conde de, 1582–1622, poet.

Villegas, Esteban Manuel de, 1596–1669, poet.

Villena, Enrique de, 1384–1434, poet, prose writer, and translator.

Yañez, Rodrigo, *fl.* fourteenth century, author of an epic work known as the 'Rhymed Chronicle,' *Poema de Alfonso Onceno.*

Zorilla, José, 1817–93, poet and dramatist.

Zurita, Jerónimo de, 1512–80, historian.

For certain other writers of Spanish nationality who did not write in Spanish, see PROVENCAL AND CATALAN WRITERS.

Spanish Succession, War of, 1701–13. Alliance of Britain, Holland, Austria, Prussia, and the Empire against Louis XIV, 1701.

Sparta or **Lacedaemon,** between 750 and 650 B.C. conquered the whole of Laconia, and by 550 the greater part of the Peloponnese. Defeated Athens in Peloponnesian War, 431–404, but after being beaten by the Thebans at Leuctra (371) the military decline of S. began, and became more rapid after about 335. It nominally retained its sovereignty after conquest by the Romans in 146. A village still exists on the site, which was the seat of a Frankish Count of S. from A.D. 1212 to 1262.

Spartacists. Organized a revolutionary movement in Germany, 1918–19. Leaders, Karl Liebknecht and Rosa Luxemburg, killed, Jan. 1919. Movement crushed, Apr. 1919, by Ebert's provisional Government, but from it modern German Communism developed.

Speaker of the House of Commons existed as an office, though perhaps not a title, from about 1326. The first member known to have performed the functions of a S. was William Trussell, who *d.* 1346, though he is not yet referred to as *Parlour* or S., a title first definitely ascribed to Sir Thomas Hungerford in 1377. Sir Thomas More the last S. to die by violence (1535). The names of all Ss. since 1600 are known. 1943, E. A. Fitzroy. 1943–51, Douglas Clifton Brown. 1951–9, W. S. Morrison. 1959– , Sir Harry Hylton-Foster.

Spectrum (solar). Treated of by Newton in his *Optics*, 1704; chemical analysis by means of a S. invented by Bunsen and Kirchhoff, 1860.

Spiritualism. Modern S. originated in Hydeville, U.S.A., about 1848.

Spitalfields (London), named after the hospital of St. Mary Spital (corruption of 'hospital'), founded 1197. Many silk-weaving Huguenots settled there after the revocation of the Edict of Nantes,

1685. Market received its original charter from Charles II in 1682.

Spitsbergen (Svalbard), so called by Dutch explorers, 1596. Placed under Norwegian sovereignty by Treaty of Sèvres, 9 Feb. 1920, to which Russia adhered, 1925. Canadian raid, Sept. 1941, destroyed mining installations and evacuated population. German naval landing, 1943. After new Russo-Norwegian agreement in 1947 the Russian mining camps were reoccupied.

Split (It. **Spalato;** Serb.-Cr. **Spljet),** Byzantine port opened c. A.D. 639 by refugees from Salona (*q.v.*). Municipal rights granted, 1239. Venetian territory from 1420 to 1797. Occupied by Italians, 1918.

Spode Chinaware, first manufactured, 1770.

S.S. (Schutzstaffel = 'Protection Squads'), militant branch of German National Socialist (*q.v.*) Party, formed by separation from S.A. (*q.v.*), 1928. Heinrich Himmler (1900–45) became commander, 1929. They served as the instrument of counter-revolution, 30 June 1934. By 1933 the distinction between *Totenkopf* (professional guards for concentration camps, etc.) and *Allgemeine* S.S. (parttime members maintaining order at rallies, etc.) units had developed. Between 1933 and 1936 new professional units living in barracks (*Verfügungs* S.S.) were formed, to act as mobile police. Out of these last were formed the cadres of the *Waffen* S.S. divisions, which first took the field in Sept. 1939 in Poland. The duplication, if not the replacement, of the civil police by the S.S. was complete by 1938, and their officers crossposted.

Stage Carriage Act, 1832, requires number of passengers carried to be painted on the vehicle. Revenue Act, 1869, defined S. C. as any public vehicle other than a railway carriage (*see also* HACKNEY COACHES). The effect of the Road Traffic Act, 1930, was to exclude motor vehicles from the category of S. C., making the term practically synonymous with trolley-bus.

Stalingrad, known until 1925 as **Tsaritsin** and since 1961 as **Volgograd.** Originally a military outpost, built in 1589 to protect farmers from predatory nomads, Tsaritsin was captured by the Cossack mutineer, Stenka Razin, 1670. During the civil war it was defended by Stalin and Voroshilov against the Whites, in the autumn of 1918. Between the end of the War of Intervention (1923) and 1939, its population increased about twenty-fold, and a huge industrial plant was constructed. The siege of S. began in Aug. 1942, and ended Nov. 1942, with

the capitulation of von Paulus and his army.

Stamp Acts. That of 1765, which was a contributory cause of the American Revolution, was repealed in 1766. Present law relating to stamp duties is contained in the Stamp Act, 1891, and in various subsequent Finance and Revenue Acts.

Standard, Royal, bore only three leopards passant in 1200, which were quartered with the arms of France in 1340. The latter were removed and replaced by the arms of Ireland, then of Scotland, 1603. From 1714 to 1837 the Royal Standard also bore the arms of Hanover until the accession of Victoria (1837), when it assumed its present form.

Standards Institution, British. Had its origins in the Joint Engineering Standards Committee formed by various engineering interests in 1901. This later became the British Engineering Standards Association. Textile, chemical, and building industries joined it, 1923–9. Granted a royal charter, 1929, as the British Standards Institution.

Standard Time. Different countries began to adopt S. T., based on a variation of a whole number of hours from Greenwich mean time, in 1883.

Star Chamber. Prerogative court going back at least to the reign of Edward III (1327–77) and abolished by Parliament, 1641.

State Department. *See* SECRETARY OF STATE (U.S.A.).

States-General (France). Last meeting before French Revolution (*q.v.*) was in 1614. It met at Versailles on 5 May 1789. The *Tiers État* declared itself the National Assembly, 17 June 1789.

States-General (Holland). Began c. middle fifteenth century, established permanently at The Hague, 1593. Abolished with convocation of the National Assembly, 1 Mar. 1796. Name used since 1814 as the title of the Dutch Parliament.

Statesmen of the Twentieth Century. The following list of political personalities, not now living, were all active in the present century, though not necessarily heads of state or of administrations:

Australian:

Curtin, John	1885–1945
Chifley, Joseph	1885–1951
Hughes, William Morris	1864–1952
Lyons, Joseph Aloysius	1879–1939
Scullin, James Henry	1876–1953

Austrian:

Bauer, Otto	1881–1938
Dollfuss, Engelbert	1892–1934
Renner, Karl	1870–1951
Schober, Johann	1874–1932

Belgian:
Francqui, Émile	1863–1935
Vandervelde, Émile	1866–1938

Bolivian:
Montes, Gen. Ismael	1860–1933

Brazilian:
Vargas, Getulio	1882–1954

British:
Baldwin, Stanley, Earl of Bewdley	1867–1947
Bevan, Aneurin	1897–1960
Beveridge, William, 1st Baron	1879–1963
Bevin, Ernest	1881–1951
Birkenhead, Earl of	1872–1930
Bondfield, Margaret	1873–1953
Burns, John	1858–1943
Butler, Sir Spencer Harcourt (India)	1869–1938
Buxton, Sydney, Earl	1853–1934
Carson, Edward, Lord	1854–1935
Chamberlain, Sir Austen	1863–1937
Chamberlain, Joseph	1836–1914
Chamberlain, Neville	1869–1940
Chelmsford, Frederic, Visc.	1868–1933
Cripps, Sir Stafford	1889–1952
Curzon of Kedleston, Marquess	1859–1925
Cushendun, Ronald, Lord	1861–1934
Deakin, Arthur	1890–1955
Ernle, Rowland, Visc.	1851–1937
Gaitskell, Hugh Todd Naylor	1906–1963
Grey of Fallodon, Edward, Visc.	1862–1933
Haldane, Visc.	1856–1928
Halifax, Earl of	1881–1959
Henderson, Arthur	1863–1935
Howard of Penrith, Esme, Baron	1864–1939
Islington, John, Lord	1866–1936
Law, Andrew Bonar	1858–1923
Lloyd George, David	1863–1945
Londonderry, C. S. H. Vane-Tempest-Stewart, Marquess of	1878–1949
MacDonald, James Ramsay	1866–1937
Morris, Edward P., Lord	1859–1935
Oxford and Asquith, Earl of	1852–1928
Pankhurst, Dame Christabel	1880–1958
Pankhurst, Emmeline	1858–1928
Peel, William, 2nd Visc.	1867–1937
Plunkett, Sir Horace C.	1854–1932
Rathbone, Eleanor	1873–1946
Reading, Rufus, Marquess of	1860–1935
Samuel, Herbert Louis, 1st Viscount	1870–1963
Snowden, Philip, Visc.	1864–1937
Stanley, Edward M. C., Lord	1894–1938
Stanley, Oliver	1896–1950
Templewood, Visc.	1880–1960
Tweedsmuir, John Buchan, Lord	1875–1940
Wilkinson, Ellen	1891–1947
Whitley, John Henry	1866–1935

Bulgarian:
Dimitrov, Georgi	1882–1949
Liaptcheff, Andrea	1866–1933
Malinoff, Alexander	1867–1938
Stambolisky	1879–1923

Canadian:
Borden, Sir Robert L.	1854–1937
King, William Lyon Mackenzie	1878–1950
Laurier, Sir Wilfrid	1841–1919
Strathcona, Donald Alexander Smith, Baron	1820–1914

Chinese:
Sun Yat-Sen	1866–1925

Czechoslovak:
Beneš, Eduard	1884–1948
Gottwald, Klement	1896–1953
Masaryk, Jan	1886–1948
Masaryk, Tomáš Garrigue	1850–1937
Spina, František	1878–1938
Stefanik, Milan Rastislav	1880–1919
Svehla, Anton	1873–1933

Dominican:
Trujillo, Rafael	d. 1961

Egyptian:
Neguib, Mohammed	1901–1958
Yehgen, Adly Pasha	1865–1933

Finnish:
Mannerheim, Carl	1867–1951

French:
Barthou, Jean Louis	1862–1934
Blum, Léon	1872–1950
Briand, Aristide	1862–1932
Cambon, Jules	1845–1935
Clemenceau, Georges Benjamin	1841–1929
Coty, René	1882–1962
Darlan, J. L. X. F.	1881–1942
Delcassé, Théophile	1852–1923
Doumer, Paul	1857–1932
Doumergue, Gaston	1863–1937
Franklin-Bouillon, Henry	1870–1938
Herriot, Édouard	1872–1957
Laval, Pierre	1883–1945
Leygues, Georges	1858–1933
Maginot, André	1877–1932
Painlevé, Paul	1863–1933
Pétain, Philippe	1856–1951
Pichon, Étienne	1857–1933
Poincaré, Raymond	1860–1934
Thomas, Albert	1878–1932

German:
Bernstorff, Count Johann Heinrich	1852–1939
Ebert, Friedrich	1871–1925
Goebbels, Joseph	1897–1945
Goering, Hermann	1893–1946

Heuss, Professor Theodor	1884–1963
Hitler, Adolf	1889–1945
Pieck, Wilhelm	1876–1960
Rathenau, Walther	1867–1922
Schumacher, Kurt	1895–1952
Stresemann, Gustav	1878–1929

Greek:

Konduriotis, Adam Paul	1855–1935
Kondylis, Gen.	1879–1936
Metaxas, John	1871–1941
Michalokopoulos, Andreas	1876–1938
Papagos, Alexander	1883–1955
Plastiras, N., Gen.	? –1953
Venizelos, Eleutherios	1864–1936
Zaïmis, Alexander	1855–1936

Hungarian:

Apponyi, Count Albert	1846–1933
Horthy, Nicholas	1868–1957
Daranyi, Koloman	1887–1939
Karolyi, Count Michael	1875–1955
Nagy, Imre	1896–1958
Tisza, Count Istvan	1861–1918

Indian:

Gandhi, Mahatma	1869–1948
Pattani, Sir Prabashankar D.	1862–1938

Iraqi:

Nuri es-Said	1888–1958
Kassem, Abdul Karim	d. 1963

Irish:

Collins, Michael	1890–1922
Hyde, Douglas	1860–1949
McBride, Maude (Gonne)	1866–1953
McNeill, James	1869–1938

Israeli:

Weizmann, Chaim	1874–1952

Italian:

Badoglio, Pietro	1871–1956
Balbo, Italo	1896–1940
Ciano, Galeazzo	1903–1944
Gasperi, Alcide de	1881–1954
Giolitti, Giovanni	1842–1928
Mussolini, Benito	1883–1945
Nitti, Francesco Saverio	1868–1953
Orlando, Vittorio Emanuele	1860–1952
Salandra, Antonio	1853–1931
Scialoja, Vittorio	1855–1933
Sforza, Carlo	1873–1952

Japanese:

Baba, Eüchi	1877–1937
Inukai, Tsuyoshi	?–1932
Tanaka, Baron	1862–1929
Tojo, Hideki	1884–1948
Yamamoto, Count	1852–1933

New Zealand:

Fraser, Peter	1884–1950
Holland, Sir Sidney	1893–1957
Savage, Michael	1872–1940

Pakistani:

Jinnah, Mohammed Ali	1876–1948
Liaquat Ali Khan	1896–1951

Peruvian:

Cerro, Luis M. S.	1889–1933

Polish:

Beck, Josef	1894–1944
Korfanty, Adalbert	1873–1939
Sikorski, Wladislaw	1881–1943
Smigly-Ridz, Edward	1886–?1939
Wojcechowski, Stanislaw	1869–1953

Rumanian:

Antonescu, Ion	1882–1946
Averescu, Alexander	1859–1938
Bukharin, N. I.	1880–1938
Calinescu, Armand	1893–1939
Duca, Ion	1879–1933

Russian:

Beria, Lavrenti	1899–1953
Dovgalersky, Valerian	1885–1934
Kamenev, Lev B.	1883–1936
Lenin, Vladimir Ilyitch Ulyanov	1870–1924
Litvinov, Maxim Maximovitch	1876–1951
Stalin, Josef Vissarionovitch Dzhugashvili	1880–1953
Tchitcherin, Georgii V.	1872–1936
Trotsky, Lev	1879–1940
Zinoviev, Grigori	1883–1936

S. African:

Botha, Louis	1862–1919
Hertzog, J. B. M.	1866–1942
Malan, Daniel	1874–1959
Roos, Tielman	1879–1935
Smuts, Jan Christiaan	1870–1951
Strijdom, Jan	d. 1958

Spanish:

Primo de Rivera, Miguel	1870–1930

Swedish:

Hammarskjöld, Dag	1905–1961

Turkish:

Atatürk, Mustafa Kemal	1881–1938
Menderes, Adnan	1899–1961

U.S.A.:

Bingham, Robert Worth	1871–1937
Bryan, William Jennings	1860–1925
Coolidge, Calvin	1872–1933
Dulles, John Foster	1888–1959
House, Edward Mandell	1858–1938
Kellogg, Frank Billings	1856–1937
Kennedy, John Fitzgerald	1917–1963
La Follette, Robert M.	1855–1925
Long, Huey Pierce	1893–1935
MacCarthy, Joseph	1909–1957
Marshall, George	1880–1959
Morrow, Dwight Whitney	1873–1931
Roosevelt, Eleanor	1884–1962
Roosevelt, Franklin Delano	1882–1945
Roosevelt, Theodore	1858–1919
Root, Elihu	1845–1937
Taft, Robert	1890–1953
Taft, William Howard	1857–1930

Vandenberg, Arthur 1884–1951
Welles, Sumner 1892–1961
Whitlock, Brand 1869–1934
Willkie, Wendell 1892–1944
Wilson, Thomas Woodrow 1856–1924

Yugoslav:

Kidrić, Boris 1912–1953
Mihailovich, Draza 1893–1946

Stationers' Hall. Incorporated, 1556.

Stationery Office, Her Majesty's, established, 1786.

Steam Navigation. *See* SHIP.

Stellaland, short-lived Boer republic set up in Northern Cape Province, 1882. Declared British protectorate, 1884.

Stettin grew up round a Wendish stronghold *c.* A.D. 1200; received municipal charter, 1243; ceded to Sweden, 1648; to Prussia, 1720. In 1945 it was ceded to Poland and named Szczecin.

Stock Exchange constitution regulated by Deed of Settlement of 27 Mar. 1802; modified by Deed of 31 Dec. 1875.

Stockholm Conference of European Social Democrats held, Aug. 1917.

Stoics. The disciples of Zeno (335–263 B.C.), whose school was held in a portico (Greek *stoa*).

Strand (London), first mentioned in Anglo-Saxon Chronicle, *sub anno* 1052.

Strasbourg or **Strassburg.** Capital of Alsace. Taken by France, 1681; captured by Germany, 1870; returned to France, 1918; Germany, 1940; France again, 1944. Contains a celebrated university, founded in 1538. Headquarters of the Council of Europe since 1949.

Stratford-on-Avon. Shakespeare Memorial Theatre built, 1877–9; burnt down, 1926; rebuilt, 1932.

Strathclyde, Celtic kingdom of the Clyde Valley and parts of Galloway, at times linked to that of Cumbria, founded *c.* A.D. 560. Became subject to Northumbria about 650, but regained independence after the defeat of King Ecgfrith by the Picts at Nectansmere, 685. Alcluith (Dumbarton), the capital, stormed by Picts, 736. King Eadberht of Northumbria conquered and annexed south-western S., 750, and temporarily subdued the whole kingdom, 756. Dumbarton sacked by the Danish king, Ivarr Ragnarsson, 870, and again invaded by him, 875 (*see* VIKING AGE). Thereafter more frequently invaded, and partly settled, by Norwegian Vikings, mainly via Dublin and Isle of Man. Submitted to Edward the Elder, King of England, about 921. Ceded by Edmund, King of England, to Malcolm I of Scotland, 946, but again became independent before 971. Last mention of a king of S. (Owen), as ally of Malcolm Canmore, 1018. Independence finally lost before 1100.

Stratosphere. Auguste Piccard and Paul Kipfer soared to height of nearly 10 miles, over Alps, 27 May 1931. World's record, at present, 72,395 ft. (13·7 miles), by Maj. Albert Stevens and Capt. Orvil A. Anderson, with an enormous balloon, from Rapid City, N. Dakota, 10 Nov. 1935. Highest aeroplane records: by Lt.-Col. Mario Pezzi (Italian), 56,017 ft. (10½ miles), 22 Oct. 1938; John Cunningham, 59,492 ft., 1948.

Street Offences Act. Came into force, 16 Aug. 1959.

Streptomycin. Isolated, 1943, by Waksman, a Russian-born scientist, who was awarded the Nobel Prize, 1952.

Stresa Conference, 11–14 Apr. 1935. Britain, France, and Italy agreed to maintain independence of Austria.

Strike, the General. *See* GENERAL STRIKE.

Stuttgart. Chartered in 1250. Became capital of the dukes of Württemberg in the fifteenth century.

Styria (Steiermark). Came under Frankish domination about 780, but only as part of Duchy of Carinthia (*q.v.*). Made a separate mark in 1056, and bestowed on Count Ottokar of Steyr, whence its name. Became a duchy in 1180, and was attached to the Duchy of Austria, 1192; belonged to Bohemia from 1260 to 1282, thereafter to the Hapsburg empire. Formed one province (*Land*) of the Austrian Federal Republics of 1918 and 1945. *See also* CARINTHIA and SLOVENES.

Submarines. First practicable submarine was demonstrated by the American Bushnell in 1775, the next by Robert Fulton in 1800; both capable of placing limpet charges. S. were first used in action in the American Civil War, 1863. First Brit. submarine launched, 1901. First nuclear-powered submarine was the U.S.S. *Nautilus*, 1955. First nuclear-powered British submarine, the *Dreadnought*, began her trials, Dec. 1962; commissioned 1963. U.S. submarine *Thresher* lost with all hands off east coast of America, Apr. 1963.

Sudan, N. Africa, sovereign independent republic since 1 Jan. 1956, formerly Anglo-Egyptian territory. The area corresponds more or less to the territory anciently called Nubia (i.e. the Nile valley S. of the First Cataract—Aswan), which was penetrated by Egyptian influence as early as the Old Empire, almost 4000 B.C. Colonies and military posts were established regularly in the twelfth dynastic period (2700–2500 B.C.), and the conquest S. to the Fourth Cataract consolidated under the eighteenth dynasty (*c.* 1350 B.C.). About 200 years later fugitive priests of Amen from Thebes founded a new state, with sub-Egyptian culture, with its capital at Napata in S. An independent Nubian civilization arose c. 800 B.C., and for a time its kings dominated Egypt (from 749 to 667). The borrowed Egyptian culture declined after the withdrawal of Nubian rulers from Egypt, and the capital Napata was supplanted by Meroë c. 300. For three centuries thereafter Nubia was virtually independent of the Ptolemaic rulers of Egypt, but the Romans who succeeded them also conquered the S., and established their southern frontier to the S. of Wadi Halfa. The Nobadae from whom the name Nubia is derived were settled on the frontier by Diocletian, A.D. 285. Only at the end of the Romano-Nubian period (c. 550) was Christianity, of the Monophysite persuasion, introduced. Moslem invasions began, 652, but strong Christian kingdoms persisted until c. 1350, and many Nubians professed Christianity until the sixteenth century. The triumph of Islam was due to direct migration from Arabia, led by the Beni Omayya tribe from the eighth century onwards. In the eighteenth century the Moslem king of Sennar finally defeated the now quite isolated kingdom of Ethiopia (q.v.). S. was conquered by Mehemet Ali, 1821. Gen. Gordon was appointed (Egyptian) governor-general, 1873–80; revolt of Sudanese under the Mahdi, 1882; annihilation of Hicks Pasha's forces, 1883; Gordon killed at Khartoum, 1885; battle of Omdurman, 1898. Anglo-Egyptian agreement on condominium, 19 Jan. 1899, determined the manner of S. administration for the first half of the twentieth century. From 1930 onwards Egypt made increasing demands for 'unity of the Nile valley' (i.e. annexation of S. by Egypt), especially after 1946. The Governor-General's Council, established in 1910, was replaced, 20 Dec. 1948, by a Legislative Assembly and an Executive Council; in 1944 an Advisory Council for the Northern S. had been set up. Demand for annexation by Egyptian nationalists, 1951, expressed in change of King of Egypt's title to 'King of Egypt and the S.' Britain refused recognition, 1952. On 12 Feb. 1953 Neguib, then Egyptian Prime Minister, signed agreement with British Government following discussion with S. political leaders: it acknowledged the right of S. to self-determination and proposed a period of three years for sudanization of defence and civil services, the population to choose, in 1955, between independence and union with Egypt. The Sudanese Parliament voted unanimously for complete independence immediately, 19 Dec. 1955, and this was agreed by Britain and Egypt, 31 Dec. 1955. An independent republic was proclaimed, 1 Jan. 1956. There was an army coup on 17 Nov. 1959, and the country has since been governed by the Supreme Council of the Armed Forces, led by Gen. Abboud. The S. Missionary Societies Act, restricting the religious freedom of non-Moslems, came into force Nov. 1962.

French S., the designation from 1920 until 1960 of Upper Senegal-Niger, a French colony formed in 1904. An Overseas Territory under the 1946 constitution. Boundaries modified, 1933, 1945, 1948. Member of the French Community from Nov. 1958; a partner (with Senegal) in the Federation of Mali, Jan. 1959–Sept. 1960. On 22 Sept. 1960 the territory became the independent republic of **Mali** (*q.v.*).

Sudetenland, district taking its name from the Sudetic Mountains in Bohemia and Moravia, and before 1945 largely inhabited by Germans from Saxony, Bavaria, and Franconia, whose immigration began shortly after A.D. 1100. Sudeten German *Heimatfront* (local Nazi and other Pan-German parties amalgamated) formed by Konrad Henlein (1898–1945), 1933. S. incorporated in German Reich, Oct. 1938. Some 3,700,000 S. Germans, out of an estimated 4,000,000, were expelled from Czechoslovakia, 1945.

Suevi. *See* SWABIA.

Suez Canal. Permission for its construction under M. de Lesseps, 1854; company formed, 1856; work begun, 1859; opened to traffic, 1869. Britain buys shares in, 1875. Under Article 8 of the Anglo-Egyptian Defence Treaty, 1938, Britain was responsible for defending the S. C. zone; but in Nov. 1955 Egypt took over. The last British troops left the zone, 31 Mar. 1956. Nasser nationalized the S. C., 26 July 1956 (concession not due to expire until 1968). Anglo-French planes began bombing canal installations, Oct. 1956, and (Nov.) invaded the zone (*see* EGYPT). Egypt blocked the S. C. and it was not opened to traffic again until 30 Apr. 1957. Shareholders of the S. C. Company accepted compensation terms offered by the United Arab Republic, July 1958. World Bank granted United Arab Republic a loan for canal improvements, Dec. 1959.

Sugar Beet Subsidy. Begun, 1934, with advance of £3,000,000.

Sumatra was a Hindu kingdom from c. A.D. 600–1300. First European (Portuguese) settlement, 1509, was replaced by Dutch settlement c. 1600. Occupation of the island by the Japanese was virtually complete by the end of Feb. 1942. Disarmament of Japanese and reoccupation of S. by Dutch and British forces took place late in the autumn of 1945.

'Summer Time.' *See* DAYLIGHT SAVING.

Sunday Observance Acts, 1625–1780, modified by the S. Entertainment Act, 1932, S. Trading Act, 1870, and Shops (Sunday Trading Restriction) Act, 1936. An attempt to liberalize theory and practice in the matter of S. O. was made in a private bill tabled by John Parker, M.P., 31 Jan. 1953, but defeated by a free vote of all parties, largely inspired by the Lords' Day Observance Society (founded, 1831).

Sunday Schools. Originally in Milan under Borromeo, 1580, and in England under Robert Raikes and Rev. Stocks, 1780. Sunday School Union (now National S. S. Union) founded 1803.

Sunspots were discovered by Galileo, 1610. Periodicity of eleven years deduced by Schwabe, 1843.

Supersonic speed, first attained by John Derry of de Havillands, 6 Sept. 1948.

Supertax first imposed by Lloyd George in Finance Act, 1909, and levied until 1929. *See* SURTAX.

Supply, Ministry of, set up in Apr. 1939. Duties transferred to Ministry of Aviation, 1959.

Supremacy, Act of, 1534, declared Henry VIII head of the English Church. Denial of this doctrine declared treasonable under Edward VI, 1457. Repealed by Philip and Mary, 1554. Restored in slightly modified form by Elizabeth I, 1559.

Supreme Council. British, French, and Italian Governments set up a S. War C. at Versailles, Nov. 1917. Its strategic functions were, during the German offensive of 1918, transferred exclusively to Marshal Foch. In 1919–20 it acted as the Executive Committee of the Peace Conference (*q.v.*).

Supreme Court of Judicature. The Judicature Act of 1873 formed one supreme court for England and Wales out of the courts of Chancery, Queen's Bench, Common Pleas, Exchequer, High Court of Admiralty, and Probate. The Bankruptcy Act, 1883, brought bankruptcy within the province of the S. C. effectively in 1884.

Surinam. *See* DUTCH GUIANA.

Surtax replaced supertax (*q.v.*) in 1929. Incomes at which S. levied raised, 1961.

Sussex, Kingdom of.

477. Aelle and his sons Cymen, Wlencing, and Cissa landed at Cymenes ora.
485. Battle between Aelle and the Britons.
491. Aelle and Cissa besieged Andredesceaster (i.e. Anderida, now Pevensey), and killed the garrison.

514. Aelle died.
661–*c.* 685. Aethelwalh, King of Sussex, killed by Caedwalla of Wessex.
c. 685. References to two kings of Sussex, Berthun and Andhun, who resisted Caedwalla. About 687 Caedwalla seems to have become effective ruler of S. *See* SELSEY.

Later history suggests that S. was ruled by a number of sub-kings, probably subject to Wessex and then to Mercia.

Suttee. Suicide of an Indian widow on the husband's funeral pile. Forbidden by the British administration, 1829.

Swabia (Schwaben), originally an ethnic rather than geographical term denoting the land of the Suevi or Swabians. It is not clear that the term Suevi when used by Tacitus (A.D. 55–120) is anything more than a vague term for nomadic tribes at a rather lower cultural level than other Germans to the S. and W.; but by about A.D. 600 Swabians had come to mean tribes speaking the western or Alemmanic variant of the High German language, and their country the rough rectangle between the Main, the Rhine, Lake Constance, and the Lech. It was a 'tribal' duchy under the Carolingian Empire (751–987) and came into possession of the Stauffen dynasty, 1079, who retained it until 1268, when it was partitioned among the local nobility. The 'Swabian League,' a confederation of Swabian cities formed in 1488, disintegrated, 1534. *See also* BADEN and WÜRTTEMBERG.

Swaziland. Independence recognized by Boer republics in Conventions of 1881 and 1884. Dual control by British and Boers set up, 1890; administration taken over by Transvaal, 1894; separate administrative services created, 1901; British protectorate declared, 1906; police force established, 1907. Elected Advisory Council for European Affairs set up, 1921; reconstituted, 1949 and 1956. New constitution, 1963.

'Sweating.' A term applied to underpaid and overworked labour. Cradley Heath chainmakers' sufferings disclosed, 1889; Anti-Sweating League formed, 1889; Blue Book published, 1890.

Sweden. S. originated in the Sver Kingdom N. of Lake Mälar and the Gothic Kingdom in south S. which coalesced after the battle of Brávalla (? *c.* 650) under the Uppsala Yngling dynasty. Swedes under Rurik found Novgorod *c.* 862. Ynglings die out and are succeeded by the Gothic Stenkil's dynasty, 1060. The Christian Sverker's dynasty follows, 1130–55, when civil war between Sverker's and Eric's dynasties follows till 1250. Folkung dynasty established by the jarl,

Birger Magnusson, 1250 till 1387. By the Union of Kalmar (*q.v.*) S. comes under Danish rule, 1397. Engelbrekt Engelbrektsen raises revolt in Dalecarlia, 1434. He calls the first Riksdag (Parliament) at Arboga, 1435, and is murdered, 1436. Sten 'Sture the Elder defeats Danes at Brunkeberg, 1471. Papal charter granted to Uppsala University, 1477. Christian II of Denmark carries out massacre at Stockholm, 1520. Gustavus Vasa raises national revolt in Dalecarlia, Jan. 1521. Elected king by Riksdag at Strängnäs, 6 June 1523. *Recess* and *Ordinantia* of Västerås establish power of the Vasa monarchy and regulate church affairs, 24 June 1527. Pact of Succession, 1544. Eric XIV deposed, 1568. S. seize Novgorod, 1611. Peace of Stolbova, 1617. Gustavus Adolfus conquers Baltic provinces, 1621–2; Pomerania, 1630. Defeats Tilly at battle of Breitenfeld, 1631. Is killed at battle of Lützen, 6 Nov. 1632. New. constitution, 1634. Abdication of Queen Christina, 1654. Defeat by Russians at Poltava, 1709, and collapse of Swedish Baltic Empire, 1709–18. Peace of Nystad with Russia, 1721. By *Riksdags ordningen* (' Parliamentary constitution '), Riksdag organized into Four Estates, 1723. Marshal Bernadotte elected Crown Prince, 1810. Norway transferred to Swedish crown, 1814. Bernadotte succeeded to throne as Charles XIV, 1818. Two-chamber legislature introduced, 1866. Union with Norway dissolved, 1905. Rise of Social Democrat Party after 1900. Universal suffrage and proportional representation, 1909. Prohibition introduced, 1922; abolished, 1955. S. neutral in both world wars, but her representatives, through the U.N.O., played a large part in solving the Israeli (1948) and Suez (1956) crises, and Swedish troops were part of the U.N. force in the Gaza Strip (1956–7) and the Congo (1960–). A Swede (Dag Hammarskjöld) was Secretary-General of U.N.O. from 1953 until his death in an aeroplane crash in 1961.

Sweden, Kings of, from c. 850–1951:

Olaf and Emund	c. 850–c. 882
Eric Emundsson	c. 882–c. 905
Bjorn Ericsson and Ring	c. 905–c. 950
Eric the Victorious	c. 950–c. 993
Period of confusion	c. 993–999
Olaf Scatt-King	999–1022
Anund Jacob	1022–1050
Emund the Old	1050–1060
Stenkil	1060–1066
Period of confusion	1066–1080
Halstan	c. 1080–c. 1093
Inge the Good	c. 1090–c. 1118
Inge II Halstansson	c. 1118–1130

Sweden. *Kings—cont.*

Sverker	c. 1132–1155
Eric IX (Saint)	1150–1160
Charles VII	1160–1167
Knut Ericsson	1167–1196
Sverker Carlsson	1196–1205 (?)
Period of confusion: rival kings	1205–1250
Valdemar	1250–1275
Magnus I Ladulas	1275–1290
Birger	1290–1318
Magnus II	1319–1365
Albert of Mecklenburg	1365–1388
Margaret (as ' Lady of Sweden ')	1389–1397
Eric of Pomerania (XIII)	1397–1439
Christopher of Bavaria	1440–1448
Charles VIII Knutsson Bonde	1448–1457
Christian I	1457–1464
Charles VIII (again)	1464–1465
	and 1467–1470
Regency under Sten Sture the Elder	1470–1497
John II	1497–1501
Regency under Sten Sture the Elder	1501–1503
Regency under Svante Sture	1504–1512
Regency under Sten Sture the Younger	1512–1520
Christian II	1520–1523
Gustavus I (Vasa) (of Sweden only)	1523–1560
Eric XIV	1560–1568
John III	1568–1592
Sigismund	1592–1599
Charles IX	1600–1611
Gustavus II, Adolphus	1611–1632
Christina	1632–1654
Charles X	1654–1660
Charles XI	1660–1697
Charles XII	1697–1718
Ulrica Eleonora	1718–1720
Frederick I	1720–1751
Adolphus, Frederick	1751–1771
Gustavus III	1771–1792
Gustavus IV, Adolphus	1792–1809
Charles XIII	1809–1818
	and of Norway 1814–1818
Charles XIV, John (Bernadotte)	1818–1844
Oscar I	1844–1859
Charles XV	1859–1872
Oscar II (renounced throne of Norway, 1905)	1872–1907
Gustavus V	1907–1950
Gustavus VI, Adolphus	1950–

Swedenborgians, followers of Emanuel Swedenborg (1688–1772), more properly called the New (Jerusalem) Church, founded in England, 1788; their propaganda organ, the Swedenborg Society, instituted, 1810.

Swedish Literature. The following is a list of Swedish authors not now living:

Almqvist, Carl Jonas Ludvig, 1793–1866, novelist.

Atterbom, Per Daniel Amadeus, 1790–1855, poet.

Bellman, Carl Mikael, 1740–95, poet.

Benedictsson, Victoria ('Ernst Ahlgren'), 1850–99, novelist.

Bengtsson, Frans, 1894–1956, novelist and biographer.

Bergman, Hjalmar, 1883–1931, novelist.

Bremer, Fredrika, 1801–65, novelist.

Creutz, Gustaf Philip, 1731–85, poet.

Dahlgren, Karl Fredrik, 1791–1844, humorist and poet.

Dahlsjerna, Gunno (Eurelius), 1661–1709, poet.

Dalin, Olaf von, 1708–63, poet and historian.

Flygare-Carlén, Emilie, 1807–92, novelist.

Franzén, Frans Mikael, 1772–1847, poet.

Fröding, Gustaf, 1850–1911, poet, critic, and novelist.

Fryxell, Anders, 1795–1881, historian.

Geijer, Erik Gustaf, 1783–1847, historian and poet.

Geijerstam, Gustaf af, 1858–1909, novelist and dramatist.

Gyalenborg, Gustaf Fredrik, 1731–1808, poet and dramatist.

Hansson, Ola, 1860–1925, poet.

Hedin, Sven Anders, 1865–1951, writer on travel.

Heidenstam, Verner von, 1859–1940, poet, novelist, and critic.

Kellgren, Johan Henrik, 1751–95, poet.

Konsenstjerna, Agnes von, 1894–1940, novelist.

Lagerlöf, Selma, 1858–1940, novelist.

Lundegård, Axel, 1861–1930, novelist.

Messenius, Johannes, 1579–1636, poet and dramatist.

Molander, Harald Johan, 1858–1900, dramatist.

Munthe, Axel Marten Fredrik, 1857–1949.

Nordenflycht, Hedvig Charlotta, 1718–63, poetess.

Petri, Olaus, 1493–1552, historian.

Rosenhane, Gustaf, 1619–84, poet.

Runeberg, Johan Ludvig, 1804–77, poet.

Rydberg, Abraham Viktor, 1828–95, poet, novelist, etc.

Schück, Johan Henrik, 1855–1945, literary historian.

Sjöberg, Erik ('Vitalis'), 1794–1828, poet.

Snoilsky, Count Carl Johan Gustaf, 1841–1903, poet.

Stagnelius, Erik Johan, 1793–1823, poet.

Stjernhjelm, Georg (Göran Lilja), 1598–1672, poet.

Strindberg, Johan August, 1849–1912, novelist and dramatist.

Swedenborg, Emanuel, 1688–1772, philosopher and scientist.

Tegner, Esaias, 1782–1846, poet.

Wägner, Elin, 1882–1949, novelist.

Wallin, Johan Olaf, 1779–1839, hymn writer.

The following though writing in Swedish were born and lived in Finland, and regarded themselves as of Finnish nationality:

Hemmer, J., 1893–1944, poet.

Lybeck, M., 1864–1925, poet.

Numers, G. von, 1848–1913, playwright (also in Finnish).

Procope, H., 1868–1927, poet.

Runeberg, J. L., 1804–77, poet.

Schildt, R., 1888–1925, novelist and playwright.

Stenbäck, J., 1811–70, poet.

Tavastjerna, K. A., 1860–98, poet and novelist.

Topelius, Z., 1818–98, poet.

Wecksell, J. J., 1838–1907, playwright.

Swiss Guard (French). Raised, 1616; ceased to exist after 1792, when they suffered heavy losses in the defence of the Tuileries.

Swiss Guard (papal). Raised by Julius II, 1506. Had heavy casualties (two-thirds of total strength) at the sack of Rome, 1527. New establishment ordered by Paul III, 1548. Disbanded in 1794, re-formed, 1825, by Leo XII. Now form part of armed forces of Vatican State.

Switzerland. Struggle for independence against the Hapsburgs (*q.v.*), thirteenth–fourteenth centuries; victories at Morgarten, Sempach, and Näfels, 1315, 1386, and 1388; overthrow of Burgundians at Granson and Morat, 1476; defeated by French at Melegnano, 1515; religious wars during sixteenth century; Calvin at Geneva, 1536, till his death; declared independent at Peace of Westphalia (*q.v.*), 1648; Peasants' Revolt, 1653; first Villemergen War, 1656; second Villemergen War, 1712; Helvetic Society founded, 1762; alliance with France, 1777; Helvetic Republic proclaimed, 29 Mar. 1798; independence secured by Treaty of Vienna, 1815; The Sonderbund Civil War, Oct.–Nov. 1847; constitution revised, 1874; Simplon tunnel completed, 1906; joined League of Nations, May 1920; S. arranged Customs Union with, and took over diplomatic representation of, Liechtenstein (*q.v.*), 1923; dispute with France over Haute Savoie 'free zones,' 1924, settled, Mar. 1928; Romansch declared an official language, 11 July 1937. Women's suffrage rejected by referendum, 1 Feb. 1959. In Apr. 1962 a referendum voted in favour of the Swiss constitution not being amended so as to prevent S. having her own nuclear weapons. For early history, *see* articles on separate cantons and WALDSTÄTTE.

Sydney, New S. Wales, was founded by Capt. Arthur Philip, 1788. S. Harbour Bridge officially opened, 1932. Capt. Cook Dock completed, 1945.

Synods. Convened formerly by the emperors, and afterwards by the Pope; rendered illegal in England except by royal permission, 1533. The Synod of Dort was held from Nov. 1618 to May 1619.

Syracuse, founded c. 734 B.C. as Corinthian colony. Beat off Carthaginians at Himera, 480 B.C.; defeated Athenian expedition, 414–413; allied to Carthage in second Punic War and taken by Romans, 212, despite brilliant defence by Archimedes (b. 287 B.C.), the chief engineer. Taken by Arabs, A.D. 878, and Normans, 1085.

Syria. Mandated to France in 1920. Lebanon Republic (or Greater Lebanon) proclaimed a state, 1 Sept. 1920. French united the states of Damascus and Aleppo, with Damascus as capital, 1924. Revolt of Druses, spring of 1925. Provisional Government of Syrian Republic formed, Feb. 1928. New republican constitution for the state of S. promulgated by French High Commissioner, June 1930. After disturbances treaty made with French Government secured independence, 9 Sept. 1936: treaty unratified. Sanjak of Alexandretta given autonomy, 1937; first Assembly, 2 Sept. 1938, when name of Sanjak was changed to The Hatay. The latter ceded to Turkey, 23 July 1939. French commander in S., loyal to Vichy Government, announced cessation of hostilities with Germany, 28 June 1940.

British, Imperial, and Free French forces carried through occupation of S. against Vichy opposition, 8 June–21 July 1941, and declared the independence of S., but in 1945 disagreements arose with the French which led to fighting. French troops finally evacuated S. in Apr. 1946. Armistice with Israel signed, Feb. 1949. Three successive army coups in 1946; the last put Shishakli in power, and he was elected first President of Syrian Republic, 10 July 1953. Another coup forced him to flee the country, Feb. 1954. Soviet influence strong in S., 1955–7. On 1 Feb. 1958 became part of the United Arab Republic (q.v.). Subsequently Syrian officials in S. were replaced by Egyptians, and economic difficulties became worse. Discontent with the union resulted in an army coup, Sept. 1961, and the union with Egypt was subsequently dissolved. The political situation remained unstable, and in Apr. 1962 there were pro-Nasser revolts in N. S., which were put down; but Egyptian influence nevertheless appeared to be increasing in S. again. In Mar. 1963 a pro-Nasser revolt was successful, and the new regime signed an agreement in Cairo on 17 Apr. 1963 which established a new federal United Arab Republic, consisting of S. Iraq (q.v.) and Egypt. Subsequent unrest in S. led to the dismissal of pro-Nasser ministers, however, and the new links with the United Arab Republic appeared increasingly tenuous.

ADDENDA

T

Tahiti, Pacific, discovered by Spaniard, de Quiros, 1607; French protectorate formally accepted by native ruler, 1847; French possession, 1880.

Tai-Pings. Followers of the Christian Hung Hsinchwan in the Chinese rebellion of 1851. Captured Nanking, Mar. 1853; Nanking retaken by the Imperialists under direction of Charles Gordon (later killed at Khartoum), 19 July 1864; and rebellion suppressed, 1865.

Taiwan. *See* FORMOSA.

Tajikistan became an autonomous republic, 1924, and a Union republic of the U.S.S.R., 1929.

Taj Mahal, India, built by Shah Jehan, A.D. 1630–52, in memory of his favourite wife, who *d.* 1629.

Takoradi Harbour, Ghana. Completed, 1928.

Tallage, a characteristically Norman tax, was placed under the control of the Commons, 1297, who abolished it, 1340.

Tallies were used by the exchequer for accounting purposes until 1826, though an Act for their abolition was passed, 1782. An unsupervised bonfire of old T. was the cause whereby the greater part of the Palace of Westminster was burnt down, 1834.

Tallin (Reval), fortress founded by Danes in 1219, joined the Hanseatic League, 1248. Ceded to Sweden, 1561, by the Teutonic Knights, who had obtained possession of T. in 1346. Ceded, 1710, to Russians, who made it the capital of the Government of Estonia (*q.v.*), 1783. Capital of the independent republic of Estonia, 1919–40. Ceded to Russia as a naval base by the independent republic of Estonia, 28 Sept. 1939. Taken by Germans, Aug. 1941, and retained until the spring of 1945 when, with the rest of Estonia, it became part of the U.S.S.R.

Talmud. The civil and religious code of the Jews. The T. dating from the fifth century is the one in use, an earlier one having become unintelligible. It is divided into the Mishna and the Gemara. The first complete copy was published at Venice, 1520.

Tammany Society. A powerful Democratic association of New York, founded in 1789; chartered, 1805. Named after Tammany, a Delaware Indian chief of the seventeenth century; the name itself means ' affable.'

Tanganyika. Formerly German E. Africa; mandated to Britain under the peace treaty, 1919. Legislative Council set up by Order in Council, 1 July 1926. Responsible government, with an elected majority, Sept. 1960. Became an independent dominion within the Commonwealth, with Julius Nyere as first Prime Minister, 9 Dec. 1961. Nyere subsequently resigned; succeeded by Kawawa, Feb. 1962. On 9 Dec. 1962 became a republic, while remaining in the Commonwealth, with Nyere as its first President.

Tangier or **Tangiers,** Morocco (*q.v.*). The Roman **Tingis.** Captured by Portuguese, 1471; given to Charles II on his marriage to Catherine of Braganza, 1662; evacuated by English, 1684; bombarded by French, 1844; terrorized by Raisuli in early years of twentieth century; policed in 1906 as a result of Algeciras Convention. By treaty of Fez (Nov. 1912) T. was to become centre of an international zone, and it was finally formed into an internationally governed neutral port, 18 Dec. 1923, by France and Britain (Spain acceded to the agreement, 1924). Spanish troops occupied T., 14 June 1940, and in Sept. T. was incorporated into Spanish Morocco. Spanish troops withdrew and former status restored, 1945. France agreed to terminate treaty of Fez, 1956. Spanish protectorate abolished, and in Oct. the powers agreed that T.'s international status be terminated as from 1 Jan. 1957, when it became an integral part of Morocco.

Tanks. British War Office began experiments, 1915. First went into action on the Somme, 15 Sept. 1916.

Taoism. One of the three religions of China. The system was founded by Lao-tsze in the sixth century B.C.

Tapestry. Introduced into Flanders during tenth century; Arras chief centre during fourteenth and fifteenth centuries; Gobelin (*q.v.*) factory founded in Paris, sixteenth century; famous T. factory founded at Mortlake by Sir Francis Crane, 1619; existed till 1703; another factory existed at Windsor, 1872–88. Revival of tapestry in twentieth century exemplified by one behind the high altar of the rebuilt Coventry Cathedral. It depicts 'Christ in Glory' and was designed by Graham Sutherland and woven, 1958–61, at the Aubusson factory in France.

398

Tara, Hill of, was the residence of the High Kings of Ireland until A.D. 560. The Danes were defeated there (see VIKING AGE), 980. Important excavations begun at, 1952.

Taranto (Lat. **Tarentum;** Gr. **Taras),** Italy, founded 708 B.C. by Spartans. Assisted by Pyrrhus in war against Romans, 281 B.C.; captured by Romans, 272 B.C.; became ally of Rome, but went over to Hannibal, 213 B.C., and on being recaptured by Fabius, 209 B.C., was severely punished. Roman colony, 123 B.C. Taken by the Saracens, A.D. 830; by the Normans, 1083. British air raid on Italian fleet, 11 Nov. 1940. Captured by British troops, 9 Sept. 1943.

Tarifa, Spain. Captured from Moslems in 1292; defended by English against French, 1811–12.

Tariff Reform League. Inaugurated, July 1903.

Tariffs (Britain). Bill to promote Imperial Preference, protect ' key industries,' and prevent dumping passed first reading, Nov. 1919, and was then dropped. Government proposals for Imperial Preference introduced at Imperial Conference, Oct. 1923. McKenna duties on certain manufactured goods imposed, 1915; abolished, 1924; reimposed, 1925. Silk and artificial silk taxed and ten-year guarantee given to preference on sugar, 1925. The guarantee extended to other preferences, ' safeguarding ' renewed for ten years, and wrapping-paper taxed, 1926. First protective measures passed by National Government, Nov. 1931. Import Duties Act, 1932. As a further ' weapon,' Reprisal Quotas (for imports) were instituted, 1934. Tariff modifications after World War II through G.A.T.T. and the European Free Trade Association (q.v.). Further international tariff reductions envisaged after G.A.T.T. conference at Geneva in May 1963.

Tarsus, Asia Minor. Founded by Ionian Greeks, c. 900 B.C. Occupied by Assyrians, 850. Birthplace of Saul (Paul the Apostle). Capital of the Roman province of Cilicia, A.D. 72. Captured by Arabs c. 660; taken by Tancred in First Crusade, 1099; under Turks since c. 1500.

Tartan. The word, which is not Gaelic and first appears in English usage in 1500, may be of French origin. The characteristic *setts* denoting clans and septs evolved probably during the seventeenth century. The wearing of T. was prohibited by law from 1746 to 1782, under the Highland Garb Act.

Tasmania. Discovered in 1642 by Abel J. Tasman. Penal settlement till 1853. Granted local government, 1856. Name then changed from Van Diemen's Land to T. United with the mainland states to form the Commonwealth of Australia, 1901.

Tatar or **Tartar Republic,** an autonomous republic of the U.S.S.R., formed in 1920 on the territory of the fifteenth-century T. kingdom of Kazan.

Tate Gallery. Opened, 1897; enlarged, 1899, 1910, 1926, 1937. Damaged by bombing during World War II. but reopened, 1946, and repairs completed, 1949.

Tattersall's. Horse mart founded by Richard Tattersall (1724–95) in 1766 at Hyde Park Corner; removed to Knightsbridge, 1867.

Taunton. Castle first built by King Ine c. 710; rebuilt c. 1100; defended by Blake, 1644–5; ' Bloody Assize ' opened by Judge Jeffreys, 1685.

Taxation (Britain). Income and property tax first levied by Parliament during the civil war, 1642. William Pitt the Younger introduced an income tax, 1798, which was repealed, 1815, and revived by Peel, 1842. Low incomes exempted and ' earned ' distinguished from ' unearned ' income, 1898. Reliefs given for dependent children, 1909. Supertax introduced, 1914–18. Surtax replaced supertax, 1929. Earnings limits at which it was levied raised, 1961.

Land tax first levied, 1690. Made perpetual but redeemable, 1798. Lloyd George introduced Land Value Tax, 1909. Abolished, 1920. Purchase tax introduced, 1940. A ' once-for-all ' Special Contribution, similar to a capital levy, imposed, 1948. Tax on certain capital gains introduced, 1961.

Tay Bridge. First opened, 1877. Famous disaster, 28 Dec. 1879. New bridge opened, 1887.

Tea. Introduced in Europe, sixteenth century, but not into England until 1657.

Tehri-Garhwal, small tributary kingdom which in Mar. 1949 the Indian Government combined with Garhwal (q.v.) as part of the United Provinces (known as Uttar Pradesh since 1950).

Tel-Aviv, founded in 1909, originally as a garden city by Jewish residents of Jaffa, received its present name in 1910. Granted municipal government, 1921. Large factories were erected in 1924, and property tax first levied by Parliament. T.-A. became the principal economic centre of Palestine (q.v.) in 1930, and the largest town in the country in 1936. It was the provisional capital of Israel (q.v.), 1948–50. Jaffa was absorbed into T.-A., 1950.

Telegraphy. Proposal to use electricity as means of communication made as early as 1753. First serviceable telegraphic device invented by Chappe (France), 1792. Ronald (England) produced his pith-ball telegraph, 1816. Morse constructed an instrument in 1835, and Steinheil in 1837. Cooke and Wheatstone's, 1837. Earliest trial, 1837, on L.N.W. Railway. First public line from Paddington to Slough, 1843; London and Paris connected, 1851. Post Office took over telegraph systems on 5 Feb. 1870. First transatlantic stations, Poldhu, Cornwall, and St. John's, Newfoundland, Dec. 1901; first installed in ships, Feb. 1902. *See* WIRELESS.

Telepathy. So named by F. W. H. Myers (1843–1901), 1882.

Telephone. Wheatstone's ' Magic Lyre ' (for reproducing sounds by means of sound-boards connected by a rod), 1831. Philipp Reis's experiments to reproduce human speech, 1861. Alexander Graham Bell (1847–1922) invented electric T., 1876; patented, 1876. Edison patented an invention of his, July 1877. The T. Co. formed, 1878; Edison T. Co. formed, 1879. Action by British postmaster-general against Edison for infringement of monopoly, 1879. National T. Co. (amalgamation of various separate concerns) formed, 1889; trunk wires transferred to Post Office, 1896; Government, by agreement of 2 Feb. 1905, obtained the whole undertaking of the National T. Co., 31 Dec. 1912. Automatic system developed in America from 1889 (Strowger's invention). Communication between London and Paris established, 1 Apr. 1891. First automatic exchange in U.K., Newport, 14 Aug. 1915. Service between New York and London opened, 7 Jan. 1927. Gradual switch to subscriber trunk dialling in Britain, 1959 onwards. First public telephone call by Telstar (*q.v.*) London–New York, 19 July 1962.

Telescope. Traditionally invented by Roger Bacon, in the thirteenth century, but no definite evidence to prove this. Giambattista della Porta probably first to construct some form of instrument, 1558; Leonard Digges is also said, in a book published in 1571, to have arranged glasses so as to obtain ' miraculous effects.' First practical instruments constructed by Lippershey and Jansen in Middelburg, 1608; Galileo constructed his first T., 1609, and began astronomical observations at the beginning of 1610. Lord Rosse's at Birr, 1844; Greenwich T. erected, 1860; Lick Observatory, California, 1880; Pulkowa, Russia, 1885; Yorkes Observatory, Chicago, 1897; Mount Palomar, California, 1949; Jodrell Bank, Cheshire, 1958. (*See also* OBSERVATORIES.)

Television was first practically demonstrated by J. L. Baird (1888–1946) in 1926, though means of transmitting images electronically had been suggested by Boris Rosing (1905) and Campbell-Swinton (1911). Still pictures were experimentally diffused by the British Broadcasting Corporation (*q.v.*) in 1928. An advisory committee counselled the B.B.C. not to transmit low-definition T. in Sept. 1935, but in Nov. 1936 a high-definition transmission station opened at Alexandra Palace. Baird system discontinued, 1937. Hankey Committee in 1943 recommended the resumption of T. after the war; recommendation accepted by government, Oct. 1945; transmission resumed, 7 June 1946. Relay station at Sutton Coldfield opened, 17 Dec. 1949. Lime Grove Studios, Shepherd's Bush, first operated T., 21 May 1950. Baird's contemporary in the same field in the U.S.A. was C. F. Jenkins. There were five stations transmitting in the U.S.A. in 1939, where T. was not, as in Europe, forced to close down during hostilities. In 1946 stations in New York State and Pennsylvania were linked by cable. Columbia Broadcasting System demonstrated coloured T., 1940, and colour T. used to a limited extent in the U.S.A. from 1949 onwards. T. cameras, not affected by radioactivity, were used to observe the Bikini tests at close range, 1946. Eurovision started, 1953. T. Act of 1954 established commercial T. in Britain, under the auspices of the Independent T. Authority (*q.v.*). The report of the Pilkington Committee, June 1962, recommended drastic changes in the organization of commercial T., but not all its recommendations were accepted by the Government. T. first shown ' live ' between Europe and the U.S.A. via Telstar (*q.v.*), June 1962. Britain to change her line definition from 405 to 625 lines gradually from 1964.

Telstar. American satellite launched from Cape Canaveral, Florida, 10 June 1962. A television picture from Andover, Maine, ' bounced off ' T. and was picked up at Goonhilly, Cornwall, at 1 a.m. on 11 July 1962, and at Brittany (even more clearly) on 12 July. Pictures from France and England transmitted to the United States via T. First live television show from United States seen in Europe via T., 23 July 1962. Subsequently the satellite's mechanism ceased to function and it went out of effective action. Telstar II launched successfully, 1963.

Templars, Knights. Order of knighthood founded under Baldwin II of Jerusalem in A.D. 1118 by Hugues de Payen and Geoffroi de Saint-Adhémar for the protection of pilgrims to the Holy Land. Statutes drawn up at the Council of Troyes, 1128. Rendered independent of any bishop's authority by a bull dated 1172. Reached England *c.* 1185. By order of Philip the Fair, Oct. 1307, the Order was persecuted in France with great cruelties, and was abolished in 1312 by the Council of Vienne. *See also* TEMPLE CHURCH (London).

Temple Bar (London). Wren's gate built, 1670-2. Removed, 1878-9. Erected at Theobalds Park, Cheshunt, 1888.

Temple Church (London). Built *c.* 1250. Severely damaged by bombing during World War II, but subsequently restored.

Tennessee, originally a part of N. Carolina, was first explored by Spaniards in 1540. Though forming part of the grant made to Sir Walter Raleigh in 1584, it was next explored by the French *c.* 1670-80. Settlement by British colonists began about 1750, and in 1776 the territory was annexed to N. Carolina under the name of Washington District, later Washington Co. T. partisans fought on the American side in the revolutionary war. Admitted to the Union as the sixteenth state, 1 June 1796. Seceded from the Union, June 1861; readmitted, 24 July 1866. Constitution (1870) last amended, 1953.

Tennessee Valley Authority (T.V.A.), created by an Act of Congress, May 1933.

Tennis. Played in France from the twelfth century onwards; popular in court circles in England from the fifteenth century. Lawn T. evolved from real T., *c.* 1870.

Ten Thousand, Expedition of the. Evacuation of Iraq by Greek mercenaries, formerly in the pay of the Persian King Cyrus, 401 B.C. The leader of the operation, Xenophon (427-355 B.C.), wrote an account of it (*Anabasis*).

Termonde. *See* DENDERMONDE.

Territorial. T. Force formed 1908 from Volunteers and Yeomanry (*q.v.*). Became T. Army, 1920. Re-formed, Jan. 1947, to include conscripts. Further reorganizations, 1956 and 1958. T. Association has administered welfare since 1908.

Territorial Waters. An Act of 1878 gives British courts jurisdiction over offenders arrested in British T. W., viz. within three sea-miles of the coastline of the U.K. In Dec. 1951 the claim of Norway to T. W. for fishery purposes of all the area three sea-miles outside an imaginary line drawn between promontories of the Norwegian coast was upheld against Britain by the International Court at The Hague. Iceland made a similar claim in 1952. In 1961 Britain accepted Iceland's claim that, for fishing purposes, her T. W. extended for twelve miles from the Icelandic coast.

Temperance League of America. *See* ANTI-SALOON LEAGUE.

Teschen (Pol. **Cieszyn;** Cz. **Tesin**), town and environs in Silesia, was a principality of the Empire, since 1290 under Bohemian suzerainty. Became part of Bohemia, 1625. Passed to Austria, 1723. Divided, 1920, between Poland and Czechoslovakia, the whole territory was seized by Poland in 1938, but recovered by Czechoslovakia, 1945. Polish population granted certain local autonomous privileges, 1947.

Test Acts of 1673 and 1678 were repealed in 1828 and 1829 respectively.

Teutonic Knights. Order of Military Knights, established 1189-91, for succouring the sick and wounded in the Holy Land; later they fought in parts of northeast Germany and the Baltic lands for the christianizing of the country; headquarters at Acre, 1191-1291, but transferred to Marienburg, 1308. Prestige hit by defeat at Tannenberg by Poles and Lithuanians, 1410. Grand Master of the Order, Albert of Brandenburg, became a Protestant, 1525, and the order was secularized; its last remaining possessions were taken by Napoleon in 1809.

Texas, first permanently settled by the French, 1685, was surrendered to Spain, 1713, and became part of Mexico when the latter declared its independence, 1821. Heavily settled by English-speaking cattle-ranchers, T. broke away from Mexican rule and declared itself independent in 1836. It joined the United States at the request of the Texans, Dec. 1845. The resultant war with Mexico over the Texan boundary lasted until 1848. T. seceded from the Union in 1861. The last battle of the civil war was fought at Palmito, T., 13 May 1865. Readmitted to the Union, Feb. 1870. The T. Rangers formed to police the cattle country, 1874.

Thailand (Siam). Present kingdom founded when Ayuthia became capital, 1350. Burmese storm Ayuthia and conquer T. *c.* 1555. Independence re-established' by Phra Naret, 1560-80. Siege and destruction of Ayuthia by Burmese, 1765-7. Phaya Tak Sin establishes new government at Bangkok, 1767-8. Succeeded by Phaya Chakri, 1782. Establishment of British interests in T. by John Burney, 1822-4. Eastern territories ceded to France, 1893. Anglo-French convention *re* T., 1895. Further cessions to France, 1902. Middle-class revolution establishes constitution, 1932. Name changed to T. from Siam, 1939.

O*

Japanese occupation, 8 Dec. 1941. King Ananda Mahidol murdered, 9 July 1946. *Coup d'état* by F. M. Luang Pibul Songgram, 9 Nov. 1947. Rising by Navy, in which Pibul Songgram was kidnapped, broke out, 29 July; put down by Army, Air Force, and police, 2 June 1951. National Assembly under new constitution confirmed appointment of Pibul Songgram as prime minister, 24 Mar. 1952. T. ratified SE. Asia defence treaty, Sept. 1954. Pibul Songgram overthrown, 1957. Further military coups, 1957-8. New constitution, 1959; temporary government by decree. Owing to deterioration in Laos situation, American marines landed in T., May 1962. A British air detachment followed. Subsequent lessening of tension led to withdrawal of British and American forces later in the year.

Thaler. *See* DOLLAR. The official unit of currency of the German Monetary Union from 1857 to 1873.

Thalidomide. Proprietary name of tranquillizing drug developed in Germany and introduced into Britain, 1958. Withdrawn by the makers as the result of evidence that when taken in early pregnancy it was liable to cause deformities in babies, Nov. 1961. In Sept. 1962 it was estimated that nearly 400 babies had been born deformed in Britain as the result of their mothers taking T.; some 300 of these survived. At the 'thalidomide trial' in Liège, Belgium, all five defendants were acquitted, 10 Nov. 1962.

Thames. Conservation of the stream given to the mayors of the city of London, 1489; twelve conservators fixed by Act of Parliament, 1857. T. Tunnel opened, 1843; closed, 1866. T. Conservancy Act, 1894; further acts, 1910, 1911, 1921, 1924, 1932, and 1950. County Council steamboat service opened, 1905; discontinued, 1909. Port of London Authority instituted, 31 Mar. 1909. River bus service started, 1948.

Thames Embankment. N. side (Victoria) constructed, 1862-70; S. (Albert), 1866-70; Chelsea, 1871-4.

Theatres (London). Licence granted to Burbage, 1576; the 'Theatre' and the 'Curtain,' 'Blackfriars,' and 'Globe' were among the T. extant in the time of Elizabeth I, and were all used by Shakespeare. Old Drury Lane opened, 1663; His Majesty's, 1705 (Sir H. Beerbohm Tree's new house built, 1897); Haymarket, old, 1720, present, 1820; Covent Garden, 1732; Sadler's Wells, 1753; Adelphi, 1806; Olympic, 1806 (demolished with Wych Street); Lyceum, 1809 (now closed); Old Vic, as Coburg, 1818 (closed,

June 1963, to reopen as temporary home of the National Theatre, Sept. 1963); St. James's, 1835; Gaiety, old, 1868, new, 1903 (now closed); Vaudeville, 1870; Court, 1871; Criterion, 1874; Savoy, 1881; Prince of Wales's (Prince's, 1911), 1884; Lyric, 1888; Shaftesbury, 1888 (now closed); Palace (originally Royal English Opera House), 1891; Duke of York's (originally Trafalgar Square), 1892; Wyndham's, 1899; Apollo, 1901; New, 1903; Scala, 1905; Waldorf, 1905, renamed Strand and reopened, 1909; Queen's, 1907; Little, 1910; Ambassadors', 1913; St. Martin's, 1916; Winter Garden, 1919 (now closed); Fortune, 1924; Piccadilly, 1928; Duchess, 1929; Cambridge, Phoenix, Whitehall, 1930; Saville, Westminster, 1931; Mermaid, 1959.

Thebes, Egypt, *fl.* 1600-1100 B.C. as capital of Upper Egypt. Partly burnt by Persians, 525 B.C., captured and sacked by Greeks, 86 B.C.

Thebes, Greece, capital of Boeotia, arose about 1100 B.C., perhaps earlier. For a short time after 371 B.C. T. became the strongest city in Greece, but lost her supremacy after 362. Razed to the ground by Macedonians under Alexander, 335, restored 316. Captured by Demetrius Poliorcetes, 290 B.C. Repatriated Greeks from Asia settled in T., 1922.

Theosophists, a sect founded by Helena Petrovna Blavatsky (1831-91), whose principal disciple was Mrs. Annie Besant (1847-1933). The Theosophical Society was founded in America, 1875. On the death of Helena Blavatsky a faction split off under William P. Judge, but the main body remained under the leadership of H. S. Olcott, its president, who was succeeded in 1907 by Annie Besant.

Thermometer. Invention of attributed to Galileo (1564-1642). General change from Fahrenheit to Centigrade in Britain begun, 1961-2.

'Thetis' Disaster. British submarine *Thetis* failed to resurface, 1 June 1939. Ninety-nine men died, and there were four survivors. Submarine was eventually beached, 3 Oct. 1939, recommissioned, and renamed the *Thunderbolt*; lost during World War II off Sicily, 13 Mar. 1943, with all hands.

Thirty-nine Articles of Religion. (*See* ARTICLES OF RELIGION (ANGLICAN)). Were agreed by the Convocation held in London, 1562, and subsequently reduced to thirty-nine and confirmed, 1571 and 1604.

Thirty Years War, 1618-48. Waged between the Protestants and Catholic Imperialists of Germany; Frederick,

Elector Palatine, the prince to whom the Bohemian Estates had offered the imperial succession which was the immediate *casus belli*, defeated at the White Mountain (*Bela Hora*), 8 Nov. 1620. English intervention against Spanish Netherlands, 1625. Protestant effort mainly directed by Denmark, 1625–30, thereafter by Gustavus Adolfus of Sweden until his death in action at Lützen, 16 Nov. 1632. Wallenstein, recalled to command imperialist forces, 1632, murdered, 1634. From 1632 French intervention became the dominant factor, and the native Protestant leadership, such as it was, devolved on Bernard of Saxe-Weimar (*d.* 18 July 1639). *See* WESTPHALIA, PEACE OF.

Thomas's, St., Hospital. Founded in 1213 as an alms-house; enlarged by the Mayor of London in 1551; rebuilt, 1693; and again in 1868.

Three Choirs Festival held annually at cathedrals of Gloucester, Worcester, and Hereford in rotation since 1724.

Thugs. Indian fanatics, a caste of professional thieves who strangled victims in honour of the goddess Bhowani (Mother Kali). Suppressed by British, 1830.

Thule. *See* FAIR ISLE.

Tibet. First king Lhato Nyan-tsen. Fourth Nam-ri Song-tsen, *d.* A.D. 630, and was succeeded by Song-tsen Gampo, who founded the secular monarchy of T. Nepalese rebellion, 703. Zenith of Tibetan power under Tisong Detsen, 743–89. War with China, 810–21. End of the dynasty of religious kings at assassination of Ral-pa-Chen, 838. Kingdom divided, 841 onwards. Dharmapala arrives from India, 1013. Atisha also, 1026. Rule of the abbots of Sakya under Mongol protection, 1270–1340. Pak-modu founds dynasty *c.* 1350. Tsong Ka-pa founds Yellow Hat Order *c.* 1370–1380. System of priestly incarnation established, 1474. Fifth Dalai Lama established as ruler of T., 1641. Chinese resident established at Lhasa *c.* 1710. War with Gurkhas, 1788–92. Chinese resident insists on closure of T. to foreigners, 1792. Dogra invasion repelled, 1841. Gurkha invasion and treaty of friendship, 1855. British attempt to open relations, 1872. Younghusband mission, after fighting, reaches Lhasa, 1906. Chinese occupation, 1910. Chinese expelled, 1911. T. requests British embassy, 1920. Telegraph established to Lhasa, 1922. New Dalai Lama enthroned, 1940; assumed full powers, 1950. Treaty of Peking signed by Panchen Lama, 23 May 1951. This gave the Tibetans the right of national regional autonomy within China. Dalai Lama and Panchen Lama visited Peking, 1954, and India, 1956. Tibetan revolt against China, Mar. 1959; T. declared herself independent. Chinese troops rapidly crushed the revolt and on 31 Mar. the Dalai Lama reached India, where he was granted political asylum.

Tichborne Case. Sir J. F. Doughty T., *d.* 1862. In 1872 a claimant to the estate, representing himself to be Sir Roger T., son of Sir Doughty, involved the T. family in litigation which cost them £70,000. In 1874 he was finally exposed as a butcher named Thomas Castro, and sentenced to fourteen years' penal servitude for perjury.

Ticino (Ger. Tessin). After the break-up of the Roman Empire the canton was part of the temporal domains of the Bishop of Como and the Chapter of Milan, taken over between 1100 and 1400 piecemeal by the secular communes of Milan and Como. The conquest of T. by the twelve ' old ' cantons of Switzerland was gradual, and complete by 1512. In 1798 the Helvetic Confederation set up cantons of Lugano and Bellinzona, which fused, 1803. to form the canton of T.

Tides. Theory of T. first made clear by Kepler, 1598, but had been studied by Posidonius of Apamea, 79 B.C.; completely explained by Sir Isaac Newton, 1683.

Tierra del Fuego, S. America, discovered by Magellan, 1520.

Tiflis, Tbilisi, capital of Georgia, founded in the fourth century A.D., and conquered by the Arabs in 645. Residence of the Christian kings of Armenia, 1121–6. From the sixteenth century until its seizure by Russia in 1801 it was disputed between Turkey and Persia. Became capital of the Georgian Republic (*q.v.*), 1922.

Tilbury Docks were opened, 1886, and extended between 1917 and 1929.

Tilsit (U.S.S.R.) is noted for the peace treaty between the emperors, Alexander and Napoleon, 1807. It was founded by the Teutonic Knights in 1288 and was renamed **Sovetsk** in 1946.

Time Measurement. *See* STANDARD TIME.

'Times, The,' Newspaper. First issued as *The Times*, 1788, but had been published as the *Daily Universal Register* since 1785. Founded by John Walter (1739–1812). Controlling interest bought by Lord Northcliffe, July 1907. On the death of Northcliffe, 1922, the paper was bought by John Walter the fourth and Maj. J. J. Astor.

Timor was divided between the Dutch

and Portuguese colonial empires, 1859, by a boundary rearranged by arbitration, 1914. Both parts of the island were occupied and used by the Japanese as an air base, 1942–5. Dutch T. became part of Indonesia (q.v.), 1950.

Tin. One of the earliest known metals, having been imported from England by the Phoenicians more than 1,000 years B.C.

Tirol (also **Tyrol**, but not locally). Trent becomes fief of Bishops of Trent, 1004. Bolzano (Bozen) and Vintschgau (Val Venosta) added, the rest of the area being given to the Bishops of Brixen, 1027. Bishops delegate authority to the Lords of T. Castle (near Merano) from which T. takes its name, c. 1100. They become counts in Trent, 1150. Acquire lands in Brixen, 1248. Finally displace the episcopal authorities, 1271. Family became extinct and T. passed to Austria, 1363. Held as an apanage of a junior line of the Hapsburgs till 1665. Ceded to Bavaria by Peace of Pressburg, 1805 Andreas Hofer's rising against French and Bavarians, 1809–10. Restored to Austria by Treaty of Paris, 1814. S. T. annexed to Italy, 1919. Fascist policy of ' Italianization ' begun, 1923. Deportation of German-spreading Tirolese agreed between Germany and Italy, 1939. Agreement between Italy and Austria on local autonomy of S. T., 6 Sept. 1946, and this incorporated into the Italian Peace Treaty of 1957. Some unrest among German elements in Italian T. from 1955 onwards, and allegations of 'Italianization.'

'Titanic.' White Star liner lost after striking iceberg near Cape Race, 14 Apr. 1912, with the loss of some 1,500 lives.

Tithes were commonly paid to monasteries up to 1215, but thereafter only to parish priests. The T. Act of 1936 was designed to replace T. by the payment of T. Redemption annuities which will cease to be payable, 1996.

Tobacco. First observed in Cuba, 1492; brought to England in 1565 or 1586 by Sir John Hawkins or Sir Walter Raleigh; cultivation in England was prohibited, 1684, and allowed in Ireland, 1779; Pure Tobacco Act, 1842; permission to cultivate T. in England under certain conditions was granted, 1886. Royal College of Physicians' Report, 'Smoking and Health,' suggested a causal relationship between cigarette-smoking and lung cancer, Mar. 1962.

Toc H (for **Talbot House**) took its name from a military chapel and soldiers' club opened at Poperinghe, Flanders, Dec. 1915. The T. H. group was formed in London, 1920, and its women's auxiliary,

the League of Women Helpers, 1922, in which year T. H. was incorporated by royal charter.

Togoland became a German protectorate, 1884. Became a League of Nations mandated territory, under British and French administration, 1920. British T. united with Ghana (q.v.) when the latter achieved independence in 1957. French T. became the independent republic of **Togo** on 27 Apr. 1960. The pro-Western President, Olympio, was assassinated on 13 Jan. 1963 and a provisional military government established.

Tokyo. Capital of Japan (q.v.) since 1868. Formerly called Yedo; castle, built fifteenth century, grew, and was capital, 1603–1868. Practically destroyed by earthquake in Sept. 1923, when Yokohama was completely demolished. Heavily bombed by the Americans, 1945, and since reconstructed on American 'skyscraper' lines. *See also* EARTHQUAKES.

Toleration, Act of, 24 May 1689, for the relief of Dissenters. Roman Catholics included, 13 Apr. 1829. *See* NONCONFORMISTS.

Tolls. The first T. in England were collected in London, 1267; toll gates were instituted, 1663; from 1827 to 1893 toll gates were gradually abolished, and now very few remain in this country. T. have, however, been applied to help finance certain new roadworks (e.g. bridges) since 1955. In the U.S.A. T. are levied to pay for several of the twentieth-century motorways.

Tolpuddle Martyrs. Six labourers living at the village of T., Dorset, convicted at Dorchester of 'administering unlawful oaths' (i.e. trade union activity), 19 Mar. 1834, and sentenced to seven years' transportation. Following nation-wide agitation, they were pardoned two years later.

Tomatoes were introduced into England, 1596, though not extensively consumed here before 1900.

Tonga or **Friendly Islands** were first explored by the Dutch under Cornelius Schouten and Jacob le Maire, 1616, then by Tasman, 1643. The first Englishman to land was Wallis (1767). Cook landed several times, 1773–7. In 1831 Tupou, the King of T., was baptized and took the name of George, his consort that of Salote (i.e. Charlotte). By 1845 he had extended his rule over the whole group; he d. 1893, aged 96. His successor, George Tupou II, signed a treaty of friendship and protection with Britain, 1900, by which only foreign affairs are conducted by a British agent, and in all other respects T. retains complete sovereignty. The reigning queen, Salote, daughter of George Tupou II, came to the throne on his death, 1918. A new treaty of friendship between T. and Britain, signed, 1958, and ratified, 1959, increased T.'s local autonomy.

Tonnage and Poundage first levied, 1371, and abolished, 1787.

Tontines. Instituted by Tonti, a Neapolitan; first used in Paris, 1653. A tontine was a fund to which a group subscribed and out of which each member received an annuity, increasing as the group diminished through deaths, until the last survivor was left with the whole fund. The last English public tontine was in 1789.

Torgau, League of. Between the Elector of Saxony and the Landgrave of Hesse to uphold the opinions of Martin Luther, concluded at Gotha, Feb. 1526.

Toronto, site chosen as seat of government for Upper Canada, 1793. Occupied by U.S. forces, 1813, and legislative buildings burned. The mace carried away on that occasion was returned by Franklin D. Roosevelt, 1934. The city, first named York, was granted municipal government, 1817, and the present name adopted, 1834.

Torpedoes. The word originally signified *mines*, and was so used till c. 1868. First T. devised by Whitehead, 1870.

Torres Vedras was captured by the Portuguese from the Moors, 1149, and was the seat of the Cortes in 1441. Wellington built a strong defensive position here, covering Lisbon, into which he retired at the end of the campaign of 1810. The French under Masséna closed up on the lines of T. V., but were unable to storm them, and having eaten the country bare were compelled to break contact in Mar. 1811.

Tory (Irish = a *persecutor, robber,* or *outlaw*). Nickname for any supporter of the Duke of York, 1679. From 1689 any opponent of the Whigs or Hanoverian party. Since about 1833 a Conservative.

Totalisator. First T. machine was set up at Christchurch, New Zealand, 1880, based on the *pari mutuel* system which was invented in France, 1872. The first machine in Europe operated at Longchamps, 1929, in Britain in the same year. In Maryland, U.S.A., T. machines were first used, 1930.

Toulon (anct. **Telo Martius**), France, docks and arsenal were begun by Vauban (1633–1707). The town was yielded to the British, Aug. 1793, who destroyed the military and naval installations before the Republicans retook them in Dec. Fire and explosion of battleship *Liberté* destroyed 200 ships in T. harbour, 1911.

French fleet scuttled in the harbour, 27 Nov. 1942, before German occupation of the port. Retaken by French troops, Aug. 1944.

Toulouse, in Roman times **Tolosa,** chief city of Gallia Narbonnensis, was colonized by the Romans in 106 B.C., became capital of a Visigothic kingdom, A.D. 419, and was captured by the Franks, 506. Became capital of Aquitaine, 630, then of a virtually independent county, one of whose rulers, Raymond IV (count from 1088 to 1105), was a principal commander in the First Crusade (*q.v.*), and refused the crown of Jerusalem. In 1271 the royal house of France inherited the county and its independence ceased.

Touraine, ancient province of France, roughly approximating to the department of Indre-et-Loire; became an independent county, 941, subject, 1040, to the counts of Anjou, and hence, 1154, to the English crown. From 1205 did homage to the French crown; won back by Joan of Arc; finally incorporated in France as a *gouvernement.* 1541.

Tours, ancient capital of Touraine (*q.v.*), was an episcopal see in the fourth century. It was captured by the Visigoths, 473, by the Franks in 507. Charles Martel defeated the Saracens near T., 732. Destroyed by Vikings, 853 and 903. From c. 1400 to 1685 centre of the silk industry in France. Seat of French Government, 13 Sept.–10 Dec. 1870, and June 1940.

Tower Bridge, built 1886–94. Proposal to demolish it in improvement scheme caused protests, 1961.

Tower of London. Begun in 1078 by William I; completed by William Rufus, 1098; additions made, 1680–5; a portion destroyed by fire, 1841, and by bombing in World War II.

Town and Country Planning. An Act of 1943 provided for the appointment of a minister to perform plannings, functions formerly devolving on the Minister of Health and the Minister of Works (*see* MINISTRY OF WORKS). The duties of the ministry were to concern the implementation of such Acts as the Town and Country Planning Acts, 1932, 1943, 1944, and 1947, and the New Towns Act, 1946. The Development Charges payable under the 1947 Act were abolished, 18 Nov. 1952, and since 1951 the Ministry of Housing and Local Government has taken over the housing and local government functions of the Ministry of Health and those formerly performed by the Ministry of T. and C. P.

Toynbee Hall opened, 1885. Named after Arnold T., 1852–93.

Trabzon. *See* TREBIZOND.

Tractarianism. Arose from *Tracts for the Times*, dealing with Church matters; published, 1833–41. All the tracts were condemned at Oxford, 1841.

Trade, Board of. *See* BOARD OF TRADE.

Trade Boards for settlement of wage disputes were authorized by the T. B. Acts of 1909 and 1918. Since 1945 their functions have been performed by Wages Councils.

Trade Marks in the U.K. are regulated principally by the T. M. Acts of 1905, 1910, 1937, and 1938, and the Merchandise Marks Act, 1926.

Trades Union Congress (T.U.C.) originated, 1868. A conference organized by the T.U.C., 1900, gave rise to the formation of the Parliamentary Labour Party (*q.v.*). The General Council of the T.U.C. formed, 1920. Withdrew from World Federation of Trade Unions, 1949. Annual Conference agreed to consider reforms of T.U.C.'s structure, etc., Sept. 1962.

Trades Unions. Instituted, 1825, to withstand the influence of capital and competition. A commission of inquiry into the working of T. U. was held, 1867; an Act to protect the funds of T. U. was passed, 1869. To counteract T. U. a Federation of Employers was founded, 1873. First agricultural T. U. founded by Joseph Arch (1826–1919), 1874. T. U. instituted in France, 1834, and U.S.A., before 1833. In the U.S.A. the American Federation of Labour and the Congress of Industrial Organizations merged, 1955. Allowed to spend funds on parliamentary representation by T. U. Act, 1913. Act passed making illegal non-industrial strikes and lockouts, and the demanding of political contributions from the members that had not volunteered to make such, 29 July 1927. This Act was repealed, 1945.

Trafalgar Square. Construction was begun, 1829, completed, 1867. Board of Trade Linear Standards in bronze placed on the N. side, 1876. Torsos of Admirals Jellicoe and Beatty erected, and N. side replanned, 1950.

Training Colleges. Established in Britain from 1840 onwards. Reorganized under Education Acts of 1902 and 1944. Two-year course extended to three years from 1960.

Training Corps, Officers'. Founded, 1908. Merged in Army Cadet Force, 1940.

Trams. First street T. operated in New York, 1832; in Paris, 1853; in London, 1861. Electric T. inaugurated in Leeds, 1891. Last T. in London ran on 6 July 1952.

Transjordan. *See* JORDAN.

Transport, Ministry of. Established, Sept. 1919, to exercise the powers and duties of various existing government departments (including those of the Road Board) relating to public aspects of transport.

Transportation was first used as a punitive measure in England *temp.* Charles II (1660–85), seven years' T. being regarded as a suitable alternative to the death sentence. It was legalized under an Act of 1719. The first shipment of convicts to Botany Bay was in 1783, the last in 1840. Convicts continued to arrive in Tasmania until 1853. The practice finally ceased in 1864. The French Government sent no new shipments of convicts to Guiana after 1927. T. nominally survives as a legacy of British rule in the Pakistan (*q.v.*) criminal code, and a sentence of T. was actually pronounced in a treason case at Karachi in 1952. T. to Siberia existed in Czarist Russia; since 1917 it has continued to be practised by the various Communist regimes.

Trans-Siberian Railway. Single track begun, 1891; completed, 1904. Railway finally finished, 1915.

Transvaal. Founded by Boers, 1836–1848; Britain recognized the independence of the territory, 1852; Volksraad elected M. W. Pretorius first president of the territory named the S. African Republic, 1857; under British protection, 1877; declared crown colony, 1879; Boers revolt and established republic, 1880; battle of Majuba Hill, 27 Feb. 1881; Orange Free State proclaimed neutrality, Feb. 1881; peace, 24 Mar. 1881; Paul Kruger president, 1883; Jameson Raid, 1 Jan. 1896; ultimatum from Boers, 9 Oct. 1899; war declared, 11 Oct. 1899; annexation of T., 25 Oct. 1900; Sir A. Milner appointed High Commissioner, 4 Mar. 1901; new constitution on representative lines, Dec. 1906; Botha Premier, 1907; became province of Union of S. Africa, 31 May 1910. *See* SOUTH AFRICAN WAR and SOUTH AFRICA, REPUBLIC OF.

Transylvania. Ceded to Rumania by Hungary, Dec. 1918. Returned to Hungary by Hitler's 'Vienna Award,' 30 Aug. 1940. Occupied by Russians, Aug. 1944. Returned to Rumania, 10 Mar. 1945, and this decision confirmed in the peace treaties between the Allies and Hungary and Rumania, 1947.

Trappists, a branch of the Cistercian order, founded, 1664, by Armand Bouthillier de Rancé (1626–1700), at the abbey of La Trappe in Normandy.

Treadmill. First used as an instrument for irrigation by the Chinese. Introduction into English prisons by Sir William Cubitt, and first used in Buxton prison, 1817; now abolished.

Treason. Defined by Statute of Treasons, 1351. Other enactments relating to T., 1495, 1543, 1555, 1695, 1702, 1708, 1790, 1795, 1800, 1814, 1817; T. felony defined by Act of 1848. Treachery by Act of 1940.

Treasury. A Board of Commissioners, appointed for the first time in 1612, instead of a Lord High Treasurer as hitherto. Lords Commissioners of the T. have functioned continuously since 1714. The practice of combining the office of Prime Minister and First Lord of the T. arose, 1721. Reorganization of T. completed by end of 1962.

Treasury Bills first introduced, 1877.

Treaties. The following is a list of major historical treaties:

Abo, 1743. Aberdaron, 1406. Aix-la-Chapelle, 1668–1748. Algeciras, 1906. Altmark, 1629. Alton, 1101. Altranstädt, 1706. Amiens, 1527, 1802. Amsterdam, 1717. Anagri, 1176. Antananarivo, 1895. Aquisgran, 1749. Aranjuez, 1752. Ardres, 1546. Arras, 1482. Athis, 1305. Augsburg, 1686.

Badajoz, 1801. Baden, 1714. Bagdad, 1955. Bagnolo, 1484. Barcelona, 1493, 1529. Bärwalde, 1631. Basel, 1499. Belgrade, 1739. Berlin, 1728, 1850, 1878. Berwick, 1560. Björkö, 1905. Blois, 1504, 1505. Bologna, 1515. Boulogne, 1550. Breda, 1667. Brest, 1435. Bretigny, 1360. Bretton Woods, 1944. Brigham, 1290. Brömsebro, 1645. Bruges, 1521. Brussels, 1516, 1522, 1948. Bucharest, 1886. Buczacz, 1672.

Caen, 1091. Calais, 1416, 1520. Cambrai, 1529. Campo Formio, 1797. Câteau Cambrésis, 1559. Charlottenburg, 1723. Cherasco, 1631. Clayton-Bulwer, 1850. Cognac, 1526. Compiègne, 1624. Constantinople, 1479, 1573, 1724, 1889, 1897. Corbeil, 1258.

Delft, 1428. Dordrecht, 1489. Dunkirk, 1947. Durham, 1136. Düsseldorf, 1624.

Edinburgh, 1560. Eisenburg, 1664. Escorial, 1733.

Ferrara, 1428. Fontainebleau, 1785. Fredericksborg, 1720. Frederickshamn, 1809. Fürstenberg, 1373.

Gandamak, 1879. Gastein, 1865. Gerstungen, 1074. Gisors, 1180. Grosswardein, 1538. Guérande, 1365. Guillon, 1360.

Hagenau, 1330. Hague, 1625, 1716, 1790. Hampton Court, 1562. Herrenhausen, 1725. Hubertusburg, 1763.

Jassy, 1792. Kalisz, 1343. Kardis, 1661. Kaschau, 1374. Khaeroed, 1613. Kuchuk Kainardji, 1774. Labian, 1656. Lambeth, 1217. Lateran, 1929. Lauf, 1453. Lodi, 1454. London, 1518, 1839, 1954. Lorris, 1243. Lübeck, 1629. Lunéville, 1801. Lyons, 1504, 1601.

Madrid, 1618, 1630, 1715. Manila, 1954 (South-East Asia Collective Defence Treaty). Meaux, 1229. Mechlin, 1513. Melfi, 1059. Mersen, 870. Montebello, 1175. Moscow (nuclear Test Ban Treaty), 1963. Mürzsteg, 1903.

Nanking, 1842. Nettuno, 1925. Newcastle, 1334. Nicolsburg, 1866. Nijmegen, 1678–9. Northampton, 1328. Noyon, 1516. Nystad, 1721. Oléron, 1287. Oliva, 1660. Olmütz, 1850. Ouchy, 1912.

Paris, 1259, 1303, 1320, 1657, 1763, 1898, 1947, 1954, 1963 (' Franco-German reconciliation '). Passarowitz, 1718. Passau, 1552. Peking, 1860, 1901. Perth, 1266. Picquigny, 1475. Prague, 1635. Pressburg, 1490, 1626, 1805. Pretoria, 1881. Pyrenees, 1659.

Rastatt, 1714. Redon, 1489. Reichenbach, 1790. Reval, 1488. Riga, 1920, 1921. Rome, 1957. Roskilde, 1658. Roxburgh, 1332. Ryswick, 1697.

St. Claire, 911. St. Germain, 1331, 1570, 1679. St. Omer, 1469. St. Petersburg, 1805. Salbai, 1782. Salisbury, 1289. San Germano, 1230. San Ildefonso, 1796. San Stefano, 1878. Saragossa, 1529. Schönbrunn, 1805. Senlis, 1493. Seville, 1729. Shimonoseki, 1895. Shrewsbury, 1267. Sistova, 1791. Stettin, 1570. Stockholm, 1720, 1724, 1959 (European Free Trade Association Convention). Stolbova, 1617. Sutri, 1111.

Tangier, 1844. Tarascon, 1291. Teschen, 1779. Thorn, 1466. Tientsin, 1858. Tilsit, 1807. Toledo, 1480, 1539. Tordesilhas, 1494. Trent, 1501. Troyes, 1420, 1562. Tyrnau, 1615.

Uccialli, 1889. Utrecht, 1474, 1712–13. Valençay, 1813. Vancelles, 1556. Venice, 1177. Verdun, 843. Vereeniging, 1902. Versailles, 1756, 1783, 1919–1920. Vervins, 1598. Vienna, 1731, 1738, 1814–15, 1864, 1955. Villafranca, 1859. Vincennes, 1330. Vossem, 1673.

Waitangi, 1840. Wallingford, 1153. Warsaw, 1955 (Eastern Security Treaty). Washington 1846, 1949 (North Atlantic Treaty). Wedmore, 878. Westminster, 1654, 1716, 1756. Westphalia (2), 1648. Windsor, 1899. Worms, 1743. Wusterhausen, 1726.

Xanten, 1614.

Zsitva-Torok, 1606. Zurawna, 1676. Zürich, 1859.

Trebizond, or **Trabzon**, the Greek city of **Trapezos**, originated, 600 B.C., in a colony from Sinope. Mentioned in connection with the retreat of the Ten Thousand (*q.v.*). At the time of the Fifth Crusade, when Constantinople was stormed by the Latins, the Byzantine refugee, Alexius Comnenus, founded an empire at T., which endured until the capture of the city by the Turks, 1462. Scene of the Armenian massacres, 1895.

Trelleborg, a unique archaeological site of the Viking Age (*q.v.*) in W. Zealand, Denmark. A large barracks or permanent camp occupied between 950 and 1050, presumably by the followers of Kings Svein Forkbeard and Knut (*see under* DENMARK), was excavated, 1932–42.

Trengganu, state of the Federation of Malaya, formerly unfederated, was a Mohammedan kingdom *c.* 1300. Did homage to the kingdom of Siam from 1776 to 1909. Entered into treaty relations with Britain, 1910, whereby a consular agent was appointed, who was replaced by an adviser, 1919.

Trent (in Alto Adige). The first Council of T. sat from 1545 to 1563; its decisions laid down the main lines of Roman Catholic development in post-Reformation times, and were confirmed by Pope Pius IV in 1564.

Trentino, another name for the region of Venetia Tridentina (*q.v.*).

Trials and Causes Célèbres:

Sir Thomas More, 1 July 1535; beheaded, 6 July.

Mary Queen of Scots: 14 Oct. 1586; executed, 8 Feb. 1587.

Sir Walter Raleigh: treason, 17 Nov. 1603; executed, 29 Oct. 1618.

Guy Fawkes and others: 27 July 1605; Guy Fawkes executed, 31 Jan. 1606.

Charles I: 20–25 Jan.; executed, 30 Jan. 1649.

Dame Alice Lisle: treason, before Jeffreys; beheaded, 2 Sept. 1685.

Lords Kilmarnock and Balmerino: treason, 28 July 1746.

Lord Lovat: treason; executed, 9 Mar. 1747.

Mary Blandy: murdered father by arsenic, 3 Mar. 1752.

Elizabeth Canning: perjury, 29 Apr. 1784; transported.

Eugene Aram: murder, 3 Aug.; hanged, 6 Aug. 1759.

Earl Ferrers: murder of his steward; executed, 16 Apr. 1760.

John Wilkes: for obscene poem *Essay on Woman*, 21 Feb. 1764 and 18 June 1768.

Elizabeth Brownrigg: murder of her apprentice; hanged, 12 Sept. 1767.

Duchess of Kingston: for marrying two husbands, 15 Apr. 1776.

Lord George Gordon: treason; acquitted, 5 Feb. 1781.

Warren Hastings: high crimes and misdemeanours, 13 Feb. 1788; acquitted, 23 Apr. 1795.

Thomas Paine: libel in *The Rights of Man*; guilty, 18 Dec. 1792.

Louis XVI in French Convention: 19 Jan.; beheaded, 21 Jan. 1793.

Marie Antoinette: 14 Oct.; executed, 16 Oct. 1793.

Wolfe Tone: 10 Nov.; committed suicide, 19 Nov. 1798.

Queen Caroline: for adultery, 16 Aug.– 10 Nov. 1820.

Thurtell and Hunt: murder, 5 Jan.; Thurtell executed, 9 Jan. 1824.

Burke and Hare: body-snatchers, 24 Dec. 1828; Burke executed, 28 Jan. 1829.

William Palmer: poisoner, 14–27 May 1856.

Rev. S. Smith: murderous assault on John Leech, 6–7 Apr. 1858.

Jessie McLachlan: murder, 17–20 Sept.; respited, 27 Oct. 1862.

Dr. Pritchard: murder of wife and mother by poison; guilty, 2–7 July 1865.

Bank Forgery: Austin and George Bidwell, George Macdonnell, Edwin Noyes, Americans, forged bills for discounting at Bank of England and obtained £102,217; 18–26 Aug. 1873.

Tichborne Case: plaintiff claimed to be Sir Roger Tichborne, lost at sea, entitled to estates worth £24,000 a year. Trial began 11 May 1871, claimant nonsuited, 6 Mar. 1872. Trial of claimant for perjury began, 23 Apr. 1872; claimant sentenced, 28 Feb. 1874.

Penge Case: Louis Staunton, his brother Patrick, Elizabeth Ann, his wife, and her sister, Alice Rhodes, mistress of Louis, for murder by starvation of Louis's wife; 19–26 Sept. all convicted; respited, 13 Oct.; Alice Rhodes pardoned; others, penal servitude for life, 30 Oct. 1877.

Whistler *v.* Ruskin: for libellous criticism in *Fors Clavigera*; one farthing damages, 25–26 Nov. 1878.

City of Glasgow Bank Directors: for fraud; all convicted, 20 Jan.–1 Feb. 1879.

Charles Peace: murder; guilty, 4 Feb. 1879.

Wimbledon Murder: Dr. G. H. Lamson, guilty, 8–14 Mar. 1882.

Adelaide Bartlett: murder of husband; acquitted, 12–17 Apr. 1886.

Florence Maybrick: murder of husband by arsenic; convicted, 21 July–7 Aug.; commuted to life imprisonment, 22 Aug. 1889.

Tranby Croft Case: Sir W. Gordon-Cumming *v.* Mr. and Mrs. Lycett Green and others. Gordon-Cumming charged them with cheating at baccarat at Tranby Croft, near Hull. Prince of Wales (Edward VII) gave evidence; verdict for defendants, 1–9 June 1891.

Dreyfus Case: Alfred Dreyfus, French soldier, for treason. Convicted, degraded, and sent to Devil's Island, 1894. Case reopened, 1898; again convicted, but sentence reduced and free pardon given almost at once. Proceedings against D. quashed, 1906.

Wilde Case: Oscar Wilde (1854–1900) v, Marquess of Queensberry, for libel, 1895; following the failure of this, he was convicted of immoral behaviour and sentenced to two years' imprisonment.

Southwark Poisoning Case: George Chapman Taylor (Severino Klosowski) for murder of Isabella Spink and Elizabeth Taylor; guilty, 19 Mar. 1903.

Moat Farm Murder: Samuel Herbert Dougal, murder of Camille Holland; guilty, 23 June 1903.

Oscar Slater: murder of Miss Gilchrist, 3–6 May; found guilty, commuted to life sentence, 25 May 1909. Released 14 Nov. 1927; given government grant of £6,000. Conviction quashed, 20 July 1928.

H. H. Crippen: murder of wife; convicted, 18–22 Oct. 1910.

Brides in the Bath Case: George Joseph Smith, for murder of Misses Mundy, Burnham, and Lofty; guilty, 22–30 June 1915.

Sir Roger Casement: treason; convicted, 17 May; executed, 3 Aug. 1916.

Désiré Landru: for murder of ten women; convicted, 7–28 Nov. 1921; guillotined, 23 Feb. 1922.

Ronald True: murder; convicted 1–5 May. Sent to Broadmoor, 8 June 1922.

Edith Thompson and Frederick Bywaters: murder of Percy Thompson; guilty, 6 Dec. 1922; both hanged, 9 Jan. 1923.

Byfleet Murder: Jean Pierre Vaquier, murder; convicted, July 1924.

Nicola Sacco and Bartolomeo Vanzetti (U.S.A.): murder; first trial, 31 May–14 July 1921. Conviction affirmed, 12 May 1926. Sentence imposed, 9 Apr. 1927. Both executed, 23 Aug. 1927.

Fred Browne and William Kennedy: murder of P.C. Gutteridge, 23–28 Apr.; guilty, both hanged, 31 May 1928.

Clarence Hatry: fraud; 20–24 Jan. 1930; 14 years' penal servitude.

Blazing Car Murder: Arthur Alfred Rouse, murder of unknown man, 26–31 Jan. 1931. Guilty and hanged.

Kylsant Case: Lord Kylsant for issuing false prospectus of Royal Mail Steam Packet Co.; one year's imprisonment, 21–30 July 1931.

Metropolitan-Vickers Trial in Moscow: Thornton, Cushny, Gregory, Monkhouse, and Macdonald; for espionage and sabotage in U.S.S.R. Thornton three years, Gregory acquitted, Macdonald two years. Monkhouse and Cushny expelled from Russia, Apr. 1933.

Lindbergh Baby Case: Bruno Hauptmann, for kidnapping and murder of child of Charles Lindbergh; guilty, 14 Feb. 1935.

Alma Victoria Rattenbury and George Percy Stoner: murder of Mr. Rattenbury, 27–31 May; Mrs. Rattenbury discharged; Stoner convicted. Mrs. Rattenbury committed suicide, 3 June. Stoner reprieved, 25 June 1935.

Dr. Buck Ruxton: murder of wife and maid; guilty, 2–13 Mar. 1936. Hanged.

Ex-Marshal Pétain: for treason; found guilty, 1945, and sentenced to death, subsequently commuted to life imprisonment.

'Lord Haw-Haw' (William Joyce): for treason by broadcasting, 17–19 Sept. 1945. Hanged, 3 Jan. 1946.

Nürnberg Trials: Nov. 1945–Oct. 1946; of German war criminals.

Japanese War Criminals' Trials: 1946–8. The seven Japanese war-leaders condemned to death were hanged 23 Dec. 1948.

John Reginald Halliday Christie: for murder of his wife, but murders of several other women on the file; guilty and hanged, 1953.

Adolf Eichmann: in Israel, for crimes against the Jewish people; 11 Apr–15 Dec. 1961; found guilty and hanged.

Gordon Lonsdale, a Soviet citizen: tried in London for espionage; found guilty and sentenced to twenty-five years' imprisonment. 1961.

Ex-General Jouhaud, O.A.S. leader: for treason, in Paris, Apr. 1962; found guilty and sentenced to death, but sentence later commuted to life imprisonment.

Ex-General Salan, O.A.S. leader: for treason, in Paris, May 1962; found guilty but due to 'extenuating circumstances' sentenced to life imprisonment.

Greville Wynne, a British business man, and Oleg Penkovsky, a Russian scientist and civil servant, in Moscow for espionage, 7 May 1963; Wynne found guilty and sentenced to eight years' imprisonment; Penkovsky found guilty and sentenced to death.

Stephen Ward, a London osteopath, on charges of procuring and of living on immoral earnings, in London. July 1963; Ward found guilty on two charges of living on immoral earnings. Verdict was reached in his absence, as he was in hospital after taking an overdose of drugs. He died on 3 Aug., and was never sentenced.

Triennial Parliaments were established by Act, 1641. The Long Parliament of 1640–63 broke this Act, and it was repealed, 1664. A similar Act of 1694 was repealed, 1716, when the limit was increased to seven years (which in turn was reduced to five by the Parliament Act, 1911).

Trieste, the Roman colony of **Tergeste,** was settled by the Romans in 178 B.C. and was an established port some time between A.D. 69 and 79. Submitted to the Hapsburg Duke Leopold III, 1382. Free port, founded 1719. Held by French, 1797–1805, and by the puppet kingdom of Illyria, 1809–13. Returned to Austria, and became an imperial city, 1849. Ceded to Italy, 1918 (*see* VENETIA GIULIA). In Apr. 1945 the German forces retreating from the Balkans passed through T.; their rearguard was driven out by two independent local guerrilla forces, Slovene and Italian, 30 Apr. On 1 May the town was entered simultaneously by the New Zealand Expeditionary Force from the W. and the Yugoslav Fourth Army from the E.; the latter occupied various towns as far W. as the Isonzo. British and American occupation continued after the signing of the peace treaty with Italy, 10 Feb. 1947, and in Sept. 1947 a Free State consisting of T. and its environs was set up. By 1948 it was clear that this arrangement was unworkable. On 5 Oct. 1954 the governments of Britain, the U.S.A., Italy, and Yugoslavia agreed that military government in both zones of T. should end; on 25 Oct. British and U.S. forces were withdrawn from their zone (T. city), which was handed over to Italy, less one small strip, which then passed, with the rest of the Yugoslav zone, under Yugoslav civil administration.

Trinidad was discovered and annexed to Spain by Columbus, 1498, but no settlement was made until the 1530s. Retained by the Spaniards, who by a new colonial policy, implemented in 1783, attracted large numbers of able foreigners to the cocoa industry, especially Frenchmen. The colony capitulated to Britain, 1797, and was formally ceded, 1802. U.S. leased defence bases there for ninety-nine years, 1941. Universal adult suffrage was adopted, 1946, and county councils set up in the same year. After

the dissolution of the Caribbean Federation (*q.v.*) the T. and Tobago constitutional conference opened in London, 29 May 1962. T. became an independent dominion of the Commonwealth on 31 Aug. 1962.

Trinity House. An institution for regulating pilots; founded in its present form by Sir Thomas Spert, who was the first master, 1512, and given its first charter, 1514. The maintenance of lighthouses and buoys is also one of the duties of the brethren of T. H.

Tripartite Pact. Extension of German-Italian Axis Pact to include Japan signed in Berlin, 27 Sept. 1940; mutual co-operation in ' New World Order.' Hungary signed, 20 Nov. 1940; Rumania and Slovakia signed, 23 Nov. 1940; Bulgaria signed, 1 Mar. 1941; Yugoslavia signed, 25 Mar. 1941.

Triple Alliance, 1668. Was ratified for the protection of the Spanish Netherlands, the contracting parties being the States-General and England (Sweden joined later) against France. Other T. As. have been: 1717, England, France, and Holland against Spain; 1795, England, Russia, and Austria; 1882, Germany, Austria, and Italy. The last came to an end, as regards Italy, in May 1915. The Germano-Austro-Hungarian Alliance was dissolved in 1918 at the end of World War I.

Tripolitania. *See* LIBYA.

Tristan da Cunha. Discovered by Portuguese, 1506. Taken over by a British garrison, 1816, during Napoleon's residence at St. Helena. When the garrison was withdrawn, 1817, Corporal William Glass and his wife elected to remain; they were joined by two ex-naval men and some shipwrecked sailors, and formed the nucleus of the T. colony. In 1904 the British Government offered to settle their descendants in Cape Colony but only three families elected to go. Attached, 1938, to St. Helena Dependencies. An administrator appointed, 1948. Crawfishing company began operations there, 1949. In Oct. 1961 the volcano on the island erupted, destroying most of the settlement. All the inhabitants were evacuated and attempts made to settle them in Britain. Subsequent visits to the island in 1962 confirmed that it was again habitable. In Dec. 1962 all but five of the adult members of the T. community voted to return; and the British Government agreed for this to be done in stages in 1963.

Trondhjem or **Trondheim.** The town of **Nidaros** (then sometimes called

Kaupangen) was founded, 996, on an existing market site by Olaf Tryggvason, who was elected king here. Kings of Norway began to be crowned here again from 1814. Name T. adoped during the Middle Ages. Seat of archbishopric of Norway from 1152, but importance waned after the Reformation. German U-boat base, 1940–4, and as a result heavily bombed by the British. Liberated, Apr. 1945.

Troubadours. Poets of Provence and Catalonia in eleventh to fourteenth centuries. *See* PROVENÇAL AND CATALAN WRITERS.

Troy. The earliest of the successive cities which *fl.* on the site at Hissarlik in Asia Minor can be dated about 3000–2560 B.C. The Homeric siege appears to have ended *c.* 1184 B.C. The site ceased to be inhabited at the end of the fifth century B.C. Excavations by Schliemann began, 1870, and lasted until 1890; Dörpfeld's from 1893 to 1894.

Truce of God (*Treuga Dei*). A device of the Church in the Middle Ages to check private warfare, by limiting the periods within which fighting would not be sacrilegious. Inaugurated at Tuluges in Roussillon by a synod, 1027. By 1041 the movement had spread all over France; soon afterwards it reached England, and, by the end of the eleventh century, only about 80 days in the year remained unaffected. Confirmed by Urban II in 1095 at the Council of Clermont. Extended to the whole Church by oecumenical council of 1179. Fell into disuse during the thirteenth century.

Truck Acts, requiring payment of wages to be made in current coin of the realm only, and not in goods, were passed in 1831, 1887, and 1896; they also forbid fines, except under special conditions. The Truck Act, 1940, forbids the provision of canteen meals in lieu of wages. One effect of the T. A. in modern society was to prevent manual workers being paid by cheque; after 31 Mar. 1963 payment by cheque in such cases is permitted, but subject to the recipient's specific agreement only.

Truro, Cornwall. Diocese re-established, 1876, and cathedral founded, 1880.

Trusteeship Council of United Nations (*q.v.*) was set up, 14 Dec. 1946. The Genera Assembly of U.N. demanded in Dec. 1949 the right to information concerning all non-self-governing territory from the administering power.

Trusts, commercial, first established by John D. Rockefeller (Standard Oil T.), 1882. Congress passed Sherman Anti-T. Act, 1890, and Supreme Court ordered dissolution of Standard Oil T., 1911.

Tuberculosis. The organism causing this disease isolated by Koch, 1882.

Tubular Bridges. The first T. bridge was built over the Menai Strait, 1846–60.

Tuileries Palace (Paris). Begun, 1564. Built by Catherine de' Medici, Henry IV, and Louis XIV. Stormed, 1792; and ransacked, 1830 and 1848. Destroyed by the Communards, 25 May 1871.

Tunis, N. Africa. Probably older than Carthage, and in 800–909 was a residence of the Agylabite dynasty. Repeatedly pillaged during tenth century. French occupation, 1881. Deep-water channel to harbour opened, 1893. Captured by Allies from Germans, 7 May 1943. Capital of independent Tunisia (*q.v.*) since 1956.

Tunisia corresponds in area with the Roman province of Africa, conquered by the Moslems in 698, and called by them Ifrikiya. Hussein ben Ali became Bey in 1705, acknowledging Turkish suzerainty, which was terminated by the Treaty of Bardo, 12 May 1881, and the Convention of La Marsa, 8 June 1883, which established the French protectorate. Important theatre of operations in World War II (*q.v.*). Nationalist agitation after the war resulted in France giving T. full internal self-government from Sept. 1955, and, by the protocol of 20 Mar. 1956, full independence. The monarchy was abolished, 1957, and Bourguiba became T.'s first president. The Algerian war caused differences between France and T., 1958–62, and in July 1961 there was heavy fighting in Bizerta (*q.v.*), where the French still maintained a naval base; this was ended by a cease-fire, 23 July, after casualties on both sides.

Tunnels. The first English tunnel for navigation was built on the Bridgwater Canal, near Manchester, in 1766. Channel tunnel begun, 1876; relinquished, 1882–3. St. Gotthard T., 1872–80. Mersey T. (rail) opened, 1886; Severn T., 1886; Simplon T., 1905; Hudson River T., 1908; Mersey T. (road), 1935. Renewed agitation for Channel T. after World War II, and indications by 1962 that government policy favoured one in principle.

Turbines. *See* SHIPS and AVIATION.

Turin. Capital of Italy, 1861–5. Besieged by the French, 1706; taken by French, 1798, but they were expelled by the Russians and Austrians in the following year; again surrendered to the French, 1800; restored to Sardinia, 1814.

Turkestan, Chinese. *See* SINKIANG.

Turkestan, Russian, was conquered by the Imperial Army, 1866–73. In 1920 the Emir of Bokhara and the Khan of Khiva were deposed and Soviet republics of Bokhara and Khiva set up. An autonomous Social Republic of Turkestan was constituted, 1921. These three states were reorganized in 1924, and their territory redistributed on an ethnical basis to form the republics of Turkmenistan, Uzbekistan, and Tadjikistan; the remaining areas of the old government of T. being attached to the Kazak, Kirgiz, and Kalpak republics.

Turkish Republic. (For previous history of the Turks *see* OTTOMAN EMPIRE.) Nationalist government set up under Mustafa Kemal Atatürk at Ankara, Oct. 1920. He refuses to accept the Treaty of Sèvres, Nov. 1920. Declares sovereign power to reside in National Assembly of the T. nation (*Kamutay*), Jan. 1921. Greek attempt to take over E. Anatolia resisted, June 1921. Greeks driven out, Sept. 1922. Mudania armistice, Oct. 1922. Sultan deposed, Oct. 1922. Sultanate abolished and Turkey becomes a republic, Oct. 1923. Moslem religion disestablished and caliphate (*q.v.*) abolished, 3 Mar. 1924. Treaty of Lausanne ratified with Allies, 1 Apr. 1924. Constitution passed, 21 Apr. 1924. Wearing of fez prohibited, 1925. Monogamy and civil marriage instituted, 1926. Atatürk re-elected president, 1 Nov. 1927. University of Constantinople transferred to Ankara, 1929. Latin alphabet supersedes Arabic, 1929–30. Joined League of Nations, 18 July 1932. Distinctive family names made obligatory, and titles abolished, 1934. Women given the vote. Refortifies Dardanelles, under League authority obtained 20 July 1936. Atatürk *d.*, 10 Nov. 1938, succeeded by Gen. Ismet Inönü, 11 Nov. 1938. Inönü re-elected president, 3 Apr. 1939. Mutual assistance pacts with Britain, 12 May; France, 23 June 1939. France cedes The Hatay, 23 July 1939. Declares war on Germany and Japan, 23 Feb. 1945. Genuine opposition parties allowed, 1945 onwards; growth of Democratic party under Menderes. T. joined N.A.T.O., 1952, and signed the Bagdad Pact (later CENTO) (*qq.v.*), 1955. In 1950 Inönü was defeated, and Celal Bayar became president. Menderes became premier and in the elections in 1954 his party virtually obliterated its opponents. Subsequently unrest grew among the military and professional sections of the public, due partly to the government's increasing political intolerance and partial attitude towards the Islamic religion, as well as because of economic difficulties. In May 1960 the Menderes regime was overthrown by an army revolt, led by Gen. Gursel. Menderes was tried for plotting against the state and executed, 1961. Parliamentary government was re-established during 1961 and various new groups adopted the policies previously held by the now-banned Democratic Party; but the army retained ultimate background control. There were unsuccessful revolts by army groups in 1962 and 1963.

Turksib (i.e. Turkestan–Siberian) **Railway,** from Novosibirsk to Tashkent, begun 1927, was connected to the Transib, 1929, and opened to traffic, 1930.

Turner's Legacies. Pictures which J. M. W. Turner, the landscape painter, bequeathed to the nation, 1851.

Tuscany, in area corresponding roughly to the ancient Etruria (*q.v.*), was in the Middle Ages a margravate of the Frankish Empire established about 800, but dissolving into a loose league of city republics of which by the thirteenth century Florence (*q.v.*) was the leader. The family of Medici, who usurped power in the Florentine republic, became dukes of T., 1532, and grand dukes, 1557. On the death of the last Medici, 1737, T. fell to the Duke of Lorraine who, as consort of the Empress Maria Theresa, bequeathed it to the Austrian crown, which retained it until 1800, when Napoleon set up the puppet kingdom of Etruria. From 1808 to 1814 T. formed part of the French Empire. The Hapsburg-Lorraine restoration lasted peaceably until 1848, after which date it was only maintained by Austrian troops, who were driven out, 1859. T. was incorporated in the kingdom of Italy, 1861.

Tussaud's, Madame. Established in London, 1833. Destroyed by fire, 18 Mar. 1925. Reopened, 1928. Damaged by bombing, 1940, but subsequently restored.

Tutankhamen's Tomb. Located near Luxor by Lord Carnarvon and Howard Carter, 1922, and opened Feb. 1923.

T.V.A. *See* TENNESSEE VALLEY AUTHORITY.

Twelve Tables, The, a code of laws collected and formulated by a decemvirate of the Roman Republic, 451–449 B.C.

Tyburn (London). Here criminals were executed *c.* 1196–1783. Many Catholics died here for their faith during the sixteenth and seventeenth centuries. The gallows were near Marble Arch.

Tyler's Insurrection, 1381. *See* PEASANTS' REVOLT.

Tynwald, parliament and supreme court of Isle of Man, meets on T. Hill, consisting originally of three estates, now effectively only of the House of Keys. A characteristically Scandinavian legislative body dating from Norse occupation (800–1266). *See* MAN, ISLE OF and VIKING AGE.

Typewriters invented by Scholes, Glidden, and Soulé, 1868. Theirs was the model which evolved into the modern Remington. It was first manufactured in commercial quantities, 1873. A patent had been granted to an Englishman called Mills, 1714, but nothing came of his invention. In 1843 Charles Thurber produced a practicable machine. The first typewriter to print both capital and small letters appeared, 1878.

Tyres, Pneumatic, were first fitted to horse-drawn vehicles by R. W. Thompson, 1845. Reinvented by J. B. Dunlop for bicycles, 1888. Pneumatic tyres for cars first made by Michelin, 1895, and for aeroplane undercarriages by Dunlop, 1910. Pneumatic tyres were first fitted to lorries, 1917, and to tractors, 1930.

ADDENDA

U

'U-2' Incident. On 5 May 1960 Khruschev told the Supreme Soviet that an American Lockheed U-2 aeroplane had been shot down over Soviet territory on 1 May and its pilot captured; on 7 May the U.S. Government admitted that the plane had been carrying out an intelligence mission. The incident was the excuse used by Khruschev to humiliate the U.S. President and break up the Summit Conference in Paris on 17 May. Subsequently the pilot, Gary Powers, was tried and convicted of espionage at a 'show' trial in Moscow; in 1962 he was released in exchange for a Russian spy held by the U.S.A.

U(ntersee)-Boot, see SUBMARINES, which were so called when used by the German Navy from 1914.

Uganda, E. Africa, assigned to Britain by Anglo-German Treaty, 1890. Civil war, 1891. Protectorate declared, 1894. Rebellion, 1897. Treaty with dominant Baganda tribe, 1900. Boundaries defined by protocol between Britain, Belgium, and Germany, 14 May 1910. Increasing internal self-government from 1920 onwards. Constitutional conference held in London, 1961. Full internal self-government attained by Mar. 1962; and on 10 Oct. 1962 U. became a self-governing dominion within the Commonwealth.

Ukraine. As the principality of Galicia-Volhynia, was independent c. 1300–20; part of Lithuania, 1321–1569; then Polish until 1772 (pro-Russian revolt under Hetman Khmielnitzky, 1648); until World War I U. was divided between Russia and Austria-Hungary. Encouraged by German Government U. declared itself independent, 20 Nov. 1917. Union of eastern and western U., Jan. 1919. Invasion by Bolsheviks, Feb. 1918. Fall of Kiev, Feb. 1918. Spoliation by German forces, 1917–18.

1918. Armistice with Soviet Russia, May; German general, Eichorn, assassinated, 30 July; Gen. Petliura and Vinnichenko drove out the government established by Germany and set up dictatorship at Kiev, Nov.–Dec.

1919. Second Soviet Government set up, Mar.; war with Poland, May; Denikin's troops upset Soviet Government, June; Soviet forces recaptured Kharkov and Kiev, Dec.

1920. Odessa taken by Soviet troops, and third Soviet Government set up, Feb.; Petliura and the Poles occupied parts of the country, May; retired before Soviet forces, June; by Treaty of Riga,

Poland and Russia recognized independence of U., 12 Oct.

1923. U. joins U.S.S.R., 6 July.

1938. On being granted self-government, the Ruthenian province of Czechoslovakia called itself ' Carpatho-U.,' Oct.

1939. Carpatho-U. annexed by Hungary, 14 Mar. The German-Soviet partition of Poland gave Polish (Western) U. to Russia, 28 Sept. Bessarabia ceded by Rumania, 1940, united to Soviet U. Carpatho-U. joined Soviet U., 1945. *See* U.S.S.R.; RUTHENIA; BESSARABIA.

Ukrainian or Little Russian Language became finally differentiated from Great Russian about the middle of the thirteenth century, although some old Russian MSS. as early as the eleventh century contain specifically U. dialectal elements. Its earliest surviving popular literature consists of seventeenth-century interludes to miracle plays. The use of U. as a vehicle of instruction in Russian schools was forbidden by an imperial ukase in 1863, and in 1876 it became a criminal offence to print or publish U. material in the tsar's dominions. The use of the written language again became legal in 1905. An official orthography was published by the U. Academy of Sciences, 1946.

Following are some better known U. authors:

Ivan Kotlyarevsky, 1769–1838, satirist.
Pantaleimon Kulish, 1819–97, novelist, poet, and translator.
Taras Shevchenko, 1814–69, poet.
Marko Vovchok, 1834–1907, novelist.
Leonid Hlibov, 1827–93, lyrical fabulist.
Oleksander Konysky, 1836–1900.
Mihailo Drahomaniv, 1841–95, philologist.
Ivan Franko, 1856–1916, poet.

Ulm, Germany. Peace signed, 1620. Cathedral built, 1377–1494. 550-ft. spire completed, 1894.

Ulster. Colonization of forfeited land, 1611. Rebellion, 1641. U. Convention against Home Rule, 17 June 1892. U. Convention League formed, Aug. 1892. Accepted under protest Government of Ireland Act, 1920, which set up two legislatures in Ireland. For later events see IRELAND, NORTHERN.

Ulster King of Arms. This office was joined to that of Norroy King of Arms in 1943.

Umbrella. Appears on Assyrian bas-reliefs, eighth century B.C. First habitual user in London was Jonas Hanway (d. 1786).

Uncle Sam, nickname for the U.S.

government, personified, first used in the *Troy Post* for 7 Sept. 1813.

U.N.E.S.C.O. (United Nations Educational, Scientific and Cultural Organization) set up, 16 Nov. 1945. Became operative, Nov. 1946.

Ungava, interior territory of Labrador, round U. Bay, joined to province of Quebec, 1912.

U.N.I.C.E.F. (United Nations Childrens' Emergency Fund), set up, 1946.

Uniformity, Act of, 15 Jan. 1549, ordered use of the Common Prayer Book. Confirmed, 1552. Repealed by Queen Mary, 1553. Restored by Queen Elizabeth, 1559. Formed basis of the stringent Act of Charles II, which came into force, 24 Aug. 1662.

Union, Act of, with Scotland, 1707.

Union, Act of, with Ireland, 1801.

Union Jack. British flag, made up of: English flag, red cross on white ground (St. George); Scottish flag, diagonal white cross on blue (St. Andrew), incorporated, Apr. 1606; Irish flag, diagonal red cross on white (St. Patrick), incorporated, Jan. 1801.

Union Jack Club. Opened by King Edward VII, 1907, for soldiers and sailors, as memorial to men killed in China and S. Africa.

Unit Trusts. First in Britain formed, 1931.

Unitarians. Sect founded by Socinus in Italy, 1546. English U. trace their descent from those mainly Presbyterian congregations whose ministers were ejected in 1662, many of whose chapels are now in Unitarian hands. The specifically Unitarian doctrines of these congregations became current *c.* 1700. International Unitarian Council, Geneva, 1905. General Assembly of Unitarian and Free Christian Churches formed, 1928.

United Arab Republic. State formed on 1 Feb. 1958 by the union of Egypt and Syria (*qq.v.*). The Yemen (*q.v.*) federated with the U. A. R. on 8 Mar. 1958. Union and election of Nasser (president of Egypt) as its president approved on 21 Feb. 1958 by plebiscites in Egypt and Syria. Britain resumed full diplomatic relations with U. A. R. (broken off Oct. 1956 at time of Suez crisis), 26 Jan. 1961. Syria seceded from the U. A. R. after anti-Egyptian revolt, 28 Sept. 1961; rejoined the U.N. as a separate member, 13 Oct. Yemen subsequently broke connection with U. A. R., but Egypt continued to be known as the U. A. R., although original federation forming it no longer existed. U. A. R. intervened in the Yemen in support of republican rebels, Sept. 1962, and sent supporting troops.

On 17 Apr. 1963 an agreement was signed in Cairo between the U. A. R., Iraq (*q.v.*) and Syria (*q.v.*), which created a new federal U. A. R. The new state was to have Cairo as its capital, and a unified military command; but anti-Nasser pressures in Iraq and Syria began threatening the union almost from its inception, and in Aug. 1963 it remained a largely theoretical concept.

United Free Church of Scotland, formed by union of the United Presbyterian Church and the Free Church of Scotland, 1900. Further united with the Church of Scotland (*q.v.*), 1929.

United Irishmen, formed, 1791, by Wolfe Tone (1763–98), organized risings in Northern Ireland, 1797 and 1798. Tone committed suicide when the latter rising failed.

United Kingdom, from 1801 to 1921, was styled 'United Kingdom of Great Britain and Ireland.'

United Nations Organization. Charter signed at San Francisco, 26 June 1945. Sufficiently ratified to begin existence, 24 Oct. 1945. First meeting of General Assembly: London, 10 Jan. 1946; New York, 23 Oct. 1946. Trygve Lie, first Secretary-General, resigned, 10 Nov. 1952. Dag Hammarskjöld elected Secretary-General, Jan. 1953. U.N.O. intervened in Korea, 1950; Suez, 1956; Congo, 1960; but powerless to influence developments in the Hungarian uprising, 1956. Hammarskjöld killed in an aeroplane crash, 1961. U Thant confirmed as permanent Secretary-General, Nov. 1962.

Secretaries-General of the U. N. :

Trygve Lie (Norway)	1946–1952
Dag Hammarskjöld (Sweden)	1953–1961
U Thant (Burma) (acting)	1961–1962
U Thant (Burma) (permanent)	1962–

United Presbyterian Church. Restoration, in 1712, of patronage in the Church of Scotland, led, in 1733, to formation of a Secession Church, which, in 1747, split over the scripturality of the burgess oath. The Burgher and Anti-Burgher Parties each split over the question of the province of civil magistrates into Auld Lichts and New Lichts. The Burgher Auld Lichts were organized, 1799; the Anti-Burgher Auld Lichts, 1806. The two New Licht churches were united, 1820; the two Auld Lichts in 1842 as the Original Seceders. Meanwhile, in 1761, the Establishment had lost, by another anti-patronage secession, a group called the Relief Church. Secession Church and Relief Church amalgamated as U. P. C., 1847. This, in 1900, was amalgamated with Free Church, the result being the United Free Church.

United Provinces (of Agra and Oudh). Designation adopted, 1902. Made a Governorship, 1921. Autonomous system of government granted, 1937. Now Uttar Pradesh (*q.v.*) (since 1950).

United States of America. First American Congress opposition to Stamp Act, Nov. 1765. Chests of tea destroyed at Boston and New York, 18 Dec. 1773. Declaration of Rights, Nov. 1774. First battle between British and Americans (Lexington), 19 Apr. 1775. Battle of Bunker Hill, 17 June 1775. Act of Perpetual Union of States, 20 May 1775. Declaration of Independence, 4 July 1776. Articles of Confederation proposed by John Dickinson, 1776. Submitted to States, Nov. 1777. Battle of Saratoga, 17 Oct. 1777. Alliance with France, 6 Feb. 1778; ratified, Mar. 1781. Lord Cornwallis surrendered at Yorktown, 19 Oct. 1781. Peace signed at Paris, 3 Sept. 1783. Constitution proposed by Convention of Philadelphia, Sept. 1787; ratified, 23 May 1788. Death of Washington, 14 Dec. 1799. Louisiana Purchase, 30 Apr. 1803. Ports closed to British ships, July 1807. Importation of slaves prohibited, 1 Jan. 1808. War with Britain, 18 June 1812–24 Dec. 1814. Missouri Compromise, defining boundaries of slave area, 1820. Monroe Doctrine proclaimed, 1823. Texas annexed, 1845. Mexican War over the annexation of Texas, 1845–8. Mormons settled in Utah, 1847. Fugitive Slave Bill, 1850. Commercial treaty with Japan, 1854. Civil war in Kansas, 1856–7. Attack on Harper's Ferry by John Brown, 16 Oct. 1859. Execution of John Brown, 2 Dec. 1859. Republican convention at Chicago, 1860. S. Carolina, State Convention passed ordinance of secession, 20 Dec. 1860. Secession of Mississippi (8 Jan.), Florida (11 Jan.), Alabama (11 Jan.), Georgia (19 Jan.), Louisiana (26 Jan.), and Texas (1 Feb.), Jan.–Feb. 1861. 'Confederate' States' delegates met at Montgomery, Alabama; elected Jefferson Davis President, 18 Feb. 1861, and formed constitution, 11 Mar. 1861. Morrill Protection Tariff adopted, Mar. 1861. Civil war began by an attack on Fort Sumter by the Confederates (S.), 13 Apr. 1861. Lincoln's call for troops, 15 Apr. 1861. Lincoln issued proclamation of blockade of southern ports, 19 Apr. 1861. N. Carolina and Arkansas seceded, May 1861. Battle of Bull Run, 21 July 1861. Battle of Ball's Bluff, 21 Oct. 1861. Jefferson Davis elected President of Southern Confederacy, Nov. 1861. Paper currency ('greenbacks') adopted, 25 Feb. 1862. Battle of Pea Ridge, 6–8 Mar. 1862. Battle of Winchester, 23 Mar. 1862. Battle of Pittsburgh, 6–7 Apr. 1862. Battle

of Fredericksburg, 10 Dec. 1862. Homestead Act passed, Dec. 1862. Abolition of slavery proclaimed, Jan. 1863. Battle of Chancellorsville, 2 May 1863. 'Stonewall' Jackson mortally wounded by his own troops in mistake at the battle of Chancellorsville; *d.*, 10 May 1863. British consuls expelled from Southern States, Oct. 1863. Fugitive Slave Act repealed, 13 June 1864. Gen. Lee surrendered to Gen. Grant at Appomattox, 9 Apr. 1865. President Lincoln assassinated, 15 Apr. 1865. Gen. Johnston surrendered at Durham station, 26 Apr. 1865. Proclamation of amnesty, 29 May 1865. End of rebellion proclaimed by President Johnson, 3 Apr. 1866. Civil Rights (of negroes) Bill passed, 9 Apr. 1866. Impeachment of President Johnson carried in House of Representatives, 25 Feb.; acquitted by Senate, 26 May 1868. Civil war in Louisiana, Feb. 1873. Race riots in Mississippi, Aug. 1874. Negro insurrection in Tennessee, Aug. 1874. Reciprocity treaty with Canada rejected by Senate, 4 Feb. 1875. Engagement with Indians at Little Horn River, 25 June 1876. Edmunds's Anti-Polygamy Act, Mar. 1882. Chinese Exclusion Act passed, Apr. 1882. Revision of tariff, Mar. 1883. Mill's Bill reducing protection duties and placing many raw materials on free list passed, 1888–9. Nicaragua Canal Bill passed, Feb. 1889. McKinley Tariff Bill (protectionist) passed, Oct. 1890. Railway strikes at Chicago, much rioting, June–July 1894. Income tax declared by Supreme Court to be unconstitutional, 20 May 1895. Request to Spanish Government to recognize independence of Cuba, 2 Mar. 1896. Senate refused to ratify Arbitration Treaty with Britain, 5 May 1897. Dingley Tariff Bill (highly protectionist) passed, July 1897. Hawaii annexed, 7 July 1898. *Maine* explosion, 15 Feb. 1898. Ultimatum sent to Spain, 19 Apr. 1898. War began, 21 Apr. 1898. Treaty of Paris between Spain and America, 10 Dec. 1898. McKinley assassinated, 1901. Panama Canal Bill passed, 26 June 1902. Alaska Boundary Treaty, 11 Feb. 1903. Venezuela dispute settled by diplomacy of the U.S.A., Feb. 1903. St. Louis Exhibition opened, 30 Apr. 1904. Riots in Chicago, May 1905. Asiatic Labourers Exclusion Act, Feb. 1907. Canadian Fisheries Treaty, Apr. 1908. Acts for reform of tariffs and for creating federal reserve of currency passed, 1913. Eight-hour Day Bill, 1916. Disputes with Mexico, 1916. Bill for reorganizing army, 1916. War declared on Germany, 6 Apr. 1917. Wilson enunciated his 'fourteen points,' Jan. 1918. Wilson, as chairman of League of

Nations Commission at peace conference, announced League constitution, Feb. 1919. Wilson presented peace treaty in Congress, July 1919; eventually rejected by the Senate, which meant that the U.S.A. did not join the League of Nations. Women's suffrage, 1920. Prohibition came into effect, 1920; repealed, 1933. Immigration quota system started, 1921. First woman consul appointed (Miss Pattie Field, Amsterdam), 1925. 1927: Sacco and Vanzetti (Communists) convicted, on doubtful evidence, of a murder committed Apr. 1920; executed 23 Aug. at Charlestown, near Boston. 1929: New York Stock Exchange slump. 1930: London Naval Treaty signed by President Hoover, 22 July. Democrat election gains on a large scale. 1931: Numerous bank failures during world trade depression. 1932: Olympic Games (10th), Los Angeles, Aug. Franklin D. Roosevelt, Democrat, elected President, on the promise of a 'New Deal.'

1933: Mayor of Chicago fatally wounded by shot aimed at President, 15 Feb.; banks closed for 5 days, 6 Mar.; earthquake in California, 10 Mar.; gold standard suspended, 5 June; fatal strike riots in Illinois, 5 Oct.; U.S.S.R. recognized, 17 Nov. Acts passed included the Economy Act; the National Industrial Recovery Act; the Agricultural Adjustment Act.

1934: Dollar reduced to 59·06 per cent of its former weight; Congress outvoted President's veto on veterans' war bonuses, 27–28 Mar.; long-term relief replaced 'civil works,' 2 Apr.; martial law in San Francisco, 6 July; the gang leader Dillinger shot dead in Chicago, 22 July; 1,000,000 cotton workers on strike, 1 Sept.; Democrats obtained control of Senate and most governorships, 6 Nov.

1935: Federal judge decided National Recovery Act to be invalid as concerned workers' rights of organization and collective bargaining, 27 Feb. (this confirmed by Supreme Court, 1936); drought and dust clouds spread ruin over Kansas, 22 Mar.–12 Apr.; National Recovery Act codes held unconstitutional, 27 May; Senator Huey Long, 'boss' of Louisiana, shot 8 Sept. at Baton Rouge, d. 10 Sept.; duties between U.S.A. and Canada lowered, 15 Nov.

1936: Supreme Court holds Agricultural Adjustment Act unconstitutional, 6 Jan.; Congress passed $400,000,000 bonus to veterans, 10–27 Jan.; floods in eastern States, 18 Mar.; tornado swept southern States, 6 Apr.; embargo on munitions for Ethiopia lifted, 20 June; Roosevelt re-elected President.

1938: Several Supreme Court decisions

in favour of New Deal (*q.v.*), 3 Jan.; Roosevelt, at Kingston, Ontario, declared U.S.A. would stand by Canada against foreign aggressors, 18 Aug.; Roosevelt sent telegram to Hitler, imploring him not to enter upon war, 26 Sept.; American ambassador to Germany and German ambassador to U.S.A. both recalled as a result of indignation over the violation of Czechoslovakia, Nov.

1939: President delivered message to Congress warning Americans of dangers from aggressor states, 4 Jan.; President's Emergency Relief Bill passed by Senate, 27 Jan.; presidential approval given for purchase by France of 600 war-planes, 31 Jan.; Supplementary Defence Bill passed Representatives, 15 Feb.; San Francisco International Exhibition opened, 18 Feb.; Representatives passed bill appropriating $500,000,000 for the War Department, 3 Mar.; U.S.A. refused recognition of German annexation of Czechoslovakia, 21 Mar.; coal strike involving 460,000 miners began, 1 Apr.; agreement with Britain whereby the Phoenix Islands should be jointly controlled by Britain and U.S.A. for fifty years, 8 Apr.; personal appeal for peace by President to Mussolini and Hitler, 14 Apr.; Naval, Air, and Submarine Bases Bill became law, 20 Apr.; New York World Fair opened, 30 Apr.; commercial treaty with Turkey came into force, 5 May; the coal strike ended in victory for United Mine Workers' Union, 12 May; inauguration of regular transatlantic air service, 20 May; King and Queen of Britain arrived in Washington, 8 June; Social Security Act Amendment Bill passed House of Representatives (more than a million additional persons brought under the old age insurance scheme), 10 June; Monetary Bill received amendment in Senate, repealing President's powers of devaluation, 26 June. Representatives decide to maintain embargo on arms and munitions for belligerents, 30 June; amended Monetary Bill became law, 6 July; Senate Foreign Relations Committee decided against the new Neutrality Bill, 11–12 July; President in a message to Congress said it would be highly advisable to lift embargo on arms, 14 July; bill to restrict policital activities of officials became law, 2 Aug.; President made an appeal for peace to the King of Italy, 24 Aug., to Hitler and the President of Poland, 25 Aug.; he signed three proclamations relating to U.S. neutrality, 5 Sept.; proclamation of 'limited emergency,' barter agreement with Britain put into operation, 8 Sept.; President called for the amending of the Neutrality Act, 21 Sept.; Senate debated Neutrality

Revision Bill and passed it, 2–28 Oct.; War Department announced that army would be expanded to full authorized peace-time strength, 7 Oct.; House of Representatives voted repeal of arms embargo, 2 Nov.; Neutrality Revision Bill became law, 4 Nov.; Mr. Sumner Welles, acting Secretary of State, made statement on American rights in the Far East and the attitude of Japan, 22 Nov.; Secretary of State announced offer of American good offices in Finno-Russian dispute, 29 Nov.; note to Britain on blockade of German exports, 8 Dec.; President sent appeal for peace to the Pope and religious communities, 29 Dec.

1940: Intensification of production for allied needs commenced, May; U.S. destroyers transferred to Britain in exchange for lease of naval and air bases in western hemisphere to U.S.A., 2 Sept.; Conscription Bill enacted, 16 Sept.; Roosevelt re-elected for a third term; Joseph Kennedy, U.S. ambassador to Britain, resigned, 1 Dec.

1941: Lease-Lend Act passed, 5 Apr. Greenland brought under U.S. protection, 11 Apr.; Atlantic charter issued by Churchill and Roosevelt, 11 Aug.; Japanese attacked Pearl Harbor, 7 Dec.; Germany and Italy declared war on U.S.A., 11 Dec.

1942: Washington Pact, 1 Jan.; Anglo-American Combined Chiefs of Staff appointed, 6 Feb.

1943: Cairo meeting, 22–26 Nov.; Teheran meeting, 26 Nov.–2 Dec.

1944: Roosevelt elected for a fourth term.

1945: Yalta Conference, Feb.; death of Roosevelt, 25 Apr.; succeeded by Vice-President Harry S. Truman; San Francisco Conference, May–June; Potsdam Conference, July–Aug.; Congress ratified the U.N. Charter, 28 July, which indicated the end of isolationism as a political force in the U.S.A.; end of Lease-Lend, 2 Sept.

1946: Atomic Energy Commission established, 1 Aug.; Republican victory in Congressional elections, Dec.

1947: Taft-Hartley Act passed over the President's veto, June; Marshall Plan inaugurated, Dec.

1948: Truman re-elected President; North Atlantic Treaty (q.v.) signed in Washington, 4 Apr. 1949. Recession and growth in unemployed, 1948–9, followed by a marked economic recovery from Oct. 1949.

1950: Mutual Defence Assistance Agreement signed between U.S.A. and Britain, 27 Jan.; Korean War (see KOREA) began, 25 June. Unsuccessful attempt on Truman's life by Puerto Rican nationalists, Nov.

1951: Constitutional amendment limiting a President's tenure of office to two terms passed, Feb.; MacArthur dismissed, Apr.; truce negotiations began in Korea, July.

1952: Dwight D. Eisenhower, Republican, elected President; McCarran-Walters Immigration Act. Inflationary pressures caused strike-waves. Rise of McCarthyism.

1953: Korean cease-fire, July.

1954: Supreme Court ruled that racial segregation in public schools was unconstitutional. Democrats regained control of Congress, May, and in Dec. a vote of censure against McCarthy was passed by the Senate, which marked the end of his real influence.

1956: Eisenhower re-elected President; Suez crisis caused severe rift in Anglo-American relations, Dec. McCarthy d., 1957.

1958: Severe business recession; Eisenhower presented largest-ever peacetime Budget to Congress—64 per cent for military programmes, Jan.; Congress passed Bill allowing exchange of nuclear weapons information with Britain, June; in response to Lebanese requests, U.S. troops landed at Beirut, July; withdrawn, Oct.; big Democratic gains in Congressional elections, Nov. U.S. four-ton missile fired into orbit, 18 Dec.

1959: John Foster Dulles resigned as secretary of state, Apr.; d. May; Eisenhower had talks in Europe, including London, Aug.–Sept.; Eisenhower made tour of Europe, Asia, and Middle East, Dec.; on 29 Dec. he announced that the U.S.A. would not extend formal suspension of nuclear tests after 31 Dec.

1960: President Eisenhower attended the opening of the Summit Conference in Paris, 16 May; Khrushchev demanded an apology for the 'U-2' incident (q.v.) of 1 May, which Eisenhower refused; on the following day the conference broke down. Britain gave permission for U.S. Polaris submarine to be established at Holy Loch, in the Clyde, 1 Nov.; Senator John F. Kennedy elected Democratic President of the U.S.A., 9 Nov.

1961: First American in space, Alan Shepard, 5 May; Kennedy visited France, Vienna (for talks with Khrushchev), and London, June; U.S.A. and Russia agreed on the principles for disarmament negotiations, Sept.

1962: First American to orbit the earth in space (three times), John Glenn, 20 Feb.; Kennedy attacked steel firms' price increases, Apr.; his Medical Care Bill rejected by the Senate, 17 June; Trade Expansion Act became law, 11 Oct.;

Mrs. Eleanor Roosevelt *d.*, 7 Nov.; Democratic successes in 'mid-term' elections, Nov.; Anglo-American differences due to U.S. proposal to cancel Skybolt, Dec.; at talks between Kennedy and Macmillan in the Bahamas, 19–21 Dec., it was agreed to supply Britain with Polaris weapons instead. The 'Mona Lisa' arrived in New York, for exhibition, 20 Dec.

1963: Kennedy announces major tax reductions, Jan; U.S. nuclear submarine *Thresher* lost off eastern seaboard, Apr.; Kennedy intervenes in racial disputes in Birmingham, Alabama, May; Kennedy visits W. Germany (including W. Berlin), Ireland, Britain and Italy, June–July; U.S.A. signs nuclear Test Ban Treaty in Moscow, 5 Aug. Kennedy assassinated at Dallas, Texas, 22 Nov. 1963. Vice-President Johnson assumes presidency.

United States Marine Corps raised, 1775.

Universities. Salerno, reputed to have been founded in ninth century, is the earliest of which there is record; Cordova, 968; Bologna, 1116; Paris, 1200; Padua, 1222; Salamanca, 1243; Rome, 1245; Sorbonne, Paris, 1253; Cracow, 1364; Vienna, 1365; Prague, 1384; Heidelberg, 1386; Leipzig, 1409; Ingolstadt, 1472 (transferred to Landshut, 1800, to Munich, 1826); Uppsala, 1477; Wittenberg, 1502 (absorbed, 1694, by Halle); Strasbourg, 1538; Jena, 1558; Douai, 1563; Leyden, 1575; Harvard, 1638; Innsbruck, 1669; Besançon, 1676; Göttingen, 1734; Bonn, 1784. (*See* CAMBRIDGE UNIVERSITY and OXFORD UNIVERSITY.) The other U. of Great Britain and Ireland are:

Aberdeen	founded	1494
Birmingham	,,	1900
Bristol	,,	1909
Dublin (Trinity College)	,,	1591
Durham	,,	1832
Edinburgh	,,	1582
Exeter	,,	1955
* Glasgow	,,	1450
Hull	,,	1954
Ireland, National University of	,,	1908
Keele	,,	1962
Leeds	,,	1904
Leicester	,,	1957
Liverpool	,,	1903
London (*q.v.*)	,,	1836
Manchester	,,	1880
Nottingham	,,	1948

* Announced in 1963 that the Royal Technical College, Glasgow, was to be given university status, and would be entitled to confer its own degrees.

Queen's, Belfast	,,	**1908**
Reading	,,	**1926**
Southampton	,,	**1952**
St. Andrews	,,	**1411**
Sheffield	,,	**1905**
Sussex	,,	**1961**
Wales (*q.v.*)	,,	**1893**
York	,,	**1963**

Further English U. are planned for East Anglia, Essex, Warwick, etc.

Some other U. of recent foundation: Sofia, 1904; Hong Kong, 1912; Frankfort-on-Main, 1914; Benares, 1916; Patna, 1917; Ljubljana, 1919; Dorpat (Estonia), reopened as an Estonian seat of learning, 1919; Lucknow, 1920; Aligarh, 1920; Dacca, 1921; Delhi, 1922; Nagpur, 1923; Jerusalem, 1925; Andhra, 1926; Agra, 1927; Travancore, 1937; Ceylon, 1942; Utkal, 1943; Bergen, 1948; Rowkee Engineering, 1949; Malaya, 1949; Karachi, 1950; Nigeria, 1960. Strasbourg University reopened under French administration, 1919.

Universities, American. Privately endowed U. include: Harvard, 1633; William and Mary, 1693; Yale, 1701; Princeton, 1746; Washington and Lee, 1749; Columbia, 1754; Brown, 1764; Rutgers, 1766; Dartmouth, 1770; Miami, Ohio, 1809; Emory, 1837; Ohio Wesleyan, 1841; Notre Dame, 1842; Wilberforce (negro), 1856; Atlanta (negro), 1865; Cornell, 1865; Des Moines, 1865; Johns Hopkins, 1876; Drake, 1881; Stanford, 1885; Chicago, 1890; Duke, 1924.

The characteristic American U. for women only are privately endowed; some of the better known are: Mount Holyoke, 1837; Elmira, 1853; Vassar, 1865; Wells, 1868; Humber, 1871; Smith, 1871; Wellesley, 1871; Radcliffe, 1875; Bryn Mawr, 1881; Barnard, 1889.

State U. are mostly of nineteenth century foundation, but a few date back to colonial times. In 1862 the federal government passed an Act setting aside public lands for the endowment of U. Owing to their being well provided with privately endowed establishments the following states have no state U.: Massachusetts, Rhode Island, Connecticut, Pennsylvania, New York; and the New Jersey State university is merely Rutgers (*see* above), re-named in 1917. The following are some of the better known state U.: Pennsylvania, 1751; Georgia, 1785–1801; North Carolina, 1789; Virginia, 1819; Alabama, 1820; Indiana, 1838; Michigan, 1841; Missouri, 1841; Iowa, 1847; Mississippi, 1848; Wisconsin, 1848; Utah, 1850; Minnesota, 1851; Louisiana, 1860; Kansas, 1866; Illinois, 1867; West Virginia, 1867; California,

1869; Nebraska, 1871; Arkansas, 1872; Oregon, 1872; Nevada, 1873; Ohio, 1873; Colorado, 1877; South Dakota, 1882; Wyoming, 1886; Arizona, 1891; New Hampshire, 1891; New Mexico, 1892; Oklahoma, 1892; Montana, 1895; Florida, 1903; Kentucky, 1908; North Dakota, 1918; Maryland, 1920; Delaware, 1921.

U.N.R.R.A. (United Nations Relief and Rehabilitation Administration). Formed, 1943. Its major tasks were virtually complete early in 1947, the first shipload of its supplies having been dispatched, Mar. 1945.

U.N.S.C.O.B., a special committee, established 21 Oct. 1947, by resolution of the General Assembly of the U.N., on the Balkans, with headquarters at Salonika, charged with the solution of problems involving Greece and neighbouring states in the confused political situation following the Communist-inspired revolt in Greece (*q.v.*).

Uppsala, or **Upsala,** Sweden. University founded, 1477. New buildings, 1879–86. The cathedral was built, 1230–1435.

Ur of the Chaldees was founded shortly before 4000 B.C. Its recorded history begins not later than 2500 B.C. Its resplendent Third Dynasty came to an end, 1960 B.C. Excavated by Taylor, A.D. 1854; Campbell Thompson and Hall, 1918–19; and Sir Leonard Woolley, 1922–1934.

Uranus, planet discovered by Sir William Herschel, 13 Mar. 1781.

Uriconium, Viroconium, near the site of the present village of Wroxeter at the crossing of Watling Street over the Severn. A Roman camp here appears to have been laid out *c.* A.D. 48 as the quarters of the XIV Legion. When the Legion was transferred to Chester in A.D. 70 the site continued in civil occupation and expanded to become the tribal capital of the Cornovii. A forum was completed by 130. Extensive damage caused by fire *c.* 300, after which the town was largely rebuilt on a less ambitious scale than before, and continued in occupation until *c.* 350.

Ursuline Nuns. Founded by St. Angela Merici, 1535; approved as a religious order by Pope Paul V, 1612.

Uruguay. In 1603 Hernando Arias, the first American-born Spanish governor of La Plata, explored the eastern bank (Banda Oriental, long the alternative name for U.) of the Plate River, and turned loose herds of cattle and horses without leaving colonists. Nomadic gauchos crossed from the W. bank every season to catch these for their hides, and when the Portuguese expedition of 1680 arrived by sea to found a settlement called Colonia there were already a few semi-permanent hide traders' stations on the Uruguayan shore. The Spaniards in 1726 erected a fort for the protection of these traders on the site of Montevideo, and in 1777 they destroyed Colonia. In 1810 the Creoles of Montevideo joined in the general rising against the Spanish royal garrisons, and besieged Montevideo with the help of republicans from the Argentine. It fell in 1814 to the Argentine Gen. Alvear. The Portuguese invaded the territory from the N. in 1816, and from 1820 to 1825 U. was under Brazilian occupation. The war between Brazil and the Argentine republic was terminated at the instance of Britain and France by a treaty of 1828, making U. independent of either. A leading Uruguayan figure of the War of Independence was José Artigas (1774–1850). Independence formally proclaimed and constitution adopted in 1919, 1934, and 1942. Entered the war against the Axis, Feb. 1945. In July 1951 a pact was signed by the leaders of the only two significant political parties—the Colorados or Batllistas and Biancos or Herreristas—agreeing to press jointly for the abolition of the presidency and its replacement by a National Executive Council of nine members, to assume office, 1 Mar. 1952.

The following is a list of presidents of U. in the twentieth century:

Cuestas	1899–1903
Batlle y Ordoñez	1903–1907
Williman	1907–1911
Batlle y Ordoñez (again)	1911–1915
Viera	1915–1919
Brum	1919–1923
Serrato	1923–1927
Campestiguy	1927–1931
Terra	1931–1938
Baldomir	1938–1943
Amezaga	1943–1947
Berreta (*d.* in office)	1947
Berres (ex-vice-president)	1947–1951
Treuba	1951

U.S.A., Constitution of, passed, 17 Sept. 1787. Came into force, 21 June, 1788 The following amendments have been made: (1) Freedom of religion, expression, and assembly. (2) Freedom to keep arms. (3) Quartering of troops illegal. (4) General warrants illegal. (5) No deprivations or punishments without trial. (6) Trial by jury secured in criminal offences. (7) Trial by jury secured in most civil cases. (8) Fines and bail not to be excessive; punishments not to be cruel or unusual. (9) Rights enumerated in the Constitution not to deny other rights retained by the people. (10) Rights not specifically given to the Union to be retained by states or people. The above, collectively known as the Bill of Rights, were passed, 15 Dec. 1791. (11) Alteration of powers of the Supreme Court, 1798. (12) Alteration of method of election of President and Vice-President, 1804. (13) Slavery abolished, 1865. (14) Definition of citizenship. Apportionment of representation in House of Representatives. Former rebels excluded from office. Confederate debt repudiated, 1868. (15) Voting rights not to be denied on account of colour, 1870. (16) Income tax legalized, 1913. (17) Senators to be directly elected, 1913. (18) Prohibition instituted, 1918. (19) Female suffrage, 1920. (20) Alteration in election and terms of office of President, Vice-president, etc., 1933. (21) Prohibition to be left to state legislation, 1933; in effect, the repeal of the Eighteenth Amendment. (22) Limiting the President's tenure of office to two terms, or to two terms plus two years in respect of a Vice-President who has succeeded to presidential office, 26 Feb. 1951. (23) Giving citizens of the District of Columbia the right to vote in national elections, 30 Mar. 1961.

U.S.A., Presidents of. Those marked V.-P. were Vice-Presidents and took office in the first instance by succession and not by election.

George Washington	1789–1797
John Adams	1797–1801
Thomas Jefferson	1801–1809
James Maddison	1809–1817
James Monroe	1817–1825
John Quincy Adams	1825–1829
Andrew Jackson	1829–1837
Martin Van Buren	1837–1841
W. H. Harrison	Mar.–Apr. 1841
John Tyler (V.-P.)	1841–1845
J. Knox Polk	1845–1849
Zachary Taylor	1849–1850
Millard Fillmore (V.-P.)	1850–1853
Franklin Pierce	1853–1857
James Buchanan	1857–1861
Abraham Lincoln	1861–1865
Andrew Johnson (V.-P.)	1865–1869
Ulysses Grant	1869–1877
Rutherford Hayes	1877–1881
James Garfield	1881
Chester Arthur (V.-P.)	1881–1885
Grover Cleveland	1885–1889
Benjamin Harrison	1889–1893
Grover Cleveland (again)	1893–1897
William McKinley	1897–1901
Theodore Roosevelt (V.-P.)	1901–1909
William Howard Taft	1909–1913
Woodrow Wilson	1913–1921
Warren Harding	1921–1923
Calvin Coolidge (V.-P.)	1923–1929
Herbert Hoover	1929–1933
Franklin Delano Roosevelt	1933–1945
Harry S. Truman (V.-P.)	1945–1949
Re-elected	1949–1952
Dwight David Eisenhower	1952–1960
John Fitzgerald Kennedy	1960–1963
Lyndon Baines Johnson (V.-P.)	1963–

U.S.S.R.
1917: Riots at Petrograd, tsar abdicated, Provisional Government formed under Prince Lvoff, Mar.; Austrian peace offer rejected, Alexeiev made C.-in-C., Council of Workmen and Soldiers formed at Petrograd, Baltic and Black Sea fleets mutinied, Apr.; Alexeiev resigned, Brusilov made C.-in-C., 4 June; Provisional Government rejected German offer of armistice, 9 June; Kerensky granted autonomy to Finland and Ukraine, June; Brusilov's advance in Galicia, 1–10 July; Russian rout at Zloczow, 19 July; mutiny among many units, 19 July; Russian retreat in Bukovina, 29 July; Kornilov succeeded Brusilov, 1 Aug.; National Ministry under Kerensky, 6 Aug.; Moscow conference of all parties, 25 Aug.; tsar and tsaritsa sent to Siberia, 25 Aug.; Riga taken by Germans, 3 Sept.; Kornilov, as C.-in-C., marched on Petrograd, was denounced by Kerensky, and surrendered, 8–12 Sept.; Russia proclaimed a republic, 15 Sept.; new Cabinet under Kerensky, 9 Oct.; military revolution (the 'October Revolution' (q.v.), 7 Nov.; Kerensky overthrown by Lenin and Trotsky, rise of Russian Socialist Federal Soviet Republic, Nov.–Dec.

1918: Trotsky announced war between Russia and Germany ended, 10 Feb.; war resumed, 18 Feb.; Germans occupied Pskoff, 25 Feb.; Treaty of Brest-Litovsk, 3 Mar.; Tsar Nicholas II and family slaughtered at Ekaterinburg, 16 July.

1919: Admiral Koltchak (leader of the Whites) failed to join hands with Gen. Ironside's Archangel force; Lord Rawlinson supervised evacuation of Murmansk and Archangel.

1920: Bolshevik revolution in Vladivostok; Koltchak surrendered and shot at Omsk; Denikin advanced towards Orel; Denikin defeated; Russo-Polish War in conjunction with Gen. Wrangel; New Economic Policy ('N.E.P.') inaugurated, 23 Nov. Petsamo ceded to Finland,14 Oct.

1921: Tukhachevsky beaten before Warsaw; Treaty of Riga between Poland and Soviet, 19 Mar.

1923: Constitution of U.S.S.R. adopted, 6 July.

1924: Soviet Republics recognized by France, Great Britain, Italy, and Sweden; Lenin d., 21 Jan. (See ZINOVIEV LETTER.)

1926: Nine governments substituted for four in Far East; much Soviet activity in China, organized by Michael Borodin.

1927: Britain withdrew recognition, 27 May; Trotsky expelled from Communist Executive c. 2 Oct.

1928: Trotsky sent to Vierney, on Russo-Chinese frontier; Central Executive Committee of the Union adopted a law on general principles of land distribution, delegation under Litvinov took part in preliminary disarmament conference at Geneva, 15–24 Mar.

1929: Tajikistan Republic (q.v.) joined U.S.S.R., 16 Oct.; Leo Trotsky exiled, 18 Feb. (murdered in Mexico, 21 Aug. 1940); decree granting atheists a monopoly of the right to teach their beliefs, and all religious propaganda forbidden, May; Russo-Chinese peace protocol signed, 22 Dec.

1930: Acute shortage of food; ruthlessness in nationalization of agriculture checked by Stalin, 2 Mar.

1931: Stalin condemned principle of equal wages for all; treaty with Turkey, Mar.; new Five-Year Plan announced for 1933–8.

1932: Nizhni-Novgorod motor works and metallurgic works at Magnitogorsk in the Urals completed; freer sale of agricultural produce allowed; Zinoviev and Kamenev expelled.

1933: Five British officials of the Metropolitan-Vickers Co. arrested, four found guilty of sabotage, two released, Apr.; recognition of U.S.S.R. by U.S.A., 17 Nov.

1934: Non-aggression pacts for ten years with Estonia, Latvia, Lithuania, Finland, and Poland, Apr.–May; entry into League of Nations, 18 Sept.; Kirov murdered, 1 Dec.; execution, therefore, of 117 persons, by 29 Dec.

1935: Chinese Eastern Railway sold to Japan, 23 Mar.; mutual assistance pact with France signed, 2 May; with Czechoslovakia, 16 May.

1936: Ships sent to Spain; skirmishes with Japanese on Manchurian border; pact with Mongolian People's Republic, 12 Mar.; strength of army raised; Black Sea closed to ships other than Russian in case of war, by authority of the League, 20 July; Zinoviev, Kamenev, and 14 others shot for sedition, 25 Aug.; new constitution adopted, 5 Dec.; 'sound money' restored; general progress.

1937: Abortive attempt at census, 6 Jan.; another treason trial at Moscow, 13 shot, 23 Jan.; second Five-Year Plan declared fulfilled, 28 Apr.; Moscow–Volga Canal opened, 1 May; many army chiefs executed, 12 June; General Election (only one candidate in each constituency), 12 Dec.; railway in E. Siberia, from Karymskaya to Khabarovsk, opened, 19 Dec.; 8 ex-ministers executed, 16 Dec.

1938: More sedition trials, 21 Feb., all pleading guilty, 2 Mar. and following days; many heads of provincial governments removed from office; tension in respect of Germany; Soviet artillery shelled Japanese lines at Changkufeng, 5 Aug. (see CHANGKUFENG INCIDENT); Yezhov, commissar of interior, disgraced, Nov.; autonomist movement in Ukraine, Dec.

1939: Diplomatic relations with Hungary severed because that country was joining in the Anti-Comintern Pact, 2 Feb.; trade agreement with Italy, 7 Feb.; trade agreement with Poland, 19 Feb.; Stalin, opening eighteenth Congress of Communist Party, reprimanded the democratic states for their continued retreat before aggression, 10 Mar.; Government refused to recognize German annexation of Czechoslovakia, 19 Mar.; Litvinov, foreign commissar, replaced by Molotov, 3 May; beginning of clashes with Japanese-Manchukuoan forces in Outer Mongolia, 11 May (see NOMANHAN INCIDENT); British ambassador and French chargé d'affaires submitted proposals for resistance to aggression, 27 May; Molotov indicated that he wished the terms to include guarantees to the Baltic states, 31 May; census of U.S.S.R., excluding Far North, 170,467,186 announced, June; more clashes with Japanese in Outer Mongolia, 2–6 July; trade agreement with China, 16 July; battle with Japanese on Khalgakol River, 25 July; settlement of Sakhalin dispute with Japan, 11 Aug.; trade agreement with Germany, 20 Aug.; Ribbentrop and Molotov in Moscow signed Russo-German pact, 23 Aug.; armistice in Outer Mongolia, 16 Sept.; U.S.S.R. invaded Poland and recognized Government of Slovakia, 17 Sept.; pact with Estonia, Soviet naval and air bases to be established there, 19 Sept.; mutual assistance pact with Latvia signed in Moscow (similar to Estonia's), 5 Oct.; Finnish Government accepted invitation to confer at Moscow and at same time prepared for defence of Finland, 8 Oct.; Lithuania made agreement whereby Vilna came again into its possession and a Russian garrison was to be established on Lithuanian territory, 10 Oct.; trade agreement with Britain signed in London, 11 Oct.; agreement for supply of grain to Germany, 21 Oct; Finnish delegates arrived in Moscow with reply to Russian proposals, 2 Nov.; Molotov reaffirmed Russian neutrality but denounced 'capitalist powers,' Comintern issued manifesto in similar strain, 7 Nov.; deadlock in negotiations with Finland, 8 Nov.; trade negotiations with Japan reopened, 24 Nov.; Soviet Government accused Finns of military aggression, 26 Nov.; non-aggression pact with Finland denounced,

28 Nov.; diplomatic relations with Finland broken off, 29 Nov.; Finland invaded by U.S.S.R., 30 Nov.; the Soviet Government set up a puppet Finnish Government at Terijoki, 1 Dec.; expelled from League of Nations, 14 Dec.

1940: War with Finland ended, 13 Mar.; Petsamo ceded to Finland and Karelia ceded to U.S.S.R., together with base at Hangö; Soviet troops occupied Rumanian provinces of Bessarabia and N. Bukovina, 28 June; Moldavian S.S.R. constituted, 2 Aug.; Estonia, Latvia, and Lithuania joined the U.S.S.R., 3 Aug. *See* BALTIC STATES.

1941: Pact of friendship with Yugoslavia, 6 Apr.; pact of neutrality and friendship with Japan, 13 Apr.; German and Rumanian attack on U.S.S.R. began, 22 June; Committee of State Defence formed, 30 June; broadcast on German aggression by Stalin, 3 July; Anglo-Russian alliance, 12 July; three-power conference at Moscow, Sept.–Oct.

1942: Anglo-Russian Treaty for twenty years, 26 May.

1943: Teheran meeting of Stalin, Roosevelt, and Churchill, Nov.–Dec.

1944: Constitution modified, 1 Feb.: each S. Republic entitled to its own ministries for Defence and Foreign Affairs; armistice with Finland, 4 Sept.; war with Bulgaria, 5–8 Sept.; armistice with Rumania, 12 Sept.; Moscow conference (Stalin and Churchill), 9–19 Oct. (*See* WORLD WAR II.)

1945: Patriarch Alexis elected by Orthodox Church General Council, 2 Feb.; Russo-Polish frontier treaty, 17 Aug.; regular passenger air services Moscow–Tashkent and Moscow–Vladivostok opened.

1946: Administrative changes affecting the number of delegates to the Council of the Union and Council of Nationalities and the status of commissars (from 16 Mar. called ministers). Fourth Five-Year Plan adopted.

1947: Peace treaty with Finland returning province of Petsamo to U.S.S.R. signed, 10 Feb.; and with Rumania, same day.

1948: Blockade of western sectors begun, 19 June. Soviet element withdrawn from Berlin Kommandatura, 1 July. Quarrel with Yugoslavia (*q.v.*) began.

1949: First section of S. Ural electric railway opened, Nov. Blockade of Berlin lifted, 12 May; airlift ended, 6 Oct. Number of trade unions reduced by amalgamation from 176 to 67. Three-year plan for livestock-rearing begun, Apr.

1950: New direct airlines to Sakhalin, the Ukraine, and Central Asia from Moscow opened, 1 May. General elections (one list), 12 Mar., polled 111 million votes. Capital punishment having been abolished, 26 May 1947, was reintroduced for treason, espionage, sabotage, 12 Jan. Defence Ministry (*see above*, 1946) split into War and Navy ministries, 25 Feb. Smaller collective farms began to be merged into larger units up to 15,000 hectares.

1951: Exchange of territory between Ukraine and the Polish Republic took place, 22 May. New state loan of 30 million roubles raised, 3 May.

1952: Nineteenth Communist Congress held in Moscow, Nov., addressed by Malenkov *vice* Stalin in his capacity as General Secretary.

1953: Stalin (*b.* 1880) *d.* 5 Mar.; succeeded as chairman of Council of Ministers by Malenkov (*b.* 1903). Considerable easing in terrorist aspect of regime which had developed under Stalin, and a *rapprochement* with Yugoslavia; promises of more consumer goods. Some revival of terrorist features after the revolt in E. Berlin on 17 June. In July Beria, Minister of the Interior, was expelled from the party, accused of treasonable activities, and executed.

1954: Struggle for leadership in U.S.S.R. becoming apparent; Malenkov's influence declining.

1955: Malenkov resigned as chairman; succeeded by Bulganin, 8 Feb. Rise to power of Nikita Khruschev, already clearly the most influential member of the 'collective leadership.' Transfer of Port Arthur to China completed, 24 Mar. Declaration of friendship and co-operation signed by Bulganin and Tito of Yugoslavia, 2 June. U.S.S.R. announced her intention to reduce her armed forces, 13 Aug. Talks between Adenauer and Bulganin in Moscow in Sept. resulted in release of many Germans still held prisoner of war in the U.S.S.R. and the establishment of diplomatic relations between the two countries. U.S.S.R. took part in foreign ministers' conference in Geneva, Oct.–Nov., but it ended without any real agreement. Bulganin and Khruschev toured India and Burma, Nov.–Dec. On 23 Nov. U.S.S.R. announced that she had exploded a very powerful hydrogen bomb.

1956: Bulganin proposed a twenty-year friendship pact with the U.S.A., 23 Jan. On 25 Feb. Khruschev denounced Stalin in a speech to the congress of the Russian Communist Party. Dissolution of Cominform announced, 17 Apr. Bulganin and Khruschev made a ten-day visit to England, 18–28 Apr., and were received by the Queen. Withdrawal began of 33,500 Russian troops from E. Germany, 16 June. Anti-Russian revolts in

Poland, 28 June. Khruschev visited Belgrade, 19 Sept. Soviet leaders visited Poland and objected to liberal measures there, 19 Oct. Russian troops and aircraft crushed the Hungarian revolt, 2–5 Nov. Revival of more restrictionist policy in dealings with satellite states. Changes in economic planning announced, 25 Dec.

1957: Khruschev ousted his chief rivals from party leadership and, as First Secretary of the Central Committee of the party, packed the Praesidium with his nominees. Further denunciations of Stalin. A meeting between Khruschev and Tito took place, Aug. 1957, which indicated an improvement in Soviet-Yugoslav relations, strained since the Hungarian rising. U.S.S.R. launched her 'Sputnik,' first earth satellite, 4 Oct.

1958: Khruschev succeeded Bulganin as chairman of the Council of Ministers, 27 Mar.; Pasternak declined the Nobel Prize for Literature after the U.S.S.R. had denounced the award as a 'hostile act,' 29 Oct. U.S.S.R. put forward proposals about Berlin, 27 Nov,. but no international agreement resulted. Khruschev admitted shortcomings in Soviet agricultural policy, 15 Dec.; more spending on science and education proposed, 22 Dec.; Soviet legal code reformed, 25 Dec.

1959: Macmillan, British Premier, visited Moscow, 20 Feb.–3 Mar. Five-year Trade Agreement between Britain and U.S.S.R., 24 May. Khruschev addressed the U.N. Assembly in New York, 18 Sept. U.S.S.R. agreed to a 'Summit Conference' in 1960.

1960: Khruschev made an eleven-day tour of France, Mar. On 5 May Khruschev announced that a U.S. 'U-2' plane had been shot down over Soviet territory on 1 May; when the Summit Conference opened in Paris on 16 May he demanded an apology for the 'U-2' incident (*q.v.*) from Eisenhower. This was refused and the conference broke up. Revival of the 'cold war', but also clear that Sino-Soviet relations worsening.

1961: Anglo-Soviet cultural agreement signed, 9 Jan. Yuri Gagarin circled the earth once in the space-ship *Vostock*, 12 Apr.; Titov made 17 orbits in another space-ship on 6 Aug. Gagarin visited London, 11 July. Soviet Union tested a nuclear bomb (first detected explosion since 1958), 1 Sept.; on 8 Sept. U.S.S.R. rejected Anglo-American proposals for a ban on atmospheric nuclear tests. On 17 Oct. Khruschev told the Soviet Communist Party that the timing of a German peace treaty was unimportant; this marked an easing in East-West tension.

1962: Sino-Soviet differences widened considerably. Spectacular space flights by Nikolayev (64 orbits) and Popovich (48 orbits), 11–12 Aug.

1963: British business man Greville Wynne tried for espionage in Moscow, and sentenced to eight years' imprisonment, May. A Russian, Oleg Penkovsky, tried with him was sentenced to death; June 16: first woman cosmonaut, Valentina Tereshkova, orbited the earth forty-nine times (*see* SPACE FLIGHTS); talks held in Moscow on ideological differences with China ended in failure, July; U.S.S.R. signed nuclear Test Ban Treaty in Moscow, 5 Aug.

Uttar Pradesh, Indian State, the name, since 1950, of the former United Provinces (*q.v.*).

Usury Laws. Interest on loans limited to 8 per cent, 1623; 6 per cent, 1651; 5 per cent, 1713. Restraint removed, 1854.

Utah. Mormons under Brigham Young entered the Salt Lake Valley, 1847. Mexico ceded the territory to the U.S.A., 1848, and territorial government was organized in 1850. State admitted to Union, 4 Jan. 1896. *See* MORMONS.

' **Utopia,**' by Sir Thomas More, published in **Latin,** 1516. In English, 1551.

Utrecht, Treaty of. Between Britain, the United Provinces, and France to end the War of the Spanish Succession, 11 Apr. 1713.

Uzbekistan admitted as an equal member of the U.S.S.R., 1925. *See* BOKHARA.

P

V

Vaccination (against smallpox). Conceived and developed by Sir E. Jenner, 1796. Made compulsory in U.K., 1853, but no longer so under National Health Service Act, 1946, which came into force, 5 July 1948. Suggested, 1962, that in future V. should be restricted to children over 2, except in cases of epidemics.

Vagrancy Acts, constituted, with the Poor Laws (*q.v.*), the greater part of English social legislation down to the end of the eighteenth century, especially under the Tudors. The Act of 1459 authorized the imprisonment of vagrants, that of 1530 whipping, that of 1535 mutilation, to which by the Act of 1597 all entertainers unless employed by some nobleman were also subject. Transportation was authorized by Orders in Council, 1603 and 1662. In 1713 previous Acts were consolidated and rationalized, and branding ceased to be legal. Previous legislation repealed by Consolidation Act, 1740, amended by Vagrancy Acts, 1822, 1824, and 1873. The Vagrancy Act, 1935, classed as vagrants only those who deliberately refuse to lodge in a casual ward, etc., when ordered to do so. Amendments of 1950 deal with persons claiming to foretell the future, etc.

Valladolid, first mentioned, 1072, as having been recovered from the Moors a hundred years earlier. Residence of Castilian kings from *c.* 1400, but after 1560 the Cortes ceased to meet at V., and decline set in. Cathedral begun, 1585.

Valona. *See* VLÖRE.

Valparaiso, Chile. Founded 1536 by Juan de Saavedra; captured by Sir Francis Drake, 1578; sacked by the Dutch, 1600; severe earthquakes, 1730, 1822, 1839, 1873, and 1908.

Vancouver, British Columbia, began to be an important commercial city about 1885.

Vancouver, Washington, U.S.A., was founded 1825 as Hudson's Bay Co. trading post; taken over by U.S.A., 1846.

Vancouver Island, British Columbia, discovered and circumnavigated, 1792, by George Vancouver.

Vandals. Earlier references to V. in Roman authors do not denote any particular people but generally all E. Germanic tribes, such as Burgundians and Goths. About A.D. 330 they were defeated by the Goths, and moved into Pannonia (now Hungary), whence in 406 they migrated via Mainz across Gaul to Spain, where they gave their name to Andalusia ('Vandalitia'), 409. Another detachment settled in Galicia, but by 429 had almost all perished. In May 429 the V. under King Gaiseric, about 160,000 strong, crossed to Africa (Tunisia) in transports supplied by the mutinous Count Bonifacius. They had captured nearly all the principal cities of Africa by 433. By treaty of 30 Jan. 435 the Emperor Valentinian ceded to Gaiseric the whole Roman territory of Africa except Carthage and its province. Gaiseric seized Carthage, 19 Oct. 439, and took and sacked Rome in 455. He built a large navy and conquered the Balearics. A treaty of 476 tolerated Catholic clergy, hitherto persecuted by Arian Vandal leaders. Carthage retaken by Count Belisarius, 533, to whom the last known Vandal king, Gelimer, surrendered, 534. No mention of V. made by historians after 536.

Vanzetti. *See* SACCO.

Varangian Guard, marine infantry corps of the Byzantine Army performing the same functions as the praetorian cohorts of the old Roman Army. Originally recruited in Sweden by Vladimir the Great, Grand Duke of Kiev, about 977–84, they were transferred by him to the service of Byzantium under Constantine VIII, 999. From then till 1066 the preponderance of recruits from Sweden and the Baltic diminished in favour of Norwegians, Icelanders, and other western Scandinavians: after Oct. 1066 Englishmen in increasing numbers joined the V. G., and eventually they and other westerners completely displaced the Swedish and Russian element; they had heavy losses against the Normans at Durazzo, 1082; Edgar Ætheling, who renounced the throne of England, joined the V. G. in 1097. In 1453 the regiment still existed, but was exclusively English.

Vatican. A Roman hill, on which a palace, commenced in 1146, became the residence of the Pope in 1377; it is said to contain 7,000 rooms. The popes made the V. their voluntary prison, 1870–1929. Established as a sovereign state, 7 June 1929, as consequence of Mussolini's concordat with the papacy. This treaty was embodied in the constitution of the Italian Republic, 1947.

Vatican Council, 1869–70. *See* COUNCILS OF THE CHURCH.

Vaud (Ger. **Waadt**), canton of Switzerland. Burgundians settled there, A.D. 443. Acquired by counts of Savoy about 1268. Invaded by Swiss Confederation, 1475; assigned as a pledge to the Confederation, 1476; redeemed, 1478. Alternated between Savoyard and Bernese rule, 1536–1617, then finally ceded to Berne. Republic of Leman declared, 1798. Entered the Confederation, 1803. Canton V. replaced designation Canton Leman, 1803.

Vauxhall Gardens. Laid out on the S. bank of the Thames, 1661. With George IV's permission called Royal, 1822. closed, 1859.

Vendée. *See* CHOUANS.

Venetia, originally the land of the Veneti, an Illyrian tribe, who entered the area between 200 and 100 B.C.; then name applied to same area, as being the metropolitan territory of the republic of Venice (*q.v.*). It consists of three regions of Italy.

Venezia Tridentina (*Alto Adige*), ceded by Austria (provinces of Trento and Bolzano, formerly part of Tirol), 1918.

Venezia proper, or *Veneto*, Austrian only from 1815 to 1866, Italian since then.

Venezia Giulia, now known as *Friuli-Venezia Guilia*, acquired in 1918, then comprised the provinces of Fiume, Gorizia, Pola, Trieste, and Zara. It was partly occupied by Yugoslav troops in 1945, and by the settlement of 1947 Istria, the Forest of Ternova, and the upper Isonzo valley passed to Yugoslavia (*see* SLOVENIA), reducing the region more or less to the boundaries of medieval Friuli (provinces of Udine and Gorizia), while Trieste (*q.v.*) and its surroundings remain under neutral occupation. The agreement of 5 Oct. 1954, however, restored Trieste to Italy, while its surroundings were assigned to Yugoslavia.

Venezuela. Became independent of Spain as part of the Federal Republic of Gran Colombia, 1811. Separated from Colombia and set up a separate constitution, 1830. Gomez became dictator, 1908. Petroleum production began, 1917. By the constitution of 1929 V. became the United States of V., consisting of a federation of twenty autonomous and equal states. Trade unions first formed in V., 1935. Social insurance authorized, 1940. Income tax first levied, 1942. Law on Hydrocarbons of Mar. 1943 provided for a state royalty on mineral oils equal to half the net profits of the industry. Exports of iron ore (by Bethlehem Steel Corporation) began, Mar. 1951. New constitution of 1953, as modified by the Electoral Law of 1955, changed V.'s name from the 'United States of V.' to the 'Republic of V.'

Venezuelan capital began to enter the country's oil industry, 1956. Four oil company power stations destroyed by left-wing saboteurs, Oct. 1962. Ex-President Perez Jimenez extradited from the U.S.A. to stand trial in V. for embezzlement, Aug. 1963.

Following is a list of heads of the Venezuelan State in the twentieth century. (It should be noted that Juan Vicente Gomez was in fact the ruler of the country from 1915 until his death in 1935; during the time when he was not actually President the office was filled by his nominees.)

Cipriano Castro	1899–1908
Juan Vicente Gomez	1908–1915
Victorino Marquez Bustillos	1915–1922
Juan Vicente Gomez	1922–1929
Juan Baustista Perez	1929–1931
Pedro Itriago Chacin	1931
Juan Vicente Gomez	1931–1935
Eleazar Lopez Contreras	1935–1936
Arminio Borjas (one week only)	1936
Eleazar Lopez Contreras	1936–1941
Isaias Medina Angarita	1941–1945
Romulo Betancourt	1945–1948
Romulo Gallegos (deposed)	1948
Carlos Delgado Chalbaud (assassinated)	1948–1950
G. Suarez Flamerich	1950–1952
Marcos Perez Jimenez	1952–1958
Wolfgang Larrazabal Ugueto	1958
Edgard Sanabira	1958–1959
Romulo Betancourt (again)	1959–

Venice, Italy. Founded *c.* A.D. 452. First Doge Paolo Zucio Anafesto, 697. Beginning naval power under D. Orso Ipato, 726. Venetian navy assists in overthrow of the Lombards, 787. At peace of Aix-la-Chapelle Charlemagne cedes suzerainty of V. to the Byzantines, 810. Seat of government moved from Malamocco to Rialto, 811. St. Mark's bones brought to V., 828. Defeat by Moslems in naval battle of Taranto, 839. Death of D. Pietro Candiano I at battle of Zara, 888. Venetian protectorate of Istria established under D. Pietro Candiano II, 932–9. D. Pietro Orseolo II conquers Dalmatia, 999–1000. 'Blessing of the Sea' first instituted, 1001. Commercial and political treaty with Byzantium concedes practical independence, 1081. Defeat of the Normans at Butrinto, 1085. Venetian fleet under D. Vitale Michiel I deserts the First Crusade, 1100. Capture and settlement of Tyre, 1124. Fourth Crusade diverted by D. Enrico Dandolo against Byzantium, 1204. Genoese defeated at Trapani, 1264. Sequins first coined, 1284. Defeat by Genoese at Curzola, 1297. The

Great Council established, 1297. Council of Ten established, 1310. Ducal palace begun, 1310. The 'Closure' (*Serrata*) of the Great Council, 1315. Complete defeat of Genoa in the War of Chioggia under D. Andrea Contarini, 1378–81. Acquisition of Padua, 1406; Ravenna, 1441. Commercial treaty with Turks, 1453. Loss of Negropont to the Turks, 1470. Turkish victory at Prevésa, 1530. Loss of Cyprus, 1570. Victory over Turks at Lepanto, 1571. Siege and loss of Candia (Crete), 1648–69. Decline of the republic after death of D. Francesco Morosini, 1694. Republic extinguished by Napoleon and ceded to Austria, 1797. Annexed to Italy, 1805. To Austria, 1814. Finally to Italy, 1866. *See also* VENETIA.

The following is a list of doges:

Paolo Zucio Anafesto	697–717
Marcello Tegaliano	717–726
Orso Ipato	726–737
Six masters of soldiers	737–742
Orso Diodato	742–755
Galla Gaulo	755–756
Domenico Monegario	756–765
Maurizio Galbaio	765–787
Giovanni Galbaio	787–804
Obelerio de' Antenori	804–809
Angello Participazio	809–827
Giustiniano Participazio	827–829
Giovanni Participazio I	829–836
Pietro Tradonico	836–864
Orso Participazio I	864–881
Giovanni Participazio II	881–887
Pietro Candiano I	887–888
Pietro Tribuno (Tron)	888–912
Orso Participazio II	912–932
Pietro Candiano II	932–939
Pietro Participazio	939–942
Pietro Candiano III	942–959
Pietro Candiano IV	959–976
Pietro Orseolo I	976–977
Vitale Candiano	977–978
Pietro Memmo	978–991
Pietro Orseolo II	991–1008
Otho Orseolo	1008–1025
Domenico Centranico	1026–1032
Domenico Flabianico	1032–1043
Domenico Contarini I	1043–1071
Domenico Selvo	1071–1084
Vitale Falier	1085–1096
Vitale Michiel I	1096–1102
Ordelafo Falier	1102–1117
Domenico Michiel	1117–1130
Pietro Polani	1130–1148
Domenico Morosini	1148–1156
Vitale Michiel II	1156–1172
Sebastiano Ziani	1173–1178
Orio Malipiero	1178–1192
Enrico Dandolo	1193–1205
Pietro Ziani	1205–1229
Giacomo Tiepolo	1229–1249

Marin Morosini	1249–1252
Renier Zeno	1253–1268
Lorenzo Tiepolo	1268–1275
Jacopo Contarini	1275–1280
Giovanni Dandolo	1280–1289
Pietro Gradenigo	1289–1311
Giorgio Marin	1311–1312
Giovanni Soranzo	1312–1328
Francesco Dandolo	1329–1339
Bartolomeo Gradenigo	1339–1342
Andrea Dandolo	1343–1354
Marino Falier	1354–1355
Giovanni Gradenigo	1355–1356
Giovanni Dolfin	1356–1361
Lorenzo Celsi	1361–1365
Marco Cornaro (Corner)	1365–1368
Andrea Contarini	1368–1382
Michele Morosini	1382
Antonio Venier	1382–1400
Michele Steno	1400–1413
Tomaso Mocenigo	1414–1423
Francesco Foscari	1423–1457
Pasquale Malipiero	1457–1462
Cristoforo Moro	1462–1471
Nicolo Tron	1471–1473
Nicolo Marcello	1473–1474
Pietro Mocenigo	1474–1476
Andrea Vendramin	1476–1478
Giovanni Mocenigo	1478–1485
Marco Barbarigo	1485–1486
Agostino Barbarigo	1486–1501
Leonardo Loredano	1501–1521
Antonio Grimani	1521–1523
Andrea Gritti	1523–1539
Pietro Lando	1539–1545
Francesco Donato	1545–1553
Marc'antonio Trevisano	1553–1554
Francesco Venier	1554–1556
Lorenzo Priuli	1556–1559
Girolamo Priuli	1559–1567
Pietro Loredano	1567–1570
Alvise Mocenigo I	1570–1577
Sebastiano Venier	1577–1578
Nicolo da Ponte	1578–1585
Pasquale Cicogna	1585–1595
Marin Grimani	1595–1606
Leonardo Donato	1606–1612
Marc'antonio Memmo	1612–1615
Giovanni Bembo	1615–1618
Nicolo Donato	1618
Antonio Priuli	1618–1623
Francesco Contarini	1623–1624
Giovanni Cornaro (Corner) I	1624–1630
Nicolo Contarini	1630–1631
Francesco Erizzo	1631–1646
Francesco Molin	1646–1655
Carlo Contarini	1655–1656
Francesco Cornaro	1656
Bertuccio Valier	1656–1658
Giovanni Pesaro	1658–1659
Domenico Contarini II	1659–1674
Nicolo Sagredo	1674–1676
Luigi Contarini	1676–1683
Marc'antonio Giustinian	1683–1688
Francesco Morosini	1688–1694

Silvestro Valier	1694–1700
Alvise Mocenigo II	1700–1709
Giovanni Cornaro II	1709–1722
Alvise (Sebastiano) Mocenigo III	1722–1732
Carlo Ruzzini	1732–1735
Luigi Pisani	1735–1741
Pietro Grimani	1741–1752
Francesco Loredano	1752–1762
Marco Foscarini	1762–1763
Alvise Mocenigo IV	1863–1779
Paolo Renier	1779–1789
Ludovico Manin	1789–1797

Venus. The American spaceship *Mariner II* sent back radio information about V., 14 Dec. 1962, before going into orbit round the sun.

Verden. *See* BREMEN (3).

Vermont, first settled by French under Samuel Champlain, 1609. English and Dutch infiltration began with the eighteenth century, and a British fort was built at Battlebro in 1724. Intensive settlement began after the cession of Canada, 1760. Between then and the revolution the territory was disputed between the states of New York and New Hampshire, and the local partisans of New Hampshire ('Green Mountain Boys') captured Ticonderoga from the British, marched into Canada, and threatened Montreal, 1775. Independence declared, 1777; but state not admitted to Union (14th) until 1791.

Verner's Law. Phonetic law propounded, 1875, by the Danish philologist, Karl Adolf Verner (1846–96).

Verona became an independent republic, 1107. Mastino and Cangrande Scaliger, Lords of V., entertained the exiled Dante, 1291–1329. Added to Milanese territory under Galleazzo Visconti, 1387; but passed to Venice, 1405. Ceded to Austria, 1797; part of Italy since 1866. The last of the Scaligers, Brunoro della Scala, *d.* at Vienna, 1434. *See also* VENICE.

Versailles. A town in NW. France near Paris; here Louis XIII built a hunting-box on the site of which Louis XIV erected a palace, 1661–87; First Treaty of V., 1783; surrendered to Germans, 1870. *See end of* WORLD WAR I for Second Treaty.

Verulamium, near St. Albans, Herts., was the tribal capital of the Catuvellauni, established about A.D. 1. Roman *municipium c.* A.D. 45. Boudicca (Boadicea) sacked V. in the Icenian rising, 61, but it continued to develop until about 200. St. Alban martyred near, 303. St. Germanus found it still inhabited in 429. The theatre was excavated in 1847; parts of the forum in 1898. In 1930 a comprehensive excavation scheme was begun,

which has made it possible to trace the complete plan of the Roman town. There have been further excavations, 1947–63.

Vesuvius. Volcano on the Bay of Naples. An eruption in A.D. 79 totally destroyed Pompeii and Herculaneum (*q.v.*). Last considerable eruption, 1944.

Viborg. *See* VYBORG.

Vice-Chancellor. The first judicial V.-C., Sir Thomas Plumer (1753–1824), appointed, 1813; two additional V.-Cs. appointed, 1841; they became judges of the High Court of Justice, 1873. The last V.-C. was Sir James Bacon (1798–1895), appointed, 1870; retired, 1886.

Vichy, France, celebrated for its mineral waters. Known to the Romans, but did not become famous till the seventeenth century. French puppet Government established here after capitulation of France, 1 July 1940, and the word V. became synonymous with 'collaborator.'

Victoria became a colony separate from New S. Wales, 1851. Following on the reports of Capt. Cook, who did not, however, land there, a party of convicts was sent out in 1785, to the site of Port Jackson. First permanent settlement by Edward Henty at Portland Bay, 19 Nov. 1834. Melbourne founded, 1835. Civil Government established, 1839. Colonial constitution proclaimed, 23 Nov. 1855.

Victoria, British Columbia, founded, 1843, by Hudson's Bay Co., and called Fort Camosun. Named Victoria, and made capital of Vancouver Island colony. 1849. Ceased to be capital when Vancouver Island was united with British Columbia, 1866; but capital status restored, 1868.

Victoria and Albert Museum. Originated as the Museum of Ornamental Art, 1852; merged in the S. Kensington Museum, 1857. Foundation stone of present building laid in 1899 by Queen Victoria; opened in 1909 by King Edward and Queen Alexandra.

Victoria Cross. For bravery in the forces, instituted, 1856. The cross was manufactured out of the cannon taken from the Russians at Sevastopol, until the supply ran out in 1942. The colour of the ribbons, originally blue for the Navy and red for the Army, was changed to crimson for all services in 1918. Royal warrant of 1920 extends eligibility to women and to civilians when serving under naval, military, or air authorities.

Victoria Falls (on the Zambesi, Africa). Discovered by Livingstone in 1855; spanned by a bridge of the Cape to Cairo railway, 1905. Hydro-electric station, 1938.

Victoria Falls Conference. 28 June– 4 July 1963, held to wind up the Federation of Rhodesia and Nyasaland (*q.v.*). It was agreed that the Federation should be dissolved by the end of 1963.

Victoria, Lake, Africa. Discovered by Speke, 1858; Messrs. Wilson and Smith first voyaged across the lake, 1877; divided between England and Germany, 1890. Germans driven from it, 1916.

Victory, H.M.S., was launched at Chatham, 7 May 1765; commissioned, 1778. Flagship of Howe, 1782; Hood, 1793; and Nelson, 1797–1805. Paid off from active service, 1812. Became flagship of C.-in-C., Portsmouth, 1825; permanently placed in dry dock, 1922, and restored throughout and re-rigged. Accommodation ship for A.A. gunners, 1939–45.

Vienna (Wien) was already an inhabited site when the Romans laid out the permanent camp of Vindobona, A.D. 180. Name appears in something like its modern form in documents of 881. The Babenberg margraves of Austria chose V. for their seat, 1142, and granted charters, 1221. Became an imperial free city, 1237. Capital of Hapsburgs, 1278. University founded, 1365. Under the federal constitution of the first Austrian republic, 1918. V. counted as a province on the same footing as other federal provinces: so under the federal republic of 1945 also.

Vienna, Congress of. Opened, 1 Nov. 1814. Closed, 8 June 1815. Representatives of all the powers of Europe, led by Britain, Austria, Prussia, Russia, and France, met to settle the internal frontiers, etc., of Europe after the Napoleonic Wars. By it Poland was placed under Russian suzerainty. N. Italy was largely restored to Austria, Prussia received the Rhineland and part of Saxony, and Hanover, E. Frisia and Hildesheim. The German confederacy was organized under Austrian presidency, and Cracow made an independent republic.

Vienne, Council of, 1311–12. Decided the abolition of the Templars (*q.v.*).

Viet Nam, at first under Japanese protection, intermittently at war with France from 1945 to 1949 when by the unification of the provinces of Tongking, Annam, and Cochin China, V. N. became an integral part of the French Union. Convention signed between France and the Emperor Bao Dai, Dec. 1949. France transferred all sovereign rights to V. N., Dec. 1954, but retained military authority there until 1956. The civil war between Communists and anti-Communists had in effect split V. N. into N. and S. zones ever since 1946, the French influence extending only over the S. zone. During 1951–3 the Communists in the N.

made gains at the expense of the S. The Geneva Agreement of 20 July 1954 brought about a cessation of official hostilities between N. and S., and stipulated that general elections should take place over the whole area in 1956. These did not take place, and the country remains (1963) divided into two separate states.

N. Viet Nam, led by the veteran Communist Ho Chi Minh, is governed by the 'Constitution of the Democratic Republic of V. N.' of 1 Jan. 1960, on lines similar to the Chinese Republic.

S. Viet Nam became a republic in Oct. 1955, after the deposition of Bao Dai, with Ngo Dinh Diem as President. There was an unsuccessful attempt to assassinate Ngo Dinh Diem in Feb. 1962. Buddhist riots and suicides in 1963, due to Buddhist allegations of religious discrimination by the governing Catholic minority, caused serious unrest in the country.

Vigilance Committee. A self-appointed body to maintain public order in San Francisco (U.S.A.), 1851.

Viipuri. *See* VYBORG.

Viking Age proper extended from the eighth to the eleventh centuries. But excursions of Scandinavian pirates, though less frequent, did occur earlier. Thus a seaborne raid of the Gautar (Geatas) under their King Hugleikr (Chocilaicus or Hygelac) was made on Frisia about A.D. 530. Irish sources describe Scandinavian raids on the Hebrides and coast of Donegal in the seventh century. Danes began intermittent land warfare with the Franks after giving asylum to Wittekind of Saxony, 777. Three ships from Hordaland in Norway raided Dorset about 790; Lindisfarne sacked, 793; Jarrow sacked, 794; Norwegians in Skye, 795; Man, 798; Iona, 802; and Sligo, 807; Armagh sacked, 832. Turgeis (Thorgest) made himself King of Ulster, 841; but drowned by Irish, 844.

Danish attacks on England began, 833; on Ireland, 849; on Holland, 833; on Seine valley, 841; on Spain, Portugal, Morocco, 844; Paris besieged, and Hamburg sacked, 845. Danes under Björn and Hasteinn first entered Mediterranean from the W., 860, and ravaged Provence, the Balearics, Liguria, parts of Tuscany and Morocco until 862. Danish penetration of Frisia and Rhineland stopped by King Lothair II (855–69). Raids in Flanders, 882–5. Paris besieged again, 885–6, but Danes defeated at Verdun in June, and by Duke Alan in Brittany, 888. Evacuated to Kent, 892. Returned, 902, reinforced by Norwegians under Rollo (Hrolfr), who did homage for the fief of

Normandy at Clair Sur-Epte, 911. Cork settled (by Danes) about 900.

Campaigns in England by the sons of Ragnar, 855–6 (mainly in Kent), by Guthrum (Guttorm), 866–78. King Edmund martyred, 870; truce in 876. Treaty of Wedmore, 878, gave most of Northumbria and Mercia to Danes. English recover London and W. Essex, 886. Campaign by Hasteinn's army (see above), 892–7; the army beaten by Alfred and disbanded. The Danelaw reconquered, 914–20. Svein Forkbeard, allied to Olaf Tryggvason (see NORWAY), attacks Ethelred, 994–1014; Svein's son Knut succeeds to English crown, 1016. See DANEGELD and SHIP-MONEY.

Norwegian: the court of the Norse king of Dublin described by an embassy sent by Abd-er-Rahman II, Emir of Cordova (d. 852). Norse settlements in Ireland plundered by Danes, 851. Olaf the White arrived in Ireland, 853; became joint King of Dublin; went back to Norway, 873. Dublin captured by the Irish, 902, and Vs. expelled, but returned, 914, to capture Waterford and (916) Dublin. Norwegians kill the High King Niall Glundubh at Kilmashogue, 919. Norse-Welsh-Scottish confederacy beaten at Brunanburh (in Galloway?), 938. Irish resistance stiffens about 940 under King Muirchertach of Ailech, and in 980 the High King Maelsechlainn II defeated the Dublin and Hebridean Norsemen at Tara. Brian Boru beats Ivar of Limerick at Sulcoit (968) and becomes King of Munster, 976, and High King, 1002. He captured Dublin, 1000, but returned it to his son-in-law, Sigtrygg Silkbeard, whom he defeated again, together with a Norse coalition, including Earl Sigurd of Orkney, at Clontarf on Good Friday, 1014. The Ostmen now ceased to be a major political power in Ireland, but retained their separate identity down to the Norman conquest of 1175.

Punitive expedition by King Harald Fairhair of Norway, following on his victory at Stiklestad (872), established his suzerainty over the W. coast of Scotland, Man (?), the Hebrides, and all N. Atlantic islands except Iceland, 873. Earl Sigurd of Orkney and Thorsteinn the Red conquer Scotland as far S. as Strath Oykel, 874. Sigurd the Thick (d. 1014) conquered Scotland as far S. as Strath Spey—Moor of Rannoch—Strath Fillan—Loch Long. The last Norse earl of Orkney d. 1231, but Scottish earls continued to do homage to the King of Norway (see LORD OF THE ISLES). Norwegian King Magnus Barelegs (i.e. 'The Kilted') was half Scottish, and ruled Norway, 1093–1103. Subsequent kings down to 1167 all had

Scottish blood or other connection with W. Scotland, especially Harald Gille (*fl.* 1130–6). Hebridean sovereignty renounced by King Magnus Hakonarson of Norway, 1266, as result of battle of Largs, 1263, which date is usually taken as end of V. A.

Swedish expansion, exclusively eastwards across the Baltic, is first recorded in 853 (attempt to reconquer Kurland from Danes, whose king, Gorm the Old, 900–40, made wide conquests in Pomerania). Danish base at Jomsborg set up by Harald Bluetooth (936–86) was destroyed, 1043, by the Norse King Magnus the Good. Russian chronicles first mention Swedish raiders in 859. Expelled in 862, they returned to Russia (to which they gave their name) at the invitation of certain Slav clans in the same year, when Rurik became prince of Novgorod. In 865 Rurik absorbed two other principalities, and Hoskuld and Dir founded Kiev, which was conquered by Oleg (Helgi) of Novgorod, 882. Commercial treaties with Byzantium, 911 and 944. Swedish-Russian habits described in detail by the Arab diplomat Ibn Fadhlan, 921. 'Varangians' mentioned for the last time in Russian chronicles, 1043, by which time (reign of Yaroslav of Kiev, 1036–54) the Scandinavian ruling class had become Slavonic in language and Greek Orthodox in religion. *See also* MAN, ISLE OF; HEBRIDES; ORKNEY ISLANDS; SHETLAND ISLANDS; FAROE; ICELAND; NORWAY; DENMARK; SWEDEN; IRELAND; NORMANDY; EAST ANGLIA; MERCIA; NORTHUMBRIA, KINGDOM OF; VARANGIAN GUARD.

Villefranche-de-Rouergue, France, was founded, 1252; fell into the hands of the Black Prince, 1348.

Vilna or **Vilnius** (Pol. **Wilno**), probably founded in the tenth century, became capital of the Grand Duchy of Lithuania c. 1323. Partially destroyed by the Teutonic Knights, 1377. Became an episcopal see, 1387 (when the Catholic cathedral of St. Stanislaus was begun); after Lithuanian union with Poland, under Casimir IV, 1427–92, V. became a centre of Polish culture. In the Third Partition of Poland (1795) V. and its province fell to the Russian share. Occupied by German troops, 1915–Dec. 1918, during which time (Feb. 1918) the independence of Lithuania was proclaimed, with V. as capital. 'Curzon Line' laid down as provisional boundary between Poland and Lithuania, 8 Dec. 1919, assigned V. to Lithuania. Handed over to Lithuanians in accordance with peace treaty of 12 July 1920 by Soviet Government, 28 Aug. 1920. Poland renounced V. by Treaty of Suwalki, 7 Oct. 1920, but Polish partisans immediately occupied the city. Dispute submitted to League of Nations without result. V. assigned to Poland by Entente council of ambassadors, 15 Mar. 1923. On collapse of Poland in 1939, the U.S.S.R. implemented the treaty of July 1920 (*see* above) by handing V. to the republic of Lithuania. Russian since 1940, except for German occupation, 1941–5.

Vimy Ridge Memorial to Canadian soldiers killed storming the ridge, 9–10 Apr. 1917; unveiled by King Edward VIII, 1936.

'Vindictive.' British cruiser which figured in Sir Roger Keyes's attack on Zeebrugge mole, 23 Apr., and was sunk in the blocking attack on Ostend, 9–10 May 1918.

Virginia, U.S.A. The first permanent English settlement in N. America, 1607, by members of the London Co., led by John Smith. Negroes first imported, 1619. Indian raids, 1622, 1644, 1676. Became a crown colony, 1624. Though royalist in sympathy, V. surrendered to the Cromwellian fleet and accepted Cromwell's governor Bennett, 1652. Williamsburg became the state capital, 1699. Seceded from the Union, 1861, whereupon Federal sympathisers set up the separate state of W. V. (*q.v.*). From 1867 until its readmission to the Union in 1870, V., as 'military district No. 1,' was governed by a Federal general. Constitutions were drawn up in 1776, 1830, 1851, 1864, 1869, 1902, but all retained some features derived from the rights of 'burgesses' laid down in the era of the London Co.

Virgin Islands, W. Indies. Discovered by Columbus, 1493. Some probably included in Charles I's grant of the Caribbean Islands to Earl of Carlisle, 2 July 1627. First settlement, Dutch buccaneers, in Tortola, 1648; ousted by British, 1672; Denmark made first permanent settlement (in St. Croix, St. Thomas, and St. John), 1672. Spain had Culebra, Culebrita, and Vieques. British islands given a representative assembly, 1774; in 1871 they surrendered the right to legislate on certain subjects to a federal legislature of the Leeward Islands. The Spanish islands passed to U.S.A., 1898. Danish islands bought by U.S.A., 1917.

Visigoths, the western group of the tribes collectively known as Goths (*q.v.*), separated from the eastern or Ostrogothic branch *c.* A.D. 376, when most of the V. followed their king Frithigern across the Danube into Moesia, at first with the consent of the Imperial Government; but soon a dispute led to war and the defeat of the Roman forces under Valens, who was killed at the battle of Adrianople,

378. By a treaty of 381 the V. entered the Roman service as *foederati*, and their king Athanaric was received with honour at Constantinople in that year. On the death of the Emperor Theodosius, 395, the V. elected Alaric (*d.* 410) king, and turned against the Empire: under his leadership the entire nation wandered across the Balkan and Italian peninsulas, fighting and plundering; after the death of the Roman (born Vandal) Gen. Stilicho, there was none to withstand them, and they besieged Rome itself in 408, 409, and 410; the last time they sacked the city. Alaric was succeeded by Ataulfus, who married the Emperor Honorius's sister, Placidia, and led the V. into SW. Gaul and to Spain, where he was murdered in 415. His successor, Wallia, set up a Visigoth kingdom, centring upon Toulouse. At the battle of Chalons, 451 (*see* OSTROGOTHS), Theodoric I, king of the V., was killed leading them against the Huns and their Germanic vassal tribes. Under Euric (466–85) the centre of gravity of the Visigoth state shifted to Spain. Though now much romanized the V. adhered to the Arian heresy (*see* ARIANISM), and in 507, under Alaric II, were defeated by the more barbarous but Catholic Franks, but protected by the Ostrogothic (*q.v.*) King Theodoric; they did not become a separate kingdom again until he *d.* in 526. The most successful Visigoth kings in Spain were Leovogild (568–86) and his son Recared (586–601), the latter of whom by becoming Catholic reconciled the Roman interests with his own, though at the cost of abandoning the Gothic language (*q.v.*), which had been used in the Arian liturgy and into which the Bible had been rendered. Now Isidore, the Catholic bishop of Seville, a 'Roman' by birth, was to be the historian of the V. down to 631. A code of Visigoth laws, issued *c.* 654 under Recceswinth, survives. The Visigoth kingdom finally perished at the hands of the Moslem emirs, 711.

Vitoria. Capital of Alava, Spain. Founded, 581, by Leovogild, King of the Visigoths. A decisive victory, which freed Spain from France, was fought here during the Peninsular War, 1813.

Vlachs, name applied to the Latin-speaking Provincials of Dacia (*q.v.*); the bulk of them withdrew southwards over the Danube, A.D. 270, and in the sixth and seventh centuries inhabited Macedonia, Thrace, and parts of Epirus. Continually displaced by Avars, Magyars, and Slavs they became pastoral nomads, and are mentioned as such by Byzantine sources in 976. They set up an independent empire which reoccupied part of

Dacia, and came to an end, 1257. Another branch inhabited Thessaly about 1050, and were conquered by the Turks, 1393. About 1150 there was a Vlach colony in Dalmatia, and another in Montenegro, elements of which wandered as far as Istria (where some survive) in the fifteenth century. *See* RUMANIA and BESSARABIA.

Vladivostok. Founded as a Russian port, 1860. Town since 1875.

Vlöne, Albania (It. **Valona**; Gr. **Avlona**; anciently **Aulon**). Occupied by Robert Guiscard the Norman, A.D. 1080. Retaken by Byzantines, 1085. Passed by marriage to kingdom of Sicily, 1295; thereafter alternately under Serbian rule or that of local despots, subject to Venice. Turkish, 1691–1912. Temporary capital of Albania, 1913. Occupied by Italians, 28 Dec. 1915 and 7 Apr. 1939. Reverted to Albania, 1945.

Volga German Republic, U.S.S.R. *See* GERMAN VOLGA REPUBLIC.

Volkssturm, German home defence force raised at the instance of Heinrich Himmler (1900–45) in his capacity as C.-in-C. Home Forces and Reinforcements, 18 Oct. 1944. Its local commanders were mostly drawn from local National Socialist (*q.v.*) party leaders, especially the Hitler Youth (*q.v.*), and instruction given by the S.A. (*q.v.*). It first came into action in the W. as soon as it was formed, and in the E. (E. Prussia) about new year, 1945.

Volgograd. *See* STALINGRAD.

Volsci. The greatest enemies of Rome during the first century of the Roman Republic; they lived in S. Latium. They were subdued by Rome, 338 B.C., and enjoyed Roman citizenship by 304.

Voltaic Pile. Invented by Volta *c.* 1793.

Volturno, Italy. The colony of Volturnum was founded here, 194 B.C., by the Romans. In 1860 the Neapolitans were defeated at the V. River by Garibaldi's army, and as a result Capua fell. German defensive position on V. forced by Anglo-American Fifth Army, Oct. 1943.

Volunteers (English). Honourable Artillery Co. granted charter by Henry VIII in 1537; V. organized on a larger scale, 1757; English and Scottish V. were disbanded, 1783, but raised again, 1794; National Volunteer force established, 1860; in 1900 V. supplied many service companies for the S. African War;

converted into the Territorial force, 1908. For Local Defence V. *see* HOME GUARD.

Voortrekkers. The Great Trek of Afrikaners out of Cape Colony began in 1836. Columns under Pieter Uys and Hendrik Potgieter defeated the Matabele king, Moselekatze, 1837. Zulus decisively defeated by Andries Pretorius at Blood River, 16 Dec. 1838. Republic of Natal proclaimed, 1840; the whole country N. to the Limpopo open to European settlement by *c.* 1848. Monument to the V. at Voortrekkerhoogte, near Pretoria, dedicated, 1949.

Vorarlberg, province of Austria, acquired piecemeal by Hapsburgs, 1375–1765, finally consolidated by Maria Theresa. Josef II amalgamated it with Tirol (*q.v.*), 1782. Ceded to Bavaria, 1805, but retroceded, 1814.

Voronezh, U.S.S.R. Founded in 1586 to rebuff Tatars, but burned by them, 1590; here Peter the Great built boats for conquest of Azov; three times almost destroyed by fire: 1703, 1748, 1773. Heavily damaged during fighting in World War II, 1942–3.

Votes. *See* FRANCHISE.

Vryheid, town and county in Natal, were ceded to a group of Boers (Lukas Beyer and others) by the Zulus, 1884, and formed an independent republic until 1888. *See* ZULULAND.

Vulgate. Latin version of the Bible prepared by St. Jerome during the last quarter of the fourth century. First printed *c.* 1455; first dated edition, 1462; critical edition issued by order of Sixtus V, 1590; superseded by that of Clement VIII, 1592; translated by Wycliffe and his followers, 1356–84. Authorized Catholic translations into English: New Testament, Rheims, 1582; Old Testament, Douai, 1609–10; by R. A. Knox, New Testament, 1943; Old Testament, 1948–9. Revision of the V. by order of Pius X, begun in Rome, May 1907, is still incomplete.

Vyborg (Rus.), **Viborg** (Swed.), **Viipuri** (Fin.), grew up round a Swedish castle built by Torgils Knutsson, 1293. Became Russian, 1710, and Finnish, 1917. Ceded to Russia, 31 Mar. 1940; recaptured by Finns in the autumn of 1941; retaken by Russians, 21 June 1944; became the capital of the Karelo-Finnish S.S.R. (*q.v.*) under the Russo-Finnish Armistice, 19 Sept. 1944. Transferred in 1946 to the Russian S.F.S.R.

W

'Wacht am Rhein, Die.' Words written, 1840, by Max Schneckenburger (1819–1849); musical setting composed, 1854, by Carl Wilhelm (1815–75).

Wadai. Once a powerful native state in the Sudan. Kingdom founded, 1635. It conquered Runga, the eastern half of Kanem, and also Borku, soon after 1860. Explored by Nachtigal, 1873; notorious as a slave-raiding state; came under French influence, 1899; annexed by France, 1909. Part of Chad Republic since 1960.

Wadi Halfa, Sudan. The British base in 1884 in the operations for the relief of Gen. Gordon.

Wager of Battle. *See* COMBAT, TRIAL BY.

Wages. First fixed by Act of Parliament, 1350. Act prohibiting payment of miners' wages in public houses, 1872; extended to wages generally, 1883. Wages payable by cheque from 31 Mar. 1963. *See* TRUCK ACT.

Wahabis. A Mohammedan Puritan sect founded by Mohammed ibn Abd al Wahhab (1703–87), son of a shepherd in Central Arabia. He converted Mohammed ibn Sa'ud, ruler of Derayeh, who married his daughter, and *d.* 1765: the Wahabi dynasty began with that daughter's son, Abd al Aziz, who with the sword spread Wahabi doctrines throughout Arabia. After seizing Mecca and Medina, Abd al Aziz was assassinated, 1803. His son, Sa'ud (*d.* 1814), and Sa'ud's son, Abd al 'lah, carried on the war; but the latter was defeated and executed at Constantinople, 19 Dec. 1818. Wahabi rule established in eastern Arabia, with Riyāz as capital, by Faizul, 1830. Wahabi Army in India was crushed at Balakot, 1831. The remnants retired to Mahában on NW. Frontier, whither punitive expeditions were sent against them in 1853 and 1858; Indian W. finally defeated at Ambéla Pass, 15 Dec. 1863.

Wailing Wall, Jerusalem. Outbreak between Jews and Moslems, Aug. 1929.

Waits. A wait was a city watchman, who sounded his pipe or trumpet during the night. As early as thirteeenth century a small band of wind-musicians maintained by a city was called W. By eighteenth century the name was applied to those that went round at Christmas time playing and singing carols.

Walcheren Island, Holland. British expedition under the second Earl of Chatham and Sir R. Strachan after capturing Flushing, 1809, came to a disastrous end through inactivity and disease, and was withdrawn. Flooded and severely damaged in the course of allied reconquest, Nov. 1944. Monument to British Commandos unveiled, June 1952. Dikes burst again, Jan.–Feb. 1953.

Waldeck, a German county of the twelfth century, was united with Pyrmont, 1621, and became a principality, 1712; joined the Germanic League, 1815. From 1919 to 1928 W. was a separate province of the Weimar republic, but was absorbed by Prussia, 1929.

Waldenses or **Vaudois.** A sect once claiming to have been established in the reign of Constantine (306–37), but founded, 1176, at Lyons by Peter Waldo. Their doctrine prohibited by the Lateran Council, 1179; and W. included in an excommunicating Bull by Lucius III, 1184. Majority driven from France at time of the persecution of the Albigenses (*q.v.*), 1209, they took refuge in Piedmont, where their persecution began, 1220. Again excommunicated, 1231. Many went to Calabria in fourteenth and fifteenth centuries. About 1532 they joined the Reformation. Those left in France again persecuted, 1545–55. Those in Piedmont attacked, 1655, when Cromwell obtained some respite for them. Persecutions recommenced, 1685, on revocation of Edict of Nantes. Many went to Switzerland from Piedmont. In 1689 they tried to recover their Piedmont valleys. Received permission to return, 1694; again exiled, 1698–?1740. They had liberty of conscience, 1799–1814. Civil and religious liberty accorded, 1848, in kingdom of Sardinia.

Waldstätte. 'Forest Cantons' Uri, Schwyz, and Unterwalden united in Perpetual League, 1291, to form the nucleus of Switzerland.

Wales. Occupied at the time of the Roman invasion, 55 B.C., by five tribes, the Gangani and Decangi, the Ordovices, the Demetae, and the Silures; Caractacus defeated by the Romans, A.D. 43, taken prisoner to Rome, 50; conquest of Silures and Ordovices by Julius Frontinus and Agricola, 78; Welsh became Christian *c.* 300, and maintained this faith when the rest of the island was repaganized; withdrawal of Romans, early fifth century; warfare with the Saxons: battle of Deorham, 577; with the Angles: battle of

Chester c. 613; battle of Hatfield and death of Edwin, King of the Angles, 633; Cadwallon slain soon after in battle; continued dissension among the Welsh princes; the N. Welsh king Rhodri the Great (844–78) defeats the Danes; peaceful reign of Hywel the Good, who drew up a code of laws, tenth century; Gruffydd ap Llewelyn became king of Gwynedd, 1039, and killed (1044) Howel ap Edwin; defeated Gruffydd ap Rhydderch and became king of all W., 1055, and was finally crushed and slain by Harold and Tostig, 1063; gradual conquest of country by William the Conqueror and his sons; expedition into under Henry I, 1121; general uprising under Ap Rhys, 1135, and victory over English at Cardigan, 1136; N. and S. divided between his sons and those of Ap Cynan; expedition into of Henry II, 1157, and peace concluded with princes of the N. and S.; later unsuccessful raid, 1169; peace made with Rhys ap Gruffydd, the ruling lord of S. W.; Llewelyn ap Iorwerth became powerful in the N. and married King John's bastard daughter Joan, 1206; joined the revolting barons, became Prince of All W., d. 1240; disputes between various claimants to the kingship, among them Prince Edward, Henry III's son; victory of Llewelyn ap Gruffydd over English at Dynevor, 1255; peace concluded with Henry, 1267, and Llewelyn declared Prince of W.; Llewelyn refused homage to Edward I; invasion by the English king, and Llewelyn starved into submission, 1277; oppression of natives by English officers, and fresh rising under Llewelyn and Dafydd; English put to flight at the Menai Straits, and Llewelyn finally slain near Builth, 1282; completion of conquest by Edward I, 1283; Statute of Rhuddlan enacted, 1284; Owain Glyndwr's rebellion, 1400–15; Richmond (Henry VII) landed in Pembroke, 1485; Council of W. under Bishop Rowland Lee, 1534; W. incorporated into England, Act of 1535; Monmouthshire detached, 1536; great sessions established, 1542: Welsh Bible translated, 1567–88; Council abolished, 1689; circulating schools, 1730; Intermediate Education Act, 1889; Welsh Land Commission, 1893–4; investiture of Prince of W. at Carnarvon Castle, 1911; Welsh National Library begun, 1911; Secretary of State for Home Affairs became also Secretary for Welsh Affairs, 1951. Cardiff made capital of W., Dec. 1955. Royal Commission suggested radical county boundary changes in W., Mar. 1963, which, if carried out, would reduce the number of counties to seven. *See* CARNARVON and WELSH LITERATURE.

Wales, Calvinistic Methodist Church of,

arose c. 1735. Its connection with English Methodism ceased before 1750.

Wales, Church in. There being no separate Welsh administration, either religious or secular, under the Tudors, its origin has the same date as the Church of England (*q.v.*). Bills for the Disestablishment of the (Anglican) Church in Wales were introduced in 1895 and 1909; a third Act, passed in 1914, did not become operative until 31 Mar. 1920. As a result of this the Welsh dioceses were increased to six by the creation of the sees of Monmouth and Swansea and Brecon in 1921 and 1923. *See also* CATHEDRALS, CHURCH IN WALES.

Wales, Princes of:

Welsh Princes only:

Maelgwn Gwynedd	?–550
Rhun ap Maelgwn	547–584
Cadvan	584–617
Cadwaladr ap Cadwallon	617–634
Idwal ap Cadwaladr	634–661
Rhodri Molwynog	661–728
Cynan and Hywel	728–755
Mervyn Frych	825–844
Rhodri the Great	844–877
Anarawd, Cadell, and Mervyn	877–943
Idwal Foel	915–943
Hywel Dda, the Good	909–950
Ieuan and Iago	948–979
Hywel ap Ieuaf	979–984
Cadwallon II	984–986
Meredith ap Owen	986–999
Idwal (II) ap Meyric ap Idwal Foel	992–997
Aedan (*usurper*)	998
Llewelyn ap Seisyll	1018–1023
Gruffydd ap Llewelyn ap Seisull	1039–1063
Bleddyn, Rhiwallon, Meredith ap Owain	1067–1073
Trahaiarn ap Caradoc ⎫ Meilir ⎬ Caradoc ⎭	1073–1079
Gruffydd ap Cynan ⎫ Rhys ap Tewdwr ⎪ Cadwgan ap Bleddyn ⎬ Iorwerth ab Bleddyn ⎭	1079–1137
Owain Gwynedd	1137–1169
Howel ab Owain Gwynedd ⎫ Daffydd ap Owain Gwynedd ⎬	1169–1194
Llewelyn (II) ap Iorwerth, the Great	1194–1240
Dafydd ap Llewelyn	1240–1246
Llewelyn (III) ap Gruffydd ('Llewelyn y Llyw Olaf')	1246–1282

From 1301 the Prince of Wales has always been the eldest son of the English sovereign.

Wales, University of. Received full charter, 1893; the university consisted of three colleges: Aberystwyth, 1872; Cardiff, 1883; and Bangor, 1884. To these have been added: Swansea, 1920; Welsh National School of Medicine (Cardiff), 1931.

Wallace Collection (London). Opened, 1900; consists of art treasures collected by the 3rd and 4th Marquesses of Hertford.

Wallachia. *See* RUMANIA and VLACHS.

Walsingham. The shrine of Our Lady of W., much resorted to by pilgrims in the Middle Ages, was built in 1061.

Waltham Abbey, Waltham Cross. The Church of the Holy Cross, founded 1061 by Harold Godwinsson, became an abbey in 1184.

Wampum. Shell money of N. American Indians, its value depending on colour; used by whites as well as Indians, and current in Connecticut in 1704.

War Crimes Commission, United Nations, established, Oct. 1943. International Military Tribunal established, Aug. 1945.

Warsaw (Pol. **Warszawa**). The date of its foundation is unknown, but a castle was erected there as early as the ninth century; not mentioned in writings before 1224; passed through many stirring periods, becoming capital of Poland, 1595; being taken by Sweden, 1655; retaken by Poles, 1656; taken again by Sweden, 1702; by Russians, 1764; and in 1806 was occupied by Napoleon's troops; taken finally by Russia, 1813; an insurrection in favour of independence took place, 1863; further insurrection, 1905–6. Surrendered, after siege, to Germany, 27 Sept. 1939. Polish rising against Germans, 1 Aug. 1944. Crushed after the Russians had refused assistance, 2 Oct. 1944. Russians entered Warsaw, 11 Jan. 1945.

Warsaw Pact. Signed between U.S.S.R. and the E. bloc countries, as a twenty-year treaty of friendship and collaboration, in Warsaw, on 14 May 1955. It represented the Soviet answer to the North Atlantic Treaty (*q.v.*).

Wartburg. A castle in Thuringia, built by Landgrave Louis *c.* 1070. A poem written about 1280 describes the 'Tourney of Grief' which, however, did not really take place. W. was seat of landgraves until 1460. Luther was brought here for safety in 1521, and here he completed his translation of the New Testament. Fabric, greatly restored in the nineteenth century, became property of W. Trust, 1921.

Washington, originally part of the Oregon territory (*q.v.* for earlier history), was ceded to the U.S.A. by Great Britain, 1846. Made a territory, 1853, and admitted to the Union, 1889.

Washington, D.C., U.S.A. Made capital of the U.S.A. by an Act of Congress, 1790. The American Government removed here in 1800. In 1814 the town

was taken by the British, and the Capitol and President's house burned. A centre of operations during the civil war. Coextensive with the District of Columbia (*q.v.*), 1895.

Washington Conference, The, on naval armaments, opened Nov. 1921; on 1 Feb. 1922, treaties for limitation of naval armaments and for prohibiting submarine attacks on merchant vessels received the assent of U.S.A., Britain, France, Italy, and Japan.

Washington, Treaties of, 1846, settled the boundary question between U.S.A. and British America; 1854, a trade and fishery treaty with Canada; 1871, with Britain for the settlement of all causes of difference; 1922, *see* preceding article.

Watches. Invented in Germany *c.* fifteenth century, when they were known as 'Nürnberg Eggs.' The greatest advance was the invention of the dead-beat escapement by T. Tompion (1639–1713), an Englishman.

Waterford, Ireland, founded by Danes or 'Ostmen' (*see* VIKING AGE), was taken from them by the Norman, Strongbow, 1170. King John gave it a charter, 1205.

Waterloo Bridge (London). Originally built by Rennie, 1811–17. Subsidence of one pier, 1923. L.C.C. propose reconstruction, 1925. Rebuilding scheme rejected by Parliament, 1932. L.C.C. persist, and begin work, 1934. Contract placed, 1937. Bridge formally opened, 1944.

Wazzan, N. Morocco. Celebrated for manufacture of coarse woollen cloth and as burial-place of the Moorish saint, Idrisi Sharif, who lived there, 1727.

Weather Forecasts, first regularly issued by the Admiralty, 1860.

Weather Ships, first permanently stationed in the Atlantic, 1947.

Weaving. First practised in China; during the tenth century the Flemings were important wool weavers, and during the fourteenth century England supplied them with most of the raw material; the first mention of W. in England is at York, 1331; early English centres of the industry were Canterbury, Colchester, and Norwich.

Wedgwood China. Josiah W. (1730–1795) first established his own pottery, 1759. Brought out patent for porcelain, 1763.

Wedmore, Treaty of, between Alfred the Great of England and the Danes, by which England was divided between the English to the S. and the Danes to the N. of Watling Street, 878.

Weights and Measures. The shekel of Babylonia and Israel is traceable back to the eleventh century B.C.; it was about one-sixtieth of a pound avoirdupois. The cubit, or length of forearm, was a favourite measure in Egypt, Phoenicia, and Greece. A king of Argos, Pheidon, was renowned as having introduced a new system, the Aeginetan, into the Peloponnesus; but even his century is uncertain, probably eighth B.C. A standard of English measure was made in 972, and kept at Winchester; the first official examination of W. and M., 1795; an Act to enforce uniformity over the U.K. was passed, 1878, and is the basis of all subsequent amending legislation; a metric system Act was passed, 1897.

Wei-hai-wei. Held by Japan pending payment of war indemnity by China, Jan. 1895, till leased to Britain, 1 July 1898, for so long as Port Arthur remained in occupation of Russia. At Washington Conference, 1 Feb. 1922, Britain offered to surrender lease on conditions. Provisional agreement, 31 May 1923; operation delayed by fall of Peking. Restored to China, 1 Oct. 1930.

Weimar, Germany. As capital of Saxe-W.-Eisenach from 1547 it *fl.* as a centre of German classical culture *c.* 1775–1828. The constitution of the German republic was drawn up here in 1919. Hence the name W. Republic.

Welland Ship Canal, between Lakes Ontario and Erie, built, 1824–9.

Wellington, capital of New Zealand, founded, 1840.

Wells. King Ine of Wessex is said to have founded first church here, 704. Work on the cathedral began before 1200, and the greater part of it was finished, 1242.

Welsh Laws. Code drawn up by Hywel Dda *c.* 943. For Statute of Rhuddlan, and later English statutes, *see* WALES.

Welsh Literature. The following is a list of Welsh authors, in chronological order, not now living:

Aneurin, *c.* 560, poet.
Taliesin, *c.* 570 (*d.* 601), poet.
Myrddin, *c.* 570, poet.
Llywarch Hen, *c.* 580, poet.
Meilyr, *c.* 1137, poet.
Caradoc of Llancarvan, *c.* 1150, historian.
Gwalchmai, *c.* 1157, poet.
Owain Cyveiliog, *c.* 1165, poet.
Hywel ab Owain Gwynedd, *c.* 1169, poet.
Einion, *c.* 1175, poet.
Dafydd Benvras, 1230 ?, poet.
Elidir Sais, 1230 ?, poet.
Cynddelw, 1250, poet.
Llywarch ap Llewelyn, 1250 ?, poet.
Einion Wann, 1200–50 ?, poet.
Phylip Brydydd, 1250, poet.
Einion ap Gwgan, 1260, poet.
Edeyrn Dafod Aur, *c.* 1270, grammarian.

Llygad Gwr, *c.* 1270, poet.
Einion ap Madoc, *c.* 1270, poet.
Y Prydydd Bychan, *c.* 1275, poet.
Howel Voel, *c.* 1280, poet.
Bleddyn Fardd, *c.* 1284, poet.
Gruffydd ab yr Ynad Coch, *c.* 1284, poet.
Gwilym Ddu o Arfon, *c.* 1300, poet.
Dafydd ap Gwilym, *c.* 1340–1400, poet.
Gruffudd ab Meredydd, *c.* 1380, poet.
Hywel ap Einion Llygliw, *c.* 1390, poet.
Iolo Goch, *c.* 1400, poet.
Llywelyn Goch ab Meurig Hen, *c.* 1400, poet.
Gruffudd Llwyd ab Dafydd ab Einion Llygliw, *c.* 1400, poet.
Rhys Goch Eryri, *c.* 1410, poet.
Sion Cent, *c.* 1410, poet.
Rhys Goch ap Rhiccert, *c.* 1420 ?, poet.
Gutto'r Glyn, wrote 1430–60, poet.
Lewis Glyn Cothi, 1440–90, poet.
Meredydd ap Rhys, *c.* 1450, poet.
Dafydd Nanmor, *c.* 1460, poet.
Howel Swrdwal, *c.* 1460, poet.
Ieuan Brydydd Hir Hynaf, *c.* 1460, poet.
Ieuan ap Howel Swrdwal, *c.* 1460, poet.
Llawdden, *c.* 1460, poet and prosodist.
Ieuan Deulwyn, 1460–90, poet.
Dr. Morris Clynnog, *d.* 1580–1, catechist.
Dr. Richard Davies, 1501–81, translator.
Sir John Prys, 1502–54, historian and miscellaneous writer.
Humphrey Llwyd, 1527–68, historian, etc.
Gruffud Hiraethog, 1530–66, poet.
Owain Gwynedd (or Owain Ifan), *d.* 1590, poet.
Dr. Thomas Huet. ?–1591, translator.
Maurice Kyffin, *d.* 1598, translator.
Dr. David Powel, *d.* 1598, historian, etc.
William Cynwal, 1530–1600, poet.
Dr. Sion Dafydd Rhys, 1534–161–?, poet, grammarian, etc.
William Llyn, 1535–80, poet.
Sion Tudur, 1535–1602, poet.
Edward Kyffin, ?–1603, translator.
Edmund Prys, 1541–1623, poet and translator.
Sion Phylip, 1543–1620, poet.
Rhys Cain, 1545–1614, poet and painter.
Simwnt Fychan, 1546–1606, poet and grammarian.
Dr. Roger Smyth, 1546–1625, translator.
Dr. William Morgan, 1547–1604, translator.
Sion Brwynog, 1550–67, poet.
Dr. Gruffydd Roberts, *fl.* 1555–95 ?, grammarian and philosopher.
Dr. Richard Parry, 1560–1623, translator.
Henry Parry, 1561–1617, grammarian.
Henry Salesbury, *b.* 1561, grammarian.
Huw Lewys, 1562–1634, translator.
Edward James, 1570–1610, translator.
Dr. John Davies, 1570 ?–1644, grammarian.
John Salisbury, 1575–1625, translator.

Thomas Prys, ?-1634, poet.

William Salesbury, c. 1575, translator and lexicographer.

William Phylip, 1577-1669, poet.

Vicar Prichard, or Rhys Prichard, 1579-1644, religious poet.

William Myddelton, or Gwilyn Canoldref, c. 1590, poet, translator, etc.

Rowland Vaughan, ?-1667, miscellaneous writer.

Richard Jones, 1604-73, translator.

Thomas Gouge, 1605-81, educationist.

Morgan Llwyd o Wynedd, 1619-59, miscellaneous writer.

Stephen Hughes, 1622-88, translator, etc.

Edward Morus, d. 1689, poet.

Huw Morus, 1622-1709, poet.

Charles Edwards, 1628-?, religious writer.

Robert Llwyd, c. 1640, translator.

James Davies (Iago ab Dewi), 1648-1722, poet and translator.

Edward Lhuyd, 1660-1709, philologist.

Elis Wyn o Lasynys, 1671-1734, author of the Barrd Cwsg.

Edward Samuel, 1674-1748, miscellaneous writer.

Griffith Jones, Llanddowror, 1684-1761, educationist, etc.

Moses Williams, 1686-1742, translator.

Theophilus Evans, 1693-1767, historian.

Lewis Morris, 1700-79, poet and miscellaneous writer.

Daniel Rowland, 1713-90, religious writer and translator (?).

William Williams of Pantycelyn, 1717-91, hymn writer.

Joshua Thomas, 1719-97, historian.

David Lewis, c. 1720, philosopher.

Goronwy Owen, 1722-69, poet.

Simon Thomas, c. 1730, historian.

Evan Evans (Ieuan Brydydd Hir), 1731-1781, poet, etc.

Thomas Edwards (Twm o'r Nant), 1739-1810, interlude writer.

Owen Jones (Owain Myfyr), 1741-1814.

Edward Williams (Iolo Morganwg), 1746-1826.

David Richards (Dafydd Ionawr), 1751-1827.

Dr. Owen Pughe, 1759-1835, lexicographer.

David Thomas (Dafydd Ddu Eryri), 1760-1822.

Edward Jones, Maesyplwm, 1761-1836, religious poet.

John Jones (Sion Glanygors), 1767-1821.

Robert Williams (Robert ap Gwilym Ddu), 1767-1850.

Robert Davies (Bardd Nantglyn), 1769-1835.

David Saunders, Merthyr, 1769-1840, translator.

Griffith Williams (Gutyn Peris), 1769-1838.

John Jones, LL.D., 1772-1837, historian, etc.

John Howel (Ioan ab Hywel), 1774-1830.

David Owen (Dewi Wyn o Eifion), 1784-1841.

David Owen (Brutus), 1794-1866.

Evan Evans (Ieuan Glan Geirionydd), 1795-1855.

William Ellis Jones (Gwilym Cawrdaf), 1796-1848.

William Williams (Caledfryn), 1801-69.

Ebenezer Thomas (Eben Fardd), 1802-63.

William Rowlands (Gwilym Lleyn), 1802-1865.

Jane Williams (Ysgafell), 1806-85.

Robert John Pryse (Gweirydd ap Rhys), 1807-89.

Reuben Davies (Prydydd y Coed), 1808-1833.

Robert Ellis (Cynddelw), 1810-75.

John Jones (Talhaiarn), 1810-69.

Rosser Beynon (Asaph Glan Taf), 1811-1876.

Roger Edwards, 1811-86, poet and miscellaneous writer.

Thomas Jones (Glan Alun), 1811-66.

John Williams (Ab Ithel), 1811-62.

Edward Williams (Iolo Fardd Glas), fl. 1839.

William Roberts, LL.D. (Nefydd), 1813-1872.

John Evans (I. D. Ffraid), 1814-75.

Edward Davies (Iolo Trefaldwyn), 1819-1887.

Edward Roberts (Iorwerth Glan Aled), 1819-67.

Thomas E. Davies (Dewi Wyn o Essyllt), 1820-91.

Evan Jones (Ieuan Gwynedd), 1820-52.

Ellin Evans (Elen Egryn), fl. 1850.

Evan Davies (Myfyr Morganwg), fl. 1855.

Thomas Stephens, Merthyr, 1821-75.

John Roberts (Ieuan Gwyllt), 1822-77.

Thomas Rowlands, 1824-84, grammarian.

Owen Wyn Jones (Glasynys), 1828-70.

John C. Hughes (Ceiriog), 1832-87.

W. Thomas (Islwyn), 1832-78.

Richard Davies (Mynyddog), 1833-77.

John Davies (Ossian Gwent), 1834-92.

Richard Foulkes Edwards (Rhisiart Ddu o Wynedd), 1836-70.

Daniel Owen, 1836-95, novelist.

John Robert Pryse (Golyddan), 1841-63.

David Griffiths (Dewi Eifion), d. 1871.

Emrys ap Iwan, 1851-96, critic.

Mary Olwen Jones, 1858-93, novelist.

Sir Owen Morgan Edwards, 1858-1920, critic.

Eivion Wyn, d. 1926, poet.

Sir John Morris-Jones, 1864-1929, poet.

Thomas Gwynne Jones, 1872-1949, poet.

H. Elvet Lewis (Elfed), 1860-1953, poet.

W. J. Gruffydd, 1881-1954, poet.

Dylan M. Thomas, 1914-53, poet.

Welwyn. See GARDEN CITY.

Wembley, British Empire Exhibitions at, 1924, 1925. Many events of 1948 Olympic Games held at W. stadium.

Wendish Literature begins with a translation of the New Testament by Jakubica, 1548. The oldest W. printed book appeared at Bautzen, 1574. The first W. newspaper came out, 1809.

The following is a list of some W. writers:

Rudolf Mjen, 1764–1841, poet.
Handrij Zejler, 1804–70, poet.
J. E. Smoler, 1816–84, poet.
J. P. Jordan, 1818–91, grammarian.
Herta Wicazec, 1819–95, poet.
K. A. Jenc, 1828–95, historian.
J. B. Tesnar, 1829–98, translator.
Michal Hornik, 1833–94, poet.
H. Ducman, 1836–1909, poet.
H. Jordan, 1841–1910, folklorist.
Matej Urban, 1846–1929, translator.
Jakub Bart ('Cisinski'), 1856–1909, poet.
E. Muka, 1857–1927, grammarian.
Jurij Winger, 1872–1916, novelist.
Jan Skala, 1889–1945, poet.
Jakub Lorenz Zaleski, d. 1939, novelist.
J. K. Waltar, 1860–1922, poet.

After 1933 the Wends were subjected to increasing persecution, and the last W. newspaper was suppressed, 1937. The retreating Germans burned down the Serbski Dom at Bautzen (W. cultural centre), 1945, but the foundations of a new one were laid under Russian auspices, 1947.

Wends or Sorbs, formerly meaning the Slavonic tribes immediately E. of the Elbe, in Pomerania, etc., now means the Slav minority in Lusatia (Ger. Lausitz), on the borders of Saxony, Silesia, and Bohemia. They are mentioned by the English missionary Winfrith (*alias* Boniface), who *d.* 754. Under German rule since about A.D. 900, they formed part of the Polish kingdom, 1002–32, and were united under the Bohemian crown from the fifteenth century until 1621 when the region was partitioned between Saxony and Brandenburg.

Wesleyans. *See* METHODISTS.

Wessex, kingdom of the West Saxons, the political nucleus of which arose out of the Gewissae (i.e. Confederates); this confederacy. military and perhaps also religious, was led into Britain, 495, by one, Cerdic, possibly a chief of mixed blood (his name is a transparent anglicization of the Welsh name Caradoc), and his son Cynric. Under 514 the Chronicles say: 'This year *came the West Saxons into Britain*' under Stuf and Wihtgar. In 519 Cerdic and Cynric 'undertook the government of the West Saxons . . . from that day have reigned the children of the West Saxon kings.' Bede. mentioning the West Saxons for the first time, a century later, says they were 'formerly called Gewissae,' and were converted to Chris-

tianity in 635 by the Italian bishop Birinus (*d.* 690). Cerdic's grandson Ceawlin obtained possession of the country between the upper Thames and lower Severn, 571–578. The territory of the Hwicce (Worcestershire, Gloucestershire, SW. Warwickshire) was lost to the militant pagan Penda, king of Mercia, 630. Somerset was conquered from the Britons of Cornwall about 660, and the Isle of Wight, 686. Ine, whose code of laws still survives, extended the W. dominions westward to include most of Devonshire, and so terrorized the kingdom of Kent as to exact a tribute of £30,000 in 694. By 726 the kingdoms of Sussex and Kent had become politically negligible, and during the next century they were eliminated and annexed piecemeal by W., which now entered into the struggle against a more formidable enemy, the Mercian kingdom, which was finally subdued and absorbed, 825–9. Thereafter *see* ENGLAND.

Wessex, Kings of, c. 552–839:

Cynric	*fl.* 552.–*d.* 560
Ceawlin	560–592
Ceol	591–597
Coelwulf	597–611
Cynegils	611–643
Cenwalh	643–645
Penda (of Mercia)	645–648
Cenwalh (restored)	648–672
(Queen) Seaxburg	672–674
Escwine	674–676
Centwine	676–685
Caedwalla	685–688
Ine	688–726
Ethelheard	726–740
Cuthred	740–756
Sigeberht	756–757
Cynewulf	757–786
Beorhtric	786–802
Egbert, KING OF ENGLAND	802–839

See further under ENGLISH SOVEREIGNS AND THEIR CONSORTS.

Western Australia was first explored by the Dutch under Dirk Hartog, 1616. The first Englishman to land was William Dampier, 1688. Formal possession taken on behalf of the English crown by Vancouver, 1791. A settlement of convicts was sent from New S. Wales, 1826. Swan River Settlement founded, 1829. Responsible government granted, 1890.

Western Union had its beginnings in a 50-year treaty signed in Brussels on 17 Mar. 1948 by Britain, France, the Netherlands, Belgium, and Luxembourg. European Council established, May 1949. In Dec. 1949 the W. U. defence organization was incorporated with the N. Atlantic Treaty command. The rejection by France of E.D.C. in 1954 was followed by the London and Paris agreements of that year, providing for joint W. European defence by the original N.A.T.O. powers plus W. Germany and Italy. The W. U. thus established was brought formally into being on 7 May 1955.

West Indies, Federation of. *See* CARIBBEAN FEDERATION.

Westminster. The abbey was founded *c.* seventh century, and refounded by Edward the Confessor *c.* 1050–65. The 'city' was governed by the abbots till 1547. St. Margaret's was founded *c.* 1100. The W. Hall was built, 1097–1100. Law Courts established in W. Hall *c.* 1200. Abbey rebuilt, 1245–69. Further additions *c.* 1350–1528, and *c.* 1722–40. The school attached to the abbey from early times was chartered by Henry VIII, but only properly endowed by Queen Elizabeth I. The abbey was converted into barracks for a time, 1643. First W. Bridge opened, 1750. W. Palace burned down, 1834. New palace completed, 1859. New bridge built, 1862. Law Courts removed from, 1883. Created a city and a metropolitan borough, 1899. Roman Catholic cathedral opened, 1903; consecrated, 1910.

Westminster Assembly. The Long Parliament, having in 1641 expelled the bishops, summoned an assembly of 121 divines, who, with 30 laymen from Parliament, formed the body that was to inaugurate a Presbyterian establishment for England and Wales. Meetings held in W. Abbey: the first, 1 July 1643; the last, 22 Feb. 1648; in all, 1,163 meetings. The assembly adopted the Solemn League and Covenant (*q.v.*), 25 Sept. 1643. It submitted to Parliament: a 'Directory for Public Worship' to supersede the Book of Common Prayer, 20 Apr. 1644; a 'Confession of Faith' and two Catechisms, both approved by Parliament, 15 Sept. 1648. The Commons ordered, 13 Oct. 1647, that Presbyterianism be tried for a year, bishops having been abolished, 9 Oct. 1646. Presbyterianism soon gave place to Independency in England. All the Assembly's work was swept away at the Restoration, so far as England and Wales were concerned; but the Confession and the Shorter Catechism remain binding in the Church of Scotland.

Westminster, Provisions of, drawn up, 1259. Re-enacted as the Statute of Marlborough, 1267.

Westminster, Statutes of.

I. 1275. A miscellaneous code on revenue, etc., matters.

II. 1285. Part of this is called *De Donis Conditionalibus*, and legalized the creation of entailed interests.

III. 1290. Part of this is called *Quia*

Emptores, and abolished further subinfeudation.

IV. 1931. This Act created the legally independent sovereign status under the crown of the British Dominions.

Westphalia, Kingdom of, created by Napoleon, 1807. Dissolved, 1814. *See* BUONAPARTE.

Westphalia, Peace of, 1648. This consisted of two treaties, which ended the Thirty Years War, negotiated at Münster and Osnabrück, and signed at Münster, 21 Oct. 1648. 1. A treaty of alliance between France, the Empire, and Sweden against Spain. 2. A treaty of peace by which Sweden received W. Pomerania, Bremen, and Verden, France received Metz, Toul, Verdun, and Alsace, and the independence of Switzerland and the United Provinces of the Netherlands was guaranteed. Religious toleration was granted to Calvinists as well as Lutherans in Germany, but the principle was not extended to the Hapsburg territories. The peace marks the failure of the Austro-Spanish effort to restore Roman Catholicism in Central Europe, and the beginning of French hegemony in Europe.

West Point Military Academy. A resolution of Congress, Oct. 1776, proposed the establishment of a military academy, but no bill was passed until 1802, despite reminders by Washington in 1793 and 1796. A further Act of 29 Apr. 1812 increased the establishment, and in 1817 a system of admitting a fixed proportion of cadets from each state was adopted.

West Virginia was admitted to the Union in 1863 by fissure from Virginia (*q.v.*). New state constitution, 1872. Petroleum first found, 1860.

West Wall, a system of fortifications, begun *sub rosa* in 1934. Between 1936 and 1940 the Germans constructed a continuous fortified belt from Lörrach in the S. to a point opposite the junction of their frontier with those of Belgium and Luxemburg. From 1939 to 1945 it was extended to protect the southern flank from Lörrach to Lake Constance.

Wexford, Ireland. Founded by Vikings in the ninth century, was taken from their descendants by the Normans, 1169; received a charter, 1318; besieged by Cromwell, 1649; held by Williamites, 1690. During the second rising of the United Irishmen (*q.v.*), 1798, W. was the headquarters of the civil administration.

Wheat, Importation of, in quantity into England first took place in 1347.

Wheel, Breaking on the. Continental form of torture first used in Germany,

1535, abolished, 1827; used in Edinburgh, 1604.

Whig. A term of contempt under Charles II, probably of Scottish origin. It eventually became the honoured party name of those who took the lead in establishing William III and George I to the throne. *See* LIBERALS.

Whipsnade Park. *See* ZOOLOGICAL SOCIETY OF LONDON.

Whisky Insurrection, 1794, in western Pennsylvania against the enforcing of the excise law by the Federal Government.

Whist is first mentioned about 1621, but only became fashionable in the latter part of the eighteenth century, being displaced towards 1900 by bridge, which evolved from it.

Whitby, so called in the ninth century by Scandinavians, who used the harbour called by the English Streoneshalh, where a monastery, built by St. Hilda in 656, was the scene of a council, since called the Synod of W., in 664, attended by St. Wilfrid (634–709) and St. Colman (*d.* 676) in the Roman and Celtic interests respectively. The extant ruins of the abbey on the E. cliff date from 1220. James Cook, the navigator, sailed in a W. brig about 1745, and the *Endeavour*, in which he set out on his famous voyage to New Zealand in 1768, was a collier of local pattern built in a W. shipyard.

Whiteboys. Irish secret organization, founded *c.* 1860. It was of the type known as Ribbonism. The Westmeath Act (1871) declared Ribbonism illegal. The movement died down about 1885.

Whitehall (London). York House, the residence of the Archbishop of York, stood on this site, *c.* 1250. It was later acquired by Henry VIII, who made it a royal residence. A new hall was designed for James I, but only partially completed, 1622; through this hall Charles I passed to execution, 1649; and when the old palace was burned down in 1698 the hall was the only part to survive. The street now called W. was called King Street until the destruction of the palace.

White House (Washington, D.C.). Built between 1792 and 1799. Partly burnt out by British troops, 1814. Condemned as unsafe, 1949; repairs were completed in 1952 and much internal renovation has since been done under the supervision of the wives of Presidents Eisenhower and Kennedy.

White Russia. *See* BELORUSSIA.

Whitley Committee. Committee under chairmanship of the then Deputy Speaker (Rt. Hon. J. H. Whitley) which in 1917 suggested joint industrial councils of employers and employed, since known as 'Whitley Councils.'

'Who's Who,' biographical reference work, first published, 1848, by Alfred Baily. Acquired, 1896, by Adam and Charles Black.

Wilhelmshaven, the chief naval station of Germany on the N. Sea, was founded in 1853, at the time of the origin of the Prussian Navy; the harbour was opened in 1869; many important additions made to the naval station from 1900 onwards; the dry dock was destroyed by the R.N. in 1948, the naval installations in general having been already heavily damaged by R.A.F. bombing between 1942 and 1945.

Wilkes's Case. Trials of John Wilkes, alderman of London, for printing obscene poem, *Essay on Woman*, and publication of *North Briton*, 21 Feb. 1764 and 18 June 1768.

Wilson Cloud Chamber. Invented by C. T. R. Wilson (1869–1959), 1911.

Winchester (Rom.: **Venta Belgarum**). A city in Hampshire. The first bishop was Hedda (*d.* 705), but no traces of the Saxon cathedral remain. Present structure begun in 1079; nave reconstructed, 1380–1400; signs of weakness manifested themselves in the cathedral in 1905, and restoration was at once put in hand. For William of Wykeham's foundation, *see* PUBLIC SCHOOLS.

Window Tax, 1697. Brought in by William III to atone for the deficiency on damaged coin; repealed, 24 July 1851.

Windsor. Family name of the British royal house, adopted 1917, when George V renounced all German titles for himself and his family, together with the dynastic names of Saxe-Coburg-Gotha, acquired through Queen Victoria's marriage with Prince Albert.

Windsor Castle. The building was begun in wood by William I; stonework begun by Henry I *c.* 1110; in 1344 the Round Tower was built, and in 1356 practically the whole castle was rebuilt by Edward III, who was *b.* there, 1312; additions were made by (*inter alios*) Henry VIII, Elizabeth I, and Charles II. St. George's Chapel was built, 1473–1519 (begun by Edward IV); it was carefully restored by George III, 1787. Extensive improvements, 1824–30.

Winnipeg, Manitoba, first reached by white travellers, 1738. NW. Co.'s trading post, founded 1810, was replaced by a Hudson's Bay post, named Fort Garry, 1822. On the creation of the province of Manitoba in 1870 its capital was sited at W., which was chartered as a city in 1873. First railway connection, 1878. Suffered severely in the floods of the Manitoba River, 1950.

Wireless. Broadcasting boom began in U.S.A., 1921. In Apr. 1922 British

Postmaster-General announced a scheme for providing licences and for broadcasting from seven stations. Long-distance wireless tested, Aug. 1922. Music from America heard in England, 28–9 Dec. 1923. Photographs transmitted, London to New York, 30 Nov. 1924. J. L. Baird makes first effective televisor, Oct. 1925. High-power station at Rugby opened, 1 Jan. 1926. Conversation, London and New York, 7 Mar. 1926; and regular telephone service begun, 7 Jan. 1927. Moving pictures transmitted (America), 10 Jan. 1927; first conversation London and San Francisco, 26 Feb. 1927; Anglo-S. African beam system opened, 3 July 1927; first broadcast from Australia to England, 4 Sept. 1927; beam service to India opened, 5 Sept. 1927. B.B.C. instituted television studio at Alexandra Palace, 1936. Regular foreign broadcasts begun, 1937. Eurovision, 1954; Telstar experiment, 1962. *See* BRITISH BROADCASTING CORPORATION; TELEVISION; TELSTAR, etc.

Wisconsin, U.S.A., was first entered by a white man, Jean Nicolet, 1634. First permanent settlement, 1701. It was admitted to the Union, 1848.

Witchcraft. A Bull against W. was issued by Pope Innocent VIII in 1484, whilst in England Acts against it were passed in 1542, 1562, and 1601. Last person to be tried under these Acts was Jane Wenham of Walkern, Hertfordshire, 1712, but a woman was actually burned alive in Sunderland as late as 1722. An Act of 1736 penalizes '*pretending* to use W., etc.' The Vagrancy Act of 1824 was amended in 1950 to cover cases of reputed W. As late as 1895 (15 Mar.) a woman was burned as a witch in Ireland, at Cloneen, County Tipperary and a case of (illegal) witch burning was reported in Mexico, June 1963.

Witenagemot or **Witan.** The Anglo-Saxon royal council; in seventh and eighth centuries separate Ws. were possessed by Wessex, Kent, Mercia, and Northumbria; there was no fixed meeting-place, but the king was always present; meetings were held three times a year: at Easter, Whitsun, and Christmas. The most celebrated meetings were at Luton, A.D. 931, and Winchester, A.D. 934.

Witney. A market town in Oxfordshire, seat of blanket-making industry, which was established in the reign of King Edgar, 909.

Wittenberg, Saxony. Mentioned, 1180; here, in the Augustinian monastery, Luther dwelt; in 1508 he was appointed professor of philosophy, and in 1517 he affixed his celebrated 95 Theses to the church door; bombarded by Austrians,

1760; taken by France, 1806; taken by Prussians, 1814.

Women's Auxiliary Air Force. *See* WOMEN'S ROYAL AIR FORCE.

Women's Colleges, English. Tennyson's *Princess*, written against women's higher education, 1847. Earliest W. C. were at London University (Queen's and Bedford), 1848 and 1849. For others *see under* CAMBRIDGE, LONDON, OXFORD UNIVERSITIES.

Women's Franchise. *See* FRANCHISE, ELECTIVE and U.S.A., CONSTITUTION OF.

Women's Institutes originated in Canada in 1897, and were introduced to the U.K. in 1915 by a Canadian, Mrs. Alfred Watt (1868–1948), who founded a branch at Llanfairpwllgwyngyll, Anglesey. The National Federation of W. I. was founded, 1917.

Women's Land Army raised, 1917. The W.L.A. came into being again in Sept. 1939, organized by committees set up in May of that year. Disbanded, 1950.

Women's Royal Air Force. 1. An ancillary service of the R.A.F., raised in 1917 and disbanded in 1919. 2. A force formed round the nucleus of certain A.T.S. (*see* WOMEN'S ROYAL ARMY CORPS) companies which had been attached to the R.A.F. since 1938, and in July 1939 were permanently transferred. It became known as Women's Auxiliary Air Force until Feb. 1949, when the present designation was adopted to signify that members could enlist for regular, as opposed to part-time, engagements.

Women's Royal Army Corps, designation adopted from 1 Feb. 1949, by the former Auxiliary Territorial Service, the formation of which was proclaimed by royal warrant, 9 Sept. 1938. First Chief Controller, with equivalent rank of major-general, appointed, 3 July 1939. Officers received royal commissions, Apr. 1941. In this year the first mixed heavy A.A. batteries were formed.

Women's Royal Naval Service. 1. Raised, 1917; disbanded, Oct. 1919. 2. Re-formed, 1939; placed on permanent basis, Jan. 1949.

Women's Voluntary Services, an association formed, 16 May 1938, by the Marchioness of Reading, and established on a permanent basis by the Home Office in May 1947.

Wonders of the World. The seven W. of the W. were: (1) the Egyptian pyramids, *c.* 4700 B.C.; (2) the tomb of Mausolus, 353 B.C.; (3) the Ephesian temple of Diana, *c.* 550 B.C.; (4) the walls and hanging gardens of Babylon, work of Nebuchadnezzar, *c.* 604–562 B.C.; (5) the Colossus of Rhodes, 280 B.C.; (6) the statue of Zeus at Olympia, *c.* 450 B.C.; (7) the pharos of Ptolemy Philadelphus, c. 282 B.C.

Wood's Halfpence. *See* 'DRAPIER'S LETTERS.'

Woolsack. The seat of the Lord Chancellor in the House of Lords; placed there in the reign of Edward III as a reminder of the importance of the wool industry; the earliest authentic mention of the W., however, is in the reign of Henry VIII.

Woolwich, England, mentioned, 1064. Already an important royal dockyard in fifteenth century. The *Great Harry* launched at, 1515. Batteries erected against the Dutch, 1667. Royal Arsenal, 1805. Royal dockyard closed, 1869. Royal Military Academy, which was established 1741, was amalgamated with the Royal Military College at Sandhurst, 1946.

Woomera Rocket Range, Australia. Developed since 1946.

Worcester became an episcopal see, 680. Benedictine church built by St. Oswald (*d.* 992), 964, extensively rebuilt by Wulfstan the bishop (1012?–95), 1084, as his cathedral church. He also founded the Hospital of St. Wulfstan, still standing now, but converted from its original purpose, 1541. Last material addition to cathedral was Prince Arthur's Chantry, built by Henry VII in memory of his eldest son. The Royal W. Porcelain Works were opened, 1751.

Workmen's Compensation. W. C. Act, 1897, introduced principle of compulsory insurance by employers in a limited number of trades, against accidents arising in course of employment. W. C. Act, 1900, brought in agricultural labourers. Both Acts repealed by W. C. Act, 1906, which largely increased scope of W. C. Amended and extended by W. C. Act, 1923, which repealed two war Acts relating to W. C. (1917, 1919). Repealed by W. C. Act, 1925, which included clerks, and also persons employed in vehicles and vessels plying for hire. W. C. (Silicosis and Asbestosis) Act, 1930. W. C. Act, 1931, amended the Act of 1925 as to persons partially recovered from effects of accident. W. C. (Coal Mines) Act, 1934. All W. C. Acts were superseded by the National Insurance (Industrial Injuries) Act, 1946.

Works, Ministry of, H.M. Office of W. first so called, 1852. Became known as Ministry of W. and Buildings, 1940; then as Ministry of W. and Planning; then (from 1943) as Ministry of W.

World Bank. *See* INTERNATIONAL BANK FOR RECONSTRUCTION AND DEVELOPMENT.

World Council of Churches, other than Roman Catholic, held its first assembly at Amsterdam, Aug. 1948.

World Health Organization. Constitution drawn up, 22 July 1946; came into effect, 1948. The W. H. O.'s status as a specialized agency of the United Nations Organization was recognized, 1950.

World War I.

DECLARATIONS OF WAR

1914: Austria-Hungary on Serbia, 28 July; Germany on Russia, 1 Aug.; Germany on France, 3 Aug.; Britain on Germany, 4 Aug.; Germany on Belgium, 4 Aug.; Montenegro on Austria-Hungary, 7 Aug.; France on Austria-Hungary, 10 Aug.; Britain on Austria-Hungary, 12 Aug.; Japan on Germany, 23 Aug.; Britain on Turkey, 5 Nov.

1915: Italy on Austria, 23 May; Italy on Turkey, 20 Aug.; Britain on Bulgaria, 15 Oct.; France on Bulgaria, 16 Oct.; Italy on Bulgaria, 19 Oct.

1916: Albania on Austria, 11 Jan.; Germany on Portugal, 9 Mar.; Rumania on Austria, 27 Aug.; Italy on Germany, 28 Aug.; Germany on Rumania, 28 Aug.; Turkey on Rumania, 30 Aug.; Bulgaria on Rumania, 1 Sept.

1917: U.S.A. on Germany, 6 Apr.; Cuba on Germany, 7 Apr.; Austria on U.S.A., 8 Apr.; Bulgaria on U.S.A., 9 Apr.; Panama on Germany, 10 Apr.; Siam on Central Empires, 22 July; China on Germany, 14 Aug.; China on Austria, 11 Sept.; Brazil on Germany, 26 Oct.

MILITARY EVENTS

France and Flanders:

1914: German invasion of Belgium begun, 4 Aug.; Brussels entered, 20 Aug.; Namur captured, 23 Aug.; Antwerp taken, 9 Oct. Battles: Mons, 23–24 Aug.; Le Cateau, 26 Aug.; Marne, 6–12 Sept.; Aisne, 12–15 Sept.; Ypres, 19 Oct.–22 Nov.

1915: Battles: Neuve-Chapelle, 10–13 Mar.; Ypres, 22 Apr.–25 May (first German attack with gas, 22 Apr.); Festubert, 15–25 May; Loos, 25 Sept.–8 Oct.

1916: Battles: Verdun, begun 21 Feb. (Douaumont, 25 Feb. and 24 Oct.); Somme, 1 July–18 Nov. (Beaumont-Hamel, 13 Nov.); Verdun, 15 Dec.; Ancre, 13–18 Nov.

1917: German retreat to Hindenburg Line, 14 Mar.–5 Apr. Battles: Arras, 9 Apr.–4 May (Vimy Ridge, 9–14 Apr.; Scarpe, 9–14, 23–24 Apr., 3–4 May); Chemin des Dames, 5 May; Bullecourt, 3–17 May; Messines, 7–14 June; Ypres, 31 July–10 Nov. (Passchendaele, 12 Oct., 26 Oct.–10 Nov.); Verdun, 20 Aug.; Cambrai, 20 Nov.–3 Dec.

1918: Battles: Somme, 21 Mar.–5 Apr.; Lys, 9–29 Apr. (Kemmel Ridge, 17–19 Apr.); Aisne, 27 May–6 June; Marne, 18 July; Ourcq, 23 July–2 Aug.; Amiens, 8–11 Aug.; Bapaume, 21–31 Aug.; Somme, 21 Aug.–3 Sept.; Arras, 26 Aug.–3 Sept. (Drocourt-Quéant, 2–3 Sept.); Saint-Mihiel, 12 Sept.; Hindenburg Line, 12 Sept.–9 Oct. (Épéhy, 18 Sept.; Cambrai, 8–9 Oct.); Argonne, 26 Sept.–2 Nov.; Ypres, 28 Sept.–2 Oct.; Selle River, 17–25 Oct.; Valenciennes, 1 Nov.; Sambre, 4 Nov.

Prussia — Poland — Russia — Austria-Hungary:

1914: Battles: Tannenberg, 26–30 Aug.; Lemberg, 1–3 Sept.; Augustovo, 1–4 Oct.; for Warsaw, 15–20 Oct., 18 Nov.–28 Dec.; Lodz, 1–5 Dec.

1915: Przemysl surrendered to Russians, 22 Mar.; recaptured, 3 June; Lemberg retaken, 22 June; third battle for Warsaw, 19 July; Warsaw evacuated by Russians, 5 Aug.; Kovno stormed, 7 Aug.; battle of Brest-Litovsk, 26 Aug.; battle of Tarnopol, 7–8 Sept.; Vilna taken by Germans, 17 Sept.

1916: Battle of Lake Narotch, Mar.–Apr.; Russian offensive in Ukraine, 4 June; in E. Galicia, 8 June; near Baronovitchi, 13 June; near Brody, 15 July.

1917: Russian offensive at Brzezany, 1 July; battle of Halicz, 10 July, 23 July; fall of Riga, 3 Sept.

1918: Odessa occupied by Germans, 13 Mar.

Rumania:

1916: Invasion of Transylvania, 28 Aug.; Silistria taken by Bulgarians, 12 Sept.; Constanza taken by Bulgarians, 22 Oct.; Bucharest occupied by Germans, 7 Dec.

1917: Evacuation of the Dobrudja, 8 Jan.; Galatz evacuated, 11 Jan.

Dardanelles:

1915: Landing at Cape Helles, 25–26 Apr.; battles for Krithia, 28 Apr., 6–8 May, 4 June; Anzac battles, 25 Apr.–30 June; landing at Suvla, 6–15 Aug.; Suvla battles, 6–21 Aug. (Sari-Bair, 6–10 Aug.). Evacuation of Dardanelles declared, 8 Dec.

1916: Evacuation completed, 8 Jan.

Italy:

1915: First battle of the Isonzo, 2–29 July.

1916: Battle of Trentino, 14 May–16 June; battle of Gorizia, 6–14 Aug.

1917: Italian offensive on Isonzo, 14 May–10 June; Italian attack between Tolmino and sea, 19 Aug.; battle of Caporetto, 24 Oct.–18 Nov.

1918: Battle of Piave, 15–23 June, 26 Oct.; battle of Vittoria Veneto, 24 Oct.–4 Nov.

Balkans:

1915: Allied landing at Salonika, 5 Oct.; fall of Üsküb, 22 Oct.; battle of Kachanik, 4 Nov.; fall of Monastir, 2 Dec.

1916: Cettinje taken, 1–3 Jan.; Durazzo taken, 24 Feb.; Monastir retaken, 23 Nov.

1917: Battle of Doiran, 24–25 Apr., 8–9 May.

1918: Battle of the Vardar, 15–25 Sept.; battle of Doiran, 18–19 Sept.; Üsküb retaken, 30 Sept.

Egypt, Palestine, and Arabia:

Operations against the Senussi, Nov. 1915–Feb. 1917; battle of Romani, 3–4 Aug. 1916; battles of Gaza, 26 Mar.–7 Nov. 1917; capture of Jerusalem, 7–9 Dec. 1917; of Jericho, 19–21 Feb. 1918; Arab rising against Turks began, 7 June 1918; Mecca taken, 10 June 1918; battle of Megiddo, 19–25 Sept. 1918.

Mesopotamia—Persia:

1915: Battle of Kut, 28 Sept.; battle of Ctesiphon, 22–24 Nov.

1916: Kermanchah taken by Russians, 26 Feb.; Battle of Sanna-i-Yat, 6–22 Apr.

1917: British occupied Bagdad, 11 Mar.; Samaria, 19 Sept.; Ramadi taken, 28 Sept.; battle of Sherghat, 30 Oct.

Africa:

E. Africa: Tanga operations, Nov. 1914; surrender of Mafia Island, 12 Jan. 1915; Tanga occupied, 7 July 1916; Dares-Salaam surrendered, 4 Sept. 1916; final surrender, 25 Nov. 1918.

SW. Africa: Luderitzbucht occupied, 18 Sept. 1914; occupation of Windhoek, 12 May 1915; German capitulation, 9 July 1915.

Cameroons: Capture of Duala, 24 Sept. 1914; of Mora, 8 Sept. 1916.

Togoland: Lome captured, 8 Aug. 1914.

S. Africa: Rebellion began, 15 Sept. 1914; surrender at Reitz, 4 Dec. 1914.

Caucasus:

Erzerum taken, 12 Feb. 1916, retaken, Mar. 1918; Trebizond taken, 18 Mar. 1916, retaken, Mar. 1918; Erzingan taken, July 1916, retaken, Mar. 1918; Batum occupied, Apr. 1918; Baku evacuated by British, 14 Sept. 1918.

N. Russia—Siberia:

Kem occupied, 7 June 1918; Irkutsk occupied by Czechoslovaks, July 1918; Dukhovskaya, 23 Aug. 1918; Archangel occupied, 1 Aug. 1918; Troitsa, 10 Aug. 1919; British evacuation, 27 Sept. 1919.

NAVAL EVENTS

1914: *Goeben* and *Breslau* reach Turkey, 11 Aug.; blockade of Kiaochow, 27 Aug.;

battle of Heligoland Bight, 28 Aug.; siege of Tsingtao, 23 Sept.–5 Nov.; H.M.S. *Aboukir*, *Hogue*, and *Cressy* torpedoed, 22 Sept.; battle of Coronel (Admiral Cradock's squadron lost), 1 Nov.; Kiaochow surrendered, 7 Nov.; German cruiser *Emden* destroyed, 9 Nov.; battle of Falkland islands (Spee's squadron sunk), 8 Dec.; Germans bombard Yorkshire coastal towns, 16 Dec.; seaplane raid on Cuxhaven, 25 Dec.

1915: Battle of Dogger Bank, 24 Jan.; German submarine blockade of Britain opened, 18 Feb.; British attack on Dardanelles forts, 19 Feb.; again, 4–7 Mar.; German cruiser *Dresden* sunk, 14 Mar.; *Lusitania* torpedoed, 7 May; *Königsberg* destroyed in Rufiji River, 11 July.

1916: Germans bombard Lowestoft, 25 Apr.; battle of Jutland, 31 May; H.M.S. *Hampshire* with Kitchener aboard mined off Orkneys, 5 June; Allies bombard Athens, 1 Sept.; blockade of Greece, 19 Sept.

1917: Suffolk coast bombarded, 26 Jan.; Germans begin unrestricted submarine warfare, 1 Feb.; H.M.S. *Swift* and *Broke* figure in a destroyer action in the Channel, 23 Apr.; Ramsgate shelled, 27 Apr.; first U.S. destroyers arrive, 3 May; British naval success in Kattegat, 2 Nov.

1918: Germans bombard Yarmouth, 14 Jan.; British blocking attack on Zeebrugge and Ostend, 22–23 Apr.; another on Ostend, 9–10 May; German naval meeting at Kiel, 10 Nov.; Allied fleet passed through Dardanelles, 12 Nov.; German fleet surrenders, 21 Nov.

ARMISTICES AND TREATIES

Armistices: Central Powers—Russia, 29 Nov. 1917; Rumania—Central Powers, 7 Dec. 1917; Central Powers—Ukraine, 9 Feb. 1918; Allies—Bulgaria, 29 Sept. 1918; Allies—Turkey, 30 Oct. 1918; Allies—Austria-Hungary, 3 Nov. 1918; Allies—Germany, 11 Nov. 1918.

Peace Treaties: Brest-Litovsk, between Russia and Germany, 2 Mar. 1918; preliminary peace between Rumania and Central Powers, Buftea, 5 Mar. 1918; ratified, 7 May 1918; annulled at Versailles, 1919. Versailles, signed by the Allies and Germany, 29 June 1919; ratified in Paris, 10 Jan. 1920. Saint-Germain, between Allies and Austria, signed, 10 Sept. 1919; ratified in Paris, 16 July 1920. Trianon, between Allies and Hungary, signed, 4 June 1920. Neuilly, between Allies and Bulgaria, signed, 27 Nov. 1919; ratified in Paris, 9 Aug. 1920. Sèvres, between Allies and Turkey, signed, 10 Aug. 1920 (never ratified). Lausanne, between Allies and Turkey, signed, 24 July 1923; ratified, autumn 1923.

World War II.

1939: Germany invades Poland, 1 Sept.; Britain, New Zealand, Australia, and France declare war on Germany, 3 Sept.; Canada and S. Africa declare war: Smuts becomes Premier of S. Africa, 4 Sept.; Russia invades Poland, 17 Sept.; Poland partitioned between Germany and Russia, 28 Sept.; *Royal Oak* sunk in Scapa Flow, 14 Oct.; Anglo-Turkish pact, 19 Oct.; U.S. 'Cash and Carry Act' repeals the arms embargo, 4 Nov.; Russia invades Finland, 30 Nov.; battle of the River Plate, 13 Dec.; *Admiral Graf Spee* scuttled, 17 Dec.

1940: *Altmark* incident, 17 Feb.; Russo-Finnish Peace, 13 Mar.; Reynaud French Premier, 20 Mar.; Germans attack Denmark and Norway, 9 Apr.; Germans invade the Low Countries, 10 May: Churchill forms coalition government, 10 May; Dutch Army surrenders and German victory at Sedan, 15 May; Belgian Army surrenders, 28 May; Dunkirk evacuation, 26 May–3 June; British evacuate Norway and Italy declares war on Allies, 10 June; Spain seizes Tangier and Germans enter Paris, 14 June; French reject British offer of union and Pétain becomes Premier, 16 June; French surrender, 22 June; Russians seize Bessarabia from Rumania, 28 June; Rumania denounces Anglo-French guarantee, 1 July; British disable the French fleet in N. Africa at Oran, 3 July; Italians invade the Sudan, 4 July; Vichy breaks off relations with Britain, 5 July; Britain closes Burma road, 18 July; Lithuania annexed by U.S.S.R., 3 Aug.; Italians invade British Somaliland, 4 Aug.; U.S.S.R. annexes Estonia and Latvia, 5 Aug.; battle of Britain, 8 Aug.–6 Sept.; Vienna award dismembers Rumania, 30 Aug.; British obtain 50 destroyers from U.S.A. in return for bases in W. Indies, 2 Sept.; beginning of the London blitz, 7–8 Sept.; Italians invade Egypt, 13 Sept.; British attack on Dakar fails, 25 Sept.; the 'New Order' Pact (Germany, Italy, Japan), 27 Sept.; Germans occupy Rumania, 7 Oct.; Italy attacks Greece, 28 Oct.; Italian fleet severely damaged by British air attack at Taranto. 11 Nov.; blitz on Coventry, 14 Nov.; Wavell opens victorious offensive against Italians in N. Africa, 8 Dec. (till 8 Feb. 1941).

1941: Italian forces placed under German control, 20 Jan.; Germans occupy Bulgaria, 9 Feb.; Britain breaks off relations with Rumania, 10 Feb.; British capture Mogadishu, 26 Feb.; Bulgaria joins Axis, 1 Mar.; U.S. Lease-Lend Act becomes law, 11 Mar.; Rommel's counterattack in Libya begins, 24 Mar.; Gen. Simovic overthrows pro-Axis government in Yugoslavia, 27 Mar.; British naval victory over Italians at Cape Matapan, 28 Mar.; Rashid Ali's pro-Axis revolt in Iraq, 3 Apr.; British capture Addis Ababa, 5 Apr.; Germans invade Yugoslavia and Greece, 6 Apr.; Germans capture Sollum, 26 Apr.; Athens, 27 Apr.; Hess flies to Scotland, 10 May; Italians surrender at Amba Alagi, 19 May; German conquest of Crete, 19 May–1 June; H.M.S. *Hood* sunk, 24 May; *Bismarck* sunk, 27 May; British and French occupy Syria, 8 June–14 July; Germany invades U.S.S.R., 22 June; U.S.A. occupies Iceland, 7 July; British and Russians occupy Persia, 25 Aug.–1 Sept.; Reza, Shah of Persia, forced to abdicate, 16 Sept.; Germans reach Leningrad, 4 Sept.; capture Kiev, 19 Sept.; second British offensive in Libya, 18 Nov.; final Italian surrender in Ethiopia at Gondar, 27 Nov.; Three-Power Conference at Moscow, 29 Nov.; Japanese attack Pearl Harbor, 7 Dec.; Japanese occupy Thailand and invade Malaya, 8 Dec.; H.M.S. *Prince of Wales* and *Repulse* sunk, 10 Dec.; Japanese take Guam and Axis declare war on U.S.A., 11 Dec.; Hitler takes immediate command of German Army, 19 Dec.; Japanese take Wake Island, 23 Dec.; Hong Kong, 25 Dec.

1942: United Nations Pact at Washington, 1 Jan.; Japanese take Manila, 2 Jan.; Japanese naval victory in Macassar Straits, 23–25 Jan.; Japanese invade Burma, 8 Feb.; capture Singapore, 15 Feb.; Rangoon, 8 Mar.; Java, 10 Mar.; American raid on Tokio, 18 Apr.; fall of Corregidor, 6 May; Japanese naval victory in the Coral Sea, 7–11 May; second German offensive in Libya opens, 12 May; first 1,000-bomber raid (on Cologne), 30 May; battle of Midway, 3–6 June; Japanese attack Aleutians, 3 June; Gen. Eisenhower C.-in-C. U.S. forces European theatre, 25 May; Germans reach El Alamein, 1 July; Germans take Sevastopol, 2 July; Americans attack Guadalcanal, 7 Aug.; British raid on Dieppe, 14 Aug.; first all-American air raid on Europe, 17 Aug.; Germans enter Stalingrad, 5 Sept.; British victory at Alamein, 23 Oct.–3 Nov.; allied landing in N. Africa, 8 Nov.; Germans occupy Vichy France, 11–12 Nov.; Russian counteroffensive at Stalingrad begins, 19 Nov.; French fleet scuttled at Toulon, 27 Nov.; Germans driven from Agheila, 13 Dec.; Russian victory at Kotelnikovo, 29 Dec.

1943: Casablanca Conference, 14–26 Jan.; British take Tripoli, 23 Jan.; Russians take Voronezh, 25 Jan.; final German surrender in Stalingrad, 2 Feb.; Gen. Eisenhower allied C.-in-C. N. Africa, 6 Feb.; Russians take Kursk, 8 Feb.; Americans finally clear Guadalcanal, 9

Feb.; battle of the Bismarck Sea, 1–3 Mar.; battle of the Mareth, 21–29 Mar.; Allies take Tunis, 7 May; Axis surrender in N. Africa, 13 May; breaching of Möhne and Eder dams by R.A.F., 18 May; Allies take Pantelleria, 11 June; Allies conquer Sicily, 9 July–7 Aug.; Mussolini resigns, 25 July; Russians take Orel, 4 Aug.; Kharkov, 23 Aug.; Mountbatten becomes allied C.-in-C. SE. Asia, 25 Aug.; Allies land in Italy and Italy surrenders, 3 Sept.; allied landing at Salerno, 9 Sept.; Russians take Bryansk, 17 Sept.; Smolensk, 25 Sept.; Kiev, 6 Nov.; Allies allowed to use Portuguese Azores bases, Oct.; Americans capture Tarawa, 21–25 Nov.; Cairo Conference, 22–26 Nov.; Teheran Conference, 26 Nov.–2 Dec.; U.S.A. and Britain give aid to Tito, 20 Dec.

1944: Ciano executed, 11 Jan.; Russian offensive in Leningrad area begins, 15 Jan.; allied landings at Nettuno and Anzio, 22 Jan.; Americans capture Kwajalein, 1–6 Feb.; battle of Cassino, 1 Feb.–18 May; Japanese defeat in Manipur, 13 Mar.–30 June; Russians reach Polish and Rumanian frontiers, 2 Apr.; capture Sevastopol, 9 May; Allies enter Rome, 4 June; allied landings in Normandy, 6 June; flying bomb attacks on London begin, 15 June; break-through at St. Lô, 27 July; Polish rising in Warsaw begins, 1 Aug.; battle of the Falaise gap, 7–23 Aug.; allied landings in S. of France, 15 Aug.; Allies capture Paris, 24–25 Aug.; Brussels, 3 Sept.; Americans take Palau Island, 15 Sept.–13 Oct.; Russians invade Hungary, 6 Oct.; Americans invade Philippines, 20 Oct.; battle of Arnhem, 17–26 Oct.; decisive Japanese naval defeat in Philippine Sea, 23–25 Oct.; armistice with Bulgaria, 28 Oct.; British land on Walcheren, 1 Nov.; last German offensive in the Ardennes, 16–22 Dec.; Hungary changes sides, 30 Dec.

1945: Russians take Warsaw, 11 Jan.; Yalta Conference, 4–11 Feb.; Russians take Budapest, 13 Feb.; Turkey declares war on Germany and Japan, 23 Feb.; Americans cross the Rhine at Remagen, 7 Mar.; Russians denounce the neutrality pact with Japan, 5 Apr.; President Roosevelt dies, 12 Apr.; Russians occupy Vienna, 13 Apr., and reach Berlin, 21 Apr.; Russians and Americans meet near Torgau, 26 Apr.; Mussolini shot, and German plenipotentiaries in Italy sign terms of surrender, 29 Apr.; Hitler's death announced, 1 May; Berlin surrenders and armistice in Italy effective, 2 May; German forces in NW. Europe surrender, 5 May; all German forces surrender, 7 May; Americans capture Okinawa, 21 June; atomic bomb on Hiroshima,

6 Aug.; Russia attacks Japan, 8 Aug.; atomic bomb on Nagasaki, 9 Aug.; Japan surrenders, 14 Aug.; Japanese forces in China surrender, 9 Sept.; in SE. Asia, 12 Sept.

PEACE TREATIES

1946: Between Britain and India on the one hand, and Thailand on the other. Between Australia and Thailand. Between France and Thailand.

1947: Between the Allies and the German satellites, signed and ratified, namely with Italy, Hungary, Rumania, Bulgaria, and Finland (the U.S.A. had not been at war with the last of these).

1951: Between Japan and forty-eight allied countries.

1955: Between Austria and the Allies.

* Up to Dec. 1963 there had been no all-German peace treaty. The Western powers terminated the state of war with Federal Germany in 1951; the U.S.S.R. did the same in 1955.

Worms, on the site of a Roman town Borbetomagus, was the capital of the Burgundian kingdom from A.D. 416 to 444. More than 100 Imperial Diets met in W., including those of 1122 and 1521 (*see* next two articles). Except for one cathedral (the oldest external parts of the present structure date from 1110, some internal parts of the structure built 1000–25) the whole town was destroyed by the French, 1689. Ceased to be an Imperial Free City, 1801, and became part of Hesse, 1815. An episcopal see, 614–1801.

Worms, Concordat of, 1122, abolished lay investiture of bishops and abbots in favour of election by cathedral chapter.

Worms, Edict of. Luther was summoned before the imperial Diet and was warned by Spalatin against entering W. His writings were recognized, but he had to remain in hiding. He was put under an imperial ban, 26 May 1521.

Writers to the Signet. Scottish law agents corresponding to English solicitors;

by an Act of 1868 they prepare all crown writs.

Wroclaw, since 1945 the Polish name of the former German city of Breslau (*q.v.*).

Wroxeter. *See* URICONIUM.

Württemberg, Germany. War between W. and the Swabian cities, 1377–88. Formation of Swabian League, 1488. W. raised to a dukedom, 1495. Ulrich Duke of W. expelled from W. by Swabian League, 1519. W. sold to the Emperor Charles V by Swabian League, 1520. Ulrich restored, with French support, 1534. Napoleon made W. into kingdom, 1806, which endured until 1918. Joined the S. German Zollverein, 1828–31. Joined the Prussian Zollverein, 1833. Fought Prussia in alliance with Austria, 1866. Fought against France, 1870. Joined German Empire, 1871. Became a republic, Nov. 1918. New constitution, 1919. In 1945 partitioned between French and U.S. zones in two provinces, but combined with Baden in a southwestern province of the German Federal Republic, 1950.

Wyatt's Insurrection, 1554. A futile revolt led by Sir Thomas W. the Younger (1521?–54), in opposition to the marriage of Queen Mary with Philip of Spain. He collected forces in Kent, marched to Blackheath, 29 Jan.; entered Southwark, 3 Feb.; then marched to Kingston, 6 Feb.; through Kensington to Hyde Park, 7 Feb.; by Charing Cross to Ludgate, turned back, and was arrested at Temple Bar, 8 Feb.; beheaded on Tower Hill, 11 Apr.

Wyoming, explored by Spaniards in the seventeenth, and French in the eighteenth, centuries, was first entered by an American, John Colter, 1807. Part of it was acquired by the U.S.A. in the Louisiana Purchase, 1803, part from the British Oregon territory, 1846, part ceded by Mexico, 1848, and part annexed (with Texas), 1854. Women were granted the vote in W. elections, 1869, and the first woman state governor in the U.S.A. took office in W., 1925. The state was admitted to the Union, 1890.

ADDENDA

X

Xanthica. Named after Xanthicus, a month in Macedonian calendar, corresponding to Apr.; it was a military festival instituted 392 B.C.

Xanthus, Asia Minor. Twice sustained sieges which ended with the self-destruction of the inhabitants; first by the Persians under Harpagus (c. 546 B.C.), and secondly by the Romans under Brutus (43 B.C.).

Xenon. Discovered by Sir William Ramsay(1852–1916), 1898.

Xeres or **Jerez,** SW. Spain. The word sherry is the English corruption of X. Roderic, the last Visigothic king of Spain, was killed here by the Saracens in 711.

X-rays. Discovered by Professor Wilhelm Konrad von Röntgen (1845–1923) in 1895.

Y

Yacht. The word was used in England in the forms yeaghe, yoathe, etc., from 1557. Charles II had a Y. named *Mary*. The first Y. club was the Cork Harbour Water Club, 1720.

Yakutsk, Siberia. Celebrated for its great trade in furs; founded in 1632; now capital of Yakut Republic in U.S.S.R.

Yale University. The third oldest university in the U.S.A.; found in 1701 by ministers selected by the churches of New Haven county. Took the name of Yale College, 1718, after Elihu Yale (1648–1721), its great benefactor. Charter, 1745. Known as Y. U. since 1887.

Yalta Agreement concluded allied conference, 4–11 Feb. 1945.

Yanaon. A former French settlement in India, founded, 1750; after many vicissitudes it was restored to France in 1815. Administration transferred to India, 1954; treaty of cession, May 1956.

'Yankee.' Used in Cambridge, Massachusetts, c. 1713, as a term of excellence. Derived by Thomas Anburey, 1789, from *eankee*, Cherokee for slave or coward; by J. G. E. Heckewelder, 1818, from Red Indian pronunciation of the word *English*. But possibly a Dutch diminutive of *Jan*: the personal name *Janke* is found in the Calendar of State Papers, Colonial Series, (1898), under date 1683. Derisively applied to the New Englander by British troops during the War of Independence; by the Confederates to the Union troops during the Civil War.

Yarkand. Chief town of Chinese Turkestan (Sinkiang); visited by Marco Polo, 1271, and by the Portuguese Goes, 1603; little known till Adolf Schlagintweit visited it in 1857.

Yellow Fever. First authentic account from Barbados, 1647. It having been shown in Havana, 1900, by Lazear, Reed, and Agramonte that Y. F. was produced by a microbe in the mosquito *Aedes aegypti* or *Stegomyia fasciata*, it was announced from Guayaquil, Ecuador, in 1918, that the microbe, *Leptospira ictoroides,* had been isolated by Hideyo Noguchi (1876–1928). A preventive serum began to be used, 1919; and in the same year, at Guayaquil, Conner devised the expedient of putting small fish into drink-ing-water reservoirs to eat mosquito larvae. These means, together with the anti-mosquito campaign that began, 1901, have put Y. F. in a fair way to extinction; though, from 1925, doubts have been thrown on the causal relationship of *Leptospira icteroides.* Recent epidemics: Sudan, 1940; Nigeria, 1946.

Yellowstone National Park, Wyo., U.S.A. Occupied by Sheepeater Indians when area was first visited by John Colter, 1807. First received publicity through account of Henry D. Washburn, surveyorgeneral of Montana, 1870. Made a public park and game preserve, 1872.

Yemen (*Arabia Felix*) settled before 1000 B.C. Conquered by Moslem tribes, A.D. 631; by Turks, 1517. Imam Yahya became independent of Turkish rule, 1918. Boundaries with Saudi Arabia determined, 1926. Treaty of friendship with Britain regarding Y.-Aden frontier, 1934. Treaty of Taif with Saudi Arabia, 1934. Tripartite treaty with Saudi Arabia and Iraq, 1936. Took part in London Conference on Palestine, 1939, and joined Arab League, 1945. Imam Yahya and the two emirs, his sons, murdered, Feb. 1948. Another son, the Emir Saif-el-Islam Ahmad ibn Yahya, succeeded, Mar. 1948. Emigration of Jewish population completed, 1949. Further agreement with Britain regarding Aden, 1951, but increasing tension on Aden-Yemeni border due to Yemeni claims after 1956. Joined United Arab Republic (*q.v.*) in a federal union, 1958, which lapsed after the defection of Syria (*q.v.*). Imam Ahmad *d.*, 19 Sept. 1962, and a week later there was a republican revolt in Y. led by Major Sallal, who subsequently took the title of President, and who was supported by the United Arab Republic. Y. threatened Saudi Arabia, Oct. 1962; and the republican regime signed a 'joint defence' pact with the United Arab Republic, Nov. 1962. Royalist forces under the new Imam Mohammed were supported by Saudi Arabia, Dec. 1962, but this support withdrawn, 1963, and by May 1963 republican regime appeared to be in control of most of the country. U.A.R. announced that her forces were being withdrawn from the Y., July.

Yeomanry (British). Mounted volunteers. First units organized under Volunteer Act of 1794; served in the S. African War in Imperial Y. battalion, 1899–1901; merged in Territorial Force, 1908.

Yeomen of the Guard. A king's bodyguard instituted, 1485; the oldest professional military body in England; properly called Y. Warders of the Tower, they were nicknamed 'Beef-eaters' *c.* 1669; their services, originally most comprehensive, are now largely ceremonial.

Yeti. *See* ABOMINABLE SNOWMAN.

Yezidis. A sect dwelling in Kurdistan, Armenia, N. Iraq, and the Caucasus; their sacred book is Al-Yalvah, interpreted by Sheikh Adi *c.* 1200. But the sect is believed to be of much earlier origin, possibly coeval with Mohammed.

Yokohama. A Japanese seaport on W. of Tokyo Bay. Opened to foreigners, 1859; it was then little more than a village. Silk and tea are the chief exports. Three-quarters of the town destroyed by the earthquake of 1 Sept. 1923. Heavily bombed by Americans, causing severe damage, 1945.

York, Archbishopric of. Date of foundation of the see uncertain: probably *c.* 625. Independent till subordinated to Canterbury by papal decree, 1073. Scottish bishops asserted independence from 1176.

Following are the dates of investiture of the Archbishops of York:

Paulinus	625	Henry Murdac	1147
Wilfrid I	664	Roger	1154
Cead	664	Geoffrey	1191
Bosa	678	Walter Gray	1215
John of		Sewal de Bovil	1256
Beverley	705	Godfrey	1258
Wilfrid II	718	Walter Giffard	1266
Egbert	732	Wm. Wick-	
Ethelbert	766	wain	1279
Eanbald I	780	John le	
Eanbald II	796	Roman	1286
Wulfsige	? 812	Henry Newark	1298
Wigmund	837	Thos. Cor-	
Wulfhere	854	bridge	1300
Ethelbald	900	Wm. Green-	
Redewald	*c.* 928	field	1306
Wulfstan	*c.* 931	Wm. Melton	1317
Osketyl	958	Wm. Zouche	1342
Oswald	972	John Thoresby	1352
Ealdulf	992	Alex. Neville	1374
Wulfstan II	1003	Thos. Arundel	1388
Aelfric	1023	Robt. Waldby	1397
Kinesige	1051	Richd. Scrope	1398
Ealdred	1060	Henry Bowett	1407
Thomas I	1070	John Kemp	1426
Gerard	1101	Wm. Booth	1452
Thomas II	1109	George Neville	1464
Thurstan	1119	Lawrence	
William	1143	Booth	1476
Thos.		Dawes Bart.	1714
Rotherham	1480	Lancelot	
Thos. Savage	1501	Blackburne	1724
Christopher		Thos. Herring	1743
Bainbridge	1508	Matt. Hutton	1747
Thos. Wolsey	1514	John Gilbert	1757
Edward Lee	1531	Robt. Hay	
Robt. Holgate	1545	Drummond	1761
Nicolas Heath	1555	Wm. Mark-	
Thos. Young	1561	ham	1777
Edmund		Edward	
Grindal	1570	Harcourt	1807
Edwin Sandys	1576	Thos. Mus-	
John Piers	1589	grave	1847
Matt. Hutton	1595	Chas. Thos.	
Tobias Mattew	1606	Longley	1860
George		Wm. Thomson	1862
Monteigne	1628	Wm. Connor	
Samuel		Magee	1891
Harsnett	1628	Wm. Dal-	
Richd. Neile	1632	rymple Mac-	
John Williams	1641	lagan	1891
Vacant	1650–60	Cosmo Gordon	
Accepted		Lang	1908
Frewen	1660	Wm. Temple	1929
Richd. Sterne	1664	Cyril Forster	
John Dolben	1683	Garbett	1942
Thos.		Arthur Michael	
Lamplugh	1688	Ramsey	1956
John Sharp	1691	Fredk. Donald	
Sir Wm.		Coggan	1961

York, City of, England (Lat. Eboracum). In Roman times the headquarters of the IXth Legion till A.D. 120. Thereafter of the VIth. Hadrian visited Y., 120. Severus *d.* at, 211. Constantine the Great proclaimed Emperor at, 306. Captured by the Deiran Angles, *c.* 520. Edwin of Northumbria baptized by St. Paulinus at, 627. First cathedral *c.* 625. Present structure built between 1070 and 1472. Stormed by Penda of Mercia and Cadwalla the Welshman, 653. Renowned as a seat of learning in the eighth century. Sigtrygg Ivarsson (*d.* 927), Danish King of Y., 921. Y. burnt by William I, 1068. Council of the North established at, 1537. Besieged by Parliamentarians, 1644. Renewed prosperity due to growth of railways after 1850. University of Y. opened, 1963.

Yosemite Valley, U.S.A. Discovered, 1851. Made a national park, 1866.

Young Men's Christian Association, founded 1844 by Sir George Williams (1821–1905). World Alliance of Y.M.C.As. established, 1855. Seventy-six countries adhered to World Alliance by 1950.

Young Plan. Despite the Dawes Plan (*q.v.*), Germany stopped paying reparations, etc., 1929. A committee of experts sat in Paris, 11 Feb. 1929, and one of their number, Owen D. Y. (*d.* 1962), of U.S.A., propounded a plan that they accepted, 7

June. With modifications made at The Hague, 31 Aug. 1929 and 20 Jan. 1930, it was signed there by fifteen nations, 20 Jan. 1930. For the first time it fixed a total, about 37 milliard gold marks, and made elaborate arrangements for payment off by 1988. The Y. P. was to have given place to the 'Lausanne Settlement' in June 1932; this was to have eased matters further, but reparation payments had ceased for good by June 1931, and in 1932 all hope of them was abandoned, largely because of the emotional opposition to the 'bondage of interest' imposed by the 'Yoonk Plahn,' a great stand-by in the oratorical repertoire of Adolf Hitler (1889–1945).

Young Women's Christian Association, founded, 1855. Independent English branches amalgamated, 1887. World Y.W.C.A. established, 1894.

Youth Hostels Association of England and Wales formed, 1930. Scottish and N. Ireland Y.H.A. formed, 1931.

Ypres, medieval capital of W. Flanders. Cloth Hall built, 1201–1342. Belgian since 1830. Belonged to France between 1678 and 1715 and between 1794 and 1814; to Holland, 1814–30. Menin Gate memorial built, 1927. *See* BATTLES.

Yucatan, Mexico. Discovered, 1517.

Yugoslavia. (For previous history *see* SERBIA, MONTENEGRO, BOSNIA, CROATIA, SLOVENIA, MACEDONIA, etc.) King Nicholas of Montenegro deposed and Montenegro united with Serbia, 29 Nov. 1918. Yugoslav kingdom under the Serbian monarchy proclaimed, 1 Dec. 1918. D'Annunzio seizes Fiume for Italy, 12 Sept. 1919. Treaty of Rapallo with Italy gives Zara to Italy and makes Fiume independent, 12 Nov. 1920. Italy annexes Fiume, 9 Mar. 1924. Treaty of Nettuno with Italy, 18 July 1925. Treaty of friendship with Greece, 18 July 1925. Diplomatic relations with Albania broken off, 4 June 1927. Treaty of friendship with France, 11 Nov. 1927. Royal dictatorship, Jan. 1929; restricted constitution promulgated, Sept. 1931. King Alexander murdered at Marseilles, 9 Oct. 1934; succeeded by Peter II and Regent Paul. Pact with Italy, 25 Mar. 1937. Government's move for a concordat with Pope abandoned, 10 Feb. 1938.

1939: Trade treaty with France signed in Paris, 10 Feb.; Paul, the prince regent, arrived in Rome, 10 May; prince regent visited Germany and (on the 1st) banqueted with Hitler, 1–5 June; announcement in Belgrade of agreement between Serbs and Croats (providing for creation of a Croatian province covering more than a quarter of total area of Y.) approved by regency, 24 Aug.; declaration of neu-

trality, 5 Sept.; pact of friendship with Hungary signed, 12 Dec.

1941: Joins Axis Pact, 25 Mar.; Gen. Simovich *coup d'état*, 26–27 Mar.; Regent Prince Paul fled and King Peter took over full royal powers, 27 Mar.; German invasion, 6 Apr.; Hungarian invasion, 11 Apr.; all official Yugoslav resistance ended, 17 Apr.; 'Independent' Croatia formed and crown offered to house of Savoy, 18 May; Dalmatia annexed by Italy, 21 May. *See* WORLD WAR II for events 1941–5. Underground resistance to the Germans became effective in Y. by the end of 1941, but was hindered by the existence of two rival groups, led by Mihailovich on the one hand and Tito on the other. Until mid 1943 Western support was given only to Mihailovich, then also to Tito. In 1944 it was henceforth given exclusively to Tito, who had had Russian support from the start, and who held control of the country when the war ended.

1945: Last German troops left Y. (Slovenia), 29 Apr; Federal Republic proclaimed, 29 Nov.; Ivan Ribar elected President, 2 Dec.

1946: National Assembly adopted new constitution, 31 Jan.; trial and execution of Drazha Mihailovich, for alleged treason and war crimes, June, July; alliance with Albania signed, 9 July; treaty with Czechoslovakia ratified, 17 July; American planes forced down, 9 Aug., and shot down, 19 Aug., over Yugoslav territory; U.S.A. threatens to appeal to U.N. Security Council, 21 Aug.; conciliatory note from Yugoslav Government, 31 Aug.; internationalization of Trieste (*q.v.*) accepted, 3 Sept.; Archbishop Stepinac of Zagreb arrested, 18 Sept., charged with war crimes, sentenced to sixteen years' hard labour, 11 Oct. (but conditionally released in 1951); Tito excommunicated by Roman Catholic Church, 14 Oct.; Greek Premier Tsaldaris accused Y. of harbouring Greek rebels in Macedonia, Nov.

1947: Ex-king and family deprived of nationality and property, 8 Mar.; Tito appeals to U.S.A. for famine relief, 14 Mar.; peace signed and diplomatic relations with Italy resumed, 17 Mar.; Five-Year Plan announced, 26 Apr.; Y. withdraws from International Labour Office (*q.v.*), 7 July; agreement with Bulgaria signed, 2 Aug., and treaty of alliance signed, 27 Nov.; with Hungary, 8 Dec.; with Rumania, 19 Dec.

1948: Any scheme for Balkan federation denounced by Moscow *Pravda*, 28 Jan.; bitter political conflict with Russia now began; census of population, 15 Mar.; Y. expelled from Cominform (*q.v.*), July.

1949: Every effort short of military force made by the U.S.S.R. to overthrow the Tito regime; twenty million dollars credit authorized by U.S. Export-Import Bank, Sept.; harshness of regime relaxed, although religious persecution continued, especially against Roman Catholics.

1950: Further credit of same amount authorized, Mar.; General Election, 26 Mar.; Ivan Ribar re-elected, 26 Apr.

1952: Orthodox faculty at Belgrade University and Catholic faculties at Zagreb and Ljubljana closed, 28 June.

1953: New constitution introduced, 13 Jan; Tito elected President of Republic, 14 Jan.; visits England, Mar.; improved relations with U.S.S.R. following Stalin's death.

1954: Tito re-elected President, Jan.; Y. a party to the agreement on Trieste (q.v.), as a result of which the former 'Zone B' came under Yugoslav civil administration, Oct.

1955–6: Tito and Bulganin, of the U.S.S.R., signed a declaration of friendship and co-operation; but renewed coolness between Y. and Russia after the abortive Hungarian revolt of Oct.–Nov. 1956. Y.'s relations with Egypt became closer after the Suez crisis of Oct.–Dec. 1956.

1957: A meeting between Khruschev and Tito took place, Aug.; Djilas sentenced to seven years' imprisonment for 'spreading propaganda hostile to the state,' Oct. (but released early); Y. recognized the German Democratic Republic, Oct.

1958: Tito re-elected President, Apr.

1960: New Five-Year Plan for 1961–5 announced, Dec.

1962: Djilas jailed for eight years for hostile propaganda, 14 May; President Brezhnev of Russia paid a state visit to Y. in Sept., but was coolly received; Tito visited Russia, Dec. Y. resumes relations with Russian *bloc* Communist parties, 29 Dec.

1963; New constitution, Jan. Severe earthquake in Skopje, July.

Yukon, Canada. Organized as a separate territory, 1898. Klondike gold rush, 1896–8.

Z

Zadar (Serb.-Cr.) or **Zara** (It.), capital of Dalmatia, taken from Eastern Empire by Venetians c. 990, from which time till 1409 Z. alternated between Venetian and Hungarian sovereignty; captured and then bought by Venetians, 1409. Became Austrian, 1797, then part of Illyrian kingdom (see ILLYRIA), 1809–13, then again Austrian. Ceded to Italy, 1918, and to Yugoslavia, June 1947.

Zagreb (Serb.-Cr.) or **Agram** (Ger.). Capital of Croatia from 1867, ceded to Yugoslavia by Hungary, 1918. Seat of (Hungarian) diocese, 1093, from which period the still extant Kaptol (fortified Old Town) dates.

Zambesi. The first European to explore the Z. was Dr. Livingstone in 1851–3.

Zante Island, Greece (ancient *Zacynthos*), traditionally belonged to Ulysses. Peopled by Achaeans c. 1390 B.C. Naval base for Athenians in Peloponnesian War. Attacked by Lacedemonians, 430 B.C. Headquarters of Dion's Syracusan expedition, 357 B.C. Seized by Philip V of Macedon, 217 B.C. Taken by Romans, 211 B.C., but restored; annexed by Rome, 191 B.C. In A.D. eleventh century it passed to the Norman kings of Sicily. After the twelfth century it belonged at different times to despots of Epirus, emperors of Constantinople, and counts of Cephalonia. In hands of Tocco family, 1357–1482; then Venetian possession till ceded to France, 1797. Briefly occupied by a Russo-Turkish fleet, 1799; then British till ceded to Greece, 1820.

Zanzibar, E. Africa. Mentioned by Arab writers, 1328; fell into hands of the Portuguese in fifteenth century, and taken by Turks in seventeenth century; proclaimed a British protectorate, 1890. Slavery abolished, 1897. Constitutional changes, 1926, 1956, and 1961, allowing for increasing self-government. Constitutional talks on Z.'s future after Kenyan independence, held in London, Mar. 1962. Z. announced her intention of joining the proposed East African Federation (q.v.)., 1963.

Zend-Avesta. The book of the religion of Zoroaster; mentioned by Hermippus in the third century B.C.

Zeppelin. See AIRSHIPS.

Zeta, or **Zero Energy Thermonuclear**

Assembly, came into operation at Harwell, Berks., Aug. 1957.

Zinc. Used in early times as a component of brass (referred to by Pliny); known to the ancients only in the carbonates and silicates called calamine. The word Z. first used by Paracelsus; and the metal was described by Libavius in 1597.

Zinder. Republic of the Niger. A trade emporium occupied by French, 1899.

Zinoviev Letter, The. Alleged to have been sent by Zinoviev, head of the Comintern (q.v.) on 15 Sept. 1924, to Russian *chargé d'affaires* in London, advising agitation for a violent revolution in Britain. Published in London press, 25 Oct. 1924, just before General Election, and possibly helped to bring about a Labour defeat.

Zionism. Congress of Basel, 1897, convened by Theodor Herzl (1860–1904), author of *The Jewish State*, 1896, who founded organization with headquarters first in Vienna, but from 1904 to 1911 in Cologne under David Wolfssohn (d. 1914). Practical work begun by actual purchase of land in Palestine, 1908, financed by Jewish National Fund, which was founded, 1901. Organization moved to Berlin for period, 1911–14. Balfour Declaration, 2 Nov. 1917, prompted by Chaim Weizmann (1874–1952) and Nahum Sokolow (1861–1936). The organization from 1917 to 1929 was identical with the Jewish Agency for Palestine, but thereafter other bodies participated in the agency. *See* ISRAEL and PALESTINE, MODERN.

Ziyanids. A dynasty which ruled Algeria (q.v.), A.D. 1235–1393.

Znaim, or **Znojmo,** Moravia. Founded, 1226, by Ottakar I of Bohemia. The armistice between Napoleon I and the Archduke Charles was concluded here after the battle of Wagram, 1809.

Zodiac, Signs of the. Names assigned by Anaximander c. 560 B.C.

Zollverein (*Customs Union*), term used especially of those economic alliances binding various German states between 1818 and 1871.

Zoological Nomenclature. First applied with any accuracy by Linnaeus in his

454

Systema Naturae, the first sketch of which appeared in 1735.

Zoological Society of London. Founded, 1826. Gardens opened, 1828. Royal charter, 1829. Whipsnade Park opened, 1931.

Zoroastrianism. Founder Zoroaster lived *c.* 800 B.C. Z. became national religion of Persia *c.* 550 B.C. to *c.* A.D. 650.

Zouaves. French African infantry. First corps raised in Algeria, 1831; saw service outside Africa for first time in Crimean War (1855).

Zuider Zee, Holland. Formed by series of storms in the thirteenth and fourteenth centuries. Bill to reclaim passed, 1918. Work on dam begun, 1924. Completed and name of Z. Z. changed to Yssel Meer, 1932. Reflooded by Germans, 1944, but largely reclaimed by the end of 1945. Flooding caused by high tides and storms, Jan.–Feb. 1953. Further reclamation set in hand thereafter.

Zululand. Annexed by Britain, 1887; annexed to Natal, 1897.

Zulus migrated southwards to the hinterland of Delagoa Bay during seventeenth century, and overran Natal, 1823, under King Chaka (*b.* 1783), who set up the military organization based on the *impi* (infantry battalion), brought about tribal fusion with the more powerful neighbouring Umtetwas, and was murdered by his brother, Dingaan, who succeeded him, 1829. About 1820 the Matabele tribe, under the dissident Gen. Moselekatze, seceded from the Zulu nation, and migrated further SW. After Dingaan's defeat at Blood River (1838) by the Voortrekkers (*q.v.*) he was deposed by his

brother Umhanda (Jan. 1840), and fled to Swaziland, where he was murdered. Civil war, 1856, won by Cetewayo, who succeeded his father Umhanda, 1873. Boundary dispute between Cetewayo and the Transvaal Republic (later Colony) settled by British arbitration in Z. favour, 1878, led to Zulu War of 1879. Cetewayo captured and deposed, 27 Aug. 1879. Restored by British. 1882; *d.* of wounds, 1884. His son Dinizulu led a rebellion, June–Aug. 1888, and was exiled, but allowed to return by the Natal Government, 1898. A rebellion, provoked by the poll tax, broke out in 1906, as a result of which Dinizulu was imprisoned, but was released in 1910 by the Union of S. Africa Government; he *d.* 1913. His son, King Solomon, *d.* 1933, when the throne became vacant until the appointment by the S. African Government of Cyrian Bhakuzulu (*b.* 1924) in Mar. 1952.

Zürich, Switzerland. Canton revised its constitution, 1336, and joined Swiss Everlasting League, 1351. Its subjects made free citizens of the Empire in 1262, granted complete autonomy within the Empire, 1400. Joined Helvetic Republic, 1798.

Zutphen, Holland. Sir Philip Sidney killed at battle of, 1586. Taken by Spaniards, 1587. Recovered by Dutch, 1591.

Zwinglianism. Followers of Swiss reformer Ulrich Zwingli (1484–1531). Now known as Swiss Evangelical Church. Since their defeat at the battle of Kappel, 1531, Zwinglian influence has been confined to Zürich and neighbouring cantons.